THE CAMBRIDGE HISTORY
OF NINETEENTH-CENTURY
POLITICAL THOUGHT

This major work of academic reference provides the first comprehensive survey of political thought in Europe, North America and Asia in the century following the French Revolution. Written by a distinguished team of international scholars, this Cambridge History is the latest in a sequence of volumes firmly established as the principal reference source for the history of political thought. In a series of scholarly but accessible essays, every major theme in nineteenth-century political thought is covered, including political economy, religion, democratic radicalism, nationalism, socialism and feminism. The volume also includes studies of major figures, including Hegel, Mill, Bentham and Marx and biographical notes on every significant thinker in the period. Of interest to students and scholars of politics and history at all levels, this volume explores seismic changes in the languages and expectations of politics accompanying political revolution, industrialisation and imperial expansion and less-noted continuities in political and social thinking.

GARETH STEDMAN JONES was formerly Professor of Political Thought at the University of Cambridge. He is currently Professor of the History of Ideas at Queen Mary, University of London. He is also Director of the Centre for History and Economics and a Fellow of King's College, Cambridge. Professor Stedman Jones has published numerous books and articles, including *Outcast London*, *Languages of Class*, *The Communist Manifesto – Penguin introduction* and *An End to Poverty?* He is currently working on an intellectual biography of Marx.

GREGORY CLAEYS is Professor of the History of Political Thought at Royal Holloway, University of London. He has edited numerous works including *Modern British Utopias 1700–1850* (8 vols.), *Restoration and Augustan British Utopias*, *Late Victorian Utopias* (6 vols.), and *The Cambridge Companion to Utopian Literature*. Professor Claeys has written several studies of aspects of the Owenite socialist movement, of the French Revolution debate in Britain, and of Thomas Paine's thought.

THE CAMBRIDGE
HISTORY OF
NINETEENTH-CENTURY
POLITICAL THOUGHT

EDITED BY

GARETH STEDMAN JONES

University of Cambridge

AND

GREGORY CLAEYS

Royal Holloway, University of London

CAMBRIDGE
UNIVERSITY PRESS

CAMBRIDGE UNIVERSITY PRESS

Cambridge, New York, Melbourne, Madrid, Cape Town,
Singapore, São Paulo, Delhi, Tokyo, Mexico City

Cambridge University Press
The Edinburgh Building, Cambridge CB2 8RU, UK

Published in the United States of America by Cambridge University Press, New York

www.cambridge.org
Information on this title: www.cambridge.org/9780521430562

First published 2011

Printed in the United Kingdom at the University Press, Cambridge

A catalogue record for this publication is available from the British Library

Library of Congress Cataloguing in Publication data
The Cambridge history of nineteenth-century political thought / edited by Gareth Stedman
Jones and Gregory Claeys.
p.   cm. – (The Cambridge history of political thought)
Includes bibliographical references and index.
ISBN 978-0-521-43056-2
1. Political science – History – 19th century.   I. Stedman Jones, Gareth.   II. Claeys, Gregory.
JA83.C24   2011
320.01 – dc22   2011003322

ISBN 978-0-521-43056-2 Hardback

Contents

Contents

Contents

Contents

Contents

Contents

Contents

Contents

Contributors

CHRISTOPHER BAYLY
Vere Harmsworth Professor of Imperial and Naval History and Fellow,
St Catharine's College, University of Cambridge

DUNCAN BELL
Lecturer, Department of Politics and International Studies and Fellow,
Christ's College, University of Cambridge

FREDERICK C. BEISER
Professor of Philosophy, Syracuse University

JOHN BREUILLY
Professor of Nationalism and Ethnicity, London School of Economics and
Political Science

GREGORY CLAEYS
Professor of the History of Political Thought, Royal Holloway,
University of London

LUCY DELAP
Fellow and Director of Studies in History, St Catharine's College,
University of Cambridge

LAWRENCE GOLDMAN
Editor, Oxford Dictionary of National Biography, Tutor in Modern History and
Fellow, St. Peter's College, Oxford

JOSE HARRIS
Emeritus Professor of Modern History and Fellow, St Catharine's College, Oxford

ROSS HARRISON
Professor of Philosophy and Provost of King's College, University of Cambridge

JEREMY JENNINGS
Professor of Political Theory, Queen Mary, University of London

DONALD R. KELLEY
James Westfall Thompson Professor of History, Rutgers, The State University of New Jersey

CHRISTINE LATTEK
Formerly Lecturer, Department of History, University of Cologne

VERNON L. LIDTKE
Emeritus Professor, Department of History, Johns Hopkins University

DOUGLAS MOGGACH
University Research Chair in Political Thought, University of Ottawa

WOLFGANG J. MOMMSEN
Late Emeritus Professor, Heinrich Heine University, Düsseldorf

JOHN MORROW
Deputy Vice-Chancellor (Academic), University of Auckland

DANIEL PICK
Professor of History, Birkbeck, University of London

FREDERICK ROSEN
Emeritus Professor of the History of Political Thought and Senior Research Fellow, Bentham Project, University College, London

EMMA ROTHSCHILD
Jeremy and Jane Knowles Professor of History, Harvard University

GARETH STEDMAN JONES
Professor of the History of Ideas at Queen Mary, University of London

JAMES THOMPSON
Lecturer in Modern British History, University of Bristol

JOHN E. TOEWS
Professor of European Intellectual and Cultural History, University of Washington

K. STEVEN VINCENT
Professor of History, North Carolina State University

ANDREZJ WALICKI
O'Neill Professor Emeritus of History, University of Notre Dame

CHERYL B. WELCH
Professor of Political Science, Chair of Political Science and International Relations, Simmons College

BEE WILSON
Formerly Research Fellow in the History of Ideas, St John's College, University of Cambridge

JAMES P. YOUNG
Emeritus Professor of Political Science, State University of New York, Binghampton

Acknowledgements

This is the last volume to appear in the *Cambridge History of Political Thought* series and it has been a long time in the making. We are especially grateful to Richard Fisher at Cambridge University Press, who has provided wise advice and patient encouragement throughout the period of preparation of the volume. We would like to extend our special thanks to the contributors who have responded so willingly to editorial suggestions.

For help and encouragement in the early stages of the volume we wish to record our gratitude to two distinguished scholars who died before their contributions could be completed; Professor John Burrow of Oxford and Sussex Universities and Professor Sir Bernard Williams of Berkeley and Oxford Universities. They provided invaluable advice on the overall shape and the content of the volume. It is also a matter of deep regret that one of our contributors, Professor Wolfgang Mommsen of Heinrich Heine University, Düßeldorf, died before this volume was complete.

Susanne Lohmann, Inga Huld Markan, Jo Maybin and Amy Price offered practical support in the making of the volume. We are especially grateful to Mary-Rose Cheadle who expertly supervised the final preparation and editing of the manuscript.

Most of the editorial work on the volume was carried out at the Centre for History and Economics in Cambridge. In this connection we would like to acknowledge the generosity of a number of foundations. We would especially like to thank the Edmond de Rothschild Foundation and its Executive Director, Firoz Ladak. We would also like to thank the John D. and Catherine T. MacArthur Foundation and the Andrew W. Mellon Foundation who provided support at earlier stages.

Finally we would like thank at Cambridge University Press, Jo North for her conscientious copy-editing, Auriol Griffith-Jones who compiled the index, and most importantly Dan Dunlavey for managing the final production process.

Introduction

The aim of the nineteenth-century volume of the *Cambridge History of Political Thought* is to provide a systematic and up-to-date scholarly account of the development of the central themes of political and social thinking in the century following the French Revolution. Its purpose is not to reinforce a canon but rather to trace the emergence of particular preoccupations and to delineate the development of distinctive forms and languages of political thinking. As in the preceding volumes, the aim will be to analyse the provenance and character of leading political ideas, to relate them to the specific historical contexts within which they arose and to examine the circumstances in which their influence made itself felt. This thematic approach has many advantages. But we do not consider it appropriate in every case. In a few instances – those of Hegel, Marx, Bentham and Mill – we have largely devoted chapters to a single author. For in assessing such major thinkers, whose influence and reputations have reached down to the present, we have considered it important that readers be enabled to evaluate their work as a whole.

A volume devoted to nineteenth-century political thought poses special problems of scope and scale not encountered in earlier historical periods. The first problem is that of scope. In the nineteenth century, the boundary between political and other types of thought cannot be drawn with the precision which may be possible in other periods. For if the definition of the *political* is too narrowly drawn, much of the most important political thinking of the nineteenth century would fall outside it. The formal boundaries of political thought were already breaking down in the eighteenth century. But the process was greatly accentuated in the period following the French Revolution in which so many inherited political categories were thrown into disarray. Natural jurisprudence which had provided a framework for so much systematic political theorising from Grotius to Rousseau and Kant was largely discarded. The juridical framework which had been appropriate to the discussion of sovereignty, contract and representation could no longer encompass new conceptions derived from political economy, medicine, social science, history and aesthetics. Novel thinking about politics to a large extent developed within these ancillary areas and some of the most important political thinkers of the nineteenth century – Marx and Tocqueville, for example – never wrote a formal treatise on politics. In the face of this intellectual shift, any attempt to confine this volume to a study of nineteenth-century political theory, narrowly defined, would have produced a seriously lopsided picture of the character and range of political thinking in the period. For this reason, considerable attention has been paid to the development of political economy, to changes in the conception of law and history, to social and natural science and to aesthetics.

The second problem is that of scale. Until the late eighteenth century, a history of political thought could by and large concentrate upon the writings of small learned groups in Western Europe with a sidelong glance at the American colonies. But in the nineteenth century, the number of authors and readers increased immeasurably. The American and French Revolutions stimulated political debate among groups and in regions where, before, it had barely existed. The spread of democratic radicalism, nationalism, socialism and feminism were in large part products of this seismic shift in political expectations. Furthermore, European expansion, the growth of world trade and the formation of new nation states spread new political ideas across the world. There were followers of Comte and Mill to be found from Brazil to China and from such tiny groupings were to develop traditions of Europeanised political and intellectual debate that interacted in various ways with indigenous political cultures. In Europe itself, the growth of population, urbanisation and the spread of literacy brought a far broader spectrum of the 'people' within the ambit of informed political discussion. The proliferation of newspapers, periodicals and tracts testified to this vast increase in demand. In sheer bulk, the volume of political writings in the nineteenth century probably outweighed that of all preceding centuries combined.

One favoured way of attempting to characterise and chart the development of nineteenth-century political thought has been to tell a story about the triumph and faltering of the idea of 'progress'. Such an idea was well established by the French Revolution, but was lent enormous impetus by scientific discoveries and inventions and a steadily rising standard of living at least for the middle classes, and after mid-century often for the working classes as well. At its peak around the middle of the century, the pervasiveness of this idea was captured particularly in notions of 'civilisation', of the sharp division between 'advanced' and 'backward' societies or sometimes between 'white' and other races, and of the vaunted superiority of the morals and manners attendant upon science, Christianity and commerce. Conversely, the period from the 1880s to the First World War is often depicted as that of a crisis of reason, in which various forms of nationalism, neo-romanticism, irrationalism, mysticism, political pessimism and cults of violence captured the imagination of the new, uprooted and restless intelligentsias thrown up by the social, scientific and political changes of the period.

There is no doubt that this approach captures some of the most significant as well as most eye-catching developments of the period. But such an interpretation, as this volume demonstrates, also has real limitations. Its vision is too selective. In the first half of the century, it underplays the traumas attendant upon the decline or loss of the religious and political hierarchies of the *ancien régime*, not to mention new Malthusian anxieties about overpopulation. Conversely, its depiction of intellectual, political and cultural developments after 1870 is inescapably coloured by a sense of the tragic denouement to come in the First World War. Consequently, it misses equally prominent expressions of optimism about education, international arbitration, peaceful economic development, social security and civic and democratic participation in the new conditions of urban life. For these reasons, we have made no attempt to construct an overarching picture of the direction of political thought in the century as a whole or to reduce the diversity of developments recounted in individual essays.

Since the size of this volume is limited, there is no optimal, let alone comprehensive, way in which all this diversity of topics can be accommodated. We have devoted more space to the literature of nationalism, socialism, republicanism and feminism than is customary in more traditional pictures of nineteenth-century political theory and we have attempted to consider the impact of Western political thought viewed from outside Europe, as well as investigating changing European conceptions of empire. Generally, we have avoided a country-by-country enumeration of forms of political thought, in favour of a more thematic organisation of the subject matter. But once again, this rule has not been applied rigidly. In certain cases, we have found a national framework to be the most illuminating way of considering a particular body of political literature. Thus the development of American and Russian political thought has been given separate treatment (Chapters 12 and 23), while other chapters discuss the peculiar problems of German liberalism and German social democracy (Chapters 13 and 22).

3

A further problem, but not one peculiar to the nineteenth century, is where to begin and where to end. This volume begins in the mid-1790s with thinkers for whom the French Revolution was generally the first and most formative event in their intellectual careers. It concludes around the end of the long nineteenth century at a point at which European expansion, industrialisation, evolutionary biology and construction of new political and constitutional forms in Europe and America had laid the basis for new types of political thinking. It reaches the critical stage of modernism, but does not cross it.

But in an enterprise of this kind, beginnings and endings cannot be made too neat. Few straight lines can be drawn from the 1790s through to the 1890s. All that can be offered is a kind of zigzag, as much generational as chronological and very roughly corresponding to turning points in political thinking. In the case of the French Revolution, the reaction of already established political thinkers has been included in the preceding volume. Therefore, this volume begins with Malthus rather than Paine, Coleridge rather than Burke, Constant and Chateaubriand rather than Condorcet and Sieyès, Fichte and Hegel rather than Kant and Herder. The end of the period is more indeterminate. There was no single commanding event comparable to 1789. But there were secular shifts clustering around the 1870s and 1880s – the Franco-Prussian War, the demise of free trade, the heightened scramble for the colonies, the great depression, the rise of socialism and the emergence of new and non-traditional varieties of conservatism. By the end of the century, the tenets of democracy met with far greater favour than at the beginning, but there were also many more, often conflicting, forms of democratic theory. There was little industrialisation in 1800; by 1900 the size and poverty of the new industrial proletariat was a central problem for all theories of social and political order, and had provoked radical theories of social change very different from those which inspired the chief actors of the French Revolution. In 1800, the great estates and orders of European society had been rudely shocked by the actions and principles of the French reformers. A century later, the commercial middle classes enjoyed widespread social and political power, while monarchies and aristocracies found themselves defending an ever less plausible principle of legitimacy. At the time of Waterloo, the foundations had been laid for the new social and economic sciences. By the century's end, these had come to displace much earlier political thinking.

The choice of boundary line in the case of individual thinkers cannot be determined exactly and has been left for the most part to the judgement of contributors. It includes Marshall and Sidgwick, but stops short at Hobhouse and Wallas, includes Jaurès but not Durkheim, Maurras or Bergson, includes Menger but not Pareto, Bernstein and Kautsky and some aspects of Nietzsche (there is further treatment of him in the twentieth-century volume).

In many respects, the attempt to map the contours of nineteenth-century political thought as a whole, and particularly on this scale, is new. Scholarly editions of the works of most of its major thinkers are still incomplete. In some cases, they do not exist. In others, they have remained, until very recently, still bedevilled by political controversy. In comparison with the early modern period or the eighteenth century, interpretative debates about the period as a whole have been rare and often dated. Until very recently most of the major interpreters of Hegel, Mill, Tocqueville, Comte, Proudhon and Marx have been more interested in the twentieth century than the nineteenth. Interpretations of these thinkers were to a large extent the pursuit of contemporary political debate by other means. It is only in the last thirty years that historians have ceased to be dazzled by the self-proclaimed modernity of the nineteenth century and have begun to investigate continuities in its political and social thinking which link it to earlier lineages of religious, political and social thought. This volume is therefore a pioneering venture since only now is it possible to attempt to redraw the whole of the scholarly map, and redefine the spectrum of nineteenth-century political thinking in terms much broader than that envisaged by the nineteenth century itself.

I

Political thought after the French Revolution

I

Counter-revolutionary thought

BEE WILSON

'The return to order', wrote Joseph de Maistre in 1797, in his plea for Restoration, the *Considérations sur la France*, 'will not be painful, because it will be natural and because it will be favoured by a secret force whose action is wholly creative . . . the restoration of monarchy, what they call the counter-revolution, will not be a *counter-revolution*, but the *contrary of revolution*' (Maistre 1994, p. 105). Maistre was fond of paradoxes, but this was not one of them. After all the 'perpetual and desperate oscillations' of French politics since 1789, Maistre argued for the need for stability, not commotion, peace, not violence, tranquillity not anarchy. Achieving this, he argued, necessitated a total separation from the political and intellectual methods of those who had favoured the Revolution. In place of de-Christianisation, was needed belief; in place of insurrection, obedience; in place of insubordination, sovereignty; in place of republic, the monarchy. In other words, what was needed in place of revolution was the contrary of revolution. This meant 'no shocks, no violence, no punishment even, except those which the true nation will approve' (Maistre 1994, p. 105). Maistre has been called a 'fanatical', 'monstrous' and 'disturbing' writer (Faguet 1891, p. 1; Cioran 1987; Berlin 1990, p. 57). Stendhal dubbed him the 'hangman's friend' because of his famous assertion, in the *Soirées de Saint-Petersbourg* that the executioner was the secret 'tie' holding human society together (quoted in Berlin 1990, p. 57). Various nineteenth-century critics accused him of terrorism, while in the twentieth century he was tainted by a supposed association with fascism. Rather than accusing his political thought of violence, however, it would be more accurate to call him a theorist who refused to imagine any political order that did not have to grapple with and contain violence and terror.[1] '[W]e are spoiled by a modern philosophy

---

[1] This interpretation of Maistre as theorist of violence rather than proponent of it is outlined in Bradley 1999.

that tells us all is good, whereas evil has tainted everything', he wrote in the *Considérations* (quoted in Spektorowski 2002, p. 287).

'He was born to hate the revolution', wrote Harold Laski of Maistre, suggesting that the spirit of reaction ran through Maistre's entire personality from birth (Laski 1917, p. 213). In fact, Maistre, like Antoine de Rivarol, Friedrich Gentz, Edmund Burke, Louis de Bonald and Mallet du Pan, along with most other thinkers that we would now classify as 'counter-revolutionaries', began his intellectual career from a position of reform and only hardened to an anti-revolutionary stance after the Revolution itself had begun. As Massimo Boffa writes, 'The counterrevolution was not defined by hostility to reform of the monarchy in 1789' (Boffa 1989, p. 641). Or, as Owen Bradley has written, 'counter-revolution was a part of the revolution itself' (Bradley 1999, p. 10). By 'counter-revolution', this chapter means not what Colin Lucas has called the 'anti-revolution' of practical and popular opposition to the Revolution (Lucas 1988), but the reaction in the sphere of ideas between around 1789 and 1830. As Jacques Godechot has shown, there was remarkably little linkage between anti-revolutionary practice and counter-revolutionary theory (Godechot 1972, p. 384). The anti-revolutionary émigrés could call for a straightforward restoration of the *ancien régime*, whereas counter-revolutionary thought was always more complicated than this. Counter-revolutionaries saw that there was no putting the genie back in the bottle (Maistre commented that you could no more reverse the Revolution than bottle the entire contents of Lake Geneva). Rather, the Revolution was the spur for new thought about how to achieve political stability. What the counter-revolutionary theorists denounced most consistently in the Revolution was its novelty, which had forced them unwillingly into sometimes novel positions. Burke inveighed against the novel abstractions of the architects of revolution. Friedrich Gentz after initially sympathising with the revolutionaries came to revile them for their unparalleled violence; where the American Revolution was in keeping with History, the French Revolution was an aggressive break from it (Gentz 1977, p. 49). For Maistre, it was that unsettling thing, an event without precedent – a horrible sequence of innovations which would necessitate novel responses. 'There is a satanic quality to the French Revolution that distinguishes it from everything we have ever seen or anything we are ever likely to see' (Maistre 1994, p. 41). The Revolution, in Maistre's view, was a 'calamity', a dreadful 'miracle', which lay outside the 'ordinary circle of crime' (Maistre 1994, p. 41).

It may be obvious, but it is also true, to say that, properly speaking, before 1789 there was no counter-revolutionary thought, in so far as this was itself the creation of the Revolution. It is possible, on the other hand, to trace numerous intellectual precursors of the counter-revolutionaries. On this score, the straightforward divine-right justifications of Bossuet were less important sources than the more ambivalent conservatism of Montesquieu, the writings on enlightened despotism of Diderot and Voltaire and, in both a positive and a negative sense, Rousseau. Isaiah Berlin made it fashionable to speak of the counter-revolutionaries as '"counter-enlightenment" thinkers', but in many respects the counter-revolutionaries were continuing rather than negating Enlightenment lines of argument.[2] Much counter-revolutionary thought can be read as an intramural debate within Rousseau studies. Counter-revolutionaries defended the 'honest', 'sincere' Rousseau who represented the socially cohesive virtue of civic religion and the politics of order, against the Rousseau of popular sovereignty and the social contract; they liked the Rousseau who attacked novels rather than the Rousseau who wrote them.[3]

It has become usual to start discussions of counter-revolutionary thought with Burke; in the case of England and Germany, this may be justified. In the case of francophone ideas, however (including Geneva and Savoy as well as France), it is less so. It is true that the *Reflections* was quickly translated into French and by the end of 1791 a very substantial 10,000 copies had been sold in five editions (Draus 1989, p. 79). It is also the case that many of Burke's themes resonated both with the moderate monarchists in the National Assembly and with the émigrés who had fled France (Lucas 1989, pp. 101ff.). Yet even if it did find an audience, the *Reflections* had very limited political influence in France. This was partly because Burkean ideas had already been expressed in France before the *Reflections* was known. As early as 1789, the Abbé Barruel had attacked the *philosophes*, just as Burke did, for their part in causing revolution by placing individual 'rights' before collective values (Godechot 1972, p. 42); Calonne – whose work on finance Burke praised (Burke 1988, pp. 116, 209) – had defended prejudice against

---

2 For various examinations of the term 'counter-enlightenment', see Berlin 1990; Garrard 1994; Mali and Wokler 2003; McMahon 2001.
3 Louis de Bonald, in fact, expressed his attitude to Rousseau in exactly these terms: Bonald 1864, II, p. 25: Bonald states that Rousseau was right to remind mothers of their domestic duties, but wrong to inflame their imaginations with his novel-writing. On Rousseau's importance for counter-revolutionary thought, see also Garrard 1994; McNeil 1953; Melzer 1996.

abstract *a priori* rationalising; in many articles in *Le Mercure* and the journal *Politique national*, Antoine de Rivarol had criticised the Declaration of the Rights of Man and Citizen and defended the throne and obedience to it in terms which may even have influenced Burke (Godechot 1972, pp. 33–4). Most substantially and influentially of all, the Swiss journalist Jacques Mallet du Pan, who from the summer of 1789 was connected with the small group within the Constituent Assembly known as 'monarchiens', had begun a thoroughgoing critique of the Revolution from the point of view of moderation. In everything Mallet du Pan wrote on politics, there was a horror of anarchy. Burke – about whom Mallet expressed ambivalence – would criticise the Declaration of the Rights of Man on the grounds of its metaphysical abstraction. Mallet du Pan's objections were more pragmatic. Either the Declaration would not be applied (and was therefore useless) or it would be (and was therefore extremely dangerous). Mallet du Pan is a good place to begin a consideration of counter-revolutionary writing, because he is the closest thing there was to that contradictory personage, namely, a pre-revolutionary counter-revolutionary.

1 Mallet du Pan and the intellectual roots of counter-revolution

Like Rousseau, Jacques Mallet du Pan approached the politics of the rest of the world primarily through the peculiar prism of Geneva. Mallet du Pan was born in 1749 in a village called Céligny twelve miles from Geneva into the patriciate, the commercial aristocracy which effectively controlled the government of Geneva. In his outlook, however, formed through education at the Collège de Génève and friendship with Voltaire during his Swiss exile, Mallet du Pan was not patrician. In his first published work of 1770, the *Compte Rendu*, Mallet du Pan wrote defending the cause of 'natifs', the descendants of so-called 'inhabitants' of Geneva, immigrant families who were without political rights. In the strange hierarchy of Genevan society, law was made in the Conseil Général, consisting of all adult males who were citizens. Outside of this were the majority of those who lived in Geneva: the 'strangers', 'inhabitants' and their children the 'natifs', who had no political existence, because being born in Geneva did not bestow citizenship. Within the body of the Conseil Général was the Small Council of twenty-five and the Great Council of two hundred. During the 1760s, the middle-class Représentants lobbied for the general body of citizens to have more power within the Conseil Géneral. In 1768, the Edict of Conciliation gave the General Council a say in electing the Council of two hundred. But nothing was done to give the *natifs* a civil existence. Moreover, an edict of February 1770 ruled that any *natif* who demanded rights beyond the privileges of 1768 could be punished as an enemy of the state. It was in this context that Mallet du Pan went into print arguing that the exclusion of *natifs* from citizenship was an act of usurpation. Geneva, he argued, was only republican in form; in reality, it was a despotism. Birth should be the determinant of citizenship. Mallet du Pan would change his mind about this in his later writings on Genevan politics. But what is interesting about this *Compte Rendu* of 1770 is that, even while arguing for expanding the citizen-body, Mallet du Pan denounced the 'natif' use of the democratic doctrine of popular sovereignty. Popular sovereignty, he claimed, was merely a fiction useful only to demagogues.

During the 1770s, Mallet du Pan strengthened his dislike of 'popular sovereignty'. In 1775, he developed an interest in the work of Simon-Nicolas-Henri Linguet, the famous lawyer and pessimist who had argued (in his *Théorie des Loix Civiles* of 1767) that liberty was a fraud, the 'primitive social contract' and 'natural law' were both lies, that positive laws were designed to protect the property of the rich against attacks from the poor, that political liberty was nothing more than the promotion of vested interest, that the intermediary bodies so beloved of Montesquieu were exploiters rather than protectors of the social body, and that as for *philosophes*, they were hypocrites who assuaged their sense of guilt at their own privilege with fancy words (Linguet 1767). Soon, by the spring of 1777, Mallet du Pan and Linguet were collaborating on a journal. After Linguet was arrested and put in the Bastille in 1780, Mallet published his own journal in Geneva, the *Annales . . . pour server de suite aux Annales M. Linguet*, which he edited until 1783, when the publisher Panckoucke gave Mallet the political editorship of the *Mercure de France*. Mallet's journalism was now impregnated with Linguet's anti-philosophism. In 1778, Mallet privately denounced Voltaire as a 'sceptical buffoon' compared to the sincere Rousseau; in public, he defended a Rousseauan theism against the Voltairean sneer. In the *Annales*, he wrote attacking what he saw as Condorcet's *gout de systême*; the passion for abstract argument, wrote Mallet, was a kind of false certainty resulting from the 'confusion of ideas, an anarchy of opinion, a universal skepticism' (quoted in Acomb 1973, pp. 68–9). By now, his writing was vehemently anti-aristocratic and he proposed a reformed, simplified French monarchy, not on physiocratic lines (he saw the physiocrats as property-serving *philosophes*) but more like the reformed French monarchy espoused by D'Argenson in 1764 in his *Considérations sur le Gouvernement de France*.

Mallet complained that 'All Europe groans under aristocracy... [being] filled with corps, orders, nobles, tribunals, all privileged, all jealous of their exemptions.' He dreamed of 'a regime... which, breaking all the barriers raised between the monarch and the people, causes their wills and their interests to coincide' (quoted in Acomb 1973, p. 76).

It might be expected from this that Mallet would have supported the Genevan *natifs*, when they revolted in 1782 against the privileged orders. In fact, however, Mallet attacked this revolt with the same counter-revolutionary arguments he would use again seven years later against the French revolutionaries. The *natif* rebellion, argued Mallet, was an example of demagogues – in this case, the middle-class Représentants – stirring up 'the people' with fictitious promises.

Republican factions come to an end sooner or later by tyranny. So, let the Prices, the Raynals and other enthusiasts who are called by giddy brains the defenders of the peoples but whom I call their poisoners – let them come stir up to effervescence the dregs of states; let them nourish restlessness and disquiet in legitimizing insurrections by the inalienable right to revolt; let us oppose them, not by argumentation, but by experience... The history of Geneva before our eyes, we shall see liberty destroying itself continually by its attempted self-aggrandisement. Twenty happy nations have received chains while looking for a government without abuses, and not one has found it. (quoted in Acomb 1973, p. 97)

In 1789, in the *Mercure*, Mallet would complain of the French Revolution in the same terms. He never assumed, as Burke did, a position of reverence towards the old regime. 'He approves of the ends of the Revolution of 1789 but rejects the means', argued Jacques Godechot (Godechot 1972, p. 75). For Mallet, it was clear that the French seigneurial system, like the Genevan political hierarchy, was in need of reform; here, he supported Jean-Joseph Mounier, who proposed transforming the Estates General into a unicameral body, in a new union of *bourgeois* and *noblesse*. What Mallet objected to was what he repeatedly referred to as the 'democracy of the rabble' (*démocratie de la canaille*). Thus, he offered limited praise to the August decrees which abolished feudal privilege, but feared the *jacquerie* accompanying it. As soon as the attack on aristocracy threatened to become a generalised attack on property, he deplored it. As the Revolution progressed, Mallet became more and more hostile to what he saw as a utopian disregard for history and experience from 'the horrible faction of Jacobins' (quoted in Acomb 1973, p. 249). 'One does not remake men like decrees', he exclaimed in a different context in March 1790 (quoted in Acomb 1973, p. 81).

He expanded on this theme in his book of 1793, the *Considérations sur la Nature de la Révolution de France*, which he wrote in Switzerland after fleeing France as an émigré in May 1792. 'Ah! When you aspire to lead men, you must take the trouble to study the human heart' (Mallet du Pan 1793, p. 71). This was exactly what the Revolutionary Convention, in his view, had failed to do, with its total neglect of experience, a side-effect of its fanatical enthusiasm. 'It is absurd to talk ceaselessly of principles, where one only finds circumstances', was Mallet's pragmatic position (Mallet du Pan 1793, p. 77). For this reason, he distanced himself as much from the royalist counter-revolutionaries as he did from the 'brigands' who had usurped France (Mallet du Pan 1793, pp. 14, 21). The royalist die-hards were far too limited and parochial in their outlook. They did not see that 'Every European is today party to this final combat of civilisation' (Mallet du Pan 1793, p. v). For Mallet, the hope was that the coalition forces might be able to save France from anarchy and save Europe from France, though he feared that the outcome of war would actually be military dictatorship (Mallet du Pan 1793, p. 74). The French had forgotten that the aim and duty of all government was 'the protection of families, public peace and settled fortunes' (Mallet du Pan 1793, p. 74).

Mallet du Pan's writing – which through the *Mercure* reached a very wide audience – encompassed many of the major themes of counter-revolutionary thought. His hatred of Condorcian systematising; his belief that history was 'experimental politics'; his love of order in general and monarchical order in particular; his fear that morals were being eroded by revolution; his dislike of popular sovereignty and natural rights theories; his defence of property; his cosmopolitan perception that the French Revolution was not merely French but necessarily European; his obsession with balance: all these motifs would be reiterated in counter-revolutionary writings across Europe for several decades. These motifs, moreover, were not in Mallet part of some irrationalism, but a continuation of the reform-minded moderation that characterised his writings before the Revolution. The example of Mallet shows that it was possible to be counter-revolutionary without being 'counter-enlightenment'. However, not all counter-revolutionaries were so moderate. Partly because of his Calvinist background, and partly because he did not share Montesquieu's or Burke's belief in intermediary bodies, Mallet du Pan was not particularly exercised by the de-Christianisation process instigated by the Revolution. While he deplored the 'pitiless fury' with which clergy were being persecuted, he had less antagonism towards their expropriation and the abolition of clerical

privilege (Godechot 1972, p. 75). For other counter-revolutionary theorists, however, religion – or irreligion – was at the heart of what was wrong
with revolution; these were those thinkers of the 1790s often dubbed the
'theocrats'.

2   Joseph de Maistre and Louis de Bonald: throne and altar

Joseph de Maistre (1753–1821) and Louis de Bonald (1754–1840) were
nearly exact contemporaries who each acknowledged the kinship they
found in the other's work. 'I have never thought anything that you had
not previously written, nor written anything that you had not previously
thought', Maistre wrote to Bonald (quoted in Godechot 1972, p. 101). Both
began their political careers from a platform of pragmatic reform. Maistre,
who was first a *Substitut*, then a senator in his native Savoy, showed himself
in his pre-revolutionary writings to be an enemy of despotism and an advocate of reformed monarchy, who hoped, in true Montesquieu-like form,
that strengthening intermediate bodies (the *parlements* in France and the
Senate in Savoy) would be enough to check the abuses of the monarchies
of Europe and thereby shore them up. 'It is necessary to repair continually
if one does not want to see the edifice collapse', he explained (quoted in
Darcel 1988a, p. 179). Bonald was more strongly reformist. As the mayor
of Millau, a town in the Roquefort-producing and glove-making Rouer-
gue region of France, Bonald spent the 1780s agitating to revive municipal
government and create a Rousseauan spirit of public service, against the
stiflingly centralised Bourbon government (Klinck 1996, pp. 25–34). He
supported both the aristocratic revolution of 1787–8 and, initially, the Revolution of 1789–90, on the ground that this was the best chance to revive
local government. He only made a final break with the Revolution in 1791,
after the controversy over the National Assembly order that clergy must take
a public oath to the new constitution. He fled with his sons to Heidelberg,
where he remained until 1795, working on his *Théorie du Pouvoir Politique*,
published in 1796. Maistre, who had an instinctive dislike of sudden change,
had broken with the Revolution much sooner than Bonald. As early as June
1789, Maistre voiced terror at the transformation of French political institutions. In September 1792, he fled Chambéry for northern Italy (first Aosta
then Turin), moving to Lausanne the following year, where he organised a
kind of spy network to provide the Savoy monarchy with intelligence and
where he also wrote the slim volume that established his reputation, the
Considérations sur la France.

These two works took quite different forms – Maistre's *Considérations* was explicitly concerned with the current affair of the French Revolution, whereas Bonald's *Théorie* was much more loftily abstract, outlining the fundamental laws of human existence since the beginning of time. Both works, however, were in agreement on the absolute interrelatedness of religion and politics. 'We are all attached to the throne of the Supreme Being by a supple chain that restrains without enslaving us', is the *Considérations'* famous opening line (Maistre 1994, p. 3). The French Revolution, for Maistre, was a fundamentally 'anti-religious' event, which through its attacks on Christianity, simply confirmed that every important institution in Europe was 'Christianised'. '[R]eligion mingles in everything, animates and sustains everything' (Maistre 1994, p. 42). Bonald agreed: civil society, for him, consisted of the union of religious and political society.[4] What this meant was the union of a revived church with a revitalised monarchy.

During the Restoration period and after, Maistre's reputation – through his book *Du Pape* (1819) – was that of the ultimate ultramontane Catholic, an orthodox defender of the papacy against the 'Gallican liberties' of the French Church. In *Du Pape*, Maistre genuinely hoped to convert atheists to faith and those of other Christian faiths to the Roman Catholic Church. He had spent the years 1803–17 at the court of Tsar Alexander where he had tried to convert many of his Russian Orthodox friends to Catholicism, with some success. Maistre's grander aim in *Du Pape* was to reinvest the papacy with the glory it had had in the Middle Ages, before it was weakened by the Reformation and the enlightened attacks of the eighteenth century. He makes the argument that the pope is the true architect of the splendour of Europe; and that France is a providential nation intended to carry on the work of Rome in a secular sphere (Armenteros 2004, pp. 103–9; Maistre 1852). Maistre lamented that French kings had become infected with Jansenism and Gallicanism, which led to uncertainty and prevented them from carrying out their vocation. Political rulers, he argued, must resdiscover their similarity to the pope – to be the entity which 'governs, and is not governed, that judges and is not judged' (Maistre 1843, p. 16). Carl Schmitt was influenced by Maistre when he wrote that the sovereign 'is by its very nature the decisive entity' (Schmitt 2007, p. 43; see also Spektorowski 2002 for the similarities and differences between Maistre and Schmitt). 'Infallibility in the spiritual order and sovereignty in the temporal

---

4 Preface to *Théorie du Pouvoir Politique*, Bonald 1864, I.

order are two perfectly synonymous words', wrote Maistre in his 'Lettre sur le Christianisme' (quoted in Lebrun 1965, p. 135).

An attachment to infallibility, however, was not the same as orthodoxy. Both Maistre and Bonald took their defence of the social utility of religion so far that it went beyond standard Catholic dogma. Maistre's outlook was shaped at least as much by youthful immersion in illuminist and Masonic writings (and practice) as it was in the orthodox teachings of the church, but he does not seem to have found the two to have been in conflict (see Buche 1935; Dermenghem 1979). The real enemy was unbelief. In the *Considérations*, he predicted a 'fight to the death between Christianity and philosophism' with the predicted result being a 'rejuvenated' Christianity (Maistre 1994, p. 47). Bonald, too, imagined half a century of increasing irreligion giving way to a new strengthened Christianity, again with some unorthodox elements. The *philosophes* were wrong to suppose that religion was an interior affair. Religion was what held a society together. Bonald continued Rousseau's dream of finding a civic religion analogous to Roman paganism; unlike Rousseau, he imagined that Catholicism could be remodelled to become this religion. In his *Théorie du Pouvoir Politique*, Bonald proposes erecting a vast civic building in the shape of a pyramid, a gigantic sign of triadic power where great national rituals such as burials and coronations would take place – a temple of providence (Klinck 1996, p. 76).

Providence and sacrifice were central to Bonald and Maistre's politics. 'With man begins religion; with religion begins sacrifice', wrote Bonald (Bonald 1864, I, p. 493). He took Condorcet's belief in the indefinite perfectibility of man and transformed it into the indefinite perfectibility of social institutions; this was what he called his 'religion of society' (Klinck 1996, pp. 97, 78). On the part of individuals – in whom Bonald scarcely believed – this would require the progressive subordination of the self into the divine whole. 'All men are unhappy, because all are mortal; thus they are all punished; thus they are all guilty; thus the will of all, the love of all, the strength of all are thus necessarily depraved or unregulated' (quoted in Quinlan 1953, p. 52). Maistre was equally preoccupied with the problem of evil. He shared with the *philosophes* a belief in the Newtonian exactness of the workings of the universe; he refers to God as the 'Eternal Geometer', a veritable cliché of the eighteenth century. Unlike them, he clung to a belief in particularised providence as well as general providence; Maistre used the enlightened deist image of God as a watchmaker (Maistre 1994, p. 3), yet also kept a fiercely anti-deist conviction that God could interfere with the timepiece of human history whenever and wherever He liked: 'Providence willed that the first blow be struck by the Septembrists, in order that justice itself would be debased' (Maistre 1994, p. 6).

This made the problem of evil an acute one. 'Evil is on the earth and it cannot have come from God', he writes in his *Examen de Rousseau*, yet how could it not have come from God, without denying God's omnipotence? (quoted in Lebrun 1965, p. 31). Maistre's answer was that evil was 'punishment'. Therefore, he writes in the *Soirées*, no evil is necessary; but given man's fallen nature, it was nonetheless constant. Man kills butterflies on pins, uses lambs' guts for harps, kills elephants for their tusks and is constantly slaughtering his fellow-man. Such slaughter can be divine, if it becomes a form of sacrifice to restore the balance in human existence. There is a big difference between war and anarchy, for Maistre. One is divine; the other, satanic.

In his anthropological essay, the *Éclaircissement sur les Sacrifices*, Maistre outlined the ubiquity of sacrifice in human existence, tracing, for example, the practice of sacrificing children and wives in Egypt, India, Greece, Rome, Carthage, Mexico, Peru and Europe before the time of Charlemagne (Bradley 1999, p. 44). The famous passage on the executioner in the *Soirées* is not a plea for the virtue of violence *per se*, but a description of the kind of blood-letting that in his view can prevent other bloodshed from becoming anarchy. '[A]ll greatness, all power, all social order depends upon the executioner; he is the terror of human society and the tie that holds it together. Take away this incomprehensible force from the world and at that very moment order is superceded by chaos, thrones fall, society disappears. God, who is the source of the power of the ruler, is also the source of punishment' (quoted in Berlin 1994, p. xxviii). Isaiah Berlin famously argued from Maistre's preoccupation with violence that he was a forerunner of fascism (Berlin 1990). Recent scholarship, however, has disputed this thesis on the grounds that Maistre – like Bonald and unlike many fascists – was deeply concerned with the question of legitimacy (Bradley 1999; Spektorowski 2002). In this light, Maistre in fact appears anti-fascist – if the label of fascist were not, in any case, an anachronism. The choice, for Maistre, was 'not between liberalism and tyranny but between legitimate authoritarianism and totalitarian tyranny' (Spektorowski 2002, p. 302). Far more terrible for Maistre than the executioner was what he called the state advocated by the 'cowardly "optimists" of the Directory, a state in which no law was enforced, in which people committed suicide out of sheer demoralisation' (Maistre 1994, p. 86).

The point of politics, in Maistre's view – which the Revolution illustrated for him in horrible detail – was to manage disorder and violence. The question, then, was which political form could perform this task best. Maistre rejected the notion that there was one form of political rule that was best for all nations. He expanded on Montesquieu's science of the relation between national characteristics and form of government: 'despotism for one nation is as natural, as legitimate, as democracy is for another' (quoted in Lebrun 1965, p. 84). But 'if one asks which government is the most natural for man, history is there to answer: it is *monarchy*' (quoted in Lebrun 1965, p. 84). Counter-revolutionaries often appealed to Egypt as proof that the first and most legitimate political form was monarchy. Bonald went further: 'There is no public society except royal monarchy' (Bonald 1859, I, pp. 34ff.). Mixed government, he called 'political polygamy' (Bonald 1845, p. 96). The great task of the current age was to reinvest the crown with sacred power, something which could not be done by following any kind of English model. Bonald had at least three objections to the British brand of monarchy: it was mixed; it had allowed 'the disorder which female succession can produce' (Bonald 1859, I, pp. 77–8); and, above all, it was *protestant*, which meant that the monarch was not a proper sovereign at all.

Bonald and Maistre shared the belief that Protestantism had sown the seeds of a fatal individualism whose logical consequence was the disorder of revolution. 'What is a protestant?' asked Maistre. 'He is a man who protests.' Protestantism was, 'positively, and literally, the sans-culottisme of religion', and therefore 'the great enemy of Europe . . . the fatal ulcer which attaches itself to all the sovereignties and continually consumes them, the son of pride, the father of anarchy, the universal dissolvent' (quoted in Lebrun 1965, p. 138). Bonald concurred that the Reformation had led inexorably to the loosening of the bonds that held society together. Protestantism was a foolish form of egoism. 'Deregulated self-love' would always lead to revolution, in Bonald's opinion, because men could only flourish in a well-ordered society founded on religion and sacrifice (Bonald 1864, I, pp. 493–6). Maistre and Bonald were both preoccupied with what Maistre called the 'generative principle' of society: where did power come from? The answer, for both of them, was that it came from God.

Their belief in the divine origins of power shaped Bonald's and Maistre's attitude to constitutions. This is not to say that scepticism about *a priori* constitution-building was the exclusive preserve of theocrats. Even without their divine-right conception of sovereignty, Mallet du Pan had already denounced the Jacobin avidity for creating laws: 'Europe cannot tolerate a legislator' (quoted in Goldstein 1988, p. 56). However, Bonald and Maistre took the argument further. Their dislike of excessive legislation was not just a question of pragmatic stability, but one of principle. If power was godly, then it must follow that men could never constitute it. Therefore, the revolutionary constitutions were at best pointless and at worst destructive. Bonald distinguished 'constituted' and non-constituted societies; the former were made by God, the latter by men. Maistre, similarly, betraying the influence of Vico on his thought (Vico's *verum-factum* principle according to which it is only possible to have true knowledge of that which one has created), insisted that 'Man can modify everything within the sphere of his activity, but he creates nothing; such is his law, in the physical world as in the moral world' (Maistre 1994, p. 49). The notion that men could create a constitution by deliberation and reflection was absurd. 'Nothing great has great origins' (Maistre 1994, p. 49). 'No constitution is the result of deliberation' (Maistre 1994, p. 49). The 'prodigious' and escalating number of laws passed by the National Convention was, to Maistre, a sign of its weakness.

Their profound antagonism towards man-made laws created a problem for Bonald's and Maistre's political thought, as well as for counter-revolutionary thought in general. Where was post-revolutionary regeneration to come from, if not from yet more laws? Blood and sacrifice provided Maistre with part of his answer. But as for the realm in which the regeneration was to take place, it was in the very fabric of society. This was the only way that the 'contrary of revolution' could be sufficiently spontaneous to accord with God's providence. It has been said that Bonald and Maistre were 'among the first to identify the social with the political realm' (Bradley 1999, p. 24). Their narrow, religious conception of power had the perverse effect of vastly widening the scope of the rest of their politics, to encompass the family, customs and economics. Having relinquished man's pretence to make constitutions, the traditionalists now focused on an area which he *could* influence (again, the echo of Vico is very strong), namely society itself. Many commentators have identified a link between Bonald and the early socialists on this basis. But what has been less often recognised is that Bonald's and Maistre's interest in society led them to a Rousseauan preoccupation with the virtue of women as a safeguard of good politics, a preoccupation which was directly contrary to the proto-feminist spirit of the Fourierists and Saint-Simonians.

3   Maistre and Bonald: women, power and mœurs

Mallet du Pan commented that, in previous eras, when there were changes in the political order, most people had remained outside the fray. Now, however, 'revolutions have penetrated to the very roots of society' (quoted in Goldstein 1988, p. 12). It was one of the original aspects of counter-revolutionary thought to 'identify the social with the political realm', to insist that 'customs and habits, gender and family relations, religion and economics' were all *political* questions (Bradley 1999, p. 24). This goes some way to explaining the affinity between the counter-revolutionaries and the early French socialists, notably the Saint-Simonians who read and admired both Bonald and Maistre. It may also explain the claims of certain twentieth-century sociologists that Bonald was a sociologist *avant la lettre* (see Nisbet 1944). In much of the *content* of their social-political thought, however, Maistre and Bonald had little in common either with nineteenth-century socialism or twentieth-century sociology. Their aim in opening up the parameters of the political was largely to close off social change, particularly for women.

Maistre and Bonald were especially upset by the way the Revolution infiltrated the family, infecting the manners of women and children. When Maistre denounced the French Revolution as 'radically bad', he cited in particular the way in which young French girls had lost their modesty, laughing at 'disgusting details' which would make men blush (Maistre 1994, pp. 38–9). The so-called 'liberty sanctioned by the revolution' had created 'horrible outrages'. 'Marriage has become legal prostitution; there is no more paternal authority, no more fear of crime, no more shelter for the indigent' (Maistre 1994, p. 86). In a work with the ironic title, *Bienfaits de la Révolution Française*, Maistre accused the revolutionary government of possessing 'an immoral principle, a corrupting power inseparable from the order of things' (Maistre 1884, VII, p. 385). Making use of various pieces of published testimony, he describes France during the Terror as a place where every aspect of the social economy is degraded, where forests are destroyed and roads rendered impassable, where prostitution is at its height, where a woman can be guillotined the day after giving birth, where revolutionary soldiers will rape women before and after they are dead, where naked girls could be used in the place of religious sacraments, where all are killed without distinction 'of age or sex' (Maistre 1884, VII, pp. 394–5, 494–5). Such debauch, argued Maistre, proved that the French Republic was fundamentally illegitimate (Maistre 1884, VII, p. 396). There was hope, however, in the character of women themselves. Maistre scorned Helen Maria Williams, a republican writer, for having written to the liberal journal *La Décade* regretting that Frenchwomen had not taken more part in the patriotic fêtes of the Revolution.[5] Maistre called Williams a 'madwoman' for thinking like this. In Maistre's view, women were 'excellent judges of honour', especially Frenchwomen, who were 'more womanly than all the women in the universe' and this was why they had remained untouched by revolutionary fervour (he conveniently overlooked here the extent to which women actually did participate in revolutionary festivals) (Maistre 1884, VII, pp. 406–7).

As this encounter between Maistre and Williams hints, the virtue of women was a fiercely contested prize in the political debates of post-revolutionary France. By the 1790s, it was a well-worn cliché that while men made laws, women were responsible for manners ('les hommes font les lois; les femmes font les moeurs'). Much has been written about the countless attempts of republicans of the 1790s to co-opt women as a tool in the regeneration of French morals. The Idéologue Jean-Baptiste Say was typical, when he expressed the hope, in his republican utopia *Olbie*, that virtuous women could republicanise the corrupt old manners of France, thereby enabling republican institutions to take root. However, the counter-revolutionaries were no less vociferous in claiming the virtue of women for their own project of social regeneration along monarchical lines. Moreover, in many cases, they drew on the same ideological sources as the republicans to make their case, most notably the conception of women promulgated by Book Five of Rousseau's *Émile*.

In *Émile*, Rousseau argues that women must always be judged in accordance with their function as mothers, even in cases when they have not in fact had children. Bonald was in complete agreement with this; like Rousseau, he claimed that the morals, and thence the political order of any society required that women recognised their vocation for motherhood. 'Every being has an end towards which it must reach', wrote Bonald. 'The natural and social end of woman is marriage, or the accomplishment of her duties, in her family, towards her husband and her children' (Bonald 1864, I, p. 84). Therefore, the entire education of women must be geared towards the instrumental role they play as wives and mothers (Bonald 1864, I, pp. 783–6). Bonald argued that licentiousness or sexual freedom was actually oppressive for women, since it prevented woman from fulfilling her natural

---

5 *La Décade Philosophique*, 1798, no. 23, p. 306.

function in life. Primarily, however, Bonald was not concerned with the happiness of individual women but with the unity of family and thence the unity of the social body. His favourite example of the way that the behaviour of women could either uphold or destroy the social order was divorce.

Du Divorce, first published in 1801, was Bonald's most widely read work and provided the main intellectual impetus behind the legislation to first modify and then repeal (in 1814) the French divorce law of 1792 (see Klinck 1996, pp. 105–14). Most of its arguments had already been stated in outline in the *Théorie du Pouvoir Politique*, where Bonald deplored divorce as 'disastrous for public morals' (Bonald 1864, I, p. 622). In *Du Divorce*, Bonald was determined to refute the idea that divorce was a private or isolated affair.

How is it possible to treat divorce, which splits up the father, mother and child, without speaking of society, which unites them? How can one deal with the domestic state of society or the family, without considering the public or political state which intervenes in its formation to guarantee stability . . . ? (Bonald 1864, II, pp. 9–10)

Marriage was, for Bonald, not a matter of individual caprice, but (and he used the phrase knowingly) 'a *truly* social contract, the founding act of the family, whose laws are the foundation of all political legislation' (Bonald 1864, II, pp. 37–8). Marriage even preceded Christianity; yet it had always been a religious act as well as a civil one. Bonald insisted that marriage related to all of the fundamental questions of power and duties (Bonald 1864, II, p. 41).

Divorce, argued Bonald, was of a piece with the democracy that had reigned 'for too long in France under various names' (Bonald 1864, II, p. 41). Divorce was political because it was directly contradictory to the principles of hereditary and indissoluble monarchy that Bonald upheld. This extreme antagonism to divorce was shared by other counter-revolutionaries. In *Du Pape*, Maistre praised the papacy for having resolutely maintained 'the laws of marriage against all the attacks of all-powerful libertinage' (quoted in Lebrun 1965, p. 148). This insistence on the marital bond was mirrored by opponents of the Revolution elsewhere in Europe. In Germany, Justus Möser lamented the efforts of the *Aufklärung* to give illegitimate children the same rights as legitimate ones and argued that 'it is unpolitical to give the unmarried condition the same condition as a married one, since a firmly united family is of far greater value to the state than a group of men and women living in fluctuating free love' (quoted in Epstein 1966, p. 332). In

Berne, Karl Ludwig von Haller argued that one of the best ways to combat revolution was to 'protect family relations, this initial germ, this initial model of all monarchy' (Haller 1839, I, pp. 134–5). Similarly, in Bonald's theory of unity, the state and the family must always be in harmony. In cases where there was order in the state and disorder in the family, one of two things would happen. Either the state would regulate the family and restore order – which was Bonald's hope; or the family would deregulate the state and give rise to 'universal materialism', an untrammelled chaos of selfishness and insubordination.

Bonald's horror of divorce was consistent with his tripartite conception of power. In *Legislation Primitive*, Bonald stated that authority structures were always trinitarian: God, Jesus, Disciples; Sovereign, Minister, Subjects; Father, Mother, Child (Bonald 1864, I, pp. 1201–20). For Robert Nisbet, Bonald's tripartite conception of power was a sign of his pluralist commitment to the social group (Nisbet 1944, p. 323). What Nisbet does not say is that, viewed from the point of view of women, it was not pluralist but profoundly anti-individualist. Bonald deplored French 'philosophy' for treating fathers and mothers as nothing more than 'males' and 'females', like animals. Bonald observed that whereas animals had no choice about reproduction, for humans, reproduction was voluntary. This was what gave it its moral dimension, and this was what made it so vital that libidinous impulses be channelled through the order of the family. The members of the family must never be seen as individuals, but always as relative beings, inextricably tied to one another. Thus, Bonald refused to speak of 'men and women', preferring always to speak of 'mothers and fathers'. There is no mother without a father, he observed, whereas a woman could exist without a man, an idea which seems to terrify him (the reviewer of *Du Divorce* in the *Journal des Débats* concluded, with some justification, that Bonald's system turned women into slaves) (Klinck 1996, p. 115). The mother in Bonald's political theory, more explicitly even than in Rousseau's, was the glue holding the whole of civil society together. She was 'the middle point' between the boundaries of father and child, 'passive for conceiving, active for producing', the pupil of her husband but the teacher of her child (Bonald 1864, II, pp. 45–6). As the nineteenth century progressed, romantic counter-revolutionaries would turn the figure of the mother into a poetic idol. Chateaubriand, who shared Bonald's opposition to divorce, heroised the Christian wife as 'an extraordinary being, mysterious, angelic' (Chateaubriand 1978a, p. 51). But for Bonald, the value of the mother is not her poetry but her role in maintaining power.

Du Divorce takes to an extreme the motif which had been used by count-less political thinkers from Montesquieu onwards of woman-as-civiliser – the idea that women were both shapers and signs of the current state of civilisation and political order. The motif would be revived in 1803 by the Vicomte Ségur in his mammoth three-volume history of women and, more radically, in 1808, by the socialist Charles Fourier in his *Theory of the Four Movements*, which made the 'progressive liberation of women' the foun-dation of all social progress. Bonald shared with these others a belief that the state of women provided a key to reading the political state. Where he departed – dramatically – from them was in his refusal to assign to women the slightest individual agency.

Bonald sees the desires of women as a terrible political threat (Bonald 1864, I, p. 785). *Du Divorce* sought to establish the principle that the state had the power to intervene everywhere. 'Government', as he wrote in the *Théorie du Pouvoir Politique*, 'can form private morals and public morals' (Bonald 1864, I, pp. 836–43). Bonald effectively eradicates any notion of a private sphere; in later works, he even suggested that the state should have the power to decide who can and cannot marry. In place of divorce, Bonald calls for a return to the old pre-revolutionary law of legal separation – *séparation de corps* – but on newer, and much harsher terms (Klinck 1996, p. 112). In such cases, neither parent would get the children, who would be taken into custody by public officials. All separated wives, even victims of domestic abuse, would be placed in religious institutions, whereas men would have no punishment except being excluded from performing public functions. Why? Because 'the same disorders are more criminal in women than in men' (Bonald 1864, I, p. 841). Bonald was quite clear about the political desirability of institutionalising women who had separated from their husbands – to 'make disappear from society the scandal of a being who is outside of her natural place, of a wife who is no longer under the authority of her husband, and of a mother who no longer exercises authority over her children' (quoted in Klinck 1996, p. 113). Such a being, for Bonald, is an enemy of the state, the equivalent of the man in Rousseau's *Social Contract* who chooses to 'renounce everything'.

Bonald's writing on women demonstrates that for all his insistence on absolute power, his real conception of power was as something fragile. His politics, like that of so many other counter-revolutionaries, was actually founded on a precarious, not to say neurotic, balance, which could be unsettled by something as slight as a woman choosing to leave her husband.

The theme of balance played itself out in a different way in the German followers of Burke, to whom we will now turn. For these Burkean counter-revolutionaries, balance – often in the form of the balance between different estates in society – was the answer to political security.

4 The German Burkeans

The concept of equilibrium or balance was at the heart of the political thought of Friedrich von Gentz (1764–1832), as befits a figure mainly remembered now as adviser to Prince Klemens von Metternich (1773–1859), Austrian chancellor at the time of the Congress of Vienna (Godechot 1972, p. 117). Gentz desired equilibrium between states – along the lines of the Metternichian system of the balance of power – but also equilibrium within the state itself. When Gentz attacked the French Revolution, it was as an event that had unsettled political balance, in a 'bottomless anarchy' that both disturbed the security of Europe and deformed the equilibrium of French society itself (Gentz 1977, p. 52). Revolutionary dreamers of a levelling equality had forgotten, Gentz argued, that society must always rest on a finely calibrated balance between intelligence, wealth and birth (Droz 1949, pp. 381–5). The only equality which mattered to Gentz – equality before the law – was secured by protecting rather than attacking the rights and privileges of corporations and the other bodies which held the nation together (Reiff 1912, p. 47).

Gentz's initial response to the French Revolution, however, was one of great enthusiasm (see Paternò 1993, p. 29). Until April 1791, his intellectual position had been Kantian (following a course of study at the University of Königsberg), something which distinguishes him decisively from Bonald and Maistre. He espoused 'the idea of an indefinite perfectibility', and defended, in the *Berlinische Monatsschrift*, the concept of natural right against the conservative thinker Justus Möser (Droz 1949, p. 374). This changed gradually after he first read Burke's *Reflections*, which he discovered, to his surprise, he preferred to 'a hundred insipid panegyrics on the Revolution' (Droz 1949, p. 374). As the so-called second French Revolution was unleashed in 1792 with the attack on the Tuileries Palace and the September Massacres, Gentz became increasingly Burkean. In 1793, the year of the Terror proper, Gentz published a translation of Burke in which he praised Burke for his astonishing clairvoyance in having seen in the enthusiasm of 1789 an embryo for the Terror of 1792 (Droz 1949, p. 375; Godechot 1972,

p. 116). In 1794, he followed this up with a translation of Mallet du Pan's *Considérations*, which he called the most powerful and profound work ever published (Godechot 1972, p. 117).

The mature position of Gentz *vis-à-vis* the Revolution is perhaps most clearly seen in a later work (published in Philadelphia in 1800 in a translation by John Quincy Adams, the future US president), comparing the 'origin and principles' of the American Revolution and the French Revolution. Just before it appeared, Gentz had attacked the belief in the identity of the two revolutions as 'one of the most widespread errors of the time'. Where the American Revolution was moderate, the French Revolution was violent. Where the American Revolution had clear, precise objectives, the French Revolution had terrifyingly amorphous aims, which allowed it to escalate into an 'offensive frenzy', a 'horrible labyrinth' (Gentz 1977, pp. 49, 70). Gentz praised the American revolutionaries for their sense of political balance, quoting with approval the Philadelphia Congress of 1776, which insisted that 'we ask only for peace, liberty and security... we demand no new rights' (Gentz 1977, p. 45). He contrasted this with the giddy claims of the Declaration of the Rights of Man and Citizen. The French 'were so proud as to think they could bend impossibility itself' (Gentz 1977, p. 69). If only the French Revolution had stayed within the bounds of law, it could have been legitimate; instead, the 'usurpers' 'dethroned the king, suspended the constitution' and 'proclaimed a republic' without 'so much as a legal pretext' (Gentz 1977, p. 41). Gentz contrasted the brash novelty of the French Revolution with the measured, empirical approach of the Americans, giving thanks that the American republic had taken on 'the mild, moderate, considerate tone' of Washington rather than the 'wild, extravagant, rhapsodical declamation of a Paine' (Gentz 1977, p. 57).

Gentz's antagonism to 'wild' democracy was mirrored by other German thinkers with rather different intellectual backgrounds. In contrast to Gentz's Prussian, Kantian *bildung*, Ernest Brandes and August-Guillaume Rehberg (who influenced the German Historical School of Law) were both Hanoverians and Anglophiles. Together with A. L. Schlözer and L. T. Spittler, two professors at the University of Göttingen, they made up the 'Hanoverian school' of 'moderate-to-conservative *Aufklärer*' who gradually rejected the French Revolution (see Beiser 1992, ch. 12). Much has been written, from Marx onwards, of the 'absence of a German political tradition' in the eighteenth century (see, for example, Reiss 1955, p. 2). The thought of Brandes and Rehberg bears this out, to the extent that their political concerns seem to have been shaped more by England and France than by Germany. In 1789, Rehberg began a deep study of the British constitution under the guidance of Brandes at the University of Göttingen (Droz 1949, pp. 360ff.). At first, the Hanoverians welcomed the Revolution. 'How wonderful', wrote Schlözer in 1789, that France had 'thrown off the yoke of tyranny', sweeping aside old feudal abuses (Beiser 1992, p. 30). However, when it became clear that the French would not adopt a British-style constitutional monarchy, the Hanoverians became much more critical. Rehberg saw the Revolution as an attempt to apply Kantian reason without the necessary supplement of a Humean sense of History (Beiser 1992, p. 305). Brandes had met Burke in England in 1785 and both he and Rehberg were influenced by Burke's ideas. Brandes lamented that very few members of the French National Assembly had been to England. He bemoaned the eclipse of Montesquieu in French opinion by a 'Rousseauist-americano-economist' clique (Droz 1949, p. 355). Like Burke, Brandes identified in the French Revolution the unfortunate consequences of rationalist doctrines and a belief in indefinite human progress. Rehberg, too, disliked the Revolution's utopian neglect of experience and accused the National Assembly of destroying the executive power, creating a dictatorship of the legislative.

In addition to Burke, Rehberg and Brandes were able to draw on older traditions within German thought to make their attacks on the Revolution. In contrast to Gentz's cosmopolitanism, Rehberg and Brandes favoured prejudice and the particularity of a nation, sentiments which long before 1789 had already been expressed by Herder with his *Volksgeist* and Justus Möser (1720–94) with his *Patriotic Fantasies*. Brandes argued that the French constitution of 1791 was so 'inadequate to the real needs of the country, that one can in no way tell if it was made for the French or for every other people of the world' (quoted in Droz 1949, pp. 359–60), words which echoed Maistre's dry comment that he had met 'Frenchmen, Italians, Russians, etc.', but he had never met Man in general (Maistre 1994, p. 53). Brandes linked the 'French anarchy' with the French love of abstraction, observing that the German respect for tradition was greater; there was no need for Brissot or Condorcet in Germany, Brandes loftily remarked.

This anti-abstract tradition of thought had a deep effect on the dominant political ideas of the next generation in Germany. Both the 'revolt against reason' of the more conservative German romantics and the Historical School of Law of Savigny provided a continuum with the Burkean antagonism towards system-building. What unified these thinkers was their defence of history and the state against novelty and the individual. Some of these themes are very clearly expressed in a lecture given by the romantic Adam Müller, a close friend of Gentz, on 22 November 1808:

Do not all unfortunate errors of the French revolution coincide with the illusion that the individual could really step out of the social contract, that he could overthrow and destroy from outside anything that does not please him, that the individual could protest against the work of thousands of years, that he need recognise none of the institutions he encounters, in brief, it is the illusion that there really exists a fixed point outside the state which anyone can reach and from which anyone can mark new paths for the great body politic, from which he can transform an old body into a completely new one, and can outline for the state in place of the old imperfect, but well tried constitution, a new one which will be perfect at least for the next fortnight. (Lougee 1959, p. 634)

This 'illusion', for Müller, as for every thinker we have so far considered, whether in France or Germany, was contingent on two other 'errors' that haunted counter-revolutionary thought: the doctrine of popular sovereignty and the idea of the social contract.

5   The attack on popular sovereignty and the social contract

Whatever else it may have been – Catholic or Protestant, secular or theocrat, Anglophile or Anglophobe, for or against intermediary bodies, moderate or extreme – counter-revolutionary thought of the 1790s was always profoundly anti-democratic.[6] In the 1990s Stephen Holmes categorised Maistre as 'antiliberal'. But as Holmes himself recognises, this is an anachronistic label (the word 'liberalism' did not come into common usage until around 1821) (Holmes 1993, p. 5). It is also problematic, given that Holmes includes Montesquieu on the side of the 'liberals' against the 'antiliberals', when, as we have seen, Montesquieu was in fact an important source for counter-revolutionary ideas. Calling Maistre and other counter-revolutionaries 'antiliberal' – like calling them 'fascist' – is, in any case, less accurate than calling them anti-democratic. Maistre himself referred to his 'antidemocratic ideas' (Lucas 1989, p. 107). Even those on the pragmatic end of the counter-revolutionary spectrum, such as Gentz and Mallet du Pan (who approved Pope's dictum that 'For forms of government, let fools contest'), were hostile to any claims of the sovereignty of the people, which

6 This observation is made by Goldstein 1988, p. 7, though he does not extend his discussion to German political thought.

Gentz, in 1809 called 'the wildest, most wicked, most dangerous of all chimeras'.[7]

How could popular sovereignty be dangerous *and* chimerical at the same time? For counter-revolutionaries, it was dangerous precisely because it was chimerical. As the Jesuit Abbé Barruel expressed it in his *Question Nationale sur l'Autorité et sur les Droits du Peuple* in 1791, the sovereignty of the people was a 'negation' of sovereignty (Goldstein 1988, pp. 21–35). The sovereign, he feared, 'will be mutilated, cut into millions of pieces, if, in order to conceive of the unity of these powers, it is also necessary to conceive of their being divided among each citizen among the people as a whole'. If government was to be *for* the people, it could not possibly be *by* the people because sovereignty required authority which required superiority and 'I am not superior to myself', insisted Barruel (quoted in Goldstein 1988, p. 26). In speeches to the National Assembly in 1791–2, Deputy Maury and Deputy Mounier repeatedly insisted that 'the sovereignty that comes from the people can never return to the people' (quoted in Goldstein 1988, pp. 61–2).

The counter-revolutionary antagonism to popular sovereignty partly derived from a contemptuous view of 'the people' as a rabble. As Rehberg had it, the French Revolution was a monstrous event because it justified itself as representing the sovereign people, when in reality the people was 'an uneducated and apathetic multitude' (quoted in Droz 1949, p. 363). It was a common counter-revolutionary trope to denigrate the people as childish. As Chateaubriand said, 'The people are children; give them a rattle without explaining the cause of the noise it makes and they will break it in order to find out' (quoted in Goldstein 1988, p. 89). Or, as Maistre quipped, 'the people' when considered as part of the government was 'always childish, always foolish and always absent' (Maistre 1994, p. 35 note).

But if the counter-revolutionary dislike of popular sovereignty was partly prejudice, it was prejudice underpinned by theory. For Maistre, the very notion that sovereignty had ever resided in the people was questionable. In his *Étude sur la Souveraineté*, he wrote:

The people is sovereign, they say; and of whom? Of itself, apparently. The people is therefore subject. Surely there is something vague here, if not an actual mistake, because the people which commands is not the people which obeys. It is thus enough to state the general proposition: 'The people is sovereign', to feel that it requires a commentary. (Maistre 1870, p. 177)

7 Quoted in Reiff 1912, p. 47; from *Aus dem Nachlasse*.

Maistre himself, needless to say, supplied this commentary: 'The people is a sovereign which cannot exercise sovereignty' (Maistre 1870, p. 178). Bonald agreed. 'Despite their pretended sovereignty, the people do not have any more right to depart from the political constitution . . . than . . . to stray from the unity of God' (quoted in Goldstein 1988, p. 50). He used the preface to his *Théorie* to show that popular sovereignty was nonsensical and not supported by history.

Men who have been honoured with the title of political metaphysicians and in whom all the metaphysics is the obscurity of a false mind, and all politics the desire of a corrupted heart, have put forward that sovereignty resides in the people. This is a general or abstract proposition; but when one wants to find the application in history, one finds that the people has never been and never can be a sovereign: because where would be the subjects when the people is sovereign? If one wishes that sovereignty resides in the people, in the sense that it has the right to make laws, it turns out that the people has never made laws anywhere, that it is even impossible that the people should make laws, that it has never done it, and that it can never do otherwise than adopt the laws made by a man called for this reason legislator: moreover, to adopt laws made by a man is to obey him; and to obey is not to be sovereign but subject, and perhaps slave. Finally, if one pretends that sovereignty resides in the people, in this sense that the people delegates the exercise of it in naming those who will fulfil the various functions, it turns out that the people does not nominate anyone . . . but that a convened number of individuals, convened to be called people, individually nominates whoever seems good to them, in observing certain public or secret conventions . . . However, these conventions are not truths; because human conventions are contingent. (Bonald 1843, I, p. 18)

As this suggests, the counter-revolutionary opposition to democracy was linked to an opposition to the concept of an original contract, and to the related discourse of natural rights. Here, the counter-revolutionaries took up where Hume had left off in his essay 'Of the Original Contract' (Hume 1994b; see also Bongie 1965). Hume had objected that the 'original contract' was an unrealistic proposition, since the kind of primitive human beings who existed in the putative 'state of nature' must have been incapable of the kind of reflection and choice needed to make a contract. The original contract, observed Hume, was 'not writ on parchment, nor yet on leaves or barks of trees' (Hume 1994b, p. 188).

Rehberg, similarly, attacked contract theory as utopian, complaining that it was based on a misreading of both history and human nature: individuals in society were simply never free and equal in the way that advocates of a social contract supposed they were (Droz 1949, p. 363). Maistre called the social contract a theory 'in opposition to the facts' of history (Maistre 1870, p. 47). 'There never has been a state of nature in Rousseau's sense, because there never has been a moment where human art did not exist' (Maistre 1870, p. 470). Or, as Calonne insisted, in terms reminiscent of Bentham, no matter how many 'pompous labels of eternal, inalienable and imprescriptable' are attached to rights, men still did not have them in the days when they 'wandered without law' (quoted in Goldstein 1988, p. 112). There were no rights without positive laws, no laws without society and no society without government.

Karl Ludwig von Haller, a Bernese professor of constitutional law (and one of Hegel's most important intellectual adversaries) who wrote the mammoth *Restauration der Staatswissenschaft oder Theorie des Naturich-geselligen Zustandes, der Chimare des Kunstlich-Burgerlichen Entgegengesetzt* (1816–34), based his entire political science on the rejection of social contract theory. He discarded not only Sieyès, Locke and Rousseau but also Montesquieu, Grotius, Hobbes and Pufendorf, announcing a 'restoration of political science' to echo the restoration of European monarchies. The effect of the social contract, argued Haller, was to render all current states illegitimate. The baneful effects of this 'false philosophy' were being seen in the revolutions in Greece, Spain and Portugal. Politics, Haller insisted, was not artifical, but both divine and natural; as was the family (Haller shared Bonald's views on the divine origin of marriage); as was monarchy (Haller 1824–75, II, pp. 22, 209). The social contract attributed legislative power to the people; but for Haller law was nothing else than 'the will of the prince', in whose person force and judgement were united. The state was founded not on a social contract but on a series of particular private-law relationships – what Haller called the 'patrimonial state'. While rejecting natural rights, Haller upheld male property and inheritance rights, speaking of the 'eternal' quality of primogeniture (Haller 1824–75, II, pp. 65ff.). States were cemented by fathers passing on to sons, whether a property-owner to his successor or a king to a prince. Haller treated the idea of an original contract as an attack on paternal authority.

Not all counter-revolutionaries were equally extreme in their attitude to contract theory and rights. For Calonne, and for Mallet du Pan, the belief that individual natural rights were specious did not entail a rejection of the individual *per se*. For the more traditionalist counter-revolutionaries, however, it did. The belief in natural rights, they argued, was a mistake with devastating consequences for the body politic, as the Revolution, they believed, had shown. For Bonald, there was no such thing as an individual, only social beings all tied, first to their families and then to the power of the state. Adam Müller denounced the state of nature as 'the unhappy doctrine that man can, at his pleasure, enter and leave the state like a house through a continuously open door' (quoted in Reiss 1955, pp. 150–1). Maistre, too, insisted that government was in 'no way a matter of choice' (Maistre 1870, p. 503). The only 'rights of the people' were those conceded by a sovereign (Maistre 1994, p. 50). Man was not, as Rousseau had indicated, naturally good. Man was both sociable and corrupt and therefore in need of government. The alternative to government – here Maistre agreed with Hobbes – was a state of war. In opposition to the natural rights of the revolutionaries, Maistre proposed the higher law of God, that cloudy law which alone was the determinant of right even if men themselves could only comprehend this higher law imperfectly.

In other words, Maistre's political thought, like that of the other traditionalist counter-revolutionaries, was an attempt to reinstate the authority of divine natural law against the revolutionary claims of individualist natural rights. Counter-revolutionaries sought to reappropriate the authority of Rousseau's *volonté générale* and to reinvest it with the religious overtones which it had lost.[8] 'In place of the general will, the divine will', wrote Haller (Haller 1824–75, I, p. xlviii). Broadly speaking, they accepted Rousseau's distinction between the will of all and the general will. The French Revolution, said Bonald, was an attempt to substitute 'particular will' for 'general will' (Bonald 1864, I, p. 338). 'Law has so little to do with the will of all that the more the will of all is involved, the less it is law', argued Maistre (quoted in Goldstein 1988, p. 47). What Maistre and his fellow counter-revolutionaries could not accept was first, that the general will was artifical and second, that the general will should be in any sense tied to the will of 'the people'. As Bonald wrote, monarchy alone could maintain the general will by rendering it perpetual through hereditary succession (Bonald 1864, I, pp. 175–84). This attachment to natural law partly explains the ultimate obsolescence of counter-revolutionary political thought. Marc Goldstein has called French counter-revolutionary writing the swansong of natural law, because the concept of natural law was 'so radically transformed after 1789 as to be unrecognisable' (Goldstein 1988, p. 15). Moreover, as mass democracy took hold and became a fact, the counter-revolutionary belief that it was fictitious seemed increasingly moribund. Robert Nisbet argued that there was not much difference between Bonald's criticism of democratic despotism and Tocqueville's (Nisbet 1944, p. 328). But there was this difference: Tocqueville recognised that he lived in a 'democratic

---

8 On the religious origins of 'volonté générale', see Riley 1986.

age'. The counter-revolutionaries had misread history; and since history, for them, was 'experimental politics', this left them with very little. In 1796, Maistre had famously bet 'a thousand to one' that the city of Washington would never be built 'and that it will not be called Washington and that the congress will not meet there' (Maistre 1994, pp. 60–1). By the time of Andrew Jackson, such a view seemed both absurd and quaint.

This is not to deny that counter-revolutionary political thought persisted long into the nineteenth century. Indeed, counter-revolutionary 'romantic' thinkers such as Chateaubriand, Victor Hugo and Lamennais, dominated French literary life during the Restoration period as well as that of the July Monarchy. But as counter-revolutionary thought became aestheticised, its political meaning became transformed. The final section of this chapter will consider the figure of Pierre-Simon Ballanche, in whose writing counter-revolutionary thought made the surprising transition from right to left.

6   Pierre-Simon Ballanche and the end of the counter-revolution

Though he was a generation younger than Bonald and Maistre, the early career of Pierre-Simon Ballanche (1776–1847) was typical of the Catholic Traditionalists. The son of a pious Lyon publisher, Ballanche and his family exchanged an initial sympathy for the Revolution with fear and hostility after the execution of Louis XVI and the de-Christianization campaign of Year II (McAlla 1998, pp. 10–17). Ballanche, a sickly young man, spent the Terror outside of Lyon at Grigny, the estate of his maternal grandparents (McAlla 1998, p. 17). On his return to Lyon after the fall of Robespierre, he was horrified at the ruination – personal, economic and architectural – that he saw. His first work, *Épopée Lyonnaise* (*c.*1795) commemorated the victims of the revolutionary siege of Lyon (McAlla 1998, p. 18). He followed this with a more theoretical work, *Du Sentiment*, written in 1797, but not published until 1801, after Bonaparte's Concordat with Pope Pius VII made the publication of Christian sentiment seem less dangerous than hitherto (McAlla 1998, p. 22).

Much of *Du Sentiment* could have been written by Maistre himself, or by Ballanche's acquaintance François René de Chateaubriand, whose best-selling *Génie du Christianisme* appeared on 8 April 1802, just after Napoleon's Concordat with Pope Pius VII was ratified, ushering in a revival of the Christian faith in France (Chateaubriand 1978b; Godechot 1972, p. 134). Later in life, the mercurial Chateaubriand became an 'Ultra', vehemently attached to monarchy and restoration. In this work, however, he stressed the idea that Christianity, as well as being beautiful and poetic and the source of all great art and literature, was the foundation of political freedom. *Génie du Christianisme* treats religious feeling not as the theocratic base of politics, but as the guarantee of liberty, of humane politics for the 'paupers and the unfortunates who make up the majority of the earth' (Chateaubriand 1978b, Book 6, ch. 5). In a reversal of Maistre's mystical executioner, Chateaubriand sees Christian worship as something that will save the masses from such frequent recourse to the executioner's blade. 'In the present state of society, can you repress an enormous mass of peasants – free and far away from the eye of the magistrate; can you, in the *faubourgs* of a great capital, prevent the crimes of an independent populace without a religion that preaches duties and virtues to all? Destroy religious worship, and you will need a police force, prisons and an executioner in every village' (quoted in McMahon 2001, p. 129). Chateaubriand's argument was not predominantly utilitarian, however. If Christianity was useful as a mechanism of social control, it was only because it was true. *Génie du Christianisme* is a plea for sincerity against those men who 'destroy everything by laughing' (Chateaubriand 1978b, Introduction).

Ballanche shared this Rousseauan attachment to sincerity. Like Chateaubriand, Ballanche defended Christian feeling and suffering – something he knew a great deal about, having endured an excruciating trepan operation that left him in constant pain – against the false, sterile rationalism of the *philosophes*. The central theme of *Du Sentiment* is Christian expiation – the salutary sacrifice that alone can lead to salvation. Like Maistre, Ballanche saw the Revolution as divine punishment for the impiety of France. Again, like Maistre – whose *Considérations* Ballanche had read closely – Ballanche insists that political and social institutions have divine origins and cannot be engineered by men, condemning these 'audacious politicians' who believe they 'have it in their power to classify the human race at their whim, and to arrange empires like sections of a garden' (quoted in McAlla 1998, p. 43). He attacks, moreover, what he takes to be the individualism of Rousseau's social contract, since 'man is born for society'. Ballanche sees the Revolution as a wholly profane occurrence, which can only be redeemed through the suffering of its victims – such as the heroes of the Lyon siege – and the grace of God's providential order. So far, Ballanche was in tune with earlier counter-revolutionaries.

During the Resoration period, however, in the years 1818–20, Ballanche modified his social theory in a direction which earned Maistre's disapproval and took him far closer to liberals such as Constant. In his *Essai sur les Institutions Sociales dans leurs Rapports avec les Idées Nouvelles* of 1818, Ballanche grafted a new component of progress on to his theory of the divine nature of social institutions. Maistre complained that Ballanche's 'excellent heart' had become corrupted by a 'revolutionary spirit'. In fact, Ballanche was still opposed to the notion of popular sovereignty, but he had now added into his political theory a notion of popular consent. Providence, he now argued, worked gradually to increase equality in the civil realm, in line with Christian equality. The only way for French monarchs to retain their legitimacy was to move in the direction of Fénelon's ideal king and away from absolutism. Those kings were most legitimate who showed the greatest Fénelonian love for their people. Ballanche famously remarked that Maistre was the 'prophet of the past' because he sought to return France to a social order whose time had passed, whereas Fénelon was the 'prophet of the future' (quoted in McAlla 1998, p. 325).

In 1827, Ballanche took the idea of social progress still further, with his new concept of 'social palingenesis', which was a self-conscious attempt to link the liberty of the liberals with the unity of the right-wing Ultras (Ballanche 1833, IV; see also McAlla 1998, Part Three, 'Social Palingenesis'). In biology, 'palingenesis' was the theory, associated with Charles Bonnet, that living beings contain within themselves a tiny pre-formed structure, which only has to be fertilised to start growing. This, coupled with some illuminist currents of esoteric history, gave Ballanche the idea that each historical era contains within itself the germ of the next age. Thus Ballanche could simultaneously hold to the notion of divine providence – because the initial germs were all made by God – and that of human progress – because certain humans (whom Ballanche called 'initiators') had the power to bring these germs to fruition. Moreover, the direction of history was democratic: each change in era brought nearer the gradual emancipation of the whole human race. The hero of Ballanche's history is not the king but the plebeian. Ballanche restores the element of individual will to 'volonté générale'. When new European revolutions took place in the 1820s – in Spain, Naples, Piedmont and Greece – Ballanche welcomed them as a sign of providentially governed social evolution. In contrast to Maistre, Ballanche now saw revolutions as part of Christian history, rather than a departure from it; Maistre and Bonald had failed, he wrote, 'to understand the new facts' of the 'new society' (Ballanche 1833, II, p. 348).

By the late 1820s, with the Restoration well underway, there was a new tradition of Catholic social thought in France emerging, sometimes labelled 'neo-Catholicism', which moved many erstwhile counter-revolutionaries far from the sentiments of the 1790s. In the days following the July Monarchy of 1830, the Abbé Lamennais, once an ultraroyalist and now a democrat, called for 'God and liberty', a fusion of democracy and religion. This was a new progressivist faith, which found support from such figures as Victor Hugo and the poet Alphonse de Lamartine, the latter calling for a 'parti social' that would transcend the constrictions of class and speak for the whole of society (see Bénichou 1977; Berenson 1989). In this era of religious revival socialist ideas mingled with Catholic romanticism. 'What is socialism?' asked Louis Blanc; the answer being 'The Gospel in action' (Berenson 1989, p. 545). The impetus for this new union of Christianity and the left came in part, as Edward Berenson has argued, from the failure of the revolutionary tradition. The abortive insurrections of 1834 and 1839 moved those on the left to reject the 'violence and conspiratorial politics' of the revolutionaries and turn towards 'a new source of change, one that would be peace-loving, unifying, and spiritual' (Berenson 1989, p. 544). At the same time, some on the right began to see the democratic potential in the fraternal ideals of the early church.

Ballanche – who found new admirers among the socialist Saint-Simonians and Fourierists – now saw the whole period from 1789 to 1830 in France as representing an 'époque palingénsique' which would usher in a new phase of peaceful social unity based on progressive Christianity. Ballanche now expressed horror at Maistre's insistence that capital punishment was an eternal feature of political society; he sensed a gathering European-wide rejection of the practice: society must cease to punish by blood (Ballanche 1833, IV, pp. 316–17). Nor could he agree, any longer, with Maistre's diagnosis of the Revolution as irreligious. To the contrary, it had provided the chance for a new religion, a new Christianity – the religion of society at large. Like Bonald and Maistre, these Catholic progressives of the 1830s wanted to bring the Revolution to an end. Unlike them, they sought not to negate it, but rather to complete it.

2

Romanticism and political thought in the early nineteenth century

JOHN MORROW

In the early decades of the nineteenth century European intellectual life was enriched by the works of composers, painters, poets and writers who were influenced in a variety of ways by the spirit of 'romanticism' (Porter and Teich 1988; Schenk 1979). Romantic ways of thinking had deep roots in early modern culture but between about 1800 and 1850 they played a particularly significant role in theoretically framed statements on fundamental political questions. Issues of definition and taxonomy bedevil the study of romanticism, but at the risk of some oversimplification it is possible to identify three concerns that were shared by a range of prominent exponents of political romanticism. These writers were all preoccupied with the epistemological and moral importance of feeling and imagination; they developed a distinctive notion of the individual; and they stressed ideas of community.

Although romanticism is sometimes associated with a rejection of reason and a preference for aesthetically conditioned intuitions, it was more common for romantic writers to claim, with Coleridge, that 'deep thinking is attainable only by a man of deep feeling; . . . all truth is a species of revelation' (Coleridge 1956–71 [1801], II, p. 709). One important insight that romantics derived from revelation was the idea that human beings were infinite creatures who possessed affective, moral and religious potentialities that could not be captured by enlightened rationalism. Furthermore, they believed that these potentialities could only be recognised within 'organic' communities, that is, historically anchored, complex social groupings reflecting the interdependence of their members and embodying values that corresponded with the requirements of their natures. Communities of this kind were unified entities, recognising the moral status of their members and appealing to them on the basis of affective values that were integral to

The author wishes to thank Colin Davis, Mark Francis, Diana Morrow, Jonathan Scott and Andrew Sharp for commenting on earlier versions of this essay; John Roberts provided invaluable research assistance.

humanity, producing harmony and symmetry in social relationships and in the inner life of individuals. For these reasons, romantic writers frequently discussed politics in language that was more often employed in aesthetic discourse.

Despite these common perceptions, romanticism did not give rise to a unified political theory. Some of the differing political implications of romanticism were closely related to the generational placement of different writers, while others can be traced to the national context. For example, a number of romantic figures in England and Germany had been broadly sympathetic to the French Revolution and were associated with radical reformism in domestic politics. However, their mature political theory (a product of the years when Britain and the German states were struggling to resist Napoleon) was both conservative and nationalistic. By contrast, certain English and French writers whose political writings were a product of the post-war years produced radical and progressive varieties of romanticism. In addition to these generational differences, one can also relate divergences in political romanticism to national context. For example, while conservative romantics in England were warmly attached to the traditional constitution, those in Germany had to contend with the taint of absolutism which had, they believed, disfigured the recent theory and practice of government in the German states. Their conservatism thus had a 'restitutive' aspect: they sought inspiration in the more distant past and were hostile to the ideas and practices of European politics immediately prior to the Revolution (Saye and Löwy 1984, pp. 63–4). The outlook of these writers differed from that adopted by French figures. In that country romantics became reconciled to the transformations wrought by the Revolution and directed their intellectual energies to identifying institutions that would serve the needs of a modern political culture.

Since generation and context are cross-cutting to some degree, the discussion of political romanticism that follows will be structured so as to take account of both of these considerations. It is arranged in three sections. The first will examine the conservative romanticism of Samuel Taylor Coleridge, Robert Southey and William Wordsworth in England, and of Adam Müller, Novalis, Friedrich Schlegel and Friedrich Scheiermacher in Germany.[1] The second section will sketch briefly the radical critique of

---

[1] Novalis was not a straightforward conservative and his political writings were products of the 1790s (Beiser 1992, pp. 266–7). He will be treated here as a writer who advanced ideas which came to play a central role in the conservative romanticism that became prominent after the turn of the century; see Beiser 1992, p. 264.

conservative romanticism produced by Lord Byron, William Hazlitt and Percy Bysshe Shelley. Progressive expressions of political romanticism in the writings of Thomas Carlyle in England, and François René Chateaubriand, Félicité de Lamennais and Alphonse de Lamartine in France will be considered in the final section of the essay. These statements were distinctive because they related romantic themes to the requirements of modernity.

1 Conservative romanticism in England and Germany, 1800–1830

Although many English and German romantics adopted conservative positions after 1800[2] they were not merely reacting against the Revolution and trying to restore what it had threatened or destroyed. To the contrary, they attributed the beguiling attractions of revolutionary doctrines to the shortcomings of prevailing conceptions of the nature and role of government. Traditional institutions were to be revitalised and restored by showing them in the light of romantic preconceptions. Of the two sets of writers, the English were far less critical of inherited political institutions because they did not have to contend with a recent history of absolute government. They were, however, as hostile to many conventional aspects of eighteenth-century thought as they were to the wild and destructive conceptions that they associated with the Revolution. Coleridge, Southey and Wordsworth were deeply alarmed by the thought that philosophical materialism was not unique to French ideologues and their English imitators, but had become part of the furniture of the modern mind. Robert Southey, for example, dismissed the previous century and a half as an age during which men 'have been reasoning themselves out of every thing that they ought to believe and feel', and he cast back to late medieval and early modern England for a model of social and political morality that was free of the incubus of materialism (Southey 1829, 1, p. 5). William Wordsworth venerated the traditional institutions of eighteenth-century England and praised the socially acquired and largely unreflective habits of Burke's 'second nature'. The doctrine of 'second nature' stressed the relationship between the intrinsic structure of the human mind and the institutional, familial and personal experiences of members of historically coherent, traditional communities (Chandler 1984, p. 162). Traditional values were imbued with 'elementary feelings of human nature'; they fostered the 'wisdom of the heart', not the mere

---

2 Beiser (1996, pp. xi–xiii) cautions against reading conservatism back into 'early' German romanticism from the 1790s.

'prudence of the head' which Wordsworth associated with the Enlightenment (Wordsworth 1974d, pp. 242, 240).

These feelings were evoked in Wordsworth's mature poetry, but unlike Southey, who upheld a simple dichotomy between 'calculation and feeling', he sought to replace sterile conceptions of rationality with an emotionally satisfying fusion of feeling and thought. For example, in the preface to *Lyrical Ballads* he claimed that the 'spontaneous overflow of powerful feeling' that marked good poetry was a product of those who, 'being possessed of more than usual organic sensibility had also thought long and deeply' (Wordsworth 1974e, p. 127). Wordsworth later insisted that his affections 'had ever been moved' and his imagination exercised 'under and *for* the guidance of reason' (Wordsworth 1974d, p. 258; cf. Southey 1829, I, p. 79). These remarks suggest a symbiotic relationship between rational discourse and second nature: both reason and imaginative sympathy were reinforced by the wisdom embodied in inherited institutions and the unreflective sense of uncorrupted humanity.

Although Wordsworth retained a place for reason in the operation of the poetic intelligence he harboured a deep-seated animus against philosophical system-building. In particular, he objected to speculative metaphysicians' penchant for fitting 'words to things' (Wordsworth 1974c, p. 103). In a notable passage in *The Prelude* Wordsworth set this criticism in a particular biographical context:

> Thy subtle speculations, toils abstruse
> Among the Schoolmen, and Platonic forms
> Of wild ideal pageantry, shap'd out
> From things well-matched, or ill, and words for things,
> The self-created sustenance of a mind
> Debarr'd from Nature's living images . . .
> (Wordsworth 1991 [1798?], I, Bk. VI,
> lines 308–13, pp. 193–4)

Later in this poem Wordsworth's critique of speculative philosophy became sharper: it was pedantic, obscurantist and related to modes of Enlightenment thinking which were destructive of traditional social and political relationships (Chandler 1984, pp. 235ff.). These charges, which one would have thought might have been levelled at Godwin or Helvetius, were actually directed at Wordsworth's friend Coleridge. They reflected a marked difference in emphasis in their respective understandings of how the Enlightenment could be most effectively combated. While Wordsworth thought that reason could be harnessed to feeling through the images of poetry, Coleridge wished to identify a philosophically coherent alternative to materialism.

At the heart of Coleridge's system lay a distinction between 'understanding' and 'reason'. The first of these terms referred to humans' calculating and discursive faculties, while the second applied to capacities of the human mind which revealed its 'spiritual and supersensuous' aspects. The 'understanding' was developed to varying degrees in different individuals, but 'reason', the source of moral feelings and moral principles of justice, law, right and the state, was common to humankind (Coleridge 1969, II, p. 104n). In *The Friend* Coleridge argued that the state was a product of reason and he traced political obligation to the (frequently unconscious) recognition of its role in promoting moral perfection (Coleridge, 1969, II, p. 126). However, while he insisted that the state was a moral agent, Coleridge strenuously resisted the idea – identified with Rousseau, but also echoing his own 'Jacobin' past – that its structure could be determined by the dictates of morality (Coleridge 1969, II, p. 127; cf. Coleridge 1971, pp. 217–29). To the contrary, questions concerning the structure of government and the distribution of political rights were subject to the influence of time and circumstance and fell within the province of the 'understanding'. Morality determined the ends of the state, but in deciding how these ends could be attained men should not ignore the lessons of experience. Recent events in France showed that political equality would destabilise unequal societies and undermine their capacity to produce the range of moral benefits of which they were capable (Coleridge 1969, II, pp. 103–4; Morrow 1990, pp. 83ff.).

Coleridge traced his conception of reason to the Christian Platonists of the seventeenth century and argued that many of the ills of his own age were a consequence of the displacement of Platonism by philosophical materialism. By the early nineteenth century materialism had left its mark on even the most sincere Christians (Coleridge 1972, p. 43, 1983, I, p. 217; Morrow 1988). This claim received its fullest treatment in the first 'Lay Sermon'. In this work Coleridge described the Bible as the 'statesman's manual', but he insisted that it would serve this function only if it was read through the lens of Christian Platonism. Since this philosophy directed attention towards those infinite forces that made moral perfection a goal for humanity, Coleridge believed that it would furnish a corrective to the materialism that was rife among his contemporaries (Coleridge 1972, pp. 43ff.).

The English romantics' response to materialism concentrated on its harmful effect on social and political morality. Southey endorsed Coleridge's claim that the development of men's moral and intellectual faculties was the yardstick of all social and political arrangements and condemned the mechanical view of humanity that he ascribed to Adam Smith. Smith's philosophy was indifferent to the 'immortal destinies' of humankind, and focused exclusively upon the '*quantum* of *lucration* of which [human beings could] be made the instrument' (Southey 1829, II, pp. 408–11, 1832f, p. 112). Wordsworth, in a similar vein, justified poor relief on the grounds that it was demanded by those 'elementary feelings' that prompted men to exalt human nature, not to degrade it (Wordsworth 1974d, pp. 242, 246). Since these feelings were fostered by traditional institutions and practices, Wordsworth was critical of radical proposals for parliamentary and ecclesiastical reform.

These criticisms dominated Wordsworth's post-war politics, but while the objects of his attention – the Church of England, the unreformed electoral system, a paternalistic state grounded in a complex of localised systems of authority and deference – were those of orthodox 'ultra' Tories, his defence of them bore the stamp of his romantic preconceptions. For example, he defended the Church on the grounds that its teachings militated against the presumptuous idea that matters of public good could be determined solely by the 'specific acts and formal contrivances of human understanding' (Wordsworth 1974d, p. 250). In an earlier address (prompted by the intrusion of metropolitan radicals into the electoral preserve of the Westmorland gentry) Wordsworth made a case for Burke's 'cloak of custom' against the insubstantial fripperies affected by reforming Whigs. The latter relied upon splendid oratorical talents and ardent feelings rashly wedded to novel expectations, when common sense, uninquisitive experience and a modest reliance on old habits of judgement, when either these, or a philosophical penetration, were the only qualities that could serve them (Wordsworth 1974f, p. 158).

At times Wordsworth deployed the language of romanticism for critical and innovative purposes. This facet of Wordsworth's political thought can be seen in *The Convention of Cintra*, written (with some help from Southey) as part of an unsuccessful campaign to induce the British Parliament to disown the agreement by which the French withdrew from the Iberian Peninsula following their defeat at the Battle of Vimeiro in 1808. Like other English romantics, Wordsworth thought that this agreement was militarily and politically unnecessary and morally tawdry. It insulted English, Spanish and Portuguese patriots whose heroism reflected the 'vigour of the human soul' which sprang from 'without and futurity'. These promptings of second nature explained the widespread opposition to the Convention in England:

it exhibited such discordant characteristics of innocent fatuity and enormous guilt, that it could not without violence be thought of as indicative of a general constitution of things, either in the country or the government; . . . it was a kind of *lusus naturae* in the moral world – a solitary straggled out of the circumference of nature's laws – a monster which could not propagate, and had no birthright in futurity. (Wordsworth 1974b, p. 292)

The Convention's promoters and supporters were dead to the principle of justice; they neither 'see nor feel'; they do not understand 'the rudiments of nature as studied in the common walks of life' (Wordsworth 1974b, pp. 281, 306). Wordsworth contrasted this moral blindness with the far-sightedness of those who looked to natural impulses to furnish an invigorated sense of human identification and political loyalty. This sense provided an effective antidote to materialism and a viable basis for politics because the impressions derived from second nature symbolised fundamental and reassuring truths about the human condition. Traditional ideas and behaviour made the present a moment in a seamless, affectively based harmony of past, present and future:

> *Enough, if something from our hands have power*
> *To live, and act, and serve the future hour;*
> *And if, as toward the silent tomb we go,*
> *Through love, through hope, and faith's transcendent dower,*
> *We feel that we are greater than we know.*
> (Wordsworth 1946, III, lines 10–14, p. 261)

Wordsworth's condemnation of a code of military etiquette that permitted a beaten foe to retire from the scene, pointed to a distinction between living and moribund aspects of tradition. Military and civil elites hid behind the past rather than using it as the basis for 'futurity'. Their 'forms, their impediments, their rotten customs and precedents, their narrow desires, their busy and purblind fears' were repugnant both to those who had received unconscious tuition in the school of humanity, and to the philosophic mind which reflected upon the fruits of human experience (Wordsworth 1974b, p. 300). These remarks could have prepared the ground for a critical, or at least an analytical, perspective on inherited institutions and practices, but this option was not taken up by Wordsworth. Traces of the critical implications of *The Convention* can be seen in his post-war support for nation states, but in this period the language of patriotism was often adopted in opposition to the progressive language of citizenship associated with the French Revolution (Cronin 2002, pp. 144–5). Any other reforming impulses that Wordsworth may have harboured gave way to an all-embracing conservatism (Cobbam 1960, pp. 149–51). Wordsworth's reluctance to allow human agency to dispense with moribund institutions and practices was indicative of this tendency. These relics, now portrayed as imaginative, aesthetically valuable backdrops to human life, were likened to

a stately oak in the last stage of decay, or a magnificent building in ruins. Respect and admiration are due to both; and we should deem it profaneness to cut down the one, or demolish the other. But are we, therefore, to be sent to the sapless tree for may-garlands, or reproached for not making the mouldering ruin our place of abode.... Time is gently carrying what is useless or injurious into the background. (Wordsworth 1974f, p. 173)

Like Wordsworth, Southey claimed that the reforms of the constitution proposed by radical publicists would damage the fabric of the state. However, his jeremiads on Catholic emancipation and parliamentary reform were accompanied by expressions of alarm at the impact of rapid and deep-seated economic and social changes (Mendilow 1986, pp. 69–79). Southey argued that in the intellectual and moral climate of the late eighteenth and early nineteenth centuries the rapid growth of manufactures had produced a population that was economically, intellectually and spiritually impoverished. This debasement was an affront to Christian morality and undercut the basis of a stable body politic. In Southey's view the state was sustained through reciprocity, a reciprocity he understood in romantic rather than rational, contractual terms. Material deprivation undercut the sense of self-identification upon which the state was based; it also reflected a general indifference – epitomised for Southey in Malthus' image of a fully occupied table – to the intellectual, moral and spiritual needs of the population. The new industrial towns and the neglected villages of rural England were fetid breeding grounds for active disloyalty to political authority and for hostility towards society (Southey 1832d, pp. 68–107, 1832e, 1832f).[3]

Although Southey emphasised the coercive and protective features of the state, these were only aspects of a form of social and political organisation that was 'patriarchal, that is to say, paternal' (Southey 1829, I, p. 105). In his excursions into history Southey identified this form of government most closely with late medieval and early modern England, but the contemporary relevance of control, protection and human development was underlined

---

3 See Winch 1996, Part III for a historically focused critique of the romantic response to Malthus' doctrines.

by his obsession with Alexander Bell's 'Madras System' of mass education. Southey described Bell's scheme as the 'fair ideal of a commonwealth' because it was based on principles of protective and regulative hierarchy (Southey 1829, I, p. 105). In Bell's schools each pupil was under the control of an older 'monitor', while in Southey's ideal commonwealth, each class within society was subjected to the benign superintendence of its social superiors (Southey 1832e, pp. 227–31).

Traditional institutions formed the basis of such a commonwealth, and Southey insisted that these must be shielded from the corrosive influences of radical agitators. In his post-war writings Southey appealed to the state to use its power to curb radical agitation. However, he also wished to undercut the basis of radical support. One way of doing this was for traditional elites to seize the initiative. Southey therefore urged the upper classes to resume responsibility for the welfare of the lower orders by promoting the regulation of working conditions, the provision of poor relief, opportunities for secular and religious instruction and internal and external immigration (Southey 1832c; Eastwood 1989). These measures, and the change in elite attitudes that was necessary to put them into effect, would ensure that the lower orders received not just the material necessities of life, but also control and guidance. Elite superintendence would foster the populace's intellectual and moral development and attach it to the state. Such attachment was not merely the basis for a *quid pro quo*. For Southey, as for other romantic writers, the benefits that the state produced were not the basis of political obligation; they were aspects of a complex relationship that was underwritten by affective and moral qualities. If the state was to be the focus of loyalty the positive links between political and social authority and the intellectual, moral and religious culture had to be restored (Southey 1829, I, p. 94, II, p. 265).

While Wordsworth pointed to the traditional constitution as a model of political and moral rectitude, and Southey wished to buttress this structure by paternalist conceptions which he discerned in the early modern state, Coleridge extolled the virtues of the Platonists of the seventeenth century. He claimed to have found in their writings the distinction between 'reason' and 'understanding' that was so important in his own political philosophy. He also identified a group of Platonic statesmen – Harrington, Milton, Neville and Sidney – who resisted the early stages of materialism in politics and whose actions were informed by an appreciation of the moral ends of the state (Coleridge 1976, p. 96; Morrow 1988). Coleridge's reverence for these 'red letter names' gave a distinctive cast to his political theory: while acknowledging the virtues of the traditional constitution of church and state, his attitude towards it was tinged with the hues of antique republicanism. He emphasised the moral and religious importance of liberty of conscience, was critical of the Laudian church, and speculated that Oliver Cromwell could have become the head of a 'republican Kingdom – a glorious Commonwealth with a King as the Symbol of its Majesty, and Key-stone of its Unity!' (Coleridge 1980–, II, pp. 1200–1).[4] In addition, Coleridge submitted traditional institutions and practices to the scrutiny of 'reason' in order to ensure that the state played its role in promoting intellectual and moral perfection. This scrutiny formed part of a theory of the state which was more critical and sophisticated than that implied by Southey's and Wordsworth's complaisant endorsement of the constitutional nostrums of early nineteenth-century Toryism.

The most complete account of this theory was presented in *On the Constitution of the Church and State, According to the Idea of Each* (1829). In this work Coleridge discussed the state in relation to the 'idea' of the constitution, that is, in terms of its *'ultimate aim'*, and he identified this with the realisation of the moral ends that he had outlined in *The Friend* (Coleridge 1976, p. 12, 1969, II, pp. 201–2). This approach was important because Coleridge allowed that historical features of the state may not adequately realise its end. It could not therefore be claimed, as Southey, Wordsworth and many other Tories did, that the existing system of government should be preserved in its entirety (Coleridge 1976, pp. 13, 19; Coates 1977, p. 502; Morrow 1990, pp. 131–2). Coleridge's analysis of the constitution rested on a distinction between the 'constitution of the state' (the legislative and executive arms of government and the 'free powers' of extra-parliamentary institutions) and the 'constitution of the nation' which embraced both the state and the national church. The 'nation' formed an organic whole that was sustained through the principle of balance, but this principle was at work also within the 'state'. Parliament focused and balanced interests connected to landed and commercial property. These interests embodied fundamental moral and social forces ('progression' and 'permanence') whose interrelationship allowed society to reap the benefits of commercial activity without abandoning the more stable, ethically directed values which Coleridge and many of his contemporaries identified with landed proprietorship (Coleridge 1976,

4 See also Coleridge 1980–, I, pp. 250, 358, 805 and II, p. 951 for criticisms of the Laudian church. Coleridge was at times exasperated by what he saw as the reactionary politics of both Southey and Wordsworth; see, for example, the letter to William Godwin dating from December 1818 in Coleridge 1956–71, IV, p. 902.

pp. 23–5). The socially beneficial balance of these proprietorial interests was facilitated by the unifying impulses produced by the Crown, and was augmented by the interaction between Parliament and the invigorating but potentially destabilising influence of extra-parliamentary forces (Coleridge 1976, pp. 41–2; Morrow 1990, pp. 133–40). 'Permanence' and 'progression' were not 'interests' in the conventional sense and were not part of a mechanical balance. Rather, they were aspects, or moments, of an organic social and political order. They were important because they embodied complementary states of mind that reflected 'progressive' and 'permanent' forces within society, not because of their physical mass. Coleridge used the language of balance as an electro-magnetic, not as a mechanical metaphor.[5]

The moral significance of landed property was emphasised in Coleridge's second 'Lay Sermon' of 1817, a work produced in reaction to the hardship and dislocation that accompanied the peace of 1815. He claimed that the ends of landed property were identical with those of the state and attributed many of the ills of post-war Britain to an 'overbalance of the 'commercial spirit' (Coleridge 1972, p. 169). These remarks reflected Coleridge's concern that the landed classes' endorsement of commercial values was undermining an essential counterpoise within the state. The cupidity and extravagance of the gentry was given an air of intellectual plausibility by the faddish 'science' of political economy, but Coleridge insisted that this discipline did not adequately specify the duties and responsibilities of statesmen or the landed gentry (Coleridge 1972, pp. 169–70, 210–16; Kennedy 1958; Morrow 1990, pp. 115–21).

At the heart of this critique of political economy and of the gentry's seduction by it, was a romantic view of the implications of enlightened rationalism. Like Southey and Wordsworth, Coleridge believed that the self-interested practical materialism of the gentry was a consequence of the

---

5 See, for example, the references to 'poles' (Coleridge 1976, p. 24 note * and p. 35). John Colmer points to a parallel between Coleridge's conception of polarity and those of his German contemporaries; 'the dynamic unity of nature, of life, and of thought was conceived as arising from a synthesis of opposing forces' (Coleridge 1976, p. 35 n3). A strong theory of polarity plays an important role in Müller's political thought (see p. 54) but I can find no evidence that Coleridge was aware of his work. Coleridge's interest in aspects of German thought has been widely studied (see, for example, Harding 1986; MacKinnon 1974; Orsini 1969), but there is little to suggest a direct link between his political ideas and those of German romantic writers. Schlegel's *Geschichte der alten und neuen Litteratur* (1815) played an important role in Coleridge's literary lectures in 1818–19, but apart from this there are only brief references to Schleiermacher's writings on prayer in his correspondence and notebooks and a short, not politically interesting comment on Novalis in his marginalia (Coleridge 1987, II, pp. 32, 46, 53–61, 1956–71, VI, pp. 543, 545–6, 555, 1980–, II, p. 958).

philosophical atmosphere of modern society, but his response to this was highly intellectual. He looked to Christian Platonism to dispel modes of thought and action that were intellectually shallow, theologically barren and politically and socially disastrous. Consequently, Coleridge called for a revival of 'austerer studies' – principally philosophy and theology – among the educated classes, and for the diffusion of the intellectualised religion and the moralised intellect that he identified with Platonism (Coleridge 1972, pp. 24, 39, 105–7, 193–5, 199; Morrow 1990, pp. 121–5).

This proposal for a revitalisation of the moral and intellectual attitudes of elites related closely to Coleridge's insistence that the 'idea of the constitution' must include a *national* church.[6] He claimed that a clear understanding of the essential features of this institution was particularly important in the moral and political climate of early nineteenth-century England. Not only was the country menaced by the overbearing attractions of an unchecked spirit of commerce, but the institution responsible for correcting this spirit, the Church of England, was threatened by proposals to remove constraints upon the political status of Dissenting Protestants and Roman Catholics. Unlike Southey, Coleridge was not implacably opposed to the repeal of the Test Acts or to Catholic emancipation, but he insisted that relief measures should not threaten the 'national' status of the Church of England (Coleridge 1976, pp. 11–12, 147–61; cf. Southey 1832b).

Although Coleridge's treatment of national churches drew heavily upon his understanding of the history and structure of the Church of England, he regarded them as necessary features of moral states (Allen 1985, pp. 90–1). The Church incorporated the 'clerisy', a body that was responsible for creating an intellectual and moral climate which encouraged secular elites to fulfil their true role within the state (Coleridge 1976, pp. 42ff.; Knights 1978, ch. 2). This role was a disinterested one which reflected the universal, moral purpose of the state (Coleridge 1990, I, pp. 187–8; Gilmartin 2007, pp. 207–52; Morrow 1990, pp. 143–6). The clerisy should identify with communal rather than sectional interests and in order to facilitate this it was endowed with property dedicated to *national* purposes. Utilising conventional claims concerning the relationship between proprietorship and independence to

---

6 This institution was quite distinct from the 'Church of Christ'; it was national rather than universal and was, as Coleridge put it, independent of 'theological dogmata' (Coleridge 1976, pp. 133ff.; Morrow 1990, p. 149). For an account of the importance of this distinction see Morrow 1990, pp. 152–4. Coleridge's ascription of a moralising and educational role to the Church and his insistence that it must be free from political interference, is very similar to the conception of the church found in some of Schlegel's earlier writings (Schlegel 1964, pp. 169–70), but this view underwent significant modifications; see below.

defend ecclesiastical property, Coleridge argued that the material endowment of the Church insulated the clerisy from the misuses of political power.
He signalled the special status of Church property by a terminological distinction; it formed the 'Nationality' while private properties were part of
the 'Propriety'. Taken together, they were the 'two constituent factors, the
opposite, but correspondent and reciprocally supporting counter-weights,
of the *commonwealth*, the existence of the one being the condition, and the
perfecting of the other' (Coleridge 1976, p. 35).

The 'Nationality' provided the means for counteracting the intellectual and moral sources of the abuse of personal property. For Coleridge,
therefore, endowed national churches had a crucial role to play in early
nineteenth-century Europe where commercial expansion reinforced existing inequalities and generated new ones. Even in the absence of such
inequality, however, national churches were an essential feature of his romantic conception of the state. This was so because, while Coleridge stressed
the clerisy's impact on elites, he also justified its existence and its privileges
by reference to its general educational role. The clerisy was charged with
the 'cultivation' of the population, with the 'harmonious development of
those qualities and faculties that characterise our *humanity*' (Coleridge 1976,
pp. 42–3). Both in its impact on the elite mind and in their role as 'cultivators', the clerisy nurtured the intellectual, moral and religious values which
lay at the heart of Coleridge's image of a just and social political condition.

After about 1800 leading German romantics took a path that was similar
in some respects to that of their English contemporaries. That is, they developed political statements that repudiated the destructive political radicalism
that they identified with the French Revolution but assumed positions that
were critical of significant aspects of the status quo. German romantics
resisted the narrowly legalistic and mechanical conceptions of government
they associated with eighteenth-century absolutism and with reform initiatives launched in response to the failure of German states to contend with
French military strength (Krieger 1972, pp. 139ff.; Sheehan 1989, pp. 260ff.).
Thus while hostility to the French Revolution and its fruits became a core
theme in German romanticism, the model of monarchy promoted by conservative romantics offered a standing rebuke to that prevalent in the eighteenth century. This point was put with great force in Novalis' claim that
monarchy in general had lost its sense of purpose and been stripped of its
legitimacy before 1789: the kings of France and of most other European
states were 'dethroned' long before the Revolution (Novalis 1969c, p. 28).
Romantics rejected the absolute state because it was incompatible with their

ideal of community and could not, because of its divorce from human values, retain the loyalty of its members. The 'poetic' state as Novalis dubbed
it, must satisfy both the heart and the mind (O'Brien 1995, p. 174). In
response to this requirement, German romantic writers sought to rehabilitate the state by urging their contemporaries to see it as a reflection of the
vital forces which underlay human life, not as the product of a contract or
of the exercise of power (Droz 1963, p. 17). They believed that the state
would only satisfy longings which had been reflected in a distorted and
destructive manner in the revolutionary era if it incorporated the aesthetically and emotionally satisfying sense of community which they associated
with the family.

Like their contemporaries in England, romantic writers in Germany
traced the shortcomings of the eighteenth-century mind to the limitations of Enlightenment epistemology, but they were also critical of the
jurisprudential conception of the state which they associated with absolutism. Romantic attitudes towards the first of these issues were captured
by Novalis' remark that while Enlightenment thinkers were fascinated by
the refraction of light, they ignored the 'play of its colours' (Novalis 1969b,
pp. 508–9). These 'mysterious' and 'wonderful' forces could only be appreciated through the intuitions of the poetic intelligence; they could not be
grasped by reason alone. Müller, whose attitude towards rationalism was
markedly more hostile than that of other political romantics, credited this
intuitive faculty with the capacity to form 'ideas', that is, conceptions of
things in relation to processes of development and as parts of more complete
'organic' wholes. The image of the world conveyed by 'ideas' was far more
complete than that produced by 'concepts' that merely arranged data and
could not capture the complexities of natural or human phenomena. This
distinction could be applied in a variety of contexts. For example, Müller
praised the rhetorical practices of the English House of Commons as expressions of '*the spirit of the living word*', and condemned both speech-reading
and 'science' for their failure to convey or discover the spirit of life (Müller
1978, p. 185; Reiss 1955, p. 156). These failures were not trivial because
Müller believed that the destructive features of revolutionary activity were a
consequence of misguided attempts to reconstruct politics upon principles
that were antithetical to the spiritual dimensions of human life (Reiss 1955,
p. 153).

Romantic critiques of the political fruits of the Enlightenment centred on the shortcomings of legal conceptions of the state. In particular, they refused to accept the claim (common both to the defenders of

eighteenth-century absolutism and to revolutionaries) that the state was a product of a contractual arrangement entered into by bearers of natural rights. They argued that the state must appeal to the affections of its subjects and not merely to their individual interests (Beiser 1992, pp. 236–9; Berdahl 1988, pp. 99–103; Krieger 1972, pp. 53ff.; Scheuner 1980, pp. 23–5). Novalis' warning of the dangers facing a state which attempted to 'square the circle' of self-interest was elaborated upon by Schlegel in a series of lectures delivered in 1804–5 (Novalis 1969c, No. 36). In these lectures Schlegel forged a sharp distinction between 'rational' and 'natural' law and dissociated the latter from individualism by making it the seed-bed of an organic state.

Schlegel claimed that while rational law deified liberty, it failed to explain why it was sacrosanct. Moreover, since it treated collective entities – the family, community or the state – as infringements upon liberty, rational law produced dissolution and discord, not harmony and unity. By contrast, natural law grew out of a unitary social entity, the patriarchal family. This institution was based on a system of authority that sprang from love and loyalty; it thus fostered the moral rather than purely natural relationships that were epitomised in the status of patriarchs. These figures were not merely heads of families; they were also symbols of God who represented the just possibilities of a natural condition (Schlegel 1964, pp. 104–6, 1966, p. 549). However, these possibilities were limited by the family's restricted scope and by the conflicts which resulted from its unilateral exercise of the natural right of revenge (Schlegel 1964, p. 123). Although these tensions were eliminated by the state, Schlegel regarded its regulatory role as of secondary importance. The most significant feature of the state was its embodiment of 'the idea of morality', that is, 'the moral education and perfection of humanity' (Schlegel 1964, pp. 111, 122; cf. Beiser 1992, pp. 255–60). This goal echoed the cosmopolitan visions of early romanticism, but after 1800 Schlegel associated it with the enlarged and unified form of community made possible by the state. The state's role in human advancement made it a moral necessity; this was recognised by its subjects and underlay their attachment to it.

The romantics' insistence that the relationship between the state and its subjects was a consequence of belief, not contract or fear, was a key element in their attempt to replace a legalistic conception of the state with one that relied upon the creation of a sense of communal identity. The state as community was based on affective, other-regarding values such as love, not on legal arrangements that were designed to protect individual interest.

For Schlegel the state was a 'great moral individual', forged by affection and belief, not a mechanical contrivance produced by contract and held together by the power of an absolute monarch or a sovereign people (Schlegel 1964, pp. 122–4; cf. Faber 1978, p. 60).

Müller endorsed these sentiments, but he treated the state as a self-subsistent totality and did not relate it to the universal goal of human perfection. The framework of this account of the state was provided by his conception of the bipolar structure of the natural and social worlds (Müller 1804; Berdahl 1988, pp. 165–6; Klaus 1985, pp. 40–1; Koehler 1980, pp. 20, 53, 59, 79–80, 86, 98; Reiss 1955, pp. 29–30). In politics the conserving and innovating principles of old age and youth, and the masculine principle of law and the feminine principle of love, produced a unity that was focused on the 'idea of the state'. It was, Müller wrote, 'the intimate association of all physical and spiritual wealth [in a] great energetic, infinitely active and living whole. The state is that point in man in which all bodily and mental interests coincide' (Müller 1922, 1, p. 39; Reiss 1955, p. 150; cf. Immerwahr 1970, p. 34).

In common with other German romantics Müller rejected the image of the state as a machine because this implied that mechanical standards could be applied to it.[7] He also resisted attempts to apply natural law doctrines to the state. The 'idea of law' resulted from a polar opposition between a physical or positive element on one side and a 'spiritual or universal and universally valid' element on the other. The coexistence of the positive and the universal produced a system of regulation which mirrored the fluid, expansive character of the state. The 'idea of law' was 'never concluded or completed, but [was] always in the process of infinite and living expansion' (Müller 1922, 1, pp. 41–2; Gottfried 1967, pp. 236–7). Like the state itself, law expressed the common consciousness of an organic community; it was a product of consciousness not the arbitrary creation of the sovereign (cf. Zilkowski 1990, pp. 95–6).

There are close parallels between Müller's critique of the legalistic basis of political individualism and Edmund Burke's anti-individualistic application of the common law tradition in the 1790s. Burke's ideas were well known in Germany and admired by Müller and other contemporaries. German

---

7 The 'mechanistic administration' of the factory state of which Novalis complained (Novalis 1969c, No. 36) had its theoretical counterpart in conceptions of the state as a mighty machine propelled by the self-interest of its subjects and controlled by the absolute power of the monarch. These images of the state were common in the eighteenth century; they are, perhaps, epitomised by August Ludwig von Schloezer's blunt statement that 'the state is a machine' (quoted in Krieger 1972, pp. 46ff., 77).

romantics, however, combined a historical understanding of law with elements that appealed to ideas which had an affinity with patriarchal theories of government (Kraus 2004, p. 203; Sweet 1941, pp. 20–3). Müller, for example, denied that the relationships between members of a state were purely legal. Law was balanced by love, a principle which imbued the state with the aura of familial affection and made it an object of beauty (Koehler 1980, p. 29). Müller believed that these feelings were epitomised in the royal family, but this belief received its most vivid statement in Novalis' paean to the young King and Queen in *Glauden und Liebe oder Der König und die Königin*.

A true royal couple is for the whole person what a constitution is for mere reason. One can only be interested in a constitution as in a letter of the alphabet. If the sign is not a beautiful image, a song, dependence on it is the most perverse of all tendencies. What is law if it is not the expression of a loved, respected person? Does not the mystic sovereign need, like every idea, a symbol and what symbol is more fitting than a splendid person worthy of love? (Novalis 1969c, No. 15)

Novalis endowed the monarch and his consort with mystical qualities to which subjects responded as an act of faith. He derived political authority from the personal, 'charismatic' qualities of the ruler (Beiser 1992, pp. 264, 272; Gooch 1965, pp. 235–6; Scheuner 1978, pp. 72, 76). Since this conception of monarchy required the state to engage the affections of its members it was related to the interest in active individuality which marked early romanticism (Beiser 1992, p. 230). Other vestiges of this concern can be seen in Novalis' disparaging references to the 'indolence' fostered by absolutism, and in Müller's comment that the sovereign should 'stimulate' as well as coerce his subjects (Meinecke 1970, pp. 53, 103–4; Reiss 1955, p. 148). The most thoroughgoing restatement of this theme appeared in Schleiermacher's writings. Schleiermacher thought that community was a product of 'free Sociality' (that is, voluntary, informal interaction) which fostered the integration of individuals who moved towards perfection by pursuing a diversity of ends (Schleiermacher 1988, pp. 183–4, 1967, II, pp. 129–30; Bruford 1975, pp. 82–4; Hoover 1990, p. 252). A pluralistic and decentralised political structure was necessary to accommodate this diversity and Schleiermacher therefore rejected the eighteenth-century model of absolute monarchy. He did not however, reject monarchy completely. To the contrary, he argued that a monarch may serve as an organ of unity reflecting a collective consciousness within a decentralised system of rule. By contrast, the rigid centralisation of the absolute state was a consequence of the weakness of its subjects' collective consciousness. Having repressed the bases of sociability, the eighteenth-century state was forced to create elaborate outward shows of unity (Schleiermacher 1845, pp. 139, 111–12; Dawson 1966, pp. 148–9; Hoover 1989, p. 310).

The fact that Schleiermacher's true monarch symbolised the collective consciousness of the people, not their membership of an all-embracing union which could be compared to the family, gave a distinctively 'liberal' cast to his political romanticism. Even for other German romantics, however, the analogy between the family and the state was not meant to bolster the absolute state by images derived from conventional patriarchal political theory. Novalis' stress upon faith, Schlegel's claim that the state was based upon belief, and Müller's concern with stimulation implied that satisfactory political relationships had to be imbued with distinctive qualities. The monarch possessed personal power that was not derived from consent, but his relationship with other members of the state was qualitatively different from that which existed between an absolute monarch and his emotionally torpid subjects. By relating monarchy to the intuitions of the poetic intelligence, German romantics sought to transform the cool, mechanical severity of the Friedrichean monarch into the authoritative, but emotionally appealing figure of an idealised royal patriarch. In so doing, they focused on the affective and aesthetic needs of human beings; they did not use the image of the family to evoke the *power* of the Father. This point was emphasised by the role ascribed to the female head of the royal family by Novalis (Novalis 1969c, Nos. 30–2, 42) and by Schlegel's remark that 'a family can form itself only around a loving woman' (Schlegel 1996b, No. 126; Beiser 1996, p. 136).

Romantics seemed to believe that by portraying the relationship between sovereign and subject in a new way they could reconcile a strong conception of sovereignty with the moral dignity of the subject (Scheuner 1980, p. 71). They ignored mechanical questions concerning the weight and direction of sovereign power and the forces which might constrain it, and focused instead on the close link between the potentialities of monarchy and the affective and aesthetic requirements of humanity and individuals' sense of identification with and participation in the community. At the height of his political radicalism, Schlegel identified true republicanism with democracy, merely allowing that monarchy might be consistent with emerging or waning republican political cultures (Schlegel 1996a, pp. 102–6). Novalis, by contrast, attempted to promote an idea of republican government that was not hostile to monarchy. This approach echoed earlier formulations of *res publica* ('the public thing') and privileged emotional and psychological identification over representation and popular sovereignty. As Novalis cryptically put it, 'the true king becomes a republic, the true republic becomes a king' (Novalis 1969b, No. 23).

Schleiermacher's identification of a symbolic role for monarchy was very similar to the position taken by Coleridge, but romantic writers in Germany produced far more elaborate accounts of kingships than their English counterparts. This perhaps reflected the practical and theoretical prominence of the monarch in German politics. Since German romantics did not wish to turn the head of state into a constitutional figurehead, it was necessary for them to formulate a radical alternative to the conception of king as state-mechanic which they identified with eighteenth-century absolutism. The novelty and difficulty of this task can be contrasted with that facing the English romantics. They generally endorsed the representative tradition of British government and could pretty much take the constitutional position and the status of the Crown for granted. The only English figure who wished to present monarchy in the guise of emotional patriarchalism was Robert Southey, but he could appeal to history and to aspects of present practice. His attachment to the cult of Charles I as 'royal martyr' provided a precedent, and in 'A Vision of Judgement' (1821), the mantle of true kingship had passed to George III (Southey 1825, chs. XVI–XVIII).

There were also divergences between German and English perspectives on other institutional implications of romanticism. Early in the nineteenth century Schlegel had presented a picture of an Established Church which was very similar to that of Coleridge, but after his conversion to Roman Catholicism in 1809 he identified a judicial and protective role for the papal head of a universal church (Schlegel 1964, pp. 148, 169–70; cf. Schlegel 1966, p. 589). This account, which harked back to Novalis' suggestion that the 'beauty' of medieval faith and the 'beneficent' influence of the Church should be recalled to bring unity to a fragmented Europe, signalled a search for political ideals that were not tainted by the modern world (Novalis 1969b, pp. 500–1, 512–13).

For both Müller and Schlegel the idea of 'estates' was a particularly valuable medieval survival, but it needed to be detached from mechanical conceptions of political representation. This feature of German political romanticism set it apart from Coleridge's attempt to integrate estates into a modern system of representative government. It also challenged those who wished to resolve Prussia's financial problems by endowing estates with a representative role in relation to taxation (Berdahl 1988, pp. 112–15, 124–7; Krieger 1972, pp. 204–5; cf. Hegel 1991, paras. 299–302). Conservative romantics in Germany did not welcome this innovation. While they thought estates should incorporate economic and social groupings, romantics stressed that these institutions were parts of the state, not organs representing sectional interests. Schlegel, for example, rejected the idea that estates should become part of a system of representation along English lines. Such an arrangement was too mechanical for his taste and was also inconsistent with the character and dignity of monarchy. The unity of the state was focused in the monarch and he should retain all political and judicial functions in his hands. He should, however, consult the various estates on matters which affected their particular interests (Schlegel 1964, p. 161).

Estates were part of an organic whole. In the modern world they were of critical importance because they provided a means of integrating individuals within the state so as to minimise the politically and socially dislocating impact of rapid commercial and industrial development. The way in which they performed this role depended on the attitude of the monarch, not upon formal legal limitations of his power (Schlegel 1966, pp. 529–33, 553–4, 584–5). Similar views were expressed by Müller. After toying with a representative role for estates, he focused instead on the harmonious interaction of the principal estates of land and trade, not on their location within a formal system of political representation (Müller 1923, pp. 51ff.). This gave his constitutional pronouncements an air of vagueness but Müller was not interested in analytic precision (cf. Berdahl 1988, p. 180; Schmitt 1986, pp. 126, 132–41). Since he believed that the structure of the state was transmitted by history, Müller did not think that it was possible or desirable for the political theorist to create neat constitutional edifices. Rather, the relics of the past could, if properly understood, serve the present. Estates were important because they provided a focus of identity that located individuals within an organic whole by attaching them to impulses that could be harmoniously related to their polar opposites.

This approach reflected a common romantic concern to imbue the economy with values that were compatible with the harmonious and communal ends of the state. Like radical romantics in the 1790s and like their conservative contemporaries in England, Müller and Schlegel were alarmed at the alienating and socially disintegrating implications of modern economic ideas and practices (Beiser 1992, pp. 232–6; Briefs 1941, pp. 283, 289; Klaus 1985, pp. 48–50; Koehler 1980, pp. 92–9). Some of these unwelcome developments were associated with absolutism, hence Novalis' critique of policies that gave priority to maximising the prince's revenues (Beiser 1996, p. 37 n.8). Others, however, were more modern. In Müller's writings these misgivings gave rise to a sustained critique of the impact of capitalism on the integrated state. The division of labour reduced labourers to 'dead cog wheels' in a mechanical process which did not recognise their humanity and undermined the basis of community; it produced a 'metaphysical chilling of the soul' (Müller 1923, p. 230; 1922, II, p. 217). In response, Müller wanted to alleviate the mechanical aspects of capitalism by evoking the relationships of medieval guilds and the *herrschaft* of a paternalistic nobility (Müller 1922, II, p. 313; Berdahl 1988, pp. 173–9; Hanisch 1978, pp. 135, 139–40).

Müller's feudalisation of society found a parallel in Schlegel's feudalisation of monarchy. He argued that the king should be 'overlord' of all property and should control foreign trade (Schlegel 1964, pp. 127–9; Meinecke 1970, p. 68). The first of these stipulations was meant to ensure that property was used in ways that were consistent with the state's educational calling, while the second not only reduced the risk of domination by those who enriched themselves through trade, but also provided a source of revenue for the state. This revenue would free the state from dependence upon taxation and undercut attempts to introduce mechanical conceptions of representation. In addition, economic dependence was to be avoided because of its harmful effect on the symbolic position of the monarch; it reduced him to the status of a paid servant of his people and thereby demeaned both him and the state by undermining its moral and spiritual dimensions (Schlegel 1964, pp. 129–30).

When those English and German romantics who had been politically active in the 1790s abandoned radical reformism and identified the organic community with the traditional order, they adopted positions which were similar in many respects to those forged by conservative critics of the Revolution. However, romantic ideas gave this conservatism a distinctive character.[8] While adopting the historical perspective on institutions and on social consciousness that was characteristic of the conservatism of the 1790s, these romantics also thought that it was important to present traditional institutions in a new light so that individuals would feel at home in their world. This light had to appeal to the sensibilities of beings whose longing for community, for a sense of belonging, was a consequence of their susceptibility to ideas and institutions that captured the values of affection, beauty and spiritual mystery which were both the products and the focus of the romantic imagination.

---

8 This parallels Nicholas Boyle's comment that in German literature early nineteenth-century romanticism formed a 'loyal opposition' (Boyle 1991, p. 23).

2   The radical reaction to conservative romanticism in the post-war years

Although Coleridge's theory of the state possessed critical potentialities which were lacking in the less systematic accounts of Southey and Wordsworth, it was still sufficiently attached to traditional institutions to confirm the conservative image of the older generation of English romantics in the minds of Byron, Hazlitt and Shelley. In the post-war years these writers reacted sharply against what they saw as the apostasy of their elders and forged a 'cult of sexuality' whose worship was part of a metaphorical, legitimacy-sapping assault on church and state (Butler 1981, p. 132; Francis and Morrow 1994, pp. 27–48; Mahoney 2002; McCalman 1988; Thorslev 1989). At the same time, however, their critique of contemporary society and government differed from that of later romantics in Britain and France. Their contemporary reputation for freethinking and materialism linked them to the liberal pro-French culture of the pre-revolutionary period (Butler 1988, pp. 38, 56) that was condemned by their successors. Moreover, Byron and his contemporaries focused on the political source of oppression and its ideological outposts. While by no means blind to economic injustice, their thinking lacked the critical focus on social and economic developments that distinguished the 'social politics' of later romantic thinkers in France and Great Britain.

Despite Byron's reputation as the *bête noire* of post-war romanticism his political theory was less egalitarian than that of either Hazlitt or Shelley (Murphy 1985; Southey, 1832e). His criticisms of the moral and religious underpinnings of contemporary society, and his search for new and complete forms of harmony compatible with the independence of individuals, yielded a conception of the state which conjured up an aesthetic image of symmetry to convey the mutually supporting interaction of reciprocating, free individuals. Byron's true commonwealth provided the political basis for a harmonious sociability that was not possible within the corrupt, repressive regimes of contemporary Europe. This state was founded on 'shared sovereignty', but its structure was not democratic. As the tragic hero of *Marino Faliero Doge of Venice* (1820) put it

> We will renew the times of truth and justice,
> Condensing in a fair free commonwealth
> Not rash equality but equal rights,
> Proportioned like the columns to the temple,
> Giving and taking strength reciprocal,

And making firm the whole with grace and beauty,
So that no part could be removed without
Infringement of the general symmetry.
(Byron 1980–6, III. ii, lines 168–75; cf. De Silva 1981;
Kelsall 1987, ch. 4; Watkins 1981)

This image of political symmetry recalled antique republics, but Byron projected it into the future, and he looked to aristocratic leaders inspired by the examples of Bolivar and Washington to create and nurture states which reflected the values that Marino Faliero had unsuccessfully attempted to restore in Venice. In his *Ode (from the French)* Byron attributed Napoleon's fall from power to his assumption of a kingly position – 'goaded by ambition's sting, / The Hero sunk into the King / Then fell; – So perish all, / Who would men by man enthral!' – and contrasted his conduct with that of George Washington. Having rid his country of tyranny, Washington presided over the birth of a republic and then retired from the scene, making way for another leader to guide the fortunes of a society of free men (Byron, *Ode (from the French)*, III. ii, lines 32–5; Add. stanza iii, lines 23–4 (1980–6, III, pp. 375–9)).

While Hazlitt shared Byron's views on the repressive nature of post-war government, he was concerned particularly with its effect on literary culture. Southey was a figure of fun for Byron, but Hazlitt regarded him in a far more sinister light. He thought that the Poet Laureate was in the vanguard of a concerted attempt to utilise the persuasive capacities of modern print culture for repressive rather than liberating purposes. Although Hazlitt portrayed individuals as bearers of inviolable natural rights, he thought that their possession of a 'moral sense' meant that personal autonomy provided the basis for a social rather than an abstract and isolated conception of individuality (Hazlitt 1931–4d, pp. 305–20). This sense, a product of what Hazlitt called the 'imagination', was essential to the formation of moral judgements, and in the modern world it was refined through the influence of literature. Because literature allowed individuals to see themselves and their actions as others saw them, it counteracted the blunting effect of self-interest and prejudice; it also created a body of 'public opinion' which modified and regulated the jarring impulses of unenlightened individuality (Hazlitt 1931–4c, pp. 47–50). For Hazlitt, public opinion was a product of the free exchange of ideas and of the sympathetic sociability that resulted from it. Its defining characteristic was tolerance, that is, a marked disinclination to apply physical, social or non-intellectual verbal weapons to those propounding views which diverged from one's own (Hazlitt 1819,

p. 318). Hazlitt believed that Southey and his friends on the *Quarterly Review* had subverted literature to the service of egotism, partiality and repression. They had set up formal and informal barriers to the growth of public opinion, thereby preventing the republic of letters from fulfilling its liberating and humanising role, and retarding the intellectual pluralism which was a precondition for the growth of a true 'public' and a true public opinion (Hazlitt 1931–4e, p. 116, 1931–4b, p. 14). This line of thinking entailed an explicit rejection of Coleridge's claim that culture should be forged by an intellectual elite and provided the focal point for a series of bitter exchanges between these two writers between 1816 and 1818 (Dart 1999, p. 238; Lapp 1999, pp. 67–112).

In responding to these threats, Hazlitt focused on the literary standard bearers of legitimism, but he also criticised the religious and political institutions to which they appealed. He thus attacked the Established Church and the principle of aristocracy and argued for a system of representative democracy (Hazlitt 1819, pp. 307, 318; Cook 1981, pp. 140–1). Hazlitt claimed that the failure to recognise the people's political rights was a corollary of an indifference to general rights. These hallmarks of legitimism could only be erased by a system of democratic representation: 'if the vote and the choice of a single individual goes for nothing so, by parity of reasoning, may that of all the rest of the community; but if the choice of every man . . . is held sacred, then what must be the weight of the whole' (Hazlitt 1931–4d, p. 308).

Shelley's critique of legitimism had much in common with those of Byron and Hazlitt, but his perception of the political implications of liberty was more visionary. In *Queen Mab* he rejected the theory of innate depravity and traced wickedness to the opinions engendered by oppressive political and social relationships:

> Let priest-led slaves cease to proclaim that man
> Inherits vice and misery, when force,
> And Falsehood hang o'er the cradled babe,
> Stifling with rudest grasp all natural good.
> (Shelley, *Queen Mab*, IV, lines 117–20
> (1965d, p. 93))

This critique echoed the arguments about the implications of necessity that had appeared in Godwin's *Political Justice*. It also pointed to the possibilities for human improvement that would be opened up by the abolition of coercive social and political relationships (Dawson 1980, pp. 76–135; Scrivener

1982, pp. 5–34). In *A Philosophical View of Reform*, Shelley advanced a highly critical history of the 1688 Revolution that traced the emergence of a parasitic 'monied' aristocracy that was an ally rather than a rival of the landed classes, and used constitutional monarchy as a vehicle for imposing additional burdens on the general population. He praised the government of the United States on the (erroneous) grounds that its constitution was subject to periodic review by the citizen body. This requirement would narrow the gap between political forms and practices and the real interests of the community that was seen as one of the unavoidable shortcomings of political and legal systems (Shelley 1965b, pp. 24–33, 10–12; Keach 1996, p. 44). But while much oppression could be eradicated through the radical reform of social and political relationships, the success of these measures and the viability of the anarchic condition to which they were a prelude, depended upon nurturing the 'imagination' (Shelley 1965b, pp. 42–55). Shelley believed that a sympathetic interest in the feelings of others was the basis for the voluntary imposition of other-regarding conduct. Sympathy was a product of non-oppressive social intercourse, of experience working on the imaginative faculty, and its development was a requirement of the effective exercise of distinctly human capacities:

Imagination or mind employed prophetically [imaging forth] its objects is that faculty of human nature on which every gradation of its progress . . . depends. . . . The only distinction between the selfish man and the virtuous man, is that the imagination of the former is confined within a narrow limit, whilst that of the latter embraces a comprehensive circumference. (Shelley 1965e, p. 75)

This faculty resembled Hazlitt's moral sense, but for Shelley it was pre-eminently a product of poetry. In his *Defence of Poetry* (1821) Shelley denied that poetry had a didactic role, but he claimed that it encouraged the development of a potentially universal feeling of sympathy. The key element here was the capacity to see others as objects of love, and this, Shelley maintained, provided the basis for non-coercive but orderly human interaction: 'The great secret of morals is love; or a going out of our own nature, and an identification of ourselves with the beautiful which exists in thought, action, or person, not our own' (Shelley 1965c, p. 118).

Love affected both perception and volition. Poetry not only engendered 'new materials of knowledge'; it also stimulated 'a desire to reproduce and arrange them according to a certain rhythm and order which may be called the beautiful and the good' (Shelley 1965c, p. 135). This perception of the role of poetry bridged the gulf between knowledge and motivation that marred Godwin's optimistic rationalism. Poetry enlightened the mind *and* galvanised the will; to 'know' through poetry was to feel the need to realise this knowledge in the moral and political world. Underlying the differences between Byron's antique republicanism, Hazlitt's democratic libertarianism and Shelley's philosophical anarchism was a shared commitment to identifying political forms which reconciled the tension between romantic interests in both active individuality, and in forms of sociability which appealed to the aesthetic, the emotional and the moral forces within human beings. Not only was this problem a distinctly romantic one, but so too were the conceptions of harmony, symmetry, imagination and love that were brought to bear upon it.

3 Romanticism and modernity, 1815–1850

In 1833, looking back from the vantage point of his sixty-fifth year, Chateaubriand, a veteran of the *ancien régime*, the early stages of the Revolution, the Empire, the Restoration and the final overthrow of the Bourbons in 1830, mused that

> I have found myself caught between two ages as in the conflux of two great rivers, and I have plunged into their waters turning regretfully from the old bank upon which I was born, yet swimming hopefully towards the unknown shore at which the new generation are to land. (Chateaubriand 1902, I, p. xxiv)

A willingness to contend with the swirling currents of modernity characterised the outlook of a number of romantic writers whose most important political writings were a product of the years 1820–50. While they lacked the iconoclastic glamour of the radical romantics, their views were distinctly modern and progressive. Whether responding to the restoration of the Bourbons in 1815, to the failure of legitimism and the Revolution of 1830, or to the impact of rapid industrial change, the writers discussed in this section accepted the fact of the Revolution, rejected emphatically the application of eighteenth-century ideas to the nineteenth-century world, and sought to find new and vital solutions to the political and social problems they perceived in post-revolutionary Europe.

Shelley and his coterie were hostile to German thought because they believed that it was reactionary, but Thomas Carlyle used its critique of materialism and utilitarianism as the basis for an influential form of radical political romanticism (Ashton 1980, pp. 95–8; Butler 1988, pp. 38–9; Harrold 1963; La Valley 1968; Lasch 1991, pp. 226–43; Morrow 2006, pp. 56–70; Vanden Bossche 1991). Carlyle identified this critique with a group of late eighteenth- and early nineteenth-century German writers that included Novalis and Schlegel and in which Goethe had a special position. Goethe was seen as the inspiration for an approach to the challenges facing modern humanity that depreciated indulgent self-consciousness and extravagant railing against the world, and focused attention on stern commitment to transformative action. Carlyle's attempt to promote German literature so as to distinguish his position from that of his British contemporaries was signalled emphatically in the clarion call, 'Close thy *Byron*; open thy *Goethe*' (Carlyle 1893j, p. 132). This call was part of a radical intellectual and political compaign in which Carlyle sought to stake his own distinctive claim for cultural authority.

The radical thrust of Carlyle's thought can be seen in his ambivalence towards Coleridge. Although Carlyle defended Coleridge against charges of incomprehensible mysticism he exhibited a marked animus to the 'sage of Highgate's' conservatism (Carlyle 1893d, pp. 183–4, 1893i, p. 52). For Carlyle, the erosion of traditional Christianity, the growth of industrial society and the redundancy of traditional institutions of government were not necessarily causes for alarm. They only became so because spiritual malaise, social disorder and the cruel deformities of life in modern industrial centres were indicative of a failure to identify an intellectual, moral and political basis from which to utilise the progressive possibilities opened up by the passing of the old order.

Carlyle sought to fill this lacuna by identifying ideas and institutions which expressed and acknowledged the infinite, spiritual dimensions of human experience. Although he believed that Enlightenment thought had been of great critical importance, Carlyle rejected attempts to forge a constructive world-view out of this philosophy. The dangers of doing so were explored in *Sartor Resartus*. This partly autobiographical work traced the tortured journey of the modern spirit from blind obedience through agonizing alienation ('the Eternal Nay') to self-affirmation (the 'Everlasting Yea'). The reaffirmation symbolised by the 'Everlasting Yea' required human beings to accept what Carlyle described as 'the God-given mandate, Work thou in Welldoing'. This mandate was framed in terms of a view of the importance of particular approaches to human action, or 'labour', that was of profound importance in Carlyle's social and political thinking. Commitment to it, however, also involved a transformation of humans' view of their world that softened and invigorated social feeling and gave an optimistic cast to Carlyle's message to his contemporaries. In terms of many contemporary discourses, these aspects of Carlyle's position involved a high degree of paradox. He insisted that neither social feeling that recognized the distinctive features of shared humanity nor a brave determination to face the future, should be confused with commonplace notions of happiness, least of all those conceptions that involved self-worship. To the contrary, life was to be approached in a spirit of 'renunciation' that required a clear sense of duty and an unbending adherence to its requirements:

There is in man a HIGHER than Love of Happiness: he can do without Happiness, and instead thereof find Blessedness! Was it not to preach-forth this same HIGHER that sages and martyrs, the Poet and the Priest, in all times have spoken and suffered; bearing testimony, through life and through death of the Godlike that is in Man, and how in the Godlike only has he Strength and Freedom. (Carlyle 1893j, pp. 132–3)

Human duty entailed a commitment to what Carlyle termed 'the gospel of labour'. 'Labour' encompassed a wide range of activities – not just productive work but also literature, prophetic religious leadership, military command, intellectual, social and political responsibilities – through which *all* human beings fulfilled their obligation to reduce chaotic nature to the condition of beneficent order that was immanent within it. Carlyle seemed to hold the view that God's creation was deliberately incomplete and that it was humanity's role to fulfil itself by perfecting it. The challenges posed by a chaotic but orderable world were tasks that destiny had contrived to foster the cultivation of the human spirit, and to give expression to humanity's infinite status.

Carlyle regarded work as the key value in a secularised metaphysics addressing fundamental religious instincts that could not be presented to modern humanity through the medium of Christian doctrine. Work was the means of salvation and the only source of consolation, one that held out the prospect of immortality because its fruits might survive to form part of the consciousness of future generations. Carlyle's statement of this position was one of the revelations offered in *Sartor Resartus* and there, and in *Chartism* (his first direct contribution to what he called 'the condition of England question'), unemployment, underemployment and the degradation of the misnamed 'workhouse' system were attributed to elites' failures to assume their obligations to the lower classes of Britain and Ireland. Governmental and social leadership was prescribed by the gospel of labour, and neglect of the duties imposed by it was seen to lie at the core of the problems facing Britain in the first half of the nineteenth century. These themes were explored most fully in *Past and Present* (1843).

In this work Carlyle sought to bring back to life the labouring achievements of Abbot Samson, the late twelfth-century head of the monastic community at Bury St Edmunds in Suffolk. The medieval focus of parts of *Past and Present* was not a symptom of nostalgia, far less of reaction; rather, it reflected Carlyle's search for images from the past that were both inspiring and salutary because they gave vivid expression to universally significant ideas that were of particular importance in light of the social, political and spiritual crisis facing his contemporaries. Samson seemed to exemplify in an admirably non-selfconscious way the timeless implications of the medieval exhortation, *laborare est orare* (to work is to pray). While his predecessor had been conventionally devout in the sense that he was committed to the life of the cloister, and the practices ('the rule') of his order, Samson concerned himself with all aspects of the well-being of the community for which he was responsible, re-establishing the economic strength of the Abbey, restoring its buildings, recovering and guarding its privileges (the 'liberties of St Edmund'), and bringing discipline, order and just purpose to its internal life. Samon's conduct was contrasted with that of modern elites, committed either to materialism or to forms of self-indulgent, highly self-conscious piety that prevented effective action and left the community prey to avarice, to the chance ordering of the market and to anarchic reactions of a working class deprived of the moral, psychological and material benefits of effective leadership. He also provided a model of leadership to inspire modern elites to commit themselves to the gospel of labour and to reaffirm it as the core of individual life and social interaction. Such a commitment entailed the essence of worship since it prompted active, positive engagement with the divinely created order of the universe.

Like Novalis, whose ideas were of particular interest to him, Carlyle stressed the need for his contemporaries to give due weight to the 'dynamic' forces at work in human history. These impulses, reflecting the 'primary, unmodified forces and energies of man, the mysterious springs of Love and Fear, and Wonder, of Enthusiasm, Poetry, Religion', were aspects of a world regulated by a system of natural law which brought human conduct into conformity with God's purposes (Carlyle 1893h, pp. 240–1; Simpson 1951). Carlyle claimed that the 'science of mechanics' had blinded many of his contemporaries to fundamental stipulations of natural law that enjoined just regulation and leadership. The first of these requirements was a consequence of the belief that the spiritual dimensions of human life could only be satisfied within an organic community; the second reflected Carlyle's belief that hierarchy was necessary for such a community. An indifference to justice was apparent in mechanical conceptions of human society, in the attention focused on the outward condition of the population and in the equally dehumanising assumptions that underlay both government policy and the attitudes of employers to their employees. These injustices pointed to a failure in leadership, one that was reinforced by the doctrine of *laissez-faire*, and was reflected in popular agitations for democratic parliaments, in trade union activity and in less well-directed acts of popular violence.

What are all popular commotions and maddest bellowing ... [but] inarticulate cries of a dumb creature in rage and pain; to the ear of wisdom they are articulate prayers: 'Guide me, govern me! I am mad and miserable and cannot guide myself.' (Carlyle 1893b, p. 144)

The progressive cast of Carlyle's thought is clearly apparent in his insistence that the hierarchy of contemporary society must differ radically from that of the old order. He thus identified a modern surrogate for the Church in men of letters; he also placed particular emphasis on the responsibilities of the emerging industrial elite, the 'captains of industry'. Captains of industry should use their economic power to maximise the populace's opportunities for labour and to participate thereby in ordering the material universe. They should also ensure that the conditions in which their troops worked and lived reflected their humanity and reinforced the interdependent, organic character of genuine forms of sociability. In so far as landholders retained a real role in modern society, they too were to resume the responsibilities, and not just the privileges, of leadership. Like other putative leaders in the modern world, the landholding classes were to be 'heroic' rather than merely traditional figures (Carlyle 1893f, p. 246, 1893e).

Carlyle insisted that heroic leaders should play a commanding role in the state. This institution symbolised the moral community and possessed the power necessary to foster co-operation and to facilitate human progression. Carlyle's conception of the state was underwritten by his belief that because political heroes grasped at least some of the underlying realities of the universe they could understand the requirements of their own age. Such figures, a Cromwell in the past and perhaps a Sir Robert Peel in the future, should not be hindered by bureaucracy, by the outmoded forms of the old world or the panacea of parliamentary democracy. In *Latter Day Pamphlets* (1850) Peel was pictured as the central figure in the 'New Downing Street', a system of administrative leadership which would direct the state by reference to the realities of the modern world (Carlyle 1893c, p. 78; Seigel 1983).

The only role that Carlyle could see for democratic institutions in this essentially authoritarian political environment was that of the sounding board: they would provide the governor of the New Downing Street with popular responses to his leadership which would allow him to determine which courses of action were feasible in the circumstances (Carlyle 1893c, pp. 204–5; cf. Rosenberg 1974, pp. 176ff.).

Carlyle's strictures on what he saw as the gross political delusions of his contemporaries, appeared originally in a series of denunciatory essays canvassing the characteristic follies of the age in sweeping, dismissive and often savage terms. Other targets included the philanthropic ethos prompting the emancipation of slaves in the West Indies and the United States and the remodelling of penal institutions at home; modern literature and drama; and the religious ethos of the modern world. The tone of these pamphlets reflected Carlyle's frustration at what he saw as the obtuseness of his contemporaries in the face of the moral corruption of their culture. They were not merely mistaken in their views but seemed to have deliberately embraced falsehood as a way of thought and life: 'All arts, industries and pursuits . . . are tainted to the heart with fatal poison; carry not in them the inspiration of God, but (fruitfulest to think of!) that of the Devil calling himself God; and are smitten with a curse forevermore' (Carlyle 1893c, p. 271). Despite this jeremiad, Carlyle did not jettison completely the air of hope that he associated with Goethe's message: with appropriate heroic leadership the residual heroism of the ordinary population might yet prompt them to put their hands to the wheel and chart a safe if unavoidably arduous course into the future.

Within English romanticism Carlyle was in some respects the heir of Robert Southey (Eastwood 1989, p. 315). Both Carlyle and Southey wrote extensively and sympathetically on the material and spiritual impact of industrialisation upon the common people and both expressed themselves in harsh, authoritarian tones. However, despite Carlyle's admiration for Southey, his progressive perspective placed the revival of pre-industrial values such as loyalty, deference and an organic and hierarchically ordered society, into a political framework that was quite different from the traditional one to which Southey appealed. In this respect, his position resembled that of post-war French romantics, but they moved towards positions whose liberal and democratic aspects stood in sharp contrast with Carlyle's authoritarianism.

The progressive concerns of French romantic writers are apparent even in their criticisms of the irreligious tenor of Enlightenment thought. They deplored what Carlyle termed the 'practical atheism' of the Enlightenment because they thought that it impeded the liberating and progressive tendencies which were the hallmarks of the modern age. Chateaubriand, for example, claimed that Roman Catholicism had always been the guardian of liberty and he related the *philosophes'* enmity towards Christianity to their fundamental intolerance: 'the true spirit of the Encyclopedists was a persecuting fury and intolerance of opinions, which aimed at destroying all other systems than their own, and even in preventing freedom of thought' (Chateaubriand 1815, pp. 388–9).

Militant atheism was a species of fanaticism, and it was this, and not Christian doctrine and practice, which was the real enemy of liberty. Chateaubriand's claim that Christianity and liberty went hand-in-hand was echoed in Lamennais' observation that the humanitarian impulses of the Enlightenment had been stifled by the *philosophes'* antipathy to Christianity (Guillou 1992, p. 10; Reardon 1985, p. 13). Lamennais rejected the one-sidedness of Enlightenment thought because it was incompatible with his belief that human life was set in a context structured by immutable, God-given laws. These laws could be known and implemented only if human beings approached them with the full range of their cognitive and active faculties. He therefore called for a renewal of the 'intimate union of faith and science, of force and law, and of power and liberty' (Lamennais 1830–1c, p. 476; Oldfield 1973, p. 220).

Lamennais' stress upon the unification of human experience was echoed in Lamartine's writings, but here it was related to the nature of poetry and the role of the poet. Although Lamartine's conception of Christianity had a strongly rationalistic flavour it was leavened by his belief that the intuitions or feelings of the 'soul' played an essential role in overcoming the limitations of unaided human reason. Rather than abandoning either reason or the emotional impulses of Christianity, Lamartine sought to fuse the two. While religion was to be stripped of its supernatural trappings, reason was to be infused with 'mystical resonances' sustained through the influence of romantic poetry (Charlton 1984a, pp. 24–6, 1984b, p. 56; Kelly 1992, p. 187; Toesca 1969, p. 281). Lamartine thought that the post-war period was distinguished by the diffusion of liberty. However, he evaluated this development in religious terms; liberty was a 'mysterious phenomenon whose secret belongs to God, but whose witness is the conscience, and whose evidence is virtue' (Lamartine 1860–6, p. 361; Fortesque 1983, pp. 78–9; Kelly 1992, p. 196). In the modern era the pursuit of liberty had produced a new kind of politics, one which sought to transpose freedom into a systematic form of social organisation. Lamartine thought that poetry would help his contemporaries to embrace and to reintegrate the intellectual, political and spiritual impulses that were glimpsed in the Enlightenment but had been fragmented by its narrow conception of rationality. Poetry was the 'music of reason' and Lamartine believed that it would make transformation possible by imbuing politically engaged minds with images of charity, compassion, generosity and morality (Dunn 1989, p. 293).

The French romantics' attempt to fuse reason and religion in the interests of social and political progress was closely related to their perception of the French Revolution. Unlike conservative romantics in both England and Germany, they gave the Revolution a verdict of qualified approval. Thus while Chateaubriand was aligned with the 'Ultra' majority in the notorious Chambre Introuvable, his defence of both the Restoration and its first elected assembly contained favourable judgements on aspects of the Revolution (Loménie 1929, I, pp. 63ff.). Although he condemned the 'moral' interests thrown up by the Revolution – obedience to *de facto* government and an indifference to honesty and justice – Chateaubraind insisted that the Restoration must preserve the proprietorial and political rights that were its most valuable 'material' contribution to posterity (Chateaubriand 1838c, p. 208). The key to this process was the general acceptance of a representative form of monarchy.

In *De Bonaparte et des Bourbons* (1814), Chateaubriand's harsh characterisations of Napoleon's regime were given a distinctive edge by his earlier association with it. He described the Empire as the 'saturnalia of royalty'. Its 'crimes', 'oppression', 'slavery' and 'folly', contrasted with the 'legitimate authority', 'order', 'peace' and 'legal liberty' of representative monarchy (Chateaubriand 1838b, pp. 13, 31). Such a regime needed the support of a hereditary aristocracy, not the complicity of a pseudo-imperial clique. Above all, it required an Established Church (Chateaubriand 1838c, p. 172). Chateaubriand insisted that this institution should not be modelled on the state-salaried clergy of the Napoleonic era. Rather, it must possess financial independence on the lines of the English Church. This conception of the Church was very similar to that of Coleridge, but Chateaubriand's view of its importance was closely related to the peculiar needs of Restoration France. A respected and viable church establishment would endow the new regime with the sanctity of traditional religion and underline the connection between liberal values and Christianity: 'The liberty which is not derived from heaven will seem the work of the Revolution; and we shall never learn to love the child of our crimes and of our misfortunes'. (Chateaubriand 1838c, p. 250).

Representative monarchy incorporated aspects of tradition but it also required certain liberal innovations. For example, Chateaubriand rejected the use of police powers for political purposes, and he also argued that a free press was necessary for a system of government founded on enlightened public opinion (Chateaubriand 1838c, pp. 175–6, 1838d, pp. 379–80). However, the feature of representative monarchy which most interested Chateaubriand was the idea of ministerial responsibility. Chateaubriand's support for this idea reflected in part the commonly held view that it would facilitate the effective criticism of the executive by allocating responsibility to removable ministers rather than to the monarch (cf. Constant 1988a, pp. 227–42). In addition, however, he claimed that this convention gave the monarch a distinctive status. By assigning the Crown a ratifying rather than an initiating role, the idea of ministerial responsibility endowed the monarch with an air of divinity: 'His person is sacred, and his will can do no wrong' (Chateaubriand 1838c, p. 163). Since the monarch only spoke with absolute authority when he ratified (and thus completed and perfected) laws produced by representative assemblies, he possessed a symbolic importance which was not available to other political actors or to the powerful but tarnished sovereigns of despotic states (Chateaubriand 1838c, pp. 170–1).

In discussing ministerial responsibility Chateaubriand dwelt on the monarch's symbolic role and utilised a romantic interpretation of a liberal constitutional mechanism to convince his 'Ultra' allies that representative government captured the essence of monarchy. However, Chateaubriand did not regard the legitimist majority in the Chamber merely as a stalking horse for the liberalisation of French government (Bédé 1970, pp. 40–2; Rémond 1969, pp. 42–4, 73). To the contrary, he believed that since the Chamber had been elected it was an authentic expression of the feelings of the nation. It thus symbolised the fusion of the old world and the new, the symbiosis of legitimist values, liberty and popular government that formed the core of representative government and was one of the most important products of the Revolution.

Lamartine's and Lamennais' understanding of the implications of the Revolution were ultimately more radical than that of Chateaubriand. In the Restoration period Lamennais' attention was focused upon the damaging effects of Gallicanism upon the liberty of the Church. The interference of the state in religious matters was very damaging because freedom was central to the reconciliation of the individual's conscience with God and humanity. Lamennais' failure to persuade either French elites or the papacy of the evils of state control pushed him towards a more general critique of traditional political and social structures (Guillou 1969). He came to regard the Revolution of 1789 was an assertion of popular liberty against repressive and disharmonious political and social structures, and that of 1830 was a reassertion of the same tendency. Lamennais described the July Revolution as:

> a popular reaction against absolutism . . . an inevitable effect of an already ancient impulsion, the continuation of a great movement which, having projected itself from the regions of thought into the political world in 1789, announced to the slumbering nations of a corrupt civilisation and an outdated order, the fall of that order and the birth of a new order. (Lamennais 1830–1b, pp. 161–2; Oldfield 1973, p. 187)

A society that combined both liberty and order had to be built anew from the isolated individuals who were the sole repositories of eternal justice and the only possible focus for Christian liberty. Since the French population had been atomised, its members could only be combined in a democratic republic (Oldfield 1973, pp. 188–90). This message (spelt out in *L'Avenir* of 1830–1) became the basis for an increasingly strident call to action in Lamennais' subsequent political writings. However, he insisted it was necessary for liberty to be a *general* feature of a reconstructed society, and also for this society to embody the principles of eternal justice. The new order would have to recognise not only political rights but also a wide-ranging set of 'social rights' which specified the social and material basis of an orderly, harmonious Christian society. As Lamennais wrote in *Paroles d'un Croyant* of 1834:

> Liberty is not a placard that one sees at a street corner. It is a living power that one feels in oneself and around oneself, the true protective spirit of the domestic threshold, the guarantee of social rights, and the first of all these rights. (Lamennais 1834, ch. 20, p. 45; Ireson 1969, pp. 27–9)

Lamartine also thought that his contemporaries must complete the reconstruction that had begun with the French Revolution. This event had been a 'tocsin to the world':

> Many of its phases are accomplished, but it has not yet concluded; nothing is finished in these slow, internal and everlasting movements of the moral life of man . . . In the progress of societies and ideas, the end is ever but a new starting-point. The French Revolution, which will hereafter be called the European Revolution . . . was not only a political revolution, a change of power, one dynasty set up in place of another, a republic substituted for a monarchy – all these things were but the accidents, symptoms, instruments and means. (Lamartine 1856, p. 496; cf. Lamartine 1848, iii, pp. 541–6)

The plasticity of political forms meant that 'men of the revolution' could be found at all points on the political spectrum, and it made the implications of the revolutionary experience a general feature of modern politics. Lamartine's conception of the ubiquity of the revolutionary experience was reflected in what Kelly calls the 'agnosticism' of his views on desirable forms of government (Kelly 1992, p. 206; cf. Charlton 1984b, p. 67). The primary requirement was that government must be strong enough to serve 'the interests and not the passions of the people'; this meant that it must be an effective expression of the social power that had first made itself felt in the revolutionary era (Quentin-Bauchart 1903, p. 403). Although Lamartine was a leading member of the second French Republic in 1848 his preference before this time was for representative monarchy. The monarch must be the 'organ and agent' of social power, not of his own personal interests (Lamartine 1860–6, p. 370). In a comment which recalled Coleridge's musings on the possibilities of a republican king in the English commonwealth, Lamartine speculated that a representative monarchy may take the substantive form of a democratic republic. The king would become 'a natural chief... who will be, at bottom, the people crowned and who will move, think, act, and reign for the ideals and interests of the people. That will be the best of republics, for it will reconcile traditions and reforms, habits and innovations' (quoted in Kelly 1992, p. 207).

There were, however, limits to this process of reconciliation and in this respect Lamartine's political thought was more radical than that of Chateaubriand. Like Lamennais, he rejected any form of alliance between the church and state. Religion was a matter of conscience and would be sullied by the inevitable temptations to corruption that would result from a close association with the state (Lamartine 1860–6, p. 373; Charlton 1984b, p. 51; Kelly 1992, p. 213). Lamartine also claimed that aristocracy was redundant. The Revolution had effectively destroyed the traditional structure of aristocratic society, the principle itself was incompatible with the egalitarian impulses of the modern age and it stood 'in contempt of nature and of the divine right of humanity' (Lamartine 1860–6, p. 371).

This remark appeared in Lamartine's *Sur la Politique Rationnelle* of 1831, a work which signalled his break with conventional legitimism and also with the more progressive stance taken by Chateaubriand (Fortesque 1983, p. 69). In the new scheme of things Lamartine's republican king was to be grafted to the stock of popular democracy based on indirect elections. This system had the advantage of recognising popular sovereignty while minimising its practical dangers, but Lamartine also wished to avoid the 'brutal individualism' that he believed would be unleashed by direct elections. Popular sovereignty was significant if it gave rise to the 'social power' generated by fraternity, responsibility and solidarity.[9] These values were the progressive core of the revolutionary idea and their realisation would be impeded by the accidental tendency for popular sovereignty to be construed in individualistic terms. The misapplication of the liberating tendencies made possible by the Revolution had to be replaced by a true expression of social power, or by what Lamartine described as 'social charity': 'Charity, acting in concert with good policy, commands men not to abandon man to himself, but to come to his aid and to form a sort of mutual assurance, or equitable condition, between the classes possessing and those not possessing' (Lamartine 1856, p. 500, 1862, II, p. 304).

The framework of 'social charity' existed in localities, families, rural values and in a social conception of property. An attachment to these ideas played an important role in conservative expressions of romanticism, but Lamartine's progressive romanticism related these apparently conventional ideas to the forces which lay behind the revolutionary demand that the state should be the organ of popular sovereignty.

In the early nineteenth century political romantics grappled with two central issues. The first concerned the relationship between the subject and the state, while the second focused on the social relationships necessary to form human beings into a community rather than an aggregation of individuals. The first of these themes was prominent in conservative attempts to endow traditional political relationships with affective and aesthetic qualities. It may also be discerned in the idea of the subject as victim that underlay post-war English critiques of legitimism, and in the attempts of Carlyle and his French contemporaries to identify political forms that would integrate individuals within post-revolutionary, non-traditional political cultures. Romantic conceptions of the implications of community were directed at economic individualism. Romantics' treatments of this problem mirrored their responses to the political individualism that they associated with Enlightenment thought. They gave rise to a marked

---

9 Charlton (1984b) suggests that French romantics were close to their contemporaries among the '*juste milieu*', an interpretation that reflects their avoidance of the party extremes of left and right and their wish for reconciliation. However, the distinctive features of French romantic perceptions of politics make Kelly's interpretation more plausible. He argues that 'ideas of fraternity and regeneration' were common to dissident legitimists, radicals, and romantics, but were 'unseemly to the men of the *juste milieu*' (Kelly 1992, p. 182).

ambivalence towards the moral implications of modern economic doctrines and practices. Conservative romantics' reactions to these developments were coloured by paternalistic images of traditional communities, but once ideas of social responsibility and community were severed from these roots they gave political romanticism a purchase on the future. Thus Lamennais' and Lamartine's rejection of legitimism propelled them into a milieu where social politics merged into democracy and socialism, while Carlyle's ideas were an important influence in the revival of British socialism that took place towards the end of the century.

3

On the principle of nationality

JOHN BREUILLY

1 Introductory comments

Nationality can be constructed as fact and value. Its construction as value presupposes its construction as fact. First, there *are* nations; second, nations *are* bearers of values. However, nations can be constructed as facts without regarding them also as bearers of values on which to base cultural or political programmes.

I define the principle of nationality as consisting of three claims: humanity is divided into nations; nations are worthy of recognition and respect; recognition and respect require autonomy, usually meaning political independence within the national territory.[1] Thus the principle of nationality contains an empirical claim, a value assertion and a political goal, each building on the previous proposition. These are *logical* relationships; they do not necessarily occur in that chronological order. This principle was constructed in nineteenth-century Europe.[2] The empirical, normative and programmatic constructions took on increasingly complex, differentiated and conflicting forms as the principle of nationality loomed an ever larger role in political culture and practice.

These considerations inform the structure of this essay. After a brief historical background I focus on how the principle of nationality was

My thanks to Monika Baar, Stefan Berger, Mark Hewitson, Peter Mandler, Gareth Stedman Jones and Oliver Zimmer for comments made on drafts of this essay.

1 This follows closely the definition of nationalism I use in Breuilly 1993, pp. 3–4 which in turn was influenced by the notion of a 'core doctrine' of Smith 1971, p. 21. It is also close to that used by Gellner 2006, p. 1 and Kedourie 1966, so this is not an eccentric definition.

2 This is a similar but not identical claim to the one asserted strikingly by Elie Kedourie in the opening sentence of his book on nationalism: 'Nationalism is a doctrine invented in Europe at the beginning of the nineteenth century' (Kedourie 1966, p. 9). The difference is that I do not claim that the invention of the doctrine was responsible for the formation of nationalist sentiments, movements and nation states. This essay is focused on ideas and doctrines but I contend these are to be sharply distinguished from nationality understood either as sentiments or political movements and organisations. For my critique of Kedourie see Breuilly 2000, and for my argument as to the distinctions to be made, see Breuilly 1994.

developed after 1800. I argue that this took place in four broad phases: nation as civilisation, as historic, as ethnic and as racial. Nationalist discourse did not so much shift from one to the next as add layers and increase public acceptance of the principle. The centrality of this principle in political culture promoted political change in the direction of nation state formation and rendered attempts to defend alternative political principles ever more incredible.

One final introductory point: nationalist doctrines have not been the work of 'great' thinkers as is arguably the case for socialist, liberal and conservative doctrines. Influential 'thinkers' are distinct from original ones. Mazzini is tedious to read as he asserts rather than argues and his 'ideas' exerted power more through personal example and action than through originality. Original thinkers often had influence far distant in time and place from themselves. Herder influenced Slav nationalism in the mid-nineteenth century more than German nationalism in his own time; Fichte's *Reden an die Deutsche Nation* had less impact in Napoleonic Germany than in Wilhelmine Germany. Some original thinking on nationality did exercise some influence; arguably this was the case with Thomas Carlyle (Mandler 2006, ch. 3). Instead the principle of nationality was developed and diffused largely by narrower and second-rank thinkers – historians, linguists, folklorists – operating in networks formed by universities, newspapers, periodicals and political and cultural associations, in close connection to the situations which also gave rise to a politics of nationalism. My essay will focus on such networks rather than individual thinkers and works.[3]

2   The national idea before 1800

Broadly 'nation' referred to political elites and institutions constituting territorial monarchies.[4] It acquired meanings to do with high culture and specific territory and its inhabitants following a long history of stable rule over a core region, as in England and France. It was deployed in internal political conflict, such as appeals to 'patriotism' by oppositional and governmental politicians in eighteenth-century Britain and France. The national idea was given collective content by Enlightenment writers who discerned

---

3 A relevant work which came to my attention too late to use in this essay but which pursues similar themes is Leersen 2006, especially the section on the nineteenth century, 'The Politics of National Identity'.

4 I list here a few relevant works on pre-1800 ideas of nationality: Bell 2001; Fehrenbach 1986; Scales and Zimmer 2005; Schönemann 1997.

stages of history, portraying progressive 'nations' bringing together political institutions and the national spirit or character. More strongly, early romanticism linked nation to collective cultural identity embodied in language, customs or values. These ideas acquired force in the late eighteenth-century revolutions in the Americas and France where the 'nation' legitimised a new state.

3 The nation as civilised

France: la grande nation

The principle of nationality initially combined high culture, individualised property rights and constitutional government. It was given sharp expression in the early phase of the French Revolution. Aspects of this liberal view of nationality were marginalised with the conversion of politics into warfare and the stress on virtue as heroic public action rather than conscientious attention to private life. This shift was acutely analysed by Benjamin Constant. He formulated a distinction between ancient and modern liberty meaning freedom *in* and *from* the state. A constant puzzle for Constant was to explain the aberration of the Jacobin/Napoleonic period with its 'ancient' stress on public virtue and heroism.[5]

French nationality came to be expressed as *la grande nation* (Godechot 1956). The concern for order marginalised democratic and republican versions of nationality. Liberal nationalists after 1815 could not disavow the Revolution although they sought to explain away 'aberrations' such as terror and wars of conquest. Liberal historians presented national history as progressive and civilising and France as a model for other nations. The liberal principle of nationality was deployed against radicals and royalists. It reached its apogee with the July Monarchy. Writers who expounded this view exercised political power, most notably Guizot (Crossley 1993).

Radicals formulated an alternative principle of nationality. Seeking inspiration from Jacobinism – with its universalist political language, classical models and its scornful dismissal of the rubbish of French monarchical traditions – presented intellectual challenges. This challenge was confronted by Jules Michelet. Michelet understood the nation as the source of spiritual values in the modern era, replacing the Church. He infused the thin notions of reason and progress with emotion, making a religion of national history

---

5 See Constant's essay 'The Spirit of Conquest and Usurpation and their Relationship to European Civilisation' (Constant 1988c). See also the essay in this book by Jeremy Jennings.

which he set within a universal historical framework. Themes of struggle, defeat and resurrection made national history understandable and attractive to a Christian readership while avoiding confessional forms. Michelet overcame 'civic' and 'ethnic' distinctions, presenting the modern French nation as a triumphant combination of Celtic, Germanic, Greek and Roman elements (Crossley 1993, ch. 6).

Nationality could be deployed by others. Louis Napoleon exploited the myth of Napoleon with massive success in his election victory in December 1848 and to justify his coup (with less success) in 1851. He invoked 'la grand nation' in promoting national causes abroad. But Bonapartism was an opportunist, ambiguous political phenomenon, difficult to relate to a coherent principle of nationality. Royalists were as yet unable to develop an influential principle of nationality.

The impact of the French Revolution in Europe

It has been claimed that the French Revolution and Napoleonic wars spread the principle of nationality beyond France. The universal mission of *la grande nation* was unattractive in the form of military imperialism. Opponents of Napoleon argued that the only way to defeat him was to emulate his mass mobilisation and warfare. This included appeals to the nation. In rejecting arguments about universal reason and the superiority of civilised nations to backward ones, thinkers formulated arguments about nations as unique and natural (Dann and Dinwiddy 1987).

This view is misleading if it means there was significant popular resistance to Napoleon inspired by the national idea. The most effective responses to Napoleon involved more efficient use of old institutions and values, such as a rejection of godless revolution by traditionalist clerics. Furthermore, Enlightenment reformers imported French principles like individualised property rights and functional state ministries. Democratic and romantic nationalists were marginalised, even if their rhetoric was exploited by governments. Where Napoleonic rule stimulated popular resistance it was guided by traditional values which did not sit easily with the principle of nationality; where Enlightenment or romantic ideas of nationality were significant, they were confined to elites. Subsequent nationalist myth-making exaggerated the importance of elite nationalism and popular resistance and yoked them together (Rowe 2003).

However, so far as nationalist doctrine is concerned, Napoleonic imperialism stimulated new ideas which, even if not politically important at the time, later had a major impact. These are associated with German political romanticism, and especially Herder and Fichte. Herder reacted strongly against Enlightenment judgements with their distinctions between backward and advanced, progressive and reactionary. He particularly detested Voltaire whose historical-moral balance sheets he constantly denounced. Herder stressed the *uniqueness* of nations. This was based primarily upon incommensurable languages but Herder extended this argument to other social practices. Instead of national character as the outcome of common conditioning (the view of David Hume 1994a) it was understood as animating spirit or principle.[6]

Herder died before Napoleonic imperialism reached its peak. His anti-Enlightenment, anti-French arguments resonated with some German elites. The most striking adaptation of his ideas to the new political situation came in lectures given by Fichte in the French-occupied city of Berlin in 1807, the 'Addresses to the German Nation'. Fichte identifies Germans as the only Teutonic nation which has retained its authentic language, an original language unlike any other. There are important arguments as to how far Fichte's nation is ultimately an ethnic one or only a cultural-linguistic one or even a civic one. Irrespective of this, Fichte's preoccupation with a natural, pre-political group, pushes the principle of nationality to a clear and extreme conclusion. However, his dilemma is that this nation has forgotten its true self (hence the inability to resist the French conquest) but this can be restored through education, building on the collective identity which resides in its language. Subsequently, other intellectuals like Jahn and Arndt sought to embody 'Germandom' in gymnastics and military volunteers, and also expressed a virulent anti-French hatred.[7]

Fichte's lectures were permitted by the French censor. They were delivered to a closed, elite audience and preached education and language reform, not guerrilla warfare or popular insurrection. They had little influence at the time. Herder's ideas, with their focus on folk culture, peasants and artisans, had more influence on small nation nationalism. In Germany it

6 A good place to start is with an English translation of Herder 2004. Here is perhaps the first use of the term 'nationalism': 'Every nation has its *center* of happiness within itself, as every ball has its center of gravity! . . . Likewise any two nations whose inclinations and circles of happiness *collide* – one calls it *prejudice*, *loutishness*, narrow *nationalism*' (Herder 2004: 29). On Herder see Barnard 1965, 2003.

7 On interpreting Fichte see Abizadeh 2005. For the original German text of the Addresses see Fichte 1845, and for an English translation see Fichte 2008. A very recent study of Prussian reactions to Napoleon is Hagemann 2002.

was a liberal fusion of progress and cultural nationality that dominated
nationalist discourse for much of the century.

Britain: civilisation rather than nationality

In post-1815 Europe the liberal national principle combining high culture, individualised property rights and constitutional government dominated. One might think this would have the greatest influence in Britain
where institutions most closely corresponded to this principle. However,
while French liberal nationality was expressed in a combative language
against threats of revolution and counter-revolution, in Britain it retained
the empirical character associated with Hume. British political thought
stressed civilisational achievement through the formation of individual elite
character (Mandler 2006, especially 'Introduction'). The national idea was
too enveloping, too democratic and inclusive, too continental. After 1848
British political thinkers discerned national genius to reside in empirical,
common-sense behaviour and piecemeal reform (Grainger 1979). This came
out of a complacent reading of the outbreak of revolution on the continent
compared to the failure of the Chartist challenge in 1848.[8] An alternative
view of nationality as inclusive, although expressed through heroic leaders,
was formulated by Carlyle but had little influence, except in contributing
to the admiration for the leaders of foreign nationalism such as Kossuth
and Garibaldi.[9] This view also explains the lack of attention to constitutional arrangements; explicit design was a continental concern, inferior to
an 'unwritten' constitution. Forceful moral-political argument in Victorian England came from radicalism and evangelical Christianity, not from
nationalism (Mandler 2000). As groups excluded from the 'nation' (i.e.
the parliamentary franchise) acquired the empirical qualities of their betters, they could be admitted. Thus franchise debates were argued in terms
of 'respectability'. Democratisation was written into history as national
progress but avoiding a doctrinaire or conflictual language. Thinkers who
deplored these values as complacent, muddled and ethnocentric – John

8 One can date almost precisely the change of establishment mood from a *Punch* cartoon of just before
   the Chartist demonstration full of anxiety to one after the demonstration mocking Chartism as
   ridiculous. See *Punch*, 14/353, 15 April 1848 and 14/355, 29 April. These are reproduced in Breuilly
   1998a. This can be accessed online. One current web link to the two cartoons is: http://web.bham.
   ac.uk/1848/comments/punch.htm.
9 Mandler 2006, p. 69 quotes Mazzini's criticism of Carlyle: 'The shadow cast by these gigantic men
   appears to eclipse to his [Carlyle's] view every trace of the national thought of which these men were
   only the interpreters or prophets, and of the people, who alone are its depositary.'

Stuart Mill, George Eliot, Matthew Arnold – actually reinforced by their criticism the sense that this *was* how nationality worked in Britain (Collini 1988; Varouxakis 2002). In this way the idea of the nation as inclusive was developed but concepts of cultural identity and national character were fragile, always likely to be trumped by those of civilisation, elite leadership and Christianity (I largely follow Mandler 2006).[10]

4   The nation as historic

Discourse

Beyond Britain and France there was not the convergence of high culture, market economy and parliamentary government which nationality as civilisation (missionary or empirical) could claim both to describe and justify. Instead the civilisational perspective of history was projected into the future.

Such ideas were taken up by elites claiming to act on behalf of culturally dominant nationalities. German and Italian nationalists claimed a national high culture worthy of respect; it remained only to bring this into a national state (Breuilly 1996, ch. 2; Riall 1994), Magyars in the eastern half of the Habsburg Empire, haunted by Herder's prophecy that they would be ground between the mills of German nationality above and Slav nationality below, in 1848–9 demanded autonomy from Vienna and assertion over non-Magyars, including in this national programme notions of commercial improvement and land reform (Barany 1968; Okey 2000, ch. 4). Polish nobility demanded freedom from Romanov, Hohenzollern and Habsburg rule on the basis of aristocratic nationality, although to appeal to liberal British and French opinion this was presented as a progressive movement for liberty (Snyder 2003).

Historic nationality claims assumed a close connection between domination and culture. In Britain and France this was asserted over Celtic regions. Political integration was at elite level. Welsh borderland gentry and the bourgeoisie of Dublin, Belfast, Glasgow and Edinburgh could be assimilated into the national ruling class. Mid-nineteenth-century France still had large numbers of non-French speaking subjects but provincial elites were thoroughly French in culture and political outlook.[11]

---

10 For a stimulating comparative study of the intellectual treatment of notions of 'national character' in nineteenth-century Britain and France see Romani 2002.
11 Weber 1976 has long been cited to establish almost as beyond dispute the lack of a standard national culture in France before the late nineteenth century. However, Weber's work may well have exaggerated diversity (e.g. it was common for elite figures to be bilingual in the local language and French)

Cultural division became a problem with democratisation. There was a demand to enforce English or French culture at a popular level. The Restoration regime of post-1815 France did not relax this policy, even if national culture was seen in Catholic and hierarchical rather than secular and democratic terms (Lyons 2006). John Stuart Mill argued that the assimilation of small, backward, peripheral cultures (Bretons, Welsh) to the dominant culture was necessary to create the public consensus needed in a liberal democracy. Mill's arguments were influential at the time and have been much discussed recently.[12]

Mill defines nationality so as to include a political demand:

A portion of mankind may be said to constitute a Nationality, if they are united among themselves by common sympathies, which do not exist between them and any others – which make them co-operate with each other more willingly than with other people, desire to be under the same government, and desire that it should be government by themselves or a portion of themselves, exclusively. (Mill 1977b, p. 546)

This leads Mill to argue for the political separation of nationalities:

it is in general a necessary condition of free institutions, that the boundaries of governments should coincide with those of nationalities. (Mill 1977b, p. 548)

However, Mill qualifies this proposition, for example in relation to geographical distributions of national populations. Lord Acton attacked Mill's argument, demanding the continued distinction between culture (nationality) and politics (independence) (Acton 1907b).

My concern is not with the presumption that a polity requires one national culture under conditions of representative democracy, but with Mill's related argument about civilisation. Mill thought that if a civilised minority ruled a less civilised majority, one could not have democracy, a position he took with regard to British rule in India.[13] Where civilised nations lived side-by-side, there should usually be political separation. Mill supported political autonomy for French Canadians on this ground (Varouxakis 2002, p. 18). However, where a civilised majority ruled a backward minority Mill's prescription was not political separation but cultural assimilation. As his most notorious passage on the subject put the matter:

and told us more about differences at the level of popular culture rather than that of elite culture or politics. For more recent studies of such issues see Ford 1993 and Lehning 1995.

12 The principal text is Mill 1977b, in particular Chapter XVI, 'Of Nationality, as Connected with Representative Government'. Varouxakis 2002 provides a reliable analysis. For recent normative arguments which draw on Mill see Miller 1995.

13 He knew India well, both his father and himself having worked for the East India Company.

Nobody can suppose that it is not more beneficial to a Breton, or a Basque of French Navarre, to be brought into the current of the ideas and feelings of a highly refined and cultivated people – to be a member of the French nationality, admitted on equal terms to all the privileges of French citizenship, sharing the advantages of French protection, and the dignity and *prestige* of French power – than to sulk on his own rocks, the half-savage relic of past times, revolving in his own little mental orbit, without participation or interest in the general movement of the world. The same remark applies to the Welshman or the Scottish Highlander, as members of the British nation. (Mill 1977b, p. 549)

We must not project contemporary understandings on to this passage. Mill was not arguing that all Breton or Welsh customs ('ways of life') be swept aside. This passage long precedes the age of mass culture and interventionist states with an extensive realm of 'public' culture and a restricted private culture. Nevertheless, this was a time when moves towards compulsory schooling in Britain raised questions about the language of instruction, indeed even how 'proper' English was to be spoken. More important is the impact of such thinking in Central and Eastern Europe.

Mill's view derives from established contrasts between the civilised and the backward but acquired new urgency with democratisation. In Central Europe 'nationality' as political concept was connected to high culture. To be a 'Pole' in 1600 was to be a privileged member of the Polish-Lithuanian Commonwealth. So Mill's arguments could be taken up by privileged groups in the political conflicts that became acute in 1848. For liberal audiences of Mill's persuasion, it was important that advocates of national causes – Greek, German, Polish, Hungarian, Italian – establish not merely that their nation existed but that it was civilised.

This acquired additional force in Central Europe with arguments about history. Hegel had taken the idea of progress and made it into world process. He notoriously asserted that Africa 'had no history'. Hegel has been roundly criticised but it was a pioneering effort to construct world history, envisaging a key nation at the centre of that history in each epoch.[14]

Such ideas were applied to mid-century Europe with the distinction between 'historical' and 'non-historical' nations. Karl Marx and Friedrich Engels used the distinction to justify support for or opposition to conflicting national claims (Cummins 1980; Nimni 1991; Rosdolsky 1986). It has

---

14 'Passing judgement on it [Hegel's 'dialectic of national minds'] today requires little effort, but it is all too easy to forget that, in spite of its metaphysical arbitrariness, this represented the first attempt to master intellectually the apparent chaos of historical events and to comprehend human history as a *developmental* process that made sense and followed its own laws' (Rosdolsky 1986, p. 130). For an English translation see Hegel 1975a.

been argued that these were pragmatic judgements about which national movements would promote or obstruct progress towards socialism, as well as expressing their fear that tsarism would exploit Slav sentiments to effect counter-revolution. However, Engels at least also argued that Slavs (excepting Poles) were ruined fragments of an earlier culture who must assimilate into non-Slav nations. Engels portrayed Habsburg history as centralising and progressive. He supported the rule of the dominant nationalities of the Habsburg Empire and their assimilation of 'non-historic' peoples.[15]

By different routes Mill and Engels discriminated between nationalities (civilised, historical) which should form states and those (backward, unhistorical) which should not. One finds similar conclusions, asserted rather than argued, in Mazzini. His 'Young Europe' programme, when mapped on to Europe, produces something similar to Hegelian projections by Engels on to 'historical' peoples.[16]

Applying the discourse

This discourse of historic nationality was central to the claims made on behalf of Germans, Italians, Magyars and Poles. Central throughout was a preoccupation, even an obsession, with modernity understood from a liberal perspective. Yet it was necessary to avoid simple emulation of French and British variations of modernity: modernity had to be given a national twist and this was achieved with the principle of historic nationality (for recent surveys not otherwise cited: see Denes 2006; Wingfield 2003).

There were important differences. In Poland there was a long-standing aristocratic conception of Polish nationality. A Polish state had existed until 1795 and there was a direct connection between that state and advocates of its restoration in the nineteenth century. Democratising the principle of nationality confronted not only the challenge of dismantling an aristocratic order but also of accommodating the many non-Polish speakers. The scale of the problem became clear in Galicia in 1846 when peasants turned against the gentry nationalist uprising and sided with the Habsburg monarchy. This revealed that the dynasties had available a populist option to use against elite nationalism (Gill 1974; Snyder 2003).

---

15 I base much of this on Rosdolsky 1986, a pioneering Marxist critique of Marx and, especially, Engels.
16 In 1852 Mazzini suggested how some fifty national units in Europe could be reduced to thirteen or fourteen larger federal groupings. In a letter of 1857 he put flesh on this idea, including a great Danubian confederation. See Smith 1994, pp. 155–6. My thanks to Oliver Zimmer for drawing my attention to this reference.

In Hungary there was an aristocratic Magyar culture, autonomy under a foreign dynasty and a significant proportion of non-Magyar speakers within the subordinate population. Unlike the Poles, however, there was a core area of Hungary with a Magyar speaking peasantry which provided a base for revolution in 1848–9, once peasant emancipation was proclaimed. Earlier independence lay further back in time than for Poland and there was more to be done in the way of constructing Magyar high culture. Hungarian nationalists had the advantage that their political demands were addressed to one dynast and not, like the Poles, to three, and there was room for compromise on internal autonomy. The Habsburgs ruled as Kings of Hungary, not Emperors. During 1848–9 the revolutionaries, on the basis of concessions made at an early stage by the ruler (the April Laws) insisted that they were *not* rebelling against their king (Deak 1979).

Magyars shared with Poles the problem that popular appeal to nationality on the basis of a shared culture and language could backfire where the rural masses were of distinct ethnicity and language or pressed for more radical land reform than elite nationalists were willing to concede. After the dualist constitution of 1867 gave internal autonomy to the Kingdom of Hungary, the official fiction of 'one and indivisible nation' was bound to trigger counter-nationalist responses.

In Italy even into the mid-nineteenth century men like Cavour preferred speaking French to Italian. Not only was Italy politically splintered but much rulership was 'foreign': Habsburgs in the north, Popes in the centre, Bourbons in the south. A few territorial states and local domination could claim to be Italian. Italy was highly localised and there was no common culture or a mutually comprehensible language. It was necessary to cultivate deliberately a high culture.[17] Mazzini ignored the problem. Italy, he asserted, had the unique advantage of being unified by 'sublime and indisputable boundaries' and a common language (Mazzini 1907, pp. 53–4).

German states were ruled by German princes and elites. German high culture had been effectively constructed. By the mid-nineteenth century this culture was entrenched in the curricula of *Gymnasien* and universities. There was a loose German political and legal system. There were dialects but they were German dialects. German nationalists were well-placed to argue that there was a distinct nationality and simple removal of fragmentation

---

17 On the diversity of Italy see Woolf 1979. For a sceptical view of the 'national' basis of Risorgimento claims see Laven 2006.

could create a national state. However, lack of alien rule deprived German nationalists of a foreign enemy while vested state interests and conflict between Austria and Prussia blocked moves to unification (Breuilly 1996; Vick 2002).

In different ways the notion of a historic nation constituted by domination and high culture could be claimed for these four nations. A shared liberal-radical vision of a national Europe in the mid-nineteenth century assumed the unification of Italy and Germany and the restoration of Poland and Hungary. The victims would be the petty states of the Italian and German lands and the Habsburg and Romanov empires. If monarchies like Piedmont and Prussia pursued this vision, however, they would have to surrender some prerogatives although it was also difficult for liberal opinion to envisage any political form other than monarchy. When Greece, Belgium, Serbia and Romania acquired political independence, a monarchical form was adopted, usually importing a king from a cadet branch of an established royal family. This demonstrates the conservative assumptions within which the notion of historic nationality operated.

There was one further potential victim of this historic-liberal principle of nationality: the 'non-historic' nationalities. A different principle of nationality was being constructed here and 1848 would accelerate and crystallise its development.

5 Nation as ethnicity

Terms such as 'non-historic' or 'historyless' were regarded by spokesmen for such nations as derogatory. Nowadays other terms are used, such as non-dominant ethnic community (Hroch 1996: 80). Indeed, the terms imply a nationalist assumption about the connection between identity and history. Naturally, therefore, nationalists who took up the cause of non-historic nationalities focused on constructing a national history.

Older notions of domination and high culture were not framed in terms of 'complete' groups but in terms of a hierarchical social order with those at the top culturally distinct from those at the bottom. If social hierarchy was sharp and cultural differences clear, as was increasingly the case as one moved from west to east in Europe, it was difficult for elite culture to generate popular appeal or for subordinate culture to present claims to domination. Social mobility was accompanied by cultural shift. A successful Czech-speaking immigrant into Prague learnt German and ensured his children assimilated into dominant German culture (Cohen 1981).

There are many reasons why and how such assimilation declined. A dynamic economy generated more upward social mobility than the traditional order could handle and the new men – farmers, merchants, manufacturers – asserted a group identity instead. Peasant emancipation was a cause of such mobility and undermined social hierarchy. Gellner developed a theory of industrialisation and unequal development to explain the emergence of such nationalist movements. Hroch has connected the impulse to formulate small nation principles to the growth of market towns in commercialising agricultural and manufacturing districts of Central Europe. Berend has stressed the role of economic backwardness and a combined resentment of and desire to emulate the 'West' (Berend 2003, especially chs. 2 and 3; Deutsch 1966; Gellner 2006; Hroch 1985).

The cultivation of national rather than civilisational arguments by dominant groups stimulated a like response from spokesmen for subordinate groups. Magyars had rejected the Josephine notion of using German as the official language and had carried on with Latin but by the 1830s were pushing for its replacement by Magyar. That stimulated Croatians to demand the use of Croatian in their assemblies (Okey 2000, pp. 121–5). With each downward step language came to be increasingly regarded as attached to group identity and interest rather than to utility of communication and administration (Lyons 2006, pp. 76–97).

Romanticism stimulated an interest in vernacular languages and traditions, a shift of focus from elite to folk culture, and provided a model for a small vanguard intelligentsia. If French or German intellectuals made so much of discovering, or even fabricating, medieval epics as indicative of the depth of the national past, why should not Scottish or Czech intellectuals do the same, especially if it impressed British or German public opinion?[18]

The growing importance of such intellectuals can be linked directly to new socio-economic interests, such as journalists catering for a demand for a vernacular press from *nouveau riche* figures who had not become fluent in the elite language. Lajos Kossuth (1802–94) came to politics through

---

18 Thus the epic poems allegedly by Ossian which James Macpherson published in the late eighteenth century and about which Goethe, amongst others, enthused, or the Czech 'Lay of Visegrad' which Josef Linda announced in 1816 (Lyons 2006, pp. 80–1). The Gothic revival in art and literature in late eighteenth-century Britain drew upon Macpherson's forgery and the *Nibelungslieder* and other such work for inspiration, something ably documented in a recent (2005) exhibition 'Gothic Nightmares: Fuseli, Black and the Romantic Imagination' held at the Tate Britain. However, one should note that if there really was some kind of oral tradition which, to gain recognition in the elite intellectual world which subscribed to the principle of nationality, had to present this tradition in a written vernacular, there could be a hazy distinction between 'forgery' and 'genuine'.

journalism. Other intellectual nationalists came from existing institutions of which the most important were churches which catered for subordinate groups such as the Catholic Church in Ireland and the Greek Orthodox and Uniate churches amongst Slavic peoples in Central Europe. Sometimes they served regional elite interests against a centralising dynasty. The Czech nationalist historian, František Palacký (1798–1876) began his career writing on Bohemian-Moravian history under noble patronage.

Such intellectual vanguards challenged notions of dominant or historical culture which denied to their national culture historic roots or equality of esteem. There was great variation in the cultural and historical resources available for pressing this challenge. Much intellectual effort went into creating more resources as well as interpreting those already available. There were three main emphases: vernacular culture, religion and political rule (for the role of such intellectual groups see Kennedy and Suny 1999).

Subordinate cultures usually had poorly developed written vernaculars. This inhibited standardisation around one dialect. The written and ritual church language (Latin, Church Slavonic) was usually separate from everyday language.[19] Secular written communication in law courts and estate assemblies was conducted in the language of the dominant culture. There was much bi- or multilingualism as well as patois forms which defied 'national' classification, such as the mixing of Czech and German (King 2002). Switches in language use were tied to social situations. In nonliterate societies this made it impossible to identify distinct languages as opposed to linguistic codes. The notion of 'a language' – a key tenet of nationalist thought – was difficult to grasp.[20]

The claim to equal recognition entailed the construction of a written form of the language of the subordinate culture. A written vernacular makes it possible to imagine language as a distinct and bounded entity possessed by a nation. The nation might even be defined as the imagined readership of a standardised written vernacular (Anderson 1991). Usually there was some earlier written form on which to draw (e.g. medieval Czech) but frequently substantial modification was required. Much work went into script (e.g.

---

19 These points do not apply to enclaves of Protestant belief in east-central Europe where direct access to the *written* word of God was a central article of faith. They apply rather to churches in which mystery and ritual mediated through an order of priests was central, that is, the Catholic and Orthodox churches.

20 For an introduction to the complexities of this subject see Fishman 1973. Extracts are conveniently reprinted in S. J. Woolf 1996, pp. 155–70. The peculiarity of the assumption that each human being possesses one essential language is well brought out in Billig 1995, ch. 2, 'Nations and Languages'.

Roman or Cyrillic), orthography and pronunciation, which dialect form to take as the norm, grammar, dictionary compilations, purging of loan words, coining of new words. There were battles to promote the language in schools and through poems, plays, novels and newspaper articles. Conflicts over the language of schools, law courts or provincial assemblies related to material interests, such as the job prospects of teachers or lawyers. Such interests only came into play once the movement for vernacular language use had got under way. Why one language succeeded and another failed was a complex matter (Berend 2003, ch. 2).

Religious differences mapped on to cultural and social distinctions. Imperial expansion in east-central Europe established differences between dominant and subordinate religions. In the Ottoman Empire Muslims ruled Christian populations. In the Habsburg Empire, Catholics ruled other Christians. Russian expansion meant domination of Russian Orthodoxy over other confessions. With the waning of the religious conflicts after the seventeenth century there was a shift away from conversion or expulsion to a hierarchy from privileged, established churches to tolerated, subordinate ones.

These churches provided an institutional basis and a small counter-elite around which subordinate cultures could construct a principle of nationality. In late eighteenth-century Transylvania Uniate and Orthodox clergy agreed on Romanian national claims (Hitchins 1969, 1977). The Uniate Church favoured a 'Roman' view of Romanian history, tracing its origins back to Trajan's conquest of Dacia and drawing a sharp distinction between Romanians, their Magyar and German rulers and Slav populations.

There was a marked difference between how these ideas were elaborated in the Ottoman Empire and the Christian empires of the Habsburgs and the Romanovs. The religious distinction was starker in the Ottoman Empire – between two opposed monotheistic religions – whereas elsewhere the divisions were confessional ones within Christianity. However, the Ottoman Empire allowed more autonomy to Greek Orthodoxy (and to Judaism) than the Habsburg Empire did to non-Catholic and the Romanov Empire to non-Orthodox confessions.

In the Habsburg and Romanov empires there was a close connection between class structure and confessional difference. (The same point applies to Ireland where populist nationalism combined with the religion of the subordinate group.) This was not the case in the Ottoman Empire where political rule was based on a bureaucratic-military system that largely left local communities alone if they provided tax revenue and obedience. Muslims were favoured but the *millet* system provided autonomy to religious communities. Such autonomy increased as the rule of the centre weakened in the nineteenth century (see for example Mazower, 2004).

The hierarchy of the Greek Orthodox church played a leading role in the running of the Ottoman Empire in the Balkans. This militated against elaborating a national principle because 'Greek' referred to a broad religious identity. Nationality was linked to religion on the basis of semi-autonomous institutions *within* Greek Orthodoxy, such as the Serbian and Bulgarian Exarchates. Greek nationalism could be framed in Hellenic terms, congenial to classically educated Western Europeans, but also as Greek Orthodoxy. Neither had much to do with the peninsula later called Greece.

These variations indicate difficulties encountered by nationalists seeking to mesh religious and nationality principles.[21] There were cross-cutting identities (Protestant Irish nationalists, Greek Orthodox Ottoman administrators). There were pressures from lay communities that did not accept the 'national' church (such as neo-Protestant converts in Orthodox territories) or the 'sacralised' nation. There was the supra-national perspective of church elites; the papacy rejected Italian nationalism and could not easily side with German or Polish Catholics. There was tension between different elites. The clergy and the secular elites based on commerce, schools and media institutions regarded each other with suspicion, drawing their authority from different sources. Nevertheless, at moments of crisis coalitions could be formed and at a popular level religious identity was the core of national identity. The fusion of religion and nationality was most likely if an imperial government acted on behalf of a privileged church against a subordinate culture that was religiously and socially distinct.

This raises the issue of rule. 'Historic' nations had political privileges: whether a recent state (Poland), control of the local state (Germans, Magyars) or class domination in the locality (Italy). Subordinate cultural groups did not have such privileges. However, some claimed a past when they did. Czech, Lithuanian and Serbian nationalists claimed medieval polities as their own and depicted the early modern period as one of defeat and decline which the nation must reverse. Some built on institutions, often

---

21 Stefan Berger has observed to me that from 1850 it does appear that the national paradigm dominates historical narratives, 'trumping' religion, class or race. However, what dominates historical writing does not necessarily work at the level of popular, political mobilisation.

granted by an imperial regime to weaken the regionally privileged elite, as was the case of Croatia in relation to Hungary. Other groups had less in the way of a definite history or institution to which their names and marks could be attached and were forced into speculative claims about the far-distant past, such as the Romanian myths about links to the Roman Empire. Slav nationalists had even less. In Lithuania by 1914 an empirical case had barely been made, let alone any movement formed.[22]

The first half of the nineteenth century saw the construction of many national histories, weaving together claims about language, culture, religion and statehood to produce remarkably similar accounts for their allegedly unique nations. The empirical claim that there was a nationality was linked to the normative claim that this nationality was worthy of recognition and loyalty. One feature of these claims was to use history, culture and other markers to turn what was often a class or some other sectional group into a 'whole' group which could be imagined as self-sufficient and complete.

Monika Baar has identified the strategies of five scholars writing the history of distinct nations. Two of these were historians of 'historical nations': the Polish historian Joachim Lelewel (1786–1861) and the Hungarian historian Mihály Horváth (1804–78), though Baar's analysis demonstrates the same intellectual strategies as those deployed by the historians of the three subordinate groups. These are Simonas Daukantas (Lithuanian, 1793–1864), František Palacký (Czech) and Mihail Kogălniceanu (Romanian, 1818–91). Influenced by Scottish Enlightenment and French Restoration romantic historical writing,[23] these men aimed to write:

a complete history of their own nation from its origins until recent times from a new perspective, one which encompassed the 'democratization' of every aspect of historiography: its subject, stage, medium and audience. (Baar 2010, p. 47)

Nation replaced dynasty as principal subject, even if the history written was about the work of dynasty. The history was written in the 'national' language, which often involved abandoning an acquired academic language

---

22 Snyder 2003 works comparatively and considers 'failures' (e.g. Belarus) as well as 'successes'. One could extend the approach and ask why, for example, to this very day it has not proved possible to work up nationalist cases for the central Asian republics which achieved nominal independence with the end of the Soviet Union.

23 Monika Baar has pointed out to me that these historians were not influenced by German historicism but rather by late German Enlightenment writers. Perhaps this indicates how difficult it is for a generalising political ideology like nationalism really to root itself in a genuine historicist view which regards each nation as quite unique.

and developing the 'national' language as the vehicle for a 'national' history. Palacký began his career writing historical works in German but shifted to Czech. Finally, these scholars looked to a national audience. Their degree of success depended on new elite formation. Palacký had a larger audience by mid-century than was available to Daukantas or Kogălniceanu.

The switch to the 'national' language depended upon the efforts of language reform movements. These were sometimes helped by new imperial rulers encouraging the use of local vernaculars, partly for utilitarian reasons (e.g. the Habsburg Emperor Joseph who wanted to raise educational standards), partly to undercut local dominant culture (as with Russia favouring Lithuanian against Polish).

National historical writing was constrained by historical materials as there was a stress on 'scientific' history based on original sources. This was a negative rather than positive constraint, fought out in arguments about forged or authentic documents but not affecting the broad thrust of the historiography, e.g. describing Slavs as peaceful and productive peoples subject to the depredations of marauding predators like Germans and Magyars.

Baar analyses the typical concerns of these historians. First, there were claims to origins, often asserted against dominant groups with their accent on Graeco-Roman and Germanic ancestors.[24] Second, there were accounts of golden ages (the Hussite period for Czechs, pagan Lithuania, the Dacian period for the Romanians). Following the golden ages comes the fall, depicted as the onset of feudalism and dynastic conquest. Feudalism turned the nation into a subordinate class. Democratisation and peasant emancipation, central points in the programme of nationalists, signalled a return to that golden age. Dynastic conquest was sometimes seen as a distinct stage, with the three dynastic empires of Eastern Europe asserting their rule in the early modern period, after the age of feudalism. Dynastic conquest was a theme the historians of dominant groups (Poles, Magyars, Italians) could take up.

Politically what mattered was whether institutions central to the history of the nation had connections to current institutions. The more thoroughly subordinate a cultural group, the weaker such connection. Consequently, greater emphasis was placed upon religion, language and ethnicity.

---

24 The German historian, Ranke, insisted on the superiority of these two 'races' over all others in Europe. A similar argument is presented by Bagehot 1876 who adds Jews (rather than Semitic peoples) as a third race type. This argument would be taken up by Moses Hess and later Zionist writers, for which see below. The emphasis of many 'small' nation historians on other origins – Celtic, Scythian – was a reaction against this focus on a small number of leading race types.

However, these should not be distinguished as types of nationalism. They all served the purpose of identifying the 'whole nation' as bearer of political rights. Nationalism switched between and combined these claims. 'Civic' nationalism takes for granted the existing dominant culture, making it the invisible medium in which national claims are couched. (Only minorities are described as ethnic, not majorities (Kaufmann 2004).) 'Ethnic nationalism' is discourse which uses apparently 'natural' markers to make a subordinate culture visible. Nationalist claims combine markers to include and exclude, to co-ordinate elites, mobilise support and legitimise political demands.[25]

There is one special case of 'subordinate' nationalism which stresses religion, language and ethnicity rather than high culture and institutions. That is Jewish nationalism. Moses Hess, in *Rome and Jerusalem* (1862),[26] was inspired by the rise and success of nationalism in Europe, especially the recent Italian victory over the papacy, seen as a fount of anti-Semitism. Hess stresses ethnic, even race identity,[27] language (Hebrew), even if this is not in popular usage, and gives priority to Jewishness as collective identity over Judaism as religion.[28] He asserts his nation is one amongst many but also unique, with a distinct world mission. Finally, like other nationalists, Hess confronts the partial and incoherent reality of the present with an imagined past when the Jews were a 'whole' people occupying their homeland and an imagined future in that reclaimed homeland. Jews can never be at home in foreign lands until they are – like other foreigners – respected guests with a country of their own. Like other nationalists, Hess is haunted by fear of assimilation to the dominant culture. A likely source of assimilation comes from *within* the nation. Hess constructed the notion of the 'self-hating Jew', the Jew who denies Jews are a nation. (Hess had been a close associate of Marx and

25 There is a long debate about polar typologies of nationalism (western/eastern, civic/ethnic, political/cultural) based on different discourses which in turn are expressive of different sentiments and politics. Apart from the critique of such typologies by Zimmer 2003, see Brubacker 2004 and Hewitson 2006. On using nationalism to co-ordinate, mobilise and legitimise, see Breuilly 1993.

26 There are a number of English translations of *Rome and Jerusalem*. I quote from Hess 1958. As Avineri 1985 points out, all these translations are incomplete and unreliable and, for those with German, Hess 1962 is recommended.

27 'All of past history was concerned with the struggle of races and classes. Race struggle is primary; class struggle is secondary. When racial antagonism ceases, class struggle also ceases. Equality of all social classes follows on the heels of equality of all races and finally remains merely a question of sociology' (Hess 1958, n.p., last paragraph of preface).

28 'Judaism is, above all, a nationality whose history, outlasting millennia, goes hand in hand with that of humanity. It is a nation which has once been the spiritual instrument of regeneration for society and today, as the rejuvenation of the historic nations is being accomplished, Judaism celebrates its own resurrection with its cultural rebirth' (Hess 1958, p. 19).

Engels. The 'self-hater' is the nationalist equivalent to the class traitor with false class consciousness.)

Zionism was confronted with a radically 'incomplete' group as Jews had been forced into occupational and geographical niches and out of their 'homeland'. The projection of the nationalist claim upon ancient Israel and the insistence, through the *kibbutzim* movement on co-operation and self-sufficiency, were ways of transforming Jewish communities into a 'whole' society, a nation, as it was imagined to have been in biblical times. This radical incompleteness makes the logic of nationalist ideology especially clear in Hess. It is a double view: the specific destiny of the Jewish nation is part of a world process of establishing nations as the essential units of humanity. He concludes *Rome and Jerusalem* stressing the fundamental centrality of *history* as world process:

> As after the final catastrophe of *organic* life, when the historic races appeared in the world, the peoples were simultaneously assigned their position and role, so also after the final catastrophe of *social* life, when the spirit of historic nations shall achieve maturity, our people too, together with other historic nations, will simultaneously assume its place in world history. (Hess 1958, p. 89)

The dynamics of Zionism were different from other cases where most members of the nation on whose behalf nationalists claimed to speak lived in the national homeland.[29] Hess exemplifies the 'demonstration effect' of nationalist discourse. As nationalist movements register political success, as in Italy in 1859–60, their discourse is imitated, with appropriate modifications, by those speaking for other nations.

Hess was the major intellectual of Zionism in the nineteenth century, Herzl its principal politician. Herzl claimed that if he had known of Hess' writing, he would not have needed to write *The Jewish State*. For Herzl Jewish nationality did not need establishing by argument but was simple fact, grounded in the rise of exclusionary anti-Semitism, and he devoted himself to developing a practical political programme.

---

29 Many nationalist writers are exiles but the nation they imagine is not an exiled nation. (Some writers have placed Zionism in a broader category of diaspora nationalisms but that only works for the activist leadership, e.g. in the overseas Chinese community. It would not, after all, make sense to refer to the overseas Chinese *nation*. Ironically the establishment of Israel produced another exiled nation: the Palestinians.) Nevertheless, one can analyse the relationship between the intellectual leadership of Zionism (mainly located in Western Europe) and the mass support it eventually mobilised (mainly drawn from Eastern Europe) in the same terms as apply to other cases of nationalism. See Vital 1999 and 1975, especially ch. 5, 'Autoemancipation'.

Early and mid-nineteenth-century constructions of diverse national languages, cultures and histories could be seen in terms of Stage A of national movements as outlined by Hroch. Small groups of intellectuals, clerical and secular, asserted the existence of nations and demanded recognition and respect. However, there was little support for such claims, let alone any political programme or movement (Hroch 1985, 1996). Stage B is when small political movements form and Stage C is when nationalism becomes a mass movement.[30] As national discourse shifts from empirical/normative arguments to forming the core ideology of political movements, so it must develop a programmatic character. This is the third element needed to complete the principle of nationality.

6   Nationality as political programme

The revolutions of 1848–9 propelled intellectual principles of nationality into politics.[31] Even if revolution 'failed' to produce national states, it put the matter on the political agenda, tested some programmes and stimulated the formulation of more 'realistic' programmes. Subsequently as successive nationalist programmes were realised, that encouraged others to formulate nationalist programmes of their own (Dowe, 2001; Sperber 2005).

As with the diffusion of the intellectual principle, the stimulus came from above, from the self-styled historical nationalities. The capitulation of princes to popular movements in the German lands in February/March 1848 led to the convening of elections on a widespread manhood franchise to a German National Assembly. It was decided that the elections must be held in the territory of the German Confederation. This included the Austrian crownlands of Bohemia and Moravia. Those speaking in the name of the Czech nation called for an election boycott. Czech speakers declared themselves loyal subjects of the Habsburg Emperor and the historic

---

30 I do not fully agree with Hroch's typology if it is taken to mean that the formulation of an elaborate nationalist ideology is a precondition for the development of a nationalist movement, whether elite or popular. Sometimes a movement can begin with little intellectual preparation and then acquire intellectual spokesmen. It is, however, useful for conceptualising the way nationalist ideas were elaborated and translated into political ideologies.

31 The French Revolution of 1789 turned the Enlightenment idea that human society could be deliberately reformed into a principle of political action. The counter-revolution both intellectually and politically sought to discredit this idea. Nevertheless, even if in limited ways, electoral contests in France and Britain in the 1830s and 1840s encouraged the formulation of programmes by competing parties. 1848 generalised the notion of political competition and programmes across much of Europe.

provinces of Bohemia and Moravia, rejecting German nationalist claims.[32] There was a swift polarisation as the conflicting nationalisms mobilised and compelled people to choose sides (Deak 1979; Havránek 2004).

The Habsburg government realised it could enlist subordinate nationalism against the more dangerous threat from dominant nationalism. Croatians and Romanians acted against Hungarian rebels. Hungarian nationalists refused to make concessions to ethnic groups they deemed might merit cultural autonomy but not political rights (Okey 2000, ch. 5). Similarly, the German National Assembly made provision for non-German language speakers but not political recognition.[33]

Where there had been mutual recognition, political crisis undermined it. Prussian liberals had supported the Polish cause before 1848 and conceded autonomy to the Grand Duchy of Posen, the part of Poland brought under Prussian rule with Polish partition. However, they retreated from this policy which sparked nationality conflicts in Posen, and led to an ethnic partition line which favoured Germans. The decision was endorsed by the German National Assembly (Breuilly 1998b; Namier 1948). Similar conflicts developed between Germans and Italians in the Habsburg Empire and between Germans and Danes in Schleswig-Holstein. Revolution stimulated the emergence of open political debate and organisation and the rapid formulation of programmes by those who had become, if only for a short time, full-time oppositional politicians.

Thus the 'springtime of peoples' turned into the 'nightmare of nations' (Langewiesche 1992). One should not exaggerate. National appeal varied regionally and had little popular resonance. A dominant national historiography has neglected social and economic issues.[34]

---

32 This was the occasion of the famous statement by Palacký that if the Habsburg Empire had not existed it would have had to have been invented. This is a good example of the way intellectuals were compelled by political crisis to formulate a programme. In this case Palacký had to recognise that simple assertion of national existence, value and autonomy could lead to the break-up of the empire which would leave small nations like the Czechs prey to their larger neighbours, in this case Germans and Russians. Thus began the formulation of a series of federalist programmes designed to combine autonomy with security in a larger territorial state.

33 See Vick 2002, ch. 4, and the imperial constitution of 1849 (translation in Hucko 1987, especially Article 188: 'The non-German speaking peoples of Germany are guaranteed their national development, namely, equal rights for their languages...' (p. 114)). Note that a 'German' was defined as a 'citizen of Germany', so these non-German speakers were, politically, Germans.

34 Rosdolsky 1986, in his critique of Engels, points out that popular Slav opposition to Polish nationalist leadership or Romanian opposition to Hungarian nationalism was mainly to do with the land, not the national question. There was no quick political revolutionary way round these social conflicts.

The rise of subordinate nationalist movements had significant long-term repercussions for dominant nationalism. Polish nationalists shifted towards a Catholic and populist emphasis. This weakened the capacity of Polish nationalists to appeal on historic grounds for support in areas of non-Polish popular culture. Politics came to focus on social tasks within different territories. Counter-revolution marginalised programmatic nationalism for decades. The rising of 1863 was confined to Russian Poland and nationalists found it difficult to co-ordinate action across the partitioned territories. Only the breakdown of imperial power in the First World War stimulated a new programme of Polish independence (Davies 1962).

In Hungary, radicals like Kossuth drew from 1848 the lesson that one must construct a federalist, multicultural programme which appealed to non-Magyars. Kossuth, however, was in exile and populist nationalism only became significant in Hungary after his death. Instead, the elite strategy, following Austria's defeat by Prussia, was to achieve internal autonomy. Within that space Hungarians pursued the forcible assimilation of non-Magyars while holding them in subordinate positions.

Hungary achieved this because of the blows to Habsburg authority, in 1859 and 1866. The consequence was expulsion from Italy and Germany. The empire appeared to be breaking into its constituent national parts as envisaged by advocates of historic nationality in 1848, although not in the form envisaged.

In the Habsburg Empire the principle of nationality justified internal conflict: between Germans and Czechs, between Magyars and their Slav and Romanian opponents. In the Ottoman Empire the creation of new polities – in Greece, then Serbia and Romania – meant that the principle of nationality served another function: legitimating statehood. The new state was seen as the core of a larger, future nation state. Its rulers used the nationality argument to justify a foreign policy which brought it into conflict with its neighbours. Nationalism in the two empires also interacted, as when Serbia and Romania made claims to 'national' territory in the Habsburg Empire or Westernised nationalist elites of the Habsburg Empire elaborated the ideology deployed by the autonomous states.[35]

---

35 There has been a huge upsurge in new research on Balkan nationalism since 1989. My suggestions in Breuilly 1993, ch. 5 about influences between the Habsburg and Ottoman empires are now very dated. For an introduction to recent work see Todorova 2004. Valuable comparative collections of essays which go across the East–West division include Baycroft and Hewitson 2006 and Hirschhausen and Leonhard 2001.

Separatist movements avoided the difficulties of formulating a programme by demanding independence and liberty against an oppressive foreigner. However, the most successful and influential nationalist movements of the 1860s were in Italy and Germany and these were unification movements. Unification is more complex than separation, requiring more than state collapse and diplomatic and military success. Unification involved co-operation between an existing state (Piedmont, Prussia) and a movement which developed the principle of nationality. To effect co-operation a key element was a constitution which extended the monarchical principle of the dominant state to the national territory whilst giving expression to the principle of nationality. The constitution included provision for an elected parliament. That entrenched 'national politics' as a routine element. This provided a model for further national movements which appealed to existing nation states to help them establish similar nation states (Breuilly 1993, ch. 4).

7 Expanding the discourse of nationality

I have traced the escalation of the principle of nationality, from civilisational claims in France and Britain, to arguments of historic nationality for Germans, Italians, Magyars and Poles, followed by subordinate cultural groups using notions of vernacular culture, popular religion and ethnicity. The increasingly populist function of political language pushed discourse in an ethno-cultural direction, even where there existed an earlier tradition of framing nationality in elite terms. The successes of German and Italian unification made the principle of nationality attractive and provided programmatic models for others. Political oppositions appropriated the principle of nationality to justify claims, even if these were mainly social or religious. Self-defined national states resorted to nationalist arguments to justify domestic and foreign policies.

Tradition and nationalism

The escalation of the principle of nationality forced non-nationalist conservatives to join in. The principle of nationality had been allied with liberal democratic and radical-populist values. Conservatives opposed those values. The Tsar was father of his people, the Habsburg Emperor above nationality. Imperial regimes meditated the strategy of unleashing nationalities against one another but the threat this posed to the ideal of order deterred them. The Habsburgs did not decree peasant emancipation in Galicia in 1846 after they repressed Polish gentry nationalism. Nor did they in Lombardy-Venetia after 1848 (Sked 1979). The British maintained the Anglo-Irish landowning class well beyond mid-century. The Romanovs did not seek to destroy the Polish nationalist elite as a landowning class after the rising of 1830–1.

It was easier for initial conservative moves to be made in nationally homogeneous territories. Rogue conservatives such as Disraeli and Bismarck saw there could be popular support for anti-liberal policies of deference at home and assertion abroad. In more radical but authoritarian form, the plebiscitary empire of Louis Napoleon undermined liberalism and democracy at home and took up the nationality principle abroad.

Principled conservatives sought to construct a national tradition on monarchy, faith and hierarchy. Burkean arguments could be rehabilitated in Britain. French and Spanish monarchists argued that the true spirit of the country resided in royalism, provincial diversity and a powerful Catholic Church. By the last third of the nineteenth century conservative figures had taken up these arguments and others, such as anti-Semitism, and deployed them against liberal and democratic principles of nationality (for a survey see Rogger and Weber 1966).

However, the irresistible rise of popular politics pushed imperial regimes into breaking with dynastic neutrality or defending dominant cultural groups. The British government under Gladstone embarked on land reform in Ireland which destroyed Anglo-Irish landed dominance and provided space for populist Irish nationalism. The tsarist government decreed emancipation of the serfs in 1861, turning this against the Polish gentry in the wake of the 1863 insurrection. It also took up a Russianisation policy against non-Russian Slavs. In the Habsburg Empire, growing Czech–German antagonism forced the government into explicit recognition of nationality distinctions (Berend 2003, ch. 6). Imperial Germany took up Germanisation policies against Poles (Hagen 1980).

Conservative sectional interests adopted nationalist language. From the 1870s increased availability of Russian and American grain put European farmers under pressure. The response was a demand for tariff protection. This was adapted to the principle of nationality with claims about the agricultural basis of the nation, the need to preserve national values rooted in the rural population, to ensure self-sufficiency, to maintain a reservoir of healthy manpower for the army.[36] Aristocratic landowners in Germany, Hungary and elsewhere who had previously disdained nationalist arguments formed pressure groups, hired popular journalists and constructed nationalist arguments. Ominously they incorporated anti-Semitic elements into their programmes: the Jew figured as parasite, non-producer and town dweller, holding honest producers in debt, a pariah group within the nation (Retallack 1988).

This is the 'nationalisation' of politics. All political groups adopt and adapt the principle of nationality. The principle becomes detached from specific political positions and one must instead consider the particular ways the principle is articulated. Presenting French or German nationality as the complex sum of its provincial identities suggests a conservative articulation. National discourse to justify expensive policies of overseas expansion can usually be located in elite liberal nationalist circles. Labour leaders argued that only full democratisation and social reform would realise the true nation.[37]

Race and nationalism

Fenton has distinguished three relationships between race and nation: race within nation, race as nation and race as civilisation (Fenton 2006). Banton has distinguished race as lineage, type and sub-species (Banton 1998).

Banton argues that much nineteenth-century race thought was in terms of 'type'. This notion of type can in turn be linked to 'race within nation'. For example, one finds many references to a division of the French between Gauls and Franks, the English between Anglo-Saxons and Normans but this is in turn based on other race ideas. Gobineau, who published a long study *Essay on the Inequality of the Human Races* (1853–5) (Gobineau 1970), distinguished between secondary and tertiary races. The white, yellow and black races were the secondary ones.[38] But they in turn gave rise to further

---

36 This rural conservative populism is also at the heart of Slavophilism. The intellectual pioneer in Germany was Wilhelm Riehl (1823–97). See Riehl 1897.

37 The Austro-Marxist politician and theoretician Otto Bauer took the argument one step further. He argued that national consciousness would become stronger with the democratisation of national culture. Bauer was responding to the particular problem of the Habsburg Empire which was the need to accommodate national difference within the socialist party while at the same time concentrating political opposition on the imperial state but his arguments could be applied to the increasingly large labour parties of the Western European nation states (Bauer 2000).

38 Gobineau reluctantly accepted a 'unitary' origin of humankind, partly through reason (the capacity for the different races to interbreed) and partly through faith (the story of Genesis) although at one point he did assert that Adam was father of the 'white race' (Gobineau 1970, p. 99).

divisions, such as Slav, Celt, Aryan and Latin races. However, nations were usually mixtures or fusions of racial types.[39] John Stuart Mill saw a mixing of Anglo-Saxon and Celtic elements as having beneficial results. Michelet argued that the modern French nation was a successful if mysterious fusion of Celtic, German, Roman and Greek ancestors (Crossley 1993, p. 205; Varouxakis 2002, p. 22). Gobineau, more pessimistically, saw such mixing as both inevitable but also having a degenerative effect on the higher race type.

This use of race – even when notions of 'blood' are used – is not biological but cultural; the terms refer to mental and behavioural qualities, not physical differences. Some writers have argued that race ideas had a class character but this does not seem to have been significant in any detailed historical or other analysis. Later, when biological reasoning was applied to class societies, it took the form of eugenics focused on the 'weak' elements within the working class, rather than being projected directly on to class difference. Nevertheless, there was a language of race difference within the nation which provided support for insisting that a racially distinct group within the national territory did not belong to the nation.

This set limits to the development of such discourse in relation to nation.[40] First, the argument had a class dimension, being applied principally to poor immigrants. Irish, Polish and Russian immigrants were depicted in racial terms, even by Max Weber who rejected biological notions of race as unscientific (Curtis 1971; Weber 1978, 1994a). But Weber did not extend the idea to all Polish speakers. In settled multiethnic states nationalist conflicts were not posed in race terms. Nationalists did not envision *within Europe* policies of expulsion or explicit separation, let alone mass murder.[41] The ideal was assimilation into the dominant nationality, incompatible with biological concepts of race which imply either fusion ('melting pot') or separation. There was a language of broad race distinction (Slavs, Teutons, Celts) and one of narrow ethnic distinction (Saxons and Normans,

---

39 As Banton 1998 points out, thinkers thoroughly confused race as lineage and race as type. There was also slippage between race as normative and race as descriptive. This makes for bad science but is precisely what is needed for ideology. The major pre-1914 obstacle to such an ideology becoming practically significant (and therefore a component of European nationalist discourse) was an inability to operationalise it. 'Scientific' racism stemming from eugenics, along with the enormous power of the Third Reich, would later provide that ability.
40 I focus here on *European* discourse. In the USA the language of race, related to Afro-American slaves and Native Americans, was much more central. See, for example, Fenton 2003, ch. 2.
41 Though the treatment of Jews in the Pale of Settlement might be regarded as an exception.

Gauls and Franks) but they were too casual, impressionistic and detached from actual political conflict to be significant. Above all, with the significant exception of anti-Semitism, such ideas were not able to generate a nationalist *programme*. Either race mixing was good (Mill, Michelet) or bad (Gobineau) but it was not something which could be made an aspect of policy. Instead, significant racist nationalism took on Fenton's third form: race as civilisation.

Overseas imperial expansion redefined race. By 1800 there was a discourse of non-European peoples as racially distinct and inferior, even if challenged by civilisational or Christian arguments.[42] By mid-nineteenth century white Europeans generally believed in a global race hierarchy with themselves at the top. At elite level there were finer distinctions: black Africans, Native Americans, Aborigines below members of decayed civilisations (Chinese, Hindus, Muslims).

During the American Civil War few on the Union side argued that Negroes were the equal of whites. The argument against slavery was based more on degrading consequences for whites and concern about the extension of slavery into new territories (McPherson 1998, especially ch. 6). Most notably, little connection was made between the ideologies purporting to explain differences between Europeans and non-Europeans and between different Europeans. This was clearest in the USA where the discourse of nativism deployed against continental European immigrants was distinct from race discourse about Negroes.[43] Even the race argument lacked elaborate biological foundation because it was such a 'natural' attitude. This distance between nationalism, race ideology and biological argument narrowed from the later nineteenth century for various reasons.

First, the rapid expansion of formal overseas empire, especially in Africa. Physical anthropology, which dispensed with culture or history as the basis of difference, flourished and was popularised through exhibitions of 'primitive' peoples and the establishment of ethnographic museums. (For the case of Germany around 1900 see Honold 2004; Zimmerman 2004.)

---

42 This was not the only or even dominant view in the first encounters between Europeans and peoples in Asia, Africa and the Americas. See for example Jackson and Jaffer 2004, a catalogue linked to an exhibition at the Victoria and Albert Museum. Of course, the story has in turn to differentiate by region and type of encounter as well as much else.

43 Partly on practical grounds as both Confederate and Union politicians hoped to enlist white immigrant support. See McPherson 2003. I have benefited from reading an unpublished conference paper: Towers 2006.

Second, race arguments acquired a new force following the publication of Darwin's *Origins of Species* in 1859.[44] Popularisation of the notion of necessary struggle, leading to 'survival of the fittest' could be applied in racial terms.[45] Whether in Darwinian or non-Darwinian form (denying common origins to races), the idea of race became explicitly biological. This radicalised and essentialised difference and justified hierarchy or separation or ultimately murder.[46]

Third, these arguments were extended into Europe, underpinning claims about Germanic, Latin and Slav peoples, or the distinct racial qualities of Jews.[47] Rapid industrial and urban growth and cross-border immigration brought together ethnically distinct peoples, often in conflict over jobs and housing. Germany became a country of net immigration from the 1890s, just as race ideas were applied to poor Polish, Russian and Jewish immigrants. Conversely, pogroms against Jews in western Russia contributed to this migration and also were justified with race arguments. The rapid development of mass politics was associated with a populist nationalism reacting against elite nationalism and the class and confessional creeds of labour and Catholic parties. Radical nationalism, including anti-Semitism, figured prominently in such populist politics.[48]

Nevertheless, perceiving national difference within Europe as a matter of biological race was still marginal by 1914. In Western Europe the

---

44 Ironically Darwin later lost influence amongst biologists because he was unable to explain the selective transmission of favoured differences, indeed his assumption that traits from parents were mixed in their offspring undermined his own argument of selection. Only after 1918, with the rediscovery of Mendel's findings on genetic selection, did the rise of neo-Darwinism begin. See Kohn 2004.

45 The phrase 'survival of the fittest' was in fact coined by Herbert Spencer in relation to competition between human beings, both individuals and societies, but acquired a pseudo-scientific meaning through its association with Darwin's notion of evolution. There is a huge literature on this subject. For a good introduction to the 'internal' intellectual history of the subject, see Banton 1998.

46 Even if one assumed – as the influence of Darwin largely led most thinkers to do – common origins and progressive evolution, the time span involved meant this had no practical significance where people perceived major racial differences. Much depended on further beliefs about how traits were inherited and what would be the consequences of racial interbreeding. Beliefs of the time tended towards purity, hierarchy and discrimination. Whereas Mill and Michelet had envisaged advantageous racial blends, this was excluded from the later discourse of biological race.

47 One telling example is how the interest in classifying peoples through skull measurement, taken up in overseas empire, was extended in Germany with a similar exercise – this time involving hair, skin and eye colour – carried out in many schools and treating Jews as distinctive in these respects. As the survey involved some six million pupils, one can imagine that it also had some impact on the attitudes of many young Germans. See Zimmermann 2004.

48 Again, the literature is vast. Generally see MacMaster 2001. For a good comparative survey for Britain and Germany, see Kennedy and Nicholls 1981. For a specific example of populist nationalism see Coetzee 1990.

assumption of advanced race mixing rendered it impossible to make such ideas programmatic and beyond Europe the sense and practice of white superiority was so embedded in imperial rule that it did not need a programme. Where one might think race ideas could be deployed in a class sense, in east-central Europe, it was rather a sense of national difference based on an amalgam of historical, cultural and ethnic factors that were used instead, though anti-Semitism was a significant exception. While nation as civilisation, history or ethnicity had become the basis of political claims and programmes, nation as race had not achieved this by 1914.[49]

8 Nationality as dominant norm

By 1914 the language of nationalism dominated political discourse. The formation of nation states in Europe advanced this process. In domestic affairs the growth of mass party politics focused on influential, if not sovereign parliaments, promoted specialised political rhetoric and organisation in which the claim to advance the interests of the electorate ('nation') was central. That rhetoric was taken up in the expanding print media by pressure groups and sectional interests.

In international affairs German unification and the growing power of the German state stimulated a reorganisation of diplomatic alignments. Foreign policy, even if still controlled by rulers and elite politicians, deployed nationalist rhetoric in justifying itself to domestic public opinion. Once an enemy had been publicly demonised (e.g. anti-German publicity in Britain after 1900) or a policy declared vital to the national interest (e.g. German battle-fleet building), it was difficult for a government to act against such opinion (Kennedy 1980).

Every group adapted nationalist language to its interests. It is pointless to discriminate between 'true' nationalism (say, ethnic or racial creeds) and other beliefs (e.g. distinctions between patriotism and nationalism, ethnic and civic nationalism).[50] Differences rather indicate interests. One French nationalist advocated overseas empire as vital, another denounced it as a distraction from revenge for 1870/71 and regaining Alsace-Lorraine.

49 There is a very large literature on the subject, less because of the significance of the subject before 1914 than because of the subsequent rise of Hitler and Nazism to power. A classical intellectual history from this perspective is Mosse 1966.
50 A good collection of essays in which a critique of this distinction is central is Baycroft and Hewitson 2006.

One German nationalist insisted on conferring citizenship on children of Germans to promote Germandom abroad, another opposed it when a German colonist married a local woman in South-West Africa (Gosewinkel 2004; Weber 1959). More significant is the consensus on foregrounding the principle of nationality in political discourse. With that established, groups shifted ground, adopting different elements of nationalist discourse as and when circumstances demanded.

The nation state itself nationalised political discourse. Tariff protectionism after 1880 nationalised economic space. Restrictions on immigration nationalised citizenship. Compulsory mass schooling promoted the teaching of national history. Welfare innovations turned pensions and medical care into national goods. Increased tensions between European powers intensified the use of nationalist stereotypes.

The behaviour of powerful nation states served as a model for others. The Tsar pursued Russianisation policies. Franz Josef acknowledged nationality differences between Czechs and Germans. Magyars imposed assimilation policies. The USA joined the drive for overseas empire. Japan justified its successful wars against China and Russia in nationalist terms. Yet one should note the limitations of nationalism. First, if everyone adopts nationalist discourse, then in everyday politics what matters are the internal differences. At another level, the very basic assumption of nationality made in the conflicting forms of nationalism, helps nationalism reproduce itself 'naturally', banally. That also shapes political values and means that in a crisis, specific appeals to nationalism can succeed (Billig 1995).[51]

Second, the nation state remained an objective rather than an achievement. Much of east-central Europe and most of the world beyond Europe was organised on non-national grounds. For many subjects of nation states, the national interest, especially abroad, was a remote matter of indifference (Porter 2004). It mattered more as one went up the social scale and got closer to state power.

In 1914 the Romanov Empire remained strong. Historians have argued that the Habsburg Empire was more stable than hindsight judgements after 1918 assumed (Cornwall 1990). The Ottoman Empire, having lost the Balkans, was energetically reforming in its remaining territory (Macfie 1998). All three empires sustained mass warfare for several years.

---

51 For the argument that constant contestation over what is 'true' national identity actually strengthens nationalism, indeed is essential to its continued importance, see Hutchinson 2005, especially ch. 4.

Yet even if not essential for political strength and stability, the principle of nationality shaped the post-war settlement. All three empires were defeated.[52] The eventual victors – Bolsheviks and western Allies – incorporated the principle of nationality into successor states. The Bolsheviks retained control of a multiethnic empire but constructed national republics (Smith 1999). The Allies created a series of nation states in the territories of the losers (Sharp 1991). That made the principle of nationality even more central to the politics of the twentieth century than it had been to that of the nineteenth century. But that is another story (Mazower 2000).

9   Concluding points

I have outlined how and why the principle of nationality shifted from the margin to the centre of political discourse. The focus of attention has been on political discourse. This might imply that discourse was the moving force in the rise of nationalism.

I do not have the space to engage with complex debates on nationalism (for a good introduction, see Smith 1998). However, it is necessary to distinguish between ideas, sentiments (that is, the emotional affect of national identity) and politics. These are closely related but they can occur independently of one another and there is no one or even dominant relationship between these three aspects of nationalism. The principle of nationality as an ideology is neither cause nor effect of nationalist sentiments or politics.

The empirical assertion that there *is* a nationality took on new form when applied to a whole society rather than just a high culture or political elite. This empirical conception of nationality is closely linked to changes that undermine fixed social distinctions, such as the rapid growth of commercial agriculture and manufacturing. It was also linked to the need for specialised political languages and institutions used to co-ordinate and mobilise diverse and larger sections of the population.

The normative assertion that nationality is a value, demanding loyalty and commitment, requires one to specify these qualities in terms of history,

---

52 What if Germany and her allies had won the war? Would the preservation of the Habsburg and Ottoman empires and the extension of German rule across Western and Central Europe have blocked the nationality principle? One can never answer such speculative questions. However, it is difficult to see nationalist movements declining in importance in the two multinational empires (just as they were taken into account explicitly in the Soviet Union). For Germany perceptive observers like Max Weber were concerned that over-extension would undermine the national character of the German state and thought it would be necessary to concede autonomy to other nationalities such as Poles and Ukrainians.

culture, language, religion and customs. The nationalist argument blends democratic with cultural claims.

Finally, the programmatic demand for self-determination requires one to envisage autonomy as a series of territorially distinct states (in some cases, federal units within a state). Only under modern conditions of sovereign, participatory states with sharply bounded and exclusive territories can such a programme become a core feature of politics.

Thus develops a political discourse which appeals to the people (democracy) in a glorifying self-referential way (the nation) and sets itself the goal of national self-determination. It is an ideological discourse which thoroughly mixes empirical and normative claims in a way that makes it incapable of disproof. It invokes different elements to identify and venerate the nation – civilisation, history, institutions, language, religion, culture, race – and can always adapt to changing circumstances by shifting emphasis from one to another feature. Its greatest success in modern times is that it is no longer considered a principle but a matter of fact.

4
Hegel and Hegelianism

FREDERICK C. BEISER

1 Problems of interpretation

Seen from a broad historical perspective, Hegel's political philosophy, as expounded in his 1821 *Philosophie des Rechts*, was a grand synthesis of all the conflicting traditions of the late eighteenth and early nineteenth centuries. Its theory of the state wedded liberalism with communitarianism;[1] its doctrine of right fused historicism, rationalism and voluntarism; its vision of ideal government united aristocracy, monarchy and democracy; and its politics strove for the middle ground between left and right, progress and reaction. Such an account of Hegel's achievement is not an *ex post facto* rationalisation; it is a simple restatement of his intentions. For Hegel saw himself as the chief synthesiser, as the last mediator, of his age. All the conflicts between opposing standpoints would finally be resolved – their truths preserved and their errors cancelled – in a single coherent system. The power of Hegel's political philosophy lay here, in its syncretic designs,

---

References to Hegel's works in this chapter are to the following editions: EPW = *Die Enzyklopädie der philosophischen Wissenschaften im Grundrisse* (1817), Heidelberg. ER = *Über die Englische Reformbill, Werkausgabe* XI, pp. 83–130. GW = *Gesammelte Werke* (1989), ed. Rheinisch-Westfälischen Akademie der Wissenschaften. Hamburg: Meiner. H = *Philosophie des Rechts. Die Vorlesung von 1819/20 in einer Nachschrift* (1983), ed. Dieter Henrich. Frankfurt: Suhrkamp – cited by page number. PG = *Phänomenologie des Geistes*, ed. Johannes Hoffmeister. Hamburg: Meiner. PR = *Grundlinien der Philosophie des Rechts* (1821). *Werke* VII – cited by paragraph number (§). Remarks are indicated by an R, additions by an A. SS = *System der Sittlichkeit*, in volume V of *Gesammelte Werke* (1989), ed. Rheinisch-Westfälischen Akademie der Wissenschaften. Hamburg: Meiner. VD = *Die Verfassung Deutschlands. Werke* I, pp. 451–610. VG = *Die Vernunft in der Geschichte* (1955), ed. J. Hoffmeister. Hamburg: Meiner. *Lectures on the Philosophy of World History: Introduction* (1975), trans. H. B. Nisbet. Cambridge. VNS = *Vorlesungen über Naturrecht und Staatswissenschaft. Heidelberg 1817/18. Nachgeschrieben von P. Wannenmann* (1983), ed. C. Becker *et al.* Hamburg: Meiner – cited by paragraph number (§). VVL = *Verhandlungen in der Versammlung der Landstände der Königsreichs Württemberg im Jahr 1815 und 1816. Werkausgabe* IV, pp. 462–597.

1 The terms 'liberalism' and 'communitarianism' are anachronistic; I use them here only as shorthand to designate some trends in late eighteenth-century thought akin to modern liberalism and communitarianism.

in its capacity to accommodate all standpoints; any critique of the system, it seemed, came from a standpoint whose claims had already been settled within it.

Some of the greatest problems in understanding Hegel's political philosophy arise from his systematic ambitions, his syncretic intentions. The most obvious problem is to provide a balanced interpretation, one that does justice to every side of Hegel's system. The flaw of most interpretations is that they are one-sided, stressing one aspect of his system at the expense of another. Hence Hegel's theory of the state has been construed as a defence of communitarianism against liberalism; his theory of right has been read exclusively as rationalism, voluntarism or historicism; and his politics has been understood as either radical or reactionary. None of these extreme or one-sided interpretations can be correct, given that it was Hegel's intention to unify all standpoints in his system.

Another even more formidable problem lies in a treacherous field, one into which few historians or political theorists like to venture: metaphysics. Metaphysics is the heart and soul of Hegel's system, the source of its unity, the basis of its synthetic designs. Since, however, metaphysics is controversial, and since it is beyond the ken of most political theorists, most recent interpretations of Hegel's politics are non-metaphysical, as if it were comprehensible in its own right apart from his metaphysics.[2] But these interpretations suffer fatal flaws. For one thing, they are viciously anachronistic: they impose a modern academic division of labour upon a more holistic era; and they force a modern positivistic spirit upon an age sceptical of positivism. Even worse, they are flatly contrary to Hegel's intention, which was to place politics on a firm metaphysical foundation.[3] Worst of all, most of Hegel's central political ideas are irreducibly and inescapably metaphysical. Hence his reason in history theme is based on his absolute idealism; his notion of freedom depends on his concept of spirit (*Geist*); his doctrine of right rests upon his Aristotelian ontology and teleology; and

---

2 For the non-metaphysical approach to Hegel's social and political philosophy, see Franco 1999, pp. 83–4, 126, 135–6, 140, 143, 151–2, 360–1 n.4; Hardimon 1994, p. 8; Patten 1999, pp. 16–27; Pelczynski 1971, pp. 1–2; Plamenatz 1963, II, pp. 129–32; Rawls 2000, p. 330; Smith 1989, p. xi; Tunick 1992, pp. 14, 17, 86, 99; and Wood 1990, pp. 4–6. For some recent protests against this approach, see Dickey 1999; Peperzak 2001, pp. 5–19; and Yovel 1996, pp. 26–41.

3 In the introduction to his 1803 *Naturrecht* essay, Hegel criticised both the empiricist and rationalist traditions of natural law for their lack of a metaphysical foundation. See *Werke* II, pp. 434–40. He saw his own distinctive contribution to this tradition as the attempt to establish just such a foundation. Never did he depart from this programme; the 1821 *Rechtsphilosophie* was its final culmination.

his methodology, which he saw as his distinctive contribution to political philosophy, demands that we grasp 'the concept' (*der Begriff*) of a thing, which is its 'formal-final cause'.

The task of this essay is to explain, as far as possible in a confined compass, Hegel's political philosophy according to its holistic and metaphysical intentions.[4] We will consider how Hegel's theory of law united voluntarism, rationalism and historicism, how his theory of the state joined liberalism and communitarianism, and how his theory of history joined radicalism and conservatism.

2 Reason in history

Any general treatment of Hegel's political thought should begin with the central event of his age: the French Revolution. Like so many thinkers in the 1790s, Hegel forged his social and political philosophy in the crucible of this epochal event. Some of the central themes of his mature political thought grew directly out of his response to the issues raised by the Revolution. Hegel himself paid handsome tribute to the influence of the Revolution on his thinking when he called it, and the quarter-century following it, 'possibly the richest years that world history has had, and for us the most instructive, because it is to them that our world and ideas belong' (VVL IV, pp. 507, 282).

When the Bastille was stormed in July 1789, Hegel was only nineteen, a student at a seminary, the illustrious Tübinger Stift. Along with his two famous friends at the Stift, F.W. J. Schelling and Friedrich Hölderlin, Hegel greeted the Revolution as the dawn of a new age and celebrated the end of the despotism, privilege and oppression of the *ancien régime*. According to legend, Hegel, Schelling and Hölderlin planted a liberty tree, formed a secret club to read new revolutionary literature and made contacts with republicans in France.[5] This was not just youthful enthusiasm, however. Although many of Hegel's contemporaries quickly became disillusioned with the Revolution, Hegel remained true to its fundamental ideals: *liberté, égalité et fraternité* and the rights of man. Even in his final years, he would toast Bastille day, admire Napoleon and condemn the Restoration.

---

4 The interpretation here has been worked out in more detail in Beiser 2005.
5 The source of the legend is Rosenkranz 1972, pp. 29, 32–4. For an appraisal of the sources, see H. S. Harris 1972, pp. 115–16 n.2.

Hegel drew three great lessons from the Revolution. First, that the constitution of the modern state should be based upon reason, not precedent or tradition (VVL IV, pp. 506, 281). Second, that its constitution should be founded upon the idea of freedom, the idea that man as such is free (PG XII, pp. 527–9). Third, that the modern state should include representative institutions, so that the people have some share in government (VD I, pp. 572/234). In short, Hegel's rationalism, his belief in human rights and his faith in representative institutions were all a legacy of the Revolution.

Although Hegel endorsed the ideals of the Revolution, he repudiated its practice. He disapproved of violent social change from below, a cataclysm that would sweep away all laws and institutions, leaving nothing to build upon. Like many of his contemporaries who had witnessed the turmoil in France, Hegel stressed the value of gradual reform from above, directed by the wise and educated.[6] All successful social and political change, he believed, should take into account the existing circumstances of a country, its economy, geography, culture and legal system (PR §§258R, 272, 274, 298A). Social and political ideals should not be imposed upon these circumstances according to some abstract blueprint, but they should evolve from them. Hegel developed this moderate attitude early, for even in the 1790s he was critical of the methods of the Jacobins and advocated timely reform to prevent revolution.[7]

The chief philosophical problem that the Revolution posed for Hegel, and indeed his entire generation, concerned the proper relationship between morality and politics, theory and practice. Should our moral principles dictate or derive from our political practice? Are these principles justifiable by pure reason alone, as Kant argued, so that they provide categorical requirements to which our practice should conform? Or are they justifiable by experience alone, as Burke maintained, so that they should conform to our actual practices and institutions? Such were the questions debated between left and right throughout the 1790s in Germany. This debate began in 1793 with the publication of Kant's famous 'Theory-Practice' essay in the pages of the *Berlinische Monatsschrift*.[8] Kant's essay was a reply to Burke's *Reflections*

---

6 See VVL IV, pp. 464–71/247–54. Cf. VVL I, p. 273 and VVL XI, pp. 86/297.
7 See VVL I, p. 273 and Hegel's 24 December 1794 letter to Schelling (Hegel 1961, I, p. 12) where he criticises '*die Schändlichkeit der Robespierreroten*'.
8 'Über den Gemeinspruch: Das mag in der Theorie richtig sein, taugt aber nicht für die Praxis', first published in *Berlinische Monatsschrift* 22, 1793, pp. 201–84; in Kant 1902, VIII, pp. 273–314.

on the Revolution in France, which had appeared in Friedrich Gentz's translation in the spring of 1793. Kant's essay sparked off an intense dispute between right and left about the role of reason in politics. While radical or more progressive thinkers, such as Kant, Fichte and Reinhold, defended an ethical rationalism, according to which theory (i.e. reason) should dictate practice, reactionary or more conservative writers, such as Justus Möser, A.W. Rehberg, Friedrich Gentz and Christian Garve, championed an ethical empiricism, according to which theory should follow from practice, which embodies 'the wisdom of generations'.[9]

Though usually ignored in secondary literature,[10] this dispute proved crucial for the development of Hegel's political thought. Hegel's response to it was the central and characteristic theme of his later political thought: reason in history. The germ of Hegel's theme is already apparent from his early essay on the German constitution, the so-called *Verfassungsschrift*, which he wrote from 1799 to 1801. In the opening passages of this unfinished tract Hegel attempts to find a middle path between the opposing parties to the dispute. On the one hand, he agrees with the left that the principles of the state should be founded on reason; but he disagrees with them that theory should dictate practice, or that these principles should be imposed on history. On the other hand, he accepts the conservative doctrine that good laws should adapt to historical circumstances, and that we need experience to know how to apply them; yet he rejects the view that the principles of the state should derive from precedent and tradition alone. How, then, is it possible to hold on to the ideals of the Revolution while still respecting history? Hegel's answer is to read these ideals into history itself. In the *Verfassungsschrift* he criticised the view, so prevalent among radicals and conservatives alike, that the ideals of the Revolution marked a radical break with the past. The ideals of liberty, equality and fraternity, he argued, were the culmination of a long historical development that began in the Middle Ages. They were the legacy of the medieval ideal of independence, of the ancient view that every vassal is the master of his own fief, having the right to represent himself in the government. It was the ideals of the medieval freeman, Hegel insists, that finally burst open in France in the heady

---

9 I have given a more detailed account of the various positions in the dispute in Beiser 1992, pp. 38–44, 80–3, 295–302, 302–9, 317–26.
10 The dispute is not considered at all by Avineri 1972, Haym 1857, or Rosenzweig 1920, the main studies on the development of Hegel's political views. The importance of the dispute has been fully recognised, as far as I can determine, only by Henrich 1983, whose account differs markedly from my own.

summer of 1789. This is a crucial insight, for it means that the radicals were as wrong to sweep away history as the conservatives were wrong to ignore reason. What the radicals and conservatives both failed to recognise is that the ideals of the Revolution lay deep in history itself.

Hence reason in history was Hegel's *via media* between the extreme positions of the theory–practice debate. While the main problem of left-wing rationalism was that it valued reason at the expense of history, the chief shortcoming of right-wing empiricism was that it prized history at the expense of reason. The faulty central premise shared by both extremes is that history consists in nothing more than precedent and tradition, that it has no structure or purpose because it is nothing more than an accident and contingency. Hegel's theme denies this crucial premise. It maintains that the fundamental ideals of reason – liberty and equality or the rights of man – are the immanent goals or ends of history itself.

As explained so far, Hegel's reason in history theme seems to derive entirely from his stance in the theory–practice dispute. It is as if his political context alone suffices to explain the origins and significance of this theme. But this impression is very misleading; for Hegel's theme had a metaphysical foundation and motivation. Hegel conceived the reason in history theme of the *Verfassungsschrift* only after sketching some of the central ideas of his absolute or objective idealism in his 1798–1800 *Geist des Christenthums*.[11] According to his absolute idealism, the entire universe is governed by the divine logos, so that everything in nature and history is an appearance of reason. The starting point for Hegel's reflections was the Johannine gospel: 'In the beginning was the word . . . ' (John 1:1); but they were also inspired by the romantic critique of Kant's and Fichte's subjective idealism and the development of an objective idealism in the late 1790s. It would take us very far afield here to discuss the full meaning of this development.[12] One point alone is relevant and of central importance in this context: the shift from subjective to objective idealism is essentially one from regarding reason as imposed on nature through our human activity (subjective idealism) to regarding reason as already within nature because of its inherent design or purpose (objective idealism). This shift went hand-in-hand with another fundamental change in Hegel's political views at this time: from attempting

---

11 The sketch of his absolute idealism appears in the manuscript *Jesus trat nicht lange vor . . .*, whose first draft was most probably written in autumn or winter 1798/99; a later draft is from 1799 or early 1800. The final draft of the *Verfassungsschrift* is around November 1802, though an earlier draft of the introduction, the manuscript *Der immer sich vergrößernde Widerspruch . . .* is from 1799/1800.

12 On this development, see Beiser 2002, pp. 349–74.

to change the world according to the principles of reason to accepting the world as it is because it already embodies or is moving towards these principles.[13] Whatever the motivations for this shift, it should be clear that Hegel read reason into history as a solution to the theory–practice dispute not least because of his objective or absolute idealism.

Apart from these metaphysical issues, the political purpose behind Hegel's reason in history theme was to justify his reformist politics. If reason is within history, it would be wrong, *pace* the radicals, to abolish present institutions for the sake of some abstract ideals; but, by the same token, if history inevitably progresses towards the ideals of reason, it would also be mistaken, *pace* the conservatives, to resist change for the sake of preserving the past. Since the ideals of reason are already latent within history, they can be realised through gradual reform, through evolution of existing institutions. *Prima facie* Hegel seems to teach nothing but resignation, since he writes in the *Verfassungsschrift* that the purpose of his doctrine is only to foster endurance and to reconcile us to the inevitable (VD I, pp. 463/145). Yet Hegel could preach reconciliation only because he believed history was moving inevitably towards the realisation of modern ideals.

Hegel never abandoned the reformist politics he sketched in the *Verfassungsschrift*. He reaffirmed his reformism, some twenty years later, in the preface to his major work on politics, his 1820 *Philosophie des Rechts*, when he wrote in some famous lines: 'What is rational is actual; what is actual is rational.' This notorious 'double dictum' (*Doppelsatz*) has been cited as evidence for both right- and left-wing interpretations of Hegel. The left seize on the first half of the dictum, because it seems to say that change will take place according to the ideals of the Revolution; the right appeal to the second half, because it seems to say that the present is already rational and need not change. Yet the dictum, once understood in the context of the *Verfassungsschrift*, involves Hegel's critique of both radicals and conservatives. The first half states that ideals are the driving forces behind history, so that it is wrong for conservatives to dismiss them as utopias or dreams. The second half holds that these ideals are already potential and latent in the present, so that it is wrong for radicals to destroy everything in the present. So, in the end, those conservative critics of Hegel who feared the revolutionary potential of his rationalism, and those radical critics who warned of the conservative implications of his historicism, both missed the point. They

---

13 On this change in Hegel's thinking, see Rosenzweig 1920, I, pp. 63–101.

failed to see that, since the ideals of the Revolution are inherent in historical development, it is necessary to realise them through gradual reform and the evolution of existing historical institutions. For Hegel, then, the main argument on behalf of the middle road of reform is that it has history on its side.

It is important to stress Hegel's reformism not least because, for generations, his political philosophy has been read as an apology for the Prussian Restoration. This reading was first put forward by Rudolf Haym in his 1857 *Hegel und seine Zeit*, and it has had many prominent followers ever since, among them Karl Popper, Sidney Hook and Isaiah Berlin.[14] One of the main sources of this interpretation was no less than Hegel himself. In the preface to the 1821 edition of the *Philosophie des Rechts* Hegel seemed to be siding with the censorship and the reactionary government when he attacked the political philosophy of his personal rival Jakob Friedrich Fries. An outspoken opponent of the government's latest reactionary policies, Fries had been persecuted by it and eventually dismissed from his position at the university. Hegel seemed to endorse Fries' dismissal, writing as if it were the deserved result of a bankrupt political philosophy that could undermine all public order. Hegel badly misjudged how his attack on Fries might be read in the current political atmosphere, which was deeply fearful of further government repression after the Karlsbad Decrees in September 1819. His disagreement with Fries was more personal than philosophical, and more philosophical than political. But Hegel had been imprudent in the opportunity he chose for attacking an old rival. As a result, even his contemporaries perceived him as a spokesman for reactionary policies; and the reputation has died a slow death ever since.

Fortunately for Hegel, there have been scholars who could rectify the damage he brought upon himself. With the benefit of hindsight, they have been able to excavate the truly reformist spirit behind Hegel's politics. Thanks to Franz Rosenzweig's pioneering *Hegel und der Staat* (1920), and thanks too to the work of Eric Weil, Jacques d'Hondt, Shlomo Avineri and Joachim Ritter in the 1950s (see Avineri 1972; D'Hondt 1968a, 1968b; Ritter 1965; Rosenzweig 1920 and Weil 1950), the reactionary interpretation has been largely discredited. Quite apart from the content of Hegel's teachings, it cannot account for the following basic facts. (1) Hegel's connections

14 See Berlin 2002a, p. 98; Haym 1857, pp. 357–91; Hook 1970, pp. 55–70; and Popper 1945, II, pp. 53–4, 62–3.

in Prussia were not with reactionary court circles but with the reforming administration of Stein, Hardenberg and Altenstein. It was indeed Altenstein who called Hegel to Prussia because he was attracted by his reformist views. (2) Rather than siding with the reactionaries, Karl von Haller and Friedrich Savigny, Hegel criticised them severely in his correspondence and the *Rechtsphilosophie*. (3) For their part, the reactionary court circles under Count von Wittgenstein harassed and spied on Hegel and his pupils. (4) Rather than glorifying the status quo, most aspects of Hegel's ideal state were far from reality in the Prussia of 1820. Indeed, Hegel's demands for a constitutional monarchy, an elected assembly, local self-government and a powerful civil service, were all defeated by Prussian reactionaries in 1819.

In fundamental respects, Hegel's mature political philosophy was indeed a rationale for the Prussian Reform Movement, which began in 1806 under the direction of Hardenberg and Stein. The purpose of their reforms was to realise, through gradual change from above, the fundamental ideals of the Revolution, namely, a constitution ensuring basic rights for all, freedom of trade and the abolition of feudal privileges. It is indeed striking how Hegel's *Philosophie des Rechts* on point after point, adopts and defends the goals of the reform programme. Like Stein and Hardenberg, Hegel champions a written constitution ensuring basic liberties, a more powerful bureaucracy, more local self-government, a bicameral estates assembly, greater equality of opportunity and more freedom of trade.[15] It is tempting to conclude that Hegel's *Rechtsphilosophie* was the philosophy of the Prussian Reform Movement. It is important to recall, however, that Hegel developed his reformism, and the outlines of his mature philosophy, *before* the formation of this movement.

3   Ethical life and the critique of liberalism

All too often Hegel is portrayed as a critic of liberalism and champion of communitarianism. Some historians regard his political philosophy as the major conceptual alternative to the liberal tradition, and they explain its historical significance in just such terms.[16]

But this common picture of Hegel distorts his true historical position. It is misleading to cast Hegel in this role partly because it better suits many

---

15 These affinities were noted by Rosenzweig 1920, II, pp. 161–7. He argues that the only respect in which Hegel's doctrine deviates from Prussian practice is with regard to the size of the army.
16 See Popper 1945, II, pp. 29, 58; Smith 1989, p. 4; and Wood 1990, p. xi.

of his predecessors and contemporaries, for example, Justus Möser, A.W. Rehberg or the later Friedrich Schlegel. Many of Hegel's criticisms of liberalism, and many of his communitarian themes, were part of the common heritage of his generation. Although, for the sake of convenience, we might consider Hegel as the chief representative of this wider tradition, we should not conclude that these ideas are original to, or characteristic of, him alone.

More problematically, this picture of Hegel falsifies his intentions. For it was never Hegel's aim to reject the liberal tradition for the sake of communitarianism. Unlike some of the more conservative critics of liberalism, such as Möser and Haller, Hegel continued to uphold fundamental liberal values, such as freedom of conscience, equality of opportunity and the right of dissent. While these conservatives denied liberal values for the sake of community, Hegel insisted upon preserving them within the community.

It is important to see, however, that even in this respect there was little new to Hegel's programme. For it was a common aim of the early romantic generation, of which Hegel was once a member, *to synthesise* liberal and communitarian ideals (Beiser 1992, pp. 222–39). What is unique to Hegel was the sustained effort to think through the romantic programme and more specifically his attempt to unite the individual to the modern state on the basis of reason. Unlike the romantics, Hegel did not believe that 'faith and love' could be a sufficient bond to wed the modern individual with the state. Since the modern individual thought for himself and questioned everything, he needed to be given *reasons* for obeying the laws. In this regard it is significant that, even in his early years, Hegel rejected the romantic programme for a new mythology, which would attempt to join the individual to the state through feeling and imagination.[17]

If we are to do justice to Hegel's intentions, we must examine how he attempts to unite the personal freedoms of liberalism with the collective ideals of communitarianism. We can do this, however, only if we first consider how Hegel accepts and rejects the liberal heritage.

The main source of Hegel's allegiance to liberalism is a single fundamental principle, what Hegel calls *the right of subjectivity*. According to this principle, the individual should accept only those beliefs or commands that agree with his own conscience or reason.[18] 'The right to recognise nothing that I do

---

17 See the fragment *Jedes Volk hatte ihm eigene Gegenstände, Werke* I, pp. 197–215, which was written in spring or summer 1796.
18 Hegel has several distinct formulations of this principle. Cf. PR §§107, 121, 132; EPW §7R, 38R; and VG p. 82/70.

not perceive as rational', Hegel writes in the *Philosophie des Rechts*, 'is the highest right of the subject' (PR §132). Hegel stresses that this principle is central to, and characteristic of, the modern state. The chief weakness of the ancient *polis* is that it did not recognise this right (§§124R, 185R, 124R). It is the special task of the modern state, he argues, to integrate the right of subjectivity with the demand for community.

Hegel appeals to this principle to justify several classical liberal values: (1) that the individual is bound by only those laws or policies to which he consents (§§4, 258R); (2) that he should have the right to participate in government, or at least to have his interests represented in it (VD 1 p. 577/238); (3) that he should have moral, intellectual and religious liberty, the right to express his opinion and to exercise his conscience (PR §§270R, 316, 317A, 319); and (4) that he should have the right to pursue his self-interest in a market economy, or that he should have the freedom of choice characteristic of civil society (§§185R, 187).

Although Hegel strongly endorses the principle of subjectivity and appeals to it to justify these basic liberal values, he still regards it as one-sided. The problem with this principle is that it is purely 'formal' because it accepts any content, i.e. *any* law or belief could satisfy it (§§136–8, 140). The principle does not tell us, therefore, *which* laws or beliefs to accept, only that whatever laws or beliefs we accept should agree with our reason or conscience. We know that a decision or belief is right or wrong, Hegel argues, from its content, from *what* it decides or *what* it believes (§137).

It is just this weakness of the principle of subjectivity, Hegel argues, that makes it necessary to transcend liberalism. To overcome the one-sidedness of this principle we must complement it with the communitarian ideal. We can give *content* to our reason, an *objective* norm to our conscience, Hegel contends, only if we place them within the ethos of the community (§§146, 148). And to determine what I should do within the community is simple, Hegel assures us, for it is only a matter of knowing my station and its duties; the individual needs to determine only 'what is prescribed, expressly stated, and known to him in his situation' (§§150R, 153R). When the individual allows the community to determine what he should do, to lay down the content of his principles, he or she becomes joined with the community. This synthesis of individual autonomy and community is Hegel's ideal of 'ethical life' or *Sittlichkeit*.

One objection to Hegel's concept of *Sittlichkeit* is that, ultimately, it cannot really provide an objective content to individual reason and conscience. When Hegel says that the individual needs to know only his or her station and its duties he seems to sanction the morality of *any* community, whether a Christian monastery, a Greek *polis*, or a national-socialist state. Hence the formality of subjectivity is simply replaced by the formality of the community, for there is no specific list of laws that give content to *Sittlichkeit*. Given Hegel's claim that individual conscience is never a sufficient criterion of morality, and given his insistence that the morality of a nation depends upon its specific historical circumstances, Hegel seems to embrace a complete relativism. We shall soon see, however, that he resists such a conclusion (section 4).

Another more serious objection to Hegel's concept of *Sittlichkeit* is that it seems to violate the very freedom of conscience that Hegel is so eager to uphold. For it seems as if Hegel expects the individual to accept, without critical reflection, whatever duties and roles the community imposes upon him or her. Hegel's first reply to this objection would be that it presupposes a false asocial conception of human nature. The objection seems to assume that the individual is a self-sufficient being which has its identity outside the community, and which has the power to assess it according to its natural needs. But it is just this conception of the self, so prominent in the liberal tradition, that Hegel wants to call into question. He argues that the very identity of the self – its basic values and its self-conception – is determined by the community. Since the self finds its meaning and purpose in life only within the community, and since it creates its identity only through performing and growing accustomed to its social roles, it does not regard its duties, tasks and responsibilities as an imposition (§§147, 153). Rather, they are the very means by which the self achieves its *self*-determination and *self*-realisation as a social being (§149).

This reply works as long as the individual does identify with his or her community. But the question remains: What if the ethos of the community violates the individual's conscience and he or she protests against it? In that case, it seems the synthesis of *Sittlichkeit* breaks down. The suspicion of authoritarianism here seems amply confirmed by Hegel's frequent insistence that the demands of the community should have priority over the right of subjectivity. It is important to see that, in addition to the right of subjectivity, Hegel also stresses a *right of objectivity*, which consists in the demand that the decisions and beliefs of subjectivity must have the *correct* content. It is striking that, whenever there is a conflict between these rights, Hegel gives priority to objectivity over subjectivity. Thus he declares that '*the right of the rational* – as the objective – over the subject remains firmly established' (§132R), and that 'the subjective will has worth and dignity only in so far as its insight and intention are in conformity with the good' (§131).

The issue of Hegel's authoritarianism arises essentially because Hegel, like Kant and Rousseau, does not take actual, but only possible, consent as a sufficient criterion of a person's acceptance of the laws. If a person *could* assent to the laws, even if he or she in fact happens to dissent from them, then the laws are still legitimate. What is decisive for Hegel is not any kind of assent but *rational* assent (§§4A, 29R, 258R). Hence a person can be regarded as having given assent to laws provided that they are rational. But then we are still left with the nagging question: rational according to whom? The suspicion of authoritarianism grows when we consider that Hegel never had much confidence in the judgement of the common man to determine whether the laws are rational, or even to know his or her best interests (§§301R, 308R, 317R). He maintains that it is the universal estate, the government bureaucracy, which alone possesses the requisite knowledge to establish rational laws and the best interests of the country. Does this not legitimate, then, an authoritarian government, and in particular a mandarinism, which lays down laws against the explicit protests of the people?

It is important to see, however, that this apparent authoritarianism is counterbalanced by some of the truly democratic and constitutional elements in Hegel's theory of the state. Although Hegel gave bureaucrats the right to determine government policy, he never held that such powers gave them a licence to infringe on certain fundamental rights, such as freedom of conscience. Hence he insisted that the state should give room for dissent, granting liberty of conscience to Quakers and Baptists whose conscience forbade them to enter military service (§270R). In his early *Verfassungsschrift* Hegel had sharply criticised the state of the *ancien régime*, because it attempted to control everything from above, not allowing any room for individual initiative or participation in government. In the *Rechtsphilosophie* Hegel argues that the individual cares about the state, and identifies with it, only if there is popular participation in it (§§260, 308R). His own theory of the state makes express provision for democratic participation by holding that no government should stay in power that is not elected, and by insisting that there should be elected representatives from the estates.

Undoubtedly, Hegel's most important criticisms of the liberal tradition are of its individualistic conceptions of human nature and of freedom. In his 1802 *Naturrecht* essay Hegel challenges this individualism with the famous dictum of Aristotle: 'That apart from the *polis* man is either beast or god' (W II, p. 505). Since it is an organism, the community is a whole that is prior to its parts; it is not only irreducible to its parts but determines their very identities. We cannot conceive of the community as posterior to its individual wills, then, for these wills are formed only through it (PR §§147, 149, 187R). The self develops its characteristic powers, especially its reason, Hegel argues, not in a state of nature but only in society. We become rational beings only by learning how to act according to general laws and principles; but we learn how to do this only by our education and participation in society. It was indeed the main argument of the famous 'Herrschaft und Knechtschaft' chapter of the *Phänomenologie* that a person becomes self-conscious as a rational being only through mutual recognition. I know that I am a rational being, someone having rights and duties, Hegel argues, only if I recognise the equal and independent status of others, and only if they in turn recognise my own equal and independent status. Hence there cannot be any rights and duties in the state of nature itself (VG p. 117/98–9).

Recognising the priority of the community over the individual provides the foundation, Hegel writes in his *Naturrecht* essay, for a completely new account of freedom and natural right from that prevalent in the liberal tradition (W II, pp. 504–6). Thanks to its individualism, the liberal tradition defined freedom and natural right strictly in *negative* terms. Freedom is the *absence* of law, constraint or coercion; and right is the permission to do whatever I want *without* the interference of others. If, however, we see the community as prior to the individual, then we are in a position to develop a more *positive* conception of freedom and right. Freedom is then not simply the absence of constraint, but self-determination, the realisation of my social nature by living in accord with the laws of the community. Right is then not just freedom from the interference of others, but the freedom to develop my nature as a social being within the community.

It is important to understand precisely what Hegel means by a positive conception of right. What he has in mind is that the individual should have the right to claim not only the *restraint* but the *assistance* of the state when this is necessary for self-realisation as a moral being. Hence the duties of the state towards the individual are not only that it protects his or her rights, but that it also creates the legal, social and economic conditions for individual self-realisation. This becomes clearer later in the *Philosophie des Rechts* when Hegel argues that the state has a duty to ensure that everyone benefits from the advantages and opportunities of civil society (§§238A, 240, 243).

So rather than giving the state powers and rights against the individual, as Hegel's critics charge, his positive conceptions of freedom and right do the very reverse: they give the individual further rights and powers against the state by allowing him or her to claim its active assistance. In this regard, Hegel anticipates the interpretation of rights in the socialist tradition.

4 The analysis of civil society

Essential to Hegel's critique of liberalism, and his attempt to wed communitarianism with liberalism, is his analysis of modern 'civil society' (*bürgerliche Gesellschaft*), that is, a society based upon private enterprise, free markets and modern forms of production and exchange. Hegel's analysis of civil society has become the focus of much attention in recent scholarship.[19] Scholars have pointed out the importance of the Scottish political economists – Adam Ferguson, James Stuart and Adam Smith – for the development of Hegel's historical and political views. They have praised Hegel for his thorough understanding and trenchant criticisms of emerging industrial society in Germany. In this respect, they see Hegel as far ahead of his time, and indeed as a forerunner of Marx. Supposedly, Hegel was the first thinker of the modern German tradition to recognise the importance of economics for social, political and cultural life (see for example, Avineri, 1972, p. 5).

However important and influential, it is necessary to place Hegel's analysis of civil society in proper historical perspective. Hegel was not the first in his generation to perceive, or even to analyse, the problems of modern civil society. Many of the young romantics did this in the late 1790s, so that in this respect too Hegel was only typical of his generation.[20] Furthermore, Hegel did not have a mastery of the technicalities of modern political economy, and in this regard was even behind some of his contemporaries. The treatment of money, labour and exchange in Adam Mueller's *Elemente der Staatskunst*, for example, is much more sophisticated than anything in Hegel. What is more characteristic of Hegel's approach to civil society is his attempt to integrate its liberties with the demand for community. It was Hegel's aim to steer a middle path between those liberals who affirmed complete *laissez-faire* and those conservatives who would use the state to regulate every aspect of economic life.

---

19 See Avineri 1972, pp. 81–114, 132–54; Chamley 1963; Dickey 1987, pp. 186–204; Lukács 1973, I, pp. 273–91, and II, pp. 495–618; and Plant 1973, pp. 56–76. See also Pelczynski 1984.
20 On the romantic critique of civil society, see Beiser 1992, pp. 232–6.

True to his acceptance of basic liberal values, Hegel praised the liberties created by modern civil society: equality of opportunity, the right to pursue one's self-interest, and the freedom to sell and buy goods in the market-place. For all his doubts about the moral and cultural consequences of civil society, he did not simply condemn it as an immoral display of egoism. Rather, he regarded the right to acquire property, and the activities of production and exchange, as crucial for the development of civilisation (§§45, 185, 187). As Marx famously remarked,[21] Hegel stressed the importance of labour for the moral development of the personality. This emphasis upon the *moral* values of civil society is indeed reminiscent of many liberal thinkers, but Hegel never drew the conclusion from it that civil society should remain completely unregulated. What is most characteristic of his position is a balanced appreciation of the moral strengths *and* weaknesses of civil society.

In his *Rechtsphilosophie* Hegel criticised civil society – 'this spectacle of extravagance and misery' – on two chief grounds. First, it creates class conflict, tension between employers and workers. Such conflict is inherent in the very laws of production, Hegel argued, because wealth can be increased only at the expense of workers (§§195, 243). Second, civil society produces, through inevitable fluctuations in supply and demand, unemployment, and so a rabble (§§241, 244). Both these factors, Hegel realised, posed serious threats to the prospects for community.

In pointing out these problems, Hegel was doing little more than affirming common wisdom. The more original aspect of his critique of civil society is his argument, stated more than three decades before the young Marx, that modern forms of production and exchange are essentially alienating, subjecting mankind to the forces of its own creation. In the 1803/04 *Geistesphilosophie* and 1805 *Realphilosophie*,[22] Hegel argued that the division of labour and the use of technology free man from the forces of nature only to dominate and enslave him. They enslave the worker by compelling him to perform dull and routine tasks, and by making him produce goods for the market-place rather than his own needs. Since the increase of technology and the division of labour creates more needs than it satisfies, the worker is doomed to a life of perpetual labour. We are never able to enjoy the comforts of life, Hegel laments, because we have to spend all our time and energy producing them.

---

21 'Kritik der Hegelschen Dialektik und Philosophie überhaupt', MEGA I/2, 404–5.
22 GW vi, pp. 321–4, and GW viii, pp. 243–4.

Given all these problems of civil society, it is not surprising to find that Hegel contests the standard liberal view that the common good and justice will emerge naturally from the play of economic forces. Although Hegel agrees with Smith that the pursuit of self-interest naturally creates social order and interdependence (§§184R, 187, 189), he denies that this order is for the common good of all. He therefore insists time and again that the market forces of civil society must be controlled and regulated by the state.[23] In the *Philosophie des Rechts* he gives two reasons why the state should control market forces: first, it will help to prevent class antagonism and the creation of a rabble (§243); and, second, it will hinder or shorten 'dangerous convulsions', economic crises such as recession and inflation (§236A). To address these pressing problems, Hegel proposed all kinds of measures: that the state should tax, or even limit, profits; that it should help the poor through public work projects (§241); that it provide for the education of the poor so that they can compete for jobs (§239); that it predict cycles of supply and demand to help the planning of industry;[24] and that it create new markets for industry through colonisation (§§246–8). Besides regulating market forces, Hegel thinks that the state should promote the public good in areas not benefited by the market. The state should provide, for example, for public health, street lighting, bridge and road building, and so on (§236A).

It was clearly crucial to Hegel's general attempt to fuse the liberal and communitarian traditions that he strike some balance between regulation and liberty in the market-place. If too little regulation would undermine community, too much would throttle liberty. Aware of this very problem, Hegel stresses the need to find some middle path between controlling everything and nothing (§236A). He denies, however, that there is some general rule that can be formulated about where to draw the boundary line between intervention and liberty (§234). He argues that this boundary line will be *per necessitatem* moving, depending upon circumstances. In general, Hegel thinks the role of the state should be to ensure fairness and stability in the market-place. He recognises that, left on its own, the market could be very unfair and unstable, impoverishing people so that they are in no position to compete for scarce jobs and resources. The task of the state is then to guarantee that everyone should have at least the opportunity to work and to provide for themselves through their own labour. Thus Hegel states unequivocally that if civil society has certain rights it also has certain

---

23 SS in GW v, pp. 354–6/170–3.   24 SS in GW v, pp. 351–2/168.

duties (§§238A, 240A). It has the duty to ensure that all have the right to work, and that they can feed themselves (§240A). Above all, it has the duty to ensure that everyone can enjoy its advantages and liberties (§243).

So far it seems as if Hegel, in arguing for the right of the state to control industry, is a proto-socialist. It is crucial to see, however, that his solution to the problems of civil society does not lie with the state alone. As much as he believes that the state has to control the market-place, he also fears granting it too much power. Hegel proposes his own non-socialist solution to the problems of the market economy: the corporation (*Korporation, Genossen-schaft*). The corporation is a group of people sharing the same trade or profession, officially recognised by the state though independent of it. Like the medieval guilds, on which it is clearly modelled, the corporation would organise, support and recognise all individuals who had become competent in their trade or profession (§252). It would address the problem of social alienation since it would become the individual's 'second family', aiding him in times of need and providing him with a sense of belonging.

Whatever its merits, Hegel's theory of corporations suffers from a fatal shortcoming. Although Hegel saw the poverty and working conditions of the emerging proletariat as one of the most serious threats to community, he failed to give workers entrance into corporations, and even disenfranchised them.[25] Thus he denied integration into society to the very group that needed it most, undermining the prospects for community.[26] Though Hegel proved to be very prescient in seeing the problems of society posed by the growing working class, he remained bound to early nineteenth-century conceptions of the limitations of the franchise. Arguably, he was still too mistrustful of the masses, too confident of the power of the elite, to ensure the community of his youthful dreams.

5   The structure and powers of the state

In the *Philosophie des Rechts* (§§283–329), Hegel provides a detailed theory of the structure of his ideal state. The central thesis of Hegel's theory is that *the* rational form of the state is a *constitutional monarchy* (§273R; H p. 238). *Prima facie* such a claim seems reactionary, and it has been interpreted along just these lines.[27] However, in the early 1800s such a claim was standard

---

25 PR §253R. Cf. SS in GW v, p. 354/171.
26 This point has been forcefully argued by Avineri 1972, pp. 98–9, 109, 148, 151–3.
27 Thus Haym 1857, pp. 365–8; Popper 1945, II, pp. 27, 53–4

reformist doctrine. It was the view of the Hanoverian Whigs and the Prussian Reformers, indeed of all those who wanted to reform the state of the *ancien régime* from above so that it could adapt to the revolutionary currents of the age. This reformist faith in constitutional monarchy has to be contrasted with the reactionary defence of *absolute monarchy*, which attempted to free the monarch from constitutional safeguards and make his will alone the source of law. The main Prussian spokesman for absolute monarchy was K. L. von Haller, whose *Restaurations der Staats-Wissenschaft* became the chief manifesto of the reactionary cause. Hegel's distance from the reactionary cause is evident not least from his lengthy polemical broadsides against Haller in the *Philosophie des Rechts* (§§219R, 258R).

Still, Hegel's strong claim on behalf of constitutional monarchy is somewhat surprising, given that he disdains disputes about the ideal constitution, and given that he endorses Montesquieu's doctrine that the proper constitution for a nation depends on its specific culture, history, climate and geography (§§3R, 273R). Hegel does not simply hold that constitutional monarchy is the best constitution for Prussia, or that it alone is suitable for its stage of historical development. Rather, he maintains that constitutional monarchy is the rational form of the state because it, more than any other form of government, realises the ideal of freedom (H p. 238). Hegel's claim becomes more comprehensible when we consider his view, expressed most clearly in his Heidelberg lectures, that constitutional monarchy alone guarantees the rights of individuality so characteristic of the modern world (VNS §§135R, 137R). Like Kant, Humboldt, Jacobi, Schiller and many others, Hegel feared that radical democracy, which gave limitless power to the will of the people, does not necessarily respect the fundamental rights of everyone alike. The crucial case in point was Athens' persecution of Socrates.

The great strength of constitutional monarchy for Hegel is that it is a *mixed* constitution, incorporating the advantages of all three forms of government. He maintains that constitutional monarchy is a synthesis of monarchy, aristocracy and democracy (§273R). A constitutional monarchy consists in three fundamental powers: the *sovereign*, which formally enacts the laws; the *executive*, which applies and enforces the laws; and the *legislative*, which creates the laws (§273). Since the sovereign is *one* individual, since the executive consists in *several* individuals, and since the legislative consists in *many* individuals, each power represents one form of government, monarchy, aristocracy and democracy (respectively) (§273R).

The main virtue of mixed government for Hegel resides in its division of powers. Since this prevents any single power from dominating others, it provides the best institutional guarantee for freedom. In this regard it is noteworthy that Hegel reaffirmed Montesquieu's famous doctrine of the division of powers because, 'understood in its true sense, [it] could rightly be regarded as the guarantee of public freedom' (§272R). While Hegel warns that an extreme separation of powers will undermine the unity of the state (§§272R, 300A), he still thinks that the modern state realises freedom only if it involves a differentiation of function and separation into distinct spheres of government (VNS §132; H p. 231).

Hegel makes a much more systematic or metaphysical claim on behalf of constitutional monarchy: that it alone realises the very idea of the state (§§272–3). Each power of constitutional monarchy represents one of the moments of the concept: since it enacts general laws, the legislative is universality; since it applies laws to specific cases, the executive is particularity; and since it incorporates in a single person both the legislative and executive, the monarch is individuality. While Hegel gives more weight to his systematic argument than any prudential consideration about the best form of government (§272), the fact remains that his systematic argument is best understood in the light of his claim that constitutional monarchy provides the best institutional safeguards for freedom. Since the idea of the state is based on freedom, and since constitutional monarchy realises freedom more than any other form of government, it follows that constitutional monarchy is the highest realisation of the idea of the state.

To understand Hegel's political values, to assess the authoritarian charges against him, and to appreciate exactly how he attempts to wed liberalism and communitarianism, it is necessary to know in some detail something about the structure of his ideal state. We should examine more closely each of the powers of a constitutional monarchy.

The sovereign

The sovereign power is the monarch. Hegel defends monarchy as a necessary part of the rational constitution because it provides the state with a single source of sovereignty. Since the monarch is one person, he is an indivisible power, and so better represents and executes sovereignty than an assembly, which could be divided within itself (§279). He maintains that a single source of sovereignty is a necessity of the modern state. The problem with the medieval constitution is that its many independent corporations and communities lacked a single source of sovereignty, and so could not act coherently even to defend itself (§278).

Hegel advocates *hereditary* monarchy on the grounds that it ensures a stable succession and stands above all conflict of factions (§281; VNS §138). Since the monarch is the highest authority, Hegel denies that he is only the highest official of the state, as if he were somehow accountable to the people and bound by a contract with them (VNS §139). He denies that the monarch can be held responsible for his actions, fixing all responsibility for them on his ministers (§284; VNS §140). Such is the exalted status he attributes to the monarch that he even expounds his own speculative form of the divine right doctrine, according to which the monarch represents the divine on earth (§279R).

Although Hegel's defence of divine right doctrine seems to give the monarch absolute power, he is very far from defending the old absolutism. Instead, his chief concern is to bind the monarch to the constitution. He stresses that in a rational state the personality of the monarch should be irrelevant, and that it is in the insignificance of the monarch's person that the rationality of the constitution lies (VNS §138). The only real powers that he permits the monarch are the right to pardon criminals and to appoint and dismiss ministers (§§282–3). He insists that the monarch possesses sovereignty only in so far as he is bound by the constitution (§278R). The monarch must follow the advice that he receives from his ministers, so that he can do nothing more than say 'yes' and sign his name to the measures placed before him (§§279R, 280A). It is for this reason alone that Hegel says that the monarch cannot be held accountable as a person (§284); for in the end, all real responsibility falls on his ministers. Ultimately, the monarch plays essentially a formal role in the Hegelian state, serving as 'the highest instance of formal decision'. Yet this symbolic role is of the greatest significance for Hegel, because it represents the unity, sovereignty and culture of the people (§§279–80).

The executive

The purpose of the executive power is to implement and enforce the decisions of the sovereign (§287). The executive power consists in the police, judiciary and civil service (§287). The cornerstone of the executive is the civil service or bureaucracy, whose main task is to mediate the particular interests of the corporations with the universal interests of the state (§289).

The bureaucracy possesses great power in Hegel's state: its advice not only binds the monarch (§279A), but it also knows the true interests of the corporations, even if they have not been voiced directly by them (§§289, 301R). Nevertheless, Hegel should not be cast as an uncritical advocate of mandarinism or the bureaucratic state. He is also aware of the dangers of corruption in the bureaucracy (§295) and of the bureaucracy becoming the dominant power in the state. Hence he stresses that its powers should be limited and its activities monitored by the monarch from above and the corporations from below (§§295, 297; VNS §145). He recommends that the opposition within the legislative have the right to question ministers because this will make them accountable to the public (VNS §149).

The legislative

The legislative power consists in a bicameral Estates Assembly on the English model (§312). There is an upper house composed of the nobility, who inherit their office; and a lower house composed of commoners, who are elected to office. Hegel thinks that such a two-tiered assembly, by creating several levels of deliberation, provides a guarantee for mature decisions and reduces chances of collision with the executive (§313). The Estates Assembly represents the two estates of civil society: the agricultural estate or the landed aristocracy, and the estate of trade and industry or the *bourgeoisie* (§§303–4). Although members of the lower house are elected through their corporations and communities, they do not receive a mandate from them (§309A). The chief role of the Estates Assembly is to develop public consciousness of political issues, and to create a link between people and the sovereign (§§301–2). They also provide an important buffer between government and people. While they protect the people from tyranny by organising and representing their interests, they shield the government from the 'mob' by controlling, directing and channelling the interests and energies of the people.

How democratic was Hegel's constitutional monarchy? There can be no question about Hegel's support for the democratic element of a constitutional monarchy. The very possibility of a common ethical life (*Sittlichkeit*) or community, he often argued, depends upon popular participation, for only when the people participate in the state do they identify with it and care about it (§§261, 308R).[28] Accordingly, the Hegelian state provides for

---

28 Cf. VD I, pp. 576–7/237–8; and ER XI, pp. 111–12/318.

some truly democratic procedures. Hegel envisages not only elected representatives in the lower house but also competing parties in the Estates Assembly (VNS §156R). These are not parties in the modern sense because they do not compete for popular votes; but they do represent opposing viewpoints that increase accountability. Hegel envisages three parties: one for the people, one for the government, and another neutral to mediate between them. He further stresses that the government should have the support of the majority party in the Estates (VNS §156R).

Nevertheless, it is important to recognise that Hegel does not advocate democracy in the modern sense of universal suffrage. All his life he was sceptical of direct democracy because he doubted the wisdom of the people, who did not have sufficient knowledge to determine their best interests.[29] Like many of his contemporaries, Hegel insisted upon a limited franchise, which excluded workers, servants and women. Furthermore, he argued against the radical view that any male of a certain age and income should be given the right to vote.[30] He put forward two arguments against this view: first, the individual does not know his best interests simply by virtue of his age and wealth; and, second, it leads to voter apathy, because the individual will feel his vote is meaningless when it is only one in millions, and when he votes for only one person in a large assembly. Instead of voting according to universal suffrage and geographic districts, Hegel advocates voting according to group affiliation or vocational interests; in other words, he thinks that a person should vote not directly as an abstract individual but indirectly as a member of a group. Hence it is the corporations, not a mass of individual votes, who elect a delegate to the Estates Assembly. Such a system, Hegel contends, has several advantages: it organises, directs and controls the interests of the people, who could otherwise turn into a violent mob; and it prevents indifference because the individual feels his vote matters as a member of a group that has much greater powers of representation than a single individual (§§302A, 303R, 311R).

Although Hegel's constitutional democracy did have some genuine democratic elements, one might well ask if these were sufficient for Hegel's ideal of ethical life. That ideal requires that everyone should identify with the state, that everyone should find the meaning of their lives within it. Hegel himself had stressed that developing such an identification, such a

---

29 PR §301R. Cf. ER XI, pp. 110–11/317.
30 PR §§303R, 308R. Cf. ER XI, pp. 110–13/317–19 and VVL IV, pp. 482–4/263–4.

sense of purpose and belonging, required participation in the affairs of state. But Hegel's limited conception of the franchise, his reservations about complete democracy, had virtually excluded large groups of the population from participation in public life. The peasants of the agricultural estate were virtually unrepresented in the Estates Assembly; if they were represented at all it was through the nobility, who were not elected (§307). Hegel also had his doubts that the businessmen of the commercial estate were sufficiently free and knowledgeable to devote themselves to affairs of state (§§308, 310A). And, as we have already seen, he stressed the importance of corporations to develop a sense of belonging only to exclude day labourers from them, thereby disenfranchising them.

So even if Hegel's political philosophy were not guilty of the worst charges of authoritarianism thrown against it, even if it did uphold basic liberal values, the question remained whether he satisfied his own ideal of community. So, oddly, it is really communitarians rather than liberals who should file complaints against Hegel. Ultimately, Hegel's grand synthesis failed not because he did too much for community and not enough for liberty, but because he did too much for liberty and not enough for community.

6   The foundation of law

The problems of doing justice to Hegel's syncretic ideals is most apparent from the many conflicting interpretations of his views on the foundation of law. Hegel has sometimes been read as a voluntarist, as someone who bases right on the will rather than reason.[31] However, he has also been read as just the opposite: as a rationalist, as someone who derives right from reason and gives it a value independent of the will.[32] Accordingly, some scholars have placed Hegel in the natural law tradition, a tradition which ultimately goes back to Aristotle and Aquinas. Finally, Hegel has also been understood as a historicist, as someone who thinks that law is ultimately based on the history and culture of a people.[33] In this respect Hegel has been placed in the tradition of Montesquieu, Möser and Herder, who saw law as one embodiment of the spirit of a nation.

---

31 See Franco 1999, pp. 178–87; Plamenatz 1963, pp. 31–3, 37–8; and Riedel 1973, pp. 96–120.
32 See Foster 1935, pp. 125–41, 167–79, 180–204; Patten 1999, pp. 63–81; Pelczynski 1984, pp. 29, 54; Pippin 1997a, pp. 417–50; and Riley 1982, pp. 163–99.
33 See Berlin 2002a, pp. 94–5, 97–8; Cassirer 1946, pp. 265–8; Hallowell 1950, pp. 265, 275–6; Heller 1921, pp. 32–131; Meinecke 1924, pp. 427–60; and Popper 1945, II, pp. 62–3.

Once, however, we take seriously Hegel's syncretic ideals, all these interpretations prove to be both right and wrong, partially correct and partially incorrect. For it was Hegel's aim to synthesise all these traditions, to preserve their truths and cancel their errors in a single coherent account of the basis of law. Hegel's theory of right was meant to be a rational historicism or historicist rationalism, a rational voluntarism or voluntarist rationalism. But such apparent oxymorons raise the questions: Did Hegel really have a coherent doctrine? Or was it simply an eclectic monstrosity? Before we can assess these questions, we must first examine the strengths and weaknesses of the opposing interpretations; we must consider exactly what Hegel accepted and rejected from these conflicting traditions.

There is much evidence in favour of the voluntarist interpretation. Hegel justifies right on the basis of freedom, which he understands as the expression of the will (PR §4A). Furthermore, he defines the good in terms of the will, as the unity of the particular will with the concept of the will (PR §129). Finally, he places himself firmly in the voluntarist tradition when he states that Rousseau was right to make the will the basis of the state (PR §258R). It is indeed of the first importance to see that Hegel denied one of the fundamental premises of the natural law tradition: that value exists within the realm of nature, independent of the will. He accepts one of the basic theses of Kant's Copernican revolution in ethics: that the laws of reason are created by us and not imposed upon us by nature.

However, there is also much evidence against the voluntarist reading. It is a central thesis of the voluntarist tradition that whatever the will values is good simply because the will values it; but Hegel protests against the purely formal and abstract will chiefly because the will alone cannot be a source of the law (PR §§135–40). It is also a basic premise of the voluntarist tradition that nothing can be good in itself or in nature, independent of human agreements or contracts; yet Hegel insists that some things are valuable in themselves, whether they are enshrined into law or recognised by governments (PR §100R). Finally, Hegel's distance from the voluntarist tradition could not be greater when he attacks the social contract theory. If we make right depend on the will of the individual, he argues, we undermine all obligation because a person will have the right to quit the contract whenever he dissents from it (PR §§29R, 258R). There is just as much evidence for the rationalist as the voluntarist interpretation. Hegel seems to endorse the central principle of rationalism when he writes that 'in a political constitution nothing should be recognised as valid unless it agrees with the right of reason' (VVL IV, p. 506/281).[34] Although Hegel bases right on the will, it is necessary to add that he defines the will in terms of reason, so that it seems to amount to little more than an imperative of practical reason. Hence he stresses that there is no separation between the will and thought because the will is really only 'a special manner of thinking': 'thinking translating itself into existence, thinking as the drive to give itself existence' (§4A). It is also noteworthy that Hegel makes a sharp distinction between the objective and subjective will, where he virtually identifies the objective will with rational norms. He then stresses that the norms of practical reason have an objective validity whether or not they are recognised by the subjective will, which consists in only individual desires (PR §§126, 131, 258R). When he stresses the objectivity of norms against the formality and particularity of the subjective will he is clear that their objectivity consists in their rationality (PR §§21R, 258R).

Still, there are at least two serious difficulties with the rationalist interpretation. First, Hegel never accepted the natural law doctrine, so central to rationalism, that norms exist in nature or in some eternal realm, independent of human activity. For Hegel, the ultimate basis of the law – and here he shows his voluntarist loyalties – lies in freedom, which cannot be understood apart from the will. Second, although Hegel insists that the will consists in and depends on thinking, he also stresses the converse as well: that thinking consists in and depends on willing (PR §4A). This is not a mere gesture on Hegel's part, a routine recognition of the equality of opposites, but reflects his teaching, developed at great length in the *Enzyklopädie* (§§440–82), that all the stages in the development of spirit are simply 'the way by which it produces itself as will' (PR §4R). True to the voluntarist tradition, therefore, Hegel assigns primacy to the role of the will in the development of reason. Reason is for him essentially a form of *practical* intelligence.

The historicist interpretation has no less evidence on its behalf than the voluntarist and rationalist readings. In his youth Hegel was deeply influenced by the historicist tradition.[35] He acknowledged that debt in the *Philosophie*

---

34 Cf. PR §132R
35 See, for example, his early Stuttgart 1787 essay *Über die Religion der Griechen und Römer* 1787, GW I, pp. 42–5, where Hegel argues that history shows us the danger of generalising about the principles of reason from our own time and place. In his 1793 *Tübingen Essay*, Hegel alluded to Montesquieu's idea of the 'spirit of a nation', and stressed how a culture is a unity, its religion, politics and history forming a living whole (W I, p. 42/27). Hegel's early interest in history is still very much in the Enlightenment tradition, however. He still believes in a universal human nature behind all the different manifestations of history, and he criticises past religions from the standpoint of a universal reason. Hegel became

des Rechts when he praised Montesquieu's 'genuinely philosophical view-point' that 'legislation in general and its particular determinations should not be considered in isolation and in the abstract but rather as dependent moment within *one* totality, in the context of all the other determinations, which constitute the character of a nation and an age'. It is within such a context, Hegel significantly adds, that laws 'gain their genuine signifi-cance and hence also their justification' (PR §3R). In the *Philosophie des Rechts* Hegel would endorse other central doctrines of historicism. First, that though they can be changed, constitutions cannot be made (§§273R, 298A). Second, that the policies of a government should be in accord with the spirit of a nation, in agreement with its concrete circumstances and way of life, not imposed from above by some leader or committee (§§272, 274, 298A).

But the historicist interpretation too has fatal problems. First, Hegel makes a sharp distinction between the historical explanation of a law and its conceptual demonstration, warning us in the firmest tones never to con-fuse them (PR §3R). To establish the moral validity of a law, he argues, it is not sufficient to show that it arose of necessity from its historical circumstances. Since circumstances are constantly changing, a historical account cannot provide a *general* justification for a law or institution. Sec-ond, Hegel also could not accept the relativism implicit within histori-cism. It is one of Hegel's striking departures from historicism – and one of his most telling endorsements of the natural law tradition – that he insisted that there are certain universal and necessary principles of morality and the state. Hence in the *Philosophie des Rechts* he states that every-one deserves certain basic rights just in so far as they are human beings, regardless of whether they are Catholics, Protestants or Jews (§209); and he is clear that there are some fundamental goods that are inalienable and imprescriptable for all persons in so far as they are free beings, such as the right to have religious beliefs and to own property (§66). Then, in a later essay, Hegel praises the monarch of Würtemberg for introducing a rational constitution that comprises 'universal truths of constitutionalism' (VVL, IV, p. 471/254). Among these truths are equality before the law, the right of the estates to consent to new taxes, and the representation of the people.

---

aware of the tension between historicism and his allegiance to the Enlightenment only much later; see the 1800 revision of the *Positivity Essay*, the fragment *Der Begriff der Positivität . . .* , W I, pp. 217–29/139–51.

The problems with all three readings raise anew the question: Does Hegel really have a single coherent doctrine, one that saves the strengths and expends the weaknesses of voluntarism, rationalism and historicism? He indeed does have such a doctrine, though it is profoundly metaphysical, resting upon his absolute idealism.

Hegel's theory about the sources of normativity are based on his social and historical conception of reason, which ultimately derives from his Aristotelian view that universals exist only *in re* or in particular things. The fundamental claim behind this conception is that reason is embodied in the culture and language of a people at a specific place and time. There are two more basic theses behind this claim, both of them deeply Aristotelian. First, the *embodiment thesis*: that reason exists as the specific ways of talking, writing and acting among a specific people at a specific time. This thesis states that to understand reason, we must first ask 'Where is reason?', 'In what does it exist?' It claims that the answer must lie in the language, traditions, laws and history of a specific culture at a specific time and place. Second, a *teleological thesis*: that reason also consists in the *telos* of a nation, the fundamental values or goals that it strives to realise in all its activities. The teleological thesis derives from Hegel's immanent teleology, which he applies to the historical world as well as the natural. Hegel thinks that just as each organism in the natural world has a formal-final cause, so each organism in the social world has such a cause, which consists in its defining values or ideals. In his philosophy of history Hegel will argue that these values and ideals play a decisive role in determining the actions of people in a culture, even if they do not pursue them in an organised and co-ordinated manner, and even if they are not aware of them.

True to his immanent teleology, Hegel understands norms and values essentially as the formal-final causes of things. The norm or law for a thing consists in its formal-final cause, which is both its purpose or essence. In Aristotle, the form or essence of a thing and its purpose or end are essentially one and the same, because it is the purpose or end of a thing to realise or develop its inner essence or nature. Hence we determine whether something is good or bad, right or wrong, according to whether it realises this purpose or essence. The good or right is that which promotes the realisation of this end; the bad or wrong is that which prevents its realisation.

It is important to see that this formal-final cause has both a normative and ontological status: a normative status because a thing ought to realise its essence; and an ontological status because this essence exists in things as their underlying cause and potentiality. It is for this reason that norms have an objective status for Hegel: the formal-final causes are in things whether or not we recognise or assent to them. It is also for this reason, however, that norms are not simply to be identified with whatever happens to exist: the norm is what is essential to a thing, and it is not necessary that it is realised in all circumstances. Since the norm has an objective status, existing inherently in things, we cannot understand it, *pace* the voluntarists, as the result of convention or agreement; but since the norm is also the essence of a thing, its ideal or intrinsic nature that it might not realise in its specific circumstances, we also cannot reduce it down to any accidental or incidental facts, such as the present status quo, *pace* the historicists. Hence Hegel breaks decisively with one of the basic premises of the voluntarist tradition: the distinction between 'is' and 'ought', between facts and values. But in doing so he never fell into the historicist camp, which virtually conflated 'ought' and 'is' by identifying the rational with *any* set of social and historical circumstances.

In fundamental respects, Hegel's Aristotelian doctrine places him very firmly in the scholastic branch of the natural law tradition. It was indeed Aristotle's metaphysics that inspired some of the classics of that tradition, such as Hooker's *Lawes of Ecclesiastical Politie* (1597) and Suarez's *De Legibus ac Deo Legislatore* (1612). Hegel was fully aware of his debt to the Aristotelian natural law tradition, and he was indeed intent on preserving and continuing it. It is indeed for this reason that he subtitles the *Philosophie des Rechts 'Naturrecht und Staatswissenschaft im Grundrisse'*. It would be a serious mistake, however, to see Hegel's theory simply as a revival of the traditional scholastic doctrine. For, in two basic respects, Hegel transforms that tradition so that it accords with his modern age. First, Hegel identifies the formal-final cause not with perfection, the traditional concept, but with freedom itself, in accord with the modern definition of humanity given by Rousseau, Kant and Fichte.[36] Second, he applies his immanent teleology on the social and historical plane, so that it applies to the entire spirit of a nation, the whole social and political organism. Thus Hegel took the central concept of the historicists – the *Volksgeist*, the spirit of a nation – and cast it in Aristotelian terms, so that it became the underlying formal-final cause

---

36 One might object: it is impossible to identify a formal-final cause with freedom because freedom consists in the power to make oneself whatever one is, and so destroys the idea that we have a fixed essence or nature. Hegel's concept of freedom, however, does not deny but implies this idea because it identifies freedom with acting according to the essence of one's own nature. *Pace* Wood 1990, pp. 18, 43, 45, we must not identify Hegel's concept of freedom with Fichte's thesis that the self is only what it posits itself to be.

of a nation. When we put both these points together – that the formal-final cause is freedom and that all nations have such a formal-final cause – we get the fundamental thesis of Hegel's philosophy of history: that the goal of world history consists in the self-consciousness of freedom. Armed with this thesis, Hegel believed he could take into account the truth of historicism while still avoiding its relativisitic consequences. Since the self-awareness of freedom is the goal of *world* history, it provides a single measure or criterion of value. We can now talk about progress, appraising cultures according to whether they promote or hinder the realisation of this goal.

Understanding Hegel's normative theory in Aristotelian terms enables us to explain what at first sight seems an irresolvable contradiction: namely, Hegel's insistence upon the objective status of value and his claim that values are made by human beings. This apparent contradiction is resolved as soon as we recall the classic Aristotelian distinction between what is first in order of explanation and what is first in order of existence.[37] While universals are first in order of explanation, because we know what a thing is only through its properties, they are not first in order of existence, because to exist they must first be in particular things. While Hegel thinks that the formal-final cause is first in order of explanation, he does not think that it is first in order of existence. It is only through the activity of particular wills, he argues, that it comes into existence. So, although having normative status does not depend on the wills of individuals, these norms are still realised or actualised only in and through these individual wills. The voluntarist then made the classic confusion: he assumed that what is first in order of existence – the particular will – is also first in the order of essence and explanation.

We are now finally in a position to understand, in summary fashion, how Hegel's social-historical teleology preserves the truths and cancels the errors of the rationalist, voluntarist and historicist traditions. The rationalists were correct that values are within nature and that they have an objective status; but they were wrong to see them as eternal norms above history or as static essences within nature; rather, these values are realised only in history and through the activity of particular individuals. The voluntarists were right to stress the central role of freedom, and to emphasise the role of the will in bringing values into existence; but they went astray in thinking that the will alone – rather than reason – is the source of normativity. Finally, the historicists were correct to see norms embodied in

---

37 See Aristotle 1971, Book v, 11m 101b, pp. 30–6; and Book ix, 8, 1050a, pp. 3–20.

the way of life of a people; but they were too indiscriminate, identifying the formal-final cause, the norm of historical change, with any specific set of social and historical circumstances. Since they did not understand history in teleological terms, the historicist confused the historical explanation of values with their conceptual demonstration: the historical explanation focuses on the factual causes, whereas conceptual demonstration accounts for the underlying formal-final cause.

So Hegel's normative doctrine was coherent after all, fusing in a remarkable fashion the rationalist, voluntarist and historicist traditions. But there should now be no doubt that the doctrine was deeply speculative and metaphysical, resting upon Hegel's Aristotelian metaphysics. Hegel made at least three basic metaphysical claims: (1) that universals exist *in re*; (2) that we can apply such formal-final causes to organisms in the natural world; and (3) that we can also apply them to 'organisms' in the social-political world. All these claims added together yield absolute idealism, the ultimate foundation for Hegel's political thought.

7   The rise and fall of Hegelianism

In the preface to his *Philosophie des Rechts* Hegel wrote in some famous lines that every philosophy is only the self-awareness of its age. This dictum applied to Hegel's philosophy too, which was only the self-awareness of its age, the era of the Prussian Reform Movement. This movement dominated Prussian political life during the reign of Friedrich Wilhelm III from 1797 to 1840. Although many of its ideals were far from reality, and although hopes for reform were disappointed time and again in the 1820s and 1830s, many hoped that their monarch would finally deliver on his promises for reform. As long as hope remained, the Hegelian philosophy could claim to represent its age, at least in aspiration if not in reality.

Thus Hegel's philosophy reigned supreme in Prussia for most of the Reform era, chiefly from 1818 to 1840. Its rise to prominence began in 1818 with Hegel's appointment to the University of Berlin. Hegel and his disciples received strong official backing from the Prussian Ministry of Culture, especially from two powerful ministers, Baron von Altenstein and Johannes Schulze. They supported Hegel's philosophy largely because they saw it as the medium to support their own reformist views against reactionary court circles. In 1827 Hegel's students began to organise themselves, forming their own society, the Berliner Kritische Association, and editing a common journal, *Jahrbücher für Wissenschaftliche Kritik*. When Hegel died in 1831, a group of his most intimate students prepared a complete edition of his works.

What did these students see in Hegel's philosophy? Why did they regard themselves as Hegelians? Almost all of Hegel's early disciples saw his philosophy as the rationalisation of the Prussian Reform Movement, whose ideals they shared. For the most part (McLellan 1969, pp. 15–16, 22–5 and Toews 1980, pp. 232–4) they viewed themselves as loyal Prussians, not out of any sense of unconditional obedience, but because they were confident that the Prussian state would eventually realise through gradual reform some of the main ideals of the Revolution. They were proud of the political traditions of the Prussian state, which seemed to embody all the progressive trends of the Reformation and *Aufklärung*.[38] Like Hegel, most of the young Hegelians believed in the virtues of constitutional monarchy and the necessity of reform from above (see McLellan 1969, p. 15; Toews 1980, p. 233). The radicalisation of the Hegelian movement would not begin until after the 1840s, after the accession of Friedrich Wilhelm IV. For almost all the Hegelians before 1840, however, Hegel's philosophy represented the genuine *via media* between reaction and revolution. It seemed to be the only alternative for those who could not accept the reactionaries' appeal to tradition or the romantic revolutionaries' call for a sentimental patriotism. To the delight of his converts, Hegel saw the ideals of ethical life embodied in the constitution of the modern state rather than in the traditions of the *ancien régime* or the emotional bonds of the *Volk* (Toews 1980, pp. 95–140).

Despite their shared sympathies, there were deep tensions among Hegel's followers from the very beginning. These became fully public and self-conscious, however, only in the 1830s. When, in 1835, David Friedrich Strauss published his *Das Leben Jesu*, which argued that the biblical story of Jesus was essentially mythical, battle lines began to form. Some regarded Strauss' argument as a betrayal of Hegel's legacy, while others saw it as its fulfilment. The basic issue at dispute concerned the proper relationship of Hegel's philosophy to religion.[39] To what extent can Hegel's philosophy rationalise the traditional Christian faith, the beliefs in immortality, the divinity of Christ and a personal God? If these beliefs were incorporated into the Hegelian system, would their traditional meaning be preserved or negated? The opposing answers to these questions gave rise to

38 This becomes most visible in Karl Köppen's tract *Friedrich der Grosse*, Leipzig 1840. See McLellan 1969, p. 16.
39 For a further exploration of some of these religious issues, see Brazill 1970, pp. 48–70; and Toews 1980, pp. 141–202.

the famous division of the Hegelian school into a right wing, left wing and centre. This distinction is not anachronistic since it was made by the Hegelians themselves. According to Strauss, there were three possible positions regarding this issue: either all, some or none of the traditional Christian beliefs could be incorporated into the Hegelian system.[40] He then applied a political metaphor to describe these positions. The right wing held that all, the centre that some, and the left that none, could be accommodated by Hegel's system. Among the chief right-wing Hegelians were Henrich Hotho (1802–73), Leopold von Henning (1791–1866), Friedrich Förster (1791–1868), Hermann Ninrichs (1794–1861), Karl Daub (1765–1836), Kasimir Conradi (1784–1849), Phillip Marheineke (1780–1846) and Julius Schaller (1810–68). Among the moderate or centre Hegelians were Karl Michelet (1801–93) and Karl Rosenkranz (1805–79). And among the prominent left-wing Hegelians were Ludwig Feuerbach (1804–72), Arnold Ruge (1802–80), David Friedrich Strauss (1808–74), Max Stirner (1806–56) and, in his later years, Bruno Bauer (1808–82). The second generation of left-wing Hegelians included Karl Marx, Friedrich Engels and Mikail Bakunin.

Although the battle lines between the Hegelians first became explicit and self-conscious over a theological issue, their religious differences were ultimately a reflection of their deeper political ones. These political tensions had been present in the early 1820s, but they became more apparent in the 1830s (see Toews 1993, pp. 387–91). The basic question at issue concerned the extent to which existing conditions in Prussia realised Hegel's ideals. Here again the Straussian metaphor proved useful to describe the various positions in the debate. The right held that most, if not all, conditions in Prussia fulfilled Hegel's ideals; the centre claimed that some did; and the left believed that few, if any, did. Although there was an apparent chasm between right and left, the dispute between them still took place within the broad confines of Hegel's reformism. All parties remained true to Hegel's basic principles and ideals; they simply quarrelled over the extent to which they were now realised in Prussia. Despite all their disillusionment, the left Hegelians continued to uphold their belief in the unity of theory and practice throughout the 1830s. They were still confident that, even if the present conditions were in conflict with Hegel's ideals, they would not remain so because of the dialectic of history.

40 Strauss 1841, III, p. 95.

These religious and political controversies within the Hegelian school were not so easily resolvable because they involved an apparently intractable problem in the interpretation of Hegel's metaphysics.[41] Namely, what is the nature of Hegel's concrete universal, his synthesis of the ideal and real, the universal and particular? Both left and right could point to some aspects of Hegel's teaching to support their case. For their part, the right argued that Hegel maintains that the universal exists only in the particular, that theory must conform to practice, and that the real is rational or ideal. This side of Hegel's philosophy seemed to show that the historical facts of Christianity, and the present conditions in Prussia, were indeed the realisation of Hegel's ideals. They objected to the left that they were creating an abstract universal, a gap between theory and practice, by too rigidly distinguishing between ideals and facts. On the other hand, the left contended that Hegel holds that the universal, the ideal or the rational, is the very purpose of history, to which everything eventually must conform. It is a mistake to assume, they replied to the right, that the ideal must exist in just these particulars when it is realised only through the whole historical process. These issues had indeed troubled Hegel himself ever since his early Jena years. The extent to which a philosophical system can explain or incorporate all the contingencies or particularities of experience proved to be an intractable problem. It seemed as if a system must *include* all particularities, because only then is it concrete and comprehensive; but it also seemed as if it must *exclude* at least some of them, since reason could never derive all the particular facts of experience. Hence, notoriously, Hegel distinguished between actuality (*Wirklichkeit*) and existence (*Existenz*), where actuality conformed to the necessity of reason but existence did not.[42] But how do we distinguish between actuality and existence? Hegel left his disciples little concrete guidance; hence the disputes among them.

This account of the disputes within the Hegelian school seems to follow, or at least confirm, that of Engels in his *Ludwig Feuerbach und der Ausgang der klassischen deutschen Philosophie*.[43] According to Engels' classic statement, the division between right and left Hegelians was essentially a split between radicals and reactionaries. While the radicals adopted Hegel's method and his dictum that the rational is the real, the reactionaries embraced his system and his dictum that the real is rational. Engels' account does contain some

---

41 Brazill 1970, pp. 17–18, seems to me to be incorrect in arguing that the divisions between the Hegelian School did not result from any ambiguity in Hegel's philosophy. This underrates the interpretative problems regarding Hegel's dictum about the rationality of the real.

42 The distinction is in Hegel 1989, §6.   43 Marx, and Engels 1998–, XXI, pp. 266–8.

important germs of truth: that the fundamental split in the movement arose from an ambiguity in Hegel's philosophy, and that it concerns the question of the rationality of present conditions in Prussia. However, it is important not to take it too literally or to draw broader conclusions from it. It is misleading in several respects:

(1) Throughout the 1820s and 1830s, the division between right and left was not between radicals and reactionaries, but between opposing wings of a broad reformist politics. The radical currents of left-wing Hegelianism developed only in the 1840s, after the accession of Friedrich Wilhelm IV; and even then there was not that much of a split between radicals and conservatives because right-wing Hegelianism virtually disappeared (Toews 1980, pp. 223–4, 234–5).
(2) The distinction between method and system is not only artificial, but also insufficient to distinguish between right and left Hegelians. After the 1840s the left rejected the method as much as the system because they lost all their faith in the dialectic of history (Toews 1980, p. 235).
(3) Engels interprets the division in *narrow* political terms, though religious differences occasioned the split in the first place (Brazill 1970, pp, 7, 53; McLellan 1969, pp. 3, 6).

What finally shattered and dissolved Hegelianism was not its internal disputes, its centrifugal tendencies alone. For, as we have seen, the debates of the 1830s continued within a Hegelian framework, never renouncing the grand Hegelian ideal of the unity of theory and practice. What did defeat Hegelianism was the very card its master most loved to play: history. In 1840 the Prussian Reform Movement came to its end. In that fateful year both Altenstein and Friedrich Wilhelm III died. Hopes for reform were raised again with the accession of Friedrich Wilhelm IV. And, indeed, he began his reign with some popular liberal measures: amnesty for political prisoners, the publication of the proceedings of provincial estates and the relaxation of press censorship. It did not bode well, however, that the new king's personal politics were very reactionary. He advocated government by the old aristocratic estates, disapproved of the plans for a new constitution, insisted upon protecting the state religion and even defended the divine right of kings. Sure enough, there were some very ominous developments. In 1841, Friedrich Wilhelm showed his political colours by inviting

Schelling to Berlin 'to combat the dragonseed of Hegelianism'. Then, in 1842, the government began to impose censorship, forcing the Hegelians to publish their main journal, the *Hallische Jahrbücher*, outside Prussia. For any Hegelian in the 1840s, then, this course of events could only be profoundly discouraging. Rather than marching forward, as Hegel assumed, history seemed to be moving backwards.

Once the forces of reaction began to assert themselves, it was inevitable that Hegel's philosophy would collapse. The very essence of Hegel's teaching made him vulnerable to historical refutation. The great strength of Hegel's system lay in its bold syntheses – of theory and practice, of rationalism and historicism, or radicalism and conservatism – for these seemed to transcend the partisan spirit, granting every standpoint a necessary, if limited, place in the whole. But the great strength of Hegel's philosophy was also its great weakness, its tragic flaw. For, as we have seen, all these syntheses rested upon a single optimistic premise: that reason is inherent in history, that the laws and trends of history will inevitably realise the ideals of the Revolution. It was just this optimism, though, that seemed to be refuted by the disillusioning events of the early 1840s. Hegel had bet his whole system on history; and he had lost.

It is not surprising to find, then, that the neo-Hegelian debates of the 1840s take on a new dimension. The question is no longer how to praise and interpret Hegel but how to transform and bury him. The publication of Feuerbach's *Das Wesen des Christenthums* in 1841 convinced many of the need to go beyond Hegel. In 1842, Arnold Ruge, a leading left Hegelian, published his first criticism of Hegel.[44] And in 1843 Marx and Engels would begin their 'settling of accounts' with their Hegelian heritage in *Die deutsche Ideologie*. Internal feuding lost its former energy and meaning. Many of the right-wing Hegelians became disillusioned with the course of events and joined their brothers on the left to form a common front against their reactionary enemies (Toews 1980, pp. 223–4). The common framework for the debates of the 1830s also quickly disappeared. Rather than reaffirming the ideal of the unity of theory and practice, many Hegelians asserted the rights of theory over practice. It seemed to Bruno Bauer, for example, that the growing gap between ideal and reality in Friedrich Wilhelm's Prussia could be overcome only by 'the terrorism of pure theory'.

---

44 McLellan 1969, p. 24. The new critical developments of the 1840s are well-summarised by Stepelvich 1983, pp. 12–15.

By the close of the 1840s, Hegelianism was rapidly becoming a fading memory. Having been the ideology for a reform movement that had failed, it could not be the ideology for the Revolution of 1848. Thus the grandest philosophical system of the nineteenth century, and one of its most influential philosophical movements, disappeared into history. The owl of Minerva flew from her roost over Hegel's grave.

5

Historians and lawyers

DONALD R. KELLEY

1 Law and political thought

How is law related to political thought in modern European history?[1] There are three different answers to this question that apply here. One derives from what may be called the legislative or statutory model of legal philosophy, which, following good classical precedent, identified law with the will of the sovereign, whether located in a monarchical or in a republican form of government. In the eighteenth century the legislative paradigm can be seen in the theory and practice of enlightened despotism and especially in the codification movement, which touched many European states, including Prussia, Austria and France (Tarello 1976; cf. Wisner 1997). European codes, modelled largely on the *Corpus Juris Justiniani* (AD 529–33), were intended to organise all private law (especially the law of persons and property) into a single system and in this way, whether directly or indirectly, to politicise it. This agenda was realised most famously in the Napoleonic Code, but it can also be seen in monarchists such as Joseph de Maistre, Louis de Bonald, and Friedrich von Stahl and Utilitarians such as Jeremy Bentham and John Austin, who defined law simply as a command of sovereign power.

The second traditional answer is associated with the rival judicial model and locates political thought within the larger field of law and jurisprudence (in the form of public law), which represents a long professional and 'scientific' tradition. C. F. Mühlenbruch's *Doctrina Pandectarum* (1838), for example, which served Karl Marx and many other law students as a textbook, begins with an introductory survey of the authoritative sources of law and a history of legal tradition going back to antiquity; then goes on to 'general' law, including its definition, divisions and interpretation; and finally takes up the 'special' part of law, that is, private law (divided in

---

[1] The following discussion draws on Kelley 1984a, 1991. In general, the most useful treatments of legal history are Fassò 1974, Landsberg 1912, Wieacker 1967, and, invaluable for bibliography, von Mohl 1855.

Roman fashion into the law of persons, things and actions, or obligations) and the larger social or institutional groupings, including the family, corporations and other 'fictitious persons', and culminating in the state (*civitas* or *respublica*). Here political authority is regarded as simply part – the highest but also the latest level – of the legal system (Mühllenbruch 1838; cf. Cappellini 1984–5, II).

The third model represents law as the expression of popular will, and of course this was associated most notably with the General Will as formulated by Rousseau (Riley 1986). This concept had philosophical and religious roots and was reinforced by the most ancient rule of jurisprudence, the *Salus populi suprema lex esto* of the Roman Twelve Tables; but it also had a more concrete expression, which was the medieval tradition of customary law (Kelley 1990, pp. 131–72, 1991, ch. 6). In 1789 the body of French customs had ostensibly perished along with the old regime, but its spirit survived the Revolution in various forms. German scholars regularly distinguished state-made law (*Staatsrecht*) from people-made law (*Volksrecht*) and judge-made law (*Juristenrecht*) (Beseler 1843). It was the second of these that inspired not only nostalgic or reactionary longings for a return to the old regime but also dreams of social justice and even a 'socialist' future in which law would be defined not as a political creation or an accumulation of individual rights but rather as an expression of social needs and ideals by which it should be judged and to which it should ultimately be subject. This view of law was associated mainly with radical critics such as Marx and Proudhon, though later it did infiltrate the legal profession in France in the form of *droit social* and elsewhere in the form of sociological jurisprudence (Gurvitch 1932).

These three legal paradigms – the legislative, the judicial and the social – may best be regarded as ideal types; for in practice, especially in the views of legal and historical scholars, few governments, not even that of Bonaparte, ever attained a state of purity. The old, still controversial theory of 'mixed government' entailed a complementary conception of law as a creation of multiple sources. So the history most familiar to jurists had taught: Roman law had been issued from popular, judicial and senatorial, as well as imperial sources until Justinian acted – though, as history also taught, acted vainly – to bring them all under imperial will. It was only in theory, the theory of an Ulpian, a Bodin, an Austin or a Stahl, that law and the law-making will were brought together in a logical and unambiguous fashion (Hinsley 1986).

These contrasting views correspond to three loci of authority in the nineteenth century – the omnicompetent state, the independent judicial establishment and 'civil society' in its largest sense. They hardly correspond to legal or political practice, but they do suggest the assumptions and rationales of the opposing positions of nineteenth-century legal, historical and political thinking. They also reflect a triangular debate which has continued in the public arena over the question of whether authority ought to rest with the state, with the people, or with some expert elite that speaks in the name of both.

What gave these questions immediacy and urgency in the nineteenth century was the experience of the French Revolution, which, however viewed, became the cynosure of historical and legal dispute. Whether celebrated by liberals and socialists as the opening of a glorious future in the name of perfectibility and progress or denounced by conservatives and reactionaries as the source of all evil in the world, whether regarded as the culmination of the forces of nationality or the despotic nemesis of national independence, the Revolution has remained the major challenge for historical explanation, model for historical theorising and test for political narrative on a grand scale (Lucas 1988).

In the nineteenth century the general concept of 'revolution' became a major presence in political thought not only as a phenomenon, which was perhaps peculiar to modern history since the English Civil War, but also as a locus of questions about social structure and political change. For historians revolution was an uncommon and dramatic set of events challenging their powers of interpretation; for lawyers it was a break in continuity threatening not only the legitimacy of existing institutions but also their own assumptions and livelihood; for political thinkers it was a point of intersection between the hardest of all test cases for political science and the most fundamental of all political value-judgements. After 1815 the discussion of the nature of revolution was carried on between two ideological extremes – one judging 1789 as the source of all modern troubles, and the other celebrating it as the great hope for the future of all mankind. In many ways it was the historians and the jurists who tried to keep this conversation on a civil and practical level.

In a long perspective the European society that emerged from the calamitous events of the revolutionary and Napoleonic periods was dramatically transformed, but perhaps less so from the standpoint of lawyers and historical scholars, who looked below the level of headline stories, diplomatic debates, political geography and constitutional theory, than from the standpoint of political observers and critics (Kelley 1994). In the law and in historical experience continuities with the old regime – continuities in mentality, social habits, legal conventions and economic arrangements – became increasingly obvious, especially to persons and groups dedicated to continuing and extending the revolutionary agenda of 'liberty, equality and fraternity'.

2 The historical and the philosophical schools

'History must be illuminated by laws, and laws by history', declared Montesquieu (Montesquieu 1751, xxx, p. 2); and this may well be taken as the motto of nineteenth-century jurisprudence – or at least as the central issue to be debated. In general Montesquieu's aphorism illustrates the amphibious nature of law, which on the one hand represents the accumulated wisdom of centuries and on the other hand must itself be judged by historical reality. The old regime lived under the rule of custom and for the most part let history illuminate the theory and practice of jurisprudence, while the Revolution judged history in the light of its conceptions of law and desires for social change. Post-revolutionary political and legal thinkers tended to cast their arguments between these two ideological poles. These two positions were defined respectively as the 'philosophical school', which drew its inspiration from ideas of natural law deriving from Grotius, Pufendorf, Barbeyrac and other 'jus naturalists'; and the 'historical school', based on 'positive law', ideas of legal development and criticism of the abstract theories of natural law (Gierke 1934, 1990; Thieme 1936, pp. 202–63; Stein 1980). The debates between these schools reverberated far beyond the confines of law and even political thought in the nineteenth century.

The philosophical school had found a home in France and, in the wake of the Revolution, a social laboratory for its theories and aspirations. In 1791 the National Assembly expressed its determination 'to make a code of civil laws common to the whole kingdom', and two years later Citizen (later Count) Cambacérès presented his first 'project' for this national code. 'The age so devoutly wished for has finally arrived to fix forever the empire of liberty and the destiny of France', he proclaimed, adding that his aim was no less than to regenerate, to perfect and to 'foresee' absolutely everything in the spirit of enlightened despotism and more immediately of Jacobin (later Bonapartist) social engineering (Fenet 1827, I). 'Legislators, philosophers, and jurists', Cambacérès declared in his 'Discourse on Social Science' of 1798; 'this is the age of social science [*la science sociale*] and, let us add, of true philosophy' (Cambacérès 1789; cf. Gusdorf 1978, VIII, p. 401; Head 1985, p. 109; Moravia 1974, p. 746). Debates between the philosophical and the historical schools – represented respectively by the radicalism of Rousseau and the historical relativism of Montesquieu – were in part a dispute over the nature of this new field (and newly coined term), 'social science'.

In the official deliberations over the Civil Code carried on by Napoleon's committee of redaction (1800–4) we can see the spirits of Rousseau and Montesquieu posthumously contending for the political soul of France (Bonnecase 1933; Gaudemet 1904, 1935). On this committee Cambacérès represented the pursuit of perfectability and codification of the General Will through an infallible science of legislation. Opposed to him was Citizen (later Count) Portalis, disciple of Montesquieu, who objected to the revolutionary and 'Robespierrist' spirit of the original plan, which for him was an 'abuse of the philosophical spirit' (Portalis 1827). 'The doctrine of the redactors is that we should preserve everything that it is not necessary to destroy' (Portalis 1844, p. 69); and he concluded, 'How can we control the action of time? How can we resist the course of events or the imperceptible force of custom? How know and calculate in advance what experience alone can reveal to us? Can foresight ever be extended to objects which thought itself cannot yet grasp?' (Fenet 1827, I, p. 469; Schimséwitsch 1936).

These questions anticipated the more extensive critique which Savigny brought in his famous manifesto of 1814, *The Vocation of our Age for Legislation and Jurisprudence* (Savigny 1831). In the eighteenth century, Savigny wrote, 'Men longed for new codes, which, by their completeness, should insure a mechanically precise administration of justice'; and the upshot was that Bonapartist creation, which 'broke into Germany, and ate in, further and further, like a cancer...' (Savigny 1831, p. 18). To throw light on these questions Savigny published passages from the preliminary debates over the text of the French Code, which took up the problems of the contradictions between legal simplicity and social complexity, referring in particular to the conservative arguments of Portalis. It was this legislative violation of history that provoked Savigny's manifesto of 1814 and led to a key question. 'What is the influence of the past on the present?' is the way he posed it, 'and what is the relation of what is now to what will be?' This was at once one of the central problems of the 'Historical School of Law' and one of the basic dilemmas of nineteenth-century political thought.

Although Hegel became the acknowledged head of the philosophical school, it was actually his intention to rise above and indeed to reconcile the historical and philosophical conceptions of law. Just as the Roman legal tradition had arisen from specific 'positive' laws and aspired to the status of 'written reason' (*ratio scripta*), so modern positive law should seek to

attain the level of natural law and civil society to find its ideal form in the
state (Hegel 1952, pp. 16–17; Kelley 1991, pp. 252–7; Lucas and Pöggeler
1986; Riedel 1984). It is this reconciliation of human will and reason on
legal terms that underlay Hegel's famous motto, 'What is rational is real
and what is real is rational.' The irony is that what Hegel brought into
unity in conceptual terms his disciples divided still more drastically – 'right'
Hegelians interpreting his slogan as a defence of conservatism and 'left'
Hegelians interpreting it as an ideal to be achieved by radical action and,
finally and again, revolution.

3 The coming of law in France

'I define the Revolution in this way,' wrote Jules Michelet: 'the coming
of law, the revival of right, the reaction of justice'; and this noble vision
persisted over many generations (Michelet 1847–53, introduction). In the
nineteenth century law and history as well as political thought were shaped,
and then haunted, by the ideologies and realities of the French Revolution.
Like political theorists, jurists and historians regularly defined their ideological positions in terms of the Revolution, whether the seating arrangement
in the National Assembly or the chronological extension of this represented
by the successive stages of revolutionary government, from constitutional
monarchy to republic to despotism and back to constitutional monarchy,
with various shadings in between. Like political theorists, too, jurists and
historians had to explain, interpret and judge the unprecedented and unique
set of events that defined the 'old regime' even as it was ostensibly brought
to a close (Kelley 1987, pp. 319–38). The difference was that historical
and legal scholars had to look more closely at the social and institutional
underpinnings of the political and constitutional structures and the realities of human relations in the context of that 'civil society' which was
increasingly being distinguished from the state. As Portalis wrote, 'New
theories are only the systems of individuals; ancient maxims represent the
spirit of the ages' (Portalis 1844, p. 84). This was a way of distinguishing not
only between legislative *science* and *jurisprudence* but also between political
theory based on general reason and utility and that based on history and
experience, both oppositions being fundamental to the history of political
thought.

As conceived by its supporters, the Revolution had claimed priority
both over the historical process and over legal convention. Such indeed
was the purpose of those 'men of law' (*hommes de loi*) who did more

than any other social group to formulate the aims of the Revolution from 1789 onwards (cf. Fitzsimmons 1987; Kelley 1994; Royer 1979). Not of course that there was any agreement on how to carry through the ideals of justice, for again there were polar extremes in the legal profession, ranging from reactionary émigrés like Nicolas Bergasse to Jacobin enthusiasts like Robespierre – lawyers both. Where the extremes finally met was in debates over the formation of a 'new judicial order' and above all a national code of laws, which Bonapartist enthusiasts hoped would bring social perfection and political unity but which conservative critics saw merely as an instrument to apply to the unending turmoil of the human condition.

For strict interpreters the Code remained an expression of sovereign will. In its preliminary discussions the committee of redaction, confronted with the problem of time lags in the communication of legislative commands, proposed an official delay of two weeks between promulgation and enforcement; but Napoleon, who attended many of these meetings, objected that this 'would be an offence to the national will' (cf. Kelley 1984, p. 43).[2] The redactors of the Code settled on a formula based on calculations for the time needed to communicate legislative orders to the provinces (one day for every twenty leagues from Paris from the first day and the *département* of the Seine from the third day). Thus the 'general will' – soon to be the imperial will – would emanate concentrically and mathematically from its legislative source and, in the form of obedience and morale, reflect back on its national foundation.

The obsession with the general – revolutionary, consular and imperial – will accounts also for Napoleon's suspicion of lawyers and judges. Like Justinian, Napoleon forbade any interpretation whatsoever of his Code; and indeed when the term was mentioned during the preliminary discussions, imperial jurists professed horror at the idea that judges could make changes in the legislative will (cf. Kelley 2001). Interpretation of a law, according to an ancient maxim, was reserved for the maker of that law. If this rule were forgotten, warned one of the Bonapartist redactors, the abuses of the old regime – 'the empire of feudal custom' – would return through the loophole of judicial interpretation (Fenet 1827, VI). To Napoleon, despite the care taken by the literalist school of interpretation, the so-called 'cult of 1804', this was exactly what appeared to happen, as the legal profession was reinstated, as jurisprudence continued to accumulate, as teachers of law in Napoleon's new *Université* disputed and altered its character, as

---

2 *Code civil*, 1803, art. 1.

historians investigated the complex history of law, and as the international debates over the nature of law undermined the simple theory of legislative sovereignty.[3]

What was increasingly apparent in retrospect was not so much what the Revolution destroyed but the survivals and continuities which emerged in the Restoration. In part this was a product of the old legal tradition, which managed to survive first unofficially under the Revolution and then in Bonapartist revival and which carried with it much of the mentality of the legal practice and theory of the old regime. Revolutionary and 'intermediate' law drew on earlier precedents, most of the substance of the Code Napoléon was based on the work of R. J. Pothier and other jurists of the old regime, and the lawyers and the magistracy of the Restoration deliberately set out to reforge links with the founding fathers of their guild (A.-J. Arnaud 1969).

In many ways jurists such as Portalis, P. P. N. Henrion de Pansey, Charles Toullier and J. P. Proudhon re-established, or reinforced, juridical conti-nuities with the feudal, corporatist and parliamentary traditions of the old regime. And French historians such as Augustin Thierry, François Guizot and Jules Michelet carried on parallel projects in the realm of historical scholarship and (in Michelet's term) 'resurrection' (Kelley 1984, pp. 93–112, 2003, pp. 141 ff.).

In part this vision of continuity had a political base, especially among opponents and victims of revolutionary and Bonapartist policies. Portalis' conservative opinions were displayed first in the heat of the preliminary discussions of the Code and elaborated further under the Restoration. He rejected the 'false doctrines concerning the social contract, sovereignty, and the false ideas about exaggerated liberty and absolute equality'. What Portalis recommended to the editorial committee formed to establish the text of the 'Code of the French People', as it was originally called, was the gradual reform of laws and institutions based on practical experience, not theoretical perfection. In opposition to revolutionary mentality that demanded utopia overnight Portalis proclaimed 'Honor to the wisdom of our fathers, who formed the national character.'[4]

For the émigré magistrate Bernardi law was not a creation of a single ruler but 'the accumulation of reason of all the centuries' and the product

---

3 Cf. Austin 1873, I, p. 334: 'In France the code is buried under a heap of subsequent enactments of the legislature, and of judiciary law subsequently introduced by the tribunals.'
4 Portalis 1844, 19: 'honneur à la sagesse de nos pères, qui ont formé le caractère national'.

of 'the great revolutions which occurred in Europe during the sixteenth century in religion, politics, and even literature', which made that age one of the first memorable in modern history (Bernardi 1803, p. 3). Bernardi invoked the names not only of Burke but also Claude de Seyssel, whose *Monarchy of France* (1515) celebrated the conservative and balanced character of the French 'constitution' (Bernardi's term) and contrasted it with Roman absolutism, counterpart of the 'Corsican domination' and 'twenty-five years outside the law' of Bernardi's time. So he dismissed the so-called (but misnamed) 'revolution' of his time.

A similar debt to the old legal tradition was owed by Henrion de Pansey, who took his inspiration from Charles Dumoulin, the sixteenth-century 'prince of legists'. Henrion praised France as a 'tempered monarchy' subject to 'fundamental laws' (Henrion de Pansey 1843; cf. Salmon 1995). During as well as after the Bonapartist period he defended the principle of life-tenure for judges, and (citing Montesquieu and others) he argued that the prince should never interfere with 'judicial authority'. Serving as magistrate under Napoleon as president of the Cour de Cassation until his death in 1829, Henrion was rewarded for his efforts by honorary membership in the 'Historical School of Law' which attracted disciples in France only after 1815.[5]

4   The new history in France

Before the Revolution lawyers were joined by historians in celebrating the glories and continuities of French history. One of the most extraordinary expressions of this traditionalism was the erudite summation of French constitutional history assembled by Marie-Charlotte-Pauline Robert de Lezardière and published in 1792 as *Théorie des Lois Politiques de la Monarchie Française*. Lezardière celebrated the Germanic heritage of the French monarchy and (in a sense similar to the contemporaneous usage of Edmund Burke) its 'political constitution' (Lezardière 1844; Carcassonne 1927). Seldom was a book more unfortunately timed, and indeed it was stillborn in the first year of the French Republic. A half-century – and two revolutions – later, however, it received new life through the efforts of Guizot, who saw to its publication in 1844, when the 'new history' of the Restoration had been established by Guizot and colleagues such as Augustin Thierry and Jules Michelet.

---

5 *Globe*, 3 (1823), 35.

In the Restoration antiquarian motives reinforced legal traditionalism, as romantic scholars turned with increasing interest to the medieval past of the nation (Gooch 1913, pp. 130ff.; Kelley 2003; Mellon 1958; Moreau 1935; Reizov, n.d.; Stadter 1948; Walch 1986). Certainly the most important politically was Guizot, who made a great reputation as a historian of civilisation before turning to a political career in 1830. As he declared in the lecture course he gave in 1820, 'It is from the midst of the new political order which has commenced in Europe in our own days that we are about to consider... the history of the political institutions of Europe from the foundation of modern states... Against our will and without our knowledge, the ideas which have occupied the present will follow us wherever we go in the study of the past' (Guizot 1852, p. 521). For Guizot, taking a deliberately Whiggish standpoint, the political lesson of history was gradualism, and for this reason, he 'was anxious to combat revolutionary theories and to attach interest and respect to the past history of France' (Guizot 1858–9, I, p. 300). Before the July Revolution of 1830, he confessed about his motives and those of other opponents of the Bourbon government, 'our minds were full of the English Revolution of 1688' (Guizot 1858–9, II, p. 17). For Guizot 1830 marked the culmination of history and the triumph of the bourgeoisie and its values – 'justice, legality, publicity, liberty'. This was the 'civilisation' which Guizot celebrated in his famous lectures and published work and which he supposed would be attendant upon the accession of the July Monarchy which he served – a government which represented not only the culmination of history but, as some observers commented, 'the victory of the lawyers'.

The real founder of the 'new history' of Restoration France was Augustin Thierry, sometime disciple of Saint-Simon, opponent of the philosophical school, and prolific writer of popular history, especially of medieval England and France (Gossman 1976; Smithson 1972). He shared entirely the Whiggish perspective of Guizot (in the sense both of presentism and of Anglophilia), and in 1836 he accepted the assignment from Guizot – significant in an ideological as well as a scholarly way – of collecting the sources for a history of the Third Estate from early medieval times. 'What is the Third Estate?' Sieyès had asked in 1789 – and had answered his own question: 'Everything', though until then it had been 'nothing' and had only wanted to become 'something'. Thierry gathered the historical materials both to answer Sieyès' question and to describe the 'something' which the Third Estate had become, which was nothing less than the Nation itself. In his introduction to his collection of 'monuments' of the Third Estate he described the rise of the communes and 'the progress of the different classes within the non-noble estate [*Roture*] to liberty, well-being, enlightenment, [and] social importance' (Thierry 1866).

For Michelet history was at once an expression of human universality, a struggle between fatalism and liberty, a national epic, a theodicy, and an allegory of self; and the writing of it gave Michelet access to the great canon of French literature. Yet Michelet had also been an explorer of the 'great catacomb of manuscripts' that had survived the Revolution; and, like Thierry, followed the meta-political story of national self-creation through the legal monuments which constituted both the last will and testament of the old regime and the prophecy of the new Nation, which Michelet believed would be the final legacy of 1789 – that triumph of law and justice which the first revolution promised. The last stage of this process came with the 'three glorious' days of that second revolution, when history would be transformed into an 'eternal July' signalling the victory of liberty over 'fatalism' (Michelet 1972, II, p. 217; Kelley 1984a). The unanswerable social question of the early nineteenth century and the events of 1848 destroyed this revolutionary dream of social fraternity – a classless Nation – as well as the constitutional monarchy; but the bourgeois ideal of a unified nation under liberal principles was preserved under other forms of government, first imperial and then republican.

In general the effect of legal and historical scholarship on politics was to qualify, to criticise or to counteract the ideals of revolutionary action on the grounds of experience and historical inertia. Revolutionary legislation, including the Civil Code, was necessarily abstract and needed not only interpretation but also application to particular cases and questions; and this was the function of the old 'science of law' and jurisprudence, which was drawn either from legal tradition or the intuitions of judges. Post-revolutionary historians also emphasised the sub-political forces which prevented the sort of direct change and control which champions of the new social science – the 'science of legislation' – envisaged. In such terms they contributed to the contemporary political debate even if they were not always attended to by constitutional and macro-political theorists.

5   The historical school in Germany

'Historical writing was old, but historical thinking was new in Germany when it sprang from the shock of the French Revolution', wrote Lord

Donald R. Kelley

Acton, adding that 'The romantic reaction which began with the invasion of 1794 was the revolt of outraged history' (Acton 1985, p. 326). Since Acton's time we have learned much more about the eighteenth-century roots of that influence 'for which the depressing names of historicism and historical-mindedness have been devised' (Acton 1985, p. 326). Long before the Revolution German scholars had inclined towards a historical view of political, constitutional and legal questions. The German *Aufklärung* was critical of the unhistorical rationalism of the French *philosophes* – legal scholars insisting on the conceptual value of 'positive law' (as distinguished from the universalism of natural law) and historians, especially those at the Göttingen School in the eighteenth century, working out ideas of national individuality and cultural development. The writings of J. S. Pütter (1725–1809) on legal and constitutional history, for example, rejected abstract systematising in favour of the study of the customs and institutions of Germany, which he understood to be 'deeply rooted in its constitution, partly in its climate, and in everything that was common to Germany's situation' (Reill 1975, p. 184; Butterfield 1955; Kelley 2003). Herder's conception of *Volksgeist* was a similar, if more philosophical expression of this view of the organic nature of society, law and political organisation.

Yet the German Wars of Liberation did provide a focus and an impulse for more intensive study of the national past; and the new University of Berlin, founded in 1808, replaced Göttingen as the centre of such historical and legal scholarship (Gooch 1913). Barthold Georg Niebuhr, Karl Friedrich Eichhorn, Karl Friedrich von Savigny and later Hegel are among the figures attracted to this new centre of national identity. Eichhorn published the first volume of his pioneering history of German law and institutions, which he saw as reflecting a national life going continuously back to Frankish times; and this work was supplemented by that on German legal antiquities by Savigny's pupil, Jacob Grimm, and especially the *Monumenta Germaniae Historica*, a systematic collection of historical and legal sources, which began appearing in 1826 and is still being produced today. Such publications formed the basis of the efforts to reconstruct a national past paralleling and reinforcing the movement towards political and legal unity of a unified German state which many of these scholars envisioned and celebrated.

The leader of the Historical School of Law in the nineteenth century was Savigny, but its true founder was Gustav Hugo (1764–1844), who had studied with Pütter at Göttingen and who taught law at the University of Heidelberg (Marino 1969; Whitman 1990, pp. 205–6; Ziolkowski 1990).

Hugo's major work was a handbook of civil law (published in many editions from 1789 to 1832) which offered a new and critical interpretation of 'natural law as a philosophy of positive law'. Hugo, who was the translator of the famous forty-fourth chapter of Gibbon's *Decline and Fall* on the history of Roman law, viewed legal history not just as a scholar but also as a theorist who disdained 'mere metaphysics' of 'dogmatic natural law' and the empty theorising of the physiocrats or *Economisten* (Hugo 1819, pp. 4, 28). He regarded the history of law and a 'juristic anthropology' as essential foundations for a legal system, or 'encyclopedia', and especially for the education of lawyers; and he saw law as a late stage of the long development of the custom of a particular society or nation. For Hugo an expert understanding of this evolution was necessary for any legal or political judgement.

After 1814 Hugo and his work were eclipsed by his younger colleague Savigny, who had been called to the University of Berlin in 1810, eight years before the arrival of his colleague and rival Hegel (Marino 1978; Meinecke 1970, pp. 158–9).[6] The historical school came into prominence with the appearance of the new journal edited by Savigny and Eichhorn, the *Zeitschrift für Geschichtliche Rechtswissenschaft*, and especially the following year with Savigny's manifesto. The premise of all of Savigny's work, including both his history of Roman law in the Middle Ages and his last book, an unfinished 'system' of civil law, was that law 'has a two-fold life: first, as a part of the aggregate existence of the community, which it does not cease to be; and, secondly, as a distinct branch of knowledge in the hands of the jurists'. Both of these aspects of law had been violated by Napoleon's international empire and its legal counterpart, the Civil Code. 'As soon as Napoleon had subjected everything to a military despotism, he greedily held fast that part of the revolution which answered his purpose and prevented the return of the ancient constitution' (Savigny 1831, p. 71). The German Wars of Liberation had ended this despotism and had created conditions under which '[a] historical spirit has been every where awakened, and leaves no room for the shallow self-sufficiency above alluded to' (Savigny 1831, p. 71).

What was at issue here were two conceptions of legal and political reason – that of the philosophical school, which identified it with abstract and universal systems, and that of the historical school, which regarded human reason as the accumulated experience of many centuries of

6 In general, see Moravia 1980.

cultural development. For critics of rationalism like Herder and Portalis history was not only an expression of this experience but also a critique (for Herder a 'meta-critique') of the 'pure reason' associated with Kant and, more vulgarly, the Jacobins and Bonapartists and radicals like Tom Paine, who, opposing Burke's anti-revolutionary 'sermon', wanted to 'lay then the axe to the root' (Paine 1989b, p. 70). This was the attitude that Savigny deplored. 'Only through her [history] can a lively connection with the primitive state of a people be kept up', he declared; 'and the loss of this connection must take away from every people the best part of its spiritual life' (Savigny 1831, p. 136). This is precisely what the Revolution had done to France and what Napoleon had dogmatically systematised and politicised.

These were some of the underlying issues of the controversy provoked by Savigny's manifesto, beginning with the pamphlets of A. W. Rehburg and especially of A. F. T. Thibaut (who was a colleague of Hugo at Heidelberg) defending the notion of a general code for Germany. In fact the real issue between Savigny and Thibaut was not history versus philosophy – for Thibaut also claimed a historical basis for his position – but rather what constituted a proper understanding of modern history.[7] Savigny did not think the time was ripe for a code, while Thibaut argued that modern civil law transcended the local constrictions of the *Volksgeist* in its earlier forms. Was Germany ready to become a unified national state with its own legal system? In the event it was only in 1900 that the German Civil Code finally resolved this problem.

Savigny had many disciples in the first half of the nineteenth century outside the boundaries both of the legal profession and of Germany. Historical linguists like Jakob Grimm (who studied with Savigny at Berlin) and political economists like Wilhelm Röscher applied Savigny's premises and prejudices to their own lines of investigation in the effort to enhance the defence and illustration of the life of the people – the *Volk* being the German counterpart of the emergent French *Nation*. Politically, the historical school resembled the philosophical school – Savigny's influence resembled that of Hegel, his great rival at the University of Berlin in that both had left-wing as well as right-wing offspring. In France in particular Savigny's followers hoped that his doctrines would be a way of completing the unfinished 'social revolution', while others associated the historicism of Savigny exclusively with the formation of the authoritarian national state (Kelley 1984a).

---

7 The essential texts are collected in Koselleck 1967 and Stern 1959.

The same divergence can be seen, even more radically, in the intellectual progeny of Hegel.

The influence of the German Historical School even reached the New World, which was ostensibly free of the burdens of the feudal past of Europe and yet which displayed a similar pattern of development. 'American law was the growth of necessity, not of the wisdom of the individuals', wrote George Bancroft (who had studied in Germany) of the period of the American Revolution. 'It was not an acquisition from abroad; it was begotten from the American mind, of which it was a natural and inevitable but also a slow and gradual development. The sublime thought that there existed a united nation was yet to spring into being' (Bancroft 1876, IV, p. 568).

In many ways German political thought was dependent on legal tradition in the wake of the French Revolution. The concept of a state based on law (*Rechtsstaat*), coined by K. T. Welcker in 1813 and popularised by Robert von Mohl, was an attractive (and in a sense non-political) alternative to the state based on absolutist or arbitrary rule (*Polizeistaat*) and that based on popular will (*Volksstaat*), associated with Rousseau and Robespierre. Such juridical statecraft (*Staatswissenschaft*), suggesting a middle path between progress and reaction, was reinforced by the work of constitutionalist jurists like K. S. Zachariae, who stood for a Germanic 'ancient constitution' and attendant liberties comparable to those celebrated by the English and French (Kreiger 1957, p. 253; Stahl 1830; Whitman 1990, pp. 95–6, 141–3).

The question that remained was on what basis such moderate government should be built, and here occurred a severe split within the ranks of the historical school and the 'new professoriate' of the nineteenth century. On the one side was Savigny and his followers, who argued that the 'reception' of Roman law beginning in the fifteenth century and the 'modern' tradition based on this reception of Justinian's *usus modernus Pandectarum* called for a Romanist legal structure. On the other side were defectors from Savigny's scholarly and professional position, including his former student Jakob Grimm, who looked rather to Germanic custom as created by the people, and his former collaborator Eichhorn, who founded his own 'Germanist' journal in 1839 (Mittermaier 1839). According to C. J. A. Mittermaier, another defector from Savigny's camp: 'Our law stands in opposition to the national consciousness, to the needs, customs, attitude, and ideas of the people.'[8] This democratic conception of law was opposed by Savigny's follower G. F. Puchta, whose book on customary law argued that custom

---

8 Remarks made at a congress of Germanists in 1847, cited in Hinton 1951, p. 100.

was really the creation of the jurists rather than the *Volk*, yet no less an expression of national spirit (Beseler 1843; Puchta 1828).

6 Conservatism and radicalism in England

In England the alliance between history and law was an ancient one, inherent in effect in the tradition of common law and the 'ancient constitution'. For Edmund Burke, on whose work Savigny drew, history was 'a great volume . . . unrolled for our instruction, drawing the materials of future wisdom from past errors and infirmities of mankind' (Burke 1969, p. 247; Blakemore 1988). Burke contrasted 1688 with 1789 in the most fundamental way. 'Our Revolution', he argued, 'was made to preserve our *antient* indisputable law and liberties, and the *antient* constitution of government which is our only security for law and liberty' (Burke 1969, p. 117). Burke drew a similar invidious contrast between the English and the French practice of law, remarking that 'the science of jurisprudence . . . is the collected reason of the ages', not an assignment to be approached 'with no better apparatus than the metaphysics of an undergraduate, and the mathematics and arithmetic of an exciseman' (Burke 1969, pp. 193, 299).

Burke was speaking of politics in the French manner, but he might well have applied his criticisms to the utilitarian doctrines of Jeremy Bentham, who had his own notions of codification that set him apart from both the philosophical and the historical schools. Bentham's conception of law was based on a theory of psychology that avoided, or evaded, any notion of collective behaviour beyond calculations of individual drives and goals. 'O rare simplicity!' he exclaimed, 'handmaid of beauty, wisdom, virtue – of everything that is excellent!'[9] Although he rejected Jacobin notions of human nature, Bentham was in agreement with some of their radical notions of legal reform, especially the euphoric suggestion of Adrien Duport, in the debates over the 'new judicial order' in 1791, that the new society could do without the legal profession: 'No more judges!' he cried. 'No more courts!'[10] This was altogether in keeping with Bentham's ideal of 'Every man his own lawyer'.

Bentham had the utmost scorn for professional lawyers and their cautious traditionalism, ridiculing the 'Wisdom of our Ancestors' as the 'Chinese argument' and the fear of innovation as 'the Hobgoblin argument' (Larrabee 1952, pp. 34, 43). To Bentham, William Blackstone was a mere expositor and an antiquary whose doctrine was not so much false as 'unmeaning'. According to Blackstone, 'That ancient collection of unwritten maxims and customs, which is the common law, however confounded and from whatever foundation derived, had subsisted immemorially in this kingdom' (Blackstone 1862, p. 16). To Bentham this was nonsense; and his first charge was 'to the science [of law] of the poison introduced into it by him' (Blackstone 1862, p. 16, cf. Bentham 2008). What Bentham wanted to do was to transform unwritten custom into written law, common law into statute law, and vague and confused legal memory into a rational system based not on the muddled ideals of justice but on the calculable goals fixed by utility and a general theory of human nature.

From these attitudes arose Bentham's projects for judicial organisation, beginning with a new plan drawn up for the benefit of the French National Assembly in December 1789 and ending with a proposal addressed in 1822 to 'All Nations professing Liberal Opinions' (Bentham 1789, 1822). Joining together 'principles of morals and legislation', Bentham assumed that individual psychology (especially the 'associationist' psychology of David Hartley) was a sufficient basis not only for social theory but also for public policy. In general Bentham's system was based on a general contempt for history, a simplistic theory of human behaviour, and a legislative strategy governed by a 'calculus' of pleasures and pains and the attendant principle of utility; and his logical-intuitive approaches offered a 'radical' alternative to both the historical and the natural-law schools of jurisprudence. To his followers, Bentham was a supreme theorist of the science of legislation; to others, such as William Hazlitt, he was a 'mere child' and an unfortunate sign of the times (Hazlitt 1828, p. 172).

Bentham's attitudes were carried more directly into the law by his disciple John Austin, whose *Lectures on Jurisprudence* were subtitled, borrowing a phrase from Gustav Hugo, 'the philosophy of positive law'. Austin was as remote as possible, however, from the ideas of the historical school and its reverence for popular custom as the ultimate source of law. Nonsense, declared Austin; custom became law not by the consent of the governed but by command of the state. Nor was 'interpretation' a qualification of this argument, for interpretation was nothing else than 'establishing new laws, under guise of expounding the old' (Austin 1873, 1, p. 27; Morison 1982). Nor was this at all objectionable. 'I cannot understand how any person who has considered the subject can suppose that society could possibly have gone on if judges had not legislated, or that there is any danger whatever in allowing them that power which they have in fact exercised, to make up for the negligence or the incapacity of the avowed legislator' (Austin 1873, I, p. 191).

Like Bodin, Austin equated law, or rather the law-making power, with sovereign will. Law was entirely dependent on what Austin called 'the superiority which is styled sovereignty' (Austin 1873, I, p. 193) and, more practically, on a 'habit of obedience'. For Austin '[T]he power of a sovereign monarch properly so called, or the power of a sovereign number in its collegiate and sovereign capacity, is incapable of *legal* limitation' (Austin 1873, I, p. 254). 'Laws proper, or properly so called, are commands', he insisted, while laws improper were those based on custom or 'mere opinion'. There was no such thing as being 'half-' or 'imperfectly sovereign' (Austin 1873, I, p. 238). Austin's mission was to define the 'province of jurisprudence'; and his conviction was that 'The matter of jurisprudence is positive law: law, simply and strictly so called: or law set by political superiors to political inferiors' (Austin 1873, I, p. 238). History played no part in this process of exerting authority, which for Austin was a matter of clear thinking and proper morality.

For Austin everything hinged on private reasoning and individual psychology, and if human relations were motivationally as clear as logic, there would be no problem with laws. Naturally, he followed the utilitarian axiom that 'Good or evil is nothing but pleasure or pain, or that which occasions or procures pleasure or pain for us' (Austin 1873, I, p. 166). This is ironic in view of Austin's own extraordinary mental irregularity that kept him in psychic pain much of his life. Nevertheless, Austin trusted hardly anyone's judgement except his own and that of his Benthamite colleagues. He cited the giants of the tradition of civil law from Gaius to Montesquieu but mainly to correct their errors, as he did with the classics of modern natural law, Grotius and Barbeyrac (though not Hobbes), especially with respect to the idea of sovereignty (Austin 1873, I, pp. 178–9, 213–14). He borrowed from Hugo's conception of positive law, but in general he found German scholarship full of 'vague and misty abstraction' (Austin 1873, I, p. 343). 'It really *is* important (though I feel the audacity of the paradox) that men should think distinctly, and speak with a meaning' (Austin 1873, I, pp. 55–6).

Among the critics of utilitarianism the most conspicuous was Thomas Macaulay, who denounced all of 'philosophical radicalism' and its 'barren theories'. Utilitarianism was based on 'mere delusion', wrote Macaulay (Macaulay n.d. [a], I, pp. 415, 447). 'Our objection to the essay of Mr. Mill is fundamental', he continued. 'We believe that it is utterly impossible to deduce the science of government from the principles of human nature.' Mill invoked history when it suited him but ignored it when it ran counter to his doctrine (the example being that in a democracy people are as likely to exploit the rich, to judge from history, as are absolute rulers to exploit the people). 'Let us not throw history aside when we are proving a theory,' Macaulay protested, 'and take it up again when we have to refute an objection founded on the principles of that theory.' Such misguided rationalism was a violation both of experience and of the 'Noble Science of Politics' (Collini *et al.* 1983).

Benthamite radicalism and Austinian legal theory were as far as can be imagined from the reverence and enthusiasm for history displayed by many English scholars of the romantic age. 'The history of law is the most satisfactory clue to the political history of England', wrote Francis Palgrave, a lawyer as well as a medieval historian (quoted in Hallam 1827, I, p. 2). 'The character of the people mainly depends on their law.' Henry Hallam began his *Constitutional History of England* (1827) by declaring that 'The government of England, in all times recorded by history, has been one of those mixed or limited monarchies' characteristic of Celtic and Germanic tradition and utterly irreconcilable with the Austinian conception of law (Hallam 1827, I; Kelley 2003). In agreement with conventional common law views going back to Edward Coke and John Fortescue, Hallam recognised a number of 'essential checks upon royal authority' (Hallam 1827, I, p. 3) including parliamentary consent for taxes and new laws, due process of law, and guarantees of individual liberties, all of which was nonsense as far as Austin was concerned. For Hallam the English constitution, though it had a common origin with those of other European nations, had an exceptionally fortunate career, producing a unique sort of security and liberty which had been 'the slow fruit of ages' and reached its present height through the 'democratical influence' which Hallam, very much like Guizot, attributed to 'the commercial and industrious classes in contradistinction to the territorial aristocracy' (Hallam 1827, I, p. 2).

Macaulay was altogether in agreement with this line of argument. In his review he found Hallam's history not only 'judicial' (if somewhat prosaic and unimaginative) but also impartial (Macaulay n.d. [a], I, p. 312; Clive 1973). 'The Constitution of England was only one of a large family', he wrote in his own *History of England*, which he began publishing over twenty years later. 'In all the monarchies of Europe in the middle ages, there existed restraints on the royal authority, fundamental laws, and representative assemblies' (Macaulay n.d. [a], I, pp. 340, 344; Macaulay n.d. [b], I, pp. 340,

344). Such were the institutional conditions of that 'progress of civilisation' which was so obvious to Macaulay in his own day. England was especially fortunate in escaping the fate of other continental states, which had fallen into absolutism. For Macaulay the lesson taught by history was not the power of reason and calculation but rather the vital force of the unwritten English 'constitution', the continuing spirit of common law, the growth of ancient and modern liberty and the pre-eminence of the revolutionary model of 1688.

7   Conclusion

The convergence between law and history signalled by Montesquieu and reinforced by the historians of the Göttingen school had a significant effect on political thought in the early nineteenth century. Law and history offered ways not only of explaining but also of legitimisng political institutions and ideas. Law was seen by the historical school both as a reflection of society and as the foundation of the state – a historically constructed bridge between the social and the political. This view gave law a context, situated it between the radical and authoritarian extremes to which doctrinaire rationalism was prone, and held out the vision of a nation in which all social classes were united under a legitimate sovereign authority – a *Rechtsstaat* in which law not only expressed the will of the people but also constrained that of their rulers.

With its 'ancient constitution', England had long reflected this ideal; and the states emerging from the revolutionary period with written constitutions were ostensibly devoted to such principles. In Restoration France the Civil Code was prefixed and as it were crowned by the Charter of 1815 to form a dual embodiment of national will. For Germany history and law (and politics) had eventually to call on military action to achieve national unity and legitimacy and to take a systematic rather than historical view to achieve a national code at the end of the century, as indeed Savigny did in his last, unfinished work (Savigny 1840, 1).

Under these conditions, or behind this pretence, lawyers continued to enjoy their pre-eminent position as interpreters of legal and constitutional tradition and umpires of economic, social and political conflict (Arnaud 1973). As members of an intellectual community which they themselves traced back to antiquity, jurists could draw on professional experience as well as legal philosophy to judge the nature and destiny of political structures. 'To study modern French political theory is to study the lawyers', wrote Ernest

Barker. 'To study German political theory is equally to study the lawyers.'[11] This is the case with France and Germany of both the revolutionary and the post-revolutionary periods. Barker did not think the same to be true of England; but such a case for this connection has been made by Stefan Collini; and indeed it is a plausible argument for the nineteenth century when one recalls the work not only of Austin and legal scholars like Maitland and Dicey but also Henry Sumner Maine and J. F. McLennan, who drew on the law for their ethnological investigations and interpretations of social and political structures.

In the early nineteenth century, history and law were most easily adaptable, perhaps, to reactionaries and defenders of the status quo; but historians and lawyers were deeply involved in political action and thought across the whole ideological spectrum. In France the liberal revolution of July 1830 has been described as a 'revolution of the advocates'; but as in the first French Revolution lawyers were also capable of a radical turn; and indeed this was a common pattern in the years before the revolutions of 1848. It was an ex-teacher of law who led the uprisings in Brunswick in 1830 and Frankfurt in 1833, and both Marx and Mazzini turned from theory to 'praxis' by dropping out of a legal career in favour of journalism and political activism. Historians as well as jurists figured prominently in the Frankfurt Parliament of 1847 before the wave of revolutions the following year which disillusioned intellectuals of almost all ideological persuasions.

The centrality of history to nineteenth-century thought was recognised by intellectuals of many ideological persuasions. As Auguste Comte put it, 'The present century is characterised above all by the irrevocable preponderance of history, in philosophy, in politics, and even in poetry.'[12] The idea of development – 'subjecting all things to that influence', Acton remarked, 'for which the depressing name of historicism and historical-mindedness have been devised' (Acton 1985, p. 543) – was well implanted before being reinforced by romantic, nationalist and counter-revolutionary sentiments. From the mid-eighteenth century the 'four-stage theory' of history converged with ideas of material progress to form a useful and satisfying historical perspective for the commercial and industrial classes (Meek 1976). The same sort of view could of course be turned to revolutionary uses; and indeed Marx conscripted the bourgeois philosophy of history, expressed by Guizot among others, to the cause of the working class and its

---

11 Preface to his translation of Gierke 1934. Cf. Collini 1993, p. 251.
12 *Politique positive*, III, p. 1, cited in Acton 1985, p. 541.

own counter-consciousness. History offered a wide choice of perspectives and genealogies for nationalities, classes, parties and groups of all sorts; and in the nineteenth century it became the chief mode of self-identification and understanding.

In the latter part of the century the study of history derived further strength from its claims to professional and scientific status. *Geschichtswissenschaft* was based not only on critical and documentary methods but ideas derived from the Darwinian theory of evolution (Blanke 1991). At the same time this 'science of history,' associated above all with the writings and teaching of Leopold von Ranke, acquired further power and prestige from its increasing associations with government service and the political elite. The aphorism that history was 'past politics' is English in origin, but it applied equally to the historical profession in other European states. In the later nineteenth century Darwinism, especially in its 'Social' form, also reinforced the central position of history in the larger view of human nature and, for better or for worse, its historical transformations.

The view from the left was a bit different. In this period of the hated 'Bourgeois Monarchy' and the German *Vormärz* – of class division and revolutionary tremors – legalism and historical gradualism became less relevant to such would-be movers and shakers and to the ideals of social and national revolution which they envisioned. To this extent political thought became estranged from conventional views of law and history and entered into an active mode. Karl Marx, for example, rejected law and jurisprudence as expressions of feudal, and then bourgeois, interests and ideology; and after 1848 he even came to doubt 'history' itself, since it had not proceeded according to his plan (LaCapra 1983, pp. 268–90).

The forces of historical change had disturbing effects on law and legal traditions in various ways. In the generation before the revolutions of 1848 many young activists had looked to the law as a basis for a continuing – that is, a 'social' – revolution to extend the political phase achieved in the 1790s. This was especially true of the new generation – the third, according to Guizot's counting – which spawned so many 'youth' movements throughout Europe between 1815 and 1848 (Guizot 1863, intro.).[13] Members of the historical school such as Pellegrino Rossi and of the philosophical school such as both the young Marx and the young Proudhon began with their juridical faith intact, hoping to achieve the ideals of social justice embodied in the old legal tradition (Kelley and Smith 1984; Proudhon 1994, intro.).

---

13 'Trois générations' being those of 1789, 1815 and 1848.

All of these (and many of their peers) were disillusioned, however, and turned away from what they regarded as the hypocritical moralism of jurisprudence and the status quo which it was in effect designed to preserve. In the late 1830s Marx railed against what he called 'the metaphysics of law' and the legalist 'opposition between what is and what ought to be'; and (turning viciously against the historical school as represented by Gustav Hugo), he rejected the law and the legal tradition as expressions of 'ideology' in his pejorative use of the term (Kelley 1978). This view was shared by many of his generation, including Proudhon, who had also taken the law as his point of departure and who likewise turned to more scientific and effective ways of understanding and confronting the looming 'Social Question'.

Abandoning the empty ideals of jurisprudence both of these young activists turned to what Marx called the 'new gods' of political economy. 'How could these men', Proudhon asked about the lawyers, 'who never had the faintest notion of statistics, calculation of value, or political economy, furnish us with principles of legislation?' (Proudhon 1993). Political economy was 'social science par excellence', declared Pellegrino Rossi; and Proudhon, who had attended Rossi's lectures in the Collège de France, could not agree more (Rossi 1840, p. 34). For Proudhon political economy represented the 'code' of bourgeois property, but it had the potential to be much more. In the right hands it could change the face of the world. 'The revolution today', declared Proudhon in 1847, '*is* political economy' (Proudhon 1960, II, p. 66).

In this way law, formerly considered a rigorous science treating 'causes' and at the same time a form of wisdom because it considered 'things divine and human', suffered a fall from intellectual grace and lost out in its rivalry with newer disciplines, especially political economy, which had the best claims to follow the natural-science model. As Cambacérès had observed at the end of the old century:

'Political economy, legislation, and moral philosophy all have the same goal, which is the perfection of social relations; but their means are not the same: the first links men through their interests, the second through authority, and the third through sentiment. Political economy considers men in terms of their physical faculties, legislation in terms of their rights, and moral philosophy in terms of their passions. (Cambacérès 1789)

In its explanatory efforts economics, drawing on the assumptions and ideas of natural law, dispensed with sentiments and human values and turned to the statistically measurable and the quantitatively calculable and on this basis could claim a method in accord with the value-free natural-science model of conceptualisation, which came to prevail in the later nineteenth century. It was also in accord with the values of both the right and the left: of both the selfish and competitive spirit of the *bourgeois conquérants* who regarded themselves as heirs of the Revolution and of the socialists and radicals who resisted such 'egoism' and looked to economic science – political or social economy – as a way of transforming society according to newer revolutionary goals.

Political science, of course, has had to come to terms with these new forces, ideals and methods, in which the gradualism, the conservatism and the moralism retained in the intellectual baggage of historians and jurists have become increasingly problematic, if not irrelevant. Instead of being central and sovereign, history and the law have in effect become observers and critics of the projects of political thought.

6

Social science from the French Revolution to positivism

CHERYL B. WELCH

Today we deliberately refer to social sciences in the plural. For much of the nineteenth century, however, writers more characteristically spoke of social science or *la science sociale* in the singular. Although there was perhaps as little consensus then as now on either the meaning of 'social' or the methods of its 'science(s)', there was an often unspoken agreement about the relationship of social science to politics: *la science sociale* would provide the master plan for a new political order. My purpose in this essay is not to canvas all the uses of social science as political blueprint, but rather to reconsider some key debates about the relationship of social science to political argument in France and England from the French Revolution, when the term *science sociale* became current, to the 1880s, when 'positivism' had come to prevail on both sides of the Channel. To this end, I will contrast the reach and resonance of the idea of 'social science' in two political milieux.

On the surface, writers in England and France shared a common discourse about social science during much of the nineteenth century. They often drew on the same sources and read each other's texts. Yet the implicit political assumptions of these writers, as well as the moral and political sensibilities of their readers, were quite different. What follows is a rough charting of these assumptions and sensibilities. Any such attempt to navigate in the treacherous channels of intercultural comparison, especially on so complex a topic, is bound to be both partial and particular. I deliberately limit myself here to comparing debates surrounding two claimants for the title of exemplary social science: political economy and Comtean positivism.[1] I hope thereby to explore several historical puzzles:

---

1 There is a large debate and literature over the term 'positivism'. Even setting aside the differences between twentieth-century 'logical positivism' and nineteenth-century 'sociological positivism', there is the problem of how best to circumscribe the latter. D. C. Charlton, for example, had in mind an ideal type of scientific analysis, and applied the term to many individuals whose ideas differed from Comte's and who were not influenced by him. Usually these writers were judged to be deficient in their positivism, and Comte himself appears as one of the worst offenders against 'pure' positivism.

Why did political economy, so integral to nineteenth-century intellectual life in England, fail to emerge as the model social science in France? And why did positivism, a quintessentially French transformation of eighteenth-century empiricism, nevertheless have a greater cultural and moral impact in England than in France? Finally, what can the differing receptions of Comte tell us more generally about what prompted the turn to a discourse centred on social science? My aim in revisiting these particular puzzles is to sharpen a sense of the ways in which inherited political vocabularies and cultures shaped the interaction of social scientific and political discourse during these years.

1   Social science during the revolutionary era

During the period of the French Revolution the distinction between 'social' and 'political' came to be articulated in France as an antagonism between the natural needs of society and the unnatural actions of governments. The term *science sociale*, i.e. the body of knowledge that would allow one to pronounce definitively on the 'natural needs of society', was heard in the salons and clubs of the moderate republicans from the early 1790s (Baker 1964). It usually signalled an attention to the natural facts affecting social life in opposition to a reliance on religious or metaphysical dogmas; a belief in self-evident principles of natural right (usually moral axioms based on sensationalist psychology); and an endorsement of the general will, the sovereignty of the people, and the French Republic.

Condorcet's conception of social science well illustrates the coexistence of these different elements. He sometimes used the term 'social science' for a collection of factual observations about social life, sometimes for the results of applying probability theory to social reasoning, but most characteristically for the set of truths revealed by introspective psychology (Baker 1975, p. 198). For Condorcet, as for other members of the so-called philosophical party, these psychological data logically implied conceptions of equal rights

---

W. M. Simon, on the other hand, confines the term strictly to the writings of Comte and his certifiable epigone. The difficulty is that contemporaries rarely used the term in either Charlton's or Simon's senses, but often much more loosely to mean something like 'a scientific thinker who denied the authority of theology or spiritual intuition, but who tried to find in service to humanity a form of quasi-religious belief free of the supernatural'. See, for example, Cashdollar 1989, p. 18. In this usage Comte was readily identified as perhaps the pre-eminent positivist of the age, though one did not have to swallow his theory whole. My use of 'positivism' generally follows this contemporary usage when unmodified; when I wished to signal a closer discipleship to Comte, I have used the phrase 'Comtean positivism'.

and universal justice. Hence, initially the attempt to ground revolutionary politics scientifically was quite easily swept up in an apotheosis of the *Declaration of the Rights of Man and Citizen*. Although never explicitly stated, the logic of the connection between the positive fact of psychological equality and equality in civil and political rights seemed obvious to Condorcet from the very definition of man as a sensate being endowed with reason (Condorcet 1847, IX, p. 14). Philosophical liberals saw a declaration of such rights as both a useful distillation of the truths of social science and a powerful political expedient.

As the Revolution progressed, however, the rhetoric of rights accelerated and broke through the tacit economic and political assumptions of moderate republicans. Frightened at the radicalising trajectory of the Revolution, and uneasy about their own earlier embrace of revolutionary slogans, many moderates abandoned talk of the rights of man (Welch 1984, pp. 23–34). During the Thermidorian reaction and the rule of the Directory, Condorcet's younger associates from the early phase of the Revolution, who emerged as a distinct group of thinkers known as the Idéologues, began to drive a wedge between 'social science' and 'revolutionary right'. Like the English utilitarians, the Idéologues self-consciously wedded *la science sociale* more closely to social utility, in the process divorcing the idea of social science from the notion of natural right with which it had been conflated in the works of such earlier theorists as Sieyès, Condorcet, Price and Priestley. Deliberately following the lead of the physical scientists in the new French Institut National, the Idéologues also resolved to be more 'positive', i.e. more exact and careful in their methodology. During the Directory years, they argued that the French Republic should use the dictates of social science – now seen as an alternative to the ideology of the rights of man rather than its complement – to establish the 'French era' in history, a union of peaceful democratic republics filled with individuals pursuing their own and society's interests in effortless symbiosis. In this way they launched the search for a new 'meta' social science that would legitimise an ever elusive political *nouvel régime* to replace the discredited *ancien régime*.[2] It has often been argued that the force of this intellectual impulse was not spent in France until a generation of scientific republicans helped to forge the political and educational institutions of the Third Republic.

---

2 James Livesey's (2001) work on the Directory continues a revisionist view of the period, a view that suggests the regime was at least potentially a viable 'republic' and that the political ideology of the period was more than self-serving opportunism or cynical exploitation of revolutionary discourse.

173

The method of enquiry underlying Idéologue versions of social science was thought to be *analyse*, i.e. the decomposition of all ideas into basic elements of sense perception and the lucid recomposition of these elements into complex ideas. Inherited from the *philosophes* and especially from Condillac, *analyse* was initially invoked as the universal method for achieving progress in the physical and social sciences. The most influential articulations of this passion for analysis were the lectures in the second class of the Institut National (Moral and Political Sciences) delivered concurrently by Pierre Cabanis and Destutt de Tracy. Cabanis lectured on the physiological aspects of 'ideology' (subsequently published as *Rapports du Physique et du Moral de l'Homme* in 1802) and Tracy examined the rational aspects in lectures later revised and published as the four-volume *Élémens d'Idéologie*.

Cabanis was a doctor whose research into human physiology ultimately proved particularly subversive of the egalitarian ideal of the *bon citoyen* that he himself continued to cherish. Presenting himself as a methodical collector of physiological facts for a history of human nature, his *Rapports* was meant to begin the task of cataloguing influences (including temperament, age, sex, disease, climate and diet) upon individual sensibility: a necessary tilling of the intellectual fields in preparation for creating (through education) a generation of more equal individuals (1956, I, p. 121). Cabanis, however, left those fields sown with the seeds of an entirely new crop of social and political ideas: biology as the indispensable context of social theorising, innate physiological differences among humans as the basis of functional differentiation, and a profoundly gendered view of the social passions and of political life. His contemporary Xavier Bichat went even further, insisting that all organisms, including humans, obey their own 'vital' laws, and that the interactions between such laws and the environment cause the emergence of three stable classes of human beings: sensory men, brain men and motor men (Bichat 1809, pp. 107–9). These organic metaphors would eventually be exploited by a new generation of social thinkers, including Saint-Simon and Auguste Comte, who integrated them in different ways into 'social science'.

2 Political economy: queen of the social sciences or dismal science?

Like the physiological *idéologie* of Cabanis, the so-called 'rational' *idéologie* of Destutt de Tracy had the paradoxical result of providing the basis for an attack on his own political ideals, and of reorienting the thrust of social science in France away from an individualist methodology. Tracy's works, however, were subject to a different set of tensions and contradictions. Though he made a real attempt to assimilate Cabanis' ideas, he was primarily concerned with a philosophical analysis of the general development of ideas and language out of sense impressions. This focus on the sensationalist theory of mind, despite important departures from earlier versions, inevitably led away from Cabanis' new appreciation of human variety to a reaffirmation of the universal elements in human nature. He proposed a universal 'logic of the will' that attempted to enthrone political economy – the science of the will and its effects – as the queen of the social sciences.

Tracy's theoretical difficulties arose from an inability to show convincingly either that this 'logic of the will' clarified existing social and economic practice or that it fulfilled liberal hopes for a new foundation for politics. Indeed, contemporary reactions to Tracy's claims for Idéologue social science serve as useful barometers of the changing climate of discussions about social science in France. If the Saint-Simonians and Comte were to draw directly on Cabanis and Bichat, they would use Tracy indirectly as foil. Arguing against his elaborate treatment of method precipitated their distinctions between 'critical' and 'synthetic' reasoning, and between the 'metaphysical' and 'positive' historical eras. Moreover, Tracy's own application of his method helped to spark a debate over the intellectual pretensions of political economy in France. A recognition of what was at stake in this debate provides us with one perspective on why political economy failed to achieve a privileged status in French intellectual life, even among 'liberal' elites.

In the first three volumes of his *Élémens d'Idéologie*, Tracy reworked the by now familiar outlines of sensationalist philosophy: the basis of all knowledge in sense impressions; the central place of pleasure and pain in the development of complex ideas; the attempt to clarify and purify ideas by reconstructing the chain from simple perception to complex thought; and finally, the conviction that philosophy is really only a well-made language. Tracy, nevertheless, decisively cut the link between a presumed equality in sensibility to pleasure and pain and equality in social and political rights. Acutely aware that there was a campaign to discredit his philosophical point of view by linking it with destructive revolutionary excesses, Tracy explicitly avoided hyperbole, illusion and metaphor, and cultivated a dry emotionless voice as an antidote to revolutionary flamboyance. Like Bentham, he portrayed the rights of man as a discredited 'means of deception' (Destutt de Tracy 1817, II, pp. 390–1).

Tracy in fact premised his entire intellectual project on a belief, analogous to that of Bentham, that his method could yield certainty about the real meaning of language and ideas. In the pursuit of this goal, however, he continually encountered unsettling doubts that led him to an unusually candid appraisal of the difficulties of such a project. Because of his rejection of the analogy to mathematics – an analogy used to great effect by thinkers as diverse as Hobbes, Condillac, Condorcet, Bentham and James Mill – his account of the association of ideas was deprived of the borrowed prestige of mathematical certainty. And because of his merciless exposure of the deficiencies of language and human memory, his own claims to have uncovered a solid chain of ideas appeared increasingly threadbare. Tracy's social thought in fact oscillated between a projection into the future of a purified natural pattern of social interactions and troubled attempts to confront inevitable human weakness and irrationality in the present. His particular appropriation of political economy exemplified these tensions, leaving his readers with the sense of a troubling gap between a science of happiness and satisfaction and an application of this science that led to misery and want.

In the final volume of the *Élémens*, entitled the *Traité sur la Volonté et de ses Effets*, Tracy placed the underlying principles of political economy at the heart of social science, defined explicitly as a system of principles indicating the way to promote the greatest amount of happiness in society (Destutt de Tracy 1817, III, pp. 380–1). This notion of invariable laws of human production (and thus of happiness), so central to the Physiocrats and to Adam Smith, was powerfully attractive to French thinkers who now distrusted revolutionary political rhetoric for its associations with the reign of terror. They wished both to return to the lessons of concrete experience and to condemn as unnatural the activist (and they thought tyrannical) governments of the Revolution and Empire. This attraction is obvious in the work of the most influential of the French political economists, Jean-Baptiste Say.[3] Tracy, not himself an original economic thinker, reworked Say's theory with an eye to elaborating its connections to a larger philosophical enquiry.

---

3 J. B. Say had published his *Traité d'Économie Politique* in 1803. It was to go through a major revision in 1814, and thenceforth to become the seminal text of the classical school on the continent. Though deeply influenced by Adam Smith, Say in some ways resisted the newer English tendencies to construe political economy within narrow limits. Rather he favoured a more expansive view of its links with 'republican' morality and manners characteristic of the Idéologues. On Say's larger political and intellectual theory see Richard Whatmore 2000, although Whatmore is not an altogether reliable guide on the complexities of Say's relationship to 'Idéologue political economy'.

Tracy prefaced his discussion of political economy with a series of 'ideo-logical' definitions of personality, property, wealth and value that emphasised the potential of economic interaction to lead to a utopian society of self-interested exchange. From the point of view of production, the most serious impediments to the ideal operation of a benevolent invisible hand were mis-guided aristocratic 'idlers', who stubbornly stood aloof from commerce and republican mores, and hence distorted a process of production that would otherwise result in gains for all. Tracy's logic of the will and its effects, then, exalted scientific laws of production and largely equated these laws with the laws of social happiness. Yet Tracy had read Malthus. Indeed, his adoption of a pessimistic Malthusian perspective on the population problem did much to popularise these ideas in France. From the point of view of the actual distribution of the social product, Tracy noted, optimism was unjustified: one had to 'recognise everywhere the superiority of needs over means, the weakness of the individual, and his inevitable suffering' (Destutt de Tracy 1817, IV, pp. 287–8). Just as radical defects in memory and language severely circumscribed the more general claims of Tracy's philosophic method, so his recognition of inevitable human limitations told against the historical emer-gence of an ideal model of social commerce in which everyone would gain. He painted a bleak picture of an unequally distributed social product that caused misery and suffering among the wage-earning class, even as he reit-erated that justice required an equal weighting of every individual's pleasure and pain. Moreover, despite the starkness of this contrast between ideal the-ory and inevitable facts, his proposed applications of social science did not go beyond the traditional pleas for education, complete liberty of trade and freedom to emigrate. In this despairing contrast between utopian claims for political economy and its inherent limitations, one begins to see why polit-ical economy failed to gain any lasting purchase on the French imagination.

It may be useful here to contrast briefly the emergence of political econ-omy in England during the early nineteenth century. By the 1830s polit-ical economy in England had achieved a certain intellectual caché as a self-contained science, the product of an active and self-conscious intellec-tual community in regular contact with both natural scientists and policy-making elites. Indeed between 1815 and 1820, it has been said, 'everyone in England who thought at all was forced to form definite opinions on a series of very difficult economic problems' (Graham Wallas quoted in Milgate and Stimson 1991, p. 8). Although political economy was often nominally sub-sumed under a broader notion of the scientific study of society as a whole, it was nevertheless celebrated as the most highly developed and useful branch of this study: the first successful 'entrepreneur of the social sciences' (Deane 1989, p. 96). Indeed, throughout the nineteenth century political economy was seen as integral to informed 'scientific' political discourse: 'its tropes and figures constantly recurred in the speeches, writings and conversation of all social classes' (Kadish and Tribe, 1993, p. 3).

The introduction to the 1836 edition of Nassau Senior's *An Outline of the Science of Political Economy* states this view of the reach of the science of political economy quite clearly. Senior contrasts most writers of the 'English school' to continental writers and a few misguided English followers. Political economy, according to Senior, studies not the science of welfare, but the science of the production of wealth. Narrow but powerfully compelling, its findings must be heeded by statesmen practising the art of government because the larger goals of statecraft naturally require the maximisation of resources. Political economy belongs, then, to the class of 'subservient Sciences' (Senior 1965, p. 3). As developed in conjunction with the utilitarian philosophies of Bentham, the Mills and Sidgwick, the view that political economy had a central but subsidiary place in public deliberations led to the practice of weighing the scientific conclusions of political economy against a larger criterion of (utilitarian) social justice. Economics itself was not expected to integrate moral norms into its science; rather, the science of economics would inform the larger tasks of political elites. A half-century later both Alfred Marshall and Henry Sidgwick articulated variations on this theme. According to Marshall in his inaugural address at Cambridge, the economic 'organon' – i.e. a scientific analysis of human motives, their grouping and interrelationships – would clarify important aspects of social life, but was only a 'machine' or 'tool' to inform the common sense that should underlie political judgement on matters of morals and politics (Sidgwick 1904, pp. 163–5). Sidgwick expressed the relationship of economics to social science in similar terms: economic science was not the whole of social science, but it, at least, had made solid progress and had something to show for itself. Political economists – unlike sociologists – were not 'always wrangling, and never establishing anything' (Sidgwick 1904, p. 189).

Political economy in England, then, rejected the task of directing a new political order through its allegedly scientific character and rejected the label of a science of human happiness. In France the claims for political economy were at once grander, more amorphous, and more evanescent. They provoked conceptions of social science that defined themselves against political economy rather than in conjunction with it.

3   The emergence of a scientific logic of the 'social'

I want now to suggest schematically the responses made to early French claims for political economy among three groups in post-revolutionary France: the Doctrinaire liberals of the Restoration and July Monarchy; Catholic reformers particularly concerned with the costs of industrialisation and with issues such as welfare and prison reform; and, finally, young radicals of the re-emerging left opposition. For different reasons, none of these milieux provided a congenial welcome for political economy. Indeed, their negative reactions conspired to inhibit the pursuit of any social science that privileged an individualist logic, and to encourage the search for an encompassing science of the 'social'.

Liberalism during the French Restoration can be defined roughly as the willingness to contest legitimist claims by demanding the rule of law and representative government. Yet these demands had to be made on grounds that were impeccably anti-revolutionary. Any set of ideas tainted by atheism or materialism or egoism – all notions linked inexorably to revolutionary excesses in the slippery slope of Restoration debate – had to be denounced. The Idéologues and their followers, however, proudly linked the methodology of French political economy to eighteenth-century sensationalism. Political economy, then, would enter the lists of Restoration debate at a disadvantage.[4] Indeed, what was most characteristic of post-revolutionary French liberalism, in George Kelly's phrase, was a 'respiritualisation of its philosophical base – a movement away from the "Idéologie" of Destutt de Tracy toward a more idealised and voluntaristic version of human freedom' (Kelly 1992, p. 2). Inspired by German philosophy, the most influential liberals, in the academy and in politics, shared the eclectic philosophical sensibilities of Victor Cousin.

By no means opposed to the legal bases of a liberal order, or to economic rights, these liberals were nevertheless hostile to the methodological temper of political economy and were repelled by the notion of focusing on self-interest as the basis of law-like regularities in social life. Their characteristic defences of property and the pursuit of wealth were shaped instead by an almost obsessive preoccupation with reconstructing the virtues of

---

4 Writers such as D'Hauterive, Storch, Charles Comte, and Charles Dunoyer – often thought of as Say's school – did continue to celebrate the benefits of economic exchange and *laisser-faire*, but they were increasingly marginalised as a 'sect'. Increasingly the proponents of *laisser-faire* in France tended towards a dogmatic style that exaggerated the utopian elements in classical economics. Perhaps the best example of this tendency is Frederic Bastiat's *Economic Harmonies* (1850).

personal responsibility and public duty. They embraced an exclusive notion of property rights, for example, as necessary for the flowering of duties surrounding husband, wife and children. Individual effort and the pursuit of self-interest were natural because they were necessary to establish the security and independence of the family.[5] Doctrinaire liberals, then, recoiled from the celebration of economic 'egoism' and reaffirmed notions of moral duty. They also launched an important critique of the methods of political economy as ahistorical and one-sided. François Guizot, for example, developed a view of history in which political and moral progress was limited by the possibilities inherent in the social state of a people: its class and property relations, economic interactions, customs and mores. The task of political thinkers was to analyse the democratic social state emerging in France and to organise an appropriate political expression of the *pouvoir social*. When considered in isolation from a more complete view of the *état social*, political economy was a sterile science. Even as the Doctrinaires' elaboration of the 'social' realm of human life reinforced its currency in post-revolution debates, however, their focus on institutional change in historical perspective led them away from any transhistorical or transcultural consideration of social laws, and indeed away from any systematic scientific approach to either society or economy.

Except for a small free-trade sect indebted to Say and the Idéologues, then, French liberals initially looked to Eclectic moral theory or to the Doctrinaires' narrative of progressive civilisation, rather than to scientific elaborations of society or economy, to bolster claims for political reforms.[6] Indeed, it was among Catholic social reformers, sometimes with impeccable legitimist ties, that the scientific claims of political economy were more often debated. It was also among this group that an explicit alternative to political economy's focus on the individual began to emerge: a conception of the 'social' as the source of a distinctive scientific understanding of human interdependence.

---

5 These sentiments can also be found in the works of the influential second generation of eclectics: Adolphe Franck (1809–93), Jules Simon (1814–96), Paul Janet (1823–99) and Elme Caro (1826–87). For a good discussion see Logue 1983, pp. 17–49. As J. S. Mill noted, Eclecticism, which had taken such firm hold of the 'speculative minds of a generation formed by Royer-Collard, Cousin, Jouffroy, and their compeers' had no exact parallel in England (1865, p. 2).

6 This is not to argue that there was a sharp divide between Eclecticism and all versions of social science. Indeed, Brooks 1998 has persuasively argued that later French innovators in the social sciences – including Théodule Ribot (1839–1916), Alfred Espinas (1844–1922), Pierre Janet (1859–1947), and Émile Durkheim (1858–1917) – were decisively marked by their spiritualist education in developing allegedly 'positivist' versions of psychology and sociology. See Brooks 1998.

Conservative French reformers interested in public charity, prisons and public health were made particularly anxious by claims that the laws of social science inevitably produced industrial poverty because, in the French context, the notion of a permanently impoverished class conjured up terrifying images of the revolutionary *peuple*. Many of these reformers became both obsessed and repelled by the English example as a harbinger of the evil consequences of unrestricted development (Reddy, 1984). They traced the new industrial plague of *pauperisme* to the transformative effects of development itself and shifted their focus from the mendicancy of the rural labourer (a frequent concern of eighteenth-century thinkers) to the dangerous condition of the industrial urban worker. Most important, they concluded that any 'science' of political economy that viewed such results as natural was in need of fundamental revision. Sismondi, for example, expertly exploited the menacing contradictions inherent in a science of pleasure that produced pain. He painted a portrait of an urban population predestined by economic laws (rather than by failure of character) to fall into the condition of a threatening modern proletariat (Sismondi 1975, pp. 158, 198). In his 'Mémoire sur la Conciliation de l'Économie Politique et de l'Économie Charitable ou d'Assistance', P. A. Dufau likened the task of specifying a method for political economy to being lost in a maze. It was contradictory and therefore unscientific, he claimed, to hold at once that modern poverty was caused by the inevitable working out of economic laws, but that the science of political economy could not and need not specify ways to combat poverty. The urgent task of social science was to find a way out of this confusion (*dédale*) (Dufau 1860, p. 106). Many middle-class reformers found the theoretical thread that would lead them out of this alleged labyrinth in a different scientific understanding, often termed *économie sociale*. In Sismondi's use, the term took on the meaning of a science that both transcended and reoriented political economy.[7]

One can discern certain common themes about the objective needs of society in the writings of the so-called French social economists of the 1830s, 1840s and 1850s. Some historians, in fact, have seen in their writings a recognisably new discourse of social intervention (Ewald 1986; Procacci 1993). A series of reports and analyses, including those by Villeneuve-Bargement (1834), DeGérando (1839), Frégier (1840), Buret (1840), Villermé (1840)

---

7 See Welch 1984, p. 220. Destutt de Tracy first used the expression *économie sociale* in order to indicate that social science should be distinct from the traditional concerns of politics (Destutt de Tracy 1817, IV, pp. 289–90). It was adopted by J. B. Say in the later editions of his works for this reason.

and Cherbuliez (1853), promoted the view that the science of social economy should focus on the well-being of the entire population, including
adequate food, clothing, shelter and welfare for the pauperised classes.
Moreover, they developed more fully the idea that pauperism was a specifically modern social threat, caused neither by individual sinfulness nor by
governmental corruption or neglect, but by the laws of economic development *tout court*. Yet they also employed and even heightened a rhetoric –
very familiar in the French context – that castigated paupers as sexually
dissolute, imprudent, lazy, ignorant, insubordinate and rebellious. On this
account, the newly pauperised classes formed a debased population bereft
of intellect and social sympathies, but imbued with a new sentiment of honour and confidence that was the unfortunate legacy of popular politicisation
during the Revolution. Like earlier images of roving beggars and brigands,
the French view of the lower classes in the early nineteenth century was
one in which the lines between the working classes and pauperised classes
were blurred into an image of dangerous hordes who 'made one tremble
for the whole order of society' (Sismondi 1975, p. 157).

In England, too, paupers were often thought of as a degraded population. Armed with a new scientific enthusiasm for social surveys that would
generate the statistics to determine what was needed and to 'rouse the community and legislature' to action, humanitarian social reformers sought to
bring the plight of these new poor before the public (Abrams 1968, p. 35).
Yet the general hope seemed to be that the community contained social
sympathies of sufficient strength to be roused. It has often been argued that
in England, the challenge of the social question was eventually met by an
expanded – though very imperfect – notion of legal inclusion, politically
created and reflecting a transformed sense that civil rights included a 'social'
dimension (T. H. Marshall 1977). In France, where the Revolution was
blamed for destroying old patterns of moral and social sympathies without
creating new ones, the rhetoric surrounding social evils was more politically charged. Paupers were perceived not only as degraded, but as politically
dangerous (Chevalier 1973; Himmelfarb 1984, pp. 392–400).

The French social economists, then, feared and despised the pauperised
classes, but were more likely than English reformers to absolve them of
responsibility for their own condition. The evils of public misery 'originate in the milieu in which individuals are placed and it is not up to them
to change it' (Dufau 1860, p. 93). The eradication of social evils was a
social obligation, rather than a matter of individual character reformation.

This obligation, however, was a duty that engendered no corresponding political right, and hence no valid legal claim. Indeed, these writers implicated the legal individualism of the Revolution, with its talk of natural right, in the very roots of pauperism: the abstract notion of the rights of economic man was fundamental to the new economic order that was generating a pauper class. To attempt to eliminate the evil of pauperism by recognising individual rights to work or to welfare would in fact only deepen the problem by intensifying individualism, destroying all intermediary associations and leaving a void between state and citizen (Cherbuliez 1853, p. 4). But how and by whom was this obligation of social reformation to be met? The social economists began to invoke both the needs and potential action of 'society', which was conceived as having its own logic and regulating force, superior to and different from economic laws. As socially conservative Catholics, many of these thinkers adopted a notion of social obligation that had clear affinities to a religious conception of the reciprocal duties that bound Christians together within a Catholic community. The idea of the 'social', however, was itself unencumbered and fluid; it had no specific theology or priesthood to give it determinate shape.[8]

In England, reformers often forged alliances with political economists in order to combat scientifically the new ills associated with industrial poverty (Abrams 1968, pp. 8–52). In France, however, debates over the social question and social reform took shape largely outside and even against the categories and claims of liberal political economy. Rather they emerged within a new discourse calling for social integration based on a larger encompassing 'science'. Indeed, to call an issue such as prison reform, child labour or poor relief 'social' in the elite political culture of the Restoration and the July Monarchy was to signal that positions on the issue would not be discussed in economic or political terms, but rather would be determined by an impartial analysis of social facts as manifested in elite expert opinion (Drescher 1968, p. 99). It was hoped that a consensus on social policy could be achieved by developing an ameliorative apolitical social science, rather than by ritualistic debates that would exacerbate fissures in the political system.

---

8 The various policy measures recommended by the social economists displayed a continuing tension between state control (such as supervision and regulation in the home) and encouragement of spontaneous co-operation and self-help among workers. See Welch 1989, pp. 179–83.

If early claims for a social science privileging political economy were rejected both by the liberals of the *juste milieu* and by Catholic social reformers largely because of divisive associations with revolutionary individualism, it was precisely those dangerous associations that first drew disaffected members of the post-revolutionary generation into a study of 'individualist' social science. Many of these younger French thinkers, initially meeting in inchoate reading circles to study the works of Tracy, Say, Cabanis, Kant and Bentham, followed tortured personal odysseys that eventually led to revolutionary conspiracy or utopian withdrawal. Like members of the Utilitarian Society in England who followed the lead of Bentham and James Mill, these young radicals sought at first to weed out the irrationalities and prejudices allegedly strangling the French polity by applying the sharp logic of utility (Welch 1984, pp. 135–53). For the French, however, this perspective often proved a way station rather than a destination. Responding sympathetically to the utopian refrain of universal happiness in a new industrial society in the works of Say, Tracy or Bentham, most soon abandoned the associated political programme, i.e. non-revolutionary democratic politics and non-intervention in the economy. Some thought of these political strictures as the faint-hearted timorousness of an older generation, and turned to versions of neo-Jacobin insurrectionism. Others faulted the Idéologues for a flawed understanding of physiology or history, or for their facile acceptance of individualist economic dogmas. Increasingly, this latter group drifted into utopian socialism, and in particular into the orbit of Saint-Simon and Auguste Comte.[9]

We are now in a position to assess the continental divide in debates over social science in the early decades of the nineteenth century. In England, political economy had emerged as the most highly developed and prestigious of the social sciences. Yet it still served as handmaiden to traditional elites who borrowed neither from economics nor social science for their political legitimacy. More pervasive in France was a morally charged condemnation of political economy, the denial of the sufficiency of its conclusions if it remained self-contained within its own sphere, and the attempt

---

9 It was among these groups of younger radicals that the term 'individualism' was first coined as a general description of methodologies – like those of the Idéologues and English utilitarians – that began from individual wants, needs and purposes. The increasing tendency to criticise individualism from the points of view of biology or history (or both) can be followed in the contributions to the Saint-Simonian journal *Le Producteur* (1826) by the then Saint-Simonian Louis-August Blanqui, 1: 139; by P. M. Laurent 3: 325–38, 4: 19–37; by Philippe Buchez 3: 462–72; and by Rouen 2: 159–64. See also the eighth session of the *Doctrine de Saint-Simon* by Amand Bazard (l958).

to subsume it within a more inclusive social science that would provide the context for the generation of new moral norms.[10] Not least among those claiming to have privileged scientific access to the social world was Auguste Comte, whose 'positivist' renovation of the rambling intellectual structures he inherited profoundly marked intellectual life in the nineteenth and early twentieth centuries. A comparison of Comte's picture of the field of social science with that of John Stuart Mill illuminates the distinct patterns of political assumptions and cultural intuitions that underlay French and English notions of social science as the master science by mid-century. It also sets the stage for a contrast of the different cultural spaces that 'positivism' would occupy in nineteenth-century England and France.

When Comte lectured on the structure of the sciences in the 1820s, lectures later published as the *Cours de Philosophie Positive* (1830–42), he tellingly omitted both the 'pseudo science' of psychology (which he associated above all with sensationalism and eclecticism) and political economy (Comte 1998, pp. 229–32). In his view, individualist metaphysical methodologies vitiated the scientific pretensions of these disciplines. Moreover, their claims to independence contradicted Comte's desire to discover the positive – that is irreducible laws of society itself (Brown 1984, p. 191). Indeed Comte shared with his mentor Saint-Simon and with the Saint-Simonians a critical attitude towards both economic liberalism and its associated 'science' that was close to that of Sismondi and the social economists (Mauduit 1929; Pickering 1993, pp. 110–12, 405–6). Comte used Destutt de Tracy's inadvertent exposure of the gap between political economy's metaphysical presuppositions and the actual facts of social experience as incontrovertible evidence that the introspective method could not be the method of social science. For example, Tracy's analyses of property, wealth and poverty were, according to Comte, patently contradictory. Though Tracy had intended to be positive, this noble intention was belied by the persistence of individualist metaphysics in his approach (Comte 1968, III, pp. 604–30 *passim*).

Comte thought more highly of Cabanis, who had argued that one must approach an understanding of the facts of social experience by presupposing

---

10 Not until the 1880s would political economy face a serious intellectual challenge from the combined front of economic historians and sociological positivists in Britain. In an echo of earlier French debates about the place of political economy within a larger social scientific project, the English positivist followers of Comte, most notably Frederic Harrison, joined the historical school in attacking the individualist and ahistorical assumptions of political economy (Harrison 1908, pp. 271–306). These attacks by no means vanquished economics, but did occasion a theoretical self-examination that pushed economics to clarify both its methods and its relationship to public purposes.

and building on the laws of human physiology. Yet Comte denied that sociological laws were derived from human physiology. Rather, they were to be sought either in the laws governing the social organism as a whole (which functions as an ensemble of interrelated parts) or from the laws governing the process by which one social organism succeeds another in history. According to Comte, the law of the three developmental stages – the theological, or fictitious; the metaphysical, or abstract; and the scientific, or positive – was the most important law of historical change. In social physics, or sociology, the initial observations that form the basis of hypothetical laws are not original sense impressions, as followers of the sensationalist theory of mind believed, but rather observations of the most general aspects of society: mores, customs and historical transformations. The initial data of social science, in short, come from the sharp eye of the social and historical observer on the alert for social patterns. These phenomena become the bases of hypotheses that are then checked against further observations. Comte's insistence that one must begin with an observation of the 'social', bracket all speculation about first causes, and be ready to re-evaluate hypotheses, has earned him canonical status as a founder not only of positivism, but of scientific sociology.[11]

John Stuart Mill explicitly reformulated his notion of the inductive/ deductive method in light of Comte's methodological discussions. More-over, he was influenced by Comte's law of historical development, in particular the view that historical factors, as opposed to biological ones, increasingly dominate human social life. Finally, he, too, wished to subor-dinate more limited human sciences to a larger integrative social science. Yet, despite Mill's claims for an overarching science that would take into account the wide variety of motives and goals that characterises actual human behaviour, he largely understood 'social science' as a synthesis or summation of discrete branch disciplines (psychology, economics and others unnamed). These branches – and here political economy provided the most highly developed model – were to provide partial laws of human nature as they operated in different fields of human society (Mill 1844, pp. 135–6). It is indeed unclear in Mill's various accounts whether he thought social science had distinctive subject matter of its own or was merely a method-ological procedure for synthesising the insights generated by its constituent parts (Brown, 1984, pp. 136–47).

---

11 This accolade is usually then severely qualified, and Comte is charged with having disastrously departed from his own methodological principles. See Charlton 1959, pp. 34–50.

4   Comtism in England and France

Let me now turn more explicitly to Comte and the place of positivism in the intellectual terrain of nineteenth-century England and France. Comte developed the outlines of his positive philosophy as a young man during a period of close collaboration with Saint-Simon. The debate regarding intellectual influence between the two men – each the founder of a new rationalist religion – has always been contentious.[12] They certainly shared much: abandonment of the revolutionary ideal of civil and political equality in favour of an organic conception of society in which harmony would result from functional differentiation; division of human capacities into rational, industrial and spiritual; and a recasting of earlier views of historical progress into a tripartite scheme of conflict, crisis and reorganisation at a higher level. Most important, they shared the view that the physical sciences and the 'science of society' were not methodologically distinct, that the primary model for social science was biology, and that social science itself was not composed of discrete disciplines but was a master science that in some sense integrated human physiology, history and politics into one set of overarching general laws. If the germs of positivism were present in the disorganised and sometimes incoherent writings of Saint-Simon, his disciple supplied the gifts of organisation and coherence, along with a much greater acquaintance with the sciences, that would turn positivism into a full-blown system. In the *Cours de Philosophie Positive*, and in the *Système de Politique Positive* (1851–4), Comte produced a body of work that – despite his repetitive, graceless and pedantic prose – was capable of moving some of the very best minds of the nineteenth century. Like Hegel and Marx, Comte offered a particular fusion of history and prophecy that supplied a compelling narrative of what had been and what was to come.

Key terms that reappear incessantly in Comte's formulations of positivism are 'unify', 'connect' or 'make whole'. Again like Hegel, he exhibited a compulsive need to resolve contradictions and restore coherence to every realm of human experience. He stimulated a response above all in those individuals troubled by the sense that something fundamental had come 'undone' in Western European civilisation, individuals who experienced quasi-romantic longings to inhabit a culture in which conflicts were

---

12 Comte's latest biographer, Mary Pickering, suggests that their shared perspective brought them together rather than resulted from the influence of Saint-Simon on the younger man (Pickering 1993, p. 101). In this she follows the classic work by Gouhier (1933–41), III, pp. 168–70.

reconciled, or at least reconcilable. Part of the story of his differential reception in Britain and France, then, has to do with differing perceptions of which conflicts had become most problematical in European culture.

Perhaps the most characteristic nineteenth-century answer to the question of what had come unhinged in European culture was the assumed link between religious faith and right action. Belief in divine purposes had long anchored moral precepts, but what God's prescience had joined together, man's science was rapidly putting asunder, at least for many in the elite classes. Yet, there were distinct national variations on this common cultural theme.

In England the phrase 'loss of faith' often can be parsed as meaning one of two things: a faltering of the conviction that one's personal selection by God would inspire the performance of social duties, or a crumbling of the underlying assurance that motives to moral action would be forthcoming because a benevolent First Cause had inevitably, if invisibly, designed human motivations in this fashion. Both varieties of 'loss of faith' undermined the belief that people could be counted on to perform their duties towards others. This loss of confidence in the sources of benevolence, combined with a strong and vital empirical tradition that privileged the egoistic drives as explanatory postulates in the human sciences, contributed to an obsessive worry about the motivations to virtuous action. Educated Victorians very often conversed in what has been tellingly reconstructed as 'the nineteenth-century idiom of egoism vs. altruism' (Collini 1993, pp. 67, 60–90 *passim*). Coined by Comte, the word 'altruism' passed rapidly into English usage. The Victorians were to be peculiarly receptive not only to Comte's new term, but also to his assurances that social evolution would not destroy the individual motivation to do one's duty.

Comte argued that the power of living for others did not wither but rather swelled with the progress of intelligence and an increasing division of labour. Indeed the nutritive and sexual instincts would steadily decrease in the face of the growth of sympathy for ever-widening circles of others. Domestic relationships and the particular affective gifts of women were not in competition with this growing altruism, but were entangled with its deepest psychological – Comte would have said physiological – roots in individual and social memory (Comte 1853, I, pp. 463–4; II, pp. 89, 106–7, 130–1, 552, 1877, pp. 18–29). Though he thought the progress of altruism was in some ways spontaneous, he became progressively more convinced that it would need the ministrations of a new religion of humanity to strengthen its hold over those born into the positivist era. Comte's, however,

188

was a godless religion that focused on the fragile nexus between moral and intellectual beliefs, and on the particular role of aesthetic and imaginative stimulation both in creating convictions and in moving people to act on those convictions.[13]

It was in this aesthetic and ethical context that Comte was to speak most persuasively to an English audience. John Stuart Mill had been influenced by Comte in the formulation of his logic of the social sciences; he was also undeniably drawn to Comte's notion of a religion of humanity (Mill 1874b). Alexander Bain, John Morley, George Henry Lewes, George Eliot and Harriet Martineau were partial adherents to Comte's positivist system; others (e.g. Matthew Arnold, Henry Sidgwick and Leslie Stephen) read Comte – often surprisingly sympathetically – because, given their particular moral concerns, he was a force to be reckoned with. From the mid-1850s there was an official positivist movement, led by Richard Congreve, and including E. S. Beesly, J. H. Bridges and the prolific Frederic Harrison.

What Harrison found most compelling in positivism was the attempt to reground the 'eternal truths of the human heart and conscience [that is] . . . resignation, self-forgetfulness, devoutness, adoration, patience, courage, charity, gentleness, [and] honour' in a theory based on scientific and historical evidence, rather than in an 'exploded mythology' (Harrison 1911, I, pp. 210, 276). He never doubted the virtues themselves; the difficulty lay in reawakening the springs of moral action and harmonising them with the requirements of modern life. Harrison's cast of mind would be particularly open to Comte's claim that 'heart' – the qualities of sympathy and energy together – would be developed by positivism and would supply a 'habitual spring of action' (Comte 1877, p. 16).

English sympathisers, John Stuart Mill among them, often greeted the later Comte's detailed religious prescriptions with distaste as authoritarian aberrations. Yet the general promise of a religion of humanity had widespread appeal. It was not through ritual, although Congreve and the English positivists held some pallid services at Newton Hall, but rather through cultural education in the widest sense that English positivists hoped to respiritualise individuals (Harrison 1911, I, p. 282). They had great hopes that George Eliot, a fellow traveller if not a communicant, would more

---

13 Peter Dale (1989, pp. 33–128) focuses on a coincidence of interest to be found between Comte (in his later works) and Lewes and Eliot. All played with the role of imagination in creating moral 'hypotheses', and in the motivating power of those hypotheses, even in the absence of the scientific validation that would turn them into 'laws'. On Comte and women see also Pickering (1993), 'Angels and Demons in the Moral Vision of Auguste Comte'.

wholeheartedly devote herself to this didactic purpose. Though she disappointed these hopes, it is perhaps in her novels that one can best appreciate the primarily ethical cluster of concerns into which Comte's social science was drawn and domesticated.

Eliot's characters – Maggie Tulliver in *The Mill on the Floss*, Dorothea Brooke in *Middlemarch*, Gwendolyn Harleth in *Daniel Deronda* – inhabit societies where their deepest moral aspirations are not 'at home'. In these contexts Eliot explores the concept of moral duty: its tangled interconnections with 'exploded religious mythologies', its emotional roots in familial memories, its uneasy relationship to necessary historical laws. In his later writings, Comte had increasingly turned to the redemptive notion that subordinating the self to social feeling, an ideal that he thought came closest to incarnation in certain exalted womanly natures, formed the highest type of moral experience (Comte 1877, p. 5). Eliot's novels, as well as George Lewes' works on psychology, also explore the 'madonna type' and the remarkable power of deeply human images, thought to have the elemental force of nature itself, to evoke unselfishness and the larger feelings.[14]

Historians and literary critics have focused on Comte's version of positivism as a particularly fruitful conduit into the nature of the religious crisis and the transformation of theology in Victorian England (Cashdollar 1989; Wright 1986) and also into the ways that the attraction to positivism illuminates the English appropriation of literature to moral purposes (Dale 1989). Indeed it is perhaps the particular nature of the Victorian moral crisis that best illuminates the surprisingly deep appeal of Comte's promise to restore moral coherence through science (Collini 1993, p. 89).

The other locus at which positivism had a major impact in England was the labour movement. If Comte had looked to the cultivation of altruism as a force of moral regeneration, it was among the working classes that he hoped positivist intellectuals would find their most important allies in the project of industrial reorganisation. Not only did he believe that the welfare of *la classe la plus nombreuse et la plus pauvre* should be the criterion of public actions, but he was among the first to argue that an alliance of intellectuals

---

14 The influence of Comtean positivism on George Eliot has been explored most fully in Wright 1981 and 1986. Eliot is particularly attractive to contemporary critics because her narratives can be read as both asserting and subverting the 'truth' that science will provide a new moral cosmology. For readings that highlight this double vision in her novels, see Beer 1986 and Dale 1989, pp. 85–101, 129–63. For a reading that explores her ambiguous relationship to social science through the prism of a confrontation with Herbert Spencer, see Paxton 1991.

and working-class leaders in a social (rather than political) movement would be able to surmount the growing antagonism between the capitalist class and the proletariat (Comte 1877, p. 136). Comte believed that the conditions of working-class life led to a greater prevalence of altruism among workers, and that their minds were less corrupted by intellectual error. Though he never attacked the individual appropriation of wealth, and indeed hoped that moralised bankers and evolved capitalists would eventually provide public leadership, he believed that wealth was social in origin and needed to be redirected to more socially beneficial ends. Above all workers needed secure employment, education and a tolerable standard of life. He urged positivist intellectuals to promote trade unionism, as opposed to involvement in corrupt parliamentary politics, and to educate public opinion through public lectures and classes.

In England, these teachings fell on fertile ground. Among the many intellectuals who influenced labour politics in the 1860s and 1870s, 'it was the English Positivists who established the closest ties with the Trade Union leaders and working-class politicians and who exercised the most decisive influence on men and events' (R. Harrison 1965, p. 251). Frederic Harrison and Beesly in particular were important in the fight to establish a legal basis for trade unionism and to change public attitudes towards this issue (Adelman 1971, p. 183; F. Harrison 1908, pp. 307–73; R. Harrison 1965, p. 277). Beesly established a working relationship with Marx and was instrumental in the founding of the International. English positivists were also tireless in their attempts to turn British workers against imperialism (Wright 1986, p. 110).

In 1908 Frederic Harrison could honestly write that he had 'taken the keenest interest in the political and social problems of the last fifty years' (Harrison 1908, p. xv). This interest, however, as well as the concerns of other official positivists, was in many ways removed from politics as understood by most of his contemporaries. The conservative Robert Lowe was not very far from common opinion when he pronounced the English positivists 'free from those complicated, embarrassing, and troublesome considerations of the collateral and future effects of measures that perplex ordinary mortals' (quoted in Wright 1986, p. 110). Indeed, if Comte's cultural diffusion in England points to the centrality of concerns about the bases of ethical action in a disintegrating Protestant culture, and to the deep anxieties produced by social unrest in a country that more and more saw itself as a pioneer of industrialism, the failure of 'Comtism' to affect specifically political modes of theorising suggests the resilience of traditional political vocabularies in Britain and their relative impermeability to the language of social science.

If one again considers the case of Mill, it is striking that his stated aspiration to absorb politics into a larger project of a historically grounded 'social science' figures so slightly in his explicitly political writings. Given his apparent openness to the positivist sociological project, one might expect that his political theory would centre not just on the scientific character of politics as a field of study, but also on the relationship between social and political science. On the contrary, 'the terms of the questions which held his attention, and even the categories under which he arranged the evidence relevant to their solution, remained... obstinately political' (Collini *et al.* 1983, p. 134; pp. 129–59 *passim*). Mill in fact never embraced the central notion of Comte's social physics, which was to interrogate society in order to find in its overmastering demands a modern calling for politics. For Mill that calling always focused above all on the human judgements and conciliations that would be necessary to create progress, and on enlarging a notion of *liberty* that was in important ways the product of a peculiarly English, rather than a generically European history.

The impact of Comtean social science in England, then, was broadly ethical, more narrowly social (in the sense that it was bound up with a specific phase of the labour movement), and scarcely at all political. At the risk of drawing much too tidy a contrast, one might say that the reverse was true in France. To his fellow citizens, Comte spoke no more persuasively than many others about the ethical, religious and industrial fragmentation of the French nation, but his contribution – or rather that of key disciples – to the binding up of its political wounds was significant.

In France, Comte was at first slower to gain adherents than in England. It has been suggested that this had something to do with the nature of periodical journalism in England, or with the long predominance of eclectic philosophy in France (Mill 1865, p. 2; Simon 1963, p. 12). By the 1860s, however, there was a definite shift among French intellectuals to religious scepticism and an appreciation of the methods of natural science. Indeed, the Second Empire and the early years of the Third Republic have often been termed the age of positivism. Much subsequent sifting of evidence has gone into assessing the role of Comte in this diffusion of the positivist spirit. While his role was certainly not negligible, the notion of a 'positivist generation' captures a much broader cultural wave, in which many expressed an anguishing loss of faith and a turn to science to restitch the fabric of their intellectual lives (Simon 1963, pp. 94–171). Sainte-Beuve tells us that expressions of loss of faith were practically mandatory to establish one's intellectual *bona fides* during the period. Renan's work on religion and Taine's studies of psychology, literature and history elevate the scientific method to a vocation and explicitly see it as replacing religion, at least for a Parnassian elite (Burrow 2000, pp. 54–5). Yet the works of these writers, so central to French intellectual life from the 1860s to the 1880s, run parallel to Comte rather than in any way responding to his particular formulation of the spiritual crisis of the age (Charlton 1959, pp. 86–157).

Comte's diffusion in France is less useful as a gauge of the larger cultural and religious crisis than was his reception in England in part because of the different spiritual sensibilities that often accompanied the experience of loss of faith in the two societies. What was felt most acutely in France was not anxiety about the soundness of what might be called Protestant moral psychology, but rather the frightening intimation of an aesthetic, moral and intellectual void, given the disappearance of the mediating functions of the Catholic Church and the fragility of French national identity. Among those who broke with the Church, there was a deeper anger at a God who abandoned His flock and a darker premonition of the dangers of true normlessness. Even among those writers most marked by the positive spirit – the conviction that knowledge comes only from observation of phenomena, and that much will remain unknowable – one is struck by a hard-bitten realism (for example in Taine), a deep cynicism (as in Louise Ackermann), or an anguished stoicism (palpable in the poems of Sully Prudhomme) that are foreign both to Comte and to the English Victorians. Though Comtean positivism has often been called Catholicism without the Church, its particular brand of substitute religion, with its emphasis on the historicity and psychology of altruism, paradoxically resonated more in a Protestant culture than in a Catholic one.

Neither did positivism make much of an impact on the French labour movement. Although Comte, following Saint-Simon, signalled the importance of industrial organisation and the concentration of industry, the particular British conjunction of a struggling trade union movement and an elite positivist group with strong affinities towards ameliorist social reform was lacking. It was not until the 1890s that French trade unions sought or achieved status as independent organisations. In the preceding years, the questions of trade union organisation and 'social' versus 'political' tactics to improve the position of the working classes, were inevitably caught up in a highly polarised political climate and structure. Under the Empire, for example, Comte's strictures against political organising had unacceptably quietist implications that they lacked in England. And during the early years of the Third Republic, working-class politics in France had to come to terms with the traumatic legacy of the Commune and its suppression. Comte himself eventually gave up his hope for conversions among the working men of the revolutionary party (Lenzer 1975, p. xlv). And one might argue that there was more general resonance among the French middle classes for Taine's pessimistic portrait of the working classes as a breeding ground for degenerate 'beasts of prey' than for Comte's picture of them as the potential saviours of humanity (Taine 1962, III, p. 113).

It was not in discussions of religion, ethics or even social organisation, then, that Comte had the greatest impact in his own country. Indeed the most intriguing twist to the story of positivism in France – given Comte's authoritarianism, anti-parliamentarianism and support of Louis-Napoléon – is his pervasive influence on the development of the hybrid political language that came to legitimise the Third Republic, a graft of certain aspects of liberalism onto the stalk of French republicanism. In the final years of the Second Empire there were a number of political figures, including Léon Gambetta and Jules Ferry, who were engaged in a fundamental examination of the bankruptcy of the imperial system. They would soon emerge among the important *fondateurs* of a new political regime. 'The influence of Comte on all of these men, mediated in general by his disciples and above all by Littré, has been formally attested to; moreover, it is easily discernible' (Nicolet 1982, p. 156). What was it that attracted these political thinkers to Comtean positivism and how did they draw on this current to legitimise the new regime?

Comte's obsession with the problem of assuring order and progress was itself a response to France's particular post-revolutionary political history. Like that of Hegel and Marx, his account of modern history gave pride of place to the French Revolution, a shatteringly destructive and mysteriously portentous event to contemporaries. For positivists, the Revolution was the climax of the transitional metaphysical age; it ushered in a new form of social organisation not only founded on science, but eventually organised by a new spiritual consciousness of unity. Comte believed that only positive philosophy, science and true politics – as opposed to the preceding metaphysical versions – could bring order out of chaos. The disorder and anarchy in French political life were rooted in the anachronistic persistence of outmoded ideas: on the one hand revolutionary dogmas about popular sovereignty, on the other theological abstractions about divine right. Positivism alone could set realisable goals for action because it alone recognised the force of evidence and experience as against sterile metaphysical argument.

Comte himself was agnostic about the transitional regime that would usher in the new positivist order. It might be a republic or a dictatorship, whichever would best diffuse the scientific knowledge that was to become the basis of the new regime. He consistently disdained, however, the parliamentary model as mired in peculiar metaphysics like 'the British constitution' or the 'rights of the people', and he envisioned the eventual establishment of an oligarchic republic ruled by a newly moralised elite on the basis of scientific opinion and the religion of humanity. This political utopia struck Mill as an appalling endorsement of intellectual subjugation and slavery (Mill 1865, p. 168). The dissonance between Comte's personal political vision and a theory of liberal democracy, however, turns out to be beside the historical point. Comte's most important followers in France, who clustered around the respected scholar and political figure Émile Littré, neglected not only his religious prescriptions but also many of his specifically political ones.[15] They found in Comte's writings other inspirations for tackling three essential tasks: taming the unruly historical messianism inherent in the French republican tradition (to which many of them, unlike Comte himself, were already attached); infusing the notion of compromise – so distasteful to generations of republicans – with the aroma of principle; and, finally, envisioning a system of lay education that could be bent to the purposes of citizenship.

For most of the nineteenth century *la République* had been the unfulfilled trajectory of the French Revolution, but it was an ideal suffused with competing and contradictory longings. The successive failures of republican political experiments had in many ways intensified the air of unreality surrounding republicanism as a political ideology. Comte's followers helped to transform this pattern of utopian failure and to make the republic thinkable by their conviction that the republic was immanent in history and by their confidence that it could be fashioned out of existing political conditions. The particular achievement of the Comteans was to invest the political

---

15 Besides contributing to major journals, Émile Littré also founded and edited the *Revue de Philosophie Positive* (1867–83), which was particularly important for the positivist republicans. See Simon 1963, pp. 15–39. Comte's followers in France were split into an orthodox group led by Pierre Lafitte, and a dissident group around Littré. The latter group broke with Comte in 1852 for political reasons and included the biologists Charles Robin and L. A. Second. It was Littré, eminent philologist and historian, author of the magisterial *Dictionnaire de la Langue Française* (1863–78), and important political figure (as deputy and then senator) after 1870, who did most to popularise Comte's doctrines in France. For the fullest analysis of this role see Hazareesingh 2001, pp. 23–83.

practices of tolerance and compromise with the prestige and authority of science.

Littré, who fell out with Comte over the latter's support of Louis-Napoléon's coup, came to reject Comte's view that the period of transition to positivism might be organised as a dictatorship. The liberties of speech, association and press that Comte recognised as necessary for progress could be effective only when combined with representative government (Littré 1864, pp. 601–3). Although, like Comte, he was opposed to the 'metaphysical' notions of the sacrosanct principles of 1789, he saw this legacy in an altogether more 'positive' light. He argued that the idea of the sovereignty of the people could be interpreted in a useful way; that its proponents were important allies; and that experience would wear the metaphysical, negative edge off such doctrines. Indeed, the certainty of vindication by history led to a re-evaluation of past republican regimes as imperfect approximations and learning experiences, rather than as disastrous metaphysically inspired mistakes.

A related innovation in political language was to seize on the positivist slogan of 'order and progress' to legitimise tainted political processes of mediation and compromise. The phrases 'politics of opportunity', 'step by step politics' and 'politics of results' were above all associated with the positivist republicans, who borrowed the experimental language of science to legitimise political experimentation. Again, Littré had early separated himself from many of Comte's political conclusions by stressing that positivism was above all a method of enquiry. In the 1870s, he drew on the prestigious notion of scientific method to rehabilitate the notion of political expediency. Comte had encouraged social experimentation and discouraged revolutionary adventurism. Because the institutions of modern society would necessarily evolve, Comte argued, 'the positive spirit will abate unreasonable expectations from them' (1853, II, p. 44). Littré and the positivist republicans transposed this element of stoic patience into the realm of politics, where they advocated a spirit of tolerance and moderation. The French Republic would always be both the definitive and provisional form of social life. It was definitive in the sense that its institutions, including universal suffrage, provided the experimental arena for resolving conflicts and conciliating interests. It was provisional in the sense that its institutions were subject to the laws of positivist political evolution. Existing social and political forces such as dynastic groups, the Church, the Jacobins and the socialists would gradually be transformed into the more rational open meritocracy characteristic of the positivist polity. In the meantime, one should not have unreasonably purist expectations of the political accommodations that were necessary in liberal politics.[16]

According to positivist republicans (as well as important others), the primary organ of transformation would be a system of national education that would eventually wean the French public from the Church and from revolutionary socialism. Despite Comte's deep admiration for medieval Catholicism, he had come to believe that France's political troubles were exacerbated by the deplorable confusion between the spiritual and temporal powers. His followers for the most part rallied under the banner of *laicisation*. Unlike England, where positivism had almost no impact on the organisation of formal education, in France it helped to shape the fundamental debate over secularisation. The claim here is not that positivism directly influenced pedagogy or curriculum – though it clearly had some impact (Simon 1963, pp. 84–93). Rather the claim is that the politically created need for a new civic education gave the views of Comte and his disciples an intellectual marketplace in which to circulate. Jules Ferry, the long-time minister of education who exemplified the regime's focus on education, was himself steeped in Comtist language. His promotion of 'positive science', *laïcité*, 'political tolerance' and 'moral virtue' illustrate a new idiom that fused the aims of education, social science and politics into a distinctively French civic language.

Comte's followers, then, used elements of his positivism in a selective and creative way to shape the ideological foundations of the Third Republic. The conventional view that the Third Republic represented the triumph of 'positivism' is surely too crude a characterisation of the complex emergence of a relatively stable republican regime in the 1870s and 1880s. Yet the adoption of elements of Comte's social physics to reinforce a liberal republican political identity was certainly a factor in the regime's success. Given the

---

16 There are ongoing debates in France about the 'liberal' vs. the 'republican' character of the Third Republic, about its debts to previous regimes, and about its legacy to the present. Yet, even in the current revival of interest in liberalism in France, there is a tendency to view the categories of liberalism and republicanism as oppositional ideal-types, and also to view them exclusively through the prism of the French intellectual tradition. Thus Mona Ozouf uses as evidence of the Third Republic's illiberalism that its founders were closer to Comte than to the Enlightenment. See 'Entre l'esprit des Lumières et la lettre positiviste: Les républicains sous l'Empire', in Furet and Ozouf eds. 1993. My account, on the other hand, suggests the mutual influence of new legitimating languages and new political practices. For an important account of the origin of liberal political practices under the Second Empire, especially around the notions of local freedom and tolerance of debate, see Hazareesingh 1998. Hazareesingh's work on the political culture of the Second Empire stresses the importance of increasing municipal political identification, and successful liberal struggles to instantiate the principles of reasoned public discussion at the local level (1998, pp. 306–21).

divisiveness of other political languages in France and the widespread yearning for 'social' unity, the eventual emergence of a political representation of a science of the 'social' is unsurprising.

5 Conclusion

For many nineteenth-century thinkers social science replaced natural law or traditional understandings as the lodestar of political thought. I have suggested only some of the complex twists and divergent turns attendant on this replacement in France and England.[17] But enough has been said to underline the power of political languages, political memory and political contingency in eliciting and shaping the interaction of social science and political practice. In France political economy emerged quite naturally from the political crucible of the Revolution as a 'scientific' and hence non-inflammatory alternative to the authority of natural rights among political moderates. The claim of political economy to be the queen of the social sciences was almost immediately challenged, however, by various pretenders who touted privileged access to 'the social' and who more successfully distanced themselves from the tainted dynamic of revolutionary discourse. The continued absence of consensus on principles of political legitimacy drove thinkers in France to seek an alternative language for settling differences outside the divisive political arena. In England the prestige of scientific sociology was to come later and to have a less pervasive effect both on the status of political economy within social science, and on the traditional languages of political life.

Paradoxically, it is the English embrace of Comte – perhaps the most arrogant and dogmatic of those who claimed to have found the scientific 'key to all [political and social] mythologies' – that best illuminates the nature of English resistance to the lure of social science. English Victorians drew on Comte for moral therapy rather than for a political cure; liberal democratic

---

17 In a longer essay, one would want to weave into these contrasting sketches the fate of Darwinism. (For a subtle discussion of the 'conversations' surrounding evolution in Germany, England and France, see Burrow 2000, pp. 31–108.) On the one hand largely appropriated to individualist and non-interventionist ends, on the other pressed into service to prove the superiority of the co-operative ends of *solidarité* and the need for governmental action, the scientific theory of natural selection clearly had more than one political trajectory. In France the language of Darwinism – in particular the notions of competitive struggle and natural selection – were widely diffused in the 1880s and 1890s. The extreme right used these ideas to legitimise racism and to combat rationalist republicans on their own 'scientific' terrain. Liberal republicans, on the other hand, argued that natural selection operated also on the level of social organisms, and favoured a co-operative society that took care of the weak (women, children and workers).

institutions were largely left to heal themselves. In France, however, the attraction of social science was intensified, as it had been in 1789, by a widespread crisis of political legitimacy. Partly via the creative variations on Comte and positivism played by republican politicians, a new political idiom was born. Increasingly contested and interrogated today, this positivist-inflected republicanism nevertheless remains deeply entrenched in French self-understandings of what it means to be a citizen of the Republic.

7

Radicalism, republicanism and revolutionism

From the principles of '89 to the origins of modern terrorism

GREGORY CLAEYS AND CHRISTINE LATTEK

1 Introduction

Modernity has been quintessentially defined by the revolutionary impulse, and our judgement, whether laudatory or critical, of the French Revolution of 1789. In the nineteenth century it would be associated with virtually all radical, republican and revolutionary movements, and, by the end of the First World War, the overthrow of many of the leading crowns of Europe. Yet the course of events which produced the overthrow of Louis XVI was not at its outset inevitably anti-monarchical, and would indeed culminate in imperial dictatorship. In association with American independence, however, the idea of revolution came to be identified with the principle of popular sovereignty as such. It was also linked to the explosion of nationalist aspirations which became definitive of the period, as well as to the causes of reaction and the creation of modern conservatism in the works of Burke, Bonald and others.[1] If the British model of limited, constitutional monarchy resting on the principle of the rule of law was central to eighteenth-century reformers elsewhere, thus, it was increasingly supplanted during the nineteenth century by the ideals which emerged from the revolutions of 1776, 1789 and 1848. 'Revolution' itself, which had once meant a restoration or rotational return to previous conditions, came to mean the violent overthrow of established regimes in the name of popular sovereignty, ethnic and national self-assertion, or both; and the conscious framing according to the principles of reason of an edifice hitherto regarded

---

1 The literature on the legacy of the Revolution is considerable. A starting point is Baker 1987 and Hayward 1991. We would like to thank Pamela Pilbeam in particular for comments on this essay, and the Minnesota State Historical Society, St. Paul, for supplying one reference.

largely as a natural, organically derived and divinely inspired order.[2] To its opponents it was also often linked to an obsessive demand for individual autonomy, the growth of commercial and societal individualism, and the wish to break from traditional forms of authority, particularly paternalism and religion.

In the first half of the century the revolutionary ideal was invoked by liberals against autocrats; in the second half, increasingly, it was by socialists, anarchists and other democrats against both autocracy, monarchy in principle, aristocratic oligarchy, and eventually, as consideration of the 'social question' gained ascendancy, liberalism in principle. Made initially largely in the name of liberty – the principle which continued to define its development in the United States – it came elsewhere to give increasing preference to equality, justice and the relief of poverty, though these too could be seen in terms of restoration as well as novelty and innovation. Driven underground, often excoriated by liberals and conservatives alike, reformers who sought a wide extension of manhood suffrage – the first and principal aim of most democrats in this period – came increasingly to link their demands to 'social' issues such as a fair wage and improved working conditions. From 1848, these were often viewed in a 'socialist' light, and the end of revolution construed not as 'freedom' or 'democracy' as such, negatively defined against despotic political rule, but as some variation of the principle of 'association', as opposed to individual economic competition (Proudhon 1923a, pp. 75–99).

Originally conceived as a sharply defined and delimited act of rebellion, revolution came to be construed as a state of mind, a continuing process to maintain a sense of virtue and self-sacrifice *en permanence*. (Negatively this would be come to be seen as an Orwellian orgy of constant agitation aimed at securing conformity by a constant threat of crisis, thus justifying dictatorship by the constant fear of threat from without.) Inspired by a Rousseauist conception of the General Will, revolutionaries would claim that that will could be represented by an elite party of committed revolutionaries ruling in the name of the majority. For some that party could in turn be represented by a charismatic or quasi-millenarian leader. Invoking historical, constitutional or moral rights of resistance to tyranny, democrats also came, often by necessity, to embrace conspiratorial approaches to political

---

2 Most modern accounts of the idea of revolution commence with Arendt 1963. For examples of varying uses of the language of revolution, see Kumar 1970.

change, and sometimes the use of individual violence, 'terror' and assassination to achieve this. The pressure for democracy, as well as increasing social
equality, were thus inexorable in nineteenth-century Europe, and eventually elsewhere. The Restoration of 1815 brought only a temporary lull in
this pressure from below for political democracy. Reaction thus became, as
it was described in the most classic statement of contemporary revolutionism, itself the further cause of still further revolutions (Proudhon 1923a, pp.
13–39).

This chapter examines the evolution of the main European radical and
republican traditions in this period; their involvement in revolutionary
underground movements; and the emergence of the strategy of individual violence or 'terrorism' as a means of fulfilling revolutionary ends, and
thus the mutation of the idea of collective struggle into that of individual
violence. While the focus here is principally on the major European and
North American traditions, some consideration is also given to their bearing
on imperial and anti-imperial developments elsewhere, and on the origins
of parallel, and particularly anti-imperial, non-European movements and
strands of thought.

2   Radical and republican traditions

Despite the American and French revolutions, and earlier examples like
Switzerland, republicanism failed to become established in most of Europe
throughout the nineteenth century. Indeed on the eve of the First World
War it had made little progress since 1870, France being the only major
European republic. After the Restoration of 1815 the Holy Alliance of
Russia, Austria and Prussia wedded the ideals of throne and altar and aimed
to suppress all anti-autocratic movements. Kingship also proved popular in
a number of newly formed states, such as Belgium. Nonetheless there were
powerful republican currents in several European nations throughout the
period, and distinctive if less vibrant movements in others. Republicanism throughout the period was initially often associated with the creation
of a constitutional or limited monarchy, and rule by law as opposed to
arbitrary will, where the republican component was thus the reposing of
ultimate sovereignty in the people, though often with a limited suffrage
based on property ownership. Opposition to aristocratic privilege, though
not necessarily elite guidance, and support for formal legal equality of all citizens, were also prominent republican themes. Resistance to increasing economic specialisation as threatening intellectual capacity and moral integrity,

a prominent theme for eighteenth-century republicans like Adam Ferguson, declined thereafter, though it reappeared in socialism. Throughout the nineteenth century, republicanism came increasingly to mean democracy, with an elected executive, and an increasingly extensive suffrage. But while the American model thus gained in importance throughout the century, that model itself underwent substantial alteration. Based initially on the ideal of a society of independent small farmers and freeholders, coexisting with slavery in the South, it evolved into an agglomeration of mass, urban, party-based political machines in which corruption was widespread, plutocracy increasingly evident, and liberty threatened by the stifling power of what Tocqueville described as the 'tyranny of the majority' (Tocqueville 1835–40; for the later period see Bryce 1899). Unlike European republicanism, American republicanism was rarely anti-clerical, and gave a marked preference to liberty over equality and fraternity, except where diluted by immigrant radicalism (Higonnet 1988). Most forms of republicanism dwelt upon the virtue of patriotism and the importance of giving precedence to the public over the private interest, though this did not exclude internationalist sympathies. Yet monarchs could also claim to embody the same virtues in kingship, and many newly created states in this period – Greece, Belgium, Serbia, Romania – chose the monarchical form when achieving independence. Monarchies could also extend their shelf-life by becoming empires, enhancing national glory and personal prestige, providing opportunities for employment and emigration while displacing growing social pressures at home. Here nationalism and the growth of empire were thus often closely wedded.

Radicalism was consequently not always republican, nor republicanism radical or democratic. Even socialists, such as Robert Blatchford in Britain, were not necessarily anti-monarchical, considering 'a very limited monarchy . . . safer and in many ways better than a republic . . . there is less risk of intrigue and corruption, and that personal ambition has less scope and power in a monarchy than in a republic' (*Clarion*, 3 July 1897, p. 212). Radicals throughout the nineteenth century indeed generally wished to extend the franchise in the direction of greater democracy, and to restrict aristocratic rule, but not necessarily to abolish kingship. Their philosophical first principles often rested on social contract and natural rights theories, but could also be utilitarian, notably in the case of the Benthamite 'philosophic radicals'. Radicals tended to be more individualist, to give greater stress to liberty as a central value, and to emphasise rights; republicans tended to give preference to community, to relative social equality, and to the virtuous performance of duty. Republicans could define their aims in terms of the purification of a monarchical ideal in which service to the public good was the king's chief duty. They could also point to numerous historical examples of classical aristocratic republics or oligarchies, such as Venice. But, in increasing numbers, they also came to reject the monarchical ideal as such in favour of one or another constitutional variants on the theme of popular democratic sovereignty.

Britain

Modern British radicalism and republicanism both commenced with the explosive debate over 'French principles' which followed the publication of Thomas Paine's *Rights of Man* (1791–2) (see Claeys 1989b, 2007a). Though no typology is uncontentious, at least five discrete if overlapping subdivisions of republicanism can be identified in Britain in this period: (1) *utopian* republicanism, in which community of goods, a tradition identified with Sparta, Plato, primitive Christianity and Thomas More, is commended as the solution to poverty and inequality (e.g., *An Essay on Civil Government*, 1793, p. 86); (2) *agrarian* republicanism, in which restrictions on landownership, once associated with the Roman republic, then the tradition revived by James Harrington, restrain inequality of wealth; this tradition includes both Paine and Thomas Spence; (3) *anti-monarchical* republicanism, in which the abolition of kingship and substitution of a republic, or 'government by election', is a central aim (Paine 1992, p. 106), which in this period is mainly associated with Paine; (4) *radical* republicanism, in which the extension of the franchise (generally to universal male suffrage) is the chief goal; and (5) *Whiggish* republicanism, in which a reform of governmental finance, the restriction of the powers of the monarch and aristocracy to interfere with and dominate the House of Commons, and a general willingness to govern with the popular good or *res publica* in mind, are central.[3] Of these forms,

---

3 Such goals can be associated with the Whig leader Charles James Fox in this period. Fox disavowed having 'stated any republican principles, with regard to this country, in or out of parliament' (Fox 1815, IV, p. 209). But this must be compared with his praise for that respect for distinction shown in the ancient republics of Greece and Rome (p. 229), and Fox's proclamation 'that he was so far a republican, that he approved all governments where the *res publica* was the universal principle' (p. 232). See also Barwis 1793: 'And as to the word *republic*, though it be usually applied to every government without a King, yet, in its original and true signification, (*the public weal*) some Kings, at least, have so well understood, and attended to the *public weal*, that their governments might much more justly merit the appellation of *republican*, than many of those which are always denominated republican, though often severe and tyrannical enemies to the *public weal*, and liberties of their countries' (Claeys 1995, VII, p. 380). Paine also argued that 'What is called a *republic*, is not any *particular form* of government.

(1) would be largely subsumed by socialism by 1840, (2) would be taken up by Spenceanism, and the later land nationalisation movement; (3) would emerge chiefly after 1848 in the writings of W. J. Linton, but thereafter virtually die out; and (4) would gradually overtake (5) throughout the course of the nineteenth and then twentieth centuries. The lineages of sixteenth-, seventeenth- and eighteenth-century republicanism into this period have been the subject of considerable controversy (see Pocock 1985). By contrast those linking the 1790s to the nineteenth century have been more neglected, partly because previous languages and paradigms disappear or become unrecognisable after the French Revolution (but see Burrow 1988; Philp 1998; Wootton 1994).

Generally speaking the term 'radical' was used in Britain during the 1790s to indicate a desire for democratic constitutional reform, and particularly the extension of the franchise, with 'radicalism', as defined by the early historiography (e.g. Daly 1892; Kent 1899), emerging *c.*1819 to describe the movement associated with such reformers. Within this group disagreements existed about how far the franchise should be extended, whether a secret ballot should be used, whether Members of Parliament should be paid, and so on. Further issues included the reduction of taxation and the expense of the monarchy and government, the extension of religious toleration, and the curtailment of patronage. Sociologically, radicalism was often associated with the plight of small producers, whether in agriculture or commerce, engaged in an often bitter, protracted and eventually usually futile competition with larger capitalists.

In Britain the plebeian branch of this movement was generally committed to universal manhood suffrage. In its early years its aims were often couched in traditional, even 'romantic' terms, more often evoking a nostalgia for a lost society of yeomanry or peasant-proprietors than seeking a new-modelled democratic republic, and hostile to Jacobinical theorising while condemning the 'Old Corruption' of an extravagant government and profligate aristocracy (see Spence 1996). Before 1820 it rallied around the prominent radicals (both disavowed republicanism) William Cobbett (1763–1835) (see Cobbett 1836, p. 159) and Henry Hunt (1770–1835) (see Hunt 1820, I, p. 505). It then re-emerged as Chartism in the years from 1836 to the mid-1850s, and helped achieve two acts of parliamentary reform

---

It is wholly characteristical of the purport, matter, or object for which government ought to be instituted, and on which it is to be employed, res-publica, the public affairs, or the public good; or, literally translated, the *public thing*' (Paine 1992, p. 140).

(1867, 1884) thereafter. But the attainment of the franchise was also widely regarded as a means to other ends, including poor law reform, the alleviation of restrictions on trade unions, factory reform and freedom of the press.

The middle-class counterpart to this movement was led by Jeremy Bentham (1748–1832) and his followers, such as Sir William Molesworth, often referred to as 'Philosophic Radicals' or 'advanced' liberals, who for a short time mustered a faction of some note in Parliament, though their influence has been claimed to have been much more extensive (Dicey 1914). Their views overlapped on some issues with those of Richard Cobden (1804–65) and John Bright (1811–89), whose radicalism focused on the peaceful promotion of free trade, extending the franchise and reducing the expenses of government, the Crown and imperial expansion. Their great legislative success was the repeal of the Corn Laws in 1846 (see Adelman 1984; Belchem 1986; Harris 1885; Wright 1988).

Amongst these movements Chartism, despite its ideological heterogeneity, was by far the largest, and in the long term the most influential.[4] Commencing in 1836, it agreed on a six-point programme, focusing on universal male suffrage, and petitioned Parliament in three great campaigns. Divided most notably over the issues of 'moral force' versus 'physical force' reform, it became associated during the mid-1840s with the 'Land Plan', a scheme for small-scale peasant proprietorship promoted by Feargus O'Connor. Plebeian radicalism faltered in England during the high Victorian period, but began to recover in the late 1860s, when the movement for female enfranchisement also began in earnest after the artisan elite received the vote in 1867 (Finn 1993; Gillespie 1927; Taylor 1995). In addition, the rapid growth of trade union organisation in the last third of the century ensured that issues important to the 'labour aristocracy' came increasingly to the fore. From the 1880s the rise of socialism divided the labour movement, but also hastened the creation of an independent labour party. From 1880 a distinctive 'Radical Programme' also emerged which identified the radical wing of the Liberal Party with Irish reform, particularly the 'three F's' of fair rents, free sale and fixity of tenure. Various 'collectivist' measures of domestic reform, notably respecting working-class housing and health, agricultural wages and tenancy, disestablishment of the state church, the extension of education and the reform of the taxation and municipal government, also

---

4 The literature on Chartism is, again, very extensive. The chief contemporary estimate is Gammage 1854. For a summary of modern scholarship, see Chase 2006 and Thompson 1986. On the leading theoretical controversies, see Stedman Jones 1983a.

became popular in this period (see Chamberlain 1885, and Toynbee 1927, pp. 219–38). A half-way house between radicalism and liberalism emerged known as New Liberalism, which combined a quasi-collectivist outlook with a basic adherence to *laisser-faire* principles (Freeden 1978). By 1880 the term 'radical' thus encompassed a wide range of both social and political reform proposals, both plebeian and middle class, but usually non-socialist, and often associated with the United States, Australia and New Zealand (Carruthers 1894, p. 6).

British republicanism

Even the most popular monarchy in Europe, celebrated for the stabilising effects of its pomp and ceremony (notably by Bagehot, 1867), had its opponents, though these were relatively few throughout much of the century (see A. Taylor 1996, 1999, 2004; Williams 1997). Indeed, the veteran Whig radical Henry Brougham lamented in 1840 that 'in point of weight from property, rank, and capacity', the republicans were 'a most inconsiderable minority' (Brougham 1840, p. 4). The tradition established by Thomas Paine's *Rights of Man* (1791 2) never entirely disappeared, with birthday celebrations continuing well into the nineteenth century. Writers like Richard Carlile, editor of *The Republican* (1819–26) (for whom republicanism meant simply 'a government which consults the public interest', *The Republican*, 27 August 1819, p. ix), kept the sacred flames alight, and assured an intimate association between secularism or freethought and republicanism in Britain (Royle 1974, 1980). During the late 1830s and 1840s a variety of Chartist writers toyed with republican themes, though the movement as a whole never embraced the ideal, and when the Chartist leader Feargus O'Connor was accused of being a republican, he retorted that he did not care whether the Queen or the Devil sat on the throne (Hughes 1918, p. 158). Many Chartists continued to embrace the American model, though disillusionment at the growth of social inequality in the United States commenced in this period. At the time of the revolutions of 1848 some associated with the movement openly avowed themselves 'ardent Republicans . . . anxious . . . to express our allegiance to the only legitimate source of authority, the Sovereign People' (Harding 1848, p. iii). After 1848 its socialist rump was led by Ernest Jones and George Julian Harney, whose *Red Republican* preached a virulent revolutionary doctrine. For many years afterwards the Chartist leader James Bronterre O'Brien would continue to champion the cause of land reform and nationalisation, his followers being particularly prominent in the International Working Men's Association, founded in 1864.

Following the 1848 continental revolutions the republican cause enjoyed a temporary surge of enthusiasm, particularly as a result of the influence of Mazzini, though the latter was principally a nationalist and little interested in constitutional forms. His great supporter was the engraver William James Linton, a leading opponent of 'the possibility of a kingly republicanism' (Linton 1893, p. 47). His *The English Republic* (1851–5), if it had a limited circulation, nonetheless revealed how far a powerful mix of charisma, religion and nationalism could enthuse British radicals with an ideal of duty based upon 'sacrifice, service, endeavour, the devotion of all the faculties possessed and all the powers acquired to the welfare and improvement of humanity' (Adams 1903, I, p. 265). Linton's republicanism subscribed to the ideals of liberty, equality, fraternity and association, and commended state education, the state provision of credit for the working classes, and an opposition to monarchy as tyranny in principle. But it also opposed socialism where the state acted as 'the director and dictator of labour', thus violating individual liberty, instead of protecting labour against capital, and giving the cultivator the opportunity of land ownership (Linton n.d., p. 2). It represented the first impressive British effort to wed the seventeenth-century republicanism of Milton, Cromwell, Ireton and Vane to that of Mazzini, Herzen, Kossuth and the causes of the Poles, Hungarians, Romanians and other subject European peoples. Auguste Comte's followers in Britain also kept the sacred flames of republicanism alight after the decline of Chartism, with Frederic Harrison insisting that the only legitimate government was republican, which was synonymous with entrusting power to those fit to rule, working in the interests of all, 'never in the interest of any class or order', and whose adoption was 'as certain as the rising of tomorrow's sun' (Harrison 1875, pp. 116–22; Harrison 1901, p. 20; *Fortnightly Review*, NS 65, June 1872, p. 613). John Ruskin, too, lent some support to the ideal.[5] Republicanism and socialism were thus distinctive if sometimes overlapping entities throughout this period.

Inspired by the downfall of the Second Empire in France, and antipathy to the 'despotic' principles of German expansionism, with which Queen

---

5 Ruskin proclaimed that 'A republic means, properly, a polity in which the state, with its all, is at every man's service, and every man, with his all, at the state's service – (people are apt to lose sight of the last condition), but its government may nevertheless be oligarchic (consular, or decemviral, for instance), or monarchic (dictatorial)' (Ruskin 1872, II, pp. 129–30). Thanks to Jose Harris for indicating this usage.

Victoria was identified by birth (McCarthy 1871, pp. 30–40), republicanism in Britain enjoyed its greatest flowering in the early 1870s, but declined by 1874. Following the foundation of the Land and Labour League in 1869, some eighty-five republican clubs were established between 1871 and 1874, and a National Republican League formed in 1872. Supporters condemned the monarchy as simply 'immoral' in principle (Holyoake 1873, p. 1), and enthused that 'great numbers of people are beginning to advocate republican principles' (Barker 1873, p. 3). Respectable radicals, catching the sense of the moment, waded into the fray. At a speech in Newcastle in 1871, and then elsewhere, Sir Charles Dilke addressed the theme of 'Representation and Royalty', and offered a critique of royal finance, moving for a parliamentary enquiry into the issue in March 1872 (see Taylor 2000). But anti-republican riots dogged his course. The increasing appositeness of the American model after the Reform Act of 1884 naturally enhanced discussion of its virtues amongst sympathisers, though even here there were dissenting voices (e.g. Conway 1872).

Charles Bradlaugh (1833–91) was the single most important British republican of the late Victorian period, and was most influential in yoking republicanism to freethought, as well as opposition to socialism (Bonner 1895; Gossman 1962). Yet his rhetoric was more extreme than his principles, and his few attempts to found any formal republican organisation were reluctant, and accompanied by disclaimers of any haste in securing their ultimate political end (D'Arcy 1982). The illness of Queen Victoria in 1871, and her return to duties after a decade of mourning, helped to restore her prestige, while Disraeli gave increasing stress to the superiority of the British constitution over the American (e.g. Watts 1873, p. 1). The decline of republicanism was clearly intimately interwoven with the expansion of empire, and with Disraeli's enhancement of the Queen's imperial role. Critics threatened that '*the day that we proclaim a Republic in this Country, our Colonies are lost, and we sink into insignificance*' (Ashley 1873, p. 19). English reaction to the Paris Commune was generally negative, and even English republicans were divided, Frederic Harrison being more favourable, Bradlaugh, increasingly opposed to the First International, less so. By 1899, it was claimed, there was only one avowed republican in the House of Commons – the Irishman Michael Davitt (Davidson 1899, p. 386, and generally Moody 1981).

Republicanism also developed in a number of British colonies in this period, at least in theory, notably in Australia. Here, as early as 1852, it was being proclaimed (by John Dunmore Lang, but without much popular support) that there was 'no other form of government either practicable or possible, in a British colony obtaining its freedom and independence, than that of a republic', which could alone promote public and private morals and 'pure and undefiled religion' (Lang 1852, p. 64; see McKenna 1996; McKenna and Hudson 2003; Oldfield 1999; and for New Zealand, Trainor 1996; see also Eddy and Schreuder 1998).

Ireland

A separate parliamentary group of Irish radicals kept up pressure for political and social (and especially land) reform there throughout the period. The leading nationalist movement of the early part of the century was led by Daniel O'Connell (1775–1847), whose chief goal was the restoration of the Irish parliament, and who famously argued that 'No Revolution is worth the spilling of a single drop of blood' (White 1913, p. 81). Rejecting the United Irish 'vain desire of republican institutions' (O'Connell 1846, II, p. 113), he promoted instead moderate parliamentary reform and liberal economic policies. Catholic Emancipation was achieved in 1828, but in the 1840s O'Connell failed to achieve 'repeal' (of the 1801 Act of Union which abolished the independent Irish parliament). His most famous successor was Charles Stewart Parnell (1846–91), the 'Uncrowned King of Ireland', president of the Land League and leader of the Irish parliamentary party in the 1880s, who promoted a policy of land reform and then, increasingly, peasant proprietorship, and an independent Irish parliament.

Irish republicanism

Nineteenth-century Irish republicanism dates from the controversy surrounding the French Revolution debate and Paine's *Rights of Man*. Its roots, however, lie in earlier 'True Whig' and 'Patriot' thought, epitomised by an opposition to the 'tyranny' of a despotic executive, standing armies and the landed oligarchy, but where English ethnic domination also played a major role in diluting a vocabulary of ancient constitutionalism and natural rights and later Catholic rights and even separatism (see Small 2002, and more generally Connolly 2000). Some reformers, like Lord Edward Fitzgerald, visited France soon after the Revolution and imbibed republican principles there (Moore 1831, I, p. 166). As the 1790s progressed other reformers like Wolfe Tone moved from seeking independence under '*any* form of government' (Tone 1827, I, p. 70) towards accepting both a broader franchise and, eventually, a more democratic republicanism. For many, particularly the Dissenters, this was synonymous with self-government (Byrne 1910, p. 4; Tone 1827, II, pp. 18, 26). With the formation of the United Irishmen in 1792, Painite republicanism and Irish self-rule fused in a mixture that was separatist by 1796 and revolutionary by 1798 (see McBride 2000). Many even of the most prominent leaders of the uprising of 1798, however, had no settled political ideas beyond a desire for national independence; the rebel General Joseph Holt admitted to being 'not very well up to republican notions' when questioned (Holt 1838, II, p. 69).

Irish republicanism in the mid-nineteenth century continued this trend. The revolutionaries of 1848 had no elaborate political theory, but aimed chiefly at nationhood. Thomas Davis, for instance, while agreeing to support a federative government, said 'If not, then anything but what we are' (quoted in Lynd 1912, p. 224), and even admitted the possibility of 'royal republics' as a viable model (Davis 1890, p. 280). When another '48-er, John Mitchel, declared for republicanism, his view was later recalled to have been 'an altogether unexpected development', since he had himself written of his comrades that 'theories of government have but little interest for them; that the great want and unvarying aim of them all is a National Government', which might include a monarchy (Duffy 1898, I, p. 262n; Dillon 1888, II, p. 130). Many were also later vexed by Mitchel's overt support of slavery and 'an Irish republic with an accompaniment of slave plantations' in the early 1850s (he went on to fight for the South in the US Civil War) (Dillon 1888, II, pp. 48–9). Even such a sophisticated social and political theorist as Michael Davitt, founder of the Land League, who favoured nationalisation of the land (with Henry George as a key influence) and state socialism (Davitt 1885, II, pp. 69–142), wrote little about republicanism as such, while hoping for the emergence of a labour party in Britain.

But the Irish Republican Brotherhood, founded in 1858, settled at least in part on a number of leading principles, though these were of course also contested. They included the expropriation of lands whose proprietors were absentees or inactive, and of church lands; the sale of such lands to create a new peasantry; the abolition of hereditary titles; the provision of an elected parliament, one-third of which would be by universal suffrage; the erection of provincial councils; and the toleration of all religions, but secularisation of education (Rutherford 1877, I, pp. 68–9). Some later Irish republicans were also principally nationalists and not necessarily anti-monarchical; Patrick Pearse for instance thought a German prince could well serve as sovereign of an independent Ireland.

France

In France a radical movement existed continuously from the time of the Revolution of 1789 which inherited the traditions of Rousseau and Jacobinism, transformed these through the writings of Babeuf, Blanqui, Proudhon and Blanc, and can be distinguished by its defence of the small producer, artisan and peasant against big capital, and the advocacy of greater democracy, social equality, civil rights and nationalism (Loubère 1974). France was the most continuously revolutionary society in Europe through the nineteenth century, experiencing moderate upheaval in 1830, and more epochal transformations in 1848 and 1871. Its radicalism was thus often republican and revolutionary, though there was no single tradition associated with the 'principles of '89' as such. Within this movement, instead, more moderate and extremist wings contended for public opinion, with Jacobins and republicans again rising to prominence during the 1848 Revolution. Radicalism spread more successfully to the countryside in the second half of the century, linking itself to wine-growing interests in the south, and pressing for constitutional reforms such as a unicameral legislature with the Senate and President abolished, though not female enfranchisement. Some radicals by the 1880s urged nationalisation of the railways, mines and banks, the regulation of working hours and conditions, cheap credit and government support for co-operatives. By the turn of the century many of these issues were identified with socialism, though of a more moderate and non-revolutionary type, and radicalism declined.

French republicanism

The French Revolution was by no means inevitably anti-monarchical in tendency, and controversy as to the advantages of retaining modified kingship was already evident in the debate between Thomas Paine and the Abbé Sieyès in August 1791. Here Paine defended republicanism as 'simply a government by representation' (Paine 1908, III, p. 9), while Sieyès indicated the dangers of an elected executive, contending instead for retaining a monarch to represent the nation as a whole (Sieyès 2003, p. 169). Such arguments would later prove compelling to many, and Sieyès' ideas would prove important under the more conservative phase of the Revolution embodied in the Directory. Beforehand, however, French republicanism inherited its chief concerns from the Convention and the first Commune of Paris, which emerged in August 1792, set the Revolution on a more radical course, and strenuously opposed both the monarchy and priesthood (see Fisher 1911; Pilbeam 1995; Plamenatz 1952; and Soltau 1931). The first Commune and the Jacobin Club organised the insurrection of 10 August 1792, and established the pattern of radical, as well as Parisian, rebellion against central government in the name of the people as a whole. An insurrection led by Marat and Robespierre on 31 May 1793 led to the National Assembly being overwhelmed by mob rule. (But to its supporters both then and later this was the sole means by which democracy could be protected; e.g. O'Brien 1859, p. 27.) The arrest and execution of the moderate Girondins, and a period of radical rule, followed. Church lands had been deemed national property in 1790, and some émigré lands sold. An even larger transfer was proposed by a decree of February 1794, but this was aborted when the Terror was overthrown on 9 Thermidor (27 July 1794). These measures were, however, populist rather than socialist, and aimed at allaying the problems of poverty and scarcity of food which threatened the Revolution itself from within. (Republicans generated their own account of political economy in the same period; see Whatmore 2000.) Universal male suffrage (though indirect) was briefly achieved at this time, and again in 1848, but withdrawn quickly.

Following the Restoration of 1815 the republicans won their next great victory with the ejection of Charles X after three days' street fighting in 1830, only to have the institution of monarchy stabilised by the accession of the Duke of Orleans, Louis Philippe. At this time the republican camp was divided into four main sections: the moderates, who were the largest group, led by Godefroy Cavaignac; the radicals or Jacobins, whose chief aim was manhood suffrage; the social reformers, many of whom, like Cabet, the Fourierists and Saint-Simonians, were anti-revolutionary and often uninterested in politics; and the revolutionaries (Plamenatz 1952, p. 39). A fifth group, the Catholic Liberals led by the Abbé de Lammenais, tried to bridge the gap between the church and democracy. But such categories were elastic rather than exclusive, and many reformers belonged to several groupings.

The Second Republic, founded in February 1848, and led by men like Ledru-Rollin, Lamartine and Louis Blanc, was also short-lived. Its leading characteristic was the popularisation of socialist ideas on a widespread scale for the first time, notably Blanc's national workshop scheme and proposals for the 'right to work'. Moderates found themselves challenged by insurrectionists, including Blanqui, in May–June, but the latter were defeated after much bloodshed, and only succeeded in tainting the radical cause in the eyes of public opinion. Following an interim government headed by

Louis Eugène Cavaignac, Louis Bonaparte was elected President. But he then staged a *coup d'état* on 2 December 1851, which resulted in the Second Empire. A period of severe repression followed, in which over 26,000 republicans were arrested and tried by special tribunals. Ledru-Rollin, Blanc and others were driven into exile, where some collaborated in the European Central Democratic Committee, formed in London (Lattek 2006, pp. 87–95). Many moderates remained in France, and succeeded in making republicanism a respectable cause over the next two decades. But disagreements over the extent of social reform needed, and correspondingly the viability of *laisser-faire* liberalism to solve social problems, continued to foster division.

The Third Republic, announced in September 1870 after France's defeat by Prussia, was formally established in 1875. With extremism discredited after the failure of the Commune, lawyers and middle-class merchants predominated amongst its supporters, with an influential sprinkling of artists like Manet, and an increasing numbers of Jews, women and Freemasons, who tended to promote a more secular approach to public culture. Its leading light was Léon Gambetta (1838–82), whose great aim was sustaining a centralised regime based on universal suffrage and free compulsory secular education long enough to build a modern democracy upon a patriotic foundation, no matter what compromises, notably in religious and foreign policy, his 'opportunist' policies demanded (see Nord 1995). In the interim, support was given to the republican ideal, amongst others, by Auguste Comte (1798–1857), whose followers, if suspicious of democracy, were nevertheless often inveterate opponents of monarchy.

The Paris Commune

An influential if much debated republican model during the late nineteenth century was that associated with the Paris Commune, the revolutionary organisation which emerged after France's defeat by Prussia in the 1870–1 war (see generally Lissagaray 1886). Following the declaration by Jules Favre, Léon Gambetta and others on 4 September 1870 of a 'Government of National Defence', and preceded by communes in Lyon and Marseille, the Paris Commune proper was declared on 18 March 1871. It was ratified by communal elections in which a number of workers and some leading members of the International Working Men's Association were returned. Inspired more by Proudhon than Rousseau, it collapsed into bloodbath in April–May 1871, only to have its republican aspirations reaffirmed by the

National Assembly in February 1875. The Commune's policy was rigorously anti-centralist. Taxation, the direction of local business, the magistracy, police and education were all to be controlled locally, and a standing army supplanted by a civic militia. Officers of the National Guard were to be elected, and liberty of conscience and work was also guaranteed. The Commune was thus a government at once republican, local, anti-centralist, in possession of its own militia and representative of working-class elements.

The Commune of Paris, in particular, indicated that such powers would be utilised in a socialist direction; provincial organisations, it was realised, might not follow suit. To the socialists, the Commune symbolised a move to divide France into a republic in which autonomous communes sent representatives to a federative council, and in which Paris was freed from the conservative weight of the provinces, a majority oppression caused by 'the dogma of universal suffrage'. To anarchists like Bakunin it was 'a bold and outspoken negation of the State, and the opposite of an authoritarian communist form of political organisation' (Bakunin 1973, p. 199). To Marx, who had caustically dismissed the commune idea in 1866 as 'Proudhonised Stirnerianism' (Marx and Engels 1987, p. 287), its popular character as a 'social republic', the 'self government of the producers', with all public functionaries elected, paid workmen's wages and directly responsible to the Commune, was the 'direct antithesis' of the old state apparatus. (Some have taken such comments as a concession to Proudhon and the anarchists, e.g. Collins and Abramsky 1965, p. 207.) It was thus the model which should be established everywhere, with rural delegates being sent to towns, and district assemblies sending deputies to Paris, thus ending 'the State power which claimed to be the embodiment of that unity independent of, and superior to, the nation itself' (Marx and Engels 1971, pp. 72–4). To some revolutionaries it also necessitated a temporary dictatorship to meet the threat from without, as in 1793, as well as from within, from a treacherous National Assembly which made peace with Germany in early 1871.

Towards the end of this period a revolutionary syndicalist movement, centred in the Confédération Générale du Travail, founded at Limoges in 1895, also arose in France (see Jennings 1990; Ridley 1970). It agreed with Marx generally on the theory of the class war, placing greater emphasis however on strikes, and especially the general strike, as its manifestation. Its ultimate aim was also the abolition of the state, bureaucracy, police, army and legal apparatus, with confederated labour supplying all these functions in the future. This strategy was to meet with support from Georges Sorel, amongst others, though the movement rapidly became reformist.

Gregory Claeys and Christine Lattek

Germany

In Germany 'French ideas' after 1789, while ambiguously accepted as imposed by a conqueror during the revolutionary wars, left a legacy of secularism, anti-parochial nationalism and an appeal to popular sovereignty which was not easily suppressed (Blanning 1983; Gooch 1927). The modern democratic movement emerged in the *Vormärz* period and reached its first apogee during the Frankfurt parliament at the time of the 1848 revolutions (see Sperber 1991). Theoretically, German radicalism also received an important impetus from the circle of 'Young' or 'Left' Hegelians to which Marx belonged, including Ludwig Feuerbach and Arnold Ruge (Breckman 1999; Moggach 2006). Some of this group, like Bakunin, became anarchists; others, like Ruge, remained radical democrats and republicans. Marx progressed to communism, promoting the necessity of violent revolution from the mid-1840s onwards. The young Engels, too, certainly exalted the therapeutic effects of proletarian revolutionary violence. Both later accepted the possibility, however, that the transition to socialism might be peaceful, where democratic processes permitted it, though this was not a view accepted by all later Marxists. By the early twentieth century the term 'radical' came increasingly also to be used in reference to right-wing movements, which association, as *rechtsradikal*, it often retains today.

In the latter decades of the century the term 'radical' came moreover in some circles to be associated with a movement of moral and cultural reform, in which the idea of surpassing or transcending existing norms, 'bourgeois' or otherwise, but especially moral restraints upon individual self-expression and creativity, was central. Some of these concepts were indebted to the more individualistic forms of earlier nineteenth-century anarchism, in Germany notably that of Max Stirner, whose *The Ego and His Own* appeared in 1845. Stirner in turn has been controversially linked to Friedrich Nietzsche, and described as presenting a 'remarkable anticipation . . . of Nietzsche's doctrine of the Superman, and the demand for a "transvaluation of all values" beyond all current standards of good and evil' (Muirhead 1915, p. 68). How far Nietzsche himself regarded the Superman ideal as 'radical' can be contested; he certainly spoke of desiring a 'radical' cure to social malaise and/or seeking 'radical' change (e.g. Nietzsche 1903, para. 534), but did not use the term positively in a primarily political sense. Some recent accounts have, however, suggested that to the degree that Nietzsche was a 'political' thinker at all, his ideas should be conceived in terms of a 'politics of aristocratic radicalism' (Detwiler 1990). Here the Superman ideal functions 'radically' to subvert democracy, and to reimpose upon the 'mass' or 'herd' a higher ethical ideal, based also in part, if again controversially, upon a Social Darwinist conception of evolutionary type. This was to be accomplished by recreating what Nietzsche termed 'the aristocratic equation (good = aristocratic = beautiful = happy = loved by the gods)' (Nietzsche 1910, p. 30), an ideal also based in part upon Nietzsche's conception of the Greek *polis* and its valuation of goodness, truth and beauty. 'Radicalism' thus describes a reversion to a purer or original moral type, in Nietzsche's case prior to a Judaeo-Christian 'transvaluation' of values, in order to avoid a 'nihilist' endpoint, God having been pronounced dead, and the subversion of all other myths being one of Nietzsche's central aims. Hence a new value was to be imposed both upon the individual, in terms of self-mastery, and upon society, in terms of the 'will to power', Nietzsche's central and much contested concept. Whatever the merits of this description of Nietzsche's aims, various of his followers certainly assumed that the master's aim could be adapted to shoring up the existing patrician order (e.g. Ludovici 1915).

In Germany republicanism emerged as a serious alternative during the 1848 revolutions, under the leadership of men like Friedrich Hecker, Carl Schurz and Gustav von Struve, though many radicals preferred the creation of an empire to that of a republic. Defeated in the Frankfurt parliament of April 1848, the republicans, whose strength lay chiefly in the south-west, were beaten in the field by Prussia by early 1849.

Republicanism enjoyed intermittent support in other European countries in the later nineteenth century. In Spain a republic was declared in 1873, but suffered four *coups d'état* and the rule of five presidents before collapsing in 1875.

The United States

All American political thought is republican in the sense of denying the efficacy of monarchy, but the democratic extension of the franchise occurred only gradually through this period. Nineteenth-century American radicalism was born from the more populist interpretation of the principles of 1776, often associated with Thomas Jefferson, and linked to the growing inequality of wealth, one critic by the mid-1830s denouncing 'what we call a Republican government' as 'sheer aristocracy' (Brown 1834, p. 43). It received an impetus from generations of foreign radical émigrés, from British democrats fleeing repression in the 1790s (Twomey 1989) to Germans after

1848 (Pozzetta 1981; Wittke 1952; Zucker 1950), and Poles, Russians and Jews in later decades (Johnpoll 1981; Pope 2001). Domestically, it evolved as a consequence of industrialisation, growing social inequality, and such issues as banking and the control of the money supply, which spawned the Free Silver and Greenback movements, and the growth of 'trusts' or economic monopolies, particularly the railways, and anti-union activity. It produced a variety of movements, from Jacksonian Radicalism in the 1830s through the radical democracy of Locofocoism and Free Democracy in the 1850s and 1860s, to Abolitionism and various forms of agrarian populism, like the Grange movement, consumer and producer co-operation, and social-ism, both domestic and foreign in inspiration. Occasionally proposals for a republican agrarian law were mooted (e.g. Campbell 1848, pp. 110–18). In the later century a number of prominent leaders emerged, notably Henry Demarest Lloyd (see Lloyd 1894), and even more, Henry George, whose single-tax theory was of worldwide influence (see George 1879). Following the example of the British experiment at Freetown, freed slaves established a variety of separatist and pan-Africanist movements, resulting, amongst other things, in the founding of the colony, then later the state, of Liberia in 1822 (Hall 1978; McAdoo 1983; Robinson 2001).

Non-European anti-imperial revolutionary and resistance movements

The nineteenth century was the period of the greatest imperial expan-sion in European, North American and Russian history, resulting in the deaths of at least thirty million people and, when poverty-fuelled famine and civil war exacerbated by foreign intervention are included, possibly 100 million. Some of these conquests were almost openly genocidal in intent; that is to say, the near-extermination of native populations, often masked by a Social Darwinist discourse on 'inferior' races, was an expected, accepted, and even desired outcome of conquest. Such expansion was, however, usually described in terms of the need for territory, raw mate-rials and new markets (see Claeys 2010). But conquest was everywhere resisted, and here European ideals of revolution, freedom, equality and jus-tice intermingled with adherence to and renovation of traditional forms of polity and social and religious organisation (Wesseling 1978 and Bayly, this volume).

In the early nineteenth century the most notable extra-European rev-olutionary developments were in Latin and South America (see Ander-son 1991, pp. 47–82; Schroeder 1998; and generally Gurr 1970). Following

Spain's defeat by Napoleon in 1808, Venezuela declared itself an independent republic in 1811, Chile proclaimed a provisional constitution in 1812, both only to suffer defeats by royalist forces. In 1821, Spanish rule was overthrown in Mexico, and by 1825, when Simón Bolívar captured Upper Peru, Spain was left with a tenuous hold on the New World, retaining only Puerto Rico and Cuba. Brazil became independent in 1822, first under a monarchy, then, from 1889, a republic. The importation of ideas of popular sovereignty, participation and representation from Spanish resistance to Napoleon assisted this process. But conservative notions of independence more accommodating to political elites, who often allied with military leaders, tended to take precedence over those based on French ideals of liberty, equality and fraternity, despite the more revolutionary aspirations of Francisco de Miranda, and others (Rodriguez 1997, p. 122). The sentiments of Bernardo O'Higgins, who proclaimed that he detested 'aristocracy . . . beloved equality is my idol' (quoted in Lynch 1986, p. 142), were thus comparatively rare. If Borbon absolutism was unattractive, political participation still remained limited to the elite, with high property qualifications for the franchise. More liberal political ideas tended to follow rather than precede rebellion, and were often resisted by both white and Creole elites fearing ethnic unrest from darker-skinned slaves, natives and peasants. Ethnic diversity, despite some social banditry and slave revolts, generally inhibited the formation of national identities in the new states, with American-born Creole elites often siding with Spain (Macfarlane and Posada-Carbó 1999, pp. 1–12). But an emergent anti-Spanish 'American' identity was also marked (Lynch 1986, pp. 1–2). Secularising trends were rare. Ideas of state intervention to promote education and prosperity, such as those proposed by O'Higgins, as well as economic protectionism, attracted greater support than those of *laisser-faire*. Republicanism was common. But even liberals like Bolívar, the first president of Columbia, who upheld principles like judicial review and a restraint of presidential power, and eventually turned against slavery, insisted on a strong executive and a franchise limited by property ownership and literacy (Lynch 2006, pp. 144–5). Caudillism, or the emergence of regional warlords hostile to centralised authority, often followed revolutionary wars. Mexico settled on an emperor, and monarchist sentiments were evident amongst leaders like José de San Martin. Insurrection centred on Caracas, Buenos Aires and Santiago, while Mexico City was initially integral to the defence of Spanish rule, and Cuba did not successfully rebel until the end of the century. The process of national independence was thus an exceptionally uneven one, with modernising elites playing a key role in determining whether wars of independence took place, and the directions in which they tended (Dominquez 1980, p. 3).

To the north, an immensely influential anti-colonial precedent was established with the overthrow of French rule in Saint Domingue in 1791 by 500,000 slaves (one-third died by 1804) inspired by the new revolutionary principles and led by the 'black Spartacus', Toussaint L'Ouverture. 'The only successful slave revolt in history' (James 1963, p. ix) led, after the defeat of French, Spanish and English armies, to the uniquely symbolic foundation of the first self-governing emancipated slave republic in Haiti in 1804 (see Geggus 2001). Revolts also occurred in Jamaica, Surinam and elsewhere (see generally Genovese 1979). In Brazil, between 1807 and 1835, they were sometimes 'millenarian', and often religiously inspired, in one case by Islam (Reis 1993). The aspiration amongst rebels of becoming peasant-proprietors was widespread. In the West Indies, Jamaica had witnessed a slave revolt in 1831 in which Baptists, including missionaries, were implicated. Here, too, an uprising of ex-slaves in 1865, generally known as the 'Jamaica Insurrection', was repressed with sanguinary fury by Governor Eyre, resulting in some 2,000 deaths, and became a *cause célèbre* (Semmel 1962). French rule was also contested in North and West Africa and Indochina (for Algeria see, for example, Laremont 1999; for West Africa, Crowder 1978; and for Vietnam, Marr 1971; Trung 1967), as was German rule, whose policy of native annihilation provoked an uprising in South-West Africa between 1904 and 1907 which was viciously suppressed. The death-toll here, when famine following the use of scorched-earth tactics is included, was in the hundreds of thousands (Stoecker 1987). A similar story could be told of Dutch rule in Java, where a war was fought between 1825 and 1830 which took some 200,000 native lives (see Kuitenbrouwer 1991). Portuguese rule was also contested (for background, see Boxer 1963). Resistance to imperialist expansion by non-European powers, notably to Russia in Central Asia and Japan in Korea, also occurred. (For Japan see Beasley 1987; Kim 1967, and Yeol 1985. For Russia see Geyer 1987.) In the United States indigenous peoples were successively isolated, decimated by war and disease and confined to reservations (Bonham 1970; Silva 2004). Exploitation and dislocation through the introduction of new methods of commerce and new technologies, relative deprivation, the disruption of village life and the displacement of native elites were common causes of discontent underlying such rebellions. Prophetic, messianic and millenarian responses to conquest were common to 'revitalisation movements' in many regions, as was the description of the pre-colonial past as a golden age. Reactions were commonly defined less by class consciousness than antagonism towards the colonial elite, whether European or co-opted natives, and less by nationalism than regional or tribal loyalty, or adherence to a charismatic, usually prophetic, leader (Adas 1987; Thrupp 1970).

In the largest European empire, rejection of British rule by native populations occurred throughout this period. Aboriginal resistance developed in Australia from the period of first occupation in 1788, led initially between 1790 and 1802 by one Pemulwuy, and continued throughout the nineteenth century. Revolts were brutally repressed, and aboriginal lands, often declared *terra nullius*, or unoccupied, were seized without compensation (Reynolds 1982). Divided by linguistic difference and tribal antagonism, lacking an authoritarian political or military structure, native peoples rarely engaged in concerted rebellion, though drilling and organisation were sometimes in evidence. 'Domesticated' natives also sometimes organised attacks on settlers (Robinson and York 1977, pp. 5, 11). Escaped convicts like George Clarke, who painted his body like a native, also occasionally assisted aboriginal raids on settlements (Robinson and York 1977, p. 120). Tribal law was sometimes used as justification for armed rebellion, but massacre and forced resettlement eventually curtailed resistance (Newbury, 1999). In Tasmania the struggle, eventually ending in genocide, lasted from 1804 to 1834. Conflict intensified during the Black War of 1827–30, and racial enmity reached new depths of bitterness. Between 20,000 and 50,000 natives probably died violent deaths throughout the century in Australia (Reynolds 1982, pp. 122–3).

Though inhibited by inter-tribal rivalry, the Maori resistance in New Zealand, lasting from 1843–72, was better organised, more prolonged, and eventually, with the cession of valuable land rights, vastly more successful (Ryan and Parham, 2002). Here resistance in the 1860s was led by the Maori-Christian hybrid religious movement, the Hau Hau, under the prophet Te Ua Haumene. Equally formidable opponents were the Zulus, who inflicted serious losses on Britain at Ishlandwana in 1879 (Chikeka 2004; Crais 1991; Jaffe 1994). In Canada, the British faced both a native population and disaffected French *habitants*, who, together with English-Canadian radicals led by William Lyon Mackenzie, staged a rebellion, with Louis Papineau, in 1837, which aimed at secession and the creation of an independent republic (see Read 1896). There was also resistance in West Africa (Pawlikova-Vilhanova 1988), Malaya (see Nonini 1992), Burma and elsewhere. Memorable thereafter as perhaps the most symbolically significant anti-imperialist victory of the period was the loss of General Charles Gordon at Khartoum in 1885.

Here Muslim revivalists conducting a jihad, or holy war, led by the Mahdi, overwhelmed British forces and established an Islamic republic which lasted until 1898 (Holt 1970; Nicoll 2004; Wingate 1968).

By far the most important instance of large-scale rebellion in the British Empire was the Indian or Sepoy Mutiny of 1857–8, also called the First Indian War of Independence. The grievances underlying it were more broadly social, ethnic and religious than political, though a sentiment of Indian nationalism was both a cause and consequence of the growing disaffection of Britain's Indian subjects. It is now widely recognised that deepseated resentment of European rule, and especially religious proselytism, were crucial sources of this war. Interference with native customs like *sati*, or widow-burning, and of course the affair of the greased cartridges, affecting Hindu and Muslim alike, the ostensible, but really only final cause of the outbreak, were also germane (see Srivastava, 1997). The reinstatement of Mughal rule, partly in response to the East India Company's treatment of the King of Delhi, was certainly also a motivating factor, though when Delhi was seized a council of twelve was erected which disregarded the King's authority (Buckler 1922, pp. 71–100). Being soldiers, the revolutionaries were far better organised than other indigenous rebels in this period, and many retained their pre-existing command structures throughout the struggle. Their professional grievances are now recognised as central to the Mutiny itself (David 2002, p. 398). Native officers, often ambitious professionals fairly anticipating greater promotion prospects under a native than the Company government, also provided a cadre of sophisticated and effective leaders, some of whom sought more directly political ends. In annexed Oudh the revolt assumed the form of a popular movement in support of king and country (Metcalfe 1974, p. 37). But recent studies, challenging the idea that the revolt was a war of national independence, have concluded that nowhere did a general anti-Europeanism emerge, though the gap between native and Briton had been growing since the 1820s (Chowdhury 1965; David 2002, p. 39; Sengupta 1975, p. 9). Though most natives remained loyal to British rule, the rebellion might well have succeeded had anticipated Persian and Russian assistance arrived. It met with sympathy from educated Russian and Chinese opinion, and provided a vital precedent for later antiimperial struggles, some of which emerged from an increasingly radical Bengali intellectual milieu (MacMann 1935, pp. 40–69; Majumedar 1962; Pal 1991). The Indian Congress Movement emerged in 1885 out of the spirit of post-Mutiny nationalism and both Hindu and Muslim revivalism, and was assisted in part by Allan Octavian Hume, the son of a prominent

English radical of the preceding generation, Joseph Hume, and later, by the socialist Annie Besant (Lovett 1920).

Various European upheavals also had an impact on other parts of the world. The revolutions of 1848 had a considerable if delayed impact, generally by encouraging greater egalitarianism, the growth of participatory politics, anti-slavery sentiments, the diffusion of socialist ideas and a 'social' critique of liberalism, in Chile, Peru, Mexico and other parts of Latin and Southern America during subsequent decades (Thomson 2002). The growth of nationalistic sentiment and 'patriotic' resistance to European imperialism sometimes spurred greater repression, however, as in the case of the partly Christian-inspired anti-Tartar (but also anti-opium) Taiping revolutionary movement (1850–65). Here secret societies attempted to create a theocracy based upon a fraternity of kings, and encouraged some redistribution of wealth to the poor. They were only defeated with Western assistance, at the cost of many millions of lives (Clarke and Gregory 1982; Cohen 1965; Michael 1966). Suppression of the fanatically anti-Christian, anti-foreign and anti-Manchu spontaneous peasant upheaval known as the Boxer Rebellion in China of 1900, which marked an important stage in China's quest for independence (Keown-Boyd 1991; Purcell 1963), also further hastened Western penetration of the region. It was accompanied by unprecedented looting and the wanton destruction of China's cultural heritage.

3 Secret societies and revolutionary conspiracies

The politics of insurrection and mass violence

An important if often blurred distinction in the politics of revolutionary violence is that between insurrectionary and terrorist violence. In the former instance, usually, an assassination (or several) is intended to provoke an uprising to overthrow what is regarded as an illegitimate regime. An act of violence, in other words, is intended to trigger a revolution, like a *coup d'état* by one or a few individuals against an established government, on the basis of a constitutionally or morally justified right of resistance (for a British instance, see Baxter 1795). By contrast *terrorist* violence is usually part of a prolonged campaign which often functions as a *substitute* for popular uprising. In this section we will examine insurrectionary ideas, and in the next, 'terrorism'. We will not consider secret organisations in this period whose function was not centrally but only marginally political (though such distinctions are often contentious), such as the Ku Klux Klan, or more obviously criminal associations like the Mafia, or political organisations which employed violence in defence of the status quo, such as the Orangemen, founded in 1794 to suppress Catholicism in Ireland, or the 'Royalist Terrorism' during the French Revolution, or the 'White Terror' which followed the Restoration. There were also a variety of underground nationalist movements in this period worth mentioning, but which cannot be detailed, notably in Turkey; amongst the Slavs; in Greece, where the Hetairia, probably founded around 1815, helped secure independence by mustering some 20,000 insurgents in 1821–2; and in Spain, where the Communeros emerged from Freemasonry to promote moderate constitutionalism. Young Europe, a loose grouping of political refugees who met at Berne in April 1834 with the aim of founding 'an association of men believing in a future of liberty, equality, and fraternity, for all mankind' (Frost 1876, II, p. 236) was a federative revolutionary democratic organisation. Its branches included Young Poland; Young Germany, which was mostly composed of German workmen resident in Switzerland, and was supposed to have about 25,000 members in 1845, with branches in twenty-six towns, but was crushed after 1849 (see Weitling 1844); and Young Switzerland. It suffered a schism in 1837, when many of the communist members, chiefly followers of Wilhelm Weitling, departed. But in 1848 it committed itself, at a meeting in Berlin, to the principle of abolishing private property in land and the means of production, credit and transportation. In Poland the Templars, founded in 1822, aimed to restore national independence. Insurrections and revolutionary agitation aiming at land reform as well as national independence were common throughout this period, notably in 1830 against Russia, in 1846 against Austria, in 1848 against Prussia, and in 1863 again against Russia (Edwards 1865; Walicki 1989). A 'Young Hungary' group suffused with French political principles emerged in 1846, with a Society for Equality emerging to lead the left-wing and republican club movement in 1848. Hungary thereafter instigated a powerful nationalist resistance movement against Austria led by Louis Kossuth (1802–94) which succeeded in emancipating the Jews and peasants, and sweeping away most of the vestiges of feudalism in the name of liberal constitutionalism (Deak 1979; Deme 1976).

France

From the early years of the Revolution the notion that the *ancien régime* had been felled by a vast conspiracy of enlightened 'Illuminati' of deist or freethinking, cosmopolitan and republican *philosophes* dedicated to 'the threefold aim of the wise – truth, freedom, and virtue' (Frost 1876, 1, p. 26), had been a popular one among the Revolution's opponents (notably Barruel 1798). That such a society, led by Adam Weishaupt, existed, and included Freemasons who opposed both despotism and priestcraft, is undisputed. (See generally Frost 1876; Heckethorn 1875; Lepper 1932; Vivian 1927.) But while little credence can be attached today to such claims respecting its role in the Revolution itself, genuine conspiracies against the Directory, Napoleon and the Restoration are well documented. These included groups driven underground by the prohibition on public political activity, like the United Patriots; the Society for the New Reform of France; the Society of the Friends of the People, which was active in the insurrection of 1830; and its successor, the Union of the Rights of Man, which staged an uprising in 1834, from which emerged the Society of the Families. A secret society known as the Friends of Truth was founded about 1818–20 as a political Masonic lodge. Some of its members became the nucleus of French Carbonarism, or *Charbonnerie* (charcoal-burners, so-called for the disguise they assumed as political refugees), which was anti-clerical and hostile to the *émigrés*, and whose main aim was the overthrow of the Bourbons (Johnston 1904). Its leading light was Armand Bazard, later a prominent Saint-Simonist.

For nineteenth-century revolutionaries the prototype of this form of conspiratorial insurrection, as well as of the type of professional revolutionary, selflessly and wholeheartedly devoted to the incandescent renewal of social virtue through violence, was François-Noël or 'Gracchus' Babeuf's abortive plot of 1796. Immortalised in the Babouvist and later Carbonarist leader Philippe-Michel Buonarroti's *History of Babeuf's Conspiracy* (1828), this aimed to overthrow the Directory, to return to the more democratic constitution of 1793, and to establish collective property in land within one generation by abolishing inheritance and establishing a community of goods via an equal division of the land (to about fourteen acres per family). Communal authorities were to supervise elected officials within each trade, and to regulate the system of production and distribution. Private employment and commerce were to be abolished, with the national government rectifying inequalities between regions (Bax 1911, pp. 125–34; Lehning 1956; Rose 1978; Thomson 1947). Babeuf (1760–97), whose first aim was to kill the five members of the Directorate, famously claimed at his trial that 'All means are legitimate against tyrants.' Buonarroti, the friend of Robespierre, agreed that 'No means are criminal which are employed to obtain a sacred end'

(Laqueur 1977, p. 23). (Critics accused them of going 'all lengths in blood, in order to go all lengths in levelling', Southey 1856, IV, p. 180.) Babeuf's scheme is sometimes described as aiming at a dictatorship as such, thus, after Robespierre, establishing the prototype of a permanent revolutionary dictatorship. Some have added that 'the absence of anything specifically popular was precisely what made it into a terrorism' (Laqueur 1977, p. 23). More detailed studies, however, emphasise the merely provisional character of the dictatorship, which was to last no longer than three months, and to be replaced by mass democracy and popular accountability, including participation by women. Thus it has been construed as not only dissimilar to the later schemes of Blanqui and Lenin, but in fact a democratic reaction *against* Jacobinical dictatorship, even 'one of the major breakthroughs in democratic theory that occurred during the revolutionary epoch in Europe' (Birchall 1997, p. 155; Rose 1978, pp. 218, 342). Nonetheless such a dictatorship of *hommes sages* 'qui sont embrasés de l'amour de l'égalité et ont le courage de se dévouer pour en assurer l'établissement' (Lehning 1956, pp. 115–16), could also be construed as existing *en permanence*, an idea Buonarroti would advocate throughout his life (Lehning 1956, p. 114). Opponents of such ideas view him as personifying the idea of 'totalitarian democracy', where the search for a perfect social order and the implementation of one true political scheme justifies practically any means (Talmon 1960, pp. 1–3, 167–248).

Doubtless Babeuf and Buonarroti created the model of the secret revolutionary organisation, rather than a proletarian party of the later Marxist type. Here the conspiracy was centralised at the top, but composed of many small groups, usually unknown to each other. This model was utilised by the Society of the Families, founded in July 1834, which was formed on a basic unit of only six members, called a family, five or six of these forming a section, and two or three sections a quarter, the chief of whom received orders from a committee of direction. Similarly its successor, formed in 1836, the Society of the Seasons, consisted of cohorts based on gradations of a Week (the lowest), with seven members composing a Month (of four weeks), three Months making a Season (88 members), and four Seasons a Year, with a triumvirate of leaders at the top. Its aim was not merely the overthrow of the monarchy; equally to be 'exterminated' were 'the rich, who constitute an aristocracy as devouring as the first', the hereditary nobility abolished in 1830 (Hodde 1864, p. 255) (but Hodde was a police spy whose veracity has been challenged).

This movement, which had some 900 members by 1839, consisted of Armand Barbès, Martin Bernard, and Babeuf's most famous successor, Auguste Blanqui (1805–81), leader of the movement known as Blanquism, and often proclaimed as the founder of the theory of post-revolutionary proletarian dictatorship associated with Marx and later Bolshevism (Postgate 1926, p. 35). (But Spitzer 1957, p. 176, denies that Blanqui ever used the phrase, the 'dictatorship of the proletariat', and views his conception of dictatorship as closer to Jacobinism than Marxism. For details of Marx's most Blanquist phase see Marx and Engels 1978a, pp. 277–87. The issue is analysed in Lattek 2006, ch. 3.) Blanqui commenced his career as an anti-Bourbon Carbonarist, but achieved fame by transmitting the tactics of revolutionary republicanism to socialism, which before 1840 was often apolitical and explicitly anti-revolutionary. The Blanquists emerged as a student society in the Second Empire, became a political faction during the Commune, languished in British exile, then regrouped in opposition to Gambetta's middle-class republicanism in the 1880s (Hutton 1981; Spitzer 1957). Their conception of revolution was essentially Jacobin, and united fervently patriotic nationalist, anti-clerical, democratic and republican aspirations. Some have emphasised that this was based on a rudimentary theory of class struggle in which the 'workers' rather than merely the poor or the 'people', would play a key role. Others, however, have contended that the masses were to be led by a disinterested elite group of conspirators constituted out of alienated elements in modern urban society, hence chiefly those Parisians who were the 'people' of Jacobin myth, rather than the industrial proletariat (Spitzer 1957, pp. 162–6). After the revolution priests, aristocrats and other enemies were to be expelled from the country, the army replaced by a national militia, and the magistracy by universal trial by jury. Private property would be retained initially, but Blanqui hoped that, after universal education, it would be supplanted by communism. The Blanquists staged one abortive insurrection in May 1839, were active in 1848, and briefly mounted another uprising in 1870.

Italy

In Italy, Spain, Piedmont and France, the early nineteenth century witnessed the rapid development of the professional underground revolutionary organisation known as the Carbonari. They are first recorded at Naples in 1807 (see Mariel 1971, and for France, Spitzer 1971). Dedicated to overthrowing Napoleonic rule, then, in France, to opposing the Bourbon restoration, the Carbonari helped to develop the idea of the morally pure revolutionary type, bound together by secret oaths (some swearing, blind-folded, dagger in hand, to wash in the blood of kings), with initiation rites and elaborate rituals akin to those of Freemasonry and the Illuminati, in this case without opposing Christianity (Bertoldi 1821, p. 22; Hobsbawm 1959, pp. 150–74). The doctrines, ritual and organisation of the Carbonari assumed many forms, but the society was generally divided into two grades, Apprentices and Masters. The assassination of traitors in their own ranks, but not necessarily their enemies elsewhere, was obligatory. Members were bound to support the principles of liberty, equality and progress, and to overthrow the rulers of Italy. They also policed their own internal morals, frowning on gambling, dissoluteness, marital infidelity and drunkenness, any of which could bring about a trial before a jury of the 'Good Cousins', and possible expulsion. The Carbonari helped to engineer revolutions in 1820–1, when 20,000 men invaded Naples, and in 1831 when linkages were established with conspirators in Germany and elsewhere; this sustained the revolutionary idea through some of its darkest days. Their aims were broadly republican, but this included a liberal or constitutional monarchy, which might in turn be more centralised, Saint-Simonian or more federalist (Spitzer 1971, p. 275). In their most theoretical exposition, the proposed Ausonian Republic, Italy was to be divided into twenty-one provinces, each with a local assembly, the whole to be ruled by two kings elected for twenty-one years (Heckethorn 1875, II, pp. 107–8).

Most of the leading Italian revolutionaries of the period were linked to this movement, which was extended to France around 1820. The most impor-tant nationalist insurgent of the early period, Giuseppe Mazzini (1805–72), began his insurrectionary life as a Carbonaro, was linked to Buonarroti in the years 1830–3, and founded Young Italy in 1831. Under the twin principles of 'Progress and Duty', this aimed to overthrow Austrian rule in Venice and Milan, unite Italy under a republic, and create a revolutionary cohort capable of bringing this about (see Hales 1956; Lehning 1956; Lovett 1982). Mazzini succeeded in establishing a short-lived republic at Rome in 1848 (Orsini was one of its deputies), was active in British exile, notably on the Central Committee of European Democracy (with Ledru-Rollin and Ruge), and remained a vocal symbol of European nationalism for some two decades thereafter. He thus established Italy as what Greece had been to the generation of Byron. Thereafter he was supplanted by his leading disciple, Giuseppe Garibaldi (1807–82), whose victorious campaign in 1860 gained Naples and Sicily for the new Kingdom of Italy (Mazzini 1861, pp. 31–47).

Germany

In Germany anti-Napoleonic resistance also gave rise to a variety of secret organisations, such as the Union of Virtue (*Tugendbund*), established in 1812 at the behest of the Prussian prime minister, Stein, and later linked to the *Burschenschaften*, or university student organisations. Here the Carbonari were also active, and established the Totenbund, or Band of Death, which was revealed in 1849 as aiming to rid the world of tyrants. A 'League of Exiles' was formed by Germans in 1834, but split and formed the League of the Just in 1836, which was inspired by Étienne Cabet and Wilhelm Weitling, and included amongst its members a number of revolutionaries prominent during the 1848 Revolution, notably Auguste Willich and Karl Schapper (Lattek 2006). Composed of cells of five to ten persons, its members used mystic signs and passwords, and each had a secret military name. The Communist League, which lasted from June 1847 until 1852, aimed chiefly to overthrow the bourgeoisie, and introduce a classless society in which private property had been abolished. It abjured the traditional rituals, secret oaths and small cell basis of the secret societies in favour of an openly democratic and centralised organisation, a scheme that would remain largely unchanged through the Bolshevik period. Its goals are described elsewhere in this volume. Before 1848 the chief theoretician of these groups was the German tailor Wilhelm Weitling (1808–71), who argued for a Christian communist vision of recapturing a lost stage of natural equality by the abolition of private property and implementation of direct democracy (see Wittke 1950).

Russia

Hints of revolutionary sentiment appear in Russia as early as 1790, with the publication of Radishchev's *A Journey from St. Petersburg to Moscow*, which has been hailed as 'the first programme of Russian political democracy' (Yarmolinsky 1957, p. 13; Venturi 1960). After 1815 a number of Masonic and literary societies were founded. The earliest underground political organisation was the Society of the True and Faithful Sons of the Fatherland, or Union of Salvation, founded in 1816, which briefly contemplated regicide. Another secret society, the Union of Welfare, followed in 1818, which aimed at spreading enlightenment and the 'true rules of morality', and was bound by quasi-Masonic oaths and rituals (Von Rosen 1872). By 1820 various Polish revolutionary societies had been formed. An early republican thinker of note, associated with the group known as the Decembrists, was Colonel Pavel Pestel. He wedded ideas of representative government based on universal suffrage to a proto- or quasi-totalitarian state which was to rely on a powerful clergy and secret police. Serfdom was to be abolished, half the land nationalised, public morals regulated and private associations, as well as drinking and card-playing, banned (Yarmolinsky 1957, p. 27). Pestel's plottings were soon linked to the Society of United Sclavonians, or Slavs, founded in 1820, with members in many noble families, which from philanthropic origins came to aim at compelling the Tsar to accept a liberal constitution, and mustered 3,000 troops for a short-lived rebellion in 1822. The Decembrists attempted a further *coup* in 1825; thereafter most were exiled to Siberia.

From this point onwards, despite a variety of populist and Jacobin currents of thought, radicalism and socialism were virtually inseparable in Russia (Gombin 1978, p. 44). In the 1830s and 1840s these trends were often linked to Alexander Herzen (1812–70), who was attracted by Hegel's analytic framework as well as the writings of communalist ideas of Fourier, Proudhon's anti-authoritarianism and Saint-Simon's renovated Christianity. Like many anarchists, Herzen's ultimate aim was the reinforcement of 'natural' voluntary associations, notably the *mir* (for peasants) and the *artel* (for artisans), in which external authority imposed upon the individual could be limited. Republicanism, in his view, could only mean 'freedom of conscience, local autonomy, federalism, the inviolability of the individual' (Gombin 1978, p. 53). While united by a desire to abolish serfdom, Russian radicalism was divided into Slavophile and Westernist factions, the latter including Herzen and Vissarion Belinsky. The revolutions of 1848 promoted socialist ideas, but resulted in the exile of a number of prominent dissidents, including Michael Bakunin, and Herzen, who continued to promote revolutionary sentiment through his journal *Kolokol* (*The Bell*, begun in 1857).

This attracted a new generation of agitators, such as Nikolai Chernyshevskii, who promoted a form of socialism based on loosely federated voluntary associations. The Emancipation of the Serfs in 1861 failed to reduce the servitude of the peasantry to the landlords, and these radicals dismissed liberal proposals for a *laisser-faire* economy and constitutional monarchy, turning instead to republican and revolutionary principles. Such views were startlingly expressed in the pamphlet, *Young Russia* (1862), which was later described as 'the first Bolshevik document' in Russian history. It called for a federal republic, distribution of the land among peasant communes, the emancipation of women, marriage and the family, the socialisation of factories under elected managers and the closure of monasteries (Yarmolinsky 1957, p. 113). One of its consequences was the popularisation of the movement mis-named Nihilism, which was in fact a critical realist, or naturalist and pragmatist critique of existing Russian conditions, especially as linked to Dmitry Pisarev, whose ideas were popularised as 'Nihilist' in Turgenev's *Fathers and Sons* (1862). Thereafter the term was widely adopted to connote a rejection of *bourgeois* opinions of marriage, religion and respectability, thus symbolising an intellectual fashion more than a political movement.

Though often ranked amongst the Nihilists or Terrorists, the Russian anarchist Michael Bakunin (1814–76) was in fact a professional revolutionary first and foremost, the epitome, in histories of anarchism, of the 'destructive urge', or belief in revolutionary action as a cathartic 'purifying and regenerative force' (Woodcock 1970, pp. 134, 162). For Bakunin rebellion would signal the apocalypse of the institutions of the old world, with the entire state, including the army, courts, civil service and police, destroyed, and all archives and official documents burned. Yet it would simultaneously embody a creative will, born of an instinctive 'sentiment of rebellion, this satanic pride, which spurns subjection to any master whatsoever' (Maximoff 1964, p. 380). While provoked by a secret elite organisation, it would produce a 'collective dictatorship . . . free of any self-interest, vainglory and ambition, for it is anonymous and unseen, and does not reward any of the members that compose the group' (Bakunin 1973, p. 193). Revolution would thus occur when the right psychological circumstances, rather than, as for Marx, the economic, combined (Bakunin, 1990). Bakunin's *Principles of Revolution* (1869) spelled out the variety of forms – 'poison, the knife, the rope, etc.' – which could be utilised to meet the end of human liberation (see Pyziur 1968). Bakunin acknowledged that many would die in any popular uprising, and counselled the death penalty for all who interfered 'with the activity of the revolutionary communes' (quoted in Pyziur 1968, pp. 108–9). Yet he also stressed that if rebellion was by nature 'spontaneous, chaotic, and ruthless', and always presupposed 'a vast destruction of property' (quoted in Maximoff 1964, p. 380), the aim of revolutionary violence was to 'attack things and relationships, destroy property and the state. Then there is no need to destroy men' (Bakunin 1971, p. 151). When victory was certain some measure of humanity could be shown to former foes, now to be recognised as 'brothers' (Maximoff 1964, p. 377).

The idea that revolutionaries should be wholly devoted to the task of destruction was outlined in the most famous tract of its type of this period. Composed for a possibly non-existent group linked to Sergei Nechayev, the 'Revolutionary Catechism' built on Bakuninist foundations, if it was not actually written by Bakunin (Carr 1961, p. 394; Laqueur 1979, pp. 68–72; Pyziur 1968, p. 91). It described the prototypical insurrectionist as withdrawn, hard, asocial and wedded solely and passionately to the struggle and its aims, which included the complete destruction of the institutions and structures of the old society. The 'Catechism' proposed to divide the upper class of Russian society into six categories, the first of which consisted of persons to be executed immediately, ranked according to their 'relative iniquities' (Woodcock 1970, p. 160). Nechayev was reputed to have founded the Nihilist society in early 1869, basing it on circles of five members, a certain number of which constituted a section, the society itself being directed by a committee which vested in itself the power of inflicting the death penalty. It circulated printed incitements to revolt in late 1874, but many arrests followed. Its social and political programme, dismissed by Marx as 'an excellent example of barracks communism', included the central supervision of production by 'the Committee', obligatory physical labour, mandatory communal dining and sleeping arrangements, and the abolition of marriage and all other forms of private contract (Yarmolinsky 1957, p. 163).

Britain

In Britain the 1790s and first half of the nineteenth century witnessed a variety of attempts at armed uprising (see Dinwiddy 1992a; Royle 2000; Thomis and Holt 1977). During the 1790s various organisations emerged as shadow revolutionary groups acting under the cover of legitimate parliamentary reform organisations, notably the London Corresponding Society, and seeking the same end of 'equal political representation' and parliamentary reform. But this could mask both republicanism and any number of possible social reforms, which were now more openly discussed than had been the case during the debate over the principles of Paine's *Rights of Man* in the early 1790s (see Wells 1986). An early group was the United Britons, based in London, who were succeeded by the United Englishmen, founded in April 1797, who adopted a system of branches, called Baronial,

County and Provincial Committees, principally centred in the Midlands, with members bound by a secret oath. North of the border the United Scotsmen fulfilled a similar role from 1797, taking over the earlier Society of the Friends of the People. The naval mutinies of 1797 had a political dimension, even if goals were rarely stated. Growing out of the United Britons and other organisations was the plot known as the Despard Conspiracy (1803), which involved a plan to assassinate the King and leading members of the government (Conner 2000; Jay 2004; Wells 1986, p. 221).

The United Irishmen, who played a prominent role in the rebellion of 1798, were the most important association of this type (see Curtin 1994; Madden 1858). Founded in Belfast in October 1791, this was not initially a revolutionary group, but aimed at 'an impartial and adequate representation of the Irish nation in parliament'. As we have seen, one of their leaders, Wolfe Tone, abjured any interest in abstract principles, and claimed that he sought not a republic, but the independence of the Irish nation; by 1796, however, Tone was committed to seeking French assistance for establishing a republic. Contemporary accounts suggest that despite many internal disagreements other members also were moving gradually towards both revolutionism and republicanism in the mid 1790s (e.g. O'Connor *et al.* 1798, p. 3). Some United Irishmen, like Robert Emmet's father, also derived inspiration from the classical republics (O'Donoghue 1902, p. 21). By 1795 the United Irish had formed a pyramid-type organisation with many small local societies based on groups of twelve persons living in the same neighbourhood. Five local societies constituted a lower baronial committee, and delegates from ten such committees formed an upper baronial committee. Above these were county and provincial committees, with a national executive at the apex. It was rumoured to have had a Committee of Assassination, though this was also vehemently denied. (By Arthur O'Connor *et al.* 1798, p. 8, for example, who asserted that the doctrine was 'frequently and fervently reprobated'. But doubt has also been placed on such assertions; see Lecky 1913, IV, pp. 80–1.) Citing the parallel of the 'Glorious Revolution' of 1688, when English revolutionaries had called upon a foreign republic to help release them from despotism, the United Irish negotiated with the French Directory through Lord Edward Fitzgerald, and a general plan of insurrection was hatched by early 1798. This resulted in the landing at Bantry Bay of French troops in 1798, who were, however, speedily routed. A further attempt at uprising, led by Robert Emmett in 1803, met with an equally dismal result (O'Donoghue 1902, pp. 121–77).

233

In the post-war period another plot, which wedded millenarianism and radical politics grew out of the land reform movement associated with Thomas Spence (see Chase 1988; McCalman 1988; Poole 2000). This involved a faction in the London Corresponding Society, led by Thomas Evans, who had been associated with the United Englishmen and United Britons, which aimed at land nationalisation and the parish management of agriculture, and which eventually became the Society of Spencean Philanthropists. It concocted the so-called Cato Street Conspiracy (1820) led by Arthur Thistlewood, which sought to provoke a general uprising in London by assassinating the Cabinet at a dinner (D. Johnson 1974). A lesser-known Spencean uprising was led by the eccentric John Nichols Tom, aka Count Moses Rothschild, aka Sir William Courtenay. In 1838, prophet-like, Tom proclaimed that he had descended from heaven, and promised to 'annihilate for ever the tithes, taxation upon all the shopkeepers and productive classes, also upon knowledge', primogeniture, placemen and slavery (*A Canterbury Tale* 1888, p. 3). He led to disaster a small band, brandishing poles on which was impaled a loaf of bread, and seeking to distribute food, and eventually land, to the poor (Courtney 1834; Rogers 1962). Generally disorganised, local, and economic in nature, was the machine-breaking campaign led by the so-called Luddites, who were particularly active between 1811 and 1816, and also formed secret organisations with illegal oath-taking (see Thomis 1972). Fuelled by poverty, but invoking a Scottish republican tradition which stretched back to 1792 and beyond, as well as recent developments in Spain, a short-lived uprising took place in Scotland in 1820 (Ellis and A'Ghobhainn 1970). Agricultural riots, often aimed at lowering bread prices, were not uncommon (Peacock 1965). The movement associated with 'Captain Swing', which aimed at the destruction of agricultural equipment and maintenance of rural wages in 1830, was similarly neither political in nature nor revolutionary in aim, though republicans were reputed to be amongst its ranks, and the French Revolution of that year clearly encouraged it (Hobsbawm and Rudé 1973).

After the 1830s trade unionism also developed a much more militant strategy in the form of proposals for a general strike, first formulated by William Benbow (Prothero 1974). The more revolutionary aspects of Spencean agrarianism were taken up by a number of Chartists, notably George Julian Harney. The Chartists also hatched a variety of schemes for violent insurrection, including a plan for burning Newcastle (Devyr 1882, pp. 184–211), a plot to seize Dumbarton Castle and, most famously, the Newport Uprising of 1839, when an attempt to rescue Henry Vincent from jail brought thousands of Chartists to converge on the small Welsh town of Newport, only to suffer rapid defeat (*The Chartist Riots at Newport* 1889; Jones 1985). Chartism in 1848 also became markedly more internationalist with the formation in the mid-1840s of the Fraternal Democrats and the Democratic Friends of All Nations, organisations that linked the Chartists to various European radicals (Lattek 1988, pp. 259–82). At the end of this period a Marxist revolutionary movement also emerged (Kendall 1969, pp. 3–83).

4 From tyrannicide to terrorism

The politics of assassination and individual violence

Historians have been unable to agree on any meaningful definition of 'terrorism', one person's 'terrorist', notoriously, being another's freedom fighter, with the use (or threat thereof) of systematic violence, usually murder and destruction, outside of formally declared wars, to achieve revolutionary ends being the common denominator.[6] But twentieth-century terrorism is usually recognised to be of a very different character from that of the preceding century in terms of both its methods and aims (general accounts include: Ford 1985; Hyams 1974; Parry 1976; Paul 1951 and Wilkinson 1974). Most nineteenth-century movements which involved or promoted acts of individual violence were adjuncts to or supportive of wider insurrectionary or revolutionary movements aimed at overthrowing despots like the Russian tsar, or usurpers like Louis Napoleon. Their anti-imperial component, central in the twentieth century, was much less important until the end of this period, with the notable exceptions of Ireland and India. (Latin and South American revolutionary movements rarely employed such tactics.) We cannot here consider state-sanctioned assassination of political opponents, which has always been common, as has been torture, which can also be considered as 'terrorist'. Not examined here, either, is state terrorism, sometimes termed 'enforcement' or 'repressive' terrorism, as opposed to 'agitational' or 'revolutionary' terrorism, such as that first initiated by Robespierre's Committee of Public Safety as the 'Reign of Terror' (1793–4), where some 17,000–40,000 people were directly executed, among them

---

6 On some definitional problems see Wardlaw 1982, pp. 3–18. Wardlaw calls 'political terrorism' 'the use, or threat of use, of violence by an individual or group, whether acting for or in opposition to established authority, when such action is designed to create extreme anxiety and/or fear-inducing effects in a target group larger than the immediate victims with the purpose of coercing that group into acceding to the political demands of the perpetrators' (p. 16).

1,158 nobles, though thousands more died of disease and neglect. This introduced the vocabulary of 'terrorism' into political language (first evidently positively by the Jacobins, then as a term of abuse, by *c.*1795), which was then extended to other regimes, like Francia's in Paraguay (see Robertson and Robertson 1839). Nor can we treat the 'normal' functioning of autocracies in which thousands may lose their lives by political repression, as in tsarist Russia, where women could be beaten to death with the knout for 'sedition', or the 'normal' mistreatment of native populations. The notion that imperial rule was as such proto-totalitarian because it institutionalised brutality on a massive scale, kept large populations *in terrorem* as a substitute for quartering much larger bodies of troops upon them, and enforced draconian penalties for minor but 'seditious' criticisms of such rule, cannot be examined here. (But the 'Negro Code' of the late seventeenth-century French, with its *routine* beatings, mutilations and torture of virtually the entire subject population, and the astonishingly cruel Belgian policy towards the Congolese in King Leopold's late nineteenth-century slave state – see Morel 1906 – were clearly 'terrorism' personified, and belong in any account of the pre-history of twentieth-century totalitarianism.) We need also to distinguish between political assassination as a means of regime change, which has been extremely common, even the norm, throughout history (from Commodus to Constantine the Great, twenty-seven out of thirty-six Roman emperors were assassinated), and the justification of the overthrow of tyrants in the name of the common good, or tyrannicide.

Nineteenth-century terrorists often took as their point of departure much older historical justifications for the assassination of tyrants by private individuals in the name of the common good. This doctrine has a lengthy pedigree which stretches back to the ancient world (see Laqueur 1979, pp. 10–46). In classical Greece, Xenophon composed a dialogue on tyranny which honoured the slayer of despots. At Rome, Cicero and Seneca, among others, lauded the killing of usurpers. An extreme anti-Roman party of Zealots engaged in individual murder and destruction as part of the Jewish resistance. Caesar was the most famous victim of justifiable tyrannicide in antiquity, Henry IV, killed by Ravaillac in 1610, of the early modern epoch. During the Middle Ages the doctrine continued that tyrants lacking a legitimate title might be killed, though legitimate rulers who became despots were a much more difficult case (Jaszi and Lewis 1957). The Renaissance and early modern period expressed such doctrines in works such as George Buchanan's *De Jure Regni apud Scotos* (*c.*1568–9), the *Vindiciae contra*

Tyrannos (*c.*1574–6) and Mariana's *De Rege et Regis Institutione* (1599). These insisted that if the contract between king and people upon which legitimate rule rested were violated the king could be removed. Amongst many mid-seventeenth-century British works were John Milton's *The Tenure of Kings and Magistrates* (written 1649), and *Killing No Murder* (1657). The French Revolution witnessed the slaying of Jean-Paul Marat by Charlotte Corday – the first modern instance, perhaps, of the use of individual 'terrorism' against state terror, and the renewed justification by Babeuf's supporters that 'Those who usurp sovereignty ought to be put to death by free men . . . The people shall take no rest until after the destruction of the tyrannical government' (Jaszi and Lewis 1957, p. 128). This was the point, thus, at which older doctrines of regicide gave way before more modern ideals of individual terror, though there would still be many attempts on European sovereigns (notably that by the Corsican Fieschi on Louis Philippe in 1835) prior to the revolutions of 1848.

In Germany philosophical justifications of terrorism have been claimed to have originated as early as 1842, when Edgar Bauer extended the method of Hegelian criticism to propose the revolutionary overthrow of the existing social and political system.[7] Romantic justifications for assassination certainly occur as early as Karl Ludwig Sand's killing of August von Kotzebue at Jena in 1819, ostensibly for being a Russian spy. The use of terror as an instrument of insurrection was considered by the League of the Just, which later became the Communist League, and was involved in Blanqui's 1838 uprising in Paris. It formally examined the proposition that individual terror might be a useful tactic in the form of Wilhelm Weitling's suggestion that 20,000 thieves and murderers could form a useful revolutionary vanguard, only to reject the idea.

Such threats palled, however, besides the theses of another German revolutionary. It was Karl Heinzen (1809–80) who provided what has been termed the first 'full-fledged doctrine of modern terrorism' (Laqueur 1977, p. 26). This took the form of a defence, in a tract entitled *Der Mord* (Murder), originally published in 1849, not merely of tyrannicide as 'the chief means of historical progress' (Wittke 1945, p. 73), but of the murder of hundreds and even thousands, at any time or place, in the higher interests of humanity. If 'the destruction of the life of another' was always 'unjust and

---

7 Luft 2006, pp. 136–65; though this account does not distinguish adequately between revolutionary violence and 'terrorism', nor sufficiently clarify whether Bauer proposed violence against possessors of state and religious power, or a much wider body of 'innocents'.

barbarous', Heinzen contended that 'If one man is permitted to murder, all must be permitted to do so.' No distinction could be drawn between war, insurrection, assassination and murder. Calculating the 'murder register of history', Heinzen estimated that the most immoral killing had been performed in the name of Christianity. In round numbers, he thought, some two thousand million people had died in the name of religion; by contrast, the number of individual murders throughout human history was minute. The leading murderers of the present day were the three great emperors of Prussia, Austro-Hungary and Russia, and the Pope; their collective message, thought Heinzen, was that 'We murder in order to rule, as you must murder to become free.' Moreover, Heinzen asserted, 'murder in the most colossal dimensions has been and still is the chief means of historical development'. Used against despots, it could never be a crime, but was only self-defence (Heinzen 1881, pp. 1–2, 5, 8, 10, 15, 24). Considering that 'The safety of despots rests wholly on the preponderance of their means of destruction', Heinzen considered 'the greatest benefactor of mankind' to be 'he who makes it possible for a few men to wipe out thousands' (Heinzen 1881, p. 24; Laqueur 1979, p. 59). He applauded every new technical means of achieving these ends, including the use of Congreve rockets, mines and poison gas capable of destroying entire cities at once. Naturally he lauded Orsini extravagantly in 1858, and reprinted *Der Mord* on the occasion.

Various efforts to associate Marx with these ideals were made (e.g. Schaack 1889, pp. 18–19). But Marx's comment on the Fenian explosion at Clerkenwell was that 'Secret, melodramatic conspiracies of this kind are, in general, more or less doomed to failure', with Engels replying that 'it is the misfortune of all conspiracies that they lead to such acts of folly' (Marx and Engels 1987, pp. 501, 505). (In 1882 Engels did, however, concede to Eduard Bernstein that while an Irish uprising did not have the '*remotest prospect of success*', 'the lurking presence of armed Fenian conspirators' might actually aid the 'only recourse' of 'the constitutional method of gradual conquest'; Marx and Engels 1993a, pp. 287–8.) The one real point at which an exception was admitted was Russia, about which Engels, writing to Vera Zasulich in 1885, said that 'It is one of those special cases where it is possible for a handful of men to *effect* a revolution ... if ever Blanquism, the fantasy of subverting the whole of a society by a small band of conspirators, had any rational foundation, it would assuredly be in St Petersburg, (Marx and Engels 1993b, p. 280). Marxism never adopted terror as a central aspect of its strategy, though mass executions (some two million by 1925) characterised the Bolshevik Revolution, heralding much greater blood-letting later in the twentieth century.

In Britain in the 1850s this controversy crystallised around the issue of the illegitimate nature of the rule of Louis Napoleon after his 1851 *coup d'état*, and specifically Orsini's attempt to kill Napoleon III on 14 January 1858. As the debate about justifiable tyrannicide grew, the secularist George Jacob Holyoake (who had helped to test Orsini's bombs) reprinted a variety of seventeenth-century tracts on the subject. A leading radical lawyer, Thomas Allsop, privately offered £100 to any would-be assassin, and helped to provide Orsini with rudimentary bomb-making equipment (Holyoake 1905, p. 41). In the best-known British defence of Orsini – whose own inspiration originally came from Tacitus (Orsini, 1857, p. 23; Packe 1957) – by W. E. Adams, entitled *Tyrannicide: Is It Justifiable?* (1858), it was asserted that

> Every moment of oppression is a state of war; every forcible denial of right is a *casus belli*. War, then, prevails wherever a despot reigns or a people is enslaved; hostilities can be commenced at any moment, whenever the people has the strength of fortitude and the hope of success; neither truce nor treaty is broken. Revolution is the ambuscade of the people. (Adams 1858, p. 6)

Young Italy was also accused of assassinations, notably of Count Rossi, but later vindicated of the charge (Frost 1876, II, p. 180). Mazzini, who had been accused of plotting to kill the Austrian emperor in 1825, and of another assassination in 1833 (Mazzini 1864, I, p. 224), now reconsidered the 'theory of the dagger' in an open letter to Orsini (a member of Young Italy). But he rejected the idea.

Systematic terrorism

Systematic or strategic terrorism as such is a product of the second half of the nineteenth century. While there were relatively small groups active in many countries, including the Ku Klux Klan in the American South, the Molly Maguires in the US labour movement, Poles, Indians, Spaniards and Armenians, the principal groups of this period were in Russia and Ireland.

Russia

Russian terrorism was intimately interwoven with anarchist doctrine, but this does not as such explain its character. Much terrorist activity in this period was directly linked to revolutionary movements, but as a leading anar-chist, Sergius Stepniak noted, it was because revolution in Russia became regarded as 'absolutely impossible' that terrorism emerged as a strategy (Zenker 1898, p. 121). Promoted by intellectuals when a peasant uprising seemed unlikely, and in the face of severe repression (Hardy 1987, p. 161), it was thus, as a modern historian puts it, 'with the *downturn* in revolutionary expectations after 1860 that the sense of separation from the mass clientele became most acute and that terrorist philosophy, in the modern sense, was born' (Rubinstein 1987, p. 145).

The most famous Russian group to advocate this strategy was Narodnaya Volya, which emerged from the populist Land and Liberty party (Seth 1966). Relatively indifferent to the form of centralised government, it aimed at the revival of the *mir*, or peasant commune, as the foundation of Russian justice and freedom. Its activities from January 1878 to March 1881 included the shooting of the governor-general of St Petersburg by Vera Zasulich, the killing of the head of the tsarist secret police, General Mezentsev, in August 1878, and most famously, the assassination of Tsar Alexander II himself on 1 March 1881. But it also justified the killing of

the most dangerous personages in the government... punishing... the most noted cases of oppression and arbitrariness on the part of the government, administration, and so on... The goal is to break the spell of governmental omnipotence, to provide uninterrupted evidence of the possibility of a struggle against the government, in such a manner as to raise the revolutionary spirit of the people (Naimark 1983, p. 13)

In the late 1880s Narodnaya Volya and social democratic thought began to merge, and the advocacy of terrorism became linked increasingly with organising the working class for socialist ends (Venturi 1960, pp. 700–2). Some Narodniki in this period, such as Abram Bakh, now dismissed terror as ineffectual, counterproductive and incompatible with true revolutionary principles (Naimark 1983, p. 230). But such views did not predominate.

A second wave of Russian terrorism followed the founding of the Social Revolutionary Party, commencing with the assassination of the Minister of the Interior, Sipyagin, in 1902, rising to fifty-four *attentats* in 1905, eighty-two in 1906 and seventy-one in 1907, then declining. This group offered an elaborate justification of terrorism which was melded with Marxist theory, the aim of terrorist acts being not the glorification of the individual act of will, but revolutionising the masses (Geifman 1993, p. 46). The many attempts to kill a succession of tsars thus fit the classic practice of tyran-nicide, which was then extended to other members of the regime, with terrorism eventually permeating the entire anarchist and socialist left in Russia. The first person to advocate conspiratorial violence as a means of arousing and educating the masses rather than as a means of seizing power was Sergei Nechayev (1848–82), widely regarded as the practical 'founder' of modern terrorism (see Rapoport and Alexander 1989, p. 70). He is often quoted for his assertion that 'The Revolutionary knows only one science – destruction... Day and night he may have only one thought, one purpose: merciless destruction' (Jaszi and Lewis 1957, p. 136); 'For him exists only one pleasure, one consolation, one reward, one satisfaction, the reward of revolution' (Zenker 1898, p. 137). To Nechayev everything could be regarded 'as moral which helps the triumph of revolution... All soft and enervating feelings of relationship, friendship, love, gratitude, even honor, must be stifled in him by a cold passion for the revolutionary cause' (quoted in Carr 1961, p. 395). The character of Raskolnikov in Dostoevsky's *Crime and Punishment* is based upon him.

The idea that 'The urge of destruction is at the same time a creative urge' was as we have seen thereafter developed practically by the principal anarchist leader of this period, Michael Bakunin, who shared a sense of historical inevitability with Marx. Its philosophical expression was further expanded by Georges Sorel (1847–1922), whose *Reflections on Violence* was published in 1912, and was indebted to the philosopher Henri Bergson (see Arendt 1969). By the 1890s, too, there emerged what we would today term the psychological profiling of the terrorist 'type' as a special brand of deviant criminal or 'anti-authoritarian' personality, in which a lust for power, sexual impropriety and anti-Semitism could be wedded into a seemingly scientific political psychology (see Kreml 1977; Lombroso 1896). This was countered by the glorification of the Robin Hood robber type, such as the Russian Stenka Razin, as a form of what Eric Hobsbawm has described as a 'primitive rebel' or 'social bandit', where the boundaries between criminal, or brigand, as Nechayev would have it, and revolutionary, are more than uncommonly blurred (Hobsbawm 1959, 1972). It was also met with the plea of the reasonableness of violent reaction to circumstances of extreme oppression and official violence or state terror (Goldman 1969b, pp. 79–108). At the end of the century some revolutionaries, such as Plekhanov, sought to restrict the use of terror to special circumstances. Others, such as Morozov, favoured 'pure terror' as a strategy superior to both individual assassination and spontaneous uprising, because it 'punishes only those who are really responsible for the evil deed' (Laqueur 1979, p. 74), though Morozov still aimed at a socialist end-point. By 1879 the latter view came to triumph in Narodnaya Volya, and met with increasing support amongst the wider public. By 1905 such tactics were used by a wide variety of political groupings, including the Bolsheviks.

Fenianism

The most important Western European insurrectionary movement throughout the nineteenth century was that linked to Irish nationalism. While there had been many groups operating in Ireland beforehand, such as the Whiteboys and Ribbonmen (Clark and Donnelly 1983; Whelan 1996; Williams 1973), the movement known as Fenianism built upon efforts of the Young Ireland party (Davis 1987; Duffy 1896). (Modern studies of the movement include Comerford 1998; Davis 1974; Garvin 1987; Newsinger 1994; Quinlivan and Rose 1982; Walker 1969.) Young Ireland emerged in 1842 around the journal, the *Nation*. It included John Mitchel, Charles Gavan Duffy, Thomas Davis and William Smith O'Brien, and left-leaning radicals like Fintan Lalor (see Lalor 1918) in 1848, and their later followers, notably Michael Doheny. Socially some of these men were fairly conservative and backward looking, romantically viewing a lost past of peasant-proprietors as a goal to be recaptured; Mitchel also opposed the French 'Red Republicans' in 1848. Later generations of nationalists were more sympathetic to seeking some compromise between capitalism and socialism, while James Connolly, though somewhat isolated, plumped for socialism *tout court* (Connolly 1917). Like the Poles, many Irish republicans also remained Catholic, by contrast to the anti-clericism of many French and Italian revolutionaries. What united them, it has been claimed, was the fact that the movement was 'avowedly republican and separatist from the very first' (Henry 1920, p. 33).

Following the failure of O'Connell's Repeal Association in the mid-1840s, and the suppression of a brief insurrection in 1848, Fenianism commenced in the United States and Ireland in the late 1850s. It was led by two Young Ireland members exiled in Paris, James Stephens, who returned to Ireland, and John O'Mahony, who went to the US. Under the name of 'Fenian', adopted from Fianna Errinn by O'Mahony (Pigott 1883, p. 99), invoking a legendary pre-Christian warrior order, and first used around 1859, it was thereafter often associated interchangeably with the 'Irish Revolutionary Brotherhood' and then the 'Irish Republican Brotherhood' (IRB), which lasted until 1924. (A 'Constitution of the Fenian Brotherhood' is dated 1865. See *The Fenian's Progress: A Vision*, 1865, pp. 68–91.) The Fenian organisation began recruitment in 1858, held its first national meeting in 1863, and became linked with another American organisation, the Clan-na-Gael, founded in 1869, by which time it had over 200,000 members. It existed separately in Ireland from 1858, under the name of the Irish Republican Brotherhood. The Fenians were organised around a 'centre' or 'A', who was supported by nine 'Bs', or captains, each of whom had nine 'Cs' or sergeants, each leading a group of nine privates, every level knowing only those immediately closest to it. This scheme Stephens probably copied from the Blanquists and other French conspirators, though it has been alleged (in a suspect source) that Stephens' plans differed from those of continental plotters in that he sought the long-term arming of a substantial portion of the population in order to defeat the British army, rather than a brief insurrection (Rutherford 1877, I, pp. 61–2). Members were sworn to secrecy, obedience to superiors and loyalty to the goal of making Ireland a democratic republic.

Associated in the first instance with an abortive attempt to invade Canada in May 1866, and an equally fruitless uprising in Ireland in 1867, the Fenians began in the early 1870s to plot a lengthy campaign of violence, but were for a time overshadowed by both the Land League and Parnell's Home Rule movement, to whom they deferred tactically (Henry 1920, p. 34; Samuels, n.d.). A plan to seize Dublin and defend it by barricades was hatched early in the struggle (Bussy 1910, p. 26). In 1873 the Fenians adopted a resolution not to attempt another armed insurrection until support from the majority of the Irish people was evident. By 1876 O'Donovan Rossa, disgusted at Fenian inactivity, mounted his own plan of violently resisting England by raising a 'Skirmishing Fund' to strike it at 'any vulnerable point' (*The Times-Parnell Commission Speech* 1890, p. 56). He was quoted as saying 'I go in for dynamite. Tear down English cities; kill the English people. To kill and massacre and pillage is justifiable in the eyes of God and man' (Adams 1903, II, p. 565). From this time onwards the 'dynamite propaganda' or 'propaganda of terrorism' (Davitt's phrase: *The Times-Parnell Commission Speech* 1890, p. 100) was to be more closely associated with Rossa than anyone else. (Davitt himself rejected the 'dynamite theory' as 'the very abnegation of mind, the surrender of reason to rage, of judgment to blind, unthinking recklessness', *The Times-Parnell Commission Speech* 1890, p. 408; see F. Sheehy-Skeffington 1908, p. 141.)

From 1878 the Fenians supported Home Rule and the policy of obstruction in Parliament, as well as the Land War, which commenced in 1879, led by Parnell's National Land League. This coalition lasted until 1882, when Parnell broke from the Fenians and established the Irish National League. The Fenians' most notorious success in this period was the assassination of the Chief Secretary for Ireland, Lord Frederick Cavendish, and his Under-Secretary, Thomas Burke, at Phoenix Park in 1882, by a secret society led by P. J. Tynan and known as the 'Invincibles'. Most of these were Dublin members of the Fenian Brotherhood or Land League organisers. They thereafter disappeared, and this ended Parnell's flirtation with the movement (Davitt 1904, p. 363). (It has been claimed, however, that this act was the result of Land League activity, and went against official Fenian policy at the time. See O'Brion 1973, p. 122, and *History of the Irish Invincibles* 1883.) In turn, however, the 'Kilmainham Treaty' by which Parnell was released in exchange for new laws promoting tenants' rights, gave an even greater fillip to the 'dynamite' propaganda aiming to make 'landlordism . . . impossible in Ireland' (Davitt 1904, p. 427). Plots were mounted to assassinate Queen Victoria, to blow up the House of Commons and to sink British shipping using a submarine (which was actually built in New Jersey). It was consequently claimed that the Fenians 'preached and put into operation the same ferocious doctrines' as the anarchists. 'It is the duty of every Irish citizen', cried an Irish orator in 1883, 'to kill the representatives of England wherever found. The holiest incense to Heaven would be the smoke of burning London' (Adams 1903, II, pp. 563–4). But agents provocateurs also infiltrated these schemes, and it was frequently denied that such tactics 'ever had the approval of the Fenian organisation in America or elsewhere' (Sullivan 1905, p. 170). An 'Assassination Committee' was supposedly established to deal with traitors within the movement, but only one man, an agent provocateur and informer, Chief Constable Talbot, met a violent end, and the very existence of such a committee was denied by leaders like Davitt (Moody 1981, p. 511). Between 1882 and 1885 some dozen explosions occurred in Glasgow, Birmingham and Dublin, but chiefly in London, where Underground stations were a favoured target. An especially powerful bomb caused great damage in the House of Commons on 24 January 1885. And the strategy seemed to work; leading Fenians quoted with approval the *Westminster Review*'s conclusion that 'Dynamite has brought Home Rule within the scope of Practical Politics' (Denieffe 1906, p. 289).

Sinn Féin ('Ourselves Alone' – meaning self-reliance) was founded by Arthur Griffith after 1899 with the aim of promoting passive resistance to British rule, a policy soon adopted by the IRB and Clan-na-Gael. Linked to the Gaelic League (founded in 1893), which did much to support cultural separatism, it also promoted Irish cultural nationalism, linguistic and cultural de-Anglicisation, and economic self-sufficiency (Henry 1920, p. 64;

O'Hegarty 1919, pp. 14–15). Emerging as a definite political grouping in 1905, Sinn Féin became a 'strictly constitutionalist' rather than a republican movement (Henry 1920, p. 51), seeking the restitution of the constitution of 1782. Under Griffith it advocated (in imitation of Deâk) a 'Hungarian policy' of abstention from parliamentary activity as a substitute for armed conflict, which was renamed the 'Sinn Féin policy' (Griffith 1918; O'Hegarty 1919, p. 18). Soon moribund, Sinn Féin was revived when its predecessor and Fenian remnant, the IRB, linked it to physical force methods and strengthened republican sentiment (Brady 1925, p. 9; Henry 1920, p. 88; O'Hegarty 1924, p. 17). Thereafter it would play a central role in the Easter Uprising of 1916, assisted by James Connolly's Irish Socialist Republican Party (founded 1896). The physical force separatist wing of Sinn Féin then formed the nucleus of what became known as the Irish Republican Army, or IRA. It has been claimed, however, that prior to 1916 the idea of physical force occupied in separatist philosophy only 'a subordinate place. It was a line of action, but it was not the only nor the main line of action; it was, rather, a last reserve . . . The use of arms, and the right to insurrect, were maintained as a matter of principle, but rather as a means of arousing the nation's soul than as a policy' (O'Hegarty 1924, pp. 104–5).

Continental and extra-European developments

Amongst the other European terrorist writers active in this period, mention should be made of Johann Most (1846–1906), who early in 1879 established the *Freiheit* in London, with the motto: 'All measures are legitimate against tyrants.' A German Social Democrat, Most was jailed in London for praising the assassination of Alexander II, but succeeded in transferring his paper, *Freiheit*, to the USA, where it became the most influential anarchist journal of the day. Most rejected the parliamentary road to socialism, contending that conspiracies led by an elite cadre aiming at the murder of the exploiters (including policemen and spies) would arouse the latent resentment of the masses.

One of the most important developments in the anarchist tradition on the continent following the Commune emerged with the theory of 'propaganda by deed'. The phrase had been coined in 1877 by a French physician, Paul Brousse (1844–1912) (Stafford 1971; Vizetelly 1911), and was linked from the late 1870s with an Italian peasant tax rebellion led by Errico Malatesta (see Richards 1965), Carlo Cafiero and the Russian Peter Kropotkin, among others, for whom its great aim was to spread 'courage, devotion, the spirit of sacrifice' (Kropotkin 1970, p. 38). The idea came to be seen as a substitute for intellectual propaganda as such. Here, too, we see the target of violence widening from a regime and its officials to a class, and not a small hereditary order, either, but potentially all property owners or *bourgeois*. Every act of violence against the established order, in this view, came to be seen as progressive; for some, such as the French shoemaker Léon-Jules Léautheir, any *bourgeois* was a fit (i.e. morally guilty) target; when the anarchist Auguste Vaillant was executed he shouted 'Death to middle-class society, and long live Anarchism!' (Vizetelly 1911, p. 153). Class could now potentially justify blood-letting on a scale as wide as race, a point Pol Pot would so vengefully exemplify in the later twentieth century.

This acceptance of a mass category of 'legitimate' targets was an extremely important step in the transformation of tyrannicide into modern terrorism (Fleming 1982, pp. 8–28). In an anti-imperial context, this could be widened to include all members of the occupying ethnic group or nation. Amongst the most important anti-imperial struggles to develop a 'terrorist' component in this period was India. There had been isolated cases of assassination in India as far back as 1853, when Colonel Mackison, the Commissioner at Peshawur, was stabbed by a 'fanatic' from Swat who intended to prevent British invasion of his ancestral lands (Hodson 1859, p. 139). In June 1897 two British officers were murdered by members of a Hindu military society, commencing a new campaign of violence (MacMann 1935, p. 43; Steevens 1899, pp. 269–78). By the end of this period political assassination became increasingly common. Mainstream nationalists were much influenced by Mazzini, and Bengali extremists received aid from Irish-American Fenians (Argov 1967, p. 3; Bakshi 1988). In 1908 a book was published entitled *The Indian War of Independence, 1857*, wrapped in a dust jacket inscribed 'Random Papers of the Pickwick Club', which justified the killing of women and children. Bomb-*parasts*, or worshippers, now became more common. On 30 April 1908, a young Bengalee, Khudiram Bose, killed a Mr and Miss Kennedy at Muzafferpur with a bomb intended for the magistrate, Mr Kingsford. The nationalist leader Bal Gangadhar Tilak, who cited the authority of Krishna in the *Bhagavadgītā* respecting the legitimacy of assassination, was arrested for extolling the use of bombs as 'a kind of witchcraft, a charm, an amulet', and convicted of sedition (Chirol 1910, p. 55). (Indigenous religious traditions were beginning to be interwoven with violent protest; see Macdonald 1910, p. 189.) This battle was also taken to the streets of London in 1909, when Lord Morley's political secretary, Sir W. Curzon Wyllie, and Dr Lalcaca were murdered. A host of other acts occurred in India shortly thereafter, and recruitment efforts overseas were renewed.

Some political violence also occurred in Egypt, including the assassination of the Prime Minister in 1910. Here nationalism and anti-British feelings, inflamed by events like the 1864 Dinshiway incident, where four villagers were executed after the accidental death of a British officer, were linked to an Islamic justification for the killing of tyrants and 'infidels' alike (Badrawi 2000).

In the late nineteenth century political violence escalated dramatically throughout the world. The 'golden age' of political assassination began in 1870s with the killing of the liberal Spanish Prime Minister Juan Prim, by right-wing opponents. By the time of the International Anarchist Congress held in London in 1881 the justification of acts of individual violence had gained wide currency, and the fusion of the image of a card-carrying anarchist and bomb-wielding *dynamitard* accomplished. This image, which remains to this day, was especially associated with dynamite, which had been invented in 1866 and had become the fashionable weapon of choice. A multitude of attempts on leading European politicians followed; victims of the *ère des attentats* at its peak included the president of Ecuador, Gabriel Moreno (1875); the Japanese prime minister in 1878; the liberal French president Sadi Carnot (1894), killed by an anarchist for whom he was a symbol of political power, rather than individually guilty; the Shah of Persia, Nasr-ed-Din (1896), killed by a Shi'ite mystic; the Spanish Prime Minister Antonio Canovas (1897), another anarchist victim; the Empress Elizabeth of Austria (1898); and the increasingly absolutist King Umberto of Italy (1900), shot by an anarchist. The American president McKinley followed in 1901, again at anarchist hands, with the King of Serbia falling in 1903, the prime ministers of both Greece and Bulgaria in 1907, the King of Portugal in 1908, the Egyptian prime minister in 1910, the Dominican prime minister in 1911, another Spanish prime minister in 1912, the president of Mexico in 1913, and Archduke Franz Ferdinand of Austria in 1914. This list could easily be doubled (see Hyams 1969). Individual acts of violence also increasingly characterised labour disputes in France and Spain. In the United States, Alexander Berkman, with the justification, 'The more radical the treatment... the quicker the cure' (Berkman 1912, p. 7), attempted to assassinate the chairman of the Carnegie Steel Company in 1892 following a bitter strike. But there were also those, like Émile Henry, able to justify the random bombing of a café, with no particular victims in mind, because society had collectively condoned injustice (Meredith 1903, pp. 189–90). Violent tactics also entered the Suffragette movement in 1912–14, though only destruction of property (window-breaking, postbox-burning) was generally sanctioned (stones thrown through windows were wrapped in paper to minimise injury). But violence as such was not glorified, and ideological inspiration seems to have been practically non-existent (Harrison 1982; Pankhurst n.d.; Raeburn 1973). The classic age of modern political assassination, whose motives thus included religion and opposition to liberalism and democratic reform as well as radicalism, ended in 1914.

There were, however, important exceptions to this trend. Many American anarchists, such as Benjamin Tucker, contended that violence could only be legitimately justified by reformers 'when they have succeeded in hopelessly repressing all peaceful methods of agitation' (Eltzbacher 1908, p. 211). A number of other prominent anarchists, notably Tolstoy and Gandhi, and including individualists like Josiah Warren and Lysander Spooner (see Rocker 1949, p. 161), also rejected violence entirely. By the 1890s Kropotkin in particular had come to deplore the loss of innocent life, denying that revolutions were made by heroic acts, while refusing to condemn their perpetrators. But other anarchists, notably the geographer Elisée Reclus (1830–1905), less hesitatingly insisted that the ends justified the means, and that every act of violence against the existing order was good and just (Fleming, 1979). (But it has been claimed that Reclus had 'nothing in common with the folly of the dynamitard'; Zenker 1898, p. 161.) The case can certainly be made that the blood-lust increasingly encouraged by political violence – but equally imperial conquest – in this period heralded and prepared the way for the vastly greater blood-baths of the twentieth century, as both fascism and communism accepted, justified and promoted violence as a means of first obtaining and then maintaining state power, thus wedding the philosophy of individual terror to attain power to that of state terror to maintain it.

Terrorism and its justification: theory and problems

It is worth briefly considering what light these developments cast on theories of terrorism, particularly in so far as the dissection of key moral issues facilitates the framing of a usable definition of the term itself. The relationship of the classical doctrine of tyrannicide to modern 'terrorism' is complex, and beset by definitional ambiguities. The propensity to condemn any armed struggle as 'terrorist' in which war has not been declared formally undermines any more precise definitions, and hinders further clarification of the subject. But according to classical definitions neither assassination as such nor the effort to overthrow by force a despotic regime, or a force of foreign occupiers in one's own country (or another's) would necessarily qualify as 'terrorist'.

Nonetheless the subject is fraught with paradox, contradiction and moral ambiguity. Much late nineteenth-century Russian political violence was aimed at the tsar, for example, who was widely recognised as an autocrat, 'the real upholder of despotism', as Victor Hugo put it, rather than a mere 'mask' like Louis Bonaparte (Hugo 1854, p. 4). Such resistance could be and was often construed by liberals as both 'legitimate' and justifiable; even John Stuart Mill would exclaim of the attempt on Napoleon III's life in 1858 that 'What a pity the bombs of Orsini missed their mark, and left the crime-stained usurper alive!' (quoted in Morley 1917, 1, p. 55). Similarly when Count V. Plehve, the Russian minister of the interior, was killed in 1904, many liberals applauded the act (Seth 1966, p. 216). But the reign of Louis Napoleon, sometimes described as the 'first modern dictator, basing his authority directly upon a carefully controlled expression of the people's will' (Packe 1957, p. 253), rested of course on a plebiscite. To his assassin, John Wilkes Booth, who famously shouted 'sic semper tyrannis' as he fired his pistol, the emancipator of American slaves, Abraham Lincoln, was also a 'tyrant'. (Southern landowners had published an offer of $100,000 to kill him two years earlier.) But the Duke of Wellington refused to admit that he possessed any right to have Napoleon Bonaparte assassinated (Browne 1888, p. 135). Nor are 'wars of liberation' aiming to free nations or peoples definable as nations 'terrorist' as such; such struggles lie more properly within the literature of the tradition known as the 'just war' (Dugard 1989, pp. 77–98). It has been pointed out, too, that most guerrillas adhere to the chief canons of war in confining their targets to the armed forces and adjuncts thereof of their enemies.

The chief theoretical issues which arose from the emergence of the tactic of individual violence as part of nineteenth-century revolutionary strategies, which would be adapted and modified in the twentieth century, include:

(1) The question of the *scope* of permitted or legitimate assassination *vis-à-vis* 'tyrants': here the problem of 'innocence', when 'killing' is not 'murder', requires a coherent definition of tyranny or despotism. If a tsar (or a Hitler or Stalin) *might* be legitimately killed (but both also enjoyed widespread popular support), what justifications permit this? And when? We should recall that temporary elective dictatorships, notably in wartime, have been permitted in most societies; hence 'dictators' cannot constitute a legitimate category for tyrannicide as such, though genocidal murder by a dictator

probably would trigger such a distinction. (But as we have seen, many European nations engaged in genocidal policies during this period. The assassination of Queen Victoria by a black Tasmanian would certainly have been legitimate according to this logic.) Additional questions include: Does 'terrorism' include the killing of 'innocent' civilians who might be family members of government officials in a despotic regime? Does it include killing such family members in an occupied colony by natives of that land?[8] Does the necessity of defending a revolution justify expanding the scope of the legitimate use of violence, such that, as Bronterre O'Brien contended, 'a large proportion of the victims' of French revolutionary terror 'deserved their fate; for they would have murdered every democrat in France, had they not been destroyed, themselves' (O'Brien 1859, p. 9).

(2) The *political context* in which terrorism is utilised where 'tyranny' is absent: Can 'terrorism' ever be justified against a democratically elected government? 'Tyranny of the majority' can assume many different and very oppressive forms (ethnic, religious). Such distinctions were drawn at this time. When President Garfield was assassinated in 1881 by an opponent of liberal treatment of the defeated South, the Executive Committee of the Narodnaya Volya condemned the act, arguing that because the will of the people made law in the United States, the use of such force was not justifiable (Jaszi and Lewis 1957, p. 138). But the assassination of President McKinley in 1901 was inspired by anarchists (Vizetelly 1911, p. 251).

---

8 It is worth noting that what a 'despot' was also underwent change in this period; as G. J. Holyoake stated, 'Formerly a man was regarded as a lawful ruler who reigned by what he called "divine right". Since representative government began, a king is regarded as a despot unless he reigns by Parliamentary right. A ruler may be good or bad, but he is still a despot if he rules by his own authority, or prevents any one else ruling by public appointment.' Thus 'tyrant killing, undertaken for public ends, with a view to temper or suppress despotism, is *not* regarded by moralists as murder. It is apparently a necessity of progress *there* and at that stage only, and is only defensible when done under such circumstances that armed resistance cannot be reasonably attempted. Where the justification of irremediable oppression does not exist, tyrant-killing is a mistake.' But he also added that 'Nevertheless the good despot who rules justly cannot be usefully killed, since one cannot be sure that an untried government, introduced by force; could rule better than he.' He then drew up four principles by which tyrannicide could be justifiable (none of which he regarded as applicable in a free country): '1. That the tyrannicide must have intelligence sufficient to understand the responsibility of setting himself up as the redresser of a nation . . . 2. He who proposes to take a life for the good of the people must at least be prepared to give his own if necessary – both as atonement for taking upon himself the office of public avenger and to secure that his example shall not generate other than equally disinterested imitators . . . 3. The adversary of the despot must not be weak, vacillating, or likely to lose his head in unforeseen circumstances, nor be deficient in the knowledge and skill needful for his purpose . . . 4. He should have good knowledge that the result intended is likely to come to pass afterwards' (Holyoake 1893, II, pp. 59–61).

(3) The issue of the nature of the *method* adopted: here the key question is the justification of violence where there is a significant risk of 'innocents' being injured; over 150 were injured, for instance, in Orsini's 1858 bombing. Many attempts involved several methods at once; the successful plot against Alexander II of 1 March 1881 proposed to assail the Tsar with explosives, grenades and finally daggers. Here, as elsewhere, the key question is whether the end to be achieved, if it can itself be justified, justifies the means adopted.

(4) The justification of *suicide bombing*: Holyoake said of Orsini that 'Those who engage in political assassination should have no hesitation in sacrificing themselves' (Holyoake 1893, II, p. 27).

(5) The problem of the relation of terrorism to *insurrection* and *internationalism*. This raises the question of the scope of those legitimately permitted to exercise such violence; in particular, *sympathisers* with a struggle as opposed to the actual victims of an oppressive regime. The willingness to fight in the cause of others, from the French in Ireland to Byron in Greece onwards, also stemmed from a sense of internationalist loyalty and devotion to principle which transcended local and national boundaries, divided loyalties and produced a sense of fragmented and contradictory political identity. Many Irish fought on both sides of the American Civil War. Escaped convicts assisted Australian Aborigines in their resistance to white violence. Some Europeans evidently took the side of mutinous sepoys in India in 1857–8 (Forbes-Mitchell 1893, pp. 278–85). Two Irish brigades as well as an Irish-American corps (plus Italians, Scandinavians, Russians, Germans, Greeks, Austrians, Bulgarians, French and Dutch volunteers) fought alongside Boers in the South African war (Conan-Doyle 1900, p. 82; Davitt 1902, pp. 300–36). (Irish taken prisoner were protected from treason charges by having previously been granted citizenship by the Volksraad.) It was easy for an Irish nationalist like Michael Davitt to condemn England's 'cowardly and unchristian' warfare in South Africa from the Boer point of view (Davitt 1902, pp. 579–90). To those who regard all forms of imperialism as *prima facie* illegitimate, such cosmopolitanism was often applauded rather than condemned (see Claeys 2010).

(6) The issue of the glorification of *violence for its own sake*, for example as 'creative', or for some psychological end which benefits the perpetrator. We need here to consider what, if any, links really exist between the destructive and the creative, and whether that 'creative hatred' which Sorel dismissed, against Jaurès (Sorel 1969, p. 275), is not an oxymoron. A related and underlying issue is the danger of moral egoism, or of a religious or quasi-theological suspension of moral norms (e.g. an anomic or

antinomian state of grace). Anarchists sometimes claimed that an individual could 'be a law unto himself' (Vizetelly 1911, p. 3) in the manner of the sixteenth-century Adamites and Anabaptists. There were precedents for this stance earlier in the modern period too; a black flag carried in Wexford in 1798 by Irish rebels carried the letters 'M.W. S.', which some have interpreted as '*Murder Without Sin*', signifying that it was no sin to kill a Protestant (Holt 1838, I, p. 89). But this has been denied, too. The glorification of violence for its psychologically liberating effects would be taken up in the twentieth century, most notably, in the context of the Algerian wars, by the French psychiatrist Franz Fanon (Fanon 1969; Perinbam 1982). The danger here that legitimate justifications for opposing tyranny disintegrate into open-ended and self-perpetuating blood-lust is evident.

5   Conclusion

Following the collapse of the Soviet Union in 1991, the secular revolutionary ideal identified with the 'principles of '89', seemed to have run its course, only to gather momentum again this century, with new challenges to authoritarian regimes everwhere. Nonetheless the idea of revolution remains tainted by the failed promise of historical necessity, and the accusation of implicit totalitarianism, the fulfilment of Proudhon's warning that those who were 'fascinated by the schism of Robespierre' would 'tomorrow be the orthodox of the Revolution' (Proudhon 1923a, p. 127). Throughout much of the world nationalist movements emerged directly from anti-colonial and anti-imperial resistance. But malformed, corrupt and failed nation states too commonly resulted, and national identities did not always succeed in transcending and mitigating ethnic, religious and tribal enmities. Even in otherwise successful and relatively mature democracies, disfranchisement of women and exploited minorities has continued even to the present. 'Radicalism' is today associated chiefly with right-wing extremist movements, rather than the extension of the franchise. Though the issue now excites little public emotion, republicanism has proven more successful in the long term, with many leading monarchies being extinguished completely in the early- to- mid-twentieth century, and others shorn of any real political or constitutional power. By contrast, debates about 'terrorism' are as heated today as in the late nineteenth century, and have subsumed much of the controversy once associated with revolutionism. By the late nineteenth century anti-imperialist and anti-colonial movements, partly inspired by the democratic ideals of European revolutions, had begun to gather momentum, and would become the focus of global politics in the coming century. After 1918, and even more after 1945, thus, the analytic thrust of the ideas and movements outlined here shifts markedly, though not completely, away from Europe to the less developed world. Here the idea of revolution has evidently far from run its course.

II

Modern liberty and its defenders

8

From Jeremy Bentham's radical philosophy to J. S. Mill's philosophic radicalism

FREDERICK ROSEN

The object of this essay is to explore the main philosophical features of Jeremy Bentham's (1748–1832) radical thought and to identify those aspects which were later accepted or rejected by John Stuart Mill (1806–73) in his conception of philosophic radicalism. It is a study in the development and transmission of a set of ideas that helped to define the nature of philosophy and its application to politics in Britain and elsewhere in the first decades of the nineteenth century. It was believed and argued that truth in numerous fields, from politics to logic, possessed great utility (see Mill 1974, *CWM*, VII, pp. 11–12). The enhancement of understanding could lead to the relief of human suffering and the advancement of happiness. It would be wrong to see these fundamental beliefs as simply a development of a universal rationalism associated with the Enlightenment. Although Mill could write that 'if there were but one rational being in the universe, that being might be a perfect logician' (Mill 1974, *CWM*, VII, p. 6), neither Bentham nor Mill expected everyone to philosophise or seek the truth. But the recognition of the utility of truth led to a new kind of politics, theoretically open to all and inspired by a philosophical concern for truth, which dared, however gradually, to transform the lives of everyone. This transformation was to be achieved through a critical vision of society, released from oppression and ignorance to find security and happiness in new laws, institutions and practices.

Several topics will not be considered here. The fairly narrow emphasis in modern scholarship on Mill's interpretation of Bentham's principle of utility in *Utilitarianism* has been discussed elsewhere (see Rosen 2003, pp. 166–206). The nature of political radicalism and the circumstances surrounding Bentham's conversion to radicalism either at the time of the French Revolution or in 1809–10 with the subsequent publication of *Plan of Parliamentary Reform* in 1817 has generated a considerable literature, but one that has not generally attempted to discover what was unique and important in Bentham's philosophical approach to politics.[1] Finally, the Benthamite contribution to the nineteenth-century revolution in government, which has focused more on influence rather than on inheritance on the one hand, and on politics and government to the exclusion of philosophic method on the other, will not be discussed here.[2]

This essay begins in 1802 with the publication of the *Traités de Législation Civile et Pénale* (henceforth *Traités*), the first of the recensions of Bentham's writings prepared by Étienne Dumont (1759–1829). Recent commentators have tended to criticise Dumont's achievement in terms of the oversimplification and even the falsification of some of Bentham's ideas (see Baumgardt 1952, pp. 324–5; Bentham 1932, pp. xxix–xxx). Although there is some truth in these criticisms, as Dumont consciously attempted to present a more readable (and less controversial) version of Bentham's thought, and may easily have missed the meaning of some of his ideas (like the theory of fictions), there is a danger in failing to appreciate the importance of the *Traités* and the other recensions in the development of Bentham's thought (see Lieberman 2000, p. 108; cf. Schofield 2003, p. 5n).[3] This issue has tended to be intertwined with another concerning the weight to be given to the *Traités* in this development. Baumgardt, for example, entitled his chapter on *An Introduction to the Principles of Morals and Legislation* (1789) (henceforth *IPML*) – 'The Main Theme' – and that on the *Traités* as 'The French Interlude' to signify the relative status of the two works (Baumgardt 1952, pp. 163, 321). Both Baumgardt (1952, p. 325) and Ogden (Bentham 1932, p. xxx) criticise earlier commentators (see Everett 1931, p. 197; Halévy 1901–4, II, p. 357) for ignoring the philosophical significance of Bentham's later writings, but they inadvertently have contributed to this neglect by failing to appreciate the new era of philosophical writing ushered in with the publication of the *Traités* itself. While it is generally agreed that the *Traités* led to the massive enhancement of Bentham's reputation throughout the world (see Dinwiddy 1992b, p. 294), what has gone relatively unnoticed is the stimulus given to Bentham's philosophical ambitions as a result of the *Traités*.

---

1 See Bentham 1817, 1999, 2002a; Burns 1966; Crimmins 1994; Dinwiddy 1975; James 1986; Mack 1962; Rosen 2004; Schofield 1999a, 1999b.
2 See Brebner 1948; Conway 1990a, 1990b, 1991; Cromwell 1966; Finer 1972; Hart 1965; Hume 1967; MacDonagh 1958; Parris 1960; Roberts 1959.
3 Besides Bentham 1802, see Bentham 1811, 1816, 1823b, 1828, from which numerous editions and translations followed (see Ikeda *et al.* 1989). See also the first collected Dumont edition (Bentham 1829–30), which was reissued in 1832 with a further edition in 1840.

In 1802 Bentham was fifty-three years old, but hardly at the pinnacle of his career. His great practical project, the Panopticon prison system, on which he had devoted so much time and energy, was doomed to failure (see Semple 1993). If one considers his writings just prior to the appearance of the *Traités*, they seem to be confined to issues surrounding Panopticon, the poor laws and economic policy (see Bentham 1984, pp. 487–8). In the decades following its publication he began a number of works of philosophical significance, such as the writings on evidence and judicial procedure, codification, education, logic, language, fallacies, religion, ethics and psychology. Much of this material, covering thousands of manuscript folios, looked back to the *Traités*, which in turn provided a window to Bentham's earliest publications, such as *A Fragment on Government* (1776) and *IPML*, which had been virtually forgotten by this time.

The *Traités* possesses an additional significance for this essay in that the answer given by Robson to the question, 'Which Bentham was Mill's Bentham?' ('if forced to answer in one word') is 'Dumont's' (Robson 1993, I, p. 206). For the *Traités*, read by Mill in 1821, was a major feature in his earliest study of Bentham (see Robson 1993, I, p. 197). Mill's interest in the *Traités* was probably enhanced by the fact that he read it after his return from France, where he acquired a fluency in that language during his visit with Samuel Bentham's (1757–1831) family (see Robson 1993, I, p. 205; see also Mill 1981, *CWM*, I, pp. 577). It is arguable that the *Traités* formed a lens through which Mill read much of Bentham, and it focused Mill's ideas in a particular manner.

To the one-word answer to his question, Robson then added a footnote: 'There is a major implication here that makes me a bit uneasy: i.e., that Mill's Bentham is the Continental (and indeed international) Bentham. Was there, in Bentham's lifetime at least, a significant English Bentham (one not seen through Dumont)?' (Robson 1993, I, p. 208n). To this further question, left unanswered by Robson, a provisional answer will be attempted here. Dumont's recensions presented Bentham mainly as a philosopher and jurist and as a bridge from the Enlightenment to nineteenth-century thought. Bentham's radical, democratic views, particularly prominent after 1809–10 in his manuscripts and after 1817 with the publication of *Plan of Parliamentary Reform*, were of little importance to Dumont (see Dinwiddy 1992b, pp. 297–9). If Mill's Bentham was that of Dumont, Mill's conception of philosophic radicalism would have to deal with this discrepancy. As we shall see, Mill attempted to reject Benthamite political radicalism (and what he saw as its narrow self-regarding foundations) while at the same time adopting and building on Bentham's philosophical ideas generally, except for the philosophic ideas not found in Dumont's recensions – such as the writings on language and logic. How Mill did this and how he was understood will be explored in several respects in this essay. We shall also consider Mill's personal response to his inheritance from Bentham and his father, which complicated his endeavours to establish 'philosophic radicalism' in the 1830s.

1 Dumont's *Traités*

The publication of Dumont's *Traités* was greeted enthusiastically by Bentham. When he received the proofs of the first two volumes in May 1802, he wrote: 'You have set me a strutting, my dear Dumont, like a fop in a Coat spick-and-span from the Taylor's' (Bentham 1988a, p. 28). Bentham had known Dumont since 1788, when, on his return from visiting his brother Samuel in Russia, he became an active member of the Lansdowne circle (see Blamires 1990). William Petty, 2nd Earl of Shelburne and 1st Marquis of Lansdowne (1737–1805) provided the resources and contacts in France that were exploited by Bentham, Samuel Romilly (1757–1818) and Dumont, leading to the publication of several of Bentham's works or parts of works by Dumont who was then also closely associated with Mirabeau (see Bentham 1999 [1816], pp. xvi–xxvi, 2002, pp. xvii ff.; Dumont 1832). Although Bentham did not have direct contact with Lansdowne after 1796 (Bentham 1984, p. 400n), and the writings for France ceased with the anti-Jacobin reaction, Bentham maintained his close friendships with Romilly and Dumont. Dumont seems to have begun editorial work on the *Traités*, at least by 1796, and some of the material was published in the Genevan journal, *Bibliothèque Britannique* between 1796 and 1798 (see Bentham 1981, p. 200n). The whole project was fraught with difficulty. Dumont had to obtain various manuscripts from a hesitant and even reluctant Bentham and transform them into readable essays. Furthermore, when a French translation of some of Bentham's Poor Law writings was to appear in 1802, Dumont feared that it would not achieve an extensive circulation. The publishers of the *Traités*, Martin Bossange, similarly feared that there might be a financial loss with the three-volume *Traités*, and only the intervention of Talleyrand, then foreign minister under Napoleon, guaranteed its publication on favourable terms (see Bentham 1984, pp. 465–7).

As we have noted, the *Traités*, together with Dumont's other recensions, achieved large sales for philosophical works at this time, were widely distributed throughout the world, and were translated into numerous languages. But what were Bentham and Dumont attempting to achieve with this first and most important of the recensions? As he had worked with Bentham for many years, Dumont was well aware of the numerous important manuscripts on legislation that Bentham had written but never completed. For a variety of reasons, they were simply left to gather dust on his shelves. Alternatively, once Bentham had made a draft or even an outline of a work, he would often abandon it for more pressing or novel tasks. For Dumont, these were valuable works, even in outline form, which should have been completed and published.

When he received the proofs of part of the *Traités*, Bentham, as we have seen, was delighted. In the course of several letters to Dumont which contained comments and corrections, he composed some notes for Dumont's 'puff Preface', which, though not used by Dumont, provide an interesting picture of Bentham's thought at this time (see Bentham 1988a, p. 24). Bentham first called attention to various thinkers who had developed a fundamental principle for morals and politics: 'some cant word, or short form of words, such as should serve as a sort of hook on which to hang the several particular opinions and tenets of which their prejudices and passions with or without the suggestion of interest had been productive . . . ' (see Bentham 1988a, p. 24). Thus, in favouring absolute monarchy, Hobbes used the idea of Leviathan and Filmer, the principle of parental power. In hoping to limit monarchy, Locke developed the 'fiction' of the original contract. Bishop Warburton used the 'fiction' of the alliance between church and state to give certain people as much power as possible in society. Rousseau invented his 'fiction' of the social contract in order to recommend democracy. The principle of utility, however, was a different sort of principle. It would at times agree and at other times disagree with the various principles of these writers. Because of this potential opposition it was often 'received with coldness[,] aversion and neglect by all parties' (Bentham 1988a, pp. 25–6).

Like many of his contemporaries Bentham regarded himself as a follower of Bacon and Newton, but he used his discipleship to highlight his concern with sensation and experience on the one hand, and observation and experiment on the other. He liked to employ the analogy with medicine and declared that many other writers on politics and morals would mistakenly expect diseases to be cured by a declaration of a right to good health. Or they would proceed (as he thought that Locke and Rousseau had done) by turning round and round in a circle, like the followers of Aristotle did in physics, by defining one word by another until they returned to the first word (Bentham 1988a, pp. 26–7). Bentham claimed to move slowly and cautiously forward observing the connection between various acts and the sensations felt by those involved:

while others were teaching legislation in matters of criminal law by declamations against individual depravity on one hand and legal cruelty and tyranny on the other J.B. was investigating the sensations produced in the breasts of the several parties affected and interested by crimes and other pernicious acts: and according to the result of the investigation in each case referring the act to its place in a system of classification in the construction of which no lawyer nor any moralist but the Limdus's [Linnaeus] the Sauvages [François Boissier de Sauvages] and the Cullen's [William Cullen] were his guides. His division of offences is the Nosology of the body politic: in it offences are classed as in the other case diseases according to the sensations produced or prevented from being produced (the painful produced the pleasurable prevented) in each case and according to the manner in which . . . the effect is made to take place. (Bentham 1988a, p. 27)

Bentham's proposed preface looked back to *IPML*, written more than two decades earlier, and called attention to two important chapters (II and XVI) in that work (also reworked for the *Traités*) (see Bentham 1996 [1789], pp. 17–33, 187–280, 1802, I, pp. 10–21, II, pp. 240ff.). In chapter II of *IPML* Bentham listed a number of phrases employed by philosophers, such as 'moral sense', 'common sense', 'understanding', 'rule of right', 'fitness of things', 'law of nature', 'law of reason', 'right reason', 'natural justice', 'natural equity', 'good order', 'truth' and 'doctrine of election', as foundations of their systems, which he simply dismissed as meaningless, reflecting only the feelings and prejudices of their authors (Bentham 1996 [1789], pp. 26n–9n). In his proposals for a preface to the *Traités*, Bentham focused more on moral and political principles (i.e. those of Hobbes, Locke, Rousseau, etc.) but dismissed them in a similar fashion.

In chapter XVI (the longest and most complex in *IPML*) he set out a complex classification of all possible offences within any society, which could then be used as the basis of a successful penal code. These chapters in turn reflected Bentham's method, which he, as we have seen, linked more with medicine and botany than with traditional political philosophy. The principle of utility was not an alternative to theories of the social contract or of rights, because it rested on different foundations, concerned with observation and experiment rather than the advocacy of particular principles or arrangements. In the material on offences he was concerned with the ways certain actions caused pain or harm to members of society and hence did or did not deserve to be considered offences. Unlike Beccaria,

Eden, Howard and others he did not take up an ideological position either in favour of or against severe punishments (see Draper 1997, 2000, 2001; Rosen 2003, pp. 144–65). The outcome in terms of leniency or severity depended on the analysis of particular offences. Established sexual or religious offences in a society might be treated with greater leniency, if they were observed to cause less pain than murder and assault, but other offences might best be treated more severely if they were to be deterred. To believe in leniency or severity in punishment would not solve the complex problems associated with designating which actions should be offences and how the offences should be punished. Much additional work would be required.

John Stuart Mill was much taken with both of these chapters. In the *Autobiography* he wrote regarding chapter II that 'the feeling rushed upon me, that all previous moralists were superseded, and that here indeed was the commencement of a new era in thought' (Mill 1981, *CWM*, I, p. 67). As for the classification of offences in chapter XVI, which he preferred in the version in the *Traités* over the more complex presentation in *IPML*, he wrote:

I felt taken up to an eminence from which I could survey a vast mental domain, and see stretching out into the distance intellectual results beyond all computation. As I proceeded further, there seemed to be added to this intellectual clearness, the most inspiring prospects of practical improvement in human affairs. (Mill 1981, *CWM*, I, p. 69)

Mill then went on to declare that when he completed the *Traités* (what Packe 1954, p. 49 has called 'a rite of initiation'), 'I had become a different being.' 'It gave unity to my conception of things', he continued. 'I now had opinions; a creed, a doctrine, a philosophy; in one among the best senses of the word, a religion; the inculcation and diffusion of which could be made the principal outward purpose of a life' (Mill 1981, *CWM*, I, p. 69).

2 Evidence

Within a year of the publication of the *Traités* in 1802, Bentham began serious writing on the theme of evidence (Bentham 1988a, p. 250 and n; see also Lewis 1990, pp. 203–4). While it is tempting to see him turning from the failure of the Panopticon project to evidence and hence to treat the work on evidence as partly politically motivated, revealing a period of transition to his acceptance of political radicalism in 1809 (see Twining 1985, p. 24), it is more plausible to suggest that Bentham was stimulated by the successful appearance of the *Traités* to undertake one of the topics necessary for the completion of his vision of a complete code of laws. The *Traités* was mainly confined to penal and civil law, and left largely untouched two main fields: evidence and judicial procedure on the one hand and constitutional law on the other.

It is not difficult to see how the law of evidence might have a strong philosophical component. By its very nature evidence and the means by which it is obtained and used in courts is related to ideas of perception, induction, theories of motivation, and concepts of proof and truth (see Twining 1985, pp. 16, 26). When Bentham wrote to his brother about the volume on evidence he was supposedly bringing to completion in 1806, that 'Metaphysics, none in this Vol', he was probably referring to the fact that much of it was highly critical of lawyers and existing legal practices (Bentham 1988a, p. 381). Indeed, the test of philosophical success in his terms would consist of the generation of human happiness through practical changes in the law. But the philosophical discussion would underpin this practical effort.

When Bentham began to write in 1806 about the completion of the work on evidence, Dumont's name also appeared in connection with it. Bentham wrote to his brother in 1806 that ' . . . about my evidence he [Dumont] plagues me out of my life' (Bentham 1988a, p. 342). The old team from the Lansdowne circle, Romilly and Dumont, paid close attention to Bentham's new philosophical venture (see Bentham 1988a, p. 356). But Bentham did not bring his own work to completion. James Mill worked on the evidence manuscripts in 1809 (Bentham 1988b, pp. 38, 47–8), and Bentham partly printed the 'Introduction to the Rationale of Evidence' in 1812 (see Lewis 1990, p. 209; Bentham 1838–43, VI, pp. 1–187). Dumont produced his one-volume version in 1823 with English translations appearing in 1825 (see Bentham 1823b, 1825). According to J. S. Mill, Dumont's work omitted the material concerned with English practice and made it more suitable for continental readers (J. Bentham 1827b, I, pp. v–vi). Nevertheless, it would be J. S. Mill who completed the five-volume *Rationale of Judicial Evidence* in 1825–7. Lewis suggests that in undertaking this burdensome chore, on which James Mill had worked, the young Mill 'was as much fulfilling a task of genuine filial duty' towards his father, 'as he was undertaking a work of piety in respect of his intellectual father, Bentham' (Lewis 1990, p. 216).

Mill's brief preface for this massive work somewhat surprisingly focused less on the nature of Bentham's achievement (which he probably thought would speak for itself) and took up several political issues concerned with reform. His main argument was that piecemeal reform in a technical legal system would produce a worse system than reform on what he called 'a comprehensive plan', even if that plan had to be introduced suddenly rather than gradually (J. Bentham 1827b, I, p. xiv). Mill admitted that 'the public mind is not yet entirely prepared' for so major a reform in its legal system but that 'it is rapidly advancing to such a state of preparation': 'It is now no longer considered as a mark of disaffection towards the state, and hostility to social order and to law in general, to express an opinion that the existing law is defective, and requires radical reform' (J. Bentham 1827b, I, p. xv). Mill pointed to Peel's recent proposals for law reform, and to the work of Humphreys, as supplemented by Bentham, on the reform of the law of real property (see J. Bentham 1827a; Humphreys 1826; Sokol 1992, pp. 225–45). Mill then used these clear developments towards reform in the 1820s to call attention to a new group of young lawyers who were active in the cause of reform, even though their pecuniary interests would oppose it (J. Bentham 1827b, I, pp. xv–xvi). This showed, for Mill, that the problem of reform was not only one of overcoming 'sinister interests' (in Bentham's phrase) but also one of seriously learning about the possibilities of an alternative system (J. Bentham 1827b, I, p. xvi). In the field of evidence, Mill declared, the subject 'has now for the first time been treated philosophically' (J. Bentham 1827b, I, p. xvi).

Book I of Mill's edition was devoted to 'Theoretical Grounds' and began with an exploration of the nature of evidence and facts. Bentham took the view that a concern with evidence was part of all studies, including those like mathematics and religion, where empirical evidence, at any rate, did not appear to be directly important. According to Bentham, 'a great part of the business of science in general, may be resolved into a research after evidence' (J. Bentham 1827b, I, p. 21). Mill seemed to accept this view, though he also sought to distinguish between a purely experimental subject, like chemistry, on the one hand, where evidence was based on matters of fact and these in turn were based on sense impressions, and mathematics on the other hand, where evidence was based on general reasoning. 'To point out the peculiar properties of these two kinds of evidence, and to distinguish them from one another, belongs', Mill added, 'rather to a treatise on logic than to a work like the present' (J. Bentham 1827b, I, p. 20n). Thus, as early as 1827, Mill set out his stall regarding the study of logic and linked it with evidence. This link is perhaps reflected in the full title of his own work on logic, *A System of Logic Ratiocinative and Inductive Being a Connected View of the Principles of Evidence and Methods of Scientific Investigation* (1843). As Kubitz

(1932, p. 23) has written, 'the standpoint of Bentham's *Rationale* regarding evidence may, accordingly, be taken as one of the first circumstances to influence the development of Mill's logical doctrines'.

3 Codification

Bentham's vision of a complete code of laws, accepted by one or more states, epitomised his conception of the ideal relationship between philosophy and politics (see Bentham 1998). To draft such a work, governing the public life of a society, and aiming at increasing human happiness or at least diminishing unhappiness, and covering all branches of the law, would require all of his philosophical skill and imagination together with an acceptance of the laws by the society concerned. As in the analogy with medicine, the ultimate object was wholly practical, in this case, the happiness of the individual and society. For Bentham, to attempt to understand human happiness, without a grasp of how laws impinged upon such happiness and how they might be changed to increase it, was pointless and self-indulgent.

Bentham never actually wrote a complete code of laws (despite receiving an acceptance from the Portuguese Cortes in 1822 to an offer to draft penal, civil and constitutional codes for Portugal) (Bentham 1983b [1830], pp. xiff., 1998, pp. xxix–xxx). But throughout his life, from his involvement in the Penitentiary Act of 1779 (for which he wrote a critical commentary on the proposed bill, entitled *A View of the Hard-Labour Bill* (1778) (Bentham 1838–43, IV, pp. 3–35; see Rosen 2003, p. 161), to his contribution to the Anatomy Act of 1830 (see R. Richardson 1986, pp. 22–33, 2001, p. 112), he took a keen interest in all forms of legislation and wrote at length on numerous topics. The philosophical vision was also never abandoned, and in his later years, his commitment to it intensified.

Bentham turned to codification in a major way in 1811 with a letter addressed to James Madison, President of the United States of America, offering to draft a complete code of laws (or *Pannomion*) to replace the Common Law (see Bentham 1988b, pp. 182–215, 1998, pp. 5–35). The letter was written in consultation with Dumont (Bentham 1998, pp. xii–xiii), and, in addition, Bentham was perhaps stimulated to undertake this second major philosophical project (after evidence) with the appearance of the second Dumont recension, *Théorie des Peines et des Récompenses*, which was published in the same year (see Bentham 1811). In the letter to Madison (and in numerous subsequent letters to leading figures throughout the world) Bentham referred to the *Traités* as containing a plan and an example of a rationale ('a mass of *reasons* accompanying in the shape of a perpetual commentary' on the proposed laws) (Bentham 1988b, p. 184). Bentham also pointed out that the *Traités* were mentioned in Napoleon's *Code d'Instruction Criminelle* (1807) and *Code Pénal* (1810) as well as in the penal code authorised by the King of Bavaria (see Bexon 1807, Pt. I, pp. lxvi, lxvii, lxx; Pt. II, pp. iv, lvii, lxxxvii, cxxii, cxxiv; Bk. II, p. I; see also Bentham 1998, pp. 11–12 and nn). Whatever provided the precise stimulus for Bentham to take up codification in a major way in 1811, it is clear that the *Traités* remained the main anchor and model for his new venture. In his letter to Simon Snyder, the governor of Pennsylvania, in 1814, when he turned from the federal government to the state governments to obtain his commission, he referred to the two Dumont recensions and also back to *IPML*, which, he declared, was 'the forerunner' of the *Traités* (Bentham 1988b, p. 390, 1998, p. 69).

In his efforts at obtaining a commission to produce a complete code of laws, Bentham did not omit to consider the possibilities for codification in Britain. In 1812 he approached Henry Addington, Viscount Sidmouth, who had just become Home Secretary, with a proposal to draft a penal code (see Bentham 1988b, pp. 247–51). At this time (as elsewhere) he referred to Bacon and wrote: 'Since the days of Lord Bacon, the sort of offer I am making to your lordship is what has never, from that time to this, been made to any public man' (Bentham 1988b, p. 249). This reference was not to Bacon in his role as a philosopher, but to his proposal to James I to make a digest of the laws (see Lieberman 1985, pp. 7–20, 1989, pp. 183–4, 241–51, 254–6). In explaining to Sidmouth what he expected from him with regard to such a proposed code, Bentham did not envisage anything so grand as the actual acceptance of the code. He thought instead that 'it should be received, and employed, and made of use in the character of a *subject of comparison* – a subject or object of comparison, capable, on occasion, of being referred to – referred to for good provision or for bad provision, for good argument or for bad argument, for approbation or for censure' (Bentham 1988b, p. 248). One might see here Bentham's distinction between the expositor and the censor in comparing law as it is with that as it ought to be (Bentham 1988c, pp. 7–8). The proposed penal code might, in his view, be accepted to play this role of standing alongside the existing law and generating the truth through a detailed comparison between the two versions of the law.

Bentham was continually engaged at this time in making proposals for reform, for example, from an attack on the evils surrounding transportation, to a critique of sodomy in the hulks, from opposition to capital punishment to proposals for tattoos for identifying prisoners. These diverse proposals appeared in his writings and correspondence at the same time as he undertook his philosophical projects that equally aimed at the reform of existing practices. One cannot distinguish between his philosophical and other proposals for reform in terms of what objects he sought to accomplish, as both had as objects the relief of pain and the enhancement of pleasure and happiness. The difference was more in the completeness of the vision of human life and motivation involved in the philosophical works alongside a method for achieving an understanding of them in their application to practice. The method also required a vision – a vision he associated with Bacon and Newton – which could establish the study of law, politics and ethics as practical sciences in their own right and as complete and rigorous as medicine, botany and engineering. Such an achievement would sweep away the vast but supposedly useless body of existing philosophical commentary in these fields.

In Bentham's writings on codification one is provided with the principles on which such codification would be based and examples of Bentham's method of logical division and organisation that would guide his work (see Bentham 1998). He was well aware that progress in the field of codification, particularly in the attempt to provide a complete code of laws, faced formidable obstacles. First, those lawyers and politicians who would have to approve such a venture had most to lose by giving such approval and little incentive to do so. Bentham noted that no government or nation had ever attempted to survey all of its laws, let alone proceed towards comprehensive codification, and much codification thus far consisted simply of digests of existing customary law and statutes, with similar defects as that which they replaced or supplemented (Bentham 1998, p. 139). Second, the work of codification, for Bentham, was highly complex and even technical. Not only was it necessary that the final product should be easily accessible to the average person, but underlying such work were complex logical operations and the development of a new technical language to express the process of logical division and distinction. The two goals were difficult to reconcile, and one basis for the widespread criticism of Bentham in these later writings was his need to adopt a difficult technical vocabulary to express the logic of the important distinctions he sought to make (see James Mill 1835, pp. 127–8). While some critics during his lifetime and at the present time see this use of language as a stylistic defect (see Hazlitt 1969, pp. 33–4;

Thomas 1979, p. 23), for Bentham, it was part of his philosophical attempt to apply logic to the law, a logic that he saw analogous to the use of algebra in science.

4   Ford Abbey

Bentham's sojourn at Ford Abbey in Devon from 1814 to 1818 enabled him to concentrate on numerous aspects of his new philosophical projects, even though he had begun some of these years earlier (see Bentham 1932, pp. xxxii–xxxiii). The first reference to his manuscript for *Chrestomathia* (meaning 'useful learning' – printed in 1815, published in 1816 and 1817), his major work on knowledge and education, appeared in his correspondence in 1814 (see Bentham 1983a, 1988b, p. 403 and n). This much-neglected work is of considerable philosophical importance, containing a series of appendices and tables dealing with classification, logic, language and mathematics, as well as the details of the proposed Chrestomathic School. In the work on codification where he was providing an example of the application of his method to different codes of law, he referred to his 'Encyclopedical Table, or Art and Science Table' in *Chrestomathia*, where he provided a classification of all branches of the arts and sciences (see Bentham 1983a, pp. 178–9, 1998, pp. 139–40). Here was proof of how one might set about classifying vast topics, such as law, and possess at a glance a complete view of the various elements that made up the totality of knowledge. Not all commentators have found much of value in Bentham's achievement. Bain, for example, in referring to the tables in *Chrestomathia*, recognised a connection with the earlier French Encyclopaedia, but concluded that 'very little attaches to this now; and I doubt if it was of much use at the time' (Bain 1882a, p. 143). George Bentham (1800–84), on the other hand, called attention to Bentham's achievement in rejecting the scholastic view that there can be a science without an art or an art without a science, and linked it with Whately's argument, developed slightly later, that logic could not be only an art, as the Schoolmen had believed (G. Bentham 1827, p. 12; see also Mill 1974, *CWM*, VII, p. 4). For Bentham, science accompanied art, as truth accompanied logic and classification.

One might trace from *Chrestomathia* the development of Bentham's writings on logic and language. The first reference to the work on logic occurred in 1814 in a letter to his brother, Samuel (Bentham 1988b, pp. 410–11). Within a year Bentham was printing *A Table of the Springs of Action* (published in 1817), his work on motivation, and, more particularly, on the language used in describing motivation (see Bentham 1983c, pp. 1–115). His work on fallacies in debate, *The Book of Fallacies* (1824), first appeared, in part, in a French edition, produced by Dumont, *Tactique des Assemblées Législatives, suivie d'un Traité des Sophismes Politiques* (1816). Furthermore, when one adds to this significant corpus of work, the material on ethics, much of which was written at this time (see Bentham 1983c, pp. 119–281), and the massive material on religion, such as *Church-of-Englandism* (1818), the period at Ford Abbey may be seen to be highly productive, and philosophically significant.

In what ways did Bentham produce a philosophical legacy? Pringle-Pattison, reflecting the Idealist reaction to utilitarianism, quotes Leslie Stephen's remark that Bentham 'got on very well without philosophy' (Pringle-Pattison 1907, p. 18). On the other hand, Bain compares Bentham's 'extraordinarily ambitious mind' with Aristotle's – both of whom sought to 'remodel the whole of human knowledge' (Bain 1882a, p. 144). J. S. Mill seemed ambivalent about Bentham's legacy in philosophy. Anyone with a tolerable acquaintance with Bentham's major writings will see reflections on many pages of Mill's writing both in the language and ideas employed. Moreover, it should be appreciated that Mill and George Bentham, Bentham's nephew and the future distinguished botanist, were working on Bentham's evidence and logic manuscripts respectively at the same time, and both works were published within a few months of each other by the same publisher. Nevertheless, there seems to have been little contact between them, except on the theme of botany, even though Mill lived with the Bentham family in France for many months just seven years earlier, and was then often in the company of George Bentham (see Mill 1988, *CWM*, XXVI, pp. 1–143). While in France Mill attended the lectures of M. Gergonne at l'Académie de Montpelier, took extensive notes (see Mill 1988, *CWM*, XXVI, pp. 191–253), and even drafted a 'Traité de Logique' (1820–1) in French (Mill 1988, *CWM*, XXVI, pp. 145–90). Several years later in 1823 George Bentham published a French translation of Bentham's most important appendix to *Chrestomathia* (*Essai sur la Nomenclature et la Classification des Principales Branches d'Art-et-Science*) (see Bentham 1823a, 1983a, pp. 139–276). Furthermore, when he first discussed the preparation of a major work on logic with Bentham in 1826, George Bentham learned that James and J. S. Mill had supposedly studied the papers on logic and that James Mill was planning to write a work on logic based partly on Bentham's manuscripts (G. Bentham 1997, p. 244).

George Bentham had first hoped to produce an edition in French, as he was more comfortable in that language and did not want to compete with the Mills. But Bentham was enthusiastic about George Bentham making his fortune and reputation through editorial work on logic, and he began to work on this project, while at the same time being forced by lack of funds to begin the study of law (G. Bentham 1997, p. 247). Unfortunately, while Bentham decried the study of law and even though George Bentham and his sisters would inherit the bulk of Bentham's estate in 1832, Bentham would not provide his nephew with sufficient funds so that he would not need to enter the legal profession. Due to these circumstances the volume on logic had to be somewhat hastily produced. Nevertheless, it was received enthusiastically by Bentham: 'My uncle is much pleased with my work; he says that *in Logic, I have already gone beyond him*' (G. Bentham 1997, p. 270). If one compares Mill's *Rationale of Judicial Evidence* with George Bentham's *Outline of a New System of Logic*, they will strike one as very different works. Mill's five volumes are a major testament to Bentham's achievement. Mill deferentially kept his own ideas out of the text and expressed them only occasionally in editorial notes (see Mill 1963, *CWM*, XII, pp. 18–19). George Bentham provided a fair summary of Bentham's ideas, together with ideas of his own, and a critical reading of Whately's *Elements of Logic* (see Whately 1826).

When Mill was asked to review the *Outline* in the *Westminster Review*, he declined the offer, even though he had already published an article on Whately in the same journal a few months earlier. In his letter to John Bowring (1792–1872), the editor, he was highly critical of George Bentham's work. While recognising his talent, Mill thought that the critique of Whately failed to show a superior grasp of the subject and contained arguments that were at times 'altogether groundless' (Mill 1963, *CWM*, XII, pp. 23–4).

What Mill omitted from this letter (and from his own *A System of Logic*) was any reference not only to Bentham's ideas in the *Outline*, but also to Bentham's writings on logic and language, which first appeared in the Bowring edition of the *Works* (Bentham 1838–43, VIII, pp. 192–357), and nearly a century later achieved wide circulation through C. K. Ogden's edition, *Bentham's Theory of Fictions* (1932). Furthermore, George Bentham had stated his object clearly to justify his early publication of the *Outline*. He was writing a preliminary work, that is to say, an outline, following the order of Whately's logic, and comparing Whately's position with that of Bentham's on the topics Bentham considered. At the same time, he would add his own ideas on subjects which Bentham did not cover (see G. Bentham 1827, p. vii). Such a procedure was not overly ambitious for someone fairly new to the subject. George Bentham also alluded to the fact that his circumstances, probably his pecuniary circumstances, were such that a full study of logic would have to be delayed. It should be noted that his later botanical studies, involving complex classifications, amply fulfilled his early promise in logic. Furthermore, the later recognition of the importance of his chapters identifying the 'quantification of the predicate' for the first time in modern logic earned for him a significant, if minor, footnote in the history of logic (see G. Bentham 1997, pp. 271, 484–6).

Why was Mill so scornful of the *Outline* and apparently so dismissive of the logical studies of both Benthams? An answer to this question would require a full study of Mill's *System of Logic*, which cannot be undertaken here (see, for example, Ryan 1987). Nevertheless, while Bentham's ideas were ubiquitous in Mill's *System of Logic* and while both were attempting to establish inductive systems, Mill seemed to draw on other sources and different strategies. This is due in part to the development of his early study of logic in France, his studies with his father, debates with friends at meetings at the home of George Grote (see Mill 1981, *CWM*, I, p. 125), and his reading of Bentham through Dumont, as well as the simple fact that he worked on Bentham's papers on evidence rather than on the papers on logic. Nevertheless, even though no full version of Bentham's writings on logic and language was available until 1843, one would have thought that he might have explored some of Bentham's ideas either through George Bentham's *Outline* or through the manuscripts themselves. Even where he discussed the quantification of the predicate in *An Examination of Sir William Hamilton's Philosophy*, no reference to George Bentham, negative or positive, appeared (Mill 1979, *CWM*, IX, pp. 385ff.).

Although Mill's standing as a logician was generally high throughout the nineteenth century, and Bentham was mainly neglected, it would be wrong to assume that Mill's neglect of Bentham's ideas was based solely or even partially on their being defective. William Stanley Jevons (1835–82), for example, not only defended Bentham's utilitarian philosophy in general and intervened over the issue of the quantification of the predicate (see G. Bentham 1997, pp. 271, 485–6), but he also criticised Mill as a logician, as in a letter written in 1876: 'Great as my respect for Mill's straightforward and zealous character is, I fear that his intellect if good originally was ruined in youth. At any rate I find after long study that his Logic is an extraordinary tissue of self-contradictions' (Jevons 1972–81, IV, p. 167; see also IV, pp. 101–2, 116, V, p. 24). These contradictions, in Jevons' view, were mainly in the sphere of the methods of geometry as well as in his account of utility.

The revival of interest in Bentham, stimulated by the republication of the writings on language and logic by C. K. Ogden also testifies to the importance of his logical thought (Bentham 1932; Ogden 1932). As Hart has noted, 'Bentham anticipated the ideas of Logical Constructions, Incomplete Symbols, and Definition in Use which are a marked feature of Bertrand Russell's philosophy and the forms of analytical philosophy which stem from it' (Hart 1982, p. 43, see also pp. 128–31; see also Harrison 1983, pp. 47–76). For Harrison (1983, p. 64), Bentham also made an important discovery in his theory of fictions – leading on to the work of Russell and Carnap. According to Quine, Bentham developed the thesis 'that to explain a term we do not need to compose a synonymous phrase. We need only explain all sentences in which we propose to use the term' (Quine 1995, pp. 6–7). Quine calls this procedure 'contextual definition' and links it with developments made by Boole.

The point of making these observations is not to establish Bentham or his nephew, George, as great logicians, but to suggest that the work being done by Bentham at Ford Abbey was both serious and philosophical. Its importance has been obscured by the fact that however much it might have contributed to analytical philosophy in the twentieth century, analytical philosophy itself turned away from its roots in the wider Epicurean tradition to provide a narrower conception of philosophy, and perhaps one more focused on logic. Thus, while Ogden could see a wider application for Bentham's philosophy in linguistics and in psychology, analytical philosophers were content simply to acknowledge Bentham as an important but distant ancestor (see Wisdom 1931).

Within the broad tradition in which Bentham was working, he provided an important philosophical legacy for James and J. S. Mill, but it was not taken up by them and certainly not by J. S. Mill. As we shall see, the only reason for this explicit neglect, when the signs of his acceptance of many of Bentham's views are everywhere, may well be based on his loyalty to his father and to his father's reputation as a philosopher. James Mill became an important figure in Bentham's life at this time, and the presence of father and son may have compensated for the departure of Samuel Bentham to make his home in France (see M. S. Bentham 1862, pp. 308ff.). Bentham would not see him until 1827, and given their ages in 1814 (Jeremy was 66 and Samuel was 57), they might never have met again.

Nevertheless, the nature of the relationship between Bentham and James Mill has never been clearly or fully defined. Mill worked on a number of Bentham's projects, as well as his own *History of India*, and considered himself a devoted disciple. But when Bain compared Bentham's *Chrestomathia* with James Mill's essay on education (see James Mill 1992b, pp. 137–94), written for the Supplement to the *Encyclopaedia Britannica* (1819), he commented: '... it is very curious to remark how few signs of action and reaction between the two minds their respective products bring to light; there is hardly any appearance in either treatise to show that the subject had undergone discussion between the two authors' (Bain 1882a, pp. 142–3). Bain continued:

In fact, Mill could have been little more than an approving listener, in all those numerous conversations: with his admirable tact, saying nothing, when he found that he could make no impression. We have to look to his own article on Education to see that he pursued a distinct track; agreeing with Bentham always in spirit, but not dwelling on the same topics. (Bain 1882a, p. 144, see also Ripoli 1998, pp. 111ff.)

Mill, himself, discounted their discussions in a revealing passage in his *A Fragment on Mackintosh*:

It may be safely affirmed, that no man ever derived his opinions from the lips of Mr. Bentham. It is well known, to all who are acquainted with the habits of that great man, that conversation with him was relaxation purely. It was when he had his pen in his hand, that his mind was ever raised to the tone of disquisition; and he hated at any other time to be called upon for the labour of thinking. Except in the way of allusion, or the mention of some casual circumstance, the doctrines he taught were rarely, if ever, the subject of conversation in his presence. (James Mill 1835, p. 123)

Mill's comment might provide an explanation for Bain's perplexity at Mill and Bentham sharing the same room for work at Ford Abbey, when they might easily have occupied separate rooms in the grand house (see Bain 1882a, p. 135). Despite their separateness their physical proximity might be a symbol of a close philosophical relationship.

By all accounts the two men had become very close. Two years earlier, in a letter to Mill, written half in jest, Bentham proposed that if James Mill met an untimely death, Bentham might be appointed the guardian to the young Mill who was then six years old. Among his duties would be to teach him 'to make all proper distinctions between the Devil and the Holy Ghost, and how to make Codes and Encyclopaedias ...' (Bentham 1988b, p. 253). Mill replied that he was not about to die, but he would seriously accept the offer so that the young Mill would become 'a successor worthy of both of us' (Bentham 1988b, p. 255). In September 1814, however, when both were at Ford Abbey, Mill wrote to Bentham an extraordinary letter designed to diminish the closeness of their friendship for the sake of the future of their philosophy. At first glance the letter might be seen solely as a protest against Bentham's possessiveness (increased perhaps with his brother's departure) and pettiness (with his objections to Mill riding with Joseph Hume (1777–1855) to see the countryside rather than taking his customary walk with Bentham) (see Bain 1882a, p. 141). According to Mill:

The number of those is not small who wait for our halting. The infirmities in the temper of philosophers have always been a handle to deny their principles; and the infirmities in ours will be represented as by no means small, if in the relation in which we stand, we do not avoid shewing to the world that we cannot agree. (Bentham 1988b, p. 417)

Mill seems to be proposing here that to avoid the scandal of a public breach the two should remain together for the sake of their offspring, in this case, philosophy.

The concern here was with a philosophical legacy. It is somewhat ironic that although James Mill was twenty-five years younger than Bentham, and on the grounds of age might feel that he would be Bentham's successor, he in fact lived only four years longer. At any rate, Mill believed that Bentham was the author of a 'system of important truths' and that Mill was 'a most faithful and fervent disciple, hitherto I have fancied, the master's favourite disciple'. He then gave three reasons for believing that 'no body at all [would be] so likely to be your real successor as myself'. First, he did not know of any other person who had 'so compleatly taken up the principles, and is so thoroughly of the same way of thinking as yourself'. Second, there were few others who had acquired the philosophical discipline to obtain a knowledge of the system. Finally, Mill was willing to devote his life 'to the propagation of the system' (Bentham 1988b, p. 417). He concluded this estimation of his qualities as a disciple by congratulating Bentham for his good fortune in having encountered himself: 'I have often reflected upon it as a very fortunate coincidence that any man with views and propensities of such rare occurrence as mine, should happen to come in toward the close of your career to carry on the work without any intermission' (Bentham 1988b, pp. 417–18). Despite Bentham's advanced age, it would be highly misleading to believe that he was at the close rather than at the height of his career. Nor does it make sense to regard Mill as Bentham's only disciple at this time. One might refer simply to Romilly and Dumont among many others.

We do not know Bentham's response to Mill's letter, but Mill's plan to leave Queen's Square for Scotland and then France was not realised, and despite some conflict between James Mill and Bentham, the philosophical breach never took place. But James Mill seems to have assumed that Bentham's philosophical legacy would first be inherited by himself, with his son to receive his inheritance from him rather than directly from Bentham (cf. Robson 1964, pp. 253ff.).

5   Philosophic radicalism

There is considerable confusion surrounding the terms 'philosophic radical' and 'philosophic radicalism'. One view links them with the thought of Bentham and its development by James and J. S. Mill. Elie Halévy writes simply that 'in Jeremy Bentham, Philosophical Radicalism had its great man' (Halévy 1928, p. xviii; see also Dinwiddy 1992b, pp. 286ff.; Finer 1972, pp. 11ff.; Schofield 2004, p. 401). Others confuse utilitarianism generally with philosophic radicalism, and can write of three generations of the doctrine (led by Bentham, James Mill and J. S. Mill) beginning in the early nineteenth century (see Pringle-Pattison 1907, pp. 3–6, 23ff.).

A second conception takes a more limited view of the philosophic radicals and their doctrine. They were supposedly a small group of mainly radical parliamentarians formed after 1832 and led unsuccessfully from outside parliament by J. S. Mill as editor of the *London and Westminster Review* during the 1830s (see Stephen 1900, III, pp. 29ff.). It has been doubted that the philosophic radicals formed either a coherent group or were even disciples of Bentham and James Mill (see Thomas 1974, pp. 53ff., 1979, p. 11, 1985, p. 50). This view, largely correct, has several variations. Hamburger, for instance, uses the example of the philosophic radicals to challenge Bagehot's view of English politics as existing without dogmatism. On the contrary, he finds that the small group of radicals took some of Bentham's ideas and 'fashioned a rationale and a guide for reshaping a particular regime – what we would call an ideology' (Hamburger 1965, p. 1; see Thomas 1974, p. 53n). To show that this group possessed ideological coherence, Hamburger then uses James Mill's 1814 letter to Bentham, discussed above, to show how Mill sacrificed his feelings for the sake of the ideological movement (Hamburger 1965, p. 3). If little of this approach seems correct nowadays, at least

Hamburger does not simply combine philosophic radicalism and Benthamite utilitarianism as a single doctrine.

J. S. Mill seems to have coined the terms in 1834 in essays published in the *Monthly Repository* (cf. Thomas 1979, p. 2). At this time he clearly had in mind a fairly restricted group, as when he referred to 'the little band of enlightened and philosophic Radicals' or to 'the little knot of philosophic radicals' (Mill 1982, *CWM*, VI, pp. 191, 212). He used the terms to identify a particular group of radicals in Parliament after the passage of the Reform Bill, who did not always succeed in carrying on the process of radical reform. Mill decided to take up the burden of leadership by becoming editor (and later proprietor) of the *London and Westminster Review*. He wanted the journal 'to awaken the slumbering energy of the radical leaders, and to force the Whigs to take a decided part', i.e. to support radical causes (Mill 1963, *CWM*, XII, p. 316). The philosophic radicals were men like George Grote (1794–1871) and John Arthur Roebuck (1801–79) and latterly Charles Buller (1806–48) and Sir William Molesworth (1810–55). J. S. Mill became the chief exponent in the press, writing mainly for the *Examiner* and, as we have seen, the *Monthly Respository*. In April 1835 Molesworth started the *London Review* to rival the *Westminster Review*, and in 1836 he bought the *Westminster Review* and merged the two journals to form the *London and Westminster Review*. Mill began as editor and in 1837 became proprietor which lasted until 1840 (see Stephen 1900, III, pp. 30–1). According to Bain, Mill published seven or eight of eighteen numbers of the review at an estimated personal cost to him of £1,500 to £2,000 (see Bain 1882b, p. 58).

In the autumn of 1834 when Molesworth was planning the *London Review*, he and his friends were delighted with the involvement of J. S. Mill. Molesworth reported to Harriet Grote that 'John is in such spirits that he says he would make it succeed single-handed', to which he added that 'Old Mill will write, consequently we shall be *respectable*' (Grote 1866 p. 8). Harriet Grote acknowledged that Molesworth had a promising editor: 'a young man whose talents were then dawning upon the world of intellect – Mr. John Stuart Mill' (Grote 1866, p. 9). James Mill contributed to the first number and to subsequent numbers up to April 1836, a few months prior to his death (see Mill 1981, *CWM*, I, p. 209n).

Within three years Mrs Grote would doubt that the *Review* could be 'the engine of propagating sound and sane doctrines on Ethics and Politics under J.M. . . . I only wonder how the people contrive to keep improving, under the purveyance of the stuff and nonsense they are subjected to' (Bain 1882b, pp. 56n–7n). The problem and change of heart were concerned with the nature of radicalism, and, to an extent, with the use of the phrase, 'philosophic radical'.

The article in which Mill first developed the phrase, 'philosophic radical', was a review of Albany Fonblanque's *England Under Seven Administrations* (1837) and was published in the *London and Westminster Review* in 1837 (Mill 1982, *CWM*, VI, pp. 349–80). Here he declared simply that 'Fonblanque's opinions, it need scarcely be said, are those of the philosophic radicals' (Mill 1982, *CWM*, VI, p. 353; see also Fonblanque 1874, p. 6). Mill began his discussion by distinguishing the philosophic radicals from four other kinds. He called the first the 'historical radicals, who demand popular institutions as the inheritance of Englishmen, transmitted to us from the Saxons or the barons of Runnymede'. The second were termed 'metaphysical radicals' who believed in principles of democracy derived from 'some unreal abstraction' such as natural liberty or natural rights. A third group consisted of 'radicals of occasion and circumstance' who opposed the government over particular issues at particular times. The fourth were 'radicals of position' who were radicals simply because they were not lords. The philosophic radicals, different from these other kinds:

are those who in politics observe the common practice of philosophers – that is, who, when they are discussing means, begin by considering the end, and when they desire to produce effects, think of causes. (Mill 1982, *CWM*, VI, p. 353)

Mill went on to say that people with this philosophical disposition became radicals when they perceived the need to oppose the aristocratic principle in government and society. He referred to this group as a 'party' and seemed to suggest that Fonblanque was its bravest warrior, if not its leader (Mill 1982, *CWM*, VI, p. 353). Fonblanque did not base his radicalism on deductions from *a priori* principles but rather on seeing things as they are – 'for taking a just view of the existing influences in society, as they actually operate' (Mill 1982, *CWM*, VI, p. 355). Nevertheless, in a subsequent altercation with Fonblanque it was clear that 'philosophic radical' was a highly contentious phrase even among the 'little knot' that constituted the group. Then editor of the *Examiner*, Fonblanque wrote on 28 January 1838, under the heading, 'Mr. E. Bulwer and Mr. Grote':

The name of 'philosophical Radicals' was bestowed [on] themselves by the gentlemen whose opinions are represented by the London Review... To us it appeared better... that the world should find out that they were philosophical, than that they should proclaim it of themselves. But this is a matter of taste, and they are fond of calling themselves by good names, and like ladies, seem glad to change them; so they have been 'philosophical Reformers,' and 'thorough Reformers,' and 'earnest Reformers', and better still, 'entire Reformers'. (Mill 1963, *CWM*, XIII, pp. 369n–70n)

Mill was stung by this attack on him and on the journal. He protested that the phrase, 'philosophic radical', was never bestowed by the journal on its 'own writers or upon the people whom Bulwer called so in his speech'. According to Mill, 'philosophic radical' was a name given 'to the thinking radicals generally'. He wanted to distinguish them from other radicals: 'from the demagogic radicals, such as Wakely, and from the historical radicals of the Cartwright school, and from the division of property radicals if there be any'. Mill had thought that the *London and Westminster Review* would be the review representing 'this large body' and that the *Examiner* would be its newspaper. But he particularly objected to his being classed with reformers like Grote and Roebuck and pointed out that his radicalism was 'of a school the most remote from theirs, at all points, which exists' (Mill 1963, *CWM*, XIII, pp. 369–70; see also *Hansard's Parliamentary Debates* 1838, 3rd Series, XL, pp. 398–9; Thomas 1979, p. 202).

Although Bentham would not have objected to Mill's account of philosophic radicalism in terms of 'the common practice of philosophers', Mill had adopted a very different agenda from that found in Bentham and his followers (see Kinzer 1991, pp. 185ff.). Indeed, he wrote in the *Autobiography* that he was pursuing two objects in the journal:

One was to free philosophic radicalism from the reproach of sectarian Benthamism. I desired, while retaining the precision of expression, the definiteness of meaning, the contempt of declamatory phrases and vague generalities, which were so honourably characteristic both of Bentham and my father, to give a wider basis and a more free and genial character to Radical speculations; to shew that there was a Radical philosophy, better and more complete than Bentham's, while recognizing and incorporating all of Bentham's which is permanently valuable. In this first object, I, to a certain extent, succeeded. (Mill 1981, *CWM*, I, 221)

The second object was the attempt to reinvigorate radical politics, which he admitted was for the most part a failure (Mill 1981, *CWM*, I, pp. 221–3).

Mill's belief in the practical success of his work in the *London and Westminster Review* in freeing radicalism from the narrower confines of Benthamism must be interpreted in conjunction with the essays on Bentham and Coleridge which he published at the end of his involvement in the review. But in the *Autobiography* Mill also distinguished between Bentham and James Mill and credited the latter with a greater influence on the development of philosophic radicalism than the former. Mill wrote concerning his father:

This supposed school, then had no other existence than what was constituted by the fact, that my father's writings and conversation drew round him a certain number of young men who had already imbibed, or who imbibed from him, a greater or smaller portion of his very decided political and philosophical opinions. (Mill 1981, *CWM*, I, p. 103)

Mill dismissed the view that Bentham was surrounded by a body of active disciples; Bentham's influence, Mill maintained, was through his writings, and, presumably, those who surrounded him were mainly engaged in assisting him with his writings. Mill recognised that Bentham was 'a greater name in history', but believed that his father was the greater figure in conversation, and through the force of his character, he exerted great influence on a number of younger individuals whom Mill associated with philosophic radicalism (Mill 1981, *CWM*, I, pp. 103–5).

Mill referred to his father's essay, 'Government,' as 'a masterpiece of political wisdom', which had a considerable influence on this youthful group, even though many disagreed with a number of its doctrines, such as the exclusion of women and those under the age of forty from suffrage (Mill 1981, *CWM*, I, p. 107; see also Bentham 1973, pp. 311–12). As Mill stated in the materials he supplied regarding his father for Appendix C of Edward Bulwer Lytton's *England and the English* (1833), 'the Essay on Government, in particular, has been almost a text-book to many of those who may be termed the Philosophic Radicals' (Mill 1981, *CWM*, I, p. 594). Mill did not refer here to the first volume of Bentham's *Constitutional Code*, published in 1830, which was far more comprehensive and philosophical, if less widely read than his father's brief essay (see Bentham 1983b).

Mill's elevation of his father over Bentham, in the context of his account of radicalism, does not make much sense, because, by his own admission, both Bentham and his father subscribed to what in his terms was this narrower radicalism. Although Mill never publicly criticised his father, a clear personal tension in their relationship became evident in the 1830s. Even earlier, during his close friendship with Roebuck and George John Graham, Mill stood up to his father, when the latter disapproved of his new friends. Roebuck (1897, p. 29) wrote that while James Mill was 'a severe democrat', he 'bowed down to wealth and position', and dismissed those young men, like Roebuck and Graham, who at that time possessed neither ('he was rude and curt, gave us no advice, but seemed pleased to hurt and offend us'). This led to a falling out between father and son, with his mother fearing that J. S. Mill would leave the house (see Bain 1882b, pp. 39–40). The father then 'succumbed', but the friends no longer met at his house, and gathered instead at the home of Harriet Grote (Bain 1882b, p. 40; Roebuck 1897, p. 29; see Green 1989, pp. 263–5).

In spite of this declaration of independence, Mill remained essentially loyal to his father. As we have seen, he even sought to elevate James Mill's importance in the 1830s, even though his own brand of radicalism attempted to break away from that of the earlier generation. Roebuck observed with considerable insight:

But John Mill took especial care to confine his criticism to Bentham, and always avoided calling in question the views of his father. This led him, in my mind, to much wavering and uncertainty; and he wanted one main quality for an original thinker, and that was *courage*. (Roebuck 1897, p. 37)

If Mill's mental crisis occurred in 1826, when he was editing Bentham's *Rationale of Judicial Evidence*, he also became seriously ill in the 1830s at the time of the death of his father in 1836. According to Bain, 'he was seized with an obstinate derangement of the brain' – with symptoms of 'involuntary nervous twitchings in the face'. This condition, continued Bain, was due to the fact that 'he had ceased to give his father his confidence both in bodily and mental matters' (Bain 1882b, pp. 42–3). It is believed that he was ill for a considerable period, and Bain noted that 'he retained to the end of his life an almost ceaseless spasmodic twitching over one eye' (Bain 1882b, p. 44).

The simple contrast between Benthamite utilitarianism and philosophic radicalism does not make much sense. As we have seen, if Mill's conception of *philosophic* radicalism was based on the 'common practice of philosophers', 'who when they are discussing means, begin by considering the end, and when they desire to produce effects, think of causes', it would easily apply to Bentham. Furthermore, to favour his father's philosophical radicalism over Bentham's also does not make much sense, as James Mill became and continued to be a faithful disciple. Mill clearly desired to break out in a new direction, but he also sought to take the legacies of his father and Bentham with him (cf. Semmel 1998, p. 51). Nevertheless, if Mill failed to lead a radical party in the 1830s, he produced some important essays on how he defined the philosophical portion of his radicalism. Three of these essays will now be briefly considered.

6 'Remarks on Bentham's Philosophy'

Mill's first substantial essay on Bentham (it was preceded by the brief 1832 obituary published in the *Examiner* (Mill 1969, *CWM*, x, pp. 495–8)) appeared as an appendix to Bulwer's *England and the English* (1833), which also contained the appendix on James Mill for which J. S. Mill had supplied the notes. In the *Autobiography* Mill referred to this essay as his first attempt in print to state both a favourable and an unfavourable estimation of Bentham's doctrines 'considered as a complete philosophy' (Mill 1981, *CWM*, i, p. 207).

As for the favourable side Mill linked Bentham's project in legislation to that of Bacon. 'What Bacon did for physical knowledge', Mill wrote, 'Mr. Bentham has done for philosophical legislation' (Mill 1969, *CWM*, x, p. 9). Yet, Bentham had gone further than Bacon – he 'did not merely prophesy a science; he made large strides towards the creation of one'. Mill praised Bentham for being the first person to attempt 'to declare all the secondary and intermediate principles of law, by direct and systematic inference from the one great axiom or principle of general utility'. In addition, Bentham was praised ('the first, and perhaps the grandest achievement') for his work in discrediting the technical systems in law. Law ceased to be a mystery and became a matter of 'practical business, wherein means were to be adapted to ends, as in any of the other arts of life'. 'To have accomplished this', Mill continued, 'supposing him to have done nothing else, is to have equalled the glory of the greatest scientific benefactors of the human race' (Mill 1969, *CWM*, x, p. 10).

Mill particularly focused on Bentham's achievements in three spheres, that of civil law, penal law and judicial procedure. In civil law (confining his remarks apparently to the *Traités*), Bentham 'proceeded not much beyond establishing on the proper basis some of its most general principles, and cursorily discussing some of the most interesting of its details' (see Kelly 1990). In penal law 'he is the author of the best attempt yet made towards a philosophical classification of offences. The theory of punishment . . . he left nearly complete' (see Draper 1997; Rosen 2003, pp. 152–65, 209–19). In the realm of evidence and judicial procedure (on which Mill had worked for the *Rationale of Judicial Evidence*), he wrote that Bentham ' . . . found [it] in a more utterly barbarous state . . . and he left it incomparably the most perfect. There is scarcely a question of practical importance in this most important department, which he has not settled. He has left next to nothing for his successors' (see Twining 1985). Mill also noted that Bentham suggested how to cut 'nine-tenths of the expense and ninety-nine hundredths of the delay of legal proceedings' (Mill 1969, *CWM*, x, p. 11).

Despite this praise of Bentham's achievements, Mill omitted at least four important spheres of Bentham's thought, about which he would have known and on which he might have commented. The first was constitutional law on which Bentham had been busily working for the last decade of his life. Mill would have known of the publication of the first volume of *Constitutional Code* (1983b [1830]), and did mention it critically in the later essay on 'Bentham' (see Mill 1969, *CWM*, x, 106). His omission here, however, possibly reflected his view of the importance of his father's essay, 'Government', as well as a general disapproval of Bentham's apparently limited approach to government. The second omission concerned Bentham's logical writings, which are crucial to an understanding of Bentham's own philosophic radicalism. Although Mill, as we have seen, could write enthusiastically of Bentham's classification of offences, based on this method, he provided no analysis of the logical method itself. He had certainly read *Chrestomathia* and would have been familiar with the various tables based on logical division and the essays on classification and related topics (see Mill 1981, *CWM*, i, p. 572; Bentham 1983a). Nor did he mention the theory of language and the empirical connection between language and the world, developed in the theory of fictions (see Bentham 1932).

The third omission concerns Bentham's writing on codification itself, its objects and methods, which was an important achievement in its own right, apart from its use in particular fields of law (see Bentham 1998). The project of a complete code of laws might easily be regarded as the culmination of his philosophical project. A final omission was to neglect Bentham as a theorist of liberty not only in *Defence of Usury* (Bentham 1952–4 [1787], i, pp. 123–207), which had been widely debated in the 1820s (see Rosen 2003, pp. 114–30), but also in numerous works, where, for example, Bentham distinguished between spheres of private ethics and public legislation or emphasised individual security in relation to law and politics (see Bentham 1996, pp. 281ff.; Rosen 1992, pp. 25–76, 2003, pp. 245–55). These omissions are mentioned here less to criticise Mill but more to attempt to understand his criticisms of Bentham. Mill had his own agenda, which was to prise radicalism away from Benthamism and link its theoretical basis with his father and philosophic radicalism generally with himself. The reference to the work of David Hartley (Hartley 1749), for example, was used almost as code for James Mill, whose work on psychological association (James Mill 1829) was used to distinguish Bentham from James Mill, particularly in pointing out defects in Bentham as a moral philosopher. Unlike Bentham, Hartley (and presumably Mill's father) recognised the importance of feelings of 'moral sense', whereas Bentham, while considering sympathy, omitted feelings of duty, conscience, and generally right and wrong as *independent* motives for happiness (Mill 1969, *CWM*, x, p. 13).

On the whole Mill was most critical of Bentham as a moral philosopher, and, by implication, as a philosopher of mind. Bentham was criticised for ignoring character in his ethics, particularly in the chapters on motives and dispositions in *IPML* (Mill 1969, *CWM*, x, pp. 8–9; Bentham 1996, pp. 96–142). Bentham and his followers, he contended, emphasised the consequences of actions alone and 'rejected all contemplation of the action in its general bearings upon the entire moral being of the agent' (Mill 1969, *CWM*, x, p. 8). Furthermore, Mill wrote:

As an analyst of human nature (the faculty in which above all it is necessary that an ethical philosopher should excel) I cannot rank Mr. Bentham very high. He has done little in this department, beyond introducing what appears to me a very deceptive phraseology, and furnishing a catalogue of the 'springs of action', from which some of the most important are left out. (Mill 1969, *CWM*, x, p. 12)

Mill went on to criticise Bentham's conception of motives and interests in relation to virtue in the sense that a person 'recoils from the very thought of committing an act; the idea of placing himself in such a situation is so painful, that he cannot dwell upon it long enough to have even the physical power of perpetrating the crime' (Mill 1969, *CWM*, x, p. 12). Mill should have known that Bentham's idea of disposition (based on habit) could and did accommodate the concept of virtue, and while Mill was not able to read a decent version of *Deontology* (even Bowring's highly defective edition was not published until 1834; see Bentham 1834), he might have seen how the idea of virtue could easily fit into Bentham's system as a combination and completion of the work of Hume. But Mill at this point sought a more earnest and uplifting morality than he would find in either Hume or Bentham (see Rosen 2003, pp. 29–57). He criticised Bentham for using the language of interests, when such a language tended to be understood as purely self-regarding interest (see Mill 1969, *CWM*, x, p. 14). Bentham's philosophy provided no moral message and uplifting theme. Mill wrote:

Upon those who *need* to be strengthened and upheld by a really inspired moralist – such a moralist as Socrates, or Plato, or (speaking humanly and not theologically) as Christ; the effect of such writings as Mr. Bentham's . . . must either be hopeless despondency and gloom, or a reckless giving themselves up to a life of that miserable self-seeking, which they are there taught to regard as inherent in their original and unalterable nature. (Mill 1969, *CWM*, x, p. 16)

As if such a sin of omission, the failure to provide an uplifting moral doctrine, was not bad enough, Mill also asserted that 'by the promulgation of such views of human nature, and by a general tone of thought and expression perfectly in harmony with them, I conceive Mr. Bentham's writings to have done and to be doing very serious evil' (Mill 1969, *CWM*, x, p. 15).

In his theory of government Mill not only ignored *Constitutional Code* (Bentham 1983b [1830]), other writings on government (e.g. *A Fragment on Government* (Bentham 1988c [1776]) and those on parliamentary reform, but he also criticised him for failing to go beyond a theory of legislation to develop a 'theory of organic institutions'. Such a theory would include 'the great instruments of forming the national character; of carrying forward the members of the community towards perfection or preserving them from degeneracy' (Mill 1969, *CWM*, x, p. 9; see also Varouxakis 1998, 2002a). He also criticised Bentham for not giving due weight to what he called 'the historical recollections of a people' in so far as these 'recollections' formed the basis of political institutions (Mill 1969, *CWM*, x, p. 17).

These criticisms on their own do not seem adequate. Mill ignored Bentham's emphasis on the continuity of traditional institutions in grounding government on a 'habit' of obedience within the people (Bentham 1988c [1776], p. 40). Furthermore, Bentham regarded his *Constitutional Code* (Bentham 1983b [1830]) as setting out the institutions that could lead to perfection and preserve the populace from degeneracy. In addition, Bentham might well have argued that the object of moral and political philosophy was not to provide moral uplift, but to seek the truth through the analysis of the language and concepts employed in argument, and an assessment of their contribution to human happiness. He meant his philosophy to be a critical doctrine, seeking truth by first exposing error and then by developing alternative arrangements.

Mill, however, set these concerns aside, as he wanted to conclude not that Bentham had a reply to these criticisms, but that Bentham was correct as far as he went. His philosophy was 'one of the faces of the truth, and a highly important one'. More specifically, Bentham's doctrines concerned with government and morality 'are still highly instructive and valuable to any one who is capable of supplying the remainder of the truth; they are calculated to mislead only by the pretension which they invariably set up of being the whole truth' (Mill 1969, *CWM*, x, p. 18). It is clear from the discussion thus far that he regarded the remainder of the truth as best supplied by his father's philosophy and his own attempt to build on that philosophy.

7 'Bentham' and 'Coleridge'

Many of the themes first stated in the 'Remarks on Bentham's Philosophy' were developed further in the two substantial essays, 'Bentham' and 'Coleridge' (Mill 1969, *CWM*, x, pp. 77–115, 119–63), published in the *London and Westminster Review* in 1838 and 1840. The essay on Bentham was ostensibly a review of the early volumes of the new edition of Bentham's *Works*, but from the outset the two essays were conceived as being related to each other (Mill 1969, *CWM*, x, pp. 76, 77). Rather than providing a full account of these important texts (see, for example, August 1975, pp. 74ff.; Robson 1968; Ryan 1975, pp. 53–8), my object here will be to explore them mainly in terms of the issues already raised in the present essay. One issue is concerned with how Mill saw the intellectual legacy he inherited from Bentham and his father. The second is Mill's conception of philosophic radicalism and how it differed from Bentham's own philosophically inspired radicalism.

Although James Mill had died in 1836, just after the publication of the 'Remarks on Bentham's Philosophy' and prior to the publication of 'Bentham' two years later, J. S. Mill did not use this occasion to provide as critical an assessment of his father's thought as he did of Bentham's. Indeed, in 'Bentham', though understated in some respects, the younger Mill seemed to inflate his father's role in completing the 'metaphysical' side of Bentham's philosophy. In linking the 'negative' philosophy of the eighteenth century with the work of David Hume, and assessing Bentham's role as a follower of Hume, he wrote: 'If Bentham had merely continued the work of Hume, he would scarcely have been heard of in philosophy; for he was far inferior to Hume in Hume's qualities, and was in no respect fitted to excel as a metaphysician.' Mill then continued by turning to his father 'who united the great qualities of the metaphysicians of the eighteenth century, with others of a different complexion, admirably qualifying him to complete and correct their work' (Mill 1969, *CWM*, x, p. 80). In contrast, Mill insisted that Bentham's mind was 'essentially practical' and that it was roused to speculation and hence 'to carry the warfare against absurdity' by the abuses he saw in practical arrangements, and mainly in the law (Mill 1969, *CWM*, x, p. 81). Although Mill appreciated the significance of Bentham's achievement, as one of the two seminal minds of his generation, his comments about his father gave the impression that Bentham's legacy was seriously deficient. However, Mill emphasised in 'Bentham' that Bentham's method was original and philosophically important:

It is the introduction into the philosophy of human conduct, of this method of detail – of this practice of never reasoning about wholes until they have been resolved into their parts, nor about abstractions until they have been translated into realities – that constitutes the originality of Bentham in philosophy, and makes him the great reformer of the moral and political branch of it. (Mill 1969, *CWM*, x, p. 86)

Mill insisted on the genuine originality of Bentham's method by arguing that it was not part of the utilitarian tradition rooted in ancient Epicureanism:

The application of a real inductive philosophy to the problems of ethics, is as unknown to the Epicurean moralists as to any of the other schools; they never take a question to pieces, and join issue on a definite point. Bentham certainly did not learn his sifting and anatomizing method from them. (Mill 1969, *CWM*, x, p. 87)

Mill was not entirely fair to the Epicurean tradition, as he seemed to refer mainly to the discussions in Cicero's *de Finibus*, and not to the more 'scientific' modern version associated with Gassendi and linked to Hobbes, Locke, Hume, Smith, Helvétius and Bentham (see Rosen 2003, pp. 15–28). Without denying its originality, one could more easily see Bentham's method emerging from this more modern tradition. Furthermore, the darker truths of man's inhumanity to man, as part of the whole Epicurean tradition from Lucretius onwards, motivated Bentham to use his method to protect individuals against such evil by attacking abuses of power and showing how one might reduce suffering in society. His method, then, was closely linked to his Epicurean conception of utility. Nevertheless, in making this contention regarding Bentham's method, Mill enabled James Mill's 'metaphysics' to fill an 'empty' space in modern thought.

In 'Coleridge', when Mill came to the point where he had to choose between the eighteenth-century philosophy of Bentham and the nineteenth-century 'Germano-Coleridgean' philosophy that opposed it, he clearly and emphatically came down on the side of Bentham:

It [Mill's opinion] is, that the truth, on this much-debated question, lies with the school of Locke and of Bentham. The nature and laws of Things in themselves, or of the hidden causes of the phenomena which are the objects of experience, appear to us radically inaccessible to the human faculties. (Mill 1969, *CWM*, x, p. 128)

If Mill rejected the doctrine of transcendental truth in Coleridge and others in the 'German' school, he nonetheless found it very valuable on another level. The development of Locke's theory in the eighteenth century had been uneven with most attention given to the theory of knowledge rather than to his psychology. The system of Condillac, Mill believed, was inadequate, even useless. Hartley's highly original and important work had been ignored. However, the attack by Reid and members of the 'German' school on Locke's psychology forced those who were followers of Locke to reconsider the work of Hartley who might otherwise have been forgotten and whose associationism solved numerous problems in Locke's psychology (Mill 1969, *CWM*, x, 129–30). In a footnote to the original 1840 edition Mill added a reference to James Mill's *Analysis of the Phenomena of the Human Mind* as 'the greatest accession to abstract psychology since Hartley' (Mill 1969, *CWM*, x, p. 130n). Hence, thanks to Coleridge and the 'German' school whose doctrine forced those in the Lockean school in a sense to keep truth alive and repair its deficiencies, James Mill came into his legacy as the 'metaphysician' that completed the doctrine of Bentham. If Bentham's longevity prevented Mill from becoming his master's successor, the son has nonetheless enabled him to realise his inheritance not only as a leader of the philosophic radicals but also as a leading metaphysician in his own right.

One might wonder why Mill did not contrast James Mill and Coleridge rather than Bentham and Coleridge. But the two essays on Bentham and Coleridge have few philosophical objectives and are written from within the perspective of radicalism. This thesis requires some explanation, as by this time Mill seemed to have abandoned the project of intellectually leading a party of radicals. Although the two essays were published in the *London and Westminster Review*, the phrases 'philosophic radical' and 'philosophic radicalism' did not appear in them. Nevertheless, Mill's agenda remained the same. He sought to point out the weaknesses and limitations of Benthamism as a foundation for radical political reform, and indicate how these failings might be remedied through the study of Coleridge.

As Robson has remarked, 'the roots of Mill's comparison of Bentham and Coleridge in the opening pages of the essay on the latter, probably go back to arguments with Coleridgeans in the London Debating Society' (Mill 1969, *CWM*, x, p. cxxi). It is also fair to say that the comparison between the two thinkers was not restricted to the level of philosophical ideas, even though Mill began with an image of two closet-philosophers secluded 'by circumstances and character, from the business and intercourse of the world . . . ' and regarded 'by those who took the lead in opinion (when they happened to hear of them) with feelings akin to contempt'. But Mill's initial point of contrast between the two was as 'progressive' and 'conservative' thinkers. These appellations were more political than philosophical, though Mill did not hesitate to refer to Bentham as 'a Progressive philosopher' and Coleridge as 'a Conservative one' (Mill 1969, *CWM*, x, pp. 77–8).

But were Bentham and Coleridge 'the two seminal minds of England in their age' (see Bain 1882b, p. 56; cf. Colmer 1976, p. lxiii)? Note that despite the emphasis on the 'German' school of philosophy, Mill confined his attentions to England. Even Scotland, whose eighteenth-century philosophers, like Hume and Smith, were the greatest of the age, and which also contained important representatives of the so-called 'German' school, such as Reid, seemed to be excluded. When one recalls the attack on Bentham as a thinker in the earlier 'Remarks', and the fact that Coleridge was known more as a literary man than as a philosopher (cf. Morrow 1990, p. 164; Snyder 1929), the choice of Bentham and Coleridge as the two seminal minds seems even more problematic (cf. Mill 1980, pp. 9ff.). Indeed, the whole enterprise of comparing these two thinkers does not make much sense unless it is seen as an attempt to define a new political radicalism, based on a combination of Bentham and Coleridge, which is designed to replace the synthesis between philosophy and politics achieved by Bentham and his followers.

When Mill discussed these essays in the later *Autobiography*, he maintained that his criticisms of Bentham were 'perfectly just'. Nevertheless, he added the following comment:

but I have sometimes doubted whether it was right to publish it at that time. I have often felt that Bentham's philosophy, as an instrument of progress, has been to some extent discredited before it had done its work, and that to lend a hand towards lowering its reputation was doing more harm than service to improvement.

Mill continued by conceding that in the essay on Coleridge:

I might be thought to have erred by giving undue prominence to the favourable side, as I had done in the case of Bentham to the unfavourable. In both cases, the impetus with which I had detached myself from what was untenable in the doctrines of Bentham and of the eighteenth century, may have carried me, though in appearance rather than in reality, too far on the contrary side. But as far as relates to the article on Coleridge, my defence is, that I was writing for Radicals and Liberals, and it was my business to dwell most on that in writers of a different school, from the knowledge of which they might derive most improvement. (Mill 1981, *CWM*, I, pp. 225–7)

What is striking about these remarks is that they are set forth in the context of creating a new political radicalism, one detached from Benthamism, but also one addressed to those who, as radicals, might never have hitherto thought of studying Coleridge's moral and political writings. Mill might have argued simply that radicalism needed to add some of the insights of Coleridge to those of Bentham, for example to be less opposed to the Church by considering the role of a clerisy, or to see in Coleridge a liberal and progressive force not opposed to improvement, rather than simply a conservative (see Edwards 1995). To argue in this manner would allow Mill to remain in the Benthamite camp and to 'improve' that position by adding some of the doctrines of Coleridge.

For example, if Bentham did not appear to provide answers to questions regarding government such as 'to what authority is it for the good of the people that they should be subject?' or 'how are they to be induced to obey that authority?', but only to questions concerning the abuse of power and authority, one might simply add this material to Bentham's doctrine (Mill 1969, *CWM*, x, p. 106). This would be one way of improving Bentham. If Bentham failed to give due weight to 'national character', it would appear to be a fairly simple matter to add considerations of national character to Bentham's own conceptions of the public interest and public opinion (see Rosen 1983, pp. 19–40).

Mill, however, did not take this route. In the essays on Bentham and Coleridge he sought to establish a new perspective from which to create a new approach to the two thinkers, which would probably not appeal to any follower of Bentham (see Wallas 1951 [1898], p. 91) and possibly not to most followers of Coleridge. If in the London Debating Society, Benthamites and Coleridgeans were bringing out the negative and positive aspects of both thinkers, it was only Mill, as far as one can determine, who decided that future improvement required a new understanding and combination of the two. He did so, not for the sake of philosophy (for his position was settled there), but for the sake of the future of a radicalism that was philosophically inspired not only to replace that of Bentham but also to carry forward Bentham's perspective of a radicalism not based on envy or opportunism but on analysis and a programme for improvement (cf. Pringle-Pattison

1907, pp. 31–2). The perspective was thus philosophical in a limited sense, though the substance, political.

Mill began to develop this perspective by taking an independent position and regarding the two thinkers as fundamentally incomplete, but when brought into proximity, they provided a new perspective. Both were questioners of established arrangements. If Bentham asked 'is it true?', Coleridge asked 'what is the meaning of it?' Bentham stood outside as a stranger, while Coleridge looked at issues from within (Mill 1969, *CWM*, x, p. 119). If Bentham tended to discard an idea he found not to be true, for Coleridge, the fact that the idea had been believed for generations was 'part of the problem to be solved, was one of the phenomena to be accounted for'. As Mill put it in a bold assertion:

> From this difference in the points of view of the two philosophers, and from the too rigid adherence of each of his own, it was to be expected that Bentham should continually miss the truth which is in the traditional opinions, and Coleridge that which is out of them, and at variance with them. But it was also likely that each would find or show the way to finding, much of what the other missed. (Mill 1969, *CWM*, x, p. 120)

Just how 'each would find or show the way to finding much of what the other missed' is not entirely clear, but for Mill it depended on their being exact contraries of each other. Logicians would say that they 'are the farthest from one another in the same kind' (Mill 1969, *CWM*, x, p. 120). But what did Mill mean by such remarks and, particularly, by 'the same kind'? For Mill, there must be important points of agreement between them. He set these out in several propositions. First, they were the two men of their age who most agreed on the importance and necessity of philosophy. Second, both proceeded by linking opinions to first principles and examining the grounds and evidence for such opinions. Third, they both took the view that sound theory was a necessary basis for sound practice. Fourth, they both believed that the foundations of all philosophy had to be in philosophy of mind. Finally, although they used 'different materials' these materials were based on observation and experience. Thus, the two could supplement each other, because, for Mill, they were of 'the same kind', but, even more, they were each other's 'completing counterpart': 'the strong points of each correspond to the weak points of the other. Whoever could master the premises and combine the methods of both, would possess the entire English philosophy of their age.' If Coleridge in his *Table Talk* could divide people, 'by birth', into Platonists or Aristotelians, so Mill could assert that 'every Englishman of the present day is . . . either a Benthamite or a Coleridgian'

(Mill 1969, *CWM*, x, p. 121). In Mill's hands, however, the two might be combined but not to achieve a new 'truth' in philosophy of mind, for Mill remained on the side of Locke, Bentham, Hartley and James Mill. Mill seems more concerned with English national character, which, in his hands, would not reflect Bentham or Coleridge, but the two together with each providing what the other ignored.

One might be excused for still wondering what Mill was attempting to achieve. Mill clearly did not choose one side over another (cf. Semmel 1998, p. 50). Nor did he provide 'a vivid portrait of the liberal, or free and complete, mind' (Berkowitz 1998, p. 24). Bain saw in it 'a noble experiment' in combining opposites and maintaining 'a perpetual attitude of sympathy with hostile opinions'. But in the end, he saw in Mill's essays no lasting benefit: 'The watch-word in those days of the Review, was – Sympathise in order to learn. That doctrine, preached by Goethe and echoed by Carlyle, was in everybody's mouth, and had its fling' (Bain 1882b, pp. 57–8). The philosophical origin of this enterprise, if there was one, might be in the early Socratic dialogues of Plato, where, despite *aporeia*, what was achieved was the recognition that one only possessed an opinion of the truth, not the whole of it and possibly not the truth at all. Similarly, Mill could write that 'the besetting danger is not so much of embracing falsehood for truth, as of mistaking part of the truth for the whole'. Mill continued by asserting:

It might be plausibly maintained that in almost every one of the leading controversies, past or present, in social philosophy, both sides were in the right in what they affirmed, though wrong in what they denied; and that if either could have been made to take the other's views in addition to its own, little more would have been needed to make its doctrine correct. (Mill 1969, *CWM*, x, pp. 122–3)

Mill's doctrine looks more to tolerance than to Socratic ignorance. Nevertheless, one might say that Mill placed a social and political version of the Socratic dialectic at the heart of his new conception of philosophic radicalism (see Rosen 2003, pp. 201–2). He did not expect and did not present a final fusion of Bentham and Coleridge to provide a new doctrine to replace Benthamism (see O'Rourke 2001, pp. 51ff.). The dialectical process was ongoing and, in his later striking arguments in *On Liberty* as well as in 'Coleridge', Mill used the example of Rousseau's thought which set an imposing challenge to those who championed the virtues of civilisation by extolling the virtues of independence (Mill 1969, *CWM*, x, p. 123). Both had merit in their positive doctrines, but their weakness rested with mistaking part for the whole and failing to see either the negative side of their own doctrines or to appreciate the positive side of the other's doctrine. Mill then suggested that with regard to partial truths, there were always two conflicting modes of thought, one that tended to give the truth too large and the other, too small a place in public debate. '[A]nd the history of opinion is generally an oscillation between these extremes' (Mill 1969, *CWM*, x, p. 124).

The 'Germano-Coleridgean' doctrine represented a severe reaction against the philosophy of the Enlightenment. It was ontological, where the latter was experimental, conservative as opposed to innovative, religious as opposed to infidel, concrete and historical as opposed to abstract and metaphysical, and poetical rather than matter-of-fact. But Mill then claimed that this reaction was not as severe as those which preceded it, particularly not as severe as that triumph that brought the philosophy of the eighteenth century to prominence and 'so memorably abused its victory, over that which preceded it'. Mill was even willing to propose a general proposition regarding human progress calling it 'the general law of improvement':

Thus every excess in either direction determines a corresponding reaction; improvement consisting only in this, that the oscillation, each time, departs rather less widely from the centre, and an ever increasing tendency is manifested to settle finally in it. (Mill 1969, *CWM*, x, p. 125)

The full nature of the improvement and the location of truth in this oscillation that may eventually end, but still requires free expression, open debate and the continued challenge of arguments simply to keep truth alive, cannot be explored further within the scope of this essay. Nevertheless, Mill had clearly found in Coleridge's thought (see O'Rourke, 2001, pp. 42ff.), together with an adoption of a Socratic method (see Demetriou 1999, p. 243) that allowed him to combine the thought of Bentham and Coleridge as 'completing counterparts', a radicalism that he thought he could use to remedy the deficiencies of Benthamism. For the most part Mill's radicalism remained one of ideas. It was philosophic radicalism but, paradoxically, it would not provide any leadership to the radicals whom a few years earlier Mill sought to lead (see Stephen 1900, III, p. 38), and, additionally, it represented no lasting contribution to philosophy. But it is also fair to conclude that his search for another way of doing philosophical ethics and politics continued in his subsequent writings from the *Logic* to

On Liberty, Utilitarianism and other works. If it lacked the decisiveness and even the philosophical coherence and grandeur that he recognised earlier in Bentham's philosophical radicalism, its challenge to that form of radical philosophy led utilitarianism to explore aspects of life and thought that were never on Bentham's original agenda.

9

John Stuart Mill, mid-Victorian

ROSS HARRISON

Looking back on John Stuart Mill, we see him as the most important English philosopher of his century. For us, he fits naturally into what we think of as a British empiricist tradition between Hume in the previous century and Russell in the next. Yet this is not how Mill himself would have thought of his work. 'Empiricism' was something he criticised and wished to avoid. Nor did he look back to Hume. Instead, he looked back to his father, James Mill. His father, he thought, provided the most advanced analysis of the human mind, which for Mill was the central key to all philosophy. And, again following his father, he looked back before him to the account of the mind in David Hartley, building on Locke.

A common ambition in all these thinkers (including Hume) is to construct a science of the human mind. 'Science' in Mill is specifically contrasted with 'empiricism'; so, in his own eyes, Mill was not an empiricist but, to use a word newly coined by his rival Whewell, a scientist. More precisely, he was not so much an active scientist as a profound analyst of how science ought to operate. His most significant early work, the *Logic* of 1843, is primarily a philosophy of science. Its culminating Book VI is entitled 'The Logic of the Moral Sciences'. This crown, towards which the whole work drives, is a study of the proper method of investigation in the 'moral' (that is, the human) sciences. Among these sciences is political science. Study of the correct way to know should produce correct knowledge about politics; and such knowledge in turn should guide us in the best political behaviour. By knowing how to know, we should end up knowing how to do; or, in Mill's terms, the 'art' of politics should be based on the 'science' of politics. The art, the practice, the real action, is for Mill always the final test. All his life he

References to Mill in the form (*CWM*, A.b) are to *The Collected Works of John Stuart Mill* (Toronto, London and Indianapolis, 1963–1991), cited by volume and page number. In the case of *On Liberty* this is preceded by an alternative citation giving chapter and paragraph number.

kept in close touch with it. For him, it is the point of thought. Otherwise we have mere metaphysical dreams.

This chapter will discuss Mill's attempt to create a logical framework for the science of politics, and so a foundation for the emerging mid-Victorian liberalism. It starts with further consideration of Mill's development of previous thought. Then, after discussion of the logical framework and the problems of a science of human nature, it concludes with consideration of Mill's mature and most significant political philosophy. This is presented in *On Liberty*, the *Considerations of Representative Government*, and the long, last, chapter on justice in *Utilitarianism*. These three works were published close together between 1859 and 1861 (when Mill, born in 1806, was in his mid-fifties), after he had been writing significant work for thirty-five years.

One curiosity about Mill is that these works that are most significant for us, the late political and moral writings, are not the largest or most serious works that he wrote. *A System of Logic, Ratiocinative and Inductive* is what initially gave him his reputation as a thinker. The *Logic* of 1843 and the *Principles of Political Economy* of 1848 have a toughness of argument, an exhaustiveness of range, and an academic approach unlike any of the later, better known, political and moral works. Nor is this merely a function of Mill's age. For after the well-known trio of the early 1860s, Mill wrote in 1865 another enormous work, the *Examination of William Hamilton's Philosophy*; this time its length and seriousness was devoted to metaphysics. (Both the Mills ended their careers with a highly critical account in which a Scotsman is torn into excessively many shreds; his father, James Mill, died the year after he published his *Fragment on Mackintosh* but Mill survived until 1873 after examining Hamilton.)

1   Intellectual and biographical context

Mill started as a disciple of his father and Jeremy Bentham, fully on song as a utilitarian. Then, as he describes captivatingly in his *Autobiography*, he departed to some extent from the faith of his fathers and constructed a theory and practice of his own. This was still, like them, utilitarian. He was still, like them, an advocate of representative democracy. However, it was done with a difference, and both the differences and continuities are important in understanding his thought.

Growing up the son of Bentham's secretary, living next door to Bentham, and going on extended visits to Bentham's country house, Mill's education was designed to make him the perfect Benthamite (or utilitarian). And, indeed, that is how he started his adult activities: editing Bentham's monumental *Rationale of Evidence*; founding a discussion group to discuss utilitarian principles (which initially met in Bentham's house); mistakenly thinking that he had invented the word 'utilitarian'; going to public debating societies to propound the Benthamite cause against the Owenites; and so on. His early journalistic writings are exactly from the school, in tone, vocabulary and content. His first was one he wrote jointly with his father, an extended analysis and criticism of the Whig periodical, *The Edinburgh Review*.

After this early period of active enthusiasm, Mill became a more semi-detached Benthamite, as he met up with the young, Cambridge-educated followers of Coleridge and became a friend and temporary admirer of Carlyle (even attempting to copy the style until he realised that no one but Carlyle should write like Carlyle). Even in this period he remained identifiable with the cause and later, particularly in his *Utilitarianism* of 1861, he became the most conspicuous expounder and defender of the utilitarian position. However, as will be seen, this was a new, richer, more complex utilitarianism, benefiting from Mill's contact with its critics.

Ever since he described it in his *Autobiography*, Mill's education has been notorious. Started on Greek at three, he was educated by his father on the newly fashionable monitor system, by which James Mill educated John as the oldest child, and then John in turn educated his siblings (and was responsible for their defects). Designed, as seen, to produce a perfect Benthamite, it was not in fact an education of cram; and the method survives better than the content. This was to argue for positions in dialogue, and probe matters by discussion. The classical authors, and particularly Plato, were important; and Mill was getting more of this (and a more philosophical grip on it) than if he had been conventionally educated at public school and Cambridge.

He translated Plato early, but again it is the method that is important. The emphasis is on dialogue, dialectics and discussion. The Socratic method is the perfect educational tool. Mill walked with his father, discussing political economy, in much the way Socrates is represented by Plato in dialectical discussion with young Athenians. He later published translations of several Platonic dialogues and the dialectical method remains important throughout. As he puts it in *On Liberty*, 'mankind can hardly be too often reminded, that there was once a man named Socrates' (2.12; *CWM*, XVIII, p. 235). A different strand from the ancient world (here quoting his Coleridgean friend,

John Sterling) is the remark in *On Liberty* that 'Pagan self-assertion' is one of the elements of human worth, as well as 'Christian self-denial' (3.8; *CWM*, XVIII, p. 266).

There are several aspects of this early work which remain typical of Mill and help to understand the later, major, work and his contribution to the political thought of the mid-Victorian generation. Firstly, there is an interest in balance, synthesis and eclecticism; of learning from the other side. Always his temperament and practice, it became erected into a principle in *On Liberty*. Earlier, in his period of semi-detachment from Benthamism, he wrote a balanced pair of essays on Bentham and Coleridge (published in 1838 and 1840, respectively). For Mill, both of these thinkers are partially right; they are correct in their affirmations but wrong in their denials. Benthamism, therefore (the doctrine of his father), is only a partial truth. In chapter 2 of *On Liberty*, Mill identifies three conditions an opinion can be in with respect to truth and proves that in each case there is a benefit in liberty of thought about, and discussion of, the view. The two obvious cases are when the opinion is true and when it is false. However, Mill spends more time on (and is more interested in) the case where an opinion is partially true. This is the case, he thinks, with most political theories. This seems for Mill even to apply to liberty itself; it is a partial truth. At all times, Mill gives the sense of pushing an opinion to redress the balance because its rival has too much sway. But, at other times, the rival would be supported. Yes, he declares; yes to liberty and democracy. But, in Mill, 'yes' tends to be followed by 'but'.

This balancing is one standing characteristic. Another is a constant interest in practice. For Mill, the test of principles is how important they are in the actual business of living. This is true of his thought, but it is also true of his life. Mill was never an academic, dispassionate or otherwise. He had to earn his living elsewhere. This was in the India Office in the City of London, which was in control of the government of India. Mill, who ended up as the chief of this office, accumulated a lifetime of experience in practical administration (of the actual workings of government by bureaucracy). Outside the office, he did not only discuss economics, philosophy of mind and politics, but attempted practical promotion on the ground. When a young utilitarian he promoted birth control by leafleting, an activity for which he was briefly arrested. The theory behind it is neo-Malthusiasm: population is a primary problem in preventing the maximisation of welfare. However, unlike Malthus, Mill and his friends went for physical rather than moral restraint.

Also, and very importantly, there was the journalism. In the later 1830s Mill was a sort of leader from outside Parliament of the philosophic radicals, attempting to push their work forward by journalistic prompting. Here he was not just a mere commentator on politics or political theory. He also attempted to drive the actual, messy, process forward. The journalism was directed at particular political projects. It should be remembered that this is still the context of the mature works of political philosophy, which are today read for their own sake and independent of context. *On Liberty* tries to persuade a contemporary public of a particular position. It aims at a particular political and social effect in a particular context. *Utilitarianism* is also designed as a popular work, intended to influence contemporary public opinion, and thereby political practice. It first appeared in a sequence of issues of a general periodical; exactly like, indeed as a part of, the higher journalism.

2   The logic of the moral sciences

The 'philosophic radicals' (Mill coined the term) formed a third party after the 1832 Reform Bill. But the seeds of this late 1830s journalism lie earlier. The extensive criticism of the *Edinburgh Review* that Mill wrote with his father was produced in 1824. It is in the first year of the new utilitarian journal, *The Westminster Review*, which had been founded by the Benthamites to provide a third journalistic force to rival the Whig *Edinburgh Review* and the Tory *Quarterly Review*. A third journal gave the intellectual shell of a third party and, whatever its varying fortunes on the practical political ground, a third form of political theory.

Attacked, the *Edinburgh* became an enemy. In 1829, a series of influential and crushing articles in it by Macaulay specifically took as its target James Mill's most conspicuous work of political theory, his *Essay on Government* of 1821. Mill had already been through his 'mental crisis' (a crisis of the kind that was not noticeable to family and friends); he had already felt that if he devoted his life to Benthamism, it would not make him happy; he had already been subject to the seductions of the bright young Coleridgeans; and so he was ready for new, or any diverse, intellectual experiences. Nevertheless, the effect on Mill of this effective attack on the citadel of his old faith was severe. His reflection on it leads to his enquiry into the correct manner of proceeding in political science incorporated in the 1843 *Logic*. Mill's mature political thought can be tracked by seeing how he both agrees and disagrees with the political thought of his father, which was well known at the time.

James Mill's *Essay on Government* is a rigorously deductive argument, deriving the desirability of representative democracy as a perfect system from two premises, one descriptive and one evaluative. The evaluative premise is the utilitarian one; that the proper end of government (and, indeed, anything else) is to promote the general happiness. The descriptive premise is that people are activated by their self-interest. Given these, it is easy to prove that the only people who will promote the interests of the people as a whole are the group that have an interest in the people as a whole, that is the people themselves. The conclusion is deductive, certain; and since the premises are taken to be universally true, the conclusion is also true for all times and places.

This is the argument that Macaulay brilliantly and effectively ridiculed, principally attacking on the basis of history and experience James Mill's assumption of universal self-interest. Mill's later account has less surface brilliance, but it responds to the real problems in his father's account that Macaulay led him to see. Indeed the two methods discussed in chapters 7 and 8 of Book VI of the *Logic* may be taken to be accounts, respectively, of Macaulay and James Mill. They are both taken to be wrong, or, at least, only partially right, leading to Mill's preferred method.

The chapter that is effectively a criticism of Macaulay is entitled 'The Chemical, or Experimental, Method'. What is wrong with this is the attempt to derive conclusions in political science from mere accumulation of experience. For Mill, this is an incorrect invocation of Bacon (a much-revered figure at the time, particularly among the Whigs) and is mere, mistaken, empiricism. The chapter that is effectively a criticism of his father is more interesting. It is entitled 'The Geometrical, or Abstract, Method'. Mill does not mention his father here, preferring, so far as any particular individuals are mentioned at all, to let eighteenth-century French thinkers take the oppositional strain. What is wrong, he thinks, with the method of his actual or spiritual fathers was that it aimed to be rigorously deductive; it was what he calls a 'geometrical' method because it derived theorems deductively from axioms. Instead, Mill thinks, claims and conclusions have to be sensitive to circumstances.

This relativity to context is something that typifies all Mill's later work, including his most important mature thought. Mill is a well-known defender of liberty. But, as will be seen, liberty is not for him a universal prescription, true for all circumstances. Mill is also a well-known defender of representative democracy. But, again, this is only for people in certain cir-cumstances. His father's supposed axiom of universal self-interest is not, he says, always (or axiomatically) true. Rulers, he says in the *Logic*, are influ-enced 'by the habitual sentiments and feelings . . . which prevail throughout the community of which they are members' (vi.viii.3 *CWM*, viii, p. 891). This may, or may not, be what is in their own interest. Hence the impor-tance for Mill of the 'historical' method, and of Coleridge, who showed him the importance of history and of variability of circumstance. He repeats passages from his 1840 essay on Coleridge in his chapter on the 'historical' method in the *Logic*.

3   Harriet

Coleridge was one influence but, on Mill's own account, the chief influence on the central part of his life was a woman, Harriet Taylor. *On Liberty* opens with a fulsome declaration that the work is dedicated 'to the beloved and deplored memory of her who was the inspirer, and in part author, of all that is best in my writings' (*CWM*, xviii, p. 216). Mill first met his inspiration in 1830. Unfortunately for them both, Harriet was married to someone else. Mill wished to dedicate his *Political Economy* to her, but her husband naturally resisted and prevented such a public declaration of association. However, after Mr Taylor died, they were free to marry and did so, some two years after his death, in 1851. The marriage lasted seven years until Harriet's sudden death in 1858.

Throughout this time, Mill published very little, although he continued to work at the India Office, governing India by correspondence and then fighting to preserve the Company against take-over by the British state after the Indian Mutiny. Mill was defending his patch, as his job required. However, the argument rings true to his general thought. This was that gov-ernment by educated, supposedly impartial bureaucrats in Platonic fashion was superior to government of a foreign country by English MPs responsive to their domestic democratic pressures.

Although Mill published little in the 1850s, he worked with Harriet planning a series of essays in which they would condense their thoughts. (They constantly feared death and wanted to get it down as 'mental pem-mican' for posterity.) Chief among these was an essay on liberty and the essay with this title was indeed published in 1859, after Harriet's death with the dedication just cited. It was explicitly Mill's monument to his wife. (Because he declared it as a monument to Harriet that he would not alter, unlike his other works it did not change in other than minor grammatical alterations in the editions brought out through his lifetime.) Both then and since, it has indeed been regarded as Mill's main work in political theory. It has been regarded as one of the founding texts of the Western world, the world that is framed by an ideological attachment to liberty. It has also been argued over ever since its appearance, both as to what it means and its possibility of application. A deceptively simple work, *On Liberty* has been much misunderstood.

4 On what *On Liberty* is about

The difficulty in understanding *On Liberty* is not immediately obvious on first acquaintance. Instead, it seems to be one of those useful works in which the author clearly states the central point at the outset. In the first chapter Mill says that 'the object of this essay is to assert one very simple principle' which he immediately specifies. This is helpful, even though the principle has not seemed simple from Mill's day to the present; interpretation has always been required. It should also be noted that when Mill describes *On Liberty* in his *Autobiography* he again says that it has a single aim. It is, he says there, 'a kind of philosophic text-book of a single truth'. The trouble is that the 'one very simple principle' of chapter 1 is quite different from the 'single truth' of the *Autobiography*. So, again, the story is more complex than it initially seems, or than Mill says it is.

The 'very simple principle' of chapter 1 is that 'the sole end for which mankind are warranted, individually or collectively, in interfering with the liberty of action of any of their number, is self-protection' (1.9; *CWM*, xviii, p. 223). This does sound simple enough, particularly since Mill immediately proceeds to clarify it by continuing, 'The only purpose for which power can be rightfully exercised over any member of a civilised community, against his will, is to prevent harm to others.' 'Harm' has become the key word in interpretation, so that Mill's 'very simple principle' has come to be called the 'harm principle'. This is that only prevention of harm to others justifies interference.

So what is the 'single truth' of the *Autobiography*? It is 'the importance, to man and society, of a large variety in types of character, and of giving full freedom to human nature to expand itself in innumerable and conflicting directions' (*CWM*, I, p. 259). It is a plea for liberty as a plea for individuality, as a means of producing diversity. Nor is this a mere autobiographical reflection; it is in line with the epigraph of *On Liberty*, a quotation from

Von Humboldt saying that the 'grand, leading principle . . . is the absolute and essential importance of human development in its richest diversity' (*CWM*, xviii, p. 215).

These hints at a final goal, or leading principle, of the work have here to be put together to see how the prevention of harm, individuality, development and diversity are blended in Mill's mind and what they have to do with liberty. Mill supports his 'simple' principle with argument; he illustrates it with applications; and he explicitly outlines its goal, or point. So the material is there to resolve the question.

5   More misconceptions

On Liberty has been understood as an extreme promotion of individualism, of the rights of the individual against the state. But this is to understand it in too limited a way. It does claim that there is some part of an individual's thoughts and actions that should remain private in that it is entitled to remain exempt from state interference. However, to think of the work as only about this would be too negative. Mill in *On Liberty* says that 'liberty is often granted where it should be withheld, as well as withheld where it should be granted' (5.12; *CWM*, xviii, p. 301). So he thinks that there is often too much liberty and therefore wishes at times to reduce liberty as well as protect it in other circumstances. His self-appointed task, about which he is quite explicit, is to draw the line in the right place.

The state, which by threatening punishment restricts people's liberty, is therefore as important for Mill as it was for Bentham. In both cases, it is only by its great punishing power that people can be made to do what they should to achieve the common aim of maximising utility. Liberty has to be restricted to increase utility, and neither theorist is in any sense an anarchist, or concerned to maximise the liberties of individuals against the state. Indeed Mill goes further than Bentham (in, for example, *Political Economy*) in recommending how the state may also work positively to promote utility. As well as punishing, it can work by encouragement and example, as a co-ordinator of activity, and as a provider of public goods that would not be supplied by the market.

In chapter 4 of *On Liberty*, Mill explains how someone should be treated when we think that he has done something imprudent or distasteful. He then immediately goes on to say, 'It is far otherwise if he has infringed the rules necessary for the protection of his fellow-creatures.' In such a case 'society . . . must inflict pain on him for the express purpose of punishment, and must take care that it be sufficiently severe' (4.7; *CWM*, xviii, p. 280). We have here (as what 'must' happen) the Benthamite, terrifying, state; the state that protects rights by enforcing duties through fear of punishment; the state that sees that its threats are sufficiently severe to ensure adequate deterrence. We therefore need both aspects to understand Mill; that is, both where state power should keep out but also where state power is needed and should come in.

Another way to make Mill's argument too negative is to miss, or misrepresent, the point of state limitation. Here the *Autobiography* description should be remembered (and the *Autobiography* was another work that Mill and Harriet were cooking in their short marriage; it dates from the same time as *On Liberty*). Getting the state out of the way is not an end in itself. It has a point, a positive point. This is to allow variety of behaviour, experiments in living, a variety that, on Mill's theory, will promote the general good. The negative message, so far as it applies, is based on positive promotion of a particular end.

Another common misrepresentation is to think that Mill's concern is exclusively with the state; with what it should (or should not) do. He is read as promoting a position about how the law ought to be. This is natural from the uses of Mill in public policy arguments in the following century, such as with respect to the legalisation of homosexuality or pornography. (Although these are matters in which his name has been centrally cited, they are not matters about which he specifically wrote.) Yet Mill is quite clear, in the negative part of his message, that a serious threat to individuality comes from the moral force of public opinion as well as from the legal force of the state. In chapter 1 of *On Liberty* 'law' is constantly twinned with 'public opinion' as the repressive forces invading appropriate liberty. What he wants to control is 'the disposition of mankind, whether as rulers or fellow citizens, to impose their own opinions and inclinations, as a rule of conduct on others' (1.15; *CWM*, xviii, p. 227). Indeed, he thinks that in the England about which he is writing, the force of public opinion, particularly of middle-class opinion, is a more important threat than state-backed legal sanctions. It is 'a social tyranny more formidable than many kinds of political repression' because 'it leaves fewer means of escape' (1.5, *CWM* xviii, p. 220).

So Mill's message is not merely the negative one that people should be left alone. In chapter 4 of *On Liberty* he remarks that 'it would be a great misunderstanding of this doctrine to suppose that it is one of selfish indifference, which pretends that human beings have no business with each other's conduct in life' (4.4; *CWM*, xviii, pp. 276–7). By contrast, he remarks that 'there is need of a great increase of disinterested exertion to promote the good of others'. Mill clearly therefore is not recommending that people leave each other alone. But how is interference permissible beyond the application of appropriate legal and social sanctions? This is where Mill provides subtle treatment of how we should treat people with whom we disagree but who have not invaded the rights of others. We may offer 'considerations to aid his judgement, exhortations to strengthen his will' (4.4; *CWM*, xviii, p. 277). This is problematic; the line is fine between helpful persuasion and improper social pressure. But what is clear is that we should concern ourselves with others, even when 'whips and scourges, either of the literal or the metaphorical sort' are inappropriate.

6   Value base

The doctrine of *On Liberty*, therefore, is not that people should as far as possible be left alone but, rather, that interference should happen in the right place in the right manner and for the right reason. Near the start, as part of his criticism of contemporary thought and practice, he says that there is 'no recognised principle by which the propriety or impropriety of government interference is customarily tested' (1.8; *CWM*, xviii, p. 223). The question is one of demarcation, of the proper area in which people should be exempt from interference and the proper area for control. This involves a proper account of the proper, and here Mill bases the particular argument on a more general epistemology and theory of value, such as occur throughout his work. The epistemology, of which the *Logic* is the centrepiece, is the substitute of science and observation for intuition and feeling. This is the thrust of his early attack on the moral doctrine of the Cambridge philosopher, Whewell. It is the substance of much of the first chapter of *On Liberty*. Here he wishes to expose how people depend for their conclusions on 'sympathies and antipathies' rather than 'interests' (1.6; *CWM*, xviii, p. 221); how they depend on their 'sentiments'; how law follows the 'sentiment of the majority'. Later, considering applications, he wishes to show particularly how wrong conclusions are based on feelings, in particular feelings of disgust at particular kinds of conduct.

If Mill, like Bentham before him, wishes to substitute 'reason' for 'sentiment', then, again like Bentham before him, he needs a basis for his value theory so that the line between proper and improper interference can be based on 'principle' rather than mere instinct, or feeling. And, like Bentham, the value theory that does the work is utilitarianism. This is quite specific in *On Liberty* where Mill states that 'it is proper to state that I forgo any advantage that could be derived to my argument from the idea of abstract right, as a thing independent of utility. I regard utility as the ultimate appeal on all ethical questions' (1.11; *CWM*, xviii, p. 224).

The ethical or evaluative basis is not duty or rights, let alone sentiments. It is utility. Shortly after *On Liberty* Mill wrote *Utilitarianism*, a defence of the doctrine of his father and Bentham. It contains, as half of its text, a chapter on justice, which was originally intended as a separate essay, another part of the pemmican condensation of the 1850s, and, like *Liberty*, an application of utilitarianism to a topic more of political than individual morality. The name is the father's name, but the doctrine is worn by Mill with a difference. In chapter 2 of *Utilitarianism* he famously says that 'it is quite compatible with the principle of utility to recognise the fact, that some *kinds* of pleasure are more desirable and more valuable than others. It would be absurd that while, in estimating all other things, quality is considered as well as quantity, the estimation of pleasures should be supposed to depend on quantity alone' (*CWM*, x, p. 211).

Mill's utilitarianism therefore does not consist in merely adding up sums about pleasure. In both works it is the kind of utility that counts. Hence the importance of the central, third, chapter of *On Liberty*. This gives a fuller exposition of the value theory behind the work, of why exactly liberty is of value. And what we find here is not that we will get a greater quantity of pleasant sensations if we promote liberty. Instead, we find that we get people of more valuable character. We need liberty to gain individuality; 'Of individuality, as one of the elements of well-being' is the chapter's title. Here we remember the 'single truth' of the work as described in the *Autobiography* (the importance of large variety in types of character). We remember the quotation of Von Humboldt used as the epigraph on the importance of diversity. By the 'experiments in living' that Mill promotes in this chapter, he hopes to discover the better kinds of utility, seeking quality rather than quantity.

7   Utility old and new

Mill said that he wished to combine the best of the eighteenth century and the best of the nineteenth century. This is exemplified by the way that utility forms the foundation of *On Liberty*. Utility is itself very much an eighteenth-century theme, with Bentham applying the thought of other eighteenth-century thinkers such as Helvetius and Beccaria. From Mill's perspective it was all too mechanical. For them, the state was a machine constructed to maximise pleasure and minimise pain. It was just like Bentham's famous prison, the Panopticon: a suitable arrangement of matter would cause people led by their natural drives to their own pleasure and avoidance of pain to do what was needed to maximise overall satisfaction, impartially considered.

This structure of motive and desired result, this use of law and government, is, as we have seen, still true of Mill. He accepted this part of his inheritance. But the elements entering into the machine and the way that it was meant to operate are different. Instead of the metaphors and analogies being mechanical, for Mill they are organic. Rather than forces being aligned on dead matter (as in that other eighteenth-century development, the accurate watch), we have the conditions appropriate for growth. The metaphors are horticultural. Cultivation is the key and development, especially self-development, is the end. Rather than maximising the occurrence of a particular kind of sensation, we need the development of the whole person. We need values that do not simply reduce to a sum of atomistically considered sensations. Above all, we need to consider what Mill calls character.

The more valuable kinds of utility in *Utilitarianism* are those that distinguish people from animals. Hence Mill's remark that it is 'better to be a human being dissatisfied than a pig satisfied' (*CWM*, x, p. 212). Mill's different way of understanding utility is quite specifically flagged in *On Liberty* itself. Immediately after he makes the remark, quoted above, that his ultimate appeal is to utility, he continues, 'but it must be utility in the largest sense, grounded on the permanent interests of man as a progressive being'. (This is one of the few points where corrupt texts in circulation have caused confusion; a printer's mistake in an early edition, inserting 'a' before 'man' has been extensively copied, leading to misquotation of this remark. Mill is concerned with the nature of people as such, not with specific individuals.)

Liberty is valued not for itself but because it has a point. So also representative democracy in Mill's *Considerations on Representative Government*. In both cases, the forms of law or government are to be valued because they lead to the right kind of people, and are only to be valued so far as this is the case. Character is the key, here and elsewhere in Mill. So the question frequently asked, of whether his thought on liberty is compatible with his utilitarianism is easily answered, at least from his point of view. There is only one overall goal, not two competing ones. This is utility. It must, however, be utility properly understood ('utility in the wider sense, founded...'). Everything else of value (such as liberty or democracy) is of value because it promotes this goal.

For this to work, two things are needed and Mill aims to provide them in the crucial, central, third chapter of *On Liberty*, the hinge on which the whole work turns. The first is an account of this more general value, of character, of the most desirable kind of person. The second is an explanation of why liberty tends to promote this value. The two are linked by energy, by activity. The more desirable sort of character is the one that tends to arrive by self-development rather than being made. Rather than being mechanically manufactured by others, it grows of itself. Hence the horticultural metaphors. But it only grows of itself if it has the appropriate conditions, among which are government, and the right sort of government. It is a government that provides, protects, and enforces liberty. It is a government that moves by representative democracy. It is a government that understands the line between when it should interfere and when it should leave people alone.

8 Civilisation

The energy that Mill wishes to release by liberty brings up another aspect of his thought, and another matter in which he thinks that the thought of his father is limited. The cultivation extolled here would, it would seem, go with civilisation, and Mill much earlier (in 1836 when he was more detached from Bentham and his father) published an important essay entitled 'Civilisation'. He followed this up in his 1840 'Coleridge' essay, part of which, as we have seen, he repeated in his *Logic*, giving it the imprimatur of his self-consciously major work. In this repeated part, Mill says that the eighteenth-century thinkers ignored the problem of government. He claims that they were so involved in working out the good that government might do that they tended to ignore that government itself poses a problem. (However untrue generally of eighteenth-century thinkers, this could be taken to apply to the early Bentham who worked on many kinds of law before he realised that he had also to work on constitutional law.) Yet Mill himself thinks that there is a problem about whether to have government at all, which can be put in terms of energy and character. How is government possible without it also being enervating?

We have here, albeit as a mere sketch, Mill's version of the state of nature story. The original social contract problem is what people would have to gain by contracting into government. The problem as put by Rousseau is how people starting with liberty might have government yet remain as free as before. The way that Mill specifically puts this is in terms of energy. How may people, starting with energy, have government and still have as much energy as before? The state of nature type of device that Mill uses to pose the problem is the 'savage' which he defines (in both essays) as someone not engaging in co-operative activity. How, with these energetic savages, is government possible? As he puts it (in 'Coleridge' and the *Logic*), 'the difficulty of inducing a brave and warlike race to submit their individual *arbitrium* to any common umpire, has always been felt to be so great, that nothing short of supernatural power has been deemed adequate to overcome it' (*CWM*, VIII, p. 921). So no contract, or rational move will do it; we need supernatural terror (an already existing Leviathan in heaven). An echo of this is in *On Liberty* when he says, 'there has been a time when the element of spontaneity and individuality was in excess, and the social principle had a hard struggle with it. The difficulty then was, to induce men of strong bodies or minds to pay obedience to any rules which required them to control their impulses' (3.6; *CWM*, XVIII, p. 264). To get government and society we have to bear down on individual will (*arbitrium*) and energy.

Hence, as Mill puts it particularly in this third chapter of *On Liberty*, we have now run into the reverse problem of lack of energy, which he maps at length. In the much earlier 'Civilisation' essay the decline of energy that civilisation produces is similarly mapped at length. In both cases, energy is taken to have moved from the individual to the mass, and the thought is expressed in similar ways. Thus in *On Liberty* he says, 'at present individuals are lost in the crowd . . . it is almost a triviality to say that public opinion now rules the world' (3.13; *CWM*, XVIII, p. 268). Over twenty years earlier he says, 'the individual becomes so lost in the crowd, that though he depends more and more upon opinion, he is apt to depend less and less upon well-grounded opinion' (*CWM*, XVIII, p. 132). Both writings are concerned with, as he puts it in the earlier one, how the 'growing insignificance of the individual in the mass . . . weakens the influence of the more cultivated few over the many' (*CWM*, 133–4).

So in both cases he wants to promote the weakened individual, to rebalance the story by returning some power from the mass to the individual. He wants to restore the energy of individuals in civilisation to something more like the primitive power of the individual 'savage' who existed before government. But, given that we have government (or 'civilisation'), is this possible? Mill thinks that it is, but only if we adopt his specific prescriptions.

We avoid the miseries of anarchy by keeping government for its good task of defending rights. But we restore primitive energy by keeping government (and the public opinion of the dreadful mass) away from what individuals wish to do when they are not harming others.

This sounds like a universal answer. Yet it has been put in terms of a historical story ('time was when . . . '). Whether Mill's preferred form of government is right is a function of context. Another, related, aspect in which Mill made a point of his thought going beyond his eighteenth-century mentors is in sensitivity to history and circumstances. What is right varies according to time and place. Appropriate conditions are needed for cultivation, and what flourishes in one context will wither in another. So in *On Liberty*, Mill is quite specific that this is only a prescription for particular circumstances. 'Liberty, as a principle,' he says, 'has no application to any state of things anterior to the time when mankind have become capable of being improved by free and equal discussion' (1.10; *CWM*, xviii, p. 224). Before then people need dictators, and they are 'fortunate' if they find one as good as Akbar or Charlemagne. No point savages being left free to practise self-cultivation; they need to be fiercely pruned into shape.

9   The harm principle

Let us return to the central ground. Obviously the application of Mill's principle depends on how 'harm' is to be understood. If it means anything affecting someone else's interests in a negative way, then it is easy to see how the principle follows from utilitarian principles. For if, as a generalisation, people left alone can be supposed to advance their interests, then leaving people alone in those matters that do not affect others will tend to improve overall utility. (The person left alone will tend to improve their own utility and, because this does not affect others' utility negatively, their gain will not be purchased at the cost of a greater loss elsewhere.) The trouble is, as Mill himself recognised, there is no kind of action that may not affect others. 'No person is an entirely isolated being', he says in chapter 4 of *On Liberty*, allowing that if somebody does something 'seriously or permanently hurtful to himself' others such as his 'near connections' will also be negatively affected (4.8; *CWM*, xviii, p. 280).

Hence, if the principle is to have any kind of practical application, as Mill not only wants but also illustrates in the last two chapters of the work, 'harm' cannot mean merely an action that affects others. Judging from Mill's examples, he thinks that it follows from his principle that adults who know what they are doing should be free to purchase drugs or alcohol, should eat what they wish, and may engage in sexual activity between consenting adults. Yet, as he also recognises, some of these practices may affect others. People caring about, or depending on, a drunkard may be seriously affected by their drunkenness. People may be revolted (and therefore upset) by the gastronomic or sexual practices of other people. So actions that have negative effects on others are clearly held by Mill to be allowed by his liberty principle.

The principle therefore has to be limited in some way so that only certain kinds of effect are suitable grounds for attempting to prevent an action by the forces of law or public opinion. Yet, although it is clear that there has to be some such limitation, it is not clear from the text what Mill thinks it is, and different suggestions have been attempted in interpretation. It might be actions that affect those interests that are so important that they can be considered to be rights; or that affect only those who choose to be affected; or that affect others merely in a distant or secondary way.

Soon after his first statement of the principle, he describes the kind of action that he wishes to protect as one 'which affects only himself, or if it also affects others, only with their free, voluntary, and undeceived consent and participation' (1.12; *CWM*, xviii, p. 225). Here the crucial element would seem to be choice; if you consent to be affected, then you cannot complain. But such would not be sufficient to cover the cases just described; the drunkard's family destroyed by his drink, the person shocked by another's tastes, do not choose to be engaged in the situations that upset them. Mill adds the gloss, 'When I say only himself, I mean directly, and in the first instance: for whatever affects himself may affect others through himself.' Now the crucial criterion seems to be the directness of the causal chain between agent and negative effect. But this cannot be adequate to draw the line that Mill wants; someone causing someone else to shoot a third party is harming them only by indirect means but we still think that they should not be at liberty to do it.

However this is adjudicated, by excluding indirect or chosen effects Mill gives himself more room that might at first be expected to apply his principle to protect kinds of conduct from interference by law or public opinion. But he also moves in the other direction, not protecting areas that might at first sight to fall clearly under his central principle. This is because, especially when considering particular applications, he invokes another consideration that limits its scope. This is that people have to know what they are doing if they are to be considered as acting freely. Information is a utilitarian good, and the stress on labelling is appropriate to Mill's general liberal stance. For him, purchase of poisons and other harmful drugs is to be freely permitted. But, if you are free to take poison, you must also be able to know that this is what you are doing. Therefore, he holds, dangerous products have to be labelled and (for the preservation of criminal evidence) their sale recorded. This is from the last, 'Applications', chapter of *On Liberty*.

So far so good, and Mill's central principle seems to provide a wide area of protection. But another example in this chapter that also depends on the importance of information could reduce it. This is the example of the unsafe bridge. Here Mill allows an official to prevent someone crossing it even though this is what they wish. For, as he puts it, 'liberty consists in doing what one desires, and he does not desire to fall into the river' (5.5; *CWM*, xviii, p. 294). This seems unexceptional on general liberal principles. The person forcibly prevented from crossing does not know that the bridge is unsafe and so may be said to be mistaken about what they want. Therefore, by being interfered with, they are given what they really want (not falling in the water) rather than what they think that they want (crossing the bridge). However, the example leaves much wider scope for interference than Mill's principle would at first sight seem to allow. It would permit paternalist interference in all cases where people could be taken not really to know what they are doing. (The drug will make you dependent and someone doesn't want to be dependent, therefore . . .)

Another example in this chapter that could have a similar extensive limiting effect on the application of the central principle is contracts of self-enslavement. Mill says that his principle would not permit the validity of contracts whereby people enslave themselves. For, as he puts it, 'The principle of freedom cannot require that he should be free not to be free' (5.11; *CWM*, xviii, p. 300). Again, at first this sounds unexceptionable. The principle is to promote liberty, so it can't also sanction its removal. But, again, the thought behind the example could be given a much wider application, preventing kinds of cases that Mill explicitly wishes to permit. (The drug will make you dependent, so you won't be free to stop taking it. Hence freedom to take the drug would be freedom to be unfree, which is not real freedom. Hence . . .)

10 Act and rule

Utilitarianism is a balancing philosophy. Things are not bad or good in themselves but bad or good according to the consequences. So different circumstances can make what is normally a bad act into a good one or vice versa. So Mill's argument in the end may be purely a generalising argument. On the whole, liberty tends to promote so many good consequences that the presupposition has to be that we should leave people free except in those cases where the freedom clearly has even greater negative effects. So if we formulate rules about it, we should only act to prevent those kinds of cases in which, as a kind, the negative effects are clearly predominant. We can say that this is so if people were left free to rape or murder. But not (for Mill) if they are free to speak, think, eat or drink. Sometimes such behaviour may seriously negatively affect others. But this is not so as a generalisation; and it is particularly so in those cases where the persons affected may choose not to be.

Therefore another factor in making utilitarianism and liberty compatible is that Mill is a rule, rather than an act, utilitarian. That is, instead of every single action being evaluated individually by the overall end of greatest utility, actions are taken by kinds, or classes, and the rules promoting or forbidding these classes are evaluated. This means that the evaluation of a particular action happens in an indirect, or stepwise, manner. First it is subsumed under a rule (such as 'do not murder'; 'keep your promises') and then the rule itself is evaluated (so that, for example, the rule that people should keep their promises might be taken to promote overall utility). So in the present case we can understand Mill to be proposing a rule that people should be allowed liberty except when their actions harm others. A particular action is evaluated in accordance with this rule and the rule is justified on utilitarian principles.

This means that Mill only has to show the general beneficial tendency of liberty and his argument is immune to the occasional counter-example. Sometimes, no doubt, greater liberty will lead to greater harm. But all Mill needs to show is that this is generally not the case. As with other examples of rule utilitarianism, knowledge is important in the argument. The rule provides general knowledge about utility and we don't have sufficient independent knowledge to depart from it confidently in particular cases.

A similar point about knowledge comes from the claim frequently made against utilitarianism, that it involves excessive calculation. But if we can rely on the rule, then we do not need to calculate afresh in every individual case and so know enough for action without any such time consuming, or impossible, operation. The analogy that Mill uses to bring this out in *Utilitarianism* is that of the nautical almanac. We do not go to sea, Mill says, having always to calculate afresh because the calculations are already made ahead for us in the almanac. Similarly, by seeing whether an action is against the liberty principle or not, we can tell ahead whether it should be proscribed or permitted without any additional examination or calculation.

Putting this in terms of rules plays naturally into the area of law, which tends to work by rules, formulating and enforcing generalisations about behaviour. But it might be thought to ignore Mill's claim that he is as concerned with moral as with legal force. However, we need here to understand an unusual aspect of Mill's thought about morality, which is that he thinks of it on the analogy of law. One index of this is how he brings punishment into his understanding of the moral. 'The truth is', he says in *Utilitarianism*, 'that the idea of a penal sanction, which is the essence of law, enters not only into the conception of injustice, but into that of any kind of wrong' (*CWM*, x, p. 246). 'We do not call anything wrong,' he continues, 'unless we mean to imply that a person ought to be punished . . . for doing it.' Contemporary political philosophy is often held to be applied ethics, in which independently formulated moral principles are applied to the political domain. But for Mill (as with other earlier thinkers) the direction is rather the reverse. It is after we understand the processes of law and punishment that we can understand morality; we start with the legal *ought*, understood in Benthamic manner in terms of liability for punishment. Only then, with this in place, do we reach an understanding of the moral *ought*.

The section of *Utilitarianism* from which this comes (chapter 5) is concerned not just with rendering justice compatible with utility but also in distinguishing justice from other moral obligations. This Mill does by using the old distinction between perfect and imperfect obligations. On the way he delineates what he calls a *right*. A right is 'something which society ought to defend me in the possession of' (*CWM*, x, p. 250). But all this (perfect and imperfect obligations; moral and legal *oughts*) is to be distinguished from other measures of value. Apart from these, there are other reasons for action. For Mill (in a doctrine, or classification, that he first proposes in his *Logic*), morality is only part of the 'art of life'. As well as the legal and moral, there is the aesthetic and the prudential; all are evaluative reasons. This makes it easier to associate the moral (as distinguished from the other kinds) with the idea of a rule. And liberty is a rule, both for law and also for moral public sanctions. Apart from these areas where liberty should rule there are other aspects of life about which recommendations can be made. These further areas covered by the 'art of life' may be evaluated, but not by the rules arising from the public moral or legal principle of liberty.

11 Paternalism

Thinking of Mill's thought in terms of rules, or generalisations, resolves some of the puzzle about how Mill, basing his argument on utilitarianism, nevertheless argues against paternalism. When, in his central statement of his principle in *On Liberty*, he says that 'the only purpose for which power can be rightfully exercised over any member of a civilised community, against his will, is to prevent harm to others' he immediately continues, 'His own good, either physical or moral, is not a sufficient warrant' (1.9; *CWM*, XVIII, p. 223). But if, as a utilitarian, Mill's central aim is to promote, or maximise, the good, then it would seem that all possible good should be promoted that does not come with the cost of a greater harm. So if by interfering (and stopping someone, for example, getting hooked on drink or drugs) we can do them good, it seems that we should. The aim is to promote the good, so it would seem that anyone's good should be promoted.

So why not interfere to do good to others? Here it is worth remembering, as was pointed out above, that Mill himself said that his doctrine was not one of selfish indifference and that his aim was very much not the merely negative one of people leaving each other alone. Victorian law tends to be critical about the so-called officious bystander, who interferes with others in matters that are not his concern. But with Mill, rather than being merely officious this seems instead to be an office; it is a duty to be performed. He says about advising others that 'it were well, indeed, if this good office were much more freely rendered than the common notions of politeness at present permit' (4.5; *CWM*, XVIII, p. 278). We have muscular interference for people's good, which also seems logically to fit with the utilitarian, evaluative, base. So why not paternalism? How can we allow Mill's simple principle? (Unless, of course, as many have suspected, Mill wants liberty for its own sake, independent of consequences.)

Part of the answer again involves knowledge, which here enters Mill's specific argument. He relies on the familiar principle that, as a generalisation, people have better understanding, or knowledge, of their own interests than they do of other people's. They are both better placed and also more motivated to acquire it. The person himself is 'the person most interested in his own well-being' (4.4; *CWM*, XVIII, p. 277). So we can promote a rule. It is not that people are invariably right about their own good but just that, as a rule, they do it better. And this is for good, general, reasons, based on generalisations about people's knowledge and interests. Given this, we can formulate the rule not to be paternalistic in the wrong way, which would be to submit people we think to be improvident or stupid to moral or social sanctions. We should instead offer the good office of advice and education.

Since it is only the cumulative, general, effect that counts, we do not have to be right in every instance. And it helps if it is the case that we are better able to generalise about kinds of harms than kinds of pleasures. If so, we can construct general rules about what kinds of action to prohibit and sanction to prevent harm, but adopt also the rule that we should leave pleasures as far as possible for people to find in their own individual and eccentric ways.

12   Feminism and other unpopular causes

Mill was also an important figure in the development of English feminist thought. This is the subject of another chapter and so does not need to be examined in detail here. Classified in retrospect, he is part of liberal rather than radical feminism, seeking to extend the same advantages to women as are already possessed by men. In particular, for Mill, this is the opportunity to vote for Members of Parliament. Typically, Mill acted as well as wrote. The first motion in the British Parliament that the vote should be extended to women was made by Mill in person when he was a Member. (This was as a proposed amendment, which was defeated, to the 1867 Act which gave further classes of men the vote.) Mill proposed substituting the word 'person' for 'man', making precise that he was arguing for the same advantages; the same property qualifications limiting the eligibility of men would also have limited women.

After his defeat in the 1868 election, Mill continued to campaign particularly for this cause. It was another monument to Harriet. He reprinted a paper on 'The enfranchisement of women' in the *Dissertations and Discussions* collection of his selected papers that he brought out after her death (in 1859, the same year as *On Liberty*). This time he prefaced it with a fulsome dedication saying that the chief work was Harriet's and that his share was 'little more than that of an editor and amanuensis'. Ten years later (1869) he published *The Subjection of Women*. His chief argument here turns upon the influence of environment and education; that is, on the malleability of character. It is too soon to tell, Mill holds, what women are capable of. Again, the feminism is liberal rather than radical, based on potential gender similarity rather than gender difference. The central thought is that women can, and should be entitled to, do what men do; that given the same initial advantages they can make similar use of them.

It is in the context of Harriet that one of Mill's thoughts that has come in for later criticism should be considered. This is his assumption in the *Subjection* that women will carry on with the same different and more domestic roles, even after political liberation. But he himself thought of Harriet and himself working as partners in thought, their chief work. After Harriet's death, her daughter Helen Taylor took up much of her position. She lived with Mill, and after his death edited his substantial posthumous publications. He helped Helen run the public campaign for the vote. They also travelled, camped and took long walks together in some of the wilder parts of Europe. In his own domestic practice, Mill did not confine females to the domestic sphere.

Votes for women was only one of the causes Mill took up in his brief parliamentary career that made him a butt for satirists (where he was portrayed in cartoons as 'Miss Mill'). By taking up unpopular causes, he became the object of vehement public opposition. He was during this time the secretary of the Governor Eyre committee, attempting to bring the governor of a West Indian colony to justice for mistreatment of the natives. He wrote a much-hated and greatly denounced pamphlet in defence of Ireland. Women, blacks, the Irish; all lesser-regarded groups. In each case Mill was driven by a passion for fairness for people of lesser standing. Given the prejudice of the period, it was a sufficient combination of unpopular causes to ensure his defeat at the next general election.

Mill quite consciously made it even worse for himself by subscribing to the election expenses of Bradlaugh, an overt atheist. So he also had the church against him. *On Liberty* had been read as an anti-church tract, and much of the immediate opposition came from the church. Mill's particular practical examples in proposing the liberty of thought and discussion was the liberty to publish atheist opinion without the threat of imprisonment. It was only after his death that his *Autobiography* could be read, with its claim that 'I am thus one of the very few examples, in this country, of one who has, not thrown off religious belief, but never had it' (*CWM*, i, p. 45). It was in this very late period of his life that Mill in his *Examination of Hamilton* (1865) attacked on moral grounds the opinions of one of Hamilton's followers, Mansel, with the ringing (and controversial) credo that 'I will call no being good, who is not what I mean when I apply that epithet to my fellow creatures; and if such a being can sentence me to hell for not so calling him, to hell will I go' (*CWM*, IX, p. 103). *On Liberty* is a passionate argument against the coercive power of public opinion. The chief coercive power at the time Mill wrote was church opinion. We may wonder, on looking back at the boldly expressed views of the confident Victorians, at what Mill could be talking about when he described this suppressive fear of opinion. The answer is atheism. Disbelievers kept their views private to avoid public obloquy and Mill could see this both with his friends and also with himself.

Among these unpopular causes, votes for women was in a relatively favourable position. It was defeated in the House of Commons, but the vote showed a somewhat surprising level of support and it looked as if ten years of campaigning might be sufficient to gain the prize. Yet it was only in 1928, sixty years after Mill's initial proposal, that voting equality for women was obtained in Britain. After the successful parliamentary vote, the women immediately repaired to Mill's statue near the Thames to celebrate. Sixty years on, Mill was still thought of as the initiator and leader. Just as at the start of his adult life, when he had been imprisoned for campaigning in an unpopular cause, Mill was an active thinker. The thought was practical thought, utilitarianism. The ambition was to think utilitarianism with a difference, with humanity but also with logical precision. And, as a practical thinker, Mill also engaged in the practices that, as a man of letters, he wrote to promote.

10

The 'woman question' and the origins of feminism

LUCY DELAP

This chapter situates the 'woman question' as an expansive and flourishing set of debates within political, literary and social thought in the nineteenth century. These debates represented an interrogation of the basic components of liberal and republican political argument – citizenship, property, access to the public sphere and political virtue. To talk of the 'woman question' is perhaps misleading, because there were many such 'questions'. To name but a few, there were questions of single (or 'surplus') women, of the status of married women, of authority and the 'struggle for the breeches' in plebeian culture, of political rights, of professional status, of rationality, and of education. This chapter gives a schematic overview of the century, and cannot possibly do justice to the complex debates unfolding in each national context. I aim therefore to show the main currents of argument in Europe and the United States, pointing to national distinctiveness and divergence as well as shared transnational arguments and emphases. As a result, the treatment is only loosely chronological; arguments are grouped together thematically and different dimensions of the 'woman question' are discussed in turn. I outline some historiographical trends in examining 'woman question' debates, and point to the literature available to those seeking more concrete information. Specific campaigns that were highly influential for the women's movement (concerning property, child custody, higher education, prostitution or suffrage) can only be mentioned briefly, for the 'woman question' was a broader discourse than the summed activism of the 'women's movement'. It represented a space for political argument in which the nature, implications and origins of sexual difference might be debated, and was regarded as intensely significant for both its symbolic and its practical import. In John Ruskin's words, 'There never was a time when wilder words were spoken, or more vain imagination permitted, respecting this question – quite vital to all social happiness. The relations of the womanly to the manly nature, their different capacities of intellect or of virtue, seem never to have been yet measured with entire consent' (Ruskin n.d. [1865], p. 49).

The nineteenth-century elaboration of the woman question (or questions) allowed women to lay claim to new identities, or think of themselves in a new way, as, for example, 'the people', *citoyennes* or as members of 'the Public'. This was aided by women's ability from the late eighteenth century onwards to inhabit new spaces – the theatre and the National Assembly for Olympe de Gouges, the speaker's platform for Josephine Butler or Ida B. Wells, the intellectual salon of Margaret Fuller's Boston 'Conversations', the space in print offered by the women's periodicals and the novel, and by the end of the century, the new urban spaces of the department store, the settlement house, mass transit systems or the music hall (Crossick and Jaumain 1999; Hamilton and Schroeder 2010; Walkowitz 1992, p. 42, 46). A key feature of the woman question was to place under review how women might inhabit the public spheres of formal politics, political argument or print culture, and what their qualifications were to do so. The woman question was a broad field, but sometimes gave rise to identities that might now be read as 'feminist', though this term has been controversial since it must always be applied anachronistically in the nineteenth century. Historians have been divided over whether to talk of the activism around questions of gender and equality as 'feminism'. While the term was available in France, it did not connote the organised movement that it implies today.[1] Some historians have used 'feminism' to give a sense of the cohesiveness and breadth of vision of the nineteenth-century campaigns for women's education, property rights, freedom from state harassment and right to work (Isenberg 1998; Levine 1994; Offen 2000). I have preferred to use the 'woman question', to suggest a reading of the debates that is less laden with present-day assumptions about the nature of such activism. 'Feminism' carries with it a great deal of twentieth-century connotations concerning the assumed 'bedrock' concerns of feminism (such as equality, public activism, primacy of gender as a personal identity) which are not attributable to some of the thinkers discussed below.

1 The origin of the term 'feminism' is commonly but mistakenly attributed, in its French form of '*féminisme*', to the early nineteenth-century utopian socialist, Charles Fourier. Instead, it was first used in French in 1837 as a pejorative term, to indicate 'the illness of womanly qualities appearing in men' (Wilson 2002, p. 9 n.30). Early uses in Britain date from 1895 and onwards, though its meaning was variable (see Caine 1997, p. xv; Ethelmer 1898). American periodicals began to use 'feminism', mostly in discussion of European affairs and often in quotation marks, from around 1904. 'Feminism' was included in the *Oxford English Dictionary* only in 1933, where it was defined as 'advocacy of women's rights' (Cott 1987, pp. 3–6; Evans 1977, p. 39 n.1).

Three historiographical trends have made the ascription of 'feminism' problematic. First, historians have examined nineteenth-century women-only spaces and cultures – the women's settlements, colleges, schools, and the sentimental friendships that flourished within them – that were initially read as regions of exclusion and confinement, the ultimate enactment of 'separate spheres' (Harrison 1978; Welter 1966). The work of Carroll Smith-Rosenberg and Martha Vicinus offered a revised reading of these sites, arguing that they enabled the solidarity and activism amongst women that later made organised Edwardian feminism possible (Smith-Rosenberg 1985; Vicinus 1985). The scope of the 'pre-history' of feminism has therefore been significantly widened from the 'liberal' campaigns for property and equality, and the origins of 'feminism' must be recognised as highly diverse. At the same time, the controversial idea of 'separate spheres' has been re-evaluated as a more complex phenomenon than an ideology of women's oppression.[2] Second, the divide between 'feminist' and 'anti-feminist' has been found to be more complex and less polarised than had been previously thought. Studies of the work of writers such as the British anti-suffragist and novelist Mary (Mrs Humphrey) Ward have termed her a 'social feminist', despite her opposition to equal political rights (Sanders 1996, Sutton-Ramspeck 1999). 'Feminists' have been found to share key ideological assumptions with 'anti-feminists'; a definitive set of 'feminist' beliefs has become impossible to find. To this end, suffrage has been decentred as the 'high point' of feminist radicalism, and other kinds of claims have been admitted as equally 'radical' (Bush 2007; Delap 2005; Holton 1986, p. 5). Suffrage by no means defined the political terrain of the woman question, and in some European national contexts it barely registered as a nineteenth-century campaign. Finally, recent interest in the history of masculinity has brought another unsettling dimension to studies of gender and 'feminism', or attempts to delineate 'separate spheres'.[3] As Ben Griffin has argued, it was the attitude

2 The concept of 'separate spheres' has been an important heuristic device for historians of gender, giving a descriptive label to the changes in morality and concepts of space that followed the evangelical revival of the early nineteenth century (Davidoff and Hall 1987; Poovey 1988). Following recent scholarship, it must be read as a complex phenomenon without a clear political valency. 'Separate spheres' has come under sustained attack for eliding and de-historicising a number of gendered dualisms. It has also been argued that the idea flourished in didactic literature, but that this tells us little about actual practices which were less governed by gender separation or a divide between 'public' and 'private' (Davidoff 1995; Klein 1995; Vickery 1993).
3 The work of John Tosh on 'domestic masculinity', for example, has challenged anew the idea of 'separate spheres', by making it clear that men moved freely between the so-called 'spheres', and used their domestic existence as an important source of self-identity as men (Tosh 1999; Kimmel 1987, pp. 121–53).

of nineteenth-century writers to masculinity as much as to femininity that defined their politics (Chernock 2010; Griffin 2011). 'Feminism' does not adequately convey the scope of the questions raised by issues of 'women's rights', and the inclusion of men as gendered beings has dramatic implications for how we study the gender politics of the nineteenth century (Francis 2002).

There was, nonetheless, a breadth to the 'woman question' debates in this period that allows us to trace the intellectual trends that made the invention of 'feminism' possible in a range of countries in the first decades of the twentieth century. Recent scholarship has therefore stressed the organised, transnational nature of the debates and activism around women's rights (Bolt 1995, 2004; Harrison 2000; McFadden 1999; Offen 2000, 2010). Karen Offen has also pointed to other major developments surrounding the nineteenth-century woman question. These include the increasing literacy of women, the growth of nation-state formations and their concerns over population, the entry of women to the urbanised workforce, and the growing divergence between feminism and socialism, which became especially marked after the founding of the 1889 Second International. Drawing on her work and others, this chapter surveys a pre-history of feminism, without claiming that the individuals described were themselves 'feminists'. I aim to show the way in which thinkers within different political perspectives – liberals, republicans, radicals, idealists, socialists and Marxists, all engaged with the 'woman question' and grappled with how women might be represented within their different political orders.

Eighteenth-century writings on women tended to stress the failings of women in the realm of manners, and to prescribe their traditional duties as a solution to their frivolity and hedonism (Taylor 2003). Responses to the French Revolution in the 1790s, however, marked a relatively new turn in the 'woman question', a point at which concerns with gender became more central to modern politics. Women came to be newly identified as an 'oppressed group' in the 1790s, as well as a group with political agency (Coole 1993). In France, women's clubs and *sociétés fraternelles* briefly provided new spaces for the popular discussion of women's rights, and speakers such as Pauline Léon, Etta Palm d'Aelders and Théroigne de Méricourt became prominent in interrogating revolutionary politics on the question of sexual difference and citizenship. The playwright and 'active citizen' Olympe de Gouges (1745–93) had responded to the *Declaration of the Rights of Man and Citizen* with her own *Declaration of the Rights of Woman and Citizens* (1791). Influenced by the Marquis de Condorcet's support for women's civic rights (Condorcet 1912), de Gouges recognised that under revolutionary law, women had an anomalous status. While recognised as civic individuals in some aspects (marriage, divorce), they were still excluded from full political rights. She claimed that women were individuals, and that by the universalist logic of the Revolution, they should therefore be equal citizens. She proposed a new 'social contract' to regulate the union of men and women in marriage, as well as full voting rights. As Joan Scott has argued, de Gouges based her claims about women, and her claim to be an author (which was not a status open to women under revolutionary law), on the basis of her active and creative imagination, her ability to dream, in the style of the *philosophes*, Diderot, Voltaire and Rousseau (Scott 1996, pp. 22–30). These thinkers had stressed that women had no active imagination – de Gouges' adoption of this mode of thinking represented a resistance to the conventional bounds of sexual difference, and a contrast to the more prevalent 'feminist' mode of claiming women's powers of rationality and reason.

De Gouges was comfortable with sexual difference between citizens – she did not claim that equality had to rest on sameness, though she did think that women could be active citizens as defined within the republican tradition. Nonetheless, the attributes of republican 'activism' – military service, political deliberation, honour and independence – had been coded as masculine, and it was not easy to argue that women could also be 'active'. In her own person, de Gouges attempted to enact the activism of citizenship, as a patriotic and public figure. But her arrest and execution in 1793 revealed the way in which this could be mistaken as a treasonous and transgressive imitation of men. In this same year, women's clubs were outlawed. Republicanism, in its different constructions in France and the United States, became explicitly constructed as underpinned by a sexual division of labour, whereby women's role was to act as good mothers and wives without an autonomous presence in the public sphere.[4] The fear of lawlessness and the Terror which fuelled the counter-revolution in Britain and other countries was deeply formative for the development of political thought, and gender figured prominently in this. After their high-profile revolutionary involvement, women could be figured as politically dangerous, socially volatile forces, and writers of the nineteenth-century woman question were divided between perceptions of women as morally elevated or politically threatening.

---

4 On 'republican motherhood' see Kerber 1980. Offen (2000, pp. 46–8, 91–2) discusses the uses European feminists made of motherhood.

Republican ideas and the language of the Enlightenment continued, however, to structure the woman question. The English writer Mary Woll-stonecraft (1759–97), a visitor to France shortly after the 1789 Revolution, offered a different register in which to situate the post-revolutionary 'woman question'. Her writings were based within the radical dissenting circles of Joseph Johnson, Richard Price and William Godwin. In Britain, there were few popular spaces in which women's rights might be debated, and participation in radical circles was limited to very small numbers of women writers such as Mary Hays and Elizabeth Inchbald, often writing fiction and drama.[5] These writers were committed to the moral progress of humanity through the use of reason. In 1792, Wollstonecraft wrote *A Vindication of the Rights of Woman*, a political and educational reform tract which denounced sentimental appeals to the passions and sympathies of women, and stressed their individual rational will, to be sustained and developed through the discipline of education. Wollstonecraft made what has been read as a key 'feminist' insight, in her linkage between private relationships and public power. She argued that 'sensibility' and social mores formed the basis of a systemic and tyrannical 'sexual aristocracy' (Shanley 1998). Wollstonecraft aimed her work on gender against that of Jean-Jacques Rousseau, who had famously portrayed women as naturally frivolous and weak, and destined for the virtuous life only in domesticity, in *Émile* (1762). They did, however, share a critical position towards the women they saw around them, leading some scholars to attribute to Wollstonecraft a 'feminist misogyny' (Gubar 1994). But though Wollstonecraft accepted that women were currently constituted as corrupt and ignorant, in abstract terms, she held that women's virtue was identical to men's. It lay in the exercise of reason and the control of the passions, leading to an 'authenticity of self' equally open to both sexes (Taylor 2003). This was the divine capacity that humans had been granted by the Creator, and Wollstonecraft situated the 'woman question' as one of how women could cultivate virtues for religious motives. But she stressed that women could not be expected to become virtuous until they had been given their 'natural rights' – independence and individuality. She concluded 'take away natural rights, and duties become null'. In her unfinished novel, *The Wrongs of Woman* (1797), Wollstonecraft spoke against the despotism of marriage, and the sexual hypocrisy of her society. Her 'female revolution in manners' was intended to change the public world through

---

5 Clark 1995 offers a broader account of how gender was addressed and constructed within British radical and plebeian culture.

giving women equal civic status and the possibility of work, though she saw them as primarily domestic. The woman question for Wollstonecraft was understood to relate to 'gentlewomen', since 'the most respectable women are the most oppressed'. Her novels, however, revealed more sympathy with the condition of working-class women, and she claimed to be speaking 'for the improvement and emancipation of the whole sex'. Wollstonecraft's 'revolution' was not constructed as furthering the greater good of the state or republic, but was for the individual self-development of women. 'Speaking of women at large, their first duty is to themselves as rational creatures, and the next, in point of importance, as citizens, is that which includes so many, of a mother' (Wollstonecraft 1993, pp. 227, 230, 262, 226).

1 The passionate languages of utopian socialism

Mary Wollstonecraft agreed with her husband William Godwin that sexual freedom should not be celebrated as a part of feminine emancipation, but was detrimental to this project. Nor did she recommend passionate love as the basis of marriage, preferring 'rational fellowship' and friendship (Wollstonecraft 1993, p. 231). But only a few years later, a diverse range of what are retrospectively read as socialist writers were to make quite different arguments that would dominate the 'woman question' for the following four decades. Ironically, while free sexual union was discussed, the trend in the nineteenth century was towards more formalised marriages, with fewer of the separations, pragmatic trial marriages and other kinds of temporary relationships that had marked early nineteenth-century matrimonial culture (Taylor 1983, pp. 193–4). But while marriage became more formalised and free sexuality more constrained, some new languages developed which enabled 'advanced' discussion of sexual matters. 'Socialism' in its early forms was one such language. Robert Owen (1771–1858), a textile manufacturer who advocated factory reform and gave his own workers 'model' working conditions, became influenced by William Godwin. Owen turned his industrial fortune towards social experimentation in Britain and America from the late 1810s. He became a critic of capitalism, not just as an economic mode but in its emotional and psychological effects, and advocated 'co-operation' as an alternative principle of living. At the heart of his thought was a commitment to sexual equality, which he believed could be achieved by an appeal to benevolence and rationality. Owen's ideas concerning the ideal organisation of society appeared in an early form in 1813 in *A New View of Society* and were developed over the next twenty years

(Owen 1991, 1993). His key insight was that human character was not predominantly self-given, but externally imposed by social circumstances. He could therefore agree with his contemporaries that women's nature was narrow, vicious, artificial and deceptive, but argued like Wollstonecraft that this was not innate but a result of 'immoral' social institutions. The competitiveness, individualism and artificiality Owen diagnosed as characteristic of early nineteenth-century society were seen as ruling out social harmony, and could only be transcended in communal living. The main institutions and systems of society that for Owen reproduced and transmitted 'immoral' values were the family and marriage system, religion and private property. He regarded 'single-family arrangements' as inevitably competitive and individualistic. Women, especially in their role as mothers, were central to Owen's vision of the 'New Moral World'. Marriage was seen as 'a pure unadulterated system of moral evil' which perpetuated the property system and effectively made women into prostitutes. Owen preferred to emphasise the 'natural' expression of sexual love outside of conventional marriage. But despite his extraordinary commitment to sexual equality, Owen did not radically challenge the sexual division of labour. Barbara Taylor's extensive study of the involvement of women in his socialist utopia reveals their frustration at their lack of voice and labour-exploitation in the Owenite communities (Taylor 1983), as do similar studies of American Owenite women (Kolmerton 1990). Women in the communities Owen inspired and financed in Britain and the United States were given a certain range of jobs to perform outside of the domestic sphere, intended to emancipate them from the roles of wives and mothers (Owen 1993, 1, p. 150). But crucially Owen did not ask men to share in domestic tasks, thus leaving women with a double burden which exhausted them. Moreover, sexual libertarianism often rebounded against the more vulnerable women Owenites.

Owenism was, like other utopian socialisms, never a mass movement, but it did offer one of the first practical experiments in alternative ways of living, and was therefore very influential for how the woman question might be understood. It also offered an intellectual framework that others might develop, and some Owenites did express more far-reaching commitments to sexual equality than did Owen himself. Perhaps as influential as Owen was the career of Fanny Wright (1795–1852) a literary woman born in Scotland, and strongly influenced by the moral philosophy of the Scottish Enlightenment. Wright's writings and unconventional personal life gave her a prominence in cultural and political affairs. She supported a flamboyant version of Enlightenment rationalism, and expressed this in support for dress reform, communal living and a desire for free sexual unions. Inspired by American republicanism, her travels in the United States from 1815 onwards gave her a transatlantic influence and her writings and activism in both countries became, like Owen's, a conduit between Britain and the United States. She had met Robert Owen at his New Harmony community in 1824, and became influenced by Owenite socialism, founding her own Tennessee community for freed slaves at Nashoba in 1825. The free sexual union basis on which the community was founded caused scandal and internal conflict, and Nashoba was dissolved in five years. Despite her antagonism towards marriage, Wright became unhappily married to another Owenite activist. She spent her final years in legal wrangles over her lack of control of her property and earnings, also attracting immense notoriety for her 'unwomanly' public lecturing (Taylor 1983, pp. 65–8).[6] Wright saw women's emancipation as a component of a wider social change, and showed little interest in women such as Lucretia Mott, who was becoming an influential leader of the newly active 'middle-class' women's movement. Unlike Mott, Wright was a religious sceptic, and based her reforms on an Enlightenment belief in human plasticity. She therefore stressed the need for education based on the inherent moral equality of all. In practice, she felt this could best be expressed through communal living, though in broad terms, the experiments she and others made with this were not successful. Despite its centrality in the early decades of the nineteenth century, there was a turning away from reformed domestic living arrangements in the 'woman question' of later decades.

In France, the sexual liberation promoted by Robert Owen and Fanny Wright was voiced in quite different terms. The late eighteenth-century writer Charles Thérémin had declared in his *De la Condition des Femmes dans les Républiques* that sexual liberty would grow stronger as republican government grew more advanced. He did not, however, think that women should take on a political role as voters, and his work indicates the limits of what has been called 'republican feminism'. The context of the Napoleonic *Code Civil*, from 1803, was in any case extremely inhospitable to women's liberty. Women became legally classed as minors and deprived of property rights; divorce was curtailed and the sexual double standard was given

---

6 See also Eckhardt 1984. Free unions and the legal status of married women continued to be foregrounded within the 'woman question' debates, within the personal lives of individuals such as Flora Tristan and Emma Martin, or reflected in the declaration of renunciation of his 'marital rights' made by John Stuart Mill on his marriage to Harriet Taylor. On the important issue of nineteenth-century marriage and property rights, see Holcombe 1983; Phillips 1991; Shanley 1989.

legislative standing. Perhaps because of this climate, the major text of the 'woman question' from this period adopted a new mode of discourse, passionate and visionary rather than rights-based. The work of Charles Fourier (1772–1837) looked to sexual liberty as a major part of the solution of the 'woman question' as well as all social questions. Like so many writers of his century, Fourier sought to outline a holistic 'social science' which would provide the key to the ordering of human affairs.[7] He completed his major work, *Théorie des Quatre Mouvements* (*Theory of the Four Movements*) in 1808, though his ideas did not attract an organised movement until the 1830s (Fourier 1996). Nonetheless his work provides an early refutation of the republicanism of Thérémin, as well as a rejection of the sexual equality claimed by revolutionary women such as de Gouges. Instead, Fourier outlined an intensely original 'socialist' conception of how social harmony could be achieved, through domestic reorganisation rather than revolution. He placed women's condition as the index of social progress – which Bee Wilson identifies as a restatement of an eighteenth-century cliché rather than a novel discovery on his part (Wilson 2002). Fourier indicated by this statement his belief that women displayed the chief evils of the current state of society ('civilisation'), as well as being its chief victims and therefore the most likely agents of change.

Fourier regarded permanent marriage and commerce as the great evils of civilisation, and as having the greatest impact upon women. He called for a wholesale reversal of the values of 'civilisation', to be achieved through a recognition of the 'scientific laws' of 'passionate attraction' which Fourier believed to govern human nature. His 'discovery' led him to postulate 810 different personality types, and he argued for all kinds of individuals, male and female, to be represented in all human activities, and for each individual to be free to undertake many different pursuits. He held that men and women did not form two groups with contrasting features – instead, humans were to be grouped by a much more complex, non-gendered formula. Fourier abandoned the discourse of natural rights that had predominated in late eighteenth-century calls for women's freedom. His solution was communal living in *phalanstères*, or in 'Harmony', in which each, whatever age or inclination, could express and fulfil their diverse passions, in both work and sexuality. Passions were God-given, and therefore could not be immoral or evil, in Fourier's theodicy. Women's sexual partners

---

7 My account of Fourier's thought draws heavily upon the recent work of Wilson 2002, and I am indebted to her. See also Beecher 1986; Goldstein 1991.

might include husband, co-parent, favourite, or 'plain lover'. Men and women (and children forming a 'third sex') were not to be understood as complementary and interdependent, but as rivals and individuals. Most importantly, and most unusually, he viewed women as potentially non-maternal (Wilson 2002, p. 146). This was a major shift in the 'woman question' discourse, but due to Fourier's relative isolation, did not become an acceptable part of nineteenth-century political discourse, and most writers, whether for or against women's emancipation, continued to class them as essentially actual or potential mothers. Through their passions, Fourier believed that women could become the motors of change from 'civilisation' to 'Harmony' – though he did not clarify what would cause this historical transition. Furthermore, he did not consistently view women as the agents of change, sometimes preferring a rich *fondateur*, or the intervention of workers, to achieve 'Harmony'.

Fourier's followers attempted to downplay the radicalism of his ideas about gender, preferring to portray him as a kind of political economist. His ideas about sexual emancipation were reworked by his follower Victor Considérant, to represent a moderate claim for the validity of divorce and voluntary union in marriage. Fourier's most explicit work, the *Nouvelle Monde Amoureuse* (1818) remained unpublished until 1967, and thus the full impact of his ideas was limited in nineteenth-century debates. In contrast, the followers of Henri de Saint-Simon (1760–1825), the constructor of an industrial utopia, made women's emancipation, including sexual emancipation, more central to their doctrine than it had been for Saint-Simon himself. Drawing on Fourierist ideas, the Saint-Simonians of the 1820s gathered around Prosper Enfantin, and proclaimed that the regeneration of humanity would depend on the emancipation of women, particularly on the substitution of 'moral marriage' or free union for legal marriage. Equality did not mean similarity in function, and Enfantin articulated a conception of God as Father and Mother, representing reason and senti-ment. While sentiment was celebrated as the higher value and women were to participate in all public offices, the sexual dualisms of their time remained intact, as well as the hierarchical structure of the movement, which tended to marginalise women. Nonetheless, Saint-Simonian support for commu-nal living and a romantic, erotic politics did introduce a number of French women to a language and a movement that foregrounded issues of gender (including Flora Tristan, Jeanne Deroin and Suzanne Voilquin), and the Saint-Simonians were also influential in Britain, through the patronage of Anna Wheeler and Robert Owen (Forget 2001; Taylor 1983, p. 46).

Though originally secular, the Saint-Simonians came to organise themselves as a church in 1829, and adopted from the millenarian groups preceding them in the 1780s the belief in *la femme messie* – the female messiah. Fourier condemned this abstract female, preferring his 'actual' women, with their bodily desires. As Claire Moses has argued, the belief in the female messiah did not empower actual women Saint-Simonians, who became progressively more excluded from the movement (Moses 1984, pp. 56–63). The followers of Enfantin became absorbed in the *Attente de la Femme* and the transnational search for her, and became an increasingly passive and introspective movement. Some of the less prominent Saint-Simonian women responded by developing a separatist voice, founding their own women-run newspaper and gradually moving away from the Saint-Simonian identity. This newspaper, originally *La Femme Libre*, but after much experimentation with title, *La Tribune des Femmes*, was published from 1832–4, and became an important site at which working- and lower middle-class women could articulate their views on gender and sexuality. The lack of consensus on a title and subtitle (*La Femme Nouvelle*, *La Femme de l'Avenir*, *Affranchissement des Femmes*, *Apostalat des Femmes* were all in play) suggests that in the 1830s there was as yet no clear language in France with which to articulate what later became known as *feministe* or *éclairiste* claims.[8] The discourse of the 'woman question' still tended to fall into either mystical or reactionary terms, and more progressive writers struggled to articulate their ideas; the 1789 Revolution had left an ambiguous legacy and did not provide an accepted language of 'women's rights', though it continued to inspire individual women such as Flora Tristan, who addressed French workers as 'sons of '89'.

Flora Tristan (1803–44) was one of the women on the periphery of the Saint-Simonian movement who went on to call for much wider roles for women than Enfantin had been willing to consider (Dijkstra 1992; Gordon and Cross 1996, pp. 19–27; Moses 1984, pp. 107–16). Tristan, an illegitimate working woman herself, was motivated by the need to improve working-class conditions, particularly for women, through 'association'. Campaigning between 1835 and 1844, she stressed women's rights to work, and called for a liberalisation of marriage and divorce laws. She had suffered within an unhappy marriage, and the Napoleonic civil code gave her husband the authority to determine his wife and children's location, full custody

---

8 The late nineteenth-century adoption of *les éclaireures* as an alternative, more avant-garde term to 'feministes' or 'new women' is discussed in Roberts 2002.

of the children, and to take their earnings. The destruction of marriage was not, however, Tristan's aim, and an egalitarian, intellectually satisfying heterosexual union remained her ideal. Tristan became an influential writer and lecturer, travelling widely and commenting on social affairs in Britain and Peru. She became associated with Fourier, Owen and some British Chartists, though like many of the 'utopian' writers of her period, she was not interested in formal political questions of the organisation of the state. In her 1843 *l'Union Ouvrière* she outlined an autonomous politics of working-class solidarity that could be extended to the women's struggle, but did not easily find a language that could express women's interests while addressing 'workers', despite her insistence that women be included in that category. As the Chartists had experienced in Britain, the 1840s in France witnessed an increasingly formalised and male-dominated movement of workers and producer co-operatives, and it became harder to insert women's claims into this milieu (Moses 1984, p. 109; Rogers 2000). Tristan's political and organisational isolation meant that she did not construct a movement around her claims. From 1835, more repressive laws made it even harder to articulate a language or organise around women's or workers rights in France, until the revolutions of 1848 allowed for fresh developments within the woman question. Tristan's attempt to construct a socialism into which sexual equality was built did not carry much resonance and the traditionalist version of socialism of Pierre-Joseph Proudhon (1809–65) or Ferdinand Lassalle (1825–64) was to become the dominant European socialist mode in the later decades of the nineteenth century. Lassalle, a leading socialist politician in Germany, opposed women's suffrage, and urged male workers to strike against the entry of women into industry. The First International, a loose coalition of socialist and Marxist activists operating from 1864 to 1876, did not fully oppose women's paid work, but did call for protective legislation that would in some cases exclude them from the workplace. While women's trade unions were allowed to affiliate, they were not actively supported; nor did the Second International (1889–1914) offer any deeper commitment to women workers. German socialists continued to recruit women as wives of workers rather than workers in their own right for the closing decades of the nineteenth century (Evans 1977, pp. 156–70).

Proudhon's *Qu'est-ce que la Propriété?* (*What is Property?*) was written in 1840, and declared that between the sexes there could be no real companionship. Proudhon envisaged a 'mutualist' socialism of small, independent family-based production, in which men directed the workshop and thus their wives' labour. He rejected Fourierist and Saint-Simonian versions of

331

socialism, and constructed a radical position that was based on women's return to domesticity. This call was popular amongst French working-class socialists, as more and more women came to work outside the home in the industrialising 1850s, and ideals of domesticity seemed threatened. Though Proudhon's misogyny became so overt that he lost credibility as a writer on the 'woman question', he nonetheless created a space within left-wing socialism for a highly reactionary gender politics, a space that was later to be inhabited by Ernest Belfort Bax (1854–1918), a prominent British socialist activist within the Social Democratic Federation (Andrews 2006; Moses 1984, pp. 152–8; Offen 2000, pp. 128–9).

In Britain, the construction of 'social sciences', and the intimate relation of this to the 'woman question' was advanced most forcefully by William Thompson (1775–1833), in his *Appeal of One Half of the Human Race, Women, Against the Pretensions of the Other Half, Men, to Retain Them in Political and Thence in Civil and Domestic, Slavery*, published in 1825. Thompson wrote his *Appeal* as an answer to James Mill's 1825 *Government*, in which Mill asserted that women, having the same interests as their male relatives, did not need political rights. Thompson was appalled that so central a figure in the radical utilitarian movement could hold such a view. Inspired by his conversations with Anna Wheeler (1785–1848),[9] and by his knowledge of Robert Owen's theories of social co-operation, Thompson offered a view of women as entirely equal contractors to men, in marriage and in political rights. Thompson argued that Mill, having assumed that all holders of unconstrained power would use it to their own advantage, could not then make an exception to this rule of half the human race. To assume that all women could count on an identity of interests between themselves and their husbands or fathers would undermine the entire utilitarian case for democratic self-government. In any case, some women spinsters and widows were not under the protection of men and Thompson believed they should be enfranchised and given equal civic status. Moreover, it was corrupting for both wives and husbands to assume shared interests. By gaining equal civil and political rights, all women would gain an 'expansion of the mind, of the intellectual powers, and of the sympathies of benevolence' (Thompson 1997, p. 178).

Such calls for self-development were to become a crucial part of the unfolding nineteenth-century woman question. Thompson held that equal

---

9 Anna Wheeler maintained and mediated contacts between (among others) Robert Owen, William Thompson and Charles Fourier (McFadden 1996, pp. 204–14).

civil rights alone could not achieve this personal development, since women were permanently disadvantaged in terms of strength and reproduction. He therefore argued for a radical change in social organisation. Like Fourier, Owen and the Saint-Simonians, he used his intervention into the woman question to make a much broader claim – that co-operation must replace competition as the basis for all social organisation. Women, disabled by their physical reproductive capacities, would always suffer in any competitive society. Instead, Thompson advocated the equal distribution of wealth and property held in common as a precondition to women's full equality. And under such conditions, Thompson predicted that masculinity would be as altered as femininity: In a co-operative world, 'Man, like woman, if he wish to be beloved, must learn the art of pleasing, of benevolence, of deserving love.' But he was not such a utopian as to dismiss gains in the contemporary, competitive world. He advised women in sweeping terms: 'Until the association of men and women in large numbers for mutual bene-fit shall supersede . . . individual competition, assert everywhere your right as human beings to equal individual liberty, to equal laws, political, civil, and criminal, to equal morals, to equal education . . . ' Under these conditions, Thompson assumed that women would still 'become the respectable and respected mothers and instructors of men . . . ' (Thompson 1997, pp. 205, 207). Women were the agents of change in Thompson's resolution of the woman question, but still within quite conventional roles. As for how change would come about, Thompson called on women to simply reflect on their situation – such reflection would inevitably lead to women's refusal to act as the chattels of men, and 'the collective voices of your sex raised against oppression will ultimately make men themselves your advocates and debtors'. Though Thompson assumed that sexual inequality had its origins in the biological differences between the two sexes, he still portrayed all male oppression as remediable by better education and reflection. To men, Thompson advised: 'Be rational human beings, not mere male sexual creatures! Cast aside the ferocious brute of your nature. Give up the pleasures of the brute, those of mere lust and command, for the pleasures of the rational being' (Thompson 1997, pp. 208, 146–7).

Nonetheless, the *Appeal* contained some quite explicit discussion of sexual pleasure. Thompson (1997, p. 101) had written that 'Woman can demand no enjoyment from man as a matter of right: she must beg it, like any of her children, or like any slave, as a favour.' He sought instead 'esteem and confidence between equals, heightened by the glow of sexual attachment'. But under current conditions, women could not even admit to their sexual feelings. While she must serve as 'the obedient instrument of man's sensual gratification, she is not permitted even to wish for any gratification for herself. She must have no desires: she must always yield, must submit as a matter of duty, not repose upon her equal for the sake of happiness: she must blush to own that she joys in his generous caresses, were such by chance ever given' (Thompson 1997, pp. 101–2). But as Barbara Taylor points out, women socialists and radicals were often less convinced of the regenerative and positive power of sexual passion than their male comrades. Anna Wheeler herself had written to Robert Owen's newspaper, *The Crisis*, in 1833, noting that women's love for men was a sign of her 'vicious and slavish training', and needed to be rationalised 'by the invigorating influence of a co-operating reason' (quoted in Taylor 1983, p. 47). Wheeler's emphasis on reason over passion was more characteristic of women writers on the woman question than Owen, Fourier or Thompson's preference for erotic liberation.

2 Mid-century debates: liberalism and sexual difference

Thompson's *Appeal* had been written in the absence of a sustained commitment to women's rights within the utilitarian movement, and in the face of James Mill's clear opposition to women's suffrage. His work influenced what has been regarded as the 'manifesto' of the Victorian and Edwardian women's movements, John Stuart Mill's *The Subjection of Women*, published in 1869 after the founding of the first women's suffrage society in 1866 in which Mill and his stepdaughter Helen Taylor were politically dominant (Rendall 1985). Mill's book had a profound international impact; it was immediately reprinted in the United States and translated into nearly every European language. Mill's argument was based on his commitment to individuality and self-development for women, only possible, he argued, within conditions of egalitarian relationships. Marriage, in particular, was the focus of his arguments for reform, and he believed it should become an equal and voluntary relationship, without legal intervention, as he stated in his own voluntary 'marriage contract' renouncing his 'rights' when he wedded Harriet Taylor in 1851 (Mill and Mill 1970, pp. 45–6). A new model of marriage would benefit individual women, but also (in utilitarian terms) society as a whole – the corrupting influence of belief in male superiority would be removed, and women would be able to absorb a wider, more public-spirited and disinterested morality. Mill placed moral regeneration, which was so important to other 'woman question' writers, as a secondary goal, achievable only when equality and justice prevailed in sexual relation-ships, and when women had voting rights and access to all public offices. Mill's argument came to supplant older, more popular radical arguments that had initially motivated claims for women's suffrage, about the repre-sentation of 'the people', and the struggle against 'the aristocracy'. Instead, the ideal woman voter became portrayed as rational and respectable, paying rates and taxes, in similar terms to the breadwinning working man. This argument was successful in gaining women the vote at the municipal and School Board levels around 1869 in Britain.

Unlike Thompson, Mill and his collaborators (wife and stepdaughter Harriet and Helen Taylor Mill), all emphasised the need for passion to be subjected to the powers of reason. None were positive about the powers of sexual attraction as a force for social and personal change. Previous societies had been based upon the dominance of the physically stronger, Mill believed. This principle survived still in gender relationships, but only as a relic of former times: 'The principle of the modern movement in morals and politics is that conduct and conduct alone entitles to respect: that not what men are but what they do constitutes their claim to deference . . . It is totally out of keeping with modern values to have ascribed statuses . . . individual choice is our model now' (Mill and Mill 1970, p. 58). Mill's work has been read as a classic statement of nineteenth-century liberalism, but in fact on the topic of women's rights, he was isolated amongst his liberal contemporaries (Griffin 2011). Mill argued that 'woman's nature', so often used as an argument for restricting their political rights, was eminently artificial: 'What women are is what we have required them to be.' He therefore left open the question of women's essential qualities, and laid a large stress on their unexplored capacities. Nonetheless, he did believe that women were best employed as household managers, and he did not comment on the necessity of paid work for most working-class women, nor the nature of the work, paid or unpaid, they might do and how this might conflict with equality in public roles. Given the context of the debates over the Factory Acts and the 'protection' they offered to women workers, as well as the stress on opening up new fields of employment to women in the women's movement of the 1860s, this was a curious omission (Rendall 1985, pp. 287, 290). His text was more useful to those who came to address women's entry to suffrage and public offices, and did not help to resolve the very significant splits that developed within the women's movement over the questions of employment (Malone 1998; Lewis *et al.* 1995). The 'suitability' of women's employment, and whether they should be given a free labour market or a state-regulated one, were perhaps the most contentious of the 'women questions' of this period – Mill's text was perhaps only able to become a 'bible' of the movement because it did not address these points in any depth.

Despite the boldness of William Thompson and John Stuart Mill's statements of egalitarian sexual relationships, in Britain and the United States of the 1830s and onwards, public opinion on women's status and roles had become shaped more by a sense of 'woman's mission', 'sphere' or special influence, which persisted into the 1880s (Helsinger *et al.* 1983, p. xvi). Though in the 1830s women's suffrage was raised by Chartists and other radicals, and was discussed at American women's rights conventions in the 1840s, it was divisive and controversial and did not yet inspire an organised movement. Instead, the early nineteenth-century evangelical revival had encouraged women in Britain and America to take on philanthropic work, in prisons, schools, temperance and abolition. Abolitionist women drew up petitions, raised funds and lectured in public – and this work has long been seen as setting in motion the conditions that led to an organised 'women's movement' later in the century, though recent scholarship has emphasised the lack of any predetermined transition from philanthropy, to abolition, to 'feminism' (Billington and Billington 1987; Hewitt 2010; Mathers 2002; Melder 1977). The language of evangelism, and the opposition they encountered in their abolition work, gave women such as Lucretia Mott and the Grimké sisters the ability to articulate an egalitarian politics of gender, as in Sarah Grimké's *Letters on the Equality of the Sexes and the Condition of Women* (Grimké 1988 [1838]; Lerner and Grimké 1998). But evangelism could also work to contain and restrict women's freedoms. The ambiguity of this discourse is demonstrated in a British text, Sarah Lewis' highly influential book *Woman's Mission*, first published in 1839. Lewis had drawn on Rousseau's ideas about women's education, via the intermediary of Louis Aimé Martin's book, *De l'Éducation des Mères de Famille, ou la Civilisation du Genre Humain par les Femmes* (1834) (Helsinger *et al.* 1983, p. 4; Lewis 1839). Like the work of Martin, *Woman's Mission* argues against women's political rights, and advises women to confine their influence to the domestic realm, rather than philanthropic work in the 'public sphere'. Nonetheless, Lewis believed that women were morally superior, and had a role to play as moral and spiritual regenerators. Maternal love was the bedrock of women's influence, and the highest expression of Christian principles. The expression of this love in the home represented 'an inexhaustible field of effort, an inexhaustible source of happiness; and here women are the undoubted agents,

336

and they complain of having no scope for exertion!' Lewis concluded: 'Till the philosophy of domestic happiness has undergone a thorough reformation, let not women seek to invade the sphere of the other sex' (Lewis 1839, p. 121). Lewis and Martin were expressing ideas that were highly influential (if less clear when put into practice) in nineteenth-century Britain, the United States and France, that the two sexes were not rivals, nor situated in a hierarchical relationship within the common sphere of humanity, as eighteenth-century writers had stressed, but reigned supreme in separate spheres (Clark 1995, p. 2). It was polemically declared that women's only political role was to influence their male relatives to adopt values of duty and self-devotion. While this belief in 'woman's mission' ran counter to the egalitarian values articulated by Fanny Wright, Flora Tristan or John Stuart Mill, the idea of 'woman's influence' was one that some within the women's movement found strategically useful, or ideologically appealing. As Karen Offen has argued of European debates, 'complementarity of the sexes was central to feminist perspectives during this period. Most feminists accepted some type of sexual division of labour in society. What they rejected was the assertive gendering of the public/private division of spheres as male and female' (Offen 2000, p. 102). French Saint-Simonian women of the 1830s, for example, emphasised maternity as the unique capacity which united women and framed their contribution as 'mother-educator' to the state and civil society. 'Maternity' had a diverse political valency; in German cities, it was idealised in the active women's kindergarten movement, and more broadly, the 'mother-educator' became associated with the reviving or sustaining of national languages and religious cultures (M. A. Taylor 1991).

Arguments about the regenerative force of women, or mothers, could take many forms, and historians have recently stressed that it was not only egalitarian doctrines that provided the impetus for thinking about the status of women or prompted activism. In Britain, Caroline Norton (1808–77) conducted an immensely influential campaign for child custody rights for women from the late 1830s, drawing agency from concepts of maternal duty and love (Poovey 1988). Writers such as John Ruskin in Britain drew on Lewis' idea of separate domains in his 'Of Queens' Gardens' (1865), a popular essay by a writer whose influence extended across the Anglo-American world. Like so many Victorians, Ruskin saw women as a major vehicle for social change, though he appeared to be arguing for the limitation of their aspirations and role to one of a harmonious helpmate to men – 'a *guiding*, not a determining, function' (Ruskin n.d. [1865], p. 58). He adopted a paternalistic approach to the woman question, seeing women as essentially pure and childlike. Nonetheless, Ruskin extended Sarah Lewis' idea of women's mission to the concept of their 'queenly power' that must be also exercised outside of the home (Mclloyd 1995). He therefore sought women's education and an expansion of their philanthropic mission – to propagate domestic values throughout society. It is not easy to place his ideas politically – they can be read as simultaneously reforming and conservative, though conservatives such as Anthony Trollope read him as a dangerous radical. He offers an example of why 'feminist' is so unhelpful an identity for this period, since his ideas gave women compelling arguments for expansion of their 'sphere', as a reviewer writing in the women-run Langham Place *Victoria Magazine* recognised, while also drawing on a socially conservative understanding of the essential nature of femininity.[10]

The work of Margaret Fuller (1810–50) in the United States gives an example of the displacement of egalitarianism from the heart of the 'woman question' and substitution of other goals – in her case (as in Ruskin's), the goal of moral and spiritual regeneration of humans through the agency of women. Fuller was active within the Boston Transcendentalist movement, edited its journal, *The Dial*, and became a well-known critic, salon hostess and writer on the woman question. In 1845 she published *Woman in the Nineteenth Century*, an extension of an earlier journal article in *The Dial*. In this text she stressed the self-dependence and cultivation of the inner intellectual life needed by women, though she later became more interested in social questions and was active in the Italian revolutions of 1848.[11] The rambling and eclectic *Woman in the Nineteenth Century* emphasised the stunting of 'woman' as currently socialised, and envisaged a heroic and intellectually expansive future for women. Fuller was less interested in legal or social equalities, and offered a more utopian contribution to the woman question. She imagined a future state in which men might express maternal love and care for children, while women were open to intellectual genius and physical enterprise. Influenced by Fourier's conception of non-gendered diversity in occupation, she famously wrote 'if you ask me what offices [women] may fill, I reply – any. I do not care what case you put; let them be sea-captains, if you will.' Nonetheless, like Thompson and Mill, she did expect most to become mothers, and to be attracted to domestic duties, though she argued that 'a being of infinite scope must not be treated with

---

10 'Mr Ruskin on Books and Women', *Victoria Magazine*, 6 (1865), pp. 131–3, quoted at length in Helsinger *et al.* 1983, pp. 99–101.
11 On women's role in the European revolutions of 1848 and the repression of the counter-revolution, see Offen 2000, pp. 108–20.

an exclusive view to any one relation'. All human powers must be perfected as ends in themselves, not as means to the satisfaction or companionship of others, and Fuller therefore regarded 'old maids' on a par with mothers, in epitomising her ideal of self-dependence and as potential agents of the new order (Fuller 1971, pp. 174, 34, 96, 97).

Fuller did not direct her writing towards what were to become the established campaigns of the women's movement in the second half of the nineteenth century – the campaigns around women's education, professional opportunities and political rights. Instead, she was interested in encouraging women to explore their dual 'Minerva' and 'Muse' creative qualities. These represented a mingling of masculine and feminine energies, expressed in all humans; ideally neither would dominate, though historical circumstances required women to explore their neglected 'active' Minerva side before they could gain true balance. As Otto Weininger was to argue in Vienna in the next century, Fuller believed that ultimately, 'there is no wholly masculine man, no purely feminine woman...' But this was not a commitment to androgyny; were women free, Fuller predicted, they would 'develop the strength and beauty of Woman; they would never wish to be men, or man-like' (Fuller 1971, p. 116). Despite her later experiences in Europe, her vision in 1845 was of the United States as the place where women's freedom could be achieved, sustaining a Jeffersonian belief in America's special mission: 'here is a less encumbered field and freer air than anywhere else' (Fuller 1971, p. 108). Women in America, less convention- and tradition-bound than elsewhere, were to be the agents of regeneration of male society. This would occur, initially, through their withdrawal from male society and freedom to 'find their peculiar secret' through establishing a personal relationship with God – 'I wish woman to live, *first* for God's sake', she wrote (Fuller 1971, p. 176). Though Fuller remained critical of how the Christian Church had treated women, her religious commitment was as influential on her own work as the egalitarian claims being made for women by Fuller's contemporaries. Her work reflects the way in which Protestant and Dissenting sects had provided intellectual communities and spaces in which to speak for many of the influential and politically active American women (Bartlett 1994).

In contrast to the counter-revolutionary oppression in Europe in the 1850s, the late 1840s and 1850s in the United States witnessed an upsurge of interest in the woman question, prompted by the new political space made available through women's rights conventions. The 1848 Seneca Falls and the 1850 Worcester conventions explicitly addressed the issue of how to represent sexual difference in a democracy. The 'Declaration of Sentiments' drawn up by Elizabeth Cady Stanton and presented at Seneca Falls in 1848 has been seen as a founding treatise of the organised women's movement, modelled explicitly on the American Declaration of Independence and admired in Britain and continental Europe. This document and the resolutions of the convention claimed for women the right to divorce, to freedom of employment, to speak and preach in public, and to vote. The suffrage issue was divisive for the convention, and was by no means the keystone that it was to become in later years. Temperance and abolition were regarded as intimately linked to the cause of the antebellum women's movement, which was also (as in Britain) sustained by Unitarian and Quaker networks. Women's rights to keep their maiden names, and their citizenship rights on marriage became points of activist reform, as did the linkage of taxation to representation. Instead reform of marriage was initially seen, as Paulina Wright Davis put it, as 'the starting point of all the reforms the world needs' (Rendall 1985, p. 303). Divorce, however, was not yet acceptable to all within the women's movement, and this became increasingly controversial in the years prior to the Civil War. Nonetheless, at the mid-century, the women's movement seemed preoccupied with questions of the state of marriage – the ownership of property by married women, their custody of infants and right to work.

3 'Redundant women' and social democracy

Demographic, economic and cultural changes led to a shift in focus towards the second half of the century. The existence and visibility of growing numbers of single women in the nineteenth century, and particularly the single middle-class woman living on her own earnings, outside of the framework of masculine authority, became an important 'woman question' in its own right, famously articulated by W. R. Greg's article 'Why are Women Redundant?' in the British *National Review* (Greg 1862; Vicinus 1985, pp. 3–6). The physical, social and moral consequences of the autonomy of these women was debated across Europe and the United States, and contributed to the sense of sexual crisis that dominated the final decades of the century, as the 'new woman' was invented in literature and political polemic (Evans 1977, pp. 26–7; Faure 1986; Richardson 2003; Roberts 2002; Showalter 1992). While women's employment became central to the woman question in Europe, population issues also became important. Population occupied an especially prominent place in imperial Germany, where the *Frauenfrage*

('woman question') became dominated by concern over the female population surplus (the *Frauenüberschuss*) in the later decades of the nineteenth
century, and thus by the figure of the *alte Jungfer* or 'old maid' (Dollard
2000). This perceived population crisis across Europe, as single women
became more visible amongst the urban middle classes, led to opportunities
to restate and rethink women's place in German society – with proposals
ranging from the commitment of 'surplus' women to religious institutions, to wider professional opportunities for them. However, the German
women's movement, hampered by the oppressive (anti-socialist) association
laws that were only repealed in 1890, and limited by the widespread social
acceptance of women's *kulturaufgabe* as limited to patriotic work within the
home and family, did not gain institutional or political momentum. It was
fatally split between the socialist activists of the *Sozialdemokratische Partei
Deutschlands* (SPD) and the *Bürgerliche Frauenbewegung*, the philanthropic-
minded women of the middle classes who looked to outline a wider public
role for themselves, along the lines that Ruskin had suggested in 'Of Queens'
Gardens'.

The SPD hosted its own versions of the 'woman question', as part of a
flourishing debate within European Marxism. In earlier texts by Marx and
Engels such as the *Paris Manuscripts* and *The Holy Family*, women served as
symbolic factors rather than active agents, with their status showing the stage
of historical development of society. The focus on production in Marxist
writing left reproductive relations insignificant to historical materialism, and
Marx made little attempt to explain why the initial state of patriarchy had
come about. August Bebel (1840–1913) had developed the Marxist analysis
of the woman question more substantially, making a firm commitment to
women's rights in his 1879 *Die Frau und der Sozialismus* (*Woman and Socialism*), a book that later socialists such as Alexandra Kollontai described as
the 'woman's bible' (Bebel 1879; Coole 1993, p. 161).[12] Bebel offered a
more visionary picture of future transformations of gender relations, and
was relatively warm to the goals of the 'women's movement' – suffrage and
professional advancement for women. While he retained the primacy of

---

12 Kollontai, a Soviet revolutionary, was shaped by the influence of the Russian nihilists and populists.
Inspired by Nikolai Chernyshevsky's 1863 novel *What is to be Done?*, which advocated sexual
liberation as part of a movement 'back to the people', the Russian revolutionary tradition was always
relatively open to women activists. Kollontai and her colleagues, often working in exile, gained the
acquaintance of European socialists such as Bebel and Zetkin, and encouraged women in twentieth-
century Russia to take a leading role in the revolutions (Engelstein 1992; Kollontai 1977; Stites
1978).

economic factors in women's oppression, *Woman and Socialism* was quite graphic about the nature of women's oppression, ranging from the obstructive dress, dependency and triviality suffered by bourgeois women to the double burden and brutal treatment of proletarian women. While Bebel felt that socialist men were to be potentially the agents of women's emancipation, he also expressed an early formulation of what twentieth-century feminist writers came to variously call the 'Turk Complex' or 'patriarchy'.[13] He recognised that men enjoyed the sense of power and self-importance that their dominance over women gave them. Nonetheless, he provided an alternative vision of the future inspired by Fourier, involving pleasant, changeable work, and the use of technology to lighten all labour. Unlike Fourier, Bebel disliked contraception, and his vision of emancipated women was closely tied to the assumption that most women were to be mothers, and that reproduction was still their primary responsibility.

Bebel's work raised the profile of the woman question within Marxism, and inspired Engels to produce his *Origin of the Family, Private Property and the State* in 1884 to describe the historical evolution of male domination. Engels drew upon the anthropological work of Lewis Morgan's *Ancient Society* (1877), and offered a materialist account of the 'pre-history' of 'civilisation', before men had come to dominate women and productive relations dominated society. His work in historicising the family and gender relations was influential for the socialist construction of the woman question, though he allowed certain phenomena such as the 'incest taboo' and women's desire for monogamy to retain their natural status. Engels postulated a period of 'mother-right', in which women gained power through lineage being traced through the maternal line, while paternity was still uncertain and men were the mobile factors between communities. Men worked outside the home, while women ruled it, in Engels' scheme. But women's desire for permanent couplings and advances in agriculture and animal domestication lead to the reversal of the situation, as men came to generate an economic surplus and desired to pass it on to their children. It was the material wealth of the father that became determinate as society moved into 'civilisation'. This 'world historical defeat of the female sex' thus enacted the first class oppression, and class antagonism remained the

---

13 The former term was coined by a British 'feminist', Eleanor Rathbone, to describe what Virginia Woolf had also noticed, men's psychological dependence on women's subordination (Rathbone 1924; Woolf 1996).

key frame that Engels and many socialists were to use in discussing the 'woman question'. The solution was to make women's labour productive: 'The emancipation of woman will only be possible when woman can take part in production on a large, social scale, and domestic work no longer claims anything but an insignificant amount of her time' (Engels 1940b, p. 184).

Engels' theory was based upon a natural and unexplained division of labour that enabled men to control the first private property. Though Proudhon-inspired calls for all women to be returned to their 'natural' work in the home persisted in the movement, it became an alternative Marxist solution to the woman question that women should be returned to 'public industry'. Domestic labour could then be socialised and free but monogamous sex-love would emerge while marriage became irrelevant. While Engels foresaw a 'gradual growth of unconstrained sexual intercourse and with it a more tolerant public opinion in regard to a maiden's honour and a woman's shame', he also felt that 'sexual love is by its nature exclusive . . . The equality of woman . . . will tend infinitely more to make men really monogamous than to make women polyandrous' (Engels 1940b, pp. 82, 88). The 'utopian' sexual liberation of Fourier had been marginalised within the socialist tradition. Moreover, this solution made the oppression of working (proletarian) women obscured, and Engels saw the remaining 'brutality' they might suffer as insignificant, a left-over super-structural habit from a former mode of production.

Two years later, Eleanor Marx and Edward Aveling elaborated on Engels' and Bebel's work with their essay the 'woman Question: From a Socialist Point of View' in *The Westminster Review* (Aveling and Marx 1886). They argued, like Bebel, that class and not sex relations were the issue, and only after the revolution could gender equality prevail, through women's material independence of men. The goals of the contemporary women's movement (suffrage, repeal of government licensing of prostitution, higher education, freedom to work) were validated, but Marx and Aveling argued that the 'bed-rock of the economic basis' of society was not understood by bourgeois activists. The reforms sought by women would not fundamentally change sex-relations, which could only achieved by the abolition of private property and the state. In an interesting aside, the authors argued that women must seek emancipation 'from themselves. Women will find allies in the better sort of men, as the labourers are finding allies among the philosophers, artists and poets. But the one has nothing to hope from man as a whole, and the other has nothing to hope from the middle-class as a whole' (Aveling and Marx 1886, pp. 210–11). This seemed to imply a certain autonomy for the women's movement that was highly controversial for Marxist organisations, and this question of the autonomy of women's struggle continued to be among the most contentious of the 'woman questions' for socialists.

Seeking to transcend the damaging possibility of division between women of different classes, in Germany, Lily Braun, a leader of the bourgeois women's movement, had joined the SPD in 1895 and sought an alliance with socialist women. However, the implacable opposition of Clara Zetkin (1857–1933) meant that there was no sense of unity between working and bourgeois women. Zetkin, editor of *Die Gleichheit* (the SPD women's newspaper) was extremely influential in shaping the German woman question as needing to be differentiated by class status. Zetkin was interested in women as socialist agents, organised in semi-autonomous party structures. She was frustrated by the views of reactionary socialists influenced by Proudhon and Lassalle who wanted to abolish women's work, but she made few concessions to the 'women's rights' agenda, and repulsed attempts at collaboration. She conceded that for bourgeois women, men were the primary enemy, while for proletarian women, their economic interests were genuinely united with men of the same class. Cross-class sisterhood therefore could not be productive. Zetkin and the other late nineteenth-century socialist writers on the 'woman question' did not publicly call for any change in the division of labour between the sexes, and preferred to demand women's economic independence, without fundamentally changing their status as wives and mothers alongside their role as workers. Seeing women workers as having different needs from male workers, Zetkin supported protective labour measures, also intended to prevent their cheap labour from undercutting men. But in contrast to Marx and Aveling's concession to the validity of women's struggle, Zetkin argued 'We recognise no special woman question ... We expect our full emancipation neither from women's admission to what are known as free trades, nor from equal education with men – although the demand for both these rights is natural and just – nor from the granting of political rights ... The emancipation of women, together with that of all humanity, will take place only with the emancipation of labour from capital' (Zetkin 1983, p. 90; Coole 1993, pp. 167–9). Despite the recognition given by Bebel, Eleanor Marx and Zetkin to women's distinctive oppression, none of these thinkers managed to resolve the tensions within the 'Marxist solution' to the woman question, and all tended to stress monogamy and traditional families within their version of liberation.

4 Character and individualism

The nineteenth-century woman question developed in a troubled dialogue with the activism that periodically arose around women's status and free-doms. Should we regard the 'woman question' as the discourse that made possible the invention of 'feminism' in the twentieth century? Was it the 'woman question' which prepared the ground that allowed women to gain full citizenship rights and to claim reproductive and economic freedoms? Historians have frequently tried to trace one ongoing conversation that links the 'two waves' of twentieth-century feminism to their nineteenth-century forebears. There were indications of shared intellectual concerns between 'woman question' writers and feminists. There was a persistent idea, for example, that women must struggle not against men, but against their own social construction as 'silly' or dependent creatures. Mary Woll-stonecraft described most women as doll-like, formed like courtiers to love pleasure and trifles: women's 'senses are inflamed, and their under-standings neglected, consequently they become the prey of their senses, delicately termed sensibility, and are blown about by every momentary gust of feeling' (Wollstonecraft 1993, p. 130). Louise Otto (1819–95), an activist and writer based in Saxony, accused women of 'characterlessness'. The London-based and women-run *Victoria Magazine* argued in 1865 that women should look within themselves for their emancipation: 'Woman can be what she makes herself; her power lies within her own grasp...' (cited in Palmegiano 1976, p. xliii). Frances Power Cobbe (1822–1904) also described women as dolls, and saw 'idle women' as the biggest obstacle to women's emancipation (Cobbe 1870). Emily Pfeiffer, a British poet and writer on women's rights, argued in 1881 in the *Contemporary Review* that character was the key concern of the 'woman question' (cited in Lewis 1987, p. 381).

A stress on the development of feminine character – and the *self*-emancipation this process could entail – persisted in discussion of the 'woman question' into the twentieth century. While the nineteenth-century women's movement has often been characterised as liberal, their rights-claims were often motivated by a sense of the emancipation of character. Liberal political thought tended to define freedom as absence of accidental obstruction or external coercion; women's movement activists, however, identified individual freedom as entailing the absence of both external and *internal* constraints, and also included psychological factors as potential bars to freedom. A contributor argued in the British journal *Blackwood's* in 1897 that 'the psychology of the feminist' involved 'dissecting [her soul], analysing and probing into the innermost crannies of her nature. She is for ever examining her mental self in the looking glass' (Stutfield 1897, pp. 105, 104). Those writing at the *fin de siècle*, who had tentatively begun to identify themselves as feminists – writers such as the American Charlotte Perkins Gilman (1860–1935), or the South African Olive Schreiner (1855–1920), spoke of women's parasitism as the most powerful object keeping them enslaved. It became characteristic of Edwardian/Progressive Era feminism to fix the feminist gaze firmly on women's own character or 'personality', rather than on external institutions and the habits of men. This grew out of the insights of earlier writers on the woman question, who had long debated the social and psychic construction of femininity.

In discussing woman's 'character', most nineteenth-century writers deployed a language of political duty and service, stressing the contribution women might make and comfortable with the distinct qualities women were believed to offer the state. One British suffragist, Ray Strachey, for example, acknowledged the influence of 'individualism and love of liberty', but saw the nineteenth-century heritage as one of the moral character of women's emancipation: 'it was not primarily a fight between men and women, *hardly even a matter of "rights" at all*. What they saw in [the cause], and what they wanted from it, was an extended power to do good in the world' (Strachey 1928, p. 305). Where a rights-discourse was prominent, as in the work of Mary Wollstonecraft, a great deal of attention was devoted to the duties and political virtues that were consequent on the rights of women (Halldenius 2007; Sapiro 1992). Towards the end of the nineteenth century, when the discourse of idealism became prominent in Anglo-American political philosophy, the idealist stress on social organicism and character carried strong resonances with the women's movement.[14] Self-generated desires and lusts might impinge on an individual's freedom, and idealists advocated strong moral control over the individual psyche (Stears 2002, 101–6). Many in the women's movement found this appealing, and were critical of the abstract, self-oriented versions of liberal freedom.

14 The work of the British feminist writer May Sinclair made this resonance explicit (Sinclair 1912, 1922). See Den Otter 1996 on idealism more generally.

Idealists continued to frame their arguments using older languages of ethics and character; their contribution can be seen as a transitional one in political argument, opening the door to the development of ideas of personality that became so influential for later feminists and political argument more generally. Newer generations of feminists used the new idea of personality to articulate a distinct vision, neither of service, nor of liberal individualism. The 'new woman' or *éclaireuse* of fiction and political argument of the 1890s and the iconoclastic feminists of the early twentieth century preferred a political vision that stressed personality over character, individual development over service and duty, and psychological introspection over external activism. While stressing individualism, their focus is better read as a contribution to the politics of early modernism than a renewal of nineteenth-century liberalism. Their values were the egoist values of self-development and uniqueness, rather than the individualist values of privacy and *laisser-faire* (Francis 2002). Influenced by the frank acknowledgement of women's dissatisfaction with domesticity by the Norwegian playwright Henrik Ibsen, and his embrace of 'natural aristocracy', feminists came to share with modernists an interest in elites – in Nietzschean terms, in the superwoman – rather than the egalitarianism feminism is commonly associated with (Delap 2004). The writings of Friedrich Nietzsche and Max Stirner began to circulate in European and American intellectual and feminist circles in the early years of the twentieth century. Stirner's neo-Hegelian account of the master–slave relationship became a resource to understand the confrontation between the genders. For Stirner, the slave was oppressed through his own attitude of servility towards the master, and emancipation lay in simply refusing to recognise the power of the master. While Stirner used this idea to reject state power over individuals, feminists such as Dora Marsden (1882–1960, editor of the British *Freewoman* periodical), Russian-American anarchist Emma Goldman (1869–1940) and in Austria, Rosa Mayreder (1858–1938), understood women's subjectivity in terms of 'slave morality', and spoke of an egoistic transcendence of male oppression (Mayreder 1913; Delap 2007). Nietzsche's *Thus Spake Zarathustra* had been translated into English in 1896, and its influence can be seen on a minority of Anglo-American feminists of the early twentieth century who came to understand themselves as 'disciples of Nietzsche', and to look for the social renewal of a 'revaluation of all values' (*Current Opinion*, Jan. 1913; Farr 1910). It became possible for Emma Goldman to argue that for women: 'true emancipation begins neither at the poll nor in courts. It begins in woman's soul . . . [Woman's] freedom will reach as far as her power to achieve her freedom reaches. It is therefore, far more important for her to begin with inner regeneration...' (Goldman 1969a, p. 230). This, however, was a controversial position; writers such as the Swede Ellen Key wrote critically of 'the feminism which has driven individualism to the point where the individual asserts her personality in opposition to, instead of within, the race; the individualism which becomes self-concentration, anti-social egoism...' (Key 1912, pp. 222–3).

The early twentieth-century feminist focus became highly introverted, sceptical of state power, and occasionally racially informed by anti-Semitism (Stone 2002). Feminist interest in the psychological dimension of the 'woman question' reflects a broad intellectual change in late nineteenth- and early twentieth-century culture, where psychological introspection became validated not only by idealist thought, but by the relatively new fields of psychology and psychiatry (Soffer 1978; Susman 1996, pp. 271–85). This shift caused a great deal of controversy amongst feminists as to what their focus could be, and even the suffrage struggle could not unite women around a single vision. The more 'avant-garde' feminists tried hard to distinguish their position from suffragism, and this led to bitterness and conflict amongst women activists. While gender remained a source of fascination and controversy in the twentieth century, and while pacifism, human trafficking and employment remained key feminist issues, all were controversial and divisive. There were few concerns that could be constructed in monolithic terms as the 'woman question' after the First World War. 'Woman' fell out of favour as a term of political argument, and until the 1970s, feminist writers became wary of offering sweeping analyses and solutions to gender controversies.

II

Constitutional liberalism in France

From Benjamin Constant to Alexis de Tocqueville

JEREMY JENNINGS

1   Introduction

When Madame de Staël wrote her *Considérations sur la Révolution Française* one of the central questions she raised was the following: 'Did France possess a Constitution before the Revolution?' (de Staël 2008, pp. 96–111). Her answer was that France had been 'governed by custom, by caprice but never by laws' and that of all modern monarchies France had undoubtedly been the one 'whose political institutions had been the most arbitrary'. This is a portrayal that France's monarchs might have challenged – they certainly felt themselves to be constrained in their actions by a set of fundamental laws that they might not transgress – but the fact remained that by 1789 there existed a widespread demand for a written constitution that would set out clear limits to the actions of government and that would define the rights of all citizens. It was in this context that the meaning attributed to the idea of a constitution changed irrevocably, and with radical implications. Henceforth it was to be understood as the set of arrangements that were to determine the manner in which institutions of the state and of public authority operated. Moreover, given the descent of the monarchy into what was widely perceived to be despotism, the demand was increasingly made that these arrangements should correspond to the deliberate choice of the nation.

What form this constitution was to take and how the views of the nation were to be expressed were questions that were to preoccupy France's legislators for much of the next decade. These passionate (and immensely sophisticated) debates were to be decisive in shaping much of France's future political history, in part for the simple reason that they were premised upon an outright rejection of the claim that the monarch alone embodied the sovereign public will. That doctrine, widely propagated by the Crown itself in its struggles with the *parlements*, had made sense in the context of a society which was both divided and parcellised and where therefore it appeared that not only was a strong state necessary in order to secure civil peace but where also that state could claim to embody the generality, as opposed to the particularity, of society's interests. The preoccupation, as witnessed in the writings of Bossuet and many others, had been at one and the same time that of denying that sovereignty had its origins in the people and of seeking to render royal power more truly public. Seen thus, *la monarchie absolue* positioned itself as an instrument calculated to enhance, rather than to diminish, the liberty and security of the individual. From this followed a suspicion of all those intermediary powers and voluntary associations that later French liberals were to consider as one of the all-important guarantees of liberty. Even when defended by Montesquieu such institutions came to be conflated with aristocratic power and what became known as the *thèse nobiliaire*.

In the summer of 1789 a dramatic transfer of power took place, with the new-found political and ideological ascendancy of the Third Estate receiving its clearest articulation in the writings and speeches of the Abbé Sieyès. For Sieyès, the only legitimate source of power was located in the nation: all other forms were contrary to the common interest. The problem remained, however, of providing institutional expression for that power. Initially, the intellectual leadership of the Revolution fell to those who became known as the *monarchiens*. They showed themselves to possess a perceptive awareness of the dangers of arbitrary government, be it in the form of the despotism of either a single individual or of the multitude. They recommended representative as opposed to direct democracy, advocating the establishment of a two-chamber parliamentary system so constructed as to give voice to the diverse interests of the whole country and to secure sound and responsible legislation. Similarly, the *monarchiens* proposed the separation of executive and legislative power. 'In order to avoid tyranny', Jean-Joseph Mounier argued, 'it is absolutely indispensable to ensure that the power to make laws is not in the hands of those who implement them.'[1] In short, they argued that the preservation of individual liberty demanded the division of sovereignty and that this could best be achieved by a system of representative and constitutional government. Seeking to draw upon the experience of the past, rather than to reason from first principles, their constant point of reference was the English constitution. The institutions of government, Mounier further opined, had to take into account 'the weakness and the passions of men'.

---

1 *Archives parlementaires* 8 (1875), Paris, p. 560.

By the late summer of 1789 the proposals of the *monarchiens* – in particular, the call for a two-chamber parliamentary system – had been overwhelmingly rejected. The prevailing view was that as France had now been divested of privilege and of the aristocratic prejudices of the past there was no need for a system designed to accommodate diverse and conflicting interests. What, Sieyès asked rhetorically, had the nation, possessed of a unitary will, to fear from itself? Rabaut Saint-Étienne set out the institutional logic which applied to such a situation. Given that the power to govern itself belonged to the nation in its entirety, '[t]he sovereign is a single, simple thing, since it is made up of the collective whole without exception; therefore legislative power is single and simple; and if the sovereign cannot be divided, nor can legislative power'.[2]

The same logic informed the conviction that legislation was not to be subject to judicial review. The framers of the new political order deliberately set out to weaken the capacity of the judiciary to curtail the legislative and executive branches largely on the grounds that sovereignty, one and indivisible, could be located in the will of the citizens alone as articulated through the single-chamber National Assembly.

How might these important developments be summarised? First, breaking with the traditions and practices of the *ancien régime*, it was quickly established that a constitution should have a clearly written and coherent form. Its authors were to be the nation acting as sovereign through its representatives. Next, although in form a monarchy, the constitution that came to be promulgated in September 1791 effectively transferred power to an assembly in the name of the people. Crucially, it was assumed that, if a people were sovereign, then this was a sufficient condition to ensure that it was free and therefore that the rights of the individual would be protected. Accordingly, those framing the constitution paid scant attention to the need for a separation or balance of powers.

The die was now cast for what was to follow. The constitution of 1791 retaining the monarchy died stillborn. The (Jacobin) constitution of 1793 reaffirmed the sovereignty of the people and did so by granting them the rights to both insurrection and legislative veto. Distrustful of the very process of representation, Robespierre's ambition was to fashion a new assembly which would be 'pure, incorruptible', peopled by 'virtuous men'. Private, local or sectional interest was equated with faction and opposition to the Revolution. The English constitutional model was deemed fit only

---

2 Ibid., p. 569.

for a nation of slaves. With the constitution suspended until 'the return of peace', France then experienced revolutionary government and with that came the rapid descent into the reign of Terror, an experiment which only came to an end with the execution of the Jacobin leadership.

After Thermidor there followed a further attempt to establish the Republic upon a secure foundation, largely through the introduction of a complex set of executive and legislative arrangements designed to limit the exercise of popular sovereignty. A much-reduced suffrage giving power to the propertied classes was combined with two legislative chambers, for example. The constitution of 1795 proved only slightly more enduring than its two predecessors. Assailed from all sides, the Directory of five members it spawned was reduced to increasingly desperate (and unconstitutional) measures in its determination to keep hold of power. No sooner was he elected to its membership than Sieyès began, with typical calculation, to plot its overthrow. His protégé, the young Napoleon Bonaparte, duly performed the necessary act with the *coup d'état* of the *18 Brumaire*. Technically the Republic still existed, although in 1802 Bonaparte had himself proclaimed Consul for life, further extending his already-considerable powers and reducing the power of the legislative branch. At this point, as Jacques Godechot remarked, 'Napoleon was already more powerful than Louis XIV' (Godechot 1995, p. 166). Two years later Napoleon crowned himself Emperor. In this way did the experience of the First Republic reach its sorry conclusion, the doctrine of popular sovereignty not only having eluded embodiment in a stable constitutional form but now associated as a consequence with Jacobin Terror and Bonapartist dictatorship.

It was against this depressing backdrop that writer after writer sought to draw lessons for France's future. If those like Joseph de Maistre and Louis de Bonald concluded that the whole experience had been an almost satanic enterprise and that there was no alternative but to return to the dual (and unchallengeable) authority of throne and altar, there were others such as Destutt de Tracy and his fellow *Idéologues* who sought to reduce the radical potential of the language of rights by developing a more consistently utilitarian conception of liberty. Still others endeavoured (against the odds) to formulate an understanding of liberty and of constitutional government that would be appropriate to a modern, commercial age. In the nineteenth century such people were to be characterised as liberals.

Properly to understand this frame of mind, we need first to return to the eighteenth century and in particular to Montesquieu. Much has been written about Montesquieu's discussion of the English constitution, and in particular about the vexed question of whether he was providing a description of how the English constitution actually worked or an ideal type of the 'constitution of liberty' (Montesquieu 1989, pp. 156–66). Whatever the answer, it is beyond dispute that Montesquieu sketched out what he took to be a tripartite division of the executive, legislative and judicial branches of government and that he saw England as a system of mixed government in which power was shared between monarch, Lords and Commons. From this he concluded that a system of division and balance was indispensable for the preservation of liberty and that the essence of good government was not only moderation but also a system which recognised that 'power must check power by the arrangement of things' (Montesquieu 1989, p. 155). The worst of all situations, as evidenced by the Ottoman Empire, was one where the enjoyment of liberty depended 'upon the caprice of the legislator' (Montesquieu 1989, p. 155) and upon the arbitrary power of the despot. Just as importantly, Montesquieu recognised (like Voltaire and others before him) that the governing principle of societal relations was in the process of fundamental transition. The pursuit of glory was being replaced by the spirit of commerce. 'Commerce', Montesquieu wrote, 'cures destructive prejudices, and it is an almost general rule that everywhere there are mild customs, there is commerce and that everywhere there is commerce, there are gentle mores' (Montesquieu 1989, p. 338). The natural effect of commerce, in short, was to lead to peace. Moreover, 'commerce is related to the constitution'. Under a 'government by one' its aim is the provision of luxury; under a 'government by many' it aims modestly, and by dint of continuous effort, to produce a level of wealth that will permeate across society. 'In short', Montesquieu wrote, 'one's belief that one's prosperity is more certain in these states makes one undertake everything, and because one believes that what one has acquired is secure, one dares to expose it in order to acquire more; only the means for acquisition are at risk; now men expect more of their fortune' (Montesquieu 1989, p. 341). It is here that England again figured positively in Montesquieu's argument. England, he wrote, 'has always made its political interests give way to the interests of its commerce' (Montesquieu 1989, p. 343).

This in turn begged the question of whether France should seek to emulate the English experience and example. Such was the extent of Montesquieu's conviction that laws should be in tune with the 'spirit of the nation' that this seemed no more than a hypothetical question incapable of resolution but it was nevertheless a question that would be repeatedly posed in the century following the publication of *De l'Esprit des Lois*. One conclusion could, however, be drawn for certain: the liberty of the individual was best preserved through the contrived balance of governmental institutions and competing social interests, each grounded upon the *mœurs* engendered by commerce.

Participants in the Revolution of 1789 did not hesitate from citing both Montesquieu and Rousseau, sometimes almost in the same breath. However, the rejection of the constitutional proposals of the *monarchiens*, as Bernard Manin has observed, marked 'the defeat of the teachings of Montesquieu taken in their entirety' (Manin 1992, p. 329). For the next few years, as the idea of using the state as a moral agent in pursuit of the creation of a 'new man' (Ozouf 1989, pp. 116–57) gained in popularity, the moderation associated with a system of balances and contrived institutional equilibrium had little purchase upon public debate.

2   Benjamin Constant

It was nevertheless in this decade that a young Benjamin Constant began the publication of a series of pamphlets that sought to draw lessons from the experience of revolution. By general agreement Constant's reflections on politics start to reach their maturity around 1806, the year in which he began writing his *Principes de Politiques Applicables à tous les Gouvernements*. His early essays define his pro-republican but anti-Jacobin position and do so often by making the comparison between the English experience of revolution in 1660 and 1688 and that of France in 1789. 'Arbitrary power', he concluded, 'is the great threat to liberty, the corrupting vice of all institutions, the deadly germ that one can neither mutate nor moderate but which must be destroyed' (Constant 1797, p. 94). Constant supported the Directory on the grounds that it was the regime most likely to 'terminate' the Revolution and he was briefly reconciled to the Consulate, but by 1802 his opposition to Napoleon Bonaparte was such that he was effectively forced into exile.

It would be both easy and tempting to conclude that the defining experience for constitutional liberalism in France was that of the descent of the Revolution into the nightmare of the reign of Terror. Constant's essay of 1797, *Des Effets de la Terreur*, might seem proof enough. Such a conclusion would be unwisely to ignore the impact of the Bonapartist regime upon the thinking of French liberals. What Constant perceived (arguably before anyone else) was the sheer novelty of this form of government. It was not to be confused with either monarchy or the despotism of the past. It was rather an example of government as usurpation. Here, for example, is his comparison between the monarchy of England and the Bonapartist regime. In the former, 'we see that there all the rights of citizens are safe from attack, notwithstanding some abuses, more apparent than real; that popular elections keep the body politic alive, that freedom of the press is respected, while talent is assured of its triumph, and that, in individuals of all classes, there is the proud, calm security of the man protected by the law of his country' (Constant 1988c [1814], p. 163). This, by contrast, is Constant's account of what is to be expected under the regime of a usurper. Usurpation exacts 'an immediate abdication in favour of a single individual'. Treachery, violence and perjury are routinely resorted to. Injustice and illegality become the norm. The usurper engages in 'incessant warfare' and is forced to 'abase' all those around him for fear that 'they may become his rivals'. More than this, in one important respect usurpation was even 'more hateful than absolute despotism'. Usurpation, in parodying liberty, demanded the assent and the homage of the enslaved. Despotism, Constant wrote, 'rules by means of silence and leaves man the right to be silent; usurpation condemns him to speak; it pursues him to the intimate sanctuary of his thoughts and, forcing him to lie to his own conscience, deprives the oppressed of his last remaining consolation' (Constant 1988c, pp. 96–7).

Crucially Constant believed that usurpation could not long survive for the simple reason that, in an age of commerce, it would look increasingly like an anachronism. As war had lost both its charm and its utility, so '[t]he sole aim of modern nations is repose, and with repose comfort, and, as the source of comfort, industry' (Constant 1988c, p. 54). Nevertheless it was to this condition that France had been reduced and this, Constant believed, was because '[the] liberty which was offered to men at the end of the last century was borrowed from the ancient republics' (Constant 1988c, p. 102). It is for this argument that Constant has become best known.

Although found in many of Constant's writings, the key text is his essay *De la Liberté des Anciens Comparée à celle des Modernes*, first given as a lecture in 1819 (Constant 1988b, pp. 307–28). 'Since we live in modern times', Constant proclaimed, 'I want a liberty suited to modern times' (Constant 1988b, p. 323). As the ambition of the moderns was 'the enjoyment of security in modern pleasures', it followed that liberty should be defined in terms of the 'guarantees accorded by institutions to these pleasures' (Constant 1988b, pp. 310–11). Accordingly, modern liberty consisted of

the right to be subjected only to the laws, and to be neither arrested, detained, put to death or maltreated in any way by the arbitrary will of one or more individuals. It is the right of everyone to express their opinion, choose a profession and practice it, to dispose of property, and even to abuse it; to come and go without permission, and without having to account for their motives or undertakings. It is everyone's right to associate with other individuals, either to discuss their interests, or to profess the religion which they and their associates prefer, or even simply to occupy their days and hours in a way which is most compatible with their interests or whims. (Constant 1988b, pp. 310–11)

Ancient liberty, by contrast, consisted 'in exercising collectively, but directly, several parts of the complete sovereignty; in deliberating in the public square . . . in voting laws, in pronouncing judgements' (Constant 1988b, p. 323). This 'collective freedom', Constant argued, countenanced 'the complete subjection of the individual to the authority of the community'. (Constant 1988b, p. 311). All private actions were subject to a 'severe surveillance': the individual was constrained, watched over and repressed, 'a slave in all his private relations'. Constant's next point was to suggest that we could no longer enjoy the liberty of the ancients and, furthermore, that it could be transposed to the modern age only at our peril. By seeking to do so Rousseau in particular (Mably is also cited) had 'furnished deadly pretexts for more than one kind of tyranny' (Constant 1988b, p. 318).

Read thus, Constant appears as a defender of a purely negative conception of liberty (a view confirmed by his statement elsewhere that 'there is of necessity a part of human existence which remains individual and independent and which is of right beyond social control'). The truth of the matter, as Stephen Holmes has commented, is that 'though Constant had no illusions about modern freedom, he saw no alternative to it . . . Radically communal alternatives seemed less attractive still' (Holmes 1984, p. 14). His concern was that, in an age of commerce, we would completely abandon the 'active participation in public power', and that consequently 'we should surrender our right to share in political power too easily' (Holmes 1984, p. 14). The not insubstantial challenge, therefore, was that we should renounce neither kind of liberty but rather 'learn to combine the two together'. As Constant announced in the last paragraph of his speech: 'Institutions must achieve the moral education of the citizens' (Holmes 1984, p. 14). Governments, in short, had both to respect the rights and independence of individuals whilst at the same time encouraging them to exercise influence over public affairs.

How best such a state of affairs might be realised became the abiding preoccupation of the last two decades of Constant's life. To begin, what meaning did Constant attach to the idea that individuals possessed rights? Stephen Holmes (1984, pp. 53–4) has correctly observed that Constant endorsed 'a contextual theory of individual rights'. Rights were not timeless ideals but had arisen within the cultural and institutional environment of modern society. This did not diminish their importance as mechanisms capable of affording protection to both individuals and society from oppressive government. This was most clear in Constant's repeated rejection of Bentham's utilitarian critique of the language of natural and inalienable rights. To subject rights to the principle of utility, he argued, was like subjecting 'the eternal rules of arithmetic to our daily interests' (Holmes 1984, pp. 53–4). Actions became the outcome of selfish calculation rather than moral duty. And nothing – least of all the appeal to utility – could excuse a man who assisted a law he believed to be iniquitous, a judge who sat in a court he knew to be illegal or a henchman who arrested someone he knew to be innocent. 'Citizens', Constant declared, 'possess individual rights independently of all social and political authority, and any authority which violates these rights becomes illegitimate' (Constant 1988a, p. 180). Constant further specified these rights to be those of individual and religious liberty, freedom of speech, the possession of property and protection from arbitrary interference.

Next, Constant broke with a conception of power that had informed both the absolute monarchy of the *ancien régime* and the worst excesses of the Revolution. In constructing a form of government which would respect these rights, he believed, limits had to be placed not upon a particular form of sovereignty but upon sovereignty itself. This was no truer than in the case of the sovereignty of the people. Those who 'in good faith' had bestowed it with 'boundless power' had made the mistake of focusing their anger upon the former holders of power rather than upon the nature of power itself. Rather than destroying unlimited sovereignty they had simply replaced it and given it a new (and, in truth) more dangerous form. 'The universality of citizens', Constant wrote, 'is sovereign in the sense that no individual, no faction, no partial association can arrogate sovereignty to itself, unless it has been delegated to it. But it does not follow from this that the universality of the citizens, or those who are invested with the sovereignty of them, can dispose sovereignly of the existence of individuals' (Constant 1988a, pp. 176–7). In terms of theory, the principal culprits were Hobbes and Rousseau.

This argument led Constant to an important conclusion. 'The vice of almost all constitutions', he wrote, 'has been to fail to create a neutral power, and to place instead the total sum of power with which such a power ought to be invested in one of the active powers' (Constant 1988a, p. 185). The particular strength of a constitutional monarchy, therefore, was not that it was separated into three branches, as Montesquieu had believed, but rather that it was distinguished by the existence of five powers: royal power, executive power, hereditary power, a popularly elected assembly and an independent judiciary. Royal power was a neutral power in the sense that the monarch had no other interest than that of the maintenance of order and liberty. Royal power as such was 'above the four others, a superior and at the same time intermediate authority, with no interest in disturbing the balance' (Constant 1988a, p. 185). Liberty was preserved because royal power could ensure that none of the four active powers gained an exclusive hold over the authority of the state. 'This reality', Constant affirmed, could be found in the English monarchy.

Constant perceived several other distinct advantages from such a system of constitutional monarchy. Ministers were responsible, not just before the law, but before the tribunal of public opinion. Openness of parliamentary debate would engender a spirit of enquiry and 'a constant participation in public affairs' (Constant 1988a, p. 239). The independence of the judiciary, trial by jury, and 'a constant and scrupulous respect' for due procedure would offer protection to the innocent. Liberty of the press would subject authority to informed criticism and publicity. The army, reduced to its proper function of repelling foreign invaders, would no longer pose a threat to individual liberty. Most importantly, Constant recommended the independence of municipal and local authorities. Here was a 'fundamental' truth: 'until now local power has been regarded as a dependent branch of executive power: on the contrary, although it must never encroach upon the latter, it must by no means depend upon it' (Constant 1988a, pp. 251–2). If this truth is ignored 'general laws' are badly implemented and 'partial interests' poorly protected. Municipal power, in short, needed to be more than 'a mere ghost' thereby preserving the liberty of 'the life of groups', their 'internal arrangements' enjoying 'perfect independence' for as long as they do not harm 'the whole collectivity'. Similarly Constant was emphatic that of all the liberties that warranted protection amongst the most important was religious liberty. The prescription of religion, he argued, always caused harm. Even more controversially, he continued by arguing that the 'multitude of sects, of which some are so frightened, is precisely what is most healthy for religion' and therefore, by implication, for society (Constant 1988a, p. 285).

Such a system of constitutional government, Constant believed, would provide the 'positive safeguards' and 'bastions' capable of guaranteeing the liberty of the individual and of protecting against the arbitrary power that would destroy morality, security and commerce. 'What prevents arbitrary power', he concluded, 'is the observance of procedures . . . procedures alone protect innocence . . . Everything else is obscure; everything is handed over to solitary conscience and vacillating opinion. Procedures alone are fully in evidence; it is to them alone that the oppressed may appeal' (Constant 1988a, p. 292).

Yet there clearly had to be more to constitutional government than the exercise of a neutral power and the existence of constitutional procedures guaranteeing individual and local freedoms. At the heart of the debates that had structured the revolutionary decade had been a disagreement about the politics of representation. Was it the monarch or the people who spoke for the nation? Constant veered towards an intermediary position, importantly denying any one person or category this exclusive privilege. He defended a hereditary chamber possessing 'constitutional and well-determined prerogatives' as a means of counterbalancing a popularly elected chamber. As for the latter body, Constant was convinced that if its membership was to be decided upon by direct election then it should also rest upon a property qualification. 'It is desirable', Constant wrote, 'that representative offices should generally be occupied by men, if not from the wealthy classes, at least in easy circumstances' (Constant 1988a, p. 212). Leisure alone made possible the acquisition of understanding and therefore property made men capable of exercising political rights. Less easy to specify was the precise nature of the appropriate property qualification, especially with regard to the relative merits of landed and industrial property. Of two things, however, Constant was certain. Property as such was inviolable and during the Revolution 'literary men, mathematicians, chemists', separated as they were from the lives of other men, had indulged 'in the most exaggerated opinions'. The 'liberal professions', he concluded, needed to be connected to property in order to ensure that their impact upon political debate was not again to prove destructive (Constant 1988a, p. 220).

These views were formulated by Constant in the years following 1806 and they continued to inform his writings and actions in the years until his death in 1830. Upon Napoleon's return to France in 1814 he somewhat unwisely offered to write a new constitution for the Emperor and then, with the return of the monarchy and the 'granting' of the new constitutional charter, found himself repeatedly seeking to push the political order of the Restoration in a liberal direction. In 1822 Constant reaffirmed many of his guiding principles in his unduly neglected *Commentaire sur l'Ouvrage de Filangieri*. 'The functions of government', he wrote, 'are negative: it should repress evil and leave the good to operate by itself' (Constant 2004, p. 316).

The general motto of all governments, he concluded, should be '*laissez faire et laissez passer*'.

3 The *doctrinaires*

The most important recent analysis of the character of French liberalism, Lucien Jaume's *L'Individu Effacé ou le Paradoxe du Libéralisme Français* (Jaume 1997), seeks to establish a three-fold typology which distinguishes distinct traditions within liberalism in France. The third, and in our context least important, tradition is that of Catholic liberalism. Associated with the names of Lamennais and Montalambert, it sought to reconcile the claims of the Catholic Church with those of the state. The first, and according to Jaume, minority tradition is one that stressed the constitutional protection of individual rights, if necessary against the state. Its leading representatives, according to Jaume, were Germaine de Staël, Constant, and later Alexis de Tocqueville and Anatole Prévost-Paradol. It advocated a 'liberalism of the subject'. The dominant tradition, according to Jaume, was that associated with François Guizot, the so-called *doctrinaires*, and the 'orleanist galaxy'. This tradition stressed the importance of governability and the subordination of the individual to the state. When expressed philosophically, as in the writings of Victor Cousin, it amounted to a 'form of anti-individualism'. It was a liberalism of the notables. Moreover it was this liberalism that guided the politics of the July Monarchy (1830–48) and which informed the institutional compromise of 1875 that so effectively established the Third Republic upon a conservative basis. As a consequence, this account suggests, liberalism became associated in the French mind with the supremacy of the upper bourgeoisie and it is this which in part explains the failure of liberalism in France.

There is much to be recommended in Jaume's detailed reconstruction of the universe of nineteenth-century French liberalism. It is true that liberalism came in different forms and that the voice of liberals like Constant was often drowned out by those who came to hold power during the July Monarchy. It is true too that the collapse of that regime in 1848 left liberalism and its representatives with a reputation for corruption, incompetence and repression. Yet it could be argued that Jaume both underestimates the achievements of Guizot and his colleagues – especially in the field of educational reform – and that he overemphasises the differences between the two main traditions. In particular – as recent works by Craiutu and Garnett illustrate (Craiutu 2003; Garnett 2003) – such a sharp distinction ignores the impact that the *doctrinaires* had upon Tocqueville. Not only did Tocqueville attend Guizot's lectures at the Sorbonne between April 1828 and May 1830 but it was from him that he came to realise, amongst many other things, that society was moving irresistibly towards an equality of conditions. For this reason alone we ought, if only briefly, to consider the views of this remarkable and unduly neglected group of men.

The *doctrinaires* were writers, scholars and men of action, throwing themselves into the political fray for three decades or more. They were historians who realised that there could be no return to the *ancien régime* and that the France of the Restoration was the product of a long evolution of European society. As Charles de Rémusat remarked: 'The French Revolution was in no way an accident but rather the necessary outcome of the entire past century' (Rémusat 2003, p. 39). They were, for the most part, Anglophiles, believing not that English institutions could be transported wholesale to France but that much could be learned from English history and political practices. They also saw that a 'new France' had emerged, a France divested of privilege and of absolutism, and moreover that a 'new means of government' was required for this new order. This, to refer again to Rémusat, was to be 'the science of constitutional government' and at its heart was to be the 'representative system' (Rémusat 2003, p. 77: see also Rémusat 1860, pp. 276–328).

The *doctrinaires* laboured long and hard to elucidate both the principles and the practices of such a system of government and representation. They did so in the face of constant opposition from those who sought to make a return to the old order. Crucially they also did so from the floor of the parliamentary chamber, frequently carrying the argument despite their insignificant number. From the outset they opposed the spirit of party, recognising both that in France the existence of parties had preceded the advent of representative government and that this had contributed to the excesses associated with the popular assemblies of the revolutionary era. Against their opponents, they struggled to impose and to assert their interpretation of the constitutional charter of 1814 as a text which could be read as the foundation of a constitutional and parliamentary monarchy. Given the ambiguities of the text and the fact that it had been graciously 'conceded' to France by a benign Louis XVIII, this was to prove a far from easy task.

Their most eloquent advocate was Pierre-Paul Royer-Collard (see Royer-Collard 1861). A philosopher by training, Royer-Collard taught at the Sorbonne from 1811 to 1814. In 1815 he was elected deputy for the Marne and remained in this office until 1839. His parliamentary addresses focused upon many themes but he returned repeatedly to the subject of representation, famously arguing that the word itself was to be understood at best as a 'metaphor'. 'We have had', Royer-Collard commented, 'the sad privilege of having learned what nations gain from being fully and wholly represented. The Revolution... [was] nothing else than the doctrine of representation in action' (Royer-Collard 1861, p. 231). In other words, not only would a 'truly representative' system prove to be extremely dangerous but in the absence of universal suffrage and a binding mandate upon those elected it was entirely incorrect – 'a lie, a chimera', Royer-Collard proclaimed – to imagine that an elected deputy could be described as a representative of the people. As such, the deputy could be said to represent neither the will of the electors nor their opinions. The deputy had a function to perform, namely that of deliberating freely and without the restraints of party, upon the interests of the country, and to that extent the function of the elector was to choose a person capable of performing that role. The right to cast a vote, therefore, had to be based upon the possession of an appropriate aptitude and independence in the elector. Of necessity this entailed a limited franchise.

Royer-Collard's doubts about turning the direction of government over to the vagaries of popular opinion and the sovereignty of the people were such that he initially denied the wisdom of leaving the composition of government to the discretion of an elected chamber. On that day, he announced in 1816, 'we shall be in a republic' (Royer-Collard 1861, p. 217). With time he softened his position, acknowledging the principle of ministerial responsibility before the Chamber of Deputies. In 1830 it was Royer-Collard who presented the so-called *Address of the 221* protesting at the abuse of power by Charles X, thereby precipitating the subsequent revolution. Nevertheless, what remained unchanged was his central conviction that over and against the sovereignty of the people had to be posited the sovereignty of reason and that this was best realised through the institutionalisation of stable, constitutional government.

It was this latter theme that was taken up most persuasively by François Guizot in a stream of writings from 1816 onwards (see Rosanvallon 1985). He approached it from at least three angles: the philosophical, the historical and the sociological. The philosophical aspect of Guizot's argument was best expressed in an unpublished and unfinished text entitled *Philosophie Politique: De la Souveraineté*, written between 1822 and 1823 (Guizot 1985, pp. 305–89). Contradicting Rousseau, he argued that the will of the individual should not be the source of a sovereign's legitimacy and power because if this was so the outcome would be the dissolution of society itself. Moreover, it was palpably absurd to believe that 'man should be absolute master over himself, that his will should be his legitimate sovereign, that at no time and by no right does anyone have power over him if he does not consent' (Constant 1988a, p. 366). In Guizot's opinion, it should rather be the case that the 'solitary will' of the individual should be constrained by the eternal dictates of 'reason, truth, justice'. Only a government which conformed to the laws of reason could be legitimate.

The argument from history drew upon several distinct sources. Guizot's *Histoire de la Civilisation en Europe* (Guizot 1985 [1846]), initially given as a set of lectures and one of his most widely read and influential texts, set out the broad framework of interpretation. The advance of European civilisation, he argued, had been characterised by two overarching trends: the emergence of nation states and the emancipation of the individual from religious tutelage. The evident tension between the two – between the practice of centralisation and the principle of liberty – was to be resolved through representative government. By way of example, Guizot explored in intricate detail the evolution of representative government in medieval England (Guizot 2002, pp. 328–38). Here, he contended, had been an electoral system that had 'summoned every capable citizen' to its ranks, thereby gathering together the 'scattered and incomplete fragments' of reason that were dispersed throughout society. From this experience he drew three important conclusions. The principle that attached electoral participation to capacity was 'universal in nature'. Nevertheless, the definition of capacity would change over time. The English electoral system, for example, had become unjust at the moment when it ceased to embrace all those capable of exercising political rights. Thus, electoral law should respond to the emergence of 'new capabilities' as they become known within society.

The precise details of the electoral arrangements preferred by Guizot can be passed over but it followed from the above that the proper object of election was to bring forth 'the most capable and best accredited men in the country', thereby 'bringing to light the true, the legitimate aristocracy'. The explicit assumption was that it would be in this way that 'public reason and public morality' would be realised and brought together to constitute a government. 'Power', Guizot wrote, 'is only legitimate in so far as it is conformed to reason' (Guizot 2002, p. 296).

Guizot devoted considerable attention to the exploration of the course of English history (Guizot 1826–7, 2002). He saw clearly that its medieval representative system had been overturned by the rise of the despotic Tudor monarchs and that it had taken fifty years of political revolution – from 1640 to 1688 – to re-establish the ascendancy of the Commons. This in turn had led to the rise to political prominence of a new, commercial class and to the dominance of a reformed religion which recognised liberty of conscience. Out of this had flowed 'free government' and 'abundant prosperity'.

Guizot, like nearly all his fellow French liberals, was always alive to the contrasts and comparisons with France afforded by the English experience. 'It is', he wrote, 'the examination of the causes that in England have determined the success of the representative system which seems to me to be the shortest and safest way of explaining their failure in our land' (Guizot 1823, p. 371). From the thirteenth century to the present, everything in England had tended towards the triumph of parliamentary government whilst in France everything had tended towards the triumph of 'pure monarchy' (Guizot 1823, pp. 511–17). This in turn provided fertile terrain for comparisons between 1688 and 1789, with the *doctrinaires* in general believing that the French Revolution would only come to an end when, as in England, liberty had been given a secure and durable institutional framework. In Guizot's eyes, 1789 had marked the culmination of a war between what had amounted to two distinct peoples within French society, and as such it denoted the triumph of equality over privilege and of the Third Estate over the nobility. The Revolution, of course, had been derailed by the theorists of popular sovereignty but in these two achievements lay its legacy.

Here was the clue to the sociological dimension of Guizot's argument. For all his admiration of the achievements of England, Guizot saw grounds for optimism with regard to France and he did so because the account of French history he offered was premised upon the ultimate triumph of the middle classes. It was this group that had emerged out of the process of revolution as that which represented the 'new interests' in French society. Unlike the aristocracy, it was not a closed caste but an open and expanding class capable of absorbing all those with the talent and determination to enrich France both materially and spiritually. Its interests thus coincided with the broad interests of France as a whole. It embodied public reason. The intention of a representative system of government, therefore, was to grant power to 'new superiorities who will prove that they merit it and who will exercise it in the interest of those people who have come to accept them' (Guizot 1821, p. 165).

The argument ran along the following lines. It was not a question of deciding what was the best form of government in the abstract but rather of deciding what form of government was most appropriate in the circumstances. For the new France, according to Guizot and his fellow *doctrinaires*, this was representative government. How did this feed into the argument for constitutional government? If representative government embodied the sovereignty of reason, it also gave form to another vital principle: 'the radical illegitimacy of all absolute power' (Guizot 2002, p. 226). The 'art of politics' and the 'secret of liberty', according to Guizot, lay in the provision of 'equals for every power for which it cannot provide superiors' as all power without equals would soon become absolute. This end was to be attained by a variety of means. First came a recognition of the 'individual rights of citizens'. These would allow individuals 'to superintend, control, and limit' the activities of the 'central supreme power'. Amongst these rights Guizot gave priority to freedom of the press and what he described as 'publicity of all kinds'. Next came the 'distinct and independent' existence of such secondary powers as municipal and judicial authorities. Finally, and most importantly, Guizot recommended the organisation of 'the central power itself in such a manner as to make it very difficult for it to usurp rightful omnipotence'. Here Guizot principally had in mind the division of legislative power into two chambers and the separation of legislative and executive power (Guizot 2002, pp. 371–6). Guizot, in short, appended a theory of representative government as the sovereignty of reason to what amounted to a modified version of a balance and separation of powers argument.

In broad political terms, during the period of the Restoration Guizot and his fellow *doctrinaires* sought to ensure that the constitutional charter of 1814 was implemented along these lines. Their ambition was to steer a course between monarchical reaction and revolutionary republicanism, to establish a *juste milieu* based upon 'order, legality, and constitutional liberty'. In this they were fighting against the odds, especially after the arrival on the throne of Charles X in 1824. However, in 1830 the old order was to come crashing to the ground. Louis-Philippe was crowned 'king of the French'; the constitutional charter was revised so as to reduce royal prerogatives and extend the electorate; and the Revolution again appeared to be over. More than this, Guizot and his colleagues were now effectively to dominate French politics for the next eighteen years (Rosanvallon 1994).

4   Alexis de Tocqueville

Before we consider the important contribution made by Alexis de Tocqueville to constitutional liberalism in France one final aspect of the thinking of the *doctrinaires* needs to be highlighted. We have already seen that, according to Guizot, the course of European civilisation had been characterised by the rise of the nation state. This had meant the centralisation of government, especially in France. Pierre Rosanvallon has argued that the *doctrinaires* were not against centralisation *per se* but rather that they wished to establish 'a new type of centralisation' appropriate to a society where it was no longer possible 'to dissociate the centre from the periphery, civil society from the State, local power from central power' (Rosanvallon 1985, pp. 59–60). Nevertheless, they were alive to the damaging and detrimental impact of the administrative centralisation associated with the *ancien régime*. If this is evident in the work of Guizot, so it is clearly visible in the parliamentary speeches of Royer-Collard and the writings of Rémusat and of Prosper de Barante. The latter's *Des Communes et de l'Aristocratie* described not only the crushing of the *communes* by centralised, monarchical power but praised local government on the grounds that it provided the opportunity to deliberate and decide upon issues of immediate and particular concern, gave citizens 'strength' and 'wisdom', freed them from 'isolation' and 'apathy' and taught people 'to know and to love public order' (Barante 1821, pp. 18–19). Moreover, it provided an indispensable schooling for the affairs of life in a free society. This defence of local government, it should be noted, preceded that offered more famously by Tocqueville by more than a decade.

It was when the likes of Barante came to consider the practicalities entailed in reinvigorating local institutions that the scale of the problem they faced became most evident. On this account, the monarchy of the *ancien régime* had progressively and successfully deprived the aristocracy of its historic functions, producing the intellectual, moral and spiritual impoverishment of France. Hope, however, lay in rekindling practices of association and, in line with the general position of the *doctrinaires*, in the emergence of a 'new aristocracy' of 'social superiors'. Some continued to look (longingly) towards English traditions of *self-government*. Tocqueville, on the other hand, found another model in America.

Tocqueville visited America for ten months between April 1831 and February 1832 (see Pierson 1996; Schleiffer 1980). The first volume of *De la Démocratie en Amérique* appeared in 1835; the second in 1840. There has for long been a debate about the level of continuity and discontinuity between the two texts, with some critics going as far as to suggest that there occured a radical change in perspective (Drescher 1964; Lamberti 1989). Of late doubt has been cast about how much Tocqueville actually saw and knew of the country with which his name is now irredeemably associated. He knew little of American industrial life and probably even less about the South (Wills 2004). Nor, indeed, can *De la Démocratie en Amérique* be properly regarded as a major work of political theory in the conventional sense. It lacks terminological clarity and is frequently ambiguous in its conclusions. Nevertheless, the hyperbolic praise has continued. Two of its recent editors felt able to announce that '*Democracy in America* is at once the best book ever written on democracy and the best book ever written on America' (Mansfield and Winthrop 2000, p. xvii).

In Tocqueville's words, *De la Démocratie en Amérique* was written 'under the pressure of a sort of religious terror in the author's soul'. That terror was produced by the sight of 'an irresistible revolution that for so many centuries has marched over all obstacles and that one still sees advancing today amid the ruins it has made'. In short, a 'great democratic revolution' characterised by 'the gradual development of equality of conditions' was taking place. This fundamental transformation of society, Tocqueville insisted, was a 'providential fact'; 'it is universal, it is enduring, each day it escapes human power'. The grave danger, however, was that through ignorance of the nature of this process democracy had been 'abandoned to its savage instincts'. We have democracy, Tocqueville announced, 'without anything to attenuate its vices'. With this in mind Tocqueville arrived in America, not only to satisfy his curiosity, but also 'to find lessons there from which we could profit'. Once there he 'saw more than America' (Tocqueville 2000, pp. 3–15).

Here, in brief, are the essential elements of Tocqueville's argument. In America men are more equal in wealth and in intelligence than anywhere else in the world. The aristocratic element has been destroyed to the point of extinction and thus it could be said that 'the people govern in the United States'. The principle of the sovereignty of the people dominated all aspects of American society. By dint of circumstance, this had produced 'conciliatory' government, founded upon the 'enlightened will of the people' and the moderate and responsible behaviour of individual citizens. Yet, 'although the form of government is representative, it is evident that the opinions, the prejudices, the interests and even the passions of the people can find no lasting obstacles that prevent them from taking effect in the daily direction of social life' (Tocqueville 2000, p. 165). Herein lay a potential problem of enormous magnitude: the tyranny of the majority.

In America this could take a variety of forms. 'It is of the very essence of democratic governments', Tocqueville wrote, 'that the empire of the majority is absolute' (Tocqueville 2000, p. 235). The interests of the many were to be preferred to the interests of the few and the people had a right to do anything they wished. The 'dire and dangerous' consequences of this were as follows: it increased legislative instability, because the majority insisted its desires be indulged 'rapidly and irresistibly' in the form of law. It likewise favoured the arbitrariness of the magistrate, because the 'majority, being an absolute master in making the law and in overseeing its execution, having equal control over those who govern and over those who are governed, regards public officials as its passive agents' (Tocqueville 2000, p. 243). Most importantly, the tyranny of the majority existed as a 'moral force' exercised over opinion. 'I do not know of any country', Tocqueville wrote, 'where less independence of mind and genuine freedom of discussion reign than in America.' The majority drew 'a formidable circle around thought' (Tocqueville 2000, p. 243).

If then freedom was ever to be lost in America, the fault would lie with the omnipotence of the majority. Yet to date, Tocqueville argued, the effect of the tyranny of the majority had had little influence upon political society, the distressing effects being limited to its impact upon 'the national character of Americans'. This was so because the threat of democratic despotism was curtailed by the existence of a series of all-important constitutional limitations upon majoritarian power. First amongst these was the federal system of government, the division of the legislative body into two branches, and the existence of an independent, if weak, executive. Next came the absence of administrative centralisation, and with that the inability of central government 'to regulate secondary things in society'. Even if it had the desire to do so, government could not 'make all citizens in all places, in the same manner, at the same moment, bend to its desires' (Tocqueville 2000, p. 250). The third counterbalance came in the form of judicial power and the character of the legal profession. In a democratic society lawyers, possessing 'the tastes and habits of aristocracy', formed 'the sole enlightened class that the people do not distrust'. If they prized freedom, they placed legality before it, fearing arbitrariness more than they feared tyranny. They were the natural friends of order and the opponents of innovation and thus had a tendency 'to neutralise the vices inherent in popular government'. More than this, they had the right to declare laws to be unconstitutional. The judge, Tocqueville wrote, 'cannot force people to make laws, but at least he constrains them not to be unfaithful to their own laws and to remain in accord with themselves' (Tocqueville 2000, p. 257).

There was, however, an important non-constitutional element to the protection of freedom. America was in part preserved from the tyranny of the majority by 'the manners and customs of the people'. This had several dimensions. For example, Tocqueville commented upon the 'public spirit' of Americans and their respect for the law; but he focused in particular upon the impact of religion upon American life (Antoine 2003). Religion acted to elevate the aspirations of the majority whilst at the same time diminishing the element of caprice in their actions. Religion among Americans, Tocqueville concluded, 'should therefore be considered as the first of their political institutions; for if it does not give them the taste for freedom, it singularly facilitates their use of it' (Tocqueville 2000, p. 280).

What lessons could be drawn from this American experience for Europe and for France in particular? On this Tocqueville was unambiguous. America proved that one should not despair over democracy and that it could be regulated for the better by laws and by social customs. However, Tocqueville did not contend that France should simply copy America but he did believe that, unless France could succeed in gradually introducing democratic institutions and in securing 'the peaceful empire of the greatest number', then sooner or later a people with no experience of freedom would fall under 'the unlimited power of one alone'. The stark choice, in other words, was between 'democratic freedom or the tyranny of the Caesars' (Tocqueville 2000, pp. 298–302).

All of the above appeared in Volume One. Five years later the second volume received less critical acclaim. There was undoubtedly a subtle change in tone. Increasingly alert to the enthusiasm of Americans for physical well-being, Tocqueville now provided a more sombre appraisal of the character of democratic man. Individualism – the 'reflective and peaceable sentiment that disposes each citizen to isolate himself from the mass of those like him and to withdraw to one side with his family and friends' – was his chief characteristic and vice (Tocqueville 2000, p. 482). At first it sapped the source of 'public virtues' but in time it produced outright 'selfishness'. Gone were the 'common bonds' that held society together. However, the Americans, according to Tocqueville, had combated individualism and had defeated it. They had done this through the practice of association in civil life. 'Americans of all ages, all conditions, and all persuasions,' Tocqueville wrote, 'constantly unite.' Through this they acquired the habit of pursuing activities in common and became aware of the interests they shared with others. The art of association, therefore, taught people the all-important principle of 'self-interest well understood'. This did not call forth heroic virtues or great acts of public virtue, but 'suggests little sacrifices each day' and 'forms a multitude of citizens who are regulated, temperate, moderate, farsighted, masters of themselves' (Tocqueville 2000, p. 502). Underlying this, however, was an awareness that despotism prospered in a situation characterised by the isolation of men and, therefore, that its emergence was particularly to be feared in democratic societies. Specifically, Tocqueville noticed that democratic societies were capable of producing a new form of despotism that was milder but more extensive than its predecessors, which 'would degrade men rather than torment them'. Our leaders would resemble schoolmasters and we would console ourselves with the thought that we had at least chosen them ourselves. State control would become ever more intrusive and all initiative would be taken away from the private individual. The 'great cause' of this growth of government activity was 'the development of industry'.

In 1839 Tocqueville entered Parliament, where for the most part he focused his attention upon foreign affairs and the French Empire, combining a commitment to the abolition of slavery with a defence of colonial expansion. From his private correspondence we know that he continued to follow developments in America and that his admiration for American institutions was largely undiminished (Tocqueville 1990; Craiutu and Jennings 2004). He became increasingly dissatisfied with the political affairs of the July Monarchy and then, in 1848, found himself not only re-elected to serve in the Second Republic but also at the very centre of the constitutional debates which followed.

Here we might briefly contrast the response of Guizot and Tocqueville to these events. Exiled in England, Guizot poured forth his venom in *De la Démocratie en France* (Guizot 1849). France's 'greatest weakness', he argued, was that of 'democratic idolatry'. Everywhere the individual liberty of citizens faced the 'single will' embodied by the numerical majority of the nation: the result would be 'revolutionary despotism'. 'It is this idea', Guizot wrote, 'that has to be eradicated' and this could be done by rallying 'all the conservative forces of social order' to hold back the advancing tide. Tocqueville, on the other hand, defended a constitutional project that bore a striking resemblance to that of his *monarchien* forebears of 1789. His emphasis fell upon seeking to ensure, through a two-chamber system, that legislation was subject to scrutiny by different groups of people who would moderate the potentially impetuous and ill-advised actions of a single chamber possessed of the belief that it alone spoke in the name of the national will. Moreover, he persisted in arguing that France still had something to learn from American constitutional arrangements (Craiutu and Jennings 2009, pp. 382–4). Here, as with much else, he was to be disillusioned. The election to the presidency of Louis-Napoleon led almost inevitably to the *coup d'état* of 1851. With this came Tocqueville's brief imprisonment and also the emergence of the precise species of despotic regime which he had for so long feared could be the product of democracy. '[T]he outward forms of popular election', he wrote to one of his American correspondents, 'had served only to establish a more absolute despotism than any other that has ever appeared in France' (Craiutu and Jennings 2009, p. 133).

The 1850s were bleak years for Tocqueville. In 1850 the first symptoms of the tuberculosis which killed him nine years later were diagnosed. There remained only the task of writing his *Souvenirs* and his final masterpiece: *L'Ancien Régime et la Révolution* (Tocqueville 1952 [1856]). The basic argument of this famous text is well known: the centralised administration of France was not the creation of the Revolution of 1789, as many had believed, but the product of the old monarchical order. That regime had eliminated all intermediate authorities and stripped the provinces of local autonomy. Paris became the 'master of France'. France was not only reduced to being the country in which 'men were most like each other' but also where people had been split up into 'small, independent, self-regarding groups'. There was, Tocqueville wrote, 'a kind of collective individualism which prepared people for the real individualism with which we are familiar' (Tocqueville 1998, p. 163). This was not to say that the French were prone to servility and subservience. The French were attached to freedom but it was an ill-adjusted, intermittent, ill-assimilated and unwholesome liberty to which they adhered. Necessary for the vital task of overthrowing despotism, such a mind-set 'perhaps made them less capable than any other people of founding in its place the free and peaceable empire of the law' (Tocqueville 1998, p. 179). Crucially, the desire for reform took precedence over the desire for freedom whilst the absolute power of the state was seen as something to be used rather than destroyed. The French, Tocqueville continued, came to see 'the ideal society [as] a people without any aristocracy other than government officials, a single and all-powerful administration, director of the state, guardian of individuals' (Tocqueville 1998, p. 216). Hostility to religion also became a fierce and intolerant passion.

It was this argument that allowed Tocqueville to provide his clearest definition of liberty. Liberty, he wrote, 'is the pleasure of being able to speak, act, and breathe without constraint, under the government of God and the laws alone' (Tocqueville 1998, p. 217). Second, liberty was to be valued as an end in itself. Whoever sought private gain from freedom was made for slavery. Third, therefore, liberty was not to be confused with 'a narrow individualism where all public virtues are smothered'. Liberty alone could free men from 'a love of material well-being'.

The second part of the argument explored the impact of the failure properly to understand the nature of liberty upon the course and outcome of the Revolution itself. In short, if the outbreak of Revolution was inevitable, so too it was doomed to failure. Two passions, Tocqueville insisted, drove on the Revolution: an intense hatred of inequality and the less powerful desire to live as free men. When the first 'virile generation' of the Revolution's leaders faded away the ideal of freedom lost much of its appeal and then the scene was set for the 'return of absolute government'. 'We returned to centralisation in its ruins', Tocqueville wrote, 'and restored it' and hence 'from the very bowels of a nation the monarchy suddenly surged forth a power more extensive, more detailed, more absolute than that which any of our kings had exercised' (Tocqueville 1998, p. 245).

Here then was a work of history written for deeply political purposes. Tocqueville's intention was to explain to his readers why it was that France had not been able to establish an enduring political regime characterised by the liberty of the individual. His short answer was that the French had come to prefer governments which flattered their desire for equality rather than those which gave them freedom, and thus they were ripe for despotism. Napoleon had fallen but successive attempts to destroy absolutism had only succeeding in 'placing liberty's head upon a servile body' (Tocqueville 1998, p. 245).

5   Conclusion

Tocqueville concluded *L'Ancien Régime et la Révolution* with a statement to the effect that it was his intention next to study the Revolution itself. We also know that he had plans to examine the Empire and the manner in which Napoleon's project had been incorporated into French political culture. Neither was to see the light of day. Having briefly occupied the position of posthumous leader of the liberal party, after 1870 Tocqueville was quickly forgotten (Mélonio 1993). In the difficult political climate of the 1860s the voice of liberalism could, however, still be heard. A work such as Odilon Barrot's *De la Centralisation et de ses Effets*, published in 1861, continued to voice traditional liberal concerns about an over-mighty state and did so by making explicit reference to the ideas of Montesquieu. Prévost-Paradol's 1868 text, *La France Nouvelle*, located his demands for the administrative and political reform of France within an undisguised admiration for English parliamentary and municipal practices. Most impressive of all was the work of Édouard Laboulaye. Long an advocate of the merits of the American constitution (see Laboulaye 1848, 1850), not only did he edit Constant's major political writings, but in *L'État et ses Limites* and *Le Parti Libéral, son Programme et son Avenir*, both published in 1863, he reworked the latter's distinction between ancient and modern liberty as part of a self-conscious liberal tradition that ran from the *monarchiens* to Tocqueville. In so doing Laboulaye set out a liberal agenda for a 'new generation' freed from the illusions and disappointments of the past and one, he announced, that was a 'programme for modern democracy'.

Nevertheless, it has been argued that the project of liberalism was 'inadequately attuned to the imperatives of the time' (Hazareesingh 1998, p. 229) and that it failed to capture the public imagination in a period when public opinion was increasingly polarised. It is thus somewhat ironic that the constitutional compromise that came to mark the institutions of the Third Republic after 1875 was broadly in line with long-established liberal demands for a balance of power.

It is only in the last twenty-five years or so that in France renewed attention has been devoted to the major figures of liberalism discussed in this chapter. Why this has been so in itself merits investigation. However, a century of neglect cannot diminish their astonishing originality and intellectual brilliance. It is easy to point out the naïvety of their faith in bourgeois rule, their tendency towards aristocratic nostalgia for a society resting upon social hierarchy, as well as the political insensitivity of their criticisms of universal suffrage but, by the same token, their great achievement was to realise, probably before anyone else, that democracy and equality of conditions could spawn an entirely novel type of despotism. In its mild form, it could take the shape of the tyranny of the majority described by Tocqueville. Less benignly, it could take the character of the Bonapartist usurpation described by Constant. Given France's post-1789 political turmoil, French liberals were best placed to discern the danger and ideally situated to reflect upon the constitutional mechanisms that might alleviate it. In so doing they provided invaluable insights into the nature of modern politics.

12

American political thought from Jeffersonian republicanism to progressivism

JAMES P. YOUNG

1 Introduction

One of the peculiarities of nineteenth-century American political thought is that it exists on a relatively low level of abstraction. There is no American equivalent to Rousseau or Hegel or even John Stuart Mill. Of course all important political theory has historically been related to the great events of the time when it was produced. But though thinkers like Plato and Thomas Hobbes were responding to contemporary politics, they still often relied extensively on ontological, metaphysical or epistemological arguments in trying to deal with them. But in nineteenth-century America the debates over political ideas were as a rule conducted on a level much closer to day-to-day political action, due perhaps to the fact that the polity was closer to democracy than any other at the time. In any case, until after the Civil War much of the most important work was produced by major political actors. Even then, the thought of academics like William Graham Sumner remained fairly close to the ground. For much of the century, if one wants to explore the nature of American political thought one turns to the same thinkers who created the politics they theorised.[1] Therefore, methodologically one must pay unusually close attention to ongoing political events if one is going to understand the ideas surrounding them.

But this characteristic need not lead to the deprecation of American political thought. One could argue, in common with such recent American theorists as Michael Walzer and Judith Shklar, that political ideas are enhanced when conducted on a lower plane, not reaching far out of the Platonic cave and displaying a principled aversion to metaphysics (Walzer 1983, p. xiv). Shklar's position is well described by Rogers Smith. She distrusted

I would like to thank George Kateb, Carey McWilliams, Gregory Claeys, Gareth Stedman Jones, Bob Harris, and Larry Berlin for their comments on an earlier version of this essay.

1 Of course this is much less true of the twentieth century.

'metaphysical pretensions' and found them to be 'politically pernicious'. Shklar studied political thought, Smith says, 'chiefly as a way of revealing the characteristic meaning that different political institutions, commitments, and ways of life expressed and fostered'. Like Tocqueville, 'she believed that in America, more than anywhere else in world history, one could discover the human fruits and perils of living within broadly democratic institutions, trying to make them work, and trying to make sense of the lives they shaped'. Shklar was sometimes less than enchanted with the results, but she did think that American political thought contained many insights into what democrats 'can and cannot hope for' (Smith 1993, p. 188). Such an approach provides a useful context within which to consider American political ideas.[2]

The nature and sources of the characteristic style of American thought has been the subject of much spirited discussion. It has long been recognised that liberalism occupies a central place in American thought and politics. My own view of liberalism is that it is a rather loosely structured body of ideas that stresses the right of putatively equal individuals to pursue their own self-defined interests within a framework that guarantees these rights and the rights of other members of society. In 1948 Richard Hofstadter published his paradigm-setting work, *The American Political Tradition*. In this revisionist study, he rejected the reigning theory of American history dating back to the progressive movement of the early twentieth century which saw a constant battle between haves and have-nots, agrarian versus commercial interests, Jeffersonians and Hamiltonians. Instead he saw a wide consensus embracing these contestants. What bound Americans together was an 'ideology of self-help, free enterprise, competition, and beneficent cupidity', which, in spite of all differences, led to a shared belief in 'the rights of property, the philosophy of economic individualism, the value of competition . . . and an acceptance of the economic virtues of capitalist culture as necessary qualities of man'. There was, said Hofstadter, 'a strong bias in favor of equalitarian democracy, but it has been a democracy in cupidity rather than a democracy of fraternity' (Hofstadter 1973, pp. xxiii, xxix, xxx).[3] This is a theory of a liberal American consensus that has the great merit of placing the values of liberal capitalist political economy at its centre, where, I think, they properly belong. The central, indeed virtually unchallenged, faith in capitalism is

2 For an interesting earlier discussion of this issue see Diamond 1957 and McCloskey 1957.
3 It should be noted that twenty years later Hofstadter retreated from his emphasis on consensus on the ground that it merely outlines the limits of conflict in American politics (Hofstadter 1968, pp. 450–5). Even in this weakened form, the theory is a useful contribution.

indeed a facet of what is often termed American 'exceptionalism'. There are other, and more controversial, dimensions to this term, but it is important to insist on the validity of this aspect.[4]

Equally notable, and more controversial, was the attempt to interpret American thought and politics in Louis Hartz's *The Liberal Tradition in America* (1955). Combining Tocqueville with Marx, Hartz argued that, since Americans were born equal rather than having to become so, as Tocqueville had observed, they had escaped feudalism and had been born a liberal capitalist nation (Tocqueville 1968, p. 509).

In Hartz's view, American thinkers were in the grip of an 'irrational' commitment to the thought of John Locke, taken as a symbol of middle-class, liberal, capitalist individualism. The key to American thought was its acceptance of 'atomistic social freedom', as its 'master assumption' (Hartz 1955, p. 62). Hartz's sense of Locke's thought is not well developed, but he certainly intended the notion to include some form of individualist, rights-based, egalitarian democracy. This view of Locke is oversimplified and it clearly cannot be made to account for everything in American political history. There are powerful currents of non-Lockean thought in the American tradition. For example, Hartz ignored the influence of seventeenth-century Calvinism, and, in fact, religion in general, always a powerful force in American life and politics.[5] Moreover, eighteenth-century variants of ancient republican thought were an influence as well, though on this last point it must be said in his defence that he wrote before the assertion of the importance of civic humanist republicanism by Bernard Bailyn, J. G. A. Pocock and Gordon Wood (Bailyn 1992; Pocock 1975; Wood 1969). Moreover, no theory of an overriding consensus can explain the Civil War, which is, by any standard, the central event in American history.

---

4 Some writers attribute to the United States a special historical mission, as in the Puritan idea of the 'city on a hill', or see in American institutions the signs of providence working itself out in the course of the national history. One need not endorse these conceptions of exceptionalism but still see significant differences between American ideas and practices and those of the rest of the world. Kammen 1997 argues that 'different' is a better term than 'exceptional', since the latter suggests the existence of a 'norm' from which the United States deviates. Without accepting this, he believes that the United States is significantly 'different', but that the differences become 'less exceptional' over time. The literature is much too large to discuss here. For two good recent discussions see Kammen 1997 and Rodgers 1998b.

5 On religion generally see Morone 2003. The Puritans, who were neither democratic nor liberal, historically preceded Lockean liberalism. On the complex relations between Puritanism and liberalism see Young 1996, pp. 13–21.

Still, in spite of the fact that the Puritans were by no means liberal, their ideas contributed, even if unwittingly, to the emergence of an individualistic, competitive capitalism and a belief in the rule of law, both closely associated with liberalism (Young 1996, pp. 13–21). Moreover, civic humanist republicanism never succeeded in dominating American thought to the extent suggested by the more ardent proponents of the 'republican synthesis' (Hulliung 2002). In addition, most supporters of the synthesis accept that republicanism rapidly began to give way to a more completely liberal political culture as the nineteenth century dawned; the only real question is when the dominance of liberalism was established. Puritanism and civic republicanism are still limitations on the theory of liberal domination, to which must be added the continued and even more important presence of a set of ascribed race and gender characteristics that undermine the theory of a dominant liberalism and often led to sharp conflict (Smith 1997, pp. 13–39 *passim*). And surely Shklar is right to point out that as long as slavery existed, America was neither liberal nor democratic, though she concedes that institutions were in place that were 'capable of becoming so and to an unequaled degree' (Shklar 1991, p. 92). However, if the early triumph of liberalism in American politics cannot account for everything, it can explain a great deal, in particular the failure of any significant socialist movement to take hold in the political culture, which was a major concern for Hartz. Any full theory of this peculiarity of American history must take into account a range of other factors including immigration, racial and ethnic conflict, the nature of the party system, and the relative success of the capitalist economic system, but the depth of the liberal tradition is certainly a major factor (Lipset and Marx 2000). And if socialism has failed in the United States, traditional conservatism has not fared much better. What else could be expected in a nation whose 'official' ideology is liberal? Reinhold Niebuhr was not far from the mark when he commented that American conservatism is 'nothing more than a decadent liberalism' (Niebuhr 1961, p. 34).

During the 1960s, the high level of social and political conflict weakened acceptance of the theory of liberal consensus, as did the discovery of the 'republican synthesis'. In his comprehensive interpretation of American political thought Russell Hanson (1985) focused on democracy more than on liberalism, while Judith Shklar rejected the theory of liberal dominance (Shklar 1998, esp. p. 92). But in one version or another, particularly among social scientists and political theorists, the theory of a liberal ideology has been strongly reasserted in much recent scholarship. Wilson Carey

377

McWilliams (1973) stresses the centrality of enlightenment liberalism, while finding, below the surface so to speak, a tradition stemming from Puritanism and nineteenth-century literature which is critical of liberal individualism. J. David Greenstone (1993) also found a dominant liberalism, though a body of ideas much more complex than what Hartz described. Isaac Kramnick (1990) sees a mixture of ideas in the founding period, but his concept of bourgeois radicalism is advanced as part of a critique of the republican synthesis and leaves pride of place to liberalism. And with no little regret the historian John Diggins (1984, 2000) repudiates the republican synthesis in rather harsh terms. One of the strongest restatements of the theory of liberal consensus, though oddly without reference to Hartz, comes from Michael Zuckert (1996) who pushes civic republicanism into the background and argues that the United States is a natural rights republic, stemming from Locke by way of Jefferson. And more recently Mark Hulliung has argued that in the United States 'liberalism, not republicanism, is the master word in our political vocabulary', though he also, like Rogers Smith, finds a 'deeply ingrained illiberalism' in the American tradition (Hulliung 2002, pp. 160, 183). Recent scholarship makes it clear that liberalism, though not the only tradition in American thought, is certainly central, especially in the nineteenth century.[6] The idea of consensus is not popular today and, at present, is arguably crumbling, but as Clifford Geertz suggests, it is possible to have 'identity without unison' (Geertz 2000, p. 225). After all, democratic politics is about disputes and their resolution. Thus, consensus theory should not be taken to mean that there is no conflict within the consensus. Sheldon Wolin is right to argue that 'This is the basic dilemma of political judgments: how to create a common rule in a context of differences?' (Wolin 2004, p. 56). And, as Geertz asks, 'What is a culture if not a consensus?' (Geertz 2000, p. 224 and pp. 224–31 *passim*). In a different terminology, this discussion points to a 'collective identity' (Wolin 1989, p. 140), a set of 'shared understandings, that shape American politics' (Walzer 1983, p. xiv;

6 Cf. also Young 1996. There I also consider the complex fate of the tradition in the twentieth century. See also Block 2003. This is an important study that appeared too late for me to consider fully. It is likely to be the subject of much discussion and debate. The major recent attempt to reinterpret the American political tradition in civic republican or communitarian terms is Sandel 1996. While important and provocative, this study is unconvincing. Sandel basically ignores the Declaration of Independence, which is a fatal flaw by itself. Cf. Hulliung 2002, p. 184. Hulliung argues that whatever the intent of Bailyn and Wood, they have often provided inspiration for New Left, neo-conservative and communitarian critics of the liberal tradition (cf. p. xi).

cf. Young 1996, pp. 1–2).[7] In the nineteenth century, perhaps more than today, the liberal tradition, though constantly changing, serves, as suggested above, as an 'official' ideology which can, and sometimes has, functioned as the basis for a critique of the frequent deviations from that tradition.[8] What can be done here is to sketch an outline of the mainstream of the liberal consensus, particularly as related to the seminal thought of Thomas Jefferson, while giving some consideration to its main challengers.

2 Jeffersonian republicanism

To understand Jeffersonian politics, it is necessary to offer a brief sketch of the political and constitutional situation at the time of his election in 1800. If we accept Abraham Lincoln's word, the beginning of American national history is signified by the Declaration of Independence of 1775. The Declaration, with its insistence on the equality of all men and its individualistic assertion of natural rights, notably 'life, liberty, and the pursuit of happiness', is clearly liberal and essentially democratic by implication, though it is clear that to its principal author 'men' meant white men and not women, blacks or Native Americans. Jefferson had no thought of extending those democratic implications to members of these groups. And, since the Declaration says nothing about institutions, it needed to be supplemented by a constitution. The constitution framed in 1787 is also a liberal document reflecting a deep distrust of the powers of the state in its elaborate institutional devices designed to make decision-making extremely difficult without wide-ranging support. The original document contained a significant set of rights, mostly unavailable elsewhere at the time, prohibiting bills of attainder, *ex post facto* laws, requiring jury trials, carefully

---

7 This linkage should not obscure the fact that there are significant differences between Wolin and Walzer.

8 For the concept of 'official' as used here see Miller 1993, p. 209. He suggests that the official claims a privileged position for itself whether its description of a society's values and norms is accurate or not. It claims legitimacy and is often aspirational. It may sometimes be complacent, but it is more than just a sham: 'The official represents those kinds of public statements in which a culture images itself, and as such it bears no small role in reproducing the culture that produces such official discourses.' What I suggest here is the sort of 'connected criticism' theorised in Walzer 1988. For another, not very optimistic example, see Smith 1996. Of course someone who finds the 'shared understandings' of the liberal tradition to be inadequate could argue that this form of political criticism is likewise inadequate because it fails the test of universalisation. Walzer attempts to answer this criticism by contrasting the thick description based on local understandings with a 'thinner' theory carrying higher level meanings which are closer to universal norms and those I have called official. Cf. Walzer 1994, esp. pp. 1–20.

defining treason, banning religious tests for public office, limiting the executive's war power, etc. These rights were expanded by the adoption of the Bill of Rights shortly after ratification of the constitution, which included rights of free speech and press, freedom of religion, freedom of assembly, a due process of law and fair trial guarantee, bans on self-incrimination, double jeopardy, excessive bail, fines, and cruel and unusual punishment (Kateb 2003, pp. 585–6).[9] But the constitution fell short on a number of liberal and democratic criteria. First, it tacitly accepted slavery, in violation of any theory of natural rights, while at the same time counting three-fifths of all slaves in apportioning congressional representation among the states, thus giving disproportionate power to the slave-holding southern states. As Abraham Lincoln remarked in 1854, 'The slaves do not vote; they are only counted and so used as to swell the influence of the white people's votes' (Lincoln 1989a, p. 331). There was no right to vote as such, with the suffrage requirements being left to the states, nor was there any question of women, African-Americans or Native Americans having the suffrage. (In fairness, it should be added that such groups were not allowed to vote anywhere else either.)[10] The President was chosen indirectly by an Electoral College rather than by direct popular vote, and the Senate was initially elected by state legislatures, again without a direct popular vote. All states were given two votes in the Senate, thus giving another disproportionate grant of power, this time to states with small populations. Moreover, a complex and not very well-defined separation of powers between the legislative, executive and judicial branches made majority decision-making very difficult and the distribution of power between the nation and the states was, if anything, even less well-defined, a fact that contributed to the Civil War and which continues to be a subject of contention to this day.[11] This open-ended character of the constitution, the fact that its authors agreed on the text but not the meaning of the document, makes it, as Sheldon Wolin has argued, an invitation to hermeneutical politics (Wolin 1989, p. 3). And, as Abraham Lincoln understood, one of the fundamental American political problems is to reconcile the tensions between the Declaration of

---

9 There has even been a systematic interpretation of the constitution as a libertarian document with a natural rights base, though it should be treated with caution. See Barnett 2004; cf. Lazarus 2004.
10 The extent to which white males were entitled to vote is unclear and varied from state to state. The suffrage was no doubt higher than in Britain at the same time. See Keyssar 2000, p. 7.
11 Dahl 2003, pp. 15–18. For a less institutional, more theoretical, critique see Wolin 1981, pp. 9–24 and 1989, esp. pp. 82–117.

Independence and the constitution.[12] In spite of these tensions, and with some reservations, Jefferson accepted the constitution and its rather more conservative theoretical justification in the *Federalist Papers* whose principal authors were his friend James Madison and his despised enemy Alexander Hamilton (Jefferson 1984, pp. 914–18, 479, 1176).

Jeffersonian liberalism is absolutely central to nineteenth-century American thought and politics. Whatever weight we might attach to the theory of civic humanist republicanism as a force during the colonial and revolutionary periods, those ideas, without quite disappearing, rapidly receded into the background with the dawn of the new century and Jefferson's ascent to the presidency. The society that emerged from the founding period was individualistic, commercial, interest oriented, rapidly expanding in population and territory, and on the road to liberalism and democracy, though neither was close to full achievement (Appleby 2000; Wood 1992). The only real issue is the question of precisely when this change occurred. A new sense of national identity began to develop, though because of the sectional divide over slave versus free labour, these characteristics gave liberalism a strong northern cast (Appleby 2000, pp. 239–66). Jefferson represented many of these tendencies and his succession to the presidency, by undermining, though not dissolving, the link between social and political power, foreclosed the possibility of an entrenched upper-class Federalist elite controlling the political system (Appleby 1984, p. 104, 2000, p. 6).[13]

This transition took place peacefully, though not without danger of serious disruption. The leaders of the founding generation were a combative lot and there were deep personal rivalries among them. Only George Washington stood more or less above the battle. The other leaders of the founding period often displayed fierce personal antagonism to one another and the emergence of a competitive political party system during the 1790s testified to the growing tensions (Davis 2001, pp. 165–77; Elkins and McKitrick 1993; Ellis 2000; Silbey 1999).[14] Richard Hofstadter was doubtless right to claim that the crisis of 1794–1801 was 'at least as real and decisive for

---

12 Wolin 1981 emphasises the tension between the Declaration of Independence and the constitution. Cf. esp. 11–19.

13 In spite of Jefferson's claim that the election of 1800 was a triumph of democracy, it has been alleged that Jefferson won because of the extra electoral strength he drew from the three-fifths clause noted above. See Wills 2003, esp. pp. 1–4. For a harsh critique of Wills see Wilentz 2004.

14 Silbey 1999 is an excellent collection of sources illustrating nineteenth-century ideological struggles, often vituperative, but within the liberal capitalist framework.

the early union as that which had been successfully passed in the 1780s' (Hofstadter 1969, p. xi).

Jefferson himself was seen as a dangerous man by his Federalist opponents, yet when the election of 1800 ended in an electoral vote tie between Jefferson and Aaron Burr, the Federalist leader Alexander Hamilton put aside his dislike and distrust of Jefferson and sided with him against Burr, thus swinging the decision in the House of Representatives in Jefferson's favour. As Hamilton, writing to James A. Bayard, gauged Jefferson's character, he rightly saw that his rival would not be violent, but would be inclined to temporise rather than risk his popularity by undermining the new political system (Hamilton 2001, pp. 977–8; cf. Hofstadter 1969, pp. 134–40).

At least on the surface, Jefferson seemed to go out of his way to foster harmony and put the Federalist opposition at ease. In his Inaugural Address, Jefferson put on the mask of a consensual leader. 'But every difference of opinion is not a difference of principle', he intoned. 'We are all Republican, we are all Federalists' (Jefferson 1984, p. 493). However, this conciliatory language ought not to be taken quite at face value. Writing to Judge Spencer Roane in 1819, Jefferson claimed that the election of 1800 was 'as real a revolution in the principles of our government as that of 1776 was in its form' (Jefferson 1984, p. 1425). Or, as he put it more bluntly in an 1802 letter, 'I shall . . . by the establishment of republican principles . . . sink federalism into an abyss from which there shall be no resurrection for it' (Elkins and McKitrick 1993, p. 754). Doubtless this was closer to his true feeling than was his public rhetoric. As Henry Adams wrote, 'He wished to soothe the great body of his opponents, and if possible to win them over; but he had no idea of harmony or affection other than that which was to spring from his own further triumph; and in saying that he was in any sense a Federalist, he did himself a wrong.' In Adams' understanding, 'The two parties were divided by a bottomless gulf in their theories of Constitutional powers' (Adams 1986, p. 136, p. 140).

Jefferson's thought is of great importance in the history of American political culture because his ideas were sufficiently diffuse to be able to give aid and comfort to a wide range of opposed political positions. This is partly due to the fact that he did not have anything like a unified political theory, in addition to which his actions frequently were in flagrant contradiction to his thoughts. He was a man full of ideas, but they did not coalesce into a single, systematic, coherent form. He wrote only one book, the *Notes on the State of Virginia*, and much of that deals with non-political matters. Aside from that, we have a brief fragmentary autobiography, his state papers and a huge mass of letters. But his very lack of system makes it all the easier for a wide range of Americans to draw on Jefferson and create an icon to their own liking (cf. Peterson 1960).[15] The issues he raised are so central to much of the subsequent thought and politics of the nineteenth century and beyond that he requires special attention.

At the foundation of Jefferson's beliefs are two ideas. One was the belief in self-evident natural rights proclaimed in the Declaration of Independence.[16] The influence of John Locke seems evident in his famous language about the self-evident truth of a right to pursue 'life, liberty, and the pursuit of happiness'. Judith Shklar is surely right to remark that, for all his confusions and the deeply troubling departures from his principles, particularly regarding slavery, he will be remembered as he wanted to be. 'This is the man who put human rights on the map forever' (Shklar 1984, p. 35). And whatever we think of Jefferson's apparent hypocrisy, the Declaration is at the heart of what I have called the 'official' American ideology and as such has real force. On this foundation of natural rights Jefferson built a large syllogism in which the middle term is made up of a sometimes unfair series of charges against George III, leading to the conclusion that the colonies must declare their separation from the Crown (cf. Becker 1958). None of this is terribly original nor did Jefferson claim it to be so. As he wrote in a letter late in his life, his object was 'not to find out new principles', 'but to place before mankind the common sense of the subject' (Jefferson 1984, p. 1501). The importance of the Declaration lay instead in its rhetorical power, which fully justifies Shklar's encomium.

A second major key to Jefferson's thought is a certain restlessness, an impatience with any status quo, which is arguably an American characteristic. This is clear in his frequent statement of the idea that 'the earth belongs to the living', so that decisions of earlier generations have no binding force (Jefferson 1984, pp. 953, 963, 1401–2, 1493–4; cf. Matthews 1984, pp. 19–29). And pursuing the same line of thought, he advanced what Shklar rightly called the truly 'daft' proposal there could be no perpetual constitution or

15 Jefferson's reputation has declined sharply since Peterson wrote due to a renewed focus on his slave-holding with its attendant hypocrisy and the now quite generally accepted evidence that he fathered children by his slave Sally Hemmings. Cf. Onuf 1993a, 1993b. For a spirited rebuttal which admits Jefferson's flaws but insists on his greatness see Wilentz 2004.

16 Pauline Maier debunks Jefferson's claim to be the author of the Declaration of Independence and stresses the extensive editing of his work by the Continental Congress. This seems part of the general tendency to downgrade Jefferson's achievements. On the other hand, Michael Zuckert argues that the crucial phrases on natural rights are in Jefferson's original draft. Cf. Maier 1997 and Zuckert 1998. Zuckert seems clearly correct.

perpetual law so that every constitution should expire after the length of a generation or nineteen years (Jefferson 1984, p. 963; Shklar 1998, p. 96).[17]

But it is the conception of rights that stands out. This idea was linked in his mind to a deep aversion to monarchy that permeates his work coupled with a constitutional theory that was strongly opposed to centralised government or a strong executive power. This was the core of his conception of democratic republicanism. Personal considerations aside, his hatred for the Federalist Party grew out of his belief that it was made up of secret monarchists. To him, most of the Federalist policies, embodied by Alexander Hamilton operating as party leader from his position as President Washington's Secretary of the Treasury, including the commitment to a national bank, the hopes for a strong manufacturing sector in the economy, the insistence on a loose construction of the terms of the constitution, the urban roots of the Federalist political base, and Hamilton's belief in a standing army, coupled with his presumed militarism, all pointed in a direction Jefferson desperately wanted to avoid.

For his part Jefferson favoured an agrarian society. In *Notes on the State of Virginia* he wrote, 'Those who labour in the earth are the chosen people of God.' He believed corruption among agrarians to be unknown. Those who desert the soil risk becoming dependants, a condition that breeds 'subservience and venality... The mobs of great cities add just so much to the support of pure government, as sores do to the strength of the human body' (Jefferson 1984, pp. 290–1). And in a letter to James Madison he argued that as long as there was open land in America, national virtue would be secure. To him the conclusion was clear: the development of large cities must be avoided. Therefore, he argued, 'Let our workshops remain in Europe' (Jefferson 1984, p. 918).

Jefferson and his followers saw the literal construction of the constitution to be particularly crucial. As Henry Adams wrote, 'The principle of strict construction was the breath of his political life. The Pope could as easily trifle with the doctrine of apostolic succession as Jefferson with the limits of executive power' (Adams 1986, p. 362). An early interpretative

---

17 Jefferson also displayed a remarkable enthusiasm for revolution. 'A little rebellion now and then is a good thing', as necessary as storms in the physical world. More flamboyantly he wished never to go more than twenty years without a rebellion. 'The tree of liberty must be refreshed from time to time with the blood of patriots and tyrants' (Jefferson 1984, pp. 882, 911). One must suspect that these statements were purely rhetorical since at about the same time he worried to James Madison about the 'instability of our laws' (Jefferson 1984, p. 918). As President he made no proposals consistent with these views. It should also be said that as President he compiled a rather weak record as a civil libertarian. Cf. Levy 1963.

crisis arose over the Alien and Sedition Acts, passed by the Federalist government in 1798 in response to French provocations. These were acts of
the national government giving it the power to deport aliens and prosecute
seditious libel. The Jeffersonian position as expressed in the Kentucky Resolutions drafted by Jefferson and the Virginia Resolutions drafted by James
Madison was full of portent (Jefferson 1984, pp. 449–56; Madison 1999,
pp. 391–2; cf. Adams 1986, pp. 96–9; McDonald 2000, pp. 40–3). Both sets
of resolutions rested on the assumption that the American constitutional
union was founded on a compact between sovereign states which had delegated certain specific powers and no others to the national government.
Since, in their view, Congress had not been delegated such powers by the
states, and in fact had been forbidden such powers, the Alien and Sedition
Acts were, in Jefferson's repeated usage, 'altogether void and of no force',
so that the offending legislation could be 'nullified' by the states, while
Madison asserted the states' authority to 'interpose' their powers so as to
'arrest the progress of the evil'. Jefferson went still further by mounting an
argument against the important constitutional clause giving Congress the
power to make 'all laws which shall be necessary and proper' to carry out
its vested powers. He insisted on a very narrow interpretation saying that
the clause itself, if freely interpreted, 'goes to the destruction of all limits
prescribed to their power by the Constitution' (Jefferson 1984, p. 452).[18]
For the next hundred years and more, these contentions were to be central
to many of the major debates in American politics. In particular, southern leaders were to use these arguments about the nature of the federal
union in the developing controversy over slavery that culminated in the
Civil War.

However, once in office, Jefferson was far less scrupulous in the application of his strict constructionalist principles than the rhetoric of the Virginia
and Kentucky Resolutions would lead one to expect. The major event of
Jefferson's first term in office was the purchase of the Louisiana territory
from France, which even he said made 'blank paper' of the constitution,
not to mention of the Virginia and Kentucky Resolutions as well (Jefferson

---

18 Late in life, in a series of letters to friends, Jefferson proposed an even more radical scheme of
decentralisation, arguing that the country should be divided into wards of such size that all citizens
could attend meetings and act in person. This was to encourage a sense in the citizens of genuine,
participatory self-government. While these letters doubtless expressed his deep feelings, Jefferson
understood that the system would not work beyond the scope of New England town meetings
(Jefferson 1984, pp. 1225–7, 1377–81, 1391–1402). The greatest impact of these thoughts was on
important twentieth-century thinkers such as Hannah Arendt (Arendt 1963, pp. 252–60; cf. Matthews
1984, pp. 81–91 and Young 1996, pp. 86–7).

1984, p. 1140; Adams 1986, p. 366). And, once the territory was acquired, he imposed a system of rule on the inhabitants that was deeply undemocratic (Adams 1986, pp. 381–6). The sweep of events simply overcame his principles. The opportunity to purchase the vast territory was too tempting as a means to further his dream of an agrarian empire for Jefferson to pass up. In the process he displayed a flagrant disregard for the 'principles of ninety-eight', as they were called, and, in acquiring the territory by treaty rather than by a constitutional amendment he undermined his commitment to a strictly limited national government. This was a momentous event. As Henry Adams observed, 'The doctrines of "strict construction" could not be considered as the doctrines of the government after they had been abandoned in this leading case by a government controlled by strict constructionists' (Adams 1986, p. 386). The theory remained current and important, but it became clear that in practice it could be ignored in the pursuit of a particular policy. Jefferson established the norm. Historically the theory of strict construction has proved to have some considerable rhetorical force, but it is rarely adhered to in a way satisfying to constitutional purists.

But at least in the case of the Louisiana Purchase the policy Jefferson pursued had merit and was successful. During his second term he held fast to principle and the result was disaster. By nature Jefferson was a pacifist, so that when it appeared that something had to be done to counter British interference with American shipping Jefferson imposed an embargo rather than resort to force. What followed was not what he expected. His own southern base suffered economically and the need to turn to domestic production to replace the cut-off of imports stimulated the manufacturing industries of New England. Alexander Hamilton could hardly have wished for more. By 1816 Jefferson came to understand, however grudgingly, 'that manufactures are now as necessary to our independence as to our comfort' (Jefferson 1984, p. 1371). In the end, he even came to accept the Bank of the United States, a private institution with close connections to the government, over whose constitutionality he had debated with Alexander Hamilton during the administration of George Washington (Hamilton 2001, pp. 613–46, esp. pp. 613–16; Jefferson 1984, pp. 416–21; McDonald 2000, pp. 30–1). Indeed, James Madison, his successor and disciple, agreed to the re-chartering of the Bank of the United States in 1816. On this matter, Jefferson was the clear loser, since the Supreme Court, in the vitally significant case of *McCulloch* v. *Maryland* (1819), accepted Hamilton's interpretation of the necessary and proper clause of the constitution and endorsed the bank Jefferson so distrusted, while rejecting his strict constructionist theory of constitutional interpretation. One could argue that the expansion of national governmental power underwritten by the holding in *McCulloch* that governmental power need only be 'implied' rather than explicitly granted by the constitution is the single most important decision in the history of American constitutional law. This opened up a theory in which government represents the people rather than the states, a nationalist position which in turn stimulated an enormously significant revival of states' rights arguments (Davis 2003, pp. 49, 45–9).

Jefferson was caught up in forces beyond his control. He could neither resist the enormous opportunity offered by Napoleon's willingness to sell the Louisiana territory, nor cope with the economic problems created when he attempted to pursue his foreign aims by means of the embargo. Perhaps the most striking interpretation of Jefferson's presidency was offered by Henry Adams. In effect, Adams contended, Jefferson out-federalised the Federalists. 'It was hard', he wrote, 'to see how any President could be more Federalist than Jefferson himself' (Adams 1986, p. 354). As Joyce Appleby has argued, matters are really more complex than that, since Jefferson did in fact enact a good deal of his domestic programme, so that he cannot be said to have completely gone over to the opposition, but there is still much to be said for the Adams thesis if we consider the constitutional issues inherent in Jefferson's exercise of executive power (Appleby 1984, p. 103, 2000, p. 31).[19] The extent to which the Jeffersonians, in spite of their rhetoric, came to accept so much of the Hamiltonian programme, even after the demise of the Federalist Party, lends real support to the idea of consensus in spite of Henry Adams' remark about the great divide separating the two.

One more consideration remains, a concern that adds a tragic dimension to any account of Jeffersonian thought and practice. Jefferson was, of course, a slave-holder, as were many of the founders of the American republic. But he was simultaneously the single most prominent spokesman for a theory of natural human rights. The contradiction was huge and he was fully aware of it. He repeatedly expressed foreboding over the continued existence of slavery. In *Notes on the State of Virginia* he reflected, apropos slavery, that God's justice 'cannot sleep forever', and, late in life, he likened slavery to a 'fire bell in the night'. 'We have the wolf by the ears', he wrote, 'and we can neither hold him, nor safely let him go. Justice is in one scale,

19 For a fuller treatment of the Adams thesis see Young 2001, pp. 53–5.

and self-preservation in the other' (Jefferson 1984, pp. 298, 1434; cf. Miller 1977). But he himself was unable to answer the bell, largely because of his deep-seated belief in the natural inferiority of the black race, not to mention his personal economic dependence on slavery. Not only are slaves black, but monotony 'reigns in [their] countenances' and the 'Oranootan' prefers black women over those of his own species. They are more tolerant of heat and less of cold, he opined; they have a 'disagreeable' odour, and while often brave, this may be due to 'a want of forethought' (Jefferson 1984, pp. 264–5, 288). The Negro is happy and simple-minded and benefits from contact with whites, 'but their inferiority is not the effect merely of their condition of life' (Jefferson 1984, p. 265). He conjectures that nature has slighted them in the 'endowments of the head', though not of the heart or the 'moral sense' (Jefferson 1984, p. 269). His tentative 'suspicion' is that 'the blacks, whether originally a distinct race, or made distinct by time and circumstances, are inferior to the whites in the endowments both of body and mind. It is not against experience to suppose, that different species of the same genus, or varieties of the same species, may possess different qualifications' (Jefferson 1984, p. 270).

Jefferson viewed the slave system as a danger to the virtue of the republic. It is an 'unhappy influence', leading to a 'perpetual exercise of the most boisterous passions, the most unremitting despotism on the one part, and degrading submission on the other'. 'The man must be a prodigy', he continued, 'who can retain his manners and morals undepraved by such circumstances' (Jefferson 1984, p. 288). Following the Revolution Virginia flirted with emancipation, but deep down Jefferson thought the idea to be impossible if it required the former slaves to live among the whites. Any interest he had in abolition was largely 'theoretical' (Davis 1975, p. 178). His strongest convictions arose when he wrote, 'Deep rooted prejudices entertained by the whites; ten thousand recollections, by the blacks, of the injuries they have sustained; new provocations; the real distinctions which nature has made; and many other circumstances, will divide us into parties, and produce convulsions which will probably never end but in the extermination of the one or the other race.' If slaves were ever to be freed they must be removed, that is 'colonised', to some other suitable place (Jefferson 1984, p. 264). Part of Jefferson's tragedy, and of the nation's, is that, with the exception of his apocalyptic conclusion, his fears were not that far off the mark and were shared with so great and ultimately successful an anti-slavery leader as Abraham Lincoln. Jefferson's thinking on this subject was not original but important because it is so typical of his time as to be symptomatic (Jordan 1968, p. 429).[20] His failure proved to be the nation's failure as well, a failure that could be rectified, if only in part, by the Civil War. But before taking up this issue, it is necessary to give some consideration to the legacy of Andrew Jackson and his followers.

3 Jacksonian democracy

The 'Age of Jackson' was not primarily an intellectual movement, though it produced some interesting ideas and was of great significance politically, socially and economically. It showed the possibilities of populist presidential leadership and was the first approximation anywhere of a mass-based political movement acting in electoral politics. It is perhaps the most American of all political periods, since as Gordon Wood writes, 'The Jacksonian era was the period that defined the basic elements of America's individualistic and egalitarian get-up-and-go materialistic culture' (Wood 2001, p. 49).

A central theme of Jackson's presidency was the fight against concentrated power in the economy and above all the Second Bank of the United States. Supportive journalists such as Walt Whitman and the editors of the Jacksonian *Democratic Review* enthusiastically endorsed the principle that the government that governs least governs best, while journalist William Leggett in particular was a militant advocate of *laissez-faire* economic principles (Blau 1954, pp. 131, 27, 66–8).

In his 'Political Testament', Jackson himself inveighed against monopoly and exclusive privilege while arguing on behalf of 'the agricultural, the mechanical, and the labouring classes' (Blau 1954, pp. 17–18). Such language introduces the sense of class conflict stressed by Arthur Schlesinger, Jr. in his paradigmatic *The Age of Jackson* (Schlesinger 1945). But this should not be taken to suggest that Jacksonian democracy can be seen as starting a campaign for a modern welfare state. Writers like Leggett made it quite clear that once equal competitive conditions had been achieved, 'As a general rule, the prosperity of rational men depends on themselves' (Blau 1954, pp. 76–7). Therefore, it is quite plausible for Richard Hofstadter to see Jacksonianism as an episode in the development of liberal capitalism (Hofstadter 1973, pp. 44–66). But Hofstadter's emphasis on rising capitalism and Schlesinger's on class conflict are complementary rather than contradictory. These perspectives point to the possibility of serious debate even within

---

20 Jordan 1968 is the starting point for any discussion of Jefferson's ideas on race. See pp. 429–81. Cf. Dain 2002, pp. 26–39 and Davis 1975, pp. 164–84.

the confines of a liberal capitalist system of the sort posited by Hofstadter and Hartz. As Hartz observed, 'You do not get closer to the significance of an earthquake by ignoring the terrain on which it takes place' (Hartz 1955, p. 20). The conflict was real though it often took the form of highly competitive individualism rather than class-oriented collective struggle.

From this viewpoint, Jackson was being perfectly consistent when he attacked the 'money power'. Marvin Meyers comments, 'There is in these words undoubtedly some appeal against the rich.' But this, he argues, is a secondary meaning. The specific language is important. Jackson castigated the 'money power', but not the rich, a position quite consistent with the thinking of Jefferson. The real enemy was corporate paper money; hence the assault on the monopoly power of the 'monster bank', as Jackson liked to call it (Meyers 1960, p. 23). The capitalism that Jackson endorsed was small-scale, non-monopolistic and highly competitive, a conclusion consistent with recent historical research which strongly suggests that the tensions of the Jacksonian era were a response to the rapid emergence of a market economy, a view quite consistent with Schlesinger's classic study (Schlesinger 2000, p. 371; Sellers 1991).

Two other aspects of Jacksonian democracy are also very important. The widening of the right to vote led to a marked increase in what Judith Shklar called one of the major 'emblems of public standing' (Shklar 1991, p. 3). As far back as the colonial period, white male suffrage was fairly widespread, and during the Jacksonian movement most of what remained of property qualifications disappeared, though of course, as Shklar insists, the existence of slavery and the disenfranchisement of blacks and women hung like a dark cloud over the nation (Shklar 1991, esp. pp. 43–7). Equally important was the emergence of what might be called a producerist ideology which stressed the right to earn, the work ethic and the importance of free labour, positions which were to be of major importance in the emerging struggle over slavery (Shklar 1991, pp. 63–79; Young 1996, p. 97).[21]

4 Antebellum reform

Coterminous with the events of Jacksonian democracy was a major set of interrelated reform movements, not specifically Jacksonian in character,

21 For a good contemporary discussion of the major forces at work in Jacksonian America see Masur 2001. Of course, the classic work on the subject remains Alexis de Tocqueville, *Democracy in America*, a masterpiece somewhat marred by excessive reliance on upper-class informants.

the most important of which were anti-slavery and women's suffrage. It is also important to take into account the deep currents of evangelical Protestantism which powered these movements (Lowance 2000, pp. 49–84; Morone 2003, pp. 144–68). A convenient place to begin is 1831, which saw Nat Turner's bloody slave rebellion in Virginia that was so terrifying to slave owners, and the publication of William Lloyd Garrison's flamboyant first editorial in his influential anti-slavery newspaper *The Liberator*. Then, in 1833 the American Anti-Slavery Society, the first organisational movement of its kind, was founded under the leadership of Garrison and the Lane Seminary debates were held in Ohio and became a major source of anti-slavery sentiment (Dumond 1961, pp. 158–65).

Anti-slavery was a very complex cause. Thus it was possible for someone like Abraham Lincoln to be anti-slavery without being an abolitionist, because he believed the national government lacked both the political power and constitutional authority to abolish slavery, while at the same time criticising slavery as a violation of the Jeffersonian theory of natural rights. Broadly speaking, there were two wings to the anti-slavery movement, reformers and radicals. Reformers saw slavery as an excrescence on a basically sound system while radicals, like Garrison, attacked the constitution and called for a root and branch reconstruction of both society and politics (Kraditor 1969, p. 8). Garrison, though anti-clerical, was deeply moralistic and might be said at least to have a religious temperament. He was also profoundly anti-political with a total belief in achieving his goals through moral suasion and a refusal to see that he might need allies who might not fully share his ideals. Slavery was an evil, and so too was the constitution, a 'covenant with death, and an agreement with hell', as he put it in 1844. The official motto of the American Anti-Slavery Society was 'No Union with Slaveholders'. It would, he thought, be better for the North to secede from the South than to corrupt itself by continuing to be bound together with slave-holders (Thompson 2004, pp. 230–45).

Aside from the belief that slavery was wrong, little else was generally accepted within the movement. Particularly in the early years, Jefferson's thought being a good example, there was much support for emancipation followed by colonisation of the freed slaves in Africa or Latin America, though this idea declined due to its impracticality and the belief of the Garrisonians that it too was inherently racist and wrong (Lowance 2000, pp. 92–4, 108–12, 117–19). There were arguments from religion and economics, debates over whether the constitution was anti-slavery or pro-slavery, proposals for political action set against the belief that relief was

beyond politics, passionate attacks on the inhumanity of slavery and frequent appeals to 'higher law', particularly the Declaration of Independence,
which became a potent ideological weapon[22] (Dumond 1961, pp. 232–3).

The problem of the meaning of the constitution with respect to slavery,
the humanitarian critique and the bearing of the Declaration of Independence on slavery are particularly important. Some of those opposed
to slavery considered the constitution to be flawed due to such clauses as
that giving slave states a base for representation that included three-fifths
of the slaves, the provisions for the return of fugitive slaves, and the ban
on prohibiting the slave trade until 1808. But nonetheless this group saw
opportunities in the constitution to choke off the institution of slavery by
controlling its expansion and placing it under 'official odium'. Radicals such
as the Garrisonians looked at the same clauses and saw a different constitution, 'conceived in compromise and dedicated to the perpetuity of slavery'.
Still others saw it as a thoroughly anti-slavery document which included the
right to abolish the institution (Kraditor 1969, pp. 185–6). Whether anti-
slavery people chose to work within the political system or agitate from
outside obviously was much affected by the hermeneutical stance adopted
towards the constitution.

The humanitarian critique was important and powerful. Theodore
Dwight Weld's *American Slavery As It Is*, a long, well-documented chronicle
of atrocities, was widely read and was the best selling anti-slavery tract until
the publication of Harriet Beecher Stowe's famous sentimental novel *Uncle
Tom's Cabin*. Weld also tirelessly propagated the idea of the higher law (Weld
1838). So too did the increasingly famous author of *Narrative of the Life of
Frederick Douglass, an American Slave, Written by Himself*, the first of three
important autobiographies published by Douglass. His graphic description
of the horrors of slavery derived great power from the fact that it was a well-
written first-hand account and it too sold very widely in the United States
and abroad (Douglass 1994, pp. 1–102).[23] Douglass' great speech 'What to
the Slave is the Fourth of July?' was also a powerful appeal to the abused
ideals of Jefferson's Declaration, an appeal symbolically delivered on the
fifth of July rather than the fourth to signify his sense of the betrayal of the

---

22 The anti-slavery literature is large and widely scattered. For surveys of these and other issues see the
documents in Lowance 2000; Pease and Pease 1965; and Thompson 2004. The Thompson volume
is especially interesting because it is edited by a political theorist with an interest in ends/means
relationships.

23 The importance of Douglass' book is indicated by the fact that it was published with prefatory
material by both William Lloyd Garrison and his fellow militant abolitionist Wendell Philips.

promise of the Declaration inherent in the continued existence of slavery (Douglass 1994, pp. 431–5).

Douglass' career is particularly notable as it took him from slavery to a position as close to the political establishment as possible for an African-American in his time. He moved from being a stout advocate of Garrisonian rejection of the constitution, to a flirtation with the violence of John Brown (Hyde 2002; Menand 2002; Stauffer 2001), to a political position which required him to argue, rather unpersuasively, that the constitution was anti-slavery and which closely linked him to the complex politics of Abraham Lincoln (Thompson 2004, pp. 144–56). In the end it was not the anti-political position of Garrison, but the activities of the Liberty Party and the Free Soil Party, which combined with the remains of the Whigs and came together to form the new Republican Party which, under the leadership of Abraham Lincoln, finally abolished slavery (Dumond 1961, pp. 290–305, 357–64; Foner 1970).

The anti-slavery movement was also closely linked in many instances with the drive for women's suffrage. The perfectionist ideology and the anti-clericalism of Garrison were particularly appealing to Elizabeth Cady Stanton, Susan B. Anthony and their feminist colleagues, as, of course, was Garrison's commitment to women's suffrage (Lowance 2000, 122–5; DuBois 1999, pp. 31–40; Davis 2001, pp. 359–76). Douglass too was a staunch supporter of women's rights (Douglass 1976). Stanton even remarked that anti-slavery was a source of the women's rights movement 'above all other causes', not because women discovered their own oppression through their encounter with slavery, but because they learned from the anti-slavery crusade how to turn their cause into a political movement (DuBois 1999, pp. 31–2).

Stanton's particular cause became the achievement of women's suffrage. In the present context, the most interesting document is the 'Declaration of Sentiments', drafted largely by Stanton and delivered at the first women's rights convention in 1848 at Seneca Falls, New York. Modelled closely on Jefferson's Declaration, its most crucial passage is Jefferson's text with the addition of two crucial words. She begins, 'We hold these truths to be self-evident: that all men *and women* are created equal . . .' (Stanton 1881, pp. 71–4). At the heart of the message was a Jeffersonian natural rights liberalism and the central goal was the drive for women's suffrage, a truly radical position since, while not denying that women had special familial responsibilities, 'the demand for the vote challenged the male monopoly on the public arena' (DuBois 1987, p. 130). Surely this was part of the logic of Jeffersonian republicanism, though Jefferson himself would surely not have agreed, since in an 1807 letter to his Secretary of the Treasury Albert Gallatin, he firmly announced his opposition to the appointment of women to office, and, one supposes, to their voting as well (Jefferson 1999, p. 545). But the goal of suffrage went beyond the achievement of political leverage and looked forward to a transformation of women's consciousness. As Stanton put it, 'Nothing adds such dignity to character as the recognition of one's self-sovereignty' (quoted in DuBois 1987, pp. 132–3; cf. pp. 127–38 *passim*).

Unfortunately the story does not have a happy ending. When the Thirteenth Amendment was passed women and former slaves were left in the same anomalous position. They were citizens without political rights (DuBois 1999, p. 62). For decades reformers had debated the question of how broad the movement should be, whether limited to anti-slavery or expanded to include other goals such as women's suffrage and temperance. The dominant position after the war was stated by Wendell Phillips: 'This hour belongs to the Negro' (DuBois 1999, pp. 59). The suffrage movement split and some of the leaders, including Stanton and her close colleague Susan B. Anthony, made seriously racist remarks about the former slaves on whose behalf they had struggled (Davis 2001, p. 370; DuBois 1999, pp. 53–78; Shklar 1991, pp. 57–61; cf. Stauffer 2001, p. 211). Not until 1920 was the vote extended to women.

The emphasis on natural rights is also clear in the anti-slavery writings and speeches of Henry David Thoreau and Ralph Waldo Emerson. Neither was a particularly political writer, but both were deeply engaged by the slavery issue. Each believed in the Jeffersonian maxim that the best government governs least and Thoreau went on to add, 'That government is best that governs not at all' (Thoreau 1996, p. 1; Emerson 1983, p. 567). Thoreau puts their position well when he says, 'I ask for, not at once no government, but *at once* a better government' (Thoreau 1996, p. 2). And clearly a better government required an end to slavery. But the constitution was a problem; it was, in fact, as Garrison also thought, an evil (Thoreau 1996, p. 9). But while Thoreau accepted, perhaps even admired, representative government, he dismissed voting as merely a form of 'gaming' and believed that it might simply be necessary to wash one's hands of evil. This may appear to lead to a prescription for passive civil disobedience and Thoreau's great influence has been as a defender of that position. But it is important to note that the much quoted essay 'Civil Disobedience' was originally more edgily titled 'Resistance to Civil Government'. And since Thoreau was a supporter of the violent campaign of the martyred abolitionist militant John Brown, it is clear that for Thoreau resistance might justifiably take violent form because of the evil of slavery and the constitution that accepted it (Hyde 2002; Kateb 1992, p. 103; Thoreau 1996, pp. 137–69).

Emerson's writings were more complex and much more extensive than Thoreau's. Like his younger friend, Emerson was a determined individualist who urged American thinkers to break free from the influence of old thoughts and practices, particularly those of European origin, so as to become independent, self-reliant thinkers and actors (Cavell 2003; Emerson 1983, pp. 53–71, 259–82; Kateb 1995). Emerson was an essayist rather than a systematic thinker. In this he, like Jefferson, was prototypically American though his range was international, his influence extending even to Friedrich Nietzsche (Solomon and Higgins 2000, pp. 142–3; cf. pp. 45, 181). His intense individualism and admiration for great men arguably could underlie a regime of competitive capitalism, yet he detested the results of that system and his intense moral commitments make him a 'real prophet of the progressive tradition' (Aaron 1951, pp. 3–20). Politics was necessary and could not be ignored, but he saw it as in many ways a second-rate activity and Emerson was also sceptical about the importance of law, leading him to the edge of anarchism. 'The law', he tells us, 'is only a memorandum', and 'Good men must not obey the law too well' (Emerson 1983, pp. 559, 563). But in the face of great outrages men may be required to act. This condition was reached in the 1850s as a consequence of the repeal of the Missouri Compromise of 1820 which had banned slavery from the northern territories as the United States expanded westward. For years Emerson opposed slavery and he had delivered annual addresses to celebrate emancipation in the West Indies, but for him the last straws were the passage of the Fugitive Slave Act in 1850 and the Kansas–Nebraska Act of 1854.

Emerson saw the Fugitive Slave Act as a violation of the 'Higher Law', a law endorsed by jurists from Cicero to Coke to Jefferson, according to which immoral laws were void (Emerson 1995, p. 59). From the Declaration of Independence on, he claimed, the mind of America was possessed by the idea of liberty (Emerson 1995, p. 104). But the constitution was flawed because of its 'monstrous' concessions to slavery which had 'blocked the civilization and humanity of the times up to this day' (Emerson 1995, p. 127). The consequence was that political action became necessary. Without rejecting his belief in the 'independence and the inspiration of the individual', but faced with the horror of slavery, he felt the need for a collective response; he could but 'exalt the social action' (Emerson 1995, p. 103).

As Len Gougeon suggests, the slavery issue became a 'central issue of Emerson's intellectual life' (Emerson 1995, p. xlii). Very critical of subsequent American history, he felt the need to go back to the Revolution of 1775 to find grounds for praise (Emerson 1995, p. 143). Like Garrison, who welcomed southern secession because 'the covenant with death is annulled, and the agreement with hell broken', Emerson also celebrated the breakup of the Union (Emerson 1995, p. xlviii). And like his friend Thoreau, he also came to the defence of John Brown. For Emerson, 'The end of all political struggle, is, to establish morality as the basis of all legislation.' This and not freedom, republicanism or democracy is the end; the more immediate political considerations are but means towards 'a state of things which allows every man the largest possible liberty compatible with the liberty of every other man' (Emerson 1995, p. 153). Emerson and Thoreau are exemplars of what George Kateb calls 'episodic citizenship', defined as the citizenship of 'loosely and temporarily associated individuals who seek to protest and end great atrocities' (Kateb 1992, p. 103).[24] Slavery was such an atrocity and only with its end could a more normal course of action be resumed.

5 The pro-slavery arguments

The pro-slavery arguments are the antithesis of the anti-slavery position, a veritable 'reactionary enlightenment', as Hartz called it (Hartz 1955, pp. 145–77). They entail a total rejection of the Jeffersonian theory of natural rights. In much southern argument, such as Senator John C. Calhoun's, slavery was defended as a positive good. In this view, the slaves had been rescued from barbarism, converted to Christianity, provided with good homes, and in exchange they provided the material base for a great new civilisation (Dumond 1961, p. 44; Hofstadter 1973, p. 78). Beyond this Calhoun masked his support of slavery in the guise of a defence of minority rights. But Calhoun's theory rapidly became incoherent. Like John Locke,

---

24 For an exploration of the philosophical substructure of Emerson's view of slavery see Cavell 2003, pp. 192–214. This paper, a meditation on the essay 'Fate', raises issues which go far beyond what can be considered here. See Emerson 1983, pp. 943–68. For Cavell on Kateb see Cavell 2003, pp. 183–91. See also Cavell 2004 for a deep Emersonian exploration of many political and other issues. This important study appeared too late for me to give it careful consideration. Emerson, and Lincoln too, in their emphasis on the Declaration of Independence, seem outstanding examples of Walzerian connected critics. Consider this from Cavell: 'When Emerson speaks of seeking our unattained but attainable self, I cannot but hear him speaking of America as our unattained but attainable commonwealth' (Cavell 2004, p. 69).

though much less successfully, Calhoun tried, in two posthumously published works, to argue from first principles. He rejected Locke and the Declaration of Independence and, in fact, heaped heavy-handed ridicule on Jefferson's view that all men are created equal (Diggins 2000, p. 29). Arguing more systematically, in the *Disquisition on Government* he avoided state of nature arguments and asserted that man was by nature social. But there was always the danger that individual feelings would override social concerns. Thus, he feared that government might be controlled by selfish men so that there was a tendency for it to abuse its powers. The first means to counter this was the vote (Calhoun 1992, pp. 5–13). But voting in itself is insufficient and is subject to the abuse of majority power. The answer to this dilemma is the theory of the concurrent majority, a majority that takes conflicting interests into account. Repressive policies would be possible unless the majority of each section and interest was consulted before action could be taken (Calhoun 1992, p. 35). Ultimately, in the *Discourse on the Constitution and Government of the United States*, he called for a dual executive branch with each section controlling one segment and the assent of both required to act (Calhoun 1992, pp. 275–7). But this system is 'profoundly disintegrated', as Hartz wrote, since its logic required protection of minorities within minorities, so that the eventual result is the veto power of each individual (Hartz 1955, pp. 161–2; cf. Hartz 1952, pp. 82–5). This intense, deeply buried individualism says something about the power of the American liberal tradition by showing the 'inability of the Southerners ever to get completely away from it' (Hartz 1955, p. 154).[25] Of course, such a system would have left the nation without a usable decision rule, but more importantly, the moral strangeness of the argument is all too obvious, since the minority right Calhoun aimed to protect was the right to enslave another minority. The result is to reduce politics to a Hobbesian jungle.

George Fitzhugh at least had the virtue of consistency that Calhoun lacked. Fitzhugh was rigorous in his rejection of any form of natural rights to which a minority could appeal. Instead of Locke, he was influenced by Sir Robert Filmer against whom the *Second Treatise* was aimed. Against Jefferson he argued that most people had an inalienable right to be slaves. The problem with northern society was *laissez-faire* capitalism with its duplicitous system of allegedly free labour, under which wage labourers were slaves without

---

25 Consider this from Hartz: 'If the South was neither decently revolutionary nor decently conservative, the North was decently both.' Garrison was 'jabobinical' but appealed to the tradition of the Declaration while forcing the South to refute it, though in denouncing the constitution he could hardly play the 'sober traditionalist' (Hartz 1955, p. 155).

knowing it. Though he did not explicitly propose to enslave northern workers, that was the logic of his position and he believed that ultimately slavery would be instituted everywhere or abolished everywhere (Fitzhugh 1960; Genovese 1988, pp. 118–234; cf. Hartz 1955, pp. 145–200). This proved to be an important argument which was noticed in the North, not least by Abraham Lincoln, whose 'House Divided' speech took up Fitzhugh's theme and argued that sooner or later the United States would cease to be divided and one system or the other would triumph (Lincoln 1989a, p. 426). Unsurprisingly then, free labour became a rallying cry in the North, even among those who cared nothing for the travails of slaves as such.[26]

6   Lincoln's synthesis

The anti-slavery argument reached its moral and rhetorical climax in the thought and practice of Abraham Lincoln who combined his theoretical and historical analysis with the degree of political skill needed to bring an end to slavery and to reconceptualise the nature of the American Union. Beyond that, he achieved a powerful synthesis of most of the major lines of American political thought that had preceded him.

Consider first Lincoln's argument on behalf of free labour. In this he embraced the slogan 'Free Soil, Free Labor, Free Men', which energised the anti-slavery movement in the 1850s (Foner 1970). His thinking is rooted in Locke's theory of property, the Protestant work ethic and the producerist ideology of the Jacksonians. In an 1859 speech Lincoln argued that labour was the source by which all human wants were satisfied. He argued further that 'labour is prior to, and independent of, capital; that, in fact, capital is the fruit of labour...' Therefore, 'labour is the superior – greatly the superior – of capital' (Lincoln 1989b, pp. 96–7). And in an 1859 letter he argued that in case of conflict between personal and property rights the man must come before the dollar (Lincoln 1989b, p. 18).

Lincoln believed that it was constitutionally and politically impossible simply to abolish slavery. That power had been given to the states and in the states the votes needed to amend the constitution were not yet available. But he also believed, rightly or wrongly, that slavery would die if it could not expand into the territories, arguing in his constantly repeated phrase that it would be placed 'in the course of ultimate extinction' if it could be

---

26 For a good collection of other pro-slavery arguments see Faust 1981.

contained. It must be contained, he believed, because it was morally wrong and because it violated the fundamental principles of Jefferson's Declaration. In his 1854 address on the Kansas–Nebraska Act, he denounced the denial of consent inherent in slavery, saying, 'no man is good enough to govern another man, *without that other's consent*'. And he went on to call consent 'the leading principle – the sheet anchor – of American republicanism', at which point he quoted the Declaration on the necessity to obtain the consent of the governed (Lincoln 1989a, p. 328, italics in original). In the rhetorical and moral climax of his speech he says, 'Our republican robe is soiled, and trailed in the dust . . . Let us turn and wash it white, in the spirit, if not the blood of the Revolution . . . Let us re-adopt the Declaration of Independence, and with it, the practices, and policy, which harmonise with it' (Lincoln 1989a, pp. 339–40).

Lincoln was not a saint. He shared, at least in public statements, many of the racial prejudices of his time and place. His first instinct, like that of so many others, was to free the slaves and return them to colonies in Africa. But he recognised the impracticality of this while at the same time he shrank from accepting the slaves as equals. Beyond this, he recognised that the great majority of whites would also not accept this, noting, in a passage reminiscent of Jefferson, that 'A universal feeling, whether well or ill-founded, can not be safely disregarded' (Lincoln 1989a, p. 316). Nevertheless, four years later, in the first of his great debates with Stephen Douglas, he asserted that the Negro is entitled to all the rights enumerated in the Declaration *even if, as Douglas argued*, he was not morally or intellectually equal to whites. Founding his argument squarely on free labour, Lincoln said, 'But in the right to eat the bread, without leave of anybody else, which his own hand earns, *he is my equal and the equal of Judge Douglas, and the equal of every living man*' (Lincoln 1989a, p. 512, italics in original).

On these issues Lincoln's moral and rhetorical strategy is crucial. He recognised the limitations of his own racial beliefs and those of his audience and by accepting them he put himself in a position to transcend both. Lincoln honoured Jefferson for placing an 'abstract truth, applicable to all men and all times' at the heart of the Declaration (Lincoln 1989b, p. 19).[27] But he overcame Jefferson's hesitation by insisting on the egalitarian implications of the Declaration, putting himself, and perhaps his audience

---

27 In Maier 1997 the author argues that Lincoln misconstrued Jefferson's argument, but, even if so, Lincoln's reading has become the historical standard.

too, in a position where the logic of equality must be accepted because it is implicit in the logic of the Declaration (Burt 1999, pp. 692–3).

The Declaration of Independence also played a large role in Lincoln's theoretical reconstruction of the relations of state and nation under the constitution. The key is the reference at the start of the Gettysburg Address to the founding of a new nation 'four score and seven years ago'. Thus, Lincoln argued that the Declaration marked the beginning of the history of a 'nation' rather than a union of essentially sovereign states. On this point he was in opposition to Jefferson and his intellectual descendants such as Calhoun. Pursuant to the theory of nullification developed in the Virginia and Kentucky Resolutions, Calhoun, in what proved to be essentially a trial run for the defence of slavery, had actually proposed nullification of a tariff in 1832, but in this he was firmly resisted by Andrew Jackson, who on that issue abandoned his Jeffersonian principles and adopted a nationalist position. However, the idea of a radically decentralised compact between states was nevertheless advanced with renewed intensity as the controversy over slavery deepened in the thirty years before the Civil War.[28]

The southern position was that the constitution was essentially an agreed institutional framework from which the parties could withdraw at will. Following the election of the anti-slavery Lincoln as President in 1860, southern states began to act on their theory. In his First Inaugural Address Lincoln firmly denied their right to secede on grounds of both constitutional and democratic theory. The Union, he argued, was older than the states. It was formed by the Articles of Association in 1774, matured in the Declaration of Independence, and further matured in the Articles of Confederation of 1778. And he pointed out that the constitution was ordained and established 'to form a more perfect union'. It follows that no state can leave the union on its own motion (Lincoln 1989b, pp. 217–18; cf. pp. 254–9). But beyond this constitutional history, he argued that there were powerful democratic considerations. The central idea of secession, Lincoln argued, is 'the essence of anarchy'. A constitutionally constrained majority is the only 'true sovereign of a free people'. Unanimity is not possible, and minority rule is inadmissible, so that if majority rule is rejected, the alternatives are anarchy or despotism (Lincoln 1989b, p. 220). The doctrine of states' rights waxes and wanes, and the validity of Lincoln's constitutional

---

28 See Hartz 1952. See also Davis 2003, p. 79.

history is debated, but on the issue of secession his position triumphed.[29] The doctrine of states' rights had been 'stretched to' and 'beyond its limits' (McDonald 2000, p. 191). As the war went on, Lincoln referred more and more to the nation instead of the Union and the nature of the United States was transformed (McPherson 1990, p. viii; Wills 1992).

Initially the problem for Lincoln had been to preserve the Union, contain slavery, and thereby put it on the path to extinction. But note that preservation of the Union, as he saw it, was a means to end slavery within the terms of the existing constitution. However, a new war aim, the abolition of slavery, began to replace preservation of the Union. This aim transformed the nature of the struggle and also circumvented Lincoln's concern that the constitution made outright abolition impossible. He argued that opponents of emancipation 'cannot experiment for ten years trying to destroy the government, and if they fail still come back into the Union unhurt' (quoted in McPherson 1990, p. 36). This empowered him to issue the somewhat limited Emancipation Proclamation of 1862 which applied only to territory not in Union control, followed by the Thirteenth Amendment to the constitution which finally banned slavery, a measure which Lincoln, in spite of earlier hesitation based on constitutional limitations, energetically backed (Vorenberg 2001, pp. 180–2, 198–9).

Lincoln achieved his synthesis of the main currents of American political thought in language that echoes the terms of the ideological consensus described by Hofstadter and Hartz. Locke's labour theory of property is there, as well as the Protestant work ethic derived from the Puritans, and, in spite of the fact that Lincoln had been a Whig, the producerist ideology of the Jacksonian Democrats. Above all Lincoln drew on the central egalitarian idea of Jefferson's Lockean Declaration. As David Bromwich suggests, the promise of the constitution could only begin to be realised 'by being rendered consistent with the Declaration' (Bromwich 2001, p. 24). But if anything Lincoln went beyond Locke and Jefferson in that he hinted at a willingness to extend equality and rights beyond white men (Diggins 2000, pp. 31–2). Moreover, Lincoln subtly reinterpreted the Lockean idea. Locke had postulated an equality in the state of nature which began to be lost in society. But for Lincoln, society 'is constituted by a movement *toward* a condition in which the equality is actual' (Jaffa 1959, p. 321).[30]

29 Samuel Beer sides with Lincoln, Forrest McDonald with the compact theory. See Beer 1993, pp. 8–15; McDonald 2000, pp. 7–11.
30 For a fuller statement of my understanding of the relation of Lincoln to the American political tradition see Young 1996, pp. 114–25.

There is therefore a potential radicalism in this version of natural rights egalitarianism.

And yet the war did not lead to radical egalitarianism. The Garrisonians, for all their anti-political limitations, turned out to be right. It took revolution, war and a repudiation of the old constitution to end slavery. But that alone was not enough. It turned out that the eradication of slavery had to be root and branch, that racist ideology ran deep, and that failure to eradicate that ideology would fail to achieve a full emancipation from the trauma of slavery (Woodward 1971, pp. 143, 161; cf. Kraditor 1969 and Young 1996, pp. 122–5).

7   The new nation

No one has ever presided over a more fundamental transformation of the United States than did Lincoln. In fact the transformation was greater than perhaps he understood. Neither side in the Civil War achieved what it hoped for. Lincoln essentially had tried to preserve Jacksonian America, 'the world of the small shop, the independent farm, and the village artisan', a world that was swept away by the modernising force of the war. The South had tried and failed to preserve slavery, but succeeded only in creating a soon to be lost opportunity for the pre-modern classes, poor whites and ex-slaves to band together in opposition to planter control. This, Eric Foner writes, 'is the tragic irony of that conflict. Each side fought to defend a vision of the good society, but each vision was destroyed by the very struggle to preserve it' (Foner 1980, pp. 32–3). The South lost its slaves, but Reconstruction, after a promising start, was a failure, the Fourteenth and Fifteenth Amendments to the constitution, designed for the benefit of former slaves, fell into desuetude for that purpose, and instead became bulwarks for the defence of corporate rights, while former slaves continued to be degraded and sentimental myths about the southern 'lost cause' were triumphant (Blight 2001; Du Bois 1992; Foner 1988; H. C. Richardson 2001; Woodward 1966). And there were major intellectual consequences as well, since the horrors of the war seemed to undermine the moral certainties that fuelled the abolitionist movement, thus opening the way for the later emergence of pragmatism (Menand 2001, esp. pp. x–xii, 3–68).

With the destruction of the most deeply anti-liberal American social institution, the liberalism Hartz saw as dominant from the start triumphed in theory, though frequently not in practice. In practice, the plight of the slaves was rapidly forgotten while the nation was faced with the explosive growth of industrial capitalism, rapid urbanisation, waves of immigration and deep economic and political corruption (Adams 1958, pp. 159–89, 1963, pp. 268–83; Fine 1956, p. 24; Hofstadter 1973, pp. 162–82; Josephson 1963). A new legitimating theory was required for the new order and it came in the form of an English import, Social Darwinism.

Among the wealthy, Herbert Spencer, Darwin's great populariser, enjoyed an enormous vogue in nineteenth-century America (Hofstadter 1992, pp. 31–50). His primary American disciple was the Yale University social scientist William Graham Sumner. The spirit of Sumner's thought is aptly captured by the title of his essay, 'The Absurd Attempt to Make the World Over' (Sumner 1963, pp. 168–80). Sumner pursued this theme by welding together a mix of fiercely competitive individualism, *laissez-faire* economics, and a Darwinian theory of social struggle (Hofstadter 1992, p. 51). He rejected natural rights egalitarianism in Jefferson's sense, claiming that rights 'do not pertain to results, but only to chances'. Thus, he embraced the pursuit of happiness, but rejected guarantees of other rights (Sumner 1989, p. 141). What remained was struggle. In Sumner's world, the fittest would survive, the nation would prosper, and the accumulation of large fortunes was not to be regretted. To set limits on accumulation 'would be like killing off our generals in war' (Sumner 1989, pp. 47–8). Without much consistency he simultaneously worried about the development of plutocracy which he considered to be the enemy of democracy. All civilised societies, he believed, tend towards plutocracy but the danger was particularly acute in the United States. He saw clearly the threat of untoward interest group pressure: 'The lobby', he prophetically wrote, 'is the army of plutocracy.' But government can be of no help. The nature of the problem was clear. 'How can we get bad legislators to pass a law which shall hinder bad legislators from passing a bad law?' (Sumner 1989, p. 94). Given the unlikelihood that this could successfully be accomplished, he thought it better to do nothing.

The greatest vice of plutocracy was 'jobbery' in the form of dubious 'legislative charters, watering stocks, etc., etc', conditions which were indeed rampant and which he saw with some clarity (Sumner 1989, p. 122). The loser from such machinations or any attempts to regulate them was likely to be the 'forgotten man', a phrase to be resurrected later for quite different purposes by Franklin D. Roosevelt. The forgotten man was the 'honest, sober, industrious citizen, unknown outside his little circle, paying his debts and his taxes, supporting the church and the school, reading his party newspaper, and cheering for his pet politician' (Sumner 1989, p. 126). But given

Sumner's animadversions against government he could offer no way out for his small-scale hero. His thought represents the triumph of the property-oriented 'Whiggery' on the right wing of Hartz's liberal tradition. As Russell Hanson wrote, 'Reconstruction and the Gilded Age were but two aspects of the more general process by which the capitalist mode of production was reproduced in America on an extended scale' (Hanson 1985, p. 183). What emerged at this time is the peculiar American form of 'conservatism' which scorns tradition and embraces the relentless change inherent in capitalist dynamics. In this sense, nineteenth-century American conservatism was very much part of the competitive, individualist, *laissez-faire* liberal tradition described by Hofstadter, but as Robert McCloskey noted, it was not the liberalism of Locke, but rather of Hobbes which lurked in the background, so that in Sumner's world 'selfishness is raised to the status of an absolute good: the Hobbesian man becomes the moral ideal' (McCloskey 1951, p. 47).

Though it falls largely outside the scope of this essay, this was not the last version of Darwinism to be a force in American thought and politics. It was not long before a variety of thinkers noticed that if natural selection was to be invoked to explain the survival of the fittest, it did not necessarily follow that the competitive struggle pitted man against man. Why could not members of the same species band together to adapt collectively to the problems posed by nature? As E. S. Corwin wrote, 'Instead of the creature being adapted to the environment, the *environment had to be adapted to the creature*' (Corwin 1950, p. 191). This reform Darwinism, as Eric Goldman called it, developed in the late nineteenth century, though it was not until the progressive movement early in the twentieth century that it began to be politically influential (Fine 1956, pp. 167–369; Goldman 1956, pp. 66–81; Hanson 1985, pp. 208–18; Hofstadter 1992, pp. 66–169).

More immediately relevant was the emergence of populism, considered as a style of thought, a political movement and a political party. As a style of thought, populists tended to see not so much class conflict as a conflict between the mass of the people and a small number of conspiratorial vested interests. This was coupled with a belief in the essential goodness of the people, a strong theory of majority rule and a commitment to participatory politics. Thus, populists came to be critical of the American system of checks and balances and its accompanying legalism which they believed tended to make popular control more difficult (Young 1996, pp. 138–40).

Nineteenth-century American populism was an agrarian movement. A fundamental truth of American history is that, 'The United States was born in the country and has moved to the city' (Hofstadter 1955a, p. 23). Farmers were the victims of a prolonged agricultural depression throughout much of the late nineteenth century, though, as Hofstadter's remark suggests, the problems went much deeper than immediate economic distress. Populists were caught up in the rapidly changing social position of agriculture and this, as much as economics, created deep anxieties.

As a political party populism was institutionalised first in the Farmer's Alliance and then, in 1892, in the People's Party which ran James B. Weaver for President. The Omaha Platform of the People's Party is a central document of populism (Pollack 1977, pp. 59–65). The platform complained of a 'vast conspiracy against mankind' on the part of propertied interests (Pollack 1977, pp. 60–1). Echoing Locke, the producerist ideology of the Jacksonians, and Lincoln, the platform argued that, 'Wealth belongs to him who creates it.' To deal with the problems and to bring the situation under control, the platform called for, among other things, government to be strengthened, the railroads curbed or nationalised, the monetary system altered, the reform of banking, a graduated income tax and direct election of senators (Pollack 1977, pp. 63–5; Young 1996, pp. 140–1).

The other major populist document was Henry Demarest Lloyd's *Wealth Against Commonwealth*. Lloyd was an atypical populist, since he was not a farmer, but instead a graduate of Columbia University and the editor of the *Chicago Tribune*, though his radical views ultimately cost him his job. The book begins and ends with an ethical critique of the new corporate economy. Denouncing the ethics of the conservative Darwinists, Lloyd argued that if the doctrine of 'survival of the fittest' were to be adopted in families or by citizens, the result would be 'a monster and would be speedily made extinct' (Lloyd 1894, p. 495). Wealth, he claimed, was destructive of liberty (Lloyd 1894, p. 2). The basic problem lay in the economic liberal's devotion to the principle of self-interest. This position ignored the fact that men are social beings. In a true *laissez-faire* system, we must let 'the individual do what the individual can do best, and let the community do what the community can do best'. In Lloyd's view, 'Civilization is the unceasing accretion of these social solutions' (Lloyd 1894, pp. 496–7, 506). Civilisation can be destroyed by barbarians from above. 'Believing wealth to be good, the people believed the wealthy to be good.' In believing this, Lloyd argued, we breed pharaohs (Lloyd 1894, pp. 510, 515). This was an analysis of industrial capitalism in the form of a critique of the 'atomistic social freedom' which Hartz saw at the heart of the American liberal tradition, a conclusion that led Lloyd to socialism as it did not for the populists he supported (Young 1996, pp. 142–4).

Lloyd offered more than the backward-looking nostalgia Richard Hofstadter was inclined to see in populism (Hofstadter 1955a, p. 23; cf. McWilliams 1973, pp. 396–406). His thought was an attempt to adapt Jeffersonian–Jacksonian ideology to the new realities of political economy, and its harshly critical view of that system pushed against the limits of the liberal consensus. Lloyd insisted that mere reform was impossible and that more fundamental change must come (Hanson 1985, p. 214; Lloyd 1894, p. 533). At the same time, populists *did* exhibit a certain nostalgia for earlier times; they yearned for the never to be recovered world that was destroyed in the Civil War. Additionally, in spite of poor economic conditions and the declining position of agriculture, most farmers did not become populists. If not simple nostalgia, the agrarian movement did display a certain provincialism so that farmers had difficulty in dealing with the plight of the urban working class. Any hope for a real farmer–labour coalition died. Lloyd's radical critique of the new economy failed to take hold in the cities, while the farmers continued to be significantly influenced by Jeffersonian liberalism, particularly in the southern states (Young 1996, pp. 143–5).

Nonetheless, many populist reforms were ultimately adopted, and in the early twentieth century the leaders of the progressive movement made a more convincing theoretical attempt to come to terms with Jefferson's legacy. Significantly, this was an urban movement one of whose major intellectual leaders was an enthusiastic follower of Theodore Roosevelt, the journalist Herbert Croly. Croly offered his theory in the form of an argumentative interpretation of American history. Like Lloyd, he too was concerned by the reign of powerful economic interests which he attributed to the dominance of Jeffersonian individualism, resulting, he claimed, in a 'species of vigorous, licensed, and purified selfishness'. The result was a system which made for 'individual bondage' (Croly 1965, pp. 49, 409). For relief Croly turned to the thought of Alexander Hamilton, Jefferson's old adversary, who was, he thought, a finer statesman and thinker than Jefferson, and more honourable as well. But Hamilton's major flaw was that, unlike Jefferson, he did not really understand his countrymen, which led to a fatal error, namely 'making the Federalists a bulwark against the rising tide of democracy'. It was Theodore Roosevelt's mission, thought Croly, to 'give a democratic meaning and purpose' to Hamilton's tradition

(Croly 1965, p. 169). This was a major reconfiguration of the mainstream of American political thought. It is often said that Croly and Roosevelt were pursuing Jeffersonian ends by Hamiltonian means; there is something to that, but Croly's move, by repudiating everything Jefferson stood for except democracy, went well beyond such a transformation (Sklar 1988, p. 401). It opened the way for state-based reformist liberalism. Even progressives who continued to revere Jefferson, such as Woodrow Wilson and his adviser Louis Brandeis, saw the need for a stronger government to regulate the activities of corporate capitalism. On this populists and progressives alike agreed (Cohen 2002; Goldman 1956, pp. 82–179; Hofstadter 1955a; Young 1996, pp. 149–68).[31] In the twentieth century the New Deal and the Great Society were direct descendants of these movements.

It is important to insist that American liberalism is not, as Daniel Rodgers suggests, flat and timeless (Rodgers 1992, p. 38). Liberalism is not static; it is a loose label under which a great many ideas can fit. There is a consensus broad enough for positions within it to migrate from one political camp to another. Thus, during the Progressive movement, the tradition of Jeffersonian liberalism was transformed by a fusion of Hamiltonian managerialism with Jeffersonian democracy. Liberalism in its familiar contemporary sense began to emerge. The states' rights position associated with Jeffersonianism was increasingly adopted by 'conservatives', as members of the more property-oriented wing of American liberalism came to be called, while these same conservatives continued to hold *laissez-faire* liberal ideas on political economy. In this way the theory of a liberal consensus retained much of its power, though in a changed form. The same basic elements continued to be present, but they were restructured into a new pattern, a process that has occurred more than once in American history. The progressives, later to be called 'liberals', continued to support an individualistic, competitive, capitalist economy, with a commitment, often honoured largely in the breach, to individual rights, but with a new sense that the ends of the individual might be best served by a stronger government committed to the regulation of the economy by the state. The characteristic form of American politics is an example of what the greatest scholar of American political parties called 'dualism within a moving consensus' (Key 1964, pp. 222–7).[32] The

31 For comparative perspectives on the transformation of liberal reform see Kloppenberg 1986 and Rodgers 1998a. On the general transformation of American life, thought and politics at the end of the nineteenth and the beginning of the twentieth century see Wiebe 1967, which remains a classic.
32 The historian Alan Dawley, though sceptical of the consensus theory, and a sharp critic of the theory of American exceptionalism, nevertheless sees that the evolution of liberalism is characterised by

historical norm in the United States is one of two-party competition which tends to draw the parties towards the centre. However, over time the centre tends to move under the stimulus of events, the response of party leaders to them, and sometimes the agitation of ideologues on the fringes or outside the bounds of political respectability, thus expanding the scope of political conflict.[33] Consider, for example, the abolitionists and populists who, while not immediately successful in ordinary electoral terms, nevertheless moved the consensus to the left. Were liberalism simply a monolithic, unchanging block of ideas it would be even more difficult than it is to gain leverage for critical positions. Through most of American history this has not been an essential problem; within liberalism there has been real room for debate.

With the advent of progressivism the 'long nineteenth century' in American politics came to a close. Only later in the twentieth century would the individual rights of minority groups again become a matter of state concern as they briefly were during Reconstruction. W. E. B. DuBois exaggerated but slightly, if at all, when he wrote in *The Souls of Black Folk* that, 'the problem of the twentieth century is the problem of the color-line' (DuBois 1986, p. 359). This has been a major problem within the liberal tradition that neither Jeffersonianism nor progressivism has successfully addressed, and it was indeed to become a major theme in the last half of the new century.[34]

'change within continuity' (Dawley 1991, p. 11). The consensus Key refers to is a general agreement to the rules of the game which probably refers to the liberal tradition, though without specific reference to the Hartz thesis or any other general theory.

33 Consider the brilliant, though now somewhat neglected work of E. E. Schattschneider 1960 who described the struggle at the margins of politics to expand the scope of the political system to include broader participation of previously excluded groups.

34 Nor did they successfully cope with the dramatic development of science and industrial technology, though the late writings of Henry Adams, who did not join with the progressive reformers, fruitfully opened that topic. Taken together, Adams' works can be read as a commentary on the entire nineteenth century, ranging from his masterful historical study of the Jeffersonians, to his journalism following the Civil War, to his autobiographical reflections which culminate in one of the earliest meditations on the increasingly rapid pace of social and technological change (Adams 1958, 1963, 1986; Young 2001).

13

German liberalism in the
nineteenth century

WOLFGANG J. MOMMSEN

Conventionally German liberalism is held to be one of the main reasons why Germany in the nineteenth century never managed to break the fetters of an authoritarian political system and why it eventually came to be the breeding ground for extremist movements on the right, notably radical nationalism and finally National Socialism. The history of German liberalism has always been seen as an aspect of the so-called *German Sonderweg*, a departure from the path towards modernity and liberal government which had succeeded elsewhere in Western Europe. In this approach, the failure of liberalism to impress German society with its values was considered a key factor. Recent research has shown, however, that this was at best a partial view. First, the parallels in the development of German and British liberalism are considerable. Secondly, the achievements and the failures of German liberalism ought to be compared with those of other European countries, notably Italy, Austria and Hungary. Such a comparison produces a far more diversified picture of German and European liberalism (Langewiesche 1988b).

I   Enlightenment, war and reform from above

In 1957 Leonard Krieger argued in an influential book *The German Idea of Freedom* that German liberalism largely originated in a movement of intellectuals without deep roots in the middle classes as such (Krieger 1972). These intellectuals propagated liberalism as a set of idealist principles, not as a political message of an emancipatory kind by which the middle classes could free themselves from authoritarian rule and bureaucratic control. In a predominantly agrarian society with few urban centres the core of the liberal movement indeed consisted of intellectuals, notably those in public office. However, liberal ideas were to be found in many quarters. A substantial number of the key spokesmen were aristocrats, often in influential social positions. Nobility did not play a role in Germany comparable to that of the Whigs in Great Britain; there were not enough of them around, and generally they did not occupy the independent social position enjoyed by their peers in Great Britain. But they certainly exercised substantial influence and were able to induce the princely or monarchical administrations to implement at least parts of the new liberal agenda. During and after the Napoleonic wars there emerged a liberal bureaucracy that was prepared to meet liberal demands in part, if only to strengthen government positions in a period of transition and unrest.

The civil servants who opted for a modernisation of the governmental systems in Germany, notably in Prussia, were impelled by Enlightenment ideas. After the upheaval of the Napoleonic wars a thorough reform along liberal lines of governmental structures, especially in the smaller and medium principalities, in line with liberal principles, seemed to be overdue. Notably the introduction of legislative bodies, either as assemblies of the traditional estates or as representative assemblies, was thought necessary in order to bring about greater cohesion of those principalities whose territories had been redesigned by the Congress of Vienna. Furthermore the patriotic attitude of the burghers to their rulers during the Napoleonic wars needed to be rewarded, if only to a limited degree. The constitutional reforms implemented by Freiherr vom Stein in Prussia from 1807 were designed to bring about a higher degree of participation of the burghers in public affairs, though only at a local level. Stein introduced a new system of self-government for the cities and towns, whereas in the countryside the power of the local nobility was by and large left intact. Similarly all governmental activities were now subjected to the rule of law. These reforms stopped far short of the demands of the nascent liberal movement but they pointed in the same direction, namely towards a greater degree of participation of the people, or rather of the bourgeois classes in the affairs of government.

Such measures from above initiated by an enlightened state bureaucracy were inspired by the philosophy of Immanuel Kant and centred on the principle of the self-determination of the autonomous individual (Merchior 1991, pp. 85–7). Although Kant did not introduce the principle of individuality into the public arena, he nonetheless demanded from the state that its actions must obey rational procedures and respect the life-sphere of the individual whose ultimate task was to realise himself as a rational human being guided by moral principles. Even though Kant did not coin the notion of *Rechtsstaat*, state of law, in substance this principle had already been fully developed in his philosophy. Later the principle of *Rechtsstaat* became a battle cry of the German liberal movement with the claim for the protection of the individual against arbitrary action of any sort. Although this benevolent bureaucratic liberalism did not go very far, it certainly paved the way for the liberal movement, if only of a moderate kind. The civil servants considered themselves not as the tools of the princely governments, but in Hegelian terms, as a 'universal estate' exempt from the web of interest politics pursued by the different estates. They claimed to represent the general interest of the state and – increasingly so – of the nation, and this encouraged them to work for legal, administrative and, to some degree at least, constitutional reforms.

This constellation led the liberals to assume that administrations could gradually be made to conform to liberal principles by public opinion. It should be noted that intellectuals inside and outside the administrative apparatus, notably those in academic positions and in the 'free professions', not least in the judiciary, shared much the same world-view and, to some degree, the same social interests. However, the early liberal movement was by no means a movement of intellectuals only; on the contrary it enjoyed the support of sizeable sections of German society (Sheehan 1988, pp. 22ff.). Certainly the lawyers, professors and journalists who enjoyed a high degree of *Abkömmlichkeit* (namely the ability to engage actively in political life), played a dominant role in the early liberal movement, but their views were shared by artisans, shopkeepers, merchants, master craftsmen, sometimes even by the owners of larger peasant holdings, that is to say the middling classes in general, and also the still marginal industrial entrepreneurs. This was also true for the Catholic part of German society. Initially there was a strong involvement of some Catholic intellectual elites in liberal policies. For example, Joseph Goerres, the well-known editor of the *Rheinischer Merkur*, came to be an important spokesman of reform. Only later did the Catholics dissociate themselves from the liberal movement, a process that eventually culminated in the *Kulturkampf* of the 1870s.

2   The emergence of a liberal movement

What were the main tenets of German liberalism in its early stages? A prominent place was given to the demand that all citizens be treated as equal, regardless of their status within the social hierarchy. All legal claims that were not in line with this principle were to be abrogated, although possibly with adequate compensation of the former beneficiaries. All remnants of arbitrary rule were to be abandoned and government subjected throughout to the rule of law. The individual was to be freed from all arbitrary restraints in society, and given liberty to pursue his or her own interests within the limits of the law, while the state was to retreat to the role of a guardian of public interests. Wilhelm von Humboldt argued in a famous pamphlet *Ideen zu einem Versuch, die Grenzen der Wirksamkeit des Staates zu Bestimmen* that within the limits of the law the state had no right whatsoever to interfere with the behaviour of the individual; it must not weaken the personal responsibility and the creativity of the individual citizen in conducting his affairs and caring for his well-being. Furthermore, citizens were generally to be given the right to form their own associations of whatever kind without control by the state authorities. These essentially negative principles were supplemented by moderate postulates of a political nature. Citizens were to be granted the right to participate in legislation and taxation by means of freely elected legislative bodies. These bodies were not supposed to take over control from the government; they were merely to ensure that the rulers and their governments would accept public opinion as the guiding principle of their policies. The experience of the French Revolution appeared to convey a clear message in this respect. In fact the liberals did not wish to interfere with the operation of the executive as such, let alone to install their own leaders in office. They were convinced that although it should conform to the demands of public opinion, a strong bureaucratic state was indispensable in the implementing of liberal principles in society at large. Their demands therefore stopped short of challenging the authority of government. However, the relative weakness of the liberals on the parliamentary level was compensated to some extent by their predominance in local government. As a rule local parliaments and city councils were firmly in the hands of the liberals.

This was certainly a modest programme, not least because the liberals were themselves afraid of potential revolutionary upheavals. J. Fr. Benzenberg argued in a treatise *Über Verfassung* (On the Constitution) published in Düsseldorf in 1816: 'It is not the purpose of the parliamentary assemblies to govern. Instead they ought to bring to bear pressure upon the government always to govern in line with public opinion . . . although in a reputable and law-abiding manner. The constitution guarantees that public opinion is officially brought to the attention of the government via the instrument of parliament' (Mommsen 1971, p. 239). On this basis there developed in the southern German principalities a specific version of constitutional rule that on the one hand recognised the autonomous positions of the prince and his government, while on the other insisted that the government should secure a parliamentary majority in matters of legislation and in particular of taxation. Needless to say a rather narrowly defined suffrage based upon taxable wealth ensured that the members of the assembly came only from the upper sections of society, an arrangement resulting in the chamber possessing a high proportion of office-holders. This dualistic type of constitutional government carefully respected the principle of the separation of powers and in no way objected to the rulers freely choosing their own ministers.[1]

In the first decades after 1815 this rather tame system of liberal constitutionalism, usually known as *Kammerliberalismus* (chamber liberalism) worked quite smoothly in the majority of south German states, albeit with the exception of Prussia which even refused to establish a representative body for the Prussian state as a whole, and instead maintained rather traditional regional representative bodies. This new constitutional form became the seedbed of German liberalism. It wasn't until the 1840s that Robert von Mohl broke with this dualistic doctrine of constitutional government. He argued with reference to English experience that the 'unfortunate dualism' between the government and the people could only be overcome if the ministers were chosen from the parliamentary majority (Angermann 1962, p. 407). This view was not yet, however, shared by the majority of liberals. The most they envisaged was that ministers who had violated the constitution should be liable to prosecution in a special constitutional court.

The liberal movement had a variety of different roots. South German constitutional liberalism was largely informed by French and Belgian examples, and derived its political claims from the philosophy of the Enlightenment and in particular the theory of 'natural rights'. Rotteck and Welcker`s *Staatslexikon* in many ways came to be the Bible of this variety of south German constitutional liberalism. But there also existed, as in Great Britain, a strong group basing its claim for constitutional rule on historical premises, namely the alleged status of free communities in early medieval times. Constitutionalism was considered by this group as nothing less than the overdue recognition of the ancient rights of the free burghers by the princes. This view was by no means radical; respect for traditional rights and hereditary monarchical authority was part of their message. This position is perhaps best represented by Friedrich Christoph Dahlmann, who was a staunch adherent of the English model; he praised the balance between the powers of the Crown and of the people as an ideal solution. More radical was a group of liberal writers who were mostly from east Prussia, notably Johann Jacoby, a physician, who on grounds of 'natural reason' demanded the right

---

1 For an impressive description of early Liberalism see Langewiesche 1988b, pp. 12–27.

of independent citizens to participate in the affairs of the state. Perhaps most outspoken were the liberals in the Rhineland who were strongly influenced by the Belgian example, and who feared with good reason that, unless the Prussian government would in time give way to the demands of 'public opinion' and grant a progressive constitution for all Prussia, the revolutionary spirit would sooner or later cross the Rhine and engulf the country in revolutionary upheavals. As early as 1830 David Hansemann, a successful Rhenish entrepreneur, pleaded strongly in a memorandum forwarded to the Prussian King Frederic William III for constitutional reforms that would give the propertied classes a say in the running of public affairs, according to the Belgian and French pattern, in order to replace the inefficient bureaucratic governmental apparatus of the day (Hansen 1919, pp. 111 ff.).

In the 1840s these different strands of the liberal movement began to coalesce, pulled together by what was referred to as the national idea. The idea of merging the still numerous small principalities into a German nation state, with a liberal Prussia taking the lead, became a universal battle-cry of liberal groups throughout Germany. It was assumed that the achievement of national unity would also lead to the triumph of liberalism. The cultural elite took the lead; numerous cultural events, in particular the popular Schiller festivals, as well as scientific congresses, commercial and even sports gatherings served as powerful platforms for promoting the ideas of constitutional reform and German national unity. The governments tried hard to suppress this agitation by means of censorship and the dismissal of persons in public service who had publicly demanded fundamental change. But this could not prevent a wide-ranging liberal network in the public arena from emerging. This network maintained close links between the proponents of reform in the assemblies, the institutions of local government, the various commercial bodies and the universities (Gall 1975, pp. 105 ff.). Bureaucracies themselves, especially in Prussia, seemed no longer capable of introducing overdue economic and constitutional reforms. They were widely held responsible for the growing stagnation in society and the economy: they made no effort to abolish old-fashioned privileges or to remove restrictions, which might have helped to stimulate economic growth and hold in check the growing poverty of the majority of the population.

The liberals demanded constitutionalism, the rule of law, the upholding of the rights of the individual citizens as well as the abolition of ancient and obsolete privileges, freedom of religion, freedom of association and above all freedom for the press. However, the great majority of the liberals were not as yet in favour of unrestricted free trade, fearing that this might lead to a class-ridden society; on the contrary they wanted to bring about a 'classless society of individuals of middling economic status [*einer klassenlosen Bürgergesellschaft mittlerer Existenzen*]'.[2] They envisaged that in due course the middle classes would encompass the whole nation. Just as the idea of parliamentary government was not considered by some to be applicable to German conditions, so there were many who rejected Adam Smith. As late as 1870 Heinrich von Treitschke argued in the then very influential journal *Preußische Jahrbücher* in a series of powerfully written essays under the title 'Das Constitutionelle Königtum in Deutschland' that the English example of parliamentary government would never do for Germany (Treitschke 1971, pp. 427ff.).

The 1830s and 1840s were a crucial period for the formation of liberalism as a political movement in Germany. Its operations were still hampered by the authorities, though perhaps no longer quite as harshly as a generation earlier, when Count Metternich had used the Deutsche Bund as an instrument to keep the activities of liberalism under control. Seen as a force for the future, liberalism drew strength from its appeal to the idea of the nation state, which seemed to be on the cards throughout Europe. Guiseppe Mazzini's nationalist message also made a considerable, if only indirect, impact upon public opinion. This mixture of national and liberal ideas strongly appealed to the educated classes, particularly Protestants, but it also found strong support among the lower classes, especially the artisans. By 1845, the demand that Prussia should establish an all-Prussian representative assembly instead of the regional parliaments was voiced more strongly than ever before. A joint representative assembly of the Prussian people might provide the nucleus for a future German national representation.

It was the increasingly prominent radical wing of the liberal movement in particular which embraced the national idea most strongly. Nationalism and radicalism amalgamated into a pseudo-revolutionary ideology that dreamt of overthrowing the established principalities all over Europe in favour of a republican order in Germany and beyond. The radical democrats showed great sympathy for the struggles for national emancipation of the Poles and other subject nations. Already in 1832 the Hambacher Fest, attended by some 20,000 people, had provided a rallying ground for radical liberalism. It had invoked in moving language a vision of the 'united free states of Germany' as part of a future republican confederation of Europe (Mommsen

---

2 Gall 1975, 1978. For the ensuing controversy see Mommsen 2000 or see also Gall 1997.

2000, pp. 53–4). At this stage such radicalism was largely rhetorical. Radicals intended to win over public opinion for their views, on the optimistic assumption that this would suffice in order to transform the established political order. Even so, the moderate liberals became increasingly worried about the rising tide of popular unrest that played into the hands of the radical democrats and signalled a potential revolutionary threat to the established order of things. A revolution was the last thing which the great majority of the liberal middle classes wanted; instead they pleaded for gradual reforms that would not endanger the governmental authorities as such. But by now they began to realise that the reform process ought to be accelerated for otherwise the masses of the population might be recruited by the radical democrats into a programme of revolutionary action.

3   Liberals, Radicals and the Revolutions of 1848

The separation of the radical democrats from the main body of the liberal movement was a slow process. It reached a critical stage just before the Revolution swept the country in the spring of 1848. With the promulgation of the so-called Offenburg Programme that was acclaimed by a large public rally at Offenburg in Baden on 10 September 1847, the radicals attempted to force the hands of the liberals. With unrest among the population mounting Karl Struve and Friedrich Hecker, the authors of this memorandum, intended to push the liberal movement to the left, and to abandon their cautious policy of compromise with the established authorities (Hubert 1961, pp. 261–2). The Offenburg Programme contained most of the liberal demands that were in everybody's minds at the time, in particular individual freedom, freedom of movement and association, freedom of conscience and the free pursuit of religion, and in particular freedom for the press. They also demanded a national representation of the people and the establishment of national unity. Only the demand for a republic was wisely omitted. They demanded the replacement of bureaucratic administrations by popularly elected governmental bodies. But at crucial points they moved beyond the list of liberal demands. The standing armies should be replaced by the arming of the people; furthermore, existing armies should take an oath to the constitution. This demand reflected the distrust of the armies among a population that had been harassed by them time and again. Even more spectacular was the notion that the existing system of taxation should be replaced by a progressive income tax, but – a rather modern idea – sparing the personal income essential for an individual's livelihood.

Otherwise the social demands of the radical democrats were unspecific: they pleaded for the 'equalisation of the unequal relationship between labour and capital'. Accordingly the society was 'obliged to elevate and protect labour'. These proposals were rather nebulous, and far from revolutionary. However, at the time they amounted to a radical challenge to the existing social order. The group which the radical democrats wanted to mobilise was not so much the proletariat – industrialisation in Germany was still in its infancy and the number of factory workers fairly small – but the lower middle classes, the artisans and shopkeepers, and possibly also the farm-workers. The key issue was whether to demand a republic. Undoubtedly, the reputation of the rulers of the smaller German states among the public was anything but good, and the Prussian king, Frederic William III, had behaved in such a manner as to totally undermine the prestige of the Hohenzollern Monarchy. For these reasons the ordinary people sympathised with the idea of removing costly royal households and establishing a republican system according to the model of the United States of America.

The liberals were alarmed. Their model of constitutional government based upon co-operation between the liberal assemblies and the governments was at stake, and also their predominant role in the political process. The radical proposals would have destroyed once and for all the chances for a peaceful agreement with the governments for which the liberals had been working hard and diligently. Moreover, the radical democrats now demanded the introduction of universal male suffrage. It is true that the liberals hoped to raise the lower orders to a middle-class status, but they were adamant that only persons with higher education and a certain level of wealth (which allegedly guaranteed independence of judgement) should play an active role in politics.

In October 1847 at Heppenheim, the liberals from south-west Germany drew up an informal programme of their own (Hubertt 1961, p. 262). It outlined the line of action of the liberals in the months that followed, since everybody expected major developments in the political arena to be in the offing. In particular there was the expectation of the establishment of a national representation of the German people, either a 'German Federation' or a Customs Association – *Zollverein* – that now was demanded by the assemblies of the smaller states. The Heppenheim Programme reiterated the political reform proposals of the liberals in considerable detail, whereas it was virtually silent about the social demands of the radical democrats, notably 'measures against impoverishment and misery'. Apparently no agreement could be reached on these highly controversial issues. The national issues were at the forefront of everybody's minds, whereas the liberals were quite happy to postpone decisions on the social question.

In principle two different strands of liberal politics had emerged: moderate liberalism and democratic radicalism. Tensions between these two alternative conceptions would determine the characteristics of the liberal movement until the First World War. Moderate liberals hoped to bring about far-reaching social change through a continuous evolutionary process that involved repeated compromises with the governments. Governments, it was hoped, would have to give way step-by-step when confronted with the constant pressure of a powerful public opinion, expressed by the various parliamentary assemblies, the representative bodies of local government, the press (which was largely controlled by the liberals) and numerous private associations. Thanks to the universally accepted principle of the rule of law the judiciary was expected to keep the governments on a constitutional course. Abolishing all unjust privileges and obsolete restrictions on the economy would instil new dynamism in society and create badly needed economic growth. All this should be crowned by the establishing of a German nation state which would harmonise the numerous legal and economic regulations in the various principalities, while maintaining the traditional diversity of regions and countries through a federalist constitution.

The radical democrats, for their part, hoped to mobilise the masses for decisive action against the princes and monarchs by appealing to a programme that included universal suffrage, the general arming of the people and far-reaching though unspecified social reforms that would bridge the gap that had opened up between 'labour' and 'capital'. They opted for a clear break with the past, both on political and socio-economic questions. They dreamt of establishing a German republican state on a federalist basis, in some way similar to the constitution of the United States of America, or possibly even as a part of a federation of the democratic nations of Europe.

A few months later the Revolution of 1848 spilled over from France and Belgium into Germany and pulled the ground from under the feet of the established governments. Liberals were strongly sought after in order to forestall a further advance of the revolutionary process. The liberals had worked hard to forestall the Revolution, but now that it was upon them, they were determined to take the lead. Hastily the German Federation agreed to arrange the election of an all-German National Assembly that eventually met in Frankfurt on 18 May 1848. Likewise, Prussia and the smaller principalities took the spokesmen of the liberal movement on board, and speedily introduced new constitutions that by and large met the liberal demands of the day. Initially it was not considered significant that the governments had succeeded in retaining control of the armed forces, as they proved not reliable enough to confront the revolutionary population directly. The 'March governments' which maintained control until late autumn 1848 succeeded in fundamentally modifying the structure of state and society in the individual states. They also took the lead in the Frankfurt National Assembly. Wisely they co-operated with the radical democrats on many issues, notably the introduction of universal suffrage for men with only a few restrictions. Largely in co-operation with the more moderate sections of the radical democrats they also drew up the Frankfurt imperial constitution which, although in the end scrapped ignominiously once conservative forces had regained control, remains one of the most impressive and magisterial documents of German liberalism. They even managed to establish a provisional Reich executive. The liberals were determined to get their way on two points: (a) to go for a compromise with the German princes, which included introducing constitutional government in the federal states, and (b), as per their slogan at the time, 'to bring the revolution to an end' Some sections of the radical democrats rebelled against this course of action by force. In April 1848 Hecker and Struve organised a revolutionary uprising in southern Germany, which, however, soon collapsed, and likewise an attempt to storm the Paulskirche on 5 September 1848, after it ignominiously had agreed to accept the armistice with Denmark. In the eyes of the public these actions largely discredited the left.

Even so the radical democrats sought to rally their supporters with all the means at their disposal; pamphlets, posters, public agitation and the organisation of popular associations. From 14 to 17 June 1848 they held an impressive rally in Frankfurt in which most of the prominent radical democrats, among them Andreas Gottschalk, Moses Hess and Ludwig Feuerbach, participated. Despite this their fervent pleas for a democratic republic as the only durable solution to the 'German Question' made little impact.

During the Revolution the initially rather fluid political divisions hardened into formal political parties. The radical democrats founded Democratic Associations throughout the country, whereas the moderate liberals tried to rally their supporters in Constitutional Associations. However, both the radical democrats and moderate liberals now had to cope with a formidable movement of conservative associations, and also with the beginnings of a socialist movement. Until April 1849 the newly founded political associations mobilised a considerable section of the population behind their banners. During the brief campaign to rescue the Frankfurt Reich constitution the liberal and radical associations operated together, although ultimately to no avail. While the liberals considered military resistance against the reaction futile, the radical democrats resorted to armed uprisings in Saxony and in south Germany. But they could not hold their own for long against the professional armies of Prussia and the other German states.

The political associations that had been formed in the later stages of the Revolution of 1848–9 must be considered as the beginning of an organised political party system, and the liberals had played an important part in it. However, after the violent suppression of the Revolution these associations dissolved without trace. They were to resurface under different names in the early 1860s. Officially the Revolution of 1848 remained anathema to liberals. It was only the social democrats who later celebrated the memory of the German Revolution of 1848. Bourgeois parties, liberals of different persuasions included, regarded 1848 as a youthful mistake that had badly miscarried.

The failure of the Revolution had been a severe shock for liberals and democrats alike. However, in the longer term all was not lost. The liberal constitutions that had been introduced in Prussia and most of the smaller states were substantially revised. In Prussia a new first chamber was established. The introduction of the three-class suffrage was supposed to end the domination of the chamber of deputies by the liberal bourgeoisie once and for all. Constitutional guarantees were scaled down in a conservative fashion and in some cases totally rescinded. Admittedly, for the time being, the position of the liberals was severely weakened; they had a hard time maintaining a hold in the assemblies, and they chose to compromise rather than get involved in new conflicts with the authorities. However, to some degree the representative bodies of local government and the commercial bodies served as a refuge for liberal politics. The democrats also steadfastly opposed the repressive legislation of the governments. This resistance earned them little respect, however, and in Prussia led to their virtual disappearance from the political arena.

Even so most of the German states, not least Prussia, remained constitutional states. The liberals had been defeated, but in crucial areas of state and society liberal principles survived. There was no return to pre-Revolution bureaucratic absolutism. Thus the apparently sudden revival of liberalism in the early 1860s was not quite as sudden as it might appear.

4 The 'new era', the constitutional conflict and unification

In 1858 the prince-regent William announced the beginning of a new era; Prussia was determined to make what he called moral acquisitions and a wise legislation and the promotion of a greater degree of German unity (Hubert 1986). The monarch appeared willing to co-operate with the liberals who in turn proceeded in a moderate fashion in order not to push him back into the conservative camp. Similarly in Baden in 1860, a liberal government was installed under the leadership of two prominent politicians, and in the next decade it became the model of such government. Indeed the experience of liberalism in power left its mark throughout Germany. The dawn of a new liberal era seemed to have arrived. This new departure was greatly assisted by the developments in the international arena. The Franco–Italian War of 1859 and the foundation of the Italian nation state had had a profound impact upon the political climate in Germany. Now all of a sudden the issue of national unity was on the agenda again, and the governments were expected by an excited public to respond to this new situation with more than just words. In 1862 the Nationalverein was founded as a joint organisation of German liberals across the state boundaries with the aim of promoting a united Germany. The public expected a liberal Prussia to take the lead in this process. It would appear that the liberals in Prussia now had a unique chance of achieving substantial reforms under a new liberal administration.

However, their attempt to push through a reorganisation of the Prussian army along liberal lines met with unexpected resistance on the part of Prince William. The demand to maintain the *Landwehr* law and to abolish the mandatory three years' military service led to a severe constitutional conflict between the Prussian government and the Chamber of Deputies in which the newly founded Progressive Party possessed a huge majority. As a last resort the Crown eventually appointed Otto von Bismarck as head of government. He did not establish a dictatorship, but he was not prepared to give an inch to the parliamentary majority. The conflict developed into a fundamental clash over whether there should be parliamentary or royal control of the armed forces. Bismarck repeatedly dissolved the House of Deputies, yet the Progressive Party majority that enjoyed the overwhelming support of the press could not be broken. The liberals for their part were determined to see things through and eventually achieve a decisive victory over 'this wretched Junker', as Heinrich Treitschke put it at the time. Bismarck defied the resolutions of the parliamentary majority and carried on with the army reorganisation, appealing to the famous theory of a gap in the constitution – that it did not state what was to be done if government and parliament could not agree. Furthermore he went on to censor the press and reprimand those civil servants and judges who had sided with the parliamentary majority. Step by step he thereby removed the constitutional conditions that guaranteed the rule of law.

Bismarck had realised that support for the liberals in the country was not as solid as it appeared to be. In fact, the parliamentary strength of the liberals was largely due to the effects of the three-class suffrage that massively favoured the representation of the upper middle classes. The liberals, in their turn, were not in a position to mobilise the masses of the population against the government, even if they had wished to do so; revolutionary action lay beyond their political horizon. Bismarck had exposed the weak spot in the armour of liberalism, namely the assumption that when conflict arose, the government would eventually give way, thanks to the force of public opinion. In Prussia, the roots of the liberals among the populace were weak. The liberals could only count on organisations of notables and office-holders. By contrast, the conservatives had successfully built up so-called People's Associations throughout the country. Hence a revolutionary appeal to the people would have been fruitless.

Finally Bismarck's surprising victories in the wars against Denmark in 1864 and Austria in 1866 totally undermined the political position of the Progressive Party in Prussia. All that was left to the Progressive Party was the meagre satisfaction of noting Bismarck's request for an indemnity from a House of Deputies no longer dominated by the liberals. This marked an acceptance in principle that the constitution had been violated by his policies. Prussian politics had undergone a fundamental reversal. The progressive wing of the liberals had suffered a crushing defeat, with long-term consequences for the position of liberalism in the nascent German nation state. The triumph of the Prussian armies over Austria cleared the way for the establishment of a North German Federation, the first step towards national unity. The enthusiasm of the public, the liberals included, was boundless. Now a new party was founded that declared that its predominant task was 'energetically to support the government in its endeavour to erect a united and powerful North-German state' (Miquel 1911, p. 19). The

National Liberals – as they now called themselves – were fully aware of the fact that in doing so they would have to forfeit for the time being important liberal objectives: 'The age of ideas is over. German unity has come down to us from the dreamland into the prosaic land of reality' (Miquel 1911, p. 19). But they hoped that they might in due course be able to establish a truly constitutional form of government in line with liberal principles. So far they were not yet prepared totally to succumb to the doctrine of *realpolitik*.

Bismarck's policies of unification were guided not least by the consideration that the passionate demand for a German nation state had to find some sort of fulfilment. Bismarck successfully directed the public desire for a united Germany on to a conservative track. For the time being he received the enthusiastic support of public opinion for this policy. Even so, he could not manage without the co-operation of various liberal factions in establishing the North German Confederation. This association of the states north of the Main under Prussian leadership provided the framework for the German Reich that came into being after the Franco-Prussian War of 1870/71. It was achieved with the loyal co-operation of the National Liberals and the other liberal factions in the North German parliamentary assembly which was duly elected on the basis of the suffrage that had been agreed upon in the Frankfurt *Paulskirche* twenty-two years earlier. The National Liberals came to be the leading faction in the North German Reichstag, and they managed to draw up the constitution of the North German Confederation in a tough but constructive struggle with Bismarck. However, they failed to achieve their main goal – that of establishing a genuine constitutional system with a cabinet of ministers individually responsible for running their departments. They had to put up with a pseudo-constitutional system that granted Bismarck, as Reich Chancellor and Prime Minister of Prussia, exceedingly wide-ranging powers. From the very beginning the new constitution was a compromise between the liberal idea of constitutional government and Prussian-German authoritarian rule; and this was especially true of parliamentary control of military expenditure. On the one hand, the new constitution was, by international standards, surprisingly democratic. This was because of the universal suffrage, which was disliked by the liberal parties because they believed that in this way Bismarck tried to mobilise the support of the underprivileged sections of the people against them. On the other hand, all direct participation of the parties in running the government was excluded. In 1871 this complicated pseudo-parliamentary constitution which left many issues unresolved was extended to the Reich without substantial alterations. Although the constitutional structure of the Reich looked quite impressive it never got beyond this compromise between authoritarian and liberal principles.

In domestic affairs the period from 1867 to 1879 was an era of liberal rule. Bismarck gave the liberals considerable leeway in legal, financial and commercial matters. Important national institutions were established: a national currency, a central bank, a comprehensive commercial code, the harmonisation of criminal law in accordance with liberal principles, to name the most important. However, such legislation always encountered opposition from Bismarck whenever the rights of the government and notably of the Emperor could have been affected. Similarly, the press, although on the whole free, remained subject to some arbitrary restrictions. The balance sheet seen from a liberal point of view was certainly a positive one; but the liberals never succeeded in closing the loopholes that allowed recourse to authoritarian ways of government where necessary. Furthermore, Bismarck pushed important legislative projects, like the social insurance system, through Parliament despite the liberal parties, even though the liberals did succeed in inserting liberal principles of equity and rationality into these complex legislative projects, and in having them adapted to the requirements of a modern society based upon the rule of law.

The National Liberal Party considered itself the party of German unification, and as such it was determined to support Bismarck's foreign policies unreservedly. In domestic affairs it worked for a gradual completion of the constitutional order established in 1867 and 1870. But it had internalised the experience of 1848 and of the Prussian constitutional conflict of the early 1860s. Henceforth it would not risk any frontal collision with the Chancellor not least because his great personal prestige had to be taken into account as a major factor. Banking on this support, Bismarck drew the National Liberals into a major confrontation with the Centre Party that had emerged in the 1870s as a serious political rival. The National Liberals violated the principle of equality by supporting exceptional laws against the Catholic clergy. Even more seriously they voted for the anti-socialist legislation which Bismarck introduced after two terrorist attacks. The National Liberals were let down by their own supporters who had dismissed their initial reluctance to enter upon the path of anti-socialist legislation as a violation of their liberal principles. Obviously the liberals were in a quandary. Unlike in Britain, German liberalism had from the beginning failed to retain the nascent working-class movement within its political camp. The Progressive Party remained faithful to classic liberal principles, and accordingly fought against Bismarck's policies tooth and nail, as a continuation of the democratic republicanism of the 1840s. But they also feared the competition of the Social Democratic Party, all the more so as in many ways the socialists could be considered the true heirs of the radical democracy of the Revolution of 1848/49. The eloquent struggle for liberal principles in open conflict with Bismarck won them few followers, although they were supported by an influential section of the liberal press. Generally the Progressive Party was reduced to 'negative policies'. In the parliamentary system that developed after the foundation of the Reich its influence was marginal.

5   Liberal divisions in imperial Germany

In 1879, Bismarck decided to break once and for all with the National Liberal Party. He opted for a new policy based upon an alliance of conservative forces in Prussian-German politics under the banner of protectionism. In order to do so he now did not hesitate to enlist the support of the Centre Party. This new departure split the National Liberal Party, which so far had been in favour of free trade, and also its supporters in the country. Despite this the National Liberals tried hard to hold on to their role as an informal government party. Gradually one section became a party of Bismarck-followers despite the indifference of the Chancellor. Bismarck's marked swing to the right led to the breakaway of the left wing of the National Liberal Party. The new *Freisinnige Vereinigung* was decidedly for 'free trade' and it refused to enter into further compromises with Bismarck. Instead the energetic defence of the liberal achievements since 1867 was now their main objective. At this stage there was still some hope that the unity of the liberal movement might be restored in due course. However, this proved a vain hope, for what actually happened was a process of progressive fragmentation of the liberal movement. The National Liberals, especially in Prussia, shifted even further to the right. They now hoped to save themselves by embracing an aggressive imperialist nationalism and making a rapprochement with the Prussian Conservatives (see Winkler 1978, pp. 5–28). In 1884 the various factions of the liberal left joined forces in the *Freisinnige Partei*. However, constant quarrels about the correct political course between the different factions continued unabated, mainly because of the utter powerlessness of a party that found itself squeezed between the policies of the government and the agitation of the socialists. Generally, they were reduced to a representation of the lower middle classes, notably the artisans and shopkeepers, although they enjoyed a substantial following among the intelligentsia and even the financial community that disliked the tariff policies of the imperial government.

By now, liberals of all persuasions were in real trouble. Their main objective – to bring to completion the programme of liberal constitutionalism on the national level – had failed, and it was not likely that it would be achieved in the near future. Many liberals, among them Max Weber, attributed this to Bismarck's policies. The Chancellor had thwarted the crystallisation of liberalism into a self-conscious political party because he would not allow anyone beside himself an independent position. 'His entire policy was based on the effort to prevent the consolidation of any strong and thereby independent constitutional party' (Mommsen 1984, p. 164). The great generation of National Liberal leaders, so Weber maintained, had been succeeded by weak politicians, because in the atmosphere created by Bismarck strong-willed personalities were not allowed to grow. 'The majestic sun that stood at Germany's zenith and made the German name shine in the farthest corner of the earth was almost too big for us and burned out the bourgeoisie's slowly evolving capacity for political judgement' (Mommsen 1984, p. 86). Indeed, this became the basis of the traditional view that German liberalism had been weak and undecided throughout and that it always had been too ready to make its peace with the authorities.

In the 1990s this interpretation was challenged on various grounds. In the first place, seen in an international context, German liberalism had been by no means as timid as these interpretations (variations of the so-called *Sonderweg* thesis) would have it. Subsequent scholarship on German liberalism has come up with far more diversified explanations. M. Rainer Lepsius (1966) had suggested that the domestic constellation of imperial Germany was largely determined by three fairly sharply distinguished socio-cultural milieux to which comparatively stable forms of social conduct corresponded: the traditional conservative milieu, the Catholic milieu and subsequently the working-class milieu. These milieux hardened into fairly stable structures that were unfavourable to dynamism and change. In the liberal camp there did not exist an equivalent to these stable socio-cultural milieux, even though there always existed a considerable degree of correlation between Protestantism and a bourgeois mentality that favoured liberal attitudes (Hübinger 1994). In this respect, liberalism that for some decades had been considered the dominant ideology of the day, was clearly worse placed than its political rivals.

In a way it could be said that liberalism suffered from its former successes. The great objective of the liberal movement, namely the creation of a constitutional nation state organised in accordance with liberal principles, had lost its magic power over the electorate. For this reason Max Weber and his generation felt themselves to be 'epigones' of the great pioneer generation of liberals who had helped to establish the German Empire. But perhaps this was too harsh a judgement. For even though the liberals had not comprehensively succeeded in their policies at the level of the central government, their impact upon society as a whole had been far greater than is usually admitted. The liberals did leave their imprint upon German society. Imperial Germany had become, notwithstanding its pseudo-constitutional constitution, very much a bourgeois society.[3] Even though the serious splits in their ranks substantially impaired their political clout, the liberals managed to gain and maintain considerable power positions in some of the federal states, and even more so in local government. For more than forty years they played a crucial role in local government, in particular in the cities. It is true that their relatively strong position was to a considerable degree due to the three-class suffrage which favoured the propertied classes. But they did a remarkably good job in running the new urban centres often against the bitter opposition of the Catholic Centre Party and the social democrats. They created a socio-cultural milieu that benefited their own clientele in particular: the educated upper middle classes and also the business circles. But the other sections of urban society also profited not only from the cultural infrastructure that the liberals created but also from the wide-ranging social benefits of the municipal socialism that was implemented by far-sighted city councillors and mayors.

Even so, the tide had turned against the liberals. A clearly discernible liberal strategy no longer existed. With the rise of a mature capitalist economy and a structural crisis in the agrarian economy, together with the persistent problems faced by the traditional artisans and shopkeepers in a rapidly developing industrial society, no political strategy could have suited the ideal and material interests of the liberal constituency in its entirety. Therefore, the political activities of the various factions of liberalism varied according to region, time and circumstances. The liberal parties were forced to enter into different coalitions, either on the right or on the left, and this drove the various factions of the liberal movement even further apart.

In Wilhelmine Germany liberalism presented itself in fragmented form. Already in their Heidelberg Programme of 1884 the National Liberals had declared their main political objective to be the defence of the established

---

3 This point has been made recently most strongly by Geoff Eley in Jarausch and Jones 1990.

order against the challenges from the right, but even more from the socialist left. They now also opted for a pronounced nationalist policy in order to hold the different factions in the party together. They prided themselves on being staunch supporters of the new *Weltpolitik* that in 1894 was launched by Prince Bülow and William II, and supported both the rearmament policies of the imperial government and in particular the policy of constructing a strong German battle fleet. When the drive for a strong German Empire overseas did not immediately yield the anticipated successes, the National Liberals demanded from the government that it should not refrain from using the weight of the military might of imperial Germany as a diplomatic weapon, and it should not shrink away from war if there was no alternative.

In Prussia the National Liberals now co-operated with the Conservatives, as far as possible, rather than joining forces with the Progressive liberals. A reform of the Prussian suffrage law was now out of the question even though it was overdue, especially after progressive taxation had been introduced in 1891. Johannes von Miquel, who by now had changed his position as leader in the National Liberal Party for the post of Prussian finance minister, thought that the National Liberals ought to become the standard bearer of a plebiscitary national monarchy under the leadership of William II thus exploiting the popular support for the monarchy (though not necessarily the person of the monarch himself). It goes without saying that the National Liberals were now prepared to support new anti-socialist measures again. Furthermore, Max Weber suspected that the German bourgeoisie would have welcomed a populist plebiscitarian regime under William II which would protect them against the socialist threat and likewise against new social reforms. With utmost contempt he stated in May 1895 in his famous Freiburg Inaugural Lecture: 'It is all too obvious that a part of the upper bourgeoisie long for the rise of a new Caesar who would protect them against rising masses from below, and likewise against the projects of social policies which seem to be pursued by some of the [smaller] German dynasties' (Weber 1984a). However, for some years, if only up to a point, the strategy of co-operation with the Conservatives in Prussia worked out. The formation of the so-called 'bloc' of the Conservative and Liberal parties under Count Bülow in 1906 seemed to herald a new era of success in overseas policies, and moderate progress in constitutional matters. Three years later this dream was rudely shattered; German policies were again dominated by an alliance of the Centre Party and the conservatives, while liberals of all persuasions were left out in the cold once again.

The Progressive liberals that formed the core of the new *Freisinnige Partei* had always been energetic opponents of aggressive foreign policies and colonial acquisitions which appeared neither to be viable nor in the interest of their supporters. Likewise they had been staunch opponents of military armaments, if only because in military matters the power of Parliament over the budget was severely restricted. However, in 1892, and again in 1893, Count Caprivi declared himself ready to end these relics of the Prussian military state, and to grant normal parliamentary budgetary rights to the Reichstag even in military affairs, provided that the Progressive liberals would vote for a moderate army bill. The progressive wing of the party thought it advisable to give up their fruitless radical opposition in this field. Eventually they separated from the party and founded the *Freisinnige Vereinigung*. They thought that the radical opposition to the government had not led anywhere and pleaded for limited co-operation with the government in order to trade in reforms concerning constitutional and other material issues, for instance the reform of military justice. The conflict between faithfulness to the principles of orthodox liberal doctrine and concessions on tactical grounds was a permanent one, but the strategy of the Progressive liberals was to some degree successful.

Besides, many otherwise left-minded liberals found it futile, if not utterly unjustified, that the Progressives stuck to their former doctrinaire opposition to armaments and a 'sensible' German *Weltpolitik* (Weber 1984a). Max Weber belonged to those who believed that only a strong future-oriented policy of overseas expansion could overcome the lethargy of the liberal movement and provide the dynamism for a second liberal era. In England Weber had detected a very different attitude both of the liberals and of the working class to the state. He attributed this 'to the reverberations of a world power position which constantly faced the state with great tasks in power politics and which involved the people in constant political education', something which during Bismarck's reign had been sadly neglected (Weber 1984a, p. 88). Weber argued that a policy of imperialist expansion overseas was no more than the continuation of the foundation of the German Empire. 'We must grasp that the unification of Germany was a youthful spree, indulged in by the nation in its old age; it would have been better if it had never taken place, since it would have been a costly extravagance, if it was the conclusion rather than the starting point for German power politics on a global scale' (Weber 1984a, p. 69). Indeed, an influential minority among left-wing liberals became determined supporters of German imperialist policies, among them Friedrich Naumann and Paul Rohrbach. But

429

though it prevented the liberals from becoming totally marginalised, the assumption that this would solve the basic dilemma of German liberalism in the post-liberal age proved unfounded. In fact neither the National Liberals nor the Progressives ever succeeded in reconquering the centre-ground of parliamentary politics at the national level.

6　Moves towards realignment and the First World War

The crucial problem was the attitude to the working classes and in particular the Social Democratic Party. By the turn of the century it had become clear that a policy of suppressing the social democratic movement would not work, and that social democracy was here to stay. Lujo Brentano had been one of the few liberal thinkers who had argued that the liberals must come to terms with the industrial working class. He pleaded for social reforms, and for the recognition of the trade unions as the legitimate representatives of the working class, and for a social order in which strikes would be considered legitimate weapons in the struggle between industrial workers and employers. Likewise, he maintained, the legislation that had so far been weighted heavily in favour of the entrepreneurs should be thoroughly revised. The younger generation of scholars in the *Verein für Socialpolitik* – the so-called 'socialists in the chair' – took the same line. Max Weber, for one, condemned the plans of the imperial government to make the incitement to strikes a criminal offence; this was 'a law for old women' rather than for self-conscious members of the working class. This message was not lost on the liberals. In particular Theodor Barth of the *Freisinnige Vereinigung* and Friedrich Naumann with his *National-Soziale Verein* acted as influential spokesmen for a programme of progressive social legislation. Naumann argued first in a series of publications and then after he joined the Progressive Party in 1906 on the floor of Parliament that the future of progressive liberalism in industrial society could only lie in close co-operation with the Social Democrats, especially with their moderate wing, the Revisionists.

The pleas by Brentano, Naumann and Theodor Barth were not without effect. Both parties progressively abandoned the traditional free trade ideology which had argued that self-help of the individual, not state assistance, was the only way to salvation. The National Liberals were more reluctant to embark upon this path. But even among them, notably in Saxony, the National Liberal Party under the leadership of Gustav Stresemann changed its traditional outlook and became the 'party of industry' (see Pohl 1995, pp. 195–216). Although Stresemann championed above all the interests of commerce and industry, in sharp opposition to the Conservatives he also sought to attract not only the votes of the white-collar workers, but those of the industrial workers as well. Hence the Saxon National Liberals looked for ways and means to mediate between the entrepreneurs and the people employed in trade and industry, and in this respect gave a lead for the National Liberal Party as a whole. In contrast to the reluctance of the National Liberals, the Progressives were deeply engaged in issues of social reform. They succeeded in introducing liberal principles into Wilhelmine social legislation, notably the comprehensive insurance system established in 1911. It is a myth that the liberals failed in the field of social policy. On the contrary, during the pre-war years their impact upon social legislation was substantial (Tober 1999).

But what is true is that the political fruits of these policies never ripened, not least because of the outbreak of the First World War. The fervent hope that in due course the liberals might regain political control via a coalition 'From Bassermann to Bebel' never materialised; only in Baden did a *Großblock* of the liberal parties and the Social Democrats assume power for a few years. The fear of the alleged socialist danger among the supporters of the liberal parties still precluded any far-reaching political arrangements with the Social Democrats, except in individual electoral districts. Thus in some federal states, notably in Saxony, the National Liberals managed to gain a hegemony in Parliament, while in others the Progressives maintained a strong position. This was true in particular at more local levels of government, notably the city governments that for the most part continued to be controlled by liberals of either party. The attempts to join forces with the Conservative Party were abandoned. By now liberalism in its different forms considered itself a modernising force in German politics, whereas the Conservatives were seen as an outdated party.

Such tendencies also made themselves felt at the imperial level. After the landslide victory of the Social Democrats in 1912 a different parliamentary constellation emerged, namely informal co-operation between the National Liberals and the progressive wing of the Centre Party that crystallised around a young and energetic figure, namely Matthias Erzberger, who eventually succeeded Ludwig Windthorst as the grand old man of German political Catholicism. Both parties now worked energetically for a modernisation of the system of rule in imperial Germany, in constant struggle with an unwilling government and an Emperor who disliked all party interference with his 'personal rule'. During the First World War this informal co-operation gradually hardened into a substantive political alliance. Instead of trying to change the constitution and possibly introduce a parliamentary government in accordance with the British pattern, they chose an indirect approach to strengthening the influence of Parliament: in crucial government departments committees were appointed in which the majority parties were represented and which would ensure that the increasing frustration of the public about the conduct of the war was at least taken into account by the government. In 1917 these endeavours were crowned by the establishment of a special parliamentary committee – the *Interfraktionelle Ausschuß* – with the aim of gaining effective control over the policies of the government, especially on the question of government peace initiatives. In this committee their leaders represented the so-called Majority parties, including both Liberal parties, with Stresemann becoming a key figure. However, this body failed mainly because the General Staff refused to accept its decisions as binding on them. Still, their power stopped short of the military authorities. The old cancer of the German political order came once again into the open. However, a firm understanding between the party leaders had now been formed and this was to provide the basis for more constructive parliamentary policies in the future. By the autumn of 1917, imperial Germany had moved a good deal closer towards a parliamentary democracy. Eventually, in 1919, the same party leaders who two years before had gathered in the *Interfraktionelle Ausschuß* formed the first parliamentary government of the Weimar Republic.

14

Visions of stateless society

K. STEVEN VINCENT

To be GOVERNED is to be kept in view, inspected, spied upon, directed, legislated, regulated, prosecuted, indoctrinated, preached at, controlled, estimated, valued, censured, commanded by those who do not have the right, the wisdom, nor
the virtue to do so . . . To be GOVERNED is to be at each operation, at each
transaction, at each movement, noted, registered, counted, taxed, stamped, measured, numbered, assessed, licensed, authorised, annotated, admonished, forbidden,
reformed, corrected, punished. It is, under pretext of public utility, and in the
name of the general interest, to be placed under contribution, trained, ransomed,
exploited, monopolised, extorted, pressured, mystified, robbed; then, at the slightest
resistance, at the first word of complaint, to be reprimanded, fined, run down, harassed,
tracked, abused, clubbed, disarmed, bound, imprisoned, shot, machine-gunned, judged,
condemned, deported, sacrificed, sold, betrayed; and, to top it all off, mocked,
ridiculed, outraged, dishonoured. That is government; that is its justice; that is its
morality! (Proudhon 1923b, p. 344)

Like worn-out old men, their skin shriveled and their feet stumbling, gnawed at by
moral sicknesses, incapable of embarking on the tide of new ideas, the States of Europe
squander what strength remains to them, and while living on credit on their past, they
merely hasten their ends by squabbling like aged gossips. (Kropotkin 1992, p. 24)

The Anarchists are simply unterrified Jeffersonian Democrats. They believe that 'the
best government is that which governs least' and that that which governs least is no
government at all. (Tucker 1969, p. 14)

1   Moral and rational foundations

The state has traditionally been viewed as important for a variety of reasons:
as an inescapable condition of order; as an efficient and expert instrument
to co-ordinate affairs of the economy and society; as the locus of community and moral unity. This essay is concerned with those who rejected
these identifications and who believed that the idea of justice required the
abolition of the state and of all other authoritarian institutions not based
on some form of co-operative agreement among autonomous individuals.
Central to this stance – often referred to as anarchism – was the belief that

433

human beings possessed sufficient rational capacities or powerful enough moral sentiments to hold society together; institutions like the state were considered artificial, unnatural and oppressive.

While the theoretical roots of these visions of stateless society can be traced back to the ancient Greek philosopher Zeno of Citium and followed through utopian and millenarian religious movements like the Brethren of the Free Spirit of the thirteenth century and the Anabaptists of the sixteenth century, modern anarchism is rooted in the reorientation of socio-political thought that took place in Europe following the outbreak of the French Revolution.[1] This challenge of the Old Regime opened the gates to numerous and profound examinations of states and other institutions on the grounds of basic principles – religious, republican, natural rights, social utility. Stimulated by revolutionary hopes for fundamental moral and socio-political regeneration, thinkers imaginatively reformulated these basic principles into competing visions of stateless societies.

One thesis of this essay is that nineteenth-century anarchist thinkers were moralists and economists first and only secondarily concerned with politics – indeed they found political practice distasteful and morally compromising, and they viewed traditional political institutions as inept and corrupt. In their eyes, regeneration required the elimination of traditional political institutions like the state and of traditional political practices like elections.

This does not mean that anarchists rejected all organisations that co-ordinated collective actions or that they denied the significance of all interactions that we would consider 'political'. They were anti-political in their rejection of traditional political institutions, but they remained political in their concern to foster just human communities. Characteristically, they looked for ways to bring individuals together in voluntary associations in order to co-ordinate production and to provide social solidarity for other specific purposes. In the words of Jean Grave (1854–1939), the most prominent French anarchist journalist of the late nineteenth century, anarchists wished to demonstrate 'that individuality cannot develop except in the community; that the latter cannot exist unless the former evolves freely; and that they mutually complement each other' (Grave 1893, p. 3). States, however, were unacceptable associations in their eyes because they were coercive, punitive, exploitative, and destructive. And because state action

---

1 Most histories give cursory coverage of pre-revolutionary movements, but the emphasis is on the nineteenth century. See, for example, Guérin 1970; Joll 1964; Préposiet 1993; Woodcock 1970. Most analysts note, however, that anarchism did not become a widespread movement until the late 1870s. On this point, see Cahm 1989; Fleming 1979; Maitron 1975.

was identified with politics, hopes for progress were predicated on the absorption of this political realm into the moral and economic realms.

Before turning to the variety of ways this replacement or absorption of politics was envisioned, it is necessary to stress the moral stance upon which anarchist opposition to the state was based. Anarchists believed living the 'good life' required the complete development of the rational and moral potentialities of individuals. This entailed a rejection of the position that viewed any constraint on individual actions as an impediment to liberty. They believed that the moral life implied a respect for other individuals and for the larger social context; they insisted that fulfilment was intimately connected with the utilisation of one's rational capacities.

This moral dimension needs emphasis because many traditional accounts have assumed that anarchists were dedicated to an absolute ideal of liberty that implied the absence of impediments to whatever the individual wished to do, and that this 'negative' liberty (to use Isaiah Berlin's terminology) was the value to which all other values needed to be subordinated. This, however, proves to be an exaggeration. Anarchists accorded high respect to liberty, but they were dedicated to a type of 'positive' liberty which evaluated actions in accordance with conceptions of the true or essential self – that is, in terms of obedience to normative conceptions of reason and morality (Crowder 1991). Another way of stating this is to point out that 'negative' liberty needed to be subordinated to the moral and rational imperatives of living the 'good life'.

The intellectual traditions that informed the moral thought of anarchist thinkers were numerous; there were intertwinings of secularised religious ideals, normative 'natural laws' believed to be inherent in the universe, and republican beliefs in the importance of altruistic virtue. Pierre-Joseph Proudhon (1809–65), for example, embraced a view of immanent justice which may be interpreted either as a secularised version of Christian morality or as a development of the republican ideal of socio-political virtue – or, perhaps more accurately, a combination of the two (Vincent 1984). When, in 1840, he adopted the label 'anarchist', Proudhon insisted that society must be infused with a social morality that would lead people to recognise the dignity of their neighbours and that would promote the general interests of society over the egoistic interests of isolated individuals (Proudhon 1926b, p. 335).

The failure to recognise the centrality of the moral dimension of anarchist thought has led many to assume that proponents of stateless societies were hopelessly dedicated to disorder. In fact, anarchists disliked chaos, and argued that anarchy, in the words of Elisée Reclus (1830–1905), was 'the highest expression of order' (Reclus 1925). Anarchists believed that stateless societies did not imply disorder because, in their eyes, humans could most successfully achieve rational and moral fulfilment in arenas of human interaction not identified with the state.

Where anarchists differed from other political thinkers was in their belief that the rational and moral capacities of individuals were vigorous enough – or could be improved sufficiently through education – to permit the elimination of the threat and use of force associated with states. There is an obvious assumption here that morality and rationality are not related to state politics; indeed they are diametrically opposed. Anarchists viewed states as poisons that contaminated social relations with impersonality, distrust and resentment. And they argued that it was the inherent nature of states that produced the evil, not a particular form of state control as might be suggested by liberal or socialist theorists. 'Under whatever form that the state exists and functions', wrote Octave Mirbeau (1848–1917) in 1893, 'it is degrading and deadly to human activity: because it prevents the individual from developing his normal sense' (quoted in Carr 1977, p. 38). Michael Bakunin (1814–76) stated this conviction succinctly when he wrote that 'despotism lies less in the form of the state or of power than in their very principle' (Bakunin 1961–81, II, p. 327).

Social authority, therefore, to the extent needed, was to be exercised by local bodies or replaced by non-institutional action like public censure. William Godwin (1756–1836) favoured the context of conversation – of close interpersonal discussion – as the best means of fostering both the growth of reason that makes individuals independent and the expansion of sincerity that ties individuals together. Proudhon favoured the association of the workshop and, in his later federalist phase, regional communities as the appropriate loci for stimulating respect and the altruistic concern for others. Bakunin and the anarchists connected with the Jura Federation during the 1870s, like Reclus and Paul Brousse (1844–1912), also searched for social solidarity in the context of trade and industrial groupings (*corps de métier* or *la corporation*), organised federally and by contract. Brousse, however, distinguished himself by emphasising that the commune was the privileged agent for the achievement of a stateless society.[2] During

2 As David Stafford points out, this is the basis for Brousse's later transition from anarchism (which he embraced between 1873 and 1878/80) to 'reformism', a stance that also focused on the Commune (Stafford 1971).

the 1880s, Pëtr Kropotkin (1842–1921), Reclus and Grave translated anarchism into a language of solidarity and mutual aid, emphasising extended neighbourhoods that fostered benevolence and reciprocal support. After the mid-1890s, anarchist-syndicalists like Paul Delesalle, looked to syndicates as the context for education and libertarian organisation (Jennings 1990; Julliard 1988; Maitron 1985, pp. 62–102).

Central to all anarchist visions was the conviction that the growth of solidarity, neighbourhoods, free associations, syndicates, etc., would lead to the development of moral and rational individuality and would stimulate co-operation and community. And, all of this would make coercive social authority, especially that connected with the state, less and less necessary. It was this categorical opposition to the state which separated anarchists from their closest ideological neighbours: from public service socialists like César De Paepe, who argued that some administrative concerns extended beyond the competence of local bodies like communes and required a federative body that one could legitimately call a state; from reformist socialists like Jean Jaurès, who argued that in some contexts militants should operate within the existing political system to achieve concrete reforms; and from Marxists, who shared the goal of 'an association, in which the free development of each is the condition for the free development of all',[3] but who believed that the elimination of capitalism required the intervening stage of proletarian dictatorship.

2 Scientific assumptions

During the nineteenth century, the anarchist stance in opposition to the state and in favour of non-authoritarian associations was closely connected to two assumptions. The first was that social and moral laws could be discerned through a reasoned examination of human nature, human societies and the larger universe. This stance was connected to what appears to us today as an inflated belief in the efficacy of science. Nineteenth-century anarchists believed that, just as Champolion had discovered the key that unlocked the mystery of the Egyptian hieroglyphs, so they would discover the secrets of human behaviour and social interaction that would permit a scientific view of politics and economics. It speaks volumes that Charles Fourier (1772–1837) referred to himself as the 'Messiah of Reason' and that Proudhon

---

3 This quote comes from the end of section II of Marx and Engels' 'Manifesto of the Communist Party', originally published in 1848.

argued that 'all that which is the material of legislation and of politics is an object of science, not opinion . . . Justice and legality are two things as independent of our assent as mathematical truth' (Beecher 1986, p. 497; Proudhon 1926a, p. 45). Brousse summarised his analytic method in typical nineteenth-century terms: 'to impartially reunify the facts, to deduce from them a general law which permits the future to be foreseen'. He referred to anarchism as 'a scientifically constituted society' (quoted in Stafford 1971, pp. 61, 78).

Such beliefs in 'science' were common throughout the century, though the scientific model from which social science was extrapolated changed in the late nineteenth century, as Darwinian and evolutionary theories replaced the more static imagery associated with Newtonian mechanics, physiology and mathematics. Reclus, for example, who was a professional geographer, believed that the progressive evolution of humanity was based on 'laws' which could be discovered through observation – laws like solidarity and brotherhood, which were destined to burst through current institutional restraints (including state-imposed 'laws' which, Reclus insisted, violated the laws immanent in human nature). Kropotkin and Grave, also reflecting the influence of evolutionary theory, argued that anarchism conformed to the physiological and psychological nature of man and therefore enjoyed the stature of scientific truth. 'Anarchy,' Grave wrote in 1899, 'is a theory supporting itself on rational bases.' Anarchists are distinctive, he claimed, because they support themselves 'on their observations, [and] they deduce logical, natural laws for the organisation of a better society' (Grave 1899, pp. 2–3).[4]

The second assumption, closely connected with the first, was that moral and rational advancement would occur. There was a general faith in historical progress – a confidence that things were improving and would continue to get better. This optimism was a legacy of Enlightenment thought, but it also reflected a widespread nineteenth-century belief in secular and scientific advancement. Some of our thinkers went through pessimistic periods when it seemed to them that humanity was destined temporarily to regression,

---

4 Anarchists are often characterised as woolly-minded romantics who rejected science and the modern world. Albert Lindemann, for example, writes that anarchists 'were distrustful . . . of modern progress and of "scientific" or deterministic answers to what they considered the ultimately unpredictable situations of life' (Lindemann 1983, p. 158). This descriptive statement fits only a minority of anarchist writers, most notably a group of late nineteenth-century cultural anarchists. This is not to deny that anarchist thinkers differed concerning the importance of science. Marie Fleming correctly points out, for example, that spiritual descendants of Bakunin like Reclus and Kropotkin added a 'scientific' dimension that was largely absent from the writings of Bakunin himself (Fleming 1988, p. 22).

and most of them fully recognised that history was not an uninterrupted story of improvement, but in general they sustained a belief that moral truth would prevail, that rational advancement would continue, and that states would wither away. 'It is incontestable', wrote Reclus for example, 'that humanity advances in the direction of progress' (quoted in Fleming 1979, p. 39). This was a view of progress that included an abounding faith, shared by most of their contemporaries, in limitless natural resources. Anarchists were critical of the inequitable distribution of natural and social wealth, but they did not express any anxiety concerning the plentiful extent of the earth's riches.

Like most other nineteenth-century political thinkers, in short, most anarchists believed that it was possible to recognise and discover moral and social 'laws' – 'laws' that were at the same time descriptive and normative. And they assumed that once these laws were conceptualised and articulated, progress would result. However foreign such beliefs sound to our more sceptical and cynical modern ears, they were common elements of nineteenth-century socio-political thought.

3   Strategy

The existence of moral and social laws that presaged a better future did not mean that human effort was not needed. Anarchists believed that progress would result only when individuals came to understand the need for moral actions and social co-operation, and when significant numbers began to act on this understanding. The central importance of education is a natural outgrowth of this assumption. Anarchists often saw their role as that of a teacher: Proudhon, for example, insisted on the importance of articulating the 'worker idea' (Proudhon 1923c, I, pp. 74–5, 1924, pp. 89ff.); Reclus conceived in the 1870s a plan for a 'scientific socialist education' (Fleming 1979, pp. 163–8); Grave wrote of the need to disseminate 'propaganda' to emancipate people from prejudice, ignorance and the intellectual supports of the bourgeois system (Grave 1893, pp. 34–8).

Beyond calls for education, there were significant divergences concerning strategy within anarchist thought. One common generalisation, however – that they were akin to 'primitive' messianic religious rebels of earlier centuries[5] – must be rejected. However strongly their theories bore the

---

5 This is the argument of Joll 1964, pp. 17–27 and of Hobsbawm 1959, p. 83.

imprint of a religious legacy (and there is no doubt that some, like Godwin and Proudhon, reinterpreted and assimilated religious elements within secular frames of reference), nineteenth-century anarchists did not have the millenarian expectations nor the depth of religious belief that such generalisations suggest. They were secular thinkers (Tolstoyan anarchists excepted) who believed in the likelihood of progress towards higher moral consciousness and less authoritarian societies.

But they imagined a large variety of means – all, of course, dismissive of traditional forms of political activity and of state-regulated economic strategies. Early anarchists like Godwin and Proudhon disapproved of revolutionary upheavals, believing that rational discussion, education and (for Proudhon) credit reform and productive co-operation based on contracts were the appropriate means for ushering in the stateless society of their dreams. Later anarchists like Bakunin, Brousse, Kropotkin, Reclus and Grave believed that education, monetary reform and workers' associations were insufficient and that popular revolt was necessary.

One of the most controversial concepts to emerge among anarchists was 'propaganda by the deed', a notion that can be traced to anarchists in Italy and Switzerland during the 1870s and which became current after the Berne demonstration commemorating the Paris Commune on 18 March 1877, and the Benevento uprising of peasants in southern Italy in April 1877. In 1881, at an international meeting in London called by anarchists and social revolutionaries, 'propaganda by the deed' was formally adopted as a tactic.[6]

Whether 'propaganda by the deed' was confined to insurrection or sanctioned acts of terrorism was a hotly debated issue. Many late nineteenth-century anarchists believed in the necessity of violent insurrection – here they differed from their 'rationalist' (Godwinian) and their 'mutualist' (Proudhonian) predecessors. But most did not support individual acts of political terrorism. The outbreak of terrorist actions during *l'ère des attentats* (1892–4) – when self-professed anarchists like Ravachol, Auguste Vaillant, Emile Henry and Santiago Salvador French set off bombs in public places and in the homes of public figures – is telling in this regard, for most anarchist writers were embarrassed with the association and condemned the acts, even if they were reluctant to condemn the actors who were depicted as driven to action by circumstances (Carr 1977, pp. 56–82; Maitron 1964). In 1891, Kropotkin wrote that 'it is not by heroic acts that revolutions are

---

6 For an extensive analysis of the development of the idea of 'propaganda by the deed', see Cahm 1989.

made . . . Revolution, above all, is a popular movement.'[7] And Jean Grave defensively stated that 'we are not among those who preach acts of violence' (Grave 1893, p. 210). But, it is also clear that Kropotkin and Grave were disturbed only by violence directed at individuals; violence that attacked institutions and that was part of a revolution was entirely justified. 'Once the struggle has begun', wrote Grave, 'sentimentality will have no place, the multitude will distrust all phrase makers and unmercifully crush all who try to stand in the way' (Grave 1893, p. 275).

Reclus and the majority of Italian anarchists refused to make these distinctions between insurrection and terrorism. They advocated 'propaganda by the deed' in the late 1870s; they defended anarchist 'thefts' in the 1880s; they wrote admiringly of the terrorists of the 1890s. Similarly, the American anarchist Emma Goldman (1869–1940) argued in 1911 that virtually every act of anarchist violence could be understood and justified in a moral context; desperate individuals were 'impelled' to act 'by the tremendous pressure of conditions making life unbearable' (Goldman 1983, p. 266). The popular image of the anarchist as a bomb-throwing extremist, not surprisingly, grew accordingly.

For most anarchists, however, individual acts of violence were not viewed as likely to lead to any positive transformation. Anarchists were forced, therefore, to consider other means of achieving the stateless society – means that covered the spectrum from relying on reason and education (Godwin, especially, but also the others), through financial reforms like the 'People's Bank' (Proudhon) and the elimination of inheritance (Bakunin), to mass violence and revolutionary action.

Related to the issue of strategy was the question of appropriate economic change. Here, too, there were significant divergences. Thomas Hodgskin (1787–1869), proto-libertarian political economists like Jean-Baptiste Say (1767–1832) and individualist anarchists like Stephen Pearl Andrews (1812–86) believed that justice and prosperity would emerge from a market economy, protected from any intervention by the state. Others, like Bakunin and Kropotkin, desired a system of common ownership in which goods would be produced by workers' associations and independent communes and would be distributed either on the basis of labour (Bakunin's ideal of 'anarchist collectivism') or on the basis of need (Kropotkin's ideal of 'anarchist communism'). Still others, like Proudhon, can fairly be placed between these two positions: he recommended a 'mutualist' position in

---

7 *Le Révolté*, no. 32 (18 March 1891).

which private stewardship was appropriate for some types of production like agriculture, but where associative control was needed in industry. What all anarchists shared was a belief that decentralised production was preferable to production that was controlled by the state.

4 William Godwin and rationalist anarchism

William Godwin was the first writer to make a reputation condemning government. Godwin believed that through education and through the use of reason, men and women could make wise, benevolent and virtuous decisions, and that these decisions would make government unnecessary. In his most famous work, *Enquiry Concerning Political Justice*, first published in 1793, Godwin argued that moral truth was eternal and immutable, not relative to human passions, and that this truth was able to be discerned by men and women who used reason and judgement. This faith in reason was coupled with an optimistic view of human nature. Godwin believed that once truth was perceived, it would be freely applied. Indeed, he argued that our capacities for reasoning and our grasp of truths had grown progressively as time had passed; history, in sum, was a record of improvement. Governments, unfortunately, obstructed the full exercise of private judgement that was synonymous with moral improvement and the full growth of independence. Based on force and stasis, governments had to be condemned in favour of the right and duty of each individual to act according to the full and free exercise of his private judgement.

Godwin's stance was largely a secularised version of Rational Dissent, which both shaped his moral-rational philosophy and nurtured his distrust of government (Claeys 1983; Philp 1986; Stafford 1980, 1987, pp. 121–45). It was the collision of Godwin's deeply rooted Dissenting moral and intellectual dispositions with Enlightenment thought and with the French Revolution that resulted in the distinctive anarchist stance of Godwin's books of the 1790s.

Godwin was the son of an East Anglian Congregationalist minister and was educated at Hindolveston by a Dr Samuel Newton, who adhered to a sect close to Congregationalism called Sandemanian.[8] Sandemanians wished to return to a pure Calvinism, but unlike many of the other Dissenting sects (the Methodists, for example) they rejected emotionalism and mass enthusiasm in favour of rationalism and strict morality. Godwin insisted that he

8 For biographical details, see Marshall 1984; Philp 1986; Woodcock 1989.

was still a strict Calvinist and Sandemanian when he emerged from his formal education in 1778, and he briefly became a minister. However, reading texts of the French *philosophes* and of the Socinian Joseph Priestley stimulated new religious doubts, and by 1787 he had given up the ministry and lost his faith. What he had not lost was his attachment to many of the beliefs that characterised his Calvinist roots: his ascetic dislike of worldly pleasures; his assertion of the value of independence and distrust of institutions; his praise of candour; his faith in reason; his focus on conduct and duty. Throughout his life, Godwin retained a belief that we are obliged and motivated to act in accordance with truths perceived through public discussion and private judgement. These moral truths are objective, immutable, timeless. Through the full exercise of reason, which is dependent on feeling but not a slave to feeling, one can discern these truths, which it is then a duty to enact. Godwin retained a stern rational moralism that is difficult not to interpret as a secular version of Sandemanian Calvinism.[9]

Godwin's exposure to French Enlightenment thought reinforced many of these stances. Reading Montesquieu and Rousseau, for example, introduced Godwin to conceptions of independence and political morality that had been central to republican thought since Aristotle (Monro 1953, pp. 57–132; Pocock 1975). Like Montesquieu and Rousseau, Godwin believed that individuals must overcome selfishness and had a duty to place the interests of others over their own interests. Godwin's development of this idea consisted in giving republican notions of virtue a utilitarian twist: he suggested that disinterested action – which he termed benevolence – was the occasion for experiencing the most exquisite form of happiness. Benevolent sacrifice did not entail a renunciation of pleasure; rather, Godwin suggested that 'no man reaps so copious a harvest of pleasure as he who thinks only of the pleasures of other men' (Godwin 1976, Book IV, xi, p. 395).

Eighteenth-century republicans generally assumed that the exercise of virtue or benevolence required independence, rigorous honesty and the avoidance of the over-refined affectations of luxurious urban living. Godwin, deeply influenced by Rousseau, was no exception.[10] Like Rousseau, for example, Godwin was critical of the unauthenticity of social mores which prevented individuals honestly speaking their minds; Godwin's defence of 'candour' is strikingly similar to Rousseau's preference for the

---

9 Max Beer has pointed out that Godwin's 'criticism is one long Nonconformist sermon, vivacious, diffuse, and sometimes powerful, but always based on abstract reasoning' (Beer 1948, p. 115).

10 For an interesting analysis of the influence of Rousseau on Godwin – one that differs in some particulars from that presented here – see Crowder 1991, pp. 40–73.

transparency of *amour de soi-même*. Also like Rousseau, Godwin was fearful of the possible dependence of one individual on another, something that was fostered by associations and other co-operative organisations. Godwin once wrote to Shelley that the 'pervading principle' of his book *Political Justice* was 'that association is the most ill-chosen and ill-qualified mode of endeavouring to promote the political happiness of mankind' (Godwin to Shelley, 4 March 1812, cited in Marshall 1984, p. 296).

Where Godwin parted company with Rousseau was in the latter's belief that governments were not necessarily identified with dependency. Rousseau had suggested that a positive form of politics was possible, if it were based on law and if the particular wills of individuals were replaced by the sovereignty of the general will. Such a political association could avoid personal dependency. To clarify this distinction, Rousseau contrasted 'dependence on things', which was natural and affected all humans equally (dependence on the law of gravity, for example), with 'dependence on men', which was unnatural and harmful to freedom and morality. Rousseau believed that the morally debilitating dependence of one human being on another could be avoided in a political system that relied on a morally benign dependency that paralleled the natural 'dependence on things' – namely in a political system that located supreme political authority in all the members of the community.[11] Godwin, on the other hand, made no such distinctions, and in what became a classic anarchist position, he concluded that all governments inevitably fostered personal dependence and worked at the expense of making men virtuous. All governments, therefore, should be eliminated.

There was a convergence of republican themes and Calvinist principles in Godwin's thoughts concerning the interrelationship of dependence and politics. Both traditions praised independence and condemned luxury, and both traditions were critical of existing governmental institutions. The result, in Godwin's case, was the transferral of the concern for promoting justice from the political to the moral realm. Or, to use the terminology of republicanism, the focus shifted from 'principle' to 'spirit' – from faith in political institutions to faith in socio-political mores, mores which in Godwin's case were to be based on reason and private judgement. As he put it in *Political Justice*, 'virtue demands the active employment of an ardent

---

11 Rousseau contrasts these two types of dependence in *Émile* (Rousseau (1970, IV, p. 311). Also see the discussions by Durkheim and Grimsley (Durkheim 1960, pp. 88–95; Grimsley 1973, pp. 101ff.).

mind in the promotion of the general good' (Godwin 1976, Book I, vii, p. 153).

The moral basis of Godwin's philosophy is evident in his stance that duties were to take precedence over rights. Unlike his contemporary Thomas Paine, who argued that duties depended on the prior existence of rights, Godwin emphasised duties, and argued that rights depended upon man's fulfilment of the duty to act in conformance with justice.

There is no sphere in which a human being can be supposed to act, where one mode of proceeding will not, in every given instance, be more reasonable than any other mode. That mode the being is bound by every principle of justice to pursue . . . If then every one of our actions falls within the province of morals, it follows that we have no rights in relation to selecting them. No one will maintain, that we have a right to trespass upon the dictates of morality. (Godwin 1976, Book II, v, p. 192)

There was also no room in Godwin's system for self-interest, a position that was highlighted in Godwin's ongoing argument with Thomas Malthus (Rosen 1987, pp. 120–43).

The event which, in Godwin's case, served as the catalyst for bringing into focus all of his thoughts about politics and morality was the French Revolution. This was true in two ways: it stimulated him intellectually to embark on theoretical works like *Political Justice*; it also created the environment for more practical writing about English political and constitutional issues. He wrote essays, for example, defending reformers who had been arrested by the English government and tried for treason. Indeed, it was the defence of English liberties – liberties which Godwin judged the government to be endangering – that provided the enduring focus for Godwin's practical political writings. He wrote an especially impassioned defence of liberty when the government introduced the Treason and Sedition Acts in 1795.[12]

One notable aspect of these essays is their repudiation of appeals to popular opinion, an indication of the moderate nature of Godwin's stance. His 1795 pamphlet against the Treason and Sedition Acts, for example, was published under the name of 'a lover of order', and it contained passages warning against 'the headlong rage of faction' and critical of organisations like the London Corresponding Society that would 'not endure to hear of any cautionary restraints upon freedom' (Godwin 1993, Book II,

---

12 William Godwin, *Considerations on Lord Grenville's and Mr. Pitt's Bills Concerning Treasonable and Seditious Practices, and Unlawful Assemblies*, in Godwin 1993, II, pp. 123–62.

pp. 123–5). In 1797, in a reference to English enthusiasts of the French Revolution (including himself), he lamented that 'the friends of innovation were somewhat too imperious in their tone' (Godwin 1993, Book v, p. 78). And in 1801, he described the reign of Robespierre as 'atrocious and inhuman' (Godwin 1993, Book II, p. 167). By 1806, he was writing that change in England should be 'gentle, temperate, almost insensible' (Rosen 1987, p. 198). This moderation also informed theoretical works like *Political Justice*,[13] but it is particularly pronounced in his more practical writings. For all the apparent radicalism of Godwin's repudiation of dependence and government, therefore, he consistently warned against violent change. Godwin suggested that reason and benevolence were the appropriate paths to political reform and social transformation, and he argued that the appropriate locus for the flowering of reasoned consideration of these issues was intimate conversation.

The French Revolution confirmed Godwin not only in his insistence that reform was to be achieved by philosophy and reason rather than by agitation; it also pushed him towards a more critical, but also more conservative, position concerning the issues of property and economic well-being. In the revised edition of *Political Justice* published in 1796, Godwin commended the increased prosperity created by commercial society and reaffirmed his position that the state should play no role in economic concerns. But he also reaffirmed his critical stance towards luxury and gaudy ostentation, continued to insist that all had a right to subsistence and expanded his criticisms of the inequality, avarice, and greed fostered by commercial society. His proposals for effecting change, however, remained extremely moderate. He made it clear that reform should come about peacefully and that some physical property inequities were justified. In his consideration of how private modes of the expenditure of wealth would benefit the poor (public expenditure was precluded because there was to be no state), he concluded that inequities were justified if they led to beneficent expenditure – if wealth was 'applied to cheer the miserable, to relieve the oppressed, to assist the manly adventurer, to advance science, and to encourage art' (Godwin 1993, V, p. 159).

What was needed to overcome poverty, therefore, was to change the opinions which had predominated in the past and which continued to

---

13 In the *Enquiry Concerning Political Justice*, Godwin writes that 'Revolution is instigated by a horror against tyranny, yet its own tyranny is not without peculiar aggravations. There is no period more at war with the existence of liberty' (Godwin 1976, IV, ii, p. 270).

control understanding in the present. What was needed, in short, was more reason and more enlightened education. Especially pernicious, in Godwin's mind, were those faulty opinions that were insinuated by the presence of government, and to counter these Godwin advocated more liberty and less government.[14] Suspicious of all associations larger than the intimate rational conversation between two equals, Godwin discounted civil and political liberty for intellectual liberty. He had the belief – common in the late eighteenth century but unusual in the nineteenth – that rational intellectual growth would produce justice and happiness. 'Make men wise', he wrote, 'and, by that very operation, you make them free. Civil liberty follows as a consequence of this; no usurped power can stand against the artillery of opinion' (Godwin 1976, Book IV, i, p. 263).

For Godwin, therefore, the exercise of intellectual liberty would serve as a bridge between the individual and the social. This eighteenth-century, pre-sociological account of how individuals combined and operated as social wholes gave immense privilege to education and to literary and verbal skills. It was based on the conviction – some would prefer to call it a pious hope – that conversation, reason and enlightened commerce would be sufficient to improve the human condition.

5 Thomas Hodgskin and individualist anarchism

Thomas Hodgskin shared with William Godwin an antipathy towards government, but the focus of his writings was not political justice but political economy and the harmonious natural order that he believed God had provided for mankind. The free market replaced private judgement and public discussion as the context for the exercise of liberty and the realisation of justice.

A naval officer who saw service in the Napoleonic wars, Thomas Hodgskin got into a dispute concerning military discipline when he was twenty-five years old, which led to his being placed on half pay and eventually to his exit from the service. He travelled on the European continent

---

14 To the extent that Godwin considered institutional organisation, he preferred limited democracy with most decisions left to the prerogatives of small communities. This, he believed, would be the regime that would best allow reason to broaden. He spoke with approval of communities which 'were contented with a small district, with a proviso of confederation in cases of necessity', and contrasted such communities with those that aspired 'to embrace a vast territory, and [to] glut their vanity with ideas of empire' (Godwin 1976, VII, iii, p. 644). But such institutional concessions were made only reluctantly by Godwin, who clearly preferred the more intimate context of rational conversation.

after the end of the Napoleonic wars (1815–18), lived for some years in Edinburgh, and then moved to London, where he worked on various journals and wrote the books that made his reputation as a critic of government and a founder of proletarian economics.[15]

Hodgskin's most famous publication was his 1825 book (first published by *Mechanics' Magazine*) *Labour Defended Against the Claims of Capital*, where he challenged the view that capital was productive. His economic doctrine is based on the distinction between labourers and idlers and on a critique of what he judged to be the unjustified power given to the latter group by governments and legal conventions. Workers 'are the main pillars of the social edifice', according to Hodgskin (Hodgskin 1922, p. 50). They produce all value, and commodities ought to be exchanged in proportion to the quantity of labour which their production has cost. Unfortunately, labourers have been prevented from enjoying this value because of social regulations and laws that favour the accumulation of riches by landowning and capitalist idlers.

The distress our people suffer... and the poverty we all complain of, is not caused by nature, but by some social institutions, which either will not allow the labourer to exert his productive power, or which rob him of its fruits. (Hodgskin 1966, pp. 267–8)

Hodgskin's books of the late 1820s and early 1830s (in addition to *Labour Defended*, he published *Popular Political Economy* (1827) and *Natural and Artificial Right of Property Contrasted* (1832)) were devoted to defending this position against economists who argued that land and capital were productive, and against Malthusians who claimed that population growth entailed subsistence wages (or worse) for labourers. Against the economists, Hodgskin argued that it was not landlords and capitalists who stimulated growth by their investment and directions; all benefits attributed to these in fact 'arise from co-existing and skilled labour' (Hodgskin 1922, p. 19). Labour created value, and if the exploitative relationship between labour and capitalist were eliminated a 'natural' order of free exchange would allow labourers to enjoy the fruits of their efforts. Against the Malthusians, Hodgskin claimed that there was no evidence that population growth led to economic and demographic disaster; rather, growing populations were the natural source of all progress and improvement.

15 G. D. H. Cole suggests that Hodgskin 'founded... proletarian economics' (Hodgskin 1922, p. 17). Max Beer recommends Hodgskin's *Labour Defended Against the Claims of Capital* as 'one of the most aggressive and closely reasoned pamphlets of the labour and socialist movement' (Beer 1948, p. 261).

Both stances relied on an underlying belief, common among deists of this era, that there was a naturally harmonious order to the world, an order that Hodgskin argued was violated by the artifice of legislative restrictions, especially the artificial rights of property. Misery and poverty are created, according to Hodgskin, by legislative meddling; laws are sinister because they are implemented for the defence of the private interests of the privileged and powerful. The so-called iron law of wages, for example, is a result not of natural competitive forces, but of the unreasonable power that legal arrangements have given to capitalists and landlords. Hodgskin believed, in his own words, 'that all law-making, except gradually and quietly to repeal all existing laws, is arrant humbug' (Hodgskin 1973, p. i).

The proper standard for all judgement, according to Hodgskin, was natural law, which was often opposed to man-made positive law. As he put it in his *Popular Political Economy*, 'there already exists a code of natural laws, regulating and determining the production of wealth' (Hodgskin 1966, p. xx). This contrasts sharply with the views of, say, Bentham and James Mill who believed that rights were the result of legislation. For Hodgskin, man is born within society and with natural rights, and human laws could not conceivably be considered as creating either. Indeed, such laws could at best record the existence of natural rights.

A similar dichotomy informs Hodgskin's view of property. He begins with a Lockean view of one's 'natural' property rights in those things with which one has mixed one's labour.

There is no other wealth in the world but what is created by labour, and by it continually renewed. This principle, now universally acknowledged, makes the right of property appear more absolute and definite than it was in Mr. Locke's comprehension, because the right to own land is in fact only the right to own what agricultural or other labour produces. (Hodgskin 1973, p. 36)

This must be distinguished from the 'artificial' right of property which is established by law:

The law . . . is a set of rules and practices laid down and established, partly by the legislator, party by custom, and partly by the judges, supported and enforced by all the power of the government, and intended as far as our subject is concerned, to secure the appropriation of the whole annual produce of labour. Nominally these rules and practices are said to have for their object to secure property in land; to appropriate tithes, and to procure a revenue for the government; actually and in fact they are intended to appropriate to the law-makers the produce of those who cultivate the soil, prepare clothing, or distribute what is produced among the different classes, and among different communities. Such is law. (Hodgskin 1973, pp. 46–7)

449

The law is controlled, that is, by the wealthy and the powerful for their own economic domination. But this 'artificial' right is a travesty of justice. 'The natural right of property far from being protected, is systematically violated, and both government and law seem to exist chiefly and solely, in order to protect and organise the most efficacious means of protecting the violation' (Hodgskin 1973, p. 53).

The solution is quite simple: eliminate the legal regime which allows non-labourers to accumulate artificial property; provide labourers the freedom to exchange the natural property which they produce. Hodgskin exemplifies what Elie Halévy has termed the 'anarchist prejudice' on issues of political systems and juridical frameworks, for he did not attack particular laws but rather the idea of law itself (Halévy 1956, pp. 171–6). It is interesting, in this regard, that Hodgskin even came to condemn workers' combinations as inappropriate interferences between capital and labour, though in his writings of the 1820s he had seen these as necessary to protect the interest of wage-earners against the demands of capitalists. As Halévy has pointed out, when confronted with the choice between bourgeois free trade and working-class 'interventionism', Hodgskin chose the former (Halévy 1956, pp. 145–7). What Hodgskin came to rely upon, therefore, was what Adam Smith had called the 'higgling of the market'. He opposed Owenite calls for the elimination of competition, a position that clearly separated Hodgskin from the socialists.[16]

Hodgskin was convinced that there were moral laws analogous to laws describing the movements of the physical universe. As he put it in *Travels in the North of Germany* (1820), 'the moral laws of nature are as regular and unalterable as her physical laws. He, who has so beautifully constructed our bodies, has not left our conduct, on which our happiness depends, to be regulated by chance . . . Regular laws are established in the moral world, and we have a capacity to discover them, and so to regulate our conduct by them, that we may diminish or destroy every species of evil' (quoted in Halévy 1956, p. 51). Such a position explains Hodgskin's opposition to Benthamite utilitarianism, which reduced moral considerations to individual prudential calculations. Hodgskin believed that there were moral promptings which inhered in all persons and which, if listened to, would provide the basis

---

16 George Lichtheim concludes that Hodgskin's theory is 'labourist rather than socialist' (Lichtheim 1969, p. 135). Some of Hodgskin's contemporaries were critical of his acceptance of individual competition. See, for example, William Thompson (1827).

for the harmonious interactions of all humanity. This too was the realm of 'natural laws'.

Hodgskin believed in the correctness of his analysis because he thought he understood the 'natural laws' which regulated the production of wealth, and because he was convinced that production was a part of 'a complicated and harmonious whole' which 'springs from a higher source than the fore-planning wisdom of man' – a higher source that he also referred to as the Master Power and God (Hodgskin 1973, pp. 261–8; see also pp. 28–35). Such beliefs – that a Supreme Being had made provisions for the terrestrial happiness of mankind and that there were scientific laws governing socio-economic relations – are a particularly stark example of a common nineteenth-century tendency that we have already noted; namely, the belief in 'laws' which were descriptive and normative, and which when discovered by the reasoned intellect would unlock the secrets of social interaction.[17] It was this optimistic scientism, based on a deistic belief in a harmonious world order, that allowed Hodgskin to, in effect, turn Malthus on his head: while the latter believed that there were secular laws of demographic and productive change that always led to want and scarcity, Hodgskin believed that these 'natural laws' were benevolent and favourable to humanity's economic development.

Hodgskin's belief in the existence of such natural laws and his conviction that these laws were at once harmonious and beneficent for humanity found echoes in other contexts, most notably the United States, where the widespread influence of natural rights philosophy and classical liberal economic doctrine provided a congenial cultural environment for individualist anarchism. Josiah Warren (1798–1874), for example, viewed government and man-made laws as the chief enemy of a free and just society, arguing that the 'sovereignty of the individual' would flourish if oppressive governmental rules and institutions were abolished. Warren – who is often referred to as 'the first American anarchist' – believed that the economic order should be based on 'equitable commerce', a system resting on the idea that the value of goods should reflect the labour expended in production. Suspicious of any associations which constrained individual sovereignty (he was an opponent even of apprenticeship), Warren expected sellers to act

17 Illustrative here is the epigraph by J.-B. Say that Hodgskin placed at the beginning of *Popular Political Economy*: 'The laws which determine the prosperity of nations are not the work of man: they are derived from the nature of things. We do not establish; we discover them' (Hodgskin 1966). On this general issue, see Stack 1998.

ethically in pricing their goods, and he expected buyers to pay this fair price and to provide information concerning their additional economic needs (Hall 1974; Martin 1957, pp. 11–34; Warren 1852). Though Warren relied less on the 'higgling of the market' than did Hodgskin, there is a strong similarity in their views of economic value and of the existence of 'natural laws'.

Even closer to Hodgskin were two of Warren's contemporaries, Lysander Spooner (1808–84) and Stephen Pearl Andrews. Spooner firmly defended 'natural law' – which he believed self-evident to all – from man-made statute law and, like Hodgskin, he also believed in absolutely unfettered competition. Pearl Andrews is best remembered for his attempt, in *The Science of Society* (1851), to provide individualist anarchism with an irrefutable scientific defence. Arguing that it is a 'natural law' that no two individuals are alike biologically, he concluded that each individual should be absolutely sovereign. The most famous exponent of individualist anarchism in the United States during the nineteenth century was Benjamin R. Tucker (1854–1939), who also believed that a truly equitable system would emerge naturally from the self-interested behaviour of individualists operating in a completely free market.

Individualist anarchism is, of all the visions of stateless society, the closest to liberal ideals of individual sovereignty and *laissez-faire* conceptions of the market, which the anarchists wished to purge of all legal and state-enforced restraints. Like Hodgskin, American individualist anarchists were partisans of private property and were committed to free market economic ideals. They believed that the system of free exchange could provide the model for all social relations.

There was an analogous intellectual tradition in France that grew out of Physiocratic economic thought of the eighteenth century. The best-known nineteenth-century exemplar of this tradition was Jean-Baptiste Say, the French political economist often credited with popularising Adam Smith's *Wealth of Nations* on the continent of Europe. By the time Say wrote his famous work, *Traité d'Économie Politique* (1803), he had shed many of his earlier hopes for a political republic and for state-directed monetary policy and, instead, focused on the science of political economy. Political economy, he argued, was to create wealth and to ameliorate the harsh inequality and dire poverty that plagued modern societies, and it was to do this independent of government. Say was also concerned with social mores, believing that it was necessary to foster a moral culture of industriousness and frugality. Unlike eighteenth-century *doux commerce* theorists, therefore, who believed that commerce fostered an advance of 'politeness' and good manners, Say argued that the growth of commerce in a society would be positive only if republican mores – industriousness, frugality, honesty, courage, temperance, wisdom, benevolence and mutual respect – were widespread. Without this culture, according to Say, commerce could lead to libertinism, moral laxity and ultimately international war. What he shared with the individualist anarchists is a belief that economic reforms must precede or replace constitution building; the economy was more central than the state.

A less 'republican' and more libertarian version of market reform was envisaged by Frédéric Bastiat (1801–50). Bastiat believed that the free market was inherently a source of 'economic harmony' among individuals, and that the role of government should be restricted to protecting life, liberty and property. Famous in France during the late 1840s for his arguments in favour of economic freedom, Bastiat also co-operated with leaders of the British Anti-Corn Law League such as Richard Cobden. In his books *Sophismes Économiques* (1845) and *Harmonies Économiques* (1850), he opposed all taxes on land and all forms of trade restrictions, endearing him to later economists of the Austrian School and presaging late nineteenth-century Social Darwinists who attacked the state.

The most famous English proponent of a proto-libertarian attack on the state was Herbert Spencer (1820–1903). In his youthful writings Spencer had argued for land nationalisation, but by the time of his greatest fame in the 1880s and 1890s, he was the leading theorist of the so-called Individualists who were defending what they viewed as the true principles of liberalism that the English Liberal Party was in the process of abandoning. State action, the Individualists argued, should be kept to a strict minimum; legal restrictions of liberty were justified only when absolutely necessary for the preservation of individual liberty. Beyond the essential duties to provide for military defence, for the administration of justice and for the enforcement of contracts, government actions were illegitimate. There should be no involvement of the state in education, religion, the economy or care for the indigent. As Spencer put it in *The Man versus the State* (1884), 'the liberty which a citizen enjoys is to be measured, not by the nature of the government machinery he lives under . . . but by the relative paucity of the restraints it imposes on him' (Spencer 1969, p. 79).

6   Pierre-Joseph Proudhon and mutualist anarchism

Pierre-Joseph Proudhon was the most famous nineteenth-century opponent
of the state. He was the first to call himself an anarchist (in his 1840 book
What is Property?) and the most successful in popularising a position critical
of authoritarian structures like the church and the state.

Proudhon was proud of his humble origins in the French Jura, never
hesitating to remind acquaintances that he was, as he wrote in 1855, 'raised
in the customs, the mores and the thought of the proletariat' (Haubtmann
1969, p. 28). The connection continued throughout his life. When he was
eighteen years old, family finances forced him to discontinue his formal
education and, yielding to the promptings of his father, he became an
apprentice printer. He worked at this trade off and on between 1827 and
1843, and with a few friends he briefly attempted to operate a printing
house in Besançon (1836–43), an unhappy experience that left him heavily
in debt. He also spent the years between 1843 and 1847 working for a
shipping firm located in Lyon, which exposed him to a wide range of
business practices.[18]

Though disrupted because of financial need, Proudhon's education was
extensive given his working-class background. During his adolescent years
(1820–7), he attended the Collège Royal de Besançon on a scholarship.
He also received, as a young man, an award administered by the Academy
of Besançon which allowed him to spend several years (1838–41) in Paris,
reading, writing and attending the classes of prominent intellectuals like
Michelet and the economist Jérôme-Adolphe Blanqui. From this time forward, he devoted himself to writing, except when forced by financial need
to take other jobs. From his late twenties he published a very large quantity
of books and articles: as one observer noted, when Proudhon found himself
with pen in hand, he seemed to have a fit of eloquence.

As a boy and young man, Proudhon was strongly religious, recalling
in *De la Justice* (published in 1858) that he had 'been thinking of God
since [he] began to exist' (Proudhon 1930, I, p. 283). It is even possible to
imagine Proudhon having remained religious, even Catholic, if the French
Church had embraced a prophetic tradition that was sympathetic to change
and to the plight of the poor. During the nineteenth century, however,
the social policy of the French Church was conservative – counselling the

18 For biographical details, see Dolléans 1948; Halévy 1913; Haubtmann 1982; Hoffman 1972; Sainte-
Beuve 1947; Vincent 1984; Woodcock 1956.

poor to accept their station in life because it was divinely ordained, and closely co-ordinating Church policy to the interests of the monarchy and the upper classes. This was especially true during the Bourbon Restoration (Proudhon's formative years), when there was a widely recognised union of Throne and Altar, and when counter-revolutionary theory was popularised by so-called 'Theocrat' writers like Bonald, Maistre, Chateaubriand and Lamennais (in his early writings).[19] Proudhon reacted strongly to the reactionary social policy of the Church and to the counter-revolutionary theories of the Theocrats, and he moved step-by-step to embrace a secular position.

Proudhon initially hoped that the Church would reform itself and adopt a humane progressive stance in favour of social equality (Proudhon 1926a). But by 1840 he was calling for 'the radical extirpation of Roman Christianity' and insisting that 'to restore religion . . . it is necessary to condemn the Church' (Haubtmann 1969, p. 120; Proudhon 1926b, p. 122). This insistence on articulating a Christian position that would support social justice – one which Proudhon assumed the Catholic Church and other Christian churches had disregarded – placed Proudhon with a significant number of French socialists of this period who saw Christ as an early social prophet and who wished to save 'true' Christianity from the reactionary position of the French Church. But unlike most of his contemporaries, Proudhon quickly moved beyond Christian socialism to a more radically secular position. By 1843, he had given up entirely on religion, and by 1846, he was insisting that 'each step in our progress represents one more victory in which we annihilate the Deity' (Proudhon 1923c, I, p. 349). All Proudhon's subsequent works attacked religion and 'transcendent morality', though he continued to recommend a secularised 'immanent' version of Christian morality.

As Proudhon's hopes for religion declined, two different themes became more pronounced: science and justice. Both were to hold at bay the spiritual and moral devastation which the renunciation of religion was assumed to entail. The first theme, science, was common in the nineteenth century, as we have seen. What is striking in Proudhon's case is how important his scientific hopes became in the years surrounding his rejection of religion. In 1839, he wrote of legislation and politics as being 'objects of science' (Proudhon 1926a, p. 45); in 1843 he made the entry of humanity into the epoch of science the major theme of his book *De la Création de l'Ordre dans l'Humanité*. 'The new science', he wrote, 'must replace religion in

---

19 The title 'Theocrats' comes from Dominique Bagge (Bagge 1952).

everything' (Proudhon 1927, p. 63n). Though he never repudiated this enthusiasm for science, in later years it received less attention, as Proudhon focused more on voluntary human action.

The transition to a secular position was smoothed as well by the presence of a tradition of republican ideas that insisted on the interaction of political institutions and social morality. This, too, assisted Proudhon in salvaging humanity's spiritual and moral side in this context of religious doubt. The institutional side of republicanism was distinctive in that the people were considered not only the ultimate repository of sovereignty, but also active participants in politics. This was easily transformed, in the thought of Proudhon, into an attachment to local institutions at the expense of any other politics, national or otherwise. But the success of a republic was dependent on more than just an institutional organisation: it required that citizens exercise 'virtue', a socio-political morality which entailed respect for law, love of country and a willingness to sacrifice immediate interests for the good of the larger community.

This moral stance strongly influenced Proudhon. Like most of his contemporaries, he had absorbed such ideas from the writings of Enlightenment luminaries like Montesquieu and Rousseau, and he was familiar with the variety of ways these ideas echoed through the Revolution and into the nineteenth century. This tradition provided Proudhon with a secular view of justice that required neither the Church nor any other religious sanction. He put forth a conception of 'immanent justice' which was based on respect for the integrity, rights and equality of one's neighbours.[20]

Justice was a central component of Proudhon's social view, as he made clear in the famous pages of *What is Property?* where he embraced the label 'anarchist'. This illustrated that, like Godwin, Proudhon's view of a stateless society did not countenance a perpetual war between egoistical individuals fighting for their respective personal gains. Justice needed to be struggling against selfish egoism for egalitarian society to operate successfully. It would provide the moral and spiritual unity which the Church and Christianity had traditionally represented, but which, in Proudhon's opinion, it was no longer able to provide. Proudhon embraced the label 'anarchist', but he insisted that society must be infused with a social morality which would lead people to recognise the personal dignity of their neighbours and which

---

20 This moral dimension of Proudhon's thought is present in all of his works; it is especially pronounced in *De La Justice dans la Révolution et dans l'Église* (Proudhon 1930).

would promote the general interests of society over the egoistical interests of isolated individuals.

This did not entail a belief in the innate goodness of mankind. Proudhon always believed that human nature was inherently depraved. 'The cause of evil', he wrote in 1846, 'must be traced...to a primitive perversion, to a sort of congenital malice in the will of man' (Proudhon 1923c, I, p. 349). According to Proudhon, it is necessary to overcome this inherent tendency through struggle and education; moral progress would be achieved by 'taming our instincts' (Proudhon 1923c, I, pp. 371–2).

Closely tied to the need to develop a socially informed morality, according to Proudhon, was the need to reorganise society. The context that informed Proudhon's vision of reorganisation was the 'associative' socialism of workers and of French writers like Charles Fourier, Philippe Buchez and Louis Blanc (Ansart 1970; Vincent 1984, pp. 127–65).

Proudhon's distinctive contribution to this tradition was to deny any role for the state and to insist on a federal structure.[21] Like other anarchists, Proudhon insisted that law and justice did not emerge from a social contract and was not associated with state structures. Proudhon insisted that the basis of law was not a political state or a political constitution, but rather the agreements that developed over time between individuals acting in the spirit of voluntarism, federalism and reciprocity (Reichert 1984, pp. 122–40). Central for Proudhon was his belief that workers should direct and control the economy and that local communities should direct and control politics. Both the economic and political side of Proudhon's theory rested on a model of small groups mediating between the isolated individual and the authoritarian and centralised state.

During the 1840s, Proudhon focused on economic issues and called for the establishment of 'progressive associations' within which workers would make the decisions relevant to the conduct and operation of their trades. He won notoriety in 1840 for his short book entitled *What is Property?*, to which his famous response was: 'It is theft.' In fact, Proudhon's position was not as radical as this familiar epigram would lead one to believe. The 'property' that Proudhon so vociferously attacked was that which provided

---

21 Until the mid-1840s, Proudhon assumed that the government had an important role to play (Proudhon 1927, pp. 387–8, 415, 422). By 1846, however, when he published *Système des Contradictions Économiques*, he had changed his mind, arguing that governments needed to be eliminated. He acknowledged the change in a note to the second edition of this work (Proudhon 1923c, pp. 388n). The federal organisation of communities was developed extensively in Proudhon's writings of the 1860s (Proudhon 1929).

an income without requiring any work: the type of ownership that was characteristic of the unproductive idle class which lived on interest and rents. Proudhon carefully distinguished this 'property' from 'possession', by which he meant the dwelling, land and tools necessary for day-to-day existence. For this latter type of ownership, Proudhon had the highest respect; 'possession' remained, according to him, one of the necessary elements of a just society (Proudhon 1926a, pp. 60, 94–5, 1926b). The elimination of 'property' would have the beneficial consequence of removing from power the *oisifs* – the idlers – who traditionally had exercised economic and political control.

The attack on property was accompanied by proposals for the creation of 'progressive associations' which were to serve as the foci of educational and economic reform.[22] On the educational front, Proudhon advocated a programme of apprenticeship within the workshops which would combine work and education. Drawing on the ideas of Charles Fourier, Proudhon insisted that apprenticeship should entail learning both manual and mental skills, and he hoped that such education would promote fraternal ties among workers.[23] On the economic front, associations would not only push aside the idle 'property owners' who inappropriately skimmed off profits, it would also eliminate the 'arbitrary' system of supply and demand by introducing exchange based on a fair evaluation of goods – that is, 'according to the time and expense' incurred in their production. In addition, Proudhon believed that these associations would stimulate workers to more productive effort because they would be working for themselves. Finally – here Proudhon differed most substantially from contemporaries like Buchez and Blanc – 'progressive association' would avoid what Proudhon termed 'community', the government ownership of property and the central control of economic and social decision-making. Such an appeal to the state, Proudhon believed, would needlessly sacrifice liberty. It would, as he put it in 1846, 'extinguish all individual initiative, [and] proscribe free labour' (Proudhon 1923c, I, pp. 246, 281–4).

---

22 In *Qu'est-ce que la Propriété?* Proudhon spoke of 'association' as the synthesis of the preceding dialectical progression leading from the thesis of 'community' through the antithesis of 'property'. 'The union of the two remainders will give us the true mode of human association' (Proudhon 1926b, pp. 324–5; also see pp. 221, 314n, 204). It is in his private notebooks that the most extensive discussions are to be found (Proudhon 1960 I, pp. 38, 74–96, 114–15, 126–9, 142–3, 145–9, 152–7, etc.).

23 Proudhon discussed such educational reforms in *Avertissement aux Propriétaires* (Proudhon 1926b) and in *De la Création de l'Ordre dans l'Humanité* (Proudhon 1927, pp. 298, 329, 338).

In 1846, Proudhon referred to this same formula for socio-economic justice as 'mutualism' (Proudhon 1923c, II, pp. 410–11).[24] And since this time, 'mutualist anarchism' has been a short-hand label for the anti-statist position that calls for education and socio-economic reform within the context of workers' associations and that recommends the avoidance of revolution and other forms of violent confrontation.[25]

Proudhon's commitment to 'mutualist anarchism' was tested and extended during the French Second Republic, initiated with the Paris Revolution of February 1848. Proudhon participated in the February uprising and composed what he termed the 'first republican proclamation' of the new Republic (Proudhon 1875, II, pp. 278–84, 291–4). But he quickly became unhappy with the new government because it was pursuing political reform at the expense of socio-economic reform, which Proudhon considered basic. He published his own prescription for reform, *Solution to the Social Problem*, in which he articulated a plan to establish a bank which would provide credit at a very low rate of interest and issue 'exchange notes' that would circulate in lieu of money based on gold (Proudhon 1868). In early 1849, he attempted to put his plan in motion by establishing a 'Bank of the People' to reform credit and exchange. It quickly failed Such fiscal reform, he hoped, would stimulate change in the direction he had been advocating in his published writings of the 1840s: namely, to facilitate the transfer of control of economic relations from capitalists and financiers to workers. The mast-head slogan of his paper in 1848, *Le Représentant du Peuple*, stated his goal clearly: 'What is the producer in actual society? – Nothing. What should he be? – Everything.'[26]

Proudhon was shocked by the violence of the June Days, and though he blamed the uprising on the forces of reaction, he never really approved of the revolt. This was in accord with his lifelong stance against violence and insurrection. He was, however, the master of verbal violence, especially in the form of cynical and combative assaults on other individuals.[27] This

---

24 In 1848, Proudhon referred to essentially the same formula as 'positive anarchy' (Proudhon 1868, p. 87). But it was as 'mutualism' that the ideal was commonly referred to during the late nineteenth century.
25 This was a prominent position within the International Working Men's Association during the late 1860s, and among French workers during the early 1870s. See Guillaume 1985, *infra*.
26 Proudhon was connected with four different newspapers during the Second Republic: *Le Représentant du Peuple* (February 1848–August 1848); *Le Peuple* (September 1848–June 1849); *La Voix du Peuple* (September 1849–May 1850); *Le Peuple de 1850* (June 1850–October 1850).
27 Maurice Agulhon has referred to Proudhon as 'a sharpshooter among the democrats' (Agulhon 1983, p. 86).

led to his isolation from others on the left and, in March 1849, to his prosecution by the conservative authorities for his aggressive newspaper attacks on the new President of the Republic, Louis-Napoleon Bonaparte. He was sentenced to a stiff fine and three years in prison. While in prison he wrote and published four books.[28] Proudhon's writings of the 1850s and 1860s built on the vision of 'progressive association' that was central to his anarchism, but now expanded to include regional organisations – it was, in effect, a geographical extension of the mutualistic ideal (Vincent 1984, pp. 209–28).

Proudhon's mutualist anarchism influenced many subsequent theorists – collectivist anarchists like Michael Bakunin and communist anarchists like Peter Kropotkin spoke highly of Proudhon's writings. More faithful to the mutualist strain in Proudhon's thought was the American anarchist William B. Greene (1819–78), who was concerned with sociability, mutuality and the provision of free credit.

7 Michael Bakunin and collectivist anarchism

To move from the world of Proudhon to that of Michael Bakunin is to experience a dramatic shift. Unlike Proudhon, Bakunin came from a background of wealth and comfort – his father was a gentry landowner with a large estate in Tver province north-west of Moscow – which provided the leisure for a broad education that encompassed European literature, painting, music and poetry. After several years in the Artillery Cadet School (1829–34) and two years in the army (1833–5), Bakunin settled in Moscow to study philosophy. Like other members of the Russian intelligentsia of his generation, he became enthralled during the 1830s with romanticism and German idealism, especially with Fichte and Hegel, and then after he left Russia for the West in 1840, with Left Hegelianism and the anarchism of writers like Proudhon. Unlike other Russian thinkers of his generation, however, Bakunin seems to have been especially impulsive and rebellious, temperamentally unable to countenance any compromise between his ideals and an imperfect world. Some analysts have speculated that this was the product of his psychological make-up – Bakunin was apparently impotent, and he carried an enduring hatred for his mother whom he claimed was

---

28 *Confession d'un Révolutionnaire* (November 1849); *Idée Générale de la Révolution au XIX Siècle* (July 1851); *La Révolution Sociale Demontrée par le Coup d'État du 2 décembre 1851* (July 1852); *Philosophie du Progrès* (September 1853).

domineering.[29] Others have stressed that the emotional support provided by the tight-knit circle he formed with his sisters at the family estate of Pria-mukhino influenced his later vision of intimate conspiratorial societies in revolt against authority (Lehning 1974, pp. 57–8). Yet others have empha-sised how his peculiar absorption of the thought of Fichte and Hegel led him to assume a radical persona in which he viewed himself as the charismatic embodiment of Reason in History (Malia 1961).

Whatever the cause, Bakunin developed an early intense dislike for state authority and institutions, especially those of his native Russia. There was in Nicholas I's Russia no opportunity for political activity or political expres-sion, even civil liberties were lacking, and as a consequence Bakunin's rebellion (again like many of his contemporaries') was channelled into an introspective and intellectualised revolt against reality that found sustenance in German idealist philosophy. Bakunin's positive ideals were a function of his revulsion in the face of the social evils and moral scandals of the world he lived in. As he put it in letters to his sisters in 1836, 'The truth, as it is, and not as adapted to particular circumstances – that is my motto.' 'Absolute freedom and absolute love, that is our aim; the liberation of mankind and the whole world – that is our destiny.'[30]

Bakunin's ideals were the antithesis of attempting to accommodate reality. Scornful of the past, his eyes were always on the ideals that the future progress of humanity could realise. As he put it in the early 1870s:

Behind us is our animality and before us our humanity; human light, the only thing that can warm and enlighten us, the only thing that can emancipate us, give us dignity, freedom and happiness, and realise fraternity among us, is never at the beginning, but, relatively to the epoch in which we live, always at the end of history. Let us, then, never look back, let us look ever forward. (Bakunin 1970, p. 21)

Bakunin's ideals were formed of the negations of the evils he desired to eradicate. Confronted with the patriarchal structure of Russian society and politics, Bakunin dreamed of a world of freedom and spiritual har-mony. Finding himself in a world where peasants and workers had no power, he idealised labour and imagined workers as central agents for social

---

29 E. H. Carr writes of his impulsive and destructive passions; Aileen Kelly analyses the relationships between Bakunin's psychological make-up and what she calls his 'politics of utopianism'; Arthur P. Mendel goes the furthest in this direction, reducing Bakunin's millennial aims to Oedipal and narcissistic complexes. See Carr 1961; Kelly 1982; Mendel 1981.
30 Bakunin to Varvara Bakunin (March 1836); Bakunin to Tatyana and Varvara Bakunin (10 August 1836); cited in Kelly 1982, p. 41.

regeneration. Faced with a world which seemed to resist all change, he recommended explosive outbursts of destructive popular violence.

After leaving Russia in 1840, he first settled in Berlin to study German philosophy and publish his first writings, then resided in Zurich, Paris and Brussels. His contact with radicals like Karl Marx and Proudhon led the Russian government to demand Bakunin's return to Russia; when he refused, he was sentenced *in absentia* in 1844 to hard labour in Siberia, which Bakunin avoided by remaining in exile. During the 1840s, Bakunin agitated for Polish national independence and pan-Slavism, and when the revolutions broke out at the end of the decade, he took an active part in the struggles in Prague in 1848 and in Dresden in 1849.[31] Handed over by the Saxons to the Austrians, and then by the Austrians to the Russian authorities, he spent over a decade imprisoned and in Siberian exile. In 1861, he escaped from Siberia to Japan, then travelled via the United States to Western Europe.

During the remaining years of his life (he died in 1876), Bakunin was particularly active in Italy and Switzerland, and it was during these years that his views finally crystallised into full-fledged anarchism.[32] He devoted much of his attention during this period to organising secret societies and plotting revolutionary conspiracies, including the dubious association Bakunin formed with the Russian terrorist Sergei Nechaev. It was during these same years that he carried on his famous struggle with Marx within the First International and wrote his major anarchist works.

What is striking about these works is their categorical and sweeping nature. Bakunin's anarchism is more general and abstract than that of, say, Hodgskin or Proudhon. He is the archetypal alienated intellectual facing an unyielding and uncaring society. His theory is principally critical, and when he turns to positive prescription, he refers to ideals of wholeness and a unified human community. 'To look for my happiness in the happiness of others, for my own worth in the worth of all those around me, to be free in the freedom of others' (Bakunin 1977, p. 92).

To bring such millenarian dreams to fruition, Bakunin believed that violence and terrorism were necessary. In a famous passage in 'Die Reaktion

31 Bakunin recounts his role in events of the 1840s in the curious confessions he wrote to Tsar Nicholas I while in prison. See Bakunin 1977.
32 There is a dispute among scholars concerning when exactly Bakunin became an anarchist. Max Nettlau sees Bakunin as impregnated with anarchism as early as 1851 (Bakunin 1932, p. 325n). It was only in 1867, however, that Bakunin declared for the first time that 'I am anarchist' (Maitron 1975, I, p. 48n; Pernicone 1993, p. 26).

in Deutschland' (1842), he exhorted the masses to 'trust the eternal Spirit which destroys and annihilates only because it is the unfathomable and eternally creating source of all life. The passion for destruction is a creative passion, too' (Bakunin 1965, pp. 403–6, 1977, p. 93). What is so startling about this statement is that it recommends violence not just because it is instrumentally important for achieving some goal – like the stateless society – but because it is intrinsically good, even liberating. This tendency to glorify violence did not abate: over thirty years later, Bakunin continued to call for a 'war to the death' between workers and the privileged classes, and referred to destruction as 'salutary and fruitful' (Bakunin 1990, pp. 20, 28).

Throughout his life, Bakunin remained convinced that only explosive popular outbursts would create the social confusion, disorder and panic that would entirely demolish authoritarian institutions like the state. Here as elsewhere, Bakunin's thought is all-encompassing: there is no allowance for incremental change in order to usher in a progressively better world; freedom is to be attained through purifying and regenerating destruction. Revolutions become the privileged means for human will to affect the course of human history; violence is assumed necessary to unleash the reason and virtue of the popular classes, presently suppressed under authoritarian regimes. Nor is revolution reserved, as it is in Marx's thought, for highly industrialised societies; Bakunin believed that revolutions were most likely to occur where the majority of people remained near subsistence level.

Bakunin demanded the liberation of individuals from the constraints imposed by all authoritarian institutions – political, religious, social or philosophical – but he reserved a special hatred for the state. 'If there is a state', he wrote in 1873, 'then necessarily there is domination and consequently slavery. A state without slavery, open or camouflaged, is inconceivable – that is why we are enemies of the state' (Bakunin 1990, p. 178). Any state represented evil; but the most dangerous were those powerful and extensive states which, because of their complex structures, were furthest from the people's interests and instincts (Bakunin 1990, p. 53). Germany was the pre-eminent example of such a powerful state in the late nineteenth century – Bakunin frequently analysed the dangerous and oppressive quality of Bismarckian Germany – but Bakunin was suspicious of any group that wished to capture the power of the state for their own specific interests.

Connected to Bakunin's analysis of different states were his generalisations concerning the mores of various ethnic groups, especially their differing proclivities for liberty or for authoritarian institutions. A crude racism

463

often shows through in these passages: Bakunin passes beyond common stereotypes in his vitriolic characterisations of Germans and Jews.

Bakunin's anti-statist attitude contributed greatly to the division between Bakunin and Marx – and more generally between anti-authoritarians and Marxists – within the First International Working Men's Association (IWA) during the late 1860s and 1870s. Marxists supported a strong central structure for the International, in this case the General Council in London that by the early 1870s was controlled by Marx himself. Non-authoritarians – or 'collectivists', as they called themselves at this time – argued for a federal structure that would leave the greatest possible degree of autonomy to local sections, many of which were controlled by Marx's mutualist and anarchist opponents. Bakunin strongly opposed the personal ascendancy of Marx and also the statist ideal for which he stood, an opposition that led to his expulsion from the IWA at the Hague Congress in 1872. In *Statism and Anarchy*, published in 1873, Bakunin bitterly attacked Marx's theory of proletarian government as a new authoritarianism – a 'despotic government of the masses by a new and very small aristocracy of real or pretended scholars'. He could only lament that 'we see the doctrinaire revolutionaries under Marx's leadership everywhere taking the side of the state and its supporters against popular revolution' (Bakunin 1990, pp. 178–9).

The only difference between revolutionary dictatorship and the state is in external appearances. Essentially, they both represent the same government of the majority by a minority in the name of the presumed stupidity of the one and the presumed intelligence of the other. Therefore they are equally reactionary. (Bakunin 1990, p. 137)

Bakunin's dislike of all forms of authority was balanced by his belief in a deep-seated social and communal instinct in people. The creation of a new and better society required only that artificial structures like the state be eliminated so that the natural social energies of the people could be released. This is what insurrection would allow, the emergence of a new society organised from the bottom up – what he often called the universal federation. 'The time will come', he claimed,

when on the ruins of political states there will be created, in complete freedom and organised from below upwards, a voluntary fraternal union of voluntary productive associations, communes, and provincial federations, embracing without distinction, because they embrace freely, people of every language and nationality. (Bakunin 1990, p. 90)

This would provide 'the sole condition for real as opposed to fictitious freedom' (Bakunin 1990, p. 13). Perhaps the most curious and disturbing element of Bakunin's thought is the residue of an authoritarianism that he himself would probably have denied. It was certainly in conflict with his self-proclaimed libertarianism.[33] Throughout his life, Bakunin seems to have been constitutionally dependent on tightly knit groups in which he was the recognised leader. After his escape from Siberia to Italy in 1861, he constructed a network of secret associations, and he believed that the realisation of liberty through the destruction of the existing order justified a revolutionary conspiratorial society in order to direct the revolution and to guard the new post-revolutionary society against any revival of state authority. His brief partnership with the Russian terrorist Nechaev is an indication of how susceptible Bakunin was to revolutionary dreams that entailed authoritarian elements (Avrich 1988, pp. 32–52; Confino 1973). It raises the troubling issue of Bakunin's willingness to countenance the transferal of coercive revolutionary power to a secret organisation – this in spite of his criticisms of Marx's notion of the 'dictatorship of the proletariat'.

There remained a tension in Bakunin's thought. On the one hand, he expected that the new federal social organisation would be a 'spontaneous and self-generated development' emerging from 'the masses [that] bear all the elements of their future organisational norms in their own more or less historically evolved instincts, in their everyday needs, and in their conscious and unconscious desires'. On the other hand, he was convinced that the masses needed 'some intelligent and honest leadership' (Bakunin 1990, pp. 135, 146). Some contemporaries were suspicious of Bakunin because they believed that his own utopian tendencies overshadowed his belief in the virtues of popular spontaneity, and that ultimately he wished to impose his own categorical ideals on the people. The French socialist Benoît Malon, for example, concluded in the late 1860s that 'instead of examining the people, as Proudhon wanted', Bakunin had 'himself formulated a preconceived ideal... that he [would] never forfeit' (Vincent 1992, p. 13).[34]

Some of Bakunin's most loyal followers were in Italy, where Bakunin spent the years 1864–7, and where Italian revolutionary traditions and aspirations became linked with Bakunin's libertarian ideals and conspiratorial

33 In 1851, Bakunin called for a 'strong dictatorial government' for Russia, and indicated that in 1848–9 he had hoped for a 'revolutionary government with unlimited dictatorial power' in a post-revolutionary Bohemia (Bakunin 1977, pp. 91, 112, 118–19).
34 Aileen Kelly points out that Herzen and Turgenev also believed that Bakunin suffered from an excessive attachment to theoretical consistency, that 'he strove with undeviating persistence to interpret and order complex historical events according to the demands of a crude dialectic to which he was faithful all his life' (Kelly 1982, p. 3).

agenda. Proudhonian mutualism had already led a few radical members of the Risorgimento like Carlo Pisacane (1818–57) to call for 'liberty and association', but it was during the late 1860s and early 1870s, when young Italian radicals became dissatisfied with Mazzini's increasingly conservative stances on social change and with his denunciations of materialism and the Paris Commune, that Italian anarchism gained its first articulate defenders. Italian anarchists initially worked within the structure of the IWA, organising workers and siding with the 'non-authoritarians' against Marx and the London General Council. Their dominance was such that at a meeting of twenty-one Italian sections of the IWA in Rimini in August 1872, a month before the showdown between Bakunin and Marx at the Hague Congress in September, they passed anarchist-inspired resolutions against political action, against participation in the Hague Congress (controlled by the authoritarians of the General Council), and for the creation of an anti-authoritarian International. In the following months, anarchists also made clear that organisation and propaganda needed to be supplemented with action – with insurrection and with what became known as 'propaganda by the deed'.

The rapid growth of the IWA in Italy during the early 1870s was due to the activities of young militants like Carlo Cafiero (1846–92), Andrea Costa (1852–1910) and Errico Malatesta (1853–1932). These men were enchanted by Bakunin, and won over by his writings that extolled the virtues of labour, attacked the capitalists, defended atheism, proposed the social revolution and denounced the state. Malatesta recounted in 1876 that 'it is to him [Bakunin], more than all others, that we owe the foundation and the early progress of the International in Italy, [and] it is to him that we owe our early revolutionary education' (quoted in Pernicone 1993, p. 106). Cafiero, following his embrace of a Bakuninist position in mid-1872, even began supporting Bakunin and his family with his inherited wealth; in 1873, he frittered away most of his inheritance with the purchase, repair and expansion of a villa near Locarno called the Baronata, initially conceived as a residence for the ageing Russian revolutionary.

The Italian anarchists placed great faith in Bakunin's vision of small conspiratorial organisations initiating revolutionary actions that, in turn, would precipitate widespread popular insurrection and bring down the state. In August 1874, they made plans for a co-ordinated series of uprisings in Bologna, Rome, Florence and other cities, but lack of popular support and early detection by the authorities led to the easy suppression of the uprisings and the quick arrest of most of the anarchist leaders. Three years later, in April 1877, there was a second attempt in the mountain villages near Benevento in the Campania; again it failed and led to a wave of government repression.

Continuing government persecution led to a fracturing of the Italian movement. Many adopted a self-defeating aversion to any organisational structure, which led to a movement with little unity or co-ordinated action. Costa converted to 'legalitarian' socialism in 1879, depriving the movement of one of its most popular leaders and effective spokesmen. Cafiero, his inheritance squandered, spent the last decade of his life (1882–92) insanely paranoid. Malatesta continued to attempt to revitalise the Italian anarchist movement into a revolutionary force, but he spent most of his years after the 1870s in exile (in such places as Argentina and London), and he never succeeded in overcoming internal dissension, government repression or the growing strength of the socialists committed to electoral activity.

Bakunin and 'collectivist anarchism' also exerted a strong influence in Spain. Anarchism was formally introduced on the Iberian peninsula by representatives of the non-authoritarian wing of the IWA in the late 1860s, especially in the years following the September revolutions of 1868 that overthrew Queen Isabella II. Until the Bourbon restoration of 1875, there was intense social turmoil in Spain, which allowed radicals of various colourations – republican federalists, Proudhonian mutualists and Bakuninist collectivists – to bid for influence among disaffected rural and urban workers. The repression that accompanied the restoration forced anarchist groups underground, giving proponents of insurrection and terrorism a stronger voice. With the establishment of the right of association in 1881, syndicalist forces within the anarchist movement became stronger, controlling the Federación de Trabajadores de la Región Española (FTRE) and its paper *La Revista Social*, edited by Juan Serrano y Oteiza (1837–86).

During the late 1880s and the 1890s, the 'collectivist anarchists' were challenged by 'communist anarchists' who called for a communal system of economic distribution, as opposed to the collectivist ideal of a worker's entitlement to the integral product of his labour. The communists also tended to support terrorism and organised violence. But the most vocal and visible anarchists – writers like Fernando Tarrida del Mármol (1861–1915) and Ricardo Mella (1861–1925) – embraced an anarchism that appealed to the strong Spanish tradition of working-class associations, unions, *circulos*, *ateneos* and similar organisations. Their so-called 'anarchism without adjectives' attempted to transcend the bitter debates between individualists, mutualists, collectivists and communists within the anarchist movement, calling for greater tolerance regarding economic questions. Their rejection of rigid economic theory appealed during the 1890s to a wide group of prominent anarchists who hoped such an ecumenical position would help unify the movement – writers like Reclus, Malatesta and Max Nettlau (the historian of anarchism, 1865–1944) in Europe; and Voltairine de Cleyre in America (Avrich 1978, pp. 144–70). In Spain, *anarquismo sin adjetivos* converged with ideas of the general strike to form the anarcho-syndicalist ideology of the Confederación Nacional del Trabajo (CNT), founded in 1910.

A similar alternation between competing anarchist stances occurred in Argentina. Made up largely of immigrant labourers from Italy and Spain, the Argentine anarchist movement reflected its European origins. The first organisations were an outgrowth of a Bakuninist Centro, formed to disseminate the anti-Marxist message of the anti-authoritarian wing of the IWA. By the 1880s, visiting Italian anarchists like Errico Malatesta were spreading the collectivist gospel in rapidly growing urban centres like Buenos Aires and Rosario. The first significant working-class support emerged during the economic crisis of the 1890s; by 1901, when the Federación Obrera de Argentina was founded, there existed an organised, militant and rapidly expanding movement dedicated to libertarian ideals. Pragmatic and activist in orientation, Argentine anarchism was a mélange of individualist and more communitarian anarchism – 'almost a stance . . . as much a symbol of outrage as an interpretation' (Yoast 1975, p. 327). It shared a federalist and revolutionary orientation with militant anarchists in Europe.

During the first decade of the twentieth century, this mass working-class anarchist movement assumed a more militant posture, leading to a Buenos Aires rent strike in 1907 and a Rosario labour strike in 1909. Escalating confrontations with industrialists and the state culminated in the uprisings and strikes of 1910 during the Centenary celebrations. Subsequent repression – a combination of legal sanctions, police and troop forces and deportations – crushed the worker-anarchist organisations and the left-wing press. This ended the golden age of Argentine anarchism, though conflicts, like the so-called *Semana Trágica* in 1919, indicated anarchism's enduring prestige and influence.

Mexican anarchism, to mention another important example, went through a similar developmental pattern. During the 1860s and 1870s, anarchist organisations grew, benefiting from the influx of European anarchist immigrants, especially from Spain, and the wide circulation of literature propagating the views of Proudhon, Bakunin, Kropotkin and others. Suppressed by the government between 1880 and 1900, anarchist organisations re-emerged in a more syndicalist guise in the first decade of the twentieth century, especially in the ranks of the Partido Liberal Mexicano (PLM), led by Ricardo Flores Magón (1873–1922) and his brother Enrique. Important during the revolutionary period, anarchism survived to influence the stance of the Confederación General de Trabajadores, founded in 1921.

In England, the split between parliamentary and anti-parliamentary forces on the left occurred in 1884, when William Morris (1834–96) and others broke away from the Social Democratic Federation led by Henry M. Hyndman (1842–1921) to form the Socialist League. For the next five years, Morris and his close associates advocated a radical change of the economy and society through education and revolution. In *Commonweal*, the paper of the Socialist League, workers were warned against compromising with contemptible politics and advised to put their faith in militant trade unionism. The battles of 'Bloody Sunday' between police and demonstrators at Trafalgar Square on 13 November 1887, and the success of the great dock strike of 1889 led some British militants to imagine that revolutionary change could be achieved through a 'universal strike'.

In the United States, finally, similar strains of working-class anarchism and syndicalism emerged, especially among workers on the docks and in the lumber mills and mines of the West. Syndicalist anarchists like Dyer D. Lum (1839–93) had insisted that violent struggle was necessary to establish worker control of factories. Communist anarchists like Emma Goldman – closer to the ideas of Kropotkin than Bakunin – had a vision of shared labour and remuneration based on need. The most visible organisation advocating direct action was the Industrial Workers of the World (IWW), founded in 1905. The most prominent exponent of such views was the chief of the Western Federation of Miners, 'Big Bill' Haywood (1869–1928). The IWW was especially active in labour disputes during the decade before the First World War. With entry into the war in 1917, 'subversive' voices were silenced by the government – Haywood, for example, was sentenced to twenty years' imprisonment for his activities opposing the war; disillusioned, he jumped bail and went into exile in Russia.

8 Peter Kropotkin and communist anarchism

Peter Kropotkin embraced anarchism after his exposure in 1872 to the non-authoritarian ideas within the International articulated by the followers of Bakunin in the Jura Federation (Kropotkin 1930, p. 287).[35] But if he proclaimed himself an anarchist only at the age of thirty, he drew from earlier experiences, including sympathies for his father's serfs, whom he knew during his childhood, and for Siberian miners, whom he observed during his military service in the 1860s. Like Bakunin, Kropotkin came from a wealthy Russian gentry family, and as a youth he was even chosen to be a page to the Tsar. When he graduated from the military academy in St Petersburg in 1862, Kropotkin obtained permission to be commissioned as an army officer in Amur in Siberia rather than take an assignment more likely to lead to professional advancement. This reflected his conviction that one should be useful to society, especially if one had the luxury, as he did, of belonging to the privileged class. He quickly became disenchanted with official service to the state, however, and was appalled at the deplorable conditions he observed miners enduring in Siberia. Though at this stage of his life he opposed recourse to revolution,[36] he came to the conclusion that the reform of Russian society through the autocracy was hopeless. It is ironic that Kropotkin's service to the state became a prelude to a lifetime devoted to opposition to all states.

Kropotkin's frustrations led him to scientific and geographical studies, including exploratory expeditions to areas of Manchuria. These occasioned his first publications and established his reputation as a geographer. In 1867, Kropotkin resigned his military service and returned to European Russia, where he devoted himself to studies in mathematics and continued to publish articles on his expeditions and on the geographical configuration of the mountains of Asia. He continued, however, to feel morally compelled to work for the liberation of the masses, a conviction that his wide-ranging reading encouraged (Kropotkin 1930, p. 240). He read, for example, Proudhon and Quinet, who convinced him that a reform of social conditions required the creation of workers' associations. When his father died in 1871, he decided to learn first-hand about workers' organisations in Western Europe. He travelled to Zurich, where he joined the First International, then visited Geneva, Neuchâtel and Brussels. It was his exposure to non-authoritarian ideas in the Jura that crystallised into anarchism his ambivalence towards authority and his frustrations with the Russian regime.

---

35 Biographical details may be found in Cahm 1989; Kropotkin 1930; Miller 1976; Woodcock and Avakumovic 1971.
36 In a letter (4 June 1866) to his brother, Alexander Kropotkin, Kropotkin cautioned against commitment to revolution without a careful consideration of the likely benefits and harms for the majority (Miller 1976, p. 68).

He returned to Russia, became a member of the radical Chaikovskii Circle (under the pseudonym of Borodin), composed a popular book on Pugachev, and advocated focusing on workers in the countryside rather than in the urban centres. He composed a manifesto in 1873 that recommended transforming capital and the means of production into common property, called for the elimination of government in favour of a federation of agrarian communes, and advocated popular revolt as the appropriate means (Kropotkin 1970a, pp. 46–116). Because of this activity, he was arrested by the tsarist police on 8 April 1874, and sent to the Peter and Paul fortress. Fourteen months later, on 30 June 1876, he escaped and made his way to Britain, settling first in Edinburgh and then in London. He was to remain in exile for the next forty years.

In January 1877, Kropotkin moved to Switzerland, where he re-established his contacts with the non-authoritarians of the Jura Federation. The Libertarian International was almost extinct by this time, however, and even the *Bulletin of the Federation* ceased publication in 1877. Kropotkin responded by co-operating briefly with Paul Brousse on the short-lived paper *L'Avant Garde* and then, in 1879, founding his own anarchist paper, *Le Révolté*. He actively advocated popular revolutionary action – mass revolt and, even, individual acts of violence if these were informed by a clear revolutionary commitment – and was closely associated with anarchists like Paul Brousse and Elisée Reclus. In 1880, at a meeting of the Jura Federation at La Chaux-de-Fonds, he became a vocal proponent of 'anarchist communism' which called not only for the elimination of all governments, but for the common ownership of the means of production and for distribution based on need.[37]

As a consequence of his revolutionary activity, he was expelled by the Swiss authorities in 1881. After another stay in England in 1881–2, he tried living in France, but in December 1882 he was arrested and, in January 1883 brought to trial in Lyon for expressing sympathy for the mine bombings in central France and for his active involvement with the International. He was convicted and sentenced to five years in prison at Clairvaux, but after serving three years he was pardoned and expelled from the country. He then made his way to London where he spent the next thirty years. This marked the beginning of the period when he wrote most of his books and

---

37 'Anarchist communism' needs to be distinguished, according to Kropotkin, from 'anarchist collectivism', which posits that remuneration should be in proportion to hours worked. This latter position was supported by James Guillaume, among others.

became an internationally renowned anarchist theorist. After the February revolution of 1917, he returned to his native Russia, where he opposed Russian withdrawal from the First World War as well as the rising power of the Bolsheviks. He was frustrated on both counts, and after the Bolshevik Revolution in October, he focused his attention on the formation of the Dmetrov anarchist commune in the village near Moscow where Lenin had banished him. He died there in 1921.

Kropotkin shared the belief in the limitless possibilities of scientific enquiry which we have already noted of earlier anarchists. Anarchism was not just a theory, according to Kropotkin, it was a form of scientific truth based on observation and analysis. It was a science, moreover, that provided the principle for positive social interaction – mutual aid – and the basis for an optimistic belief in secular change. Kropotkin believed that people, properly enlightened through education and inspired by the action and vision of revolutionary minorities, would recognise the truth of anarchist ideals and break free from the demoralising effects of contemporary society to build a society based on these ideals. With education and leadership, Kropotkin believed that popular creative tendencies could prevail over the divisive authoritarian tendencies which animated, and unfortunately dominated, modern industrial societies.

Throughout his mature years, Kropotkin insisted that co-operation and mutual aid were the norms in both the natural and social worlds. In *Mutual Aid* (1902), he attacked the Social Darwinists for arguing that the evolution of nature and human society was driven by competition. In fact, spontaneous co-operation was more important than ferocious competition in the struggle for existence, and evolution was accurately characterised as an associated struggle by the species as a whole against the environment. In this struggle as it applied to humans, mutual aid was the foundation out of which morality would emerge. Society, in the absence of state or religious authority, would not become a community of warring individuals. It would become a community within which human solidarity would grow, and out of which higher ideals of justice and equity would evolve. Mutual aid was the principle and the therapy that would overcome egoism in favour of an altruistic morality, and it would provide the framework for concrete socio-economic advances.

In spite of Kropotkin's scientific self-consciousness, therefore, he must be seen, first and foremost, as a moralist. Even his final book, incomplete at the time of his death, dealt with ethical doctrines (Kropotkin 1924). Moral imperatives were what impelled him to call for socio-economic change. In books like *The Conquest of Bread* (1892) and *Fields, Factories and Workshops* (1898), he outlined a social organisation based on a free federation of autonomous communes. One of the themes of these works is that the instruments of production are the inheritance from the common labour of humanity, and therefore ought not to be considered the property of a few. 'Each discovery, each advance, each increase in the sum of human riches', he writes, 'owes its being to the physical and mental travail of the past and present' (Kropotkin 1972, p. 46). This makes it impossible to assess accurately the productive contribution of any single individual, a judgement which led Kropotkin to two conclusions: all social wealth must be viewed as the common inheritance of humanity and distribution of goods should be based on need.

Kropotkin was convinced that the popularity of this stance – which he called 'anarchist communism' – was spreading; he believed that, little by little, authoritarian governmental principles were yielding to voluntary co-operation in a multiplicity of organisations such as trade associations, learned societies and communes. These small communities were the appropriate context for the instincts of solidarity and mutual aid to flourish. And they were the appropriate foci for education and personal growth. Assumed here was the evil nature of the state, which Kropotkin spelled out explicitly in such works as 'The State: Its Historic Role'.[38] Here, Kropotkin argued that the state had emerged victorious over free towns and communes during the sixteenth century, a victory that represented an unfortunate advance of tyranny over liberty.

> We see in [the state] the institution . . . to prevent direct association among men, to shackle the development of local and individual initiative, to crush existing liberties, to prevent their blossoming – all this in order to subject the masses to the will of the minorities. (Kropotkin 1970a, p. 259)

The state favoured 'pyramidal authoritarian organisations' and was animated by 'the spirit of discipline'; it destroyed 'the spirit of initiative and free association' that was the essence of 'the federalist spirit which had created the free commune' (Kropotkin 1970a, p. 241). Fortunately, according to Kropotkin, technological advances were making possible regional self-sufficiency which, combined with education, would support the human tendencies towards solidarity and mutual aid. The future victory of the

---

38 Originally a lecture delivered on 7 March 1896, it was published in *Les Temps nouveaux* (19 December 1896). There is an English translation in Kropotkin 1970a, pp. 211–64.

social revolution would eliminate the state and fulfil humanity's quest for freedom.

The social and moral foundations of Kropotkin's vision remained constant. But he did change his views concerning the appropriate means to achieve anarchism. In the late 1870s and early 1880s, he assumed that Europe would soon be in revolution, and he advocated revolutionary self-sacrifice by committed anarchists to stimulate revolutionary action by the masses. Though at first opposed to trade union activity, he also came at this time to see revolutionary potential here if the workers were sufficiently radical – meaning, for Kropotkin, that the workers needed to be committed to the expropriation and collectivisation of property. Kropotkin by the early 1880s, therefore, advocated a combination of individual and collective revolutionary actions that focused on socio-economic change and the elimination of traditional political institutions. Proposed actions ranged from militant strikes to violent revolt and economic terrorism. He insisted that, in addition to oral and written propaganda, violent revolutionary action was as necessary as it was inevitable (Kropotkin 1992). Much of this reflected the influence of Bakunin and his followers, who also recommended actions over sterile doctrines which could 'kill life'. And like Bakunin, Kropotkin imagined revolution as a popular revolt in the broadest sense, including elimination of all governmental bodies and the expropriation of property for utilisation by communal groups and workers' associations.

Where Kropotkin differed from Bakunin was in his opposition to tight conspiratorial organisations. Drawing from his own populist convictions and influenced by Elisée Reclus' belief in the spontaneity of the masses, he saw anarchist violence as a catalyst for broadly based popular struggle. He did not wish to see a 'vanguard elite' taking a secretive directive role. Anarchist leaders should lead popular social revolts; they should not encourage senseless terrorist violence or secret conspiratorial organisation. In this regard, Kropotkin's vision for change reflected his generally mild and benevolent personality. As Paul Avrich has put it, 'he lacked Bakunin's violent temperament, titanic urge to destroy, and irrepressible will to dominate' (Avrich 1988, p. 71).

In later years, Kropotkin seems to have had more reservations concerning terrorist violence, brought to public prominence by the assassinations and bombings of the early 1890s. He refrained from condemning individual anarchist terrorists, but he did insist that it was necessary to distinguish indiscriminate terrorism, which he opposed, from spontaneous mass violence which he believed was necessary for fundamental social change. This was a

474

position which paralleled that of Jean Grave, the editor who took over *Le Révolté* from Kropotkin in 1883.

Through his many writings,[39] Kropotkin was arguably the most prominent anarchist thinker in the years before the First World War. His call for a stateless society serves as an appropriate final manifesto:

> Breaking the chains of the state and overthrowing its idols, mankind will march towards a better future, no longer knowing either masters or slaves, keeping its veneration for the noble martyrs who paid with their blood and suffering for those first attempts at emancipation which have lighted our way in our march towards the conquest of freedom. (quoted in Avrich 1988, p. 239)

9 Conclusion

Nineteenth-century visions of stateless society seem unrealistic to the early twenty-first-century mind because we are more pessimistic concerning the efficacy of science, more anxious about the supply of natural resources, more cynical about beliefs in human progress and more despondent about the effect of local decisions on the complex environmental and social problems that confront modern humanity. The first three factors separate us from almost all nineteenth century political thinkers, for it was common before the First World War to assume (as we do not) that scientific reason could chart trajectories of socio-political change, and it was customary to feel assured (as we are not) that informed human effort would lead to social, economic and moral progress. The fourth factor – concerning the efficacy of local decisions – also separates us from anarchists and proto-libertarians of the nineteenth century and later. Most of us now believe that the highly structured and intensively interdependent nature of modern societies transcends the reach of local groups, though many of us despair that national, regional and global organisations have proven to be no more capable of containing the destruction and violence of the modern age.

What remains appealing in anarchist thought is the recognition of the danger of states – states that, unchecked, have continued to expand, to intrude and to control. Anarchists viewed as naïve the liberal idea that the state would be correspondingly reduced in importance as 'civil society' flourished. They considered ridiculous the Marxist prediction that the dialectical conflict between the forces and relations of production would

---

39 In addition to his many books, Kropotkin was associated with such prominent anarchist journals as *Le Révolté* (in Paris) and *Freedom* (in London).

lead to the progressive withering-away of the state. As these hopes and prophecies have evaporated, it is difficult not to credit the anarchists with a profound insight. States have proven to be more powerful than ever, and at times more terrible than our worst nightmares. Anarchists took seriously the power of the state as a coercive, irresistible, bureaucratic machine – not as a super-structural manifestation of a more basic socio-economic structure, nor as a benign impediment to the growth of 'civil society', but as a threatening reality. Anarchists shared with Marxists the belief that socio-economic change was more important than politics, and they shared with liberals the notion that the growth of civil society was more valuable than the growth of the state. But they cogently perceived a central problem: that some of the worst oppressions and the most hideous injustices in the modern age have been carried out by the continually self-reproducing secular bureaucratic organisations that we call states.

III

Modern liberty and its critics

15

Aesthetics and politics

DOUGLAS MOGGACH

According to Hegel, the central discovery of the Enlightenment is that everything exists for the subject (Hegel 1971, pp. 332–3). This theoretical shift, from ideas of a fixed natural or social order towards subjective utility and freedom, occurs in conjunction with political challenges to the old regime in Europe, and the emergence of modern civil society. While the underlying social changes can be treated only allusively here, the intellectual legacy of the Enlightenment is that values and institutions must be critically authenticated as corresponding to subjects' own insights (C. Taylor 1991, pp. 81–91), and that traditional forms of life must cede to relations sanctioned by reason, whereby subjects attain a growing ascendancy over natural and social processes which inhibit their autonomous self-determination.

The subject as source of values has been conceived in a variety of ways across the disciplines of modern thought. In the eighteenth century, aesthetics arises as a field of enquiry, and as a programme of political and cultural criticism, in connection with new understandings of subjective activity; it retains a pivotal role in nineteenth-century thought. The history of aesthetics is closely intertwined with the emergence and an eventual eclipse of modern subjectivity, contributing multifaceted images of subjective self-awareness, and of objective, formative action.

Most explicitly, aesthetics, deriving from a Greek term for perception or sensation, is concerned with the apprehension of beauty and the sublime, with the nature of art and with the workings of the senses in relation to the understanding. Beyond this already ambitious agenda, it examines fundamental aspects of the new subjectivity, such as spontaneity, creativity and action, asking how subjects engender objective forms, and further, how they relate to and distinguish themselves from their externalisations in the world, viewing these as manifestations or as limitations of themselves. Friedrich Schiller, one of the foremost theoreticians and practitioners of the new aesthetic, defines this simultaneous relating and distinguishing as the problem of reflection, the reciprocal relation of self and world (Schiller

479

1967, Letter XXIV. 2), which is one of the principal issues in aesthetic thought, and which can be taken as a hallmark of various tendencies within it, helping to discriminate among varieties of romanticism, for example. It is in analysing concepts of subjectivity, formative activity (Pareyson 1974) and reflection that the political charge of modern aesthetics can best be discerned.

While early eighteenth-century thinkers continued to stress an objective 'reason and fitness of things' (Bate 1949, p. 160), a given order of values and relationships, sanctioned by tradition, with which subjects' aims and actions must comply, the focus gradually shifts towards subjective spontaneity and self-definition, and the possibility of directing this freedom through self-legislation or rationally binding law. The emergence of aesthetic subjectivity is connected to the important cultural and theoretical developments initiated in the Enlightenment: a shift from the object as constituted to the creative subject, from mimemis, or reproduction of a natural order, to spontaneity and imagination, and from the transcendent and absolute grounding of values to their subjective authentication. The turn to subjectivity from the late eighteenth century onwards is not equivalent to affirming individualism, though this is prominent among its figures. Forms of subjectivity may rather be taken to delineate types or groups (Barrell 1986, pp. 3–10). This commonality or uniformity among subjects is frequently stressed, but the value of the individual and the personal also attains growing importance through the Enlightenment (Taylor 1989, pp. 286–94). Nor does the focus on spontaneity entail an unconditional denial of all transcendence, or of the divine; what now becomes vital, even within more traditionalist currents like pietism, is the personal relation which subjects assume towards the ultimate source of value, even if it remains external to them.

Illustrative of changing relationships between art, subjectivity and the social order are conceptions of what is involved in aesthetic creation. The baroque style of the seventeenth and early eighteenth centuries had depicted the work of art, in the language of classical rhetorical theory, as an *inscriptio* or *inventio*, which is less an act of free creation than an acknowledgement of existing religious and political standards (Raulet 1992, pp. 148, 154). *Inventio* here bears the sense of a coming upon or a discovery, rather than of a creative, imaginative act, because it refers to the normative order in which the work is to be inscribed, and which it is to illustrate and embellish. In eighteenth-century neo-classicism, too, the aesthetic is construed as a canon of rules for the production of objects, in which the imagination is downplayed.[1] The differentiation between 'artes qua technai', or artisanal production (depending upon accepted rules and procedures), and the fine arts as spontaneous and innovative, is effected slowly throughout the eighteenth century (Scholtz 1990, pp. 12–29; Barrell 1986, pp. 7–8, 78–9; Becq 1984, II, pp. 802–9; Mortensen 1997). This process involves the institutionalisation of art as a sphere of value and activity, and the recognition that artistic production is distinct from labour;[2] only later, in the nineteenth century, when working activity is itself interpreted in an aesthetic register, will their synthesis again be sought. The idea of a relatively autonomous aesthetic order depends on conceiving the activity of the artist as an *inventio* in a new sense, as an act of a free and imaginative consciousness (Becq 1984, II, p. 513; Starobinski 1964, p. 13) or of a spontaneous modern self. This change occurs very gradually, and is not yet complete at the beginning of the period under investigation here. In J. W. Goethe (1749–1832) or in Joshua Reynolds (1723–92), the ideal of artistic excellence stands for the mimetic reproduction and purification of essential natural types (Becq 1984, II, pp. 522–3; Benjamin 1986, pp. 165–77); though Goethe's contributions to the new romantic sensibilities and ideas of alienated subjectivity, especially through his *Werther* (1774), are highly significant. His *Faust* (1808–33) depicts the conflict between the modern overstepping of bounds, and the classical preservation of measure and place. Similarly, in the romanticism of William Blake (1757–1827), *inventio* retains its reference to a transcendent order. His term 'original' refers to the eternal pattern or model to be grasped in aesthetic vision, and reproduced in the work; the originality of artists consists in their having access to these models (Barrell 1986, pp. 225–31, 244–53), not in their creation of something without precedent. At the turn of the nineteenth century, other varieties of romanticism, together with German idealism, issue a challenge to these views of mimesis in the name of spontaneity and creation.

As a facet of this modern selfhood, the idea of spontaneity that typifies nineteenth-century thought refers to the capacity of subjects to initiate and validate changes in themselves and in the external world. The forms of their manifestation, and the establishment of appropriate limits, no longer tend to be fixed with reference to a natural order. Though this order had been frequently challenged, the Enlightenment delivered a decisive attack on it, and

---

1 Bate 1949 interprets neo-classicism as such a canon, but Butler 1981 sees it as essentially critical of the waste and excess of the pre-revolutionary order. On imagination as a response to a crisis of artistic and theoretical representation, and of culture, see Whale 2000.
2 Eagleton 1990 relates aesthetic subjectivity to the rise of capitalist relations of production and exchange.

began to think through the corresponding concepts of the subject, setting the stage for nineteenth-century developments. In opposition to the ancient ethic of circumscribed place,[3] with its view of hubris as the transgression of legitimate limits, and nemesis as the restoration of a violated natural order, the constant overstepping of bounds is a manifestation of modern freedom. The injunction in Goethe's *Faust*, never to bid the passing moment stay, exemplifies this attitude; and Fichte's *Wissenschaftslehre* of 1794–5, in a similar vein, prescribes the conformity of the world to reason through infinite approximations. In the new, dynamic subjectivity, are these transformations to be seen as capricious and arbitrary, or are they governed by rules of some general validity? How can spontaneity and autonomy (or self-limitation) be reconciled, or need they be? The problem of enlightenment assumes pointed formulation in the 'Kantian paradox': 'How can subjects themselves be the authors of a law which binds them?' (Pinkard 2002, p. 362). This ethical question is equally at the heart of aesthetics, from its earliest formulations onwards, late into the nineteenth century. The autonomy of art, as a distinct value sphere, though only relative throughout much of the period under investigation, poses a number of significant issues. Where is truth to be found in an art no longer interested in reproducing or imitating naturally given forms? How does art relate to morality: by illustrating and evoking freedom, by indifference, or by making manifest the illusory quality of subjectivity itself, and thus the nullity of the moral law?

In his powerful characterisation of ethical and aesthetic subjectivity, Hegel himself provides two distinct images of modern culture. He maintains that the great achievement of modernity is the idea of the free and infinite personality (Hegel 1991, pp. 20–1). This figure is constructed from two vectors. One is a centrifugal, vigorous outpouring of particularity, a growing differentiation of function in civil society, together with increasing demands for individual recognition. This is counterbalanced by a reflexive movement, or a self-aware return to unity in political institutions and ethical relations. This pattern can be described in aesthetic language as an extensive clarity or multiplication of meanings, conjoined with an intensive clarity, a distinct, shared, univocal meaning. The new affirmative self-consciousness of modern subjects permeates juridical relations, with the unprecedented expansion of the scope of interests and activities, and the increasing division of labour. Correspondingly, the rights to satisfy private purposes, to refashion objectivity in light of subjective ends, and to assert an autonomous

---

3 The Epicurean version of hedonism as the minimising of pain can be seen in this light.

moral conscience, gain acknowledgement as the perquisites of the modern subject. But, according to Hegel, to witness only this unfolding particularity is to have a one-sided vision, to miss the reflexive turn. Modern solidarities are also constituted by acts of freedom and recognition, which express the new understanding of the self (Hegel 1991, pp. 282–3). Reflection here assumes the sense of reconnecting the multiple into a unity, not forcibly, but in mutual affirmation.[4] This prospect is afforded by political institutions in which subjects appear as an amplification, and not only as a limitation, of one another's freedom. For Hegel, the rational state, towards which modernity tends, combines spontaneity or freedom with autonomy or self-legislation consistent with this underlying diversity.[5] This mutuality is prefigured in aesthetics, and even if, in Hegel's mature thought, art can no longer secure a genuine reconciliation among modern subjects, the background of his theory of shared ethical life is provided in aesthetic ideas of reflection deriving from Enlightenment sources.

Yet Hegel also describes modernity as a culture of rigid opposition, fragmentation or diremption (Hegel 1964, pp. 88, 90–1), an assertion of unbridled particularity, which dangerously undermines the potentiality for rational autonomy. In this image, the expansive and the reflexive motions of modern subjectivity do not harmonise with each other. They remain in stubborn opposition, and any momentarily achieved unity is highly fragile. The centrifugal forces threaten constantly to overwhelm the integrative capacities of modern institutions and relations. This image is one of mutual antagonism and separation, between understanding and sensibility, freedom and form, subject and subject, subject and object.[6] Hegel finds evidence of these intractable contradictions in the philosophy of Kant, who nonetheless struggled to resolve them, and in his own romantic contemporaries,[7] whom he saw as irresponsibly extolling the tensions and conflicts of the modern world. After Hegel, the ideal of rational self-determination is increasingly

---

4 Reflection will assume several different meanings in the authors examined here: the movement from division towards unity (Hegel); the projection of a subjective content into objective existence (expressivism); and, conversely, the withdrawal of the subject from external objects back into the self (irony). This ambiguity is unavoidable; it is present in the texts under discussion, and illustrates the central role played by reflection in this body of thought. In each case, the specific meaning will be indicated.

5 For various recent perspectives on these issues, see Siep 1997.

6 Bernstein 1992, pp. 1–65, sees in aesthetic theory a nostalgia for lost unity, but overstates the separation between aesthetics, ethics and scientific reason by the time of Kant.

7 Hegel 1964 uses the term 'romantic' to designate post-classical, Christian ideas of the subject generally, while stressing the new forms emerging from the Enlightenment. On various current definitions of romanticism, see Butler 1981, pp. 3–10.

cast into doubt, and the ideas of spontaneity and self-legislation come to diverge and conflict.

The history of aesthetics provides a clear vantage point for observing the movements of modern subjectivity. It illustrates attitudes of recognition, resignation or affirmation towards the culture of fragmentation, but also the tendency to press beyond it, to seek harmony and reconciliation. Its images of free self-determination and of particular self-assertion are intimately connected, as the very pressures and tensions of modernity constantly reawaken the desire for synthesis, and spawn new projects of reconciliation, even as these again falter. The reflexive moment of which Hegel spoke may make itself felt less in the institutions of modern ethical and political life than in the persistent discontents of modern subjects with their fragmented world. The elaboration of the images of harmony and conflict is the subject matter of modern aesthetic thought.

1   Foundations of modern aesthetics

Contributing to the decisive shift to subjectivity that constitutes modern aesthetics, G. W. Leibniz (1646–1716) dissolves objective forms into the power and motion that produce them, thus into the activity of subjects (Leibniz 1993, pp. 55–117). The movement from stable form to underlying formative process will be essential in subsequent aesthetic thought, from the romantics through Marx's understanding of labour. It is foundational for the discipline itself. Alexander Baumgarten (1714–62), widely regarded, together with J. J. Winckelmann (1717–68), as an originator of modern aesthetics, initially defines the subject (soul, or *anima*) as a *hypokeimenon*, an inert substrate bearing properties, according with the classical metaphysical meaning; but, applying Leibniz's conception of form and movement, he also suggests a new understanding of the subject, as a formative power which actualises a property, or has that property as its externalisation (Baumgarten 1739, pp. 501, 527; Menke 1999, pp. 596–7; Paetzold 1992, p. 13). When Hegel defines personality as an acquisition or an accomplishment, he is pursuing the line initiated by Baumgarten.

The concept of reflection, in the sense of the subject's relating to form and distinguishing itself from it, is at the heart of aesthetic responses to modernity. Are forms to be seen as externalisations or expressions of subjects' implicit selves, or do they raise more problematic questions of alienation, discordance and dissatisfaction? Two positions, originally largely complementary, though later opposed, were developed by J. G. Herder

(1744–1803) and Moses Mendelssohn (1729–86). Herder traces the elaboration of objective form from the powers and capacities of subjects. Form is the manifestation or expression of an implicit subjective content. Further, his placing of sensuousness and rationality not merely in correspondence, but in a genetic relationship with the more complex unities of the spiritual realm emerging from simpler, natural antecedents,[8] anticipates Schelling and Hölderlin in their quest for the original unity of thought and being (Herder 1878, pp. 3–43, 1892). In Mendelssohn, reflection attends to the self-aware enjoyment of subjective energies, as distinct from their realisation in outward forms (Menke 1999, p. 601; Paetzold 1992, p. 13). This conscious separation of subject and object marks the properly aesthetic attitude (Menke 1999, p. 603). The distinction between Mendelssohn and Herder evolves into an alternative that will be decisive for later romantic thought: reflection as locating a creative force detached from the object, the stance of irony; or reflection as working subjective forces into determinate form, the stance of expressivism.

The aesthetic theory of Immanuel Kant (1724–1804) refers aesthetic judgement neither to an empirical community of taste, as in Shaftesbury (1671–1713) or David Hume (1711–76), nor to a transcendent Platonic idea, but to a common-sense or intersubjective assessment. This reference of an objective form back to its subjective source, echoing Leibniz, is the inverse to Herder's process of outward reflection; it refers the self-aware subject not only to its own interiority, as in Mendelssohn, but to the possibility of shared judgement with others, and to the universal moral idea.[9] For Kant (1987), the autonomy of the aesthetic means that it derives its content from no pre-given norms or interests, but this autonomy is only relative, since beauty serves as a symbol of morality. Unlike the Platonic doctrine of the *Symposium*, beauty does not disclose a metaphysical structure of nature, but confirms the (inter)subjective presence of practical reason (Rüsen 1976, p. 37; Thérien 1997, p. 759). The beautiful bridges the gulf between nature and freedom; it is a symbol of ethical life, prefiguring the end of history where sensuousness stands under the command of practical reason (Pluhar 1987, pp. lxxxvi–cix).

---

8 Menke 1999 distinguishes Herder's and Mendelssohn's concepts of reflection, but sees these less as possible alternatives to each other than to what he calls the metaphysical subject model attributed to Hegel and Heidegger (p. 595). He proposes that reflexivity and not subjectivity is the more basic category of aesthetics, but concedes that reflection refers to spontaneous activity by a subject (p. 609).

9 The introduction of intersubjectivity thus offers a further development of the concept of reflection.

Kant claims that the *Critique of Judgement* completes his systematic enterprise, linking the supersensible with the sensuous, the noumenal with the phenomenal order. In the judgement of his successors from Schiller onwards, Kant's own solution fails. The problem can be traced through various understandings of reflection, and of subjective spontaneity, in relation to objective forms, and to autonomy, or rational self-legislation (Pippin 1991, pp. 153, 180 n.7). The idea of spontaneity is central to Kant's account of the freedom of the will.[10] In manifesting *Willkür* or freedom of choice (Kant 1991a, preface), the will acts spontaneously as its own cause: it admits the rule or maxim which is to govern its action, independently of any external causes which might determine it without its own compliance. But for Kant, the spontaneity of willing must be regulated by autonomous self-legislation and adherence to universal moral criteria valid for all rational subjects. This higher determination Kant calls *Wille*, the moral will. The ends of *moral* action require rational sanction unrelated to private interest or appetite; though Kant distinguishes from this more exigent standard the realm of right, which deals with the coexistence of freedoms in their external aspect, independently of motivations (Kant 1991a, pp. 68–90). In actions that count as autonomous, the spontaneity or freedom of the will comes under the command of practical reason. Such actions are guided by maxims which can be willed universally without contradiction. These maxims are derived neither from motives of sensibility or interest, nor from the supposition of a teleological order of nature, but from subjectivity itself, pure practical reason (Kant 2002, pp. 98–100). After Kant, two divergent lines can be traced, the one tending to dissociate spontaneity from autonomy, the other to develop ideas of spontaneity and autonomy into more concrete forms. This distinction roughly corresponds to that between the early romantics, and the school of German idealism from Schiller to Hegel and beyond. A second differentiation appears in the concept of reflection, as the spontaneous revelation or withdrawal of the subject in relation to objective forms.

2   Aesthetics and revolution

Traditionally, the neo-classical style of the eighteenth century has been interpreted as a formal system of rules, against which the romantics, notably in England, react by stressing, and eventually overstressing, the value of

---

10 Kant 1997, B75/A51, defines spontaneity as the mind's power of producing representations out of itself.

subjective feeling (Bate 1949, pp. 166–72); but the critical character of classicism in respect to pre-revolutionary society should also be recognised (Butler 1981, pp. 18–22). Denis Diderot (1713–84), for example, celebrates the classical ideals of gravity and simplicity against the degrading luxury of the present (Becq 1984, II, pp. 534–7). J. J. Winckelmann seeks to restore the spare beauties of classical art by recovering its animating spirit for the present. Everything accidental or extraneous in art, such as baroque ostentation, is to be eliminated, so that the permanent (Platonic) idea shines forth (Butler 1981, p. 19; Raulet 1992, p. 151; Winckelmann 1755, 1764). Balance and control are the essence of an Apollonian classicism (in contrast to Nietzsche's proclivity for the disruptive Dionysian, in his refurbished nineteenth-century version: Desmond 1988, p. 120), but the role of the creative subject is not yet highlighted. The principal difference between classicism and romanticism is not in their critical bearing, but in their understanding of the subject.

As the Enlightenment view of the modern subject increasingly permeates all fields of culture, it shatters the neo-classical restraints which are themselves an aspect of Enlightenment thought. An aesthetic revolution is launched, giving rise to the varieties of romanticism and to new forms of idealism. This revolution in culture is open to many political applications. The problem of binding spontaneity under self-imposed law is one that spans European culture, even where Kant's influence is not directly felt. It is an epochal problem that Kant poses with great insight and clarity, reflecting on the achievements of his age. Prior to Kant, Rousseau (1712–78), frequently viewed as an early romantic, seeks the solution to modern decadence and oppression in rediscovering and reactivating an uncorrupted subjective core, endowed with compassion and healthy self-love, which can furnish principles for consensus and a new social union. English romantics like William Wordsworth (1770–1850) and Samuel Taylor Coleridge (1772–1834) begin from a similar perspective, but their reflections on the course of the French Revolution lead many of them to politically conservative and quietistic conclusions. Arising from Enlightenment critique, the new thinking about subjectivity and its relations to nature receives a particular inflection under the impact of the French Revolution. In a development paralleling the evolution of Richard Wagner half a century later, Wordsworth moves from political optimism, and endorsement of revolution, to the idea that political solutions are too superficial to address the problem of modern subjectivity. In Wordsworth's case, this conclusion results from radicalising the principle of subjectivity itself. Attributing poverty to the feudal monopoly of property and power, the *'forced* disproportion of... possession' (cited in Izenberg 1998, p. 127), he initially supported efforts to overthrow this regime. He collaborated with William Godwin, whose doctrine of political justice appealed to benevolent propensities locked in the individual conscience, but as Wordsworth worked out his own version of radical freedom, it came to resemble an absolute capriciousness, a purely self-regarding spontaneity unchecked by any law or rational restraint (Izenberg 1998, p. 122; Wordsworth 1979, p. 821). In this respect, it is much like the anarchistic egoism later defended by Max Stirner (Stirner 1845). For Wordsworth, however, such an attitude was unsustainable. He detected it in Jacobin politics, and was repelled by its effects. As a partial corrective to the hubris of the modern subject, Wordsworth's later work advocates recognition of sublime, infinite nature (Wordsworth 1992). Like his contemporary German romantic A. W. Schlegel (1808; see Becq 1984, II, p. 826), Wordsworth sees the mind as marked by a duality: a dependency on the absolute creative power of nature, understood not classically, as a fixed order, but dynamically, as the source of infinite potentiality; and a self-relation by which the individual consciousness emerges and creates forms for itself (Izenberg 1998, p. 125). In a romantic reworking of the classical themes of restraint and fixed place, Wordsworth proposes that acknowledging the infinity of nature allows subjects to limit their claims of freedom, and to see their own activity in a more modest light (Bate 1991; Izenberg 1992). The movement from fragmented and disordered modern culture to unity is to be achieved not, as Hegel thought, through rational political institutions, but by a common state of natural dependency. While (as in Schopenhauer) it is proper to alleviate suffering where possible (Izenberg 1998, p. 129), the problem of subjectivity is intractable to political remedies.

Other romanticisms reaffirm traditional religion as the means of securing unity and harmony. In the wake of Enlightenment critiques of orthodoxy, new kinds of justification must be found. In *Le Génie du Christianisme*, François-René de Chateaubriand (1768–1848) stresses not the truth, but the beauty of Christianity, a religion which best promotes the arts and improves the lot of humanity. The work was published in 1802, in the climate of the Concordat between Napoleonic France and the papacy. Chateaubriand had contested the historical basis of Christianity in an earlier publication, *Essai sur les Révolutions* (1797), where he argued for the derivation of fundamental Christian dogmas from Platonic and other ancient sources, and attacked the despotic rule of the clergy (Chateaubriand 1978a, pp. 404–27). He speculated, too, on a coming end to Christianity, in either universal enlightenment or barbarism (Chateaubriand 1978a, pp. 428–31).[11] His recantation after 1799, when he began composing *Le Génie* in English exile, involved a renewed aesthetic appreciation of Christian doctrine and ceremonies, and of its vision of world order, rather than an assertion of literal truth. Christian art occupies a higher standpoint than classical, pagan art, because of its more profound grasp of the relation of finite and infinite (though the distinction is nuanced: the Greeks practised a nature religion, but their art and philosophy appealed, at their best, to the spirit, not the senses: Becq 1984, II, pp. 821–2). The deeper Christian understanding of spirituality finds expression in works of architecture, painting and literature of unparalleled richness, from Gothic cathedrals and medieval religious depictions, to the writings of Pascal and Fénelon. Christianity thus offers an aesthetic education whose effects are to promote civilisation and to tame savage passions, including those unleashed by the recent revolutionary tumults in France. The Church had originally salvaged culture from the ruins of the Roman Empire, and was still a beacon of hope in the modern world (Chateaubriand 1978b). Chateaubriand attempts to appease the new, post-Enlightenment subjectivity by demonstrating that the traditional religious order is in accord with its aesthetic aspirations.

3 Spontaneity and autonomy: Schiller and Hölderlin

In his lectures on the history of philosophy, Hegel connects the development of post-Kantian thought in Germany with the dynamics of the French Revolution (Hegel 1971, p. 314). The young Engels would echo this idea, accentuating, however, the pallor of this reflected movement. In an unfavourable comparison of Friedrich Schiller (1759–1805) with Goethe, he credits the latter with a keener insight into German political backwardness and incompetence, even though Goethe himself was unable to overcome these limits in his own work. Engels accuses Schiller, in contrast, of lacking Goethe's hard realism. Schiller, he claims, seeks flight into the abstractions of Kantian idealism, retreating into an illusory inner freedom that leaves intact the structures of political and economic oppression. Schiller thus becomes a spokesman of the German ideology in its pejorative sense. Engels depicts Schiller's idea of aesthetic education as an apolitical utopianism, masking the

11 The full title is *Essai Historique, Politique et Moral sur les Révolutions Anciennes et Modernes, Considerées dans leurs Rapports avec la Révolution Française*. Despite his radically changed viewpoint after 1799, Chateaubriand reprinted the work in 1826. His formulation of possible futures anticipates early twentieth-century ideas of 'socialisme ou barbarie'.

'prosaic wretchedness' of material conditions in Germany with a pretentious and vacuous intellectual wretchedness (Engels 1972a, p. 232).[12]

More recently, the idea of an aesthetic revolution, in which Schiller, the early romantics and the post-Kantian idealists are participants, has been applied to the German case. Here this intellectual movement appears not as a surrogate, or a consolation, for failed political action, but as a complement and guide to political transformation. The early German romantics and idealists share with Schiller an ambitious cultural programme in which religion, science and social life, as well as politics, would be profoundly reformed (Jaeschke 1990, p. 2). The political and philosophical trajectories soon deviate, and after 1799 many among the romantics come to uphold orthodoxy in church and state. Schiller did not take this conservative turn. Despite his disillusionment with the course of the French Revolution, his aim was not to repudiate politics in favour of individualistic self-cultivation, but to advocate 'a better society of interrelated human beings' (Wilkinson and Willoughby 1967, pp. lxxxii–lxxxiii), in which aesthetic education was a necessary but insufficient condition for promoting a more comprehensive ethical life.

Schiller broadens Kant's account of autonomy, and recasts spontaneity as self-formation. He proposes a system of aesthetic education in which spontaneity trains and elevates itself to a moral standpoint, where the demands of duty and of sensibility are no longer in conflict. Autonomy does not refer only to an internal condition: it is not confined to the determination of maxims for action, but sets the subject in an institutional matrix, in which freedom, intuited as real, permeates social and political relations (Pippin 1991, p. 180 n.13). Schiller thus anticipates Hegel's critique of Kant, and his elaboration of modern ethical life.

The basic problem for Schiller's *Aesthetic Education of Man*, written in 1794–5, contemporaneously with the publication of Fichte's first *Wissenschaftslehre*, is to discover connections without eliminating differences (Wilkinson and Willoughby 1967, p. lxxxviii). Schiller envisages a new kind of politics compatible with modern individuality and its differentiated forms. How is it possible to secure harmony without producing uniformity, and without suppressing spontaneity? Aesthetics provides the outlines of a solution to the growing diversity of interests in modern political and social

---

12 Cf. Lukács 1954, pp. 11–96, but, for a contrary view, Popitz 1953 and Marcuse 1955. On Schiller, Goethe and romanticism, see Sharpe 1995, pp. 52–3. The following discussion of Schiller incorporates material from Moggach 2007, with kind permission of the publisher.

life. In unifying the manifold forms of individuality, a universal interest is not to be authoritatively imposed, as the French Revolution attempted in vain, but must evolve in a spontaneous movement, whereby the particulars make themselves fit to represent a general will. They reshape themselves aesthetically in light of their understanding of a common good. As Schiller puts it: 'A political constitution will still be very imperfect if it can bring about unity only by the suppression [*Aufhebung*] of multiplicity' (Schiller 1967, Letter IV. 3).[13] Further, he affirms, 'The state ought not to honour only the objective and generic, but also the subjective and specific character of the individuals' (Schiller 1967, Letter IV. 3)[14] who are its citizens. This inability to accommodate diversity is one of the failures of the French Revolution, in Schiller's assessment. He acknowledges difference, and seeks to balance diversity with commonality of purpose. According to his political ideal, 'the triumphant form rests just as far from uniformity as from confusion' (Schiller 1967, Letter IV. 7).[15] Aesthetic education is part of the process which reconciles the particular and the universal both within subjects and in their interrelationships.

Schiller is particularly attentive to the conditions of modern subjectivity and freedom in which the problem of difference is posed. The harmony of particular and universal interests can no longer simply be presupposed, but must be created. How it is created is the decisive point. The wholeness and harmony of the Greeks represents a beautiful, given unity, largely undifferentiated in interest and function, and thus is no longer an attainable modern ideal. In present conditions, the attempt to restore this unity directly is repressive, as in the efforts to establish the uniformity and identity of citizens in the French Revolution. The French revolutionaries viewed diversity as an illegitimate differentiation in rights, privileges and juridical status among estates. Diversity was thus a bulwark of the old order and of despotic rule (Maza 2002, p. 122), to be effaced before the common identity of citizens endowed with equal rights.

Schiller resists the logic of imposition or standardisation, but he also distinguishes the inequalities of the *ancien régime* from the emergent specialisations of modern civil society. The problem of differential rights and of the arrogance of power provides the themes for Schiller's dramatic works, such as *Die Räuber* (1781), *Don Carlos* (1787) and *Wilhelm Tell* (1804). His theoretical writings stress the newer forms of social distinction. Schiller presents the problem of specialisation as a result of the growth of scientific knowledge,

---

13 My translation, DM.   14 My translation, DM.   15 My translation, DM.

and of new political and administrative arrangements, but his illustrations evoke the new technical division of labour (Schiller 1967, Letter VI. 8). Like Adam Smith, Schiller judges the modern specialisation of labour to be historically necessary, but detrimental to the individual producer, whose activity and perspectives on self, society and the world are truncated and deformed. 'Everlastingly chained to a single little fragment of the Whole, man himself develops into nothing but a fragment' (Schiller 1967, Letter VI. 7). If such specialisation benefits the species in promoting a quantitative advance in knowledge, it is injurious to the mutilated individuals who enact the process. The new diversity is highly problematic, disintegrating the personality and society, but it also contains elements of resolution, a reflexive turn to community, understood aesthetically.

Distinguishing the naïve aesthetic style, which bespeaks the immediate and transparent connections among ancient subjects, from the sentimental, expressive of the more problematic and reflexive modern self (Schiller 1984),[16] Schiller precedes Hegel in describing modernity as a culture of oppositions. Applying new concepts of determinability, he views the personality as the site of abundant and varied potentialities. The division of labour causes a reduction of this malleability, as individuals become tied to one restrictive and repetitive function. Anticipating Marx's critique of alienated labour, Schiller contends that under modern conditions, individuals face enormous obstacles in achieving a harmonious externalisation of themselves in the forms of their activity. Instead of expressing the plenitude of human capabilities, their actions become deformed and fragmentary (Schiller 1967, Letter VI). Hence arises an imperative to redress this state of alienation, to discover a kind of wholeness and integrity compatible with the discriminations of modern life.

The political implications of this analysis lie in the critical ideal of an aesthetic state of beautiful and harmonised life-conditions, and in the idea of aesthetic education. Schiller thus distinguishes, on the one hand, the modern, dynamic state of rights based upon individual self-assertion and mutual exclusion. On the other, extending Fichte's idea of reciprocity as conjunctive (Pott 1980, pp. 54, 66–70), Schiller describes a possible aesthetic state as an ideal of collaborative action and mutual recognition (Schiller 1967, Letters XIV. 1 and XVI. 1). This state designates not a final, utopian

---

16 The naïve and sentimental have also been read as members of a triad, in which the (tacit) central term, designating the present, is the culture of diremption; the sentimental would then presage the synthesis, in which reflection and harmony coexist (Sharpe 1995, p. 113).

condition, but a process of constant renewal, with invigorating effects on ethical life. It is order as produced, not given; but produced by free play, not under duress. Stressing the importance of subjective assent and collaboration, this idea also stands in opposition to the uniformity and identity of earlier republican thought, permitting a more complex account of the general will.

According to Schiller's aesthetic republicanism, 'Man must learn to desire more nobly, so that he may not need to will sublimely' (Schiller 1967, Letter XXIII. 8). It is not necessary to repress the particular identity, as sublime, rigoristic versions of republicanism will demand (Moggach 2003, ch. 7); nor may it count as immediately valid, as in juridical accommodations among existing particular interests (e.g. Kant's population of intelligent devils; Kant, 1991b, pp. 112–13). Instead, the particular self provides material for aesthetic refashioning, a spontaneously generated self-transformation. Aesthetic education elicits the idea of freedom in those who undertake it. While art is independent from direct moral instruction, it acts like morality in exemplifying freedom (Becq 1984, II, p. 848; Beiser 2003, p. 42). Schiller's position has been described not as art for art's sake, but 'art for life's sake' (Wilkinson and Willoughby 1967, p. clxxxi), enhancing individual and collective existence. Through aesthetic education, the empirical individual can correspond to the rational idea of Man, not because the ideal suppresses the empirical self, but because individuals adapt and elevate themselves to the stature of the idea (Schiller 1967, Letter IV. 2). The result is not uniformity, but harmony (Schiller 1967, Letter XIII), not a one-sided subordination and persistent internal division, but a mutual exchange and active reciprocity. This unity-in-difference designates the aesthetic condition.

Schiller proposes two concepts of freedom, corresponding to the Kantian beautiful and sublime. First, he sketches a beautiful concordance of the faculties of mind (will, understanding and sensibility) within the individual personality, implying, further, harmony with external nature and with other subjects. Aesthetic education is a process of self-formation, taming disruptive passions and controlling them, not by repressive intellect, but by cultivated taste, which can unobtrusively regulate social interactions. Secondly, he understands freedom as dignity, the sublime elevation of the self above natural causality in the determination of ends. The compatibility of these two conceptions, and Schiller's success in integrating them, have been disputed (Sharpe 1995, pp. 47–8, 63–4), but his extensions and applications of Kant were enormously influential. They depict aesthetic and political self-determination and moral autonomy as the fulfilment of the idea of spontaneity, not as its denial.

Douglas Moggach

A related theoretical current proposes other Kantian means to overcome the persistent dualisms of modern life, which the French Revolution proved inadequate to resolve. Here Kant's idea of the intuitive intellect, a conceptual understanding that produces its own corresponding objectivity, suggests an image of the new subjectivity, and of a shared realm of freedom. Among the early German idealists, Friedrich Hölderlin (1770–1843), companion of Hegel and Schelling, finds a model for this productivity of the mind in artistic practice, as defined by G. E. Lessing (1729–81), for whom not objects, but actions, or subjectivity at work in the world, provide the proper contents of art (Lessing 2003, pp. 25–129). For Hölderlin, the supersensible refers to the possibility of community among all finite spirits, and their claim of absolute freedom against powers that claim an underivative, transcendent status (Lypp 1972, p. 22 n.24). The noumenal realm of freedom is accessible in an intellectual intuition, which reveals the unity of subject and subject, and of subject and external form. The recognition of a common ground where being and freedom meet checks the dangers implicit in a boundless subjectivity. The intuition of a preconceptual identity of thinking and being, attested in art, especially poetry (Harris 1993, p. 32; Henrich 2003, pp. 279–95), brings to rest the infinite regress of subjective reflection: the constant retreat of subjectivity before its own products is a problem detected in Fichte's reformulation of Kant (Hegel 1971, pp. 415–16; Pinkard 2002, pp. 139–44). Hölderlin resists this romantic turn. In evoking a harmony of reflection and objective form, aesthetic insight can prefigure and guide more concrete political transformations.

These developments receive brief but pointed political interpretation in the anonymous, fragmentary text known as 'The Earliest System Programme of German Idealism',[17] of 1796 or 1797, which illustrates Hölderlin's influence, if not his authorship. This text attributes to Kant's aesthetics the intention of placing free goal-determination within a natural order that we can conceive, regulatively, as purposive, in accord with our own ends. The contemporary world, however, is shaped by the dull and mechanical interaction of parts (Lypp 1972, p. 20). Kant could not completely free himself from this perspective. Almost simultaneously with the 'System Programme', he would describe and endorse this mechanism explicitly in his *Doctrine of Right*, the first part of his *Metaphysics of Morals* of 1797, basing juridical relations upon constraint or unilateral exclusions

17 On the disputed authorship of this text, in Hegel's hand, see Gammon 2000, pp. 145–70; Mathy 1994, pp. 9–10.

494

from private spheres. The 'System Programme' proposes an alternative, better to realise the accord of the natural order with freedom. This ideal is the transcendence of the mechanical state, and the birth of the aesthetic state of beautiful and harmonised life-conditions. The idea remains rudimentary in the 'System Programme', but it had already figured in a work by Carl von Dalberg (1744–1817), a friend of Schiller (Dalberg 1791),[18] and, as an incentive and catalyst for reform, in Schiller's own *Aesthetic Education*. To what extent can modern life be pacified under the category of beauty? Like Schiller, Hölderlin's work is devoted to this question. Spontaneity becomes the idea of freedom as a shaping of the self and society. The aesthetic holds out prospects of social and political solidarity in an age of increasing division of labour and specialisation.

4   Spontaneity, schism and expression: Schelling and
the varieties of romanticism

Though he later diminishes the status of the aesthetic (Cesa 2000, pp. 199–217), F. W. J. Schelling (1775–1854), in his *System of Transcendental Idealism* (1800), depicts art as the organon of philosophy. It is the vehicle of an intellectual intuition, or a concept that brings about its own realisation. Schelling conceives this productivity of thought to be an aesthetic act. Art thus completes philosophy, because the content which the latter can only depict subjectively, as a concept, can be shown to have an objective presence in artistic depiction (Mathy 1994, pp. 11–12). The study of artistic works allows us, moreover, to recover the creativity of self-consciousness as it unfolds in nature, and discloses the complex inner structure of subjectivity: a consciousness operating without full self-knowledge, in that the process of creation is never entirely transparent to reflection (Bowie 2000, pp. 245–6; Bowie 1990). This partial opacity distinguishes art from science and philosophy, allowing it to escape from strict causal determination, and to originate the new, the unprecedented and the incalculable. Schelling's early work seeks to resolve the problem of how the mind relates to the external world. He takes up this problem as expressed by Spinoza, for whom there are two parallel manifestations of a common universal substance, one objective, the other subjective (Spinoza 2000). Each of the attributes of

18 Dalberg is cited by Schiller in the original publication of *Aesthetic Education* in the journal *Die Horen*. He was among the leaders of the Napoleonic Confederation of the Rhine in 1806, and was responsible for implementing significant legal reforms in these territories. Schiller 1793 is dedicated to Dalberg.

thought and extension (or objectivity) has an identical and necessary content, guaranteeing their accord, but at the price of subjective freedom, since subjects confront an entirely determined world. Their freedom amounts to adaptation to necessity. This problem will prove highly important for the romantics. Schelling's initial move is to resolve Spinoza's attributes of thought and being into a continuum, where they flow together harmoniously, and reveal their common origin at an 'indifference point', prior to the separation of subject and object. Freedom is possible in so far as the world is not entirely governed by causal laws. This is the lesson of art. While Hölderlin's intellectual intuition reveals a common project of subordinating the external world to rational freedom, Schelling's places the prospect of freedom in the indeterminate and the contingent.[19] Here idealism and romanticism begin to establish their own proper identities.[20]

From the point of view of the early romantics like Friedrich Schlegel (1772–1829), Schelling's approach to art has two principal defects. First, Schelling seeks to over-systematise experience.[21] Instead, the romantics cast doubt on ultimate foundational principles or definitive syntheses of thought and being, and celebrate multiplicity and difference over unity,[22] thus heralding contemporary 'post-modern' attitudes, whose vaunted originality is dubious. This posture involves the defence of the non-identical, though the late Schelling, too, is adamant in his criticisms of what he sees as Hegel's reduction of being to an aspect of thought.

Secondly, Schelling's aesthetics distinguish inadequately between ancient and modern art, seeing in them not distinct historical phases but merely formal variants on an identical pattern: the ancients depict the infinite in the finite, the moderns the finite in the infinite. Like Schiller and Hegel, Friedrich Schlegel stresses a break in continuity, an epochal rupture in the history of art (Mathy 1994, pp. 17, 23). After a brief period around 1795 when he upholds the classical unities against the diffuse and eclectic modern style (Beiser 2003, pp. 126–7), Schlegel writes the founding manifestos of the romantic school in 1797–9 (Schlegel 2003).[23] In conjunction with a critique of Fichte's ahistoricism, Schlegel rejects the timeless universal

---

19 Ferry 1990, pp. 113–14, derives this position from Kant 1987.
20 Hegel, however, maintains close connections to Schelling until the *Phenomenology* of 1807.
21 Schlegel also feels that the complete lack of a system is an equally detrimental attitude. See Schlegel 2003, p. 247.
22 Beiser 2003, pp. 3–5, however, sees closer affinities of the romantics with Platonism.
23 Though the term 'romantic' is ubiquitous in the writings of its members, the school acquires the name after 1805 (Behler 1992, pp. 22–3).

standards of classicism in favour of a contextual and hermeneutic approach to works of art, soon to be developed by Schleiermacher (Bubner 2003, pp. 17–28, 35–45). Schlegel differentiates nature- and art-poetry, the one a mimesis of a natural order, the other an exploration of subjective moods. Ancient literary and artistic expression depicts a direct appreciation of nature and objectivity, but it suppresses freedom, whereas modern forms celebrate an objectless liberty, the endless play of subjective aesthetic powers (Mathy 1994, pp. 17–18). This transition leads to an emphasis on the bizarre and the abnormal (which become especially the themes of later romanticism: Bohrer 1998), but it also indicates new developmental possibilities within modern subjectivity itself (Jaeschke 1990, pp. 5–6), a potential for perfectibility and so for new and higher stages of aesthetic production. Schlegel anticipates a future synthesis in the poetry of the objective, based upon neither mere subjectivity nor immediate, external nature; but the outlines of this resolution remain vague, and he is frequently understood to revel in the dissonances of modern experience (Hegel 1971, pp. 415–16). Richard Wagner will take up this programme of a new, integral art in his own compositional work.

The early efforts at synthesis by Friedrich Schlegel and his collaborators are a facet of the aesthetic revolution, the cultural transformation of individual and social life. The political demarcations traced by Heine and Ruge in the 1840s, between republican idealism and conservative romanticism, are not yet germane. Schlegel himself writes a defence of republicanism in 1796 (Schlegel 1996, pp. 93–112). While eschewing rigorous systematisation of thought, he attempts a great philosophical fusion, between the seemingly incompatible positions of Spinoza, Leibniz and Fichte. From Spinoza, as read by Schelling, comes the idea of a pantheistic nature, with thought and being as continuous and complementary outpourings from a single source; from Leibniz (and from contemporary discoveries in chemistry and physics), the idea of nature not as a mechanism, but as the play of living forces; and from Fichte, ideas of spontaneous and permanent creation, and the reference of objective forces and forms to the subject. This synthesis proves unstable, and it is the autonomy of the subject, the Fichtean dimension, that is ultimately sacrificed in romanticism (Beiser 2003, pp. 185–6). As in Wordsworth, a recognition of an engulfing natural order serves to limit the arrogations of the self. Subjective creativity is expressive of the powers of nature and not of rational freedom. Meanwhile, subjects are increasingly thrust back into their own private, inner worlds. They are thus integrated into nature, but increasingly separated from each other.

In its analysis of the workings of modern subjectivity, romantic thought confirms Hegel's view of its participation in the culture of diremption. The contradiction between the subject and society comes to permeate romantic thought (Rüsen 1976, p. 19). The idea of irony highlights this detachment. Hegel describes romantic irony as the divorce between conscious selves and their essential ends, resulting from a one-sided subjective morality which cannot make the transition to the shared values and practices of ethical life. Seeking to draw the criteria of their judgements from an abstract interiority, and not from the network of social ties and mutual recognition, subjects fall into contradiction with objectivity (Hegel 1991, pp. 180–6). Their ends become contingent and arbitrary, and while they acknowledge this arbitrariness, they are incapable of advancing to reconciliation. Their subjectivity becomes exhausted in self-absorption. A typical figure of romantic inwardness is thus the 'beautiful soul' critically described in the *Phenomenology*, a pure self-regarding consciousness which disdains to realise itself in objectivity (Hegel 1967a, pp. 658–66). This figure is distinct both from the classical 'beautiful individual' as a microcosm of the *polis*, and from the modern 'free and infinite personality', whose reflexiveness guides it back to unity with others. Friedrich Schleiermacher (1768–1834), who, after Schiller (1793), gives this image its most poignant expression, depicts the beautiful soul as the 'unmoved centre of a turning world' (Schleiermacher's *Soliloquy* of 1810, cited in Simpson 1984, p. 12), evoking an inwardness that detaches the subject from objective relations. Anticipating facets of Schopenhauer's thought, Schleiermacher distinguishes a devalued phenomenal realm from the essential and the noumenal, now conceived as the domain of a pure self-consciousness, and he subordinates the finite subject to an ineffable absolute, accessible not through rational thought, but in feelings of dependency and subordination. Thus ideas of both self-realisation and autonomy are cast into doubt. Schleiermacher, like Hamann and Jacobi, affirms religious faith as a spontaneous act of submission to a rationally inaccessible power. In contrast to Kant, the spontaneous act of the subject is not regulated by an autonomous self-legislation, but by heteronomous compliance; aspects of the Kantian self thus come to be sundered. Hegel will be severely critical of this stance: Schleiermacher's intended endorsement of Christianity is predicated upon an introspection that threatens to undermine social cohesion and unity (Simpson 1984, pp. 11, 14, 19). The recognition of this danger helps to explain Hegel's vigorous anti-subjectivist polemics of the *Philosophy of Right* (Hegel 1991, pp. 9–23).

Romantic irony attests to a divorce between the inner and the outer similar to that characterising the religious movement of pietism (Simpson 1984, p. 14), though in Novalis (Friedrich von Hardenberg, 1772–1801), this idea is linked to a defence of Catholicism, and not of Reformed Christianity (Novalis 1996). Irony is a form of reflection that dissociates subjects from their attributes or externalisations. If Herder's idea of reflection is to resolve external form into the workings of force, and thus to maintain a continuity between subject and object, Friedrich Schlegel adopts a view closer to Mendelssohn's concept of reflection as the inward turn of the subject away from its outer manifestations. Schlegel's idea of irony implies that in external forms are not to be found authentic expressions of subjective self-awareness, but merely transitory moments of creation and destruction (Menke 1999, pp. 604, 608), from which the subject stands aloof. His thought attests to complex influences from Fichte's first *Wissenschaftslehre* of 1794–5 (M. Frank 1995, pp. 65–85), though Fichte's major concern is to show how subjects assume relations towards the objective, and how they seek to rationalise it under the command of practical reason. Such practical motives are missing from Schlegel's texts. Kantian ideals of rational self-determination are also challenged by the recognition of transcendent powers, beyond the reach of subjectivity (Cesa 2000, pp. 199–217); these powers can be taken to be beneficent, as by Novalis, but increasingly they assume a more threatening mien, and they penetrate within consciousness itself, rendering the self impermeable to knowledge.[24]

The separation of the subject from externality has consequences for the understanding of being and objectivity. The early romantics incline towards a Spinozistic or pantheist view of substance as a self-causing continuum (Lypp 1972, p. 28), but this idea is difficult to harmonise with the emphasis on forms as transient and discontinuous. Against ideas of process and historical continuity, the romantics break down subjective activity into discrete and incommensurable moments, each fraught with radically different and unforeseeable outcomes (Bohrer 1998, p. 12; Mathy 1994, p. 16). Particularly in the late romantics, time is dissolved into atomistic points, each capable of initiating fundamentally new series of events (Bohrer 1998, p. 11). Causal regularity and the rule of scientific rationality are thereby dismissed. This tendency has been identified as a subjectified occasionalism (Schmitt 1924, p. 23). It represents a revival

---

24 This view persists in Freud, in conjunction with a new idea of subjectivity as multiple, construed in naturalistic or scientist terms.

in secular garb of the early modern idea of instantaneous and inscrutable divine interventions into the created order, upsetting any predictably operating natural causes. Deriving from the works of Nicholas Malebranche (1638–1715), occasionalism offers an alternative to Spinoza's formulation of the relation of thought and being. It detaches the operation of causality from physical bodies, and attributes it to a transcendent source in divine will; observable physical interactions do not really cause each other, but are merely the deceptive appearance of deeper, immaterial forces (Malebranche 1945, Book VI; McCracken 1983, ch. 3). Thus, in contrast to Spinoza, there is no necessity or determinism in nature. In subjectifying occasionalism, the late romantics stress moment over process, multiplicity over unity, unpredictability over recurrence. Unlike Malebranche's theological account, it is now the finite subject who is empowered to effect changes, and these (at least in the later romantics) follow no providential designs.

The shift towards occasionalism can be documented through views of accident and its place in a larger order. While Hölderlin's strongly anti-romantic ideal of transparency leads him to seek the subordination of contingency to rational rule (Lypp 1972, p. 19; Raulet 1992, p. 159), Novalis celebrates the contingent and the accidental for shattering routine and auguring the new: 'All the accidents of our lives are materials from which we can make what we will' (cited in Bohrer 1998, p. 12 [my translation, DM]). Freedom here lies in indeterminacy, not in rational autonomy; in *Willkür*, taken as arbitrary action, and not *Wille*, or submission to universal law. This attitude again highlights the romantic divorce between spontaneous subjective action and self-legislation. Occasionalism is not fully realised in early romanticism, however, because Schlegel holds a developmental view of history, in which the chaos of the present portends undetermined possibilities for a future synthesis of subject and object. Novalis, too, retains a teleological perspective in which the accidents of individual life are ultimately integrated. He combines a modern view of the reflexive subject with a defence of traditional values and relations, sanctioned by providence. Thus accident still figures within a potential order (Novalis in Bernstein 2003, pp. 203–38). Late romanticism shatters this order in favour of a fragmented reality, a 'substanceless punctualisation' (Bohrer 1998, pp. 12–13) of infinite and incommensurable possibilities. The fantastic, a pathological and demonic realm of inexplicable effects, comes to predominate in the work of Ludwig Tieck (1773–1853, though he is also counted among the early romantics), E. T. A. Hoffmann (1776–1822) and Edgar Allan Poe (1809–49). By a kind of *auxesis* or rhetorical augmentation (Aristotle 1926, 1368a

40f), Mendelssohn's reflexive shift away from form as constituted towards the subject as constitutive extends into a view of objectivity not as a causally governed domain, but as fields of arbitrary actions and outcomes.

A distinct current of thought generally described as romantic takes its lead not from Mendelssohn, but from Herder. Here the central concept is not irony, but expression, the authentic rendering in objectivity of an essential subjective content. Following Leibniz's translation of form into configuration, the structuring activity described by bodies themselves in their movements, Herder stresses the aesthetic, formative power of the self as an expression of its freedom (while also stressing continuity between the realms of nature and spirit). Ethically, as in Rousseau, an implicit subjectivity must give itself an authentic manifestation in the external world. This transposition of subjective content into objective and stable form encapsulates Herder's expressivist view of freedom (Taylor 1989, pp. 368–90). Further applying Leibniz's monadic doctrine, Herder considers each subject as offering a unique and irreplaceable perspective on the totality of human accomplishments, and realising an aspect of a composite human personality; these subjects appear both as individuals and as collectivities, though the relations between these levels are not always clear in his thought. Expressivism serves as a criterion for assessing the modern social order. Herder detects in modernity a growing tendency towards a mechanistic reduction, not an increase, of social differentiation: the division of labour reduces workers to standardised, interchangeable units, whose movement is imparted from without (Herder 1877, pp. 534–64). Like the early idealist 'System Programme', he equates mechanism and heteronomy. Authoritarianism is inherent in modern society as connections are severed and solidarities break down, and as the protection of intermediate bodies is withdrawn, releasing the egoistic individual as a prey to the naked power of the state (Herder 1965, pp. 27–145). In opposition to the mechanical unity of this modern state, Herder views the people or the nation as an organic entity, a shared pattern of ethical life reflecting a dynamic inner principle (Helfer 1990, pp. 367–81). The endogenous movements of these collective subjects generate a spontaneous order of increasing complexity, based upon extended interactions and recognition of multiplicity. This tendency parallels Hegel's synthesising, reflexive moment of modern freedom. Unlike Novalis' preference for hierarchy and subordination, Herder's organicism implies the diffusion rather than centralisation of power.[25] The impact of

---

25 Simpson 1984, p. 15, on organicist theories of art, society and nature.

such views in the formation of modern national consciousness has been profound, especially in the period of the revolutions of 1848. To cite a single example, Elias Lonnrot (1802–84), whose two editions of the *Kalevala*, the great Finnish national epic, appeared in 1835 and 1849, applied (though unsystematically) both Herderian ideas of expression and Hegel's theory of the epic to his compilations of folk material. His publications gave powerful voice to indigenous traditions, and catalysed the emergence of a national self-awareness under conditions of Russian tutelage (Karkama 2003; Manninen, 1996).

5   Art, modernity and autonomy: Hegel and the Hegelian School

Hegel's posthumous *Lectures on Aesthetics*, published in 1835 by Heinrich Gustav Hotho (1802–73), situate Kant within the modern culture of oppositions. Kant's philosophy recreates the conflict of thought and being, understanding and sensibility, that are characteristic of modernity; but at the same time, sensing a higher unity, he struggles to overcome these contradictions (Hegel 1964, pp. 88, 90–1). Hegel contends that there are other sites in which Kant approaches, without attaining, the vantage point of his own philosophy. Kant's new presentation of teleological reason in the Third Critique anticipates the Hegelian conception of reason's embodiment in objectivity, and, consistent with the demands of modernity, shows that this embodiment cannot be an immediate unity, as in the classical world; instead, it must be worked out through the very oppositions generated by free subjectivity. While for Hegel the *Critique of Judgement* distinctly innovates in this way, the First Critique should not be read as exclusively dualistic, either; it contains tensions like those of the Third. Hegel argues, for example, that the transcendental schematism of the *Critique of Pure Reason* places concept and intuition into intimate and dynamic harmony, but that Kant fails to follow up the implications of this insight, reverting to his formulaic distinction of spontaneity and receptivity (Hegel 1971, pp. 347–8; Pippin 1989, pp. 69, 275 n.30). The critical philosophy thus constitutes a unity, but a defective unity, which posits fixed oppositions even when it glimpses the prospect of a higher and more concrete unity (Lebrun 1970, pp. 469 n.6, 471–3). Kant's system is overly subjective, constricting reason's ability to actualise itself in the world. Kantian morality does not grasp the concrete forms of freedom, but remains mired in inwardness.

Hegel proposes to develop the rational Idea, the unity of thought and being, beyond the confines of Kantian dualism. This unity is not the static identity of the ancient Eleatics, but a process of development in which objective reality is reshaped through experiences of rational freedom. Hegel expresses this dynamism in his concept of *Wirklichkeit*, the actuality or causal efficacy of reason, its ability to fashion aspects of the objective world into the vehicle of spirit, and to perfect and transcend its previous achievements (Hegel 1975c, pp. 142, 200–2, 1975b, pp. 147–9). This sense of *Wirklichkeit* derives from Aristotle's idea of *energeia*, the presence or activity of form and end in matter, but in keeping with the primacy of freedom in modernity, the end is not fixed within a natural order, but involves free, rational self-determination. Hegel defines personality as the subjective form of this movement, the ability to determine one's own attributes, to transform given particularity into conscious individuality by investing it with reflective choice. The achievement of modernity will be to recognise the infinity of the personality, its capacity for freedom, rational autonomy and shared ethical life.

The role of aesthetics for Hegel is defined in relation to this idea of *Wirklichkeit*. The modern subject is too complex to express its content adequately in art. Simultaneously, however, artistic achievement is a facet of reason's objectivity. It is not to be seen as the mere dilution of the idea in matter (Kimmerle 1999, pp. 91–9), though pure philosophical cognition exceeds it in its insight into the rational idea. Art is rather a manifestation of this idea, its *parousia* or tangible presence in the world. Like living organisms, beautiful objects partake of a necessary ordering of their parts, and they manifest the power of reason to propel itself into objectivity. The harmony of beauty is not simply a subjectively gauged accord, but a form of manifestation of reason in its objectivity. As in Plato's *Symposium*, beauty is a mode of emergence of reason; but the rational idea is no longer a given, objective form. It is now, as modernity demands, mediated by subjective activity. Like Herder, Hegel establishes a continuity between subjectivity and the forms of expression; but aesthetic forms can no longer reveal the capacities of the subject in all their complexity. This harmony was attainable for the beautiful individual of ancient Greece, but not for the reflexive selves of modern society. At the same time, to revel in the detachment between subject and form, and to fail to grasp the possibility of a higher synthesis, is for Hegel the hallmark of a deviant romantic irony.[26] This attitude, struck

---

26 Hegel 1991, pp. 170–86, provides a description of romantic irony, and a striking critical anticipation of post-modern attitudes. See also Hegel 1971, pp. 415–16. For distinctions among types of irony, see Henckmann 1990, pp. 214–40.

by Schlegel and Novalis, marks the emptiness of a self-enclosed subjectivity. It is a tendency that Hegel assesses as profoundly destructive of the bonds of ethical life, in which alone the genuine aspirations of the modern self can be satisfied. Though its own role is not negligible, it is not art, but the rational state and the institutions of civil life, that fulfil this promise of autonomy and transparency.

Among its most noted features, Hegel's late system advances the controversial thesis of the end of art (Henrich 1974, pp. 295–301; Hofstadter 1974, pp. 271–85; Knox 1980, pp. 1–10; Kuhn 1974, pp. 251–69; Winfield 1993, pp. 131–44). The *Aesthetics* derives modern art's inability to illuminate truth from the unrepresentability of the achievements of reason, in the complex configuration which they assume for the post-classical, 'romantic' subject (Hegel 1964, pp. 30–1). As it emerges from the Christian matrix of the unhappy consciousness, the free and infinite modern personality poses the issue of aesthetic representation with particular acuity. The increasingly self-conscious and reflexive character of the modern subject is intractable to artistic representation, without shattering the unity of the artwork and overburdening it with subjective accretions; this necessary self-referentiality is the deeper truth expressed (and distorted) by romantic irony. This complexity affects not only the individual artwork, but also rules out, as insufficient and unattainable, a purely aesthetic justification of modernity, or reconciliation of antagonistic interests within the culture of fragmentation (Bubner, 1971, p. 12; Klinger 1990, p. 38; Rüsen 1976, p. 34). The solution must be sought elsewhere, in the political relations of the rational modern state, which realise concretely the demand for autonomy, and in philosophy, where the Idea, the unity of thought and being, attains fully adequate articulation. Art is not literally exhausted, and will continue to depict the creative engagement of thought with material causes. But it can no longer satisfy the highest drives of subjectivity to comprehend its relations with the world or itself. The multifaceted character of the modern subject, in its self-awareness and its diversified activities and relationships, exceeds the compass of artistic depiction, in contrast to the immediate harmony of individual and community which classical art could convey.

Hegel's thesis of the end of art bears a strongly polemical character towards contemporary romantic tendencies. First, because of the expansive particularity and conflicting interests of the modern world, art can no longer demonstrate to the individual consciousness its own universality and membership in a community, as it could do in classical antiquity. To overlook this crucial difference is to mistake the part for the whole, making art into an ideological instrument of particularistic interests disguised as universal. Nor, secondly, can the reflexive return to unity be grasped as a restoration of historically outmoded structures. Hegel's claim about the end of art is a rejection of the romantic attempt to revivify the medieval past and to reconstitute modern art on the basis of traditional religious and political conceptions (Gethmann-Siefert 1986a, pp. 69–72, 1986b, pp. xi–xiii, xxviii). Some of Hegel's students, notably Hotho, may have partly yielded to this tendency, incorporating concessions to romanticism into their renditions of Hegel (Gethmann-Siefert 1983, pp. 229–62). Recent criticism tends to stress the tension in Hegel's aesthetics between its systematic character, or its grounding in the system of absolute knowledge, and its openness to the phenomenal dimension, to works of art in their particularity and historicity (Gethmann-Siefert 1981, pp. 182–7, 1984, 1991, pp. 92–110, 1992). This tension dissipates under Hotho's editorial direction.

After Hegel's death, the struggle for a unified, republican Germany becomes intense. Under the leadership of Schelling, the late romantics take up the defence of the Restoration order. Among their adversaries was a loose affiliation of literary and intellectual figures known, by 1834, as Young Germany, on the model of Mazzini's Young Italy of 1831. Prominent members of this group include Ludwig Börne (1786–1837), Georg Büchner (1813–37), Georg Herwegh (1817–75) and Heinrich Heine (1797–1856). They criticise the political and moral bankruptcy of the existing order, promote the republican constitution and the egalitarian ideals of the French Revolution, and advocate the emancipation of women. Their realistic and satirical literary style contrasts with the growing romantic preoccupation with the abnormal and the fanciful, though a romanticism of the left is still an important force (e.g. Fourier 1889). Resident in Paris after 1831, Heine establishes close links with French socialist writers, and combines Hegelian and Saint-Simonian elements in his own critiques of the Restoration state, religion and culture.

A Young or Left Hegelian philosophical movement also emerges in the late 1830s, with increasingly explicit, though distinct, political agendas. Ludwig Feuerbach (1804–72) shares with the Young Germans the defence of sensuousness against intellectual abstraction. In his work the link of aesthetics and ethics remains strong. He contrasts aesthetic contemplation with practical egoism, contending that subjects must limit their needs and activities in order to live in harmony with the natural world, and not in competition with others (Feuerbach 1957, p. 113). Criticising Feuerbach's passivity, the young Karl Marx (1818–83) interprets labour itself as an aesthetic act, vindicating productive action as expressive of freedom and autonomy, and depicting alienated labour as subjection to heteronomous control (Marx 1975; Marx and Engels 1976). By late 1843, Marx begins to envisage a socialist reorganisation of production to overcome the modern culture of fragmentation and opposition. His early thought adapts and modifies, through a Kantian perspective, ideas of self-realisation through diversified activity, and the aesthetic transformation of work, which had been developed by the French romantic socialist Charles Fourier (1772–1837: see Fourier 1889; Rihs 1978).

Among the Left Hegelians, Arnold Ruge (1802–80) and Bruno Bauer (1809–82) are most closely associated with activist aesthetic approaches to freedom and republicanism. They follow Kant in linking spontaneity with self-legislation, and understand autonomy as the rationalisation of political relations. Objective forms are to correspond to the concept of freedom; this process involves not simply the expression of a given subjective content, but self-transformation, since subjects' particular interests, if they conflict with the general interest, are a potential source of heteronomy. Like Heine and the Young German authors, Ruge opposes romanticism on political grounds, seeing it as a conservative rejection of modernity and equality. The nostalgia for the past in writers like Novalis attests a desire to undo the liberating work of the French Revolution, and to regress to the hierarchical social forms of the *ancien régime*. Ruge underlines the contrast between the romantics and Schiller, whose work heralds personal emancipation, and advocates social harmony resting not on suppression, but on free mutual recognition (Bubner 1971, p. 10).

In his more systematic approach to aesthetics and art forms, Ruge (following a suggestion in Schiller) takes the comic to typify the emancipatory attitude of the modern, post-revolutionary subject. Unlike the ironic stance assumed by the romantics, where subjects' detachment from the ends of their activity confines them to an impotent interiority and thus shores up the old order, Ruge sees in comedy a subversive challenge to subordination and inequality. The comic conveys a sense of liberation from existing relations by showing that these are contemptibly beneath the standards of critical rationality. It reveals the disparity between the concept of freedom and the current forms of political rule, and exposes to ridicule the pretensions of the dominant elites, as the Young Germans had done to devastating effect. It also looks to the future, anticipating reconciliation and harmony among liberated and self-conscious subjects, constructing their world according to their deepening insight into the meaning of freedom (Bubner 1971,

p. 10; Ruge 1837). These views are attested throughout Ruge's corpus. His interest in aesthetics dates to his first publication (Ruge 1832).

The use of comedy and satire to undermine political and religious orthodoxy is also one of Bruno Bauer's preferred techniques. In two anonymous texts (Bauer 1841, 1842a), he adopts the guise of a pietist critic of Hegel in order to stress the revolutionary consequences of his system. The comic form in no way detracts from the philosophical seriousness of these works. Bauer's doctrine of universal self-consciousness is deeply aesthetic in inspiration, based on an idea of formative activity in which, subjectively, the beautiful unity of the self is achieved through the transcendence of particular interest, and objectively, sublime and unrelenting struggle is waged to make the outer order accord with the demands of conscious freedom. He opposes the weight of substantiality, or of unreflective historical traditions, to the form-giving and critical power of the self, as the agency of cultural and political transformation. Objectivity can be read as the record of human strivings for emancipation; the substantial represents a teleological order of freedom, in which each new stage builds upon and corrects the deficiencies of the preceding.

In contrast to his own position, Bauer criticises the passive 'beautiful soul' of Schleiermacher for its appeal to the immediacy and particularity of the subject, powerless in face of the ineffable absolute. Though Schleiermacher's position is far more subtle and complex, Bauer's attitude is reflective of Hegel's own polemics against pietism in the Preface to the second (1827) edition of the *Encyclopaedia* (Hegel 1989, pp. 5–18) and in his correspondence (Hegel 1961, p. 202). Pietism renounces reason as an instrument of liberation. It thus contributes to freezing the historical movement, and imprisoning creative spirit in its own alienated works. These consequences ensue because the universal power of shaping reality has been displaced into an alien realm beyond self-consciousness. The rigid particularity of subjects, and the transcendent absolutism of religious cults and of political power, sustain each other and support a mundane order of irrationality and domination.

Bauer reverses the theoretical priority of religion to art within Hegelian absolute spirit. In religion, self-consciousness is alienated and appears to be passive, receiving law and revelation from outside itself. Thought here succumbs to a dialectical illusion: it deceives itself about its own activities, attributing them to a transcendent source. Art, in contrast, displays the activity of thought, though confining it in a material element. In affirming productive freedom, art demonstrates its close kinship to philosophy.

While its materiality leaves the artwork partly opaque to reason, art is also emblematic of the formative power of thought, its ability to reshape objective existence. In an article on Beethoven (Bauer 1842b), Bauer stresses the common aim of art and philosophy, the awakening of the powers of spirit to untrammelled extension. Art, especially music, expresses the intuition and the aspiration of freedom, not only making accessible the content of philosophy, but arousing practical reason and action more compellingly than can theoretical speculation alone (cf. Burnham 1995). This formulation recalls Schelling's ideas of 1800, where art overcomes the one-sided conceptuality of philosophy. In his unpublished Jena manuscripts, Hegel, like Schiller, had contrasted the musical-restless sublime and the plastic-restful beautiful (Lypp 1990, p. 105). For Bauer, too, music is sublime, symbolising his theory of self-consciousness and its hold on material existence. The autonomy of the aesthetic is only partial, however, as it maintains close ties to practical reason, historical perfectionism and political and cultural change.

6 The denial of autonomy and aesthetic redemption: Schopenhauer and Wagner

As processes of social change accelerate with the onset of industrialism and its attendant problems of poverty, displacement and resistance, the culture of diremption can also give rise to despair at the prospects of reconciliation and community. A profound disillusionment with the achievements of modernity, and with the project of political emancipation, takes hold in aesthetic thinking, especially after the failed revolutions of 1848. Though he published his major work in 1819, Arthur Schopenhauer (1788–1860) anticipates this mood. To demonstrate not the autonomy but the thraldom of the individual will, Schopenhauer effects a singular combination of Kantian and Platonic conceptions, establishing what has been called the metaphysics of pessimism (Knox 1958, p. 129). In this vision, subjects are heteronomously determined by a transcendent force that impels them constantly onward in meaningless striving. The solution lies in escape from desiring, a negation of subjectivity partly achieved through aesthetic insight into the ultimate constituents of reality (Janaway 1997, p. 246; Pinkard 2002, pp. 333–45). This escape also secures a release from the mechanistic causality of Newtonian natural science, as well as from the insatiable self. Schopenhauer sees the phenomenal world as entirely governed by the principle of sufficient reason, the causal laws whereby objects are constituted and known as distinct, and situated in space and time (Janaway 1997, p. 246; Knox 1958, p. 127; Schopenhauer

1818, Book I). This outer world is grasped through concepts, which are not pure in Kant's sense, but related to empirical needs and desires, making possible the manipulation of objects, and directing them towards the evanescent satisfaction of subjective urges. Underlying this sphere is the noumenal world of the thing-in-itself. For Schopenhauer, this hidden essence is an irrational power, which he designates as the Will. This is not a personal will, even of a divine subject, but a blind and endless *conatus* or striving, acting as an anonymous force, without finality (Schopenhauer 1818, Book IV; Taylor 1989, p. 442). The Will manifests itself in the phenomenal world in subjects' own ravenous appetites. It establishes itself very differently in the noumenal realm, taking the shape of permanent Ideas concealed behind the veil of sufficient reason (Desmond 1988, pp. 101–22; Schopenhauer 1818, Book III), but accessible in art. These Ideas are not forms of subjective action, or of a supreme principle of the good, but are objectifications or patterns assumed by the voracious Will itself. They stand in a hierarchical relation depending on the quality and clarity of their manifestation of the ultimate principle (Knox 1958, p. 128).

Schopenhauer repudiates Kant's appeal to pure practical reason, the capacity for rational self legislation and autonomy. The empirical practical reason of the Enlightenment had recognised happiness or the fulfilment of need as a criterion of social progress, but Schopenhauer opts for abnegation and the elimination of desire. The aesthetic contributes to this end, releasing the practitioner of its disciplines from the grip of the phenomenal world and its delusory attractions, and from the ego itself. Aesthetics offers a kind of disinterestedness, removed from the avidity of want; this is an echo of Kant's argument about pure aesthetic judgements. In Schopenhauer, art refers beyond the phenomenal, to the deeper levels of the Will's manifestation in the permanent Ideas (Janaway 1997, pp. 243–4, 322; Schopenhauer 1818, Book III). Why this more intimate acquaintance with the Will should be construed as a liberation from it is one of the enduring mysteries of Schopenhauer's metaphysics. One solution is to maintain that seeing the world as a whole, and denying individuality, together make possible a kind of limited philanthropic attitude towards suffering, as one's own pain becomes indistinguishable from that of any other being (Janaway 1997, pp. 322, 326–7). It remains unclear why Ideas as crystallisations of the Will should have any special status in this emancipation from the self.

For Schopenhauer, the artist as genius is endowed with a surplus of representations that bursts the narrow bounds of conventional, pragmatic concepts,[27] and thus embodies Mendelssohn's conception of the sublime as the overstepping of limits, analogous to Baumgarten's extensive clarity or multiplicity of meanings (Best 1974, pp. 173–97, 207–46; Paetzold 1992, pp. 10, 21). The genius also possesses a penetrating vision into the essence of Will and the Ideas, casting aside the principle of sufficient reason. Among the art forms, music occupies the highest place, as it best reveals the overflowing energies of the Will. Tragedy becomes sublime when the destruction of the protagonists derives from no fault of their own, when their undoing appears not as the consequence of their subjective action, but as the work of an inexorable power (Janaway 1997, p. 295). If among the Left Hegelians the experience of sublimity elicits a greater exertion to establish the reality of freedom, in Schopenhauer it serves to devalue subjective action and to illustrate its utter futility.

The work of Richard Wagner (1813–83) manifests complex and contradictory philosophical influences illustrative of both these tendencies. His early operas (*Das Liebesverbot* 1836, *Der fliegende Holländer* 1843, *Tannhäuser* 1845, *Lohengrin* 1850) depict themes derived from Young Germany, and from materialist currents in Left Hegelianism, notably from Feuerbach: love as the essential social bond, self-realisation through the rehabilitation of the physical and the sensuous, and the opposition between individual spontaneity and social repression. After participating in the unsuccessful revolution in Dresden in 1848–9, together with the Left Hegelian and future anarchist Michael Bakunin (1814–76), Wagner narrowly escaped to Zurich. There he published *The Art Work of the Future* (1849), its title echoing Feuerbach's *Philosophy of the Future* of 1843. Wagner restates the romantic programme of a new mythology for the modern world, and outlines the requirements for a unified work of art, combining poetry and music, on the model of Greek drama (Magee 2000, pp. 89, 177; Wagner 1993, 1994). The harmony of Greek life, and the corresponding integration of its art forms, had been broken by fragmented modern culture, and by the dire influence of Christianity. The other-worldliness of this religion had not been beneficial to art and culture (as Chateaubriand believed), but was disastrous and repressive.

In an anonymous text attributed to Wagner, and published on the eve of the decisive confrontations of 1849, the author defends the aesthetic revolution as establishing the right to free creation, and legitimating the

---

27 Knox 1958, p. 140, observes that in releasing the artist from the principle of sufficient reason, Schopenhauer blurs the distinction between genius and madness.

forcible overthrow of state and property relations. The impending insurrection announces its aims:

I will destroy from the ground up the order of things in which you live ... I will destroy all illusions that have control over man. I will destroy the rule of one man over others, of the dead over the living, of matter over spirit; I will break the power of the mighty, of the law and of property. Let his *own* will [*Wille*] be the master of man, his *own* pleasure his only law, his *own* strength his whole property, *for what is holy is only the free man, and there is nothing higher than he* ...

Let the illusion be shattered, that makes man subject to his own work, to property. The highest good for man is his creative power. That is the source from which all happiness springs. Not in the *product*, but in *producing* itself, in the *activation of your powers*, lies your true, highest satisfaction. (Wagner 1974, pp. 114–16)[28]

These ideas are given musical expression in Wagner's operas. Describing his four-part *Ring des Niebelungen*, whose libretti he wrote between 1848 and 1852, Wagner remained consistent with his revolutionary views. He explained his intentions to evoke in the opera

an existence free from pain. But I meant in the presentation of the whole Nibelung myth to [show] ... how from the first wrongdoing a whole world of injustice arose, and subsequently fell to pieces, in order to teach us the lesson that we must recognise injustice and tear it up by the roots, and raise in its stead a righteous world. (Cited in Magee 2000, p. 58)

The original injustice is the institution of power, property and contract, which can only be maintained by constraint, and which opposes the spontaneous manifestation of love and freedom. This letter dates from 1856, when Wagner had already undergone a radical change in perspective, a conversion to the philosophy of Schopenhauer in autumn 1854 (Magee 2000, p. 133). Political emancipation could no longer address the fundamental issues of human freedom and satisfaction, as the problem of alienation was ontological, not historical. Wagner did not modify his original libretti, however, in which, seemingly anticipating his later evolution, he shows that the new order based on love cannot succeed either (Magee 2000, pp. 135–6).

Tristan und Isolde (1859/1865) and *Parsifal* (1882) are works that most clearly reflect Schopenhauer's influence, but still contain an admixture of Wagner's earlier views on the emancipation of the body. Their use of medieval tales of the Grail and of Christian symbolism depicts the deceptiveness of earthly goods and desire, while maintaining the prospect of

---

28 My translation, DM; emphasis in original.

redemption through physical love. After breaking with Wagner, his former close friend, in 1876, Nietzsche will attack him for the sickly romanticism of these works, distinguishing the Dionysian from the romantic as the difference between overflowing and impoverished life (Nietzsche 1921a).

7 Decadence, classicism and alternative modernities: from Baudelaire to Nietzsche

If it cannot be overcome in social and political life, the futility of existence decried by Schopenhauer can, however, assume an aesthetically appealing shape. Nor need one appeal to deeper realities, as Schopenhauer does. An attention to surface phenomena, and a denial of underlying ideas or forces, characterise the approach of Charles Baudelaire (1821–67) to aesthetics and modernity. For him, the modern project is not yet complete. Art remains too much under the sway of ethical and religious notions. Its own proper subject matter is inconsistent with the classical unities (Klinger 1990, p. 31); it needs to stress the ugly, the repellent and the disjointed in the experiences of the modern subject. Appeals to universality and stability must cede to contingency and alteration (Baudelaire 1964, pp. 37–45, 291–300; Pippin 1991, pp. 32–3). The hope of aesthetic reconciliation fades before an ideal of self-making (Pippin 1991, pp. 174 n.25), a spontaneity without limits, in which style or form becomes a punctiliousness about external manner and appearance (Taylor 1989, pp. 434–42). It is the expression of a highly particularised self, aware of its distinctiveness and superiority. Such an attitude stands in sharp contrast to eighteenth-century ideals of manners, which involved the suppression of particularity, with the intent that all polished individuals would behave in exactly the same way, as though they were a single person (Henry Fielding, cited in Hundert 1998, p. 332 n.82).

Revivals of classicism in the late nineteenth century offer distinct perspectives on the modern project of emancipation. Like Baudelaire, Walter Pater (1839–94) advocates an art divorced from ethical application. He represents an attitude of cultivated aestheticism, intended to preserve a domain of experience unsullied by mundane concerns (Thompson 1977, p. 147). Art is to be walled off against crass material interest, just as the personality is a wall confining subjects within their private world of impressions. Pater shares with eighteenth-century classicism an ascetic view of form as unadorned and simple (Gagnier 2000, pp. 54–6; Pater 1974, pp. 103–25, 190–8), while rejecting the idea of underlying universal forms that characterised the thought of Winckelmann. For Pater and Baudelaire, modern art was still too traditional, because it was tied to ideas of universality originating in an outmoded metaphysics. They develop instead a specific version of the autonomy of art, or art for art's sake. This autonomy had up till now been only relative, meaning the emancipation of art from dominant political or religious interests, or from the need to represent a given natural order or to dispense directly moral instruction. Yet in Kant, Schiller, Hegel and others, art had retained its links to morality in complex ways. Artistic autonomy now means the separation of form from any function extraneous to itself, whether moral, political or paedagogical (Wilkinson and Willoughby 1967, pp. clxxvii–clxxxi).

Still in a classical register, but reacting against such views of the autonomy of art, Matthew Arnold (1822–88) continues to stress its necessary connection with ethics and public service (Thompson 1977, p. 144). He views aesthetics or culture as self-regulation, promoting the cultivation of a higher self by individuals and groups, in overt tension with narrow possessive individualism (Gagnier 2000, pp. 106–7). The elevation above immediate private interest appears as the condition for social harmony in a society divided by class. This idea is analogous to the earlier view of Joshua Reynolds that art contributed to the creation of a public sphere, instituting a republic of taste, and anticipating a politically active public that was still to be constructed (Barrell 1986, pp. 69–72). With Arnold, in the distinction between aristocratic barbarians, bourgeois philistines and the populace, the awareness of division goes much deeper than in the eighteenth-century sources, and imparts a characteristic melancholy to Arnold's reflections. Not the extravagant cultural forms of the old regime, as in Winckelmann, but the miserable realities of commercial relations, become the objects of critique in this new classicism.

Avowing the social and political usefulness of an aesthetic approach, Arnold contrasts classical Greek thinking with the more rigidly legalistic approach that he traces to biblical sources, and to the Puritan tradition in England. Modern culture comprises both of these currents, but in unequal measure, and Arnold seeks to restore a balance by bringing to bear a healthy Greek scepticism on the dogmatic pronouncements of the politicians of the day. Narrow and partial perspectives on the disestablishment of the Irish Church, the question of inheritance rights and other issues can be challenged and rectified if the principles underlying them are allowed to work themselves out in their concrete implications, revealing their real animating interests. The plasticity of aesthetic thought is of greater value to the community in determining political orientation than is the unbending assertion of principles, which, on inspection, often prove to derive from an idea of absolute entitlement by an individual or group. Culture implies perfection, the development of the best self, not the assertion of exclusive private rights. It fosters individual self-cultivation, the wide dissemination of talents, and also the enlightened reform of political and social institutions. Modern industry is of value not as an end in itself, but as providing a basis for cultural development and propagation (Arnold 1993). This is a classicism in the public interest, but like many classical thinkers, Arnold fears disorder and unruly political interventions from below, which he sees as stemming from the brutality of the populace, and not from its desire to achieve a higher or worthier standard of life.

For Jacob Burckhardt (1818–97), sordid modern economic competition has supplanted the ancient agonal view of the self, based upon a consciousness of rank and the desire to excel within the hierarchical order (Jähnig 1979, p. 180; Large 2000, pp. 3–23; Sigurdson 1990, pp. 417–40). Burckhardt's studies of classical antiquity and of the Renaissance focus on heroic forms of individualism, which have been eclipsed before bourgeois acquisitiveness (Burckhardt 1860). Aesthetics affords a refuge from the intellectual and cultural squalor of the present day. Unlike transient ideas of truth and goodness, Burckhardt maintains that beauty is both time-related, in that art manifests the essential content of a mode of life, and also timeless, in that its works speak a universal language, permanently available to other cultures (Flaig 1987, p. 93; Jähnig 1979, pp. 186–7). Despite its own cultural degradation, modernity offers the possibility of a comprehensive view of previous history (Jähnig 1979, pp. 188–9). Historical knowledge elevates the observer above the senseless turmoil of mundane affairs and interests, the upheavals and menacing revolutions of the present. The sublime is not an injunction to participate in the struggles of the modern world, nor an invitation to a broadened compassion, but an attitude of serenity and disinterested contemplation (Flaig 1987, p. 92).

The late nineteenth-century awareness of decadence, from Baudelaire onward, reflects a definition of modernity similar to Burckhardt's, as an overarching standpoint that makes all past historical experience available for reflection and appropriation. The self-proclaimed decadence of Oscar Wilde affirms modernity for the variety of attitudes it makes possible (Gagnier 2000, p. 90). Here, late romantic occasionalism penetrates not only the account of the outer world, but even of the subject, which can recast itself at will. Wilde defines form as a subjective stance of insincerity, not authenticity (Calloway 1997, pp. 34–54; Gillespie 1996, pp. 61–4, 70–4,

116–32). Since there is no essential content to manifest, an expressivism like Herder's is precluded. For Wilde's characters, form is the multiplication of the personality, not its integration (Gagnier 2000, p. 111, citing Wilde 1962, pp. 154–5). It is not singular and stable, but complex, shifting, arbitrary. Subjects refashion themselves in endless spontaneous combinations. In this creative self-shaping lies their freedom.

If, in the works of Friedrich Nietzsche (1844–1900), the decadence of the modern world appears as a danger and not an emancipation, he nonetheless shares this 'decadent' idea of the multiple self. Writing of his intellectual development in 1864, the young Nietzsche gives an occasionalist portrayal of his past. Time refers not to a continuum, but to an infinity of discrete moments, each inaugurating incommensurable possible worlds. Every instant in time provides an opportunity to break with established patterns and to initiate a new movement, eradicating previous phases. The past is of value only as material for the will and for the formation of character (Nietzsche 1994a, pp. 132, 146). Even the later doctrine of eternal recurrence (Nietzsche 1968a) can be interpreted in this light: not as a dogmatic assertion of inevitable patterns of history, but as an advocacy of a life lived without resentment or regret. In his later writings, Nietzsche (1954, p. 92) recognises an affinity with Spinoza, in the denial of free will and teleology. Despite his aversion to romanticism as a sickly form of self-assertion, he retains a fragmentary, ruptured view of externalisation, of romantic origin. His agreement with Spinoza does not extend to the concept of substance as continuous, flowing without contingency from a single ultimate cause.

Not only is substance set in an occasionalist frame, but so too is the self. The individual becomes an artefact, constantly reshaping itself out of its drives and energies. Nietzsche repudiates the classical conception of the subject as a *hypokeimenon* or passive substrate; nor does he admit Baumgarten's idea of a durable subjective identity expressing itself in force. Nietzsche conceives this self anew, after the manner of contemporary science.

In the positivistic wave of the 1860s, which supplanted the influences of idealism, the dominant schools in physiology had effected a decomposition of individual identity. Drawing on the *Idéologues* Cabanis and Destutt de Tracy, they developed a vitalistic materialism, postulating an unconscious mind and a central vital core from which activity emanates (Becq 1984, II, pp. 834–41). Rejecting the unity of subjective consciousness as the seat of spontaneity and autonomy, physiologists such as Théodule Ribot (1839–1916) proposed a theory of the multiple self (Bodei 2002, pp. 65–6). Hippolyte Taine (1828–93), best known for his critiques of the French

Revolution, was influential in propagating this view. The self is an aggregation of cells or foci of energy. Its apparent unity is factitious and unstable. The effectiveness of the organism in its environment depends on levels of co-ordination among the discrete elements that comprise it, but in the human organism these constituents are largely impenetrable to conscious thought. The unity of the self is evanescent; it does not refer to a conscious and durable subjective being, but to a momentary organisation. In perception, too, objects dissolve into immaterial points of energy; this idea is reflected in artistic movements like Impressionism (Bodei 2002, p. 58). It is as though the Leibnizian monad recurs, but in naturalised form, freed from the perfectionist and theological structures which contained it in the *Monadology*.

These views provide the background to Nietzsche's agonal recomposition of the self. While agreeing with Baudelaire that the constant transgression of limits is the purview of the creative spirit, he is not averse, at least in some of his moods, to naturalising the subject.[29] Repudiating Platonic and Christian dualisms, he equates the self with the body. The body is a composite. It is composed of multitudes of organisms that submit to monarchical organisation by some central instance or drive, but only in a temporary stabilisation, since any momentary weakness in this directive power becomes an occasion to displace it as a co-ordinating authority. The monads that make up the body exhibit no pre-established harmony, but conflictual and shifting coalitions. The effectiveness of the body, or the vivacity of its life energies, is dissipated if the directive force is split or diffused. By extension, decadence can be understood as homeostasis, the sapping or levelling of energies, so that no dynamic discharge occurs;[30] it is this stagnation of the vital forces, the result of egalitarianism and resentment, that threatens the modern world. Nietzsche recognises the danger of nihilism, the reflexive undermining of values, implicit in the Kantian paradox of self-imposed law, without transcendent grounding. Resolutely modern, he does not yearn for such grounding, but presses on.[31] He sees himself not as a nihilist, but as a herald of new, redemptive values.

While for Winckelmann the Greeks embody the values of order, harmony and proportion, and Hegel and Schiller stress classical 'beautiful individuality' as the concord of character and *polis*, Nietzsche, like Burckhardt,

---

29 See Taylor 1989, pp. 393–418, on naturalism and anti-naturalism. The extent to which naturalism pervades Nietzsche's thought has not been widely remarked in recent English and French literature.
30 Bodei 2002, pp. 83–116, with numerous references to Nietzsche's texts.
31 Nietzsche's modernism is hotly contested. See, for example, Habermas 1987; Pippin 1996; Nehamas 1996.

emphasises Greek irrationalism, competitive individualism and aristocratic heroism, the reign of honour over both reason and material desire. The achievement of the Greeks, as Nietzsche describes it in the *Birth of Tragedy*, offers not a nostalgic escape or aspirational ideal, but a paradigm for shaping one's own identity out of conflicting elements and forces (Bishop 2004; Strong 1996).

The Greek experience of self-formation was undermined in antiquity by forces that continue active in the modern crisis of nihilism. Nietzsche views both Platonism and Christianity as products of an unhappy consciousness, the passive-aggressive resentment of slavish natures against their subaltern status. Unable to shake this subordination in practice, they repudiate it in theory. Platonism retreats into pallid ratiocination, preferring it to vigour and life. Christianity exacts an imaginary revenge for the afflictions of earthly existence; its heroes are martyrs, not athletes (Nietzsche 1968b [1887]). Platonic and Christian tendencies converge in substituting, for the older aesthetic distinction between the beautiful-noble and the base, a new moral distinction between good and evil, intended to constrain the powerful in their self-affirmations, and to validate the sufferings of the weak. While Chateaubriand at the turn of the nineteenth century had endorsed Christianity on the grounds of its beauty rather than its truth, this beauty is badly tarnished by century's end: Nietzsche links Christianity with asceticism and resentment, and opposes it on aesthetic grounds. His criticisms of religion grow more strident through the 1880s, though he also acknowledges a certain educative effect (Nehamas 1996, p. 245). Modern decadence, exemplified in mass society or the 'herd mentality', is depicted not as a failure of rational autonomy, itself delusory, but as a deficiency of energy and insight sufficient to found new institutions as the Greeks had done, together with a generalised sense of indeterminacy misconstrued as freedom (Pippin 1996, p. 260).

As in Burckhardt's conservative critique of modernity, though with less serene detachment, Nietzsche's classicism is an invocation of superior natures, based upon the *agon* for supremacy. His early work, strongly influenced by Schopenhauer and Wagner, portrays the interplay of Dionysian and Apollonian currents in the classical world, where form is a momentary crystallisation constantly threatened with dissolution, including the loss of self (Nietzsche 1921b; Tanner 1997, pp. 386–7). His later writings emphatically abandon this idea in favour of untrammelled self-assertion. Creative spirits are artists of their own identity (Desmond 1988, pp. 120–1; Nietzsche 1921a; Tanner 1997, pp. 386–7), overbrimming with creative energy, and sublime in their elevation above the banality of modern life. This pre-eminence need not imply overt political domination, but refers to processes of aesthetic self-shaping and self-transcendence (Tanner 1997, p. 388), a new affirmative relation to the world. Nietzsche substitutes for Hegel's master–slave dialectic the idea of a self-certifying mastery (Pippin 1991, pp. 106–12). The old dualistic metaphysics and religion had sought to stabilise the self as the site for the imputation of guilt and responsibility, constricting the vital energies and subordinating them to alien powers. Freeing oneself from these emasculating attitudes is not a matter of will, but of nature. Only some are free.

Nietzsche's cultural critique has proven highly influential in myriad circles. Castigated as conservative irrationalism by Lukács (1980, pp. 309–99) and Losurdo (2002), these criticisms of modernity have been linked with archaism and celebrated by the extreme right (on which see Strong 1996, pp. 132–3); but they have also been expounded in left-Nietzschean radical-democratic projects (Connelly 1989). Nietzsche has been described as the last metaphysician, whose doctrine of the will to power (substituting for the thing-in-itself, in Schopenhauerian fashion) is taken to be the culmination of the philosophical tradition inaugurated by the Greeks (Behler 1996, pp. 311–15; Heidegger 1991). He has been greeted as a harbinger of post-modernism (Foucault 1966); and his writings have been read as a repudiation of the Enlightenment programme of liberation through theoretical and practical reason (Habermas 1987, pp. 83–105), offering, in place of universalism, more localised and contingent aesthetic judgements and perspectival relativism (Nehamas 1996). While Nietzsche himself stoutly opposes indeterminacy, his aphoristic writings occasion the most diverse interpretations.

Rejecting the appeal to universals as suppressing the individual and the noble (Losurdo 2002, p. 718), Nietzsche denies autonomy, or the subordination of spontaneity to rational self-legislation. That is a slavish mentality, and Nietzsche will have none of it. Spontaneity instead appears as unbounded enjoyment of the self. Despite his criticisms of romantic flaccidity, Nietzsche thus completes the disjunction, initiated by the romantics, between spontaneity and rational autonomy.

8 A new synthesis?

Theodor Adorno observes that Nietzsche's depiction of modern culture as repellent, mediocre and banal might have induced in him a very different reaction, an effort to raise modern life to a higher aesthetic and ethical standard (Adorno 1974, p. 97; Tanner 1997, p. 420). That is precisely the response of William Morris (1834–96), as it had been earlier in Schiller. With Morris, we have described a circle, from the eighteenth-century distinction between art and artisanry, to a new equation that might be called the 'technai qua artes', inverting the older formula. If previous artists dissociated their work from repetitive and imitative manual labour, and considered art's disinterestedness as a liberation from service to need, Morris seeks instead to elevate labour to the level of creative artistic achievement. This fusion of art and labour now appears as an answer to the fragmentation and degradation of modern relations, the experiences described by Schiller and Hegel. Like Marx in 1844, Morris connects labour not only with the satisfaction of material needs, but with the expression of freedom, securing the harmony between subjective and objective ends, between the goals of activity and its accomplishments. To this extent, Morris, like the early Marx, remains faithful to the German idealists' legacy, the processual identity of thought and being. Hegel had considered that the Kantian system grasped this unity too formally and abstractly, and so he sought greater concreteness and determinacy, locating autonomy in social and political relations. Morris follows further along this path.[32] The central image in Morris' work is the free and infinite personality, grasped in an aesthetic register. He implicitly rejects Hegel's strictures on the impossibility of such an aesthetic reconciliation in the modern world. The aestheticisation of labour is to have wide-ranging effects: the embellishment of the community, the realisation of beautiful and affirmative life-conditions, intersubjective concord, harmony with the natural world. These ideas are illustrated in Morris' *News from Nowhere* (1890; see also Morris 1884, 1888).

Morris draws heavily upon British as well as German sources. Thomas Carlyle (1795–1881) had extolled the organic solidarity of medieval life, and denounced the reduction of all human relations to market transactions and commodity exchange. The village community had acknowledged the sanctity of labour, degraded and bestialised under modern conditions (Thompson 1977, pp. 29–32). Unlike Morris, Carlyle's is a conservative critique, proposing heroic and charismatic leadership as a solution to social ills (Carlyle 1977, 2000). John Ruskin (1819–1900) sustains the moral purpose of art, and, like Schiller, defends the ideal of wholeness against modern fragmentation; it is not labour that is divided in the modern economy, but

---

32 On Morris' opposition both to state socialists and anarchists, see Leopold 2003, pp. vi–xi.

the workers themselves, whose identity is warped and vitiated (cited in Thompson 1977, pp. 37–8). Surveying late romanticism, Ruskin identifies a distinguishing feature in modern art in its attention to the picturesque, or a delight in ruin. In its best manifestations, as in the art of Turner, this takes the form of a sublimity of tragic emotions, whose effect is to establish a community of feeling with the subject matter, and with the perceiver (Ruskin 1906). Like James Barry (1741–1806; Barrell 1986, pp. 167, 171–3), Ruskin understands the beautiful not as a single ideal form, but as distinguished into types, each displaying a characteristic, if not absolute, beauty (Knox 1958, pp. 186–7 n.9). As in Barry, this variety of types is a positive good, and underlies a social ideal of diversity, which differs from the alienating divisions imposed under market imperatives.

With Ruskin and the late romantics in Britain, Morris shares a powerful distaste for the philistinism of modern culture and the degradation of urban life. The intolerable conditions of the poor, living in the midst of abundance and waste, demand redress. Morris combines these influences into an expressivist conception of freedom, where form and subjectivity mutually confirm each other. Again as in Schiller, aesthetic education, become universal, secures a liberation from the mechanical, coercive state, and from merely instrumental relations to others and to nature. Art and ethics forge a new alliance under the sign of beauty. Morris' utopianism is an education of desire, not a mere denial of facts unassimilable to an ideal of beauty. Like Schiller's distinction of melting and energising beauty, it invokes a beauty toughened by a recognition of the sublime (Thompson 1977, pp. 83, 791).

The ideal that Morris espouses with his idealist and romantic precursors has been gravely compromised by the experiences of the twentieth century. These experiences confirm the hold of the culture of diremption, but they do not obviate the need for concord and pacification. Aesthetics records the travails of the modern subject, its aspirations, disillusion and the decomposition of its unity, but it also gives voice to resurgent hopes for a more humane life. It anticipates reflexive and spontaneous forms of interaction that might yet release the thwarted potential of the free and infinite personality, the emancipatory promise of modernity. If the Kantian paradox of self-legislation still awaits solution, aesthetics intimates that such a solution is not absolutely beyond reach.

16

Non-Marxian socialism 1815–1914

GREGORY CLAEYS

1 Introduction: 'political' and 'anti-political' socialism

The various strands of thought which would be termed 'socialism' by the early 1830s emerged from three main sources: the failure of the French Revolution to have solved the problem of poverty, particularly by securing an adequate food supply; its political degeneration into dictatorship; and the onset of industrialisation. After 1848 these problems would be widely recognised as having a characteristic 'socialist' solution that was broadly democratic, collectivist and anti-capitalist, and tended towards community of property and the rejection of 'free markets' as such. But the diversity of these responses also needs to be stressed at the outset: socialism possessed authoritarian and paternalist strands, and later in the century was sometimes combined with various forms of individualism and anarchism (in William Morris, for instance), and occasionally it proposed retaining elements of capitalism (for example in Fourierism, where rewards for investment, separate from labour, were encouraged). Moreover, the degree of centralisation appropriate to socialist ends, and whether the ideal society should be essentially communitarian, were also much disputed. For Saint-Simon and his followers, as for Marx, the nation state, if not indeed a confederation of affiliated states, was the appropriate locus, at least *ad interim*; for Owen and Fourier, the small community or *phalanstère* was to be preferred. Some writers thus decouple Saint-Simonism in particular from Owenism and Fourierism (e.g. Iggers 1972, p. xli). Hence, too, it is misleading to oppose 'individualism', or *laissez-faire*, to 'socialism', or intervention led by the 'state' as such (e.g. Ely 1883, p. 29).[1] The degree to which a more just and egalitarian society could or should encourage luxury was also a divisive issue. So too was the means, revolutionary or evolutionary, by which such a society was to be achieved.

---

1 All works cited here were published in London unless otherwise indicated.

521

Many of these issues had been explored speculatively in the utopian literary tradition, from Sir Thomas More through the 1790s, in which various schemes for limiting inequality of property ranging from an agrarian law through community of goods were mooted that reached back for inspiration to Plato's *Republic*, Lycurgan Sparta, concepts of 'natural society' and various medieval peasant rebellions (Claeys 1994, 1997b). Morelly, Mably, Rousseau, and particularly Babeuf, whose *Conspiracy of the Equals* of 1793, based largely on Morelly's *Code de la Nature* (1755) was often seen as the starting-point for the socialism of the next generation (e.g. Ely 1883, pp. 29–38), were interpreted as having proposed a return to virtuous and often communistic egalitarianism, via the nationalisation of corporate and public property and the abolition of inheritance. Collectivist elements were also rediscovered in Fichte and other writers. By the end of the nineteenth century a rich anthropological literature detailed a variety of forms of primitive communal property holding that could be seen as precedents for socialism (e.g. Lafargue 1890; Laveleye 1878), or, to their critics, evidence that an 'acquisitive instinct' proved the impossibility of such communalism precisely because of the decline of a 'herd instinct' in later historical stages (e.g. Rivers 1923, pp. 81–94). If Marx's theory of alienation was still unknown, countless millions had experienced the loss of village and small-scale community life, and its replacement by anonymity, drudgery, overcrowding, intense economic competition and widespread contempt for the poor by their notional social betters. In Russia, where Saint-Simon and Fourier were especially influential, Alexander Herzen (1812–70) was one of the most important figures to develop the socialist tendencies in the Decembrist movement, which focused principally upon defending the communal nature of the Russian peasant community, or *mir* (Malia 1961).

From the early 1880s onwards, until the First World War, a plethora of socialisms developed across Europe, more or less antagonistic or friendly to the growing force of Marxism, more or less revolutionary or evolutionary in the intended means of social transformation, more or less authoritarian or democratic in political method and aim, more or less collectivist in the ultimate design of social organisation, more or less religious in their description of the underlying moral impulse of social reform or ideological bond of the new society. A spectrum of positions ranging from authoritarian socialism to individualist anarchism thus developed which by the 1890s presented a rich diversity of alternatives, united by a commitment to greater 'association' or 'community', and economic justice for the working classes (seen as the unifying principle of early socialism by, for example, Thomas

Kirkup 1908, p. 86). (Contemporary histories include Kirkup 1892; Rae 1891. Later studies include Cole 1954, 1962; Lichtheim 1969; Lindemann 1983. The literature on communitarianism is now large; an early introduction is Gide 1928. The sole study of the political thought of early socialism as such is Taylor 1982.)

The relationship of socialism to the history of political thought in this period is consequently a complex one. All of the leading forms of early socialism expressed discontent about most traditional forms of polity, however, or were indeed explicitly anti-political in believing that partisan 'politics' emanated from the existing system of unequal property ownership, and would largely disappear once private property or competition for scarce resources had been abolished. (Marx's famous prediction of the eventual 'withering away of the state' – which was greatly indebted to Saint-Simon's assumption that 'politics' would be superseded by the 'administration' of the industrial system – shares a similar preconception, as does Weitling's proposal that 'government' would give way to 'administration'.) In a number of instances charismatic leadership or the quest for a messiah-like figure filled the void left by more traditional forms of politics. This ideal of a non-governmental form of society was thus shared by Marx, most anarchists, as well as a variety of later socialists, such as Edward Carpenter, for some of whose accounts of primitive societies (such as Melville's *Typee*) were central to the concept (Carpenter 1917, pp. 76–98). By 1900, however, this anti-statism had also declined markedly among non-Marxian writers, replaced by the view that both the local and centralised state were essential bodies for the organisation of economic forces (e.g. Macdonald 1909, I, pp. 112–20). The state could thus become, as one leading writer put it, 'what its people make it' (Hardie 1907, p. 23); it was not inevitably coercive. By this time many socialist parties had been formed that engaged in electoral politics of a traditional sort, typically proposing universal suffrage, the abolition of hereditary legislatures and frequent elections. Most forms of non-Marxian socialism were anti-revolutionary (e.g. Hardie n.d., p. 109, arguing against Hyndman's Social Democratic Federation), and some rejected Marx's doctrine of the class war explicitly; in Britain, Robert Blatchford stated that 'not one Socialist in fifty, at this day, expects or wishes to get Socialism by force of arms' (Blatchford 1902, p. 75). Many assumed that 'All active agitators of socialism want a democratic state, because they wish that control of the collectivity over the economic life should be exercised in behalf of the masses' (Ely 1894, p. 31). Many expressed cosmopolitan or internationalist and anti-imperialist sentiments, though a substantial number wanted to improve rather than dismantle the rapidly extending empires of the period (Claeys 2010).

Most types of later socialism thus presumed that some form of centralised state would persist after socialist reforms had been introduced (e.g. Gonner 1895). However, a greater stress was given in British socialism to local and municipal forms of organisation over centralised control, in France to the commune (municipality or township), in Switzerland the canton. French socialists were also suspicious of proposals for state nationalisation of the land, preferring peasant proprietorship in the interim, while German socialists rejected Bismarckian paternalist schemes of state insurance. Socialism thus gave greater stress to decentralisation, local control and trades' and federative democracy than did Marxism, which urged a substantial centralisation of state power during the period of the 'dictatorship of the proletariat'. This preference for more direct over more representative forms of democracy was thus not anti-political, but intensified political practices in proposed socialist societies. Referenda were in some cases proposed in order to secure popular assent. More importantly, and particularly in so far as feminism played a leading role in early socialism, 'politics' was extended beyond economic into personal relationships, the 'personal' effectively becoming 'political' as patriarchal assumptions of power were challenged. (On the development of feminism in early socialism see Taylor 1983; Kolmerten 1990; Moses 1993; Pilbeam 2000; Wilson 2002.)

2   Definitions, historiographic controversies and boundary issues

Throughout the nineteenth century the terms 'communism' and 'socialism' were often used more or less interchangeably in the popular as well as the reformist press. The word 'socialism' appeared first in English, French, German and other European languages from the mid-1820s onwards (see Claeys 2003; Reybaud 1840; Stein 1964). From the publication of Marx and Engels' *Manifesto of the Communist Party* (1848), however, and more emphatically from the early 1880s, Marx's followers distinguished between the earlier or 'utopian' forms of socialism, and their own 'scientific' communism, a juxtaposition that continues to dominate the historiography of the nineteenth-century socialist movement. Non-Marxists have also frequently adopted the terminology, but giving a different stress to the term, and emphasising a common belief among the early socialists in a beneficent natural order, the essential goodness of human nature, a belief in rational solutions to the social problem through the discovery of new laws of social organisation, and a faith in tactics of rational persuasion. Here the chief 'utopian' factor is 'the belief in education and in the power of the knowledge of what is good' (Sombart 1913, p. 39), which resulted in underestimating the strength of their opponents and overestimating their own (see Claeys 1989a).

In the case of Marx and Engels, the utopian/scientific distinction was held to rest on three grounds: (1) that the proletariat were merely a passive 'suffering mass', rather than the active agent of revolution; (2) the belief that society could or should be transformed by propaganda and experiments only, rather than revolution; (3) a refusal to acknowledge that the seeds of social development lay in the economic development of capitalism (as summarised in Engels 1972b). This teleological conception is, however, no longer justified. For many early socialists, like the Chartist leaders James Bronterre O'Brien and William Lovett in Britain, or the Cabetists in France, see the struggle for the franchise as a means to socialist ends, though they rarely counsel revolutionary transformation as such. Robert Owen and most of his followers also adopted a theory of economic immiseration, the centralisation of capital and recurrent commercial crises to argue that the existing economic system would usher in its own collapse. They also saw the advent of industrialisation as ensuring a higher standard of living for the working classes, and contended thus that socialism could not have been introduced in any earlier historical period. Bracketing this group of writers together, moreover, obscures their very substantial differences. In particular, the systems of property-holding proposed by Fourier and Saint-Simon offer a much greater role to private property than does Owen's; some consequently have denied the label of 'socialist' to Fourier entirely (e.g. Riasanovksy 1969, pp. 185–214). In addition, not only has 'history' failed to deliver the revolutionary outcome predicted by Marx; the notion that it is sensible to trust to spontaneous historical processes, rather than planning future development, has also been heavily devalued (e.g. by Wells 1933, p. 38). Those hostile to socialism may regard *all* large-scale collectivist schemes, particularly of the communist type, as 'utopian' in the most negative sense. Still others would term all forms of socialism 'utopian', Marxist or otherwise, in the precise degree to which they presume a fundamental improvement in human behaviour under altered circumstances, particularly the elimination of selfishness. The weight of evidence against the 'utopian/scientific' distinction is thus overwhelming. Historiographically it is clearly preferable to speak now of 'early' rather than 'utopian' socialism.

Although this chapter concentrates upon the chief early socialist schools, it is worth noting that there are substantial scholarly disputes as to who should be included under the 'socialist' rubric. Pierre-Joseph Proudhon (1809–65) is usually described as a founder of the nineteenth-century anarchist movement, because he described his ideal form of government in terms of 'anarchy', the absence of a master or sovereign. Most actual government was to be through a national exchange bank that would ensure 'mutualism', or the guarantee of an economic credit created by actual labour time. Some of his works, however, notably *What is Property?* (1840), had a marked influence on the socialist movement, especially the individualist wing of its French followers (Vincent 1984). Michael Bakunin (1814–76), too, though an anarchist, aimed at a regime of social justice and equality not dissimilar from the vision of many socialists of the period, and also had a marked influence on the socialist movements of Spain and Italy in particular. The leading British liberal writer of the period, John Stuart Mill (1806–73), who supported co-operative efforts as a type of half-way house to socialism, famously declared that his views ought to be classified 'under the general designation of Socialists', aiming thus at a

time when society will no longer be divided into the idle and the industrious; when the rule that they who do not work shall not eat, will be applied not to paupers only, but impartially to all; when the division of the produce of labour, instead of depending, as in so great a degree it now does, on the accident of birth, will be made by concert on an acknowledged principle of justice; and when it will no longer either be, or be thought to be, impossible for human beings to exert themselves strenuously in procuring benefits which are not to be exclusively their own, but to be shared with the society they belong to. (Mill 1874a, pp. 231–2)

Given the perceived importance of retaining Mill's undiluted liberal pedigree many Mill scholars have disputed this self-description (but see Claeys 1997). Similar problems arise with the classification of the ideas of Thomas Carlyle and John Ruskin, both of whom proposed collectivist (Carlyle) as well as communitarian schemes (Ruskin) indebted to, as well as influential upon, the socialist movement, but which were authoritarian, paternalist and anti-democratic. It was said of Ruskin's writings that they had 'probably done more than any other single influence to imbue English minds with sentiments and principles of a socialistic character' (Rae 1891, p. 88). Writers like William Morris have been enrolled under the Marxian banner (Thompson 1977), but are as plausibly described as non- or even anti-Marxist (Hardie 1907, p. 25; Cole 1954, p. 419). The Positivist followers of Auguste Comte (1798–1857), who had been Saint-Simon's secretary, evince a variety of socialist qualities (see Harrison 1908, p. xv), and continued Saint-Simon's insistence on the coming government of society by scientists and industrialists. So, too, do many prominent New Liberal writers, such as John Hobson, who projected schemes of a mixed private and public economy (see Hobson 1909, pp. 89–156, and generally Clarke 1978 and Freeden 1978). While plans for land nationalisation, such as that of the naturalist Alfred Russel Wallace (1823–1913), which restricted the collectivist principle to the soil alone (Wallace 1882), tended to be rejected by socialists as too limited, some had socialistic aspects (Beer 1920). A number of leading proponents of eugenics termed their proposals for state interference to ensure genetic purity 'socialist' (e.g. Pearson 1887a, 1887b).

The term 'socialism' thus became increasingly susceptible to a wide definition. It was often used synonymously with 'collectivism', including writers like the gradualist Belgian land nationaliser Jean de Colins (1783–1859), whose scheme of 'Rational Socialism' also had a large agrarian dimension. 'Collectivism' could, however, also be used more narrowly to describe efforts to restrict inheritance as well as nationalise land and capital (e.g. Laveleye 1885, pp. 244–64). In 1848 Proudhon famously said that socialism entailed 'every aspiration towards the improvement of society'. The statement by the later Victorian British statesman Sir William Harcourt that 'we are all socialists now' also indicates the degree to which collectivist or statist approaches to poverty, education, sanitation and trade unions in particular had become ubiquitous by the 1880s. Hence Dicey's well-known description of the growing appeal of collectivism, defined as 'faith in the benefit to be derived by the mass of the people from the action or intervention of the State even in matters which might be, and often are, left to the uncontrolled management of the persons concerned' (Dicey 1914, p. 258). This view thus came to be understood as having widely replaced 'individualist' approaches to poverty and social planning, notably in various forms of New Liberalism.

By the 1880s, programmatically, 'socialism' broadly came to mean collective control over the means of the production of wealth, particularly land and industry, for the benefit of the whole people.[2] More crudely expressed

---

2 For the most influential British socialist, Robert Blatchford, whose *Merrie England* (1894) sold more than two million copies, and whose *Clarion* circulated more than 80,000 copies weekly, the 'root idea' was 'That the country, and all the machinery of production in the country, shall belong to the whole people (the nation), and shall be used by the people and for the people' (Blatchford 1902, p. 84). (Cf. Graham 1890, p. xxi: 'I take the form of Socialism called Collectivism, which postulates the collective ownership of land and capital, with production under State direction, to *be* Socialism.') To Schaeffle

in terms of interests, it meant a system in which individual interest was
sacrificed to that of the community, and specifically that of the capitalist
class to the common good (Flint 1895, p. 17). Broadly speaking it entailed
a co-operative as opposed to a competitive approach to production. It was
usually contradistinguished from revolutionary collectivism or communism
(especially Marxist), and anarchism. In so far as radicalism was understood as
proposing collectivist legislation in aid of the working classes, and the limitation of private property in the name of the public weal, socialism could
be defined as its logical outcome (e.g. Besant 1893, p. 4; see Davies 1914).
A number of movements were peripheral to socialism or contained socialist
elements, including working-class political organisations such as Chartism
in Britain; trade union organisations like syndicalism, which were powerful in France, Spain and Italy; producer co-operation; and guild socialism.
From the 1880s onwards reaction against centralisation also brought several
strands of socialism increasingly into closer proximity with anarchism; a
noted contemporary commentator wrote that: 'all socialists are working for
the decentralisation of government. They look upon the present state as
too highly centralised. They wish to transfer functions from central governments to local political units, in order that the business of the people may
be near the people' (Ely 1894, p. 31).

While we cannot explore their political economy here in any detail,
socialists from Owen onwards through Karl Rodbertus (1805–75) and Marx
confronted Smithian and Ricardian political economy at some length, offering a sharp critique of competition, of the inegalitarian nature of capitalist
distribution and its inevitable tendency through the 'iron law of wages'
to increase poverty, and of dominant theories of value, especially that of
Ricardo (Claeys 1987; Thompson 1984). In its place they offered various
schemes of communal and collectivist production and distribution driven by
a theory of justice that was usually either egalitarian or, alternatively, based
upon work, and dedicated to production for use rather than profit (e.g.
Hardie n.d., p. 58). In general liberal contract theory of the sort associated

'*the Alpha and Omega of socialism is the transformation of private and competing capitals into a united collective
capital*' (1889, p. 20). To Villiers 'There is one thing, and one thing only, common to all Socialisms –
the belief in the common ownership of land and capital' (1908, p. 18). For Besant 'Socialism is the
theory which declares that there shall be no private property in the materials which are necessary for
the production of wealth', whether land or 'wrought material' (Besant and Foote, 1887, p. 6). To Ely
it was 'that contemplated system of industrial society which proposes the abolition of private property
in the great material instruments of production, and the substitute therefore of collective property;
and advocates the collective management of production, together with the distribution of the social
income by society, and private property in the larger proportion of this social income' (1894, p. 19).

with Locke was now introduced into economic argument, with a view thus of democratising the labour process, and overruling any 'laws' supposedly dictated by the market.

Contemporaries tended to divide nineteenth-century socialism into five distinct periods: (1) the aftermath of the French Revolution; (2) the 'utopian' phase of Owen, Fourier and Saint-Simon; (3) an era of decline from *c.*1849–63; (4) the years from the formation of the International in 1864, to its dissolution in 1872; (5) the epoch dominated by Social Democracy, from the early 1880s.

3   Owen and Owenism

Born in Newtown, Wales, Robert Owen (1771–1858) rose from humble origins to become one of the greatest entrepreneurs of his age, achieving both fame and fortune as a cotton-spinner at New Lanark, near Glasgow. Early alarmed by the deleterious effects of factory work on operatives, Owen in his first major published work, *A New View of Society; or, Essays on the Principle of the Formation of the Human Character* (1813–14), heralded the one great idea he never tired of reiterating: that human character was essentially the product of the environment, and was not voluntarily chosen. If that environment were ameliorated, so too would human behaviour become more orderly, sociable and 'rational'. If religion persuaded people that character was not malleable, it was, as Owen announced in 1817, the principal obstacle to humane social reform. Owen by 1815 had gained considerable renown as a sympathetic employer who endeavoured to improve conditions in his mills and the villages surrounding them. After Waterloo, social dislocation and unemployment convinced him that limited reforms, such as restricting the hours of child labour, were insufficient. Instead, by 1820, Owen became convinced that increasing mechanisation and a steady narrowing of the division of labour would destroy the character of the working class (Owen 1993, I, pp. 109–19). The causes of poverty, he asserted, lay in the injustice of the existing system of wages, which did not return to labourers the value of their produce (Owen 1993, I, pp. 287–332). His remedy, unfolded from 1817 onwards, was that a 'new moral world' should be created based upon small-scale communities of no more than 2,500 persons, living and working in common, aiming at self-subsistence, and alternating between manufacturing, agricultural and other forms of labour. By 1820 he coined the phrase the 'social system' (whence 'socialism' derives, in English) to describe his opposition to the 'individual' system of 'buying cheap and selling dear', soon to be termed 'individualism' (Owen 1993, II, p. 11). (Two-thirds of Owen's autobiography (1858) reprints his chief early writings. An annotated edition of the autobiographical section is Owen 1993, IV. The chief biographies are Booth 1869; Cole 1965; Donnachie 2000; Harvey 1949; Jones 1889; and Sargant 1860. Bibliographies of Owen's writings include *A Bibliography of Robert Owen, the Socialist* 1914 and Goto 1932–4. Essay collections on Owen include Butt 1971; Pollard and Salt 1971; Tsuzuki 1992.)

From the mid-1820s until his death Owen's chief aim was to construct a model community exemplifying these principles. The first great effort was at New Harmony, Indiana, the last at Queenwood, or Harmony, Hampshire, from 1839–45, with followers attempting a variety of similar schemes at Orbiston and elsewhere, all of which were short-lived. (On Owenism see Bestor 1950; Garnett 1972; Harrison 1969; and Royle 1998.) In the intervening years he played a role in the nascent trade union movement, helped to set up 'Labour Exchanges' in the early 1830s, where artisans were to trade directly with one another, and inspired the beginnings of the consumer co-operative movement. He also constructed, by the early 1840s, a substantial network of branches of a new organisation, the 'Association of All Classes of All Nations', which aimed at disseminating socialist propaganda as well as establishing a community (Claeys 1998). Despite his initial secular outlook, he portrayed his principles in the early 1830s in terms of a 'rational' 'new religion' that sought to promote charitable principles (Owen 1993, II, pp. 167–201).

As the 'Social Father' of this sectarian organisation, Owen tended to act in a paternalistic manner towards his followers. His eventual scheme for the political organisation of communities, as published in *The Book of the New Moral World* (1836–44), proposed the division of the community into eight age-groups, with each person following the same sequence of development through life. The first 'class', to age 5, would attend school; the next (5– 10) would assist in domestic labour; those 10–15 would learn agricultural and industrial skills. All those aged 15–20 would engage in production and the oversight of younger members, being supervised themselves by those aged 25–30. Finally, the 30–40-year-old group would govern the community, and the most mature, aged 40–60, would conduct 'foreign affairs' (Owen 1993, III, pp. 286–97; see Claeys 1989a). By institutionalising a traditional, gerontocratic principle of rule by elders Owen wished to avoid any elections or contests for leadership, as well as ensuring 'equal rights' and 'equal education and condition through life according to age' (Owen 1993, III, p. 365). Social order would be preserved in part, too, simply because the community was small enough to ensure a mutual policing of morals. 'Democracy' in the traditional electoral sense, then, was to be superseded, but what Owen took to be its rational content, a substantive plea for equality, would be realised in community. In principle this scheme was to apply as much to women as men, and feminism, with a demand for liberalised marriage and divorce laws, would emerge as a characteristically Owenite theme by the mid-1830s (see Kolmerten 1990; Taylor 1983; and Thompson 1997).

Owenite propaganda ensured the widespread introduction of the term 'social' to modify 'democracy' in British radical discourse from the late 1830s onwards, by which political ends, chiefly the goal of attaining universal male suffrage sought by the Chartist movement, became increasingly understood as entailing 'social' ends, especially the improvement of working-class economic standards. Equally impressive, analytically, was Owenism's critique of the chief models of plebeian radicalism, especially the United States, which by the mid-1830s was rapidly developing a class of poor (Claeys 1996). To Owenites this exemplified the operations of the competitive system. It also proved that democracy as such did not solve working-class economic distress, and that poverty was not caused, as radicals of a Cobbettite ilk continued to suggest, by heavy and unjust taxation imposed by a corrupt state, but derived from the injustice of the wage relationship, and the failure of the wage to reflect the value of the produce of labour. This would become, in Britain and elsewhere, one of the most significant arguments against other forms of radicalism through the end of the century. Most of Owen's followers were more committed to traditional forms of democratic rule than Owen himself, but accepted the thrust of this critique of the economic assumptions tacit in existing radical democratic theory.

Of all of the early socialist groups Owenism engaged in the most prolonged confrontation with classical political economy, producing dozens of pamphlets on the subject, and a number of major works, including John Gray's *A Lecture on Human Happiness* (1826) and *The Social System* (1831); William Thompson's *Inquiry Concerning the Distribution of Wealth* (1824) and *Labor Rewarded* (1827); and John Francis Bray's *Labour's Wrong and Labour's Remedy* (1839) (see Claeys 2005). These addressed some themes Owen himself had introduced, notably the disadvantages of competition, the harmful effects of unproductive labour, increasing specialisation, the instability of capitalism, and its proneness to promote poverty. Those inspired by Owen, however, were also relatively independent thinkers, and as early as the 1820s, notably in the writings of George Mudie and John Gray, had begun to propose the rational reorganisation of the national economy by some system of planning. This implied a vastly more complex system of production, as well as the possibility of expanding needs, rather than the stasis and renunciation of luxury associated with Owen's community proposals. By the early 1830s, Owenites also offered a relatively sophisticated analysis and critique of recurrent economic crises, which they saw as endemic to capitalism and prone to deepening working-class poverty.

4 Fourier and Fourierism

The social system proposed by Charles Fourier (1772–1837) was less a reaction to industrialisation than Owen's proposals, and more a criticism of the irrationality and injustice of the existing commercial system (see Fourier 1966–8. English excerpts include Fourier 1901, 1971a, 1971b). The son of a Besançon cloth merchant, Fourier saw his family fortune disappear during the French Revolution. He passed much of his life as a commercial traveller, broker and clerk in cloth houses in Marseilles, Rouen, Lyon and Paris, remaining a bachelor. He preferred children at arm's length (dining apart from their parents in the ideal future), but doted on cats and flowers. In the latter years of his life he returned home punctually each day to await – in vain – any capitalist, Napoleon or other *fondateur* who might call to offer support for his system. His introspection bred heady fantasy; salt water might be made to taste like lemonade, 'anti-tigers' would carry humans from place to place, and the Pole rendered fertile by cosmic light. Fourier's ideal was based on his discovery, announced in his first major work, the *Theory of the Four Movements* (1808), that the human and material worlds were being governed by one law of 'passionate attraction', of which Newton's law of gravitation was the natural basis. The development of this idea took the form of Fourier's critique of commercial selfishness, waste and individualism in the latest stage of history, 'Civilisation', which increasingly tended to empower merchants, bankers and stock-jobbers, and to promote both monopoly and speculation. His later chief writings were the *Traité de l'Association Domestique-Agricole* (2 vols., 1821), also published under the title of *La Théorie de l'Unité Universelle* (1822), and *Le Nouveau Monde Industriel et Sociétaire* (1829) and *La Fausse Industrie* (1835–6), which exemplify his theories of association.

The basis of Fourierism was the assumption that God intended a certain form of social order to secure mankind's happiness. Yet this order, if discernible by reason, was not, paradoxically, based on it. The folly of humanity hitherto consisted in having failed to recognise this. As Fourier proclaimed, announcing the psychological radicalism, hostility to repression and devotion to pleasure that distinguish his system:

> My theory confines itself to utilising *the passions now condemned, just as Nature has given them to us and without in any way changing them.* That is the whole mystery, the whole secret of the calculus of passionate Attraction. There is no arguing there whether God was right or wrong in giving mankind these or those passions; the associative order avails itself of them without changing them, and as God has given them to us. (Fourier 1901, p. 66, 1851)

Fourier described an elaborate cosmology; his religion included a belief in the immortality and transmigration of the soul. God had not intended, he insisted, that the greed and selfish aggressiveness characteristic of 'civilisation', epitomised by England as the social type and the Jews (whose emancipation he accordingly opposed) as the individual type, should be the final development of humanity. Early convinced of the essential dishonesty of the commercial system, he became persuaded that a new system that encouraged honesty, economy and association in line with human instincts needed to be designed; this became his life's task. His proposed scheme of organisation was based upon a radical view of the human passions, whose repression, unlike most of the pre-socialist utopian writers and many later socialists, he condemned utterly. The problem was rather 'to *change the direction* of passion rather than to change or repress the passions and instincts' (Fourier 1971a, p. 191). Hence Fourier has often been seen as a precursor of Freud. He assumed the community could both harmonise and satisfy human passions in a manner, under the rubric of the idea of 'associative' order (*ordre sociétaire*), that promoted happiness while abolishing poverty. More than any other early socialist writer, thus, Fourier proposed to maximise individuality while exalting the social or community bond at the same time.

The key to this scheme was 'passional attraction', by which the free play of the passions was to produce universal harmony. Fourier identified twelve 'radical passions', susceptible of 820 variations, and arranged around three types of attraction, the sensitive being based upon enjoyment, the affective, bearing on group affinity, and the familial, relating to parenthood. Eventually the Phalanx would exhibit '*Harmonism* or *Unityism* . . . an unbounded philanthropy, a universal good-will, which can only be developed when the entire human race shall be rich, free, and just' (Fourier 1901, p. 61). At its simplest level, then, Fourier's theory postulated that happiness required the satisfaction of desires for social interaction as well as those for individual self-expression. By maximising freedom, thus, these could be reconciled, and order could also be attained.

The most important application of this account of the passions was to labour, which was repulsive only because falsely organised, but which would be made attractive by recognising that here three passions needed to be fulfilled and harnessed: the *papillonne*, or need of change and variety; the *cabaliste*, or love of intrigue, rivalry and emulation; and the composite, a compound pleasure affecting both mind and the body. Fourier's communitarian ideal, called by him the 'Phalanx' from about 1800, was to involve about 1,800 persons, or 400 families, organised on a square mile of land, and living in one enormous central building some six storeys high, with two wings, called the *phalanstère*. Here unproductive labour would be minimised, by pooling resources communally and abolishing idleness. Economies of scale in community would reduce the cost of living immensely, and avoid the need for any class of servants. The system of 'attractive association' based on the 'law of passionate attraction' was to be applied to work in order to release individual creative potential. Monotony was to be avoided by a scheme of rotation between up to eight tasks daily which linked groups possessing similar aptitudes and tastes, encouraged the free choice of work, and avoided excessive labour. Industrial labour would be no more than one-quarter of the total: the phalanx, defined in 1808 as an 'agricultural association' (Fourier 1996–8, p. 10), would essentially be a market garden on an immense scale. Organisation of the community was broken down into groups of seven to nine people, twenty-four to thirty-two groups forming a 'series'. The continuing existence of capital would help to ensure the preservation of individual freedom in face of the possible tyranny of the phalanx. Here liberty and fraternity are given greater priority over equality than in the other early socialist systems; Fourier indeed described equality as 'a political poison in association', adding that

the English are ignorant of that fact, and constitute their communities of families of about equal fortune. The associative *régime* is as incompatible with equality of fortune as with uniformity of character; it desires a progressive scale in every direction, the greatest variety in employments, and, above all, the union of extreme contrasts, such as that of the man of opulence with one of no means, a fiery character with an apathetic one, youth with age, etc. (Fourier 1901, p. 128)

The phalange or phalanx was thus not to be communistic, nor was self-interest to be abolished; hence Fourier's principle of distribution is often understood as more 'realistic' than that of the communist writers. (Accommodation and dining facilities of different grades were to be available too, though 'the food sent to the ordinary people's kitchens' would 'be finer than the food we reserve for kings', Fourier 1996–8, p. 164.) The economic product was to be divided into three parts: capital receiving four-twelfths, labour five-twelfths and talent three-twelfths (but individuals might belong to each group). Freedom of inheritance would also secure existing fortunes. But despite social classes, a spirit of unity would pervade the association: for some it is thus 'Fourier's concept of community as individual self-realisation through the creation of social institutions permitting human encounters that defines him as a socialist' (Poster, in Fourier 1971a, p. 20). The wealthy would benefit by being no longer despised by the poor, and would assist in some work purely for the sake of association. Hard labour would also be better paid than pleasant work, with a generous minimum wage, each 'Harmonian' being advanced clothing, food and housing each year, to be repaid by labour (Fourier 1901, p. 191). The government of the phalanx was to be republican, with all officers elected, and coercion minimised. But details of phalangist 'politics' are sparse; the assumption again is once the great 'stumbling-block' of politics, poverty, had been abolished (Fourier 1851, I, p. 339), fundamental divisions of opinion would not create entrenched partisanship; that satisfied beings, content with, perhaps exhausted by, the exercise of rich individuality, would be less prone to disagreement, and that the passion for power over others, or the cabalist spirit of intrigue, would have been sublimated by being channelled into the passional intrigues of some thirty series.[3] By this means the rich, in particular, would be less prone to desire domination over the poor in the phalange (Fourier 1971a, p. 299, 1851, I, pp. 325–45, and II, pp. 13–27, on cabalism). Eventually all phalanges would federate and elect a single leader, resident at Constantinople. But this would not be a paternalistic world-government, for Fourier was utterly dismissive of 'the most ridiculous prejudice, the conviction that the good can be established by government action', claiming that every form of 'civilised' administration also preferred its own good (Fourier 1971a, p. 162).

---

3 '... love, a passion of which the analysis appears very frivolous to us, and which, far from being a spring foreign to the politics of harmony, will with ambition be then the most potent spring of the industrial combinations, for in harmony love is quite as powerful a vehicle as ambition to attract men to agricultural and manufacturing labor' (Fourier 1851, vol. I, p. 248). Fourier here calls love 'a lever of social politics' (I, p. 248).

Fourier also recognised that other forms of human vice besides greedy self-interest could corrupt and destroy communities. But such passions, again, were not to be repressed, but channelled in positive ways. Gluttony and the love of luxury could be accommodated, for instance, by increasing the standard of living and taste culture in food and accommodation ('the generalisation of epicurism', in other words; Fourier 1901, p. 63); while a love of disorder and dirt in children could be fulfilled by their occupations. Lust was to be sated by ensuring a 'sexual minimum' of gratification, and the vast extension of every form of sexual relationship that would occur when the 'incoherent household' of bourgeois society had been superseded. But Fourier's radical theories on sexuality and marriage or 'enslaved monogamy', which he proposed to abolish, and his urging of the necessity for universal sexual gratification, with a 'Court of Love' supervising sexual relations, were regarded as overly controversial by his disciples, and suppressed (his treatise *Le Nouveau Monde Amoureux* was not published in full until 1967; English extracts are in Fourier 1971a; and a German translation, Fourier 1977). Fourier contended, however, that only such an 'amorous corporation' could ensure the fullest freedom for women, and insisted indeed that 'the extension of privileges to women is the general principle of all social progress' (Fourier 1901, p. 77).

The Fourierist ideal of daily varied labour, five sumptuous meals, free religious worship, diverse cultural expression and copious sexual intercourse, not unsurprisingly soon found votaries. The movement spawned a number of mostly short-lived communities in France (notably Jean Godin's *Familistère* at Guise, founded in 1859) and Britain, and rather more in the United States, notably at Brook Farm, during the 1840s (Guarneri 1991). Fourier's chief disciple in France in this period was Victor Considérant (1808–93), who gave preference to the state over the phalange as the agency of social reform (Beecher 2001). In the United States Albert Brisbane (1809–90), whose *Social Destiny of Man* appeared in 1840, proved an indefatigable interpreter. Fourier's influence was also powerful on the nascent Russian socialist movement. And for a brief moment, at least (in 1845–6), and perhaps only fancifully, Marx and Engels acknowledged the attractions of being able to 'hunt in the morning, fish in the afternoon, rear cattle in the evening, engage in criticism after dinner, just as I please' (Marx and Engels 1976, v, p. 47). But this was not to be the image of communist society with which they would thereafter choose to be affiliated.

5   Saint-Simon and Saint-Simonism

The most influential form of early socialism, as far as mainstream social and political thought is concerned, was Saint-Simonism. Its founder was Henri de Saint-Simon (1760–1825), a French nobleman who fought in the American War of Independence and renounced his title at the French Revolution. Thereafter he became involved in canal construction and land development, but was ruined financially in 1804. His main writings, published between 1803–17, are neither communitarian nor, by most definitions, socialist (though see Durkheim 1959); it was his chief followers who extended his ideas in this direction, or, like Auguste Comte, built upon his analysis of industrial society. Saint-Simon himself was initially chiefly concerned, in the tradition of Condorcet, to describe human progress in terms of the perfectibility of scientific methodology (*Letters from an Inhabitant of Geneva*, 1802). He then turned to offer a solution for European national struggles by proposing a European (initially Anglo-French) confederation on liberal, parliamentary principles based on 'European patriotism' or 'Europeanism', which would aim at perpetual peace, with a central body arbitrating over national disputes (*Reorganisation of European Society*, 1814). National Houses of Commons were, however, to be composed only of economic and administrative elites, elected by their professional bodies. Deputies were to possess a landed income of not less than 25,000 francs per annum, but twenty members of a chamber of 240 members would be granted this property every ten years on the basis of merit. The initial Parliament was also to be two-thirds British and one-third French. Saint-Simon became best known, thereafter, for his description of the new form of industrial society, and for describing a means, chiefly religious, of ameliorating the lot of the poor created by its development. (His works are Saint-Simon 1865–78. Selections in English include Saint-Simon 1964, 1975, 1976. Studies include Booth 1871; Carlisle 1987; Manuel 1956; Picon 2002. On Saint-Simonism see Booth 1871; Butler 1926; Charléty 1896; Iggers 1958; Janet 1878; Jullien 1926; Reybaud 1864; Walch 1967; Weill 1896.)

The industrial epoch, in Saint-Simon's view, demanded an entirely new, commensurate, form of polity. Distinguishing between organic historical periods, when a social order was developed, and critical periods, when it came under attack, Saint-Simon took the chief crisis of the age to be one of authority; the old order was disintegrating rapidly, a new leading group needed to take its place. His endeavour to provide a new form of spiritual authority, utilising a 'new religion', called 'Physicism' (or sometimes, 'Positive Philosophy'), assumed a scientific explanation of the homogeneity of matter and mind would supersede theology. Comte would develop this into the system called 'Positivism', echoing Saint-Simon's view that the reinforcement of spiritual power was crucial to the transitional age, particularly during an intermediary stage when theology was still widely upheld. (Prior to its public acceptance, however, rejecting efforts by Bonald, Maistre and others to restore Catholicism, Saint-Simon counselled deism as a popular religion, which still presumed governance by a divine will rather than natural laws.) This emphasis on the need for a new ruling spiritual power to replace that lost by the decline of medieval Catholicism is often taken to be a leading feature of Saint-Simon's system, and can be linked to similar themes in Carlyle and Mill, among others (see Cofer 1931; Pankhurst 1957; Shine 1941).

Saint-Simon's chief contribution to socialism was thus his account of the transition of modern society from a military stage to 'industrialism' (a term he coined) and its implications for the reshaping of the modern world, notably in *L'Industrie* (1816–18). Society was here categorised in terms of three main classes: scientists, writers and artists; proprietors; and toilers. Spiritual power was to reside with the former; temporal power, or control of the state, with the property owners; and the right of election with all workers. All useful workers, not merely the bourgeoisie, whom Saint-Simon regarded as having made the French Revolution and conducted it in their own interest, were 'industrialists', since work was the basis of all virtue, and all incomes not based on work (including that of lawyers, who were to be abolished and replaced by unpaid courts of arbitration) were essentially robbery. The failure of the French Revolution lay in the assumption of power by the most ignorant, and the concentration of effort on perfecting the mechanism of government, when its chief aim should have been the subordination of government to administration as the main activity. The new spiritual power would guarantee universal peace through European government, abolish parasitism and idleness, and establish universal association and the right to labour, with reward based on merit. But governments as such would have less power and fewer financial resources than previously, and national governments would also be weakened by their subordination to European institutions, which would curb alike 'the ambitions of peoples and kings' (Saint-Simon 1976, p. 96).

Here we see that the analysis of politics, indeed the proposal of a new science thereof, in which the 'politics of power' is supplanted by the 'politics of abilities', was vastly more important to Saint-Simon than to Owen or Fourier, or for that matter most other nineteenth-century socialists. For Saint-Simon the present transitional age witnessed the natural progress of society from a governmental, or a feudal, military or predatory regime of 'idlers', nobles and lawyers, to an administrative or industrial regime of 'producers'. Soon governments would 'no longer order men about; their functions will be limited to ensuring that useful work will not be hindered' (Saint-Simon 1964, p. 71). Thus, as encapsulated in the famous phrase, 'politics is the science of production' (Saint-Simon 1976, p. 108),[4] the class of industrialists would promote the greatest production of useful things. This was, for Saint-Simon, a meritocratic ideal hostile to feudal privilege and economic interference; as such it is close in some particulars to the liberal economics of 'the immortal' Adam Smith (e.g. Saint-Simon 1976, p. 107). Saint-Simon also believed that taxes would be much reduced in the juster industrial system. Saint-Simon's *Le Politique* (1819) also advocated the abolition of standing armies, the costs of which hindered the relief of the proletariat (Saint-Simon 1976, p. 239). Much more important than political participation, thus, was economic participation, by which power was more diffused. Saint-Simon anticipated a growing interdependence in the productive process, which would promote a greater harmony of interests between the various types of industrialists, with decision-making being based less on command and obedience than persuasion and argument amongst the different organisations of producers, be they trade unions, corporations, communes, etc. National parliaments would formulate an economic 'plan', but this respected public works only; as a whole the economy itself was to remain independent of political control in order to maximise efficiency and minimise parasitism and interference. Yet if, as Durkheim supposed, the point of this scheme was 'to bind economic life to a central organ that regulates it', this could also be termed 'the very definition of socialism' (Durkheim 1959, p. 137).

In *L'Organisateur* (1819) Saint-Simon offered a plan for an industrial parliament composed of three chambers of Invention, Examination and

---

4 In the original: 'La politique est donc, pour me résumer en deux mots, *la science de la production*, c'est-à-dire la science qui a pour objet l'ordre de choses le plus favorable à tous les genres de productions' (quoted in Booth 1871, p. 48).

Execution, the first to plan public works; the second, also consisting of engineers and other educated people exercising 'spiritual power', to scrutinise such plans; and the third being great capitalists and bankers, who would retain executive power and control over taxation and expenditure, though they were supposed to be guided by the other chambers. This scheme, later criticised as dictatorial by Mill (1968, p. 168), was taken up in Auguste Comte's *System of Positive Polity* (Comte 1875–7, II, pp. 276–345, IV, pp. 315–454). In the *Système Industriel* (1821), however, Saint-Simon withdrew the power he had assigned men of letters, worrying that they would be prone to despotic clericalism, and offered it instead to positive philosophers guided and invested with power by the King. (Comte would agree that a dictator might introduce his scheme, which was however to be republican.) Saint-Simon's *Catéchisme des Industriels* (1823) emphasised the dangers of revolutionary change, and proposed government by the leading priests, savants and industrials, more or less spontaneously given power by the masses. There is nothing particularly socialistic about this scheme, unless the centrality of the 'Plan' as such defines socialism. For politically, Saint-Simon always presumed that rule by an educated elite was natural and inevitable. He did assume a degree of harmony and common interest between the capitalist and proletarian, which can be seen as the outcome of his general principle of the subordination of politics to ethics, later also a Positivist ideal. But he also had come to reject any assumption that the pursuit of individual interest spontaneously generated any common good. Saint-Simon did become increasingly aware of the condition of the working class. But he did not solve the social question as such, apparently viewing as over-optimistic his earlier classification of workers and employers together as harmonious 'industrials', without recognising antagonisms inherent in the capitalist system. Only in his later works, notably the *Système Industriel* (1821), did Saint-Simon move towards what would be later more commonly understood as socialism, mainly by proposing that the government guarantee the right of work; he also argued for temporal power to be exercised by cultivators and the proprietors of manufactories. By 1825 he was urging that priority should be given in state expenditure 'to ensuring work for all fit men, to secure their physical existence', as well as providing them education and the means of recreation (Saint-Simon 1964, p. 77). This was the first main form of statist socialism described in this period. In his final and most influential work, the *Nouveau Christianisme*, 1825, it is a reformed religion which cements these ties, with the aim of religion being the amelioration of the condition of the working class and the promotion of the single divine principle that 'Men should treat each other as brothers.' This became the basis of the Saint-Simonian religion and was again echoed in Comte's Positive religion. The social problem thus had in part a religious answer.

The most prominent of Saint-Simon's followers were the 'Supreme Fathers' of the sect, Saint-Amand Bazard, who did most to develop Saint-Simon's conception of organic and critical historical periods, Barthélemy-Prosper Enfantin and Pierre Leroux. They adopted a distinctive blue costume, and extended the master's ideas in a markedly socialist, authoritarian and feminist direction in the late 1820s and early 1830s. Their chief interpretation of his writings, *The Doctrine of Saint-Simon* (1828–9), also argued for greater equality for women, the increased facility of divorce, an expansion in national education, and both greater freedom of trade and closer integration of the state and the system of production, especially through a remodelling of the banking system (Iggers 1972). Taking the view that the exploitation of labour had followed three successive forms of slavery, serfdom and wage-labour, the Saint-Simonians insisted that the moral end of historical progress was 'universal association', which required the abolition of economic exploitation. Capital as such belonged to the community rather than the individual. Since the competitive system was increasingly prone to engender industrial crisis, it was necessary for the government, rather than, as for Saint-Simon, private enterprise, to balance supply and demand by centralising economic knowledge. The abolition of inheritance was to be introduced, followed by a principle of distribution based on the famous principle 'From each according to his capacity; to each according to his works.' Here reward according to merit was stressed, and community of goods firmly rejected as destroying the principle of emulation by giving the idle the same share as the industrious (Iggers 1972, p. 89). The state thus became the owner of land and capital, and the organiser of the entire labour force on military principles. Administration would be centralised through the banking system, with a 'central bank representing the government in the material order', extending credit to and monitoring the activities of lesser banks, thus becoming the chief economic unit (Iggers 1972, pp. 103–7). A new intellectual elite and industrial hierarchy would emerge based upon talent rather than birth, and aiming at maximising economic efficiency; in short, 'industry is organised, everything is interlinked, and all is planned' (Iggers 1972, p. 98). An expanded form of Christianity, again, in which labour and science were sanctified, was to provide an ethical bond for the new society. This scheme was later derided by some historians as an extreme form of 'scientism' (Hayek 1952, p. 135), and by others as a 'totalitarian fantasy' (Iggers 1972, p. vii), which foreshadowed a later débâcle (by unifying an ideology of order, a regimented popular movement, a party based upon a monolithic secular religion, and an absolutist leader emerging spontaneously from the masses and acknowledged for his greatness). (A critique of this view by Gita Ionescu (Saint-Simon 1976, pp. 21–2) denies that the functional aspects of a *dirigiste* or collectivist society have any intrinsic relation to the deprivation of rights and freedom associated with fascist and communist totalitarianism.) Nonetheless by 1831 it was claimed that the 'new religion' had some 40,000 adherents throughout Europe. The movement began to split, however, in part over the issue of whether a female Messiah was needed to reveal the next stage of doctrine, upon which Enfantin insisted. By the 1840s its influence had dwindled, though its philosophy of history and account of industrial society were developed by various thinkers, including Marx. Many Saint-Simonians also became prominent in France as engineers, businessmen and economists.

6 Paternalistic or feudal socialism: Thomas Carlyle and John Ruskin

The Saint-Simonian ideal was taken up in Britain by one critic of industrialism in particular, Thomas Carlyle (1795–1881). As early as *Sartor Resartus* (1831) Carlyle achieved a measure of renown as an opponent of Benthamism and classical political economy, which he accused of promoting a culture of money- or 'Mammon' worship. By the early 1840s he had come to reject the market system based on competition entirely. In Book 4 of *Past and Present* (1843), Carlyle proposed an 'organisation of labour' into industrial armies, led by an 'aristocracy of talent', chiefly captains of industry, who would be charged with instilling a new sense of chivalry and just subordination. Workers would be offered a permanent labour contract, subject to performance, and might share in the management of industrial enterprises, though Carlyle dismissed demands for democracy as merely promising further anarchy. Labourers might, moreover, also be compelled to work if they were found to be idle or shirking. Legislation would ensure greater safety and comfort in the workplace through the regulation of factories and mines and sanitary regulations. Public parks, education and assisted emigration were also to be introduced.

John Ruskin (1819–1900) is usually taken to be a disciple of Carlyle, though his 'socialism' is equally difficult to classify. It falls broadly, however, into two parts. The economic programme presented in *Unto This Last*

(1862) pleads for an equal exchange of labour for labour, rooted in Owenite and Christian Socialist argument, and is linked to a scheme for permanent working-class employment (see Anthony 1983; Cockram 2007; Henderson 2000). Second, Ruskin mounted briefly a communitarian experiment called the Guild of St George in the 1870s (Scott 1931).

Other early socialists

Amongst the other influential forms of non-Marxian socialism during the nineteenth century, mention should be made of the proposals of the communist lawyer Étienne Cabet (1788–1853), author of the *Voyage en Icarie* (1840), who founded a series of colonies in the United States beginning in 1848 and lasting until the early 1880s (see C. Johnson, 1974; Sutton, 1994). Cabet proposed a highly rationalist, and somewhat authoritarian, system of social organisation (which became democratic after his death). Its proposals for non-violent, gradual change towards egalitarian socialism attracted several hundred thousand adherents in France during the 1840s. Like Babeuf, who had proposed similarities of dress (distinguishing only for age and sex), food and education, there is an enforced uniformity in Cabet's egalitarianism, though elegance and beauty were supposed to be encouraged.

The principal early German socialist was the tailor Wilhelm Weitling (1808–71), whose first tract, *Mankind As It Is and As It Ought to Be* (1838), was composed under the influence of a secret revolutionary society based in Paris, the League of the Just (Wittke 1950). This projected a future system of organisation based upon units of 10,000 families, sub-divided into units of 1,000 families which were in turn sub-divided. Each unit would choose delegates to administer its own affairs, who would in turn elect administrators to the next higher level. Industry was to be similarly organised on the basis of an ascending series of elected bodies representing major occupational groups, organised around the small workshop rather than the factory. Weitling's main work, *Guarantees of Harmony and Freedom* (1842), described the loss of a golden age or state of nature prior to the creation of private property and examined the emergence of the modern industrial proletariat. Weitling's proposals for a communist society detailed those needs (principally for acquisition, pleasure and knowledge) that would be satisfied, including the assurance of intellectual development, and the extension of freedom to all. Basic subsistence for all, including housing, clothing and food, was to be assured; any luxuries desired could be earned by additional units of work. The production of unnecessary surpluses would be regulated by denying labour-credits to their producers until stocks were depleted. An industrial army, modelled on the military, would be the main unit of labour organisation, by which means large-scale projects could be completed. Money and private property, the bane of modern existence, were to be eliminated, and the system of exchange instead based upon labour-time. Against Owen and Fourier, Weitling placed greater stress on family life, while recognising the need for easier divorce and the extension of employment rights to women. Like Marx he agreed that socialism could be introduced by revolutionary means, and proposed that popular dictatorship would follow the revolution and precede the ultimate creation of communism. Like many early socialists, however, Weitling also sought to found his views on a radical interpretation of Christianity which included a millenarian component, as explained in *The Poor Sinner's Gospel* (English translation, 1969).

Other German socialists of note include Karl Schapper and Auguste Willich, who were linked with the French revolutionary Auguste Blanqui in the League of the Just, which after 1847 became the Communist League. The Young Hegelian Moses Hess (1812–75) was a theoretician of minor influence, and author of *The European Triarchy* and other works (Berlin 1959; Weiss 1960). Other 'True Socialists', mostly now remembered through Marx and Engels' caustic dismissal of their views in 1845–6 in *The German Ideology*, included Karl Grün and Georg Kuhlmann. Another German, John-Adolphus Etzler (1796–c.1860), wrote a number of works, notably *The Paradise Within the Reach of All Men* (1833), proposing a technologically innovative form of socialist society (Etzler 1977).

7   The revolutions of 1848

During the upheavals of 1848 it was chiefly Louis Blanc (1811–82) who popularised the principle that a democratic state could introduce socialist reforms rather than relying on local initiatives funded by capitalists or workers on the lines of the Owenite and Fourierist communities. Blanc's *Organisation du Travail* (1839) can be seen as blending Fourierist and Saint-Simonian ideas. It proposed that the state fund co-operative workshops to compete with private capitalists, and eventually supersede them by universal association. Workers might also group together once they became aware of 'the evident economy and indisputable excellence of living in common', on the basis of a 'voluntary association of wants and enjoyments' (Blanc 1848,

p. 137, 1982). Government would regulate industry for the first year of an interim period, but thereafter popular elections would introduce new leaders. Political reform was thus to be the means of social change, rather than the working classes acting independently of or with hostility towards the state. The state once reformed would act not despotically, as Blanc feared a Saint-Simonian regime would. Instead its functions were to be limited to a general supervision of the rules of production, with each branch of industry electing its own managers. Capitalists would also join the new associations, receiving the existing rate of interest on investment rather than being partners with the working classes, and gradually being won over to the associative principle. Eventually competition would be superseded entirely. Blanc dismissed Fourier's and Considérant's reliance on any conception of a cosmic 'natural order' as 'a mere mimicry of omnipotence' (Blanc 1848, p. 131). He also ridiculed the Saint-Simonians' efforts to abolish the family. Blanc's scheme enjoyed some success, but of some fifty-six state-funded associations established, only one remained by 1875.

8 Christian Socialism and the problem of religion

Most forms of nineteenth-century non-Marxian socialism saw themselves as supplanting or extending Christianity, either, like Owen, by proposing a 'new religion', a paradise on earth based upon harmony rather than competition; or, like Fourier and Comte, a metaphysical substitute. For some, it was a spirit of duty and self-sacrifice which bridged socialism and Christianity (e.g. Tuckwell 1889, p. 15). To others, the essence of socialism, 'the expression of the feeling of the brotherhood of all men among each other' (Neale 1851, p. 32), could only result from the acknowledgement of a common parent, God. Medieval Christianity could be combed for illustrations of an 'original' communistic spirit. More recent Christian communalism of the Shaker type could also furnish a useful precedent (Noyes 1870). Socialism, indeed, could be seen as *the* religion of the future, as writers like Guyau, Wells and Le Bon predicted (Kaufmann 1906, pp. 179–80). By the early twentieth century this search for a revivified secular faith had come to be seen by some as an essential psychological motive force underlying the socialist movement, where an intense desire for social equality compensated for existing inequality and distress (e.g. de Man 1928). To some, notably Le Bon, thus, it was the psychology of the mass or crowd as such, inviting manipulation by its leaders, which predominated in socialism (Le Bon 1895, 1899, 1913). For Georges Sorel (1847–1922), the great goal and motivating factor would be the quasi-mythical ideal (based on a Bergsonian concept of instinct) of the general syndicalist strike, which Sorel hoped would replace the Marxian ideal of catastrophist revolution. 'Myths' were any conception that had inspired great social movements, or could be manipulated to secure their ends, including primitive Christianity, the Reformation, Marx's theory of revolution, the French Revolution, and Mazzinian nationalism; to Le Bon, 'the reason why socialism is so powerful to-day is that it constitutes the last illusion that is still vital' (Le Bon 1895, p. 109).

The fact that religion could be construed as both the epitome of 'false consciousness' and an essential bond of communal unity meant that it remained a deeply divisive issue among later nineteenth-century socialists. Many were agnostic, and the more Marxist, like Ernest Belfort Bax (*The Religion of Socialism*, 1887) were usually overtly anti-Christian, though Bax had Positivist leanings. Some, however, preferred to ignore the issue. Robert Blatchford, the leader of the Clarion movement, proclaimed that 'Socialism does not touch religion at any point. It deals with laws, and with industrial and political government' (Blatchford 1902, p. 78). But others, probably in a majority, took an opposing view. George Bernard Shaw insisted that it was only by religion that socialism could be brought about. Prominent working-class socialists like James Keir Hardie could declare that 'the impetus which drove me first of all into the Labour movement, and the inspiration which has carried me on in it, has been derived more from the teachings of Jesus of Nazareth, than from all other sources combined' (Hardie n.d., p. 140). In Britain, between 1848 and 1854, F. D. Maurice, Thomas Hughes and Charles Kingsley promoted various co-operative and educational schemes, and were vehemently opposed to the Manchester Free Trade School of John Bright and Richard Cobden. Later the Guild of St Matthew was active in England (see Binyon 1931; Jones 1968; Kaufmann 1888; Raven 1920; Woodworth 1903). In the last third of the century, despite the influence of the secularist movement led by Bradlaugh, Holyoake and others, religion thus continued to exert a strong influence in Britain and elsewhere. Various schemes, led by Stewart Headlam and others, were introduced between 1875 and 1900, which were of substantial influence on the labour movement. Most European nations possessed organised Christian Socialist movements in this period. Germany had Catholic and Protestant Christian Socialist movements, favouring a paternal state socialism, and men like Christoph Moufang and William Immanuel, Baron von Ketteler, promoted a variety of legislative measures to protect the working classes, and to regulate capitalist speculation. In France a Christian critique of competition was popularised by Félicité de Lammenais (1782–1854), while Italy produced writers like Rafaele Mariano and Francesco Nitti (Nitti 1911).

Despite the secularist emphasis in Owenism in particular, the dividing line between socialism and Christian Socialism was never as great as secularly minded historians have tended to presume. 'Scientific socialism' rarely provided the sense of spiritual bond or community which such attempted substitutes for religion patently offered, particularly where its claims of scientific predictability based on biology and history were regarded as mere 'suppositions concerning the probabilities of human action or events' (Glasier 1919, p. vii). As the British socialist Philip Snowden suggested, thus, socialism was not for most a profit-and-loss, 'materialistic' calculation, but rather 'like a religion – the promise of a full spiritual life' (Snowden 1934, I, p. 81). Hence many non-Marxian socialists emphasised the moral aspects of socialist theory, particularly in so far as they contributed to discussions of changes in 'character' to be anticipated under socialism, resting sometimes on a quasi-Comtean moral or religious solidarity in society, or possibly embodied in the ideal of the state as such. For some indeed such considerations had primacy; to Sidney Ball the 'mere substitution of public for private administration is the shadow and not the substance. The forces required to work Collectivist machinery are nothing if not moral' (Ball 1896, p. 14). This was particularly important where, as was often presumed, large-scale private employment was to be replaced by public service 'with the stimulus of duty and esteem, instead of that of fortune-making'. Such was Sidney Webb's formulation, referring to Comte, but with Ruskin's *Unto This Last* as a principal model, underpinned by Carlyle's quasi-religious duty to labour (Webb n.d., p. 16).

9 Leading trends 1875–1914

Much continental socialism after the 1860s was Marxist, with the German Social Democratic Party eventually dominating the movement. But in Germany, besides Christian Socialism, there was also an academic socialist movement, the *Katheder Sozialisten*, or Socialists of the Chair, including Professors Schmoller and Held, who promoted various ameliorationist and associative schemes based upon state intervention to ensure fair wages, regulate trades unions, inspect factories, etc. (see Laveleye 1885, pp. 81–145; Rae 1891, pp. 195–217). Another branch of the socialist movement was associated with Bismarck's nationalisation and welfare programmes, which included schemes for accident, sickness and old age insurance. These commenced after 1878, when the Social Democratic party was suppressed. Most

French socialism from the 1860s onwards was also Marxist (Moss 1976). Following the failure of the Commune, no substantial meeting of socialists took place until 1880 at Havre, when the movement split into three strands, of which the opposite wings were termed Co-operationists, who opted for gradual improvement through the existing political process, and Anarchists. The third section became the Socialist Revolutionary Party, committed to considerable reforms, but not large-scale nationalisation. But the party split again two years later into groups led by Paul Brousse and Jules Guesde, the former favouring decentralised municipal control over industry, the latter a more centralised Marxist approach. (Another revolutionary grouping, the Blanquists, are assessed elsewhere in this volume.) In 1889 there were thirty members of the so-called Socialist Group in the legislature, supporting a programme of progressive nationalisation of industrial monopolies, communal autonomy, international arbitration, the abolition of standing armies, sexual equality, and a variety of other measures. Jean Jaurès (1859–1914), who was first elected as a Radical in 1885, stood successfully as a Socialist in 1893, and was the most important French Socialist leader at the turn of the twentieth century. Italian and Spanish socialism in this period tended also to be much influenced by anarchism, especially Bakunin, as was a substantial minority of Belgian socialists. An Italian Socialist party first emerged as a distinctive group in 1892.

The International Working Men's Association, founded in 1864, represented the trade unions, Proudhonists, Blanquists and Bakuninists, as well as Marx's followers. At Congresses held in 1866, 1867 and 1868, it agreed that the land, mines, forests, the means of transport and communication should become public property, but might be managed by workers' associations, with co-operative societies and mutual credit organisations (the Proudhonist plan) proposed to supervise industrial production. In 1869 a measure to abolish inheritance was rejected, but the growing strength of Bakuninism engendered tensions with Marx which eventually resulted in the organisation splitting in 1872. In the most prescient of the anarchist critiques of Marxism, *Statism and Anarchy* (1873), Bakunin would later accuse Marx of wishing to impose an intellectual dictatorship over the working classes. The Paris Commune, which arose at the end of France's defeat by Germany in the Franco-Prussian War of 1870–1, was clearly an attempt to reassert the principle of the local, workers' self-organising unit against excessive centralisation. Various later socialists, including Marx, would claim its organisation to be paradigmatic for socialist democratic theory; Bax and others argued that 'from the *Political* point of view, the Revolution of Paris established in France a new form of administration – Federalist Administration' (Bax *et al.* 1886, p. 60). The socialism of the Second International, from 1889 onwards, is discussed elsewhere in this series (Geary 2003).

10   Later non-Marxian socialism

Following Kropotkin (1899, II, p. 213), we may distinguish three main strands of non-Marxian socialism emerging in the later nineteenth century. With its statist emphasis, Saint-Simonism tended to develop into social democracy, while Fourierism encouraged anarchism. Owenism in turn lent assistance to trade unionism, co-operation and municipal socialism, and was less sympathetic to social democratic state socialism. The social democratic state with a mixed economy, the model which predominated in Europe after 1945, was hence indebted primarily to the more statist strands of later nineteenth-century socialism. The most important development in the theory of socialist organisation to occur after 1848, thus, was the move towards collectivism and statism and away from communitarianism of the Owenite, Fourierist or Cabetist variety. This resulted from the widespread perception that communitarianism had failed, and was in any case ill-suited to harnessing large-scale mechanical production. Marxian socialism was based upon the critique of political economy, the theory of surplus value and a historical account of the development of capitalism.

But not only did many late nineteenth-century forms of socialism continue to urge both a moral and religious appeal: they also developed anti-centralist, even romantic and individualist themes in many respects alien to Marxism. Some did so in reaction to critics of socialism who suggested that collectivism would enforce uniformity of character and curtail individual liberty, for instance in Herbert Spencer's *Man versus the State* (1884) (e.g. Blatchford 1908, pp. 178–87). Some advocated an individualist point of departure linked to a romantic ideal of creativity as the core of human identity and personality. By 1900 a few, notably in Britain, emphasised that a love of liberty springing from 'a reverence for parliamentary institutions' was 'a condition of socialist success' (Macdonald 1909, I, pp. xxi–xxv). Other socialists were sympathetic to anarchist demands for a society which maximised human liberty, even if they rejected the possibility that an anarchist society as such could ever function. Dutch socialism at the turn of the century, for example, was dominated by the personality of the ex-clergyman Domela Nieuwenhuis (1846–1919). He entered Parliament in 1888, and founded a Social Democratic League in 1889, before rejecting political involvement and opting for an anarchistical communism. But despite this trend most forms of socialism nonetheless either ignored or were hostile to the language of liberal rights, preferring to promote an intensified sense of public duty. Given the twentieth-century degeneration of Marxian socialism into totalitarianism, which occurred at least in part because of its weak theorisation of democracy, authority and leadership, such emphases repay study.

In Europe the most influential developments of this type, favouring a greater emphasis on individual liberty, were in Britain, where Marxism was weakest. Although the most influential British socialist organisation from the early 1880s onwards was H. M. Hyndman's Democratic Federation, founded in 1881, which, reincarnated as the Social Democratic Federation in 1884, became avowedly Marxist, there were many other strands of socialist thought evident in the period.

William Morris

Though sometimes claimed as a Marxist, William Morris is as easily affiliated with the anarchist or individualist wing of non-Marxian socialism (e.g. Kirkup 1913, p. 276). He began as a member of Hyndman's Social Democratic Federation, but in 1884 left to form a new organisation, the Socialist League, from which Morris seceded again in 1890 with his following to the Hammersmith Socialist Society. Morris wedded Ruskinian aesthetics to a socialist programme. Extraordinarily active as a lecturer and journalist, Morris remains best known today for his great 'utopian romance', *News from Nowhere* (1890). This was a response to Edward Bellamy's immensely popular 'cockney utopia' (as Morris termed it), *Looking Backward*, published in 1889, which envisioned the future in terms of greatly advanced mechanisation and centralisation. By contrast, Morris proposed considerable decentralisation, the dispersion of large urban populations to smaller towns, preservation of the environment, and cultivation of the arts and crafts in order to maximise individual creativity and fulfilment in work. Politics was to be primarily a local affair conducted at 'Mote' meetings (the term echoing Saxon and Icelandic institutions). Differences of opinion would no longer 'crystallise people into parties permanently hostile to one another, with different theories as to the build of the universe and the progress of time' (Morris 1899, p. 95). In determining public policy, minority opinion, when substantial, would be respected so far as to prevent majority opinion overriding it until opinion had shifted markedly towards any majority. Most causes of crime having disappeared with the abolition of private property, criminals were to be treated not as habitual offenders, but errant friends, and none but the mad and ill restrained. Toleration for individual differences of dress and personal style would be encouraged.

Like Morris, Edward Carpenter (1844–1929) also took up the theme of the 'simplification' of life, attacking the vaunted claims of 'civilisation' as such. Though his plea for 'non-governmental society' places him closer to anarchism than socialism in some respects (Carpenter 1890), Carpenter's description of gerontocratic rule in non-governmental society closely parallels Owen's proposals, but was based even more directly on the idea of primitive society (Carpenter 1917, pp. 77–8; see Tsuzuki 1980). Other prominent English socialists, like J. Morrison Davidson, also gave greater support to anarchist by contrast to statist socialism (Davidson n.d., pp. 7–8).

Fabianism

Commencing in 1883, Thomas Davidson's Fellowship of the New Life proposed a small-scale community of like-minded adherents to the refined principles of the 'Vita Nuova'. Some of its members formed the Fabian Society in January 1884, naming it after a Roman general famous for wearing his opponents down. After German Social Democracy, Fabianism was to remain one of the most long-lived of socialist groupings of the period. The Society's members included Sidney and Beatrice Webb, Graham Wallas, Sydney Olivier, Frank Podmore, Annie Besant and George Bernard Shaw. Its agenda included a commitment to gradualist, evolutionary socialism through a process of permeating the existing political system; an emphasis upon municipal rather than centralised control; and the belief that rule by bureaucratic expertise and the intellectual class generally was both inevitable and preferable. Its most important document is the *Fabian Essays in Socialism* (1889) (see Cole 1943, 1962; Mackenzie and Mackenzie 1979; McBriar 1962; Wolfe 1975). Some of its ideas were extended in Guild Socialism (e.g. Goldwell, 1918).

H. G. Wells (1866–1946) was also a member of the Fabian Society. In *New Worlds for Old* (1908) he described his aims in explicitly socialist terms (Wells 1908, p. 1), while later terming his goal the 'Great State' (Wells et al. 1912). In *A Modern Utopia* (1905) Wells put forward a scheme for a voluntary leadership body of devotees to the public good, called the 'Samurai', which is indicative of crucial problems in socialist theorisation of democratic mechanisms and organisations through this period and into the twentieth century. Wells soon became disillusioned with the Samurai ideal, fearing an inevitable decline into oligarchy of all such elitist organisations, and with Orwell and others would promote the thesis of the 'treason of the intellectuals' in twentieth-century socialist politics. Captains of industry, Hegelian bureaucrats, the enlightened tyranny of mandarin socialist intellectuals, Saint-Simonians and Comtists, had, in this view, all failed to replace traditional leadership.

The Fabians rejected Marx's theory of value, his revolutionism and his antagonism towards the state, and substituted an ideal of the exploited community for Marx's proletarian class war. They were enormously successful as a propaganda organisation, circulating 175 pamphlets before 1914, in some millions of copies. The Independent Labour Party, founded in 1893, was much indebted to Fabian ideas. Its most important theoretician was the later Labour Party leader James Ramsay MacDonald, author of *Socialism and Society*, *Socialism and Government* and other works. The miners' leader, James Keir Hardie (1856–1915), popularised socialist ideals amongst the trade unions. Also influential was Robert Blatchford's Clarion movement, whose ideals were expressed in the immensely successful *Merrie England* (1894), which proposed nationalisation of the land and other productive assets, a system of agricultural self-subsistence, reduced industrialisation, an increase in working class leisure and education, the introduction of communal laundries and kitchens in working-class districts, and a general curtailment of drudgery and waste. Of the accusation that the regulation of work by the government would be despotic, Blatchford was utterly dismissive; no despotism could be worse than the existing system (Blatchford 1908, p. 184; but contrast Blatchford 1909).

11   Extra-European socialism: Australasia and the USA

Two extra-European developments in socialist thought and activity merit special mention: Australasia and the United States. In Australia and New Zealand, as in many colonies, the advantages of collective organisation and enterprise in developing a relatively primitive economy and infrastructure where limited private capital was available (as in railway construction) were readily apparent. In Australia the Canadian-born journalist William Lane (1861–1917) gave impetus in the early 1880s to a movement that spawned initiatives to nationalise railways and introduce the eight-hour day. Old age pensions were first introduced in New Zealand in 1898, Minimum Wages Boards in Victoria in 1896, and compulsory arbitration of labour disputes in

New Zealand and South Australia in 1894, besides a variety of acts respecting land tenure, compulsory primary education and the extension of the vote to women (first in New Zealand, in 1893). (For Australia see Ledger 1909. For New Zealand, Le Rossignol 1911; Lee 1938; Reeves 1902; Siegfried 1914.)

American socialism in the early nineteenth century was dominated by an Owenite period (1824–30) (see Bestor 1950; Harris 1966), and a Fourierist phase (1840–50; see Guarneri 1991), in which over thirty mostly short-lived communities were founded, themselves indebted to earlier traditions of Shaker, Rappite and other forms of Christian communalism (Nordhoff 1966; Noyes 1870). The advantages of mutual assistance on the frontier assisted the socialist communities, which declined as private land settlement extended. The more long-lived included John Humphrey Noyes' Oneida community (1847–81), which promoted a scheme of group marriage on quasi-eugenic grounds. Leading critics of inequality of property included Thomas Skidmore, Langton Byllesby and Cornelius Blatchly. In various writers, such as Parke Godwin, socialism and anti-slavery ideals were united. By the late 1870s German Social Democracy, anarchism and a variety of domestic socialist groups also began to influence American thought, culminating in the formation of the Socialist Labor Party, whose programme was laid down in 1889. Amongst the more popular works of socialist thought, Laurence Gronlund's highly successful *The Co-operative Commonwealth* (1886) described a scheme for electing managers from the bottom up through the entire industrial edifice (Gronlund 1886, pp. 151–79.) Here 'government', as in Saint-Simon, would largely be supplanted by 'administration'. (On the origins of later American socialism, see Ely 1894; Hillquit 1903; Hughan 1912; Obermann 1947; Quint 1953; Sotheran 1892.)

Thereafter two leading figures, Henry George (1839–97) and Edward Bellamy (1850–98), emerged in the United States. A journalist born in Philadelphia, George expanded a pamphlet entitled *Our Land and Land Policy* (1871) into an enormously successful book, *Progress and Poverty* (1879), which contended that all forms of taxation except that on land should be abolished, since land ownership was invariably a function of monopoly power. While George did not call himself a socialist, many of his followers identified with the term and his ideas, and especially the view that poverty could be prevented by state activity, were extraordinarily influential in Britain and the US in particular (see Andelson 1979). Bellamy published an extremely influential utopia, *Looking Backward* (1888), which gave

Gregory Claeys

rise to a worldwide movement known as Nationalism. Bellamy described a future in which industrial organisation was highly centralised, forming one great corporation, the State. Labour was to be universal and mandatory for twenty-one years, distribution equal, and money abolished, to be replaced by a universal credit system. The advantages of technological innovation (air cars, television) are stressed. Crime would virtually disappear, and there would be no need for an army. A sequel, *Equality* (1897), was also published. Bellamy's followers were dedicated to nationalising the post, telegraphs, telephone, railways and coal mines, municipalising gas and water supplies, promoting more equal educational opportunities, and other reforms (see Lipow 1982; Thomas 1983).

12   Conclusion

Perhaps the central *political* problem faced by nineteenth-century socialism was reconciling the demands of an increasingly impoverished working class with the collapse of feudal forms of secular and Christian forms of spiritual authority. This required new types of social organisation appropriate to industrial society, as well as new bodies of political authority to promote them, which needed in turn to be reconciled with widespread demands for greater political democracy and social equality. The question of authority, and the preference for centralised versus local management, defined the relationship between socialism and the state, and is thus the crucial issue in evaluating the strands and development of non-Marxian socialism, as well as their relationship to Marxism. The more centralised this power was envisioned to be, the more concentrated and unchecked such power was likely to be. Related to this is the issue of the management, regulation or abolition of the market: in the degree to which market mechanisms were rejected by socialists, state and/or local/municipal direction of resources is clearly implied. And the more property was to be held in common, the greater would be the power invested in the new forms of authority. As we have seen, most non-Marxian socialism throughout this period was non-revolutionary and anti-authoritarian, and exhibited a preference for local and regional, or workers' self-organising, administrative units, and a suspicion of an overly centralised state or interim form of administration of the Marxian type. There are clear parallels between the Owenite and Fourierist communities and Bakunin's ideal of the free commune. The exception to this generalisation, Saint-Simonism, offered a vision of a centralised administration of the economy, albeit one in which private property was retained. Marxism clearly developed this trend.

While, as we have seen, there were significant anti-political trends in all forms of early socialism, notably by opposition to elections in Owenism, and a preference for 'administration' over 'politics' in Saint-Simonism, there was also a broadening of the scope of political activity, not merely through the exercise of democratic controls in small-scale communities, but through proposals to regulate industry through trade unions, co-operatives and other structures. This meant, effectively, that the anti-political elements in early socialism were potentially outweighed by what we might term a *hyper-politicisation* of large areas of both civil society and economic activity, where hitherto private property or traditional institutions of social order, such as the church or patriarchal family, had predominated, and defined the mechanisms of power. These domains and institutions were now objects of contention and debate, and hence politicised. Where the idea of the 'private' or 'individual' had itself become suspect, this process might include virtually all facets of social life. In 'community', moreover, the function of moral police, or the regulation and supervision of public space, and the maintenance of public order, was no longer assumed to be delegated to a separate body, but instead was reassumed by the entire community. Some of these elements were shared by Marxism, and have been condemned subsequently by its opponents as proto-totalitarian. But other aspects of non-Marxian socialism have met with greater public acclaim retrospectively. The enduring if not unchallenged legacy of nineteenth-century socialism thus lies in the widespread public acceptance of the idea that substantial areas of economic activity might and could efficiently be organised and managed by government on a non-profit basis and in the public interest, but without the danger of the complete suppression of individuality, or of the market mechanism. But early socialism also revealed the dangers created by the excessive individualism and inequality generated by unrestrained capitalism. Its value, thus, as Edward Carpenter remarked, perhaps lay less in its constructive programme than its 'searching criticism of the old society', and its enthusiasm for providing an alternative to it (Carpenter 1916, p. 126).

17

The Young Hegelians, Marx and Engels

GARETH STEDMAN JONES

1   From Hegel to Hegelianism

In *The Communist Manifesto* completed just before the outbreak of the 1848 revolutions, its joint authors, Karl Marx and Friedrich Engels, depicted communism as a theory which explained how the development of industrial capitalism would lead to a proletarian revolution. In that revolution, private property in the means of production would be abolished, the political state would be superseded, and humanity would enter into a higher state of freedom. Twentieth-century commentators, following the *Manifesto's* characterisation of modern communism, attempted to relate its genesis to the industrial revolution and the emergence of the working class.

But the *Manifesto* was polemic, not history. The connection between human emancipation, industrial workers and communism owed little or nothing to first-hand observation, and was anything but obvious. In the Rhineland town of Trier, where Marx had been born into a lawyer's family in 1818, and – except for his student years in Berlin – spent his first twenty-five years, the changes associated with industrialisation had barely begun. Paris, where he took refuge as an exile at the end of 1843, was a city of workers, but the vast majority worked in small workshops employing handicraft skills. Similarly, the 'communism' that Marx espoused from around the end of 1843 was not built upon first-hand encounters with the new wage workers of industrial Europe, but upon a series of bold speculative connections designed to escape from the impasse reached in discussions among radicals about how Germany could be 'emancipated'.

References to the works of Marx and Engels are taken from either *Karl Marx and Friedrich Engels Collected Works* (*MECW*) (1975–2005), 50 vols. (Moscow, London and New York) or *Karl Marx/Friedrich Engels/Gesamtaugabe* (*MEGA*), begun in Moscow and Frankfurt in the 1920s, under David Ryazanov, but discontinued under Stalin; resumed in Berlin by Dietz Verlag, 1975–98, then refounded under the Internationale Marx-Engels Stiftung (IMES) and published in Berlin by Akademie Verlag (1998–).

Engels, born to a merchant's household in 1820 in the cotton textile town of Elberfeld-Barmen in neighbouring Westphalia, was from an early age more familiar with the conditions of workers. He briefly described their condition in his home town as early as 1839 (*MECW*, II, pp. 7–25); and this knowledge was greatly deepened by the twenty-one months he spent in England between 1842 and 1844, representing his father's firm in Manchester. His first-hand depiction of the terrible conditions in which Manchester workers lived, *The Condition of the Working Class in England* (*MECW*, IV, pp. 295–584), has remained one of the great classic accounts of the nineteenth-century industrial city. But it is important to remember that Engels' communism was not a response to his Manchester experience. For he had already been converted to 'communism' in the autumn of 1842 before he left Germany.

In order to explain how workers came to bear the weight of such high and world-transforming expectations, it is necessary to start, not from the condition of workers, but from the condition of German philosophy, especially in the years between the end of the Napoleonic wars in 1815 and the 1848 March Revolution in Berlin – the period which German historians call *Vormärz*. In Prussia, the largest and most powerful state of the German Confederation, and particularly in its Rhineland province, newly acquired from Napoleon after his defeat in 1815, it was not industrialisation, but the legacy of the French Revolution and the political and religious turmoil unleashed by it, which explained the radicalism of the political thought that developed in the 1830s and 1840s.

The French Revolution of 1789 had appeared to vindicate in practice the philosophical hopes of Enlightened Germany, especially those of its most famous philosopher, Immanuel Kant. The French had embarked upon the construction of a constitution based upon reason. All the sharper, therefore, was the disappointment when the Revolution degenerated into terror and war. Kant's admirer, the playwright, Friedrich Schiller, best expressed the German reaction. For a moment, he wrote in 1795, there had seemed to be 'the physical possibility of setting law on the throne, of honouring man at last as an end in himself, and making true freedom the basis of political associations'. But it was 'a vain hope' and the result had been either 'a return to the savage state' or to 'complete lethargy' (Schiller 1982, p. 25).

There were many explanations for why the Revolution had ended in disaster. But most important in this context was that provided by Georg Wilhelm Friedrich Hegel. At the time of the storming of the Bastille, Hegel was an eighteen-year-old theology student at Tübingen; and he still drank to that anniversary in later life. By 1815, however, he had become the most prominent thinker in Germany and in 1818, he was called to the Philosophy Chair in Berlin, where he remained until his death in 1831. Hegel saluted the French Revolution as a decisive event in world history, but believed that it had ended in failure because a viable constitution could not be built out of the abstract and mechanical ideas of reason and freedom deployed by its leaders. Or as Schiller had remarked, 'a moment so prodigal of opportunity' found 'a generation unprepared to receive it' (Schiller 1967, p. 25).

During the debate that followed 1789, defenders of the Revolution, most notably Kant, had argued that all beliefs and institutions must be made subject to the demands of reason. Kant's argument had been a response to the criticism of Burke and his followers, that in the name of a disembodied notion of universal reason, the revolutionaries had wilfully ignored the lessons of history and experience. Hegel's response to this conflict was to find a way of bringing reason and history together. Reason, he argued, was not an abstract and timeless entity. It was embodied in language and culture, and found its concrete manifestation in 'the spirit of the people'. Since languages and cultures differed across time and space, this also meant that reason itself had a history. Therefore, far from being an arbitrary event, the Revolution represented a fundamental moment in the world-historical progress of reason.

The French failed because they were unable to reconcile 'the rights of man' with those of 'the citizen'. As a result, ideas of representative government, division of labour and modern commercial society jostled with incompatible notions of popular sovereignty, direct democracy, social equality and a revival of ideals of virtue associated with the ancient Roman republic. Hegel's aim was to get beyond these divisions. Against those thinkers, from Hobbes to Rousseau and Kant – representatives of 'modern natural law' in Hegel's terminology – who had attempted to base the state upon a contract (thus assuming that individuals might have an existence prior to, and exterior to the state), Hegel returned to Aristotle's dictum that unlike beasts or gods, man was by nature a political animal (Everson 1996, p. 14). The state was therefore neither 'provisional' (the product of a social contract), nor the means to an end (the legal and political mechanism necessary to protect life and property). As the embodiment of 'ethical life' (*Sittlichkeit*), the modern state was an end in itself. 'Union as such', he wrote, 'is itself the true content and end, and the destiny of individuals is to lead a universal life' (Hegel 1991, no. 258, p. 276).

But Hegel was equally critical of those who had hoped to revive the ethos of the ancient republic. His depiction of the modern state in the *Philosophy of Right*, published in 1821, was designed to demonstrate its superiority over the Greek *polis*. In contrast to the ancient state, which was based upon slavery, the modern state, by which Hegel meant the state after the French Revolution, was based upon the presupposition that all were free.[1] On this basis, Hegel claimed that the modern state was a political community. Through its observance of rational and universal norms in the construction of the constitution and in the conduct of public administration, the state enabled the self-conscious individual subject to will the general will of the community as his or her own.

In contrast to the Ancients, Hegel argued, modern 'ethical life' could incorporate both moral 'subjectivity' (the ability of the individual to subject moral and political demands to the judgement of reason), and self-interested 'particularity' (the ability of the individual to pursue personal ends in economic and cultural life). This was possible because, between household and political life (*oikos* and *polis*, as they had been depicted in Aristotle's *Politics*) Hegel introduced a new category, 'civil society', designed to encompass modern commercial society, as portrayed by Adam Smith (see Dickey 1987; Riedel 1984; Waszek 1988).

Ideas of citizenship went back to the heroic times of Sparta, Athens and the Roman republic. But 'civil society' had only emerged after the disappearance of the ancient *polis*. Hegel traced its emergence to the Roman Empire, in part to the notion of legal personhood brought into being by Roman law, but above all to the coming of Christianity and the idea of a 'soul' whose identity owed nothing to the polity, to which a particular individual might belong. Thus Hegel's political thought contained a fundamental Christian component, which indirectly at least linked Christianity to the individualism of modern economic life.

Not only were the 'rights of man' Christian in origin, but Christianity once properly understood provided the foundation of the modern state in which 'all were free'. From the Renaissance onwards, there had been

---

1 Hegel did not literally mean that all were now free, just as he did not literally mean that what is real (or actual) is rational and that what is rational is real. Reality or actuality (*Wirklichkeit*) in Hegel's thought did not primarily refer to the existing state of affairs, but rather to a state of development or becoming. Reality was not a state, but a process of transition from the abstract to the concrete. Thus in the case of freedom, Hegel supposed that in the modern world after the French Revolution, its principles would gradually be inscribed in the constitutions and institutions of all states. He was perfectly aware that this was not the current situation in Prussia or elsewhere in Metternich's Europe.

political thinkers, most prominently Machiavelli, who chided Christianity for its focus on the City of God at the expense of the earthly republic. Rousseau in his *Social Contract* even devised a civic religion, intended to restore the patriotic ethos of the ancient republic. In the radical phase of the French Revolution in 1793–4, hostility between the Catholic Church and the Revolution led to the Jacobin assault on Christianity and in Robespierre's case, the ambition to replace it by a Rousseau-inspired 'Cult of the Supreme Being'.

Hegel came to believe that much of this antagonism, whether derived from the Enlightenment or from the Revolution, was the result of a primitive and dogmatic reading of Christianity, which failed to recognise its civic dimensions. He argued that the freedoms associated with the modern state had first been introduced by Christianity after the fall of the Greek *polis*. Furthermore, it was the Christian notion of freedom that connected the two commanding events of modern history: the Protestant Reformation and the French Revolution. The Reformation had made explicit the essential freedom embodied in Christianity as a religion of free individuals. For 'in Protestantism, there is no *laity*, so that there is likewise no clergy to act as an exclusive depositary of Church doctrine' (Hegel 1991, no. 270, p. 299). Its notion of freedom of conscience had also been decisive in nurturing the development of civil society.[2] This was why the freedom of the modern individual was identified with the Protestant principle. But that freedom had remained 'abstract', so long as the subject was unable to discover his or her inner freedom mirrored in the institutions of the outer political and social world. This was why the French Revolution was such an important world-historical event. For although the Revolution ended in the Terror, inner feeling had been turned into a concrete external form, and henceforth would become the basis of all true social and political order.

In Protestant Germany, this convergence of spiritual and political history was now reaching fulfilment. In Prussia, a rational reform programme was accomplishing peacefully what the French Revolution had attempted to create by force. There was, therefore, no further need for a religious flight from the world. Now the state rather than the church had become 'the positive and definite embodiment of the spiritual kingdom' (Hegel 1991, no. 360, p. 380, 1956, p. 441). Religion was no longer a phenomenon set

2 'The repudiation of work no longer earned the reputation of sanctity.' 'Industry, crafts and trades now have their moral validity recognised, and the obstacles to their prosperity which originated with the Church have vanished' (Hegel 1956, p. 423).

apart from the everyday world of work, the family or the state. This was what Hegel meant by 'secularisation'; it was a 'sacred' process, through which the divine became incarnate in human culture.

Hegel's practical politics had been that of the Prussian 'Reform Era' and his credibility had depended upon hopes of a continuing process of reform ('secularisation' in Hegel's usage).[3] Within the state depicted in *The Philosophy of Right*, emphasis was placed upon constitutional monarchy, a uniform legal code and a reforming bureaucracy; the relationship between state and society was mediated through an estate-based representative system and reinforced by the organisation of trades and professions into corporations for civic and welfare ends. In the course of the 1820s, however, the balance of power had shifted against the reformers. The French Revolution and Prussian military defeat had led to an evangelical revival, which attracted many conservatives, among them the future monarch, Frederick William IV. Evangelical Christianity was to be based not upon reason, but upon revelation and faith. Its emphasis was upon original sin, divine right and the independence of the Church. Conservatives also emphasised the priority of property rights over social obligations and sought to reverse the depersonalisation of power, which they associated with rationalism and infidelity. Not surprisingly, they were deeply sceptical of Hegel's Christian credentials (see Breckman 1999; Dickey 1993, pp. 301–48; Toews 1980).

2 Hegelians, Saint-Simonians and the formation of Young Hegelianism

In July 1830, at a time of high unemployment and depressed trade, the restored Bourbon king, Charles X, made a rash attempt to dissolve the newly elected parliamentary assembly and suspend press freedom. The response in Paris was a three-day insurrection, in which the king was toppled, and the crown transferred to the 'citizen king', Louis Philippe from the House of Orléans. Parallel constitutional disturbances followed in Belgium, in the Reform Bill crisis in Britain, in parts of Germany and elsewhere in Europe. Contemporaries recognised that these upheavals brought to an end any hope of restoring the old order.

---

3 The Prussian 'reform era' began as an attempt to recover from catastrophic military defeat by Napoleon. A series of fundamental military, political, educational and economic reforms between 1807 and 1821 under the leadership of Stein and Hardenberg were designed to transform Prussia into a modern constitutional state. Hegel was invited to the professorship in Berlin to strengthen the reformers.

The French Revolution of 1830 also challenged the Hegelian position from an unanticipated direction. It highlighted the aspirations of workers, who were prominent among the fighters on the barricades. Most immediately, it raised the question of poverty or what was coming to be called 'the social question'. Concern about the rising population, the multitudes forced off the land, and the increase in the numbers of the urban poor had already begun to mount in the 1820s. But the publication of *The Doctrine of Saint-Simon* shortly followed by the July Revolution turned poverty into an acute *political* question. According to *The Doctrine of Saint-Simon*, the French Revolution had not eliminated tyranny and slavery; it had not brought to an end 'the exploitation of man by man'. Such oppression had continued in the relationship between the capitalist and the wage worker.[4]

In Prussia these arguments made a particularly strong impression upon Marx's future teacher, Eduard Gans, Professor of Law and Hegel's closest colleague and follower at the University of Berlin. In *The Philosophy of Right*, Hegel had written about poverty as a problem of 'pauperism' and the growth of the 'rabble'. He considered charity, the poor law, provision of work and colonisation as possible remedies, but made no attempt to treat workers as citizens. In the 1820s, Gans reiterated this approach. But in 1833–4, he abandoned Hegel's 'corporations' and instead proposed that workers be allowed to form associations akin to trade unions. These associations would reduce the imbalance between masters and workers and end their exclusion from political life. Gans accepted Hegel's picture of secularisation and therefore opposed 'New Christianity'. But he was deeply impressed by the Saint-Simonian stress upon the dangers of unfettered competition. His visits to France and England had alerted him to the growing disparity between wealth and poverty and the threat of class antagonism (see Gans 1995; Waszek 2006).

The attempt to establish the Saint-Simonian Church proved a tragi-comic fiasco. But the broader impact of the Saint-Simonians' critique of Christianity, especially their conception of the present, was profound. History, according to the *Doctrine*, was divided into 'organic' and 'critical' epochs. In 'organic' epochs such as those of medieval Catholicism or 'New Christianity', the picture was of 'union among members of ever widening

---

4 See Saint-Simon 1958, pp. 63–9. The *Doctrine* was intended as the founding document of the Saint-Simonian Church. It was a collective and posthumous elaboration of *The New Christianity* which had appeared in 1825. According to Saint-Simon, 'the general aim which you must present to all men in their work is the improvement of the moral and physical existence of the poorest class' (Saint-Simon 1868–75, XXIII, p. 152).

associations... towards a common goal'. 'Critical epochs', on the other hand, were 'filled with disorder; they destroy former social relations, and everywhere tend towards egoism' (Saint-Simon 1958, p. 28). The present was the last stage of a 'critical' epoch, which had begun with Luther. Current Christianity, especially Protestantism, was marked by its lack of concern for man's bodily existence. Pantheist 'New Christianity' stood for 'the rehabilitation of matter' and for the restoration of social harmony through the emancipation of both soul *and* body.

Among German admirers of 'New Christianity', therefore, Hegel's picture of secularisation found itself in competition with a rhetoric that associated Protestantism with individualism, egoism and untrammelled competition. The poet Heinrich Heine identified Christianity with indifference to material need, and linked the Saint-Simonians with a 'secret' German tradition of pantheism (Heine 1959). According to the unorthodox Polish Hegelian, August Cieszkowski, both Christianity and Hegel were guilty of considering only the soul, but not the body of man. Hegel had prematurely ended history with the attainment of Absolute Knowledge. It would now have to be complemented by an activist 'Philosophy of the Future', which would bring into being 'the social individual' based upon 'unity' in life as well as thought (see Liebich 1979; Breckman 1999, ch. 5). In a similar vein, the radical journalist Moses Hess, often described as the first German communist, thought that Christianity had generated the exploitative egoism of the 'money aristocracy'. Emancipation, the reconciliation of body and mind or the harmony between 'spiritualism' and 'sensualism', would require both 'inner' and 'outer' equality; hence both 'pantheism' and 'the community of goods' (Hess 1961, pp. 6–75).

But it was not the view from France that caused the breakup of the Hegelian School and the formation of the 'Young Hegelians'. This was brought about by the 1835 publication of *The Life of Jesus* by David Strauss, a follower of Hegel and briefly a Lutheran pastor in Württemberg. Hegel had argued that religion and philosophy were identical in content. They differed only in form. Strauss argued that the rational truth embodied in Christianity, the union of the human and divine, could only become clear once the Gospels were freed from their archaic supernatural setting. In the New Testament, the 'Idea' had been encased in a narrative about the life and activity of a single individual. That narrative had been the product of 'an unconscious mythologizing process' shaped by the Old Testament picture of the Messiah. If Christianity were to be saved for modern science, the figure of Christ would have to be replaced by the idea of 'humanity' in the whole of its history. For only the infinite spirit of the human race could bring about the union of finite and infinite, as depicted in Hegel's portrayal of 'Absolute Spirit'.

Strauss' book unleashed a storm of controversy in Prussia and divided Hegelians. The democratic journalist and former Bürschenschaftler, Arnold Ruge, a Privatdozent at the University of Halle, led radicals defending Strauss. Among these '*Young* Hegelians', as they were derisively called by their more conservative colleagues, the attributes of 'Absolute Spirit' were transferred to humanity. The historical process was now described as the coming to self-consciousness and realisation of the human species within an ethical community, in which individuals would achieve autonomy and the fulfilment of their human potential through identity with others (see Toews 1993, pp. 378–414).

The radicalism of the Young Hegelian critique was further sharpened at the beginning of the 1840s by the work of the erstwhile orthodox Hegelian Bruno Bauer, at that time attached to the University of Bonn. According to Bauer, Strauss' break with Christianity was incomplete, and his association of Christianity with Old Testament Jewish aspirations unhistorical and un-Hegelian. Christianity *did* constitute a new beginning in world history, but a false one, for its victory over 'nature' was achieved by miracles rather than science and its conception of man was self-abasing. Now, however, with the final abolition of God and its replacement by the 'I' of 'self-consciousness', the true emancipation of humanity would begin (see Moggach 2003).

Karl Marx, the son of a converted Jewish lawyer, went to the local University of Bonn in 1836 to follow his father in a legal career. But after one year, he moved to Berlin University, where he read Hegel and switched to philosophy. At Berlin, Bauer was his philosophical mentor. In 1841, they planned together to publish a journal entitled *The Annals of Atheism*. Marx prepared a doctorate probably under Bauer and accompanied Bauer back to Bonn, when the latter gained a post at the university. But in 1842 at the behest of the new king, Frederick William IV, who remained darkly suspicious of Hegelianism, Bauer was dismissed from his academic post. For Young Hegelians, this was considered a 'world-historical event' in the battle between Christianity and modern consciousness; for Marx, it meant the end of any hopes of an academic career. He therefore moved to journalism and later in that year became editor of a liberal-radical newspaper, recently founded in Cologne, the *Rheinische Zeitung*.

Despite the anti-Hegelianism of the king, 1842 was a promising year in which to embark upon journalism. It was a year of relative press freedom since for romantic conservative reasons the king declared himself keen to learn about the views of his subjects. In response, a group of liberal merchants and manufacturers in Cologne set up the *Rheinische Zeitung* to press for representative government and the extension of the Zollverein. The government welcomed what it hoped would be a Protestant pro-Prussian newspaper in the Catholic Rhineland, advocating free trade and moderate liberalism. It had not anticipated the recruitment of Young Hegelians to write for the paper and the radical constitutional agenda which they introduced. For this reason, the experiment barely lasted a year.

If religion was one great source of division among the Hegelians of the 1830s and 1840s, politics, not surprisingly, was the other. The Young Hegelians were republicans rather than liberals.[5] Liberal preoccupations such as spiritual freedom, the sanctity of the person and individual rights were not uppermost among their concerns. Their republican ideal was of a state governed by laws rather than men, of citizens inspired by the civic ideals of the ancient *polis* rather than *bourgeois* attention to private interests. It was a republicanism constructed out of Hegel and a Jacobin reading of Rousseau. Drawing upon Hegel, it could be said that unity between individual and general will was made possible by the shared foundation of reason, which enabled each individual to prescribe the law to him- or herself. But seen from a more Jacobin perspective, one major defect of Hegel's state was the smallness of the space accorded to active political participation.[6] It was, as Gans described it, 'a tutelary state'. More fundamentally, no Young Hegelian could fully accept Hegel's notion of civil society. How could a political community, the embodiment of 'ethical life', accommodate a commercial society, in which each sought to further their self-interest at the expense of the other, in which each individual treated the other as means?

Marx's early view of the state can be discerned from his time as editor of the *Rheinische Zeitung* in 1842. Like Bauer and Ruge, he continued to emphasise the rationality of the state. If the essence of the state was reason and freedom, the task of the free press was to make the existence of the state conform to its essence. What prevented the state from acting according to universal norms were, first, particular forms of religious consciousness and second, private economic interests. 'Criticism' would be victorious, it was assumed, because it was doing no more than raising to consciousness the

---

5 For the importance of republican themes among the Young Hegelians, see Moggach 2006, pp. 1–24.
6 The emphasis upon the frequency or extensiveness of political participation, although often associated with Rousseau, derived more from Jacobin political practice during the French Revolution than from Rousseau himself. See Leopold 2007, p. 267.

real desires of the people. Sooner or later, it was believed, Frederick William would have to abandon the 'Christian State', which he had imposed upon Prussia. It was, therefore, a considerable shock when in 1843 the government closed down the opposition press without encountering any real opposition from the people.[7] How then could the state be 'the actualisation' of freedom, if it persecuted philosophy and closed down the free press? How could the people collude in the suppression of their freedom? How else could the convergence between reason and reality be achieved? (see Löwy 2003). It was as a reaction to this moment of despair that Young Hegelians moved either towards a more explicit form of republicanism or, like Marx, to socialism or communism.[8]

3   The breakup of the Young Hegelian movement

Bauer and his supporters remained closest to the original Hegelian position, albeit now depicted as post-Christian and republican. As Feuerbach complained, Bauer's 'self-consciousness' was simply another word for Hegel's 'Absolute Spirit' and could only take account of man as a rational reflective being. For Bauer, the mistake of the Enlightenment and of the French Revolution had been to assume that 'sensuousness' (the pursuit of happiness) rather than rational autonomy (reason-based independence of thought) was man's essential characteristic. Only the establishment of a community of autonomous rational beings would ensure the victory of reason over nature. Cultural transcendence of nature had originally been conceived in religious terms (miracles, life after death). But now with the end of Christianity and knowledge of the rational course of history, man could take full responsibility for this process of self-making. For Bauer, its attainment meant the acquisition of a new form of self-consciousness, capable of rising above private economic interests and obsolete religious creeds. But such

7 Frederick William's government was based upon a combination of authoritarianism and individualism; it emphasised the pre-social rights and privileges of different estates and categories of property. As a believer in Divine Right, supported by the Conservative Christian philosophies of Stahl and Schelling, the king detested all forms of rationalism, especially that of Hegel. It was for this reason that he had ensured the dismissal of Bauer.
8 In the early 1840s, the various followers of Saint-Simon or Fourier were known as socialist. 'Communist' described the position of French secret societies claiming allegiance to the ideas of Babeuf. Marx was closest to a socialist position. However, later in the 1840s in order to underline the allegiance of himself and Engels to a 'proletarian' form of socialism intent upon bringing down capitalist society by force, Marx and Engels described themselves as 'communist'. But from the 1860s onwards, given working-class antipathy to the notoriety of 'communism', Marx and Engels were content to describe themselves as 'socialist'.

self-consciousness could only be an individual acquisition. It was, therefore, impossible to attribute an emancipatory role to a social class. In the case of the working class, labour did not in itself engender free subjectivity; so socialism would simply mean the organisation of workers in their present unfree state. In Bauer's view, revolution was certainly a prerequisite, but the emancipation of workers would be the result of the education provided by a rational republic (see Moggach 2000, 2006, pp. 114–36).

Bauer's main rival was another of Hegel's former students, Ludwig Feuerbach, formerly a philosophy teacher at Erlangen. Feuerbach had become famous in 1840 as the author of *The Essence of Christianity*, later translated into English by George Eliot. Among the Young Hegelians in 1842, however, he was particularly valued for his critique of Hegel himself (see Feuerbach 1972, pp. 153–75). For Feuerbach, the reality that Hegelian reason could not accommodate was nature and the bodily existence of man: 'sensuousness' or what the Saint-Simonians called 'the rehabilitation of matter'. 'Man' (i.e. the human) was not simply a thinking being. He was first and foremost a sensuous, emotional being. He was not purely active like Hegel's 'spirit', but both active and passive. Passivity meant the need of a natural being for another, for a means of life outside him/herself, expressed in physical existence and the sexual relationship. It was for this reason that 'Man' was a communal being. The essence of Man was only found in community, only in 'the unity of I and Thou'.

But Man, according to Feuerbach, had been alienated from this essence by religion, and by Protestant Christianity in particular. Unlike animals, humans could turn their emotions into objects of thought. It was in this way that Man had been led to project his own essence as a species upon a fictive being, God. This was what Feuerbach meant by 'alienation'. God was the perfected idea of the species viewed as an individual. In Christianity, this meant that the communal nature of Man, the union of 'I and Thou', had been replaced by the particular union of each individual with a personal external being: Christ, 'the mediator' who interposed himself between each individual and his or her fellow beings.

For Feuerbach, like Hegel, the point at which Christianity had manifested its true character had been the Reformation. But for Feuerbach, this meant the ever-sharper separation of spiritual from natural being. Protestantism, with its emphasis upon individual conscience and the priesthood of all believers, had dismantled the spiritual community of medieval religion and produced instead a turning to private affairs, an egoistical withdrawal from communal life and a material world divested of sanctity. In short, religion was responsible for the individualism of modern society. In the coming age, Man would reappropriate his 'species essence'. The fellowship of prayer would be replaced by the fellowship of work, and the atomised egos of modern society would reunite in a loving union no longer based upon the Christian soul, but upon 'the whole Man'.[9]

For Marx, reality was also 'sensuous'. But the sensuous reality that was to interest Marx was one in which individuals employed their mental and physical capacities in transforming the natural world as a result of their need to produce their means of subsistence. Marx was not excited by French ideas about pantheism or a new social religion. His wholly negative attitude towards religion remained closer to Bauer than to Feuerbach. He was drawn instead to French criticism of private property and the position of the proletariat. He had been impressed by P. J. Proudhon's notorious *What Is Property?* (1840), as was already apparent in his *Rheinische Zeitung* articles about the dominance of private economic interests in the debates of the Rhenish Estates. Marx's interest in socialism and the proletariat was probably first stimulated by the historical sequence of forms of property and exploitation laid out in *The Doctrine of Saint-Simon*, and was then greatly reinforced by reading Lorenz Von Stein's compendious *Socialism and Communism in Contemporary France*, which appeared in 1842.[10]

This shift in Marx's thinking can first be traced in an unfinished 'critique' of Hegel's *Philosophy of Right*, which he began after the closure of the *Rheinische Zeitung* in the spring of 1843 and continued in two essays written for the *Deutsch-Französische Jahrbücher*, the journal which he and Ruge briefly edited after leaving Prussia for Paris in the autumn of that year. The Young Hegelian hope that 'Criticism' would lead a movement towards the rational state in Prussia had not been borne out. But even had it been successful, according to Marx, Bauer's assumption that religion would disappear with the removal of 'the Christian state' was false. The flourishing of religion in the United States, where there was a separation of church and state, was sufficient to demonstrate that 'the emancipation of the state from religion' was not 'the emancipation of the real Man from religion'.

Marx was greatly impressed by Feuerbach's critique of Hegel and Bauer. Emancipation was not the product of the progress of spirit or the

---

9 For Feuerbach's break with Hegel, see especially Breckman 1999, ch. 3.
10 On the significance of Stein and other contemporary representations of the proletariat, see Marx and Engels 2002, pp. 27–39; see also Stein 2002, pp. 16–59.

development of self-consciousness. It depended upon a transformation of the relations of 'man to man', and was located within civil society. Marx chose the example of Bauer's essay 'On the Jewish Problem' to make his point. Bauer, Marx alleged, claimed that Jewish emancipation would require two steps, first to recognise the superiority of Christianity over Judaism, and then the superiority of 'Criticism' over Christianity. Marx's response was to reject this 'theological' distinction between Christianity and Judaism, and substitute a 'social 'approach. Extending an argument put forward by Moses Hess, Marx defined Judaism as 'practical need', 'egoism' and money, a position that deprived the world of all 'specific value'. But Judaism had not been enough to precipitate the full flowering of civil society.[11] This had been achieved by Christianity, which made 'all natural, national, moral and theoretical conditions extrinsic to man' and dissolved 'the human world into a world of atomistic individuals who are inimically opposed to one another'. The solution was not a reform of consciousness, but the elimination of the *social* element that made 'the Jew' possible. For religion, he argued, was not 'the cause', but only 'the manifestation of secular narrowness'. What religion revealed was the existence of a 'defect', the alienation of Man's species attributes into a fictive supernatural mediator and the negation of Man's communal capacities as a result (*MECW*, III, p. 175).

Both Ruge and Marx were also attracted by Feuerbach's notion of alienation, which they attempted to apply to Hegel's conception of the modern state. In 1842, Ruge abandoned his optimistic version of the Hegelian idea of 'secularisation', in which the Protestantism and rationalism inherent in Prussia's history would come to inform the texture of everyday life in state and society. Confronted instead by the unapologetic belligerence of the Prussian 'Christian state', he shifted towards an explicitly republican stance. Christianity, he now concluded, meant depoliticisation. Protestant 'abstraction' had turned the state into a transcendent entity. Protestantism and liberalism had not promoted 'ethical life', but a civil society in which the *bourgeois* flourished at the expense of the *citoyen*.

---

11 Despite the participation of those from Jewish or converted Jewish families like Moses Hess and Marx, or leading Saint-Simonians in France, much socialist writing in the first half of the nineteenth century contained anti-Semitic passages and was uncritical in its acceptance of anti-Jewish stereotypes. It was especially prominent in the case of Fourier and Proudhon, who regarded Jewish emancipation at the time of the French Revolution as a mistake. Later in the century, Engels at least publicly condemned anti-Semitism. See Engels, 'On Anti-Semitism', *MECW*, XXVII, pp. 50–2.

4 Marx's move from republicanism to communism

In his unfinished critique of the *Philosophy of Right* Marx's criticism of Hegel's state was more drastic. The modern state was the *mediator* between man and man's freedom, leading to an analogous 'bifurcation' between the atomised individual and the alienated species in the 'practical struggles' of mankind over 'the political state'. Marx denied Hegel's claim that there existed a higher unity between the state and the modern citizen, made possible by representative and administrative institutions, which *mediated* between state and civil society. In antiquity, the *respublica* had been 'the true and only content of the life and will of the citizens'. But now, Marx believed, 'property, contract, marriage, civil society' had developed as 'particular modes of existence' of the private individual 'alongside the *political* state' (*MECW*, III, pp. 69, 77).

What predominated in all these areas, including the state, was private property. The modern state was the creature of private property. For citizenship had become an attribute of private property (suffrage property qualifications), just as state administration had become the private property of the bureaucracy 'over against other private aims'. Similarly, the place of monarchy and primogeniture in the constitution attested to the centrality of private property and the pre-social rights that they conferred (i.e the privilege of birth). Furthermore, just as Christianity had developed alongside 'man's separation from the community' on earth, so there had been an analogous 'abstraction' of the state. Since the French Revolution, the political constitution had acquired 'an unreal universality', while at the same time, all the bonds, which had 'restrained the egoistic spirit of civil society', had been removed. Marx confirmed his interpretation with an analysis of the French revolutionary *Declaration of the Rights of Man and the Citizen* of 1789. In that document, 'political community' was turned into 'a mere *means*' of maintaining the 'so-called rights of Man', pre-eminently, the right to private property. The *citoyen* was 'declared to be the servant of the egoistic *homme*'. 'The *essential* and *true* Man' was not 'Man as *citoyen*, but Man as *bourgeois*' (*MECW*, III, pp. 162–4).

In the unfinished 'Critique', Marx had pressed for a 'democracy' by which he meant a republic based upon the re-politicisation of society through the abolition of the distinction between civil society and the 'political state'. But in the following few months, he all but totally severed any relationship with a republican position through his insistence upon social revolution and the abolition of the modern political state. The distinction between 'political' and 'unpolitical' man now seemed to him not simply the problem of Prussia or of Hegel's state, but of the modern state as such. The 'unreal universality' of the republic left the egoism of bourgeois civil society unaffected. The 'political state' was incapable of transforming civil society, because it was itself the creature and product of civil society. It was for this reason that the Jacobins had failed when they attempted to assert the independence of the state. Similarly, Marx's former ally, Ruge, was mistaken in assuming that the state could solve 'the social problem'. As proof, he cited the failure of Napoleon's attempt to abolish pauperism.[12] In short, it was the very existence of civil society that posed the fundamental obstacle to man becoming a species being in his 'everyday life'.

What was therefore needed, Marx came to think, was not a 'political' revolution, but a 'human' transformation of the 'relations between man and man', performed by a class outside and beneath civil society. This was the proletariat. For, as French socialists had already made clear, this class arose, not only from 'industrial' development, but also from the 'the drastic dissolution' of society. If civil society represented the sphere of private property, the proletariat stood for its 'negation' (*MECW*, III, pp. 186–7). The proletariat stood outside the political sphere and, as Lorenz von Stein noted, was a creation of the French Revolution. For there could be no proletariat so long as birth rather than property had been the precondition for participation in the state. This transformation had been completed by the 1830 Revolution, which had resulted in the control of the state by the bourgeoisie and the removal of everything except property as the basis of citizenship. According to Stein, this had transformed the 'propertyless' into 'the proletariat', an 'estate' defined by its exclusion from political life (Stein 1848, I, pp. 166–7).

The belief that reason and freedom were incompatible with the existence of civil society underlay what became Marx's major preoccupation in the ensuing twenty-five years: the critique of political economy. Marx's aim was to set alongside Feuerbach's notion of alienation as a means of interpreting religious belief an analogous process of alienation at work in the social relations of civil society.[13] Political economy, Marx thought, constituted the

---

12 Karl Marx, 'Critical Marginal Notes on the Article "The King of Prussia and Social Reform. By a Prussian"', *MECW*, III, pp. 189–207; for Marx's criticism of Jacobinism, see also Furet 1992.

13 Although Marx distanced himself from Feuerbachian humanism from the time of the *German Ideology*, he in no way retreated from the idea of a parallel between religious alienation in the spiritual realm and social alienation in the domain of material production. In the Economic Manuscripts of 1863–4, Marx wrote, 'The rule of the capitalist over the worker is therefore the rule of the object over the

pre-eminent theoretical expression of this alienated social world, or as he later termed it, its 'anatomy'. Marx reached this conclusion with the help of two essays submitted to the *Deutsch-Französische Jahrbücher* around the beginning of 1844.

The first article was by Hess. It shifted the focus of alienation from consciousness to activity. It defined life as 'the exchange of productive life activity' involving 'the co-operative working together of different individuals'. By contrast, in 'the inverted world' of money and private property, this 'species activity' was displaced by the 'egoistic' satisfaction of private needs; Man's species attributes became mere means towards individual self-preservation. Marx built upon this shift of perspective. In his first attempt to develop a critique of political economy – what were subsequently entitled the *Economic and Philosophical Manuscripts of 1844* – he adopted 'conscious life activity' as his starting point. For, as he argued, 'religious estrangement occurs only in the realm of *consciousness*', 'but economic estrangement is that of *real* life' (*MECW*, XXXIV, p. 297; McLellan 1969).

The second essay was by Frederick Engels, who at that time was working for his father's textile company in Manchester. It criticised political economy as the theoretical expression of this estranged world. Political economy presupposed private property without once questioning its existence.[14] As Marx developed the argument in the *Manuscripts*, political economy mistook a world in which Man had alienated his essential human attributes for the true world of Man. It conflated 'the productive life' of Man with Adam Smith's 'propensity to truck, barter and exchange', and was therefore unable to distinguish Species-Man from the estranged world in which he currently had to act.

By focusing upon the estrangement of Man's capacity to produce, Marx was once again able to connect his conception of history with that of Hegel. For in *The Phenomenology of Spirit*, Hegel had according to Marx, grasped 'the self-creation of Man as a process' and in so doing had grasped the essence of labour, the creation of Man as 'the outcome of Man's *own labour*' (*MECW*, III, pp. 332–3). This enabled Marx to distance himself from the

---

human, of dead labour over living, of the product over the producer... This is exactly *the same* relation in the sphere of material production, in the real social life process... as is represented by *religion* in the ideological sphere: the inversion of the subject into the object and *vice versa*' (Marx, 'Direct Results of the Production Process', *MECW*, XXXIV, p. 398).

14 Friedrich Engels, 'Outlines of a Critique of Political Economy', *MECW*, III, pp. 418–43. For the intellectual and political development of the young Engels, see Carver 1989; Claeys 1987; Marx and Engels 2002, especially pp. 50–69.

implicit passivity of Feuerbach's notion of 'sensuousness'.[15] Man was not merely a 'natural being', but 'a human natural being', whose point of origin was not nature, but history. Unlike animals, Man made his activity 'the object of his will'. He could form objects in accordance with the laws of beauty. Thus history could be seen as the humanisation of nature through Man's 'conscious life activity' and at the same time, the humanisation of Man himself through 'the forming of the five senses'. History was the process of Man becoming 'species being' and the basis of Man's ability to treat himself as 'a universal, and therefore a free being' (*MECW*, III, p. 280).

But if freedom was self-activity, and the capacity to produce, Man's 'most essential' characteristic, it became possible to understand why estranged labour formed the basis of all other forms of estrangement and why, therefore, 'the whole of human servitude is involved in the relation of the worker to production'. For estranged labour was the inversion of 'conscious life activity' and the greater the development of private property, the more the labour of the producer fell into the category of labour to earn a living. In other words, Man's '*essential being*' became 'a mere means to his *existence*'. The '*life of the species*' became 'a means of individual life'. It meant not only that 'the worker is related to the *product of his labour* as to an alien object', but also the 'estrangement of Man from Man'. 'The *alien* being, to whom labour and the product of labour belong . . . can only be some *other man than the worker*'; 'a man alien to labour and standing outside it'. In other words, 'the capitalist' (*MECW*, III, pp. 275, 276, 278, 280).

Just as, according to Feuerbach, it was estrangement that had produced religion, and not religion that had produced estrangement, so, according to Marx, it was estrangement that had produced private property.[16] That private property was the product of alienated labour was the 'secret' that was only revealed when private property had completed its domination over Man. It was only when private property had become 'a world-historical power', when most of mankind had been reduced to 'abstract' labour, and everything had been reduced to 'quantitative being', that the antithesis

---

15 This had been one of Marx's major criticisms of Feuerbach in the so-called 'Theses on Feuerbach': 'contemplative materialism' did not 'comprehend sensuousness as practical activity'. *MECW*, V, p. 5.
16 If the causal sequence had been reversed, the whole phenomenon of alienation would have disappeared. The translation of economic into human categories would have lost its point and there would have been no reason to place 'the *positive* transcendence of *private property* as *human self-estrangement* in the imminent future rather than at any point in the past'. On the difficulties besetting the argument, see Marx and Engels 2002, pp. 120–39.

between property and lack of property was transformed into that between capital and labour, bourgeois and proletarian.

In this way private property was driven towards self-destruction by its own economic movement. As Marx later wrote, history was the judge, the proletariat the executioner. The proletariat executed the sentence that private property pronounced upon itself. The emergence of mass labour movements in the nineteenth century – whether of the Chartists in England or of the Social Democrats in Germany – was a reaction to the desire, whether of conservatives or liberals, to exclude the working classes from the political process (see Stedman Jones 1983c, pp. 90–179). Political exclusion or subordination was originally prompted by fear of another Terror consequent upon the sovereignty of the propertyless masses. Conversely, the aim of movements of the working classes was to gain a recognised place *within* the polity, from where the aspirations of their adherents could more effectively be advanced. These aims were quite distinct from those of Marx. In Marx's view, estranged labour was heteronomous labour, the negation of freedom as self-activity, and ultimately a sign of mankind's lack of control over the forms and purposes of its material exchange with nature (see Moggach 2000, pp. 56–62). Marx's position also owed much to the vision of 'the industrial revolution' and the development of the working class put forward most powerfully in 1844 in *The Condition of the Working-Class in England* by his new, and henceforth closest political companion, Frederick Engels.[17] For this reason, Marxian and social democratic aims, while ostensibly close, were ultimately quite distinct.

As private property had advanced to 'world dominion', the condition of the proletariat had become ever more 'inhuman'. This polarisation meant that at one pole there was the ever-greater sophistication of imaginary appetite (the dietary and sexual excesses of the metropolitan rich), at the other barbarisation, the treadmill and rotten potatoes (a reference to workhouse punishment and the meagre diet of the Irish poor). But this journey of Man through the vale of estrangement had not been wholly negative.

---

17 In Engels' treatment of England, the reduction of political to social had already occurred before Marx and Engels formulated their 'materialist conception of history' in *The German Ideology*. Engels had arrived in England in 1842, already persuaded by Moses Hess that England was heading for a revolution, which would not be 'political, but social'. In an analysis of the political and legal system, he had concluded that the constitution was 'one big lie'. The Chartist battle against the undemocratic state was therefore in reality not a political battle, but a social battle against the rule of property. 'The struggle of democracy against aristocracy in England is the struggle of the poor against the rich. The democracy towards which England is moving is a social democracy.' Engels, 'The Condition of England. The English Constitution', *MECW*, III, p. 513.

First, private property had forced Man to become more productive to the point where with the aid of steam-power and automatic machinery, he/she now stood on the threshold of abundance. This was the significance of what Engels, following French commentators like Jean Baptiste Say and Adolphe Blanqui, called 'the industrial revolution' (see Stedman Jones 2002, 2004, chs. 4 and 5). First, as Robert Owen, Charles Fourier, Thomas Carlyle, Moses Hess and Engels himself had all in different ways pointed out, the old conditions of famine and scarcity had given way to a new form of crisis, what Fourier called 'plethoric crisis', the crisis of 'overproduction' – a sign of the discordance between the new possibilities of abundance and outmoded forms of property ownership.[18] Second, dehumanisation – captured most graphically in Engels' 1844 account of Manchester slums – had generated proletarian revolt. Revolutionary crisis was therefore imminent.[19]

5   Marx's theory of the advent of communism

During the years between 1844 and 1848, Marx with the help of Engels transformed this initial critique into a fully elaborated theory of communism: what was later called 'the materialist conception of history'. Its 'materialist' form originated in the need to reply to Max Stirner, another of the Berlin Young Hegelians, a schoolteacher and friend of Bruno Bauer. In his *Ego and Its Own*, Stirner attacked the quasi-religious ethos of Feuerbachian humanism (see Stirner 1995). Feuerbach's criticism of religion had focused upon the separation of human attributes ('predicates') from human individuals ('subjects') and their reassembly as attributes of a fictive God. But, as Stirner pointed out, Feuerbach himself did not return these alienated attributes to human individuals, but rather to another equally fictive creation, 'Man' or 'Species Being'. 'Man' continued to be presented to individuals as their 'vocation' or ethical goal. 'Man' was in effect just another version of the Protestant God; it was an attack made worse by Feuerbach's own admission that he had taken the term, *species*, from Strauss, who had employed it as a dynamic substitute for the place of Christ in orthodox Christianity.

18 During the 1820s and 1830s for the first time, contemporaries became aware of the relationship between factory production and the trade cycle. Investment in factory production and automatic machinery created the possibility of crises of overcapacity. The trade crises of 1825, 1837 and 1842 were each accompanied by the conspicuous presence of large quantities of unsold goods. See Matthews 1954.

19 Engels, 'The Condition of the Working-Class in England. From Personal Observation and Authentic Sources', *MECW*, IV, pp. 295–584; see also Stedman Jones 2006.

Marx was certainly implicated in this attack upon Feuerbach. In 1843, he had written in the *Deutsch-Französische Jahrbücher* that 'the criticism of religion' ended with the teaching that 'Man is the highest being for Man', and he proclaimed 'the categorical imperative to overthrow all relations', in which Man was 'debased' (*MECW*, III, p. 182). Now, rather than concede communism's ethical or voluntarist dimensions, Marx presented communism and all other ideas simply as expressions of the social situation from which they arose. Moreover, if, as Marx and Engels were to claim in the *Communist Manifesto*, 'the history of all hitherto existing society' was 'the history of class struggles', the existence of revolutionary ideas in a particular period presupposed 'the existence of a revolutionary class'. Communism, therefore, was not 'an ideal'. According to the *German Ideology* it was 'the *real* movement which abolishes the present state of things' (*MECW*, V, p. 60, p. 49).

The adoption of 'class struggle' in place of an ethical imperative enabled Marx to connect his new 'materialist' epistemology to the substantive conception of history that he had begun to sketch in his writings of 1844. For class struggle, as he later explained, could be connected to 'historical phases in the development of production'.[20] Central to Marx's new approach was Adam Smith's discussion of the division of labour. For this enabled Marx to introduce a dynamic historical principle of increasing productivity or the development of man's productive capacity (Marx's version of Hegel's account of the self-making of man in *The Phenomenology*) which could be connected to the changing configurations of private property. The terms of 1844 – 'the true natural history of man' and 'private property' – were now renamed the 'forces' and 'relations' of production. Historically, the development of man's power to produce was accompanied by a succession of social forms (property relationships), each appropriate to a particular stage in man's productive development.[21] The 'capitalist mode of production' was the last and by far the most dynamic of these social forms, whose structure had been systematically explored by political economy.

Political economy, it was claimed, took 'the capitalist mode of production' for granted. But social critics and 'utopian socialists' had noted its increasing tendency towards overproduction – a sign of its approaching end, and

---

20 Marx to Weydemeyer (5 March 1852), *MECW*, XXXIX, p. 61. Ideas of class struggle were widely used at the time. So, as Marx himself stated, there was nothing particularly innovative in his adoption of the idea.

21 For a philosophically systematic, but also historically informed analysis of Marx's theory of history, see Cohen 1978.

replacement by a higher social form. In Germany, the Historical School of Law had demonstrated that private property was far from a trans-historical feature of all human societies. As Niebuhr, Savigny and others had argued (on the basis of ancient Rome), the first forms of ownership were tribal and communal, and more generally, through most of history the owner-ship of property had been conditional upon fulfilling the duties of defence or citizenship.[22] Niebuhr listed a historical succession of property forms, which Marx followed in *The German Ideology*. An almost identical list also appeared later in Marx's famous 'Preface' to *The Critique of Political Economy* in 1859. There he mentioned 'the asiatic, ancient, feudal and modern bourgeois modes of production'. But whereas for Niebuhr, these were primarily forms of military organisation, Marx described them as 'progressive epochs in the economic formation of society' (*MECW*, v, pp. 32–5, xxix, p. 263).

The historical path traced by *The German Ideology* led to communism. But Marx's communism was not that of the 'positive community of goods' proposed in the model settlements of Owen or Fourier, or of the *Icaria* of Étienne Cabet. Instead, Marx drew upon a notion of 'negative community' found in the continental natural law tradition, and absorbed into the beginnings of Scottish political economy through translations of the works of the seventeenth-century German natural law theorist, Samuel Pufendorf.[23] In this tradition, the original condition of the earth, that of a great primeval forest, had resembled that of the sea. Man could pick fruit, hunt deer or pasture sheep just as he could still fish in the sea – without impinging upon the rights or property of others. He was therefore innocent of any notion of property, whether private or communal. That was because Man's needs were modest and his resources abundant.

With the growth of population, the satisfaction of need began to require co-operation and the division of labour. Forms of scarcity appeared and each contributor to the production process had to be apportioned an appropriate share of the product. Such organisation also necessitated the formation of an institution with the power to enforce agreed forms of distribution and to punish violations of property and person. Hence the foundation of the state.[24]

22 For the importance of the impact made by the Historical School of Law, see Marx and Engels 2002, pp. 148–62.
23 See Pufendorf 1672; on the relationship of this natural law approach to the Scottish Enlightenment, see Moore and Silverthorne 1983.
24 On 'negative community', see Hont 1989 and Tuck 1979, ch. 3.

Crucial to Marx was the notion that primitive communism had been the product of abundance. This meant that private property, justice and the state had a historical origin. They had been invented to manage the onset of scarcity. In the *Communist Manifesto*, Marx and Engels praised capitalism and the bourgeoisie for driving the world towards a new epoch of abundance, created by the industrial revolution and the world market. As Marx was later to argue in *Capital*, the universal development of productive forces, the growth of large-scale industry and the harnessing of science in the service of production caused private property to become a 'fetter' upon the further development of the forces of production and this, according to Marx in 1859, would usher in 'an era of social revolution' in which capitalism, 'the last antagonistic form of the social process of production', would be overcome and 'the prehistory of human society' would draw to a close (*MECW*, xxix, pp. 263–4).

In the aftermath of insurrectionary situations, whether in June 1848, or again in the years following the Paris Commune in 1871, Marx claimed that the 'dictatorship of the proletariat' would be the initial form assumed by this 'social revolution'. What this term meant and whether this was a momentary tactical move to please allies on the left or a more permanent change of position was a cause of long-running argument within the subsequent Marxist tradition.[25] But in either case, Saint-Simon and Comte had already described what would soon follow this interim situation as a transition from 'the government of men' to 'the administration of things'. Engels later described this as a process in which the state would 'wither away'.[26] In Marx's somewhat different conception, the current distinction between the modern state and civil society would be dissolved, and in its place there would emerge a new form of the *Respublica* ('the public thing'), in which concern for the common good would no longer be obstructed by the rule of private interests characteristic of civil society.[27] But in either case, with the end of scarcity, the need for justice, private property and the state conventionally understood, would disappear. In 'the higher stage of communist society', as Marx still maintained in the *Critique of the Gotha Programme* in 1875, 'the

---

25 Around 1849–50, ideas about the need for a transitional dictatorship were widely shared, as much among democrats like Heinzen, as among revolutionary republicans and socialists like Willich, Schapper, Marx and the Blanquists (see Lattek 2006); the idea was republican and neo-Roman in inspiration. See Draper 1977; Hunt 1975, ch. 8.

26 See Saint-Simon (and Comte), 'Catéchisme des Industriels', Saint-Simon 1966, IV (1er cahier), p. 87; Engels, 'Herr Dühring's Revolution in Science', *MECW*, xxv, p. 268.

27 Marx nearly always referred to the abolition or transcendence (*Aufheben*) of the 'modern state' rather than the state as such. See the detailed analysis of Marx's writings of 1843–4 in Leopold 2007, ch. 4.

narrow horizon of bourgeois right' could 'be crossed in its entirety' and society would 'inscribe on its banners: from each according to his ability, to each according to his needs' (*MECW*, xxiv, p. 87).

6   The critique of the state

As Marx understood his task in 1844, a theory of communism presupposed not only a critique of political economy, but also a critique of the modern state; it required the completion of the project he had begun in 1842. In late 1844, his notebooks contained a 'Draft Plan for a work on the Modern State' whose heading was *The History of the Origin of the Modern State* or the *French Revolution* (*MECW*, xxiv, p. 87). In his original plans for *Capital* in 1857, there was once again the intention to include a book 'on the state'.[28]

The most familiar formulation of the theory associated with Marx's name is to be found in the *Communist Manifesto*, where it was stated that, 'each step in the development of the bourgeoisie was accompanied by a corresponding political advance of that class . . . the bourgeoisie has at last, since the establishment of Modern Industry and of the world market, conquered, for itself in the modern, representative state exclusive political sway. The executive of the modern State is but a committee for managing the common affairs of the whole bourgeoisie' (Marx and Engels 2002, p. 221). This statement drew primarily upon English history and probably derived from Engels' elaboration of his Chartist sources. Such a conception of the state could be traced back through Cobbett and Paine to the neo-Harringtonian views of the eighteenth-century country party; a cruder version of the same thought with obvious reference to England was to be found in *The German Ideology*, which stated, 'to this modern private property corresponds the modern state, which, purchased gradually by the owners of property by means of taxation, has fallen entirely into their hands through the national debt and its existence has become wholly dependent on its commercial credit, which the owners of property, the bourgeoisie, extend to it, as reflected in the rise and fall of government securities on the stock exchange' (*MECW*, v, p. 90).

By contrast, Marx's emphasis was more upon the impotence of the modern state. In the 'Draft Plan', he wrote of 'the self-conceit of the political

---

28 The most detailed description of his plans is contained in his unfinished 'Introduction' to the *Grundrisse* of 1857–8. It would concern 'The State as the epitome of bourgeois society. Analysed in relation to itself. The "Unproductive Classes". Taxes. National Debt. Public Credit. Population. Colonies. Emigration'. Marx, 'Introduction' (*Grundrisse*), *MECW*, xxviii, p. 45; and see also Marx to Lassalle (22 February 1858), *MECW*, xl, p. 270; see also Rosdolsky 1977.

sphere to mistake itself for the ancient state', and in an attack on Arnold Ruge written around the same time, he argued that 'the *administration* has to confine itself to a *formal* and *negative* activity, for where civil life and its labour begin, there the power of the administration ends'. The modern state was 'inseparable' from 'the slavery of civil society', by which Marx meant 'the unsocial nature of this civil life, this private ownership, this trade, this industry, this mutual plundering of the various circles of citizens' (*MECW*, III, p. 198).

The moralistic tone of this denunciation was modified when Marx adopted an interpretation based upon class struggle in 1845. But the refusal to accord any independence to the political sphere did not change. Following up upon the new-found determination of the political superstructure by the current relationship between 'forces and relations of production', between 1845 and 1848, Marx and Engels committed themselves to a confident series of predictions about the coming revolution. England, which was furthest developed, was to expect the first proletarian revolution. France where there still existed a large intermediate class of peasants and petit bourgeois would have a plebeian social-democratic republican revolution. Germany, whose governments were still feudal-bureaucratic, would experience a bourgeois revolution akin to that of 1789. This whole scenario was placed in a framework of world revolutionary collapse, in which the German bourgeois revolution would 'be rapidly followed' by a proletarian revolution consequent upon the acceleration of productive forces under the aegis of bourgeois rule.

In 1848, revolutions across Europe duly occurred, but these predictions were not borne out. Chartism in England declined after the failure of the Kennington Common demonstration called to present the national petition on 10 April 1848. From the beginning, the German bourgeoisie showed itself to be fearful of unleashing popular revolutionary forces, and in the face of disorder, rallied to the pre-existing dominant class. In France, confronted by the threat of lower-class revolt, the bourgeoisie found itself unable or unwilling to rule in its own name and abdicated power to Louis Napoleon Bonaparte. By December 1848 the direction of events was clear. In Cologne in Germany, where he had resumed his editorship of the *Neue Rheinische Zeitung*, Marx recognised that the bourgeoisie was incapable of making a revolution and, therefore, changed his political strategy. Instead of working within the Cologne Democratic Society to push bourgeois liberalism to the left, he and his supporters now backed an alliance of working-class, petit bourgeois democrats and peasants to make a 'democratic revolution'.

He also encouraged the formation of a national and independent working-class party. Hopes for a renewal of revolution were no longer tied to the further development of the forces of production, but to the (unlikely) possibility that France might be provoked into war with Russia, thus pushing the French regime to the left as it had done in 1792. In place of revolution from above, hope was now invested in revolution from below. This was the context of Marx's brief advocacy of 'permanent revolution' in his two 'Addresses of the Central Committee of the Communist League' in 1850.[29]

In his subsequent writings about these years, *The Class Struggles in France 1848–1850* of 1850 and *The Eighteenth Brumaire of Louis Bonaparte* of 1852, Marx attempted to explain the course of revolution in France. His approach to French history had been shaped by the French historians of the 1815–30 period, especially the prolific historian and Orléanist chief minister, François Guizot. In order to explain the development of revolution in France and its displacement of semi-feudal rule by a new commercial society based on talent and moneyed wealth, these historians had employed an English model. Hence a historical parallel was drawn between 1640, Cromwell and 1688 on the one hand, and 1789, Napoleon and 1830 on the other. Seen from this perspective, 1848 was an anomaly – neither the completion of the bourgeois revolution of the past, nor yet the proletarian revolution of the future. Hence the singular angle of vision from which Marx judged the sequence of recent events. What was important about the revolution, he argued, was not 'its immediate tragic-comic achievements', but 'the creation of an opponent in combat with whom the party of insurrection ripened into a really revolutionary party'.[30]

Marx's aim was to uncover the fundamental existence of class struggle beneath the surface play of political and ideological events. Such an approach worked well, as it had for Restoration historians, when describing the struggle between Legitimists (supporters of the *ancien régime*) and Orléanists (supporters of the 'Citizen' or 'Bourgeois' monarchy of Louis Philippe) as a conflict between land and mobile capital. But it offered little guidance in distinguishing between one political faction and another. There were no sociological criteria to distinguish the June insurgents from the *Garde*

---

29 Marx was forced to leave Cologne and then Paris, arriving in London at the end of August 1849. For Marx's role in the exile politics of German refugees in London in the aftermath of 1848, see Lattek 2006.
30 Marx, 'The Class Struggle in France', *MECW*, x p. 47; for the impact of Guizot and other French historians upon Marx's conception of the revolution in France, see Furet 1992.

Mobile. There were no specific material interests to identify the 'bourgeois republicans', while the attempt to provide a common social foundation for the politics of the petit bourgeoisie was purely speculative.[31]

Marx's refusal to accord autonomous space to the political sphere was the most distinctive feature of these writings. Universal suffrage was treated as a form of illusion akin to the notion of the equality of exchanges in the economy or the apparent naturalisation of economic categories in what he was to call 'the fetishism of commodities'. He considered all these to be symptoms of the alienating power of commercial society. But his refusal to accord universal suffrage its full import imposed serious limitations upon his understanding of the sequence of events. It led him to underestimate the ways in which the suffrage issue pushed the revolution in directions different from anything encountered in 1789 or 1830. For Marx, writing in *The Civil War in France*, universal suffrage was simply the deflation of petit bourgeois democratic illusions, a proof that it 'did not possess the magic power which republicans of the old school ascribed to it'. Its one great merit was of 'unchaining the class struggle', of taking away from the middle strata their 'illusions' and tearing away from all sections of the 'exploiting class' their 'deceptive mask' (*MECW*, x, p. 65).

Just as almost a decade before, Marx appears to have avoided plain acknowledgement of a prosaic and disenchanting political reality by a desperate *fuite en avant*. In 1843 in response to the lack of a popular reaction to the closing down of the free press, he moved from a 'political' to a 'human' revolution. In 1850, he wrote of the sequence of events that had culminated in the implementation of universal male suffrage and a massive electoral majority for Bonaparte as the ripening of 'the party of insurrection' into 'a really revolutionary party'. He had little to say about what was to be its most indisputable consequence – that, as a result of the political demand for universal male suffrage in France in 1848, and again in Germany in the 1860s, both the liberals and the more traditional parties of order found themselves defeated, not by radical democrats on the left, but by the

---

31 On the *Garde Mobile* and the June Insurgents, see Traugott 1985. On the bourgeois republicans, Marx remarked rather lamely that 'it was not a faction of the bourgeoisie held together by great common interests and marked off by specific conditions of production. It was a clique of republican-minded bourgeois writers, lawyers, officers and officials', Marx, 'The Eighteenth Brumaire of Louis Bonaparte', *MECW*, xi, pp. 112–13. In the case of the petit bourgeoisie, Marx tried to align the views of democratic writers with shop-keepers. He admitted that in terms of education and individual position, 'they may be as far apart from them as heaven from earth', but, he went on, 'what makes them representatives of the petit bourgeoisie is the fact that in their minds they do not get beyond the limits which the latter do not get beyond in life' (*MCEW*, xi p. 130).

demagogic manoeuvres of maverick post-Legitimist leaders on the right – Bonaparte and Bismarck.

In *The Eighteenth Brumaire*, Marx brilliantly retraced the steps by which Bonaparte established his ascendancy. But he had nothing to say about the developments that looked forward to the insights of Michels and other analysts of mass democracy later in the century. He did not get beyond the thought that Napoleon's regime was just a more effective way of giving the bourgeois supporters of the 'Party of Order' what they really wanted. The Second Empire was not therefore a defeat of the bourgeoisie, but a new form of bourgeois rule and hence a new stage in the development of the forces and relations of production. It was in this sense that the relationship between the bourgeoisie and the representative state depicted in *The Communist Manifesto* was thought to have been historically superseded by 'Bonapartism'.

'Bonapartism' meant a much greater stress upon the role of state power in its own right. Towards the end of *The Eighteenth Brumaire*, Marx wrote: 'France, therefore, seems to have escaped the despotism of a class only to fall back beneath the despotism of an individual and what is more, beneath the authority of an individual without authority. The struggle seems to be settled in such a way that all classes, equally impotent and equally mute, fall on their knees before the rifle butt.' He went on to emphasise 'the enormous bureaucratic and military organisation' of this 'executive power', of 'a host of officials numbering half a million, besides another army of another half million, this appalling parasitic body which enmeshes the body of French society like a net, and chokes all its pores' (*MECW*, XI, p. 185).

The attempt to elevate 'Bonapartism' into a new and general form of bourgeois rule was also evident in Marx's English writings, where from the early 1850s, he presented Palmerston as an English equivalent of Bonaparte, and made an attempt to align the English to the French state machine. In 1866, Engels wrote to Marx, 'it is becoming more and more clear to me, that the bourgeoisie has not the stuff in it to rule directly in itself', and that therefore (apart from England where a well-paid oligarchy still ruled) 'a Bonapartist semi-dictatorship is the normal form' (*MECW*, XLII, p. 266). In 1871 in *The Civil War in France*, Marx described 'Bonapartism' as 'the only form of government possible at a time when the bourgeoisie had already lost, and the working class had not yet acquired, the faculty of ruling the nation' (*MECW*, XXII, p. 330). As the proletariat became stronger, 'the state power assumed more and more the character of the national power of capital over labour, of a public force organised for social enslavement, of an engine of class despotism. After every revolution marking a progressive phase in the class struggle, the purely repressive character of the state power stands out in bolder and bolder relief' (*MECW*, XXII p. 329).

This way of characterising the changing relationship between the bourgeoisie and the modern state proved illusory. The idea of an increasingly coercive state to contain an increasingly belligerent working class was undercut by political developments in Britain and France. In Britain, from the time of the 1867 Reform Act, a significant proportion of the male working class became enfranchised, and yet during the years of Gladstonian liberalism there was little sign of the development of a more coercive state machine. Even starker was the contrast between the Bonapartism of the Second Empire and the subsequent development of the Third Republic. In France after 1871 — whatever the problems posed by Legitimism, Boulanger or the Dreyfus affair — the legislative did reassert control over the executive, and weak government proved compatible with universal male suffrage.

Marx vainly attempted to confront these difficulties in his 1875 *Critique of the Gotha Programme*. He criticised the Social Democrats for talking vaguely about 'the present state'. Given their empirical diversity, the 'present state' was 'a fiction'. But his own presumption continued to be that despite 'their motley diversity of form [modern states] do have things in common: they all stand on the ground of modern bourgeois society'. 'They thus also share certain essential characteristics.' What were these 'essential characteristics'? Marx did not specify, and as one critic has noted, the whole passage could be called 'an impressive sounding tautology'.[32] Marx himself seemed well aware of his failure in this area. In a letter of 1862 to his admirer, Dr Kugelmann, he claimed that he had arrived at the basic principles at least from which even others could reconstruct his system, 'with the exception perhaps of the relationship between the various forms of the state and the various economic structures of society' (*MECW*, XLI, p. 435).

More basic than the various attempts to update the *Communist Manifesto*'s picture of the bourgeois state was the persistence of Marx's earlier ambition to delineate a polity freed from what he considered to be the crippling division between state and civil society. The opportunity arose when Marx in his capacity as Secretary of the International Working Men's Association took upon himself the task of defending the establishment of the Commune of Paris in April–May 1871.[33] Between the resulting text, *The Civil War in*

32 See Maguire 1978, p. 203.
33 On Marx's activities during the First International and his relations with English trade unionists, see especially Collins and Abramsky 1965.

France, and the unfinished *Critique of Hegel's Philosophy of Right* of 1843, there is a striking continuity of preoccupation. Leaving aside the question of how far the reality of the Commune corresponded to Marx's depiction of it, it is clear that his intention in *The Civil War* was to describe a new polity, what in 1843 he had called 'democracy', and what he now characterised as the political form assumed by working-class rule.[34] It was as near to a tangible political theory as Marx got.

He described a form of self-organisation that had dispensed with the institutional assumptions and procedures of the modern state. Church and state were separated, the army was dismantled, working hours were regulated, and police powers were reduced to a minimum. Most striking was the political form this polity prescribed for itself. Rousseau's arguments against representative government were repeated. There was no gap between delegates and those who delegated them. The Commune was a 'working body' and its members were paid the wages of skilled workingmen. There was no division between legislative and executive. The judiciary was elected. All delegates, both in central and local government, were instantly recallable. In 1843, Marx had written of choosing a delegate as one might choose one's cobbler. In 1871, he expanded the point, this time taking the example of employers and their choice of skilled workmen.

But the form of political organisation was only half of the story. Marx's radicalism encompassed not only the institutional structures and assumptions of the modern state, but also those of private property in the means of production and market exchange in civil society. Here Marx's analysis became more vague and evasive. The depiction of a form of social organisation that had got beyond the practices of commercial society depended upon the critique of political economy, and in this area, Marx had run into problems far more formidable than he had ever anticipated.

7 Marx's critique of political economy

Just before the Revolution of 1830, the epochal collective work of the Saint-Simonian school, *The Doctrine of Saint-Simon*, had claimed that the contemporary condition of the 'worker' and 'the woman' was the latest in a succession of different historical forms of 'the exploitation of man by

---

34 The continuity of Marx's preoccupation with the abolition and transcendence of the state between 1843 and 1871 is discussed in Avineri 1968, ch. 8. As Avineri notes, Marx used the Hegelian term, *Aufhebung* (dialectical surpassal), whose implications differed from the term employed by Engels, *Absterben*, a more 'biological image of withering away'.

man'. Republicans, and many socialists too, attributed the plight of the worker to the 'unequal exchange' between capital and labour, and thought of it as another legacy of the system of 'force and fraud', which the French Revolution had failed to overcome.[35]

In contrast, Marx's 'Critique of Political Economy' – the subtitle of his three major works between the 1840s and the 1870s – started from Engels' original claim that political economy never questioned the private property basis of commercial society; or as Marx put it, it did not distinguish between Man's material interchange with nature and the successive social forms within which that interchange was conducted. This juxtaposition was transformed into a continuous historical dialectic between matter (persons, means of production) and form (property relations).[36] Marx used this distinction to challenge those who thought that the injustice of commercial society derived from an unfair exchange between the buyers and sellers of labour. Radical denunciation of the excesses of those who 'bought cheap and sold dear' did not satisfactorily explain the proletarian condition. Marx's own critique started from the work of David Ricardo (1772–1823), whom Marx regarded as the last 'scientific' exponent of political economy before it had entered a 'vulgar' apologetic stage from around 1830. He therefore accepted that a freely made agreement ensured that labour *was* paid its value in the form of wages (that is, as Ricardo had shown, its cost of production). Rent had likewise also been defined by Ricardo as the necessary cost of bringing scarce means of production into use. So if labour was paid at its full value, and rent deducted as a necessary cost, where was the source of profit?

Marx argued that existing political economy could not answer that question, because it paid attention only to the *exchange* value of commodities. It had neglected the obvious fact that commodities were not only exchanged, but also used. While it was true to say that the exchange value of labour was determined by its cost of production (Ricardo's subsistence theory), this was quite distinct from labour's *use* value. For what the wage labourer sold was not a defined quantum of labour, but his/her capacity to labour or *labour power*. Marx argued that, while the use and exchange values of other

---

35 See for example the analyses found among English Chartist and Owenite writers in the 1830s and 1840s. See Stedman Jones 1983c, pp. 90–179.

36 The clearest exposition of Marx's conception of the relationship between matter and form and his consequent understanding of the terms 'forces' and 'relations' of production is to be found in Cohen 1978.

commodities were equivalent, in labour's case, the use value to the buyer exceeded the exchange value of the labour paid. This is why Marx placed such emphasis upon his distinction between 'constant capital' (machinery) and 'variable capital' (living labour). Machinery might be the means of increasing the amount of labour that the labourer performed. But living labour was the sole source of profit. In return for a wage, the capitalist had purchased the capacity to appropriate a surplus beyond labour's exchange value by varying the length or intensity of work performed. 'Exploitation', therefore, was located, not in mechanisms of exchange (the wage contract), but within the interstices of production (how much labour the employer could extract from the worker during the hours of work). This was the basis of Marx's theory of 'surplus value', the form of 'exploitation' specific to capitalism.

Marx's 'labour theory of value' can also be traced back to a related socialist debate which had been current in England and France from the 1820s to the 1840s, and revolved around the issue whether the labourer ought to receive the whole produce of labour. In *The Poverty of Philosophy* written in 1847, Marx derided Proudhon's ideal of the equivalence of value and price. Following Ricardo, he maintained that such equivalence was already the actual situation under capitalism. Ricardo had originally argued that the absolute magnitude, in terms of which one commodity normally exchanged against another (its equilibrium price), was determined by the 'socially necessary labour' time embodied in its production. Ricardo, however, had abandoned this theory after discovering that variations in periods of production caused equilibrium price (and therefore value) to deviate from socially necessary labour time. Marx, however, confusingly falling back upon the popular political belief (that he had elsewhere dismissed) that labour was the source of all value, quibbled with Ricardo's revision.[37] He did so not least in order to preserve a radically simplified picture of the equivalence of value and price, which he employed for purposes of exposition in the first volume of *Capital* published in 1867.

---

37 Marx claimed that the deviation was not that of value from socially necessary labour time, but of equilibrium price from value. One of the major flaws in Marx's value theory was that he did not consistently recognise that the popular idea that labour was the source of all value and the Ricardian-derived claim that value was determined by socially necessary labour time were incompatible. For while the socially determined labour time theory started from the point at which the product was marketed, the labour-source-of-all-value theory referred solely to the production of the product. See Cohen, 'The Labour Theory of Value and the Concept of Exploitation', in Cohen 1988, pp. 208–38.

These simplified assumptions piled up problems for Marx's theory of profit (which was supposed to be fully expounded in the subsequent volume of *Capital*). For if surplus value could only be generated by living labour, it would appear that the higher the ratio of machinery to living labour, the lower the profit. Yet in the real world profit rates were equalised across different sectors of the economy. In the manuscripts, published by Engels after Marx's death as Volumes Two and Three of *Capital* in 1885 and 1894, it appeared that Marx's solution to this problem was both perfunctory and arithmetically incorrect. In what became known as 'the transformation problem', Marx's opponents, led by the Austrian economist, Eugen von Böhm-Bawerk, treated this failure as a refutation of the theory as a whole (see Böhm-Bawerk 1949).

Measured by Marx's initial ambitions, however, this definitional failure was relatively minor.[38] Far more serious, though barely noticed at the time, was the fact that Marx had not produced a theoretical analysis that demonstrated that capitalism would come to an end, whether in the near or far future.[39] *Capital*'s main claim to originality consisted in its theory of surplus value. In other respects – including the celebrated passage in which the expropriators were expropriated – its image of capitalist breakdown did little more than elaborate the picture of increasing polarisation between

---

38 Technically, it was also soluble. A mathematical resolution of the problem was put forward in 1907 by Von Bortkeiwicz, and others have been proposed since. See Desai 1979.

39 During the 1889–1914 period and well into the 1920s and 1930s, there was a widespread assumption among Second International socialists that capitalism would come to an end, not so much as a consequence of working-class revolt and 'an epoch of revolution', but more as a result of systemic economic failure. Engels had originally given sustenance to this idea in *Anti-Dühring* (see citation p. 591). It was reinforced by the 1891 Erfurt Programme of the German Social Democratic Party (drafted by Kautsky), which stated that 'irresistible economic forces lead with the certainty of doom to the shipwreck of capitalist production' (Kautsky 1910, p. 117). An attack on 'The Theory of Collapse' (*Die Zusammenbruchstheorie*) formed a central feature of Bernstein's revisionism (see Tudor and Tudor 1988, pp. 159–73); the term may have originated in Engels' editing of what became Volume Three of *Capital*, published in 1894. In 1988 and 1993, Marx's original manuscript of 1864–5, from which Engels put together the bulk of *Capital*, Volume Three, was transcribed and published in the *Marx/Engels/Gesamtausgabe*, 11/4.1 and 11.4.2 Ökonomische Manuskripte 1863–1867, Teil 1 1988; Ökonomische Manuskripte 1863–1867 Teil 2, 1993. It is therefore now possible to determine how much Engels was responsible for shaping and at times re-rephrasing Marx's 'very incomplete first draft'. Engels clearly believed in the political importance of the volume, and wrote to Bebel (4 April 1885), 'Our theory ... is provided for the first time with an unassailable basis ... it will again bring economic questions to the forefront of controversy' (*MECW*, XLVII, p. 271). It was probably as a result of his resolve to produce an exposition 'in which the general line of argument comes out graphically clear' that Engels in his editing of the concluding chapter of 'The Law of the Tendency of the Rate of Profit to Fall' (centre-point of many theories of the final capitalist crisis), replaced what Marx's manuscript referred to as the 'shaking' of capitalist production by the word, 'collapse'. Marx, '*Capital*, Volume Three, *MECW*, XXXVII, p. 245. See in particular, Roth and Moseley 2002, pp. 1–10; Vollgraf and Jungnickel 2002, pp. 35–78.

bourgeois and proletarian found in the *Communist Manifesto*.[40] Indeed, in strictly economic terms, no part of *Capital*, published or unpublished, offered a model of what the breakdown of capitalism would look like. On the contrary, what models were to be found there either presented a picture of cyclical development without any tendency to deterioration or else of a model of balanced growth (see Desai 2002, ch. 5). Marx's nearest approach to a notion of capitalist decline was to be found in his discussion of 'the declining rate of profit', a prominent part of Engels' edition of *Capital*, Volume Three. There, the idea was that while surplus value could only be extracted from living labour, the development of capitalism was accompanied by an ever-increasing proportion of means of production (constant capital – machinery, plant etc.) to labour power (variable capital). The result was intensified accumulation and exploitation as capitalists fought for a proportionately dwindling bounty of surplus. Marx defined this as a 'law'. But his own list of 'counteracting tendencies' was scarcely less powerful than 'the law' itself. He therefore contented himself with the claim that 'the law and its counteracting tendencies' 'breed overproduction, speculation crises and surplus capital alongside surplus population' (*MECW*, xxxvii, p. 240).

Capital contained an account neither of capitalist breakdown, nor of its putative successor. This mattered because despite his hostility to blueprints for the future, Marx could not but delineate the basic components of his vision of a post-capitalist alternative.[41] Among the most important would be the abolition of the market, in which 'the process of production has the mastery over Man, instead of being controlled by him'. The market would be replaced by a rational plan worked out between the associated producers. But to remove the market as the means whereby needs were harmonised with resources was to remove the central dynamic feature of the modern exchange economy. In pre-capitalist societies, as Marx's own researches in the 1850s had demonstrated, the harmonisation of resources and needs was effected by non-market forces – customary norms, religious or political institutions. Needs were assumed to be static. Only within a generalised system of commodity production did it become possible for 'the economic' to become separated from other spheres of life; and it

---

40 See Marx, *Capital: A Critique of Political Economy*, Volume One, *MECW*, viii, ch. 22 'Historical Tendency of Capitalist Accumulation', pp. 748–51. The passage referring to the 'expropriation of the expropriators' and 'the negation of the negation' occurs on pp. 750–1.

41 This hostility went back to his earliest discussions of communist schemes in 1843 and seems to have derived from a quasi-Hegelian belief that the shape of a new society would not be the product of utopian invention, but was immanent within the contours of the old.

was this freedom from institutional or customary restraint that explained capitalism's enormous superiority in forwarding productive advance and the proliferation of new needs. *Capital* offered no solution to the objection that socialism might therefore simply replicate the rigid and static character of pre-capitalist economic forms.

In Volume One of *Capital* Marx had produced a cogent theory of the capitalist form of exploitation and its relation to the dynamics of the capitalist mode of production. But he had not succeeded in disclosing what one sympathetic reviewer, cited in the 'Afterword' to *Capital*, termed 'the special laws which regulate the origin, existence, development, death of a given social organism and its replacement by another and higher one'.[42] And by the early 1870s – if not before – Marx at least knew that such disclosure was not to be found in his unpublished work.

8 After *Capital*: Engels

During the 1860s, as Secretary of the International Working Men's Association, Marx had become actively engaged with European labour movements. After the Franco-Prussian War and the Paris Commune of 1871, however, Marx withdrew from front-line involvement in international affairs. He left the day-to-day management of political correspondence to Engels, who had recently retired from the family firm in Manchester and moved to London. The two men were already well known to the leaders of the newly founded German Social Democratic Party. Elsewhere in Europe and especially in Russia, acquaintance with Marx's ideas increased in the 1870s, partly following the publication of *Capital*, but more immediately as a result of the notoriety of his defence of the Paris Commune. Between 1879 and 1892, German-inspired Social Democratic parties, which were influenced to some extent by what they took to be Marx's ideas, were formed in every major European country.

It was from Engels rather than Marx that the future leaders of European socialism – Bernstein, Kautsky, Plekhanov among others – learnt what they understood as Marx*ism* during the years before 1914. The turning point was the appearance of Engels' *Anti-Dühring* in 1878. Urged by his German Social Democratic friends to write a polemical riposte to the radical Berlin *Privatdozent*, Eugen Dühring, Engels provided a general compendium of his own ideas, putatively those of Marx as well – on philosophy,

42 Marx, 'Afterword' to the 2nd German Edition of "Capital", *MECW*, xxxv, p. 19.

science, dialectics, history, economics and politics. His overall aim was to insist upon the scientific status of the socialism that he and Marx had developed.

During the twentieth century Engels was widely condemned for his elevation of dialectics into a general cosmological framework governing all change. Following what he considered to be a materialist version of Hegel's conception of the relationship between accident and necessity, Engels maintained that historical events, apparently governed by chance, were in fact 'always governed by inner hidden laws'. Cosmology had formed a major component of the 'utopian socialism' of Fourier, the Saint-Simonians and Owen. The cosmological framework elaborated by Engels situated the socialist goal, while also incidentally obscuring the fact that *Capital* lacked a theory of the end of capitalism. This was apparent in Engels' treatment of Marx's famous passage at the end of the chapter on 'Primitive Accumulation' pronouncing 'the expropriation of the expropriators', and, in Hegel's terminology, 'the negation of the negation'. Dühring generally approved of the 'Primitive Accumulation' chapter, but objected to this resort to 'dialectical crutches' to help the chapter to its conclusion. Engels did not engage with the substantive claim only with the resort to Hegel. He insisted that only once Marx had established from history that 'in fact the process has already partially occurred and partially must occur in the future', he in addition characterised it 'as a process which develops in accordance with a definite dialectical law' (*MECW*, xxv, pp. 120, 124). Elsewhere in *Anti-Dühring*, Engels repeatedly invoked the crisis-ridden career of capitalism to suggest a terminal future. 'Modern large-scale industry has called into being' a ruling bourgeoisie which 'proves that it has become incapable of any longer controlling the productive forces, which have grown beyond its power; a class under whose leadership society is racing to ruin like a locomotive whose jammed safety-valve the driver is too weak to open' (*MECW*, xxv, pp. 145–6).

There was nothing new in the theory that Engels attempted to defend. It remained that of the *Communist Manifesto*, and *Capital* so far as it accorded with the *Manifesto* vision. The transition to socialism would take place in those countries like England and Germany where capitalism and the industrial proletariat were most developed. On the question as to when this transition might occur, he was much more pragmatic. Unlike Marx, who twenty years later still stuck to Engels' original vision of England in 1844, Engels was quite clear about how economic and political change in England had accounted for the demise of Chartism. Socialism would return, he believed, when Britain's mid-Victorian prosperity was once more challenged by the growth of international competition.

For all his preoccupation with 'the dialectic', Engels' political and intellectual position remained relatively uncomplicated and remarkably constant. Socialism was the modern form of democracy; capitalism had brought to power a new bourgeois class who controlled the state and exploited the proletariat – the great majority of the people. The aim, therefore, was to establish rule by a party that represented the proletarian majority and abolish private ownership of the means of production – the main cause of the poverty of the people. Once socialism was established, the state would 'wither away', the imbalance between town and country would be redressed and the condition of women would be immeasurably improved.[43]

This democratic-socialist transformation was to be accomplished, if necessary, by force. In his early life, the legacy of 1789, an upbringing under Prussian absolutism and his experiences in 1848 all led him to associate this change with violent revolution. But in later years, as the condition of English, and to a lesser extent European, workers improved and their political rights increased, Engels increasingly turned away from the romantic insurrectionism of his youth.[44] He was generally opposed to 'anarchist', revolutionary or 'Marxist' sects and favoured mass constitutional working-class parties. Unlike Marx, he was happy to acknowledge the improvements that had occurred since the publication of his book in 1845, and to adjust his theory to the changing political situation.[45] During his last years, he was probably more preoccupied with the danger of European war than with the prospect of revolution.[46]

9 After *Capital*: Marx

In the years after 1870, there was a remarkable change in Marx's general outlook. Commentators have noticed shifts in particular areas, but rarely attempted to make connections between them. They have therefore

---

43 Engels laid out his vision of the future of women in 1884 in 'The Origins of the Family, Private Property and the State. In the light of the Researches of Lewis H. Morgan', *MECW*, xxvi, pp. 129–256. Engels' text built upon notes left by Marx, but added many reflections of his own. Engels was more deeply affected than Marx by the form of feminism to be found in utopian socialism, particularly the writings of Charles Fourier.

44 See Friedrich Engels, 'Preface to the Second German Edition (1892) of *The Condition of the Working Class in England*', *MECW*, xxvii, pp. 307–23.

45 Engels to Marx (7 October 1858), *MECW*, xl, p. 344; Engels to Marx (8 April 1863), *MECW*, xli, p. 465.

46 See Engels, 'Can Europe Disarm?' (February 1893), *MECW*, xxvii, pp. 367–94.

generally missed the subtle but noticeable changes in the character of Marx's theory as a whole. These included a retreat from the universal and unilinear terms in which he had framed his theory in 1867, a growing interest in human pre-history and the virtual abandonment of the attempt to complete *Capital*.[47] Politically, this shift was marked by an acceptance of the strategy of the Russian Populists in preference to the 'orthodox' Marxism of the group gathered around 'the father of Russian Marxism', G. V. Plekhanov in Geneva. There was a similar shift in Marx's attitude to empire.[48] In 1853, he had described 'England's destruction of native industries' in India as 'revolutionary'. In the late 1870s, however, Marx no longer praised the breakdown of traditional and often communal social structures by European merchants and colonisers (*MECW*, xxxix, p. 347). Primitive communal structures left to themselves were resilient enough to survive in the modern world, and in favourable political conditions, could even develop. But they had been prevented from doing so by European colonisation.[49] The old faith in the world-transforming advance of the bourgeoisie and post-bourgeois modernity faded. Post-capitalism yielded to anti-capitalism. The recurrent points of emphasis in Marx's late writings were that the pre-history of man had been that of primitive communities, that capitalism was an unnatural and ephemeral episode in the history of mankind, and that man's future lay in a return to a higher form of a primordial communal existence.

In his writings of the 1850s, especially the *Grundrisse*, Marx had frequently argued that the Asiatic remained nearest to the original communal form of society, but also that this form of communal property was inseparable from despotic rule. If in Asiatic and other pre-capitalist societies communal ownership was coupled with despotism, it clearly had no place

47 Clearly, the difficulty in formulating his theory of profit was one of the issues which railed him; the last substantial attempt he made to resolve these problems (directly relevant to the second volume of *Capital*, what Engels published in 1894 as Volume Three) was a 132-page manuscript of 1875 entitled 'The Rate of Surplus Value and Rate of Profit Rendered Mathematically'. Marx spent time in the 1870s revising various editions of *Capital*, Volume One, but he appears to have made no sustained attempt to correct or reformulate the 1864–5 manuscript of the putative successor volume after 1867–8. See Vollgraf and Roth 2003. When asked by correspondents about the progress of the volume around the end of the 1870s, Marx claimed that censorship would prevent its publication in Germany and that he did not wish to embark upon publication before 'the English industrial crisis reaches a climax'. See letter to Danielson (10 April 1879), letter to Domela Nieuwenhuis (27 June 1880), *MECW*, xlv, p. 354, xlvi, p. 16.

48 A more extensive version of this argument is to be found by Stedman Jones 2007a, pp. 186–214.

49 For instance, in the case of the East Indies, he no longer believed like Sir Henry Maine that the destruction of the communes was the result of 'the spontaneous forces of economic laws'. It was rather 'an act of English vandalism, pushing the native people not forwards but backwards'. Marx to Vera Zasulich (first and third drafts), *MECW*, xxiv, pp. 359, 365.

in a communist future. But after 1870, Marx discarded the assumption that communal property and despotic rule went together. The change was most obvious in his references to Russia. In 1881, Vera Zasulich from the Geneva group around Plekhanov requested that Marx make clear his position on the Russian village commune. After the emancipation of the serfs in 1861, she asked, would the commune inevitably disappear as Russian capitalism developed? Or could it, before capitalist development became unstoppable, become 'the direct starting point' or 'element of regeneration in Russian society'? In a reply that was never sent, Marx conceded that 'isolation' and an association with 'centralised despotism' was a weakness of the commune. But now he argued that 'it is an obstacle which could easily be eliminated' (*MECW*, XXIV, pp. 353, 354, 363, 368).

What had apparently convinced Marx to change his evaluation of the village commune in Russia were Nicholas Chernyshevsky's essays on the community ownership of land. Chernyshevsky dismissed the Slavophile mysticism surrounding the backwardness of Russian communal institutions, but then went on to argue that this backwardness could be an advantage. For 'in backward nations, thanks to the influences of the advanced nation', it was possible to skip 'an intermediary stage' and jump 'directly from a low stage to a higher stage'.[50] This meant Russia could proceed straight from the village commune to socialism. Marx's reversal of his original position appears to have been the result of a combination of difficulties, both theoretical and practical. The mounting theoretical problems he had already encountered can be detected by a comparison between the unmistakably unfinished character of the published volume of 1867 and the successive plans and manuscript drafts that had preceded it. In his original plan of 1857, *Capital* was presented as a logical sequence or 'organic system' modelled on Hegel's *Logic*. Like Hegel's 'concept', it developed in successively more developed and elaborated forms starting from the commodity and ending with the world market. The system was conceived as a moving circuit, in which the end point (the world market) was also a return to the point of departure (the commodity) but now universal and fully developed. 'Universality' would in turn precipitate collapse, since its progress had engendered increasingly formidable obstacles to its further development: for example, lengthening times of circulation, falling profit rates and an intensification of exploitation. But even allowing for the inevitable scaling down of

---

50 Cited in Wada 1983, p. 48. See also White 1996.

this original scheme, the 1867 publication was a poor expression of Marx's theoretical intentions. As late as October 1866, Marx stated that production and circulation would be discussed within a single volume, thereby establishing the capitalist system as a circular process based on necessary laws (White 1996, ch. 4).

The inclusion of 'circulation' would have required a discussion of the expansion of capitalist relations across the world, what Marx called 'expanded reproduction'. Since it was important to Marx to distinguish this economic process from 'primitive accumulation' (the origins of capitalism), it was necessary to explain how 'expanded reproduction' 'dissolved' earlier modes of production, and how it refashioned pre-existing societies along capitalist lines. In particular, it was important to explain the subordination of agriculture to capital. These were to be the topics covered in what Marx called 'the genesis of capitalist ground-rent', and just as England had provided the basis of the discussion of capitalist production, so, Russia, particularly after serf emancipation, would provide the basis for the discussion of the genesis of 'capitalist ground-rent'.

But these plans were not followed through. The 1867 volume did not include the intended analysis of circulation, and therefore the chapter entitled 'Direct Results of the Production Process', designed to provide a transition between production and circulation, had to be dropped. Instead the published volume ended with 'primitive accumulation', a historical account of 'the expropriation of the agricultural population from the land' by means of enclosure and 'bloody legislation' in medieval and early modern Britain.

Was this British story to be understood as part of an inevitable and universal global process in which communal ownership died out? Readers of the first edition certainly assumed so. But Marx himself was beginning to back away from this position. It was at this time – in the years immediately after the publication of *Capital* – that Marx became acquainted with the arguments of Chernyshevsky and his followers. But as he was already discovering, instances in which peasant communal production was 'dissolved' in a purely economic process were hard to find. Furthermore, researches into the history of landholding in Germany, particularly those of G. L. Maurer, suggested that peasant communal ownership was far more resilient than had previously been supposed and in some areas had survived until recent times. This form of ownership, it seemed, did not simply 'dissolve' in the face of capitalist exchange relations. It was more probable that, as in Britain, it was destroyed by force or by destructive forms of taxation.

Marx accepted Chernyshevsky's claim. In 1873 in the second German edition of *Capital*, he dropped the sneering reference to Herzen, and instead introduced a fulsome tribute to Chernyshevsky, 'the great Russian scholar and critic'.[51] Acceptance of this claim also meant abandoning the universal terms in which he had originally framed his argument.[52] In the French translation of 1875, the chapter on 'Secret of Primitive Accumulation' was amended to imply that the story of the dispossession of the English peasantry only applied to the path followed by Western Europe. This enabled Marx two years later to dissociate himself from the idea that *Capital*'s depiction of the process of 'primitive accumulation' necessarily applied to Russia.[53] It is also clear that Marx had come to endorse the politics of populism. That is, he agreed that following the emancipation of the serfs in 1861, a socialist revolution must be made *before* capitalist development in the countryside destroyed the village commune (*MECW*, xxiv, pp. 357, 360).

Marx's vision of the village commune in the 1870s should not be seen solely as a shift of position on Russia.[54] It clearly went together with other changes, political and theoretical. The prospect of anti-capitalist revolution in the industrialised nations was becoming remote, in the aftermath of the Franco-Prussian War, the defeat of the Commune, and the growth of moderate and constitutionally oriented labour movements in Western Europe and North America. Marx's hopes were now invested in the unstable

51 Marx, 'Afterword to the Second German Edition' (1873), *MECW*, xxxv, p. 15. Engels was much less predisposed than Marx to abandon the coupling between the village commune and despotism. See Engels, *Anti-Dühring*, *MECW*, xxv, p. 168; in 1894, although respectful, he continued to maintain that Chernyshevsky was not entirely blameless in encouraging 'a faith in the miraculous power of the peasant commune to bring about a social renaissance'. Engels, 'Afterword to "On Social Relations in Russia"' (January 1894), *MECW*, xxvii, pp. 421–3, 431.

52 In the 1867 first edition of *Capital*, Marx had written – and added an exclamation mark for further emphasis – that 'the country that is more developed industrially only shows, to the less developed, the image of its own future!' Marx, 'Afterword' to *Capital*, *MECW*, xxxv, p. 9. In the 1870s, Marx stealthily backed away from this claim. In the second German edition of 1873, the exclamation mark was dropped.

53 Marx drafted, but did not send, a letter to the editor of *Otechestvenniye Zapiski*, Nikolai Mikhailovsky. Mikhailovsky described *Capital* as 'a historico-philosophical theory of universal progress', which argued that every country would undergo the same process of peasant expropriation as that experienced by England and assumed that Marx's attitude to populism was summed up by his denunciation of Herzen. Marx referred him to the 1875 French edition and his praise of Chernyshevsky, implying that he shared the analysis of the populists. See Wada 1983, pp. 57–60; White 1996, ch. 5; for the letter, see *MECW*, xxiv, pp. 196–201.

54 In the twentieth century, Marx's changing view about the village commune and 'skipping a stage' was generally treated as a particular response to the Russian situation. It was also a source of embarrassment since Russian 'Marxism', both in the work of Plekhanov and in Lenin 1899 was associated with the rejection of populism.

future of tsarist Russia. At the outset of the Russo-Turkish War in 1877, he not only predicted Russian defeat, but also went on to claim that 'this time the revolution will begin in the East' (*MECW*, XLV, p. 278; Wada 1983, pp. 55–6). But this was a war that the Russians won.

This political disappointment was compounded by theoretical difficulty. Marx effectively gave up the attempt to finish *Capital*. His study of capitalist crisis was inconclusive, his attempts to resolve the relationship between surplus value and profit were unsuccessful, he was not satisfied with his theory of the modern state and he was suffering increasingly frequent bouts of ill health. But that did not prevent the growth of other interests, notably his Russian researches and an increasing preoccupation with the early history of man (see Kelley 1984b). The character of these interests also suggested a distancing from his previous perspectives. Firstly, references to capitalism, so expansive in the 1850s, became cursory and dismissive. The Russian rural commune could bypass capitalism, Marx argued, because it could appropriate its 'positive acquisitions without experiencing all its frightful misfortunes'. But the 'acquisitions' mentioned were purely technological, and there was no mention of the changes in productivity, which this technology presupposed (*MECW*, XXIV, p. 34). Capitalist production was 'merely the most recent' of a succession of economic revolutions and evolutions that had taken place since 'the death of communal property'. Despite its 'wondrous development of the social productive forces', 'it has revealed to the entire world except those blinded by self interest, its purely transitory nature' (*MECW*, XXIV, p. 361).

Conversely, capitalism's primitive communal ancestor was endowed with 'a natural viability'. 'The vitality of primitive communities', Marx claimed, 'was incomparably greater than that of Semitic, Greek, Roman, etc. societies, and *a fortiori* that of modern capitalist societies' (*MECW*, XXIV, p. 358). Or, as he noted of the work of the American anthropologist, Lewis Henry Morgan, both on the Grecian *gens* (tribal society) and on the character of the Iroquois, 'unmistakably...the savage peeps through'.[55] Marx was greatly inspired by Morgan's depiction of the *gens* as that form of primitive community which allegedly preceded patriarchy, private property, class and the state. Morgan inferred the existence of the *gens* from both his contemporary researches on the tribes of North America, especially the Iroquois, and from his classical study of Greece and Rome (Morgan 1877).

---

55 'Marx's Excerpts', Krader 1972, p. 198.

Inspired by the new world which pre-history had opened up, Marx's vision now encompassed, not 'merely' capitalism, but the whole trajectory of 'civilisation' since the downfall of the primitive community. Remarkably, he had now come to agree with the French 'utopian' socialist, Charles Fourier that 'the epoch of civilisation was characterised by monogamy and private property in land' and that 'the modern family contained within itself in miniature all the antagonisms which later spread through society and its state'.[56] 'Oldest of all', he noted, primitive community contained 'the existence of the horde with promiscuity; no family; here only mother-right could have played any role': a fact denied only by 'the donkey' or 'block-headed John Bull', Sir Henry Maine, who transported his 'patriarchal' Roman family into 'the very beginning of things'.[57]

Primitive community had preceded the subjection of women, and it had embodied 'economic and social equality'. It was thanks to these 'character-istic features' borrowed from 'the archaic prototype' that 'the new commune introduced by the Germanic peoples in all the countries they invaded was the sole centre of popular liberty and life throughout the middle ages' (*MECW*, xxiv, pp. 350, 351). Kingship and private property in land – the political realm as such – both arose from the gradual dissolution of 'tribal property and the tribal collective body'.[58] Maine did not realise that the state was 'an excrescence of society'. Just as it had only appeared at a certain stage of social development, so it would disappear again, once it reached another stage yet to be attained. 'First, the tearing away of individuality from the originally not despotic chains (as the blockhead Maine under-stands it), but satisfying and comforting bonds of the group, of the primitive commune – then the one-sided spreading of individuality.'[59] 'Civilisation', however, was approaching its term. Capitalism was now in a 'crisis', which will only end in its 'elimination' and in 'the return of modern societies to the "archaic" type of communal property' (*MECW*, xxiv, p. 349). Marx agreed with Morgan. 'The new system towards which society tends . . . will be a revival in superior form of an archaic social type.'

10 Conclusion

Reason had been at its strongest in the late eighteenth-century attack upon 'force and fraud' – upon the unfounded claims of hierarchy, privilege and

56 Ibid, p. 120. For Fourier's theory, see Fourier 1996, pp. 56–74.   57 Krader 1972, pp. 102, 324.
58 'Maine Excerpts', Krader 1972, p. 292 and 'Introduction', p. 10.   59 Krader 1972, p. 329.

feudal rule, upon the mystifications of priesthoods, and not least upon the unwarranted metaphysical pretensions of reason itself. Far less straightforward was the attempt to introduce reason and autonomy into the forms and purposes of mankind's material exchange with nature, and the forms of social relations they entailed. The type of exploitation peculiar to commercial society could not so easily be aligned with that of feudalism or slavery. For one thing it did not involve the imposition of force. It was true that commercial society was based upon private property, and as Adam Smith had accepted nearly one century before, the origins of private property like those of the state went back to force. But the consequences of Marx's identification of 'surplus value' as the root of capitalist exploitation were less explosive than he might initially have anticipated. For the fact that the labourer produced a surplus over and above his cost of production was not in itself a scandal. In every economic form, a certain proportion of the product was withheld from the producers in order to make possible investment in the future reproduction and growth of society. The real question was whether a system in which means of production were private property should be replaced by a society in which ownership was collective and production rationally planned.

According to Smith, commercial society was to be defended because despite its inequalities, its benefits to everybody greatly outweighed its costs (see Smith 1809, p. 10; Stedman Jones 2004, pp. 49–50). But in the 1830s and 1840s, these benefits were far from self-evident. Large numbers had been forced off the land, the sub-division of plots had brought the spectre of famine, hand-workers in such basic trades as shoe-making, tailoring and carpentry suffered cut-throat competition and outworkers endured declining wages, sometimes exacerbated by the threat of machines. In the new industrial towns, horrified observers, most eloquently Engels, described overcrowding, lack of sanitation, environmental pollution, child labour, industrial accidents and excessive hours of work. Angry workers protested about their conditions with increasing menace. By June 1848, these protests had turned into violent rebellion as 'more than one hundred thousand men' – most of them unemployed workers – took to the streets of Paris and engaged in what Tocqueville described as a 'sort of "servile war"' (Tocqueville 1971, p. 169).

Yet despite all these ominous developments, as Marx found in the twenty years following 1848, capitalism was not heading for self-destruction in fact, nor could he produce a convincing picture of capitalist breakdown in theory. The workers were not undergoing 'immiseration'. There were even signs of improvement – though he was loath to admit it. Furthermore, it was far from clear that the society beyond the 'modern state', which Marx sometimes invoked but never detailed, could organise itself as productively or efficiently as its capitalist predecessor.

Formed before 1848 by the anti-romanticism of Hegel, and the satire of Heine's *Romantische Schule*, Marx's writings of the 1850s and 1860s were of a resolutely modernist and anti-romantic kind. They were of a piece with his critique of political economy and his identification of socialism with a post-capitalist future, which would be heralded by a revolt of the new industrial working class. But many of these hopes had faded by the 1870s. Only this can explain why a disappointed Marx came to convince himself about the emancipatory possibilities of the supposedly archaic communal practices of the 'rural commune', and to believe that the key to the future might after all be discovered in the allegedly still living past.

IV

Secularity, reform and modernity

18

Church and state: the problem of authority

JOHN E. TOEWS

The history of thinking about the structures of human association in Western Europe during the nineteenth century was marked by a remarkable resurgence of interest in questions pertaining to the conflicting and mediating relations between the spiritual and temporal, the transcendent and immanent, the sacred and secular dimensions of human experience, as well as to the institutional, 'objective' articulation of such 'subjectively' defined relations in the renegotiations, transformations, reforms and reconstructions of the relations between state and church. Between the defeat of Napoleon and the massive social and political transformations of the last quarter of the century, it was virtually impossible to formulate questions concerning the associative life of human beings outside the framework of the field of tension and reciprocity produced by religious and political agendas for transforming emancipated strangers into members of a community of consciousness, will and sentiment. It is difficult to find a significant political or social thinker before 1870 whose discourse was not framed in large parts by this polarity.

The new centrality of church–state relations in political and social theory was obviously instigated by the sweeping legal and political changes of the revolutionary and Napoleonic era. The legal emancipation of the individual from the privileging and restricting bonds of a corporate social order and the liberation (at least in principle) of the pursuit of self-interest under the uniform laws of civil society and the exigencies of the market, raised new questions not only about social order but also about the sources of meaningful social cohesion and ethical authority. Liberal constitutional reforms that gave at least some emancipated individuals political rights in the formation and administration of their own laws raised questions about the political community as not just a collection of obedient subjects but as a communion of subjective agents, participant members of

603

a national political culture. What meaning would join the newly emancipated individuals of civil society into a common identity; what norms would regulate their actions? The role and authority of the established confessional churches in fulfilling this function of providing meanings and norms for social interaction were radically altered by the loss of traditional corporate status, property and thus autonomy (especially in Catholic continental states), by the confessional pluralism inherent in liberal reforms (freedom of thought, expression and association), and by the growing competition of aesthetic and scientific ('secular') ideologies that increasingly made bids for hegemony in the sphere of 'spiritual' authority and its cultural institutions.

These changes could not be intellectually contained or controlled by the rehabilitation and repetition of conventional, inherited discourses about church–state relations. The old arguments concerning the relations between spiritual and temporal powers were transformed by the infusion of dynamic intellectual energies and complicating tensions from new experiences and from the new consciousness of personal, communal and ontological identity that had risen to public prominence during the revolutionary and Napoleonic eras. 'Church' and 'state' as well as their relations with each other were redefined in the conceptual frames of the individual self as a dynamically evolving, embodied agency or 'subject', of community as 'inner' (subjective) identification with a system of meanings and norms shaped into the historical particularity of a cultural totality by language and tradition, and of faith as an experience of the sublime or abyssal ground of individual existence and cultural identity. In clarifying and complicating ways, arguments about the relations between church and state organised the public implications of post-revolutionary conceptions of subjective autonomy and communal being.

This chapter will sketch out four historical and conceptual 'moments' in the nineteenth-century attempt by West European thinkers to reimagine the tensions, reciprocal relations and boundaries between state and church as objectifications of 'inner' relations within the historically structured, inwardly differentiated 'totality' of human existence. The central theoretical question was not one of renegotiating boundaries between two existing institutional entities within a consensually validated world, but of achieving consensus and authorisation for the constitution of a world in which those entities would emerge with new identities.

1   Romantic reframing: church and state as expressive polarities

In the cluster of influential, canonised texts that marked the emergence of the various romantic movements in Western Europe around 1800, specific theorising about the relations between church and state played a subordinate, almost peripheral role. At the same time, the early writings of Samuel Taylor Coleridge, William Wordsworth and Robert Southey, René de Chateaubriand, Joseph de Maistre and Benjamin Constant, Friedrich von Hardenberg (Novalis), Friedrich Schleiermacher, Friedrich Schlegel, F. W. J. Schelling, Friedrich Hölderlin and G. W. F. Hegel gave shape to conceptions of self, culture and religious experience that would set the terms for the nineteenth-century debate. Church and state appeared in these writings as expressive rather than constituent forms, as the contingent appearances of the substance of personal and collective human experience, as the external 'letters' (either expressive articulations or repressive fetters) of the inner, immanent 'spirit' of individual and associative life. Four interrelated concepts or beliefs defined the cultural and ideological map constructed by the early romantic texts.

Most striking, exhilarating and disturbing was the romantic reconstruction of essential selfhood or personal identity as radical autonomy, as creative subjective agency engaged in an 'infinite' process of self-fashioning through the organisation and sublimation of its natural ground in the body and its desires and through the subjective appropriation and shaping of its particular socio-cultural, historical conditions. The model for autonomy in this romantic conception was not so much the inherited liberal notion of individual rights and interests guaranteed by universal laws of nature or reason, or the notion, most commonly attributed to Rousseau or Kant, of a self-legislating moral subject constructing the public rules governing its own behaviour, but the freedom of the poet constructing self and world as works of his creative imagination. Michel Foucault has aptly summarised the problematic tensions in this construction of selfhood in terms of the contradictions of the 'empirico-transcendental doublet' of finite subjectivity (Foucault 1971, pp. 312–43). On the one hand, the self was understood as 'essentially' embodied and historical, as always specifically and 'positively' fashioned by the anonymous structures of language and culture. On the other hand, the self was posited as the dynamic creative agency, the 'infinite' productive power for which any particular 'positive' identities were simply possible embodiments or expressions. In their dynamic element, the empirical embodiments of self-identity were like specific works of the poetic imagination, open to acts of reflective transcendence and constant transformation. They revealed, in their very particularity, the possibility of being otherwise.[1]

What kind of associative life or 'community' could constitute an appropriate 'home' for this romantic subject? Romantic politics was above all a cultural politics, a politics of meaning in which processes and institutions of subjective identification and mutual recognition superseded, and sometimes all but displaced, processes and institutions for the protection of individual rights and the regulated pursuit of individual interests. It was in the communicative interaction of social relations that the self as subject actualised its potentialities, produced itself as a specific concrete identity for others, and recognised this identity as an object of reflective transcendence through the eyes and actions of others. The medium for this reciprocal interactive sociability of a diversity of subjects was language, broadly defined in terms of the symbol systems that allowed individuals to give meaningful shape to their subjectivity and communicate with others. The conditions for membership in such cultural communities of individuated subjects or 'individualities' included general access to the means of self-objectification and communication and freedom of interaction. In this sense the cultural 'state' or community of meaning of early romantic ideology assumed both the emancipatory liberal and inclusive populist/democratic/nationalist dimensions of the transformations of the revolutionary era. Even romantic theories that looked to the past for models of authentic community were less conservative attempts to sustain a living tradition than therapeutic responses to the peculiar dilemmas of post-revolutionary homelessness.

Early romantic ideas of community were marked by the assertion that recognition of diversity, difference or subjective individuality was the condition for the reciprocal bonding of an 'organic' totality. At the same time, the mutual recognition of diverse individualities was premised on the existence of diverse *collective* subjects, cultural 'selves' that ultimately defined the boundaries of the cultural organism. After 1800 such cultural subjects tended to become identified with cultural 'peoples' or 'nationalities', but at the outset and in important ways in later decades as well, the collective subject of 'Europe' or 'Christendom' constituted an important element in

---

1 The contradictions of romantic subjectivity in the early works of Wordsworth, Chateaubriand, Friedrich Schlegel and Schleiermacher are analysed, psychologised and historically contextualised in Izenberg 1992.

romantic cultural politics. Romantics often displayed an obsessive interest in an idealised historical model of the differentiated unity of pre-Reformation European Christendom, conceived as a naïve prefiguration of the self-consciously 'organic' society of the future. The specific juridical, administrative and legislative institutions of the state proper played a subordinate role in this romantic vision, as dependent expressions of the substance of associative life that was located in social interactions of mutual recognition and symbolic identification. Legal and governmental institutions possessed importance as instruments for expressing difference and for nurturing or repressing the reality of communal identity but were not the *loci* of that identity itself. Or at least the identity of the community was only present in the institutions of government and law in a formal way, separated from the actual substance of individual life as a life of will, feeling and creative agency.

The third element in the early romantic vision of culture was the 'restoration' of religious experience and consciousness to the centre of communal life. In a 'classic' romantic formulation, Schleiermacher in 1799 defined religious experience as the unmediated 'intuition and feeling' of the 'infinite nature of totality, the one and the all', a 'childlike' encounter with the Absolute as the 'ever-fruitful womb' of Being in relation to which everything individual appeared as 'a part of the whole and everything limited as a representation of the infinite' (Schleiermacher 1988, pp. 102, 105). In religious consciousness the embodied historical individual experienced the ground of its own double life as both the subject and the object of its activity through an encounter with the foundational, primal unity of subjectivity and objectivity. Religious experience thus produced a consciousness of the infinite source of the finite subject's acts of self-expression and self-shaping. Metaphysical philosophy (and theology), art and literature, and the ordering principles of associative ethical life were all attempts to mediate religious experience of 'absolute' or 'infinite' identity with the natural and historical conditions of finite subjectivity. Religious experience provided direct, unmediated contact with the absolute centre of existence, the Being of all beings. Early romantic conceptions of the church flowed from such conceptions of religious experience as an encounter with the conditions or presuppositions of finite existence. In general terms, churches represented that aspect of culture in which individual subjects recognised, nurtured, articulated and communicated their religious experience. It was a site for giving expression to that dimension of common life in which individuals recognised in each other their shared relationship to the absolute, to that

607

infinite power which made their finite existence possible. It was a place for the language of art and for the aesthetic priests who sustained and renewed this language. Whether such churches had anything to do with the actual, existing confessional churches was not, at first, very clear.[2]

Romantic conceptions of the subject as creative individuality, of community as an identity of diversity in an organic totality, of religion as both an unmediated relation to the absolute and a mediation between the absolute ground and cultural difference, were connected and transformed by the romantic theory of history, which constructed the past as a succession of cultures in a teleological narrative moving from some originating undifferentiated identity of subjects and objects, through a process of fragmentation, individuation and conflict, and culminating in the achievement of an artificially or culturally constructed 'higher' unity that affirmed differentiation within an articulated, organic or systematic totality.[3] The merger of the secular history of peoples and cultures into the sacred history of redemption, in which a lost Garden of Eden was refound as a culturally constructed 'New Jerusalem', made all attempts to stabilise the relations between church and state, even when defined as subordinate products or objectifications of subjective cultural identities, problematical and contestable.

Amongst the array of early Romantic texts, Friedrich Schleiermacher's *On Religion: Speeches to its Cultured Despisers* (1796–9) addressed the specific problem of church–state relations most directly. As an intimate friend of the literary critic and aesthetic philosopher Friedrich Schlegel, a participant in the Berlin romantic circles of the turn of the century, and a trained theologian on an ecclesiastical vocational track within the Prussian Reformed Protestant church, Schleiermacher was perfectly situated to bring romantic perspectives on self, culture and the experience of the sublime into a critical relation with inherited conceptions of the church and church–state relations. In the Fourth Speech of the *Reden*, entitled 'On the Social Element of Religion, or, On Church and Priesthood', he noted that an understanding of the nature of subjective religious experience required a rethinking or reimagining of ideas of religious community. The 'whole idea

---

2 The German romantics Schlegel, Novalis and Hölderlin certainly wavered at first about whether or not the 'new mythology' or 'new religion' would be 'Christian'. Schlegel claimed: 'we have no mythology . . . it is time that we earnestly work together to create one' (Schlegel 1968, p. 81). Hegel and Schelling similarly played with the notion of a post-Christian religious mythology as the popular form for their philosophical innovations.

3 There is a remarkable comparative analysis of the dialectical spiral of romantic theories of development (both for collectivities and individual psyches) in Abrams 1971.

of the church' needed to be subjected to 'a new consideration, reconstructing from the centre outwards'. The 'centre' in Schleiermacher's view was
the associative life that evolved among those individual subjects who were
in the process of attempting to give shape to their unmediated intuition
(*Anschauung*) of the dependence of the individual subject on the Absolute
through communication with others in religious fellowship. Religious life
was essentially social in the sense that religious intuitions only became real
as they were articulated for other subjects, and thus emerged as objects of
reflection and further development. This fellowship of 'mutual communication of religious intuitions' was a fellowship of equal subjects without
hierarchical order and without fixed languages or symbols for defining the
never completely or transparently expressible content of religious intuitions.
It was a community in which language was always in process and individuals
continually worked at shaping the particularity of their own intuitions for
communicative interaction – an open-ended dialogue of love, rather than
a static conformity to a creed or dogmatic discourse. Such communities of
the religious were essentially 'free' and dynamic, but they also led naturally
to a search for institutions of mediation that would at least temporarily unite
the diversity of private religious languages for purposes of edification and
education of those who were seeking religious experience but did not yet
possess it. The creation of an institutionalised church with trained teachers
(clergy) was made necessary by a membership that included not only the
positively pious – those who possessed the religious experience – but also
the 'negatively' or potentially pious – those who were seeking or needed
the religious experience. In terms of the inherent logic of religious community, Schleiermacher imagined a process in which linguistic articulation
and historical institutionalisation underwent a constant process of transformation and never became fixed in creed and law. Common languages and
symbolic systems could never be more than temporary results of the communicative process, emerging like the harmonies of choral music from the
always diverse, constantly evolving and accumulating experiences in which
individuals constructed personally differentiated perspectives on their common dependence on the Absolute. What stifled the dynamics of this natural
process was the interference of states in religious society. The state, seeking to use religious society for its own purposes of establishing civil peace
among self-interested individuals through obedience to its laws, fixed forms
of language and symbol into systems with claims to exclusive and permanent
validity and organised the broader ecclesiastical society into a politicised,
legal ecclesiastical state, appropriating the historically contingent forms of

religious expression for its own tasks of fixating and stabilising identities. In 1799 Schleiermacher presented the absolute separation of church and state, the emancipation of religious society from all political interference and control, as a prerequisite for the progressive evolution of the 'true' or authentic church as a religious community.

Schleiermacher, however, did not imagine his religious society as an invisible church, as a purely spiritual communion. The reciprocal sociability, the communicative and ethical interaction, of religious individuals was a dynamic association in the world, 'a perfect republic' or a 'priestly people' in which 'each alternately leads and is led; each follows in the other the same power that he also feels in himself and with which he rules others' (Schleiermacher 1988, p. 166, 1984, p. 270). The relations of this society were imagined as potentially permeating the whole culture, emerging first in the mutual relations of family and friendship but expanding outwards in concentric circles to encompass the totality of associative life. The emancipation of religious society from the external fetters of political control would in fact allow religious experience to work transformatively within society and culture. Ecclesiastical emancipation was thus redefined in a positive way, not as an escape or refuge from the political realm, but as the centre from which the realm of politics would itself become an expression of ethical community, of an identification of free subjects. In the last pages of the fourth speech Schleiermacher intimated that the eradication of mass poverty and mechanical, necessary labour through technological and scientific control of the inanimate 'dead forces' of nature could free everyone to join in the mutual labour of expressive self-fashioning and thus enjoy the consciousness of participation in the infinite powers of the Absolute: 'then for the first time, everyone will be freeborn; then every life will be at the same time practical and contemplative, the rod of the taskmaster will be raised over no one, and all people will have peace and leisure to contemplate the world in themselves' (Schleiermacher 1988, p. 186, 1984, p. 290). Both state and church would disappear as separate institutions when all of society took on the characteristics of a church association.

As long as this utopian identification of religious society with human society remained a future hope rather than a present reality some form of separate religious society, with both exemplary functions as a model for the future and as the cultivator of religious consciousness among the 'negatively pious' was required. In 1800 it was not clear among Schleiermacher and other members of his romantic generation whether this mediating church would emerge as a reformation of existing ecclesiastical forms, or present itself in more radical revolutionary form as a 'messias in pluralis'[4] of a post-Christian future, in which the self-expression of religious experience would move beyond the limiting historical moment of European Christendom and its confessional differentiations. Where Schleiermacher's choices would fall was intimated in the *Reden* in his view of the historical evolution of religious societies and cultures. Although in principle Schleiermacher insisted that every individual intuition of the Absolute was necessarily perspectival, individually shaped in historically limited 'positive' symbolic forms, and that all collective symbolic expressions of religious experience and associative life were historically defined organisations of diversity open to constant transformation, he also presented a teleological development of religious forms in which Protestant Christianity represented a culmination that superseded other religious societies (both non-Christian and Christian) and included their perspectives within it. Christianity superseded pagan and Judaic religious forms because its mode of intuiting the relationship between finite subjectivity and the Absolute brought to symbolic objectification the essential nature of religious experience and religious society. The Christian perspective was self-reflexive and thus able to encompass all of the historical and perspectival diversity of religion within it. In Protestant Christianity the particular individual cultural form became itself the universally human, represented as an organism of dynamically mediated difference (Schleiermacher 1988, pp. 213–22, 1984, pp. 316–25).

Written with rhetorical fervour and infused with the consciousness of imminent historical transformation, Schleiermacher's *Reden*, like the aphorisms and essays of Friedrich Schlegel and Novalis, the poetry of Wordsworth and Coleridge, or the philosophical treatises of Schelling and Hegel, slid over a number of problematic areas in early romantic conceptions of religious culture, collective symbolic forms, and ecclesiastical institutions. Some of these problems were more explicitly displayed in the sprawling apologia for the historical superiority of Christian culture in Chateaubriand's *Genius of Christianity* (1799–1801). Like his early romantic contemporaries, Chateaubriand rediscovered the power of the doctrines, rituals, institutions and language of Christianity in the context of the emotional, aesthetic and cognitive needs of a finite, temporally and naturally individuated, human subject. Seeking recognition for the infinite dimension in its restless processes of self-making, the romantic subject was driven by indeterminate passions that could attain no adequate earthly objectification.

---

4 The term is from Novalis 1929, p. 364.

In two novellas originally intended as illustrative stories displaying both the need for Christianity and its therapeutic power in meeting that need – 'Atala' and 'Rene' – Chateaubriand provided exemplary accounts of the anchorless, homeless human subject (a 'stranger among men', Chateaubriand 1978b, p. 716, 1856, p. 298) driven by passions that could find no satisfactory object within the realm of finite relations. This 'unsettled' state of a soul whose passions constantly transcended their objects was unknown, Chateaubriand claimed, in ancient classical cultures. The literature, mythology and cultural institutions of Greece and Rome were inadequate to the needs of modern man. The modern subject was defined by the infinite (indeterminate, insatiable) nature of its yearning, a yearning that could only be stilled through identification with the infinite divine power that was the source of the split between desire and object, between self and world (Chateaubriand 1978b, pp. 714–16, 602–5, 1856, pp. 296–8, 184–7). The stories, doctrines, rituals and aesthetic symbols of Christian culture both recognised this contradiction of finite subjectivity, whose striving could only be stilled in the collapse of the world or the death of the self, and provided it with appropriate therapeutic solutions.

Much more than Schleiermacher, Chateaubriand presented a conception of subjectivity as an infinite and ultimately futile desire for fulfilment in the world of natural and historically determinate objects. Resolution or satisfaction of the finite subject's infinite yearnings could only be represented in aesthetic reconstructions of the primal undifferentiated unity of subject and object, self and world in prehistoric culture or the mother–child symbiosis, or through a dissolution and transcendence of the body and time. The infinite object to which the yearning of the subject was directed was necessarily transcendent, existing outside of the differentiated world of subjects and objects in time and space. Christianity's 'genius' for Chateaubriand was that it both reflected the sufferings of the modern individual subject and provided the institutions to assuage those sufferings. Its doctrines and rituals penetrated to the depths of the inherent relationship between love and death, desire and dissolution in modern consciousness and offered a transcendent redemption as the only way of stilling the infinite yearning of the finite subject.[5]

---

5 Chateaubriand's emphasis on the Christian connection between a vision of man as fallen and God as a transcendent father is especially present in Chateaubriand 1856, Part I, where he presents this Christian perspective as a purified 'natural religion' implicit in all human experience.

Chateaubriand's principled pessimism about the possibility of achieving earthly satisfaction for the self's infinite longings under the conditions of finite embodied, temporal selfhood produced a vision of the institutionalised church rather different from Schleiermacher's. For Chateaubriand the 'church' was synonymous with the institutional and symbolic forms of a unified, Catholic Christian culture as he imagined it existing in Europe before the Reformation, and to some degree up to the French Revolution. The church provided aesthetic consolations for the suffering of finitude, images of the loveliness of death as the fulfilment of life, but it also represented the discipline that the transcendent divinity imposed on finite creatures seeking to attain the infinite within the restrictions of earthly existence. As a disciplinary society, articulating the claims of the transcendent against the over-reaching passions of the finite, the church was inevitably involved in the power relations of earthly life, and Chateaubriand had no difficulty accepting the necessity of an institutionalised church as the centre of Christian culture and religious society. Only by permeating human institutions with its message of the vanity of earthly ambitions could religion moderate the consequences of the endless striving to make nature and history conform to the desire for absolute unity. The vast and complex institutional structure of established Christendom that had evolved since the era of the apostolic church, in Chateaubriand's view, was the appropriate articulation of a culture that recognised the paradoxical passions of selfhood. As modern forms of homelessness became more prevalent in the post-revolutionary era, a restoration and invigoration of these cultural institutions was urgently required. A viable church was needed to save earthly communities from the ravages of infinite desire. Chateaubriand revealed little consciousness of the inherent or potential tensions between state and church. Emancipating the church to do its cultural work of disciplining utopian hopes for secular redemption was seamlessly integrated with the political functions of maintaining peace and stability. Displaying the inherent limitations of temporal community, religious communities placed a brake on the political hopes raised by reformist and revolutionary claims.[6]

---

6 Chateaubriand 1856, Part VI is devoted to an expansive listing and praise of the services performed by the church as a civilising power in European society, in fact as the civilisation of Europe. Near the end of the book Chateaubriand claims that a reinvigorated church will overcome the degeneracy of the revolutionary era and re-establish the proper hegemony of spiritual power within society (Chateaubriand 1856, p. 643, 1978b, p. 1053).

Comparison of Schleiermacher and Chateaubriand highlights two issues that became prominent in the subsequent history of theorising about relations between church and state – the relationship between immanent and transcendent meaning, and the question of expressive and disciplinary power. Did church society simply give articulate form to the religious experience already present in the social relations of religious subjects? Or did it impose a transcendent shaping power on the formlessness of individual striving? Was the church an institutionalised expression of the substantiality of organic community implicit in natural and social life, or a disciplinary construction of order within a fallen world?

In the polemical, anti-revolutionary works of the émigré Savoyard noble Joseph de Maistre (1753–1821), these tensions took on an exemplary intensity that gave priority to the imposed discipline of institutionalised states and churches within the historical development of religious society and differentiated cultural communities. Maistre's interpretation of the infinite striving of the romantic subject was framed by traditional Christian views of unbounded hubris and sinful rebellion against divine order. 'Infinite in his desires' and inevitably discontented with any finite object or particular identity, man was a 'born despot' insatiable in his lust for power (Maistre 1971, p. 118). All claims that individuals could regulate and socialise this striving through their own intellect and moral powers were illusory and merely exaggerated the original fault. At the same time Maistre claimed that such hopes for rational self-regulation corrupted an original, natural, instinctual wisdom, grounded in recognition of the radically self-destructive tendencies inherent in the drive for self-sufficiency. Prior to its corruption by the released powers of egoistic self-interest this instinctual communal knowledge recognised that striving for radical autonomy needed to be controlled by submission to the absolute power of the group, and that rational calculation would ultimately have to submit to blind faith in the providential divine will. This communal wisdom was sedimented in historically produced traditions and languages, and especially in the institutions of state and church. In one sense Maistre seemed to present a conception of state and church as the expressive articulations of the 'directing spirit' (Maistre 1971, p. 212) working in an immanent fashion in national political cultures. He was different from writers like Schleiermacher and Chateaubriand primarily in his vision of this immanent evolution as a coercive disciplinary process marked by the violent punishment of rebellious subjectivity and ruled by the rituals of sacrifice: 'The whole earth, continually steeped in blood, is nothing but an immense altar on which every living thing must be sacrificed without end, without restraint, without respite until the consummation of the world, the extinction of evil, the death of death' (Maistre 1971, p. 253).

This shift in interpretative emphasis produced a qualitative shift in the relations between state and national community, and between religious society and ecclesiastical governance. Because the incorrigible striving for autonomy could only be controlled through total submission to absolute power, the sovereignty of the ruler became the actual, efficacious cement of the communality of the nation. It was through common recognition of the need for unrestricted power in the political sovereign that individuals affirmed the priority of the national community over their individual claims. Consciousness of community was inherently tied to the recognition that identity was enforced through the arbitrary, unrestricted will of an authority outside the individuals in the group: a 'transcendent' power actualised their immanent unity. The state thus took ultimate priority over national community. Submission to the necessity of absolute rule, rather than mutual recognition among individual subjects, articulated the structure of the social organism. Similarly, collective recognition that finite strivings for radical autonomy would only lead to self-destruction could not emerge 'naturally' as the expression of religious experience, but only as blind faith in an absolute, transcendent authority that ultimately subdued the unconscious drives for power and self-sufficiency. The disciplinary and doctrinal authority of the transnational institutionalised church and its autocratic head, the pope, created the substance of religious society out of the strangers of a fallen world.

In Maistre's political philosophy states and churches were not creations of human will but historical products of supra-personal, ultimately unknowable events and processes. As such they remained historically particular: 'every possible form of government has shown itself in the world, and everyone is legitimate once it has been established' (Maistre 1971, p. 142). At the same time this historical relativism was tempered by a belief that certain generally acknowledged and 'eternal' laws structured the diversity of historical forms. All states and churches were marked by the inherent necessity of individual submission to the governance of an absolute power transcending the individual will. In most of his works Maistre imagined state and church as analogous in structure and unified and commingled with each other in the formation and development of national cultures: 'There should be a state religion, just as there is a state political system, or rather, religion and political dogmas mingled together form a *general* or *national mind sufficiently* strong enough to repress the aberration of individual reason which is of its nature the mortal enemy of any association' (Maistre 1971, p. 108). At the same time belief in the 'eternal' rules of all such associations, the total submission of the individual to a transcendent, mysteriously operating will was enforced and not just 'expressed' in a single Catholic Church ruled with absolute, 'infallible' power by a pope who could rightfully claim the authority to override the claims of individual states if the leaders of those states rebelled against the eternal laws of divine order. 'Religious truths', he insisted, 'are only general truths manifested and made divine within the religious sphere: so that it is impossible to attack one without attacking the law of the world.' As the absolute executor and judge of divine law, Maistre's papacy was the 'great *Demiurgus* of universal civilisation', the actual legislating, constitutive subject of human culture (Maistre 1971, pp. 131, 143). The ultramontane tendencies inherent in Maistre's search to stabilise ethical norms and ontological meaning in terrestrial representatives of absolute transcendent authority gained momentum throughout the nineteenth century, and were increasingly appropriated by the papacy itself. By the second half of the century they had become strong enough to fuel major conflicts both within the various Catholic churches in continental Europe and between these churches and the various movements striving to achieve communities of national identification. When the papacy asserted its radical claim to supreme authority in matters of norms and meaning at the Vatican Council of 1870, and presented infallible papal authority as the only remaining bulwark against the hubris of modern subjectivity and historical relativism, Maistre's framework for understanding state and church emerged from obscurity to trump the apologias for ecclesiastical revival in romantic thinkers like Schleiermacher and Chateaubriand.

2 Systematisation: church and state in the totality of history and culture

During the 'Restoration' period between the external reconstruction of European states at the Congress of Vienna and the reinvigoration of the political and cultural movements for reform and revolution during the 1830s, Coleridge (1772–1834) and Hegel (1770–1831) constructed ambitious, complex theoretical syntheses which both transformed romantic visions of personal, communal and ontological identity into systematic structures of differentiated totality, and posited these systems as the true meaning of the cultural world brought into being by the revolutionary age. Their claims for theoretical closure and historical reconciliation were tenuous, problematic and contested, but they set the agenda for most discussions of church–state relations in their own national languages during the decades between their deaths and the Revolution of 1848. In France, the equally ambitious but more polemical, historically unreconciled and prophetic writings of Félicité de Lamennais (1782–1854) and Comte Henri de Saint-Simon (1760–1825) dominated discussion and set a rather different agenda for the cultural critics and activists of succeeding generations.

Coleridge's *On the Constitution of the Church and State, According to the Idea of Each* (1830) marked a culminating, though cryptic synthesis of the metaphysical and historical theory of culture that had been in the making since his participation in the historical hopes, visions and disappointments of the romantic movement at the turn of the century. The starting point of Coleridge's analysis was the romantic reformulation of the Kantian distinction between idea and concept. The elements of his analysis – 'church' and 'state' – were not considered as generalising and descriptive terms abstracted from historical particulars, but constitutive agencies, potencies defined by their 'ultimate aim'. They embodied themselves, or made themselves manifest, within historical particulars in a dynamic process of actualisation. The determination of such 'Ideas' and their process of self-actualisation and self-revelation occurred within a totality of reciprocal relations. 'Church' and 'state' defined their identities in relation to each other, as dynamic elements of a cultural totality (itself an 'Idea'), as opposing dimensions of a field of forces constituted by their polarised difference, analogous to a magnetic field. In this theoretical framework, the difference between church and state was assumed to be constitutive of human culture. Collapse of one into the other, reduction of one to the other, would destroy the 'field' of relations that their difference produced. Moreover, as 'Ideas', church and state were understood as spiritual or 'psychic' powers that operated in individuals through processes of identification (either unconsciously as action possessed by the Idea, or self-consciously as transparent possession of the Idea), rather than 'objects', or empirically delimited institutions external to individuals. Church and state became 'real' in historical individuals through processes that 'cultivated' subjective identifications. Finally, as Ideas, church and state were marked by a constant tension between potentiality and actuality and between the agency of subjective energy and the objective forms of cultural institutions. The ultimate aim defining the cultural meaning of the institution was in a constant process of self-definition; at any particular historical moment the empirical institution was in a critical relationship with its own essence. Every organised form of subjective energy was a manifestation open to further transformation.[7]

Coleridge's analysis of the relations between church and state as dynamic potencies or incarnate, self-actualising Ideas, operated on two major levels. His first and most obvious concern in *On the Constitution* was the way in which the state as the legal and political institution of governance (the state in a limited and 'narrow' sense) and the church as the institution for communal identification were defined in relationship to each other in the constitution of the historical organism of a national culture or 'realm' (the 'state' in a broader, more general sense). In this context, the Idea or 'ultimate aim' of the state was the preservation of a dynamic equilibrium between the interests of permanence and progression in so far as they were objectified in differentiated, opposing forms of private property ownership or 'propriety' (landed property on the one hand and the 'movable and personal' property of mercantile, manufacturing, distributive and professional classes, on the other) organised into the legal vessels of 'estates' and represented in the political institutions of the legislative body or parliament. Within this sphere, the executive office, or kingship, the 'beam of the constitutional scales', constituted the disinterested, or general interest of balance and equilibrium (Coleridge 1976, pp. 29–30).

The opposing power to the state within the 'realm' of a national culture was the church, defined here as a worldly, national estate or 'order' whose idea or aim was the educational one of 'educing' an incorporation of national identity within the minds and consciences of its citizens. A professional/functional class (the clerisy) constituted the national church as an estate of the realm devoted to the preservation and development of historical traditions embodying the progression of the national Idea which connected isolated individuals to their common essence. The clerisy was also ideally organised into legislative bodies (Houses of Convocation) and headed by the executive office of kingship, since the person of the king symbolically represented the nation as a unified subject of will and judgement. The clerisy was sustained materially by a national reserve or endowment which Coleridge called the 'nationality'.

In some ways the national church, because it constituted identity rather than difference in the polar tensions of the culture, had priority over the

---

7 Coleridge expounds on the meaning of his use of the word 'idea' in the first chapter of his essay. See Coleridge 1976, pp. 11–22. The concept of polarity and its magnetic analogy is discussed throughout the text, but see especially pp. 24, 31, 86 n.95.

'state'. Yet Coleridge insisted that the actual sovereign within the realm was the national Idea, implicitly presented in the unconscious will of the people and manifest in the king. The national church was an 'immanent' institution, an estate of cultural functionaries called from within the world. It consisted of both the groups of scholars and thinkers who constantly worked through and clarified the national cultural heritage and the mass of educators and edifiers who carried the national idea into every town and village. The cultivating function of 'educing' the implicit wisdom of the national idea within the individual subject or person was distinguished from the 'civilisational' task of 'instruction' which gave individuals the means to pursue their personal interests within civil society in an efficient, rational and law-abiding manner. In England the earthly vessel of this function was historically manifest according to Coleridge in the institutions of the established Anglican Church. But Coleridge did not perceive the national church as necessarily confessional. Criteria for membership were criteria of national allegiance, in both political and cultural affairs, although this did clearly exclude those Catholics who saw their loyalty to a foreign state (the papacy) or to moral injunctions (like celibacy) that prevented full participation in national life, as taking priority over their national identifications (Coleridge 1976, p. 81).

At the same time it was clear that in an 'immanent' sense the national church was aptly named a 'church' because its primary aim was connected to the actualisation of the 'divine' idea within the mind and conscience of the national population. Thus 'theology', at least in the applied sense of the study of the manifest presence of the 'Idea' in national literature, philosophy and historical institutions, remained at the centre of national education and the clerisy's function (Coleridge 1976, pp. 46–9). But this function as Coleridge defined it was a condition of all cultures, not the contingent quality of special cultures, and present in primitive cultural realms like those of the ancient Celts, as well as in Greece, Rome, ancient Israel and Egypt; it was not the distinguishing mark of a Christian culture.

The reciprocal relations of state and church within the organic totality of national cultures was framed by Coleridge within a wider context of church–state relations that encompassed the immanent and transcendent dimensions in which national cultures themselves functioned as the 'state' pole in a differentiated identity of the whole. The Idea of the 'Christian Church' was not a part of the 'essential Being' of the national churches, but 'the sustaining, correcting and befriending Opposite' of the world of organised, historically immanent national cultures (Coleridge 1976, pp. 55–6, 114–15). The 'Idea' of this 'spiritual' church was to actualise the intelligent will as a participant in the ultimate ends of divine will, to pursue redemption from earthly finitude and identification with transcendent divinity. This church was a visible community engaged in public tasks of redemptive transformation within the world, but it could have no earthly organisation, hierarchy or visible head. It constituted the spiritual pole of the relationship between the divine and the world, between the absolute creative subject and its objectification in nature and history. Coleridge defined the relationship between the spiritual and the national churches as contingent, because the religious encounter with the infinite occurred as an act of freedom. The national culture could be directed by convictions flowing from a direct encounter with the divine and thus constructed from the perspective of eternal values, but it could also form itself as an articulation of its essential inner 'Idea' without this transcendent connection. The spiritual church was universal or 'catholic' but found its earthly existence not in a Catholic organisation (this false idolatry of the spiritual as a material, earthly organisation was represented by the papal 'anti-church'), but scattered throughout existing congregations of different confessions and among certain members of the national clerisy. Coleridge thus opposed in principle all utopian notions of an organised City of God on earth and maintained the distinction or differentiated polarity between transcendent and immanent in his general philosophy of culture. Relations to the divine Idea as an immanent potency, as the incarnate spirit unifying the elements of a national culture, were not simply equated with relations to the transcendent source of that Idea. The tension in Coleridge between a definition of the church as the 'immanent' cultural institution through which the national identity was articulated and infused into the population and the church as the institution that mediated between the transcendent and the immanent in a 'contingent' manner dependent on the acts and choices of individual subjects, remained a critical issue in nineteenth-century thinking about the ultimate authority for validating ethical norms and cultural meanings.

The theory of the relations between church and state that evolved in Hegel's philosophy of culture after 1800 was grounded in an idealist philosophical discourse that Hegel shared with Coleridge. But Coleridge remained closer to the language of Schelling's absolute idealism (with its emphasis on historically immanent ideas as potencies of an ultimately transcendent, pre-conceptual Absolute Being) than Hegel, who defined himself within the German Restoration debates as the primary opponent of Schelling's residual supernaturalism. Hegel's positions revealed some significant dimensions of Coleridge's distinctions but the particular spin he gave to these distinctions produced a theory with markedly different cultural and historical implications. Like Coleridge, Hegel began from a standpoint that assumed the priority of absolute unity and posited difference as differentiation within a totality in which every element was defined through its relation to other elements in a system of differences. The individuality that structured the differences of persons and nations emerged from a primal creative ground and moved with internal necessity towards some form of self-conscious reintegration. Hegel's dialectic of development was different from Coleridge's co-inhering polarities because of the much more prominent role it gave to the processes of historical transformation and to the 'sublation' (*aufhebung*) of differences within these processes. For Hegel, at least most of the time, it appeared that the Absolute did find its own fulfilment (made itself actual and manifest) in history and human consciousness, and thus could attain the public transparency of a philosophical science of totality.

In the Hegelian system, the 'state' constituted the fulfilment of the ethical life of the cultural nation. 'The state', he insisted, 'is the actuality of the ethical idea' (Hegel 1967b, p. 115). Coleridge's occasional use of the word 'state' (in the broader sense) as the term for the national cultural organism had a more literal political meaning in Hegel. It was in the complex legal, administrative, legislative and executive institutions of the political constitution that the process of subjective identification in which the individual subject recognised its freedom through identification with the publicly articulated collective will of the community reached its final form. 'Self-consciousness', he claimed, found 'its essence and the end and product of its activity, its substantive freedom' in the state (Hegel 1967b, p. 115). The political realm was not just the site for a rational balancing of interests articulated through functional classes or estates, but was expanded to encompass the realm of ethical identification that Coleridge had assigned to the national church. All forms of community based on feeling, historical traditions and identification with symbolic 'representations' found their fulfilment in the publicly articulated order of a state of laws in which the subject could recognise its participation in the 'idea' in a transparently rational, self-conscious fashion. The inevitable pluralism of religious confessions, confessional churches and religiously defined cultural communities (grounded in the particularity of their representational speech and the 'subjective' forms of their identification) provided the instigation for a historical movement to the 'higher' universality of the state as an ethical community.

The polarity between cultivation and instruction, between the national clerisy and secular teachers of instrumental knowledge, was also, in the Hegelian system, transformed into a dialectical movement within the realm of 'scientific' knowledge. Such knowledge was sustained and propagated by a class of intelligence, which found its appropriate place as an estate *within* the state. Religious communities were free of state control as long as they restricted themselves to the communicative interaction of private individuals and the articulation of personal conviction and feeling. At the point where they made claims on the public will and universal 'objective' truth they were subordinated to the higher ethical sphere of the political community and the objective knowledge of self-conscious 'science' (Hegel 1967b, p. 170). Demands for the complete union of church and state, in Hegel's view, implied the imposition of private conviction on public reason, the fanatical, ultimately destructive domination of the objective differentiated structures of cultural life by the undisciplined subjective convictions of a particular confessional group.

At the same time, however, Hegel's system posited religious faith as a subjective appropriation of an 'absolute' truth that transcended the finite limits of rationally directed will in the terrestrial institutions of the state. In religious experience, religious language and religious communities, the human subject took as its object, as the 'other' of its subjectivity, not the communal organism of the state but the absolute truth that actualised itself in the ethical practices and institutions of historical states. 'As intuition, feeling, representative knowledge', religious experience 'is concentrated upon God as the unrestricted principle and cause on which everything hangs. It thus involves the demand that everything else shall be seen in this light and depend on it for corroboration, justification and verification' (Hegel 1967b, p. 166). However for Hegel the truth of man's relation to the Absolute was articulated in religion in a limited form, in the experience of subjective feeling, in the language of representation, and in communities of 'irrational' identification.

Religious apprehension and manifestation of absolute truth thus found its fulfilment not in religion but in the rationally affirmed, self-conscious, fully transparent and objectively 'public' truths of philosophical or 'scientific' knowledge. Hegel merged Coleridge's universal spiritual church, the Church of Christ that transcended the limitations of terrestrial national cultures and their constitutions, into public institutions of absolute knowledge and into the 'clerisy' of academic philosophers, scholars and educators who articulated and taught that knowledge. Moreover, this knowledge was not free in relation to the state. Its content was the ethical substance of the state; it was the state's self-consciousness.

Hegel was quite ready to assert that religion was the 'groundwork' of the state and that states could demand that all their citizens assume membership in some form of religious community or church. Experience of the Absolute grounding and permeating the life of the individual subject was the basis for identification with the collective will of the state. The rational ethos of the universal political community articulated and objectified the religious experience of irrational and symbolic identification in public form, just as knowledge of the Absolute in the systematic structures and rational language of science raised the cognitive content of religious faith to a form appropriate to its content. Moreover, within even the most highly developed ethical state, there would always be a need for religious communities and religious language. The majority of the population would never attain the self-transparency of systematic knowledge but would always appropriate their knowledge of the Absolute through symbolic representation and irrational identification. Similarly, in the educational development of individuals the substance of ethical life was experientially absorbed through feeling and appropriated in the representational forms of narrative and myth before it could be intellectually appropriated. But this 'autonomy' of the religious sphere and ecclesiastical institutions, was a 'relative' autonomy restricted by the disciplined control and knowledge of the state and its philosophical 'clerisy'. Hegel and his disciples claimed to have 'reconciled' state and church, religious faith and philosophical knowledge, but the metaphysical and historical dynamics of the Hegelian dialectic implied an ultimate domination of state and philosophical knowledge over the church and religious faith: 'In contrast with the church's subjective conviction, the state is that which knows' (Hegel 1967b, p. 171). In the churches the Absolute was still made manifest as a 'transcendent' reality, as 'other' to the human subject. Hegel's theories of church and state appeared to defy such limitations and brought the transcendent within the sphere of human culture. It relegated those institutions in which subjective self-consciousness related to its own essence as an external transcendent reality to the status of stages on the way to a full appropriation of the substance of the transcendent within the immanent structures of history.

In the theories of Coleridge and Hegel, metaphysics and historical meta-narrative often seemed to be at the service of a comprehensive justification of the official or established relation between state, national culture and church within their own cultural communities. The Anglican Church and Evangelical State Church of Prussia revealed their intrinsic meaning in the theories of the self-styled intellectual spokesperson of the truth of the totality. Despite the obvious differences between Britain and Prussia regarding the relations of intellectuals to state and nation, and of state and nation to each other, Coleridge and Hegel shared an unmistakably Protestant perspective. Lamennais and Saint-Simon represented contrasting views from within the French and Roman Catholic traditions. Both articulated their fear of, and opposition to, the imagined (and remembered) anarchical social consequences of the liberation of self-interested individuals during the revolutionary period with a polemical demand for the restoration or construction of a hierarchical order of spiritual and temporal authority. Both were convinced that the restoration of spiritual order, general submission to the universal validity of certain unquestioned truths about human existence, took precedence over changes in the temporal order, and that only a reinvigorated, unified spiritual power could create a stable moral order among the anchorless, atomised individuals of a post-revolutionary society. Neither Lamennais nor Saint-Simon could imagine the creation of a moral order or ethical community in terms of the diverse incommensurabilities of national cultural 'ideas', but identified ethical order with the dominance of a universal, institutional church (on the model of the Roman Catholic papal church) over the limited sphere of politics and the particularist communities of national cultures. Both simplified the complex reciprocities and dialectical relations present in Hegel and Coleridge into a dichotomous relation between a universal ethical community based on spiritual identification through submission to absolute truth and the particular claims of self-interest regulated by external force.

Lamennais set the agenda for Restoration debates in France on church–state relations with his multivolume *Essay on Indifference in Religious Matters* (1817–23). Against the notion, certainly insinuated in Chateaubriand, that the reinvigoration of religious life was a matter of feeling and imagination rather than consensual submission to correct doctrine, Lamennais' apologia for Catholic Christianity was based on the claim that the Christian church possessed absolute infallible authority in matters of doctrine, and therefore constituted the only hope for social harmony. 'Re-establish authority!' he proclaimed in the preface to the *Essay*:

Order will be entirely reborn; truth will again be set on an unshakable base. The anarchy of opinion will cease; man will listen to man, minds united by One and the same faith will dispose themselves around their centre, which is God, and will draw life again from the source of light and life. (Lamennais 1817–23, I, p. 49)[8]

Only correct belief could provide the certainty required for the ethical discipline of egoistic interests and the formation of communal identifications. The feelings or reasonings of the individual subject could never attain such certainty on the basis of evidence; it could only be provided by the power of testimony that spoke with absolute authority. Such authority had two forms in Lamennais' analysis. It was implicitly present in the general reason or common sense (*sensus communis*) embodied in popular traditions and inherited familial wisdom in all human cultures. In this sense it constituted all of those truths that were simply accepted *a priori* because human existence was impossible without them. This general reason was thus not a creation or discovery of individuals but the consequence of a primal encounter with the divine will, a product of universal revelation. Common sense emerged from recognition of human finitude and of the dependence of the individual on the whole of which he or she was a part. In response to historical deviations from this revealed general reason, through individual or collective rebellion, the Church of Christ emerged both to re-enforce common sense with a public doctrine that had infallible authority, and to provide the sacraments of grace that would make it possible for fallen individuals to order their wills in conformity with the truths of authoritative belief. For Lamennais, therefore, the infallible authority of Christian doctrine derived from its role as the fulfilment and inheritor of the immanent truth of human history. But the source of this truth was ultimately transcendent, the divine revelation of God. Ethical order among human beings was synonymous with submission to divine truth. The official spokesperson for this authority on earth, synthesising, correcting and interpreting the corrupted and obscured intuitions of common consciousness, was God's deputy – the pope.

In *On Religion Considered in its Relations with the Political and Civil Order* (1825–6) Lamennais drew out the contemporary institutional consequences of the premises established in the *Essay*. Because of the tendencies among current states and political leaders, even those who claimed to support the church, to subordinate ecclesiastical authority to their own limited goals of external order and obedience to temporal authority, Lamennais moved towards a 'liberal' position in which the independence of the church from

---

8 Translation from Reardon 1985, p. 181.

political authority was judged as a precondition for the creation of a society in which the church could exert its proper spiritual authority over the temporal realm. The church would never be able to reform itself in order to play the role of spiritual authority in the creation of an ethical order unless it freed itself from the interference of temporal interests in its internal affairs. By 1829 Lamennais was insisting on the need for the church to claim the civil liberties – freedom of conscience, press and association – that would allow it to restore its autonomy against temporal interference under the reinvigorated authority of papal leadership. The alliance with aristocratic privilege and monarchical power had cost the church its inner soul and thus ultimately its authority over the mass of individuals in society. Ultramontanism, the superiority of the institutionalised spiritual power (the papacy) over temporal authority in the control of church organisation and internal affairs, was claimed as the only position from which a restoration of European culture as a moral order could be realised. In his influential journal *L'Avenir* (1830–1), Lamennais presented himself as the prophetic leader of a religious 'enlightenment' that 'will one day bring not only the French but all Europe into Catholic Unity, which eventually and by successive advances will draw to itself the rest of the human race and will constitute it, through an identical faith, into an identical spiritual society'.[9]

During the period 1829–32, a precarious balance between transcendent and immanent theories of religious authority marked the position of Lamennais and his followers. On the one hand, the Menaissians seemed to be concerned primarily with a transformation of the international Catholic Church into a purified spiritual church. Even their liberal politics and populist propaganda were meant to mobilise mass support and public opinion under the authority of papal power and established church doctrine. Their aims were focused on the submission of the individual to the absolute truth of divine revelation, a submission that rejected any interference of temporal interests in the relation between the subject and divine authority. At the same time Lamennais continued to insist that this spiritual church was implicitly present in the common consciousness of all cultural collectivities or 'peoples', and the preaching and journalism of his followers addressed this popular audience directly, suggesting the possibility of a spiritual, universal Catholicism outside of the existing church hierarchy. Public opinion would not only be mobilised but also taught to speak the truth that it already possessed in implicit form. The populist dimension in Menaissianism was

9 *L'Avenir*, 27 January 1831, cited in Reardon 1975, p. 93.

also evident in its strong support of the Polish nationalist rebels and exiles during their years of rebellion against tsarist domination (Parvi 1992).

After the revolutions of 1830 Lamennais' apocalyptic sense of the present moment as a turning point in human history, which would inaugurate the full realisation of European Christendom as a spiritual community under the international leadership of the papacy, reached a new intensity. However, when he was rebuffed by the ecclesiastical agency that he had heralded as the infallible spokesperson of truth and the leader of a spiritual reformation of European society, the unity of the two dimensions of his theory began to fall apart. In 1832 and 1834 the papacy rejected first the alliance with liberalism and then the theory of general reason embedded in the tradition of human culture and carried by the implicit consciousness of the 'people'. In a striking popular work, *Words of a Believer* (1834) Lamennais took on himself the role of prophet and leader with a direct appeal to the masses to rise to their own responsibility, to end privilege and injustice and to establish a divine kingdom of brotherly love. Lamennais rebuffed the established Catholic hierarchy by clearly placing his hopes in the people as the agent of divine truth and presenting himself as the people's spokesperson. A new populist Catholicism, a people's church separate from both states and organised churches, became Lamennais' imagined historical agent for the transformation of Europe into an ethical community. If the papacy would not speak for and lead this movement, a new clerisy would have to be created, and Lamennais seemed quite ready to assume leadership of such a new cadre of spiritual reformers. Lamennais still imagined the ethical order as grounded in submission to divine, transcendent authority, but this authority now articulated its will in the voice of the people. Within a few years the transcendent element in Lamennais' religious prophecy had almost disappeared. In his *Book of the People* (1837), virtually all of the authority for the creation of an ethical world came from 'below', from the innate genius of national peoples and their immanent historical experience. Moreover, as Lamennais moved towards the authority of the unconscious will of the people as the foundation of spiritual community and a new church, the theory of a national church, and of people's churches organised in a federation of national movements, also emerged more prominently. With breathtaking rapidity Lamennais had shifted his role from a servant of transcendent truth and papal authority to a spokesperson for popular national consciousness.

As a prophet of the immanent ethos of national development, Lamennais' intellectual itinerary culminated in intellectual proximity to the site where that of his compatriot, Henri de Saint-Simon, had begun. Since the turn

627

of the century Saint-Simon's various historical projects had focused on the construction of a new 'organic' ethical order in European Christendom. From the time of his first published manifestos calling for a new European order in the first decade of the century, however, Saint-Simon had imagined the new truth that would organise European society and ground its ethical principles as a scientific creation, a body of verified scientific laws produced by a clerisy of scientists who would exert their 'spiritual' control over society in a secular and post-Christian 'church'. As rational knowledge displaced faith in authority as the organising principle of the social organism, secular scientists inherited the mantle of the church as carriers of the 'spiritual power' (Saint-Simon 1964, pp. 1–20).

Disappointed by the response of the scientists to his calls for an international scientific clerisy, Saint-Simon had moved towards presenting himself as the prophet of a 'New Christianity' by the end of his life in 1825. The authority of the spiritual power over temporal rulership in society and the priority of the unity of the social organism over the pursuit of individual self-interest could not be sustained by rational knowledge alone. The new meanings that would motivate ethical identification and produce the new organic order were now ascribed to a renewed revelation of the universal truth of Christianity as a religion of brotherly love. Like Lamennais, Saint-Simon saw his role as the chosen leader of a divine mission and called upon his readers to 'Hearken to the voice of God that speaks through me' (Saint-Simon 1964, p. 116). Saint-Simon's vision of the new moral order was grounded in a revealed, absolute and infallible truth, and it found its fulfilment in a universal earthly society produced through complete identification of all individuals with this truth and its representatives. The 'church' reappeared as an intellectual clerisy, not legitimated by tradition or tied to the established institutionalised churches, but taking its authority from the implicit unspoken will of the people. From the standpoint of the absolute claims of this future church society the temporal order of states could only be a fetter on the historical incarnation of spiritual community. The spiritual church swallowed up national churches and political states in its triumphant construction of an integral, 'organic' order on the foundations of a loving practice that flowed from the revelation of true doctrine.

3   Practice: the intellectual movements of the mid-nineteenth century

By 1830 the prophetic visions of both Lamennais and Saint-Simon had begun to take on the historical role of party programmes for groups of disciples. As the 'schools' of adherents grew and faced the challenges presented by political and social change, the tensions and oppositions within their intellectual positions became manifest in school divisions. Such partisan fragmentation was also the fate of the theoretical legacies of Coleridge and Hegel. In the middle decades of the century intellectual coteries, movements and 'parties' intent on bringing into historical actuality aspects of the theoretical positions inherited from the synthetic thinkers of the 1820s dominated the discourse on relations between church and state. Despite an enormous diversity of positions both within and across national cultures, some general similarities in these movements, crossing national lines, can be constructed.

The 1830s and 1840s witnessed, first of all, a significant growth in the influence and public presence of the movement for inner reform (purification, spiritualisation, unification) within the established, dominant confessional churches. This movement, led by academics, churchmen and intellectual publicists of the younger generation (born around 1800) was committed to the general aim of transforming existing churches into authentic exemplars of an ideal 'spiritual' church. In such a church the direct authority of transcendent truth would provide the organising centre for an association of believers free from the interference of state bureaucrats and secular politicians. The historical and cultural implications of the general movement to emancipate the church from state interference and inner political corruption were not always clear and produced divisions among the church reformers. The projected cultural mission of a 'free' church was to transform the atomised individuals of post-revolutionary civil society into an ethical organism. In order to accomplish this task the church needed not only 'freedom' to control its internal affairs in the making of appointments and the establishment of authoritative doctrine, but also the freedom to engage in its moralising mission through educational, publicistic and philanthropic institutions. Moreover, this moralising mission entailed direct confrontation with the state for control of the norms of the domestic sphere – especially relating to sexuality, marriage and child-rearing – as well the control of educational and charitable, social-welfare institutions. The movement to free the church from the state thus rapidly became, implicitly and often explicitly, a political movement with the aim of constructing a 'Christian State'. In the second half of the century battles were fought over the control of higher education, over the creation or rehabilitation of religious orders to fulfil the role of social and educational agencies, and over divorce and marriage laws. As democratic institutions and parties evolved after the 1860s, divergent views of the relationship between church and state and about the appropriate role of church society in shaping the ethos of a national culture became a familiar element in the conflicts among conservative, liberal and socialist movements and their political organisations.

In France, the movement for inner church reform instigated by the early work of Lamennais and expressed in the brief outburst of liberal Catholicism in *L'Avenir* illustrated the various elements of this pattern of development. Lamennais' most distinguished, active and influential disciples during the years of *L'Avenir*, Henri Lacordaire (1802–61) and Count Charles de Montalembert (1810–70), did not follow their mentor in his break with the papacy. They retained their commitment to an inner, 'loyal' reform of the Catholic hierarchy. This did not necessarily imply a complete rejection of the liberal and populist elements of Lamennais' view of church reform but it did involve the reinterpretation of these elements within a framework that rejected any immanent (cultural or natural) foundation for the spiritual truths according to which a Christian society was to be reconstructed. The truth did not come from the people but was brought to them as a transforming transcendent answer to the dilemmas of their fallen existence. Lacordaire gave a new urgency to the development of forms of worship, preaching and propaganda that would speak to the needs of the people for salvation; Montalembert appealed to the public to support religious control of educational institutions; while Frederic Ozanam (1813–53) tried to meet the sufferings of the victims of the post-revolutionary society with the recreation of ecclesiastical charitable orders. These practices presented a vision of the church informed by authoritarian populism and directed to meet the spiritual and physical needs of individuals victimised by liberal political and economic policies. By the 1840s this vision had been carried into the public discourse of political debate not only by parliamentarians like Montalembert, but also by ecclesiastical officials like the Abbé Félix Dupanloup (1802–78) and the polemical journalist Louis Veuillot (1813–83). It found philosophical expression in the work of Louis Bautain (1796–1867) who attacked the 'pantheism' implicit in the hypothesis of a *sensus communis* that found its perfected final form in Christian truth, and asserted the transcendent 'otherness' of religious truth as the only viable foundation for a Christian moral order.

As Lamennais' personal intellectual itinerary after 1834 suggests, it was difficult to sustain the viability of a universal 'people's church', a church that found its authority not in centralised hierarchy and submission to a transcendent power, but in the common identity of an immanent 'revelation' and communal ethic that pre-existed the differentiations of civil society. In France this populist version of the universal church tended, as in Lamennais' case, to lose its distinctively ecclesiastical identity and merge into religiously framed conceptions of the nation as a moral community. It was quickly swallowed up by more secular ideologies for national identity or ethical socialism that perceived the ecclesiastical movements as rivals.

The authoritarian, neo-orthodox, activist, Catholic pietism of the Mennaissian movement represented by Lacordaire and Montalembert and mobilised at a popular level by battles with the anti-clericalism of liberal and republican programmes for secular control of cultural institutions, especially after 1870, had its counterparts among the younger generation of theologians, priests and lay intellectuals in Catholic regions throughout Europe, most notably in western and southern Germany. In Prussia, and after 1871, in the Bismarckian German Empire, the movement for Catholic renewal struggled with the cultural hegemony exerted by a Protestant majority that made claim to represent the national ethos. Resistance to attempts to subordinate the institutions of the church to the political instruments of this hegemony led both to the creation of a powerful Catholic political party (*Zentrumspartei*) and a 'cultural war' (*Kulturkampf*) between the church and the national state that lasted from 1871 to 1887.[10] Ultramontane sentiments grew with the need to secure moral and institutional authority for resisting the acts of the state. A liberal commitment to rights of free speech and association was often combined with an anti-liberal, authoritarian vision of an ideal Christian state and society.

The authoritarian, neo-orthodox movement for church reform and the mobilisation of popular religiosity, however, also had significant counterparts in the established Anglican and Evangelical churches of England and northern Germany. In these areas of a nationally shaped Protestant culture, however, the vitality of the merger of church reform with the idea of a national church and a populist politics had greater sustaining power, producing a more balanced tension among and within ecclesiastical reformers between the authoritarian, liberal and populist conceptions of a Christian church society and a Christian state.

In England, the Coleridgean legacy was divided among ecclesiastical reformers between the transcendent orientation of the Oxford Movement and the more loosely defined 'broad' church reformers who retained a

---

10 For recent analysis of the Kulturkampf and its historical background see Ross 1998 and Smith 1995, pp. 19–49.

stronger sense of the immanent historical authority of a national church. The major theoreticians and public spokespersons of the Oxford Movement – John Henry Newman (1801–90), John Keble (1792–1866), John Pusey (1800–82) and Richard Hurrell Froude (1803–36) – set out with the aim of transforming the established Anglican Church into a true Church of Christ. Their self-assigned task was to purify the church of its temporal corruptions, to lead it back towards a strict submission to the authority of transcendent spiritual truth and the institutional forms which would express that submission. The autonomy of the church, its emancipation from interest politics, was as central to their sense of the church's mission to create a Christian society as it was to the Catholic followers of Lamennais.

The members of the Oxford Movement were convinced that the goals of cultivation and moralisation that Coleridge had assigned to the national church could only be fulfilled if the national church became an expression of the universal church, and asserted its disciplining control over socially disintegrative, self-interested egoism on the basis of universal and super- natural authority. Newman (before 1845) and Keble saw the Established Church of England as one branch (along with the Greek and Latin) of the universal Catholic Church (Newman 1967, p. 72). The authority of its ministry derived from apostolic succession, through the continuity of the sacrament of ordination. The church presented itself as a representative of transcendent authority over against the nation in a number of forms. In its creeds it provided 'objective' spiritual truth that was not open to subjective, individualising interpretation. The Protestant tendency to emphasise the priesthood of all believers and the authority of scripture was subordinated to the authority of the church. The process of moral 'cultivation' was redefined as submission, as self-sacrifice. Faith was not so much a subjective feeling of encounter and identification, as an act of surrender to a higher authority. In its liturgical conceptions the church was to emphasise the vertical relation to transcendent authority; the focus was on worship, prayer and ceremonies of submission. In the sacraments the presence of God as the transcendent Other was to be made symbolically manifest. The association among believ- ers was mediated through their relations to the transcendent. All immanent order was a product of this relationship to the transcendent divinity.[11]

---

11 The positions of the Oxford Movement were presented in a series of ninety 'Tracts for the Times' published between 1833 and 1841. They have been excerpted in Chadwick 1960. The implicit politics of the mission of internal church reform is analysed in an essay on John Keble in Prickett 1976, pp. 91–119, and its implications for social policy in Rowlands 1989. Roe 1966 represents at least the beginnings of an attempt to place the Oxford Movement in a European context.

The puritanical moralising zeal of the Oxford reformers, their often-intolerant demands for absolute authority as the only therapy for self-doubt and the collapse of spiritual discipline, indicated the extent to which they based their strict neo-orthodoxy on very contemporary concerns about the threatening disintegration of individual morality and social discipline. Their demands for absolute authority arose as therapeutic demands from the inner conflicts of the romantic subject. They were not so much defenders of the status quo – which they perceived as rampant with corruption – as fervent, pious, authoritarians. Despite disclaimers about any positive interest in politics, however, their missionary zeal to bring about a new spiritual discipline through submission to transcendent authority could not be separated from the 'immanent' issues of social order and national identity. They believed it was precisely the transformation of the national church into a branch of the universal church of Christ that would resolve the problematic disintegration of the nation as an ethical organism. The church was to free itself from submission to politics, in order to present itself, in purified form, as the ultimate arbiter of the political realm. Moreover, since the Oxford reformers, unlike the Menaissians in France, were prepared to alienate the 'nation' in order to purify the church (for the ultimate good of the nation) they found themselves drawn to a conservative politics, seeking protection for the church's autonomy (and monopoly of at least some of the means of moralisation) through support of the politics of traditional privilege and personal monarchical authority.

Although not 'officially' a member of the Oxford Movement, the young William Ewart Gladstone, in his first published work, *The State in its Relations with the Church* (1838), tried to draw out some of the implications of its ecclesiastical and theological positions for the task of transforming the nation into an ethical community. For Gladstone, reform of the Established Church provided an opportunity to create a new coalition of state and church for the project of constructing the nation as a Christian moral order. In his view political society and ecclesiastical society overlapped as two dimensions of a single order. The state as well as the church was a site for moralisation and the transformation of self-interest into communal identification. The state had moral ends, which were provided with transcendent authority by the church. The church was to serve ideally as the 'conscience' of the state, the subjectively internalised paternal authority that cemented the bonds of brotherhood that shaped the nation. The state thus had a legitimate interest in sustaining a unified church and a unified doctrine. But this church was fundamentally a national church; the historical reality of submission to the transcendent will operated not in some universal realm ruled by a spiritual church, but always within the positive historical development of the national community (Butler 1982; Helmstadter 1985, pp. 3–42).

Gladstone's tendency to merge the state and church was also present in the 'liberal' or 'Broad Church' wing of post-Coleridgean church reformers. The loose group of religious philosophers (Frederick Maurice) and historical critics (Connop Thirlwall, J. C. Hare) gathered under this rubric are usually perceived primarily in terms of their continuation of Coleridge's interest in the historical processes by which the divine idea manifested itself within the national community and its intellectual 'clerisy'. In general they tended to emphasise the ways in which the national church should be broadened to encompass the totality of religious positions within the culture, positions that were themselves dimensions of a historical dialectic in which oppositions were eventually grasped as reciprocal dimensions of the national organism. The function that Gladstone fulfilled in relation to the Oxford Movement (clarifying its political dimension) was provided in this case by the famous schoolmaster of Rugby, Thomas Arnold (1795–1842). Like Gladstone, Arnold was driven by a vision of the state as an ordering of social life that went beyond the balancing of interests and included the production of moral life among its subjects. Church and state were thus institutions aiming at the same end. Their institutional separation might have been historically justified in the past but it was not intrinsically necessary to the perfection of their goals. Arnold perceived an immanent historical development towards an ethical society in the history of the state. The church was a representation of this dimension as long as the state had not fulfilled its own purpose. Once the spiritual community of the church was internalised as the conscience of the nation, however, the church would become superfluous, or would simply become the real substance of the political order, now characterised as a 'Christian Kingdom': 'the state in its highest perfection becomes the church' (Arnold 1874, pp. 331–2). Unlike Gladstone however, Arnold thought that in order for the church to fulfil itself in this fashion it would have to encompass the broad spectrum of confessional difference within its doctrines and institutions. In Arnold, dependence on transcendent authority for the tasks of moral reform tended to become a 'historical' stage in the development of Christian community.

What we might called the ambivalent Menaissian inheritance was also carried forward and developed by the two most distinguished English Catholic intellectuals of the nineteenth century: John Henry Newman, who had followed the logic of the search for a secure ground for meaning and value in a 'conversion' to Catholicism in 1845, and Lord John Acton (1834–1902), who had enriched his indigenous Catholic heritage with a cultural education in both French and German traditions of Catholic church renewal and cultural reformation. Both struggled with the relationship between their own affirmation of faith in the transcendent authority of Catholic doctrine as the only stable ground for truth, meaning and moral certainty in a world of subjective interpretation, cultural relativism and historical difference and their equally strong critical consciousness of the ways in which the articulation of that authority might itself be deceptively connected to the particularities of finite subjectivity and historical contingency. Both were caught in the paradox of seeking to affirm the embodiment of absolute truth in historical revelation and historical institutions, while expressing their critical distance from any particular terrestrial claim, like that of Pius IX in his Syllabus of Errors of 1864, to fully represent this embodiment. Newman became, next to Kierkegaard perhaps, the most acute nineteenth-century analyst of the ways in which the absolute commitment of religious faith operated therapeutically to still the psychological need for certainty only if it was not actually perceived as a product of psychological need, but rather as an encounter with a transcendent reality outside the self.[12] Acton dealt more directly with the political paradox that the critical ability to assert human freedom against the terrestrial determinations of history required a conscience formed in absolute obedience to a power that spoke with the voice of transcendent truth.[13] Both remained in the Catholic Church after 1870, reluctantly subordinating their critical consciousness to the need for an absolute moral power, speaking with transcendent authority, in order to sustain their own moral 'independence' from the corrupting influence of immanent historical powers.[14]

In Prussia the inner reform of the Evangelical State Church according to the ideals of a free church operating as the deputy of transcendent authority

12 Newman's moral reasoning concerning the necessity and the paradoxical near-impossibility of religious faith and his account of the ways in which the search for the absolute certainty of faith determined his intellectual itinerary and conversion to Roman Catholicism are articulated in Newman 1870 and 1967.
13 Acton published no books during his lifetime. His views were expressed in occasional essays and lectures. Two collections that highlight his writing on liberty and the relationship between moral authority, transcendent truth and terrestrial powers are Acton 1952 and 1958.
14 There is a thoughtful comparison of Acton and Newman's responses to the papal claim to infallibility in Chadwick 1998, pp. 115–38.

became a part of the political agenda of the state after 1840. Two spokespersons for this agenda, the legal philosopher Friedrich Julius Stahl (1802–61) and the royal adviser and ministerial official Christian Bunsen, reproduced the Gladstone/Arnold tension from the perspectives of conservative and liberal political reform.

Stahl approached the question of state–church relations from the perspective that ethical communities were not produced through a process of immanent development manifesting and actualising the inherent 'idea' of the national culture, but through a double (political and religious) act of submission to authority. The political structure of the national organism was restricted to the coercive imposition of obedience to abstract norms. The subjective ethical transformation of this external obedience into a willed, internal obedience was the function of the church. The national church and the Church of Christ were synonymous. The task of interpreting the guiding principle of the national idea and cultivating it among individual subjects was not a job for the philosophers and historians of a secular clerisy but a theological and ecclesiastical undertaking, a task of interpreting and preaching the divine will of a transcendent divinity. The state became a Christian state, an 'ethical realm', when external submission to coercive force became voluntary obedience to a higher will. But this internalisation of the will of the father could never be fully accomplished within the society of finite, 'fallen' individuals. The 'ethical realm' would always remain a divided world in which internal obedience to the divine will could never fully displace the necessity for external obedience to divinely instituted coercive power.[15]

For Stahl, the purification of German Protestantism for the purposes of fulfilling its cultural function entailed a return to the absolute validity of the confessional creeds and institutions of Reformation Lutheranism. Bunsen, on the other hand, saw the development of church doctrine and institutions in terms of progressive historical development of the Christian idea. This development involved an expansion of church membership to all members of the national community and an assimilation of church doctrine to the liberal ideals of individual autonomy and voluntary communal identification. The full appropriation of the Christian idea demanded the participation of all individuals as autonomous subjects in the ethical life of the nation and state. The only legitimate authority in a free church and a

---

15 Stahl's positions were theoretically formulated in Stahl 1833, esp. II, pt. 1, pp. 70–190. The church reform component of his theory was explicated in Stahl 1840.

free state was the authority internalised by a free inward disposition. Liberty of individual conscience and therefore political liberty were prerequisites for the actualisation of the true church. On the other hand, political liberty could only be sustained by consciousness of participation in divine authority. Christianity only became real in associative life. National culture and the state were essential to the substance of the Christian idea as a life lived in full transparent participation in the community. The perfected state was the objectified ethical life of the Christian religious community. For Bunsen, as for Arnold, therefore, the perfected church ultimately overlapped with the perfected state. The goal of church reform was the union of the spiritual and temporal dimensions of being in ethical life. Its promise for and vision of the future was 'that the harmonious reciprocity of power between heaven and earth is restored, the chasm between the visible and the invisible is spanned, the barrier between the secular and spiritual is broken down' (Bunsen 1845, pp. 84–6).

Although Bunsen, like Stahl, saw himself as an heir of Schelling and the intellectual traditions of romantic historicism, his position in the 1840s and 1850s often seemed virtually indistinguishable from mainstream Hegelianism. The difference lay in his claim that the ultimate fulfilment of the divine idea on earth occurred within the actual experience of the ethical life of the community, rather than in philosophical, 'scientific' comprehension of that life. A correlate of this difference was that Bunsen also interpreted the fulfilment of the Christian idea in the state as a fulfilment within the associative life of a political organised Christian culture, but not specifically within its governmental and legal institutions. During the 1830s and 1840s, however, the Hegelian inheritance was itself undergoing a process of fragmentation and revision. Most significantly, the divisions of the school over the question of whether or not reason was fully actualised in the historical present was displaced in the late 1830s by divisions over the transcendent and immanent content of the divine idea. In the critical works of David Friedrich Strauss, Bruno Bauer and Ludwig Feuerbach the divine idea was redefined as the idea of humanity or 'human essence'. Religious experience was revealed as Man's relation to his essential self, projected into stories of the relation between mankind and a transcendent other. In this radical process of humanisation and historicisation of the relation between sacred and secular, the transcendent and the immanent, the polar relationship between church and state as two forms of community was first dissolved and then reconstituted in a purely secular fashion. Once the nature of the transcendent as a self-projection of the immanent was understood, church society dissolved into political society. In a 'free' state the transcendent became simply the essentially human, constituted as the normative identity of the political community. The representation of human essence in religious dogma and myth was translated into the secular activity of representing the evolution of mankind in its cultural forms. Politics displaced religious practice as the site of authentic ethical life, and cultural studies (literature, science, philosophy and art) displaced theology as the true self-representation and self-comprehension of that life. The language of church and state, however, could be reconstituted in metaphorical form to mark the difference between essence and existence within the realm of secular, this-worldly being. The relations of representation and rational self-understanding directed towards the meaning of the essentially human could be articulated in the activity of a scientific or aesthetic or philosophical clerisy of a 'church of humanity'. The worship of essential humanity as the normative model for individual existence and the disciplined self-conscious pursuit of the practices of human self-realisation (love and work) could become elements of a 'religion' of humanity. The concept of transcendence was restricted to a purely historical meaning – marking the distinction between the historical present and the goal of historical development, between the actuality of empirical humankind and the essential humanity that was being created through the dynamics of development within this actuality. 'Church' and 'state' thus still retained a core of meaning in referring to the difference between present and future, appearance and essence. But the persistence of this difference also required the creation of a clerisy to mediate 'Ideas' or essential ends with the realities of existing practices. The 'church' of the already illuminated and sanctified, and thus of potential educators and edifiers, could be reconstituted as an institutionalised body of intellectual midwives mediating between present estrangement and future reconciliation, present misery and future happiness, between the present gap between essence and existence and their future reconciliation. At both national and universal 'human' levels, the problems articulated in theories of church and state did not disappear in the process of their translation into secular, humanist terms. The conceptual distinctions articulated in those theories maintained their relevance within all secular ideologies and secular movements whose aim was a process of historical redemption leading to the formation of an ethical community.[16]

16 This process of translation as appropriation of substance and rejection of 'form' is very evident in three major works of Hegelian humanism: Bauer 1840, Feuerbach 1841 and Strauss 1840–1.

The translation of church–state theory into secular ideological conflict was also present in France among the heirs of Saint-Simon. Beginning with Auguste Comte's early defection in the 1820s, the school split into two 'ecclesiastical' parties. Those who went Comte's way tended to believe in the power of empirical knowledge and rational understanding to comprehend the totality of human culture in its historical development, and thus gave priestly status to men of science. By the 1840s, however, Comte was himself elaborating this science of humanity in its historical totality into an ethical practice and religious system, which mimicked the liturgical, sacramental and organisational patterns of the Catholic Church, including the construction of a clerical hierarchy presided over by a 'Pope of Humanity'. The other wing of the school, building on Saint-Simon's final prophecies of a future practical religion of fraternal love, placed their hopes in the ability of the emancipated power of the passions, of sexuality and love, to create a new ethical order. Like the Comtean Positivist Church, the Saint-Simonians created an elaborate hierarchical organisation and set of rituals around their commitment to correct theories of the idea of humanity and its historical actualisation.[17]

The theoretical and institutional separation of church and state was grounded on the perception that life in community was built on a double relationship, to the 'others' within the horizontal relations of communication, sociability and power, and to the 'other' beyond these relations, which gave them ultimate meaning, which 'grounded' them in a 'higher' truth and a 'higher' reality. To what extent was this 'other' itself historical? To what extent could this 'absolute' other be appropriated within the horizontal relations of associative life? Questions about the historicity of meaning, essence, truth, were at the core of nineteenth-century theories of the relations between church and state.

4   Historicism and church–state relations: the case of Ranke

Historical narratives of cultural development and historical philosophies attempting to mediate the dynamic relations between essential truths and particular empirical contingencies played a prominent role in the formulation and presentation of different perspectives on the church–state relation

---

17 The works of Frank Manuel provide the most sympathetic accounts of the religious and ecclesiastical components in the Saint-Simonian and Comtean traditions. See especially Manuel 1962, but also Charlton 1983.

in nineteenth-century thought. One could say that it was the problem of historicity above all that provided the central issue in the discussion of relations between the sacred and the secular, the temporal and the spiritual, the transcendent and the immanent. At both the personal and collective levels, historical understanding was the primary medium for establishing the meaning of the particular, and the historical process was imagined as the site where the ethical community was to be realised.

The historians Jules Michelet (1798–1874) and Lord Acton might serve as exemplary figures for displaying the contrast between immanent and transcendent historical perspectives. Identifying himself with the dynamic life forces of the divine idea in its national form, Michelet merged the sacred truth of ultimate identity with the divine Idea into the historical construction of the national Idea as an ethical community. The separation of ecclesiastical institutions from the cultural forms of a common national life became a hindrance rather than an aid to the ultimate reconciliation of human beings with their divine essence. Standing on the ground of faith in the transcendent reality of truth and value embodied in Christian revelation and its mediating institutions, Acton portrayed historical development in terms of the critical dichotomous relations between universal values grounded in transcendent truths that entered into historical reality through human actions motivated by the commands of conscience grounded in religious faith and the immanent contingencies and relative necessities of an associative life shaped by the interests and desires of finite, 'fallen', creatures. It was in the work of Leopold von Ranke, the 'father' of modern historiography, however, that this dichotomy was most clearly displayed as an internal dynamic of historical understanding and representation.

In 1841 Ranke was appointed official historiographer of the Prussian state, an appointment which he saw as a confirmation of his personal identification with the 'partisan commitment to the positive and historical' (Ranke 1867–90, LIII/LIV, p. 273) of the 'Christian-German' reform party that had come to power with the accession of Frederick William IV to the throne in 1840, and which included Schelling as its official philosopher and Bunsen and Stahl as two of its most prominent ideologues. Three sets of tensions marked this convergence of Ranke's historiographical perspective and the historical actuality of the Prussian regime: between national culture and state, between immanent and transcendent divinities as foundations of the church and ethical life, and between the 'positive and historical' on the one hand, and a meta-historical narrative of personal redemption and cultural reconciliation on the other.

From the time of his formative political awakening in 1816–18 and sympathetic identification with the cultural politics of nationalist student fraternities and their heroes from the Wars of Liberation against Napoleonic France, Ranke's outlook was framed within a tense duality between two models of ethical community. His most obvious commitment, at least during the 1820s, was to a conception of social relations, law and political institutions as expressive 'objectifications' of the distinctive characteristics of the innate 'national genius', the collective subjective individuality or spirit of national 'peoples'.[18] His first major historical work conceptualised modern European history as an evolving family of national individualities; his second demonstrated the impossibility of successfully imposing centralised political uniformity on the vital, intractable resistance of national cultures (Ranke 1824, 1827).

This romantic historicist conception of political institutions as the external expressive forms of the underlying, pre-rational identities of national peoples remained a critical component of Ranke's political vision, but by the early 1830s it was increasingly in tension with a different model, also traceable to Ranke's student years, a model in which ethical life was conceived as the voluntary association of autonomous individuals obeying only those laws they had freely imposed upon themselves. For Ranke this type of intersubjective identity was grounded not in the pre-rational 'nature' of the collective national subject, but in a shared commitment to the transcendent grounds of autonomous selfhood through religious faith. As Ranke became disillusioned about the prospects of a spontaneous political formation of the people into an ethical community after 1830, his works tended to emphasise the need for a transcendent foundation of ethical life. The organising force of 'Ideas' as the inherent essences of national cultures was matched by the power of transcendent 'Ideas' to intervene in the immanent historical process. In his great multivolume works of the 1830s and 1840s, *The History of the Popes* and *German History during the Age of the Reformation*, the transcendent religious 'Idea' provided the objective ground for the transformation of the national 'Idea' into the unique moral self of the state. His histories of the emergence of modern nation states were not restricted to describing the expressive actualisation of national individualities, but became histories of relations between religious universality and

18 This emphasis on innate national identity was evident from an early essay (1818) entitled 'Aus den Papieren eines Landespfarrers' in Ranke 1964–75, III, pp. 474–82 to his political essays of the 1830s like 'Ueber die Trennung und Einheit von Deutschland' (1832), in Ranke 1867–90, XLIX/L, p. 134.

national individuality, between church and state, between transcendent and immanent deities.[19]

This shift in Ranke's conceptions of ethical life towards a tense reciprocity between obedience to the inner voice of national identity and obedience to the transcendent truth of universal religion was tied to a change in his religious conceptions. His earlier loyalty to an impersonal pantheistic deity informing all natural and historical phenomena (Ranke 1964–75, I, pp. 117, 141–2) was gradually displaced by belief in a transcendent personal divinity as creator-father (Ranke 1964–75, I, pp. 119–20, 126–8, 131, 155). Religious obedience now operated primarily as a way to discipline the rebellious, sinful, fallen self, rather than to express identity with one's innate 'nature'. As Ranke, in the wake of what he perceived as the revolutionary threat of elemental forces of social disintegration and egoistic self-interest after the revolutions of 1830, turned his attention to problems of the discipline and moralisation of nature, his theology became more patriarchal, personalist and transcendent. The authentic freedom that informed the idea of ethical community as an association of self-legislators required a purifying restoration of the living essence of personhood through voluntary submission to the revealed will of a transcendent father. Ranke concluded the final volume of *The History of the Popes* with the hopeful projection that contemporary Christianity was moving towards a recovery of the original apostolic faith in 'the true and eternal principles of pure and spiritual religion'. Faith in immutable transcendent truth would 'appease and reconcile all enmities': 'High above all conflict – this hope we can never relinquish – there will yet arise from the ocean of error the unity of conviction... the pure and simple consciousness of the ever-enduring all-pervasive presence of God' (Ranke 1901, III, pp. 173–4).[20] But could this spiritual apprehension of the purified Christian idea, which informed spiritual communion under the universal rule of a transcendent father, also forge a genuine reconciliation between the concrete individualised life of national cultures and universal forms of ethical community? This, for Ranke, was the 'German Question' as addressed in his *History of Germany during the Age of the Reformation*.

In Ranke's account of the German Reformation, Luther played a heroic role in redefining the relations between the sacred and secular orders. First,

---

19 See especially Ranke 1867–90, XXXVII, pp. 1–8; and the opening pages of Ranke 1925–6.
20 This passage was excised after the first edition and does not appear in Ranke 1867–90.

he rediscovered the transcendent foundations of moral life in their original apostolic purity, freed from all of the corrupting historical accretions of material interest, overweening personal power, and centralising institutional ambition. Second, he connected the re-established relation to the transcendent to the historical demands of the German national idea as it pushed for self-determination and self-expression. The universal Christian idea organised and energised the slumbering potency of the national genius, providing it with transcendent foundations and a world-historical, universal mission. Germany made its historical bid to become an organised political self, to attain the moral personality of a state, under the guidance of universal religious values internalised as the Protestant conscience.

However, Ranke also tied the Reformation to 'the totality of the spiritual movement' from which it originated and which it infused with a new energy and an epochally significant historical form (Ranke 1925–6, II, p. 69). The Reformation was both a theological and a political event in a pan-European sense. By recovering the purity of the original Christian idea as a direct relation between the autonomous subject and its infinite source it redirected all of Europe back to its ethical foundations. By emancipating the political realm from ecclesiastical domination (separating the sphere of the state from the sphere of religion) it served as a general exemplar of the emancipation of the concrete historical life of national peoples from the chains of a centralising, hierarchical spirituality. Paradoxically, the release of personal piety from earthly mediations, its rediscovery as a direct encounter of the finite human subject with the transcendent divine personality, also released the immanent impulses animating the associations of national life. The Reformation thus projected, as a future goal and redefined historical purpose, the reconciliation of immanent and transcendent 'Ideas', of maternal and paternal forms of divinity, in the 'deeper life' from 'which they both emanated' (Ranke 1925–6, I, p. 3).

Ranke concluded his history of the German Reformation with a chapter on secular humanist scholarship and artistic culture in the sixteenth century. The religious reconstitution of the relation to transcendent authority stimulated the rediscovery of the earthly wisdom of the ancients and also promoted the free scientific investigation of the immanent relations of natural and historical life. By instigating this great movement of European scholarship, art and philosophy, Ranke believed the Reformation had played an essential role in 'universal spiritual progress', even though the completion of the Reformation project – the creation of an integrated 'positive and

historical' European culture – remained a present task and future hope
(Ranke 1925–6, IV, p. 37).

Ranke did not perceive his own time and culture as the actuality of
the reconciliation of transcendent and immanent meaning, or of the integration of church and state as forms of life lived in this double relationship. What tied Ranke to the Prussian regime was the belief that it had
reopened and committed itself to the historical agenda articulated in the
Lutheran Reformation. Ranke rejected the 'conservative' interpretations of
this agenda in which the transformation of the nation into an ethical community was tied to the domination and control of the temporal realm by
transcendent authority (as in Stahl's theory). But he was also not willing to
accept a purely immanent standpoint in which collective moral consciousness emerged simply as the self-development of the unconscious potential
of the national 'genius'. He remained suspicious of tendencies (which he
discerned in both Schelling and Bunsen) that completely assimilated the
transcendent realm to either the development of the national community
or the perfection of European philosophical or 'scientific' consciousness.
For Ranke the development of human beings from the blind existing being
of nature to the self-consciousness of moral cultured subjectivity required
recognition by the finite creature of its origins in, and dependency on,
a transcendent other, a submission of the child to the voice and law of
the creator/father. For Ranke such submissive recognition of the absolute
power of a transcendent father did not destroy, but rather emancipated
and shaped the immanent energies emerging from the maternal womb of
being.

It may seem a bit forced to treat Ranke as a philosophical thinker, but
he defined his project as historian within the cultural dilemmas posed by
post-Kantian idealist and romantic philosophy. When Ranke chose the
vocation of historian in the 1820s, it was at least in part because he was
convinced that historical knowledge could resolve the questions posed by
philosophers but that had proven to be irresolvable in their terms. The
result was a severely ambivalent attitude towards the stance of philosophy
and philosophers. On the one hand, Ranke insisted on the autonomy of
historical knowledge. As knowledge of the real it was distinguished from
and opposed to the abstract conceptual knowledge of philosophy. On the
other hand, he insisted that history was 'not the antithesis but the fulfilment of philosophy' (Ranke 1964–75, IV, p. 69). All forms of systematic,
conceptual knowledge were ultimately absorbed into historical knowledge
and communicated as a reconstruction of the embodiment of divine ideas

in historical actuality. Ideas became real in historical 'life', which was the object of historical knowledge. In this sense Ranke's views paralleled those of the Left Hegelians for whom the truth of philosophy was reduced to the positive knowledge of historical human existence in anthropology, psychology and historical sociology, and for whom the questions of philosophy were ultimately resolved in historical life or 'praxis'.

Historical writing functioned for Ranke as an unveiling of existence, a comprehension of the contextual totality of life-relations that gave individual phenomena meaning. Purified of the distortion of self-interested individual subjectivity, the documentary traces of past human life emerged as representations of individual existence whose organic interconnectedness itself manifested, though often obscurely, the foundations of individual existence in the 'ground of universal life (*Grund des Allgemeinen Lebens*) (Ranke 1964–75, IV, p. 63). However, Ranke's growing confidence in the 1830s that historiography could displace philosophy as the universal science was based on his incorporation of the transcendent dimension of philosophical theology – the comprehension of the grounds of human freedom in the eternal moral order ruled by the transcendent personality of the absolute existing subject – into the project of historical knowledge. Ranke expanded his theory of Ideas to include not only the implicit divine essences actualising themselves in the patterned totality of historical cultures, but also Ideas of transcendent, infinite reality that entered the historical process as the empirically recoverable convictions, ethical ideals, and cultural ideologies of specific individuals and groups. By tracing the emergence, diffusion, conflict and transformation of religious ideas the historian could discover how human words and deeds not only exemplified or 'expressed' the hidden organising power of the national Idea, but actually created, in the specific actions of historical events, a constructed order of their own. The source of this constructed meaning was the relation to the transcendent; its practical actualisation emerged through an appropriation of the 'Idea' as a goal of self-conscious practice.

The transcendent ground of being to which religious ideas referred was not itself an actor within history. History was not the revelation of a 'becoming God' or a progressive self-expression of the redemptive reconciliation of the finite and the infinite. The transcendent entered history through individual conviction, choice and action, as the mark of human freedom. The religious relation to the transcendent, articulated in the doctrines, liturgies and sacraments of churches, broke through the apparent necessity of the evolution of immanent relations. In the 1840s Ranke rejected

Hegelianism not only because it dissolved concrete existence in abstract thought, but also because it denied 'individual human consciousness' as the real subject of history (Ranke 1964–75, IV, pp. 187–8). Already in 1837 he had criticised a colleague for identifying 'life' and 'freedom'. 'Life', Ranke claimed, was the 'infinite all-connecting agency' that associated cause and effect in 'unbroken continuity'. In contrast, 'freedom' remained 'individual, moral, self-determined, though only in rare moments also self-originating and self-creating'.[21] In most eras and among most national cultures, freedom took the form of customary obedience and conformity to inherited religious ideas. But on those rare occasions when the reproduction of religious meaning veered into historical discontinuity and qualitative change, the words and deeds of individual human subjects would break into the ongoing necessities of 'life' and the customary forms of religious meaning and appear as 'self-originating and self-creating', providing an experience of new possibilities for the construction of the relation to the transcendent and opening new possibilities for the way human lives were lived.

The appropriate representational form for Ranke's view of the relationship among national cultural totalities, inherited discourses concerning the connection between finite existence and its infinite ground, and the free acts through which a recreation of the discourse of transcendence provided new possibilities for the direction of national cultures, was a narrative of contingent human action that only in retrospect displayed the larger coherence of divine purpose. In such narratives the immanent meanings of cultural development were set in relation to the construction of meanings based on direct experience of the transcendent sphere, in order to produce a genealogy of the contingent events that had shaped the tradition that confronted the present as a fund of inherited meaning. The narrative of Ranke's *German History* was organised around such historical conjunctures in which creative intervention and discontinuity had been possible. Many such moments remained moments of unfulfilled possibility because of the failure of individuals to grasp the new experiences and act on them with moral conviction. At the centre of Ranke's work, however, was the epochal moment in which Luther's articulation of a new religious meaning intervened in the evolution of German national culture, revised the direction of that culture on the basis of a radical encounter with transcendent truth, and produced a qualitative turn in human history.

---

21 Ranke to Heinrich Ritter, April 1837, in Ranke 1949, p. 285.

In the last volume of his history Ranke reflected on this post-romantic, 'existential' or 'positive' historicism that informed his narrative:

From the distance of centuries we can perceive the great combinations that are inherent in the nature of things; the individual action in every individual present, however, cannot depend on them. Here it is a matter of the correct handling of what is immediately given, on the good cause which one represents, on the moral force one can exert. The moments which condition the progress of world history are, I would like to say, a divine secret. The value of man is grounded in his self-determination and activity. (Ranke 1925–6, IV, p. 64)

Like so many of his contemporaries, Ranke believed that a reformation of the human relation to the divine, a recognition of the infinite ground of human action, would open up the possibility of constructing the national culture in new ways. The emergence of an ethical community of free subjects was not just the perfected expression of the immanent potentialities of the national genius, an objectification of the implicit goal of the collective cultural subject, but a constructive shaping of that culture on the foundation of an experience of the transcendent grounds of all cultures and historical possibilities, a construction that expressed the freedom of human beings to make the world conform to (or to fail to make the world conform to) divine truth through moral action.

The site of ethical community for Ranke was the 'national' state, the political world produced by the interaction of the immanent forces of ethnic and linguistic tradition and the moral convictions grounded in religious ideas about absolute, transcendent truth. In the relations between church and state, the church became the exemplar of the transcendent grounds of free action that could break the internal causal nexus of ethno–linguistic national life and produce a new moral order within the constructed forms of the state. Within the political constitution of the state the inherent necessities of the national idea were 'modified' according to a will infused with a conviction of universal transcendent truth. The national culture provided the specific contextual limitations within which such ethical construction could occur. Ranke affirmed the freedom of the moral subject as the creator of its own history. But religious convictions only manifested themselves in effective action if they conformed to the objective foundations of human existence in both the 'maternal' ground of 'natural' being and the transcendent spiritual ground of divine paternal authority. The human subject could exert its will as a free agent only by conforming to the restrictions imposed by its status as a finite creation.

In the Rankean historical constructions the description of human existence in terms of a narrative of relations between religion and nationality, church and state, became a way of expressing the contingency of historical events, the freedom of human actions in time. Within the religious consciousness of church membership recognition of human finitude and historical contingency, and thus recognition of human freedom in relation to the immanent 'necessities' of national culture and historical tradition, was inextricably connected to the experience of transcendence. It was in the sphere of the 'church' that the ultimate meaning of human existence was encountered, appropriated, internalised and expressed in actions aiming at the construction of an 'ethical' human order. Church and state framed the discussion of associative life as long as the question of that life as an expression or construction of fundamental values remained a vital and contested question, as long as politics was perceived in terms of the historical creation of an ethical community according to values derived from an experience that related the immanent relations of historical cultures to the transcendent ground that defined their possibility.

19

The politics of nature

Science and religion in the age of Darwin

DANIEL PICK

1 Introduction

Perhaps no Victorian was more startled by the implications of evolution than Charles Darwin (1809–82). Transformations of nature through natural selection were considered in his private and, eventually, very public writings; but even as they flowed from his pen, these ideas disturbed him. He was perennially torn about their moral and ethical consequences. The imagery of struggle, selection and extinction in nature that Darwin did so much to fashion was also ready-made to describe the rough passage of arguments and beliefs through history, including the struggle for survival of the evolutionary idea itself. Darwin and his followers identified themselves with a cause, but they were not always so sanguine about the social and political repercussions of their intellectual battles. This chapter situates Darwin's struggle – and his concept of struggle – in a wider context of nineteenth-century evolutionary thought and explores political and religious consequences of the claim that species (human included) are not definitively fixed in form, but undergo change over time.

The controversy generated by Darwin's most famous published works, *On the Origin of Species* (1859) and *The Descent of Man* (1871) was not only intense, but also multifaceted. Religious, political, moral and scientific objections became deeply entangled. Moreover, the debate was conducted in many styles and genres, at times light-heartedly, at others in deadly earnest. The subject of evolution became the stuff of novels and cartoons, sermons and popular pamphlets, poems and learned articles. Some commentators raised intellectual objections to Darwin's account of evolution which caused him considerable heartache. On the other hand, there were also many crude attacks on evolutionary 'morality' that he found easier to dismiss, as we see, for instance, in this flippant remark, soon after the publication of *The Origin*, to his friend, the distinguished geologist Sir Charles Lyell (1797–1875): 'I have received, in a Manchester newspaper a rather good squib, showing that I have proved "might is right," and therefore that Napoleon is right and every cheating tradesman is also right' (F. Darwin 1887, II, p. 262). The debate about the politics and ethics of Darwinism (the 'ism' word was coined as early as 1860, in a review by T. H. Huxley (1825–95)), reduced by some to a straightforward battle between the causes of the apes and the angels, or the adherents of might and right, became part of the common currency of the age.

The Victorian critics of evolutionary ideas in general and Darwinian hypotheses in particular, have often been dismissed as bigots or intellectual dinosaurs. But the range of hostile responses included not only deep religious and moral objections to such visions of nature, but also scientific arguments which, on occasion, were to be considered awkward, even devastating. There were thought to be evidential as well as ethical grounds for challenging Darwin's theory of natural selection, and the various further claims inspired by it. Moreover, internecine controversies continued amongst the evolutionists themselves. The interpretation of scientific success and failure was unclear; speculations as far-reaching and untestable as Darwin's led into a quagmire of uncertainty. Historian of science Peter Bowler has argued that there was even an 'eclipse of Darwinism' in the late nineteenth century as alternative arguments found new favour (Bowler 1983). Certainly the boundaries, credentials and consequences of all such ideas about metamorphosis in nature remained deeply unsettled throughout the Victorian period.

Even as it destabilised religious convictions and divided the scientific elite, evolutionary thought was producing its own zealots, for whom a particular text, be it by the best-known contemporary philosopher of the cause, Herbert Spencer (1820–1903), who coined the phrase 'survival of the fittest', or by the rather less ebullient Darwin himself, provided a new, hallowed truth. For many, the initial dizzying experience of reading *The Origin* precipitated a crisis. The reader's disorientation of faith was sometimes followed by a new fervent commitment to naturalism and materialism, and an insistence that such ideas be applied immediately to every facet of culture, society and politics. The genius of the author and his books became the object of worship, bordering on a cult. Some contemporaries sought to stabilise themselves by stabilising Darwin's theories (Durant 1977, 1985). At any event, for what were no doubt multiple political, emotional and intellectual reasons, many sought moral salvation, and not merely scientific education, in Darwin's books, and in an ever more militant advocacy of his claims.

The attitude of Darwin's German follower, Ernst Haeckel (1834–1919), a professor of zoology at Jena, is a case in point. He sought to have evolutionary theory enshrined in the schooling system and campaigned for this science with a fervour that smacked of the very religiosity he purported to challenge. Haeckel was by no means the only disciple to trek to see Darwin at his home in Kent, there to pay homage before the great man. Emma (Charles' wife) privately objected to the intrusion, referring to his thundering voice, but to no avail (Desmond and Moore 1991, p. 28). The style of the encounter can only be called devotional. As Desmond and Moore put it in their rich intellectual biography of Darwin, Haeckel's meeting with the English scientist, 'was an intensely religious experience' (for the former). He described Darwin as 'tall and venerable . . . with the broad shoulders of an Atlas that bore a world of thought: a Jove-like forehead, as we see in Goethe, with a lofty and broad vault, deeply furrowed by the plough of intellectual work' (Desmond and Moore 1991, p. 539). Haeckel had seen *The Origin* as a contribution to politics as much as science, and felt no compunction about extending the debate to society, seeing selection as a driving force, propelling peoples onward to greater things, whilst casting the failures aside. It was taken to offer sanction for certain government policies and warning against others. Progress was regarded as a natural but uneven law, and evolution as crucial to the fortunes of the nation state, Teutonic supremacy and the genius of the *Volk*. Neither religious orthodoxy nor moral scruples, it was argued, could be allowed to contradict the reality of evolutionary struggle.

Historians debate how far *The Origin* was specifically responsible for detonating an intellectual explosion, but clearly the foundations of Christian belief had already been severely tested by other emerging sciences, most notably geology. Darwin was the heir to eighteenth-century scepticism, and behind that, to seventeenth-century enquiries into the very nature of Nature. Darwin's account was in fact but one of many new lines of nineteenth-century intellectual endeavour that conflicted with traditional Church teachings. Christianity, of course, was no monolith. Champions of evolutionary science were as likely to align themselves with a congenial religious vantage-point as to proclaim out loud the death of God. They might perhaps find themselves confronting earnest and militant evangelical divines, who were themselves at odds with other churchmen (Hilton 1988), rather than attacking the value of faith *tout court*. Nonetheless, Christianity, as traditionally conceived, faced a variety of powerful intellectual challenges and sometimes withering analyses. It had been provocatively suggested, for instance, that God might be but the alienated construct of man (the thesis of Feuerbach's *The Essence of Christianity*, 1841). Presentations of the story of Jesus also sometimes adopted an unnervingly cool tone; notably in the historicist focus of David Strauss' *Life of Jesus* (1841), rendered into English by George Eliot in the 1840s. Even this was as nothing beside the positively icy-toned investigation of the possible psychopathological symptoms of once-revered saints to be found in the work of late nineteenth-century anti-clerical *provocateurs* in the Third Republic, such as the important Parisian neurologist, Jean-Martin Charcot. Icons were battered and some fossilised beliefs were turned over, not least by new evidence about the fossil record itself. In short, Darwin's work needs to be situated amongst numerous other jolts to conventional faith and traditional beliefs about the human species, the 'animal kingdom' and the age of the Earth.

Nowhere can the challenge be seen more clearly than in the rising tide of speculations about the flexibility of natural forms themselves. In France, the notion of species transformation had been most importantly developed by Jean-Baptiste Lamarck (1744–1829). Sympathetic to the French Revolution, he had originally been a protégé of the great naturalist Georges Buffon. Lamarck had provided an elaborate account of the historical development of nature and had used the term 'biology' to refer to the world of living things. His work homed in on the way organisms interacted with and adapted to the environment. Like the famous French physician, Marie François Bichat, Lamarck was acutely engaged by the problem of how to define the specificity of life. Lamarck's most-quoted idea was 'the inheritance of acquired characteristics', but his work was in fact far more wide-ranging.[1] His writings stimulated various important debates, not least about the time-scale of the creation of life on Earth. Lamarck's study of hydrogeology in 1802 stressed that physical changes must have taken place extremely slowly, through the agency of water. His transformist theory was first articulated publicly in lectures in 1800 and developed in *Philosophie Zoologique* (1809). Species, Lamarck contended, were subject to change and underwent adaptive alterations in order to retain the harmonious balance of nature. He believed that 'spontaneous generation' could occur, transforming the inorganic into the organic. Thus gelatinous matter formed into live creatures of a rudimentary kind where the combination of humidity, heat and substance was right. Yet Lamarck also argued that nature operated according to a plan and was

---

1 On the variety of and controversy surrounding his work, see Jordanova 1984, especially ch. 10.

subject to laws. Nature itself might appear blind, but somewhere behind it there existed an organising will.

German nature philosophy also played its part in this story, notably through the work of Johann Wolfgang von Goethe (1749–1832). He was not a 'Darwinian before Darwin' (despite later attempts to portray him as a precise forerunner). Goethe did not assume 'natural selection' as the mechanism of change. Moreover, he had no specific theory of evolution at all, although it has been argued that there are significant hints of this in his later writings. But he merits consideration because he provides an indication of the emerging representation of natural forms in continuing flux. Recognising the significance of metamorphosis, Goethe rejected rigid, stable classifications, setting himself against the tradition of dividing and tabulating plants and their parts on which an earlier botany, associated particularly with Linnaeus, had rested (Callot 1971, ch. 6; cf. Magnus 1949). Goethe was fascinated by variations and by the blurring of species borderlines. 'Nature has no system', he declared, 'it has – it is – life' (quoted in Reed 1984, p. 44). In *The Metamorphosis of Plants*, he suggested that normal change was progressive, 'ladder-like in the mind's eye'. What he termed 'retrograde metamorphosis' was abnormal (Goethe 1790, pp. 91–2). His interest lay in the processes running through structures; in movement, transition, 'morphology' (the science of developing forms). Nature became a space of 'mobile order', even if the system itself was ultimately conceived as a unity. Indeed it was the totality of these processes which enthralled him. Natural phenomena were to be viewed synthetically; 'otherwise every separate thing is only a dead letter' (quoted in Reed 1984, p. 47).

While Lamarck and Goethe believed in the tendency to progress, order and economy in nature, each insisted on the real and continuous transformations occurring within it. Darwin took these transformist ideas much further. He declared (not without trepidation) that the fixity of species, as set out in the Bible, was a myth. He acknowledged as much to his friend, Joseph Hooker on 11 April 1844:

At last gleams of light have come, and I am almost convinced (quite contrary to the opinion I started with) that species are not (it is like confessing a murder) immutable. Heaven forfend me from Lamarck nonsense of a 'tendency to progression,' 'adaptations from slow willing of animals,' etc.!, But the conclusions I am led to are not *widely* different from his – though the means of change are wholly so. I think I have found out (here's presumption!) the simple way by which species become exquisitely adapted to various ends. (Darwin and Seward 1903, I, pp. 40–1)

Such recognition of the malleability of forms ran together with controversial geological arguments about the extreme age of the planet. You could propose the latter without the former, but only with great difficulty the former without the latter. As the building blocks of geology were erected, so the discomfort increased of those scientifically intrigued Christians who nonetheless took the Bible seriously as a historical record. The Earth was simply too old, Lyell realised, to enable a literal reading of the Holy Book. His frequently revised *Principles of Geology* (1830–3) was widely read. It ran to twelve editions and offered a glimpse into astoundingly gradual sedimentary changes, a vision which replaced eighteenth-century accounts of suddenly induced and relatively recent natural catastrophes to explain the complex make-up of the ground underfoot. But that gradualist account did not lead Lyell to renounce Christianity. For the Bible itself could be read less literally than had those seventeenth-century divines who had given the precise figure for the world's beginning as 4004 BC (Oldroyd 1980, p. 40). Lyell recognised the truly ancient history of the Earth; he was talking hundreds or thousands of millions of years. But the age of the Earth was one thing; the process of human 'descent' quite another (Lyell came to accept evolution, but balked at Darwin's attempt to treat human beings as just another animal within the natural world).

The Origin, when finally published, retained a great deal of developmental vocabulary, but Darwin pictured evolution not as a ladder or a line, but rather as a branching tree-like form, bereft of a central trunk (Bowler 1989, p. 12). However carefully Darwin formulated his ideas or sought to differentiate them from earlier, wilder studies, he knew the public was ready-primed to find books about evolution at best controversial, at worst utterly disgusting. The stormy fate of a previous work, *Vestiges of the Natural History of Creation* (1844), had not escaped Darwin's notice. *Vestiges*, the brainchild of the Edinburgh publisher Robert Chambers, had appeared anonymously. It was widely and fiercely derided and denounced. If this caused Darwin himself much anguish, many others surreptitiously enjoyed the frisson of reading Chambers' notorious book. *Vestiges* became a voguish topic of conversation, whispered about at genteel dinners and argued over amongst working-class radicals in the 1840s. *Vestiges* drew attention from all social ranks, with its mix of progressionist evolutionism and such scandalous gems as the claim that man had descended, via the apes, from the primeval slime. It was a kind of frog-prince yarn for adventurous grown-ups, and some saw Darwin's as merely a more sober sequel. Indeed, the clamour surrounding Chambers' text has perhaps been too little considered, and that around Darwin's *Origin* viewed too much in isolation. *The Origin* itself became a false origin – cast by later admirers as the founding work of Victorian evolutionary debate, when in fact, as the historian of science James Secord has shown (2000), it was by no means always perceived this way.

Thus many of the elements of the Darwinian dramas of the 1860s were already powerfully evident in the scandal surrounding *Vestiges*, fifteen years earlier. Darwin's claims were more formidably researched, the tone more measured, than Chambers'; yet in both cases, so it was claimed by critics, the role of the Creator had been disturbingly sidelined or even monstrously negated. There was to be no consensus about the best response to evolutionary theory within the Church of England. In 1864, at the Anglican Convocation, evangelicals reaffirmed their faith in the harmony of God's words and works. Some set their face resolutely against Darwin (let alone Chambers); other, liberal theological voices continued to demand fresh thought about the terms of faith and to seek a dialogue about the implications of science and evolution. Contributions broadly favourable to evolution were included in the much-thumbed collection, *Essays and Reviews*, published in England in 1860, a text soon criticised as polemical, unwise and perplexing.[2] Yet strikingly Frederick Temple, one of the authors, would become Archbishop of Canterbury.

During the early nineteenth century, there had been intermittent accounts of human remains found in geological deposits so ancient that they contained evidence of now-extinct animals. Superficial deposits of gravel or boulder-clay, known as 'diluvium', could be seen as the residue of Noah's flood, the last great geological catastrophe. Many preferred to go on insisting that there could be no link between the geological and human time-scales; that people must have appeared on the scene only beyond the last catastrophe. Claims for the very existence of ancient human traces were thus countered by arguments that deliberate burial and the natural mixing-up of deposits were equally likely to be responsible for any such surprises (Bowler 1989, p. 78). Yet disturbing material that appeared to contradict the biblical time-scale continued to be unearthed. The geologist William Buckland, for instance, visited a cave near Swansea and found a human skeleton in deposits containing bones of what appeared to be died-out forms of mammals. In

---

2 The book appeared shortly after *The Origin* and included a respectful discussion of Darwin (Temple *et al.*, 1861, p. 139). Penned by Oxford professors, clergymen and the head of Rugby school, it sold more than 20,000 copies in two years and remained controversial, a famous example of a much wider tide of books that described the struggle to reconcile religious belief and practice with the findings of science.

1858, two reputable geologists, William Pengelly and Hugh Falconer, began to excavate at Brixham cave near Torquay. They located stone tools and the bones of extinct animals in close proximity and convinced themselves that human toolmakers must have lived in the very remote past. More geologists came to the cave, including Lyell, and were persuaded by the evidence. A number of papers were published in 1859 and 1860 supporting the view that the human race was of a much greater antiquity than had previously been supposed. Parallel developments were occurring in France, with discoveries by Jacques Boucher des Perthes in the gravel beds of the Somme valley. Much of the new evidence was summed up in Lyell's widely read *Geological Evidences of the Antiquity of Man* of 1863.[3] Yet when it came to *The Origin*, Lyell had profound misgivings. Nor was he encouraged when, in voicing his doubts and warning that 'the dignity of man is at stake', Darwin replied that he was sorry to say he had no 'consolatory view' to offer.[4] Indeed, if anything, Darwin expressed to his friends his regret at having hitherto offered too much by way of theological reassurance, having excessively 'truckled' to public opinion (F. Darwin 1887, III, p. 18).

The problem for Darwin, however, was not simply vicissitudes of public opinion; his often contradictory declarations about the compatibility of evolution and belief in God's design appeared to reflect a heartfelt personal conflict. He had once been greatly drawn towards the notion of divine organisation of the world and thus the language of natural theology. Later, however, he confessed that he had come, increasingly, to doubt this view. He declared that 'I had no intention to write atheistically', but owned up that 'I cannot see as plainly as others do, and as I should wish to do, evidence of design and beneficence on all sides of us.' Or again: 'There seems to me too much misery in the world. I cannot persuade myself that a beneficent and omnipotent God would have designedly created the Ichneumonidae [parasitic wasps] with the express intention of their feeding within the living bodies of Caterpillars, or that a cat should play with mice.' Not believing in

---

3 Lyell 1863, pp. 98ff. Lyell's parting remark was as follows: 'I may conclude this chapter by quoting a saying of Professor Agassiz, "that whenever a new and startling fact is brought to light in science, people first say, 'it is not true,' then that 'it is contrary to religion,' and lastly, 'that everybody knew it before'" (Lyell 1863, p. 105).

4 Desmond and Moore 1991, p. 475. Cf. Darwin's remark to Hooker (15 May 1860): 'As for the old fogies in Cambridge, it really signifies nothing. I look at their attacks as a proof that our work is worth the doing. It makes me resolve to buckle on my armour' (F. Darwin 1887, II, pp. 307–8). For Lyell's admiration of Darwin's 'close reasoning' as well as his objections and Darwin's response to the criticism, see F. Darwin 1887, II, pp. 205–15. Darwin insisted that the theory of natural selection 'implies no *necessary* tendency to progression' (p. 210).

this, he added that he could also 'see no necessity in the belief that the eye was expressly designed'. On the other hand, he immediately went on to say that he could not be contented with the view that 'this wonderful universe' and 'especially the nature of man' are 'the result of brute force'. At which point he reached once again for a compromise: 'I am inclined to look at everything as resulting from designed laws, with the details, whether good or bad, left to the working out of what we may call chance.'[5]

Perhaps Darwin sought to resolve this conflict in his final autobiographical statements, where he went the whole hog and declared his total loss of faith. Fanciful claims that he had a death-bed conversion to the church sought to push the image the other way (Desmond and Moore 1991). In any event, his status as national treasure was confirmed (after various machinations and negotiations) by his burial in Westminster Abbey. Darwin's statements often brimmed with ambiguities. Thus a multitude of commentators (atheist, agnostic or religiously devout, and ranging from the radical left to the right of politics) seized upon them and claimed some allegiance, or rather sought Darwin's allegiance to their own pet schemes. Arguments for atheism, *laissez-faire* economics and socially minded co-operation, for brute struggle and egotism, natural altruism or a mix of the two, all found some support in his remarks. Darwin's conclusions were often fluid, and his attitude vexed, as we can see, regarding the role of chance in the process of evolution.[6] Reeling from his own challenge to guaranteed and continuing improvement, to say nothing of the bleak prospect of the eventual heat death of the sun (courtesy of the second law of thermodynamics), Darwin confessed his perplexity and distress:

Believing as I do that man in the distant future will be a far more perfect creature than he now is, it is an intolerable thought that he and all other sentient beings are doomed to complete annihilation after such long-continued slow progress. To those who fully admit the immortality of the human soul, the destruction of our world will not appear so dreadful. (F. Darwin 1958, p. 65)[7]

Many of Darwin's interpreters left nothing to chance, restoring the idea that evolution did mean – indeed must mean – continuing progress and improvement (Bowler 1989, pp. 151–2). The specific theory of natural

---

5 Letter to Asa Gray (22 May 1860), in F. Darwin 1887, II, pp. 311–12. Darwin gloomily concluded 'Let each man hope and believe what he can', (p. 312).
6 Darwin and Seward 1903, I, p. 321. cf. Ospovat 1980, p. 194n. For a study of the variety of ideas of chance in the evolutionary tradition, see Shanahan 1991.
7 Spencer reacted with similar personal disquiet when told of the thermodynamic theory by the physicist Tyndall (Spencer 1908, p. 104).

selection was frequently ignored by his readers, at least until much later; perhaps the theory was not fully given its due until the 1920s and 1930s, when population biologists and laboratory geneticists 'rediscovered' the book's most crucial argument (Secord 2000, p. 516). By extension from the notion of the natural improvement of nature, through evolution, it was argued that social and political progress were inevitable. Spencer, for one, had already vigorously insisted that this might be a 'natural law'.[8] There were always those, including at points Darwin himself, who could translate the story of our chancy existence into an assured moral as well as technological advance, as was proposed, for instance, in John Lubbock's study, *Prehistoric Times* (1865). This was a paean to our development from rude beginnings, our ascent from apes and savages. At the 1867 meeting of the British Association, Lubbock confronted Archbishop Richard Whately of Dublin on the subject of evolution and progress, using archaeological evidence to dispose of any belief that the earliest human beings were directly given civilisation by God.

Such views were countered by Whately and his supporters such as the Duke of Argyll, Secretary of State for India. An amateur naturalist and author of *Primeval Man* (1869), the duke argued that the archaeological record could only prove technological not moral progress. He could not accept the proposition that man had risen unaided from a 'low condition' of 'utter barbarism'. Instead he contended that mankind had sunk from some higher state. Man's place in nature, he declared, was the great 'battle-ground', for 'No man can run up the natural lines of Evolution without coming to Christianity at the top' (Argyll 1869, p. 439). Others were insistent that history witnessed both moral and physical advance. But here again evolution was finessed into the more palatable terms of a tough but rewarding struggle to the top, be it for individuals alone, or groups working together, images that were congruent with Victorian homilies about our just rewards, the moral virtues of physical exertion and personal sacrifice, for instance in team sports or Alpine conquests. In Henry Drummond's uplifting tome, *The Ascent of Man* (1894), faith and science once again shared the summit, and the darker clouds of Darwinism were spirited away.

The good news that the religiously faithful and the socially concerned might legitimately become Darwinians had been spread by 'muscular Christians' such as the novelist and social commentator Charles Kingsley since

8 Spencer's evolutionary arguments, even after the publication of *The Origin*, cannot be simply run together with Darwin's; see Crook 1994, pp. 41–7; Peel 1971.

the 1860s. He had welcomed evolution precisely because he felt it enabled us to abandon the idea of an excessively meddling God. But this was clearly not, for him, in order to choose atheism. As he wrote to the Reverend F. D. Maurice in 1863:

I am very busy working out points of Natural Theology, by the strange light of Huxley, Darwin and Lyell. I think I shall come to something worth having before I have done... Darwin is conquering everywhere, and rushing in like a flood, by the mere fact of truth and fact. The one or two who hold out are forced to try all sorts of subterfuges as to fact, or else by evoking the *odium theologicum*... But they find that now they have got rid of an interfering God – a master magician, as I call it – they have to choose between the absolute empire of accident, and a living, immanent, ever-working God. (Kingsley 1877, II, p. 171).[9]

While the Genesis story was increasingly understood to be (at best) a metaphorical rendition of events, evolutionary theory provided a new language of history in which the problem of final origins could be suspended. All individuals and civilisations were subject to evolution and lay at different points on its trajectory, but science could not be sure how it all began – maybe a divine designer set it in motion, maybe not. But other high-minded, scientifically literate Christians expressed far more personal dismay than did Kingsley at the direction in which Darwin was taking them. The Catholic scientific writer and admirer of Darwin, St George Jackson Mivart (1827–1900), for instance, found himself on the horns of a terrible dilemma. Although Darwin did not openly denounce Christian faith in his *magnum opus*, Mivart did not know how to save him from the charge of materialist subversion. The author's insistence that there was 'grandeur' to the view of life he presented would not do, at least not for this particularly excruciated onlooker. Mivart found too little glory and nobility in his account of nature, concluding that Darwinian evolutionary theory reflected (or perhaps even added to) the moral perniciousness of the times. Darwin apparently lent himself easily to prevailing beliefs in the collective advantages of self-interest, even to the endorsement of capitalism, utilitarianism and *laissez-faire*. Karl Marx, also an admirer of Darwin, made similarly caustic interpretations about the ideological dimension of this evolutionism, although he reached very different conclusions to Mivart's.[10]

9 There are various admiring letters from Kingsley to Darwin in the same volume.
10 Soon after the publication of *The Origin*, Marx commented on its importance even as he wryly drew attention to its questionable ideological assumptions. He considered it remarkable how the naturalist recognised among beasts and plants an English society marked by division of labour, competition, the aggressive opening-up of new markets and the Malthusian 'struggle for existence'. Marx and

In the Munich Brief of 1863, the Pope had declared that while Catholics might cultivate sciences, explain them, and render them useful and certain, on the other hand they could not do so if this conflicted in any way with 'the infallible intellect of God as revealed in Christianity' (Gruber 1960, p. 46). Mivart did his best to find a middle way, but his difficulties continued. Pope Pius IX's *Syllabus of Errors* soon appeared, a warning shot across the bows of those who might attribute more weight to new scientific ideas than to the secure teachings of the church. By the late 1860s, Mivart was in the midst of a major crisis, not keen to break with members of the Darwinian circle (whose society he valued), but very unwilling to make the kind of Faustian pact that Darwin seemed to invite, indeed privately to have been rather excited about, when he had daringly allowed himself to muse: 'What a book a Devil's chaplain might write on the clumsy, wasteful, blundering low and horridly cruel works of nature!'[11]

If Mivart was nonplussed by the atheistical flirtation of the old master, he was positively horrified by the positions of some of his supporters. He could not shake off the idea that there was something horribly sordid here, a kind of pornography of nature. Wandering about Italy, he had been 'amazed and saddened' to see a work by Darwin's vociferous lieutenant, T. H. Huxley, on sale at 'most of the railway stations amongst a crowd of *obscenities*' (quoted in Desmond and Moore 1991, p. 569). Huxley's explicit attacks on the Roman Church as 'our great antagonist' made him shudder; but even this was mild stuff when placed alongside the blistering anti-religious writings of some of Darwin's continental admirers, like the German Carl Vogt, exiled after 1848 to Geneva, whose provocative *Lectures on Man* (1863) were unmistakably contemptuous of Christian sentiments.[12] Truth and reason belonged to science, Vogt taunted. Religious cowardice made clerics obfuscate. They were unwilling to stare our simian history boldly in the face, he contended, much as Huxley had witheringly dealt with Wilberforce's enquiry about whether the monkey pedigree was to be found on the paternal or maternal side of the family.[13]

Engels 1936, pp. 125, 198, 201, 237. For Engels' musings on evolution, adaptation, regression and so forth, see Engels 1940a, for instance at p. 236 and Salvadori 1979, at p. 24.

11 Letter to J. D. Hooker (13 July 1856), Darwin 1990, VI, p. 178.

12 The English edition of Vogt's work, the full title of which was *Lectures on Man: His Place in Creation, and in the History of the Earth*, was edited by James Hunt. Vogt's text was printed for Hunt's recently established Anthropological Society.

13 This occurred during Huxley's set-piece debate with Bishop Wilberforce at the British Association in Oxford in 1860, an event often caricatured at the time as a straightforward choice between the voice of reason and dogma (Di Gregorio 1984; Lucas 1979; Richards 1989). In fact Wilberforce

When Mivart's book, *The Genesis of Species* appeared in 1871, a breach with Darwin became unavoidable. The latter told his erstwhile admirer that *The Genesis* was a travesty. Further discussion between them was to be abruptly curtailed.[14] But the urgency of the task of critique, as Mivart understood it, could not be doubted any more than could Matthew Arnold's horror shortly before, in contemplating political agitation in the 1860s and the wider moral vacuum of the age. Arnold railed against the barrenness of *laissez-faire*, the thin gruel of utilitarian philosophy, the urgent need for the sweetness of light and culture to bind and heal, to create moral uplift in an age where orthodox religion was not to be relied upon. Mivart also dreaded that England might be approaching a religious decay similar to that of the middle of the eighteenth century in France for which Frenchmen were paying in 'blood and tears'.

A number of Darwin's critics would seize on similar points. They wanted to understand the history of the world as an unfolding design (a concept Darwin himself had, as we have seen, reluctantly, and perhaps never quite wholeheartedly, given up). They spoke up for the intended beauty and spiritual significance of plumage and nature's rich colours – all these brilliant God given patterns. Beauty could not be explained away through the merely useful or the random. Why one tint for the feather rather than another? Was there always merely some 'use' at stake – camouflage or sexual signpost? Darwin replied that while the initial variations had arisen by the way, selection always followed. But surely there was some irreducible realm of loveliness, caused and designed by our maker, argued critics such as the Duke of Argyll or Mivart, that was not simply to be understood in the language of evolutionary advantage. Arguments about art and aesthetics were distinct, but in this respect strikingly similar to such critiques of Darwinism. Beauty, anti-Darwinian naturalists as well as aesthetes in the circle of Pater and Wilde would have agreed, was never simply to be understood in terms of social utility or some other pay-off.[15]

had been carefully primed for the debate by scientific opponents of Darwin, including Richard Owen. Other examples of militant evolutionists thumbing their nose at the church include the aforementioned anti-clerical Haeckel. His ridicule of the Christian God as a 'gaseous vertebrate' was just the kind of thing to rile the faithful. Haeckel denounced the pernicious effects of religion and supported Bismarck's *Kulturkampf* against the Catholic Church. The papacy was dismissed as a swindle, its despotism founded on an unscrupulous and labyrinthine system of lying and deceit.

14 In a letter to Hooker, Darwin complained that Mivart had cut him 'into mincemeat'. Mivart continued to express regret that their 'philosophical' quarrel had become so wide; see Darwin 1985, p. 332, item 7710 and p. 354, item 8145.

15 On Darwin's version of utilitarianism, see Richards 1982, p. 57.

The representation of the nineteenth century as an epoch dominated by narrow-minded utilitarian beliefs was culturally powerful; it can be traced through the work of Carlyle, Dickens, Ruskin and many others. There are famous, much-quoted passages from such writers, in which the beauty of a flower or the value of a person is seen to be brutally denied by a cold, utilitarian analyst. The value of nature, art or humanity could not simply be explained through decomposing the whole into its constituent parts and processes, they complained. The sense of spiritual inadequacy and psychological impoverishment, even of personal crisis, this philosophy might lead to was, of course, eloquently and movingly set out by John Stuart Mill in his *Autobiography*. Whether anyone actually went so far as to claim that a flower had no meaning beyond the strict analysis of its properties (as Ruskin implied that his contemporaries did) matters less than the fact that in their scathing accounts, such critics seemed to have identified a kind of bankruptcy in the prevailing views of the age.

Darwin has been seen by various commentators as a kind of naturalist utilitarian. Much earlier, the idea that nature could best be viewed as a cornucopia of useful traits had been explored in the work of that highly influential natural theologian, the Reverend William Paley. His *Natural Theology: or, Evidences of the Existence and Attributes of the Deity Collected from the Appearances of Nature* (1802) had been much appreciated by the young Darwin. Paley's account nicely restated a number of familiar eighteenth-century arguments: crucially, he accepted that the day-to-day operation of nature was devoid of magic. Life proceeded without any chronic divine meddling. But these laws and processes were themselves intended, set in play by God. It was indeed a miracle that so many useful natural materials should be provided, and that the system should all work together like clockwork, but once it did, no more help was required. Crucially, however long the chain of natural causes and effects, behind it all was a designer who had the ultimate utility of the scheme in mind, and had set the whole sequence in motion. To imagine no such creator or 'artificer' was to enter into the 'absurdity' of atheism, the 'irrationality of irreligion', in the historian John Hedley Brooke's phrase (1991, p. 151).

Some commentators see Darwin's renunciation of natural theology as a reflection of social conditions themselves: the brutal evidence of industrial and urban change in England in the nineteenth century placed Paley's vision of 'contented' nature and design under intolerable strain.[16] There is something in this, but it would, nonetheless, be misleading to imagine that *either* Paley *or* Darwin simply encapsulated the cultural 'mood' of their time. Darwin's grandfather Erasmus penned verses which undid the 'benign' view of nature long before Charles joined the fray: 'One great Slaughter-house the warring world!' (E. Darwin 1804, p. 107). The vision of violent nature, its continuing 'vegetable war' (p. 106), was not erased by Erasmus Darwin's simultaneous admiration for the temple of nature (p. 113). Conversely, Paley's own rather reassuring story continued to be influential (his work indeed reprinted and recycled) well after *The Origin of Species* appeared.

Any broad-brush characterisation of shifting 'moods' on nature across the century is likely to distort, erroneously unifying the beliefs of what were ideologically and spiritually disparate times. The world may well have been, in Desmond and Moore's phrase, 'turned upside down in fifty years' (1991, pp. 449–50), but there were numerous ways to construe such material changes. Contemporaneous with Paley's work, and perhaps even more significant to Darwin, was Thomas Malthus' *Essay on the Principle of Population* (1798) which was often identified with political and moral pessimism, a rebuttal of the upbeat words about 'human nature' and 'progress' which the author had detected, *inter alia*, in the writings of Godwin. But in Malthus' case, no less than in Darwin's, there is a risk of producing mere caricature; we are well advised to avoid instant descriptions of his law of population as 'bleak', 'dark' or 'stern' (Winch 1987; La Vergata 1990).

Malthus' work challenged the eighteenth-century commonplace that population increase necessarily reflected and stimulated progress and prosperity. His work led to countless debates about the precise relationship between the expansion of numbers and the future adequacy of resources. Some later commentators continued to combine the population warnings of Malthus with the benign constructions of Paley, thus to provide 'natural theological' rationales for the reproductive mayhem and indeed for the burgeoning increase in population evident during the nineteenth century.[17]

16 Desmond and Moore's *Darwin* reads as follows: 'The world had been turned upside down in fifty years. Seen through Paley's rose-tinted spectacles, it was a continual summer's afternoon, with the rectory garden buzzing with contented life. But no longer. An expanding industrial society meant that more and more people were herded, hungry and angry, into factory towns. Those on the sharp end began hammering away at Paley's image for ages' (1991, pp. 449–50).

17 Extravagant exercises in providential 'number-crunching' claimed, for instance, that the system of nature was divinely arranged to ensure that every woman could find a husband without recourse to the 'unnatural' practice of polygamy. Mathematicians busied themselves in formulating the ideal

Both Paley and Malthus afforded Darwin much food for thought; 'nature has scattered the seeds of life abroad with the most profuse and liberal hand', Malthus had declared. Slaughter, it could be argued, was utterly necessary. For otherwise each tiny square of Earth would be overrun by millions of clamouring creatures. Malthus' lesson: infinite multiplication and crowding are *necessarily* held in check by waste, sickness, destruction, misery and vice: population, unchecked, *necessarily* outstripped resources: 'I see no way by which man can escape from the weight of this law which pervades all animal nature' (Malthus 1988, p. 72). For Darwin, the imbalance between population and resources is not to be understood as a flaw in the system of nature; on the contrary, it constitutes the necessary mechanism, the very precondition of natural selection.

2 Science and authority

In the age of Darwin, words such as 'science' and 'scientist' were often invoked to convey a sense of moral and political impartiality. 'Scientist' was eventually to suggest a member of a trained, professional (salaried) caste, but it was also to be adopted to connote a particular kind of neutral stance. Such credentials were strongly claimed, for instance, by Darwin's polymath cousin, Francis Galton (1822–1911), even as he advocated policies that were anything but value-free. Darwin, who had thought very highly of some of Galton's earlier work,[18] died before the latter's full eugenic ambitions had become apparent, and we can only speculate on whether he would have considered these equally admirable.[19] Galton coined the word 'eugenics' in 1883. It set the seal on his already prolific enquiries into heredity, genius,

natural design which led to the (not precisely equal) ratio of the sexes. Many commentators insisted on the indissoluble link between fecundity and the best possible economy of nature (La Vergata 1990). Thus social and physical ills that stymied reproduction were really a blessing in disguise. Prostitution was deemed by some writers to be a necessary antidote to excessive fecundity whilst even venereal disease was occasionally mooted as helpful, since indirectly it might curb the population.

18 Darwin offered some encouragement but did not directly endorse his relative's more specific ideas and proposals. Galton could not accept the implied equation of fitness with fertility, given that the poor were the most fecund. The struggle for existence, he suggested, as he looked darkly at the Victorian city, 'seems to me to spoil and not improve our breed'. On this correspondence, see Himmelfarb 1952, pp. 326–7; Jones 1980, p. 100; cf. Forrest 1974. For reflections on these issues in *The Descent*, see Darwin 1871, I, pp. 177–8.

19 Darwin occasionally urged his family as well as colleagues to think twice before drawing sharp political or atheistical conclusions from science. 'I venture to advise you not to carry the degradation principle too far', he wrote, characteristically, for example, to the zoologist Anton Dohrn (letter, 24 May 1875, in Dohrn 1982, p. 63).

animal breeding, 'nature and nurture' (his phrase) and much besides since the 1860s (Bulmer 2003; Forrest 1974).

Deep-seated fears of socio-biological decline as well as exalted hopes of evolutionary improvement and collective 'regeneration' informed such discussions. In the eugenics movement, to which so many early twentieth-century intellectuals were to be drawn, a science of racial engineering aimed to offer appropriate blandishments to 'the fit', whilst providing necessary disincentives to 'the unfit', in order to stem the pathological tide. Eugenics was supposed to provide a demystifying and liberating corrective to superstition, sentimentalism and religion, a rational, planned approach to population, in response to the contemporary bio-political crisis so widely feared.[20] Galton's ideas, combined with those of other European and American theorists and activists, produced a notable scientific flurry, now copiously documented in a secondary literature, which traces the sharply differing national nuances of the movement. There were journals, lobby groups, university posts, essay prizes, laboratories and conferences. There were elaborate explorations of the eugenic implications of new research or argument, such as Weismann's theory of the 'continuity of the germ plasm'. Further complicating the picture (eventually) was the path-breaking work on inheritance of traits in pea plants by a priest from Austrian Silesia, Gregor Mendel (1822–84). His findings languished in obscurity until 'rediscovered' in 1900. Mendel's work paved the way for twentieth-century 'genetics' (the word itself coined by William Bateson in 1905).

Often it was the failure of eugenic movements to effect legislative change that was its most striking feature. Nonetheless, in the USA and later (with far greater consequences, and on an altogether more violent and appalling scale), in Nazi Germany, a version of radical eugenic thought was put into practice. Various American states pioneered laws enabling compulsory sterilisation of the so-called 'feeble-minded', often claiming the very best of motives, but with cruel and tragic personal consequences. Whatever the motives of early eugenic pioneers in the USA, their policy proposals (and successes) attracted notice, admiration and sometimes emulation amongst some European politicians and opinion formers. A full history of the global consequences of such ideas about compulsory sterilisation during the twentieth century remains to be written, although of course the central modern European catastrophe, namely the 'racial state' that was created in Nazi

---

20 See Kevles 1985; Searle 1976, 1981. For recent discussion, surveys and further reading lists, see *New Formations*, 2007.

Germany, is widely documented. The success of eugenic lobbying in the period before 1914 was no doubt far more modest than some of its more extreme campaigners hoped, but some of the outrages that were perpetrated later on in the name of eugenics, or the necessity of collective 'hygiene', even in non-fascist polities, well into the post-war period, only became fully apparent towards the end of the century.

Karl Pearson (1857–1936), who became Galton's equally energetic successor in London, argued that 'only a very thorough eugenic policy can possibly save our race from the evils which must flow from the antagonism between natural selection and medical progress' (Pearson 1912, p. 29). Pearson had come from a middle-class English Quaker background. After mathematics at King's College Cambridge, he had studied law, philosophy and mathematics in Berlin and Heidelberg. He changed his name from Carl to Karl and wrote *The New Werther* in homage to Goethe. He suffered a personal crisis of faith and wrote a passion play that attacked Christianity. Having held a chair of mathematics, he became, under Galton's patronage, the professor of eugenics at University College London. Influenced by Fichte's view that the interests of the people were best expressed by the state, Pearson would come to see himself in the British context as an iconoclastic rationalist, able to draw German thought, particularly of the left, together with Darwinism into a socialist advocacy of imperialism. He was in his own eyes a member of a caste of experts whose views were above the petty factionalism and distortions of party politics; characteristic publications were *The Ethics of Freethought*, which appeared in 1881 and *The Grammar of Science* in 1892. Elected to the Royal Society, Pearson was awarded the Darwin medal in 1898 (Kevles 1985).

Not all eugenicists agreed with Pearson's views that the state should do away with class struggle so as to be better able to fight the *necessary* war between nations. He argued (with the Boer War in mind) that when such violence ceased, mankind would no longer progress, for there would be nothing to check the fertility of inferior stock (Pearson 1905). Early twentieth-century eugenics provides a complicated story in its own right; Janus-faced, it turned between anxious laments on the degeneracy of today and visions of a regenerated and more disciplined tomorrow. It demonstrated an extreme propensity for 'mismeasurement' and the naïvety of the attempt to rise clean above the mud of politics whilst wading neck-deep. Its assertion that science could deliver such value-free guidance, and moreover that the eugenics movement could constitute itself as the representative for the 'scientific point of view', was always contested. Its fanciful aspirations and utopian aspirations are nicely exemplified by Galton's plans for a novel set in the land of 'Kantsaywhere' (Pearson 1914–30, IIIa, pp. 411–25).

Galton, Pearson and their associates extolled science as a means to provide a rational basis for future state population policies. Science was also advocated as a way to achieve a profound moral awakening of the masses. Here the eugenics movement had been prefigured by earlier stalwarts of evolutionary politics, such as Spencer and T. H. Huxley. The latter, for instance had forcefully suggested that science might be both an antidote to superstition, and an alternative moral agent to religion, a source of inspiration to all toiling labourers. He declared that he wanted 'the working classes to understand that Science and her ways are great facts for them – that physical virtue is the base of all other and they are to be clean and temperate and all the rest – not because fellows in black and white ties tell them so, but because these are plain and patent laws of nature which they must obey "under penalties"' (L. Huxley 1900, I, p. 138).[21]

Huxley became an indefatigable Sunday Lecturer, the doyen of working men's colleges as well as a stalwart of the Royal Institution (where, from 1856, he had been Fullerian Professor). In his lectures, he emphasised human nobility: we are from the brutes, but not of them. He envisaged a morally awakened science battling for the souls of the people with a corrupt dogmatic church. Yet he also argued for the full separation of evolutionary study from ethical questions (Huxley 1894). Importantly, he suggested that the progress of civilisation might involve challenging rather than imitating nature. The separation proposed here, however, between science and social belief was to prove hardly less chimerical than in Galton's case. Huxley drew the lesson that political moderacy flowed naturally from his biology. His strictures were directed against particular political positions (of the left and right) rather than against moral or political extrapolations from nature *per se*. Evolution might bring good or bad tidings: 'Retrogressive is as practical as progressive metamorphosis' (Huxley 1891, p. 17).

Elsewhere, Victorian evolutionary theory was to feature within grand and sweeping histories of ideas. Although recent historians have greatly refined such broad-brush interpretations of the clash between 'Science' and 'Religion', Victorian writers often conceptualised their century as engaged in a fight to the death between two antithetical modes of thought. Henry Thomas Buckle (1821–62), for example, described the 'terrible struggle between theology and science, which, having begun in the persecution of

---

21 The natural scientific approach was to be extended to history as well as to politics.

science and in the martyrdom of scientific men, has in these later days, taken a happier turn, and is now manifestly destroying that old theological spirit, which has brought so much misery and ruin upon the world'. 'It is by science, and by science alone, that these horrible delusions are being dissipated' (Buckle 1861, II, p. 596). There appeared to be no place in this formulation for the emancipatory potential of political thought, still less for the novel, drama or poetry.

Buckle sought to produce a new science of history, freed from mythology. An exceptional linguist, traveller and autodidact, his controversial *History of Civilisation in England* was first published in 1857, going through various subsequent enlargements. It argued that beneath the apparently random individuality of human actions lay regular social currents that could be addressed scientifically. He cited statistics on crime and death, including suicide, as well as birth and marriage rates, to illuminate the underlying, impersonal patterns and the viability of systematic analysis. A fully scientific history, declared Buckle, would take in soil, climate and food resources as well as the chemistry of the body itself.

The war for truth was set out in a different, but no less ambitious synthesis a few years later by Friedrich Lange, businessman, teacher, journalist and philosopher.[22] Lange became a professor in Zurich in 1870 and then at Marburg in Germany from 1872. He died in 1875, ten years after producing a monumental study of the history of materialism. Here, knowledge itself was understood in relation to the principle of struggle. History appeared as a vast trial for supremacy between religion, idealism and materialism. Lange noticed how materialism often foundered, lured back towards mysticism. Science could bring intellectual emancipation but, in this respect like Friedrich Nietzsche (1844–1900), Lange wanted to show how it could easily become trapped in the very spiritual fetters that it believed it had shaken off. Nonetheless, Lange admired Darwin's achievements, considering him perhaps the greatest of modern demystifiers and describing the tragedy of waste and death which the great Englishman, building on the foundations of political economy, had shown to operate throughout nature. 'The struggle for a spot of earth, success or non-success in the persecution and extermination of other life, determines the propagation of plants and animals. Millions of spermatozoa, eggs, young creatures hover between life and death that single individuals may develop themselves' (Lange 1925,

22 Marx considered Lange's work confused, 'sham-science', a mixture of 'bombastic ignorance and intellectual laziness' (Marx and Engels 1936, p. 201).

bk. 2, p. 35). Nature moved forwards on an immense funeral pyre of redundant 'unfit' individuals. We have to recognise our world as an 'ocean of birth and death', an 'eternal slaughter of the weak' (Lange 1925, bk. 2, p. 36). It was a short step from such descriptions of nature's waste-disposal system to the endorsement of war as a natural event, even a necessary form of collective catharsis. Treitschke, Von Bernhardi and even, on occasion, Nietzsche, would notoriously draw evolution this way, linking prolonged periods of peace with lethargy and decay (Moore 2002a; Pick 2003); there were writers of other nationalities, French and British amongst them, who spoke in similarly brazen terms.

Wild militarist claims were undoubtedly made in the name of Darwin; yet one must also ask what it was about his work that so easily lent itself to such appropriation in the first place.[23] A memorable war metaphor had appeared after all in the famous concluding passage of *The Origin*:

> Thus, from the war of nature, from famine and death, the most exalted object which we are capable of conceiving, namely, the production of the higher animals, directly follows. There is grandeur in this view of life, with its several powers, having been originally breathed into a few forms or into one; and that, whilst this planet has gone cycling on according to the fixed law of gravity, from so simple a beginning endless forms most beautiful and most wonderful have been, and are being, evolved. (Darwin 1964, pp. 459–60)

At that point in his discussion, Darwin was anxious to insist that he was not providing an *ignoble* conception of the world, after all those ferocious 'dog eat dog' descriptions in his text, but many late Victorian and Edwardian readers were more impressed by the bellicose than the pacific references and sympathised with Darwin's own increasingly gloomy socio-political intimations in *The Descent of Man*.[24]

Nietzsche's attitude to Darwinian ideas was to prove especially important, as well as particularly complex and malleable. Scrutiny of Nietzsche here may also serve to underline the point that the intellectual assault that took place during the second half of the nineteenth century on orthodox morals and religion derived from a variety of philosophical positions

23 Debate about the bellicosity (or otherwise) of Darwin's work in particular, and evolutionary thought and eugenics in general has been studied in various monographs (for instance, Crook 1994; Stepan 1987).

24 In *The Origin*, Darwin proposed that one might 'look with some confidence to a secure future of equally inappreciable length' and had insisted that 'natural selection works solely by and for the good of each being, all corporeal and mental developments will tend to progress towards perfection' (Darwin 1964, p. 489), but *The Descent* was tinged with doubt about the years to come: 'We must remember that progress is no invariable rule' (Darwin 1871, I, p. 177).

and cultural sources, quite apart from Darwin. Some aspects of Nietzsche's shattering diagnosis of Judaeo-Christian values in *The Genealogy of Morals*, for instance, could be reconciled, no doubt, with other militant forms of scientific materialist thought in this period, but its intellectual roots, purposes and consequences ran far wider. Nonetheless, Nietzche's thought clearly drew upon, and entered into dialogue with, the ideas of Darwin and Spencer. He kept abreast of contemporary natural science and had followed recent developments in psychiatry and criminology as well. He had paid sharply close attention to Lange's history of materialism and often seemed to rely on it for his information about modern science (Stack 1983). But if we compare Nietzsche's thought with that of any of the immediate Darwinian circle, it is the differences of ambition, argument, implied reader, style, rhetorical purpose, intellectual context and sensibility that seem ultimately more striking and significant than the similarities.

Certainly references to natural selection, struggle for existence and the possibility of bio-medical degeneration seasoned many of Nietzsche's broadsides against weak will and slavishness (Moore 2002a, pp. 126–7). He also admired Darwin's devastating assault on teleological thinking. On the other hand, Nietzsche sometimes rejected what he took to be a kind of anthropomorphism in the evolutionists' accounts of nature and decried the pettiness, grubbiness and superficiality of what he believed that they so often found there. Thus in *The Gay Science* (1882), amidst aphoristic revelations about the death of God and the possibility of eternal recurrence, he took a swipe at the 'incredibly one-sided doctrine of "the struggle for existence"' and suggested that this reflected the relatively humble social origins of many natural scientists. Born of the common people – their ancestors poor and lowly folks, who 'knew all too intimately the difficulty of scraping by' – they conceptualised a nature in their own image – governed by distress, scarcity and want. Instead the philosopher stressed abundance, preponderance and force. The very intensity and passion of Nietzsche's style and argument seemed to echo his argument: the drive towards expression, growth and domination operated inside us, and remorselessly in nature itself. He painted a landscape in which creatures were not merely intent on survival and struggle, but gave free rein to the will to power (Nietzsche 2001, bk. 5, section 349, p. 208).

Although Nietzsche applauded scientific methodology for its bracing and liberating potential – bringing myths, and indeed all commonplaces, radically into question – he also implied that the quest for 'truth', as extolled by the likes of T. H. Huxley, was a disguised version of the metaphysical faith that science supposedly eschewed: 'even we knowers of today, we godless anti-metaphysicians, still take *our* fire too, from the flame lit by the thousand-year old faith, the Christian faith which was also Plato's faith, that God is truth; that truth is divine' (Nietzsche 2001, bk. 5, section 344, p. 201; Nietzsche's emphasis). But what, Nietzsche mused, if this were to become more and more difficult to believe, if nothing more were to turn out to be divine except error, blindness, the lie? What if God himself were to turn out to be our longest lie? Throughout, Nietzsche wrestled with different conceptions of science, pulled between 'rejection, enthusiasm and ambivalence' (Moore and Brobjer 2004, p. 15). Some have sought to periodise his attitudes to the natural sciences. Thus the metaphysician of the early phase, influenced by Schopenhauer and inspired by Wagner, railed against all vestiges of Socratic rationalism (*The Birth of Tragedy*). Then, having broken with Wagner, Nietzsche sought a cure for his youthful romantic pessimism in the hard truths of science (*Human, All too Human, The Gay Science*) (see Moore 2002a, 2002b; cf. Moore and Brobjer 2004, p. 15). Finally came the reassertion of art over science, or at least of a new conjuncture of art and science. In the *Late Notebooks*, the tragic view of existence predominated and the desiccated rationalism of modern culture was once again eschewed: science risked fatally stripping the world of all meaning; art stood a better chance of doing justice to the contingent nature of existence.[25] Yet shifts and ambiguities occur more locally too. The very idea of the 'will to power' was both metaphysical, a universal force more basic than natural selection, and also, in another vein, an attempted internal revision of Darwinism itself (Richardson 2004, p. 12). Nietzsche perhaps found his own moments of consolation in privileging Lamarck over Darwin: internal effort and striving could thus count in the transmisions to future generations (Stack 1983, 180; cf. Moore and Brobjer 2004).

A less well-noted affinity between Nietzsche and Darwin may lie rather in their shared, ambivalent struggle to accommodate the materialist ideas and model of natural selection. Just as Nietzsche restlessly shifted his ground in pondering evolutionary science, so Darwin worried away at his findings. Some of the harsher and more 'Nietzschean' moments in Darwin's texts contrast with softer sentiments he expressed in notebooks and letters; elsewhere the reverse. Inevitably, the more Darwin is explored in detail, the more received images of his outlook can look like caricature. Drawing on voluminous correspondence, biographers have carefully teased out his varying reactions to specific Victorian campaigns, from birth control and

---

25 On Darwin, biology and Nietzsche's 'will to power', see Richardson 2004.

vivisection to chimney sweeping: 'It makes one shudder to fancy one of one's own children at 7 years old being forced up a chimney – to say nothing of the consequent loathsome disease, and ulcerated limbs, and utter moral degradation.'[26] We can note his passing comments on slavery (a 'sin');[27] track his sympathies for nations involved in specific wars;[28] or identify his attitude to Governor Eyre, the man who had violently put down a rebellion in the British West Indies in a scandal that led John Stuart Mill to organise a campaign for his prosecution (Darwin subscribed £10 to the costs of the action against him).[29] And in these miscellaneous opinions on the issues of the day, we can establish the causes with which he sympathised and those that disgusted him. But the gaps and contradictions, or sometimes the sheer lack of comment on domestic and world events, are just as striking. There are moments where Darwin changed the stream of conventional thought about race, evolution and nature; other occasions where he seems more thoughtlessly to have reproduced the platitudes of his time: hence the plausibility of Nietzsche's praise for the pioneering, demystifying Darwin *and* his criticism of the evolutionist's too narrow acceptance of contemporary beliefs.

3 Nature and inequality

Philosophy was by no means the only field in which Darwinism influenced, but certainly did not bring into existence, harsh critique of morals and religious orthodoxies. Racial anthropology was another. The popular furore in Britain surrounding the aforementioned Governor Eyre or, a few years

---

26 Darwin 1989, v, p. 84. Darwin had been reading Mayhew on chimney sweeping at the time (March 1852) and became a contributor to a society set up to prosecute those who break the law on the matter; see ibid.

27 Darwin 1945, p. 36 and Colp 1987, p. 24. Fitzroy, captain of the *Beagle*, on the other hand condoned slavery, which had led to several quarrels between him and Darwin. For Darwin's relatively progressive belief on this matter, alongside Mill's, as to the need to impeach Governor Eyre after the Jamaica Massacre, see Semmel 1962. In his private correspondence, Darwin sometimes saw himself as a slave, or in his word, 'nigger', dominated by his work, isolated, labouring to prove his worth to hostile colleagues. This word was also used, queasily for us, but comfortably for them, as a term of endearment; he called himself Emma's (i.e. his wife's) 'nigger'; she replied fondly to 'My dearest N.' See Colp 1987, p. 25.

28 Take this remark on the Franco-Prussian War in a letter to H. Settegast 29 September 1870): 'Every one whom I know in England is an enthusiastic wisher for the full and complete success of Germany' (Darwin and Seward 1903, I, p. 324). When Paris fell, however, Darwin expressed his sorrow for the French people; see Desmond and Moore 1991, p. 578.

29 Note that Wallace, Darwin, Lyell, Huxley and Spencer were all on the same side in this debate. See Desmond and Moore 1991, p. 540.

earlier, the 'Indian Mutiny' reflected and shaped new increasingly determinist attitudes to race. From around the mid-nineteenth century, 'race'
was indeed becoming a more significant and central concept in Western
thought, ascribed major explanatory significance in understanding political
and social questions – everything from economic inequalities to national
crime statistics, from the justice of imperial conquest to the capacity (or
lack of it) for creative thought and artistic achievement. Whilst neither the
concept of race nor the existence of racial prejudice were new, gathering
'scientific' interest in and fear about the immutable causes and effects of
human racial difference were evident in many quarters. Whatever disagreements followed, the utility of the concept of race itself was often placed
beyond argument.

The end results of racial mixing (miscegenation) constituted the central preoccupation in Gobineau's *Essay on the Inequality of the Human Races*
(1853–5), a French work whose direct influence, negligible at the time,
grew stronger by the last quarter of the century. Natural racial laws could
not be gainsaid, declared the Scottish author, Robert Knox, sometimes
dubbed in the twentieth century 'the father of British racism'. It is perhaps true that his book, *The Races of Men*, first published in 1850, has been
more carefully scrutinised by recent historians of race than by his immediate contemporaries, but his contention that 'race is everything: literature,
science, art – in a word, civilisation depends on it' pithily characterised an
increasingly commonplace view. Richard Wagner's contemporaneous anti-
Semitic study, *Judaism in Music*, was another striking production. We may
now see it as an ominous landmark of racist invective, presaging worse to
come. Yet its intellectual significance was by no means widely hailed at the
outset.

As this suggests, an inventory of late Victorian commentators who took
such authors, or at least some aspect of their more strident personal views,
to task, might well be longer than a list of those who simply extolled
them. Nonetheless, in diverse ways, biological and anthropological myths
were insidiously reshaping assumptions about the shared physical, moral
or psychological features of humanity. In the history of anti-Semitism, for
instance, a substantial shift (evident in fiction, social and political commentary, and the sciences) can be observed across the nineteenth century from
a primarily religious definition of the Jew (in which allegiance, 'belief', was
understood to be determining of identity) to the notion of the Jew as member of a 'race' marked apart for ever by inheritance and given character. In
parallel, national identification was less and less to be understood in terms

of choice (as say in the French Revolutionary notion of the foreign sympathiser 'becoming' a citizen, even being elected to the Assembly), more and more in terms of inheritance, blood, soil and inalienable roots (Hobsbawm 1990).

In the second half of the nineteenth century, criminology and psychiatry were consolidated as distinct disciplines and in each case drew heavily on ideas of evolution and of its reverse. They became centrally concerned with innate biological factors in the make-up of personality. Political agitators were sometimes subjected to forensic appraisal, as likely to be labelled as degenerates, recidivists or evolutionary 'throw-backs' as rational opponents. Each individual criminal case could be understood as the subset of a particular degenerate type, demanding close bodily investigation. Fear and folklore went scientific and claimed a new unassailable objectivity as the supposed inferiority and peculiarities of, *inter alia*, colonial subjects in India or new immigrants to London, Paris and New York, were solemnly charted. Fingerprint samples, studies of handwriting, diagnosis of the art of the insane, even medico-psychiatric analysis of tattooing became popular. Claims to have created a science of the criminal – replete with images of the thief's handle-shaped ears and the murderer's monkey-like torso – were developed most spectacularly by Cesare Lombroso (1835–1909) and his circle of followers inside and outside Italy. But this was only the most dramatic of many such endeavours, claiming some allegiance to Darwin (alongside other scientific luminaries), and aiming to provide a reliable guide to biological and moral differences (Gibson 2002; Pick 1989).

Deviants emerged from the womb, according to several prominent Italian criminologists in the last three decades of the nineteenth century. Alternatively the criminal was warped by the noxious 'brew' of the social milieu. This was claimed by various French specialists in a long-running argument about the 'born criminal' and the wilder claims of the 'Italian school'. Either way, it was feared that modernity was in the grip of biological decay. Lombroso and some of his followers argued for preventive detention of the *potentially* most dangerous types, in advance of their crimes – ideas that were to fascinate novelists ranging from Conrad to Tolstoy. The proposals gained considerable traction later on, for instance, in fascist Italy. In the earlier period, however, such policy recommendations were often met with opposition and rejection, leading the theorists either to find ever more ingenious justifications and classifications for their science, or sometimes to tone down their more strident claims. In Lombroso's final years, the intense focus on criminal bodies gave way to a new preoccupation with spiritualism: he conducted a series of experiments in a bid to make contact with his dead mother.

Many specialists in criminal science or more generally in racial anthropology saw their target as the sentimental ideas about equality or the human *tabula rasa* to be found within the Enlightenment. Science proves that humanity is not a democracy, thundered the anthropologist James Hunt in England, as he excoriated 'sentimentalism' on behalf of other 'races' (or as the polygenist Hunt believed, other species). Thomas Carlyle had fulminated about much the same thing in his notorious *Occasional Discourse on the Nigger Question*.[30] But Hunt gave the scathing anti-sentimentalist view a powerful new scientific patina. Committed to the view that there were distinct species rather than races, Hunt and his associates at the newly founded Anthropological Society (1863) did not find Darwinism congenial.[31] Only after Hunt died in 1869, was the impasse between monogenist and polygenist theory overcome, when the Ethnological Society and the Anthropological Society merged to form the Anthropological Institute of Great Britain and Ireland (1871).

Darwin himself remarked blithely that he expected the 'less intellectual races' to be 'exterminated' in the course of time (F. Darwin 1887, II, p. 211). Yet Darwin did not accept this notion (à la Hunt) of separate species of man, corresponding to contemporary racial categories. Nor could he countenance the idea that any bodily feature or psychological trait was historically immutable. But the polygeny argument did not simply vanish once Darwin began to publish; only slowly did the view of separate human species retreat. It should be added that the assumption that all people were part of the same species still lent itself perfectly well to theories of racial inferiority and superiority. Other races might be seen not as irredeemably

---

30 First printed in *Fraser's Magazine* in 1849, the polemic was subsequently published in revised form in 1853. For John Stuart Mill's ardent critique of Carlyle's views, see Mill 1850. The dispute exposed the two thinkers' fundamentally different assumptions about law and the moral basis for Western rule, and indeed about the nature of deeper human affiliation itself, across the so-called races. Their distinct arguments and styles exemplified ideological divisions in Victorian thought that can in turn be traced back through various conflicting strands of Enlightenment and romantic theory (Stepan 1982). Mill considers his own complex relationship to Carlyle's style and thought in his *Autobiography*. For an exploration of shifting utilitarian views of race, assimilation and conquest in Anglo-Indian relations, see Stokes 1959. For analyses of the intellectual argument, social context and sexual politics of the Mill–Carlyle exchange, see Hall 2002.

31 There is an extensive secondary literature on the uses of evolution and the language of race in the history of anthropology and medicine. Helpful older surveys include Lorimer 1988; Melman 1991; Stepan 1982; Stocking 1987. For an illuminating recent regional study see Anderson 2002.

backward (anatomy as destiny), but rather as less biologically (as well as culturally) evolved. As Huxley declared in a speech relating to the American Civil War, the abolition of slavery was right, not on the grounds that all are equal, but rather on the grounds that the superior white man should show moral compassion. Non-whites would be unable to compete with their 'bigger-brained and smaller-jawed rival', in a contest which is to be carried on 'by thoughts and not by bites'. The highest places in the hierarchy of civilisation, he added, 'will assuredly not be within the reach of our dusky cousins, though it is by no means necessary that they should be restricted to the lowest' (Huxley 1865). Innate inequality of intelligence and morals was widely treated as immutable scientific fact. Thus the French writer, Georges Vacher de Lapouge (1854–1935), author of *Social Selection* (1895), said that the slogan *liberty, equality, fraternity* ought to be replaced with the words, *determinism, inequality, selection* (Burrow 2000, p. 94). The political disputes that underlay the many variants of such Social Darwinism could not be resolved by science itself not least because the unit of analysis was so arbitrary. Some sought to discuss evolution at the level of the individual body; others spoke of groups, cities, nations, races or continents. In short the so-called biological data tended to be manipulated to fit the required hypothesis (Burrow 2000, pp. 92–108).

The cluster of beliefs now referred to under headings such as the new scientific racism or Social Darwinism certainly provided new positivist rationalisations of older social hatreds and hierarchies, but they also restyled in powerful ways Western understandings of international relations, laws and institutions. Images of atavism and degeneration haunted the peripheries of empire and the heart of the European city. And in the final years of the nineteenth century the sense of bio-medical crisis was often cranked up. Thus parasitism was to fascinate biologists, social investigators and racial theorists alike in the 1880s and 1890s. Degeneration theory has a complex history of its own, and its widely recognised founding text had been produced in 1857 by the Catholic psychiatrist, Dr Benedict-Augustin Morel (1809–73). He worked in Rouen in Northern France. As the date of his most significant treatise suggests, this text was written independently of the impending Darwinian tradition. By the last decades of the century, however, books with titles such as *Degeneration: A Chapter in Darwinism* (Lankester 1880) sought to consolidate the debate in terms of evolutionary naturalism and natural selection.

Who were 'the degenerate' and 'the unfit'? These groups, whilst variously designated, included prisoners and inmates of mental hospitals. Sometimes the terms were used with anti-aristocratic innuendo (the effete and pathetic privileged class, as pictured for instance in Huysmans' tale, *Against Nature* or in H. G. Wells' *The Time Machine*), but generally they were taken to refer to specific subgroups amongst the socially disadvantaged, the casual poor or new immigrants, the 'residuum' and 'outcast' of the cities (or sometimes remote 'uncivilised' rural hinterlands), the white or black 'trash' so often conjured in American hereditarian thought. Ideas about culling the unfit (or sending them to labour colonies) were openly discussed at scientific congresses. In various countries, militant 'new women' who placed career or politics before motherhood and marriage aroused worry and contempt amongst eugenic lobby groups. Robust, intelligent and socially privileged women were urged to do the appropriate thing – marry and replenish the 'stock' with a plentiful supply of babies to support the requirements of the economy, the army or the empire (Kevles 1985; Richardson 2003; Ronsin 1980; Semmel 1960). Meanwhile militarists echoed Hegel's more chilling formulations about the tonic effects of war (as set out much earlier in *The Philosophy of Right*) and combined them with the language of Darwinism and sometimes with shrill pronatalism.

Romantic endorsements of or damning attacks upon the modern state were equally possible through a Social Darwinist lens. These arguments were certainly pervasive, but were also significantly affected by local cultural concerns and political anxieties in different countries.[32] An individualistic reading of the science had been most influentially elaborated by Herbert Spencer and reached its fullest extension in the United States. It was here that Spencer had his greatest audience and achieved the most dramatic sales (cf. Bannister 1979; Peel 1971; Wiltshire 1978). He had attacked state intervention remorselessly. He had viewed various forms of charity, for instance, as anathema to progress and seemed to accept the need for the natural wastage of the 'inferior'. Civilisation was its own worst enemy, retarded by its supposedly humane policies, stymieing nature's broader tendencies to betterment. The tone was generally rather optimistic; the future, Spencer believed, belonged to the 'industrial' rather than the 'militant' form of society. Peace and progress were inextricably tied together; trade was the catalyst of progress and formal empires were unnecessary. By the 1880s and 1890s, even Spencer had his doubts about the pacific intent of the nations

---

32 The literature covering the global reception, diffusion and elaboration of these arguments and models is now copious. See for instance, Bannister 1979; Conry 1974; Dikötter 1992; Engs 2005; Gasman 1971; Glick 1972; Hofstadter 1955b; Kelly 1981; Kohn 1986; Pancaldi 1983; Pusey 1983; Vucinich 1988.

of modern Europe, including Britain. To his horror, he came to see that these two supposedly distinct 'types' of society, the industrial and the militant, were converging, as even Britain became increasingly 'Prussianised' (Spencer 1876–1896, III, ch. 24).

A pioneering study of the American context of Social Darwinism by Richard Hofstadter (1944) generated much historical enquiry in its wake.[33] Hofstadter showed how a class of rich businessmen drew on evolutionary ideas to rationalise economic procedures. Thus John D. Rockefeller: 'The growth of a large business is merely a survival of the fittest.' Business was perceived as the working out of nature, although in practice, as has been pointed out by Peter Gay (1994), Carnegie and Rockefeller seemed to prefer mergers and monopolies to cutthroat competition. Amongst the American apostles of free trade evolutionism, W. G. Sumner provides a particularly striking example. He argued fervently that society ignored Darwin's law at its peril. 'If we do not like the survival of the fittest', he told the Free Trade Club in 1879, 'we have only one possible alternative, and that is the survival of the unfittest' (quoted in Gay 1994, p. 58). In a piece on state interference in 1887, Sumner acknowledged his extreme scepticism about the value of state 'meddling' with nature (Sumner 1911, p. 213). This was *laissez-faire* with a vengeance. The title to another of Sumner's polemics against intervention in 1894 was 'The Absurd Effort to Make the World Over'. Egalitarianism, he argued, was mere wishful thinking.

The French translator of *The Origin*, Clémence-Auguste Royer, derived not only a *laissez-faire* moral, but also a distinctly anti-clerical message from the text (J. P. Clark 1984; Conry 1974). In Germany, statist versions of Darwinism were perhaps more typical.[34] In Italy, the first translation of *The Origin* appeared in 1864 and Darwinism, whilst remaining highly contentious, especially when materialist theoreticians and doctors challenged lawyers and priests as to the idea of free will, was nonetheless quickly to find some resonance in nationalist ideology (Landucci 1981; Pancaldi 1983).

---

33 Hofstadter made clear that the notion, widely disseminated in the period of the two World Wars, that social Darwinism was a bellicose philosophy largely emanating from Germany, involved an extremely partial reading of the history. Arguably, however, he oversimplified the American situation by focusing so much on the free-trade ethos and so little on other models. For a critique of Hofstadter, see Bannister 1979 and, in turn, for a critical response to the latter's work, see Jones 1980. Hofstadter stimulated other historians to trace Darwinism in diverse national cultures.

34 Studies of German Social Darwinism also show the remarkable range of political claims that were made upon Darwin. Feminists and anti-feminists, liberals, conservatives and socialists, imperialists and internationalists all sought to find some support in his work. For comparative comments on the national reception of Darwinism, see Glick 1972; cf. Gasman 1971; the useful appendix, 'Social Darwinism' in Crook 1994, pp. 200–6; Crook 2007; Kelley 1987; and Kohn 1986.

In Spain, various novelists and painters took up the Darwinian theme with relish, although the Catholic Church was perhaps to prove more effective than in Italy at mobilising intellectual and political opposition to these new ideas (Paul 1972).

Even as argument raged, and Darwinists of left and right offered their own competing interpretations, many fundamental assumptions were really shared. Karl Kautsky (1854–1938), for instance, a Marxist enthusiast for Darwinism, appeared to assume the real existence of superior and inferior races, despite his trenchant opposition to early twentieth-century blood myths and his endeavour to substitute the term 'peoples' for 'races' (Kautsky 1926, *passim*, 1988, pp. 52, 127, 143). Evolutionary naturalism and political prophecy went hand in hand. Kautsky's Marxism, as Eric Hobsbawm writes, was the 'definer of its orthodoxy' in its phase of triumphant late nineteenth-century confidence: 'It was materialist, determinist, inevitabilist, evolutionist, and firmly identified the "laws of history" with the "laws of science".'[35] Kautsky's assumptions were in fact generally Lamarckian, but this presented no problem, as he viewed Lamarckian and Darwinian perspectives as much the same thing (Kautsky 1988, p. xxxiii).

'Darwin, Spencer and Marx' were placed side by side, in the subtitle of a noteworthy book by the Italian socialist politician, and follower of Lombroso's criminology, Enrico Ferri (1905 [1896]). In Russia, some Marxists were critical of Social Darwinism, although others – Plekhanov is the best example – were attracted to the view that Darwin's principles constituted a natural corollary of Marxism (Vucinich 1988, pp. 356–66). Darwin's theory, Plekhanov claimed, was impressively dialectical (Plekhanov 1934, p. 172). Naturally, both Plekhanov and Kautsky were more critical of the politically gradualist conclusions many other commentators had drawn from Darwinian materials (Plekhanov 1969; Salvadori 1979, pp. 23–4). The struggle for existence, they insisted, should be conceived not in terms of the individual but collective efforts. Even the Great War was understood merely as a temporary deviation on the general march of socialist and evolutionary progress (Kautsky 1988, p. xxxvi). English Fabianism's far from trivial flirtation with Social Darwinism or eugenics involved many of the same presumptions; the unit of evolutionary analysis was no longer the individual, but the class, society or nation (Jones 1980). Economics, physiology

---

35 Hobsbawm 1987, p. 267; cf. Salvadori 1979, p. 23. On the origins of the 'Darwinian left', see Stack 2003.

and heredity were run together in a new hybrid form of diagnosis: physiological 'capital' was said to be vital in the struggle for survival of nations, whilst racial 'expenditure' demanded the keenest actuarial scrutiny; society, one commentator explained, must be analysed in terms of 'biological economics' (Geddes 1886, p. 1166).

Thus the celebration of individualism that can be gleaned sometimes in Darwin's work, and far more stridently, in Spencer's, was countered by a later generation of evolutionists who stressed the indispensability of groups and insisted on the advantages of social co-operation over struggle. The Fabian-leaning David G. Ritchie (1853–1903) wrote a characteristic work of the time, *Darwinism and Politics* (1889), in which he sought to ally progressive policy ambitions (social justice, a greater role for education and so forth), with the logic of evolution. Societies, he suggested, advance through imitation and co-operation, not simply through the brute force of individual will. In organised communities, social sympathy could mitigate the 'internal strife' of bloody nature. Ritchie's work exemplified the spirit of a new 'reform Darwinism' (Hawkins 1997, ch. 7), evident in the motley pronouncements of various anarchists, socialists and 'new liberals'. L. T. Hobhouse (1864–1929), a prominent journalist, did much to champion this new view. Governments were urged to think about 'the community', and to do far more to tackle the problems of modern poverty, ill-health and industrial inefficiency, in the interests of all (Freeden 1978).[36] Welfare was no longer a dirty word. References to altruism and co-operation, and also a certain reverence for nature, in Darwin's own accounts were now eagerly taken up and drawn out. We see this new focus in the work of an obscure clerk from the British Civil Service, Benjamin Kidd (1858–1916), who quietly penned *Social Evolution* (1894), only to discover he had a best-seller on his hands. Here religion made a come-back, now seen as evolution's best friend, its values extolled as those best adapted to ensure socio-biological progress.

4   Uncertain futures

Friedrich Lange pointed out how Darwin wanted to jettison the supernatural and the unknowable in favour of the natural and the comprehensible. Whilst this is true, such an account does not quite capture the fluidity of Darwin's thought nor the bold imaginative gambles that he took. Despite

---

36 For related discussion of political philosophy in France, and specifically on the emergence of biomedical ideas about social solidarity and social defence, see Nye 1994.

the congruence of some of his pronouncements with those of Galton and company, the style, tone and capacity for self-doubt were different. We also know, as Lange could not, that Darwin's thought was by no means encompassed by his best-known, formal works. The range of his writing, published and unpublished, was much wider. In addition to his private correspondence, he filled a series of notebooks with an extraordinary range of speculations. The first notebook entitled 'The Transmutation of Species' had opened in July 1837; such scribblings continued unabated into the subsequent decade. Darwin cannot be seen in conventionally defined terms as a political firebrand any more than he can be dubbed a consistent reactionary. Undoubtedly he was appalled by some social and political disorders he witnessed in his lifetime, but his work also displayed a remarkable openness of thought and a willingness to probe boundaries of many types. He deployed materialist terms even where this allied him uncomfortably with politically revolutionary ideas. These jottings, bold in conception, shy of publicity, ranged across sexual desire, inheritance, theology, the moral sense, evil as a function of our biological descent, God as human projection, morality as a function of the influences to which we are subjected, and many other matters. Darwin probed the materialist origins of our behaviour, yet he also dreaded where the work was taking him. The potentially subversive implications of this trajectory were clear enough to their author but he was unable to censor his 'free associations' any more than he could the saliva, which, he declared in a notebook, ran freely at moments of sexual desire, whether consciously willed or not.[37]

Several recent commentators have suggested that materialism rather than evolutionism caused the deepest moral disturbance, both for Darwin himself and his critics. It was this aspect of his work which Victorian readers either failed to grasp or refused to countenance (Bowler 1989, pp. 86–7). But Darwin was not comfortable with the idea that he might provide ammunition to radical political dissenters, low-life anti-clerics and other extremists. The prospect of being associated with outright hostility to the church or state

---

37 'Sexual desire makes saliva to flow / yes, *certainly* / curious association: I have seen Nina licking her chops. – someone has described slovering teethless-jaws as picture of disgusting lewd old man. One's tendency to kiss, and almost bite, that which one sexually loves is probably connected with flow of saliva, and hence with action of *mouth* and jaws. – Lascivious women are described as biting : so do stallions always. – No doubt man has great tendency to exert all senses, when thus stimulated, smell, as Sir C Bell says, and hearing music, to certain degree sexual. – The association of saliva is probably due to our distant ancestors having been like *dogs* to bitches.' Grubar 1974, p. 338. 'Nina' was one of Darwin's dogs.

appeared to made him wretched, indeed to make him retch.[38] Through the
1820s and 1830s, some political radicals and medical men had sought to use
evolutionary ideas as well as materialist arguments as part of a wider campaign against current political arrangements as well as orthodox morality.
Darwin's modern interpreters have debated the timing of his move from
theism to 'agnosticism' (Huxley's word) and have argued over the degree
to which he continued to believe in a preordained design, even if the very
notion of such a blueprint went against his own most challenging formulations (Ospovat 1980). How had his teachers and associates, in Edinburgh,
Cambridge or London, affected him? To what degree did his family's fate
and values impinge upon his scientific views – from the enduring religious
faith of his wife, to the devastating loss of his daughter, Annie? That death,
it has been argued, caused him to discard the last vestiges of the Christian
creed.

It is now and then claimed that Darwin, in the end, definitively accepted
that the world was entirely devoid of God. But to seek that final resolution
of Darwin's beliefs is to conjure away the contradictions that mark his
oeuvre and to travesty this most complex of modern Victorians. To see
evolutionism at large as necessarily at war with religion also underestimates
the ingenious accommodations that have continued to be made long after
Darwin's death (see Lustig *et al.* 2004, ch. 1). One very significant merit
of the greater literary and metaphorical emphasis that was to mark late
twentieth-century studies of Victorian evolutionary thought has been a
greater appreciation of the plurality of connotations, the rich novelistic
and imaginative quality of Darwin's work and more generally of scientific
communications.[39] Sometimes Darwin's public references to religion have
been interpreted away as mere rhetorical subterfuge. But it seems doubtful
that we can make so crude a distinction in Darwin's case between a genuine
belief in and a cynical deployment of God. The language of religion, even of
demonology, sometimes informed the very insights in which he shook the
faith. Indeed even in his notoriously 'blasphemous' notebooks, it is striking
how often Darwin brings in metaphysics and religious images, even as he
seeks to make them redundant. Darwin's equivocation on such matters was
matched by the twists and turns of faith evident in many of his scientific
contemporaries. His concessions to religious belief were arguably exceeded

38 Darwin's chronic experience of illness has prompted extensive interpretation and a rich vein of
speculation; see Bowlby 1990; Colp 1977; Desmond and Moore 1991.
39 See Beer 1983; Levine 1988. For Darwin's 'metaphor', see Young 1985. Other works on literary
Darwin or the Darwinian strain in literature (in Hardy or Conrad, for example) have followed.

by those of Spencer, who generally had a 'let-out clause' for the materialism which shaped his pronouncements.

Darwin's autobiographical remarks lend some weight to the view that he became increasingly disillusioned with religious, providential and natural theological explanations of nature, but he remained famously cautious about open dissent and continued to doubt himself. He would advise his son George to 'pause, pause, pause' before writing an article which uncompromisingly attacked religion (Desmond and Moore 1991, pp. 602–3).[40] Expediency and moral confusion remained difficult for anyone to disentangle. As he declared on one occasion to Hooker, 'My theology is a simple muddle; I cannot look at the universe as the result of blind chance, yet I can see no evidence of beneficent design, or indeed of design of any kind, in the details.'[41] In the autobiographical sketch which he produced for his children in 1876, he vividly described the internal struggle he had in overcoming orthodox religious philosophy. He admitted to them his growing realisation that with the theory of selection, natural theology 'which formerly seemed to me so conclusive, fails' (F. Darwin 1958, p. 63). To spell out the conclusion: 'There seems to be no more design in the variability of organic beings, and in the action of natural selection, than in the course which the wind blows' (F. Darwin 1958, p. 63). Darwin told his children that belief in an intelligent God must be drawn from 'deep inward conviction and feelings which are experienced by most persons'. But he confided that the religious sentiment had never been very strongly developed in him (F. Darwin 1958, p. 65). Interestingly, however, he cast his agnosticism as a *loss* of perception, rather than as a firm conviction. It was like being colour-blind (F. Darwin 1958, p. 65).

---

40 The moral problem of speaking out on the subject of religion, Darwin considered 'frightfully difficult'. For his view that overt attacks on religion were counterproductive, and to be avoided, see Desmond and Moore 1991, p. 26. Despite his diffidence, it seems likely that the damage his work inflicted on orthodox faith was a major factor in preventing him from being knighted. When the idea was mooted by Palmerston (the incoming Prime Minister in 1859), the idea was blocked, probably through the intervention of the Bishop of Oxford, Wilberforce.

41 Letter to J. D. Hooker (12 July 1870) (Darwin and Seward 1903, I, p. 321). A young science lecturer, Dr Edward Aveling, asked Darwin if he might dedicate a book to him. The work in question was due to appear in the International Library of Science and Freethought, under the editorship of Annie Besant and Charles Bradlaugh, MP. Darwin replied that although he was a strong supporter of free thought, he thought it best to avoid discussion of religion and had always 'confined myself to science' (quoted in Desmond and Moore 1991, p. 26). On the other hand, to take a conflicting example, note Darwin's (cautious) support in the 1870s for *The Index*, an American weekly from the radical wing of the Free Religion Association, a grouping of Unitarians and philosophical unbelievers who demanded freedom from dogma and promoted a humanistic 'free' religion (Desmond and Moore 1991, p. 591).

Evolutionism as such was not necessarily a materialist philosophy, but Darwin's frequently was (Sanderson 1990). Had he given full vent to the ideas in the notebooks he might have expected a more stormy response than the somewhat bland reception that his first communication on natural selection, alongside that of Alfred Russel Wallace (1832–1913), received at the Linnean Society in 1858.[42] Later, Wallace would join the ranks of those who balked at the materialist implications of evolution. It is worth setting out Wallace's intellectual formation and social position here as they were so strikingly different to Darwin's own background. Indeed Darwin's comfortable social origins and status (be it as the well-connected young voyager, or the settled country squire in Kent) has often served to define a broader image of the leisured, gentleman evolutionist. Wallace had a very different start to life. He was the eighth of nine children, born in Wales and brought up in genteel but very modest circumstances. He left school at fourteen. His knowledge of botany, astronomy, evolution and politics was picked up 'on the hoof', as he proceeded, not without difficulty, to make his way in the world. If Wallace was untypical in his exceptional qualities as a thinker, traveller and writer, his desire for intellectual betterment and for enlarged moral horizons was also exemplary of a large world of self-taught working-class and lower-middle-class workers, whose leisure time was devoted to political clubs, institutes and lecture halls, and who devoured an ever-expanding popular scientific literature.

When his family moved to London, young Alfred and his brother John began to frequent the 'Hall of Science' in central London where they learnt about the ideas of Robert Owen and Thomas Paine. Alfred began an apprenticeship as a surveyor in 1837, but gradually, despite family pressures, and a chequered career as surveyor and schoolteacher, it was his love of travelling, nature writing and scientific speculation that won out. An invitation to accompany the naturalist Henry Walter Bates to the Amazon in 1848 was but the start of a remarkable adventure that took him to the wilder spots of South America and Asia. He studied the latest works on

---

42 The Darwin–Wallace presentation (made in the absence of both men) had consisted of a short essay by Wallace, extracts from a sketch by Darwin from 1844 and from a letter to Asa Gray of 1857. The lack of opposition expressed may well have owed something to the intimidating presence of Charles Lyell and Joseph Hooker (Loewenberg 1959, p. 33). The President of the Linnean Society, Thomas Bell, was later to remark that the year which has passed 'has not, indeed, been marked by any of those striking discoveries which at once revolutionise, so to speak, the department of science on which they bear; it is only at remote intervals that we can reasonably expect any sudden and brilliant innovation which shall produce a marked and permanent impress on the character of any branch of knowledge, or confer a lasting and important service on mankind' (Bell 1859, pp. viii–ix).

plants and animals, and was an avid admirer of Darwin's *Journal of the Voyage of the Beagle* (which he read in the early 1840s), Humboldt's narratives of his travels in South American, Coombe's studies in phrenology and, perhaps most crucially, Malthus' *Essay on the Principle of Population*. He had a taste for political radicalism and could never accept that it could be just or acceptable for one child to be born a millionaire and another into a life of poverty. He called this a crime against God. Wallace became a fellow of the Royal Society in 1893 and continued to write prolifically on a large range of subjects, from evolution to spiritualism. His readers would find him at one point speculating about the outer reaches of the universe, at another, discoursing on the iniquities of this world and pondering the nitty-gritty of social policy reform. In 1881, at the start of a decade in which his espousal of socialism was becoming far more pronounced, he was appointed as the founding president of the Land Nationalisation Society.

The degree to which natural selection could explain our fundamental humanity was an issue which would soon pull apart the temporary convergence of thought between Wallace and Darwin in the 1850s. 'Natural selection' had apparently come to the former whilst in a fever, and increasingly he sought to hedge in this potentially pathological argument with important caveats. Wallace distanced himself from the shared approach with Darwin, moving progressively towards a 'spirit'-centred evolutionism (as well as radical land reform projects and other intriguing political hobby-horses) which Darwin found deeply worrying: 'I hope you have not murdered too completely your own and my child', he wrote to the erstwhile fellow parent of natural selection. On seeing a piece in the *Quarterly Review*, outlining Wallace's revisionist ideas in the late 1860s, Darwin had added and triply underlined the word 'No'. Wallace concluded that the human mind could not be explained in materialist, evolutionary terms; a gorilla's brain would have sufficed for our needs, he argued, whilst the human being had an excess capacity, for which selection, dealing only with the utility of the here and now, could not account. Wallace came to recognise an unseen spiritual hand and admitted to Darwin that his views had been altered by studying 'the existence of forces and influences not yet recognised by science' (quoted in Desmond and Moore, 1991, p. 569).

Philosophical unease with the imperialist claims, missionary zeal and quasi-religious fervour of natural science can be picked up in a variety of settings in the late nineteenth century. Rationalism and empiricism were themselves placed under the intellectual microscope, as we saw earlier in the case of Nietzsche.

But at stake was not simply the adequacy of one method over another, in the scrutiny of humanity, or the animal world, but growing dread about the nature of the human mind itself, and the dire consequences of bringing those minds together in new, politically powerful aggregates. In England, commentators divided as to whether national character might free the nation from the extremes of disorder and convulsion evident on the continent, for instance most recently in the Paris Commune of 1871. Walter Bagehot (1826–77), author of *Physics and Politics* (1872), influenced many of his contemporaries with his exploration of the power of imitation and instinctual reflexes in the formation of national character. Bagehot drew upon Darwin as he warned that politics was a delicate science. In his work, society appears a fragile organism and civilisation a rare achievement, not some inevitable destiny. 'Only a few nations' he warned in 1872, 'and these of European origin, advance; and yet these think – seem irresistibly compelled to think – such advance to be inevitable, natural and eternal' (Bagehot 1872, p. 42).

Whilst they castigated radical and popular political movements of the past and present for their delusions of rationality, the new 'scientific' historians and political theorists often glossed over questions about the rationality or neutrality of their own procedures and assumptions. Yet reason itself was now sometimes seen as an altogether frail instrument. For the influential French historian, Anglophile and keen student of modern science, Hippolyte Taine, it had an unmistakable responsibility – with its sins of omission and commission – for the horrors of the French Revolution. Whilst he reviled Rousseau, Taine was as committed as anyone to the proposition that the nature of society could be laid out and investigated upon the philosopher's table. But for Taine, dry and abstract eighteenth-century 'reasoning' had been overtaken by the 'scientific' findings of investigators such as Broca, Lombroso and Charcot. He was intent on getting to the violence out there in the revolution and diagnosing the psychopathology of the crowd. As he baldly admitted: 'J'ai horreur de la foule.' Eighteenth-century philosophy was viewed as something sterile and systematic, an artificial imposition upon reality. Science on the other hand derived from observation, experiment and induction; it accepted incompleteness and the provisional nature of conclusions. For all the ambition of cool scientific appraisal, his own descriptions sometimes erupted into passion and fear. There was nothing provisional about Taine's evolutionary verdict on French revolutionary atavism as he glimpsed springing forth 'the barbarian', 'the primitive animal', 'the grinning, sanguinary, wanton baboon, who chuckles while he slays, and gambols over the ruin he has accomplished' (Taine 1878–85, 1, pp. 52–3).

In political theory as in historiography, there was growing attention to the psychological incoherence and hysterical propensities of massed populations. Huge gatherings and militant (let alone violent) protest movements came increasingly to be portrayed in quasi-psychiatric terms. Indeed in the thirty-year period after the Paris Commune in 1871, a range of historians and crowd psychologists wrote deeply critical, forensic, analyses of group hysteria or psychosis, convinced that there was no real 'moral economy' to be found in the crowd. Le Bon, Tarde, Sighele and a variety of similar commentators explained at length why the reader had every reason to be worried that we were now living in what was quickly dubbed 'the age of the crowd'. The anti-democratic leanings, clichés, sensationalism, self-promotion, snobberies, racial tropes and gender prejudices that run through this literature have been amply contextualised and appropriately analysed since (see, for example, Barrows 1981; Ginneken 1992; Nye 1975). But even leaving aside Le Bon and company's original intellectual significance, the course of subsequent mass group phenomena (the spectacle of the Nuremberg rallies being but the most notorious case in point) means that such pioneer enquirers remain complex and often double-edged sources, not simply one-dimensional figures to be dismissed with mirth.

Collective 'unreason' and 'atavism', much raked over in the political theory, history-writing and social psychology of the *fin de siècle*, were also to be the launching pad for new probing fictions about the uncanny. The field of the primitive and the regressive, as well as the ghostly and the telepathic – horrors and wonders of heaven and earth insufficiently dreamt of in nineteenth-century scientific naturalism – returned to the fore in those final decades. Such pursuits often had a borderline quality; the investigator poised between scepticism about and enthusiasm for the fleeting and the fantastic. It was the age of Henry James' *The Turn of the Screw*. In the mid-1890s, Henry's elder brother William would become the president of the Cambridge society established for the pursuit of psychical research. In *The Varieties of Religious Experience* William James declared 'the exploration of the subliminal region' the essential task. The Society for Psychical Research, now much studied, recognised the limits of conventional science and sought to probe 'beyond'. But whether this was to be a rationalist pursuit of the unknown or whether the methods of enquiry would themselves need to be in some sense 'irrationalist' remained very much in question. Freud (who was to become a corresponding member of the Society) would provide a dynamic route out of this particular conundrum, but his contribution to political thought will have to await the next volume of this series.[43] Freud famously declared that Copernicus and Darwin had struck the first two great blows against human narcissism; psychoanalysis, he suggested, had provided the third, showing that even the ego was not master in its own house. Let man visit the orang-utang in captivity, Darwin had declared in one of his private notebooks much earlier, let him see its expressive whine, its intelligence, its affection, passion, rage, sulkiness and despair and then 'let him dare to boast of his proud preeminence'.[44]

In these years, new understandings of the 'unconscious' were emerging, often poised between a kind of 'ape in man' post-Darwinian trepidation and intuitions of unconscious meaning, whose exploration went beyond biological concerns with 'selection', struggle and survival. Novels such as Stevenson's *Strange Case of Dr Jekyll and Hyde* (1886), Du Maurier's *Trilby* (1894) or Bram Stoker's *Dracula* (1897), entangled in the nomenclature of apish spite, racial endowments or criminal brains, were also able to popularise a new shadowy language of dream and desire. Shaw's theatrical work, *Man and Superman* (1903) illustrates the difficulty in hunting out straightforward Darwinian influences and beliefs in the work of novelists or dramatists. The title itself played on a very contemporary nerve and Darwin himself was cited in the preface. But in solemnly cataloguing references, we may fail to see the comedy, the intellectual ferment, the 'playing with', rather than simply endorsing of, the author of *The Origin*, or, for that matter, in this playwright's case, Nietzsche, Wagner and Ibsen, not to mention Don Juan himself upon whose myth he aimed, without concessions to prudery or stultifying convention, to cast a new and open light. The *fin-de-siècle* creative thinkers and artists whose work has survived to be appreciated by later generations surely displaced and hybridised, as much as they absorbed and condensed, the familiar Darwinian debates of their day.

I will leave aside here the question of whether the 'two culture' division implied immediately above between scientists and artists is quite tenable for this period, and merely note that a concern with limitations and misapplications of natural selection were to haunt no small number of the theorists of evolution itself. Thus Darwin's supposed one-time intellectual bedfellow, Alfred Russel Wallace, turned increasingly away from the theme of natural selection, in search of other forms of knowledge and explanation. A preoccupation with the invisible and the ineffable, the eternal and the

---

43 Hughes 1979a. On Freud's relationship to Darwin, see Ritvo 1990.
44 'C Notebook', line ref. C79, Grubar 1974, p. 449.

cosmic marked his late work. Wallace's study *Man's Place in the Universe: A Study of the Results of Scientific Research in Relation to the Unity or Plurality of Worlds* (1903) was characteristic of this shift of focus. It was not simply a question of seeking a new vista – the stars above, rather than the earth below – but of politics, ethics and the meaning of science. Wallace had become dissatisfied with the hegemony of 'utilitarian' ideas in Darwin's account (Wallace 1891, pp. 35, 89, 188–94). For all his copious imaginative and reasoning powers, perhaps Darwin had illuminated but one side of life and its struggles, failing to attend sufficiently to others. Even Friedrich Lange, in his very admiring history of materialism, had painstakingly drawn attention to the blind spots in our capacity to see. He included, tellingly, a reference to the theory of the blind spot, suggesting perhaps by way of analogy the hole that needed to be punched in our confident vision of nature (Lange 1925, II, p. 224). Attempts to rewrite materialism in more complex and adequate forms or to challenge it decisively proliferated. Later nineteenth-century psychologists, for instance, sought to move beyond romantic intuitions, and also beyond what has subsequently come to be known as 'psychiatric Darwinism', towards new and still mysterious accounts of 'automatism', 'multiplex personality', hypnotism and other very puzzling psychic phenomena. Thus a new intense concern with meaning and language, dreams and fantasies, and above all with the dynamic relationship of conscious and unconscious mental functioning, rather than a preoccupation with hereditary taints and lesions of the brain, marked the central clinical shift from Charcot to Freud. A vision of the interior world, already presaged earlier, crystallised around 1900, dealing not so much with the visible 'expression of the emotions', still less with the degenerate body, but rather with the intra-psychic complexity of the subject.

Victorian readers who had sought to have the last word on the politics and ethics of Darwinism found themselves quickly superseded, as rivals emerged to claim the science. *The Origin* has always suffered its inadequate snap 'verdicts'. Harriet Martineau, who knew the Darwin family, quickly offered her own endorsement: 'What a book it is! – overthrowing (if true) revealed Religion on the one hand, and Natural (as far as Final Causes and Design are concerned) on the other. The range and mass of knowledge takes away one's breath.'[45] Her ardent message was sufficiently indiscreet as to cause her to add: 'Please burn this scrawl.' But our resting place should

---

45 Martineau 1859 to her fellow campaigner, George Holyoake, British Library Add. Ms 42, 726 f. 26. She regretted the theological elements which remained.

not be Martineau's decisive statement, but rather her caveat, 'if true'. This was perhaps more faithful to Darwin, who never quite got over his own burning doubts. His letters are punctuated by the fear of imperfection, fits of the 'wibber-gibbers', the terror of scandal, of prematurely rushing into print; the dread of being 'horridly imperfect and with many mistakes, so that I groan and tremble when I think of it' (Darwin 1990, pp. 109, 135–6, 142). If his hesitating nature could be deemed a personal affliction, it was also a prerequisite for his exceptional talent, and for the sophistication of his synthesising endeavour. His capacity to move boldly back or forth across ideas, and to tolerate, despite misgivings, their open expression, provided the royal road to his extraordinary intellectual achievement.

20

Conservative political thought from the revolutions of 1848 until the *fin de siècle*

LAWRENCE GOLDMAN

1 The emergence and definition of the conservative tradition

Like so much of the vocabulary of modern politics and social science, the term 'conservative' can be traced back to the early nineteenth century (Vierhaus 1973, I, pp. 477–85). Its first use was apparently in the title of the weekly journal founded in 1817 by Francois René de Chateaubriand (1768– 1848) and Louis de Bonald (1754–1840), *Le Conservateur*. Its declared mission was to uphold 'religion, the King, liberty, the Charter and respectable people [*les honnêtes gens*]'.[1] In Britain the term was first used as a synonym for the Tory Party in 1830.[2] It rapidly became a part of the vocabulary of politics during the Reform Bill crisis of 1831–2. Daniel O'Connell, the political leader of Irish Catholicism, noted the new coinage in 1832: 'Conservative – that is the fashionable term, the new-fangled phrase now used in Polite Society to designate the Tory ascendancy.'[3] It was being used pejoratively against conservatives in Germany by the late 1830s, but there, as elsewhere, the political formations opposed to change came to accept and employ the term themselves. By the middle of the nineteenth century the term was in universal use and it is the purpose of this essay to explain the different ideological positions, groups and individuals who were embraced by it. The essay will consider the different conservative reactions to the mid-century European revolutions and the emergence of mass politics. It will also examine the ways in which conservatism changed over time from the anti-revolutionary creed of 1848 to the more complex, intellectualised

---

1 *Le Conservateur*, 5 October 1818, p. 7.
2 'We now are, as we always have been, decidedly and conscientiously attached to what is called the Tory, and which might with more propriety be called the Conservative Party.' 'Internal Policy', *Quarterly Review*, 42, January 1830, p. 276. The quotation has been attributed traditionally to the Tory politician and journalist, J. W. Croker, but there is some doubt about this. See Houghton 1966, p. 709, and Blake 1985, p. 6.
3 Daniel O'Connell, 'Public Letter to Edward Dwyer', *Freeman's Journal*, 25 May 1832, O'Connell 1977, 418n.

and yet irrational forms it had adopted by the end of the century. Because there was no single, dominant conservative thinker in this period the essay will examine different variants of the creed from the United States to the Russian Empire – from the South Carolina of John C. Calhoun to the St Petersburg of Dostoevsky. And because it will be argued that conservatism was more a set of attitudes generated by specific historical situations than a systematic ideology, the treatment will closely relate conservative thought to the history of the era.

The conservative intellectual tradition can be traced back to the eighteenth century and to related reactions against Enlightenment optimism and the French Revolution. In France, Joseph de Maistre (1753–1821) and Louis de Bonald gave it a distinctively catholic and legitimist character, based, in Maistre's case, on a Christian pessimism about human nature, expressed most famously in his *Considérations sur la France*, written in the mid-1790s at the height of the Revolution. God's authority over men, and the beneficent forces of tradition and family, were elevated all the more by Maistre in the light of man's evident inability to rule himself. Scepticism, not to say contempt in Maistre's case, for human social arrangements and the capacity of men to govern themselves, was a defining feature of the conservative mentality in this era (Lebrun 2001). In Maistre's view, men should be governed by absolute authority, to which they should offer absolute obedience. In conformity with this view Bonald was an apologist for both the Napoleonic Empire and the Bourbon Restoration which followed. He also took the part of the artisan and craftsman whose livelihoods were threatened by encroaching mass production: the defence of traditional communities, and of traditional social relations within them, was a characteristic theme of nineteenth-century conservatism in France, as elsewhere (see Godechot 1970). Conservatism in Germany on the other hand had a secular rather than theological basis in its respect for, and subservience to, the state as the embodiment of human will and the vehicle for social emancipation. In the century defined by the emergence of the nation state, the idealist tradition generated another variant of conservatism distinguished by its loyalty to constituted authority and its intolerance of liberal individualism (Berdahl 1988; Epstein 1966). In Britain, meanwhile, the conservative tradition was formalised by Edmund Burke (1729–97) in his *Reflections on the Revolution in France* (1790) which was different again. Indeed, not only did Burke predate the emergence of conservatism, but he was himself a Whig with a consistent record of support for reform in his approach to imperial questions in the 1770s and 1780s (America, India and Ireland) and to the composition and functions of the British Parliament. Burke's conservatism owed little to the obedience humans must show their maker, as in the French tradition; nor did it elevate obedience to the state. Rather, it derived the anti-revolutionary case on empirical grounds, from the observation of what, in Burke's view, was conducive to social stability, political order and human contentment (Cobban 1960; O'Gorman 1973; Pocock 1982, pp. 331–49).

Burke was not as widely read or admired in the nineteenth century as in the twentieth: he was less of a presence than is sometimes imagined. Nevertheless, his ideas recur in many different forms of conservatism in this period, whether acknowledged or not. He countered the disorientating effects of liberty which he believed he saw in the very earliest stages of the French Revolution (and which were undoubtedly present in its later stages) with an emphasis on order, tradition and gradualism. He countered social levelling and equality with hierarchy, deference and the acceptance of self-evident human (and thus social) differences. The friends of liberty welcomed a new age of reason: Burke reminded his readers of the foibles and intellectual limitations of humankind. Against the twin French diseases of statism and internationalism, Burke famously lauded localism, the attachment to community first and foremost, for this was the natural and original location of the spirit of civic-mindedness. 'To be attached to the subdivision, to love the little platoon we belong to in society, is the first principle (the germ, as it were) of public affections' (Burke 2003, p. 40). His was a cautionary message – an attempt to remind mankind that as morally flawed and intellectually limited creatures, they should not seek to overthrow the inherited wisdom and the institutions of the ages. But Burke was not, in the manner of Maistre, a reactionary, or a conservative utopian seeking a return to the past. In this he helps us differentiate between conservatism and orthodoxy which latter position rejects all change and the calculus of human advantage that might lead the conservative to accept moderate reform. Burke accepted social progress based on due respect for custom and tradition: as he recognised, 'a state without the means of some change is without the means of its conservation' (Burke 2003, p. 19). But he emphasised that slow-maturing change based on collective wisdom would prove more durable and beneficial than change dictated by the theories of 'sophisters, economists, and calculators' (Burke 2003, p. 65). As he wrote elsewhere in relation to 'the French revolutionists', 'to innovate is not to reform' (Burke 1991, p. 156). Legislation would not make men good, nor lead to lasting improvement: 'Manners are of more importance than laws. Upon them, in great measure, the laws depend' (Burke 1904, p. 310). He rejected the democratic principle, which could become the tyranny of the majority: 'It is said that twenty-four millions ought to prevail over two hundred thousand. True; if the constitution of a kingdom be a problem of arithmetic' (Burke 2003, p. 44).

While conservatism in the second half of the nineteenth century focused on other themes beyond this Burkean inheritance, and while we must note that this form of Anglo-Saxon conservatism cannot stand for all types, the essence was always, as in Burke's case, anti-revolutionary. And that anti-revolutionary case usually comprised some at least of Burke's arguments (Muller 1977, p. 25). Nineteenth-century conservatives stressed human imperfection; they counselled, therefore, an epistemological caution because we cannot know all we need to know, or would like to know, in fashioning society. They placed their faith in institutions, whether religious or secular, as necessary restraints on human irresponsibility. *Pace* Rousseau, men were civilised by institutions rather than enchained by them: they were born bad rather than free. Hence the utility of religion: while many conservatives embraced Christianity in true faith, others saw its usefulness in impos-ing moral, and by extension, political restraints on men and women, and reminding them of their fallen nature. That social institutions had endured was taken as evidence of their fitness for purpose rather than a reason for their reform: the past was a surer guide to political wisdom than the unknown future that liberalism rushed to embrace. According to Chateaubriand, 'The past is a fact, a fact that cannot be destroyed; while the future, which is so dear to us, does not exist.'[4] Conservatives were suspicious of theorising, both because no theory can account for the vagaries of human will, and because theories applied to the crooked timber of humanity must ignore the historic, the local, and specific, and might then become tyrannous. Thus the universalist deductions of nineteenth-century liberal political economy were as much anathema to the conservative as to the socialist: in figures like Thomas Carlyle and John Ruskin moral and emotional opposition to lib-eral economics led to an ambiguous stance, allowing them to be claimed by both left and right. Conservatives were suspicious of liberal contractualism as a way of understanding and organising society because this degraded the complex relations and loyalties that held actual societies together. The use of organic imagery in conservative discourse ('webs', 'skeins', 'nets', 'fabrics') was an affirmation of the interdependence of social groups and institutions, and an implied critique of those who would disturb the complex work

---

4 'Études Historiques', Chateaubriand 1859, pp. 21–2, quoted in Tholfsen 1967, p. 188.

of time by shallow, because ideologically inspired, reform: this would rend the social fabric, and, in upsetting social order, lead to unanticipated and disturbing consequences.[5]

Nineteenth-century conservatism was reactive rather than purposive, therefore. It thus accords with the views of those who have argued that conservatism is always better understood as a set of attitudes (or a 'disposition' as Michael Oakeshott put it) than an ideology (Oakeshott 1962, pp. 168–96).[6] Unlike liberalism and socialism, it did not present itself as an all-encompassing solution to human ills, it did not aspire to universalism. It emerged in response to specific threats in specific social situations (and has thus been termed a 'positional ideology' by Samuel P. Huntingdon).[7] And in so far as it was localist in mentality, emphasising particular and contextual features, it varied considerably in different national contexts, and, within nations, in different regional contexts (Pocock 'Introduction', in Burke 1988, pp. vii, xlix). The so-called 'conservatism' of the industrialising northern states in America in the late nineteenth century may be contrasted with the quite different conservatism of the agrarian American South.

2 The development of conservatism: European politics and society after 1848

The 1848 revolutions confirmed the prejudices of many observers. At one extreme Joseph de Gobineau's abhorrence of democracy led him to embrace and disseminate his degenerative theories of racial mixing. At the other, Macaulay's Whig triumphalism was reinforced: that Britain was untouched while the rest of Europe was in turmoil was evidence of the superiority of British institutions, built on the wise governance of whig-liberal elites since the Glorious Revolution had secured order and representation in 1688 (Macaulay 1864, II, pp. 239–43). But the well-known description of the 1848 revolutions as the historical turning point where history did not turn, gives a clue to understanding the conservative response to these events.

---

5 For a general definition of conservatism see Scruton 1980, 1991, pp. 1–28.

6 Conservatism has been defined as 'an attitude of opposition to disruptive change in the social, economic, legal, religious, political, or cultural order', Rossiter 1968, pp. 290–1. Though see Karl Mannheim's distinction between traditionalism and a true ideology of conservatism in Mannheim 1971, pp. 132–222.

7 'The articulation of conservatism is a response to a specific social situation. The manifestation of conservatism at any one time and place has little connection with its manifestation at any other time and place.' Huntingdon 1957, pp. 454–73 (quotation at 468).

For if initial conservative reactions took the form of Burke's response to the Revolution of 1789, later and calmer reflection gave reason to believe that the revolutionary movement was weak and that that weakness might be exploited. The history of several European states over the next two generations and more may be understood as the exploitation by conservative elites of the paradoxes and contradictions of liberalism.

These were not lost on conservatives. The peasants and artisans who took up arms were often fighting against the destruction of a traditional economic and social order by liberal capitalism. The liberals failed to represent the whole of the middle classes but only the professional groups – lawyers, professors, students, officials – among them: the property-holding and commercial bourgeoisie was much less in evidence. Only the nationalistic uprisings in Italy and Hungary were large in scale and truly threatening to established authorities. Outside of Paris, and perhaps not even there, the new industrial proletariat played almost no role. In general, revolutionary incidents were triggered by traditional problems, most notably crop failures and the price of bread. Monarchy and order were reimposed with relative ease across the continent. The divisions within liberalism on social and also national lines (as exposed in the Frankfurt Parliament) and the lack of decisive liberal leadership in almost all the revolutionary situations were plain to see. Further crucial divisions that emerged between the bourgeoisie and the working classes in several of the German states and in the violence of the 'June Days' in Paris demonstrated the fragility of inter-class unity. Catholic, peasant France voted in 1848 under the universal suffrage of the Second Republic for a conservative Chamber and for a Bonaparte, Louis Napoleon, as President. All these features suggested strategies and possibilities that could be exploited by conservatism in the future, be it in imperial, monarchical, aristocratic, papal or populist form. The real lesson of 1848 was that popular revolution could be averted by the astute management of different and opposed social groups and the manipulation of popular, and above all, national sentiments (Agulhon 1983; Evans and von Strandmann 2000; Price 1988; Sperber 2005).

In addition, changing intellectual, economic and social structures offered conservatives opportunities among new social groups and explain the fundamental historical transition in conservatism during the second half of the nineteenth century from an elitist preserve to a popular force. At a political level, as liberalism evolved to embrace a new, redistributionist social agenda by the 1880s and 1890s, so conservatism adopted the classical *laissez-faire* liberalism of an earlier era and appealed to disaffected property-holders fearing the taxes that social liberalism would impose. Where once conservatism was synonymous with landed interests it could now depend upon the support of an urban business class. Indeed, in many societies a consolidated class of the propertied began to emerge, no longer divided by considerations of status and landed background, whose members reflexively turned to the right. This trend was accelerated by the agricultural depression from the 1870s which affected all rural populations, and which spurred landed families to diversify their assets where they could by investing in urban property and industrial stocks. The traditional liberal policy of free trade was often unpopular among farmers and peasants, and also among urban workers who feared for their jobs under a regime of unrestricted imports. Indeed, declining rural incomes from Texas to Russia gave rise to deep resentment on the land towards traditional urban liberal elites, especially bankers, who were blamed for the downturn, and by extension, towards Jews. In a situation in which world markets were awash with cheap commodities, it suited landholders just as much as their tenants and peasantry to impose tariffs – as it also suited industrial interests in regions developing after the mid-century and facing price competition from the imports of more and earlier-established industrial nations. Thus was born the so-called 'Rye–Iron' alliance in Germany, an intrinsically conservative association between large landholders and capitalists in favour of import tariffs. The emergence and growth of a petit bourgeoisie between the urban liberal middle classes and the workers was another opportunity to be exploited. Owning a little property, they had much to gain from the politics of order and respectability, and much to fear, or so they believed, from the rise of organised socialism. The combined impact of the rise of working-class movements; the consolidation of the class of large property-holders; the emergence of a lower middle class in the new service-based economies of the more advanced cities; and the immiseration of small farmers and peasants on the land created tensions, resentments and fear that worked in favour of conservatism. For their part, conservative leaders learnt to embrace mass democracy, which they found, despite the dire predictions of the early nineteenth century, could be manipulated and led in the interests of elites – though these elites were now very different from the traditional aristocracies of the *ancien régime* (Weiss 1977, pp. 71–3).

Forms of conservative populism were evident in Britain from the 1870s, in France, during the Second Empire, and in Germany after 1871 in the Second Reich. In Britain, in a genuinely plural political culture (if not yet a fully democratic system) where the differences between liberal and conservative were narrower and more muted than almost anywhere else, the

Conservative Party of Disraeli and Salisbury attracted disaffected middle-class voters on the rebound from the more radical liberalism of Gladstone's party after 1868 (Cornford 1963, pp. 35–66). Liberal political dominance during the mid-century was followed after 1874 by a string of Conservative electoral successes based on a soothing rhetoric of constitutionalism, social stability and imperialism. Though the debate over the character of the French Second Empire between 1851 and 1870 continues, there are good reasons for taking Louis Napoleon as a new type of conservative able to sustain his regime by the manipulation of a mass electorate. This was achieved by exploiting threats of revolutionary subversion; conciliating the many different conservative interests in French society including the Catholic Church and local notables, as well as the various right-wing political factions, Legitimist, Orléanist and of course, Bonapartist; encouraging prosperity through state intervention as an antidote to popular discontent; and using an ambitious foreign policy (albeit one that failed miserably) in Italy, Mexico and the Far East, to encourage patriotic support (Bury 1965; Plessis 1985; Zeldin 1958). Meanwhile, in the new Germany, building on a wave of popular exultation for the new Reich, these and other tactics were employed to control, in the conservative interest, a complex and fissiparous nation riven by regional, religious and class division (Craig 1978; Sheehan 1978; Wehler 1985). Sham constitutionalism gave the illusion of democratic accountability in Germany. It was reinforced by the alliance of the most powerful urban and rural conservative interests; the suppression of ideological and social 'enemies of the Reich', notably the socialists between 1878 and 1890; the marginalisation of liberal interests and opinion in both the state itself and wider civil society; the blandishments of a social welfare programme from the 1880s; and the promotion of a militaristic and nationalistic internal culture as the corollary of an aggressive foreign policy. In these ways it has been argued that an unreformed and essentially pre-industrial elite was consolidated at the apex of German society reliant upon the support of property-holders who, a generation before, looked as if they were lost to the conservative cause (Goldman 2003, pp. 97–113).

Sustaining this elite, and conservative interests across Europe in general, was made all the easier by the transformation of nationalism from a liberal to a conservative force (Hobsbawm 1990; Kohn 1968, pp. 19–20; Mosse 1975). The change is vital to an understanding of nineteenth-century political thought in general. Nationalism, the corollary of the first French Revolution, and adopted by liberal intellectuals in many different parts of Europe after 1815, had emerged as a genuinely radical and popular movement in its support for national self-government as opposed to localist particularism, and in its opposition to dynastic rule based on hereditary, or supposedly divine, rights. But the 1848 revolutions had revealed its darker, atavistic heart, and demonstrated that a powerful and emotive ideology designed to differentiate and separate one group from another had no inevitable connection to liberal principles. As John Stuart Mill opined (with prescience) in 1849, 'in the backward parts of Europe, and even (where better things might have been expected) in Germany, the sentiment of nationality so far outweighs the love of liberty, that the people are willing to abet their rulers in crushing the liberty and independence of any people not of their race and language' (Mill 1849, p. 347).

As Mill could now see, nationalism was not only a force for international discord, but might be used by unscrupulous (and otherwise unpopular) rulers as a tool for the internal control of the people, co-opting them in a process in which popular liberties were stalled or undermined. Because there were real enemies abroad in an age of increasing national economic and political competition, it was also comparatively easy to associate the left, characterised by internationalism and anti-militarism, with an absence of national feeling, and even treason, as in the famous Dreyfus case of the 1890s in France (Bredin 1987; Johnson 1966). And because this competition compelled European nations to raise and sustain large armed forces, they were able to socialise generations of young men and their families in the anti-democratic culture of military service and 'preparedness'. The conservative historian Jules Michelet apparently told Matthew Arnold, who quoted him approvingly, that 'France was a nation of barbarians civilised by conscription' (Arnold 1960, pp. 75–6; Weber 1976, pp. 292–302). The history thus tells of a rightward drift, or lurch in some cases, across Europe after 1848. By the manipulation of the new mass politics; by judicious political alliances; by magnifying the threat of internal subversion; by the invocation of 'the national interest'; and by virtue of increasing international tension the means were devised to maintain or reinstall conservative interests, groups and classes in power.

3 Conservative cultural and political thinkers in Britain

There was no single corpus of conservative political thought in this period, but a series of reactions varying according to national location and the character and situation of specific writers. The spectrum of opinion was wide, running from the outright rejection of modernity by the orthodox, through those conservative thinkers who focused on specific themes, such as the moral and material degradation caused by liberal capitalism, and the cultural declension caused by mass culture, to those later figures, largely outside the Anglo-Saxon frame of reference, who embraced various forms of pseudo-scientific justification for radically asocial and 'irrational' ideologies often based on racial rather than conventional social categories. For ease of understanding, these reactions can be divided nationally and the remaining discussion will focus on British, American and European forms of conservative thought in that order.

Paradoxically perhaps, we might begin this discussion of conservative philosophy by explaining the questions at issue through the work of two impeccable liberal theorists whose work nevertheless betrays anxiety over the nature of nineteenth-century social development, Alexis de Tocqueville (1805–59) and John Stuart Mill (1806–1873). In both cases we are dealing with thinkers who expected this development to end in full democracy and who supported such an outcome. Yet both registered the type of reservation that conservatives around them were also expressing. The reservations are caught at the very end of the second and final volume of Tocqueville's *Democracy in America* (1840):

The nations of our time cannot prevent the conditions of men from becoming equal, but it depends upon themselves whether the principle of equality is to lead them to servitude or freedom, to knowledge or barbarism, to prosperity or wretchedness. (Tocqueville 1945, p. 352)

Freedom and individualism could be threatened by the force of majority public opinion, by the political will of the majority deployed against a minority, or by the tendency towards cultural mediocrity intrinsic to the egalitarian mentality of democracies. Tocqueville feared the development of a powerful government providing material comfort and assistance to the many, and able thereby to dictate to the mass of equal individuals, unchallenged by any intermediate institutions or interest groups. This was what he called 'democratic despotism'. Unsurprisingly, his political legacy was ambiguous and Tocqueville was later claimed by both liberals and conservatives. He had foreseen this, writing in 1835 that 'Some will find that at bottom I do not like democracy and that I am severe toward it; others will think that I favour its development imprudently.'[8]

---

8 Alexis de Tocqueville to Louis de Kergolay (January 1835), in de Tocqueville 1985, p. 95. See also Jardin 1988; Welch 2001.

On Liberty (1859), Mill's text written a generation later, develops many of these ideas, especially Mill's concerns regarding social and cultural uniformity and their negative effects on individualism:

there needs protection [also] against the tyranny of the prevailing opinion and feeling; against the tendency of society to impose, by other means than civil penalties, its own ideas and practices as rules of conduct on those who dissent from them; to fetter the development, and, if possible, prevent the formation, of any individuality not in harmony with its ways, and compel all characters to fashion themselves upon the model of its own. (Mill 1977a, p. 220)

By the 1850s it was clear to Mill, as to many others, that the expansion of the British suffrage and reform of Parliament in 1832 would be followed by further measures of democratisation. As he wrote in 1861, 'it is evident, that the only government which can fully satisfy all the exigencies of the social state, is one in which the whole people participate' (Mill 1977b, p. 412). Mill's anxiety concerning the effect of this on the quality of government and the coherence of measures expressed itself first in his support for plural voting based on education and attainment, and then in his support for an electoral reform that might improve the calibre of legislators. If they were to have more authority, and if they were to be elected by the less educated classes, let them at least vote for men of ability. Mill in his *Thoughts on Parliamentary Reform* (1859) endorsed a so-called 'fancy franchise' that allocated votes according to the citizen's level of education and occupation; some might have five or six votes, others but one, so as to equalise the contest in mid-Victorian society between 'brains and numbers'. He then became an enthusiastic convert to a suggested scheme of voting, essentially a type of single transferable vote, devised in the 1850s by the lawyer Thomas Hare, which promised the election of men of intellectual ability.[9] His concern to give power to the best men led him also, in *Considerations on Representative Government* (1861), to devise administrative structures within government such as drafting committees and legislative councils, staffed by policy experts, that would remove the taint of ignorance and amateurism from democratic government. If Britain was to have a democracy, let it be a skilled one (Goldman 2002, pp. 278–89). Mill was contemptuous of the pretensions of aristocratic government to direct affairs intelligently and efficiently: if he had doubts about popular administration he was even more hostile to rule by privilege. Yet these strains of conservatism within Mill's liberalism

---

9 J. S. Mill to Thomas Hare (3 March 1859), Mill 1972b, pp. 598–9. See also Hare 1858.

illustrate very effectively the challenge of democracy: if the proponent of liberty could fear its consequences, how much more so the defenders of property?

Despite this ambivalence, 'Mill's pontifical authority', as the liberal politician and higher journalist, John Morley, referred to it, was an obvious target for conservative criticism. In the famous critique by the jurist James Fitzjames Stephen (1829–94), a series of essays collected and published as *Liberty, Equality and Fraternity* in 1873, many of the themes that characterised nineteenth-century conservative thought were deployed in an attempt to undermine not only liberal conclusions, but first principles and assumptions also. Stephen, drawn from a famous evangelical dynasty, was a severe rationalist and religious sceptic (a position he shared with his brother, the Victorian man-of-letters, Leslie Stephen) and a well-known voice in the reviews and journals of the mid-Victorian era (Colaiaco 1983). His essential argument was encapsulated in a letter of 1872 in which he remarked that Mill's *Liberty* was dependent on a 'concept of human nature [which] appears to me to be a sort of unattractive romance'.[10] Mill would grant as much individual freedom as possible, consistent with doing no harm to another. In Stephen's view, echoing Burke, this was a fatally optimistic view of human nature: 'The condition of human life is such that we must of necessity be restrained and compelled by circumstances in nearly every action of our lives' (Stephen 1991, p. 59). Since 'there are and always will be in the world an enormous mass of bad and indifferent people', so 'compulsion and restraint' will always be required. And given the degree of their moral failings, no conceivable grant of liberty would 'in the least degree tend to improve them'.[11] Mill's fundamental principle would also negate 'every existing system of morals', for these, by their very nature, guide and compel right conduct and disapprobate actions that the community may condemn, whether or not the consequences of such actions are harmful to individuals. The principle of liberty, in other words, is not a sufficient foundation for social ethics.[12] To Stephen, Mill's defence of liberty encouraged moral disorder and also social insubordination by undermining 'a proper sense of the importance of the virtue of obedience, discipline in its widest sense'.[13] Stephen's arguments depended quite as much as Mill's on a particular view of human nature, though Stephen could claim that he, at least, had openly articulated

---

10 Stephen to Lady Edgerton (24 April 1872), in Smith 1988, p. 161.
11 Ibid., p. 72.   12 Ibid., p. 58.   13 Ibid., p. 169.

his psychological assumptions. In doing so, his critique was, in essence, a restatement of long-standing conservative themes.

Those who rejected liberalism sometimes found the certainties that Catholicism offered, and its orthodox rejection of the present and future, a consolation and an attraction. The case of John Henry (Cardinal) Newman (1801–90) is perhaps the best-known example in the English-speaking world, reminding us that while conservatism did not mandate religious belief of any sort, or membership of any particular denomination, it was frequently associated with Christianity and its defence (Ker 1989; Newman 1956, 1961–2008). In Newman's complex case, he was driven Rome-wards by a multiplicity of factors, many of them historical, scholarly and doctrinal, emanating from prolonged and extensive study of the Church Fathers. But the ease with which the British state could alter the religious arrangements of the nation (as in Catholic emancipation in 1829 and the subsequent suppression of Irish bishoprics) and its erastian imposition on the Anglican Church in the early 1830s, forcing it towards institutional rationalisation, demonstrated to Newman and his bother 'Tractarians' in the so-called Oxford Movement that clerical independence was a pretence; that spirituality and holiness were menaced by the new gospels of statism, efficiency and utility; and that the Established Church in England was complacent and apathetic. Their campaign to respiritualise Anglicanism and the nation failed, undermined by a liberalism that, in their view, diluted and routinised the faith. When the leader of the Conservative Party, Sir Robert Peel, delivered a speech in 1841 that seemed to favour the replacement of religion by education as the ethical guide to social development, Newman's ironic riposte in a series of letters to *The Times* ('The Tamworth Reading Room') reaffirmed faith as the enduring basis of moral action. The rejection of liberalism thus took the form, in Newman's case, of a reversion to the one true church which he joined in 1845, and later to a famous discussion of the ills of modernity, alongside a vindication of his beliefs and actions, in his autobiographical *Apologia Pro Vita Sua* of 1864.

But there were other forms of outright rejection and other destinations for anti-liberals drawn, sometimes despite themselves, towards conservatism. In the case of Thomas Carlyle (1795–1881) his utter detestation of the doctrines of, and the consequent social arrangements created by, liberal political economy led to a corrosive social criticism – corrosive of his own reason as well as early Victorian society (Froude 1882–4; Kaplan 1983). And when that criticism was reinforced by a growing contempt for the inadequacies of liberal parliamentarianism and democratic procedures (though he remained sympathetic to the common worker and even the deluded Chartist radical) his rejection turned to a new faith in the capacity of the great man and leader to bring order and reason through a benevolent authoritarianism to the generality of inadequate humans incapable of governing themselves. Carlyle's remarkable essay, 'Signs of the Times' (1829), demonstrated his intuitive understanding of the dehumanisation intrinsic to the processes of industrial civilisation and a 'mechanical age': 'men are grown mechanical in heart as well as head'. *Past and Present*, published fourteen years later, was a torrent of hostility and invective at what he had earlier called 'the cash nexus'[14] and its destruction of human relations and moral conduct, carefully counterposed to an idealised picture of life in a utopian twelfth-century community. To 'work sore and yet gain nothing; to be heart-worn, weary, yet isolated, unrelated, girt-in with a cold universal Laissez-faire' was the lot of everyman in the present (Carlyle 1903, pp. 210–11). By the time that his essays were published in *Latter-Day Pamphlets* (1850) Carlyle was implacably critical of self-government, even in Britain where it might be said to have established the strongest and longest roots, and prepared to endorse slavery itself as more desirable than an alienated and aimless freedom. Editing the letters and speeches of Oliver Cromwell (1845) and writing his biography of Frederick the Great (1858–65) were more than exercises in historical scholarship, therefore: liberalism was a dangerous delusion and the role of the great man in history was to save us from ourselves.

Carlyle's erratic insights, which were so arresting to his contemporaries but sometimes so difficult to discern amidst the recalcitrant written style of an Old Testament prophet, informed and coincided with the development of other conservative movements and thinkers. The rejection of *laissez-faire* was an especially strong theme in British conservative thought between the 1830s and 1850s, and the Young England movement through which Disraeli (1804–81) expressed his views in the early 1840s echoed Carlyle's invocation of a better, juster and moral past in their equally idealised view of medieval paternalism (Blake 1966, pp. 167–89; Faber 1987). For Young England, not only were the social arrangements of pre-Reformation England superior to the flux and social instability of the present, but their animating spirit was taken as a model by which to outflank the bourgeoisie, both ideologically and politically. The accommodation of the aristocracy and the people, who

---

14 'In these complicated times, with Cash Payment as the sole nexus between man and man...', Carlyle 1904, pp. 168–9.

would follow the conserving paternalism of their superiors, was held up, half-seriously and half-fancifully, as an alternative to liberalism. That this was also a quite specific critique of the leadership of the Conservative Party by the liberal-tending Sir Robert Peel, a son of the middle classes who seemed to revert to type as prime minister between 1841 and 1846, and thus had a narrow party-political rationale, should not obscure the imaginative hold of a romanticised Tory benevolence over many opponents, both rich and poor, of industrial civilisation and *laissez-faire*. Disraeli's trilogy of novels, *Coningsby*, *Sybil* and *Tancred* (1844–7) gave substance and form to this outlook and strategy: while scholars will continue to debate their relevance for an understanding of his political thinking, they doubtless embody an important, though unrealised and unrealisable strain in the Conservative tradition (Blake 1966, pp. 190–220; Vincent 1990, pp. 81–104).

Coincidence with Carlyle's ideas can also be discerned in the work of John Ruskin (1819–1900) who famously described himself as a 'violent Tory of the old school'[15] – though an earlier self-description that he was 'by nature and instinct a Conservative, loving old things because they are old, and hating new ones merely because they are new'[16] may be more faithful to Ruskin's true spirit, and helpful also in understanding the general conservative psychology. Ruskin is unusual in the history of social thought (where he has a place, but in which he is not usually included), for his social and political ideas developed from his aesthetic sensibility and his vocation as a critic of art and architecture. But the deadening reach of *laissez-faire* liberalism extended very far – even to the quality of Victorian design and craftsmanship and the nature and experience of work itself under capitalism. As Ruskin came to see that the architectural record provided a moral history of mankind – that how and what we build and make are projections of our deepest values and reflections of the organisation of our society – so he became more critical of the shallow materialism of Victorian style, the destruction of the natural environment, and the exploitation of men and women that were each the cause and effect of this moral degeneration.[17] His magnificently original essays on political economy, *Unto this Last*, published in 1862, were paradoxical. They emanated from an enraged conservative spirit that presented the social and economic philosophy of liberalism as

---

15 *Fors Clavigera*, 1st Letter, January 1871, in Ruskin 1903–12, XXVII, p. 14.
16 Ruskin to Henry Acland (27 April 1856), in Ruskin 1903–12, XXXVI, p. 239.
17 Ruskin's moral-historical ideas were set out first in *The Seven Lamps of Architecture* (1849) and *The Stones of Venice* (1853). See Hilton 1985; Hunt 1982.

ungodly and inhumane, but they became classical among the emerging labour movement at the end of the nineteenth century, and inspired the ethical anti-capitalism that animated the founders of the British Labour Party. Ruskin was the single most widely read author among the first cohort of Labour Members of Parliament elected in 1906 (Goldman 1999, pp. 57–86). That Ruskin (and Carlyle also) were revered by working men of a later generation should not surprise us, however: the conservative and the socialist could find common ground in their shared protest at the consequences of economic and social liberalism – though in what they proposed to do about it they differed widely. No self-conscious and politically astute working man could be drawn to the static, hierarchical and paternalistic society beloved of the conservative critics.

Ruskin thus exemplifies another theme within the conservative tradition, so-called 'cultural conservatism' whose focus was less on the political effects of modernity and more on its consequences for public taste, learning and behaviour. In some degree it may be seen as a retreat: having lost the battle against *political* liberalism in the 1840s, during which period the Conservative Party was torn apart by internal disputes over its responses to social and economic change, many conservatives turned instead to the preservation of traditional values in art, religion and education. It is a strain of conservatism, running from Coleridge through Carlyle to Ruskin and Matthew Arnold, which is best exemplified in a specifically English context, and it has attracted notable and influential scholarly attention.[18] Like his contemporary, John Stuart Mill, Matthew Arnold (1822–88) was a self-confessed liberal who believed in many of the progressive principles of the age: democracy, self-improvement, reform and the administration of experts.[19] But in *Culture and Anarchy* (1869), his flawed and opinionated lectures from the end of the 1860s, he presented the most famous, if not necessarily the best account of cultural conservatism in the English-speaking tradition. Accepting that democracy was now embedded (and it is noteworthy that the essays were stimulated by some minor disturbances caused by a public demonstration in Hyde Park in July 1866 in support of the extension of the suffrage)[20]

---

18 Williams 1958, pt. 1, 'A Nineteenth-Century Tradition'.
19 Arnold 1960, p. 41: 'I am a Liberal, yet I am a Liberal tempered by experience, reflection, and renouncement, and I am, above all, a believer in culture.' See also, M. Arnold, 'The Future of Liberalism', 1880 in *Complete Prose Works*, IX, p. 138. See, in general, Collini, 1988; Honan 1981.
20 See the allusion to the 'Englishman's right to do what he likes; his right to march where he likes, meet where he likes, enter where he likes, hoot as he likes, threaten as he likes, smash as he likes' in Arnold 1960, p. 76. On the so-called 'Hyde Park Riots' of 22–23 July 1866 see Harrison 1962, pp. 354–6.

Arnold's theme was how to make it tolerable, how to make it cultured. As he had written somewhat earlier, 'The difficulty for democracy is how to find and keep high ideals.'[21] Though culture itself was never very satisfactorily defined in *Culture and Anarchy*, Arnold presented it as an inheritance of order, stability and civilised values which the finest art embodies. 'Without order there can be no society, and without society there can be no human perfection.' Culture was, indeed, 'a study of perfection', and 'the best that has been thought and said' (Arnold 1960, p. 45). But few aspired so high in mid-Victorian Britain. Arnold was especially critical of the vulgarity and 'the bad civilisation' – the philistinism – of the nonconformist (i.e. Protestant non-Anglican) middle classes, slaves to what he termed 'Hebraism', a doctrine and lifestyle of materialism, provincialism and confining biblical moralism, of 'money and salvation'. To this he counterposed the spirit of 'Hellenism', derived from the classical sense of the complete, balanced and fulfilled life.[22]

Arnold was no snob: no man who was for thirty-five years an inspector of schools, travelling the country in the dutiful pursuit of social improvement, and who passionately advocated the elevation of the quality of secondary education in England, can be dismissed in this way.[23] But Arnold, though humane, high-minded and a political realist, demonstrated nevertheless the weakness of the conservative case for culture. For his famous lectures were delivered in his own university, Oxford, barely a decade after it had been opened up to non-Anglicans in 1854 for the first time since the Reformation, and at a time when teaching and professorial posts there, and in Cambridge also, were still closed to all but members of the Established Church. If high culture was threatened by philistinism; if the lower classes lived unenlightened and spiritually impoverished lives; if anarchy threatened (though in nineteenth-century Britain of all places, it did not) what responsibility did cultural elitism and deliberate exclusion bear for all this? Arnold was convinced of the harm done to national culture by the 'isolation from the main current of thought' of dissenting communities (Arnold 1998, p. 382). But as one 'philistine' put it in reply, Oxford 'might look down with regret, no doubt, upon the flippancy and thoughtlessness, upon the gigantic Philistinism, which everywhere prevail, but they have no right to regard it with scorn unless they are prepared to deliver us from it' (Watson

---

21 Matthew Arnold, *The Popular Education of France* (1861), in Arnold 1960–77, II, p. 17.
22 'Hebraism and Hellenism' in Arnold 1960, pp. 129–44.
23 On secondary education see *The Popular Education of France* (1861) and *A French Eton or Middle-class Education and the State* (1864) in Arnold 1960–77, II, pp. 3–211, pp. 262–325.

1871, pp. 365–6).[24] It must be allowed that Arnold, through exemplary public service and writing *was* so prepared. But the paradox of cultural conservatism, and its great disability, was that the very thing it feared – the dilution of high culture by the masses – was caused by the very thing that defined and characterised it, the preservation of high culture by means of social and intellectual exclusion.

4 The conservative tradition in America

These varieties of conservatism within a British context show considerable variation in the way they were expressed, in the focus of their concern – whether religious, aesthetic, social or cultural – and in the solutions suggested. But they were articulated within a stable political culture where the spectrum of ideological difference was relatively narrow, and in a society that experienced only minor disturbances to its social order from the 1840s onwards. Conservative ideas could be advanced in the safe assumption that the deluge was unlikely. This was not the case in either the United States or continental Europe. In America, their centrality to the defence of sectionalism and the 'peculiar institution' of black, chattel slavery, gave them an altogether different significance: they provided the basis for the South's defence of its society and its secession from the Union. In continental Europe, where the threats to social order were demonstrably more serious, conservatism took a more virulent form.

It has sometimes been contended that America has no true conservative tradition.[25] In an argument made famous by Louis Hartz, the absence of a monarchy, of a feudal class and of an established church in the United States gave conservatism no natural institutional or social focus (Hartz 1955). In addition, democracy and industry emerged in the early nineteenth century and developed together as natural ways of American life, conformable with the liberal spirit, political individualism and representative institutions which, in this interpretation, had led the Revolution and been enshrined in the federal and state constitutions at the end of the eighteenth century. Given the relative weakness of social radicalism among a 'people of plenty' with remarkable resources to exploit, there was no substantial challenge from the left to give rise to an indigenous conservatism (Sombart 1906).

---

24 Spence Watson, from the north-east of England, was a leading figure in late Victorian provincial liberalism.
25 On the difficulty of defining conservatism in the United States see Crick 1955, pp. 359–76.

But this view has been challenged by a more recent generation of scholars for neglecting the essential conservatism of the American Revolution, a conflict undertaken by the colonists to preserve a status quo under threat from British administrative and fiscal innovation in the 1760s and 1770s. In that conflict, the strongest arguments were those founded on the traditional rights of subjects of the Crown, and on an older understanding, based on Whig ideology of the late seventeenth and early eighteenth centuries, of the powers of government to tax the people (Bailyn 1967). In turn, the founding fathers of the republic who framed the federal constitution in 1787, demonstrated a wholly cautious psychology based on a realistic appraisal of human nature. They feared the accretion of centralised power, which was therefore divided between different branches of government and offset by the authority of the states; they ensured that the unmediated power of popular election applied to only one branch of the central legislature, and not to the executive or judiciary; they designed a political structure that balanced carefully between individual freedoms and restraints; they accepted that men were driven by cupidity and sought to harness that selfishness for the good of the Union in systems of public credit.[26]

While the label 'conservative' has sometimes been applied to the social philosophies that emerged in the United States to validate the monopoly capitalism of the late nineteenth century, the commitment to economic individualism and *laissez-faire* that they all shared placed them securely within the liberal tradition. But in the antebellum South a true American conservatism took root, compounded of agrarianism, racism and paternalism, and the style (if not the substance) of seigneurialism (Genovese 1996, pp. 22–3, 31, 98). Southern conservatism was premised on a belief in the natural inequalities of races and classes. Though the great planters were themselves great capitalists, investing in land and cotton to produce essential commodities for a world market, and amassing great profits in the process, the Old South was loudly critical of the 'free labour', *laissez-faire* system of the Northern states which, it contended, was careless of the welfare of the new urban and industrial workers employed there. Northern individualism and exploitation were contrasted with Southern organicism and paternalism. In the South, it was argued that labour and capital had identical interests and were not at war. How could it be otherwise, when labour – slaves – were literally capital in themselves, valuable assets which it would be irrational to

---

26 Hofstadter 1973, ch. 1. 'The Founding Fathers: An Age of Realism'. See also Elkins and McKitrick 1971.

treat other than humanely? It was claimed as well that the social structure of the South, with its leisured class of wealthy planters, provided for a higher and nobler civilisation than that which had emerged in the venal, liberal North. According to the self-generated legend of the 'Old South', 'its social pattern was manorial, its civilisation that of the Cavalier, its ruling class an aristocracy coextensive with the planter group' (Cash 1991, p. xlix).

Some of these arguments were designed to dignify and justify the holding of slaves; nevertheless, the Southern conservative tradition was authentic rather than simply self-serving. It can be traced back to the agrarian republicanism of Thomas Jefferson, expressed in his *Notes on the State of Virginia* (1787), which hymned the life on the land as morally superior to any other – though Jefferson endorsed a society of yeoman farmers rather than one dominated by a 'plantocracy', and in so many other respects was a quintessential revolutionary liberal (Shalhope 1976, pp. 529–56). It was carried forward into the nineteenth century by, among others, John Taylor of Caroline (as he was known) (1753–1824) in his *Inquiry into the Principles and Policy of the Government of the United States* (1814), and by John Randolph of Roanoke (1773–1833) through his speeches in Congress. They were critical of the growth of a commercial society in the North whose accretions of wealth and influence over government threatened the liberties of the people; they defended the agrarian, patrician order of the South from which they came; they were both increasingly anxious about the fate of slavery in a modernising republic; and for these reasons they opposed the growth of federal power, falling back to the doctrine of state sovereignty. By the 1840s the Southern defence of its 'difference' had mutated into the argument that slavery was a 'positive good', both for slaves, who wanted for nothing on the plantations, and slaveholders. It had also been transformed into an aggressive critique of the ills of Northern political economy. Among the many Southern conservatives of the mid-century who developed these ideas, George Fitzhugh (1806–81) and John C. Calhoun (1782–1850), Senator for South Carolina and former Vice-President, stand out.

Fitzhugh, a lawyer, author and journalist, was influenced by his reading of Carlyle and of British periodicals in the 1840s from which he formed his view of the immoral, exploitative and unstable nature of industrial capitalism. He also admired Disraeli. In *Sociology for the South; or the Failure of Free Society* (1854) and *Cannibals All! Or, Slaves without Masters* (1857) he took further the conservative critique of atomistic liberalism, defending slavery by reference to the degraded, immiserated condition of the 'wage slaves' in the North and vindicating Southern paternalism in comparison to the social anarchy of the free states (Genovese 1969, pp. 118–244). To Fitzhugh, liberty was 'an evil which government is intended to correct' (Fitzhugh 1854, p. 170). Free labour placed 'all mankind in antagonistic positions, and put(s) all society at war' (Fitzhugh 1854, p. 23), whereas slavery was 'a beautiful example of communism, where each one receives not according to his labour, but according to his wants' (Fitzhugh 1854, p. 29). Once again we note the anti-liberal kinship of conservatism and socialism: indeed, arguments very similar to Fitzhugh's, using the same terms, were deployed by Northern working men in New York and Boston in the 1840s in their complaint that the wage slavery of the North was more exploitative than chattel slavery in the South (Goldman 2000, pp. 177–233). But Fitzhugh was no nostalgic: though he denounced the cities of the North, he could see the need for numerous small towns in the South to complement a rich countryside and to provide both a home market for Southern commodities and a domestic manufacturing base to relieve the region's reliance on imports.

Fitzhugh was interested in social organisation and the diverging social values of the two sections. Calhoun, on the other hand, was a politician and political theorist who sought to defend the South's peculiarity by finding a means to preserve minority rights within a democracy. The defence of minorities was a classically liberal theme at this time (as Mill's work makes clear): the paradox of mid-century America was that this principle was required to defend conservative interests. Calhoun's defence of Southern difference had begun in 1828 when he justified the right of a state to 'nullify' a federal law which threatened its vital interests – in this case a new tariff – in his papers drafted for South Carolina's legislature and known as the *South Carolina Exposition and Protest* (1828). In his Fort Hill Address of 1831 ('On the Relations of the States and Federal Government') he first proposed the idea of a 'concurrent majority' to protect minorities by granting significant interests the power to veto the enactment or implementation of a public law. In his posthumously published *Disquisition on Government* and *Discourse on the Constitution* (both 1851) he took this idea further, developing a political theory applicable to a plural society with many different economic and social interests that would protect those differences from federal interference and the tyranny of the numerical majority (Calhoun 1992; Niven 1988). Given that the political, economic and territorial 'balance' and 'equilibrium' of the Union had been progressively upset to the detriment of the South, he proposed in the *Discourse* a dual executive to represent both slave and free states, and argued for the right of a local majority to withhold consent to the laws of the numerical majority in Congress (Hartz 1955, pp. 158–66; Niven 1988, pp. 328–34; Spain 1951). The problems with such rights and mechanisms in practice are obvious, and would have disabled any coherent national government, be it in the United States in the 1850s or elsewhere at any time. But though Calhoun died in 1850, his ideas more than those of any other Southerner generated and legitimated the secession of the Southern states from the Union in 1860–1 after Lincoln's election. The Civil War that followed was about many things and had complex roots: but at some level it was about the struggle of a more conservative society against a more liberal one. It was, as J. Barrington Moore has argued, a type of modernising revolution in which a backward, agricultural and paternalistic society was vanquished by a more dynamic, industrial and commercial one.[27] As Eugene Genovese has argued, the South was the one society in the nineteenth-century world to have actively resisted liberal capitalism (Genovese 1992). Its military and political defeat did not end that ideological resistance, as the history of the failure of Northern 'reconstruction' in the South after 1865 and the institutionalisation of Southern racism in the 1880s and 1890s demonstrate.

5   The 'revolt against positivism': conservative irrationalism in late nineteenth-century Europe

Southern conservatism developed in very different political and economic contexts from those in which nineteenth-century British conservatism took root, though the two movements shared ideological positions and social instincts, as is clear. But in its overt racism, which actually seems to have grown in virulence with the destruction of slavery during the Civil War and the attempted introduction of free labour after it, and in the crude justifications of the racism that underpinned the entrenched system of legalised discrimination under the 'Jim Crow' laws from the 1890s, the South shares some characteristics with types of conservatism found in continental Europe from the 1870s. Partly this is a question of a shared tone – virulent, uncompromising and intolerant – and partly a question of the type and style of argument advanced: as several authors have noted, European conservatism became increasingly anti-rational and vulgar (by the distortion and cheapening of ideas) towards the end of the century, emphasising instinctive behaviour, intuition rather than reason, and the subconscious, where

---

27 Moore 1966, ch. 3, 'The American Civil War: The Last Capitalist Revolution'.

formerly it had placed its greatest emphasis on epistemological empiricism, political realism and naturalistic explanations of human conduct.[28] H. Stuart Hughes has referred to this as 'the revolt against positivism' (Hughes 1979a, pp. 29–30, 37).

The vulgarisation of ideas was evident in the movement known as Social Darwinism. Natural selection as explained by Darwin in *On the Origin of Species* (1859) was a random and amoral process: the capacity of a species or an organism to survive and thrive depended on the chance possession of certain favourable characteristics. This was one of several reasons why Victorians who held to the belief that they lived in a universe in which justice was assured, found the doctrine so deeply shocking. But Social Darwinism, adapting natural science to provide a basis for social science, made explicit linkage between worldly success and the supposedly superior features, attributes and talents of those – be they individuals, classes, nations, races or species – who came out on top. In this way, the 'fittest' – those most deserving – survived and prospered, while the morally, intellectually or racially degenerate did not. It was a crudely circular argument, designed to rationalise existing social and political structures, including rule by elites and the control of inferior peoples by their supposed superiors, by defending inequality or subordination as 'scientifically' determined. While the emphasis on competition and struggle in Social Darwinism would suggest a natural affinity with *laissez-faire* liberalism – and its most famous exponents like Herbert Spencer were extreme partisans for that creed – it was a malleable doctrine that could be employed in many different situations, and which influenced a diverse range of political theorists, including socialists. But it was especially useful to elites attempting to 'conserve' their position, be they American 'robber barons' justifying their wealth, or imperialist statesmen justifying colonialism (Burrow 1979; Dickens 2000; Hawkins 1997; Hofstadter 1955b; Jones 1980).

One source of ideological conservatism unlike anything within the Anglo-Saxon world was papal orthodoxy, which sought to dictate the thinking of millions of Roman Catholics worldwide, and was notorious in the second half of the nineteenth century for its implacable hostility to liberalisation and nationalism. Pius IX had seen Rome occupied by a succession of foreign armies since 1848, his papal domains annexed by the new Italian state, his political authority challenged. In retaliation he denounced liberal Catholicism, the attempt to bring the Church into some sort of

---

28 Burrow 2000; Hughes 1979a, pp. 17, 35–7, 63–4; Weiss 1977, p. 106.

relationship with the world around it, as a heresy. In 1854, in the face of a more sceptical, empirical and materialist age, he promulgated the doctrine of the immaculate conception of the Virgin Mary (Coppa 1998, p. 96). A decade later came the papal encyclical, the Syllabus of Errors, condemning socialism, liberalism, modern scientific thought, and even Bible societies, and asserting the absolute authority of the pontiff (Coppa 1998, p. 108). There followed in 1871 the doctrine of Papal Infallibility, designed to stifle all discussion – and hence to smother liberalism – within the Church (Coppa 1998, p. 111).[29] Rome had declared war on the age itself and would not reconcile itself to earthly powers or the march of mind.

Another source of uncompromising conservatism was the nationalism of right-wing governments and movements after about 1870. If the revolutions of 1848–9 had first shown how nationalism might counter rather than complement liberalism, and had opened up the possibility of right-wing manipulation of the national idea for ulterior political ends, the multiplication of national movements throughout Europe in the second half of the century, and especially within the Austro-Hungarian Empire, had two consequences. First, there were more, and more serious, challenges to the very integrity of the European empires in the late nineteenth century; and second, there was increasing competition, friction and antagonism between national groups themselves. Both developments allowed reactionary statesmen to pursue conservative policies designed to suppress disorder and impose uniformity, be that uniformity linguistic, cultural or religious. They were assisted by ideologues in all nations whose support in print and at the lectern could be assured. Heinrich von Treitschke's historical lectures at the University of Berlin in the 1870s and 1880s were attended by the imperial elite. As a professor, a member of the Reichstag (1871–84), and editor of the *Preussische Jahrbücher*, Treitschke was the apotheosis of German nationalism (though under Prussian control), militarism, authoritarianism, anti-socialism and anti-Semitism (Davis 1973; Dorpalen 1957). Tactically it was easy to play off one national minority against another, or to refocus partisan feeling on alien groups resented by all: it is no coincidence that anti-Semitism developed at this time (and was often encouraged by the authorities, as in Russia) as a type of diversionary manoeuvre, a form of negative integration designed to keep otherwise divergent political and ethnic groups in harmony. Loyalty to the state and regime could be enhanced by encouraging chauvinism at home and prejudice abroad. A movement like Russian

---

29 For a sympathetic portrait of Pius IX, see De Mattei 2004.

pan-Slavism as exemplified by Fyodor Dostoevsky was characterised by hostility towards specific national, ethnic and religious groups (Poles, Jews, Roman Catholics); towards socialism, liberalism and the middle classes; and towards the West in general. Dostoevsky's travels in Europe in the early 1860s led to a conservative, Russophile, reaction.[30] In *The Brothers Kara-mazov* (1880) Western rationalism was famously counterposed by a deeper tradition of Russian spirituality and mysticism. With such a pedigree, pan-Slavism was absorbed easily into the reactionary state ideology of Alexander III and Nicholas II from the 1880s (Kohn 1953).

In similar fashion the optimistic and enlightened ideas about race that the nineteenth century had inherited from the eighteenth were transmuted from the 1850s into a pseudo-science premised on the natural inequality of races and the moral right of the supposed superior to control the inferior (Poliakov 1974; Stocking 1968). Eighteenth-century environmentalism had encouraged the belief that racial difference was neither genetically determined nor permanent, and that Africans might indeed be turned into Englishmen given the right education and opportunities. The 'noble savage' was different certainly, and intellectually undeveloped, but he was not morally or personally inferior to the European. But later nineteenth-century racial theory emphasised a strict hierarchy of races, each with its distinct abilities, and with Aryan whites at the top. In part this change was the consequence of greater anthropological investigation and information at this time, which seemed to suggest remarkable racial diversity and which gave credence to the view that Englishmen and Africans were inassimilable. It also owed something to the prevalence of Social Darwinist theories premised on competition, and to the belief that only the most accomplished and adaptable races would survive that competition. Racism could also be employed to justify imperialism: the backwardness of some races provided the excuse for European colonisation and the 'civilising mission'. Interestingly, the so-called 'father of racism', Joseph Arthur de Gobineau (1816–82), author of the four-volume *Essai sur L'Inégalité des Races Humaines* (1853–5) had been *chef de cabinet* to Tocqueville when the latter was briefly Foreign Minister in the Second French Republic in 1849 – and Tocqueville was among his sharpest critics (Biddiss 1970; Gobineau 1970). Gobineau abhorred democracy for the usual conservative reasons, but was concerned further that it would encourage racial mixing, and hence the moral and

30 Dostoevsky 1965, *Winter Notes on Summer Impressions*. This was originally published as an article in Dostoevsky's own journal, *Vremya* ('Time') in 1863.

intellectual degeneration of the higher races and the extinction of civilisation in an age of uniformity and mediocrity. Tocqueville's response was impassioned and prescient:

Don't you see how inherent in your doctrine are all the evils produced by permanent inequality: pride, violence, the scorn of one's fellow men, tyranny and abjection in every one of their forms? . . . There is an entire world between our beliefs.[31]

Though Gobineau complained bitterly that he was ignored by his contemporaries, his ideas were subsequently influential, notably and ominously in Germany (Gobineau 1915).

In Maurice Barrès (1862–1923) the spirit of conservative irrationalism found a characteristic proponent among *fin-de-siècle* men of letters. Along with the historian and commentator Hippolyte Taine and Louis-François Veuillot, the editor from 1843 of the newspaper *L'Univers Religieux*, Barrès forms a link between Maistre at the beginning of the nineteenth century in France and Charles Maurras, the extreme right-wing editor of *L'Action Française* (and Nazi collaborator) in the early and mid-twentieth century. Barrès mixed the individualism and instinctivism of his trilogy *Le Culte du Moi* (1888–91) with protest against the moral decline of France under the liberal Third Republic in the sequence of novels entitled *Le Roman de l'Énergie Nationale*. The first of these, and the best known, *Les Déracinés* ('the uprooted'), was published in 1897 and depicted a group of students 'uprooted' from their religion and traditions, in part by secular education. In this series he contrasted the values of provincial France, fixed in the land and the church, and in contact with ancestral tradition through them, with the cosmopolitan hypocrisy and corruption at the nation's political and financial centre (Hughes 1979a, p. 54). Unsurprisingly, liberals, Jews and Germans were among his favourite targets: the foreigner in general, as a threat to French tradition, was scorned (Doty 1976). A supporter of General Boulanger (who had briefly threatened to overwhelm the republic in a quasi-Bonapartist coup at the end of the 1880s), Barrès represented several different constituencies in the French chamber, including Les Halles in Paris, until his death in 1923.[32]

In Gustave Le Bon (1841–1931) meanwhile, the irrational found its pre-eminent social theorist. Like Gobineau, Le Bon was a natural racial

---

31 Alexis de Tocqueville to J. A. de Gobineau (17 November 1853), in Tocqueville 1959a, p. 229. See also de Tocqueville 1959b.
32 On the French conservative tradition see Nisbet 1978, pp. 80–117. On Barrès see Tiryakian 1978, pp. 209–10.

hierarch who asserted the scientific superiority of the Anglo-Saxon race over all others, and the inferiority of groups he did not favour or held in contempt, including socialists. Trained in medicine and with strong interests in archaeology and anthropology, he turned to what would now be called social psychology, and his most important work in this field, *The Crowd*, appeared in 1895 (Pick 1989, pp. 90–3). Le Bon's theory is premised on the essential irrationalism of social life: ideas become influential not because they are true or good, but by virtue of their psychological hold over us. That hold can be established by techniques of repetition, or by the submission of the crowd to mass persuasion and mass suggestion – 'mental contagion' as he called it. Masses – be they nations, religions, races or social groupings – react in ways different from the reactions of individuals, establishing thereby a 'collective mind'. They are suggestible and come to define themselves through their shared sentiments and beliefs: this was the 'law of the mental unity of crowds' (Le Bon 1979, pp. 58–9; Merton 1963, pp. v–xxxix). And these beliefs determine how social institutions function, rather than the reverse: institutions reflect rather than determine consciousness. One implication of these ideas is that political arrangements must harmonise with national or group psychology if they are to be successful. Another is that the attitude of the crowd, or of the masses over longer periods of time, can be manipulated towards a desired end. Hence Le Bon focused on the persuasive power of the leader. His fear, and the anxiety of those influenced by him, was of the socialist agitator capable of subverting the reason of individuals and substituting for it the dangerous mentality of the levelling crowd (Le Bon 1898). In the event, Le Bon's insights into collective hysteria and its manipulation were as useful to the right as the left in the twentieth century. As the sociologist Roberto Michels observed in 1930, 'Although public opinion may lose its balance and become extremely radical it has been correctly called the headquarters of conservatism. Public opinion is always fanatic and devoid of all basis of real thinking' (Michels 1930, p. 231). European history in the next few years was to demonstrate this only too dramatically.

The conservative theorists of the mid-nineteenth century had tried to counter liberalism in terms of its own discourse: they had questioned the belief in natural human rights, debated the impact of democracy, tried to refute the iron laws of political economy, lamented the destruction of paternalistic social relations, worried about the dilution of high culture. In Britain these issues and styles of exchange continued to characterise the native conservative tradition into the twentieth century (Quinton 1978). In the United States we can discern continuity from the antebellum Southern conservatism of the 1830s through to the so-called Southern Agrarians of the 1930s, including Robert Penn Warren, John Crowe Ransom and Allen Tate, who continued to champion the lost cause of a Jeffersonian South, most notably in their co-authored volume of 1930, *I'll Take My Stand*. But continental European conservatives of the late nineteenth century rejected any engagement with the forces of change, and rejected the very social and economic categories used by their opponents. In opposition to the reasoned and systematic forms taken by liberal political economy and 'scientific socialism', they threw up arbitrary and highly individualistic categories like the will, instinct and faith. They justified their conservatism without reference to facts or examples, but in relation to the soil on which they lived, the nation for which they spoke, the spirit in which they would do battle, the blood they were willing to shed.

In their irrationalism it must be acknowledged that they were part of a more general trend in European thought at the end of the nineteenth century. Writers and thinkers of all types were subject to these changes as the very concept of the calculating and self-conscious individual, who had been placed at the heart of nineteenth-century political economy and liberal theory, was broken down. Theorists became more interested in the behaviour of groups as subjects of study and as the dominant force in mass politics (Biddiss 1977). The model of the rational individual was also undermined by new medical and psychological studies of the unconscious, with consequent effects on art and literature: the fragmentation of personality and consciousness is as much a theme in Cubism as in the modernist writings of James Joyce. But the change in the nature of conservative thought may also be related to the more fraught position in which conservatives found themselves at this stage, as the challenge from the masses, now organised in trade unions and socialist parties, grew more threatening; as the international situation became more unstable from the 1880s; and as the economic downturn from the mid-1870s began to undermine their incomes and the integrity of their estates. At this stage they seem to have given up rational engagement with their critics, and turned to the manipulation of public opinion and national politics through the use of a new and dangerous vocabulary of struggle and hate (Hughes 1979a, pp. 65–6).

There are respectable academic arguments for treating European fascism after the Great War as *sui generis* and hence unrelated to preceding national and intellectual history.[33] But in so far as fascism and Nazism strove to control and direct the masses in the interests of conservative elites by using the new techniques of modern mass politics, we can see the roots of this manipulation in the late nineteenth century in continental Europe. Conservative theorists there and then attempted to analyse mass psychology and explain how it might be influenced; conservative regimes used explosive forces like nationalism, religious difference and racial prejudice in their efforts to hold off democracy and socialism. That the dictators of the 1920s and 1930s were the more effective in exploiting such factors should not blind us to the continuities.

33 Richard J. Evans, 'Wilhelm II's Germany and the Historian' and 'From Hitler to Bismarck: Third Reich and Kaiserreich in Recent Historiography' in Evans 1987b.

21

Modern liberty redefined

JAMES THOMPSON

1   Introduction

This chapter is devoted to British liberalism in the latter part of the nine-teenth century. These years have commonly been viewed as an era of transition. Mid-Victorian liberalism has been widely seen as individualistic, and suspicious of state intervention. The close of the century, however, saw the emergence of a new liberalism, which departed from the earlier individualism, and advocated an enhanced role for state action.

The historiography of new liberalism has been much informed by con-temporary political and theoretical concerns. It has been suggested that the presumed dichotomy between liberalism and communitarianism in recent political theory can be transcended through the examination of the new liberal reconciliation of the two (Simhony and Weinstein 2001). Similar claims have been made for new liberalism as a fruitful marriage of liberal and social democratic priorities (Clarke 1978). Later nineteenth-century liberalism, including the later Mill, has been depicted as a powerful fusion of liberal and republican perspectives (Biagini 2003). Dialogue between the-ory and history in accounts of new liberalism is not, however, novel. New liberals were themselves concerned to demonstrate the evolutionary nature of their relationship to earlier thinkers, often in response to attempts by libertarian critics to categorise the new collectivism as a betrayal rather than an extension of the liberal tradition.

The historiographical battle lines were largely laid down in the early 1880s. Legislation passed by Gladstone's second government aroused an agitated response from those individualist liberals who regarded themselves as the keepers of the true faith. The Ground Game Act, the Employers' Liability Act and the Irish Land Act were vigorously castigated as a dan-gerous assault on property rights and freedom of contract. In 1884, the evolutionary philosopher Herbert Spencer published a series of articles in the *Contemporary Review*, subsequently issued as a book, in which he argued that the current political tendency meant that 'most of those who now pass as Liberals, are Tories of a new type' (Spencer 1969, p. 63). Individualist critics of constructive liberalism were similarly unimpressed by the extension of the franchise to the agricultural labourers in 1884 and the subsequent redistribution of parliamentary seats in 1885. H. S. Maine's jeremiad on *Popular Government* reflected his distance from the governing liberalism of the mid-1880s, but its distressed diagnosis of the implications of democracy for the conduct of politics resonated with individualists who continued to identify themselves as liberals (Maine 1885).

In a famous lecture on freedom of contract, delivered in 1881, the Oxford philosopher and activist T. H. Green responded to parliamentary critics of the Ground Game Act and the Employers' Liability Act. He acknowledged the apparent departure from mid-century liberalism, and recognised the role household suffrage had played in fostering greater interventionism. However, Green asked his listeners to question the notion that these Acts ran counter to the cherished liberal value of freedom. 'True freedom', he urged, was extended rather than extinguished by the elimination of circumstances that prohibit 'the free exercise of human faculties' (Green 1885–8, III, p. 371). Green's case was that statutes restricting freedom of contract actually advanced real freedom, and hence did not destroy, but instead developed, liberal principles. The argument that enhanced state action advanced rather than retarded liberalism was to become a recurring motif of new liberalism, which received extended enunciation in L. T. Hobhouse's celebrated account of *Liberalism* (Hobhouse 1911).

Both individualists and collectivists produced assessments of mid-Victorian liberalism coloured by their own preoccupations. The preservative claims of late nineteenth-century individualist liberals and the modernising rhetoric of their opponents have had an enduring impact on the historiography of Victorian and Edwardian liberalism, not least because many of the founding works in that historiography were themselves part of this debate. Taylor has plausibly suggested that this inheritance has encouraged historians to underestimate the novelty of individualist argument and to present new liberalism as a natural and appropriate deepening of liberal thought in response to the revival of the condition of England question in the last two decades of the nineteenth century (Taylor 1992, pp. 38–9).

The pivotal figure in narratives of late nineteenth-century liberalism has undoubtedly been John Stuart Mill. Mill presented himself in the *Autobiography* as a radical, often embattled figure, but there is a palpable sense in much of the book of his intellectual evolution personifying larger trends and anticipating future developments (Mill 1989a, p. 190). In much turn-of-the-century writing, Mill's status, for better or worse, as a transitional figure in the history of liberalism came to be firmly established. This picture of Mill was most influentially drawn in the work of Barker, Dicey and Leslie Stephen in the twenty years before the First World War (Barker 1915b, p. 20; Dicey 1981, p. 432; Stephen 1894, pp. 398–9).

This narrative of late Victorian liberalism proved hugely influential. In recent years, it has come under increasing pressure. Dicey's depiction of an individualist mid-century consensus, heavily indebted to utilitarianism, has been subjected to considerable criticism. Many historians have stressed the limited purchase of utilitarian ideas, and, in the work of Collini especially, a differing portrait of mid-century liberalism, as more concerned with the cultivation of character than the maximisation of utility or justice, has emerged (Collini 1993, p. 189). Important work on the moral language of nineteenth-century liberalism (Collini 1993, pp. 91–128), the significance of the radical inheritance (Biagini and Reid 1991), and the intellectual substance of Whiggism (Parry 1993) has significantly revised older accounts, especially of mid-Victorian liberalism. The emergence of a more complex and convincing account of the relationship between and development of utilitarianism and idealism has deepened our understanding of the philosophical underpinnings of late nineteenth-century liberalism (Den Otter 1996, pp. 88–119; Simhony and Weinstein 2001, pp. 159–84; Weinstein 2007).

While much recent writing has challenged the stylised contrasts that ordered earlier portraits of nineteenth-century liberalism, real differences remain over how best to narrate nineteenth-century intellectual history. Some emphasise the legacy of the eighteenth century and the enduring search for 'a science of politics', whereas others stress the novelty of nineteenth-century arguments and the deflating impact of evolutionary modes of thinking upon mid-century political philosophy (Collini *et al.* 1983; Francis and Morrow 1994). Differing approaches can lead to contrasting chronologies. While the late nineteenth century has been seen as heralding a revival of formal political theory, others have focused more upon continuities in underlying moral vocabulary extending into the twentieth century (Francis and Morrow 1994; Collini 1993).

This chapter provides a multidimensional analysis of late nineteenth-century liberalism. It builds upon previous work revealing the limitations of atomistic accounts of mid-century liberalism; but it also stresses the enduring diversity of liberal argument throughout the period. Rather than treat the close of the century as merely the prelude to the new liberalism, it demonstrates the variety of liberalisms in these years. While due attention is paid to the disputes over liberty and the remit of the state tackled by the first historians of late Victorian liberalism, proper consideration is also given to debates about the health of representative government and the qualities of the citizenry.

While the discussion is organised thematically, it pays careful attention to questions of chronology. Three phases receive particular scrutiny: the mid-Victorian period often seen as the high-water mark of nineteenth-century liberalism; the 1880s debates about representation and state action; and the charged conflicts of the 1900s which did so much to shape the historiography. In each of these cases, the range of issues discussed is emphasised and the interaction between ideas and contexts examined. The body of the chapter falls into three parts. The first section analyses late Victorian debates about liberty, good government and state intervention. The second part examines ideas about citizenship, democracy and the constitution. In the final section, an assessment is provided of change and continuity in liberalism during these years

2   Liberty, good government and the state

Arguments about the meaning of 'liberty' were at the heart of discussions among late nineteenth-century liberals. The most celebrated account of the history of ideas about liberty is undoubtedly Isaiah Berlin's essay 'Two Concepts of Liberty' (Berlin 2002b, pp. 166–218). Berlin adumbrated a contrast between 'negative' and 'positive' liberty that has been the subject of much discussion, both theoretical and historical, in the ensuing years. His essay draws upon the history of liberalism in the nineteenth century. There are, however, grave difficulties in casting late nineteenth-century debates in terms of his two concepts of liberty. These difficulties are both historical and theoretical. References to 'negative' and 'positive' liberty can certainly be found in the period, but their appearance was less frequent than is often suggested, and likely to involve the distancing use of quota-tion marks. Where they did deploy these terms, contemporaries were, as Marc Stears has noted, generally adopting them as shorthand for complex positions importantly different from those made familiar by Berlin (Stears 2002, p. 25). These considerations do not entail the impossibility of using Berlin's concepts as a heuristic device for organising late nineteenth-century discussions of liberty, though they do suggest some of the potential dangers in doing so.

Berlin's sketch of 'positive' liberty details a variety of conceptions of liberty ranging from autonomy and self-realisation to political participation. These are, as we shall see, importantly distinct kinds of claims that are not best understood as species of positive liberty. Quentin Skinner has offered strong evidence that negative accounts of liberty need not define liberty purely in terms of the absence of restraint, and that what he calls neo-Roman theories of liberty cast political participation and vigilance as essential to the maintenance of the free state, without which liberty was extinguished (Skinner 1998, p. 18, 2002). The emphasis placed in some histories of republicanism on the view that liberty was the obverse of domination, rather than interference, further reveals the limited purchase of Berlin's famous contrast for comprehending the complexity of historical accounts of liberty (Pettit 1997, pp. 21–41). Berlin's insistence that liberty should not be confused with the conditions of its exercise draws a sharp divide between economic and political liberty. In Berlin's terminology, defenders of 'effective' liberty mistook considerations about the conditions of liberty for contributions to its definition (Berlin 2002b, p. 169). However, this division is far from clear, and was forcefully contested by many late nineteenth- and twentieth-century advocates of state intervention to enhance liberty. Historical reconstruction is thus hampered by undue reliance upon Berlin's account.

Mill's paean to liberty has often been taken as a definitive statement of mid-century opinion. In *On Liberty*, Mill distinguished between self- and other-regarding actions. Liberty in self-regarding action was crucial to the development of individuality and progress. Mill acknowledged the extent of other-regarding actions, but argued that restrictions on liberty were justified only where these harmed others (or perhaps the interests of others). He did not, however, offer in *On Liberty* an exhaustive analysis of harmful actions, nor was the book intended as a comprehensive account of his views on the related but distinct question of state action (Mill 1989b, pp. 14–15, 94, 95–6). Mill's purpose in *On Liberty* was to assert the value of liberty and, in particular, to demonstrate the threat posed by the development of mass opinion to the social diversity on which progress depended. Mill contrasted social conformity with the virtues of vigorous individuality, energetic activism and rational self-fashioning – attributes close to, but subtly different from, those celebrated in contemporary accounts of 'character' (Mill 1989b, pp. 61, 63–5). This preference is equally evident in his recasting of utilitarianism, through the distinction between 'higher' and 'lower' pleasures (Mill and Bentham 1987, pp. 276–83). It is not, consequently, preexisting wants that necessarily demand satisfaction, since the cultivation of higher pleasures is crucial to the maximisation of utility and the attainment of progress. Liberty fosters individuality, and with it, progress. The value of ring-fencing self-regarding actions is the space this creates for the development of the 'higher' pleasures. These goods are the preserve of the autonomous and rational individual, capable of reflecting upon and progressively revising his or her own ends (Skorupski 1998, pp. 43, 45). The protection of individuals from interference in their own projects serves the larger goal of fostering those virtues essential to the enjoyment of higher pleasures (Jones 2000, p. 31).

Mill's distinction between self- and other-regarding actions means that his discussion of the former in *On Liberty* needs to be supplemented by his view of liberty with regard to the latter. Mill attributed great importance to active citizenship in fostering the individuality of the populace by 'strengthening their active faculties, exercising their judgment, and giving them a familiar knowledge of the subjects with which they are thus left to deal'. Mill argued that 'these are not questions of liberty', as defined in *On Liberty*, but proceeded to warn that 'without these habits and powers a free constitution can neither be worked nor preserved; as is exemplified by the too-often transitory nature of political freedom in countries where it does not rest upon a sufficient basis of local liberties' (Mill 1989b, pp. 109–10). This recognition of the significance, and demands, of maintaining 'political freedom' was amplified in the *Considerations on Representative Government*, where Mill discoursed upon the educative value of political participation and its necessity for the preservation of what he terms 'free government'. Mill insisted that 'the most important liberty of the nation' is 'that of being governed only by laws assented to by its elected representatives' and commends that 'popular suffrage which is essential to freedom' (Mill 1977b, pp. 377, 432, 527). For Mill, civil and political liberties were complementary (Urbinati 2002, p. 12; Urbinati and Zakaras 2007). He argued in *The Subjection of Women* that, after material necessities, 'freedom is the first and strongest want of human nature', and that social duty and freedom were mutually reinforcing in civilised communities which embraced 'the liberty of each to govern his conduct by his own feelings of duty, and by such laws and social restraints as his own conscience can subscribe to' (Mill 1989b, p. 212). Finally, freedom could and indeed must be enjoyed by all, as 'the freedom of one has no solid security but in the equal freedom of the rest' (Mill 1977b, p. 610).

Mill's view that political participation and the freedom to pursue one's own ends were parts of a whole resonated widely in mid-Victorian Britain. Rooted in radical accounts of aristocratic power and the value of 'independence', popular liberalism in the 1860s and 1870s attributed great importance both to widespread involvement in politics, not least through the suffrage, and to reducing the scope of the feudal state. The former was regarded as essential to achieving the latter. Popular conceptions of liberty prized self-determination, for both persons and nations, and sought the creation of a polity that fostered equally the values of political participation and personal independence. These kinds of concerns are also apparent in the conceptions of liberty upheld by advanced liberals, and embodied in some of the arguments about political reform in the 1860s and 1880s.

Debate about enfranchisement between the 1850s and 1880s was complex and exhibited a variety of approaches to drawing the boundaries of the electorate. Many of the arguments were conducted in terms of the relationship between taxation, property and representation, or through the more radical but equally traditional appeal to alleged ancient constitutional proprieties. The positions propounded by Robert Lowe and William Gladstone provided prominent targets in the debate. Many of the university liberals who contributed to *Essays on Reform* in 1867 were concerned to counter Lowe's utilitarian case against reform by urging the superior credentials of a wider suffrage for producing good government. Gladstone's moral case for incorporating those fit to exercise the vote both reinforced and reflected a broader preoccupation with 'character' as the prerequisite for possession of the suffrage. Millian links were made between liberty and the vote. Radicals such as G. J. Holyoake connected freedom with assent, whether direct or indirect, to the laws and compared the voteless to slaves (Biagini 1992, p. 258). The contributors to *Essays on Reform* offered a range of arguments for extending the franchise. Dicey's essay on the balance of classes argued that belief in 'free government rests ultimately on the conviction that a people gains more by the experience, than it loses by the errors of liberty', and Kinnear's account of redistribution charged oligarchical government with destroying freedom by subordinating the many to the authority of the few (Guttsman 1967, pp. 65, 99).

In recent years, the perfectionist aspects of Mill's view of liberty have come into increasing focus (Biagini 1996b, pp. 36–7; Jones 2000, pp. 36–7; Ryan 1998, p. 519). Mill's insistence that opinions should be subjected to active criticism was integral both to his arguments for free speech and to his account of the pursuit of the good (Ryan 1998, p. 509; Urbinati

2002). It was, though, essential for Mill that individuals should be allowed to follow their own conception of the good, though the nature and extent of Mill's pluralism, given his utilitarian allegiances, has proved intensely controversial (Mill 1989b, p. 16). These aspects of Mill's thought have led many commentators to describe his account of liberty as, at least in part, a 'positive' one (Jones 2000, p. 36; Pyle 1994, p. xiii; Ryan 1998, p. 509). Mill's attitude to less developed societies, along with his advocacy of self-criticism and engaged debate, presumed that it was a certain kind of individual whose pursuit of the good would be protected by the liberty principle. Much of the wide-ranging criticism of Mill's position in *On Liberty* distinguished, in deeply un-Benthamite fashion, between liberty and licence (Pyle 1994; Rees 1978). These commentaries, which often utilised the language of 'character' and stressed the importance of shared values, reveal the limited pluralism of much mid-century liberalism. Value pluralism, whilst some-times apparent, for instance in the work of Acton, did not occupy the central position that it came to assume in much twentieth-century lib-eralism (Acton 1907b). Perfectionist positions were correspondingly more popular. Acton himself married recognition of the importance of variety, embracing advocacy of the multinational state, with a moralised conception of liberty as the 'reign of conscience' (Watson 1994, p. 61).

Many of the most common criticisms of Mill's *On Liberty* were elaborated with great vigour by Fitzjames Stephen (Stephen 1873a). In *Liberty, Equality, Fraternity* Stephen emphasised the interconnectedness of persons and the imperious demands of morality in the face of human weakness and division. Stephen upheld an especially strenuous conception of manliness in which 'to be less strong is to be less of a man' (Stephen 1873a, p. 221). Deeply impressed by Hobbes' theory of language, Stephen argued that the only meaningful definition of liberty was 'absence of restraint' (Stephen 1873a, p. 172). Such liberty was, however, 'a big name for a small thing' (Stephen 1892, p. 64), merely a question of 'who wants to do what, by what restraint he is prevented from doing it, and for what reason it is proposed to remove that restraint' (Stephen 1873a, p. 182). For Stephen, liberty depended upon power, and was not an end in itself. Mill's enthusiasm for diversity was misplaced, and his belief that liberty was compatible with utilitarianism mistaken. Stephen offered a rebuke to Mill from one 'trained in the school of Locke, Bentham and Austin' (Stephen 1873a, p. 196).

The Millian rejoinder to Fitzjames Stephen was delivered by John Morley (Morley 1873, 1874). Predictably, Morley fastened on Stephen's presentation of liberty as a negation, countering that Mill rightly championed liberty 'as one of the most powerful positive conditions of attaining the highest kind of human excellence' (Morley 1873, p. 238). Less predictably, Morley also criticised Stephen's methodology, complaining that 'he does not practice the historic method' (Morley 1873, p. 252) but treats society like a mathematical puzzle. Morley was not, in fact, entirely enamoured of the historical method, arguing that in practice it had encouraged a debilitating form of relativism by focusing attention on how beliefs arose rather than whether they were true. His appeal to the historical method against Stephen reflects the mid-century prestige accorded the comparative approach, which was increasingly conflated with evolutionary perspectives. Stephen had in fact cited the foremost exponent of the historical method, his mentor Henry Maine, and had attacked Mill precisely for his overly sanguine use of history. Yet Stephen, like Morley, while acknowledging the historical method as distinguishing the nineteenth century from the eighteenth, insisted on the need for rigorous reason and moral vision in the conduct of politics.

The reception of Mill's work provides a crucial backdrop to the emergence of idealist accounts of liberty later in the century. The relationship between Mill and the idealists has often been obscured by their tendency to attack his individualism and, consequently, to challenge his account of harming the interest of others. These accounts, in turn, propagated a particular view of the sharpness and character of the divide between mid-century and later conceptions of liberty. Real differences certainly existed between Mill and the idealists, and the latter's accounts of Mill are an important part of their work, but these should not be taken as wholly adequate accounts of ideas of liberty in the period. This point can be developed by a consideration of the most influential and significant of the idealists, namely T. H. Green.

Green was one of the suspects rounded up by Berlin in his account of 'positive' liberty (Berlin 2002b, pp. 180, 196). Recent work has, however, done much to demonstrate the complexities of Green's perspective (Brink 2003, pp. 82–3; Kelly 2006; Nicholson 1990, pp. 116–22). In his discussion of the different senses of freedom, Green described three forms of freedom: formal, juristic and real. The first of these simply denoted the freedom of the will in moral matters. The second referred to society's recognition of formal freedom, which was essentially a matter of law in nineteenth-century Britain. The law provided and protected equal juristic freedom for all by guaranteeing certain legal rights, but did not, generally speaking, enforce particular actions. Real freedom in contrast must be exercised to be enjoyed, and required self-realisation through participation in the common good (Green 1885–8, II, pp. 308–33). Green's affinities with Kant are manifest in his focus upon the good *will* as constitutive of real freedom, and in his highly inclusive account of the moral community.[1] His Aristotelian perfectionism is apparent in his insistence that only through the process of self-realisation, which was only possible in the polity, could real freedom be attained (Brink 2003, pp. 44–50; Kelly 2006, p. 530). His Hegelian and Pauline debts are evident in his historicist and immanentist account of the content of the common good (Boucher and Vincent 2001; Vincent and Plant 1984, pp. 6–18).[2] Green's absolute idealism underwrites his belief in the harmony of interests evident in his proposed identity between self-realisation and the common good (Nicholson 1990, pp. 54–64).

Green's championing of real freedom led him to insist that 'when we speak of freedom as something to be so highly prized, we mean a positive power or capacity of doing or enjoying something worth doing or enjoying' (Green 1885–8, III, p. 371). It is this stress upon freedom as dependent upon a positive power to act that was most significant in late nineteenth-century debates. The broader significance and response to Green's views can best be understood by addressing the issue of effective freedom, which played a key, if controversial, role in liberal argument in the period.

In his introduction to Samuel's restatement of liberal principles of 1902, Herbert Asquith argued that freedom 'in its true meaning' could not be confined to the removal of constraints, as 'the true significance of Liberty' lay in enabling individuals 'to make the best use of faculty, opportunity, energy, life'. This realisation, he suggested, was apparent in liberalism's new emphasis upon 'education, temperance, better dwellings, an improved social and industrial environment' (Samuel 1902, p. x). The claim that social reform extended opportunity, and thus increased freedom, was central to new liberal argument. L. T. Hobhouse argued that 'freedom to choose and follow an occupation, if it is to become fully effective means equality with others in the opportunities for following such occupation' and made repeated use of the notion of effective liberty (Hobhouse 1911, p. 32). His fellow new liberal J. A. Hobson proclaimed that the creation of 'equal opportunities for

---

1 There is a valuable discussion of Green's relationship to Kant in Brink 2003, pp. 92–107.
2 On Green and religion, see De Sanctis 2005, which emphasises his 'Puritanism', and Leighton 2004 for a reading that downplays the importance of the German theological tradition of Strauss and Baur.

self-development' expressed 'a fuller appreciation and realisation of individual liberty' (Hobson 1974, p. xi). This emphasis on liberty as equality of opportunity proved highly controversial. Edwardian individualists portrayed such reformism as a socialist betrayal of liberty, denying that absence of material resources constituted a lack of liberty.

Moralised conceptions of liberty certainly could, but need not, support more extensive conceptions of state action. Hobhouse's relationship to Green was complex, but his developmental understanding of liberty presumed the existence of 'a possible ethical harmony' (Hobhouse 1911, p. 129). Both Hobhouse and Hobson defined rights and duties in terms of the demands of the common good. It is important, though, to recognise that perfectionist and activist accounts of liberty did not necessitate advocacy of enhanced state action. Differences over effective freedom often had greater implications for views of the state. Green's emphasis upon liberty as capacity was invoked in accounts of liberty in terms of equality of opportunity, but this move was resisted by some idealists, like Bosanquet, who championed a highly moralised conception of liberty (Bosanquet 1923, pp. 116–41). In order to comprehend better these disputes, it is necessary to investigate changing liberal views of the ends of government.

The debates about reform in the 1860s reveal the continued purchase of notions of 'good government' in liberal argument. This ubiquitous phrase requires, however, some scrutiny to determine its meaning. As historians like Parry have demonstrated, the governing ethos of mid-century liberalism cannot be defined exclusively in terms of *laissez-faire* (Parry 1993, pp. 195–227). Good government was required to embody and encourage a virtuous society (Stephen 1862, Stephen 1873b). Arguments about the relationship between church and state were centrally concerned with how best to encourage Christian morality (Parry 1986). Widespread support for a limited, if not minimalist, approach to central government rested upon the notion that character was chiefly fostered in civil society and local government. Legislation to enforce contracts or bankruptcy laws established the requisite responsibility to ensure good and bad character received their just rewards (Hilton 1988). These moral arguments could be combined with economic arguments that emphasised the progressive credentials of market society. Adherence to the moral economy of free trade appealed on a number of grounds. Free trade promised a reduction in the power of the landed interest through cheaper food, but it also embodied a broader vision of a purged and moralised state (Trentmann 2008). Acclaim for Gladstonian budget-making reflected the common liberal view that free and fair trade were identical, and that a socially just balance between indirect and direct taxation was founded on the economically beneficial reduction of tariffs (Biagini 1992).

Whilst fostering liberty was always central to liberal accounts of the ends of government, it was never the sole aim. The suppression of harm provided a significant argument for state action, whose scope advanced liberals repeatedly sought to extend (Hobhouse 1911, p. 92). Radicalism, particularly in the hands of Joseph Chamberlain, advocated social reform by appeal to the greatest happiness of the greatest number (Biagini 1992, p. 267; Taylor 1992, p. 56). Such rhetoric was not, of course, invariably accompanied by rigorous utilitarian analysis, but it was precisely the looser egalitarian and consequentialist dimensions of utilitarianism that proved its most significant legacy. Explicit argument about justice became more apparent in the later part of the period. Utilitarians from Mill to Sidgwick addressed the issue, but it was the new liberal theorists, concerned about poverty and inequality, for whom its demands loomed largest (Mill and Bentham 1987, pp. 314–38; Sidgwick 1891, pp. 107–18). For writers like Hobhouse, the requirements of justice limited the extent to which the interests of individuals could be sacrificed for the greater good, and distinguished his approach to the common good from that of thoroughgoing utilitarianism (Hobhouse 1911, pp. 72–3). The publication of Spencer's volume on justice in 1890 supplied a further impetus to a developing discussion about justice, equally apparent in the writings of Sidgwick. Turn-of-the-century debates about taxation, poverty and redistribution are illuminated by examination of the long-standing and persistent dispute over the land question.

Radical assailants of the status quo drew upon an established critique of aristocratic control of land (Taylor 2004). For centuries, it was argued, aristocrats had enclosed the common land of the people, and flouted the biblical insistence on common ownership. Plebeian hostility to the Game Laws expressed, particularly in its more confrontational forms, a communitarian understanding of rightful ownership (Biagini 1992, pp. 87–93, 56–7). Land ownership was highly concentrated in Victorian Britain, and reflected a history of dubious appropriation and restrictive inheritance laws. Opposition to the existing regime of ownership united many liberals, extending beyond the ranks of plebeian activists. The popularity of Henry George's proposals for land taxation, and the advocacy of land nationalisers, reveal the resonance of such arguments (George 1879; Taylor 2004). The notion of rent, developed by political economists, was widely taken to suggest that the profits of land ownership were unearned.[3] In the last quarter of the century, the status of urban land proved increasingly controversial, with radicals frequently attributing huge increases in site values to social development rather than the actions of owners. The concepts of rent, and the unearned increment, were applied by new liberals to other sources of wealth, notably shares, in ways that echoed traditional contrasts between the productive and the idle.[4]

Criticism of the prevailing distribution of land and property drew upon established classics in political thought. Locke's account of appropriation, sometimes regarded as a cornerstone of liberal individualism, could have more radical implications, as new liberals like Hobhouse noted (Hobhouse 1913). The focus upon labour as the source of property claims, and the requirement to limit appropriation in the light of the claims of others, were mobilised to challenge the status quo. Radicalism had long presented property as essential to the independence upon which a just political order depended (Stedman Jones 1983a). Such arguments were traced back to the Aristotelian emphasis upon the necessity of private property for the development of individuality, and their redistributive implications correspondingly emphasised. Incarnationalist theology, with its focus on building heaven on earth, fostered an appreciation of theological arguments for common entitlement, at least in conditions of scarcity, which were similarly used to highlight the travails of the landless and the dangers of oligarchical control of resources (Gore 1913). Liberal defences of the existing distribution did not disappear, but the issue of land posed particular problems for such accounts, apparent in the support of some individualists for land nationalisation, and the difficulties experienced by those, like Spencer, who sought, abandoning his earlier radicalism on this issue, to protect the status quo on grounds of justice. Widespread support for free trade in land, modification of inheritance and the establishment of commons demonstrates the enduring and changing appeal of land reform to late Victorian and Edwardian liberals. These debates embodied a wider set of arguments about state action, which require further attention.

Collini has drawn a clear distinction between the extent of state action in Victorian Britain and the basis upon which it was justified. He argues that the record of legislative and government interference must be

---

3 The work of Henry George, and the doctrine of rent, proved highly controversial. On the relationship between George and the socialism of the 1880s, see Wolfe 1975. On Fabian ideas about rent, see Bevir 1989. For new liberal approaches, Clarke 1978 and Collini 1979 are helpful.
4 On the idea of the surplus due to the community, see Hobhouse 1911, p. 194.

distinguished from the terms of debate, since mid-century *laissez-faire* principles were concerned with the grounds rather than the extent of state action (Collini 1977, p. 239). Liberal preference for self-help, whether individual or collective, over government action, rested as much on moral as economic arguments (Collini 1979, pp. 29–30). Anatomies of mid-century liberalism have rightly come to emphasise the organic, rather than atomistic, character of its individualism, but this needs to be combined with acknowledgement of liberal recognition of communities, apparent in attitudes to redistribution of seats, and praise for associationalism (Jones 2000, pp. 2–3). Municipal activism was accordingly more congenial than central government intervention, which awakened fears of centralised bureaucracy. Centralisation was often identified with the imperialist excesses of the Second Empire, and held to undermine the sociological underpinnings of liberty in the dispersal of power, destroyed by Bonapartism in France. Similarly, analyses of the dangers of bureaucracy were frequently illustrated with Prussian examples (Parry 2001). Some mid-century liberals, including Bagehot, observed that British celebration of localism, while an essential antidote to worship of the state, could be excessive (Bagehot 2001, p. 182; Fitzjames Stephen 1873b). Acclaim for associational and civic activism importantly inflected attempts to defend an enhanced role for central government. The development of such arguments was also shaped by the acceptance of exceptions to the general preference for societal over state solutions.

Much ink has been spilt outlining the increasing limitations to *laissez-faire* principles within political economy, particularly in the work of Mill (Collini 1977; Hollis 1983). Mill was concerned in particular to demonstrate the range of state action that was non-coercive. He noted the role that government could play in fostering rather than dictating outcomes, not least by the provision of information. He distinguished between complementary and exclusive state services. Famously, he detailed those valuable services, such as lighthouses, that would not be offered by a market of self-interested agents but would benefit all. His awareness of non-optimising market behaviour informed his discussion of state regulation of working hours (Mill 1965a, pp. 937, 968, 956–8). Mill's sympathy towards peasant proprietorship, his use of public benefit arguments, and his recognition of national differences, notably between England and Ireland, provided much support for radicalism on the land question (Readman 2008). Millian political economy examined the strengths and weaknesses of *laissez-faire* on the basis of a hedonistic psychology and a utilitarian benchmark. The latter could, however, support various degrees of state action, depending primarily on interpretations of the nature of market competition (Jevons 1882). Growing emphasis upon the rise of monopolies, and the role of the state as an engine of economic development, led some new liberals to emphasise a greater role for government and co-operatives (Hobhouse 1974, pp. 72, 77–8). The advent of marginalism reinforced the view that max-imising utility required attention to distribution, particularly through the taxation system. Late Victorian individualists often relied upon an outmoded view of political economy, which took little account of the implications of both marginalism and Marshallianism (Taylor 1992, p. 49).

Moral arguments, however, especially those cast in terms of the dic-tates of character, continued to exercise real influence. Proponents of state action sought to demonstrate that their proposals would facilitate rather than frustrate the development of character (Collini 1993, pp. 92–3). This was especially evident in the emphasis of Hobson on the detrimental impact of environment upon character, and in criticism of the Charity Organisation Society (hereafter COS) for neglecting the dangers to character imposed by the idleness of the wealthy (Hobson 1974, pp. 206, 199). Moral con-cerns could, of course, also justify intervention in the face of suffering and incapacity. Attitudes to state provision of education provide useful insights into the changing contours of debate. Mill retained real doubts about the extent to which government should intervene in education, but his stress on the power of education to elevate morality and to develop individuality seemed to many of his successors to require an enhanced role for the state in propagating education (Mill 1965a, pp. 947–50). Liberal doctrines of char-acter stressed the importance of informed choice and self-development, and economic realities suggested the dangers of leaving education to parental choice and the market. The politics of education policy was shaped by reli-gious differences over the place of the Established Church. Nonconformist perspectives played a significant role in determining liberal opposition to measures like the 1902 Education Act that appeared to privilege Anglican interests. These confessional cleavages, evident in conflict between Dis-senting and Catholic trade unionists, should not, though, distract from the growing conviction that the state had an essential part to play in elevating educational standards and empowering those groups traditionally excluded from full access to knowledge.

The proper role of the state was the subject of considerable debate amongst liberals in late Victorian and Edwardian Britain. This discussion was complex, but some general features of the rapprochement between some forms of liberalism and the state may be noted. The increasingly broad basis for the suffrage served to defuse some kinds of hostility to state action which were rooted in suspicion of aristocratic power, though for some liberals doubts about plutocracy and the impartiality of the judiciary endured. In charting more abstract developments, much emphasis has been placed upon idealism and evolutionary doctrines in fostering a more organicist view of the relationship between the state and the people (Collini 1979; Freeden 1978). Idealists, like Green, Ritchie and Bosanquet, were certainly prolific and significant contributors to late nineteenth-century debates. Evolutionary motifs are prominent in the work of Ritchie, Hobhouse and Hobson. There are, however, two difficulties in evaluating the impact of these intellectual trends. First, both idealist and evolutionary perspectives were taken to support a range of positions, both within liberalism, as the contrast between Bosanquet and Ritchie suggests, and also outside liberalism, as manifest in the work of the conservative political commentator, Arthur Boutwood (Green 2002, pp. 63–4). Second, these fashionable idioms may have been deployed to bolster positions essentially adopted for other reasons, rather than acting as independent sources of new thinking. Historians have differed, on a case-by-case basis, about both the relative impact of idealist and evolutionary tropes, and over the status of liberal appeals to these strands of thinking. It should not be assumed, however, that new trends in political argument were important only if they led liberals consciously to recast their positions. Constructing political language constitutes an important element of political debate in itself, and the impact of novel modes of argument in changing the terms of debate was often both pervasive and lasting.

The rise of more strongly organicist approaches to politics importantly altered the character of arguments about the relationship between the people and the state. This occurred in two main ways. First, revisionist liberals came to portray the work of their predecessors, most obviously Mill, as vitiated by an undue emphasis upon the separateness of persons. This historiographical manoeuvre, as we have seen, underestimated the significance of sociability in earlier liberal positions, and came in a variety of forms, ranging from the more abrupt account of Ritchie to the more appreciative assessment apparent in some of Hobhouse's work (Ritchie 1891, p. 12; Hobhouse 1911, p. 107). Organicist approaches were used to challenge the distinction between self and other-regarding action, and to advance the claims of the community. Hobson and Hobhouse in particular stressed the social creation of wealth and the entitlement of the community to its proper share in that wealth. This claim of the community related to the second aspect of organicism, which emphasised the role of the state as the fulcrum of an ethical polity. Idealist progressives like Ritchie portrayed central government as the embodiment of the ethical life of the community (Ritchie 1891, pp. 16–17, 22). Evolutionary organicists presented the state as the highest expression of moral progress, and often gave special attention to the claims of expertise in guiding state action. Changing attitudes to the state did not, however, eliminate arguments about bureaucracy, expertise and democracy. It is to these debates that we now turn.

3 Citizenship, democracy and the constitution

The late nineteenth and early twentieth centuries witnessed a protracted discussion amongst liberals about representative government. The scope of the franchise, the role of the second chamber and the relationship between parties, representatives and voters were keenly contested. Debate was accompanied by and contributed to significant changes in the boundaries of the franchise, the powers of the House of Lords and the relationship between executive and legislature. Historians have often analysed these developments and disputes in terms of the emergence of democracy, the rise of cabinet government and the advent of mass parties. In recent years, important modifications have been made in our understanding of the political history of this period. Greater emphasis has been placed on the restrictions in the franchise before 1918 (Parry 1993). Historians of party have noted increasingly the limits to party power, and the widespread scepticism about mass organisation (Lawrence 1998, 2009). Older narratives of the rise of democracy have shaped much of the historiography of liberalism in this period, which has often stressed liberal disquiet in the face of popular government. Recent emphasis on continuity over change in the political history of the period suggests the need to reconsider liberal perception of and prescription for developments in representative government.

Liberal constitutionalism supplied an enduringly powerful language for discussing political structures and processes. Established liberal conceptions of the constitution emphasised its adaptability and functionality, often by contrast to arrangements elsewhere, especially the USA and France (Parry 2006; Varouxakis 2002b). Whig histories of the constitution traced the development of liberty though the proper ordering of political forms (Burrow 1981, p. 35). Radical conceptions of the constitution had traditionally emphasised the loss of popular liberties, and the need for constitutional renovation (Stedman Jones 1983a; Taylor 1995). While Whigs lauded the Reform Act of 1832 for its supposed incorporation of the middle classes into the polity, radicals and Chartists bemoaned its exclusion of labouring people. However, the repeal of the Corn Laws and the passage of the 1867 Reform Act served to reconcile many radicals to an optimistic view of constitutional progress. This was facilitated by the more populist and inclusive tenor of late nineteenth-century constitutional history (Burrow 1981, pp. 72–3).

Tensions remained, however, within the family of liberal understandings of the constitution. Attitudes to the judiciary nicely encapsulate these. Whig historians applauded the rise of common law, often contrasted with Roman law abroad, as a safeguard of liberty superior to the whims of autocratic government. Liberal acclaim for the rule of law could, though, sustain strong criticism of judicial tyranny in earlier centuries, especially the seventeenth. Radicals retained a strong sense of the failures of 'judge-made law'. This was very apparent in the popular reaction to the Taff Vale decision in 1901, which fanned radical disdain for the class law of the judiciary (Thompson 1998). In his influential textbook on constitutional law, Dicey, by contrast, cast judicial sobriety and independence as the chief bulwark of liberty and constitutional progress (Dicey 1915, p. 192).

The most celebrated liberal portrait of the constitution from this period has, of course, been that of Bagehot. It is, however, important to recognise that Bagehot's account was less novel than it purported to be, and that its immediate reception was considerably more muted than its subsequent reputation might suggest. Eighteenth-century conceptions of the separation of powers, and of the mixed constitution matching in its tripartite form the divisions within society and between types of government, were firmly in retreat before Bagehot's attack on them (Bagehot 1867). By mid-century, eulogies of the mixed constitution had yielded to more dynamic accounts of the balance of social forces within the House of Commons, evident in the work of Earl Grey which also anticipated Bagehot's emphasis on fusion between the executive and legislative branches (Vile 1967). Bagehot's famous book was intended as a contribution to two debates: the first on parliamentary reform, the second on the relative merits of presidential and ministerial government. Aside from his financial expertise, Bagehot's contemporary fame as a political writer lay as a comparative analyst of social and political forms as given more theoretical form in his *Physics and Politics* (Bagehot 1872). Drawing upon evolutionary ideas and informed by his view of the American Civil War, *The English Constitution* celebrated the greater coherence of parliamentary over presidential government (Bagehot 2001; Craig 2007a). In this, as well as its distinction between the dignified and the efficient aspects of the constitution, it married functional analysis with a modish evolutionary idiom.

Much late nineteenth-century debate focused on the role of party. Suspicion of party, particularly amongst radicals, endured, but widespread recognition existed, especially amongst advanced liberals, of its necessity for effective executive government (Biagini 1992; Lawrence 1998). This was combined, however, with the enduring attraction of the 'independent' member, and a Burkean understanding of party that stressed the importance of shared principles (Hawkins 1989). Liberals frequently portrayed the Conservative Party as merely a creature of organised interests, but tended to view their own party as embodying, or needing to embody, the living faith of its creed. Arguments over the caucus in the 1880s often turned on whether organisational development was perceived as broadening or narrowing the distribution of power within the party. Opponents of the caucus often argued that its rise would convert representatives into delegates, and so damage the operation of representative government. Comparisons with the machine politics of American cities abounded. Enthusiasts for the caucus, however, saw organisational reform as an instrument of direct democracy, which rather than replicating the politics of Tammany Hall, would provide an Athenian sense of connection between leaders and led within the party (Biagini 2007; Owen 2008).

New work on nineteenth-century conceptions of 'civil society' has insisted on the primarily political connotations of the term in Britain, and hence distinguished strongly its use in the nineteenth century from contemporary invocation of civil society as a realm distinct from formal politics (Harris 2003, pp. 14, 22, 26, 29). It was once commonly argued that the nineteenth century witnessed the supplanting of traditional political theory by a new emphasis on the social (Wolin 1961). Much recent work on nineteenth-century political thought has emphasised instead the widespread aspiration towards a science of politics, while acknowledging the challenge posed by a growing awareness of social and economic development. This sort of approach, apparent in the work of Collini, Burrow and Winch, noted the impact of historicism and the discovery of the 'social', but dissented from the view that the political was reduced to the social in this period (Collini *et al.* 1983). Much light is shed on these debates by an examination of the role of 'public opinion' in liberal conceptions of parliamentary government.

Constitutional history, as epitomised by Erksine May's canonical volumes, set great store by the rise of 'public opinion', usually located in the second half of the eighteenth century (May 1871, II, p. 268). 'Public opinion' was the organic product of a process of debate and deliberation in which views were weighed rather than counted. In a series of articles on the revolution of the nineteenth century, published in 1870, J. R. Seeley clearly articulated these assumptions. Seeley's work drew upon the legacy of liberal Anglicanism, supplemented by an admiration for the achievements of Bismarck, but his account of 'public opinion' embodied more widely shared doctrines about social and political change. He insisted that 'public opinion . . . is not merely the sum of the opinions of the individuals composing the public'. This was because 'the individuals must be brought into relation with each other, and be formed into some sort of organic whole, before anything worthy to be called a public opinion can spring up among them' (Seeley 1870, pp. 349–50).

The implications of this approach were made plain in the Gladstonian liberal George Carslake Thompson's anatomy of attitudes to Disraeli's foreign policy in his study of *Public Opinion and Lord Beaconsfield*, issued in 1886. Carslake Thompson insisted that true public opinion required volume, persistence, reasonableness and earnestness (Thompson 1886, I, p. 32). The first two of these are reasonably familiar from contemporary evaluation of 'public opinion', though his emphasis on persistence already begins to reveal the normative character of his conception of 'public opinion'. The latter attributes, however, exemplify the distinctive nature of nineteenth-century liberal understandings of 'public opinion'. Thompson's emphasis on the requirement of 'reasonableness', which should not be conflated with the stricter demand for rationality, registers the legacy of earlier accounts of 'public opinion' as the embodiment of the new political intelligence forged by commerce and urbanisation. His advocacy of 'earnestness' reflects liberal respect for deeply held and publicly displayed convictions, which were both more influential and more worthwhile than weaker, private beliefs. This insistence on the primacy of reasonable and bravely articulated convictions was both common and enduring in liberal circles. Liberal sympathy for platform politics, especially evident on, but not restricted to, the left of the party, was coloured by the importance attached to the clash of strongly held ideas in the agora of public debate (Thompson 2000, pp. 108–90).

While late nineteenth-century liberals appealed to a broadly shared account of 'public opinion', the meaning and reference of the term was variously defined. Opponents of the ballot presented open voting as a crucial mechanism for incorporating 'public opinion' into the constitution (Cox 1854, pp. 216–17). Some supporters of the ballot, like Thorold Rogers, rejoined that the 'public opinion' of the hustings was merely that of a mob (Guttsman 1967, p. 113). It was more common, however, to argue that open voting subjected holders of the franchise to the tyranny of the powerful rather than ensuring accountability to the public (Kinzer 1982). There was broad acceptance amongst liberals of the claim that 'public opinion' was the fourth component of the constitution.

Discussion of the duties of voters to the public entailed that the scope of the latter exceeded those of the former. Political notions of 'public opinion' rarely treated the public as synonymous with the population as a whole. The ranks of the political public were often defined, as by Mill in 1848, in terms of reading and debate (Mill 1965a, p. 764). This intellectualist way of conceiving of the public was apparent in mid-century discussion of the intelligent artisan, and inflected later debate about women and the suffrage. These portraits of the public often placed, in Aristotelian fashion, middle-class male opinions at its core. They tended to do so, however, by weighting such opinions more heavily rather than by equating the public with the middle classes. Many liberals, including Gladstone, emphasised instead the political wisdom of the masses over that of the classes (Gladstone 1879, III, pp. 138–71, 176–213). Intellectualist approaches became more inclusive in gender, as well as class, terms over time. Of course, some opponents of female enfranchisement argued throughout our period that women were intellectually and emotionally incapable of proper political deliberation. Proponents of the suffrage unsurprisingly differed, often emphasising, as did the conservative Lord Robert Cecil, that women's membership of the public demonstrated their possession of the qualities needed in a voter.[5] More interestingly, some anti-suffragists, such as Dicey, argued that since women already contributed to the formation of public opinion, they had no need for the vote (Dicey 1909).

Nineteenth-century observers differed especially over the location of 'public opinion'. The leading candidates were the constitutional triumvirate of press, platform and petition. There was considerable debate over their relative importance and changing character. The growth of a mass readership daily press, and the declining significance of petitioning, altered views. At the end of the century, popular support for the Boer War led many liberals to argue that the public had become a mere crowd. There was, however, a significant revival in the reputation of the public among liberals following the 1906 election. Considerable faith, apparent in

---

5 *Hansard*, 5th series, XIX (1910), col. 102.

discussions of industrial bargaining, was invested in the moral efficacy of 'public opinion', increasingly distinguished from the less cerebral movements of 'mass opinion' (Thompson 2000, pp. 279–336). The importance attributed to 'public opinion' was apparent in liberal emphasis, drawing on the celebrated example of the Anti-Corn Law League, upon the mobilisation of popular support through campaigns and associations. The constitutional significance of opinion lay in its ability to link government to the public, and to align political developments with social change. It is thus the language of 'public opinion', rather than discussion of 'civil society', that best illuminates the relationship between politics and society in this period.

The debate about 'public opinion' is crucial to understanding arguments about the suffrage and about the changing nature of politics in Britain. Historians have differed over the extent to which Britain was viewed as a democracy in the period before 1914. While Pugh and McKibbin argue that democracy was generally seen as something that happened elsewhere, and probably for the worse, Jones and Nicholson have suggested that by the 1880s Britain was widely regarded, for good or ill, as a democracy, or at least a democracy in the making (Pugh 2002, p. 4; McKibbin 1998, p. v; Jones 2000, p. 63; Nicholson 1990, p. 288). All these commentators acknowledge the variety of ways in which democracy was defined in the period. 'Democracy' could be used to refer to a particular social group, as in 'the democracy', which was identified with the mass of the population; talk of 'the growth of democracy' often denoted a reduction in deference and an increase in 'the self-consciousness of the masses' (Stephen 1875). 'Democracy' was also employed in more explicitly political terms, but, again, these differed. It could be deployed to refer to full adult, or at least male, suffrage, or to direct rule on the Athenian model. It could be utilised, less precisely, to denote rule by the poor, or the many. Further complications arise from the tendency of contemporaries to combine these variants. After 1884, rather than 1867, discussion of the advent of democracy, or popular government, certainly became more prevalent. By the Edwardian period, reference to democracy had become common, although by no means universal.

Many historians, influenced in particular by Harvie, have emphasised the disillusionment of educated liberals confronted by the consequences of an enlarged suffrage and the related emergence of organised mass parties. Harvie has traced the growing consternation of university liberals, like Sidgwick and Dicey, about the evolution of politics (Harvie 1976, pp. 141–74;

Von Arx 1985). It has been suggested that this produced a more favourable attitude to the limitations on the popular will imposed by the separation of powers and judicial review in the American system (Tulloch 1977). Many mid-century liberals were certainly unimpressed by the new politics, and Dicey's famous study of law and public opinion gave influential expression to this disappointment. However, some members of this generation, notably Green and Bryce, were more sanguine about popular government (Tyler 2003).

It is important to distinguish scepticism about institutional developments from pessimism about the moral health of the electorate. Those liberals affected by the second, like Sidgwick, were more likely to adopt the first, and, furthermore, more likely, as Sidgwick did, to gravitate towards liberal unionism. Social liberals, such as Hobson and Hobhouse, whose faith in the popular judgement, while scarcely unvarying, was more robust, viewed institutional issues differently. Like many radicals, they argued energetically for reform of the second chamber, especially after 1909, and, unlike most radicals, they advocated the use of referenda in Britain (Hobhouse 1911, pp. 245–6; Hobson 1974, p. 32). Support for the referendum was generally confined to a small and diverse minority. Some, like Dicey, urged its adoption, partly in order to blunt the power of party government, and so protect the constitution and the union (Qvortrup 1999, p. 533). For its new liberal proponents, however, the referendum reflected greater faith in the popular judgement on well-defined issues. New liberals worried by the power of party leant towards proportional representation rather than the written constitution, fearing that the latter would provide a basis for reaction, much as they thought it had in America.

Liberal support for enfranchising women grew in the late nineteenth century. Mill's attachment to votes for women had proven highly controversial. Some liberals, including commentators on Mill like Stephen and Dicey, regarded his position as impractical and sentimental. Many liberals, however, came to advocate some form of enfranchisement, whether on terms comparable with those current for men, or as part of a move towards universal adult suffrage. The growth of education for women, a cause dear to many liberals, challenged previously dominant conceptions of female abilities and potential. Evidence of successful participation by women in local politics became increasingly relevant as the national agenda moved towards more social issues. The complexities of party politics, combined with differences over the form enfranchisement should take, obstructed parliamentary action on the issue. This was exacerbated for some liberals by the spectacle of suffragette action. Overall, however, there was a clear growth of support for some measure of reform.

The labour question emerged with renewed force as an issue in British politics from the 1880s onwards. Liberal engagement with these developments offers significant insights into the changing character of liberalism in this period. The return of labour issues to the top of the political agenda presented a significant challenge to liberals, raising questions about the state, civil society and social justice. There were a number of dimensions to the ensuing debates. The role of trade unions within the polity came more sharply into focus with the rise of new unionism and a series of high-profile industrial disputes. Research into poverty, especially by Booth and Rowntree, produced troubling evidence of its extent in urban Britain (Booth 1902; Rowntree 1901; see also Englander and O'Day 1995). Growing awareness of unemployment as an economic problem, evidenced by the increased use of the term, produced sustained discussion of its causes, consequences and possible remedies (J. Harris 1972). The appearance from the 1880s of socialism, previously considered by liberals a primarily continental phenomenon, ignited discussion on the role and capacity of government to effect social change. This debate ranged from the significance of Marx's labour theory of value to the validity of Henry George's proposals for land taxation and nationalisation, with the latter provoking the more intense response amongst liberals. The challenge of socialism intensified the need to formulate distinctively liberal answers to the labour question.

Liberal attitudes to trade unions reveal the intermingling of social, political and economic aspirations. By the late nineteenth century, craft unions commanded considerable respect amongst liberals. Marshall described these organisations as 'a greater glory to England than her wealth'.[6] Liberal observers, influenced by the work of the German historical economist Lujo Brentano, regarded the Amalgamated Society of Engineers as the model for a new breed of disciplined and peaceful trade union. Trade unions were praised for their welfare functions, for their role as schools of collective action, and for their adherence to collective bargaining in the sphere of civil society rather than the German adherence to more politicised methods. Economists, like Marshall and Langford Price, emphasised the beneficial impact of unions upon industrial relations. The kind of skills safeguarded and fostered through apprenticeship by craft unions were presented as a

---

6 Marshall to Caird (5 December 1897), in Marshall 1925, p. 400.

legitimate form of property. Economic discussion of trade unionism was much influenced by the prevalence of high wage theories, often explicitly traced back to Adam Smith. In the aftermath of the demise of the wage fund doctrine, many liberal economists accepted the argument that high wages produced productivity gains through physical and mental improvement. More individualistic liberals often continued to uphold variants on the wage fund, but their analysis relied upon an outmoded appeal to a previous era of economic thought. However, the growth of organisation amongst the unskilled was less open to justification by the tenets of contemporary economics. Marshall in particular was deeply concerned by strikes, such as by the engineers of 1897, which he regarded as designed to obstruct necessary technical innovation. In fact, many of the new unions struggled to retain members in the 1890s and 1900s. Prior to the labour unrest of 1911–13, industrial relations appeared to remain relatively peaceful (Thompson 1998).

Liberal analysis of why this was the case drew especially upon the idea that 'public opinion', conceived in primarily consumerist terms, exercised real influence on bargainers. This view underpinned the publication of statistics on industrial relations by the Labour Department of the Board of Trade and provides a recurring motif in royal commission reports, parliamentary debates and press coverage of industrial relations through the late Victorian and Edwardian period. Its prevalence reinforced the willingness of liberals to exclude industrial relations from legal and state regulation through statute (Thompson 1998). Political economists of differing political perspectives, including Marshall, Price and Nicholson, attributed considerable power to public opinion as a regulator of industrial life. This view accorded with a preference for separating economics and politics, but it also linked the economy to social forces. Invocation of 'the consuming public' as a regulator proved problematic for those more concerned with the interests of producers, and more sceptical about the capacity of the weak to shape public opinion. This was particularly apparent in the response of syndicalists to criticism of miners in 1912 for 'sweating the public'. Mainstream labour politicians upheld the right of miners to a living wage, and the duty of consumers to pay for this, but argued that workers and the public should unite against the robbery of the coal owners (Thompson 2007). Liberals, however, continued to argue that 'public opinion' could justly regulate industrial disputes, and to uphold the interests of consumers through adherence to the moralised economy of free trade.

The 'discovery of poverty' and unemployment raised acute questions about the success of Gladstonian liberalism in ensuring the material well-being of significant sectors of the industrial workforce. Liberals responded in a range of ways. Free trade retained its appeal, in part because of its perceived success in delivering cheaper food and liberal votes. Theorists and politicians, however, emphasised that free trade was not identical with minimal state action (Trentmann 2008). Radicals, like Chamberlain, advocated the state provision of assistance in old age, on the grounds that it was unrealistic to assume working-class wages were sufficient to secure adequate funds for old age. It was commonly argued, though, that this should supplement rather than replace the expectation that individuals would save for their retirement, and hence stimulate rather than stifle thrift. Voluntarism, whether individual or collective, remained preferable for many to state action (Roberts 2004). The politically powerful friendly societies fitted well with this model of provision. Organised charity was, however, the subject of sustained debate. Bernard Bosanquet, the idealist philosopher and bastion of the COS, insisted upon the importance of case work and the damage to character wrought by doles, whether state or private (Bosanquet 1895, pp. 103–18). Hobson strongly criticised COS thinking, arguing that their understanding of character took insufficient account of the formative role of environment. More radically, and more unusually, Hobson's underconsumptionist analysis led him to suggest that excessive saving was counter productive, and that poverty was a systemic economic problem requiring significant state intervention (Hobson 1974, pp. 192–218). Mounting evidence of the limitations of charity in addressing poverty, combined with examination of social policy abroad, encouraged liberals in the view that the state could supplement private provision, through national insurance schemes.

Differences over ends in social policy had implications for discussion of means. The poverty surveys of Rowntree rested upon a need-based analysis of the minimum adequate wage. Some new liberals, including Hobson and Hobhouse, defended the right to a minimum income, which while building on the established notion of a right to life, defined the living wage in terms of the ability to participate fully in the life of the community (Thompson 2007). Many of the issues featured prominently in liberal interventions in the Edwardian debate about Poor Law reform, culminating in the reports of the Royal Commission on the Poor Laws in 1909. The majority report, shaped by Helen Bosanquet and reflecting COS concerns, insisted upon the baleful consequences of poor character but did allocate a role for social policy in nurturing independence. The minority report, dominated by the Fabianism of Beatrice and Sidney Webb, advocated a more extensive programme of general public services, and viewed character deficiency more as the result than the stimulus for poverty (Harris 1993, pp. 240–1; McBriar 1987). This approach was closer to that favoured by the more interventionist breed of new liberals, epitomised by Hobson and Hobhouse. It is thus apparent that in the early twentieth century lively debate reigned on the broad left of British politics about social policy (Jackson 2007). These discussions demonstrated, however, important developments within liberalism, as progressives in particular attempted to forge a revised liberalism more adequate to the perceived challenges of a new century.

4   Conclusion

Liberalism in the second half of the nineteenth century was a complex and varied body of ideas. Mid-century liberalism cannot be reduced to *laissez-faire*; new liberalism was far from unchallenged amongst Edwardian liberals. Nor, however, is the period marked solely by continuity, whether on the radical left or the individualist right of the liberal spectrum. Polarising narratives of the transition from individualism to communitarianism, or *laissez-faire* to state intervention, clearly overstate the extent of change by identifying contrasting ideal-types at the start and end of the period. The historiographical revisionism of the last thirty years has elucidated the essentialism of the first generation of historians of late nineteenth-century liberalism. This chapter has sought to convey and build on these developments, by emphasising both the emergence of social democratic concerns within new liberalism and by attending to arguments about the constitution, civil society and 'public opinion'.

In a well-known essay, Larry Siedentop contrasted British and French liberalism in the nineteenth century, arguing that the latter displayed a sociological sophistication absent in the former (Siedentop 1979). John Burrow has suggested the limitations of this characterisation of British liberalism in the first half of the century (Burrow 1988). This chapter has suggested some of its weaknesses with respect to the liberalism of the latter part of the century. Elsewhere, Siedentop has contrasted the rich debate about political forms in nineteenth-century liberalism with the neglect of constitutional questions in contemporary philosophical liberalism. He stresses the important role ascribed by nineteenth-century liberals to constitutional arrangements in mediating between social change and political outcomes

(Siedentop 2001). This chapter has argued that such concerns were central to British liberalism from the 1860s to the 1900s, and were intimately involved in better-known debates about liberty, and the relationship between individuals and the state. Late nineteenth-century liberalism, simultaneously strange and familiar, remains both historically significant and intellectually provocative.

22

Political economy

EMMA ROTHSCHILD

I Introduction

The nineteenth century was from the outset an 'economical age' or an age of 'sophisters, oeconomists, and calculators' (Bishop 1796, II, p. 296; Burke 1790, p. 113). The 'administration of things has been perfected at the expense of the administration of men', the French conservative Louis de Bonald wrote in 1802, of the governments of the new century, and Adam Smith's work was 'the bible of this material and materialist doctrine' (Bonald 1802, II, pp. 89–90). By the end of the century, in the description of the Indian jurist Mahadev Govind Ranade, the great questions of the times were 'more Economical than Political'; a 'conflict of practice with theory, not in one, but in all points, not in one place or country, but all over the world' (Ranade 1906, pp. 5–6).

The history of political economy is difficult to distinguish, in these circumstances, from the more capacious history of political thought. The definition of political economy was itself a subject of intense interest in the new epoch that was described as 'the age of economical science' (Miller 1805, III, p. 291). The lawyer George Pryme introduced the first course of lectures on political economy at the University of Cambridge by explaining the distinctiveness of political economy, in relation to 'pure Politics'; 'though it may seem less interesting than Political Philosophy, its utility is more extensive, since it is applicable alike to a despotism and to a democracy' (Pryme 1823, pp. 3, 6). For the historical schools of political economy of the later nineteenth century, by contrast, economic thought was intricately engaged with politics, culture, history, geography and law; an 'economic cultural history' (Hildebrand 1863, p. 3) or an 'éthico-historico-psychologico-statistico-inductive' investigation (Guyot 1914, p. viii).[1]

---

1 On the frontiers between legal, political, religious and economic thought, see the chapter by Donald R. Kelley in the present volume (Chapter 5).

Nineteenth-century political economy is difficult to define, too, in relation to the now well-established distinction between the 'high' or scientific thought of intellectuals, the intermediate thought of publicists or politicians, and the 'low' thought or ways of thinking of almost everyone; of a public which had by the end of the nineteenth century been extended, at least in prospect, to women as well as men, to the dependent, to former slaves and to colonial subjects. The loftiest economic thought of the nineteenth century was in many cases the thought of individuals who were involved in the ordinary life of politics, or political journalism. They were participants in a vast and novel enterprise of economic popularisation or economic ideology, in the new media of weeklies, parliamentary reports, petitions, encyclopaedias and semi-scientific economic conceptions, from *Manchestertum* and *protectionnisme* to *Egoizumu*.[2] There was a new world of what Walter Bagehot described in 1860, in an obituary of his father-in-law, James Wilson, the founder of *The Economist* – who had died of dysentery in Calcutta in the course of introducing the income tax to India – as '"middle" principles' or 'intermediate maxims' (Bagehot 1860, pp. 1289–91).

The economists and economic publicists of the nineteenth century were preoccupied, in turn, with the economic thoughts, or the inner lives, of large numbers of individuals. The laws of political economy, in John Stuart Mill's account, were 'moral or psychological laws', and the most successful of all the economic movements of the late nineteenth century, the marginal revolution of the 1870s and 1880s, was known at the time as the 'psychological school of political economy' (Mill 1836b, p. 318; Böhm-Bawerk 1890, p. 265). The economists' most enduring political conflicts were over opposing conceptions of human nature, including the self-interestedness or sensuality of the poor, and the incapacity of colonised peoples. This interest in psychological states is one of the most unfamiliar characteristics of nineteenth-century political thought, in part because the psychological theories are themselves so unfamiliar, whether in respect of the science of 'hedonimetry' on which the 'mathematical psychics' of the 1880s was supposed to be founded, or the 'social fevers' of late Meiji Japan.[3] But political economy is itself an interesting illustration of the nineteenth-century politics of the mind. It was for the English economist Alfred Marshall 'a history of man himself' (Marshall 1897, p. 120).

---

2 On the invention of protectionism, see Todd 2008a; on late nineteenth-century Japanese ideas of *Egoizumu* and *kosumoporitanizumu*, see Gluck 1985, p. 110.

3 On hedonimetry, see Edgeworth 1881, and on ideas of social fevers in late nineteenth-century Japan, see Gluck 1985.

Nineteenth-century political economy was even difficult to distinguish in relation to the frontiers between different nations, or national spirits. Political thought, which is thought about the *polis*, has an enduring relationship to the nation, or the national state, as the principal site of political participation. There was a considerable amount of thought, in the course of the nineteenth century, about supra-national political institutions, from the Congress of Vienna to the Latin Monetary Union of 1865 and the International Sanitary Convention of 1892. There were also theories of sub-national or village or local government, or of what the legal historian F. W. Maitland described in 1888 as the 'shallows and silences of real life'.[4] But political thought, in this epoch of empire and commerce, was for the most part resolutely national. It could be divided, as it is in the present volume, into American and German and Russian political thought; one of its characteristic enquiries was into the comparative virtues of different (national) forms of government.

These frontiers of the political imposed a particularly self-conscious reflection in relation to the history of political economy. Economic thought was conspicuously, by the beginning of the nineteenth century, an investigation of national economies; of the wealth of nations. It was identified as 'political' economy because it was concerned with the policies of national states, and the expression *Économie Politique* was translated into German, as early as 1807, by the neologism *Nationaloekonomie*.[5] Economic thought, even more than the political thought of which it was a part, was divided into national schools – American, Austrian, English, French, Italian, Dutch, German, Russian and Spanish, among others – in Palgrave's *Dictionary of Political Economy* (1899).

But economists were at the same time criticised, as they were throughout the course of the century, for what the German economist and publicist Friedrich List, an exile successively in the United States and in France, described as a 'boundless *cosmopolitanism*', or a 'cosmopolitical idea of the absolute freedom of the commerce of the whole world' (List 1909, pp. 97, 141). One of the principal preoccupations of political economy was with the relationships between individuals, companies and nations over very large and sometimes oceanic distances; relations of commerce, colonisation,

---

4 'It requires only a slight acquaintance with our classical literature and our current politics to understand that here we mean to speak of county government...' (Maitland 1911, I, p. 467).
5 Jean-Baptiste Say's *Traité d'Économie Politique* was translated into German, in 1807, as *Abhandlung über die National-Oekonomie*. Say 1807.

finance, empire and influence. 'In which epoch will society disappear?' René de Chateaubriand asked in 1841, of the economists' new world, in which the technologies of commerce 'will have made distances disappear [and] it will not only be commodities which travel, but also ideas which will have recovered their wings': 'how will we find a place in a world extended by the power of ubiquity, and reduced by the little proportions of a globe which is everywhere polluted?' (Chateaubriand 1973, III, pp. 714, 715, 721).

2 A universal science

The history of nineteenth-century political economy was classified, in the many retrospects of the end of the century, into three large phases.[6] There was a founding epoch of economic science, or of 'abstract economics', in which the ideas of Adam Smith were simplified into a vast system of thought, principally by Jean-Baptiste Say and David Ricardo; and expressed, in turn, in policies of *laissez-faire* in national politics, and freedom of trade in international relations. In a second phase, starting in the 1840s, there was a historical or historicist counter-revolution against the system of what came to be known as Smithianism, or *Smithianismus*, initially in Germany, and then across Europe, North America and Asia. In a third phase, there was a counter-counter-revolution against the historical schools of political economy, and the policies of social protection with which they were associated. This began, in the 1870s, with the mathematical and psychological theories of W. S. Jevons, Carl Menger and Leon Walras, or the 'Marginalists' who were later identified as the founders of twentieth-century economic theory (Ashley 1907, p. 476; Fetter 1901, p. 237).

This triple scheme is itself an interesting illustration of the nineteenth-century idiom of a purely scientific history of economic science, in which the doctrines of successive founding figures are refined, diffused and eventually transcended. It leaves out several of the political questions with which nineteenth-century economists were most preoccupied, including money, financial crises, empire and race. It has an odd and disorienting relationship to the political dichotomies of the times, of radicalism and conservatism, or

---

6 There were more than 200 histories of economic thought published between 1880 and 1914. The Hollis Catalogue of the Harvard University Libraries lists 146 works published over the period on the subject of the history of economics; there are 233 articles on the subject, published over the same period, listed in the JSTOR database of predominantly English-language journals and pamphlets.

liberalism and socialism, or the left and the right. It is also a drama, as will be seen, of the nature of human nature.

Adam Smith died in 1790, and he was transformed, within a very few years, into a stateless fiction; an adjective ('Smithsche' was used in 1795, and 'Smithian' in 1800); an unproper noun (the German publicist Friedrich Gentz was described by the *Morning Chronicle*, in 1802, as 'the German Smith'); or a verb (Coleridge referred to 'a rich man perfectly Adam Smithed & Mackintoshed').[7] Smith was also identified, confusingly, with both English and French politics. For the French diplomat Alexandre d'Hauterive, writing in 1800, the new economic theory of the times – 'what is called, in my opinion, rather too pompously, the science of political economy' – was an adjunct of English power, in which the 'vessels of England cover all seas; she sends soldiers, arms, money, agents to the four parts of the Earth'; little more than a pretext for 'interfering in the most important relations of the social, administrative and political organisation of all nations' (Hauterive 1800, pp. 140, 150–1, 255).

For the Prussian/Austrian economist Adam Müller, Smith was by contrast almost French. The 'onesideness' of the new political science was for Müller a repudiation of 'national feeling,' in the interest of private property. Adam Smith and his followers conceived of the state as a 'useful enterprise', and not as an object of reverence: as a *wilde ehe*, a 'wild marriage', or a relationship without commitment. Smith was thereby identified with French power, and with the origins, in the philosophy of the French Enlightenment, of revolutionary destruction. His system was in Müller's description a 'theory of the absolute *tiers-état*'; 'Smith's cosmopolitan views and his concept of freedom could only bring happiness at the moment of greatest decline for all nationalities in Europe' (Müller 1931, p. 86, 1817, I, p. 228, 1936, p. 305). The Edinburgh publicist William Playfair found it necessary, in a new edition of the *Wealth of Nations* published in 1805 and embellished with extra chapters and obnoxious footnotes, to defend Smith against the charge of having been in agreement with the 'French Oeconomists' (or physiocrats) of the 1760s: 'I must, and do attribute to them, and those with whom they associated, most of the terrible transactions of the last sixteen years' (Playfair 1805, I, pp. 297, 308).

---

7 Article of 22 December 1802 in the *Morning Chronicle*, enclosed in a letter of 18 January 1803 from Gentz to Karl August Böttiger, in Gentz 1909, p. 264; entry from July–September 1808, in Coleridge 1973, III, text, 3565; and see Rothschild 1998.

The oddest comparison of all was between Smith and Napoleon. The 'systems of political economy of Adam Smith and his disciples' were as 'disastrous' as Napoleon's 'law of elections', in Bonald's description of 1810; war, plague and famine were unable to destroy the moral order of society, 'and a book is sufficient to overthrow it'.[8] Smith was '*more* than a co-sovereign of Napoleon', the Berlin intellectual Rahel Varnhagen wrote in 1811 (Varnhagen 1966, pp. 93, 102), in an image later made famous by Friedrich List: 'they are both the two most powerful monarchs on earth' (List 1841, p. lvii). Even the Emperor himself seemed to have been pleased with the association. When he paused at the Chateau de Rambouillet in 1815, on his way to his final exile, he selected a five-volume translation of the *Wealth of Nations* to take with him; in Saint Helena, he was reported to have discussed Smith's ideas ('he avowed them to be true in principle, but demonstrated that they were false in their applications') and Smith's descriptions of the English (a nation of '*boutiquiers*', in one translation of Smith's 'nation of shopkeepers', or a '*nation de marchands*').[9]

The transformation of political economy into a universal science, in the early decades of the nineteenth century, was a repudiation of these revolutionary and counter-revolutionary disputes. 'Until the moment when *Smith* wrote, *Politics* in the strict sense, the science of government, was confused with *Political Economy*', Jean-Baptiste Say wrote in 1803. But even the *Wealth of Nations* was insufficiently orderly, in Say's description; a 'vast chaos of just ideas, pell-mell with pieces of positive knowledge' (Say 1803, I, pp. i, vi). The subsequent reordering of political economy was a matter of highly self-conscious effort, on the part of Say, David Ricardo and others. There was a 'silent revolution', as Beatrice Webb wrote in a manuscript of 1886 on the history of English economics, between the publication of the *Wealth of Nations* in 1776 and of Ricardo's *On the Principles of Political Economy and Taxation*, with its conception of society as 'a collection of gold-seeking animals', in 1817; 'What, then, were the changes in events and ideas that transformed the crusade of the 18th century against the oppression of the Many by the Few, into the "Employer's Gospel" of the nineteenth century; and substituted, under the shelter of a common name,

---

8 'Sur l'Économie Politique' (1810) and 'De la Richesse des Nations' (1810), in Bonald 1859, II, pp. 297, 308.
9 Letters of 16 June 1840 from Napoleon's valet Louis-Joseph Marchand to Mme. Guizot and Mme. Dosne, in Bibliothèque Nationale de France, Reserve P. R. 379; Las Cases 1968, p. 1441; O'Meara 1824, I, p. 391, II, pp. 159, 160.

a set of abstract principles for the conduct of financial business, for the scientific observation of one aspect of human life, the Economic nature of man?'[10]

Ricardo's *Principles* and Smith's *Wealth of Nations* were strikingly different, in size and shape and idiom. The *Wealth of Nations* was a large, discursive, historical investigation. It was, in the description of the American statesman Woodrow Wilson, 'a book of digressions – digressions characterised by more order and method, but by little more compunction, than the wondrous digressions of Tristram Shandy' (Wilson 1893, p. 16). There were by contrast no digressions in Ricardo's *Principles*. There were almost no proper names of persons, with the exception of the names of writers on political economy; or of places, except in an idiom of counterfactual example ('if Portugal had no commercial connexion with other countries...'). Even the numbers were counterfactual ('if my income is 1000l. per annum...') (Ricardo 1817, pp. 157, 321). Approximately 500 pages of the final edition of the *Wealth of Nations* were concerned with colonial and commercial companies; Ricardo's chapter on colonial trade was of no more than fifteen pages.

'I was the spiritual father of [James] Mill, and Mill was the spiritual father of Ricardo', Jeremy Bentham wrote towards the end of his life, and the idiom of Ricardo's *Principles* was in substantial part Mill's invention. It was an enterprise, in James Mill's description, of sorting and classifying; a kind of post office of thought, not unlike his own business office, in the English East India Company, of Assistant Examiner of Correspondence. 'You want some practice in the art of laying down your thoughts', Mill wrote to Ricardo in 1815; the objective 'is, when all the ideas are on paper, then to put them together in their proper parcels'. 'What I want to see, in the first place, is – all the ideas', he wrote again in 1816; 'we will then lay our heads together, to see how it may be sorted and shaped'.[11] The scientific organisation of political economy was for Mill a constituent, in turn, of an even vaster ordering, or sorting, of all the sciences of political life. The objective of Mill's own book of 1817, his *History of India*, was no less than that of 'laying open the principles and laws of the social order', as he wrote to Ricardo. His eventual plan was yet more awesome, he wrote in another

---

10 Beatrice (Potter) Webb, 'The History of English Economics', 3: 16, 3: 23, 'Diary', 8 August 1886, x, p. 695: Passfield MSS, London School of Economics.
11 Bentham 1838–43, x, p. 498; letters from James Mill to David Ricardo, in Ricardo 1951–73, VI, pp. 321, 330, VII, pp. 73, 99, 108–9.

letter of 1817: 'If I had time to write a book I would make the human mind as plain as the road from Charing Cross to St Pauls.'[12]

But the new scientism of economic thought was in no respect a rejection of the public world of politics. Ricardo, Bentham and James Mill were all virtuosos of political, economic and financial information; Ricardo as a stockbroker, Member of Parliament and investor in East India Company obligations, Mill in the Company's correspondence office, and Bentham as a sort of one-person Worldwide Web, with his network of correspondents from Honduras to Bengal, and his indefatigable secretaries, John Bowring and others.[13] The enthusiasm for science, in the 1810s, 1820s and 1830s, was also an enthusiasm for the public understanding of science; for all the innovations in popular knowledge, from halls of science and conversations about chemistry to travelling exhibitions and pocket encyclopaedias, which were such a conspicuous characteristic of the post-revolutionary world. As the apostle of free trade Richard Cobden asked in 1835, 'We have our Banksian, our Linnaean, our Hunterian Societies; and why should not at least our greatest commercial and manufacturing towns possess their Smithian Societies?' (Cobden 1835, p. 30).

Even the vast ocean would soon be covered by newspapers, reviews, journals, statistical information and 'severe economic studies', the Italian poet Giacomo Leopardi predicted; a 'Ganges of political writings' of the new century, from 'Morocco to Cathay' and 'from Boston to Goa'.[14] Jean-Baptiste Say followed his *Traité d'Économie Politique* of 1803 with a *Catéchisme d'Économie Politique, ou Instruction Familière* in 1815, two volumes of economic notes (on Ricardo and on the Russian economist Storch), and a *Cours Complet d'Économie Politique Pratique*, in seven volumes, in 1828–33. Ricardo's friend Mrs Jane Marcet proceeded from *Conversations on Chemistry* to *Conversations on Political Economy*; her books were estimated to have sold well over 200,000 copies (Polkinghorn 1993, pp. 3, 35). Economic thought, in the new media, was a middling or medium sort of thought; the 'business of everyone', in Say's description, and in particular of 'la classe mitoyenne', the individuals working in offices, the heads of very small administrations,

---

12 Letter of 19 October 1817 from James Mill, in Ricardo 1951–73, VII, p. 196; extract of a letter from James Mill to Francis Place, British Library, Add. Mss. 35153 (Place Papers, vol. 84), f. 29, and see Halévy 1901–4, II, p. 173.
13 On Bowring, see Todd 2008b; on Bentham, Rammohun Ray and revolutionary Guatemala, see Bagchi 2005, pp. 250–62.
14 'Palinodia al Marchese Gino Capponi', 1835, in Leopardi 1993, I, pp. 38–40.

upon whom the prosperity of provinces depended (Say 1803, 1, pp. xxvii–xxix).

The abstract propositions of economic science were invoked in practical politics, and the successes of policy were invoked in support of economic abstractions. Scientific political economy was associated, in particular, with two sets of policies, which were in each case reforms of the elaborate systems of 'protection', external and internal, that the post-revolutionary governments of the nineteenth century had inherited from their disparate old regimes. It was 'the immense success of Free Trade as an experimental proof of the current doctrines of *laisser faire*', Beatrice Webb wrote in her history of economics, which, together with the reform of the English Poor Laws, explained 'the self complacent dogmatism that overcame the minds of the Political Economists in the first half of this century' (Webb 1886, 3: 33–4).

The invention of free trade and its 'other', protectionism, was the outcome of disparate coalitions in different countries; evangelical and radical (in England), Catholic and colonial (in France), slave-owning and Anglophile (in the United States). It was a religious movement, in the sense that several of the most prominent of its exponents, including Richard Cobden (an Anglican and phrenologist) and Frédéric Bastiat (a devout Catholic, who died in Rome), identified the universal laws of society with universal religion. It was religious, too, or almost religious, in its identification of natural, social and providential laws (see Hilton 1988; Todd 2008a). But the free trade movement was cold-hearted, in the view of its opponents. It was the expression of English insincerity, for Friedrich List, in which national interest was concealed within the cosmopolitan arguments of Adam Smith, with their 'spirit of sophistry – of scholasticism – of obscurity – of dissimulation and hypocrisy' (List 1841, p. lviii).

The disputes over the reform of social protection were even more spirited. Thomas Robert Malthus' *Essay on the Principle of Population*, in its successive editions from 1798 to 1826, was a bitter attack both on French revolutionary proposals for social protection or social security – 'that a fund should be established, which should assure to the old an assistance produced in part by their own former savings' – and on the 'pernicious system' of English poor relief, with its consequences of 'wide-spreading tyranny, dependence, indolence, and unhappiness'. Malthus' principle of population, or 'the acknowledged tendency of the human race to increase faster than the means of subsistence', was the basis, in turn, of a dismal prospect of endless penury; of wages that would never rise, more than fleetingly, above the level of subsistence (Malthus 1826, II, pp. 4, 42, 337, 347). The 'monster Malthus' and his followers were the theorists, in the journalist William Cobbett's description, of the 'unfeeling oligarchs and their toad-eaters', or of 'a grinding, an omnipresent, never-sleeping *oligarchy of money*' (Cobbett 1830, p. 356, 1831, II, no. 5, p. 119).

The political economists were inculpated, eventually, in what was described as an awesome enterprise of moral and spiritual destruction. The study of political economy, William Godwin wrote in 1820, was considered to be responsible for 'the heart of flint that has disgraced the beginning of the nineteenth century' (Godwin 1820, p. 112). The critique was in a part a continuation of the polemics of the early years of the century; the denunciation of the economists for their disrespectful view of the state, and of the state's responsibility for religious and moral improvement. But it also turned, more insidiously, on a conflict of conceptions of human nature. The poet Robert Southey described Smith as a Diogenes of the modern employee, poised to 'pluck the wings of his intellect, strip him of the down and plumage of his virtues, and behold in the brute, denuded, pitiable animal, the man of the manufacturing system!' (Southey 1812, p. 337). The effect of materialist doctrines, the French Catholic theorist Félicité de Lamennais wrote in 1820, was to transform society into an anarchy of interests and desires. The new economic society would be a universalisation of England; a country that was dead because of its morality or mentality, a corpse galvanised only by the convulsions of cupidity, or by 'an unquiet and prodigious activity, which some take to be life, and which is life, as fever is life, as the contractions of a galvanism are life' (Lamennais 1820, I, pp. 74, 375).

The tendency of political economy, on this view, was to destroy the moral foundations of social existence and individual virtue. The economists were criticised for being cold and hard-hearted in the policies they proposed, and for having a dismal view of the future of society. They were criticised, too, for their dismal view of the nature of men in general, and of the working classes in particular: 'inert, sluggish, and averse from labour', and induced by vice into 'inextricable unhappiness', in Malthus' description of 1798; or stimulated by the desire for money, with 'self-love for the mainspring of the great machine' (Malthus 1798, pp. 70, 207, 363). The consequence of all this coldness, in turn, was even more sinister. The economists were putting forward a description of society, and in the view of their critics, they were at the same time changing societies, and changing individual dispositions.

The theorists of political economy were closely involved, thereby, in the most profound of all the political discussions of the times, over the nature of the human mind. 'The first question in regard to any man of speculation is, what is his theory of human life?' John Stuart Mill wrote in 1838; 'every Englishman of the present day is by implication either a Benthamite or a Coleridgian'. The Benthamite theory, with its 'idea of the world [as] that of a collection of persons pursuing each his separate interest or pleasure', was inspired, in Mill's account, by the French philosophy of the eighteenth century. The 'Germano-Coleridgian' theory of the 'culture of the inward man [and] the formation of national character' was inspired by Herder and Goethe. These were universal conceptions and they posed a universal, dire dilemma: 'sensualism is the common term of abuse for the one philosophy, mysticism for the other. The one doctrine is accused of making men beasts, the other lunatics.'[15]

It was this conflict of conceptions of human nature, in an extended dialectical process, which shaped the subsequent course of nineteenth-century political economy. The early nineteenth-century depiction of 'Smithian' political economy was a parody, at least in respect of Smith's own writings, which were only occasionally abstract, and almost excessively preoccupied with the inner lives of excise officers. Even Malthus, with his vista of beastly vices, was closely involved in theories of conscience and prudence (see Winch 1996). But it was this parody, Bonald's or Southey's travesty, which the political economists of the 1810s and 1820s embraced. It was an 'unconscious generalisation of one type of man, the city man', in Beatrice Webb's description; Ricardo 'accepted as axioms of human nature certain generalised facts of one aspect of human nature, the economic aspect and he tacitly asserted that no other side of it existed' (Webb 1886–7, pp. 690–1).

John Stuart Mill's own essay on the definition of political economy, which he published in 1836, the year of his father's death, is a poignant illustration. Political economy, in his account, was obliged to abjure any interest in 'the whole conduct of man in society'. It was concerned with 'him solely as a being who desires to possess wealth . . . [and] makes entire abstraction of every other human passion or motive'; it 'considers mankind as occupied solely in acquiring and consuming wealth'. This was the Faustian renunciation required of modern science: 'not that any political economist was ever so absurd as to suppose that mankind are really thus constituted, but

---

15 John Stuart Mill, 'Bentham' (1838) and 'Coleridge' (1840), in Mill and Bentham 1987, pp. 151, 155, 180, 185, 200–1.

because this is the mode in which science must necessarily proceed' (Mill 1836b, pp. 318, 321–2). Mill himself, some years later, came to renounce his youthful renunciation. 'It was one of my father's main objects to make me apply to Smith's more superficial view of political economy, the superior lights of Ricardo', he wrote in his autobiography, of his own initial and 'thorny' instruction. In the end, he chose 'the practical and popular manner of Adam Smith' over 'the abstract manner of Ricardo and my father', and sought, in his own *Political Economy*, to 'bring in, or rather to bring out, a great number of opinions on incidental matters, moral and social'.[16] But the dialectic of thesis, in the form of abstraction (or Smithianism/Benthamism), and antithesis, in the form of the morality of society, had by then assumed its own, virtually global momentum.

In the illustrated children's series of 1841, *The Private and Public Life of Animals*, there was a story by Balzac about the search for the best form of government. The hero of the story, a philosopher-sparrow, was given to reflection on such political questions as 'our rights, our duties, and our future' ('where are Sparrows going? where do they come from? why can they not weep?'). He had been chosen by the birds of Paris as a special envoy to investigate the difficult governments of the world. He travelled far: to an absolute monarchy (the kingdom of the Bees), whose motto was 'PUBLIC ORDER'; to a Spartan republic of absolute equality (the Lupian Republic); and to a neighbouring island, the Formic Empire.[17]

The regime of the Ants, or the Formicalians, had been described to the philosopher-sparrow as a model form of government. It was a society in which the people obeyed the laws, and were the servants only of their own morality, or mentalities. The first sight which greeted him was of the 'marvellous activity of this nation', 'everywhere the Ants were coming and going, loading and unloading commodities'. But the ants were all the same, as depicted in the artist Grandville's illustration of steam engines, ships, porters, carriers, tunnel-diggers and ant-labourers unpacking crates of opium: 'they were all black, very clean as though varnished, but without any individuality'. As one of the patricians, a queen ant, explained, 'our worker ants are very proud to belong to the Formic Empire, and work with good heart, singing *Rule, Formicalia!*' ([Balzac] Sand 1977, pp. 149, 151–2, 156).

---

16 *Autobiography*, in Mill 1981, p. 31; letters of 1844 and 1847, in Mill 1963b, pp. 642, 708.
17 [Balzac] Sand 1977, pp. 146, 164; letter of 1841 in Sand 1964–95, V, pp. 322–4.

The prosperity of the empire was founded, the philosopher-sparrow concluded, on a 'shocking inequality' at home, and on unjust aggression overseas. The Formicalians were endlessly setting off for or returning from expeditions of conquest. You have grain, and we have wood, they would say to distant sovereigns; 'it is not permissible to keep commodities which are in abundant supply, while we have shortages: this is against the laws of good sense. Let us exchange.' If the foreign ants refused, the Formic Navy would set sail, as required by 'formic honour and commercial freedom'. 'I departed', the philosopher-sparrow recalled, 'really afflicted by the perfection of this oligarchy and the boldness of its egotism' ([Balzac] Sand 1977, pp. 153, 155, 157).

3 Economic cultural history

The outset of the counter-revolution of historical political economy was generally identified, in late nineteenth-century histories of historicism, with the publication, in 1843, of the lecture notes, on subjects from 'income' and 'luxury' to 'giro-banks', of the Göttingen professor Wilhelm Roscher. It was Roscher's three and a half page preface, the economic historian W. J. Ashley wrote in 1894, which 'sounded the first clear note of the new movement'. Political economy (*Staatswirthschaft*) was a political science (*eine politische wissenschaft*), Roscher told his students, and its objective was 'to pass judgement on men, to rule over men'. It did this by representing 'what nations have thought, willed, and felt in the economic field'. It proceeded in the closest union with legal history, political history, and cultural history; it understood that nations were not only the mass of individuals living at any particular time. It sought to compare all nations, 'so closely entwined with one another' in modern times, and to make the responsibilities of legislators and administrators more rather than less complicated (Roscher 1843, pp. iv–v; Ashley 1894, p. 100).

The 'historical method' in political economy was remote from the 'school of Ricardo', Roscher concluded. It was closer to Malthus, and it was inspired, above all, by historical jurisprudence. Its duty, he explained a little confusingly, was to provide to history 'somewhat the same service as histology and organic chemistry render today to natural history'. The study was itself organised in the manner of a textbook; it concluded with a bibliography of the 'reaction against Adam Smith', from the work of a Venetian monk writing in 1771 (*Errori Populari Intorno all'Economia Nazionale*), to Alexander Hamilton's reports on trade, and to the 'extreme socialists', including the *Catéchisme des Industriels*, and Saint-Simon's plans of 1814 for reorganising 'European society' into a 'single political body' (Roscher 1843, pp. v, 149–50).

The investigation of the new economic-cultural history was within a very few years a matter of considerable political importance, in Germany and elsewhere. The Marburg professor and later member of the Frankfurt Parliament Bruno Hildebrand identified the reform of economic thought, in 1848, with a revolution, long overdue, against the philosophy of the Enlightenment. Smith, or the 'Smith'sche Schule', was once again the object of obloquy, for its cosmopolitanism – 'a sort of universal political economy for the world and humanity' – its atomism – an 'economic ratio-nalism', associated with the constitutional theory of the enlightenment – and its 'materialism' – a 'deification of private-egotism'. So too was the English model of industrial inequality, as depicted, for Hildebrand, in Friedrich Engels' *Condition of the Working Classes in England*. The philoso-pher Proudhon, in Hildebrand's account, had demonstrated 'the relativity of all economic institutions', and the 'one-sidedness' of the application of abstract concepts to 'concrete cases' of economic policy; he showed 'the necessity of a historical method in economic science' (Hildebrand 1848, pp. 27, 30–4, 52, 275, 326–9, 1863, p. 3).

The historical method of the mid-nineteenth century was anti-Ricardian, in the sense of refusing the supposed abstraction of English or French political economy. It was Hegelian, in the sense of identifying the spirit of nations as the most important object of economic investigation, and the state as the 'most important incorporeal capital of every nation' (Roscher 1882, I, p. 154). As Marx wrote in 1847, apropos Ricardo, Hegel and Proudhon's historical method, 'if the Englishman transforms men into hats, the German transforms hats into ideas' (Marx n.d. [1847], pp. 87–8, and letter of 1846, pp. 152–4). But the historical political economists were also, for the most part, practical and enterprising men. They were historians of railways, forests and rivers; specialists of what Roscher described as 'the stages of economic development', or the 'laws of the development of the economy of a nation' (Roscher 1882, I, pp. 87, 293).

In the almost worldwide economic expansion of the 1850s and 1860s, the historical economists were theorists of the state and its role in economic development; of 'dominion over nature', in the expression of the Irish economist Thomas Cliffe Leslie, inspired by a visit to the Ruhr, in a 'world of change and progress' (Cliffe Leslie 1870, pp. 230, 241, and see Hobs-bawm 1975). They were theorists, too, of the natural capital of Germany, expanding to the east, or of the United States, expanding to the west. Capital was abstract, financial and international, in the historical economists' parody of English or Ricardian political economy: men into hats, hats into bonds, and bonds into men. It was national and natural, in their own vista, embodied in the destinies of historical nations.[18]

Historical political economy, in the course of the economic expansion of the mid-nineteenth century, became a dominant mode of economic thought, in Germany and eventually elsewhere. The successive historical schools were extraordinarily efficient in the enterprise of ideological invention, or popularisation, with which James Mill and Jean-Baptiste Say had been so involved in the 1820s. They were far more solidly established in university life in Germany than the opposing 'schools' in France or England; they were schools in a literal sense, as Roscher explained in his celebrated preface, for young men who aspired to an administrative career. They were supported, as the Ricardians and Cobdenites were in Britain, by a prolific universe of committees, journals, charities and associations, notably the *Verein für Sozialpolitik*, created in 1872 by Hildebrand and others, including the most powerful of all the younger historical economists, Gustav Schmoller, to promote social reform in the new German Empire. They were responsible for a new language of popular economic thought, with its own codes and mnemonics. Almost a century of disputes over Adam Smith's economic ideas was thus summarised, from the 1860s, in the new concept of *Smithianismus*. *Smithianismus* was opposed to culture, society and law itself, its leading critic, the Rostock law professor Hermann Roesler explained in 1868; his dire conclusion, which he described as 'at first glance astonishing', was that 'Socialism is the pure consequence of *Smithianismus*' (Roesler 1871, p. 36).

The institutional successes of historical political economy extended far beyond Germany. The yearning for an economic-cultural history of nations was itself international. The economists of the world made their way to Germany; Richard Ely, the principal founder of the American Economic Association, who went to study in Germany in 1877, recalled a 'joyous expansion', 'the feeling when I went there that I had entered into a new heritage of freedom'. He and the other young Americans were weary of 'endless harangues over paper money', they were inspired by 'the idea of relativity as opposed to absolutism', and they aspired to base their thoughts 'on the world's experience instead of conventional English ideas'; the 'warm

18 On the German and American frontiers, and the spirit of mastery over nature, see Blackbourn 2006.

humanitarianism of the German theorists moved the Americans of my day deeply' (Ely 1910, pp. 68, 69, 77, 78, 80; Grimmer-Solem and Romani 1998).

The American Economic Association was founded, in 1885, on the model of the *Verein für Sozialpolitik*. A young Japanese law professor, Kanai Noburu, who had studied in Heidelberg, like Ely, in Halle together with Max Weber, and in Berlin with Schmoller, founded the *Shakai Seisaku Gakkai* (Association for the Study of Social Policy), also on the model of the *Verein* (Marshall 1977, p. 85; Pyle 1974, p. 139). The German economists, meanwhile, made their own way to the world. Professor Roesler of Rostock, having been dismissed from his post in the conflict between Bismarck and the Catholic bishops, was appointed as one of the earliest foreign legal advisers to the Meiji court in Japan, with special responsibility for the commercial code to be promulgated in connection with the new constitution of 1889. He remained in Japan until almost the end of his life, an exponent of 'social law' in the internal discussions over the Meiji constitution, and a representative of the emperor in negotiations in Belgium and China; he was described as an 'enthusiastic Japanese' and 'persona ingratissima' in England, who 'of all the foreigners who influenced the making of modern Japan, played the greatest role' (Siemes 1968, p. xi; Suzuki 1941, pp. 61, 78).

In India, too, the historical political economy of the German theorists was identified as a prospect of freedom. The new discipline which the Bombay jurist Mahadev Ranade introduced as 'Indian Political Economy', in 1892, was to be national, historical, and inspired, above all, by Friedrich List; a theory of the 'full and many-sided development of national productive powers'. India had been an experimental object in 'laissez-faire policy', or in 'the so-called maxims of rigid Economical Science', in the description of the Indian historical economists. There was a 'levelling up of Oriental Institutions to the requirements of the most radical theorists in Europe', or to the circumstances of 'happy England' (Ranade 1906, pp. 20–1, 36, 314–15, and see Ambirajan 1978; Goswami 2004; Mehta 1999; Stokes 1959). The new 'Indian' political economists of the later nineteenth century were inspired, in contrast, by the Indian-ness of India; by everything that was un-English and un-European in India's national past and future.

The characteristic idiom of political economy, in its new, historical role, was the statistical series. It was to be an 'economic cultural history in the context of the history of the total political and legal development of nations, and statistics', as Hildebrand wrote in the first issue of the *Jahrbücher für Nationalökonomie und Statistik* (Hildebrand 1863, p. 3). It was also an effort to depict the 'full empirical reality' of economic life (Grimmer-Solem and Romani 1999). Economists associated with the multiple historical schools, from Germany, Hungary, Ireland and England to India, Japan and the United States, were actively involved in the invention of local, regional, national and international statistical offices, and in the collection and dissemination of statistical information (see Grimmer-Solem 2003 and Studenski 1958). The duty of both 'historical' and 'orthodox' economists was no longer, in Beatrice Webb's description, to lecture 'politicians on the worn out text of *laisser-faire*', and to 'imagine themselves to be the schoolmasters of the universe'. It was rather to provide scientific advice on factory legislation, employer's liability acts, compulsory registration of friendly societies, merchant shipping bills, 'Charity commissions, Societies for the prevention of the enclosure of commons &c., &c' (Webb 1886, 3: 35, 37, 52).

The idioms of statistical reasoning were common, by the late nineteenth century, to Germans and English, free-traders and protectionists. Even James Wilson, the founder of *The Economist*, had very little taste for the 'more refined abstractions' of the 'more specially scientific Political Economists'. He had 'what may be called a business-imagination', his son-in-law, Walter Bagehot, wrote in 1860; 'he had a great power of conceiving transactions'. Wilson had founded *The Economist* in 1843, as a 'weekly Free Trader'. It became profitable, influential and widely imitated; it included a 'bankers' gazette', a 'railway monitor', and copious statistical information; 'the best shape of communicating information had to be invented in detail', in Bagehot's account. It employed a redoubtable collection of journalists, many of them with connections to other economic media, including Bagehot himself, Herbert Spencer, who was sub-editor from 1848 to 1853, and R. H. I. Palgrave, later of Palgrave's *Dictionary of Political Economy*. But *The Economist* was also a new kind of medium between economic doctrines and a public opinion, English and worldwide, which was transfixed by economic news, economic statistics and economic 'questions', ideologies, or '-isms'. 'He was a great *belief producer*', Bagehot wrote of Wilson; he diffused the truths, or the ideas, which were '"in the air" of the age' (Bagehot 1860, pp. 1289–91, 1293; Edwards 1993, pp. 4, 15, 143–51).

4   Abstract and deductive ideas

The 'belief in the Historical Method' was by the 1880s 'the most widely and strongly entertained philosophical conviction at the present day' (Sidgwick 1886, p. 203). But the moment of triumph of historical-statistical political economy was also a swansong. The historical or 'social' school of economic thought became fairly suddenly, in the course of a few years, the subject of destructive criticism (Guyot 1914). In the continuing dialectic of the economic side of human life, the German economists' parody of *Smithianismus* was embraced, by a new generation of counter-counter-revolutionaries, as scientific truth. Just as John Stuart Mill, in the 1830s, had accepted the romantic parody of late eighteenth-century political economy, so the new, 'psychological' school of the 1870s and the 1880s committed themselves to the abstract and egotistical individuals of the historical economists' dire imagination. As the late nineteenth-century history of economic thought was summarised, on behalf of the American Economic Association, in 1901, 'this sudden revival of abstracter or deductive economics, just as such studies seemed to be growing into discredit, is one of the most remarkable chapters in economic theory' (Fetter 1901, p. 237).

The initial moment of what was later identified as the revolution of the 'marginalists' passed almost without notice.[19] The three treatises with which the movement was subsequently most identified were in three different languages (*Grundsätze der Volkswirthschaftslehre* by Carl Menger, published in 1871 in Vienna; *The Theory of Political Economy* by W. S. Jevons, published in London, also in 1871; and *Éléments d'Économie Politique Pure; ou, Théorie de la Richesse Sociale* by Léon Walras, published in 1874 in Lausanne) and they were the outcome of three different sets of circumstances, in the expanding world economy of the times. Menger had grown up in Galicia, on the estate of his maternal grandfather, a merchant who had moved east from Bohemia after making a fortune during the Napoleonic wars; he went to the universities of Vienna, Prague and Cracow, and in 1871 he was a civil servant in the 'press department of the Austrian "Ministerratsprädium"' (Hayek 1934, pp. x–xi). Jevons grew up in Liverpool, the ninth child of an iron merchant, and emigrated as a very young man to Australia, after the failure, in 1848, of the family business. He returned to England in 1859, where he devoted himself to preparing a 'Statistical Atlas' of diagrams and plates of historical statistics; in 1871 he was a professor in Manchester (Jevons 1972–81, I, p. 180). Léon Walras was in 1871 a professor in Lausanne; he had grown up in Normandy, and was successively a mining engineer, an economic journalist, and a novelist (*Francis Sauveur*, published in 1858, was a narrative, inspired by Balzac, of the 'generation of 1848' and of

---

19 It was the historical economist and economic historian W. J. Ashley, in 1907, who identified Jevons, Menger, Böhm-Bawerk and Wieser as 'the marginalists'. Ashley 1907, p. 476, and see Winch 2009.

'nature... tortured with a ferocious energy') (Walras 1858, pp. ix, xviii; Jaffé and Walker 1983).

The most conspicuous innovation of the new theories, in the view of contemporary observers, was a preoccupation with the psychological foundations of economic thought. 'It would not at all surprise me if in the future this school should come to be called the "psychological school of political economy"', the Austrian economist Eugen von Böhm-Bawerk, at the time a high official of the ministry of finance, wrote in 1890 (Böhm-Bawerk 1890, p. 265). The science of political economy must be concerned with the 'Measurement of Feeling and Motives', in Jevons' account (Jevons 1888, p. 12). The Irish barrister Francis Y. Edgeworth called his own treatise of 1881 *Mathematical Psychics*, and it was an essay, in his description, in 'the application of mathematics to the world of soul' (Edgeworth 1881, p. 9). One of the prominent young Austrian economists of the turn of the century, Ludwig von Mises, was later criticised, as an 'extreme devotee of the psychological school', for seeking to identify even the foundations of monetary theory in the 'unknown strata of self' (Lutz 1913, p. 146).

A second common concern, much commented upon at the time, was with the economic theory of consumption. Ricardian political economy was a theory of production, and of the three 'classes of the community', owners of land, owners of capital and owners of labour (Ricardo 1817, p. iii). Menger's *Grundsätze* was to a striking extent concerned with the 'causal connections between things and human welfare'; with needs, desires and the 'world of goods'. It started with individuals and their ideas about a multiplicity of goods, including telescopes, opera glasses, 'medicines for diseases that do not actually exist', winter clothing, horse and water for flower gardens. Walras' central concern, too, was with 'people and things'. Economic life, for the theorists of the 1870s, was very much like the world they had observed (in the information service of the Austrian ministry, or the Australian mint, or the Paris commercial press); a world of millions of consumers and millions of producers, connected by 'the cotton reports of Ellison and Haywood' in relation to 'America, India, Eygpt', in Menger's illustration, or, in Walras' expression, a 'world [which] may be considered as a vast general market' (Menger 1976, pp. 53, 70, 74, 93; Walras 1926, pp. 18–19, 44–5).

The counter-counter-revolutionaries of the 1870s were concerned, thirdly, to demonstrate, once again, the possibility of a science of political economy. Only Carl Menger, of the new psychological economists, was engaged in any sustained way in the continuing disputes over the methods of historical and non-historical economics (in the *Methodenstreit* of 1880s, during which he was subjected, by Gustav Schmoller, to the double insult of '*Manchesterthums*' and '*Mysticismus*') (Menger 1884, p. 84). But the objective of the 'psychological school' was to show that political economy was a science, as much as physics, or chemistry, or mechanics, or psychology. It was an exact science, of universal validity. It was not national, and it was not concerned, in particular, with national policies; it was a science, even more than the sciences imagined by Jean-Baptiste Say and John Stuart Mill, of pure rationality.

These preoccupations with science, finally, were a return to John Stuart Mill's old spectre, of man considered 'solely as a being who desires to possess wealth'. All the 'marginalist' revolutionaries of the 1870s made declarations of faith, in an abstract and universal conception of individual existence. Economic theory was concerned with 'economising men', in Menger's description (Menger 1976, pp. 48, 173), and it was unempirical in the way that chemistry was unempirical. The 'theory here given may be described as *the mechanics of utility and self-interest*', Jevons declared, and its 'method is as sure and demonstrative as that of kinematics or statics' (Jevons 1888, p. 21).[20] Walras described economics, in a letter of 1901 to the physicist and mathematician Henri Poincaré, as a 'mathematical science with the same claim as mechanics or astronomy', to which Poincaré responded that 'in mechanics, one often ignores friction and considers bodies as infinitely polished. As for you, you consider men as infinitely egotistical and infinitely farsighted' (Poincaré 1960, pp. 11, 13). If the rationalists of the late eighteenth century were the first revolutionaries, and Lamennais, Müller and Southey the counter-revolution, and Ricardo and the Mills the counter-counter-revolution, and the historical schools of political economy the counter-counter-counter-revolution, then the course of nineteenth-century economic thought had returned, here, to its universal origin.

5 Money, empire and race

Political economy, by the end of the nineteenth century, had become the new, conquering discipline of academic life, in much of Europe, North

---

20 Kinematics is the science of motion, as in, to take a modern example, the kinematics of undulatory swimming in the American alligator.

America and Asia. 'In every sphere we find that the economic way of looking at things is on the advance', Max Weber said in 1895, in his own inaugural lecture as professor of political economy at Freiburg; 'we economists have "come into fashion"' (Weber 1994b, pp. 17–18). Economists were no longer vaguely French or vaguely subversive. They were employed, in their thousands, in public administration, in statistical offices, in private and public enterprises, and in imperial government. 'In some respects economic science is now at the height of its prosperity', and 'the trained economist to-day finds a great and growing demand for his services', the President of the American Economic Association, Arthur Hadley, said in his end of the century address. But the turn of the new century was also a time of anxiety. For the economists had experienced, with their new prosperity, a 'loss of economic influence'. 'In one vital respect the conditions are far less satisfactory', and 'our practical politicians . . . have an ill-concealed contempt for a class of men whom they regard as theorists and visionaries', Hadley lamented; 'economics and politics have grown apart in the immediate past' (Hadley 1899, pp. 194–5).

The great political questions of the early twentieth century – about money, empire and race – were to a disorienting extent both economic and non-economic. They were the outcome of extraordinary or exogenous circumstances, which were at the same time of determining importance for the organisation of economic life. The separation of economics and politics was a consequence, for Arthur Hadley, of 'the excessive use of psychological terms and conceptions'; economics had become 'a subordinate department of psychology rather than politics' (Hadley 1899, pp. 198–9). But the psychology of financial and monetary crises, like the psychology of empire, was non-economic, in the terms of contemporary economic thought. It was external to the large dialectical history of economic science, and even to the opposition between theoretical (or psychological) and practical (or historical) political economy.

The periodic fluctuations in financial markets had been an illustration, throughout the century, of the limits of economic understanding. The crisis of 1797 was in David Ricardo's account one of 'those extraordinary occasions, when a general panic seizes the country', and '"which baffles ordinary speculations" . . . I think it utterly impossible to provide against the effect of panic, on any system of banking whatever' (Ricardo 1951–73, I, p. 358, V, p. 410). In the aftermath of the crises of 1825, 1837, 1866, 1873 and 1893, the collision of economic forces or laws with the melodramas of economic opinion was again the occasion for painful reconsiderations of the science of political economy. Even the history of financial crises was a flourishing genre of nineteenth-century economic thought. As the American economist Henry C. Carey wrote in 1864, 'the essential characteristic of barbarism is found in instability and irregularity of the societary action' (Carey 1864, p. 4).

The related political question that was of consuming importance to nineteenth-century economists, and which has been of much less subsequent interest to historians of economic and political thought, was money. Of the many thousands of publications on economic subjects of the times, there was a profusion of works on the gold standard, bullion, seigniorage, inconvertible paper money, bimetallism, brassage and currency unions; more than 200 works of which the titles contained the word 'money' in the 1890s alone. Money was a subject, throughout the century, of the highest and the lowest politics; even of the century's most heroic enterprise in supranational politics, in the monetary union of the 1860s, which extended, at least in prospect, from Greece to England, and from Sweden to Brazil (Einaudi 2001). It was also a subject of political excitement. William Jennings Bryan was nominated for President of the United States in 1900, by 'yelling and perspiring delegates', as a Hercules of bimetallism, who had strangled the monster of imperialism by rising above 'the selfish, worldly plane of greed and gold' (Bryan 1900, pp. 21, 24). The demonetisation of silver in India, and the Chinese–Mexican currency agreement, were matters of intense excitement. 'Cecily, you will read your Political Economy in my absence. The chapter on the Fall of the Rupee you may omit. It is somewhat too sensational. Even these metallic problems have their melodramatic side', Miss Prism declares in *The Importance of Being Earnest*; 'Horrid Political Economy! Horrid Geography! Horrid, horrid German!' (Wilde 1895, act 2, scene 1).

The even vaster political question of the nineteenth century – of war and empire – was the object, too, of intense investigation by economists. One of the endlessly repeated charges against the 'cosmopolitical school' of political economy was to have spoken only 'incidentally' of war – this was List's accusation against Smith – and to have founded entire theories on 'the idea of a perpetual state of peace' (List 1909, pp. 98, 107). But the laws of exchange and the laws of naval conquest were not entirely distinct, as was evident in Balzac's Formicalian empire, and the economists of the nineteenth century were preoccupied, like other political writers, with wartime mobilisations, pre-war expectations, and post-war expansions. The 'peacefulness of the modern spirit' was much overrated, Thomas Cliffe Leslie wrote in 1860 (in an essay called 'The Question of the Age – Is it Peace?'); he counted no fewer than 337 'Wars &c' in the post-Napoleonic period (Cliffe Leslie 1879, p. 72).

The political economists of the nineteenth century had been involved with the administration of empire since James Mill's and John Stuart Mill's organisation of the East India Company's correspondence, or Malthus' lectures at the Company's Haileybury College for officials on their way to India, or Bentham's exhortation to *Emancipate your Colonies!* (Bentham 1830). Wilhelm Roscher published a long study of colonies, colonial policy and emigration in 1856, revised in subsequent editions; an enquiry into 'German colonial policy, a postulate of German cultural and economic policy' (Roscher and Jannasch 1885, p. 357). The French economist Michel Chevalier proclaimed in his inaugural lecture at the Collège de France that 'Europe subjects everything to its rule . . . to direct this civilizing invasion, governments must wish to hear the advice of a sound political economy' (quoted in Todd 2009).

But the 'general principles' of colonial political economy were elusive, even for the 'Committee on Colonies' which the American Economic Association established in 1899. A quarter of the entire 1900 volume of the publication which later became the *American Economic Review* was devoted to a study called 'Essays in Colonial Finance', which ranged from French taxes on dynamite in Senegal to the Oriental Seminar in Berlin, colonial companies in the Bismarck Archipelago, the *verponding* or tax on fishponds in Java, the role of 'race-pride and "megalomania"' in Italian Eritrea, the *'Casa de contracion*, or India House' in Seville in 1503, constitutional provisions for the use of Danish in the lesser Antilles, the 'swarming negroes' in Dominica, 'the evils of internationalism' in respect of cesspools and indebtedness in Ottoman Egypt, the 'hut tax' in British Bechuanaland, and municipal revenues from 'boiling offal' in Singapore. 'By the sanguine imperialist the collection will not be found exhilarating reading', in the summary of *The Economic Journal*.[21]

Political economy, like all the social sciences of the time, was by the last decades of the century deeply involved with biological theory in general,

---

21 'Essays in Colonial Finance' 1900, pp. 405, 420, 431, 438–9, 469–70, 494, 505, 532, 571, 573, 643–6, 658; Reeves 1901, p. 60.

and racial theory in particular.[22] *Physics and Politics*, the little book published by Walter Bagehot in 1872, which was one of the publishing sensations of the age, was a good illustration. Its objective was to apply the new 'physical knowledge' of the nineteenth century – of natural selection, the relationship between man and his environment, and Herbert Spencer's philosophy of the will and the world – to the two 'old sciences' of politics and political economy. It was a drama of the improvement of the economic mind, which was also the English mind. But it was expressed, to a striking extent, in the language of empire and race. The 'mixture of races' was full of danger, and 'the union of the Englishman and the Hindu produces something not only between races, but *between moralities*'. The experience of the English in India showed that it was very difficult to change the characters of men; 'the higher being is not and cannot be a model for the lower'. The progress of mind and form, in which 'the English not only possess better machines for moving nature, but are themselves better machines', was an aspiration for everyone without exception; 'we need not take account of the mistaken ideas of unfit men and beaten races' (Bagehot 1873, pp. 1, 70–1, 145, 183, 208–9).

The economist Alfred Marshall was the most prominent exponent of what he described as 'the biological view of the science', and his *Principles of Economics* of 1890 was the embodiment of these ideas of mental and moral progress. Its language, too, was strikingly racialist. There was anxiety, as in the assertion that 'good is mixed with the evil . . . especially in the case of a parasitic race'.[23] There was sublimation, as in Marshall's succinct history of industry and race; 'meanwhile the English character was deepening . . . life became intense and full of awe'. There was economic history ('race history is a fascinating but disappointing study for the economist') and the history of economic thought; David Ricardo, Marshall wrote, was 'often spoken of as a representative Englishman: but this is just what he was not . . . nearly every branch of the Semitic race has had some special genius for dealing with abstractions'. The great drama, once more, was of the mind and the economy. The 'special character' of the book, Marshall wrote in his preface of 1890, lay in its concern with 'ethical forces'. It was inspired, he wrote, by the 'Principle of Continuity', in its biological (or Spencerian)

---

22 See the chapter by Daniel Pick in this volume (Chapter 19).
23 'The fact that there is an economic demand for the services of Jewish and Armenian money-dealers in Eastern Europe and Asia, or for Chinese labour in California, is not by itself a proof, nor even a very strong ground for believing, that such arrangements tend to raise the quality of human life as a whole.' Marshall 1890, pp. 71, 303–4.

and historical (or Hegelian) manifestations, which could be expressed, in turn, in the mathematical continuity of marginal quantities. The ultimate promise was that the "'economic man'" of 'abstract science', who was also the Englishman of the nineteenth century, would evolve, continuously, into a lofty and social nature; 'unselfishness then will be the offspring of deliberate will' (Marshall 1890, pp. vi, 34, 47, 60, 71, 248). There was a 'growing perfection of scientific machinery in economics', Marshall wrote. But the enduring concern of economists should be with 'the direction and the rate of growth of human nature in the future'; with 'social science or the reasoned history of man, for the two things are the same' (Marshall 1897, pp. 117, 121).

These were the preoccupations, too, of the American Economic Association. The association had in 1896 published an extended study of the 'race traits' of the 'American Negro', which predicted the 'gradual extinction' of the black population in consequence of the 'immense amount of immorality, which is a race trait', referred in passing to the opinion of a French surgeon in Algeria that the 'native Mussulman population would rapidly disappear', and was memorable principally as the occasion for one of the earliest and most brilliant reviews by W. E. B. Du Bois of the 'unscientific use of the statistical method' (Hoffman 1896, pp. 95, 176, 196, 318; Du Bois 1897, p. 133). At its turn of the century meeting in December 1899, the association established a new committee on the economic condition of the American Negro; the result was another very long study, published in 1902, of 'The Negro in Africa and America', of which the conclusion, as summarised by Du Bois, was that 'the slave trade and slavery were a species of natural selection in which "the race probably made a gain"'.[24]

6   The politics of political economy

The histories of economic and political thought were intertwined at every turn, as has been seen, in the course of the economic century. But political economy had an odd and even subversive relationship to the most imposing classifications of nineteenth-century politics: to the opposition between

---

[24] The study declared in the first paragraph that 'by excluding the Chinese we have avoided one threatening phase of heterogeneity. But unfortunately no African exclusion act was passed in the days when such action might have delivered us from the black peril.' 'Council Meetings', in *American Economic Association Quarterly*, 1900, p. 43; Tillinghast 1902, p. 1; Du Bois 1903, p. 695.

right and left, or religion and doubt, or nationality and universality, or reverence (for established institutions) and disrespect. The posthumous and ever-shifting renown of Adam Smith was only the most incongruous illustration. The cold-spirited economists of the *laissez-faire* system were criticised, at one and the same time, for their almost religious faith in the benevolent consequences of self-interested actions, and for their lack of faith in human benevolence. The Irish historical economist John Kells Ingram accused Adam Smith, in 1888, of having been 'secretly led' by '*a priori* theological ideas' about the harmoniousness of nature, and of 'a certain deadness to the high aims and perennial importance of religion', a failure to 'keep in view the moral destination of our race' (Ingram 1967, pp. 102, 106).

The political positions of the various historical schools, and of their critics in the 'psychological school of political economy' were similarly difficult to classify. The historical economists had in common, for the most part, a concern with the 'social' (and in many cases the 'national') as an object of investigation and an object of policy. Some were socialists, and some, like Hermann Roesler, saw in *Smithianismus* the origins of socialist extortion. Carl Menger pointed out the extreme oddity of a tendency which on the one hand espoused extensive social reforms, and on the other hand favoured the epistemology of the historical school of jurisprudence, with its conception of a higher nation whose 'unconscious wisdom . . . stands high above meddlesome human wisdom', and from whose 'conservative basic principles' were derived multiple political consequences, 'highly useful to the ruling interests' (Menger 1883, p. 84).

The political setting of the marginal revolution was itself very odd, in the terms of late nineteenth- and twentieth-century distinctions. The heroes of the new discipline whom Jevons described ironically as the 'obnoxious subject of mathematico-economic science' were not, in general, conservatives (Jevons 1888, p. xl). Walras' hope was that 'while being scientifically entirely socialist', he might 'still find a way to be politically as deeply and as sincerely liberal as it is possible for anyone to be' (Walras 1896, p. 16). To set the individual, and his or her consciousness, at the centre of economic thought was, as Menger observed, to do something very different from, and in some respects more subversive than, the historical investigation of social and political institutions. It was to be less than reverent in respect of at least some of the policies of established institutions. One of the earliest charges against 'Smithian' political economy was that it conceived of the state as a 'useful enterprise', or an illicit union. The marginal or psychological economists, too, found themselves dissecting the state; looking to some sides of the state (the monarchy, the military, monetary institutions) with reverence, and to others with reforming and even revolutionary disrespect.

Nineteenth-century political economy had an odd relationship, at the same time, to the familiar classification of kinds of thought: into high or scientific thought; the 'middle principles' through which, as Mill wrote of Bentham, the ideas of speculative philosophy 'diffuse themselves through these intermediate channels' over 'the ocean of mind'; and the low thought of large numbers of people (Mill and Bentham 1987, pp. 132–3, 235). The effort to distinguish a science of political economy was at the heart of nineteenth-century economic thought, as has been seen. The scientific models in question included chemistry, anatomy, astronomy, physiology, histology, comparative jurisprudence, celestial mechanics, kinematics, biology, historical philology, physics, psychics and successive sciences of the mind from phrenology to associationism, Herbartianism (from the Göttingen educational psychologist Johann Friedrich Herbart), and the microscopy of morality of 'these English psychologists', in Friedrich Nietzsche's description ('people tell me they are just old, cold, boring frogs') (Nietzsche 1994b, p. 11). But all these nineteenth-century sciences were themselves engaged with a larger semi-scientific world of public influence and public understanding.

The shifting frontier between scientific and 'intermediate' thought ran through the lives of almost all the economists with whom this chapter has been concerned. David Ricardo, who was identified as one of the 'highest' or most abstract of nineteenth-century economists, was a kind-hearted stockbroker, who was continually being interrupted by visitors, intimidated by the dire father–son duo of Bentham and James Mill, and distracted by invitations to make speeches about bullion, or become a director of the East India Company. Carl Menger, one of the other indisputably philosophical nineteenth-century economists, was successively a press information officer in the Austro-Hungarian ministry, tutor to the Austrian crown prince Rudolf, and a prolific contributor to the *Neue Freie Presse* in Vienna.

In respect of 'popular science,' too, political economy was a model of inventiveness. The most widely read writer on political economy of the first half of the nineteenth century was probably 'Mrs Marcet', or Jane Haldimand Marcet, the daughter of an Englishwoman from Spitalfields and a Turin-born Swiss silk merchant, mother of four children, friend of Ricardo and Say, and the author of thirty-two books, including *Conversations on Political Economy*, *Conversations on Vegetable Physiology*, *The History of Africa* and *Willy's Holidays: or, Conversations on Different Kinds of Governments*. Her friend Harriet Martineau (*Illustrations of Taxation, Poor Laws and Paupers Illustrated, Letters on Mesmerism*) was similarly prolific; even by late in the century, political economy was a subject for women writers, including Margaret Benson (*Capital, Labour and Trade*) and Millicent Fawcett (*Tales in Political Economy*). Richard Ely found German historicism (or German social theory-cum-social policy) so exhilarating, he recalled, because the only economic instruction for undergraduates at Columbia University in the 1870s had consisted of weekly recitations from 'Mrs. Fawcett's "Political Economy for Beginners"' (Ely 1910, p. 70).

The statistical idiom of writing on social reform constituted a different model of intermediate thought, or of the diffusion of ideas. The historical school of Gustav Schmoller's associations and yearbooks and bureaux was unified, if at all, by the use of statistics, and by a political rhetoric which sought to convince with numbers (see Grimmer-Solem 2003). In England, social reform was itself a distinctively feminine subject. The French historian and psychologist Hippolyte Taine observed that psychology, statistics and political economy were proceeding together in England, and that the 'social sciences' were substantially a concern of women; he mentioned Louisa Twining, Barbara Collett, Mary Carpenter, Florence Hill, Florence Nightingale, Bessie Parkes, Sarah Remond, 'Mistress Wiggins' and Jane Crowe (Taine 1872, pp. 99, 338). For Alfred Marshall, it was rather 'general economic principles' of a 'dictatorial sort', which were associated with women writers; 'never again will a Mrs Trimmer, a Mrs Marcet, or a Miss Martineau earn a goodly reputation by throwing them into the form of a catechism or of simple tales' (Marshall 1897, p. 117).

The diffusion of economic ideas was important, above all, to the rise, over the entire course of the century, of large-scale political movements. The nineteenth century was an age of '-isms': *Philoguillotismus, Demokratismus* and *Antirevolutionairrismus*, as the historian Bartold Niebuhr complained in the 1790s; *Obscurantismus, Enthusiasmus, Sophisticismus, Fanatismus,* and *Egoismus*, according to a work of 1802 about enlightenment and revolution (Niebuhr 1926, I, pp. 7, 32, 35, 37; Salat 1802, pp. 162, 187, 193). These were abstract nouns which identified political or religious opinions. But the most successful abstractions of the later nineteenth century identified (or collected together) economic opinions. Like the religious ideologies or '-isms', they had a connotation of *Catechismus*, and its etymology of oral instruction, or of resonance and downwardness. This process of instruction in turn required the simplification of complicated ideas into single concepts. It was a process, too, which required extensive material resources;

the organisation of parishes and printed catechisms in the case of religious instruction, and of weekly newspapers, monitors, encyclopaedias, public meetings and statistical registers, in the case of the production of economic beliefs.

The history of 'intermediate' political economy in the nineteenth century is a remarkable illustration of this sort of institutional and organisational inventiveness. It is also an illustration of the extent to which the imposing simplifications of economic thought were concerned with collections of ideas which were of different local origins, which were exchanged across very long distances, and which were transformed in the course of international exchange. *Smithianismus* is only an extreme example, as a German noun that described a school or direction, in Germany and elsewhere, which had very little relationship to Adam Smith, and which was committed, or so it was believed, to the universalism of the human spirit. There was also *Cobdénisme*, and *Germanismo italiano*, and the *Richtung Burke-Savigny's* (the Burke-Savigny direction), described by Carl Menger; there were, above all, the twin ideologies of free trade and protectionism, in which *The Economist* had its origin, and its 'other'; the ideas, in Bagehot's expression, which were '"in the air" of the age' (Menger 1883, pp. 205, 207, 212; Bagehot 1860, p. 1291).

The politics of nineteenth-century political economy was odd, most of all, because of its relationship to the ideas of those whom Marx described in *The German Ideology* as 'the real living individuals themselves' (Marx and Engels 1978b, p. 47). The great drama of nineteenth-century economic thought, as has been suggested in this chapter, was the dialectic of the understanding of human nature; of the supposedly 'Smithian' conception of cold-spirited and self-interested men, which was successively rejected, embraced, re-rejected and re-embraced over the entire course of the long nineteenth century. But this dialectic was itself part of a more imposing drama, of political destiny. The great question of early nineteenth-century politics was thus of whether the novel of the French Revolution (in Napoleon's expression) was really over; of what the people were really like, and whether they could be restrained by religion, or the executioner, or public instruction. One of the great questions of 1848, and of subsequent debates over the extension of the suffrage, was of what the new men of an incipiently universal politics would really be like. One of the great questions of the end of the century was of racial difference and racial heroism, and of what the conquerors and the conquered were really like, in a world filled with empires. Of all the anxieties of nineteenth-century political thought, these are now among the most archaic. They were associated with psychological, religious and historical theories that were almost forgotten by the 1920s. But they were the setting in which the economists' own political drama unfolded.

The economists' conception of human life was in Mill's early account no more than an act of abstraction. For Carl Menger, too, the 'so-called "dogma" of human self-interest' was an abstraction, like a mathematical surface or the chemist's idea of pure hydrogen (Menger 1985, p. 87). It was a 'postulate', in Walter Bagehot's account of 1876. As Bagehot added reprovingly, 'modern economists know their own limitations; they would no more undertake to prescribe for the real world, than a man in green spectacles would undertake to describe the colours of a landscape'. But the conception that Bagehot described as the 'standard of economic man' was at the same time very much more grandiose. Bagehot explained that 'in some very large scenes of our present English life, Political Economy is exactly true'. It was a description of the world, 'in a society of grown-up competitive commerce, such as we have in England'; a commerce which is 'about the most definite thing we have, the thing which it is most difficult to help seeing' (Bagehot 1908, pp. 2, 7–9, 22, 104, 109, 126). For his obituarist, Bagehot's achievement was 'to prove as against the historical school that there is an age and society – the whole business world of England at the present time, and a large part of other modern communities – in which the assumptions of English political economy are approximately true in the concrete as well as in the abstract. We are in an economic age, and the leading assumptions of political economy are applicable with comparatively little friction, so that the abstract doctrines can be applied to a concrete world' (Giffen 1891, p. lxxiv).

The worldwide drama of self-interested man was thus in substantial part a drama about Englishness, and the English mind. 'Mr Bagehot felt so strongly the inapplicability of the assumptions of the system to the greater part of the world', Cliffe Leslie wrote in 1879, 'that he actually limited political economy to England at its present state of commercial development, and to the male sex in England' (Cliffe Leslie 1879, p. 399, and see Bagehot 1908, p. 28). India, even in James Mill's *History*, had been widely described as an economising society; 'the Gentoos are indefatigable in business', and 'they are the acutest buyers and sellers in the world' (Mill 1818, I, pp. 317, 328). But a generation later, for Sir Henry Maine, India was a land of wayward children; 'this is a society in which, for centuries upon centuries, the imagination has run riot . . . What the Native Mind requires, is stricter criteria of truth' (Maine 1881, pp. 275–6). For Bagehot himself, India, like China, was unmodern and uncommercial. The 'imperfect but thickly populated civilisations, like those of China and of India', he wrote in a startling description of new, old and modern peoples, were no more than economic obstructions, fit only 'to cumber the ground' (Bagehot 1873, p. 122).[25]

It was this prospect of perfection that was so much in question by the last years of the century. The psychological idiom of late nineteenth-century political economy is by now unfamiliar, with its Herbartianism and its Spencerism. But the political idiom is even odder. Political institutions, in these turn of the century economic prospects, were understood not as ends in themselves, but as means to the more important end of political culture, or political civilisation. Hermann Roesler, the nemesis of *Smithianismus*, commented in his observations on the Meiji code that the general object of a constitution was to elevate the people, and to secure the civilisation of the state; 'the enjoyment of political rights, and the security of civil rights based thereon, strengthens the development of human forces, moral, intellectual and economical' (Siemes 1968, p. 51). Even the liberal idyll of an 'age of discussion', or of 'government by discussion', was identified, in Bagehot's *Physics and Politics*, as an instrument of progess, a 'principal organ for improving mankind', a polity which 'tends to diminish our inherited defects' (Bagehot 1873, pp. 162, 179, 200).

The nineteenth century was an economic century in the sense that the study of political economy was transformed from a mildly subversive form of political writing into the conquering academic and administrative discipline of the 1890s; and in the sense that economic relationships were vastly more extensive than in any earlier period. It is 'the true London maxim, that every thing is to be got with money', Jane Austen wrote in *Mansfield Park*, and the entire world, in the course of the century, had come to be depicted as a vast London (Austen 1985, p. 90). There were vistas of endless economic life, and of endless disruption, as in Marx's and Engels' prospect of international and industrial capitalism in *The Communist Manifesto*; 'constant revolutionising of production, uninterrupted disturbance of all social conditions, everlasting uncertainty and agitation distinguish the bourgeois epoch from all earlier

25 Bagehot's reference was to the 'strange chance which has un-peopled so great a part of the world just when civilised people wanted to go there. It is strange to think how different would have been the fate of this and coming generations, if America and Australia had possessed imperfect but thickly populated civilisations, like those of China and of India. In climate, and in all external circumstances, America seems as fit for an early civilisation as India. Happily, it did not possess one, nor did Australia. There is nothing there now left to cumber the ground.'

ones . . . the need of a constantly expanding market for its products chase the bourgeoisie over the whole surface of the globe. It must nestle everywhere, settle everywhere, establish connexions everywhere' (Marx and Engels 2002, p. 223).

But the nineteenth century was also an economic century in a different and less familiar sense, the sense with which so many of the nineteenth-century economists were themselves preoccupied, of the transformation of sentiments and minds, or ways of thinking. The economists enquired tirelessly, like Balzac's philosopher-sparrow, into the nature of existence; where are men going? where do they come from? why can they not weep? They were involved, like the editors of *The Economist*, or like Hermann Roesler in Meiji Japan, in the immense nineteenth-century enterprise of the production of beliefs. They were on all possible sides in the great political questions of the times. They were completely confused, above all, about how it might be possible to invent a science of, or to write the history of all these endlessly changing sentiments, ideas and conditions of mind. In this, at least, they are very much like the economists, or the historians, of later times.

23

German socialism and social democracy 1860–1900

VERNON L. LIDTKE

I Origins of socialist political thought

It might have been expected that the political thinking of German social democracy would build upon a variety of European socialists who wrote before 1848. However, that was seldom the case. To be sure, German intellectuals knew something of the ideas of Fourier, Saint-Simon, Cabet, Proudhon, Simonde de Sismondi, Owen, Blanqui and Blanc, but it is difficult to show that those ideas guided the later organisations of the German labour movement. People familiar with the polemical literature in German, notably that produced by Karl Marx and Friedrich Engels, often gained their knowledge of early socialist thought second hand. The intention of Marx and Engels, of course, was not to disseminate the ideas of those they labelled 'utopian', but to discredit them. To be sure, in 1888, August Bebel published a very sympathetic account of Fourier's ideas, but he also stressed the weaknesses of the 'utopian's' thinking.

If we look within Germany itself, it is also true that the ideas of socialist thinkers of the early nineteenth century – with the exception of Marx and Engels – resonated only to a limited degree in the German labour movement after the 1860s and did not serve as a foundation for the political thought of social democracy. Although Wilhelm Weitling gained recognition with the publication of *Guarantees of Harmony and Freedom* (1842), his influence waned in Germany when he emigrated to the United States. Among the Young Hegelians Ludwig Feuerbach proved to be a great stimulant for Marx's critical thinking, but he provided no foundation for the political thought of the socialist movement. Other Young Hegelians on the left, notably Bruno Bauer, Moses Hess and Karl Grün, did influence socialist political thinking, but only to a very limited degree. The individualistic anarchism of Max Stirner was diametrically opposed to the collectivist orientation of most socialist thought. In retrospect it is striking that despite the number of socialist thinkers of the first half of the nineteenth century, they appear only sporadically in social democratic discourse in the later decades of the century.

Early social democratic political thought grew much more directly out of the liberal and democratic movements in Germany than from the theorising of early socialist thinkers. This is exemplified in several ways in the revolutions of 1848–9, when, for the first time, one can speak of a labour movement that reached throughout most of the German-speaking states. A variety of organisations appeared in 1848–9, but some of the most important were the Workers' Educational Societies (Arbeiterbildungsvereine). Of these, the Workers' Brotherhood (Arbeiterverbrüderung) in which Stephan Born was especially prominent, manifested the importance of liberal and democratic ideas for the emerging labour movement. Two principles were central at that time: the right of free association and workers' education. For 'education' they preferred the German term *Bildung* in order to indicate that in addition to transmitting elementary knowledge, their programmes were designed to promote the cultivation and development of the free individual. The failure of the Revolution and return to reactionary policies by 1849–50 meant the suppression of most associations and public meetings. For a decade German public political life stagnated. With few exceptions, the voices of labour, liberalism and democracy were silenced within Germany (Birker 1973, pp. 191–7; Noyes 1966, pp. 124–53; Roth 1998; Welskopp 2000, pp. 29–33).

Despite the great disappointment and pessimistic implications of failure, the revolutions of 1848–9 also left a positive legacy. Liberalism and democracy had set the agenda, if only for a short time; a progressive constitution for a unified Germany had been drafted, though not implemented; artisans and workers had learned how to create organisations to promote their goals; demonstrations, meetings and elections had created for the first time a truly animated public sphere; and seminal social and political ideas had been spread throughout much of the population. Within little more than a decade the positive lessons drawn from this legacy would help to revitalise public political life in Germany.

As the political atmosphere in Prussia, and Germany, relaxed gradually after 1858 when Wilhelm I became regent, many Workers' Educational Societies were revived and new political associations created, including the liberal Nationalverein (1859) and organisations of democrats, especially in south Germany. Although these democrats, whose leaders included Ludwig Eckardt (Karlsruhe), Karl Mayer (Stuttgart) and Ludwig Büchner (Darmstadt), held conferences beginning in 1863 and thought of themselves as a Demokratische Volkspartei (Democratic People's Party) they could not create a unified organisation because the Württemberg group, one of the strongest, held extreme federalist views and initially opposed the establishment of a central national party. When these particularist obstacles were finally overcome in September 1868, Johann Jacoby (Königsberg), a prominent democrat of 1848, and Leopold Sonnemann (Frankfurt am Main), owner of the *Frankfurter Zeitung*, were leaders in founding the Deutsche Volkspartei (German People's Party) that, though never large, maintained a presence in German national politics until the early years of the twentieth century. The programme of the Deutsche Volkspartei embodied principles that were rooted in the revolutions of 1848 and widely shared by democrats throughout Germany. They called for parliamentary government, universal manhood suffrage, a people's militia to replace standing armies, separation of church and state, and unrestricted right of association. They fiercely rejected German unification under Prussian dominance (most of them also opposed Austrian control), but demanded a federal structure in which all German states would be equal. The party also called for legislation to improve the condition of workers, rejected the strict *laissez-faire* capitalism embraced by most German liberals, and maintained a close relationship with the emerging labour movement (Elm 1968; Mayer 1912; Weber 1968).

The liberals in the Nationalverein assumed that artisans and workers would be loyal followers, but in fact the members of the Workers' Educational Societies favoured the politics of the democratic left and collaborated closely with the Volkspartei. When Ferdinand Lassalle, in 1863, called on the Workers' Educational Societies to reject collaboration with other parties, including liberals and democrats, a substantial number agreed and helped form the new party, the General Association of German Workingmen (Allgemeiner Deutscher Arbeiterverein). However, many of the Workers' Educational Societies declined to join the Lassalleans. Instead they established a league of their own, the Union of German Workers' and Educational Societies (Verband Deutscher Arbeitervereine) which, although not strictly a political party worked closely with the democratic Volkspartei. At the annual congresses of the Union between 1863 and 1869 educated middle-class leaders continued to articulate a programme of workers' education, co-operatives and democratic political principles. Some of the most prominent of these included Leopold Sonnemann, Dr Emil Roßmäßler, Dr Max Hirsch, and Friedrich Albert Lange, philosopher and author of numerous books. August Bebel greatly admired Lange, and devoted three appreciative pages to the philosopher in his memoirs (Bebel 1911–13, I, pp. 97–100).

For the most part, the participation of these educated middle-class leaders ceased when, first at the Union's congress in 1868, Wilhelm Liebknecht and August Bebel persuaded the delegates to affiliate with the First International, and second in 1869 (at Eisenach) when they dissolved the Union and created the Social Democratic Labour Party, commonly referred to as Eisenachers (Dowe 1980, pp. 149–65, 187–8). This meant splitting from the Volkspartei organisationally, and an intention to enter the German political arena as an independent workers' party with a socialist orientation. There were thus two socialist parties, Lassalleans and Eisenachers, competing for the allegiance of workers and artisans.

2 Ferdinand Lassalle

No one influenced the political thought of German socialism in the early decades more than Ferdinand Lassalle, but it is also true that even during his lifetime and subsequently the worth and implications of his ideas have been sharply debated. Although it is impossible to say how the labour movement would have developed had he not met an untimely death, one can assume that Social Democrats would have been more flexible on the potential of the existing state to implement social reforms that would genuinely benefit workers. It must be emphasised that Lassalle's political programme, no less than Marx's, did not stand alone, but was interlinked with his ideas about history, legal systems, economics and society. Although much influenced by Hegel, notably with respect to the state, Lassalle was an intellectual of broad learning who drew easily on the work of a wide range of thinkers. He often cited the works of Jean-Baptiste Say, Simonde de Sismondi, Adam Smith, David Ricardo and many others. He particularly admired John Stuart Mill, who, he declared in 1863 was 'the greatest living English national economist' (Lassalle 1919–20, III, p. 188). In one of his speeches on constitutions, he praised England as a 'country in which there is a real constitution', that is, in contrast to sham constitutions for which he had so much contempt. To him the repeal of the Corn Laws in England was a model of how to bring about progress through sustained agitation. He even implied that his ongoing demand for universal manhood suffrage might turn out to be comparable to Cobden's campaign against the Corn Laws (Lassalle 1919–20, IV, pp. 129–34).

Lassalle believed strongly that the intellectual and moral foundation on which acquired rights and privileges rested had to be thoroughly destroyed. That meant that he had to engage critically with some of the principles of the historical school, a major current of legal thinking throughout most of the nineteenth century, not only in Germany but in Europe generally. It was expounded initially by Gustav Hugo, but promoted most effectively by Friedrich Karl von Savigny, a prolific historian of law and influential professor at the University of Berlin, where he and Hegel were competing colleagues. Savigny first came to prominence in 1803 as an opponent of codification and someone who distrusted all efforts to base legal systems on rationalist principles or notions of natural law. He argued that properly understood, law is the product of particular customs, accumulated rights and privileges, and popular traditions of the people, and cannot be imported on the basis of abstract principles.

The published product of Lassalle's encounter with this conservative view of law was one of his major works, *The System of Acquired Rights*, which appeared in 1861 (coincidentally, the year of Savigny's death). It was a sustained attack on the conservative view that lawfully acquired rights, whether based on inheritance or personal acquisition, could not be abolished or diminished by any new law. This conservative tradition meant that even the harshest feudal rights could be abolished only, if at all, by buying out the privileged group. Lassalle directed some of his sharpest criticism against the legal views of Friedrich Julius Stahl who called for the creation of state statutes that would make acquired rights unassailable. At great length Lassalle argued that traditions of the past cannot under any circumstances exercise authority over the present and that perpetuating acquired rights would be equivalent to recognising the independent sovereignty of individuals (Lassalle 1919–20, II, pp. 303–45; Bernstein 1893, pp. 81–90). Although Lassalle wrote these two volumes as a scholarly contribution to legal theory, his real motive, as he told Franz Duncker, was to create a legal system that would be a 'mighty fortress' for revolution and socialism (Oncken 1912, p. 188). He was determined to subvert the legal theories that supported conservative, or even liberal political structures in order to clear the way for the legitimation of democratic and socialist principles.

In much of his political thinking, Lassalle forcefully focused attention on the decisive role played by power, from whatever source, in determining how institutions, laws and constitutions were shaped. In much of his political and social thinking Lassalle was a fully-fledged realist, though his optimistic nature also encouraged occasional flights of fancy. In his lecture of 1862, *On Constitutions*, he argued that the nature of constitutions is always determined by power relationships, and he specifically meant the power of economic and social classes (Lassalle 1919–20, I, pp. 36–8, 52). In a blunt statement of the overriding significance of power by itself, he declared that 'basically questions of constitutions are not questions of law, but questions of power; . . . written constitutions are only of lasting value when they are an accurate expression of real power relationships in society' (Lassalle 1919–20, I, p. 60). Lassalle warned that authoritarian monarchical government might grant written constitutions that allowed a minuscule amount of power to the representatives of the people, but would not permit them to share power or to implement the 'will of the people' in any meaningful way. In a second speech on constitutions, *What Now* (1862), he urged German liberals that they had to expose this kind of 'sham constitutionalism' and fight it relentlessly (Lassalle 1919–20, I, pp. 102–5).

Lassalle articulated much of his political thinking in speeches and pamphlets designed to provide the new labour party with a body of relevant knowledge on history, economics, politics and social theory, and to set forth the fundamental principles, goals and strategies of the movement. Many members of the socialist labour movement, like Bebel, first learned about socialism by reading Lassalle's speeches and writings and only years later turned to the works of Marx and Engels (Bebel 1911–13, I, pp. 130–1). Two speeches were particularly significant as an illustration of Lassalle's political ideas as they related to the incipient labour movement. The first was 'On the Connection of the Current Epoch with the Idea of the Workers' Estate' which he gave to an artisan association in a Berlin suburb (April 1862), and then published simply as *The Workers' Programme*. The second was the 'Public Letter to the Central Committee' (March 1863), a detailed and creative response to the invitation to address a forthcoming congress of associations of artisans and workers in Leipzig. As explications of principles and goals, and as calls for action, these are superb examples of Lassalle's command of the art of political communication. Even in print today, one senses the force of his brilliant mind and spirited personality and can imagine the excitement of listeners, for he was a charismatic orator.

Lassalle's political thinking should always be understood in relation to his fundamental and lasting commitment to what he called 'pure and uncompromising democracy' (Lassalle 1919–20, II, p. 79), though it is also true that he sometimes failed to make this explicit and thereby left an impression that he may have strayed to a more conservative outlook. At the core of his thinking, both for his own philosophy, and as a central principle for the burgeoning labour movement, was the demand for universal manhood suffrage, with direct and secret elections. This was an absolute necessity for any democratic philosophy; a political system with less than universal suffrage could never claim to be a democracy. Strategic considerations also recommended stressing universal suffrage. In *The Workers' Programme* Lassalle explained in a long discourse on the phases of historical development that the time had arrived when the social and political principles associated with the *Arbeiterstand* (Workers' Estate) should become the dominant force in society. Just as the modern bourgeois principle (capitalism) had displaced the principle of the nobility, so the *Arbeiterstand* was on the threshold of transforming society according to its democratic and social principles. But at present it possessed no means to implement its goals. For Lassalle, universal manhood suffrage would be that instrument. Since the *Arbeiterstand* constituted the vast majority of the population, implementation of one-man one-vote would mean that no serious obstacles would stand in the way of acquiring control of state power (Lassalle 1919–20, II, pp. 147–202). (It might be noted that Lassalle's use of the term *Arbeiterstand* in these speeches did not mean that he identified with a feudal view of the social order, but participated in a common usage of the time. He frequently used 'working class' and one can see that he often thought of the terms as interchangeable.)

But why would the working class fail to do what previous dominant classes had done, that is, use the power of the state to create privileges for themselves and impose burdens on other social groups? Lassalle assured his audience that the 'moral content' of the principle of the working class was itself universalist and its benefits extended to all humans. This was possible, he argued, because workers owned nothing that they would seek to preserve once they gained dominance. The working class stood in harmony with the 'development of all of the people', 'the progress of culture' and the 'advance of freedom'. Its cause is the cause of 'all humanity'. Here Lassalle had given way to his strong sense of optimism but also, perhaps, to a feeling that workers needed a degree of self-esteem that was unknown to them. A vibrant belief in the moral superiority – which is what Lassalle claimed – of the principles of the *Arbeiterstand* could do much to legitimate a blatant drive for power. It is important to emphasise that Lassalle's insistence on the centrality of universal manhood suffrage meant that he believed that a parliamentary form of government was completely compatible with a socialist programme. He did not argue that parliamentary government was a particularly bourgeois political form that would not survive into a socialist historical epoch. Although Lassalle would sometimes utter broad notions about a future socialist society, his ideas were not based in historical or economic determinism. For all of his Hegelianism, he always stressed the need for voluntarist human action to achieve socialist goals.

It is appropriate to note two points that separated Lassalle and the Marxists. Where he assumed that parliamentary democracy would function as part of a socialist society, Marxists maintained that parliamentary forms belonged only to a bourgeois-liberal phase of historical development and would be discarded under socialism. There was also a striking difference between Lassalle and the Marxists on how to conceive of the state theoretically and with respect to its place in a socialist society. Lassalle did believe with Marx and others that historically and in the present, all states were controlled by a dominant class, or a coalition of classes. Where the two parted company was on the issue of what would happen to the state when the working class had achieved its goal of dissolving social classes. To the Marxists that meant that there would be no class dominance and no reason for the state to exist. In time, the state would vanish. Lassalle did not speculate about the withering of the state. On the contrary, he remained closer to his Hegelian heritage, but continued to believe that democratic forces could transform the state into an instrument to achieve the highest goals of humanity. It is true that Lassalle's formulations can leave the impression that 'state' means any state. When he writes, for example, that 'the state is [the institution that] has the function to bring about . . . the full freedom of humanity' he fails to add that he did not believe that the Prussian state under the Hohenzollern dynasty would carry out that mission (Lassalle 1919–20, II, p. 197). Far from it, he was through and through a sharp critic of the Prussian state. When he speaks of the purpose of the state, he refers, on a philosophical level, to the moral and cultural goals that a state should seek to realise, not to the possibility that they may have done so in historical reality. 'The purpose of the state', he wrote, 'is to bring about the positive and progressive development of humanity, in other words . . . to give real existence to the culture of which humanity is capable.' But then in the following sentences he makes it clear that he has been speaking of a democratised state under the guidance of the labour movement: 'Thus a state which is dominated by the idea of the *Arbeiterstand* would no longer do what all others have hitherto done, . . . but would with the highest degree of clarity and with complete awareness take as its task to realise the moral nature of the state' (Lassalle 1919–20, II, p. 198).

In Lassalle's view it was absolutely essential for workers to gain control of the state. One reason derived from his understanding of the operation of the wage system in a capitalist economy. His key notion was that there was an 'iron law of economics' that always keeps wages at approximately the subsistence level. If wages rise for a period, workers and others are likely to feel confident to raise larger families, which over time will expand the labour supply to a point where wages will decline again. On the other side, wages cannot drop below subsistence levels because entrepreneurs need able-bodied workers. How can this vicious cycle of the 'iron law of economics' be broken? The only way according to Lassalle is for people who belong to the class of non-propertied and non-holders of capital to take control of the state. In that way they can become their own employers, and when there is no longer a difference between employer and employee the problem will be solved. For Lassalle, the state and political action were crucial for solving the social question of the time. The deprivations of workers could be removed, not through the self-help associations, such as consumer societies, proposed by left liberals like Hermann Schulze-Delitzsch, but only through the kind of political action that would lead to control of the state by the *Arbeiterstand*. The logic of his starting point – that the interests of the social classes were in conflict and the disinherited must gain control of the state – led Lassalle to conclude that the political interests of workers could not be harmonised with those of bourgeois liberals. Even well-intentioned liberals, such as as Schulze-Delitzsch, promoted remedies that fell far short of the goals that workers had to pursue if they were going to gain sufficient control of the state to use it to annul the 'iron law of economics' and achieve emancipation. That is why Lassalle expended great effort to write his long polemic against Schulze-Delitzsch – *Herr Bastiat-Schulze von Delitzsch* – which turned out to be his most important publication on economics (Lassalle 1919–20, v, pp. 27–339; Na'aman 1970, pp. 688–99). Schulze-Delitzsch's sympathy for the plight of the *Arbeiterstand* and his ideas for solving the social question of the time appealed to many workers and artisans who looked to liberals with a social conscience as their political friends and leaders. That is why in the 'Public Letter' Lassalle warned the organisers of the workers' association in Leipzig against further collaboration with the liberals and pressed them, successfully, to constitute themselves as an independent political party that would make the demand for universal manhood suffrage its central tenet (Lassalle 1919–20, III, p. 47).

3   The *Volksstaat*

The members of the Workers' Educational Societies who declined to join Lassalle's General Association of German Workingmen eventually created the Social Democratic Labour Party at their congress in Eisenach in 1869. Three political issues were prominent among the Eisenachers: their relationship to liberal and democratic thought; the influence of the Marx-led First International with which they were affiliated; and their conception of the state, both as it existed and what it would be in a socialist society. On all these and other topics, Bebel and Liebknecht were the recognised leaders of the Eisenachers and their speeches and writings were accepted as authentic expressions of the party as a whole. Although close political partners and friends for nearly four decades, Liebknecht and Bebel were also a study in contrasts.

Liebknecht came from an educated family of pastors and officials, studied philology and philosophy for a time at the university in Marburg, and earned his reputation as a democratic radical with communist leanings in the revolutions of 1848–9. Bebel, fourteen years younger, the son of a low-ranking army officer, lost both of his parents by the age of thirteen, but because of his native ability and self-discipline became a master wood turner at the age of twenty-four (1864) and was elected chairman of the Leipzig Workers' Educational Society a year later. In the early years of their collaboration, Bebel was the pupil and Liebknecht the teacher and mentor. Not only had Liebknecht the advantage of formal education, but in London exile in the 1850s he became a personal friend of Marx and Engels, a relationship that gave him a certain aura in Germany as an authentic representative of their ideas. By the end of the 1870s, however, through his intelligence, industriousness, intellectual curiosity and talent as a speaker and writer, Bebel surpassed Liebknecht in the eyes of Marx and Engels and also as the more effective and esteemed leader of the socialist labour movement. The Eisenachers were no less committed than Lassalle to radical political democracy, perhaps even more so, and their version was rooted in the views of the Volkspartei as embodied in the idea of the *Volksstaat*. Conceptions of the state, as with Lassalle, played a major role. This concept was so central and important to them that they named their party newspaper *Der Volksstaat* (1869–76). They conceived the *Volksstaat* as a fully democratic system, with a parliament, based on universal, direct and secret manhood suffrage, as well as in elections to all other representative bodies. (In the 1860s the socialist movements did not yet advocate votes for women.) It would also introduce the principle of direct legislation by the people which, in practice, would involve initiative and referendum. To ensure that persons of limited means could serve in parliament, deputies were to receive *per diem* allowances, a feature unknown in most political systems of the time, but already put forward by the Chartists. Although most discussions of the *Volksstaat* did not declare explicitly that it would also be a republic, that was understood implicitly. At their trial for high treason in 1872, Bebel and Liebknecht forthrightly stated that their movement understood the *Volksstaat* to be a republican form of government (Leidigkeit 1960, pp. 142, 165).

The Eisenachers spelled out the features of the *Volksstaat* in even more detail. They affirmed that it would do the following: abolish all privileges based on property, birth, class and religion; prescribe the separation of church and state, as well as the separation of church and public schools; replace the standing army with a people's militia; provide free public education and make primary school education obligatory; create an independent court system with juries and free legal services; and rescind all laws that put restrictions on the press and the right of free association. Leaders of the Eisenachers frequently elaborated on their conception of the *Volksstaat*. In his references to the *Volksstaat*, Bebel stressed that his party, in contrast to the democrats in the Volkspartei, believed that the acquisition of political power by the workers' movement and the democratisation of the state constituted a preliminary stage to the implementation of their socialist programme. In the people's state, socialist measures would be instituted by the people themselves, not by a ruling class, and that would mean that 'in such a state, self-help is people's help, people's help is state-help; self-help and state-help therefore are identical; there is no contradiction'. Bebel also wanted to avoid the impression that the Eisenachers aimed to help only workers, so he explained that under 'working class' he included not only dependent wage earners, but also 'artisans and small farmers, intellectual workers [*geistiger Arbeiter*], writers, elementary school teachers and lower civil servants, all of whom suffer under present conditions . . . and fall victim to modern developments' (Bebel 1870, pp. 10–11).

The *Volksstaat* continued to be the key political concept not only for the Eisenachers, but all of its defining characteristics were retained in the Gotha programme adopted when the Lassalleans and Eisenachers united into one party in 1875. The new party now preferred the term *Freistaat* (Free State), but the substance was the same. In this way the unified party continued to manifest its roots in the political thought of German liberalism and democracy, a point denounced by Marx in his extremely harsh critique of the Gotha programme. Engels too had access to the preliminary draft of the Gotha programme, and in a letter to Bebel (March 1875) two months before the unity congress met, remonstrated strongly that all mention of the 'state', 'people's state' and 'free state' should be omitted from any and all socialist programmes. Engels' arguments ultimately influenced Bebel to alter substantially his political thinking about the state, and this new view was gradually disseminated throughout the socialist movement. Engels explained to Bebel that because 'the state is only a transitional institution which is used in the struggle, in the revolution, in order to hold down one's adversaries by force, it is pure nonsense to talk of a free people's state: so long as the proletariat still *uses* the state, it does not use it in the interest of freedom but in order to hold down its adversaries, and as soon as it becomes possible to speak of freedom the state as such ceases to exist. We would therefore propose to replace *state* everywhere by "community" [*Gemeinwesen*] a good old German word which can very well represent the French word *"commune"'* (Marx and Engels 1955, II, pp. 41–2). This was strong medicine indeed. Engels explicated a view of the state that must have seemed very strange to Bebel. He called upon Bebel to discard, or drastically revise, all of the principles of political democracy as he knew them. Could Bebel easily absorb the sweeping implications of the theory of the withering away of the state? What could Bebel and his comrades have done to introduce 'Gemeinwesen' or other synonyms for 'Commune', or 'Commune' itself, as the foundation on which to build a large framework of political thought?

It is true that the Commune resonated with German socialists. Both the Lassalleans and Eisenachers had expressed strong support for the Parisian Communards and the principles of the Commune as they understood them. Bebel spoke forcefully in defence of the Communards. In May 1871 he told the deputies that 'the whole European proletariat and everyone who still loves freedom and independence looks to Paris. Gentlemen, if in this moment Paris is suppressed, then remember this much, that the struggle in Paris is only a minor outpost skirmish, that the great issue in Europe is still before us and that before a few years pass the battle cry of the Paris proletariat, "war on the palaces, peace for the cottages, death to misery and laziness!" will become the battle cry of the whole European proletariat' (Bebel, 1911–1913, II, pp. 348–69). In later years Bebel continued to herald the greatness of the Paris Commune (Lidtke 1966, pp. 41–2). This total identification with the cause of the Paris Commune contributed greatly to the popular image of the socialists as radical revolutionaries who would take to the barricades when they chose to act.

But to praise the Commune was one thing – to build on it another. Despite all of his speaking and writing, Bebel never attempted to base a political conception of socialism upon the Commune. The same is true of others. Karl Kautsky, social democracy's chief theorist and disseminator of Marxism, tells us that from the time of the Commune, for which he had sympathy (he was about seventeen at the time), he was attracted to socialism. Although Kautsky seems to have believed that the Commune should be viewed as a model for socialism, he too never explored what that meant theoretically or practically (Kautsky 1960, pp. 182–6; Steenson 1978, p. 20).

Instead of immediately taking up Engels' recommendation on the Commune, Bebel held onto the *Volksstaat*, and years passed before he absorbed and then passed along some of the views Engels had presented to him in 1875. In the first edition (1879) of *Woman and Socialism* Bebel used *Volksstaat* as he had before, but in the 1883 edition he replaced it with a concise account of the doctrine of the withering away of the state. From about that time, *Volkstaat* also vanished from his speeches and writings without, however, being replaced by *Gemeinwesen* or any other political concept with historical meaning or theoretical clarity.

In following Marx, and, at the time particularly Engels, social democratic thought embraced the speculation that a socialist society of the future would not need a political state, that nothing more would be required than non-political administrative structures necessary to carry out the basic functions of production and distribution. Engels spelled out this message of the withering away of the state in much greater detail in his polemical book, *Herr Eugen Dühring's Revolution in Science* (1878), three chapters of which were published independently as *Socialism: Utopian and Scientific* (German edition, 1883) which became the most popular source in Germany for understanding Marxism in the last two decades of the nineteenth century. (In the 1870s, Eugen Dühring, a Privatdozent at the University of Berlin, with vaguely socialist inclinations, promoted a 'socialitary system' of harmony between capital and labour and gained a following among young Social Democratic intellectuals chiefly because of his battles with the university authorities. Dühring's popularity, though it proved to be temporary, nonethless made Engels extremely anxious and impelled him to write an extensive refutation, known commonly as *Anti-Dühring*, which, ironically, is the only reason the name of the Privatdozent continued to appear in socialist discourse.) Engels explained that 'as soon as there is no longer any social class to be held in subjection . . . nothing more remains to be repressed, and a special repressive force, a state, is no longer necessary . . . State interference in social relations becomes, in one domain after another, superfluous, and then dies out of itself; the government of persons is replaced by the administration of things,

and by the conduct of processes of production. The state is not "abolished".
It dies out' (Marx and Engels 1955, II, pp. 150–1).

By the early 1880s Bebel and other Social Democrats were broadcasting
this argument almost word for word. In the extremely popular *Woman and
Socialism*, Bebel included a short chapter on the 'abolition of the state' which
illustrates how he understood Engels' precepts.

Together with the state will vanish its representatives: ministers, parliaments, standing
army, police, courts, lawyers and district attorneys, prison officials, collectors of taxes
and duties; in short, the entire political apparatus. Armories and other military buildings,
palaces of justice and administration, prisons, etc. will then serve better purposes. Tens
of thousands of laws, decrees and regulations will become just so much waste-paper;
their only value will be a historical one. The great and yet so petty parliamentary
struggles, during which men of the tongue imagine that by their orations they rule and
guide the world, will disappear. They will make room for colleges of administration
and administrative delegations whose purpose will be to consider and determine the
best means and methods of production and distribution, to decide how large a quantity
of supplies is required, to introduce and utilise new appliances and improvements in art,
science, education, traffic, etc., to organise and direct industry and agriculture. (Bebel
1910, pp. 435–6)

Bebel's utopian vision of socialism implied that political thinking was of
no real consequence for social democracy, but could be relevant only with
respect to tactics during the era of capitalism. Political thought did not
vanish from socialist discourse, to be sure, but for many it was of marginal
interest. In the 1880s, as the Social Democrats discarded their commitment
to the ideal of the *Volksstaat*, they were seriously weakening one of their
most important links to the traditions of European political democracy and
liberalism, a rupture that, rather than leading to increased theoretical clarity,
resulted more often in uncertainty and ambivalence. The no-state theory
left Social Democrats on a terrain that was difficult to chart.

Women's issues played an important role in Bebel's thinking already in
the 1860s and 1870s, years before a socialist feminist movement existed.
The demands of the bourgeois feminists at the time focused on improving
educational and occupational opportunities for women, especially for those
who were single. Louise Otto-Peters, for many years the bourgeois movement's most eminent leader, believed that such benefits should be shared
by working-class women as well as those of affluence. Bourgeois feminists
did not call for political rights or social equality, but emphasised female
difference, set forth a doctrine of 'spiritual motherhood', and promoted
the Kindergarten movement. Within the early socialist labour movement,

the Lassalleans, who were not particularly sympathetic to feminist causes, opposed female employment because of the 'iron law of wages' – increasing the supply of labour with women would drive down wages – and argued that the improvement of the male working class was a precondition for bettering the condition of women. Even the Eisenachers allowed for female employment chiefly because women in need, especially those who were single, might otherwise turn to prostitution to earn a living. Bebel's thinking on women's issues then progressed far beyond both the views of most socialists and the demands of bourgeois feminists. In a short pamphlet, written while incarcerated in the 1870s, he detailed the injustices suffered by women in most aspects of their lives. Then, in successive editions of *Women and Socialism* he elaborated on these themes, and his arguments exerted a broad influence in the socialist movement. After the fall of the anti-socialist law, the Erfurt Programme of 1891 incorporated many of the changes in thinking about the position of women, calling broadly for equality with men, women's suffrage and equal access to education. At about the same time, a dynamic socialist feminist movement emerged that pressured the male-dominated Social Democratic Party to put women's rights high on its agenda. However, the reigning theory even among socialist women subordinated feminism to the emphasis in orthodox Marxism on the dominant role of social class and the class struggle. This view, expressed repeatedly and forcefully by Clara Zetkin, their most prominent leader, contended that genuine female liberation could only be achieved as part of the emancipation of the whole working class. Class came before gender (Allen 1991, pp. 95–104; Quataert 1979, pp. 90–117).

4   State socialism

Social democratic discourse seldom felt a need to engage directly with conservative German political thought, except for brief polemical denunciations and the fact that socialist Reichstag deputies routinely lashed out at the conservative parties on specific issues. However, a conservative doctrine of state socialism appealed to some members of the labour movement and thereby aroused serious debate. What came to be called 'state socialism' grew particularly strong in the 1870s and 1880s. In this specific form, state socialism recognised the 'social question' as the main problem confronting German society and advocated that the state should take strong action to improve the condition of workers and the poor. State socialists were often sharp critics of capitalism and liberalism, which they linked together, and they looked to the state, especially on the national level, to intervene decisively in the economic realm. In politics, state socialists favoured monarchy and traditional religion, disapproved of democratic and liberal principles, and hoped to persuade workers to be loyal to the existing system. The strength of state socialism lay in the fact that its advocates included a number of learned and talented intellectuals – often trained in economics and social science – who explained their vision in numerous publications. These included Johann Karl Rodbertus, Hermann Wagener, Albert Schäffle, Rudolf Meyer and Adolf Wagner, as well as two Protestant pastors, Rudolf Todt and Adolf Stöcker, the latter a chaplain at the Hohenzollern court. State socialists aimed to influence the state directly and made few efforts to institutionalise their movement, though for a few years they did publish a newspaper, *Der Staatssozialist*. Only Adolf Stöcker, later joined by Rudolf Meyer, formed a political party – the Christian Social Party – which for a few years in the early 1880s attempted, with only minor success, to attract workers away from social democracy.

Had state socialism remained primarily a theoretical system, only a few socialist intellectuals would have been interested. State socialism became a pressing issue by 1881 when Bismarck initiated the national programme for accident, sickness and invalidity insurance. In this context, a number of intellectuals associated with social democracy showed a growing fascination with the ideas of Rodbertus, who had died in 1875, and whose cause was advanced at the time by other state socialists like Adolf Wagner and Rudolf Meyer. The fact that Ferdinand Lassalle had an extensive correspondence with Rodbertus, which Adolf Wagner edited (1878), appeared to give Rodbertus special credibility as a theorist of socialism. Moreover, Rodbertus enjoyed considerable respect as an economist, though he published his ideas chiefly in scattered essays and failed to bring together his theories in a comprehensive treatment. Thoroughly grounded in the works of the classical economists, Rodbertus accepted the labour theory of value as the foundation for much of his thinking. The state, he firmly believed, should intervene with measures that would improve conditions by regulating wages and hours. In his analysis, capitalism was just one phase of long-range economic development, and would necessarily be followed by socialism. But he wanted above all to preserve the monarchy and to avoid violent revolution. By moving the economy in the direction of state socialism, he believed, revolution and serious social upheaval would be avoided. As Rodbertus summarised his view in 1872, he stood for a 'German social-conservative party', whose principles could be summarised in three words:

'monarchical, national, social' (Rodbertus-Jagetzow 1880, 1, p. 178; Lidtke 1964; Lindenfeld 1997, 151; Meyer 1882, 1, pp. 57–72).

The intense debate among Social Democrats, including a vigorous intervention by Engels, revealed that some were willing to compromise their democratic principles in the interest of social reforms. A small group of intellectuals, for example, Moritz Wirth, Georg Adler, Max Quarck, Hermann Bahr and Max Schippel, who were close to social democracy, expressed their fascination with Rodbertus. They ranked him as a major theorist, but did not believe that he alone had all the answers. Carl August Schramm, who had been a member of the Social Democratic Party for several years, published a small book, *Rodbertus, Marx, Lassalle* (1885) that aroused the intense hostility of Engels, Kautsky and Eduard Bernstein. According to Schramm, Rodbertus, Marx and Lassalle were the founders of modern socialism, but Lassalle was the 'greatest' of the three. Schramm rejected Marx's ideas and used Rodbertus as a source for counter-arguments. 'It is my deepest conviction', he wrote, 'that the social question will not be solved only by legal acts from above, as Rodbertus believes, or by violence from below, as preached by Marx, but through a long and irresistible forward development' (Schramm 1885, p. 83). The wave of enthusiasm for Rodbertus, it is fair to conclude, was driven only partially by high esteem for his ideas, but also by those who looked with anxiety on the growing influence of Marxism and wanted to find theoretical obstacles to hinder its advance.

5 Parliamentary participation

The issue of parliamentarism in socialist thought had three distinct dimensions. In the first place, it was the practical question of how the party should relate to the existing German parliaments. What were the benefits of entering elections and participating in parliamentary activity? The second dimension posed the question whether socialists would be able to use parliament to take political power and build a socialist society. The third raised the broader theoretical question, whether representative bodies, including the Reichstag, would be retained in a socialist society.

The practical issues concerning parliamentarism began in earnest in 1867 when the constitution of the North German Confederation specified that elections to its parliament were to be based on universal manhood suffrage. Suddenly, leaders of working-class organisations had a realistic opportunity to win seats in the Reichstag and play a public role at the national level.

In fact, Bebel, as a candidate for the Saxon Volkspartei, won a seat to the constituent assembly, but he and Liebknecht contemptuously rejected the new Confederation chiefly because they opposed German unification under Prussian leadership. Although both won seats, again as candidates of the Saxon Volkspartei (1867), for the first regular session of the new Reichstag, they believed that socialists should use their positions primarily as a forum for criticism, not for positive legislative participation. Liebknecht in particular launched vehement attacks against the parliament and in 1869 declared as an absolute principle that socialism and parliamentarism were completely incompatible. If elected to the Reichstag, he believed that a socialist deputy should make a series of vigorous protests and then leave the building to go to the working class. On this occasion, Liebknecht linked his denunciation of parliamentary action with a rhetorical declaration in favour of violent revolution, asserting that 'socialism is no long a question of theory, but simply a question of power, which, like any other question of power, cannot be decided in parliament, but only in the streets, on the battle-field' (Liebknecht 1959, pp. 26–8). Liebknecht's hard line seemed excessive to Bebel who believed that for tactical purposes, at a minimum, socialists should exploit the Reichstag in every way possible; and even Liebknecht never consistently followed his own advice.

A pattern emerged after 1875 that lasted to the end of the century: on the one hand the socialists exploited the Reichstag for agitational pur-poses, but on the other they deliberated seriously and sometimes entered legislative proposals. Some socialists, again especially Liebknecht, contin-ued to rail against the Reichstag as a sham and to emphasise that the party's deputies should exploit it tactically for criticism. However, by early in 1878, just before the anti-socialist legislation was passed, the socialist deputies introduced a substantial number of bills, and not just for agitational purposes. Contrasting attitudes were now evident between moderates and radicals in the party. Moderates did not participate in the rhetoric of anti-parliamentarism, but desired to engage in positive legislative activity to the extent that was possible. The radicals, who were more successful in shaping the public image of social democracy, developed a less consistent posture. They continued to complain that the Reichstag was a sham and to contend that no substantial gains for workers could be won by participating in it, but some of them perfected parliamentary politics to a high degree. This was especially true of August Bebel.

During the twelve years of the anti-socialist law (1878–90) the issue of parliamentary participation underwent a paradoxical development.

Bismarck exploited two assassination attempts on the life of Emperor Wilhelm I in 1877 and 1878 as justification for demanding legislation to ban the Social Democratic Party, though there was no evidence to prove that the party was behind the attempts. It seems clear that Bismarck genuinely believed, even feared, that the socialist labour movement would become an influential political force and was determined to stop its growth as early as possible by using a carrot-and-stick approach. The legislation banning the party organisation and its affiliates passed in October 1878, but the law, owing to the constitutional conscience of numerous deputies, did not prohibit persons who professed socialist beliefs from running for seats in local and national elections. As a consequence, individual Social Democrats were candidates for parliamentary seats, and those who won and entered the Reichstag enjoyed a certain immunity as deputies and constituted an unofficial executive committee of the party. The outcome, paradoxically, was not only that Bismarck's stick turned out to be a fragile whip, but that the existence of the Social Democratic Reichstag delegation actually helped to preserve the viability of the socialist labour movement. On the other side, Bismarck hoped to draw workers away from the Social Democrats by sponsoring a broad programme of social welfare, which he did in the 1880s. However, Social Democratic deputies used the debates on the social welfare legislation, and all other debates as well, as occasions to attack the inadequacy of Bismarck's programme and to expound their socialist principles and goals. Since Reichstag debates were reported extensively in the newspapers, the speeches of Social Democratic deputies reached a wide audience and served a prominent agitational function. In practical terms, therefore, during the anti-socialist law parliamentarism became more rather than less significant for the survival and growth of social democracy (Lidtke 1966, pp. 70–105, 326–31).

6 The road to power

Social Democrats, especially those who claimed to follow Marx and Engels, faced a significant question: Could socialists use parliament to take political power and build a socialist society? Or could they come to power only through revolution? Their answer was supremely ambivalent, an ambivalence that grew with the spread of Marxism. A striking expression of this ambivalence was to be found in the preface to the published minutes of the party's congress in Copenhagen (March 1883). Written by radicals at the congress, the statement claims that Marxism guided their reasoning:

We are not a parliamentary party, we do not send our deputies to the various representative bodies to parley – but also we are not makers of revolutions [*Revolutionsmacher*]. German Social Democracy is proud that its attitude is always to follow the principles of its great master Marx, who would have nothing either of parliamentarism or of the making of revolutions [*Revolutionsmacherei*]. We are a revolutionary party, our aim is a revolutionary one, and we permit ourselves no illusions about its accomplishment by parliamentary means. But we also know that the manner in which it will be achieved does not depend upon us, that we cannot make the conditions under which we fight, but that we have to study those conditions and we know that our task in conjunction with this knowledge consists simply in acting in accord with what we know. (Lidtke 1966, p. 153)

It is certainly a stunning statement: they sent deputies to parliament, but were not a parliamentary party; they were revolutionaries, but did not engage in revolution. Their task was to study conditions.

Marx and Engels had not been ambivalent when they wrote the *Communist Manifesto*, but passionately called proletarians to revolution. Even Lassalle, who also could lay some legitimate claim to being a revolutionary in 1848–9, did not advise workers to use revolutionary force, but counselled them to gain political power through the full use of the ballot and parliament. By contrast, Marx and Engels spoke of 'violent revolution' that would overthrow the bourgeoisie and of 'sweeping away by force' the old relationships of production. They intended to incite fear, concluding that 'the Communists ... openly declare that their ends can be attained only by the forcible overthrow of all existing social conditions. Let the ruling classes tremble at a Communistic revolution. The proletarians have nothing to lose but their chains. They have a world to win' (Marx and Engels 1955, I, pp. 45, 54, 65). There is certainly no ambiguity in the *Manifesto* about the need to use revolutionary force.

A political party, already under a legal ban, that hoped to avoid complete suppression, could scarcely inscribe the rhetoric of the *Manifesto* in its official programme without endangering its survival. The dilemma was most troublesome for the radical wing of the party. One solution was to remove violence and force from their definition of revolution. As early as 1871, Wilhelm Liebknecht set forth a view, not new with him, that stressed the pervasiveness and gradualism of revolution. 'All of human history', he said, 'is a continuous revolution. History is the revolution in permanence – it is becomingness, growth, change, progress – perpetual transformation, because life is perpetual creation. As long as a human lives, he is a revolutionary ... The revolution, movement is life – the non-revolution, stasis is death.' This sounds mild, and it is, but Liebknecht wanted also to take his stand with revolution, so he simultaneously declared himself a revolutionary, insisting that force would be used only if absolutely necessary (Liebknecht 1883, pp. 18–19). Others shared Liebknecht's general attitude towards revolution, but with variations. By the mid-1880s Bebel had studied Marx, especially his analysis of the internal contradictions of capitalism. He therefore interpreted revolution within a highly deterministic framework. He believed firmly that a revolution would take place at some time, probably in the near future. It might even involve a violent struggle, but not necessarily, and he minimised that possibility. More significantly, he emphasised that socialists could not, and would not, create the revolution. It would come upon them when the social evils had become intolerable and capitalism's internal contradictions had totally undermined it (Bebel 1910, pp. 363–6). He never professed to know what the revolution would be like, but believed that Social Democrats had to be prepared so that they could act at the appropriate time, but here too he had few, if any, ideas about how to prepare for an active role. As a result, Bebel fell into a very passive conception of revolution. In a letter to Engels in 1881 he wrote that 'when things develop further, which is not to be doubted, I hold it possible that in a certain moment the ruling classes will find themselves in a kind of hypnotic state and will let everything take its course almost without opposition' (Bebel 1965, p. 106). This was certainly Bebel's hope, formulated as a positive interpretation of revolution which he believed to be based on Marxism. His influence on the political thinking of socialists can scarcely be overestimated and he often repeated his passive view of revolution. In the well-known Reichstag debate on the socialist state of the future (1893), after outlining the inevitable collapse of capitalist society, he explained that 'at present there is nothing more for us to do than to make sure that we have enlightened the masses on the essence and nature of bourgeois society' (Bebel 1893, p. 12).

This passive conception of revolution was derived from an understanding of the Marxist analysis of capitalism as put forward by experts, most notably Kautsky. By the mid-1880s Kautsky was social democracy's leading authority on Marxist historical and economic theory and, as a prolific writer and editor of the movement's theoretical journal, *Die neue Zeit* (founded 1883), an intellectual mentor for younger members of the movement. Although Kautsky often commented on political issues, political theory was only of marginal interest to him. Gary Steenson does not exaggerate when he says that at times Kautsky's political views were 'very simple and even dogmatic. Politics for him [Kautsky] was the class struggle, and all states were class states which ruled for the dominant economic class' (Steenson 1978, p. 76).

Kautsky's understanding of socialist theory, and of Marxism in particular, was informed in considerable part by his familiarity with the theories of Charles Darwin and Ernst Haeckel, and to a lesser extent Thomas H. Buckle. He read their works in his early twenties. Two broad ideas found in Buckle appealed to the young Kautsky: the belief that by discovering the laws according to which societies function, the study of history could be transformed to resemble a natural science; and the hypothesis that the widespread dissemination of knowledge, chiefly of natural science, was the foundation and pre-condition for social and political (democratic) progress. Kautsky understood Buckle to mean that the possibility of social improvement, or revolution, rests upon the spread of a new *idea*, and the lesson he drew was that propaganda was the most important task for socialists. At about the same time, Kautsky was delving into the work of Ernst Haeckel, an eminent zoologist in his own right and, in books like *Die Natürliche Schöpfungsgeschichte* (1867), Germany's most prominent and prolific advocate of Darwin's theories. Kautsky was also deeply impressed by Haeckel's concept of monism, which claimed to be a coherent world view with a theory which could overcome dualisms. When applied to the social world, monism offered a means – on a theoretical level – for overcoming such dualisms as the gap between capitalists and workers and rulers and the ruled. Kautsky incorporated Haeckel's monism into his own outlook (Holzheuer 1972, pp. 14–19; Kautsky 1960, pp. 172–3, 224–5; Steenson 1978, pp. 24–30).

But it was ideas drawn directly from Darwin that most thoroughly permeated Kautsky's thinking throughout his most productive years. Although he had learned about Darwin by reading authors like Haeckel, he first read *The Descent of Man* only after it appeared in German translation in 1875. Immediately he set about incorporating Darwinian ideas into his thinking, adapting them in several instances to fit into a framework of thought influenced by general socialist principles as well as by notions taken from Buckle and Haeckel. He drew heavily on Darwin's conception of humanity as a social animal and of social instincts as the foundation of morality. When aspects of evolutionary theory did not fit easily with socialist principles, Kautsky modified Darwin's formulations. He shifted the concept of the struggle for survival from a competition between individuals to one between groups, for example, classes and nations. Darwin's view of social instincts became in Kautsky an argument for group solidarity. In adapting Darwin's idea of social instincts to his emerging socialist outlook, Kautsky contended that proletarians have communist instincts that form the basis for class solidarity and are so strong that they guarantee working-class victory in the future. All of this, Kautsky believed, corresponded to the laws of nature, the foundation on which to build a new social system and which the socialist movement had to follow to reach its ultimate goal. This schematic outline of Kautsky's assimilation and adaptation of Darwinian thought gives just a hint of the extent to which images and words drawn from biology and the natural world are scattered throughout his writing and give a naturalistic cast to much of his interpretation of Marxism. In contrast to his absorption in Darwinian thought, Kautsky never immersed himself deeply in Hegelian philosophy, the starting point for Marx, and his limited appreciation and knowledge of Hegel also affected his approach to Marxism (Holzheuer 1972, pp. 19–25; Kautsky 1960, pp. 379–81, 518–22; Pierson 1993, pp. 187–8).

Kautsky's Darwinian orientation was present even as he consistently emphasised Marxism as a system of economic determinism, but he also argued for a multilayered understanding that included voluntarist elements. He explained that 'we [Social Democrats] do not mean that the social revolution will be accomplished of itself, that the irresistible, inevitable course of evolution will do the work without the assistance of man; nor . . . that nothing is left to those who suffer . . . but idly to fold their arms and patiently to wait for its [capitalism's] abolition'. The revolution could take various forms, he explained: 'It is by no means necessary that it be accompanied with violence and bloodshed . . . Neither is it necessary that the social revolution be decided in one blow; such probably was never the case. Revolutions prepare themselves by years or decades of economic and political struggle' (Kautsky 1910, pp. 89–91; Pierson 1993, pp. 60–9, 231–5).

A deterministic or passive conception of revolution did not exclude the possibility that peaceful parliamentary action could also be the road to socialism. Party moderates, inclined to reformism, had been sympathetic to this view from the early 1880s, but the radical wing tended to dismiss it as an illusion, especially in view of the restricted powers of German representative institutions. However, by the end of the 1880s, there were hints that on this matter the attitudes of the Marxist-influenced leaders were also shifting. Wilhelm Liebknecht, who earlier had expressed extreme contempt for parliament, is a good example. By 1890 he appeared to have shifted his ground substantially. Social democracy, he argued, had matured from a sect to a party, and with that transformation came a changed perspective on the means to achieve power and socialism. It was necessary to recognise that revolutions require time, that they take place gradually, without people noticing what is actually going on 'and the transition from this bourgeois society to the socialist society', he counselled, 'will be realised just as organically, just as gradually, and just as irresistibly'. He concluded, therefore, that it was possible that the road to socialism would be through parliamentary reform, though he still maintained that no absolute answer could be given (Liebknecht 1890, p. 33).

Kautsky, more rigorous than the impulsive Liebknecht, actually came to a similar conclusion around the same time. In explaining the Erfurt programme of 1891, Kautsky would not flatly say that socialists would gain power through parliament, but he clearly believed that if the working class, through the Social Democrats, showed strength, they could use parliament to gain control. Furthermore, proletarian participation improved parliament. 'Whenever the proletariat engages in parliamentary activity as a self-conscious class, parliamentarism begins to change its character. It ceases to be a mere tool in the hands of the bourgeoisie. The very participation of the proletariat proves to be the most effective means of shaking up the hitherto indifferent divisions of the proletariat and giving them hope and confidence. It is the most powerful lever that can be utilised to raise the proletariat out of its economic, social, and moral degradation.' At this point Kautsky began to sound like a genuine advocate of parliament as an instrument for gaining power, as he stressed that 'the proletariat has, therefore, no reason to distrust parliamentary action; on the other hand it has every reason to exert all of its energy to increase the power of parliaments in their relation to other departments of government and to swell to the utmost its own parliamentary representation' (Kautsky 1910, pp. 186–8).

A year later Kautsky appeared to be more impressed by the role that parliament might play in the socialist drive to power, but now he gutted it of its liberal and democratic qualities. He viewed parliamentary power by socialists as a way to establish the 'dictatorship of the proletariat'. He speculated that a 'genuine parliamentary regime can be just as good an instrument for the dictatorship of the proletariat as it is an instrument for the dictatorship of the bourgeoisie' (Kautsky 1893, p. 118). This is striking! It is one of the few instances in all of the political discourse of social democracy in the nineteenth century that embraces the dictatorship of the proletariat. Though sometimes mentioned in passing, the concept never appears as an important feature of social democratic discourse. This is not at all surprising. They could not fail to see that the idea of a dictatorship of the proletariat clashed directly with their long-standing commitment to democratic principles. They could attempt to water down the meaning of 'dictatorship', to make it less offensive or even contend that it was compatible with democracy, as some scholars have argued. But a political party needed doctrines that did not require appeals to overly subtle or paradoxical explanations. In this matter, Marx and Engels also were not very helpful. They themselves used the phrase sparingly, and only in a few instances offered brief explanations of what they meant (Hunt 1975, I, pp. 284–336).

7   The socialist society of the future

Would a future socialist society have a place for liberal and democratic institutions? What kind of political form was envisaged? Would there be a state? A republic? On these issues the thinking of socialists was seldom unambiguous, though they sometimes sought to give answers. The usual place for Social Democrats to spell out the principles of a socialist society was in the official party programme, a new version of which was adopted at Erfurt (1891). But in a fundamental way the Erfurt programme itself reflected the uncertainty of the Social Democrats as to the political form of a socialist system. The Erfurt programme, drafted largely by Kautsky and often viewed as evidence of the dominance of Marxism, made no mention of the withering away of the state or of the political principles of a socialist society. The first part of the Erfurt programme summarises the widespread understanding of Marx's analysis of capitalism and of the outcome of class conflicts. The second part is a list of current demands, many of which are substantively the same as points that appeared in the earlier programmes of 1869 and 1875, though now universal suffrage was extended to everyone over twenty years, including women. If one assumes that the second part of the Erfurt programme included all of the fundamental economic, social and political demands, one could interpret it to mean that Social Democrats were implying that the Kaiserreich could be transformed into a democratic state that would work for and achieve the emancipation of all humanity.

But that surmise, though logical, is incorrect. On crucial political principles the drafters of the programme were indecisive, or, at least not explicit. The most notable lack was any mention of a republic as a political goal. In 1891 this omission was more striking than the failure of the Gotha programme (1875) to call explicitly for a republic. That earlier programme had set forth the *Volksstaat* as its political ideal, and it was commonly assumed that this meant a democratic and republican form of government. In 1891, on reading in advance a draft of the Erfurt programme, Engels wrote an extensive critique which he sent to leaders in Germany – it was not published until ten years later in *Die neue Zeit* – and he specifically criticised the omission of 'republic'. But Engels' recommendation created difficulties of its own. He explained that socialists could only gain power by means of a 'democratic republic', which, he elaborated, is the 'specific form of the dictatorship of the proletariat' (Engels 1901/02, p. 11). For Engels a democratic republic was only an intermediate goal, not the final political form for a socialist society. Bebel and those around him explained to Engels that it would be impossible under present conditions in Germany to call explicitly for a republic, which likely would provoke severe repression (Bebel 1965, p. 424). But Engels' suggestion posed still another difficulty that Bebel did not mention. How could the Social Democrats advocate a democratic republic if they had to explain to their followers and the public that it was merely an intermediate goal and, moreover, that it would be the instrument for establishing a dictatorship of the proletariat? If Engels had proposed including 'democratic republic' in the programme as a genuine goal of social democracy, it would have been easily comprehended, even if it aroused hostility, and in the context of the Kaiserreich it would have been perceived as an authentic revolutionary demand.

In order to get some notion of how socialists of Marxist persuasion understood the Erfurt programme's political implications for a socialist society, we can turn to Kautsky's widely circulated commentary. Although he included a section on 'The Structure of the Future State', he offered few particulars. Kautsky argued, wisely perhaps, that it would be foolish to try to describe the socialist society of the future, and so he declined also to talk about the place of democratic and liberal institutions. He grasped again for a determinist interpretation, affirming that 'social science has proved . . . that . . . the history of mankind is determined . . . by an economic development which progresses irresistibly, obedient to certain underlying laws and not to anyone's wishes or whims'. Except for refuting the accusations by enemies of social democracy that socialism would be oppressive, Kautsky always resisted the temptation to give a picture of the future, except for general statements about a classless society and improved welfare of all humanity (Kautsky 1910, pp. 112–26).

Not so for Bebel. He claimed to know much about the future socialist society. We have seen above that Bebel, drawing directly on Engels' writings, concluded that there would be no state and therefore nothing one could call a political system: 'Together with the state will vanish . . . the whole political apparatus.' Consistent with this argument, Bebel had little or nothing to say in *Woman and Socialism* on those topics that are conventionally considered to be political. On other topics, however, he did not shy away from providing a long list of the most detailed features of a future socialist society.

The expositions of Kautsky and Bebel illustrate the degree to which those influenced by Marx and Engels had abandoned, on the theoretical level, the commitment to the political ideals and institutions of liberalism and democracy. On the level of political practice, however, they were deeply embedded in the work of liberal institutions, notably the Reichstag and local representative bodies, and Bebel, ironically, more than almost any other Social Democrat embodied the exceptional skill displayed by Social Democrats engaged in parliamentary work.

8   Eduard Bernstein

Moderate and reformist socialists believed that the party should use all legal means to bring about the kinds of economic, social and political reforms that would gradually improve the lives, not only of workers, but of all people who were disadvantaged by the unrestrained workings of capitalism. Although this reformist outlook had been widespread throughout the history of the German socialist labour movement, it lacked a coherent and forceful statement of its principles that could be deployed in internal debates against orthodoxy's revolutionary doctrines. Reformist sentiment had also lacked an articulate and persuasive leader, one who understood Marxist theory thoroughly and whose socialist credentials were beyond doubt. Eduard Bernstein had excellent credentials when he began in the early 1890s to harbour doubts about the validity of important parts of orthodox theory. As editor of the party's quasi-official newspaper, *Der Sozialdemokrat* (1879–90), he belonged to the inner circle of Marxist-oriented leaders who immersed themselves in socialist literature and corresponded regularly with Marx and especially Engels. Upon moving the editorial office of the newspaper to London in 1888 – he was expelled from Switzerland – Bernstein became a close and trusted friend of Engels, demonstrated by the fact that the elder statesman of the Marxist movement chose the younger comrade to be his literary executor. In London, first through the close association with Engels, and then on his own, Bernstein came in contact with a wide range of English socialists, radicals and intellectuals. It is difficult, if not impossible, to sort out the specific influence that particular people or groups exerted on Bernstein, but it is clear that his British experience contributed in some measure to a gradual change in his outlook. Some scholars have concluded that the Fabians, with whom Bernstein associated despite initial misgivings, shaped much of his thinking. However, Bernstein always played down the influence of the Fabians, though he particularly admired Sidney Webb. He was present at the founding meeting of the Independent Labour Party in 1893, and among others, his acquaintances and friends included Kier Hardie, Ramsay MacDonald and William Morris. Contact with socialists and intellectuals may have been less important for his later development than his generally favourable impression of the British social and political environment, particularly the effectiveness of parliamentary government and the fact that compromise and collaboration between liberals and labour was possible. In some significant sense, Bernstein's years in London, as well as his appreciation of thinkers like John Stuart Mill, revived his youthful attachment to liberalism (Carsten 1993, pp. 47–80; Steger 1997, pp. 12, 66–71, 143).

As Bernstein examined the contemporary capitalist world, empirical evidence suggested strongly that actual economic and social trends often contradicted the expectations of Marx and Engels. After the death of Engels in 1895, Bernstein assembled his critical thinking in a series of articles in *Die neue Zeit* under the general title 'Problems of Socialism'. From that point on he began to question central tenets of Marx's theory. Bernstein made a series of observations that contradicted the forecasts of Marx and Engels: the internal contradictions of capitalism were being moderated rather than intensified; the working class was not getting poorer but in numerous places making headway; industrial societies were not being polarised, and the middle class was growing not decreasing. Then, with his rigorous questioning of the claim that Marxism constituted a 'scientific socialism' he debunked a major tenet of Marx and Engels and their orthodox followers (Bernstein 1901b, pp. 32–7).

According to Bernstein's analysis, contemporary capitalism was proving to be both more resilient and more flexible than Marx and Engels had believed. That led him to argue that it would not be necessary to abolish capitalism totally in order to achieve working-class emancipation. On the contrary, it had become apparent that capitalism could be changed gradually through legal reforms. Where Marx and Engels made abolition of private property a precondition for the achievement of socialism, Bernstein argued that the total abolition of private property would be impossible in practice and that, in any case, the right of ownership could be harmonised with the basic principles of socialism.

If the theory of capitalist collapse could not withstand critical scrutiny, Bernstein reasoned, neither could most of the political conclusions that assumed the truth of economic determinism. Bernstein based his own political outlook on a deep and sustained commitment to democracy, and indeed his view of how to achieve socialism emphasised the need to employ all legal means to advance the cause of political democracy. Elections and legislative action were keys. The labour movement should call insistently for the introduction of universal suffrage in elections on all levels, not just for the Reichstag. Although Bernstein did not in any one place elaborate a full theory of democracy, certain principles were essential. He stressed that democracy called for self-government of the people and left no room for the dominance of privileged social groups. Democracy meant, he emphasised, the abolition of class government, 'a state of society in which no class has a political privilege which is opposed to the community as a whole' (Bernstein 1993, p. 140). He would not embrace theories of direct democracy which, he believed, were impracticable for large political units, but called for the implementation of the will of the community through representation in parliament, that is, in a parliamentary democracy. Democracy assumed universal suffrage, a precondition for the possibility that all members of a community could become participants in the fullest sense (Bernstein 1993, pp. 142–4).

Most importantly, for Bernstein political democracy and socialism were linked together in a tight reciprocal relationship. There could be no socialism without democracy, and political democracy would not realise its fullest development until it was combined with socialism. Democracy was an unambiguous goal of socialism. 'Democracy is both means and end. It is a weapon in the struggle for socialism, and it is the form in which socialism will be realised' (Bernstein 1993, p. 142). Bernstein thus rejected completely Engels' argument for the overlap between a democratic republic and the dictatorship of the proletariat. Instead, Bernstein insisted that 'the dictatorship of the proletariat' was a totally outdated concept 'at a time when representatives of Social Democracy have in practice placed themselves wherever possible in the arena of parliamentary work . . . and in the struggle for popular participation in legislation, all of which is incompatible with dictatorship. The phrase is nowadays so out of date that it can be reconciled with reality only by stripping the word dictatorship of its actual meaning and giving it some kind of diluted significance' (Bernstein 1993, p. 145).

Parliament thus became a key institution for Bernstein, both in theory and for socialist practice. As early as 1890, while still editor of *Der Sozialdemokrat*, he distanced himself totally from the ambivalent parliamentarism of leaders like Bebel. 'The road to full political freedom', he wrote, 'goes by way of parliament, not around it. Despite all of its weaknesses, parliamentarism is still the most modern public institution in present-day Germany, and no doctrinaire grounds should cause us to overlook that' (Bernstein 1901a, p. 25). He pointed repeatedly to the fact that Social Democratic participation in the German parliament, for all of the Reichstag's limitations, had been the key to the party's enormous growth and, he expected, would continue to be in the future. The negative and intransigent posture of many socialist Reichstag deputies in the early years had gradually given way to a realisation that, as their numbers grew, they could become crucial shapers of legislation. He went further and speculated on the possibility that in some countries with strong labour movements and effective parliaments, socialist deputies might have to face the uncomfortable choice of participating in coalition governments. He did not shy away from that prospect but thought in fact that it would be beneficial for socialists to work together with left liberals (Bernstein 1896, pp. 44–55).

It followed that Bernstein strongly recommended that social democracy should moderate its habitual battle against liberalism and attempt to understand the positive historical and theoretical relationship between the two movements. Socialism had in fact evolved from liberalism and should still build on its fundamental principles, particularly on personal freedom and civil rights. He emphasised the flexibility and adaptability of liberal institutions, making them excellent instruments for gradually introducing socialism. It should be recognised, he stressed, that socialism was the 'legitimate heir' of liberalism, not just chronologically, but also in several matters of principle and theory. To be sure, Bernstein rejected most of the principles of classical liberal economic theory that were so closely intertwined with capitalism. But as the heir to political liberalism, socialism had to complete the tasks that liberals left unfulfilled, the 'principled struggle against militarism, against the privileges of birth, and further the removal of corrupted legal institutions – all things that first imply an expansion of the power of parliament, that is, of the Reichstag' (Bernstein 1901a, p. 24).

Bernstein highlighted other links between liberalism and socialism. Both wanted to see the development and secure position of the 'free personality'. Even liberal economic thinking had something to recommend it, namely, because historically liberalism had the task of breaking economic chains. 'Socialism will create no new bondage of any kind whatever. The individual will be ... free from any economic compulsion in his actions and choice of vocation.' Bernstein gave a great amount of attention to the value of self-government on the regional and local level, for these were institutions that also contributed to the advancement of democracy (Bernstein 1993, pp. 147, 150, 155–6). Clearly, Bernstein intended to select from liberalism what he found most valuable for the advancement of socialism and democracy.

It follows as well that Bernstein dispensed with Marxist notions of the withering away of the state, but believed fervently that a socialist state should take the form of a democratic republic. Moreover, in his optimism, Bernstein believed that even the German Kaiserreich, despite its authoritarian features, still possessed institutions – for example, the Reichstag – through which it could gradually be transformed into a system of liberal democracy. Bernstein's contemporaries and later scholars believed that he overestimated the adaptability of the German imperial system, and that is probably true (Steger 1997, p. 142). Still, he firmly believed that once liberal socialists – as against intransigent socialists – were in control of parliament they would be able to abolish, gradually, the privileges of the dominant classes so that it would no longer be possible to speak of the state as simply the instrument of class rule. Although his contemporary orthodox Marxists colleagues in the Social Democratic Party greeted Bernstein's theories with dismay, anger and bitterness, on balance historians at a later time, with the exception of those in the former German Democratic Republic, have interpreted his life's work and his contributions to socialist political thought as a highly positive heritage (Carsten 1993, pp. 196–200; Steger 1997, pp. 253–60).

24

Russian political thought of the nineteenth century

ANDREZJ WALICKI

1 The epoch of Alexander I

The first years of the nineteenth century in Russia were a time of great hopes. The new emperor, Alexander I, hated the arbitrary despotism of his assassinated father, Paul I, and vowed to make Russia a law-abiding state, a legitimate representative of universal civilisation, playing an important part in European affairs and realising thereby a universally significant imperial mission. The educated strata of the Russian society shared this mood. They felt that a great historic change was imminent and wanted to participate in it. Expectation of a new beginning united the old-fashioned rationalists of the Enlightenment with the members of the mystical freemasonry, known as Illuminati, or Martinists.

The first group, represented by the Free Association of the Lovers of Literature, the Sciences and the Arts, included two thinkers greatly influenced by the Scottish Enlightenment: Ivan Pnin, author of *An Essay on Enlightenment Concerning Russia* (1804) and Vasilii Popugaev whose main work bears the self-explaining title *On the Firmness of Constitution and Laws*. They developed the conception of a civil society (*grazhdanskoe obshchestvo*), based upon private property and legally safeguarded rights of man, supporting the constitutional ideas of the young emperor and urging him to complete the transformation of Russia from a military to a commercial state. The other group, the Martinists, expected a religious regeneration of humanity, deriving this messianic hope from a universalist, supra-ecclesiastical interpretation of Christianity. Both currents of thought, secular liberalism and political mysticism, were interconnected in the ideas of Mikhail Speranskii (1772–1839) who in the years 1807–12 played the role of Alexander's prime minister in fact. His constitutional project, submitted to the emperor in 1809, combined a liberal programme of introducing to Russia the rule of law, the division of powers and the principles of self-government, with the idea of the Christianisation of political and social life – the chief idea of the socially oriented, millenarian mysticism. Very characteristic of his time was the fact that he drew his ideas from the most different sources, such as the Napoleonic Code, on the one hand, and the occult mystics, especially Jacob Boehme and Saint-Martin, on the other. He even consulted the legacy of the Church Fathers.

Speranskii did not call for the formal abolition of autocracy; he preferred to reinterpret the meaning of autocracy (the Russian *samoderzhavye*) in the spirit of true monarchy, combining the elevated position of the monarch with his submission to the law. Neither did he envisage the immediate abolition of serfdom, choosing to leave the solution of the peasant question to a slow, gradual process. Nevertheless, the very idea of a legal limitation of autocracy, as well as the acknowledgement of the need for the emancipation and enfranchisement of the peasantry, aroused the ire of the gentry's conservatives. Their main spokesman became Nikolai Karamzin (1766–1826), the well-known sentimental writer who had cleansed the Russian language from Church-Slavonic archaism and the official historiographer of the Russian state. In his confidential *Memoir on Ancient and Modern Russia* (1811), given to Alexander to counteract Speranskii's constitutional project, he claimed that the absolute power of the monarch, together with the historical rights of the gentry, is an inalienable part of Russia's national tradition. At the same time, however, he sharply distinguished between absolutism and arbitrary despotism, arguing in particular that the Russian monarch had absolute and indivisible power only in the *political* sphere, but not over the social and private life of his subjects. This view enabled him to combine a resolute rejection of political liberty with an equally resolute defence of civil liberty, safeguarded by moral laws and unwritten rules of tradition.

Soon afterwards Speranskii was attacked by conservative nationalists who acccused him of a hidden support of Napoleon. As a result he was deprived of his post and sent into exile. The year of his dismissal – 1812 – is usually treated as the beginning of the second part of Alexander's reign, characterised by the growing influence of reactionary forces. In fact, however, the change was not abrupt and the emperor, the true Hamlet on the throne, continued to be exposed to influences from different quarters. After all, at the Congress of Vienna (1815) he created under his rule a small but autonomous Kingdom of Poland, giving it a liberal constitution and a parliamentary form of government which was to be a model for Russia proper.

The spectacular victory over Napoleon tremendously increased the international prestige of Russia, conferring on it the position of first arbiter of

Europe's destinies (Malia 1961). Alexander saw this as a step towards real-isation of his larger vision of Russia's mission – a vision formulated at the beginning of his reign by his close Polish friend, Prince Adam Czartoryski (who in the autumn of 1802 took the post of Deputy Minister of Foreign Affairs and in January 1804 was given full control of this department, with the rank of Acting Minister). In his extensive memorandum on the political system to be adopted by Russia (1803), approved by the emperor, Czarto-ryski endowed the Russian Empire with a mission of creating a society of states, based upon the law of nations, adopting liberal institutions, and aim-ing at the implementation of the idea of eternal peace. Similar ideas were developed by Czartoryski's close collaborator, Vasilii Malinovskii (1765–1814), in his treatise *Reflections on Peace and War* (1803) and in an unpub-lished memoir submitted to Russia's Foreign Ministry. He postulated the creation of a European Union, based upon the principle of national self-determination, establishing rule of law in international relations, and com-mitted to radical social reforms in the spirit of agrarian socialism. A part of the European Union was to be a federation of Slavonic nations, liberated from the Austrian and Turkish yoke.

Malinovskii was probably a Martinist and some of his liberal views on Russia's calling could be given a religious interpretation. This happened in the case of the emperor who, in 1812, underwent a mystical, chilias-tic conversion. Three years later – on 26 September 1815 – he signed the proclamation of the Holy Alliance – a document heavily influenced by the Russophile German mystics (Baroness von Krüdener, Jung Stilling and Franz von Baader), and only reluctantly accepted by the monarchs of Austria and Prussia. It promised to treat the peoples of Europe as a single Christian nation under the rule of the Saviour, to ignore denominational boundaries dividing Christians, and to institutionalise Christian morality in international relations.

In practice these lofty ideals were used to justify the policy of supporting conservative legitimism in Europe and suppressing the movement for reform within Russia. This resulted, of course, in the growing dissatisfaction among the progressive Russians – especially among the officers of the army, who vividly remembered the glorious days of Russia's triumph of 1814 and did not want to see their country as a pillar of European reaction. They organised themselves in secret societies and embarked on revolutionary activities, resulting – after the death of Alexander – in the abortive military uprising of December 1825. Hence, all participants of this movement were named by historians as the Decembrists.

The political ideology of the Decembrists had two main variants. The most important document of the Northern Society of the conspirators was the draft constitution prepared by Nikita Muraviev. It visualised the future Russia as a decentralised constitutional monarchy, which restricted popular sovereignty by property qualifications giving peasants personal freedom but retaining for a transitional period their labour obligations to the landlords. The leader of the Southern Society, Colonel Pavel Pestel, was much more radical: his constitutional project entitled *Russian Justice* described the post-revolutionary Russia as a centralised egalitarian republic of the Jacobin type. A peculiarly Russian element in it was the proposal to divide land into two equal parts: one held as alienable private property, the other reserved for communal ownership, modelled on the existing village communes in Russia.

Even more radical were the leaders of the Society of United Slavs – the Borisov brothers (Andrej and Pëtr) and a Pole, Julian Lubliski, who wanted to create a democratic Slavonic federation, uniting Russia with the peoples of East Central Europe. Unlike the Decembrists, they were in favour of a popular revolution of the masses rather than a military revolt.

As befitted revolutionists of the gentry, the Decembrists tried to link their political ideas with the past, presenting their aim as the restoration of the ancient Russian liberty. Typical in this respect was the poet Konstantin Ryleev who, in opposition to Karamzin's historical views, sided with the Muscovite boyars in their struggle against the emerging autocracy and praised the ancient liberties of the Cossacks.

2   The Nicholaevan Russia

The Decembrist uprising had a fatal influence on the new emperor. Nicholas I decided to eradicate the revolutionary infection from Russian life by isolating Russia from the West and, at the same time, actively supporting the most conservative forces in Europe. The official ideology of the new reign was summarised in three principles, proclaimed in 1833 by the minister of education, Sergei Uvarov: orthodoxy, autocracy and nationality.

For the emerging Russian intelligentsia this victory of reaction was a terrible blow, undermining their belief in Russia's European identity and its praiseworthy historical mission. The most extreme expression of these pessimistic moods was the *Philosophical Letter* of Pëtr Chaadaev (1794–1856), published in 1836. It described Russia as a country forgotten by Providence, a country without past and without future, a strange nation lacking the supra-individual continuity of tradition, isolated from humankind and playing no part in universal history.

The ultimate cause of this predicament was the religious schism which separated Russia from the universal Church. Following the French traditionalists (Maistre, Bonald and Lamennais of the Atheocratic period), Chaadaev saw the Roman Church as the purest expression of Christian universalism. Hence the lack of the Catholic past amounted in his eyes to non-participation in universal history.

No wonder that the *Philosophical Letter* aroused extreme indignation in official circles and among nationalist Russians. Chaadaev was declared mad and put under medical surveillance. In the next year, however, he modified his views, making them more palatable for Russian patriots. In his *Apology of a Madman* (1837) he recognised that the lack of history might be a kind of privilege: without the burden of the past Russia would meet no obstacles in learning from Europe and building its future on purely rational foundations.

An elaborated answer to Chaadaev pessimism about Russia was provided by the so-called Slavophiles. This term, originally a nickname, designated a group of educated landowners who criticised the Westernisation process and preached a return to the truly Christian and Slavonic principles of pre-Petrine Russian life. The main representatives of this current were: Ivan Kireevskii (1806–56), a philosopher, who developed a sophisticated Russian version of conservative romanticism; Aleksei Khomiakov (1804–60), a lay theologian, who elaborated the concept of sobornost', i.e. free unity and conciliarity (from the Russian words sobor – *council*, and sobirat' – *bring together, unite*), defined by him as the inner essence of the Orthodox Church; Konstantin Aksakov (1817–60), an extreme romantic anti-legalist, treating law and state as alienated, artificial forms of social life, acceptable only as a necessary evil; and Iurii Samarin (1819–76), best known for his political activity in preparing the land reform of 1861.

The Slavophile contribution to political thought consisted in providing elaborate arguments for reversing the Westernisation of Russia, returning to the native roots, and replacing the Eurocentric model of development – accused of bringing about destructive rationalisation and atomisation of life – by the Russian way, based upon the communitarian values of Orthodox Christianity and the peasant commune. Challenging Chaadaev, the Slavophiles stressed that the true guardian of Christian universalism was the Eastern Church, and not the Church of Rome. This enabled them to claim that the Russian values had universal significance, representing the truly Christian spirit in its struggle with the pagan rationalism of the West.

The opponents of Slavophilism, called Westernisers, set against Slavophilism the ideal of the free, autonomous personality, seen as the final product and central value of European progress. The main figure among them was the famous literary critic Vissarion Belinskii (1811–48). In the 1830s he was a Right Hegelian, trying to reconcile himself with the Russian reality, as a necessary phase in the unfolding of the objective Reason of History. At the beginning of the 1840s he rebelled against this historiosophical theodicy, vindicating the value of individual freedom and the role of negation in historical processes. The logic of his philosophical position led him to open conflict with Slavophile romantic conservatism. In contrast to the Slavophile concept of an integral, pre-individualised person, he conceived personality as a radical negation of unreflective faith and tradition, saw the essence of history in the growing individualisation of people and rationalisation of society, accepting – although not uncritically – the bourgeois progress as a means to the further Westernisation of Russia. The reforms of Peter the Great were for him not a national apostasy but a turning point in the transformation of the patriarchal Russian people (*narod*) into the modern Russian nation (*natsiia*).

Similar ideas were championed by the liberal historian, Professor of European History at the University of Moscow, Timofei Granovskii (1813–55), who saw history as a process of the individualisation of the masses by means of thought. Granovskii's disciple, Konstantin Kavelin (1818–85), applied this conception to Russian history, arguing in his 'Survey of Juridical Relations in Ancient Russia' (published in the journal *Sovremennik*, 1847) that the Russian historical process consisted in the gradual dissolution of patriarchal bonds and their replacement by the juridical order of the centralised state, which made more room for individual freedom. Seen from this perspective, Peter the Great appeared as the first completely emancipated individual in Russian history.

Another current of Westernism was represented by the Petersburg circle of Mikhail Butashevich-Petrashevskii, active from 1845 to 1849. Its members combined the socialist utopianism of Charles Fourier with the anthropological materialism of Ludwig Feuerbach: in both doctrines they found the idea of a rehabilitation of matter and of an imminent regeneration of humanity (Fourier's Harmony, Feuerbach's idea of the disalienated God-like man of the future). Unlike Fourier, who showed no interest in political forms, they tried to link their socialism to constitutional and republican tendencies. From the point of view of the tsarist government – especially in view of the revolutionary events in the West – this combination of ideas seemed to be extremely dangerous. The main members of the circle – among them the young writer Fyodor Dostoevsky – were arrested and (in December 1849) sentenced to death. Only in the last minute before the execution was this horrible verdict commuted to hard labour in Siberia.

The greatest thinker of the Nicholaevan epoch was certainly Alexander Herzen (1812–70). In the 1840s he was a Westerniser and a Left Hegelian, trying to transform Hegelianism into a philosophy of action, centred around the concept of a free, conscious activity, changing the world in the desired direction. However, his travel to the West in 1847, especially his negative impressions of France under Louis-Philippe, undermined his Westernism and Hegelian optimism. The culmination of this disappointment in the West was the victory of the bourgeoisie in the Revolution of 1848. This was for him a violent shock, more than sufficient to destroy his faith in an inevitable, teleologically conceived progress. In the book *From the Other Shore* (1850) he proclaimed his final break with Hegelian belief in the rational laws of history. He developed in it the view of history as an eternal improvisation which never repeats itself; as a process guided not by reason but by chance and blind forces. The belief in progress, seen in this light, turned out to be a dangerous idolatry, demanding human sacrifices in the name of ideological fictions.

Having arrived at the conclusion that socialism had no chance in Europe, since Europe had already found its equilibrium in the bourgeois system, Herzen set forth a doctrine of Russian socialism, developed mainly in his works *Du Développement des Idées Révolutionnaires en Russie* (1850), *Le Peuple Russe et le Socialisme* (an open letter to J. Michelet, 1851), and *La Russie et le Vieux Monde* (letters to W. Linton, 1854). We find here some characteristic ideas of Chaadaev, of the Slavophiles, and of the liberal and democratic Westernisers of the 1840s. Like Chaadaev, the creator of Russian socialism asserted that Russia was a country without history, a country where no burden of the past would hinder the introduction of a new and better social organisation. Like the Slavophiles, he saw the immense superiority of Russia over the West in the peasant commune and in the lack of a firm juridical tradition of individual property. At the same time he remained faithful to the values of the Westernisers, epitomised in the word 'personality'. He believed that the idea of personality, which had developed in the West at the expense of the communal principles, was firmly rooted in Russia among the intelligentsia of the gentry. The task of Russian socialism was thus to reconcile the values of the Westernised Russian intelligentsia with the instinctive communism of the Russian peasantry: to preserve the commune and to render the individual free.

In spite of his disillusion with the West, Herzen chose to emigrate, settled in London and organised, with the help of Polish emigré democrats, the Free Russian Press. From 1856 he was aided in this undertaking by his closest friend, Nicholai Ogarev (1813–77). In the first years of the reign of Alexander II his publications – especially his journal *Kolokol* (The Bell) – exerted a strong influence on public opinion in Russia. It was carefully read even at the Imperial court.

3   Liberals and radicals of the period of reforms

Russia's humiliating defeat in the Crimean War, together with the unexpected death of Nicholas I, created a situation in which important social and political reforms – above all the emancipation of the peasantry – could no longer be delayed. Hence the first years of the reign of the new emperor, Alexander II, inaugurated the period of the so-called Great Reforms. These reforms were prepared in the atmosphere of a political thaw, which permitted the rise of a relatively strong public opinion with clear-cut political divisions.

A free forum for independent political opinion was provided by Herzen's publication *Voices from Russia*. In its first issue (1855) an open letter signed 'Russian Liberal' appeared. It was written jointly by two liberal historians, disciples of Granovskii, representing the Étatist School in Russian historiography: Konstantin Kavelin and Boris Chicherin (1828–1904). They declared their full support for liberal reforms from above, in accordance with the main thesis of the Étatist School, which claimed that in Russia the state had always been the leading organiser of society and the most important agent of progress.

Soon afterwards, however, the two liberals parted company. Chicherin thought that the government should be allowed to implement reforms without the constant pressure from the left; in particular, he became very critical of Herzen's radicalism, accusing him (in an open letter published in *Kolokol* in December 1858) of revolutionary impatience and of relying on poetic caprices of history. Herzen reacted to this by describing Chicherin as an old-style Hegelian, worshipping the state and believing in an inflexible historical necessity. Kavelin sided with Herzen seeing Chicherin's Open Letter as a betrayal of political opposition and support of the government.

The emancipation of the peasantry, announced on 3 March 1861 (19 February, Old Style), put on the agenda the problem of political changes. Some wealthy nobles, grouped around Senator Nikolai Bezobrazov, demanded an oligarchic constitution, which would compensate them for the loss of control over the peasantry and for the increased influence of bureaucracy. In the broadly conceived liberal camp the constitutional issue proved to be deeply divisive. The provincial assembly of the Tver' gentry, led by Alexis Unkovskii, surprised the government by renouncing the class privileges of the gentry and demanding a convocation of a popularly elected constitutional assembly. An even more radical position was taken by the emigré aristocrat, Prince Pëtr Dolgorukov who (in his pamphlet *O Peremene Braza Pravleniia v Rossii*, Leipzig, 1862) demanded the immediate transformation of Russian autocracy into a constitutional monarchy with representative government. Kavelin, however – this time in full agreement with Chicherin – strongly opposed such views. In his brochure *Dvorianstvo i Osvobozhdenie Krestian* (Berlin, 1862) he argued that the necessary prerequisite of political liberty must be a strong middle class and a good, well-entrenched system of civil law.

A similar differentiation of opinion existed among the Slavophiles. Alexander Koshelëv, invoking the precedent of seventeenth-century Land Assemblies in Russia, advocated the convocation of a national Land Duma which would act as an advisory body and counterbalance St Petersburg officialdom. Samarin criticised this proposal as serving the particularistic interests of the nobility and set against it the ideal of a centralised and bureaucratic social monarchy.

However, the most important political force of the period of reforms was the newly emerged democratic radicalism. It expressed the ideas and attitudes of the nonconformist elements among the *raznochintsy*, i.e. the intelligentsia of non-gentry social background, the educated commoners. The chief organ of these radicals was Nikolai Nekrasov's journal *Sovremennik*, and its ideological leaders were both sons of provincial priests: Nikolai Chernyshevskii (1828–89), a journalist with a scholarly, encyclopaedic mind, and his disciple, the literary critic Nikolai Dobroliubov (1836–61). In their philosophical views they represented materialistic scientism and critical rationalism. The concepts of reason and nature served them as powerful means in the struggle against the institutions, traditions and prejudices of a semi-feudal society, a struggle similar to that once waged by the thinkers of the French Enlightenment; for that reason they were given the name of Russian Enlighteners.

The most sophisticated version of this materialistic outlook were the views of Chernyshevskii, who considered himself a disciple of Feuerbach; his *Anthropological Principle in Philosophy* (1860) was an attempt to combine naturalism with some elements of Hegelian dialectical historicism. The crudest version was the militant utilitarianism of Dmitrii Pisarev (1840–68), publicist of the journal *Russkoe Slovo*. In his articles he advocated the attitude of thinking realists whose literary prototype he saw in Bazarov, the nihilistic hero of Turgenev's novel *Fathers and Sons*; in defiance to the generation of the fathers, i.e. the generation of Belinskii and Herzen, he called himself a nihilist – in the sense of a radical rejection of everything that could not be justified from a realistic, utilitarian standpoint. He was especially obsessed with a struggle against aesthetics; that is, the creation and consumption of non–utilitarian, merely artistic products. He went so far as to proclaim that Pushkin was not worth reading and Raphael was not worth a brass farthing. This aggressive iconoclasm in the domain of art was a sort of compensation for the moderation of his social programme, which was reduced to organic work for material and intellectual progress. But, obviously, it was very easy to transform his nihilism into a tool of revolutionary destruction.

Chernyshevskii's importance for Russian political thought lay mostly in his critique of liberalism and in his conception of a specific privilege of backwardness which (in his view) enabled Russia, and the backward countries in general, to skip the capitalist phase of development. In his critique of liberalism, developed mostly in his essays on French political history, Chernyshevskii distinguished sharply between liberals and democrats. The first, he maintained, were concerned with political liberty, which could benefit only privileged classes, whereas the latter saw forms of government as unimportant, because what really mattered were the relations between social classes and the material welfare of the people. This conception of democracy exerted a profound influence on Russian populist thought, but, ironically, it was not Chernyshevskii's final word. In his *Letters without Addressees* (1862), addressed in fact to the emperor, he described political freedom as a necessary condition of Russian progress and supported constitutional demands of the gentry liberals of Tver'.

In his articles on political economy (which were known to Marx and highly appreciated by him) Chernyshevskii set against bourgeois liberalism a conception of the political economy of the working people. He recognised the progressiveness of capitalist development in the West but wanted for his country a more humane, non-capitalist progress, based upon communal property relations. In his *Criticism of Philosophical Prejudices against the Peasant Commune* (1859) he argued that Russia, like other latecomers to the arena of history, could benefit from the accumulated experience and scientific achievement of the West in order to skip the intermediate phases of development or at least greatly reduce their length. His argument for the Russian peasant commune was based on a dialectical view of progress. He claimed that the first stage of any development is similar in form to the third; thus primitive communal collectivism is similar to the developed collectivism of a socialist society and enables a direct transition to it.

The evolution of Chernyshevskii's thought was interrupted by his arrest (1862), followed by trial and deportation to Siberia for his alleged revolutionary activities. In prison, awaiting trial, he wrote the novel *What is to be Done?*, describing the new people of Russia, fully emancipated and wholeheartedly devoted to the cause of progress. Owing to the oversight of a censor, the novel was printed in *Sovremennik* and became a source of inspiration for several generations of Russian progressive youth.

4   Populism and anarchism

The end of the 1860s was marked in Russia by the emergence of a specifically populist revolutionary movement. The word 'populism' (*narodnichestvo*) referred originally to revolutionaries who wanted to work in the villages in the name of the authentic ideals of the peasantry (as opposed to the abstract notions of socialism, imported from the West). This tendency culminated in the great upsurge in the people's movement of 1874 and in the activities of the revolutionary organisation Land and Liberty in the second half of the 1870s. In broader, contemporary usage the term 'populism' is the common name for all currents of Russian agrarian socialism, aiming at Russia's direct transition to socialism on the basis of the peasant commune. The first fully articulated expressions of populist ideology were Pëtr Lavrov's (1823–1900) *Historical Letters* and Nikolai Mikhailovskii's (1842–1904) *What is Progress?* – both published in 1869.

Lavrov, a philosopher and sociologist who in 1870 settled in the West and became one of the recognised leaders of the Russian revolutionary movement, wrote in his *Historical Letters* about the price of progress and the debt to the people. The luxury of talking about progress, he reasoned, had been purchased by the hard labour and terrible sufferings of many generations of heavily exploited masses. The intelligentsia, i.e. the critically thinking part of the privileged minority, should make every effort to discharge this debt through revolutionary activity. Its members should be guided by the ethical ideal of the development of the individual and the gradual embodiment of truth and justice in social institutions. Hence they should reject all theories which claimed that progress was objective, inevitable and automatic. In Russian conditions such theories were just a convenient tool for apologists of capitalist development, who sanctioned and justified the sufferings of the people by referring to the objective laws of history. Against such objectivism Lavrov set his vindication of a self-conscious subjectivism. He meant by this a principled defence of ethicism in social theory, coupled with the belief in the great, sometimes decisive, role of the subjective factor in historical processes.

It is understandable that Lavrov's ideas had enormous appeal to the young idealistic intelligentsia, tormented by the feeling of social guilt, dreaming about heroic self-sacrifice and believing in the greatness of its progressive mission.

Mikhailovskii, an influential literary critic and the main representative of the populist subjective sociology, supplemented Lavrov's ideas with a theory of progress as a gradual approach to the integral, all-round personality. Opposing Herbert Spencer, and referring positively to the critique of capitalism in Marx's *Capital*, Mikhailovskii sharply contrasted true progress with capitalist development. All-round individuals, he claimed, were possible only in conditions of the least possible division of social labour; hence the natural economy of peasant communes represented a higher *type* (although not a higher *level*) of social development than the capitalist industry, maximising the division of labour in the interest of productivity and thus mercilessly transforming individuals into mere organs of the social whole. This was a skilful argument against the liberal view that capitalism had liberated the individual. It appeared in this light that the village commune was worthy of defence not only as a safeguard of egalitarianism but also, and above all, for the sake of the many-sided, all-round development of human personality, utterly impossible in the capitalist system.

Yet another variant of populism was presented in the seventies by Pëtr Tkachev (1844–86) – the leading theorist of the Jacobin, or Blanquist, current in the Russian revolutionary movement. In his social views he was a belated disciple of the primitive communism of Babeuf, vehemently rejecting bourgeois individualism. He attacked from this viewpoint Lavrov's principle of individuality, seeing it as a dangerous concession to the enemies of the people. In his programmatic article 'What is the Party of Progress?' (1870), he demanded the greatest possible levelling of individualities, the physiological, intellectual and moral equality of individuals, as the precondition of social happiness. This extreme egalitarianism was bound up in his ideology with an equally extreme revolutionary elitism. His ideal of communism was to be implemented by a vanguard party of professional revolutionaries who, having seized state power, would organise a paternalistic dictatorship, concentrating all efforts on creating a completely new type of human being.

Within the populist revolutionary movement Tkachev's position was seen, above all, as a decisive break with the view that socialists should carefully distinguish between social and political tasks, concentrating on the first and leaving political struggle to bourgeois radicals. Under the influence of Tkachev's Jacobinism, the revolutionary party People's Will declared a war against government and organised a series of terrorist attacks on its representatives. The culmination of this terrorist activity was the assassination of the emperor, accomplished on 1 March 1881.

Besides populism, another characteristic current of Russian socialist thought of the second half of the nineteenth century was anarchism. It differed from populism in seeing the source of all evil and, therefore, its enemy number one in the state.

The father of Russian anarchism was Mikhail Bakunin (1814–76). He began his revolutionary career as a Left Hegelian, during the Springtime of the Peoples represented revolutionary pan-Slavism, and at the end of his life became the recognised leader of the European anarchist movement, the chief antagonist of Marx in the First International. His main theoretical works – *The Knouto-Germanic Empire and the Social Revolution* (1871) and *Statism and Anarchy* (1873) – were passionate polemics against Marx, whom he accused of German statism and Jewish intellectualism, and whom he fought on behalf of the revolutionary spontaneity, inherent, he believed, in the character of the Latin and Slavonic peoples.

Bakunin's anarchism was not individualist, but collectivist. It was based upon a sharp distinction between society and state: the first is a natural milieu of people while the second is always an alienated power, bound up with legal compulsion and the institution of private property which destroys the innate social instincts in people's hearts. Society can perfectly dispense with the state and with all forms of intervention from without. The ambitions of intellectuals to subject social life to scientific control are especially dangerous. The scientific socialism of Marx would be necessarily bureaucratic and authoritarian; it would result in a tyranny of abstract thought over real life, in a dictatorship of the learned over the unlearned workers.

Bakunin's best-known disciple was Prince Pëtr Kropotkin (1842–1921), a revolutionary populist who in 1876 managed to escape from the Peter and Paul Fortress in St Petersburg, settled in Switzerland and became one of the leading theorists of European anarchism. He was less radical than Bakunin, concentrating on the constructive tasks of communal self-government and co-operation in social life. In his classic work *Mutual Aid as a Factor of Evolution* he protested against the capitalist, competitive model of society and against its ideological justifications in Social Darwinism. Himself a naturalist and evolutionist, he tried to show that biological evolution and social history were moved not only by the struggle for existence but also by powerful factors of co-operation. Although suppressed by statism, mutual aid was still the main force of ethical progress and would flourish in the communist anarchism of the future.

Bakunin (influenced in this respect by Feuerbach) and Kropotkin (a positivist) were decidedly anti-religious, seeing the idea of God as an expression of human alienation and a corollary to the coercive power of the state. A completely different, religious and programmatically non-revolutionary variant of anarchism was represented by the famous writer, Count Lev Tolstoi (1828–1910). Having passed through a spiritual crisis at the end of the 1870s, he developed a doctrine of Christian anarchism, drawing mostly from the Sermon on the Mount and preaching non-violent resistance to evil. This doctrine, presented by the writer in his *What I Believe* (1884), *What Is To Be Done?* (1886), *The Kingdom of God is Within You* (1893) and other treatises, was a blend of utterly rationalised, non-confessional Christianity with radical social utopianism, forcefully attacking the state and law, as institutionalised violence, condemning also the institutional churches and the entire social order based upon inequality, competition and private property. Some features of this powerful call to a return to evangelical simplicity were strikingly similar to the idealisation of the village communes in the populist utopia of Mikhailovskii.

Of course, Tolstoi treated politics with contempt and never saw himself as a political thinker. Nevertheless, his radical delegitimisation of the existing social order and of modern civilisation in its entirety exercised great political influence on the Russian intelligentsia, contributing thereby to the overall crisis of the old-regime Russian state.

5 Ideologies of reaction

Political polarisation during the period of reforms brought about the emergence of the revolutionary organisation Land and Liberty and, consequently, the consolidation of the conservative wing within the government. Soon afterwards the Polish uprising of January 1863 united Russian liberals and conservatives under the nationalist banner. Even many Russian radicals proved susceptible to demagogic arguments portraying the insurrection as a reactionary movement of the gentry, aiming at the restoration of Polish rule over Lithuania and Ukraine. Herzen, who supported the Poles on moral grounds – despite his serious doubts about the timing of their uprising and the likelihood of its success – was violently attacked for his alleged betrayal not only of Russia but also of socialism and democracy. The circulation of his *Kolokol* dwindled rapidly and never again reached its previous high level.

The chief ideologist of the chauvinistic anti-Polish campaign in the Russian press was a former liberal Mikhail Katkov (1818–87), editor of *Moskovskie Vedomosti* and *Russkii Vestnik*. Very soon he came to be the most influential spokesman of Russian conservative nationalism. He embraced the idea of transforming Russia into a unitarian national state on the French model. He saw this task as modernisation of the state but stressed at the same time that in order to fulfil its nation-building role Russian autocracy must abandon its experiments with reforms and instead strengthen itself at the expense of decentralising liberal forces. He did not hesitate to proclaim that Russian politics must be based on brutal force in the service of outspoken national egoism.

In the domain of foreign policy the main ideology of Russian nationalist expansionism was pan-Slavism. Its pioneer was the conservative historian Mikhail Pogodin (1800–75). His favourite dream was the creation, under Russian hegemony, of a powerful union of Slavonic peoples, having its capital in Constantinople and resurrecting thereby the ancient Byzantine Empire. Nicholas I, deeply committed to the principles of dynastic legitimism, refused to embrace such ideas, but the Crimean War offered Pogodin a chance to advocate pan-Slavism as a natural and permanent programme for Russia's foreign policy. The ideological justification of this programme was reduced to a self-contradictory mixture of conservatism with nationalism. Despite his deeply ingrained social conservatism, Pogodin supported revolutionary nationalism among the Balkan Slavs, invoking the principle of national self-determination; on the other hand, however, he refused the right of self-determination to the defeated Poles (even suggesting the deportation of patriotic Polish nobles to ethnic Poland, or to distant places within the Empire). He also proclaimed the urgent need of the Russification of the Baltic peoples, including their conversion into Orthodoxy. His pan-Slavism, therefore, had almost nothing in common with the idealistic projects of a free federation of Slavonic peoples, which were developed by progressive thinkers of the first quarter of the century.

A somewhat different kind of pan-Slavism – trying to make use of the Slavophile legacy – was represented by the influential journalist, editor of several Slavophile newspapers, Ivan Aksakov (1823–86). He was sometimes very critical of the government but, on the whole, advocated a conservative, religiously oriented ethno-nationalism, extremely hostile towards the Poles and the Jews, whom he perceived as the most dangerous national minorities in Russia.

The chief theorist of pan-Slavism as a form of the self-conscious Russian nationalism was Nikolai Danilevskii (1822–85). In his book *Russia and Europe* (1871) he grounded his views on Russia's historical mission on naturalistic foundations, rejecting the Christian universalism of classical Slavophilism and replacing it by a theory of self-contained and incommensurable civilisations, which he called historico-cultural types. This led him to conclude that in politics there is no place for ethical idealism, that the Slavs, under the Russian leadership, should think only about the interests of their historical type, abandoning the utopian aim of universal Christianisation of life and ceasing to see themselves as serving the cause of an imaginary Humanity. The European or Germanic-Romanic civilisation had already entered the period of decline, but the Slavs, fortunately, did not belong to Europe – they were destined to create, under Russian hegemony, a civilisation of their own, more powerful and many-sided than all previous ones. To achieve this end Russia should capture Constantinople, liberate the Slavs from Turkish and Austrian yoke, unite them under the wings of the Russian eagle and thus become an invincible political power. This policy of external expansion should be supported by strengthening the Russian state from within, by suppressing the destructive influences of the decadent West and limiting the effects of the newly introduced liberal reforms.

Danilevskii's theory of the pluralism of civilisations was taken up and developed by Konstanin Leontiev (1831–91) a romantic reactionary who for several years had served as a Russian consul in Turkey. His philosophy of history (presented most fully in his *Byzantinism and Slavdom*, 1875) set forth a conception of the triune process of development. Each of the multiple civilisations ascends from an initial simplicity to the stage of flourishing complexity through the individualisation of its parts and their integration in a despotic unity of form. After this, development passes into the stage of decay – the individualised parts become again homogeneous, the cultural whole undergoes a destructive process of secondary simplifications and levelling interfusion, resulting in its final dissolution and death. The modern capitalist West is a sad example of a dying culture; Russia can still avoid this gloomy fate, on condition, however, that it bases itself on Byzantinism, whose legacy has been preserved in its autocracy and in the Orthodox Church.

Unlike Danilevskii, Leontiev was not a pan-Slavist. He saw nationalist movements among the Balkan Slavs as purely tribal, culturally impotent, serving in fact the cause of Westernisation and, therefore, not worthy of Russian support. He thought that Russia should concentrate its efforts not on external expansion but on internal regeneration, through the policy of salutary reaction. But he shared the pan-Slavist belief that if Russia had a historical mission, it could consist only in the future conquest of Constantinople and restoring the ancient Byzantine Empire.

The assassination of Alexander II by the revolutionaries from People's Will was followed by a period of sweeping reaction, promoted and symbolised by Konstantin Pobedonostsev (1827–1907) who (in the years 1880–1905) held the position of Director General of the Holy Synod. He was very influential already in the 1870s, as member of the Council of State and the private tutor of the heir to the throne, the future Alexander III. He believed, following the German Historical School of Law, that each nation evolves according to laws specific to itself and rooted in the collective unconscious of the masses, so that imitating other nations is always unnatural and injurious. Russia's native principle was the inviolability of Orthodoxy and autocracy. Practical implementation of these views was seen by him as encouraging anti-Semitism and conducting a policy of Russification that systematically restricted the rights of religious and national minorities in the empire.

Among Pobedonostsev's closest friends was Fyodor Dostoevsky (1821–81). As the editor of the conservative journal *Grazhdanin* (Citizen) he used to visit Pobedonostsev every Saturday for long discussions and even asked his advice when he was writing *The Brothers Karamazov*. He was also an admirer of Danilevskii and, on the whole, there is no doubt that as the author of *The Diary of a Writer* he did enough to be regarded as a conservative nationalist, distinguished mostly by his anti-Catholic obsessions. But, nonetheless, it is impossible to treat him as a conventional representative of reactionary trends of his time. Even his imperial messianism, proclaiming that Constantinople should be Russia's, had a profoundly idealistic, universalistic dimension, sharply contrasting with Pobedonostsev's reactionary isolationism and Danilevskii's *realpolitik*. As a writer of genius he stood above the political divisions of his time. His masterful analysis of the crisis of modern individualistic humanism, shown in his great novels as a theomachic struggle for the achievement of Mangodhood (as opposed to Christian Godmanhood), strongly influenced a number of highly diverse thinkers in Russia and in the West. Its political importance increased after the Bolshevik Revolution because it became widely recognised as a prophetic foreboding of revolutionary totalitarianism and a profound insight into its nature.

6   Vladimir Soloviev and Boris Chicherin

An important aspect of Dostoevsky's justification of imperial messianism was his belief in the universalism of the Russian soul, requiring a truly universal Orthodox-Christian state. Vladimir Soloviev (1853–1900), who was to become the greatest religious philosopher of Russia – and who was very close to the author of *The Brothers Karamazov* in the early period of his life – developed these ideas in the spirit of Chaadaev's religious Westernism, diametrically opposite to Dostoevsky's anti-Catholic bias. His philosophy of history defined Russia's great mission as the creation of a universal, freely theocratic empire, uniting the Eastern Church with the Latin Church under the authority of the pope and thus bringing about the reconciliation between East and West (see Soloviev 1888, 1889). He visualised this empire as a state deeply committed to the liberal ideals of the rule of law, tolerance and equal rights for religious and national minorities. He saw Katkov's and Danilevskii's nationalism as profoundly non-Christian and incompatible with political unity of a multinational state. In a series of articles published between 1883 and 1891 in the liberal *Vestnik Europy* (later collected in two volumes under the title *The Nationalities' Problem in Russia*, 1891) he attacked all forms of ethnic nationalism, as well as the Slavophile idealisation of Orthodox Christianity, claiming that true patriotism had nothing in common with national exclusivity and that commitment to Christianisation of political life should not be confused with confessional fundamentalism.

In his system of ethics entitled *A Justification of the Good* (1897), together with the small volume *Law and Morality* (1897), Soloviev made another contribution to Russian liberal thought: his conception of law as an enforceable minimum of morality gave law a function of ensuring for everyone a minimum of positive freedom, including the minimum of welfare necessary for a dignified existence. Soloviev saw dignified existence as a new right of man, something legally claimable, and interpreted it very broadly: as including not only rights to employment, to proper working conditions and proper earnings, but also to rest and free time. He exhibited also ecological concerns, demanding legal safeguards for the preservation of the natural environment.

In this manner classical liberalism of the free market and absolute private property was transformed into a new social liberalism. No wonder that Boris Chicherin, the most consistent representative of classical liberalism in Russian thought, strongly disapproved of Soloviev's position. In his view Soloviev's definition of law misinterpreted the nature of both law and morality. Law, backed by the coercive power of the state, defines only the limits of liberty, whereas morality defines dictates of moral duty, which cannot be legally enforceable. Hence, if law and the state were conceived as serving moral aims, the inevitable result would be boundless tyranny, suppressing freedom of conscience and, therefore, recalling the practices of theocracy. Seen from this perspective, Soloviev appeared to Chicherin as legitimising theocratic despotism and deserving to be called a modern Torquemada.

In his own legal theory, set forth in the two volumes of his *Property and State* (1882–3), three volumes of *A Course of Political Science* (1894–8) and in *Philosophy of Law* (1900), Chicherin combined economic liberalism with Hegelianism. Following Hegel, he conceived of civil society as a sphere of conflicting private interests, a sphere of individualism and economic freedom, regulated by private law, seen as the purest expression of the idea of law in general. He accused legal positivism of blurring the fundamental difference between private and public law, at the expense of the former. He insisted that this led to an illegitimate expansion of the legislative authority of the state, thus paving the way for socialism (which he saw as a total bureaucratisation of life and, therefore, a full suppression of private freedom).

As a political thinker Chicherin held the view that transition to constitutionalism in Russia should be preceded by the introduction of universal citizenship through the liquidation of the separate status of the peasantry, that is, through the transformation of millions of peasants from the status of wards of the state, attached to the compulsory rural communes, to the status of individual proprietors, subjects of private law, equal before the law with other members of civil society. He developed this view in a programmatic manuscript *The Tasks of the New Reign*, written in 1881 for the new

Emperor. Alexander III, however, chose to embark on a completely different policy. The tasks of a new agrarian reform, outlined by Chicherin, were undertaken only by Pëtr Stolypin – much too late and in very unfavourable political conditions. At the end of his life Chicherin came to the conclusion that the arbitrary rule of Russian bureaucracy could not be broken under the absolute power of the tsar. Under this conviction he published in Berlin (1900) a brochure entitled *Russia on the Eve of the XXth Century*, proclaiming the urgent need of transforming Russian absolutism into a constitutional monarchy.

Despite all differences, Chicherin and Soloviev had something important in common. Both of them paved the way for the anti-positivist revolt in Russian culture, a part of which was the impressive development of philosophical theories of law and the state. Hence they deserve to be treated as the founding fathers of modern liberal constitutionalism in twentieth-century Russia.

7 The controversy between populists and Marxists

The Russian revolutionary movement at the beginning of the 1880s was marked by the emergence, in Geneva, of the Emancipation of Labour Group (1883) – the first Russian organisation to derive its programme from the theoretical foundations of Marxism. Its leader and chief theorist was Georgii Plekhanov (1857–1918), formerly the leader of the Black Repartition – a populist organisation which opposed the terrorist activities of People's Will.

In fact the populist reception of Marxism did not begin with Plekhanov. Marx's *Capital*, which appeared in Russian translation in 1872, was widely read by all populists: Marx's description of the atrocities of the capitalist development in England horrified them and endorsed their belief that everything should be done to avoid capitalism in Russia. Plekhanov, however, was the first revolutionary theorist who discovered in Marxism the old Hegelian idea of objective historical necessity and used it against populist subjectivism. He emphatically rejected the favourable populist idea (formulated already by Herzen and Chernyshevskii) of skipping the capitalist phase and moving directly to socialism (although he knew, from Marx's letter to Vera Zasulich of 8 March 1881, that Marx himself was inclined to share this populist hope). This meant in practice that Russian socialists should accept, as historical inevitability, all the cruelties of capitalist development, including the destruction of the rural communes and painful proletarianisation of the peasantry.

In its application to the problems of Russian revolutionary movement the objectivist theory of history meant that the revolutionaries should postpone their struggle for socialism to an indefinite future, concentrating instead on the struggle for political freedom, that is, on the tasks of a bourgeois-democratic revolution. In his first Marxist books – *Socialism and Political Struggle* (1883) and *Our Differences* (1885) – Plekhanov linked this conception to programmatic Westernism, seeing the Western type of social development as the universal norm and endowing Russian Marxists with the mission to complete the work of Peter the Great. True socialism, Plekhanov argued, was impossible without a high level of economic development; hence a successful Westernisation of Russia was a necessary precondition of the victory of socialist ideals in the future. The Blanquist idea of the seizure of political power, in order to impose socialism on a backward country from above, could result only in disastrous deviations from the normal historical evolution.

In his philosophical book entitled *On the Question of the Development of the Monist View of History* (1895) Plekhanov claimed to be the most consistent and vigorous Marxist. In reality, he offered a one-sidedly deterministic interpretation of historical materialism, coupled with an attempt to formulate, in a dogmatic manner, the main tenets of dialectical materialism, deriving the necessities of history from the dialectical laws of the universe.

In the milieu of People's Will Plekhanov's position was seen as tantamount to a betrayal of socialism. More important, perhaps, was the fact that his populist antagonists could borrow arguments not only from subjective sociology but also from a theory which claimed to be entirely objective and even offered its own interpretation of Marxism. This was the theory of Vasilii Vorontsov (1847–1918), the leading representative of legal, non-revolutionary populism, set forth in his book *The Fate of Capitalism in Russia* (1882).

Capitalism in Russia, argued Vorontsov, was an artificial phenomenon, depending entirely on government subsidies. It could not successfully compete with the capital of the more advanced industrialised countries: foreign markets were already divided up, while the home market could not be extended because of the growing poverty of the masses, which was unavoidable in the early stage of capitalist development. In the West capitalism had performed a great progressive mission; in Russia, however, and in all other backward countries, it was merely a form of the exploitation of the masses for the benefit of a small, parasitic group of the population. Hence a successful industrialisation of Russia could be achieved only by means of socialist planning through the agencies of the government. Vorontsov expected, of course, that this socialist industrialisation would be less painful, more humane than the capitalist variety.

Vorontsov's ideas were developed and modified by another legal populist, Nikolai Danielson (1844–1918). He was the Russian translator of the first volume of *Capital* and considered himself to be a Marxist; his main book – *Outline of Our Social Economy after the Enfranchisement of the Peasants* (1893) – was written at the suggestion of Marx himself. He tried to apply the Marxian method to the specific problems of a backward country, formulating his task as follows: how to raise Russian industry to the high level of Western industry, increasing the welfare of the people, without falling into economic dependence on the more civilised countries. He differed from Vorontsov in advocating more radical means: he was sceptical about such half-measures as cheap credit for the peasants and co-operatives for artisans, putting more emphasis on large-scale modern industry, created and managed by the state.

From Plekhanov's point of view, Vorontsov and Danielson implied acceptance of the existing authoritarian state and, for this reason, deserved to be called police socialists. The populists, in their turn, treated Russian Marxists as disguised apologists of capitalism. The controversy between the two currents reached its climax in the 1890s, with the emergence of the so-called Legal Marxists. The leading figure among them was Pëtr Struve (1870–1944) whose *Critical Notes on the Economic Development of Russia* (1894) contained the famous sentence 'We must concede that we lack culture and go to the school of capitalism.' After Struve's book, Legal Marxists became influential allies of Sergei Witte's programme of capitalist industrialisation of Russia, having its own periodicals and representatives in universities and other institutions of higher education.

For the average Russian *intelligent* at the turn of the century Marxism in Russia began not with Plekhanov, but with Struve. At the first congress of Russian Social Democrats in Minsk in 1898, it was Struve who was invited to write the party's *Manifesto*. Nevertheless, it is difficult to deny that the Legal Marxists (as Struve himself later admitted) were essentially liberals, interested above all in economic growth and constitutional freedom. Even in their theoretical constructions they were, from the very beginnings, very unorthodox. Struve anticipated in his *Critical Notes* some of the crucial ideas of Bernstein's revisionism and openly stated that Marxism lacked as yet a proper philosophical foundation. At the end of the 1890s he took an active part in the German revisionist movement. In his study *Die Marxische*

Theorie der Sozialen Entwicklung (1899) he accused Marx of utopianism and described social revolution as an essentially evolutionary process.

Around 1900 the majority of former Legal Marxists broke their association with Russian social democracy and joined the ranks of the emerging liberal movement. Some of them, under Struve's leadership, organised in Switzerland the Union of Liberation which was to become the nucleus of the Constitutional Democratic Party.

In addition to the Emancipation of Labour Group and the Legal Marxists there also existed in the 1890s a third variant of Russian Marxism: revolutionary Marxism, developing in the provinces, especially in the Volga area, and continuing in many respects the revolutionary tradition of the People's Will. In the 1880s a typical representative of this transitional, semi-Marxist, semi-populist intellectual formation was Alexander Ulianov (1866–87), executed in 1887 for an abortive attempt on the life of the emperor.

His younger brother, Vladimir Ulianov – the future Lenin – soon became a fully-fledged Marxist. His Marxism, however, differed in many respects from Plekhanov's orthodoxy. These differences were very visible in his polemic treatise *The Economic Content of Populism and its Criticism in Mr. Struve's Book* (1895). Unlike Plekhanov, the young Lenin from the very beginning suspected Struve of being a bourgeois liberal and accused him of putting too much stress on winning the support of the bourgeoisie while completely disregarding the need of a revolutionary alliance with the peasantry. He cut himself off from Struve's objectivism, setting against it the spirit of the party commitment (*partiinost'*). In accordance with the populist legacy, he vindicated the great role of subjective factors – revolutionary consciousness and organised will – in historical processes. Finally – in contradistinction to both Struve and Plekhanov – he treated Russian capitalism not as the social order of the future, which could fully develop only in conditions of political freedom, but as a structure definitely established under autocracy and sufficiently ripe to justify a relentless class war against it.

At the threshold of the twentieth century all participants of the great debate of the 1890s were ideologically prepared to organise their own political parties, actively engaged in the struggle against autocracy. The views of Vorontsov and Danielson, modified to suit revolutionary aims, became the ideological foundation of the neo-populist party of the Socialist Revolutionaries, established in 1901 and headed by Victor Chernov. Legal Marxists, as already mentioned, underwent an evolution towards liberalism (combined, as a rule, with transition to philosophical neo-idealism) and provided ideological direction to the Constitutional Democratic Party. Social Democrats at the Second Congress of the Party (1903) divided themselves into Mensheviks, who remained faithful to Plekhanov's deterministic Marxism, and Bolsheviks, who embraced Lenin's voluntaristic credo – which had evolved by then into his pre-totalitarian conception of the vanguard party.

25

European political thought and the wider world during the nineteenth century

CHRISTOPHER BAYLY

As this volume demonstrates, Western political and social thought in the late eighteenth and nineteenth centuries is a vibrant area of study. Yet scholarship has for the most part remained confined to political and philosophical developments in the European and American heartlands. This is strange because one of the most important dimensions of European thought during this period was the manner in which it achieved an international reach, and in some areas, a near hegemony over the minds of extra-European intellectuals. To an extent even greater than in the case of earlier expanding 'world religions', Islam, Christianity and Buddhism, European state-theory ideology, liberalism, and later, integral nationalism, 'scientific' racism and communism, became the currency of political debate for elites across the world. These ideas also influenced a wider range of popular movements, so that, by 1900, the leaders of anti-government protests in places as far distant as Santiago, Cape Town and Canton invoked the notion of their 'rights' as individuals and as representatives of nations.

This is not to suggest that historians of European empires and extra-European nations or language groups have failed to produce powerful studies of political ideas. John Pocock early and resolutely set his study of late civic republicanism within an Atlantic framework. In British imperial history, the study of the appropriation by administrators of utilitarianism and liberalism in extra-European contexts, begun by Eric Stokes (1989), has been developed by Mark Francis (1992), Lynn Zastoupil (1994) and Uday Mehta (1999), among others. David Armitage (2000) has extended the study of imperial ideology backward in time to its roots in ideas about British domestic sovereignty. Historians of legal norms, such as Lauren Benton (2002), have demonstrated how Whig ideas about the primacy of private property were generalised across the world and were in turn modified by the expansion of European empires.

There are also to hand expert studies of liberalism and republican ideologies in one country or cultural area. Notable among these are Albert Hourani's *Arabic Thought in the Liberal Age, 1789–1939* (1970) and David Brading's *The First America* (1991). Finally, throughout the nineteenth and twentieth centuries Asian, African, European and American scholars continued to consider the great bodies of political and social theory which emerged from the classical traditions of Asian and Islamic civilisation. These remained of significance even for those extra-European intellectuals who began to use and adapt Western ideologies. Typical here was P. V. Kane's massive *History of Dharmasastra* (1960–8) which provided an exhaustive analysis of classical Indian political theory and social thought. Similarly, the Reverend James Legge and many later Chinese commentators revised and interpreted the 'Analects of Confucius', while Middle Eastern scholars continued to study and comment on the works of the classical Arabic theorists, such as Ibn Khaldun.

It remains true, however, that while the history of science, economics and political practice have already taken the 'global turn', the 'global history' of Western political thought remains quite fragmented and localised. By a global history of Western political thought I mean a study of the generation, reception and transformation of European and American political ideas by intellectuals and administrators in public debates across the rest of the world. The field would also encompass the reception and transformation of non-European social, religious and political ideologies in the Western world. This chapter can do little more than suggest some directions which might be taken to remedy that deficiency. It represents an initial survey, rather than a substantive study. The longer-term aim of historians must be to begin to bring together the large quantities of excellent work in nineteenth-century political thought, which lie isolated in different national historical traditions. First, however, it will be useful to consider some of the difficulties of this project and suggest some ways in which they could be negotiated.

Ironically, the reason for the European- and American-centred character of the history of political thought seems attributable, in part, to one of the field's great strengths. The 'hermeneutic turn' in political thought, associated with Pocock and the 'Cambridge School', insisted on the need to understand the intentions of the authors of major political ideas – and the wider meaning of their writings – in context. These 'great works' had to be seen against a rich canvas of recessed ideology and what today would be called 'political discourse'. It was no longer good enough to reduce political thought to the study of the lineages of influences on major thinkers, on the one hand, or to see it mainly as a reflection of broad social and political conditions, on the other.

In theory, this approach should be very congenial to historians of the non-European world. As early as 1979, J. Ayo Langley began to try to apply the 'hermeneutic turn' to the wider world in his valuable work, *Ideologies of Political Liberation in Black Africa, 1856–1970* (1979). Langley showed that pan-Africanist thinkers appropriated European liberal ideologies and adjusted them to deeply held ideas of African religious or 'racial' uniqueness. Previously, if they had considered the extra-European world at all, historians of political thought often seem to have assumed that there occurred a relatively simple process of diffusion. In this process, the doctrines of Western thinkers were slowly spread across to those elite members of non-European societies who knew European languages. The power of persuasion lay in the ideas themselves rather than in the meanings attributed to them by the Asian or African thinkers who received them.

If the 'hermeneutic turn' is taken for global intellectual history, however, great conceptual, cultural and linguistic problems come into view. We have first to understand the meaning of authors such as Mill, Spencer or Comte and how European and American intellectuals and political leaders understood them. We have then to analyse the reception and transformation of such ideas by extra-European intellectuals and the publics to which they spoke. Extra-European intellectuals operated in a complex conceptual space. Most, though not all, read English, German or French. But they interpreted what they read with reference to indigenous concepts and moral sensibilities. These were rooted in ancient ideological and religious systems and influenced by popular discourses of morality and virtuous practice. In order to achieve the transformation, Asian, African and Latin American thinkers reinvented and adjusted these traditional concepts. The whole process, therefore, involved at least three transformations of meaning.

Where, again, do differentials of power fit into these transformations? Western ideas gained wider currency during the nineteenth century, in part, because they were a reflection of Western military and economic power. They were imposed by colonial regimes through educational institutions, newspapers and public political debate. Asian, African and Latin American minds were undoubtedly 'colonised' to some degree. Even in these cases, however, intellectual domination was not a simple process. To be adopted, Western doctrines had to be persuasive. They had to speak to people's conditions, but they also had to be translated, metaphorically as well as literally, and adjusted to modes of debate in other societies. Even where Western political ideas and languages of debate were quite novel, rupturing previous understandings of political good, they were subtly altered, adjusted and set to new purposes by indigenous writers and intellectuals.

Sometimes, appeals to the ideas of Western intellectuals acted merely as symbols of modernity for new classes of lawyers and state servants. In other cases, though, as for instance with *Hind Swaraj* ('Free India') and M. K. Gandhi's other early writings, non-European intellectuals were able to blend ideas from Western thought with themes or motifs from Asian or African ones. This produced bodies of hybrid doctrine, which were politically empowering because they had the capacity to subvert colonial claims to authority, but at the same time resonated with indigenous sensibilities and even bodily practices. The case of Gandhi is particularly significant. Quentin Skinner appears to suggest that, from Thomas Hobbes broadly through to Henry Sidgwick at the end of the nineteenth century, political liberty in Britain was generally understood as a negative good. Liberty consisted of an absence of restraint or coercion. Earlier thinkers from Aristotle, through the Church Fathers to the Renaissance moralists had associated liberty with a more active form of virtue, he implies (Skinner 2002, p. 104).

Yet liberty, or its analogues, had always been an active good in the major non-Western tradition of political and social thought. Gandhi himself was writing for Western as well as Indian audiences when he insisted on an active interpretation of liberty in *Hind Swaraj*. For him, self-rule or independence (*swarajya* or *swatantrata*) could only exist as a corollary of moral self-making (*satyagraha*, often loosely translated as 'soul force'). Here Gandhi had interwoven themes taken from European concepts of the good society with Hindu ethics.[1] The point, however, is that this was a transformation at the international and not simply the European level. An Asian intellectual interpreted Western ideologies in the context of Indian traditions and had then redeployed them in the Western arena of public debate (Kapila 2011; Skaria 2002).

In the longer term, indeed, one of the consequences of the internationalisation of European political ideologies was to de-centre intellectual authority and restart a flow of political doctrine from Asia, Africa and Latin America back into Europe and America themselves. Since the late Middle

---

1 Gandhi 1997, editor's introduction.

Ages, when Greek political philosophy and science had been received in Europe from Arab sources in a modified form, there had been little direct intellectual influence passing from the East or the South to the West. It was not until the early twentieth century, with the reception of Gandhianism, Maoist Marxism and the pan-Africanism of Franz Fanon and others, that the East–West flow of political ideas was initiated once again. In the nineteenth century, only theosophy and some other forms of spiritualism among Western doctrines reflected the impact of Eastern religion and philosophy. Theosophy could perhaps be regarded as a political as well as a religious system but, while it was typical of the period, it was hardly central to its thought.

Non-European influences did, however, act on and react with European thought in less direct ways. From William Robertson through to the works of Marx and Gobineau, closer observation of non-European societies and their forms of knowledge inflected the way the evolution of polity and society was understood by European theorists. German and French scholarship which used oriental texts also influenced the development of European historiography. So, even if the flow of ideas in the nineteenth century was more unidirectional than it was in earlier or later centuries, those ideas were changed in quite novel ways when they moved to Asia, Africa and Latin America, just as they were constantly being transformed within Europe and America themselves.

This chapter builds on and generalises approaches that are drawn from the history of science. Not only was physical science itself a critical backdrop to non-Western appropriations of European political thought during this period, but historians of science have been relatively more successful in inscribing indigenous agency into a picture of Western ideological domination than most other sub-disciplines. The chapter aims, then, to account for the reception and rejection of radical concepts derived from the learned and political worlds of Europe with reference to the intellectual formation of different societies across the world. Liberalism, socialism, positivism and social evolutionism obviously spread initially from Western sources. Yet they widely mingled with and were empowered by ideas derived from indigenous rationalistic and ethical traditions. The chapter also considers how intellectuals and activists in Asia, Africa and Latin America created radical ideologies for change which spoke directly to their own condition, without a similar degree of indebtedness to Western ideas. The chapter ends with two case studies, on South Asia and the Caribbean-African worlds respectively.

1   Righteous republics worldwide

In the later eighteenth century, scholars and administrators across the world continued to interpret the abstract political ideas embedded in the great Asian and African traditions: Islam, the Indian Sanskrit tradition, the Confucian and the Buddhist traditions, among others. Many of the most famous of these works were expositions of state craft and *realpolitik* addressed to kings and generals. In these civilisations, as in the West, there was, however, another and more practical style of moral and political thinking that bore on local governance and administration. One quite general preoccupation was the form of the 'righteous city' and the dangers to good government posed by corruption and tyranny. This was a widespread theme throughout Eurasia, Africa and the Americas. Developments since the 1970s in the historiography of Western political thought have made it easier to see both linkages and analogies in global political thought during the age of revolution and the first period of worldwide imperial expansion. It is worth briefly considering these varied understandings of righteous society, because they provided, as it were, the matrix of doctrine and sensibilities to which modern liberalism and rights theories were later adjusted.

John Pocock and Bernard Bailyn argued that thinkers in the civic republican tradition[2] emphasised the importance of the patriarchal household rather than the market and highlighted the obligation of the individual citizen and of the republic to pursue virtue. In the civic republican tradition, the enemies of virtue were corruption and luxury, particularly the corruption and vices of the royal court and its mercenary hangers-on. In the British and North American worlds, this tradition was associated with what Pocock called the 'country party' which opposed the tyranny and idolatrous religion of the 'court party'. Rather than being the harbingers of a free market commerce, the tradesmen, the usurer and the hoarder were figures of detestation to many American and French radicals.

In a similar vein, David Brading, writing in 1991, discerned an older tradition of 'creole patriotism' working within the movement to Latin American emancipation from Spanish rule. This persisted even while the early liberal economists were constantly on the lips of the leaders of opinion

---

2 I emphasise the European civic republican tradition here not because it was the only or even the dominant tradition of political and social thought which predated the liberal age. Traditions of *realpolitik*, divine monarchy or millenarian levelling, were equally important. What has come to be called civic republicanism was in many ways, however, the lowest common denominator of European thought and the one most commonly invoked by its dominant oligarchies.

and the Church Fathers continued to inspire conservatives. Figures such as the mercy-giving Mexican Virgin Mary, Our Lady of Guadalupe, and a myth of descent from the old Aztec Empire were prominent symbols of this tradition. Creoles, such as Fray Servando Teresa de Mier, the Dominican theologian and patriot (Brading 1991, pp. 582–602), based their case on an ideology of righteous conquest and summoned up the spirit of the land in their support. These were themes which sit uneasily with modern liberal political theory based on individual rights of property.

This re-evaluation of political theory and its representations in Europe and its former American colonies is an important development for the writing of global history. It has the effect of diminishing the distance between Western ideas and the major strands of non-European political thought. Indeed, ideas analogous to European traditions of civic republicanism had flourished in many world societies. Anthropologists, for example, have shown how pre-colonial Africans used ideologies of good kingship to justify the overthrow of wicked and ineffectual rulers. J. D. Y. Peel (2000) has demonstrated this particularly effectively in the case of the West African Yoruba, a people who recorded their struggles to maintain a harmonious society and wise kingship through bardic myths which stressed the role of the honourable householder and the role of friendship in structuring the polity. Wise counsel, care for the toiler and the desire to be ruled by virtuous patriarchs were, quite understandably, the social goods sought by intellectuals in all agrarian and early commercial societies before industrialisation. In contrast, what was perceived as corruption, although understood differently in the various traditions, seems to have legitimised dissent almost universally.

In Japan, the violation of the rights of the 'noble peasant' by a corrupt court, which had diverged from the norms of the classic Confucian writings and their respect for the ancestors and the workings of nature, was a potent theme. Ogyu Sorai, probably the most influential thinker of eighteenth-century Japan, attacked samurai corruption and merchant violations of moral economy. He saw this as a way of safeguarding the regime (Totman 2000, pp. 264–5; cf. Yashinaga 1992). His early nineteenth-century followers elaborated this critique at the same time as they became aware of the need for self-strengthening against the West. In China, the rise of royal despotism and corrupt officials were taken to be the outward signs of the decay of a political order. Before the impact of Western ideas was registered, nineteenth-century Chinese intelligentsia, working within a Confucian framework, called for the monarchy to relinquish some of its autocratic power in the interests of the body politic. They argued that officials should be able to admonish the rulers in cases of bad government. Intellectuals such as Wang T'ao (1828–97) drew on 'A Plan for the Prince' of Huang Tsung-hsi (1610–95). This work in turn looked back to the consensual form of government that supposedly characterised the Han period, rather in the way that European civic republicans looked back to the Roman Republic (Cohen 1974, pp. 43–4). The theme of the improvement and empowerment of a civil bureaucracy stands in contrast to the European classical notion of *res publica*, of course. But it is noteworthy that Wang T'ao also wished to consult 'public opinion' on the promotion and transfer of officials. This was on the grounds that 'ordinary people might be simple, but they were the most fair-minded' (Cohen 1974, p. 41).

These are cases where we can find analogies to Western ideas of the good city in other complex, non-Western polities which sought to inflect the principle of power with a concern for justice. Elsewhere, as in the case of Islam, the connections were more direct. In Muslim polities, the doctrine of holy war, the 'lesser *jihad*', was always at hand for rebels and resisters against European rule. Yet scripture tightly constrained its invocation. Instead, much early Muslim nationalist and pan-Islamic thought harked back to the medieval Arab and Persian scholars' attempts to reconcile Aristotle's civic morality with the Prophet's norms of the godly life. These had been expressed in the ethical literature of the Islamic world (in the *akhlaq* tradition) (cf. Thompson 1839 and Tusi 1969). One feature of what has been called the 'Ottoman renaissance' of the seventeenth century was the translation of Aristotle into the Ottoman language. Many editions of his works were printed in the nineteenth century. Nineteenth-century Arab, Persian and Javanese (cf. Florida 1995) thinkers argued that Western invasion and corrupt forms of indigenous governance spread the evils of bad counsel, usury, the violation of men's homes and the dishonouring of women.

Here one can glimpse a direct, if distant connection between the archaic European traditions of civic republicanism and the political ethics of an extra-European society. Aristotle was common to both civilisations. Even radical conservative ideologies within the Muslim world, such as purist Wahhabism, which emerged in eighteenth-century Arabia, looked to the restoration of the ideal *madina* or *polis*, governed by God's revelation. Abdul Wahhab and his followers across the Muslim world sought to purge the cities of polytheistic innovation (Al-Rashid 2002).

But their doctrine was also directed to ending the oppression of the poor by the rich and reinstating the Prophet's traditions of charity and benevolence. It was this tradition within Islam of 'purging the city' which made Aristotle so congenial to its medieval thinkers and their eighteenth- and nineteenth-century interpreters. As in the thought of American patriots, so too, some traditions of Islamic thought, especially within its Shi'a branch, held that since religious authority was eternal, it should be protected from the intrusion of the state.

There are good reasons for treating these varied political traditions as analogues to, or even distant relatives of European civic republicanism. Though they were inflected with religious ideas and imagery, all these traditions were distinct from the millenarian religious ideologies that existed in most cultures. Though they could accommodate kings, and in the case of the *akhlaq* tradition were patronised by kings, to one degree or another they sought to limit royal power by emphasising the king's pivotal role in a wider republic of virtue. Of course, the similarities between them lay more in their application, than in their overarching cosmology. Hindu Buddhist ideas of 'cosmic retribution' (*karma*), for instance, or Confucian ideas of 'harmony' stood on quite distinct ideological foundations from those of the Aristotelian *polis* or Christian commonwealth. Yet benevolent patriarchy, good council, the idea of humoral balance in land and people along with hatred of corruption and luxury were common to all.

This was not because the political thought of all traditions 'evolved' in a similar direction. It was instead because these traditions of thought were reappropriated and reinvented in different societies to fill similar 'ecological niches', in Ian Hacking's phrase (Hacking 1998). With the global spread of commerce, luxury and large-scale states in the early modern period, people across the world perceived similar moral and political dangers. They feared respectively courtly corruption in Europe and the American colonies, the 'reign of King Silver' in China and the pollution of the land by the 'drunken butlers of the Europeans' in India. Arguments for the restoration of the 'virtuous city' spoke to people's conditions in all these now interlinked contexts. In the course of the nineteenth century, they bonded with and transformed incoming Western ideologies.

2   The advent of liberalism

The ideas of liberalism, nationalism, secularism and the self-determination of peoples were closely connected in that they all presupposed the action of rational individuals singly or as collectivities. A new language of politics was created by the French and British thinkers of the eighteenth century and its practical implications were made clear in the first libertarian spring of the American and French revolutions. As conventional as this theme may seem, the writings of contemporaries leave no question of the carrying-power of such ideas. Young people, not just in Western Europe and North America, but across the world, woke up and saw their situation afresh. The movement of Russian liberal nobles in 1825, which was dedicated to securing a constitution from the autocratic tsar, reflected this ideological tumult. The reforming nobles invoked older notions of the virtuous republic alongside the rights of man, the checks and balances of the American constitution and the glorious tableaux of radical nations under arms, which they had recently glimpsed in Naples, Portugal and Spain (Dixon 1999, p. 208). One of their key intellectuals declared:

This divine law was decreed for all men in equal measure, and consequently everyone has an equal right to its fulfilment. Therefore the Russian people is not the property of any one person or family. On the contrary, the government belongs to the people and has been established for the good of the people and the people does not exist for the good of the government.[3]

In a very different context, Ignacio Altamirano (1834–93), the Mexican Indian radical, urged his countrymen to 'love the patria and consecrate themselves to science', singling out the ideals of the French Revolution as a permanent goal for Mexico (Brading 1991, pp. 663–4). French-speaking Ottomans had quickly become aware of the ideas of the revolution through the *Gazette Française de Constantinople*. By 1837 Sadik Rifat Pasha, an Ottoman ambassador to Vienna, was writing about the relationship between 'liberty' and classical Islamic notions of justice (Lewis 2002, p. 51).

The works of John Stuart Mill became a bible for Latin American liberals in the 1850s and 1860s. In Brazil, the abolitionist, Joaquin Nabuco stated: 'I am an English liberal... in the Brazilian parliament' (Graham 1972, p. 263). The Meiji reformers of the 1870s in Japan secured copies of the life of George Washington. Low-caste western Indian reformers of the 1850s read Hume, Voltaire, Tom Paine and Gibbon (O'Hanlon 1985, p. 83). Munshi Abdullah, the first modern writer of the Malay world, drew on Western liberal themes and Muslim notions of enlightenment when he attacked the ignorance and corruption of the Malay rajas in the 1820s (Milner 1994, pp. 10–31).

All these emerging varieties of political thought appropriated and reworked the classical European ideologies of liberalism: the stress on

3 P. I. Pestel cited in Vernadsky *et al.* 1972, p. 514.

individual rights, property, and the rule of law and the morality of the market. They developed these themes, however, to a much more limited degree than the European writers. This was in part because liberal thought itself registered an enduring tension between the concept of absolute individual rights and reverence for traditions and the spirit of nations, as writers as varied as Berlin, Himmelfarb and Ryan have pointed out. In the writings of many continental European thinkers the struggle for individual liberties was subsumed into an argument for the integrity of nations, their culture and language. Here Johann Gottfried Herder was an enduring influence. It was the activist Giuseppe Mazzini, however, who was most widely translated into Chinese, Japanese, Bengali, Hindi, and many other languages. Liberalism therefore made its journey overseas already wrapped in the integument of an organic view of the nation. In the British tradition, too, rights theories were tempered by ideologies of paternalism. The John Stuart Mill of *On Liberty* took a strikingly more radical approach than the Mill of the 'Spirit of the Age'. This latter essay took the view that most men, even systems of representative government, should 'fall back on the authority of still more cultivated minds, as the ultimate sanction of the convictions of their reason itself' (Himmelfarb 1990, pp. 40–1).

Sentiments like these 'bonded' with understandings of hierarchical civil virtue in the political traditions of other societies, to the extent that they generally eclipsed the more radical formulations of individual rights. So liberal imperialism among colonial writers was matched by liberal patriotism among non-Europeans. Despite the attacks of James Fitzjames Stephen on Mill's supposed radicalism, Mill himself doubted that Asian and African peoples could properly exercise their individual rights except in the context of European tutelage. It was out of this conviction that the liberal imperialist doctrine of 'trusteeship' emerged in the late nineteenth century. Yet this conservative turn was common to early Asian and African nationalists as well. They also insisted on the role of tutelage by virtuous elites, a theme which had been prominent in the earlier traditions of the 'righteous city'. In his later works, the Chinese reformer Wang T'ao, mentioned above, asserted that China's survival as a nationality and a culture depended on the cultivation of learned experts to guide the people. Wang applauded the consultative nature of the English constitution and the French Third Republic. Yet this was because he saw Britain and France as benevolent oligarchies, not as incipient democracies. Throughout his writings he advocated the need for 'men of ability' trained in the Chinese classics and also alert to Western science. He wrote to the modernising governor of Canton,

Li Hongzhang, in 1865 'Men of ability are to a nation what energy is to a human being' (quoted in Cohen 1974, p. 161).

This is not to say that the more radical interpretations of individual rights associated with the French Revolution, Paine, Wollstonecraft and Gouges had no effective influence on the nineteenth-century extra-European world. It is true that most active movements of resistance against European imperialism adopted neo-traditional forms of cultural protectionism as slogans for activism. All the same, groups of reformers working in the interests of slaves, low-caste people, peasants and women echoed the Rights of Man. They did so against the background of linguistic shifts similar to those that created the sense of 'rights' as absolute truths, rather than the gift of kings, in Western Europe. For instance, the Sanskrit-derived term *adhikar* originally meant power devolved by, or derived from a sovereign and had a meaning similar to *recht* in medieval Europe. In south India, for instance, there was a form of local official called an *adhigari*. In the hands of radical Indian reformers this word, too, came to mean an absolute and self-evident right.

Apart from catalysing such changes in meaning, European rights theories stamped a degree of uniformity and mutual translatability onto diverse sets of sentiments by which subordinated groups in non-European societies claimed moral worth. For instance in Japan, Shinto-Buddhist ideas of *karma* and regeneration gave rise to the idea of the 'noble husbandman'. A stoic, peasant-patriot, in the wider moral cosmos, he was worth as much as any other being, however socially lowly. The husbandman figure was often compared favourably with deceitful samurai and court hangers-on in the literature of the Tokugawa period (*c.*1600–1868). Modernising reformers in Japan in the 1870s and 1880s sought to give the new Meiji constitution a more popular basis by blending these older ideas with transformed Western concepts. They sang the praises of the noble husbandman, but they also distributed Japanese translations of Mill's *On Liberty* and Samuel Smiles' *Self-Help* during their political campaigns (Sukehiro 1989, pp. 480–6). In a sense, Mill was incorporated into the pantheon of Shinto ancestor-deities.

This hybridising of rights theories took a different form in the case of low-caste people in India. Here, those who were ritually low in the Hindu ranking scheme commonly claimed a more elevated lineage on the basis of caste legends. They might assert, for instance, that they were descendants of rulers or Brahmin priests or noble warriors who had lost caste as the result of malign fate. In western India during the 1860s and 1870s, low-caste reformers associated with Joti Rao Phule constructed rights arguments from a number of different sources. They drew on indigenous traditions of devotional religiosity (*bhakti*) which proclaimed the soul's equality before God (O'Hanlon 1985). They pointed to their historic importance and later degradation as a result of Brahminical or, sometimes, Muslim tyranny. Yet they also made direct references to Tom Paine and to Christian missionary preaching on spiritual equality. These European references energised and generalised indigenous claims to respect. They did not create them *de novo*.

It was perhaps in the world of abolitionism and of freed African slaves that rights theories had their most unambiguous impact. The Declaration of the Rights of Man and of the Citizen led directly to the temporary abolition of slavery in France and its colonies. Condorcet, Sieyès and Mirabeau, among others, built their opposition to slavery on Enlightenment theories of absolute human rights, even if their practical efforts mirrored the Christian humanism of Wilberforce. The 'Black Jacobins' of the West Indian slave revolts of the 1790s and 1800s localised these arguments and developed them into a theory of government for the liberated plantations. Hereafter, in the Americas and the Caribbean black and white anti-slavery activists deployed both natural rights theories and Christian humanism against slave-owners. North American slave-owners, in their defence, appealed to something like Burke's organic view of the commonwealth. Conservative churchmen and magnates in central and south America appealed to Aristotle on the 'naturalness' of slavery.

Natural rights theories were also received and transformed by Creoles and people of mixed European and Indian race in Mexico and Peru. Here, theorists blended them with indigenous forms of civic republican patriotism. Mexican rebels against Spanish rule as well as post-independence reformers argued that men were born free. Yet they also enlisted the idea that Mexicans and Peruvians as a whole inherited the sovereignty of ancient Aztec and Inca kingdoms to buttress their claim against Spanish despotism. Mexican soil was not only a land of free peoples originating in Asia, it was also visited by the Virgin Mary in the form of Our Lady of Guadalupe. These doctrines, did not, of course lead to a rapid emancipation of Indians, let alone black slaves. Yet they did provide a pool of indigenous radical thinking which persisted down to the time of the Mexican Rebellion of 1911–15.

3   From liberalism to cultural protectionism

The previous section argued that classical liberal rights theories were often received in non-European societies in a manner that embedded them in indigenous traditions of civic virtue. These local traditions were all, to one extent or another, imbricated with religious concepts. Indigenous thinkers generally selected the more conservative elements of liberal ideology which emphasised the history and organic unity of human communities, rather than those which asserted unmediated rights. These fitted well into local understandings of hierarchy and order. More importantly, they spoke to the need for self-strengthening which spread across all extra-European civilisations, subject or partially independent, as European dominance of the world reached its high point after 1850.

One area where this was particularly clear was in the reception and use of classical political economy. In general, even those Asians, Africans and Latin American writers who argued for human rights were firm in their opposition to free trade. Of course, European thinkers in the tradition of Adam Smith and Condorcet understood free trade as the analogue of 'moral independency' and political freedom. It was a moral as well as a political theory, as Emma Rothschild (2001) has emphasised. A few writers such as Ram Mohun Roy and Alexander Crummell, both of whom are discussed below, accepted the need for free trade on the grounds that it afforded protection against the violence of armed monopoly companies such as the East India Company and the various Africa companies. Roy even argued that the European emigration into the subcontinent which would follow free trade might create a kind of Indian Brazil in which the common interest of Anglo-Indian Creoles, Indian indigenes and mestizos would guarantee some constitutional freedoms to all Indians (Ghose 1887, II, pp. 613–19).

In general, however, economic protectionism was quickly associated with cultural self-preservation. It was therefore Friedrich List and other advocates of national political economy who were pressed into service. The assault on 'Smithianismus', or 'animal political economy' (Rothschild 1998) was more or less contemporaneous in Prussia, Hungary, Brazil and India. List was read in Bengal by the 1840s. Calcutta intellectuals also noted those passages in the writings of Adam Smith and J. S. Mill which conceded that war and national protection might be valid arguments against free trade. It is not clear when List was translated into Chinese, but Wang T'ao, Feng and Kang Youwei all marshalled strong arguments against free trade which worked in the interests of Britain and wiped out indigenous industries. In works written after he had visited England and France, Wang compared the modern international system to China's early period of 'warring states', before the universal rule of Confucian norms had been established by the empire. In such conditions, nations had the right and duty to protect their industries and artisans. In 1865, he wrote to Li Hongzhang that the problem of getting the European barbarians in hand was two-sided. It involved establishing Chinese 'economic control' and the promotion of China's 'national dignity' (Cohen 1974, pp. 60–70). Both these themes were entirely compatible with earlier Chinese norms of statecraft. The Ming had attempted to discipline 'King Silver' and promote righteousness by closing the country. The Qing had created the state monopoly, the Cohong, and sought to exclude British opium imports for similar reasons. From Meiji Japan to Brazil and Argentina economic and cultural protectionism went hand in hand. The idea of a virtuous royal or natural monopoly to ensure that artisans and workers secured employment and a just price emerged in different political languages. The concept bonded in different ways with the inheritance of List.

Alongside free trade, another key doctrine of nineteenth-century radicalism was the expansion of electorates towards a universal franchise. Here again the hierarchical and paternalistic elements within the liberal formulation were in perpetual tension with the dictates of universal rights. Outside Europe, both colonial administrators and indigenous literati adduced further arguments to temper such radicalism. Even advanced liberals, headed by John Stuart Mill, broadly denied the capacity of Indians, Chinese or Africans to rule themselves on the grounds that their domestic life was defective and that centuries of oriental despotism had inured them to autocratic rule. This was a view they inherited from eighteenth-century writers. Native self-rule could only follow on from enlightenment over the longest possible term. The most radical European reformers, such as Allan Octavian Hume, founder of the Indian National Congress, resorted to the fiction that Indians were fit for self-rule because they were 'Aryans', honorary white men, in a sense. Where the British introduced tiny non-European electorates, as in India, Egypt and the Caribbean after 1883, these were seen as adjuncts to the mechanisms of taxation, or sops to rising nationalist opinion, rather than as schools for self-government. The New Zealand measures after 1867, which gave seats in parliament and later voting rights to some Maori, seems to be a partial exception here. Yet these Maori were seen as a civilising agency for their less tractable brothers (Belich 1996, pp. 265–6). Here the concept of tutelage surfaced again.

Indigenous literati quite often tacitly supported these positions. Islamic theory contained the theory of the shura, technically a representative body of all believers. The Koran, Hadiths and medieval reworkings of Aristotle emphasised the importance of consultation and good counsel. Yet the tradition also gave much weight to the advice of the learned (the *ulama*) and people of property. Both conservatives and populists within the Ottoman Empire and its dependencies argued against the 'parliaments' that were periodically established after 1840 on the grounds that they tended to oligarchy and corruption and interfered with good government. In other traditions, the superior weight of Brahmins, Buddhist monks or samurai was similarly recognised.

Philosophical objections to extending the franchise reached their most intense in the case of women's votes, indeed in reaction to any form of participation by women in public life. British and other European theorists argued against women's votes on the grounds that it would divide families as well as because of women's mental incapacity. Where women franchises were conceded, as in South Australia or Wyoming, leaders argued that women might domesticate their savage frontier males. Women's right to representation was only conceded very late, if at all. The position of Muslim reformers illustrated this very well. In Egypt, Qasim Amin wrote of 'the emancipation of women' and said Muslim treatment of them violated Islamic beliefs. He was vigorously attacked (Badawi 1978, p. 90). The reformer, Rashid Rida, wrote 'A Call to the Fair Sex' in which he claimed that women were better treated in Islam than in Western societies and had unspecified political rights. But when a woman in one of his audiences said that women should be able to mix with men on a freer basis, Rashid Rida denounced her as an apostate (Badawi 1978, p. 111). These reformers were mainly concerned with the rights of subject populations and of nations, not those of individuals, male or female.

4 National essences and race

After 1860 classic liberalism had passed its peak in Europe. Social Darwinism stressed the development of societies as organisms, not as bodies bound by social contract. Many theorists, including self-styled liberals such as Fitzjames Stephen, argued for a greater role of the state. Idealist philosophers returned to virtue and downplayed rights. This shift was even more apparent outside Europe and the United States, where liberalism had already been reinterpreted to suit local conditions and local philosophies. A major factor here was the feeling in Asia and the Middle East that the virtue of whole civilisations was under threat from increasing Western military and economic dominance. In different ways theorists as varied as Kang Youwei in China, Nakae Chomin in Japan, M. K. Gandhi in India and Jamal al-din al-Afghani in the Islamic lands invoked religion, nation and culture as entities to be served and protected. At the same time, surviving predispositions within non-European political philosophies determined the reception, 'capture' and use of these new Western theories.

A classic case was the reception of the thought of Auguste Comte in the extra-European world, as it has been described by Geraldine Forbes (1999). Positivism was conceived as a radical prophecy of the passage of humanity into a new age of reason and science. Even in Britain and France, however, positivists quickly transformed the doctrine into a kind of secular religion, emphasising Comte's transcendent deity rather than the coming age of reason. In Japan, Comte was understood as a critic of what they saw as the 'feudalism' of the old order. His followers, however, saw no incompatibility between this and advocacy of a new form of devotion of the emperor and exaltation of Shinto spirit worship. In India, positivists read Comte's works on the banks of the Ganges as if they were sacred scripture. In Latin America, they were annexed by military modernisers who wanted to break the residual hold of the 'Spanish feudal spirit'.

Herbert Spencer stands comparison with Comte as the English-speaking world's most celebrated thinker among non-Europeans in the second half of the nineteenth century. In Europe and America it was Spencer's individualism and radical *laissez-faire* philosophy which attracted most attention. His *The Man versus the State* took late nineteenth-century liberals to task for becoming paternalistic interventionists, as Tories had once been. The emerging class of industrial magnates on both sides of the Atlantic, notably Andrew Carnegie, took this to heart.[4] Outside Europe and the United States, however, it was Spencer's understanding of polity and society as evolving organic beings which resonated best with local political sensibilities. Kang Youwei and other Chinese reformers, for instance, used early translations of Spencer to argue that the Chinese people would evolve through struggle to a new racial and national perfection. For them, Spencer seemed to hearken back to Confucian and Daoist notions of the polity as a harmonious and sentient being. His radical individualism and *laissez-faire* principles were given much less attention in their analyses. Spencer's organicism, like the racial ideologies of some of his contemporaries, seemed to find an ecological niche in societies whose leaders searched for unity where caste-like divisions of status were prominent.[5]

4 Spencer 1969, editor's introduction.
5 For Japan see Brown 1955, a study written in the shadow of the Second World War, but still valuable.

This type of appropriation was later to overtake classical Marxism. Where non-European thinkers took up Marx's notions it was the primitive communist ideal of sharing within the ideal polity which came to the fore. Class struggle and the rights of the alienated worker received much less emphasis before the radical movements of the 1920s. The struggle against colonialism became the struggle of cultures, not of classes. In China, too, the young radicals who began to espouse Marxism in the dismal 1890s fell back on the traditional denunciations of corruption and the oppression of the poor which echoed in the Taiping and Boxer rebellions. They thought that what they believed to be the growing 'power of the rich', people outside the quasi-Confucian moral community, could be halted by strikes, as had apparently been the case in the Tsarist autocracy (Spence 1999, p. 260). Here, as in Italy or in revolutionary Mexico, agrarianism, socialism and populist conservatism developed in the same breeding grounds as what was later to be called fascism. In China, though, new political ideas were also subtly adapted to prevailing doctrines. Hu Hanmin, an early collaborator of Sun Yatsen, wrote of socialism in 1905:

Not all collectivist theories may be applied to China in her present state of development. But in the case of land nationalisation we already have a model in the 'Well-field' system of the Three Dynasties [a very early form of joint holding and irrigation of land] and it should not be difficult to practice something indigenous to our racial consciousness in this period of political change.[6]

5   Liberalism and culture in South Asia

This chapter now goes on to consider two case studies in somewhat greater detail. These concern colonial India and early pan-Africanist political thought. In the Indian case, we see the reception of first British and, later, wider European political and social thought against the background of an intrusive form of colonial rule. British administrators and missionaries tried consciously to mould the minds of a small Indian elite by inculcating 'reason', science and, if possible, Christianity, by means of a limited expansion of Western-style education. What is striking, however, is the virtuosity with which Indian thinkers adapted Western doctrines to their own circumstances. First liberalism and later versions of idealism and even racialism were adopted and set working to national ends before the end of the nineteenth century.

6 Hu Hanmin cited in Bernal 1976, p. 71.

Between 1750 and 1900, Indians continued to pass down and adapt traditions of good government which had some common points of reference with European civic republicanism. Mughal emperors had once prized works in the Islamic-Aristotelian tradition, such as the Akhlaq-i Nasiri. The rulers of the post-Mughal successor states continued to patronise this style of text which advised on the right conduct of princes and householders. The evidence of early nineteenth-century petitions and vernacular newspapers suggests that these notions of good counsel remained central to the political language of the last semi-independent Indian kingdoms and those clerical people who went into British service.[7] It should not be thought, of course, that this tradition was necessarily an inclusive or harmonious one. In the hands of Muslim purists of the transitional period, such as Shah Wali-Allah and Shah Abd al-Aziz of Delhi, it was deployed with some ferocity against both Hindus and Shi'ites. Wali-Allah maintained the ideal of good counsel and civic virtue, but argued that the ideal city had no room for idolaters and heretics (Rizvi 1980, 1982). A parallel, Sanskritic tradition of righteous rule continued to develop in works such as the *Ajnapatra*, an eighteenth-century text on good government from Maratha western India (Puntambekar 1929, pp. 81–105, 207–33). Works such as this stressed the role of the king more centrally than the Indo-Muslim equivalent and conceived the virtuous polity in terms of a proper ordering of castes. Only after the mid-century, and partly as a result of the influence of Western conceptions of *realpolitik*, did the more 'Machiavellian' Indian tradition associated with the *Arthasastra* of Kautilya attract the attention of Indian literati.

Traditional understandings of ethical government continued to mark popular political discourse and the ideology of Hindu and Muslim reformers throughout the nineteenth century. For instance, Sir Sayyid Ahmad Khan, later founder of the Mahomedan Anglo-Oriental College at Aligarh, drew on the *akhlaq* tradition when criticising the British for unjust rule and listening to bad counsel before the Rebellion of 1857 (Khan 1858). But over time, his formulations became much more eclectic. He drew on St Paul in urging the need for friendship between ruler and ruled. He also modified European theories of the eugenic decline of races in a call for Indian Muslims to regenerate themselves through education and physical prowess, one thing which he had in common with his Hindu contemporaries.

In the meantime, Bengalis, in particular, had been engaging more directly with the liberal ideologies they read about in British books and newspapers.

---

7 These themes are explored in greater detail in Bayly 1998, pp. 64–85.

The major figure here was Raja Ram Mohun Roy, who is still rightly regarded as the first modern Indian political philosopher. Roy came from a Persian-writing Mughal service family and was influenced by Muslim monotheism and Christian ethics. He read voraciously in English and later French and died in England in 1833 while upholding the 'rights' of the now powerless Mughal emperor and condemning the abuses of the East India Company (Ghose 1887, II, pp. 525–79). Ram Mohun Roy argued for the freedom of the press and in favour of free trade, which, he believed, would banish the corruption associated with the Company's monopoly. His writings display a cosmopolitan vision quite striking by comparison with the Mills or other English contemporaries. He argued for the rights of peoples to self-determination. He supported the revolutions in Genoa, Spain and Portugal. He championed Catholic emancipation and praised Daniel O'Connell, though there is no evidence that the compliment was returned.

By contrast, Ram Mohun Roy appears to have adopted Bentham's view that the concept of absolute abstract rights was theoretical nonsense. What he advocated was an extension of Blackstone's eighteenth-century English constitutionalism to India. This was reinforced by Montesquieu's notion of the separation of powers and the rule of law (Majumdar 1934, pp. 16–17). Parliament should displace the Company and reassert good government. He thought that the British rulers should be advised by councils of learned Europeans and Indians. Local magnates, powerful merchants and intelligentsia who knew the 'sense of the country' should comment on proposed legislation (Ghose 1887, II, pp. 554–5).[8] In my view this represented not only an appeal to Whig paternalist theory, but also a reappropriation of the Mughal tradition of good counsel. This had long been epitomised by a form of representation called the *mahzar* in which the 'sense of the locality' was conveyed to the ruler through the petition of learned men, persons of good lineage and respectable merchants. Roy did not demand freedom of the press as an absolute right, but in order that the rulers should be informed of the errors committed in 'managing the affairs of a vast empire' (Majumdar 1934, pp. 64–5). Press editors were to fulfil a role similar to that of the news-writers of the Mughal regime, warning the ruler of corruption and oppression.

A more robust liberal tradition emerged quite early at the Calcutta Hindu College. A group of young men of mixed race and Bengali descent drew

---

8 This was originally Roy's evidence to the Parliamentary Select Committee on Indian Affairs, 1831.

more directly on the thought of Tom Paine and the French revolution. Called 'philosophical radicals' by the historian B. B. Majumdar, Henry Derozio, Rasik Krishna Mullick (1810–58) and their followers derided Brahminism and 'casteism' while demanding civil rights from the British (Majumdar 1934, pp. 78–155). Equally significant, was the response of a group of their neo-traditional elders who had come together in a body called the Dharma Sabha (Society for Righteous Religion) in 1830. These men were also drawn from the new intelligentsia and burgher class of Calcutta. Yet they complained bitterly against British intervention to suppress the custom of widows burning themselves on their husbands' funeral pyres (*sati*). Ram Mohun Roy had supported this intervention on the grounds of humanity, even while he rejected other attempts to change Hindu inheritance practices.

The leaders of the Dharma Sabha, however, also found themselves in opposition to Roy on the issue of free trade and colonisation. Roy believed that upright British settlers would help temper the Company's despotism and bring English liberties to India. Publicists associated with the Dharma Sabha argued that colonisation had destroyed Ireland and indigenous peoples in North America and Australia. But this early anti-colonialism was given a particular Indian inflection. The argument was made that European settlement would compromise the caste purity of Hindus. Moreover, Hindu merchant people were allegedly debarred from overseas travel because their caste would be polluted. It was only fair that they should be left undisturbed in control of Indian commerce. For both reasons, national political economy, not *laissez-faire* was suitable for India's condition. This pairing of economic and cultural protectionism appeared later even in the thought of a modernising liberal such as Bhola Nath Chunder Ghose. It anticipated Gandhi's pairing of *swaraj* (self rule) and *swadeshi* (home industry) with the idea of Hindu purity (Chunder 1869, I, p. 169). It provides another good example of the way in which nineteenth-century European political thought was adapted and transformed in the non-European world when it could adjust to particular ecological niches.

These themes and the tensions between them resurfaced in the ideologies of the Indian National Congress and its affiliated reforming associations after that body was founded in 1885. On the face of it, the Congress was a typical British liberal institution (Wedderburn 1974, pp. 1–5). Its early leaders, European and Indian, used old Whig arguments against the curse of the military-fiscal state to imply that the Government of India was starving Indian peasants in order to carry on aggressive frontier wars. On the one hand, Congressmen displayed a disinclination to consider any measures of land redistribution and argued for a permanent settlement of land revenue to encourage responsible land ownership. On the other hand, they urged the establishment of agricultural credit co-operative societies and measures to control rents. Congressmen wished to move rapidly towards a Dominion Status model of Indian government. If the issues of the rights of women and low castes were addressed at all, it was from a position of high paternalism. Low castes would have to give up their dirty habits and achieve self-control before they could take part in the political process. In this interpretation, women ought to be guided by their husbands. Conceptions of embodied worth derived from Indian classical texts were here adjusted to colonial conceptions of tutelage.

The break towards a more radical position was associated with the Liberal Member of Parliament, Dadabhai Naoroji, who argued for national political economy and protectionism, using reams of data drawn from parliamentary Blue Books. Broadly, Naoroji's position was an echo of Friedrich List and of earlier European and American advocates of protectionism. More distinctive trends of thought were, however, emerging under this sober and Victorian surface. The early Congress was implicated in the localities with various movements broadly called Hindu revivalist. Chief among these was the Arya Samaj, a modernising association whose leaders rejected 'polytheistic' medieval Hinduism and wanted to return to the pure religion of the Vedas, the most ancient Sanskrit texts. Yet for activists in the mould of the Samaj's founder, Swami Dayananda Saraswati, the Hindus were a race and a nation as well as a religious group (Saraswati 1927). Dayananda urged the coming together of all Hindus, implicitly excluding both Christians and Muslims from a central role in the Indian community. The protection of Mother Cow was a central concern of the Arya Samaj. They argued for an end to cow-slaughter on the authority of the Hindu scriptures, also adapting Western eugenic arguments that the cow was essential for the physical and economic health of Indians. Dayananda's prescriptions for marriage and sexual hygiene similarly drew on a variety of European and Indian sources. He reiterated earlier Indian ideas about the proper conditions for breeding, while at the same time adapting colonial conceptions of masculinity.

Another emerging late nineteenth-century tradition of religious and social thought, which ultimately became politicised, was the Bengali movement associated with the Vaishnavite religious teachers, swamis Ramakrishna and Vivekananda. The pioneer of the Ramakrishna social service movement, Swami Vivekananda, had read Comte, Mill and Spencer

(Vivekananda 1960, p. 77). He was initially attracted to ideas that stressed the ineffability and unattainability of Deity. Later, however, Vivekananda came to reinstate and refurbish a belief in the human need for divine love for and devotion to the Great Mother and her associated manifestation, the God Krishna. This was not so much a 'revolt against reason', as John Burrow has termed its analogues in the European context, but an attempt to energise political and social life by subsuming reason within cosmic religious passion. Vivekananda's appearance at the Chicago World Parliament of Religions in 1893 was decidedly an act of national political self-assertion. The Eastern holy man had come to prove the superiority of India's divine love and mysticism over the greedy and aggressive polities of the West.

Vivekananda's thought was covertly political and organicist as well as social and religious. He told a disciple that there were four castes in India and likewise four castes in the world. The role of the highest, the priestly Brahmin caste was fulfilled by India, while the warrior function was fulfilled by the Roman Empire and modern military states. The role of the merchant (the *bania*) was played by England, while the United States with its democratic pretensions was the realm of the *shudra* or common man (Vivekananda 1960, p. 564). A more overtly political stand was taken by Aurobindo Ghose, ideologue of nation-building through self-sacrifice (Aurobindo 1958). Worship of the Mother and opposition to the corrupting Western presence came together in the ideas of the so-called *swadeshi* (or 'Indophile') period of 1905–10, when Bengali youth turned to mass rejection of Western styles and Western goods, and instigated at the fringes a cult of terrorism against British officials. The so-called 'extremists' of this period rejected constitutional agitation for a cult of violence, which drew on Russian anarchist and Irish Fenian precedents. Their aim was a free Indian nation, but increasingly that nation was defined as a Hindu nation (Sartori 2008).

Many Indian intellectuals now take this to have been the dominant trend of south Asian ideology in the later nineteenth century. In the twentieth century it easily evolved, they believe, into what is commonly regarded as the 'Hindu fascism' of Vinayak Damodar Savarkar and the integralist RSS. This, however, would be to homogenise and caricature Indian political thought around 1900. Countering this tendency was the communitarian and antistatist thought of Mohandas Karamchand. Gandhi wove together themes from Ruskin and Tolstoy with pacifist and vegetarian Gujarati Vaishnavism. For him, as pointed out above, self-rule had to be predicated on the basis of self-control; moral, sexual and dietary. A national community in a sense was what it ate, what it wove and how it deported itself. Popular versions of this inclusive ideology, which appeared to incorporate Muslims and Christians into the body politic, had emerged in the Indian regions. In Bengal, for instance, where Muslims spoke the vernacular and used the Sanskrit-derived script, the Mother Goddess was seen in her nurturing as well as in her militant form as Kali (Bose 1997). So, too, in 1900, India supported a secular network of voluntary associations, which paralleled the Ramakrishna missions. The ideals of a body such as the Servants of India Society urged educated men to devote themselves to service of the poor in order to create a true national community. The Indian concept of *sewa*, the service of a lord or deity, had been translated into the idea of common service of the body politic. Here again, we see an example of a linguistic and conceptual transformation brought about by contact with Western political thought. Yet it was one which had already been anticipated in indigenous traditions of spiritual love (*bhakti*).

6   The African triangle: religion and emancipation

Over most of Asia and North Africa, intellectuals adapted European political ideas against the background of sophisticated indigenous traditions of thought which also claimed universal validity. In sub-Saharan Africa ethical traditions were oral and particularistic. Early pan-African political thought evolved instead in the triangle of slavery between Western Europe, West Africa, the Caribbean and the USA. Here African intellectuals seized on European theories of human rights. But, once again, these were adjusted to the sensibilities of African Christianity, and later to early anthropological understandings of the African continent itself.

European political thought had little direct impact on sub-Saharan Africa before 1900 for the simple reason that most of Africa was not conquered until after 1870. Of course, Dutch settlers in the Cape had evolved both a conservative Christian ideology of the Chosen People and a 'liberator' ideology of natural rights by the 1790s. But the Western education of Africans themselves was restricted to tiny pockets on the west and southern African coast. By the 1880s black Christian churches were springing up in several parts of the continent. These showed great virtuosity in adapting Christianity to indigenous sensibilities. They replaced the European emphasis on redemption with an African concern with mental and spiritual healing, for instance. Biblical ideas of the Chosen People were also adapted to what might be called 'Hottentot patriotism' of mixed-race and semi-acculturated

Africans on the Cape of Good Hope. Nevertheless, before the end of the nineteenth century it was mainly in the old 'slave triangle' connecting West Africa, the West Indies and the United States that something which could properly be called modern African political thought developed.

Initially, this took the form of a religious and millenarian vision of black emancipation and participation in the Christian republic. Eighteenth-century preachers among 'free people of colour' in the northern British American colonies pondered on the text of Psalms 68:31, 'Princes shall come out of Egypt and Ethiopia shall soon stretch out her hands unto God.' Loyalist blacks, escaping to Jamaica in 1783, took the message of liberation and redemption to the West Indies.[9] These prophetic themes were, however, overwhelmed and transformed by the impact of Black Jacobinism and the rise of the anti-slavery movement in Britain and France.[10] The unequivocal statement of human rights for blacks announced by Toussaint L'Ouverture in Saint Domingue, by Wilberforce in the British Parliament and by the black republican, Jean Baptiste Belley, in the French Assembly, galvanised communities of free blacks and, more distantly, slave societies. The connection was clear since Toussaint had several subordinate commanders who had fought in the French or American revolutions. No less a figure than Thomas Jefferson tried to censor reporting on Haitian proclamations of liberty in the USA.

Over recent decades, under the influence of 'Black studies' several historians tried to suggest that the great insurrection owed relatively little to European influence. Instead they depicted it as a form of *grand marronage*; a large-scale slave 'break for freedom' of the sort which had populated large parts of the Caribbean with communities of free blacks since the seventeenth century (e.g. Fouchard 1989). It was suggested that *vudun* or 'voodo', the neo-African religion, lay behind the millenarian and patriarchal form of government which emerged in Haiti. It must certainly be true that Jacobin principles were meaningful to Haitians because they spoke to existing systems of beliefs. Nevertheless, the political language of the rebels and of the later free government of Haiti was heavily imprinted with the ideas of the Declaration of the Rights of Man and it was in this form that other black and white activists understood and used them.

---

9 The best brief account is by Kwame Anthony Appiah, 'The Black World', 'Pan Africanism', www.africana.com/Articles/tt_658.htm.
10 The classic study remains James 1989.

The message was quickly received in North America. John Brown Russworm,[11] born in Jamaica in 1799, graduated from Bowdoin College, Brunswick, Maine, in 1826 as the second black graduate of a US university. In the same year he celebrated the half-century of the American revolution with a speech on the virtues of revolutionary transformation. But the revolution he spoke of was the Haitian revolution. He went on to participate in two abolitionist newspapers, *Freedom's Journal* and *Rights of All*. About the same time, Daniel Walker published *An Appeal to the Colored Citizens of the World, but especially to those of the United States of America.* This tract came close to advocating the need for a just war against oppression. It was, however, the notion of a Christian rather than a Jacobin republic which had the greatest purchase amongst American abolitionists, both black and white, and which registered its earliest impact on the African continent itself. The foundation at the turn of the century of the freed slave colonies of Liberia and Sierre Leone provided a context within which a small African-American intelligentsia could emerge. Alexander Crummell, founder of the first Negro Academy in the United States (1897), had experienced racialism in America. He moved in abolitionist circles in Britain, where he took a Cambridge degree, and had experience of teaching in Liberia (Langley 1979, pp. 23–31).

Crummell had much in common with Ram Mohun Roy. He was unconvinced by the idea of absolute natural rights and also rejected the 'atonement' idea that blacks had earned freedom through suffering (Crummell 1861).[12] He held instead that the colonisation of Africa by educated black Christians was part of God's plan to create a worldwide republic of virtue (Crummell 1856). Crummell's vision of the Christian civilising mission appears to have been heavily influenced by Bishop Butler's ethical thought. Again, this 'black Zionism' echoed some of the earlier Ethiopian discourse. But it more obviously drew on liberal imperialist and free trade doctrines. As with Roy, Crummell believed that commerce would banish the oppression associated with monopoly and ignorance.

As in India and China, though, this was a relatively brief phase. Before the end of the century black writers began to argue a relativistic case. The culture and history of the 'Negro Race', it was said, constituted a particularly favourable environment for true Christianity. Imperialism and

---

11 'Julius S. Scott on John Brown Russworm, Africans to Americans', www.pbs.org/wgbh/aia/part 3/3i3131.html.
12 Crummell was one of the first religious and political thinkers to make a transition from the atonement idea to the idea of Jesus as social exemplar, see Hilton 1988.

European domination was a destructive rather than a creative force. Edward Blyden was a West Indian-born Christian preacher (Langley 1979, pp. 35–41). He lived in both Liberia and Sierra Leone and became one of the earliest ideologues of pan-Africanism. Blyden held that the Negro race was characterised by a 'communistic' patriarchy[13] which found both Western industrialism and individualistic versions of Christianity repellent. In his book *Christianity, Islam and the Negro Race* (1887) he argued, in effect, that Islam suited African conditions better than Christianity, especially in its European missionary version. Orishatukeh Faduma (alias W. J. Davies), a Yoruba born in British Guyana, developed a more scientific version of the argument (Moore 1996). He was influenced by Liberal Protestant Theology, which had begun to postulate the need to accept African and Asian cultures in their own right. Animated by the sense that faith and reason were immanent in all cultures, liberal theologians came to stress the idea of cultural and racial difference. But they rejected the type of hierarchical racism promoted by Gobineau.[14] Faduma carefully delineated the thought underlying the 'ancient constitutions' of the Yoruba and Asante kingdoms of West Africa, displaying the movement's kinship with early anthropology. He argued that God uses the evolution of races and cultures to advance the corporate life of mankind, echoing a theme of Herbert Spencer. Africans had once created the civilisation of Egypt and, through it, Greece. They would once again rise to sanctify the world. He wrote:

The fundamental principles [of Christianity and reason] will ever remain the same, while in their application to meet the necessities of the human race, adaptation is a desideratum. This is as fair as it is scientific. Upon the Hebrew mind there is, and ought to be, a Hebrew coloring; upon the Negro mind, a Negro coloring, upon the European mind a European coloring. (Moore 1996, p. 79)

The intellectual position of Blyden, Faduma and their generation is reminiscent of that of Vivekananda. This is no mere coincidence. Protestant liberalism and pan-Africanism both flourished in the atmosphere created by the 1893 Parliament of Religions. Vivekananda, of course, elaborated his socio-political ideology in a context where the living traditions of Vaishnavite ethics and practice were all around. Blyden and Faduma viewed Africa from a distance. Their world was the world of the slave triangle and abolitionism. But pan-Africanism was not simply an invented tradition. It

---

13 Much of Blyden's sociology of Africa was written in journals after 1885. It was synthesised in Blyden 1908.
14 For specific refutations of Gobineau by pan-Africanists, see Mathurin 1976.

drew on early anthropological observation of African societies and on the memory and experience of African converts to Christianity.

Within those African societies themselves, as was observed at the beginning of this case study, Christianity was the almost exclusive form of Western thought to make an impact in the course of the nineteenth century. John and Jean Comaroff have argued that African reception of Christianity was a form of 'colonisation of the mind' which involved the erasing or total transformation of earlier ideologies. By contrast, J. D. Y. Peel and his pupils would retort that Africans and Europeans met on terms of discursive, if not material equality. Peel's major study of the Yoruba represents the most exhaustive work on African political thought yet written. Certainly, as early as the 1830s Africans in the west and south of the continent were 'converting' the Christian message. Africans downplayed the redemptive message of European Christianity. They stressed instead Christ's role in cleansing the body politic, a distant echo of African religion. They saw Christianity as a means of affirming the proper social order, organised through elders, age sets and friendship. Above all, biblical ideas of the Chosen People and the Mosaic Law provided ideological legitimation for the emergence of new forms of nationality. Amongst the Yoruba, a series of educated converts, of whom Dr Samuel Johnson was the most famous, created a new narrative of Yoruba history which was compatible with Christianity. These men erased the memory of earlier ethnic and political conflict within the 'nation'. They transformed earlier deities into historical figures. They drew on the example of Saint Augustine's conversion of the pagan English into a Christian nation (Peel 2000, pp. 278–309). The upsurge of healing cults, community-based forms of prayer and church organisation pointed forward to the way in which African churches would become the basic units for emerging African nationalism and its ideologies of *Negritude*.

7   Conclusion

A short chapter on a vast topic such as this can only hope to challenge the student of Western political thought by pointing to a seemingly obvious fact. This is that people outside Europe consistently and creatively grappled with abstract political thought during the nineteenth century. The story is one of how they received and transformed European ideologies within 'ecological niches' created by Asian, African or Latin American philosophical traditions and local socio-economic conditions. This created new schools of thought that were neither 'Western' nor Asian and African, but spoke to a common global modernity. Broadly, during the nineteenth century at least, ideologies of individual rights in the extra-European world were subordinated to ideas of order, stability and hierarchy to an even greater extent than in Europe. But there is a broader conclusion here. The very discipline of the history of European political thought might itself be transformed by a consideration of the extra-European career of these ideologies. Political ideas must certainly be understood in the light of the intention of their authors and their meaning within a wider field of discourse and public debate. Yet the history of political thought cannot really be divorced from the history of religion and the history of science, either outside or within Europe. The category 'political thought' is self-limiting. This is especially true of the nineteenth century when conceptions of polity were inflected once again with universalising religious themes[15] and expressed in terms of metaphors derived from science. Finally, the career of political ideas outside Europe makes it clear that even before the rise of modern socialist and democratic ideologies, political practice and popular conceptions of purity and justice fed back into and transformed theories of government constructed by elites. To this extent, the 'hermeneutic turn' in political theory has only just begun and the study of transcultural hermeneutics will be a discipline for the future.

15 Hilton 1988; see also Marx and Engels 2002, editor's introduction.

26

Empire and imperialism

1 Introduction

Empire is one of the most contested terms in the modern political lexicon. Over the centuries it has carried a multiplicity of meanings; today it still lacks a clear and consistent definition. Like so much of our political vocabulary, its etymological roots lie in the ancient world. It originates with the Latin term *imperium*, which designated initially the right of command (held by magistrates) within the Roman state, and which was subsequently extended to denote, in the age of Julius Caesar and Augustus, the physical space occupied by the territorial acquisitions of Rome, the *Imperium Romanum* (Richardson 1991). Subsequent European empires never fully escaped the obsession with ritual, virtue and glory, the sanction of religion, or the claims about spreading civilisation, which had been central to the Roman vision. Until the eighteenth century, when it began to be applied to foreign conquests and modes of rule, the term was employed almost exclusively in European political thought to encompass either the Holy Roman Empire or to designate the sovereign territories of individual states.[1] However, the conceptual field of empire has mutated over time, as have the practices associated with it, assuming different forms across diverse national and regional contexts.

In this chapter my focus will be limited to the political thought of European expansion during the nineteenth century. I explore, that is, some of

I would like to thank the following for providing helpful comments on earlier drafts of this chapter: Robert Aldrich, Peter Cain, Gregory Claeys, Istvan Hont, Beate Jahn, Karuna Mantena, Julia Skorupska, Gareth Stedman Jones, Casper Sylvest, and Michael Taggart. All the usual disclaimers apply.
1 On the history of the concept, and that of cognate terms such as 'colonialism' and 'imperialism', see Burbank and Cooper 2010; Armitage 2000, 2002; Duverger 1980; Finley 1976; Koebner and Schmidt 1964; Muldoon 1999; Pagden 1995; Pocock 1990. For useful historical surveys of imperial forms, see Alcock *et al.* 2001; Bayly 2004; Lieven 2000.

the theories that confronted, justified and challenged the seizure and government of non-contiguous territories during a period that witnessed a massive extension in the physical scale of empires. In 1800 the European powers between them controlled 35 per cent of the landmass of the planet; by 1878 this had grown to 67 per cent; by 1914 it reached a staggering 84 per cent (Kennedy 1987, pp. 148–9). I will not be exploring the legacies of 'empire' in the European context – for example the Holy Roman Empire, dissolved by Napoleon in August 1806 – or non-Western modes of imperialism. For much of the century, the military and commercial dominance of Britain set the terms for much of European (and later American) discourse about empire. For this reason I will focus chiefly, although not exclusively, on British political thought. Although individuals from all points on the political spectrum offered arguments in favour of empire, the most rigorous theoretical accounts, as well as the most ambitious visions, tended to emanate from self-described liberal writers. For this reason I focus mainly on liberals. The relationship between liberalism and empire was complex and variable: it escapes casual generalisation. Forged in the political and intellectual fires of the late eighteenth and early nineteenth centuries, liberalism was a multifaceted and constantly evolving constellation of positions, intermingling and often fusing philosophical ideas (some old, others new) and political-economic practices.[2] Liberals were amongst the most ardent imperialists; they also offered many powerful criticisms of empire. Despite claims to the contrary (Jahn 2005; Mehta 1999) there was no singular or inherent liberal imperial 'logic', 'impulse' or 'urge'. This line of argument seems to suggest, minimally, that a special act of will or theoretical circumspection was (and is) required to stop liberals from becoming imperialists. Whilst true of some specific articulations of liberalism, this does not paint an accurate portrait of the liberal tradition, which was itself internally contested and diverse. European liberal thought was, in general, theoretically indeterminate in regard to imperial expansion and rule.

Questions of empire were woven through the fabric of nineteenth-century political thought. Sometimes they were addressed directly, for example in the discussions about the means and ends of despotic

---

2 On the difficulties of viewing liberalism simply as a normative political theory, see Geuss 2002. For variations on a liberal theme see also the chapters in this volume by Bayly, Claeys, Harrison, Jennings, Mommsen, Rosen, Thompson, Vincent and Young.

government over subject peoples found in the writings of John Stuart Mill and Alexis de Tocqueville, or in the withering criticisms of empire offered by Benjamin Constant or Herbert Spencer. But empire also permeated, in a less direct but no less important sense, many other aspects of social and political thought, helping mould conceptions of liberty, nationality, gender and race, supporting assumptions about moral equality and political rationality, framing debates over the scope and value of democracy, and underpinning analyses of the nature of political economy, progress, civilisation and the self. Imperial ideology was diffused across an array of mediums and articulated in a variety of registers, including the creation of colonial 'knowledge' – anthropological, cartographic and technological. It shaped the development of the sciences, natural and social. It infused literature and the visual arts. Such polyphonic variation and ideological pervasiveness is hardly surprising given the pivotal role of empires in structuring world order. But the tenor and tone of imperial thought differed widely between individuals and theoretical positions, and often according to the relative power of the communities from which it emanated. Nineteenth-century European thinkers tended to exhibit great confidence, and frequently unabashed arrogance, in the perceived cultural and material achievements of their own 'civilisation(s)' in comparison with more 'backward' forms of life. This often translated into a claim about moral superiority – and hence, for many, to the justification of suzerainty. There were nevertheless significant national variations. For most of the century the British were relatively secure in their assertion of imperial power, although this was often accompanied by a nagging sense in some quarters that decline (and possibly fall) was threatening, even imminent, especially towards the end of the century; the French, on the other hand, frequently directed an envious gaze across the Channel, the universalistic aspirations of post-revolutionary republicanism tempered by a recognition of political realities. Later in the century, this combination of insecurity and emulation pervaded much German, Italian and, to a lesser extent, American political thinking. By the turn of the twentieth century many in Europe were watching nervously, torn between admiration and envy, as the United States grew in political, economic and military might. A new and potentially vast empire was looming on the horizon. The desire to compete successfully, both in economic and geopolitical terms, drove many of the debates over imperialism.

In order to illustrate the variety of imperial thought, I briefly outline the views of four influential thinkers: John Stuart Mill, Alexis de Tocqueville,

Herbert Spencer, and J. A. Hobson.[3] Before doing this, however, I explore some of the general issues motivating and giving shape to conceptions of empire in the nineteenth century.

2 Mapping the imperial imagination

Nineteenth-century European thinkers often viewed the world through a bifocal lens. Whatever their particular conceptions of empire, and independently of their location on the political spectrum, they tended to divide the peoples of the world into two categories: the civilised and the non-civilised ('savage' or 'barbarian'). This distinction did not preclude considerable variation within each category – it allowed, for example, the construction of elaborate hierarchies of the 'civilised' states, as well as between the different types of 'savage'. But the most important line carved the world into two spheres. This dualistic logic reached back to the Greek distinction between those who spoke Greek and those, the 'barbarian' (*barbaros*), who did not. It played a central role in the political thought of the eighteenth century, where it was given sophisticated historical-sociological form by the stadial theorists of development, most notably in Scotland (Hont 2005, Pocock 2005). During the nineteenth century it was crucial. Each sphere was subjected to different political, legal and ethical arguments. This bifocal world-view was, in turn, given formal expression by the majority of international lawyers during the century (Anghie 2005; Koskenniemi 2001; Pitts 2007). However, there existed no consensus about the definition of civilisation. It could be characterised according to the dominant understandings of religion found in a society, levels of technological sophistication, ascribed racial properties, economic dynamism, the structure of legal and political institutions, posited gender roles, and perceptions of individual moral and intellectual capacity, or (as was typically the case) some combination of these. This division often underpinned the justification of empire. It did so in two ways. First, it meant that 'non-civilised' political communities lacked the same protective rights of sovereign independence as the 'civilised' powers; second, that in the name of universal progress, or of a providential God, it was legitimate, and even necessary, to aid the 'immature' peoples of the world reach 'maturity'. The

---

3 Each of these thinkers is introduced in greater depth elsewhere in this volume, and for that reason I will avoid providing general accounts of their political thought. See especially the chapters by Harrison, Rosen, Jennings, Thompson and Vincent.

second did not automatically follow from the first, but they were often yoked together.

It was not only British and French liberals who spoke the language of civilisation, or employed it to defend imperialism. It was also a common theme in socialist thought.[4] Although critical of the aggressive nationalism displayed by many of his compatriots, Eduard Bernstein, a leading 'revisionist' theorist of evolutionary socialism, argued in his polemical *Vorausset-zungen des Sozialismus* that there was no good reason to view the acquisition of colonies 'as being reprehensible as such'. And he proceeded to argue that 'we can recognise only a conditional right of savages to the land they occupy. Higher civilisation has ultimately a higher right' (Bernstein 1993, pp. 169–70).[5] Ensconced in his own long British exile and reflecting on the awesome powers of capitalism, Karl Marx frequently employed forms of civilisational classification. In the *Communist Manifesto* Marx and Engels argued that the 'bourgeoisie, by the rapid improvement of all instruments of production, by the immensely facilitated means of communication, draws all, even the most barbarian nations, into civilisation' (Marx and Engels 2002, p. 224). Although he was bitingly critical of most facets of European imperialism, highlighting both the pernicious motivations and the frequently cruel results, Marx offered a qualified defence of the modernising dynamics of empire. His views on this topic, which underwent a significant change towards the end of his life, were never fully developed, and are scattered throughout his vast corpus of writings. In the early 1850s his arguments about the British Empire in India, published in a series of articles in the radical *New York Daily Tribune*, were shot through with ambivalence. On the one hand, he castigated the brutality, oppressiveness, and greed of the British – and indeed of all Western empires. He wrote that the 'profound hypocrisy and inherent barbarism of bourgeois civilisation lies unveiled before our eyes, turning from its home, where it assumes respectable forms, to the colonies, where it goes naked' (Marx and Engels 1960b, p. 81). The British were falsely cloaking their gluttony in the vocabulary of benevolence. On the other hand, the empire in India, and in particular the unleashed vigour of capitalism, had generated beneficial unintended consequences, most notably in catalysing a 'social revolution' that was reshaping

---

4 On the varieties of British 'socialist-imperialism' see Claeys 2010.
5 From 1887–1901 Bernstein lived in London, having fled an arrest warrant in his native Germany. Initially a close friend of Engels, his writings generated the 'revisionist controversy' over the future direction of socialism during the late 1890s. His views on colonialism were attacked by Karl Kautsky and Rosa Luxemburg, amongst others.

a stagnant caste-bound society. The underpinnings of 'Oriental despotism' were being eroded, allowing for the future expression of the 'grandeur and historical energies' of the Indian people (Marx and Engels 1960a, p. 36). British civilisation was, he stated, 'superior' to that of the Hindus (Marx and Engels 1960b, p. 77). Above all else, the British brought with them railways, bureaucratic rationality and industrial modernity. 'Modern industry, resulting from the railway system, will dissolve the hereditary divisions of labour, upon which rests the Indian castes, those decisive impediments to Indian progress and Indian power' (Marx and Engels 1960b, p. 80). The empire was making the world afresh. In his chapter on 'The Modern Theory of Colonisation' in *Capital* (1954b, p. 758), meanwhile, Marx lambasted capitalist practices of imperial acquisition while suggesting that the colonisation of 'virgin' lands could in principle secure the freedom of labour. From the 1870s onwards, however, Marx's argument shifted in important ways; his vision of empire was transformed as part of a general theoretical reorientation. He now theorised a transition from 'post-capitalism' to 'anti-capitalism', from conceiving of capitalism as a destabilising albeit necessary step on the road to a socialist future to seeing it as almost wholly destructive. Marx instead searched for, and eventually found, the best model for human association in primordial communities. As such, and under the influence of the ethnological writings of (amongst others) Lewis Henry Morgan, Marx's views on the effects of empire shifted from ambivalence to outright hostility (Stedman Jones 2007b).[6] But they did so only by returning to a mythopoeic pre-industrial idyll.

Civilisational arguments, then, were not confined to liberalism; they helped to structure various forms of universalistic thought. And nor were they new, or unique to the West. The distinction between civilisation was also common in Japan, China and the Islamic states (O'Brien 2006, p. 18). Such accounts did not lead inevitably to the advocacy of empire, although they certainly helped to justify it. Civilisation was also a key category for those critical of expansion. This argument took (at least) three forms. First, it could be argued that the attempt to export civilisation would invariably fail given the intrinsic difficulty of the task, and in particular the perceived recalcitrance of the target communities. This argument was increasingly popular towards the end of the century, as anthropological and

---

6 The main target for much of Marx's musings on ethnology was the 'blockhead John Bull' Henry Maine, whom Marx came to regard as fundamentally mistaken about the nature of ancient 'village communities' (Marx 1972, p. 324). On Maine, see Mantena 2010.

sociological accounts of the structure of 'native' communities became prominent in imperial debate (Mantena 2010). Alternatively, even if the spread of civilisation was both possible and universally beneficial, there were more efficient and humane modes of transmission – a case made by Richard Cobden, and many later liberal internationalists, for whom the primary engine of transformation was international commerce (Hobson 1968, chs. 8 and 13; Morley 1910, pp. 333–4). Finally, and most commonly, it could be argued that even if empire was an effective vehicle for spreading civilisation it inevitably damaged the imperial metropole, politically, economically, socially and morally. The very quest for empire was, as such, self-defeating as it challenged the forces of progress, and even the accomplishments of civilisation itself. This was the lesson that many post-Renaissance Europeans drew from the fall of Rome, and it formed a key element of the criticisms of empire offered by Bentham, Constant, Cobden, Spencer and a long line of nineteenth-century radicals.

Civilisational binaries were frequently complemented, supplanted and occasionally undermined by other attempts to classify and order the world. This often resulted from the difficulties faced in incorporating liminal societies, those that fell awkwardly between the categories of 'civilised' and 'barbarian'. China, Japan, Russia, the rapidly declining Ottoman Empire, the independent republics of Latin America freed from the mantle of a disintegrating Spanish empire between 1808 and 1826, even the countries of Southern Europe – all generated contentious debate. Other ways of dividing up the world cut across normative accounts of civilisation. For example, it was also common to judge states within the civilised world according to their purported levels of 'greatness', a label that was often but not always related to physical size, or according to whether they were among the select group of militarily dominant 'great powers'.

It has recently been argued that during the early decades of the nineteenth century there was a 'turn to empire', a move characterised by increasing support for imperial expansion and rule, especially amongst liberals. This represented a radical break from late eighteenth-century political thought, a period of 'enlightenment against empire' defined by the views of thinkers such as Bentham, Condorcet, Diderot, Herder, Hume, Kant, Smith and Voltaire (Muthu 2003; Pitts 2005). There was, however, substantial continuity between the two periods. Firstly, numerous late eighteenth-century commentators (albeit often those who fall outside of the retrospectively constructed canon) were proud adherents of the beneficial 'civilising' effects of empire. Burke was an ardent defender of a munificent vision of empire, arguing, for example, that the spread of Christianity was vital to lift indigenous populations, in particular in the West Indies and slaves in the Americas, out of their moral and political slumber (Kohn and O'Neill 2006). Adam Ferguson, another stern critic of Warren Hastings, defended a simultaneously monarchical and commercial empire. William Robertson, the author of an extremely popular history of Charles V and the Spanish Empire, argued in a manner that prefigured later liberal imperialism. Even Jeremy Bentham, who was generally sceptical of empire, occasionally resorted to outlining some of the possible benefits of colonisation. The poetry of the era can be seen in the same light: even in its most zealous anti-imperial articulations, and most obviously amongst dissenters and evangelicals, it left space for 'moral rehabilitation as a language of revitalised imperialism' (O'Brien 2001, p. 292). And second, throughout the nineteenth century numerous liberals vented stinging criticisms of empire, often in terms similar to those adumbrated during the eighteenth century. There is, nevertheless, something to be said for the argument that there was a turn towards empire, at least in so far as confidence in the ability of European powers to conquer and to rule effectively increased throughout the first half of the century, generated by (and generating) a further strengthening of the belief in the moral superiority of European political institutions and culture. During the nineteenth century the European powers vastly increased their economic and military dominance over the rest of the world, and this helped underpin an increasingly common argument that the 'civilised' had a duty – and not simply a capacity or right – to directly intervene to assist the 'backward'. This view was summarised by the British radical politician and imperialist Joseph Chamberlain in 1897: 'the sense of possession has given place to a different sentiment – the sense of obligation. We feel now that our rule over their territories can only be justified if we can show that it adds to the happiness and prospects of the people' (Chamberlain 1897, p. 3).

The same assumptions about European civilisational superiority were usually shared by enthusiastic imperialists and critics of empire, although they interpreted them in different ways. (This is one reason why the labels 'pro-imperial' and 'anti-imperial', whilst perhaps unavoidable in some instances, are usually too crude for satisfactory historical and theoretical discrimination.) Allied with other political and intellectual developments, surveyed elsewhere in this book, including the increasing popularity of theories of race, ideas about progress, and the development of the social sciences, the material and normative foundations of imperial expansion became ever more secure and deeply embedded over the course of the century.

European political thought both reflected and helped reinforce the increased confidence in the potentially transformative powers of empire.

Empire assumed many different political and legal forms. British thinkers tended to differentiate between settler colonies, such as those founded in Australia, New Zealand and Canada, and the 'dependent' empire, including most prominently India but also encompassing territories in the Caribbean and Africa. The two categories were both imagined and ruled in a very different manner, especially during the second half of the century; the former seen essentially as civilised (or at least semi-civilised) outposts of the 'mother country'; the latter as 'backward' communities in need of generous but firm rule. As the historian J. R. Seeley wrote in his best-selling tract, *The Expansion of England*:

> The colonies and India are in opposite extremes. Whatever political maxims are most applicable to one, are most inapplicable to the other. In the colonies everything is brand-new. There you have the most progressive race put in the circumstances most favourable to progress. There you have no past and an unbounded future. Government and institutions are all ultra-English. All is liberty, industry, invention, innovation, and as yet tranquillity. (Seeley 1883, p. 176)

The settler colonies, that is, were already embedded within the sphere of civilisation, and the most pressing concerns were not over how to drag them to enlightenment but rather about the most efficacious ways to regulate relations between the settlers and the indigenous communities – a theme running through many liberal accounts in particular – and to secure colonial loyalty to the 'mother country'. Both forms of empire were frequently justified using versions of a long-standing defence of territorial acquisition, which stressed that 'unoccupied' or poorly utilised land could be claimed.[7] Property rights were thus derived, at least in part, from modes of production and forms of political organisation. The perceived differences between the empire of settlement, which during the late nineteenth century was often termed 'Greater Britain' (Dilke 1868; Bell 2007), and the other aspects of empire was further reinforced by the introduction of colonial

---

7 This is often referred to as a *terra nullius*, but it is important to recognise that this is an anachronistic usage, and that the term (though not the concept or the practice) is of recent coinage (Fitzmaurice 2007). See, for uses of the concept, in historical context, Tuck 1999 and Tully 1993. It was not only liberals who drew on such arguments. In his defence of colonialism Bernstein wrote that '[i]t is not conquest but the cultivation of land that confers an historical right to its use' (Bernstein 1993, p. 170). On British socialist uses of the argument, see also Claeys 2010. Another line of argument suggested that at least some indigenous populations (most commonly Australian Aboriginals) were heading inevitably for extinction, a process that should be lamented but accepted as a necessary dimension of human progress: Brantlinger 2003.

'responsible government' (essentially limited representative institutions) in the mid-Victorian period. But the distinction between 'dependencies' and 'dominions' was not always clear-cut.[8] Caution is thus required in generalising about 'the' British Empire; in essence, there were a variety of different though interpenetrating empires, the boundaries of which were sometimes hard to discern.

Political thought during the era relied on a habit of comparison, the imperial gaze stretching across the world and back through time. Other empires, past and present, provided templates for ways of ruling, practices to emulate, as well as lessons about what to avoid. The most common historical reference point was Rome, which was utilised to bolster an array of competing and sometimes contradictory political arguments. The most common contemporary target was the British Empire, which generated both envy and derision, albeit with the former predominating. Just as French constitutional thinkers, at least since Montesquieu and up through Constant and the *doctrinaires*, had looked across the Channel for a model of balance and restraint, so French imperial thinkers frequently looked to the British for lessons in empire, both positive and negative. In considering the best policy for Algeria Tocqueville sought to learn from the experience of the British in India, as well as from the American campaign of internal colonisation. One of the key factors motivating Wilhelmine German imperial 'Weltpolitik', the quest for a 'place in the sun', during the 1890s was the belief that it was necessary to compete on equal terms with the great European empires, and in particular Britain.[9] At the end of the century numerous American imperialists also looked to Britain for guidance on how to acquire and govern their new territorial possessions, including Hawaii and the Philippines (both annexed in 1898). Indeed, one of the key texts of American imperialism, Alfred Thayer Mahan's *The Influence of Sea Power Upon History, 1660–1783* (1890), sought to model future American politics on the lessons that could be drawn from the rise of the British Empire. It was in turn fêted in Britain. But the traffic was not all one-way. Hobson drew heavily on both American imperialism (especially in the Philippines) and American economic writings to underpin his account of the roots of late nineteenth-century imperialism (Hobson 1997, pp. 76–9).

---

8 The difficulty of clearly delineating and labelling the elements of the British Empire was a recurrent theme: Cornewall Lewis 1841; Mill 1977b, p. 562; Mills 1856; and Jenkyns 1902, pp. 1–9.
9 For a striking example of this, see the writings of the scholar and imperialist Carl Peters (Perras 2004).

Critics of empire drew different lessons from the past. One of the fiercest detractors of French imperialism, the political economist and parliamentarian Amédée Desjobert, reached the opposite conclusion to Tocqueville, arguing that the British experience highlighted the ruinous expense of empire (Pitts 2005, pp. 219–25, 185–9). It was popular to point to the decline of previous European empires, especially the Spanish, and to utilise the long-standing argument that Roman liberty had ultimately been destroyed by the quest for empire. The symbolic capital of the ancient world, though, could be spent in different ways. Numerous British commentators, including Thomas Carlyle (1971, p. 202) and the historian J. A. Froude (Froude 1886, pp. 8–10; Bell 2009) were inspired by the annals of Rome, whilst others, notably James Mill, John Stuart Mill and William Ewart Gladstone, preferred the alternative model of settler colonisation presented by Greece (Gladstone 1855; James Mill 1992a; John Stuart Mill 1843). Even as the late Victorian proponents of 'Greater Britain' hymned the novelty of the British (colonial) empire, they tended nevertheless to look to America for inspiration, viewing it as a model for an expansive federal polity. Seeley (1883) even saw America as providing the template for an Anglo-Saxon 'world-state'.

Comparison could also be employed as a strategy to 'deflect moral anxiety' about the actual practices of empire (Welch 2003, p. 254). The brutality of conquest and imperial rule could be relativised, and thus downplayed, either by comparing it favourably to the gross atrocities of past empires or by arguing (as was widespread in British debates over India) that the subject populations were better off governed by the British, whatever their defects, than by another more violent imperial state. Seeley wrote of the 'unjustifiable means' by which the East India Company acquired power, adding the equally common qualifier that their behaviour was 'not as bad as many others', and stressing that such 'crimes' as had been committed, 'have been almost universal in colonisation' (Seeley 1883, pp. 135–6). It could also be argued that the imperial rulers had done so much damage to indigenous political structures that if they withdrew the resulting chaos would be devastating. For the radical politician Charles Dilke, even if the British Empire in India was secured illegitimately it was essential to remain, because after withdrawal India would fall prey to 'Russia or to herself' (Dilke 1868, II, p. 383). This was an argument that Marx also raised, without offering a clear answer. 'Indian society has no history at all, at least no known history', he proclaimed in the early 1850s. 'What we call its history is but the history of the successive intruders who founded their empires on the passive basis of that unresisting and unchanging society. The question therefore is not whether the English have a right to conquer India, but whether we are to prefer India conquered by the Turk, by the Persian, by the Russian, to India conquered by the Briton' (Marx and Engels 1960b, p. 76). The implication was that the British were acting as the 'unconscious tool of history' in bringing about social revolution (Marx and Engels 1960a, p. 37).

Much imperial thought was driven by the logic of international competition. The power and status of a country were often seen as a function of its physical size and global reach. Combined with a patriotic desire for national greatness, the concern with size and military strength led to a widespread belief in the value, indeed the necessity, of imperial expansion.[10] The obsession with scale, territory and the control of key strategic points catalysed the late nineteenth-century emergence of the field of geopolitics, popular especially in Germany, although such topics had been central to debates over empire throughout the century. Imperial discourses were also infused, although unevenly across national contexts, with 'Social Darwinist' ideas about perpetual struggle and harsh inter-state (and often interracial) competition.[11] But the political repercussions of evolution were rarely straightforward, as proponents of 'peace biology' argued that it pointed towards increasing levels of international harmony and co-operation, and virulent forms of evolutionary racism could be used to argue against imperial expansion on the grounds that this led to dangerous interracial mixing (Crook 1994; Hawkins 1997). Added to the concern with scale was the belief, still strong in the late nineteenth century, although often challenged by historians today, that great empires generated great wealth. It should be noted, however, that economic gain, whilst usually important, was far from the only or even the most prominent reason offered to justify empire. Even leading promoters of the economic benefits of empire, such as Joseph Chamberlain, stressed the role of glory, virtue and character in defending expansion (Cain 2007a). Indeed many imperialists lamented the standing given to economic calculations, seeing them as debased and lacking in the true spirit and grandeur evoked by the imperial mission.

---

10 For a good example of this, which threw in for good measure an account of the civilisational powers of commerce, see the French economist Paul Leroy-Beaulieu's, *De la Colonisation chez les Peuples Modernes* (1874). In 1880 Leroy-Beaulieu became Professor of Political Economy at the Collège de France.

11 For further discussion of race see Pick (in this volume); Rich 1986 and Mandler 2000.

3   Liberalism and empire: glory and civilisation

John Stuart Mill and Alexis de Tocqueville played crucial roles in the evolution of European liberal thought. They were also immersed in imperial
affairs, as both theorists and political actors. Although their conceptions of
liberalism overlapped on many points, their justifications of empire differed
considerably.

Following defeat in the Napoleonic wars, and under the terms of the
Congress of Vienna (1815), France was stripped of most of its imperial
possessions. This was the humiliating conclusion to a series of imperial
conflicts with Britain that had raged throughout the eighteenth century, a
period that Seeley labelled a 'second Hundred Years' War' (Seeley 1883,
p. 24). Donning the mantle of Alexander and proclaiming himself liberator
not conqueror, Napoleon Bonaparte had invaded Egypt in 1798, only to be
driven out by 1801. During the ensuing century foreign conquest appeared
regularly on the agenda of French thinkers, who often looked back wist-
fully to Napoleon's brief foray into extra-European expansion (Pitts 2005,
pp. 163–96). Benjamin Constant, the Swiss-born anatomist of the 'liberty
of the moderns', regarded Napoleon's rule as the embodiment of the 'Spirit
of Conquest' (1814). In common with most European nineteenth-century
critics, Constant viewed empire from two angles. He lamented the unjust
denial of self-government to those living in the conquered societies. 'It is
one thing', he wrote, 'to defend one's fatherland, another to attack people
who themselves have a homeland' (Constant 1988c, p. 69). And echoing a
long-standing theme in European political thought (Armitage 2002), he also
feared that the pursuit of empire challenged domestic stability and progress,
and in particular that the state centralisation and militarism necessary for
successful empire building threatened liberty. Conquest was a 'gross and disastrous anachronism', an option suited to the world of the ancients not that
of the commercially vigorous and increasingly liberal moderns (Constant
1988c, p. 55, 1988b).

As the century unfolded, this sceptical attitude, inherited from the eighteenth century, became increasingly rare in France, although it never disappeared entirely. From the 1830s French liberals, disappointed by their failure
to enact radical transformation at home and fearful of the fragility of the
country, looked increasingly to empire (Pitts 2005). Mid-century French
liberal imperial ideology was influenced in particular by Jean-Baptiste Say
and followers of Saint-Simon, most notably Michel Chevalier who drew
heavily on British and American imperial examples to advocate a global

civilising role for France (Todd 2011, pp. 175–6). Throughout the century the idea of civilisation played an important, though shifting, role in the French imperial imagination: the universal claims of the post-revolutionary French political model should, it was argued, be spread to the benighted corners of the world. This ideological projection bolstered Napoleon's North African expedition and the creation of the Institut d'Egypte in 1799, and it pervaded the official reasoning behind the conquest of Algeria, which had begun with the capture of Algiers in 1830. But it was in the second half of the century and in particular during the Third Republic, that its hold on French thought was strongest (Giradet 1972). A core aspect of the argument focused on 'mastery': 'To be civilised was to be free from specific forms of tyranny: the tyranny of the elements over man, of disease over health, of instinct over reason, of ignorance over knowledge and of despotism over liberty' (Conklin 1997, pp. 5–6). The self-proclaimed possession of such mastery opened the door to empire. Science and the 'philosophy of scientism' were also central to this vision, as influentially articulated by the republican French prime minister and colonial advocate Jules Ferry during the 1870s and 1880s (Petitjean 2004). In a speech to the Chamber of Deputies in 1884 he argued that 'the superior races have a right because they have a duty. They have the duty to civilise the inferior races' (Ferry 1884, p. 210). Many French thinkers, administrators and politicians embraced the grandiose claims of *la mission civilisatrice*. But as in Britain, intellectuals did not speak with one voice, and many remained highly critical of imperial aggression (see, for example, Louis 1905).

Tocqueville's views on empire need to be seen in relation to the post-Napoleonic political status of France and the vicissitudes of an emergent French liberalism. As much a man of the eighteenth century as the nineteenth, he combined aristocratic republicanism with liberalism. The crucial function of empire in Tocqueville's thinking has often been ignored or downplayed, with Isaiah Berlin even claiming that he was opposed to 'every form of rule by outsiders no matter how benevolent' (Berlin 1965, p. 204). Best-known for his insightful analysis of American and French democracy, Tocqueville was also an ardent proponent of French colonialism in Algeria (Boesche 2005; Pitts 2005; Richter 1963). Like his friend Mill, moreover, he was an active participant, serving as an expert on Algeria in the Chamber of Deputies (1839–51), visiting the colony on a number of occasions, and writing parliamentary reports on military and political strategy. But Tocqueville's vision of empire was not primarily motivated by a desire to civilise. Unlike Mill and also unlike many later French writers, he justified empire mainly in terms of securing national glory and on the revivifying effects of colonialism on French society. Strong national 'morale' and an active citizenry were, after all, antidotes to the dangers heralded by the spread of democracy (Kelly 1992, pp. 31, 54, 65). Power politics and republican virtue provided the foundations for conquest and colonial government. Striking a neo-Roman note, he wrote in his *Recollections* (Tocqueville 1959c, p. 79) that 'war almost always enlarges the mind of a people and raises their character. In some cases it is the only check to the excessive growth of certain propensities that naturally spring out of the equality of conditions, and it must be considered as a necessary corrective to certain inveterate diseases to which democratic communities are liable.'[12] The project of empire performed a similar function.

The colonisation of North Africa would establish the material and moral foundations for national greatness. Concerned with the moribund state of French society, which he viewed as deficient in patriotism, increasingly materialistic, and lacking adequate social cohesion and moral purpose, Tocqueville sought to reinvigorate the *patria* through foreign conquest. With 'time, perseverance, ability, and justice', he prophesied, 'I have no doubt that we will be able to raise a great monument to our country's glory on the African coast' (Tocqueville 1837b, p. 24). His conception of colonialism changed over time.[13] In his two 'Letters on Algeria' (1837) he offered an account of the possibility of slowly and sympathetically integrating, and then assimilating, the assorted indigenous populations with the French settlers, foreseeing them all living eventually under common laws and bound by mutual respect and tolerance. Following his visit to Algeria in 1841, however, he became more pessimistic about the prospects of assimilation, arguing in his 'Essay on Algeria' (1841), which was only published posthumously, that the French colonists should remain separate from, and dominant over, local communities. He turned increasingly to address questions about strategy and imperial governance. As the French became embroiled in a brutal war, he prescribed violence against those who resisted (Tocqueville 1846, 1847a, 1847b). 'In order for us to colonise to any extent', he proclaimed, 'we must necessarily use not only violent measures, but visibly iniquitous ones', and this meant that it was sometimes justified to 'burn harvests . . . empty silos, and finally . . . seize unarmed men, women, and children' (Tocqueville

---

12 Published posthumously, Tocqueville's *Recollections* are a highly selective account of his thoughts and actions during 1848–9.

13 See especially Pitts 2005, chs. 6–7, to which this overview is indebted; and also Richter 1963 and Welch 2003.

1841, pp. 83, 70). These cruel observations should be read alongside his sympathetic yet ultimately ambivalent account of the American extermination of the Amerindians in *Democracy in America* (Tocqueville 2000, pp. 302–91). It was only towards the end of his political career, in his parliamentary reports on the state of Algerian policy (Tocqueville 1847a, 1847b), that he exhibited disillusionment with the methodical violence of the occupation and acknowledged its counterproductive nature, although he never turned against the project of colonialism itself. It was here that he invoked, in desperation as much as with confidence, the universal creed of the republic. 'Let us not, in the middle of the nineteenth century, begin the history of the conquest of America over again', he warned. 'Let us bear in mind that we would be a thousand times less excusable than those who once had the misfortune of setting such examples; for we are less fanatical, and we have the principles and enlightenment of the French revolution spread throughout the world' (Tocqueville 1847a, p. 146). Instead he offered vague suggestions, modelled on British experience, for indirect rule via co-opted local elites, stressing the coincidence of interests between the colonised and the colonisers.

Tocqueville, then, saw a double movement, outwards and upwards, as an escape route from France's troubles: the quest for empire would force the metropolitan *citoyen* to face outwards, substituting a solipsistic and politically neutered individualism with a wider conception of the public (national) good; and France would climb upwards, promoted from a dethroned and demoralised great power to a resurgent force in global politics. Tocqueville's imperial vision highlights the dissonance, typical of many nineteenth-century liberals, between a belief in the principle that people have a right to rule themselves and actual support for foreign conquest. It also demonstrates the different ways in which liberals could justify empire. There was nothing inherently liberal in Tocqueville's arguments; they could have been, and have been, made by non-liberals. Indeed they displayed more than a passing resemblance to a far older language of republican imperialism. Such arguments were anathema to many liberals, including Tocqueville's British friends and correspondents, who were at pains to criticise them, for his position was grounded more explicitly in a straightforward concern with national interest than with the purported welfare of the subject populations.

In Britain, as in France, debates over the nature and justice of empire led to unusual intellectual alliances as well as to significant divergences between otherwise comparable thinkers. Political radicals, for example, offered contradictory accounts of empire. Meanwhile, people with distinct theoretical and political perspectives often converged on similar justifications for empire. A common point of agreement was the argument that the legitimacy of the imperial project derived primarily from the benefits it generated for subject populations. For example, the utilitarian 'philosophical radical' James Mill argued in 1810 that even if the British occupation of India failed to produce any economic benefits (indeed even if it resulted in significant losses) it was nevertheless warranted if it improved the lives of those it ruled over. 'If we wish for the prolongation of an English government in India, which we do most sincerely, it is for the sake of the natives, not of England. India has never been anything but a burden; and anything but a burden, we are afraid, it cannot be rendered. But this English government in India, with all its vices, is a blessing of unspeakable magnitude to the population of Hindostan.' He concluded, in a passage that simultaneously acknowledged the history of European brutality while dismissing it as of secondary importance, that '[e]ven the utmost abuse of European power, is better, we are persuaded, than the most temperate exercise of Oriental despotism' (Mill 1810, p. 371). Such views were not limited to ambitious radicals, or to utilitarians. Thomas Babington Macaulay, Whig parliamentarian, popular historian and fierce critic of Mill, offered a complementary defence of empire in a speech in July 1833 addressing the renewal of the East India Company charter. He argued that India was not yet capable of self-government, but that at some (unspecified) future date this would change, and that when this momentous transition occurred it would be the result of well-intentioned and skilful imperial 'good government'. The British would be able to congratulate themselves on a magnificent deed. 'To have found a great people sunk in the lowest depths of slavery and superstition, to have so ruled them as to have made them desirous and capable of all the privileges of citizens, would indeed be a title of glory all of our own' (Macaulay 1833, pp. 585–6).[14]

The paradigmatic defence of this 'benevolent' vision of empire can be found in the writings of John Stuart Mill.[15] Following in the footsteps of his father, Mill worked for most of his adult life in the offices of the East India

---

14 Macaulay was the author of a famous intervention in the debate between 'Orientalists' and 'Anglicisers' over how best to allocate money for the teaching of languages in Indian higher education (the former group favoured Sanskrit and Arabic, the latter preferred English). His Anglicising 'Minute on Indian Education' (2 February 1835) argued, as James Mill had also done, that the English language should be supported because it conveyed the teachings of a superior civilisation.

15 Mill's views on empire have been the subject of considerable scholarly debate. See, for example, Bell 2010; Jahn 2005; Kohn and O'Neill 2006; Mantena 2010; Mehta 1999; Mori *et al.* 1999; Pitts 2005; Sullivan 1983 and Zastoupil 1994.

Company, rising to senior rank and leaving only when the government stripped it of its charter in 1858 following the Sepoy Rebellion (1857). His life and work were inextricably entwined with empire.

Mill can be interpreted as one of a long line of utilitarian advocates of empire (Stokes 1959), an arch proponent of what Bernard Williams termed 'Government House Utilitarianism' in light of the elitism, esoteric nature, and 'important colonial origins' of the doctrine (Williams 1995, p. 166). Many utilitarians were indeed ardent imperialists, including Mill, James Fitzjames Stephen and Henry Sidgwick (Sidgwick 1891, pp. 311–28, 1902, p. 236). Stephen, a judge and jurisprudence scholar who also served as Legal Member of the Viceroy's Council in India (1868–72), sought to defend a reformulated liberalism that would govern with a 'liberal imperial spirit' (Stephen 1862, p. 82). And he argued in *Liberty, Equality, Fraternity*, his stinging assault on John Stuart Mill, that a patriotic citizenry should bask in the glory of military victories in India (Stephen 1990, p. 113). His authoritarian liberalism exemplified yet another modulation of imperial political thought. But while Stokes was correct to argue that utilitarianism had a profound effect on the government of India, not all utilitarians were staunch imperialists. Bentham was, in general, critical of empire. In offering (unsolicited) advice to the leaders of the new French Republic, he wrote that '[c]olony-holding is a species of slave-holding equally pernicious to the tyrant and the slave' (Bentham 2002b, p. 202). And in his pamphlet 'Emancipate Your Colonies!' – written originally in 1793, but only published in 1830, and aimed primarily at the post-revolutionary state[16] – he argued that emancipation was essential on the grounds of '[j]ustice, consistency, policy, economy, honour, [and] generosity':

> You will, I say, give up your colonies – because you have no right to govern them, because they had rather not be governed by you, because it is against their interest to be governed by you, because you get nothing by governing them, because you can't keep them, because the expense of trying to keep them would be ruinous, because your constitution would suffer by your keeping them . . . If the happiness of mankind is your object, and the declaration of rights your guide, you will set them free. (Bentham 1830, pp. 312–13)

This advice was not only applicable to France, but also to Britain and Spain. Indeed if the French emancipated their colonies, the British might

---

16 The document was renamed *Emancipate Your Colonies!* for its publication, under Bentham's guidance, in 1830.

be forced to follow them (Bentham 1830, p. 310). The choice between setting a positive example and coercing reluctant subject populations was stark.
'Reform the world by example, you act generously and wisely: reform the
world by force, you might as well reform the moon, and the design is fit
only for lunatics' (Bentham 1830, p. 310). He was similarly critical of Spanish imperialism in his exhortatory 'Rid Yourselves of Ultramaria' (1820–2).
But in common with virtually all self-professed critics of imperialism, Bentham was not above defending some aspects (or an idealised version) of
empire. During his long career, and to some degree influenced by shifts
in his wider economic and constitutional thought, there were times (for
example in 1801–4 and later in 1831) when he did lend heavily qualified
support to specific colonial policies. At the turn of the century, a period
in which he viewed the political world through a dark prism, he offered
some positive comments on the social and economic benefits of settler
colonisation. And towards the end of his life, and inspired by the writings of
the maverick political economist Edward Gibbon Wakefield, he produced
an unpublished plan for a new colony in South Australia (Schofield 2006,
pp. 199–220; Semmel 1970). Herbert Spencer was, as we shall see, another
utilitarian who despite his vociferous criticisms of imperialism was nevertheless willing to occasionally justify, and indeed encourage, limited colonial
ventures.

Utilitarianism, like liberalism, was theoretically indeterminate in regard
to empire. Mill's formulation of liberal utilitarianism, on the other hand,
consecrated imperial rule. He argued that in providing a global public good
the empire benefited the greatest number, bringing progress to the backward and helping to secure the stability of the international system. It was
an engine of 'improvement'. As such, the empire can be seen as providing
an enormous laboratory for his 'ethology', the science of individual and
collective 'character' that he sketched in the *System of Logic* (Mill 1974,
VII, pp. 861–75). But empire was only justifiable, he maintained, if it ultimately benefited those subjected to it. 'Despotism is a legitimate mode of
government in dealing with barbarians', he wrote in *On Liberty*, 'provided
the end be their improvement, and the means justified by actually effecting that end' (Mill 1977a, p. 224). A Tocquevillian defence of empire was
illegitimate. The connection between his cult of expertise and his views
on empire is also apparent. Mill regarded expert knowledge as the basis
for stable and judicious government, as witnessed in his discussion of the
balancing mechanisms necessary to constrain the excesses of parliamentary
democracy (Mill 1977b, pp. 448–520). He was likewise keen to stop the

national government interfering in the operation of imperial affairs. The government of India, he argued, should be left free of the fetters imposed by invidious political partisanship, bureaucratic amateurishness and moral myopia, and instead left in the hands of experienced, disinterested imperial administrators – men like himself.

Mill's understanding of the benefits and burdens of civilisation was structured by a notion of universal and sequential progress. Civilisation was a rare and fragile achievement, a level of development attained by only a very few communities (Mill 1836a; Kelly 2010, pp. 174–218). National self-determination, that other liberal shibboleth, was likewise reserved only for those who demonstrated the necessary and sufficient conditions of nationality. His famed definition of liberty, the 'one very simple principle' that governed his ideal conception of society, did not apply to those who had failed to reach the 'maturity of their faculties'. Children, the mentally disabled, and those 'backward states of society in which the race itself may be considered as in its nonage' were not included within its embrace. 'Liberty, as a principle, has no application to any state of things anterior to the time when mankind have become capable of being improved by free and equal discussion' (Mill 1977a, p. 224). Only a select few states had reached this level of maturity. Mill followed his father's view of the 'backward' condition of India, a view elaborated famously in *The History of British India* (1818), although his position oscillated throughout his career, moving from a harsh attitude to race and Indian development in his youth to a more sympathetic approach in the 1830s–40s, darkening again in the aftermath of 1857 (Zastoupil 1994, pp. 153–4). And like his father, Mill never visited India, preferring to judge it from afar. And judge he did. '[B]arbarians', he stated, 'have no rights as a *nation*, except a right to such treatment as may, at the earliest possible period, fit them for becoming one' (Mill 1859a, p. 119; see also Mill 1836a, 1977a; 1977b, pp. 566–7). This was because they were incapable of reciprocity and of following rules, and as such were not to be accorded equality with more advanced states, wherein the cognitive and moral qualities of individuals were more highly developed. The 'minds' of those lacking civilisation, he wrote, 'are not capable of so great an effort' (Mill 1859a, p. 118). This argument simultaneously denied 'barbarians' any rights against imperial conquest and supplied a justification for conquering in the first place. Mill argued, then, that the primary duty of an imperial occupying power was, through a combination of coercion (primarily legislative) and example setting, to help drag the indigenous population into a position where it was 'capable' of responsible self-government; to guide, in the common familial metaphor of the age, the children into adulthood. As he wrote in the *Considerations on Representative Government*, the imperial

mode of government is as legitimate as any other, if it is the one which in the existing state of civilisation of the subject people, most facilitates their transition to a higher stage of improvement. There are . . . conditions of society in which a vigorous despotism is in itself the best mode of government for training the people in what is specifically wanting to render them capable of a higher civilisation. (Mill 1977b, p. 416)

During the closing decades of the century, and especially in the wake of the Sepoy Rebellion and the controversy that followed the brutal suppression of a rebellion in Morant Bay, Jamaica in the 1860s, both the value and the plausibility of the civilising mission were increasingly challenged in Britain.[17] In his exposition of *Liberalism* Herbert Samuel, 'new liberal' thinker and later senior politician, praised the civilising potential of imperialism. 'A barbarian race may prosper best if for a period, even for a long period, it surrenders the right of self-government in exchange for the teachings of civilisation' (Samuel 1902, p. 330). Reflective colonial administrators such as Evelyn Baring, Earl of Cromer, also remained dedicated to the mission to civilise (Owen 2004, pp. 183–349). In the hands of thinkers such as Henry Maine and Seeley, however, there emerged a somewhat less ambitious, disenchanted vision of empire that sought to defend conquest more in anthropological, sociological and historical terms than in the name of universal morality and relentless progress (Mantena 2010). This occurred at the very time when French thinkers were placing an ever-greater emphasis on the civilising potential of empire, although the problems that had been faced in Algeria often tempered their optimism (Conklin 1997, pp. 21–3).

One theme that has often been overlooked in exploring Mill's thought is the importance he placed on settler colonisation. Whilst it is true that much of his attention was taken up with India, he also wrote widely and passionately about the economic and political value of colonies (Bell 2010). Mill was associated early in his career with the vocal 'colonial reform movement', which was influenced by the philosophic radicalism of his father and Bentham. He saw colonisation not as the imposition of 'civilisation' on the 'barbarian', but rather the formation of new and already civilised communities throughout the world. As he wrote of Wakefield's proposed settlement in Australia, 'Like the Grecian colonies, which flourished so rapidly and so

---

17 On the Eyre controversy, which involved many of the leading intellectuals of the day, including (on opposite sides) Mill and Thomas Carlyle, see Kostal 2005 and Semmel 1962.

wonderfully as soon to eclipse the mother country, this settlement will be formed by transplanting an entire society, and not a mere fragment of one' (Mill 1843, p. 739). In the early part of his career he focused chiefly on the socio-economic benefits of an 'enlightened view of colonisation' (Mill 1834, p. 733), arguing in particular that planned (and self-financing) emigration to the colonies would help to alleviate the poverty of the British working classes, while strengthening the economy as a whole (Mill 1965a, bk. 2, pp. 962–8). While this remained an abiding theme in his vision of colonisation, in the last twenty years of his life he placed considerable emphasis on a mix of socio-economic and geopolitical factors. In the *Considerations on Representative Government*, for example, he argued that colonies were valuable for at least three reasons (Mill 1977b, pp. 565–6). First, they reduced the probability of war by minimising the number of potentially aggressive sovereign units in the international system. Second, they helped to keep the markets of the world open, preventing 'that mutual exclusion by hostile tariffs, which none of the great communities of mankind, except England, have yet completely outgrown'.[18] Finally, the colonies offered a shining example to the world: 'in the case of the British possessions it has the advantage, specially valuable at the present time, of adding to the moral influence, and weight in the councils of the world, of the Power which, in all existence, best understands liberty'. Despite this optimism Mill, like Tocqueville, was critical of the actual behaviour of many settlers, especially in relation to indigenous communities (Mill 1977b, p. 571). This was a fairly common lament, and it could even act as a further justification for the extension of empire. At the turn of the century George Bernard Shaw (1900) offered a Fabian socialist defence of imperialism in Southern Africa, arguing that states, like landlords, had no special rights over the land they controlled; political action had to be justified in the name of a wider humanity. Consequently, in the absence of a world state or federation benevolent imperialism was warranted in order to protect indigenous populations from tyrannical rulers, in this case the Boers.

Mill's vision of the colonies ultimately complemented his views on despotic rule; both helped spread British values, liberty and good government in particular, around the world. Both, that is, fed the flames of progress. He conceived of the political connection with the settlement colonies as a

---

18 Mill's general views on the political economy of colonisation were influenced by the writings of Wakefield, who as well as providing inspiration for Bentham also served as a target for Marx (Wakefield 1968; Mill 1965a, pp. 120–2, 735–6 and 958–9; Marx 1954a, ch. 33; Pappe 1951).

voluntary one, however, to be rescinded the moment either party dissented. This view presupposed parity between metropole and colony in two key domains: individual rationality and political culture. This parity was entirely absent from his conception of 'barbarous' communities.

4   Liberalism and empire: ambivalence and critique

While liberals were amongst the most fervent defenders of empire, many also launched harsh assaults on what Constant had labelled the 'spirit of conquest'.[19] Two leading figures in the evolution of British liberalism, the individualist philosopher Herbert Spencer and the 'new liberal' political economist John Hobson, illustrate some of ways in which liberals of different stripes came to view empire and imperialism critically. They also articulated some of the common liberal ambivalences about empire.

Herbert Spencer has a good claim to being the most widely read philosopher of the nineteenth century, his views filtering widely throughout and beyond Europe (Harré 2003, p. 24; Bayly in this volume, Chapter 25). One of the reasons for this popularity, especially outside Europe, was the vehemence of his opposition to imperialism in virtually all of its forms. From his earliest writings in the 1840s through to his last, often desperate, outpourings in the wake of the South African War (1899–1902), he lambasted the greed, arrogance and hypocrisy of empire (Bell and Sylvest 2006; Weinstein 2005). As public attitudes and imperial thought mutated, and as 'jingoism' took hold of swathes of the British intellectual elite, Spencer remained steadfast in his opposition. His criticisms of empire should be seen as an integral element of his wider critique of political authority.

In *The Proper Sphere of Government* (1842–3), Spencer derided the 'evils' of war, and in particular wars of conquest, which diverted attention and resources away from industry and commerce, the underlying mechanisms of progress. Violence was 'inconsistent with the spirit of Christianity', retarding the 'civilisation of the world' and acting as the 'grand bar to the extension of that feeling of universal brotherhood with all nations, so essential to the real prosperity of mankind' (Spencer 1992, pp. 212–13). Although he later argued that war was an essential engine for the original development of human communities, he contended that in the modern world it had been rendered obsolete, a throwback to a darker age and a threat to the

---

19 The most consistent critics of imperialism in Britain were the positivist followers of August Comte, such as Frederic Harrison and F. S. Beesly (Claeys 2010). Many of the positivists (including Harrison) were liberals.

hard won transition from 'militant' to 'industrial' society (Spencer 1992, pp. 658–731). In an emblematic British radical idiom he decried imperialism as the preserve of the governing elite, the aristocrats, military, clergy and politicians, all of whom he routinely castigated for their mendacity.[20] The empire was a financial drain on the country, the wealth it generated ending up in the hands of a select few. 'But who are the gainers? The monopolists. And who are the monopolists? The aristocracy' (Spencer 1992, p. 220). '[A]rtificial colonisation is injurious in each of its several influences', he argued, and 'colonial trade has always been turned into a monopoly for the benefit of the aristocracy' (Spencer 1992, p. 261). Spencer's originality lay in anchoring these long-standing arguments in an idiosyncratic 'synthetic philosophy', a non-Darwinian evolutionary account of human development.[21]

In an interesting twist on the common trope of 'civilisation versus barbarism' Spencer argued that the pursuit of empire threatened the 're-barbarisation' of Britain (Spencer 1902b). It was both a cause and a symptom of the wider re-barbarisation – manifested also in the popularity of bloodthirsty literature, jingoism over the war in South Africa, the fetishisation of competitive sports (he loathed football), and the general 'regimentation' of church, schools and political life – that he thought was 'carrying us back to medievalism' (Spencer 1902c, p. 138). If left unchallenged, imperialism promised to return Britain to a state of barbarous militancy. '[M]ilitancy' and 'imperialism' were, he warned, 'different manifestations of the same social condition' (Spencer 1902a, p. 113). In 1896 he wrote to his French translator,

The truth is that, of all the feelings I entertain concerning social affairs, my detestation of the barbarous conduct of strong peoples to weak people is the most intense . . . To my thinking the nations which call themselves civilised are no better than white savages, who, armed with their cannon and rifles, conquer tribes of dark savages, armed with javelins and arrows, as easily as a giant thrashes a child, and who, having glorified themselves in their victories, take possession of the conquered lands and tyrannise over the subject peoples. (Duncan 1908, pp. 399–400)

Not only was European imperialism cynical, hypocritical and cruel, it was also, he argued, a type of 'political burglary' that was 'diametrically opposed to human progress' (Duncan 1908, pp. 399–400). It was a throwback to a more primitive age. Like Bentham, Spencer was not in principle opposed

---

20 On radical attitudes to empire, see Cain 2007b; Claeys 2007b; and Taylor 1991.
21 For further details see Francis 2007; Taylor 1992; and Weinstein 1998.

to colonisation when it was understood as a non-violent act securing and populating 'new' territories. But state involvement in such colonisation was never justified, as it led inevitably to state militancy, provided a poor deal for emigrants, and guaranteed the unjust treatment of indigenous populations. 'Our colonial history, to our shame be it spoken, is full of the injustice and cruelty, to which the original possessors of the soil have been subjected', thus demonstrating the 'inhumanity attendant upon state colonisation' (Spencer 1992, p. 224). This was an 'artificial system'. Given his numerous arguments in favour of a minimal state his opposition to government involvement in colonisation was unsurprising. But he was not opposed to a 'natural system' of colonisation, whereby people emigrated to form new communities without any government involvement, as long as this was the result of private initiative, free from the machinery of the state. This would simultaneously prevent all the dangers attendant on state 'interference' and lead to the just treatment of indigenous populations; Spencer pointed to the experience of the English in Pennsylvania as an admirable example (Spencer 1992, pp. 225–6). Such emigrants, however, were no longer to be regarded as British citizens and they could not claim 'protection from the mother country' (Spencer 1992, p. 221). No gunboats would come to their rescue.

A leading new liberal thinker and a self-professed 'economic heretic', J. A. Hobson also drew heavily from the well of radicalism in order to proffer a sophisticated and influential critique of imperialism. His account of the causal dynamics of imperialism shifted over time, as did his normative assessment of the value of empire. Here, however, I will focus on his views up to and including his seminal *Imperialism: A Study* (1902), a text that helped to set the terms for much twentieth-century debate, especially through its influence on V. I. Lenin's *Imperialism: The Highest Stage of Capitalism* (Lenin 1917; see also Lenin 1968).[22] Hobson started his career as a fairly conventional free trading liberal unionist, and indeed as a qualified defender of empire, only metamorphosing into a new liberal critic of imperialism in the early 1890s, selectively combining elements of Fabian thought, Spencer's political sociology of industrial modernisation and Ruskin's conception of organic economic society (Cain 2002). By the late 1890s he became convinced that the 'new' imperialism, unfolding mainly in 'the tropics' (Africa and Asia), represented an overriding threat to British democracy.[23] 'Imperialism', he warned, 'was not only unnecessary, it was positively harmful' (Hobson

---

22 On his link with, and differences from Lenin, see A. M. Eckstein 1991; and Long 1996.
23 For 'new liberal' criticisms of the 'new imperialism' see also Hobhouse 1972, pp. 13–56.

1898, pp. 31, 46). As with most radical critics of empire throughout the century, his primary concern was not for the victims of empire abroad but rather with the potential (and actual) damage at home. The new imperialism challenged 'peace, economy, reform, and popular self-government' (Hobson 1997, p. 126), bringing in its wake militarism, reaction and jingoism.

Hobson was motivated to write *Imperialism* by the war in South Africa. It was his third book on the topic, and the themes that it developed were partly prefigured in *The War in South Africa* (1901c) and *The Psychology of Jingoism* (Hobson 1901a). Its ambition and scope were, however, considerably grander. It offered a multicausal explanation for the emergence, since roughly 1870, of the '[e]arth hunger' (Hobson 1997, p. 13) that had gripped Britain, Germany, France and the United States. The 'leading characteristic' of this novel mode of imperialism was competition between great capitalist empires (Hobson 1997, p. 19). Its main stimulus was investment. The 'taproot of imperialism' (as he named a famous chapter) lay in the combination of over-saving amongst capitalists and under-consumption by the masses, resulting in the inability of the rich to spend or invest their money profitably in the domestic market. In search of a high rate of return they pushed for the opening of new markets abroad, which in turn required territorial acquisitions. His most powerful illustration of this point came not from the recent history of British imperialism, but from the American attack on the Philippines (Hobson 1997, pp. 76–9). Hobson's account of the underlying economic logic of the new imperialism, grounded in the 'under-consumption thesis', attributed great political influence to small groups of prominent individuals within society, and especially to financiers: 'the business interests of the nation as a whole are subordinated to those of certain sectional interests that usurp control of the national resources and use them for their private gain' (Hobson 1997, p. 46).[24] This was not Spencer's clique of traditional aristocratic monopolists, but rather a new breed of financial aristocrats, 'parasites upon patriotism' (Hobson 1997, p. 61) intent on manipulating politics for their own gain:

the motor-power of Imperialism is not chiefly financial: finance is rather the governor of the imperial engine, directing the energy and determining its work: it does not constitute the fuel of the engine, nor does it directly generate the power. Finance manipulates

---

24 Like many contemporary critiques of finance capitalism, Hobson's views were tainted with anti-Semitism (Cain 2002, pp. 84 and 92–3). On earlier socialist and radical accounts of finance imperialism, see Claeys 2007b; Claeys 2010.

the patriotic forces which politicians, soldiers, philanthropists, and traders generate; the enthusiasm for expansion which issues from these sources, though strong and genuine, is irregular and blind; the financial interest has those qualities of concentration and clear-sighted calculation which are needed to set Imperialism to work. (Hobson 1997, p. 59)

Echoing Bentham and Spencer, he argued that imperialism was '[i]rrational from the standpoint of the whole nation', although 'it is rational enough from the standpoint of certain classes in the nation' (Hobson 1997, p. 47). Utilising various forms of manipulation and misleading propaganda, this profit-driven imperialism was disguised as necessary government policy; it was a 'calculating, greedy type of Machiavellianism' wrapped in the evocative language of 'national destiny' and the spread of 'civilisation' (Hobson 1997, pp. 12–13). His analysis of the social psychology of imperialism, articulated most clearly in *The Psychology of Jingoism*, resonated with wider European developments in 'crowd psychology' (Bellamy 2003) and anticipated Joseph Schumpeter's analysis in *Zur Soziologie der Imperialismen* (1919) of the regressive, atavistic tendencies generating imperialism.

Hobson's critique of imperialism fitted his priorities as a 'new liberal' reformer. The surplus capital driving imperialism, he argued, could be spent more efficaciously on domestic social reform. Unlike Lenin, Hobson was no critic of capitalism *per se*; he sought instead to redirect capitalism in a broadly social democratic direction, bringing it under increased levels of state control in order to dampen its most destructive effects. 'It is not industrial progress that demands the opening up of new markets and areas of investment, but mal-distribution of consuming power which prevents the absorption of commodities and capital within the country' (Hobson 1997, p. 85).

Hobson's views on empire were considerably more ambivalent that those of Spencer. Empire itself was not the problem, only its malignant forms. Not only had he started out as a liberal imperialist, even when he moved into his most radical phase of critique he remained a staunch defender of certain forms of empire, including the settlement colonies, insisting on the 'radical distinction between genuine colonialism and Imperialism' (Hobson 1997, p. 36). Whereas the former represented the progressive spread of civilisation, the latter comprised the 'expansion of autocracy' (Hobson 1997, p. 27). One of the many problems with the new imperialism was that it stood in the way of imperial federation – the further unity of the British state and its settler colonies – which would simultaneously benefit the individual units and the wider world. Indeed it could help act as a brake on imperialism

(Hobson 1997, pp. 328–55).[25] At one point he argued that 'inter-imperial' federations would help to pacify world politics.

> Holding, as we must, that any reasonable security for good order and civilisation in the world implies the growing application of the federation principle in international politics, it will appear only natural that the earlier steps in such a process should take the form of unions of States most closely related by ties of common blood, language, and institutions, and that a phase of federated Britain or Anglo-Saxondom, Pan-Teutonism, Pan-Slavism, and Pan-Latinism might supervene upon the phase already reached . . . Christendom thus laid out in a few great federal empires, each with a retinue of uncivilised dependencies, seems to me the most legitimate development of present tendencies and one which would offer the best hope of permanent peace on an assured basis of inter-Imperialism. (Hobson 1997, p. 332)

Without the implied political centralisation of an imperial federation, however, the colonies themselves risked turning into semi-autonomous imperial powers, seeking to dominate the 'lower races' in their regions and dragging Britain into hazardous entanglements with other aggressive imperial states. The dangers were the same as in the 'mother country': the influence of local cohorts of financiers pushing for market expansion and plotting the 'subversion of honest, self-developing democracy' (Hobson 1997, p. 345).[26]

5 Conclusions

The story of empire is in part the story of modernity. The nineteenth century saw a number of European powers, led by Britain, continue a centuries-old policy of aggressive expansion throughout the world, culminating in the 'Partition of Africa' in the 1880s. Nineteenth-century political thinkers were unsurprisingly concerned, sometimes obsessively, sometimes less directly, with questions about empire. In this chapter I have highlighted some of the overarching themes that united many European thinkers during the century, as well as illustrating the variety of different types of arguments about empires offered by liberals in Britain and France. As the reach of the Western empires expanded, so new ideologies spread in the wake of the conquerors and colonisers, adapting to local circumstances, and subsequently

---

25 For Spencer's opposition to imperial federation, see his letter to J. Astley Cooper, 23 June 1893 (Duncan 1908, p. 328).

26 Hobson later retreated from this position, horrified as he was by Chamberlain's Tariff Reform campaign. He called the remaining followers of imperial federation 'the dupes of Kiplingesque sentimentalism' (Hobson 1909, p. 238).

modified and mobilised by indigenous agents. Amongst the ideological traditions that found favour across the elites of the non-Western world were forms of Marxism, nationalism and liberalism. The leaders of anti-imperial protests 'in places as far distant as Santiago, Cape Town and Canton invoked the notion of their "rights" as individuals and as representatives of nations' (Bayly in this volume). The Western project of modernising empire contained within it the seeds of its own destruction, a bloody process that was to be played out over the course of the twentieth century. Its effects are with us to this day. The European empires were hollowed out from within, and ultimately the costs – human, moral, geopolitical and financial – of sustaining them proved too much to bear, precipitating withdrawal, retreat and often the reshaping of the imperial polities themselves. Albeit in modern form, the curse of the Romans returned to haunt their distant heirs.

Epilogue

French Revolution to *fin de siècle*: political thought in retrospect and prospect, 1800–1914

JOSE HARRIS

1 An overview from 1900

Commentators writing in various countries between 1900 and the eve of the First World War disagreed profoundly about what had been the core themes and trends in the evolution of political thought over the course of the past century. In Edwardian Britain there were those who interpreted the predominant political ethos of the previous hundred years as marked by ever-increasing voluntarism, privacy, personal liberty and the progressive limiting and 'discrediting' of the powers of the state. And there were others who saw the history of the period in exactly the opposite terms, as signifying the eclipse of 'individualism', the decline of ancient self-governing communities and corporations, and the inexorable rise of the 'collectivist state in the making' (Barker 1914, pp. 102–21, 1915b, pp. 236–8, 248–51; Davies 1914, *passim*; Figgis 1914, pp. 54–98; Dicey 1914, pp. 259–88). In the Wilhelmine Reich there were likewise some who emphasised the deepening tensions between authoritarianism and mass democracy, whilst others pointed to the growth of a much more progressive liberal and reformist 'Rechtsstaat' (Eley 1991a, pp. 316–46; Guillard 1915, pp. 254–353; John 1989, pp. 105–31; Kepp 2000, pp. 215–66; Mitzman 1987, pp. 15–36; Naumann 1905, pp. 197–220; Tönnies 1914, pp. 65–70). Similarly in turn-of-the-century France, there were enthusiasts who identified the Third Republic with the advance of 'solidarism' and 'public spirit'; critics to whom it seemed an abyss of cultural corruption and 'utilitarian mediocrity'; whilst an embattled minority viewed the inner structures of French state power as largely unchanged since before the Revolution of 1789 (Agathon 1911, pp. 21–118; Hayward

I am grateful to Joshua Cherniss, Louise Fawcett, Joanna Innes, Julia Moses, Marc Mulholland, Anna Vaninskaya, and particularly to Stella Moss for help with tracking down certain obscure references used in this essay.

1961, pp. 19–48, 2007, pp. 253–7, 285–97, 299–304; Sorel 1916, pp. 107–16; Sternhell 1996, pp. 32–89). Throughout Western Europe the growing provision of public social services from the later decades of the nineteenth century appeared to some contemporaries as the distinctive hallmark of a new democratic age; whereas to others it signalled a dangerous relapse into an earlier epoch of stagnation, patriarchalism and serfdom (Belloc 1912, pp. 29, 143–6, 148–53, 179–94; Spencer 1982, pp. 487–518; Webb 1910, pp. 730–65; Weber 1994b, pp. 68–9). And in all Western countries there were political commentators who assumed that female emancipation had already advanced to its furthest limits, whilst others emphasised the continuing legal, constitutional and practical exclusion of women from all aspects of the public sphere.

Turn-of-the century opinion about who had been the key political thinkers and philosophers of the previous hundred years was similarly divided. Benthamite utilitarianism as a touchstone of moral philosophy had largely fallen out of fashion since the 1860s and 1870s. But the rigorous analytical positivism associated with Jeremy Bentham's legal and administrative ideas remained influential among lawyers and social reformers in many parts of Europe, the British Empire, Latin America and the United States; while Bentham's famous 'felicific calculus' (designed to chart the collective sum of individual human happiness) came to be seen as an important strand in the rise of 'marginalist' political economy (Hutchison 1953, p. 14; Stark 1946, pp. 583–608). John Stuart Mill was still widely revered as a pioneering feminist and public moralist, with *The Subjection of Women* remaining his most internationally famous work; but by 1900 Mill's views on liberty and the scope of 'state intervention' had come to be viewed in many progressive circles as unduly 'negative' and old-fashioned (Collini 1993, pp. 328–36). *The Communist Manifesto* continued to circulate widely among socialists and radicals, and Karl Marx's more theoretical writings attracted increasing attention among continental philosophers; but most turn-of-the-century readers, including many socialists, dismissed Marx's vision of the post-revolutionary eclipse of the state as belonging to a now largely vanished age (Hughes 1958, pp. 68–89; Tudor and Tudor 1988, pp. 45–6, 84–5, 90–5, 218–23; Wells *et al.* 1912, pp. 21–4). Indeed in much of Western Europe and North America the very term 'socialism' had come to be identified, for good or ill, with state provision of public social services: a prospect derided by Lenin as 'pompous projects for miserable reforms' (Lenin 1961–6, v, p. 354). The late nineteenth-century upsurge of philosophical 'idealism' in Britain, France, Italy and the USA had reawakened interest in the writings of Hegel and Kant, but as reference-points in current political thought both remained secondary to the abiding influence of Plato and Aristotle; and many turn-of-the-century idealist thinkers were in any case less interested in the political powers of states than in the moral character and duties of good citizens (Caird 2002, pp. 20–37; Den Otter 1996, pp. 47–50, 168–75; Nicholson 1990, pp. 23–39). Amongst other nineteenth-century schools of thought, the evolutionary positivism of Herbert Spencer continued to command a wide following in India, Japan and parts of the United States and Latin America, but after 1900 Spencer's works in his native Britain were increasingly unread and ignored. A more all-pervasive, though often under-acknowledged, influence throughout Western Europe and both North and South America was that of the French positivist philosopher, Auguste Comte, whose ideas on science, modernity and the 'religion of humanity' permeated the thinking not just of self-confessed 'positivists', but of many progressive Christians, social reformers, internationalists and ethical socialists as well (Godard 1900, pp. 17–103; Harp 1995, pp. 5–6, 58–60, 212–14; Levy-Bruhl 1903; Wright 1986, *passim*). The works of the Swiss federalist theorist Jacob Bluntschli had been adopted as path-breaking exercises in modern political science when the subject was first introduced into the universities of Oxford and Cambridge in the 1870s. But Bluntschli had largely receded from public debate by the early twentieth century (suggesting perhaps that dons were bad judges of intellectual significance, or else that 'modernity' itself was changing faster than many had imagined).[1] The writings of Mary Wollstonecraft, Madame de Staël, Harriet Martineau, Harriet Taylor, George Sand, and more recently Millicent Fawcett and Elizabeth Cady Stanton, were acknowledged even by their detractors to have made powerful contributions to debate on the political status of women. But before the 1890s there were few contemporaries, even among active feminists, who identified such works not simply as brilliant campaign literature but as part of a long-standing intellectual tradition of systematic political theory (below, pp. 919–21).

More recent historians of nineteenth-century political thought have likewise tried to identify certain seminal themes and 'classic' philosophical texts, on a par with those believed to have sparked the English revolutions of the 1640s and 1680s, the American Revolution of the 1770s, or the French

---

1 Bluntschli's work was dropped from the Oxford political thought syllabus in favour of Rousseau's *Du Contrat Social* in 1908, though he continued to be a major influence in international law and in the early genesis of ideas about a possible 'federal' Europe.

Revolution of 1789. But consensus about such core themes and texts has again proved elusive and contentious. On the contrary it has been suggested that, although nineteenth-century political conflicts certainly provoked a ceaseless torrent of both systematic and polemical ideas, they produced – by contrast with earlier centuries – no grand theoretical paradigms, comparable with those found in the writings of Machiavelli, Locke, Rousseau or the founding fathers of the American republic. Instead, so one recent commentary on British thought has argued, nineteenth-century political debate constituted a mere 'patchwork quilt' of many distinct and disjointed narratives, often of major historical interest in their own right but providing no magic clue to the overarching political character of the epoch. There were thus no 'Machiavellian moments' in nineteenth-century British politics, no crucial points of intellectual engagement when major theorists of many different persuasions joined battle, in ways that crucially defined and shaped the history of their own times (Bevir 1996, pp. 114–27, and *passim*; Francis and Morrow 1994, pp. 1–8). Historians of political thought in nineteenth-century Europe have been no more able to agree on the great master narratives of the period, but have focused instead upon the diversity of ideas and controversies within different national cultures (Castiglione and Hampsher-Monk 2001, pp. 1–9, and *passim*; Di Scala and Mastellone 1998, pp. 15–143). Even more surprisingly, the powerful ideological strands that clashed in the American Civil War produced no great classic work of political analysis comparable with the Federalist Papers of eighty years before. And from a rather different perspective another critic has suggested that the 'strange death' of modern political theory, often associated with Western culture after 1945, had already been well underway in Britain and North America during the later nineteenth century, precipitated in part by the loss of a sense of politics as a 'philosophic' activity and its replacement by a quest for political knowledge as a form of exact social and behavioural science (Tuck 1993, pp. 72–3, 76–9).

Such posthumous critiques of nineteenth-century political thought clearly bear some relation to the dense and diverse character of the period. Nevertheless the negative tone of such judgements (as though something else much more ambitious and coherent ought to have happened) may perhaps be called into question. One obvious caveat is that some of the most powerful generators of nineteenth-century political ideas (among them Mill, Marx, Ricardo, Tocqueville, Nietzsche and Weber) were not to find their fully-fledged mass audiences until a much later era (with many of Marx's most subtle political writings, for example, remaining substantially unpublished until the fourth decade of the twentieth century). Another is that these judgements relate to a time when throughout Europe and the wider world, many new institutions and ideologies were bursting out of the inherited structures of past centuries, while many older ones were being dissolved or drastically reconstituted under the impact of industrialisation, science, migration, international trade and both formal and informal empire. Both the range of political ideas and the public auditoriums in which they were being acted out were therefore potentially much vaster and more variegated in the nineteenth century than had been the case even in 1789, let alone in the much more narrowly circumscribed contexts of the American Revolution or the English civil wars. Moreover, throughout the century the discourse of political thought in many countries was moving simultaneously in a number of quite contrary and clashing directions. Theorising about politics was becoming, at one and the same time, both more academic and more populist, more international and more intensely nationalistic, more deeply penetrated by other theoretical disciplines and more self-consciously informed about its own intellectual heritage, than had been the case in earlier centuries. In much nineteenth-century political writing (including that of many authors and movements discussed earlier in this volume), an enhanced awareness of the multitudinous forms of human difference – in the shape of class, nationhood, race, sex, culture and basic individuality – was emerging simultaneously, and often in deep tension, with both older and newer notions of an overarching common humanity. Thus theorists of politics who for many centuries had plausibly been able to work with the model of a single 'republic', 'commonwealth' or 'state' as a self-contained unit of analysis, now found themselves having increasingly to take account of the diversity of the globe. The absence of the kind of well-honed abstraction found in the writings of Thomas Hobbes is therefore unsurprising.

Given these many complicating pressures, what is perhaps most striking about the political thought of the nineteenth-century epoch is not that it seems less focused and coherent than that of earlier periods, but that – however precariously – so many familiar benchmarks of classical, early modern and 'Enlightenment' thought did remain recognisably intact. As in earlier centuries, political theorists in many countries continued to engage with long-standing questions about laws, property, religion and civic virtue, whilst at the same time relating those themes to much newer concerns about public opinion, evolution, mass democracy, market forces, cultural nationalism and advancing knowledge about the individual human psyche.

As in many earlier periods, 'geometric' models of 'man' or 'mankind' (in the works of Ricardo or James Mill, for example) competed with those that engaged with rough historical reality (as in the accounts of Joseph de Maistre, Ludwig Feuerbach or Sir Henry Maine). Answers given to such questions by different thinkers over the course of the nineteenth century have been explored in detail in earlier chapters of this volume. This concluding essay will aim to pin down some of the most important of those new developments, and ways in which they were incorporated into (or broke the mould of) the images and languages of more traditional political thought. And since it is now a commonplace that the 'long nineteenth century' did not end until 1914, some attention will also be paid to the torrent of new trends, policies, problems and prophecies that were emerging after 1900, during what may be called the 'long *fin de siècle*'.

2   Issues and problems

Despite the continuities identified above, by 1900 both the context and content of political thought in Europe, America and the wider world, were in many respects unrecognisably different from the familiar landmarks of a hundred or even fifty years before. A field of enquiry that had long flourished largely outside formal academic institutions (other than in Scotland and northern Germany) had become since the 1870s a standard component of university degree courses in history, law, philosophy and political and social science throughout Europe, the United States, Britain and the British dominions (Burrow *et al.* 1983, pp. 341–63; Karl 1974, pp. 44–7). Over the course of the century the authors of many classic political texts, from Aristotle to David Hume, whose writings had once been virtually inaccessible except in private libraries of the well-to-do, had become potentially available to a much wider readership through numerous cheap editions, scholarly commentaries, popular summaries and translations into many languages. And the same was increasingly true of theorists of contemporary political processes, both academic and more populist. The rise of representative institutions, organised political parties, revolutionary and reform movements, and ever-expanding opportunities for paid government employment, had all in their different ways generated new popular audiences for sustained political argument, far more extensive than anything that had existed even at the time of the French Revolution of 1789. This latter event, with all its competing connotations of liberty and democracy, tyranny and terror, had nonetheless continued to act throughout the nineteenth century as a major imaginative catalyst for the trickling downwards of a discourse that had once been the exclusive province of courtiers, lawyers, learned country gentleman and coffee-house pamphleteers.

Over the same period the disciplinary content and frame of reference of political thought had also been modified or transformed in numerous different ways. Many core political concepts (such as 'citizenship', 'sovereignty', 'civil society' and 'policy') had subtly shifted in meaning; while many newer ones (such as 'public opinion', 'pluralism', 'feminism', 'social justice' and 'social welfare') had been added to the vocabulary of politics in many languages. The word 'citizen', for example, which in England in the early 1800s was often equated with sympathy for Jacobinism and radical subversion, a hundred years later had become a signal for notions of respectability, civic duty and devotion to the public good (Harris 2004a, pp. 84–6). The concept of 'liberty' or 'freedom' had likewise acquired several fresh nuances over the course of time. Traditionally in continental Europe a 'liberty' had meant a special 'privilege' (as in 'freedom of the city'), and even in the Declaration of the Rights of Man it had carried overtones of 'a special privilege that everyone ought to have', rather than the more 'negative' connotation of freedom as the right to do anything not explicitly prohibited, more common in Anglo-Saxon parlance. And with the rise of idealist discourse a third nuance came into play in the form of 'positive' liberty, which implied freedom for a higher purpose such as self-improvement or performance of duty or the 'desire of perfection for its own sake' (the latter a notion that in turn harked back to classical and biblical understandings of the term, as in the Stoics and Saint Paul) (Green 1911, pp. 2–27; Hobson 1901b, pp. 29–30).[2] The very terms 'political thought' and 'political theory' were themselves neologisms of the later nineteenth century. They had crept unobtrusively into French and English usage, as less formal alternatives to the more contentious notions of 'political philosophy' and 'political science' (the latter label being increasingly identified in some quarters with the attempts, mentioned above, to align the study of politics with 'positivism' and natural science) (Bonnot de Mably 1849; Cornewall Lewis 1832; Haigh 1878; Kawakami 1903; Merriam 1903).

Moreover, some major strands of political thought had shifted their identity over the passage of time and by the later nineteenth century had become attached to causes with which allegiance would earlier have been

---

2 A theme that deserves much closer historical documentation and scrutiny than there is space for here, but the classic (retrospective) formulation is in Berlin 1998. For the ongoing debate see Skinner 2001.

unthinkable. 'Republicanism', for example, which in 1793 had seemed inextricably linked with Jacobinism and regicide, was to re-emerge over the following century in alliance with a much wider spectrum of both older and newer meanings. A 'Roman' model of republicanism, derived from the writings of Livy and Cicero, pervaded nineteenth-century constitutionalist thought in many European countries, and was by no means incompatible with the vogue for constitutional monarchy – provided always that individual kings and queens practised civic virtue and obeyed popularly ratified laws.[3] And a more idealised version of 'republicanism', emphasising the prime duty of rulers to care for the welfare of their people, was inspired by Plato's *Republic* and the *Laws*. These two powerful foundation texts of European political philosophy were to become increasingly available both in Greek and in vernacular languages, and their ideas impregnated 'modern' educational, civic and welfare policies through numerous unexpected channels (Biagini 1996a, pp. 21–44; Harris 2004a, pp. 343–60; Ruskin 1903–12, XXIX, pp. 177–8, 226–41, 253–4; Turner 1981, pp. 369–446). All three visions of a republic – Jacobin, Roman and Platonist – together with some new ones were present in Latin America, where throughout the continent from Cuba to Peru diverse strands of republican thought grappled with the intractable problems of post-colonial nation-building (Belaúnde 1938, pp. 63–100, 148–68; Collier 2003, pp. 3–20, 145–6; Jaksic 2001, pp. 124–8, 153, 176–7, 219–20; Posada-Carbo 1998, pp. 1–33, 61–106). In the United States, by contrast, the republican tradition (once deeply hostile to such 'old world' corruptions as cosmopolitanism and 'moneyed interests') had been absorbed over the course of the nineteenth century into an organised Republican party that was increasingly linked, not just to local communities and notions of the 'common weal', but to protectionism, big business and industrial and finance capital (Merriam 1923, pp. 25–9; Meyers 1960, pp. 3–15, 24–8, 74–97, 207–12).

Other important bodies of ideas that appeared outwardly similar likewise often significantly diverged within different national cultures. Liberalism itself, although still widely associated with personal freedom, internationalism, free trade and *laissez-faire*, had acquired during the latter half of the

---

3 See Bertrand Russell's account of his upbringing by his grandfather, Lord John Russell, who was himself the great-great-grandson of one of the regicides of 1649, and twice Queen Victoria's Prime Minister: 'I was taught a kind of theoretic republicanism which was prepared to tolerate a monarch so long as he recognised that he was an employee of the people and subject to dismissal if he proved unsatisfactory. My grandfather, who was no respecter of persons, used to explain this point of view to Queen Victoria' (Russell 1956, pp. 7–8).

century increasingly 'state-interventionist', 'social-reformist' and/or 'nationalist' wings in Germany, Britain, France and the United States (Brouilhet 1910, pp. 71–163; Freeden 1978, *passim*, 2005, pp. 60–77; Karl 1974, pp. 61–81; Sheehan 1966, pp. 64–94, 155–77, 1978, pp. 189–218, 260–7, 272–83). Likewise in much of 'Latin' Europe Roman Catholic political thought continued throughout the nineteenth century to be closely attached to conservatism and the 'party of order'. But elsewhere in Europe and the wider world, Catholic theorists had become increasingly engaged with the assertion of personal liberties, rights of free association, and resistance to statist or entrepreneurial oppression (Nitti 1895, pp. 180–98, 214–33, 242–57, 267–310; Vidler 1964b, pp. 14–18, 35–51, 126–7). Protestant thought embraced an even wider spectrum of political ideas within different national contexts, varying between groups who supported a very close liaison between church and state through to those for whom any suggestion of secular interference in church affairs was anathema. Indeed in some countries (most notably in the four kingdoms of the British Isles) the strongest pressures for institutional 'secularisation' in the nineteenth century came not from principled opponents of religion but rather from devout Congregationalists, Methodists, Quakers, free Presbyterians, and both Roman and Anglo-Catholics: all wanting to separate their conception of true Christianity from the coercive power of the state and secular society (Brown 1982, pp. 292–349; Figgis 1914, pp. 3–53; Laski 1917, pp. 27–210; Skinner 2004, pp. 101–22, 133–8). Indeed for some British theorists the vision of a secular state had itself a quasi-religious significance, as a body that could transcend confessional divisions by forming 'a new and larger City-State, having everlasting foundations and whose builder and maker is God' (Amos 1883, p. 483). Likewise Freemasonry, which in much of continental Europe remained a social philosophy closely attached to free thought, rationalism and (reputedly) radical subversion, in Britain, the British Empire and North America had developed along quite different lines, as a philanthropic, civic and paternalist movement whose patrons included lord mayors, captains of industry, public school headmasters and royal dukes (Gould 1931; Hazareesingh and Wright 2001; Sherren 1914). The militant women's suffrage movement, which in Germany and Russia was primarily a socialist or revolutionary cause, in late nineteenth-century Britain, Ireland, France and North America also included many liberals and conservatives (Caine 1992, pp. 131–72; Caine and Sluga 2000, pp. 130–6; Hause and Kenney 1984, pp. 61–7, 81–6; Stites 1978, pp. 89–154, 233–77). Socialism also had evolved along what appeared to be a range of mutually exclusive routes, which stretched from big-statism to anti-statism, from religious millennialism to scientific positivism, and from the archaic communitarianism of Fourier and William Morris to the technological ultra-modernism of Lenin, H. G. Wells and Georges Sorel.

At its most abstract and ambitious level, theorising about politics remained in the nineteenth century what it had always been, as in the writings of Plato, Aristotle, Hobbes and Locke; this was a discourse concerned less with substantive institutions and policies than with trying to articulate certain 'universal' truths about the nature of government, law, political obligation, human association and individual psychology. And bisecting these concerns was a long-standing current of methodological debate, about whether such truths were best discovered by *a priori* reasoning, or by empirical investigation of laws, commands, customs, institutions and history – or by a dialectic between the two. Such debates had raged with unabated force – in many other spheres of knowledge no less than in political thought – throughout the nineteenth century (Burrow 1979; Lively and Rees 1984; Mill 1865b; Seward 1909). But, even for theorists who insisted that political theory was about axiomatic truths, the empirical details of institutional and material life had become much more pressing and wide-ranging than those addressed by earlier generations. Down to the later eighteenth century much systematic political-theory writing had been largely a juridical and/or theological exercise. It had deployed concepts and examples borrowed from civil, common and canon law, and its only major material concerns had been with the use of force and the rights and duties of property – the latter exemplified by Archdeacon Paley's *Principles of Moral and Political Philosophy*, which remained by far the most widely circulated work of political thought in England until the early 1850s (Paley 1785, pp. 91–105).[4] These juridical and theological roots were to remain strong in many nineteenth-century treatises, including some that vigorously disclaimed any such ancestry. But nonetheless political theorists of all complexions had been increasingly obliged to take account of many newer kinds of information and explanation.

---

4 Paley's preface acknowledged his debt to Locke's *Two Treatises on Government*, portraying his own work as a more 'practical' exposition of Locke's principles. But Paley's work was to run into nineteen editions between the 1780s and 1850s, together with many reprints, whereas over the same period there were only two editions of the *Two Treatises*. Paley's extensive readership stemmed from the fact that his work was a prescribed text on moral and political philosophy for candidates for Holy Orders in the Church of England. By the 1870s his book had been replaced on ordinands' reading-lists by, surprisingly, J. S. Mill's *A System of Logic*.

The most important of these new bodies of knowledge related, first to the ever-expanding impact of material production and 'markets', and second to the emergence of the new and somewhat mysterious phenomenon known as 'society' (an entity to be discussed in more detail below). Assumptions, material examples and a model of human rationality borrowed from political economy had been increasingly incorporated into political writing since the time of Hume and Adam Smith, and were to be progressively reinforced over the nineteenth century by developments in other fields of knowledge such as psychology, anthropology, ethnology and evolutionary biology. Under the influence first of Herbert Spencer and later of Darwin, biology came to be viewed by writers on politics as much more than just a convenient 'organic metaphor', but as a concrete determinant of human behaviour and of differential outcomes in private and public affairs (Burrow 1979, pp. 97, 112–13, 187–90). And 'history' likewise became an increasingly powerful category of political explanation, not just as an empirical discipline that helped to explain the origins of organised human life, but – in the eyes of some – as a disembodied, almost metaphysical force, that was actively driving and shaping the destinies of individuals, cultures, classes, races and nations.

These shifts of emphasis in ways of analysing political life had been compounded throughout the nineteenth century by the massive accumulation of knowledge about alternative political cultures. Even the political systems of classical Greece and Rome – an abiding template for European political thought since the early Middle Ages – had become known about in much greater depth and detail through advances in academic scholarship (stemming particularly from the universities of Germany). The growth of historical, archaeological and philological research, the widespread post-Napoleonic extension of Roman law, and the proliferation of critical and popular editions of major Greek and Latin texts, all vastly extended knowledge about the ancient world and its political, philosophical and religious ideas, far beyond the limited range of classical texts previously available (Jenkyns 1980; Mommsen 2007; Stein 1999, pp. 104–32; Turner 1981). The imaginative impact of such scholarship on contemporary thought had gone far beyond mere 'futile classicism', derided by critics like Thorsten Veblen as designed simply to throw sand in the eyes of the lower orders (Veblen 1970, pp. 252–8); indeed many of its exponents were among the master theorists and protagonists of advanced political modernity. J. S. Mill's vision of modern 'representative institutions', for example, was explicitly designed to inseminate into the prosaic and privatised culture of mid-Victorian Britain the disciplined, altruistic, public-spirited values that Mill associated with the Athenian *polis* (Biagini 1996, pp. 21–44; Mill 1960, pp. 205, 210, 216–17, 310, 319–20); while Karl Marx's analysis of private property borrowed not just many underlying ideas but much technical terminology ('alienation', 'expropriation,' etc.) from Roman civil law. John Ruskin's advocacy of public 'social welfare' policies in *Unto this Last* was likewise derived, not just from its obvious sources in the Old and New Testaments, but from the models of enlightened paternalism set out by Plato in the *Republic* and the *Laws* (Ruskin 1903–12, XVII, pp. 1–114). Didactic novels and treatises written in the form of 'Platonic' dialogues about virtuous government, social justice and the 'good life' became a popular literary and political medium throughout Europe during the later nineteenth and early twentieth centuries; while, even at the very end of the period, a classical education was still widely regarded as no mere antiquarian exercise, but the very 'cradle of modern statesmanship' (Feiling 1913; HMSO Special Reports 1910, pp. 1–56; Lowes Dickinson 1905; Mallock 1975; Soloviev 1915, pp. 5–179).

Nor was the quarrying of political concepts from earlier times confined to the classical era. Similar appropriations of historical models were derived from works such as Sismondi's history of the late-mediaeval Italian republics, Burkhardt's *Civilisation of the Renaissance in Italy*, new editions of the Icelandic Eddas and Norse sagas, anthropological studies of early village communities and the roots of the Indo-European family, and the massive body of historical scholarship on the English common law (Burckhardt 1958; Maine 1871, pp. 128, 1893, pp. 185–224; Palsdottir 2001; Pollock and Maitland 1895; Sismondi 1832; Wawn 1994, 2000). Late nineteenth-century studies of medieval and early modern constitutional history were deployed by radicals and feminists to suggest that early political franchises had been by no means so exclusively arms-bearing, landowning and masculine as many modern commentators had previously believed (Rogers 1885; Stopes 1907a). And in Ireland in particular a powerful synthesis of themes drawn from classical republicanism, European romanticism and the Gaelic cultural revival had continually fuelled the political ideology of the Irish nationalist movement (Lyons 1979, pp. 31–52; Moran 2006; Small 2002, pp. 31–52, 59–83). Such reference-points supplied political theorists throughout Europe and beyond with a cornucopia of historical data, modes of argument and visionary myths about older political cultures, together with a wide range of critical and sometimes revolutionary perspectives on current political arrangements of the nineteenth century.

No less important than these models from past times had been the impact of new knowledge about political cultures of the contemporary age beyond the boundaries of Europe. Since classical times Western political thought had, unsurprisingly, been overwhelmingly Eurocentric in outlook, with extra-European polities such as Persia, China, Turkey, Utopia, even America, all being invoked mainly to illustrate various political stereotypes both adverse and favourable. Political writings of the early modern era had on the whole been sympathetic to the view that 'civilised' political structures could be found in well-ordered non-European polities (though not, by definition, in 'savage' or 'primitive' ones). For much of the eighteenth-century British, French and Dutch transactions with the residents of China and India, though on occasion brutal and violent, had not generally been construed as encounters with 'inferior' civilisations (sometimes indeed quite the reverse). But the growth of more detailed information about remote cultures, together with the rapidly widening technology gap between 'Western' and other nations, had made it increasingly difficult to sustain the one-size-fits-all model of politics and civil government earlier employed by theorists such as Hobbes and Locke. During the early and mid-nineteenth century some European ethnologists had used evidence of 'backwardness' to question the common species-identity of the human race; but by the end of the period this belief was far less common than the view that 'backward' peoples and their institutions were in process of scaling the lower rungs of the same evolutionary ladder that had once been ascended by nations of the 'progressive' West (Burrow 1979, pp. 128–34, 242–51; Stocking 1987, pp. 259–73).

Such assumptions were in turn called into question, however, by disturbing extra-European phenomena, such as the dynamic political regime of post-Meiji Restoration Japan. In Japan from the 1860s 'modern' bureaucratic, military, scientific and educational institutions, together with notions of 'rights' and 'personal freedom', and even Marxian and Christian socialism, had coexisted with the survival of ancient political, religious and family codes quite different from anything known in the nineteenth-century West (Kawakami 1903, pp. 93–106, 114–45, 187–93; Tsunoda *et al.* 1958, pp. 131–210). Russia too, with its strange conjunctions of the medieval mir and a rapidly developing oil industry, its absolute monarchy and self-governing zemstvos, its liberal penal reforms and savage racial pogroms, its mass illiteracy together with its extensive system of higher education, and its deep-rooted penchant for both nihilism and Christian piety, all constantly baffled and confounded the expectations of political observers from countries further west (Drage 1904, pp. 18–42, 70–1, 125–33, 167–9, 585–7, 642–6;

Kovalevsky 1902; Mitzakis 1911, pp. 11–13, 62–9; Thompson 1896, pp. 265–72). And the United States in particular, formerly depicted in early modern thought as little more than a convenient museum of primitive humanity ('in the beginning all was America'), now figured in nineteenth-century European works in a quite different and much more complex fashion. Down to the 1840s America was widely viewed as a burgeoning paradise of equality, self-government and rough-hewn civic virtue (flawed only by petty corruption). But then, as the century progressed, it re-emerged in much more ambiguous terms – still as the land of 'freedom' for migrants and refugees from Europe, but also increasingly as a powerhouse of aggressive economic expansionism, materialism and future world domination (Cox 1902; Seeley 1883; Tocqueville 1968, I, pp. 58–105, 271–9, 290–8; Wells 1906). Moreover, in Japan, China, Russia, Mexico, Venezuela, Chile and elsewhere, scholars, lawyers and intellectuals by the latter half of the century were generating systematic accounts of political norms and behaviour within their own regimes, that certainly showed evidence of interaction with European thought, but were nevertheless also culturally distinctive and *sui generis*. Indeed by the end of the nineteenth century there were many signs that the avant-garde in such speculative activities was migrating away from Western Europe, to the major universities of the USA, to dissident and revolutionary groups in imperial Russia, China and Latin America, and to the new models of ultra-nationalism and disinterested public service being advanced by Samurai intellectuals in Meiji Japan[5] (Bary *et al.* 1960, pp. 51–97; Kawakami 1903; Tsunoda *et al.* 1958, pp. 147–50, 158–93, 252–7).

3   New wine in old bottles

Throughout the latter half of the nineteenth century these multifarious global developments had posed challenges for contemporary theorists in many countries, as they strove to make sense both of the dynamic and decaying elements in their own cultures and of an ever-changing and expanding wider world. In the great metropolitan centres of the world, from Berlin, Paris and London to St Petersburg, Kyoto and New York, coteries of intellectuals, underground activists and defenders of established order had continually reflected upon modern variants of the questions classically posed by Aristotle: namely, who should wield political power, for

---

5 Not to be confused with H. G. Wells' Samurai in *A Modern Utopia* who, though also a dedicated order of superior human beings, saw their mission as global, not nationalistic (Wells 1905, pp. 258–317).

what purposes, and whether the norms and practices contained in power politics were unique to particular cultures or (like the laws of physics) were everywhere fundamentally the same.

One of the most pressing of these newer versions of old problems related to how far established regimes should resist, incorporate or surrender to the burgeoning new socio-economic classes and under-classes created by commercial and industrial expansion, most spectacularly in Western Europe and North America, but to some degree throughout the international trading and imperialised world. Class conflict of a 'factional' kind had a long history in political thought as far back as ancient Athens and beyond. But the post-Napoleonic war period had seen the appearance of seminal works by several major European theorists such as Guizot, Hegel and Ricardo who, though in other respects profoundly differing from each other, nevertheless concurred in highlighting a new kind of 'functional' class division as a central building-block of modern political economies and hence of the social relations of modern states (Guizot 1997, pp. 31, 53, 128–32; Hegel 1991, pp. 261–7, 453–4; Ricardo 1973, pp. xvii, 52–63). By the mid-century the analytical category of 'class', most powerfully purveyed in the writings of Marx and Engels but by no means confined to them, had everywhere come to permeate the language of political thought (though often complicated and blurred by the fact that many subtle nuances of class terminology were lost or distorted in translation from one culture to another).[6] And closely linked to the theme of class was debate about the relation between political rights and 'property', as definitions of the latter subtly shifted over time to include not just the ancient notion of possession of land, offices and privileges, but commercial and industrial capital, the fruits of labour both physical and intellectual, and – more speculatively and contentiously – the primal notions of selfhood, self-development and human 'personality' (Herbert 1893, pp. 1–8; Proudhon 1994, pp. 5–6, 10–12, 52–4, 124–5; Ryan 1984, pp. 5–6, 10–12, 53–4, 124–5; Stein 1964, pp. 47, 59, 166–7). It was this latter dimension that offered most scope for development of a specifically 'feminist' political thought, a point implicit though not always fully spelt out in much political writing by women (Caird 1913, pp. 1–11; Stopes 1907b; Wills 1913). Class issues thus affected the very nature of the state, as economic and political pre-eminence in many countries increasingly migrated

---

6 Thus terms like Bürger, bourgeois, middle-class, proletariat, lumpen-proletariat, working-class, peuple, menu-peuple, tières-état, gentleman – to name but a few – not only carried different shades of meaning when transposed into other languages, but also shifted over time within their original cultures.

away from hereditary ruling castes, whose status had for many centuries been generically defined by ownership of land as the exclusive qualification for defence, honour, public order and the holding of public office.

Other related issues had likewise cropped up again and again in political theory both within and across the boundaries of many political cultures. These included such themes as the nature and limits of 'state intervention'; the competing loyalties and identities of 'kinship', 'community', 'nation-hood' and wider 'humanity'; the totally new kind of human culture and civilisation being widely generated by large-scale industry and the growth of great cities; and the impact of economic change upon patriarchy, gender roles, and the structures of family life (Tönnies 2001, pp. 24–9, 34–5, 48–51, 209–10, 252–3). And looming on the mental horizon of thinkers in many countries over the latter half of the century was the political integration or exclusion of individuals and peoples belonging to 'alien' or 'minority' races. This issue had been brought to the fore in practical politics by the American Civil War, by the rise of ethnic and linguistic nationalism in Europe, Asia and Latin America, and by the epoch of unprecedented international mass migration that had been set in train since the 1870s and 1880s. But it had been addressed most systematically as a problem in social and political theory by writings on the much older question of the role and status of European Jews, and the many divergent strategies proposed on this theme over the course of the nineteenth century. These had included various forms of religious and cultural pluralism; the total immersion of all separate ethnic and religious identities within a wholly inclusive secular state; the nascent vision of a Jewish territorial homeland; and the collective incorporation of Judaism as a sect within the Roman Catholic Church – the latter a solution at one time contemplated by Theodore Herzl, the later theorist of Zionism (Marx 1974, pp. 212–41; Schorske 1981, p. 121; Sombart 1913). No other single issue demonstrated more sharply the profound ambiguities that lurked in contemporary political thought on racial questions, nor more clearly foreshadowed the seismic shifts involved in the long-drawn-out transition from the era of feudalism and dynasticism through to the politics of nation-statism, democracy and mass modernity.

All these newer questions coexisted and to some extent intersected with the continuing salience of many much older themes. These included the rights and duties of different forms of citizenship; the nature of territorial 'sovereignty'; and the relation of national politics to the international claims of the papacy (the latter a particularly pressing problem after the pope's loss of territorial power through Italian unification). The issue of sovereignty (in the sense of a state's right to defend itself against encroachment by other powers)[7] had become increasingly divorced over the course of the nineteenth century from notions of personal kingship. But 'sovereignty' was nonetheless a central tenet both of the positivist jurisprudence that permeated constitutional thought in many Western countries, and of early twentieth-century 'rational-liberal' theories of the state (Dicey 1885, pp. 134–76; Laski 1917, pp. 1–25). It was also a deeply contested notion in a political environment shaped by large-scale expansion of empires, nationalist liberation movements, mass migration across national frontiers, and the continual expansion of free trade in capital and consumer goods. And it was further challenged by ideas dimly emerging in some quarters during the latter half of the century about the erection of regulatory powers above and beyond those of the individual nation state. Such ideas included movements for the setting-up of an international court, compulsory arbitration in interstate disputes, codification of the 'laws of war', and the very tentative formulation of notions about supra-national sovereign authorities and inviolable 'human rights' (Comte 1865; Holland 1908; Hook 1891; Laity 2001).

For many writers and theorists about politics, the major theatre of action throughout the nineteenth century had nevertheless remained the cluster of institutions known as 'the state'. This was true no less of Great Britain than of any other contemporary polity, despite the oft-repeated (though almost wholly unfounded) claim that nineteenth-century Britons had little or no conception of 'the state' or contact with its institutions.[8] The century had seen the construction of many new states, involving very diverse constitutional structures, in Europe, Latin America and the settler territories of the British 'commonwealth'; and, despite the rise of 'internationalist' discourse towards the end of the century, there seemed little reason to suppose that, in any foreseeable future, the state would ever be seriously superseded as the apex of political life. Indeed – notwithstanding libertarian and radical critiques of state power – by the end of the century the role of the state appeared to have become more rather than less important in the lives of nations, as more and more subordinate communities began to claim

---

7 On the related but separate issue of internal sovereignty – of who held ultimate power within an independent state – see below.

8 A claim classically made by Taylor 1965, p. 1, despite the fact that the number of nineteenth-century British authors, from Gladstone downwards, who wrote about 'the state' in one or other of its many guises is almost uncountable, and that around 50 per cent of the population at some time in their lives were claimants for public relief under the statutory Poor Laws.

self-government and national autonomy from older supra-national dynastic and territorial empires (see below).

Nevertheless, though states grew in number (and some of them in size) there was ever-increasing diversity of opinion about their proper functions and powers. From the writings of Bentham at the end of the eighteenth century and of John Austin in the mid-nineteenth century through to those of Max Weber in the early twentieth, there was a powerful strain in the cross-national culture of political thought that defined the essence of the state in implicitly Hobbesian terms: as a 'political society' ruled by whichever power held ultimate or 'absolute' command over the use of force within a given territory (Austin 1965, pp. 212–93; Bentham 1970b, pp. 5–6, 18–30, 196–208, 289; Weber 1954, pp. 338–48, 2005, 126–49).[9] This model of state power, as rooted in 'sovereignty' (and in the cognate though not identical concepts of 'domination', 'rulership' or 'Herrschaft') was widely disseminated by many British and continental theorists, who saw it not as an endorsement of state tyranny but as an objective, 'scientific' account of ordered political existence, even in a polity where the mass of the people was sovereign, and as inexorably 'true' of any constitutional order as the law of gravity in Newtonian physics (Comte 1851–3, pp. 432–5; Stephen 1892, pp. 16, 30; Tocqueville 1968, pp. 68–71). As even J. S. Mill, celebrated as the prophet of personal liberty, put it, 'government is always in the hands . . . of the strongest power in society, and . . . what this is does not depend on institutions, but institutions on it' (Mill 1981, p. 169). This so-called 'Hobbesian' perspective had been regularly criticised, however, from many quarters, as despotic, historically outmoded or logically flawed. Such criticisms came, not just from classical liberals like Lord Acton, who denied that properly constituted states ever had need of 'absolute' or arbitrary powers. They came also from representatives of various strands of philosophical 'idealism', ranging from Immanuel Kant earlier in the century who – despite largely endorsing Hobbes' account – thought that formal rationality required sovereign rulers to be bound by universal moral law; through to T. H. Green, Bernard Bosanquet and the young John Dewey at the end of it, who emphasised the state's role as the medium of collective moral life, rather than (or at least in addition to) organised legal coercion (Bosanquet 1910, pp. 172–8; Dewey and Tufts 1910, pp. 473–85; Green 1911, pp. 121–5, 206–16, 230–47; Kant 1998/9, pp. xxvi–ix). Dissent came likewise from some late nineteenth-century feminists, who

---

9 Bentham's treatise on this subject was not published until the 1940s, but his views were widely known in utilitarian circles, and were closely replicated by Austin.

interpreted the claim that the state was an institution inherently rooted in force as part of the false reasoning that excluded the so-called 'weaker sex' from substantive political power (Caird 1897, pp. 190–1). And similar objections were raised by many romantic conservatives and liberal nationalists, who portrayed the state not as the crude mediator of superior brute strength but as the institutional embodiment of a nation's historic, linguistic, corporate and religious identity (Moran 2006, pp. 96–114; Seton-Watson 1915, pp. 5–31).[10]

Pressures upon the state of a quite different kind had also come from a range of theorists, many of whom fully or partly endorsed its legitimate 'coercive' role, but who nevertheless looked to public authorities to perform a much more extended range of 'welfare' functions than in past eras, going far beyond the traditional boundaries of public order and national defence. Since the late eighteenth century nearly all 'civilised' governments had continually extended their 'police' activities: 'police' being a term that originally implied not just powers of arrest and surveillance, but provision of public services such as highway maintenance, street-lighting, drainage and primary education, all of which helped to make communal living more civilised, ordered, healthy and 'polite' (France 1992, pp 60–1; Gordon 1994, p. 72). It was on this plane – in the creation of an infrastructure of social, economic and environmental services to support and civilise their growing populations – that many nineteenth-century nations had seen the most dramatic expansion in the role, functions and (in the eyes of some) fundamental identity of the modern state, even during decades supposedly committed to economic liberalism and administrative *laissez-faire*.

In this process of state-expansion, political theorists and publicists in many countries had been sometimes merely the interpreters of institutional change, sometimes its active agents, often a mixture of the two. Such involvement was by no means confined to any one point on the political spectrum, but had included conservatives, liberals, socialists, nationalists, Bonapartists, revolutionaries and other dissidents (including some who were in principle profoundly hostile to the very notion of state power).[11]

---

10 It may be noted that proponents of this latter view did not always preclude domination over others when practised by their own favoured nation. One of Moran's most bitter complaints about Britain was that British rule in Ireland had prevented the Irish from establishing their own overseas empire. And Serbian nationalism was likewise notably hard-headed about the romantic nationalist aspirations of lesser minority groups.

11 For examples of contemporary authors who were both theorists and active protagonists of state-building processes, see Emminghaus 1870; Simon 1897; Stein 1962.

Moreover, very disparate ideological groups often unexpectedly echoed or borrowed political ideas from each other. In France, for example, the (deeply Catholic) Society of St Vincent de Paul, whose English branch in the 1850s and 1860s had inspired the family-welfare theories of the (strongly anti-statist) Charity Organisation Society, went on in the 1880s and 1890s to provide a working model for the public–private social welfare partnerships that were a feature of the (militantly secularist) French Third Republic (Layet 2005, pp. 30–40; Vidler 1964b, pp. 24–5, 52, 64–7, 89; Zeldin 1977, pp. 1015–21). And, no less paradoxically, Pierre-Joseph Proudhon, more unswerving than Karl Marx in his belief in the corruption of all current states and redundancy of future ones, had nonetheless put forward theories of welfare reform that were to form the bedrock of French 'solidarism' and the long-term development of French state social security (Hayward 1960, pp. 33, 39; Jabarri 1999, pp. 12–16). Likewise in Germany, Lorenz von Stein, whose pioneering writings on French socialist movements had anticipated and influenced Marx, had been a prime author of the new fiscal, social and administrative structures introduced from the 1840s and 1850s by the Prussian 'welfare monarchy'; while later in the century such state-building policies were further fostered by both the protagonists and the bitter ideological critics of the Bismarckian and Wilhelmine empire (Steinmetz 1993, pp. 123–45). In Britain a long line of very diverse populist theorists over more than a hundred years, from Tom Paine in the 1790s, William Cobbett in the 1820s and John Ruskin in the 1860s, through to New Liberals and Fabians in the 1890s and 1900s, had advanced a long series of proposals for using state power to regenerate the economy through public employment schemes, social services and progressive redistribution of income and wealth (Money 1905, pp. 291–325; Paine 1989a, pp. 223–6, 232–54, 259; Ruskin 1903–12, XVII, pp. 1905, 21–114). Until the last quarter of the nineteenth century, however, the guiding philosophy of central government in Britain had owed less to such economic populism than to the more austere doctrines of Ricardo, who had believed there was nothing that states could do to boost national prosperity, other than maintaining a strong currency, keeping supply lines open, pursuing global 'comparative advantage' and fostering civic peace. It was the tacit acting out of these rigorous doctrines of fiscal and monetary management (involving strict central controls over local government expenditure rather than direct provision of new public services) that had played the most important role in developing and fine-tuning the deceptively invisible infrastructures of the nineteenth-century British state (Gladstone 1971, pp. 132–57).

It will be noted that many of these newer conceptions of state power related directly or indirectly to the 'social' sphere; and although the state remained central to political thought, its role as the overarching institution in collective human life had been progressively modified over the course of the nineteenth century by the emergence of the much more elastic and elusive phenomenon of 'society'. The significance of this latter development, though often ignored or misinterpreted, can scarcely be overemphasised. Although 'society' was a very ancient term (derived from the Latin word *societas*), prior to the late eighteenth century it had usually referred to the coming together of human beings in small, finite groups, set up for some particular purpose, such as business partnerships, charity, art and learning, or for mere neighbourliness and 'sociability'.[12] Within this frame of reference, the state itself was often seen as simply another form of *societas*. It was that 'society' charged with the special civic role of maintaining public order, hence its characterisation as what was known as 'civil society' (Cornewall Lewis 1832, p. 240; Harris 2003, pp. 12–19; Kant 1998/9, p. 119). These precise and limited meanings of 'society' remained in use throughout the eighteenth and nineteenth centuries (and indeed have continued to do so down to the present day). In writings of the Scottish Enlightenment and French revolutionary eras, however, there had emerged a newer and much more ambitious understanding of 'society', as a phenomenon that embraced the multiplicity of human relationships on a much grander scale, extending throughout a whole national polity or even potentially throughout the whole of humanity. This was what Adam Smith had called the 'great society' or, more evocatively, the 'great chess-board of human society', on which individuals were not just passive 'pieces' but autonomous 'players', subject to 'rules' but at the same time working out their own private moves within the complex totality of interlocking human affairs (Smith 1974, p. 234; Merz 1896–1914, IV, pp. 182–4).

This newer, more macroscopic conception of society had been slow to penetrate the language, and indeed the imagination, of political thought, and was to be the subject of continuing confusion and perplexity to many thinking people throughout the nineteenth century (Merz 1896–1914, IV,

---

12 E.g. Mr Darcy: 'In a country neighbourhood you move in a very confined and unvarying society'... Mrs Bennet, 'As to not meeting many people in this neighbourhood, I believe there are few neighbourhoods larger. I know we dine with four and twenty families' (Jane Austen, *Pride and Prejudice*, 1954 [1813], pp. 49–50). Mrs Bennet, though deemed socially deficient in many other respects, here perfectly understood the meaning of 'society' in late eighteenth/early nineteenth-century vernacular usage.

pp. 545–90). Its all-encompassing existential reality in many cultures was often better captured by novelists, painters and imaginative writers (by Elizabeth Barrett Browning in *Aurora Leigh*, for example, or by the novels of Balzac, Dostoievsky and Dickens) than by mere political or even 'social', theorists. Lorenz von Stein, one of the first theorists to grasp the importance of this new form of human grouping, had nevertheless emphasised in the 1840s its still very sketchy and imperfectly formed identity, both as a social phenomenon and as a sociological idea (Stein 1956, pp. 17–51; Tönnies 1974, pp. 121–82). John Stuart Mill had aspired to write a great work on the subject, as a sequel to his *A System of Logic*, but notoriously failed to do so; while his colleague Herbert Spencer was to spend a lifetime of largely fruitless effort in trying to uncover the workings of society's causal laws. Its most effective exponent in a specific historical context was Alexis de Tocqueville, whose *Democracy in America* very graphically portrayed the workings of a polity in which, not a 'great society' but hundreds of 'small societies' appeared to be spontaneously performing at a very low-key level many of the co-ordinating and policing functions elsewhere authorised by an overarching 'state' (de Tocqueville 1968, I, pp. 78–81, II, pp. 657–76).

A very different account of recent socio-political change was given a generation later by the German theorist Ferdinand Tönnies. Writing in the 1880s, Tönnies sharply differentiated between 'society' and 'community', as terms that in everyday speech were often used interchangeably, but more properly referred to two starkly contrasting kinds of collective organisation, each involving two quite different forms of human rationality and subjectivity. Tönnies suggested that 'communities' were rooted in relationships that evolved incrementally and unselfconsciously, and were 'given' or 'grown into' rather than 'chosen'; whereas 'societies' were the product of conscious construction, 'atomistic' social relationships and individual rational choice. This antithesis he portrayed as penetrating all layers of human culture, from government, politics, law and economic exchange, through to religion, aesthetics, sexual relations and modes of subjective perception. All human interaction in all historic periods, Tönnies argued, combined elements of both these models. But the enormous explosion of markets since the early eighteenth century, together with the rise of rational-positivist theories of politics and law, had tipped the balance dramatically against 'community' and in favour of 'society', the latter being a way of life that would ultimately merge into a single homogeneous 'global civilisation' (Tönnies 2001, pp. 247–61).

The idea of 'society' as a self-regulating network of interlocking human relationships, operating independently of the rise and fall of governments, and subject to its own generic behavioural laws, had been most fully articulated in France, where from the 1830s the Positivist movement and particularly the writings of Henri Saint-Simon and Auguste Comte had generated the notion of a new 'science of society' or 'sociology'. This was a science, so its protagonists claimed, that not only made it possible to identify law-like regularities in social behaviour, past, present and to come, but also revealed the extent to which all other, seemingly autonomous, historical movements, intellectual disciplines and forms of knowledge were simply the products of societal processes and laws, summed up in the philosophy of Positivism (Comte 1975, pp. 91–2, 195–217, 248–52; Saint-Simon 1976, pp. 18–19, 38, 108–9). Many contemporaries were sceptical, however, not simply of the claims of positivist sociology, but about whether 'society' in this larger, more all-encompassing sense really existed at all. Without a framework of government 'there would be no such thing as society', affirmed the British jurist, James Fitzjames Stephen; instead there was simply the aggregate sum of exchanges and interactions between individual human beings (Stephen 1892, p. 74).[13] And the German sociologist George Simmel likewise argued that, unlike the world of nature, society was cumulatively 'invented' by the purposive thoughts and acts of individuals (and was thus beyond the reach of French-style positivist social science). Nor in Simmel's view was society an all-embracing phenomenon. On the contrary, individual human beings lived in deep tension between private identities and ever-changing social forces; while society itself was constantly defined and redefined by people on its margins who were patronised, ostracised or excluded by mainstream social groups. Among those excluded, or teetering on the edge, were migrants, strangers, adventurers, prostitutes and the poor – the latter not confined to the working classes, but occurring in all social strata (Simmel 1971, pp. 36–40, 121–6, 143–9, 161–73, 187–94). Nevertheless, during the 1840s, 1850s and 1860s the newer conception of society as an all-encompassing collectivity had become a colloquial commonplace in much of Europe and North America; suggesting that, at some spontaneous and intuitive level, many people in those countries had clearly begun to

13 There is no reason to suppose that Fitzjames Stephen's point (made in an article on Thomas Hobbes) was being consciously echoed in the later and much more famous use of this phrase by Margaret Thatcher (*Woman's Own*, 31 October 1987). But there can be little doubt that the then prime minister was endorsing exactly the kind of 'aggregative', rather than 'organic', sociability that Stephen (and indeed Thomas Hobbes before him) would have had in mind.

think of themselves as living in a 'society' in the enlarged Adam Smithian sense of the term. And in the writings of Comte and his disciples in many countries, theorising about politics had itself become a branch of sociology, with government being redefined as the educational and 'organizing' branch of 'society', charged with 'co-ordinating' rather than 'commanding' its citizens, who would themselves be imbued with a sense of 'spontaneous order' that precluded the need for either force majeure or juridical right (Comte 1975, pp. 195–217, 274–5, 334–71, 429–41).

4   Political thought on the brink of the twentieth century

By the end of the nineteenth century political thought in one guise or another had thus become an activity that was much more diverse and multilayered than it had been a hundred years before. Although Western political cultures were still extensively transplanting their ideas across the globe, theorists and political activists in many non-European settings were now vigorously adapting various strands of European thought to their own purposes, and at the same time discovering alternative traditions within their own historic cultures (Bary 1960, pp. 60–93; Owen 2003, pp. 149–75; Weiming 1996, pp. 21–91, 132–54). And just as non-European intellectuals in Japan, India, China, Persia, Turkey, Latin America and elsewhere were asserting the validity of their own political ideas, so there were many theorists in 'advanced' countries who were seeking to recover or emulate the past traditions and cultural purity of so-called 'backward' ones. Iceland, Albania and Serbia, for example, as well as Greece, Rome and the high Middle Ages, all figured as idealised models and reference points in British utopian writings of the turn-of-the century period (Flanagan 2006; Morris 1896–7; Palsdottir 2001). And, conversely, a strangely prescient lecture on the recurrent spectre of 'decadence' that haunted advanced societies in every epoch was delivered in Cambridge in 1908 by the philosopher and former British prime minister, Arthur Balfour. Balfour suggested that Western states could no longer assert their hegemony over 'decayed' or 'backward' nations on cultural, religious or even political grounds. Their claims to ascendancy lay if anywhere solely in the 'material' sphere – in superior scientific knowledge, greater efficiency in reducing scarcity, and more effective advanced technology (Balfour 1908, pp. 38–41, 46–59).

The global penetration of 'Western' political thought as a form of cultural discourse did not therefore necessarily entail a 'global' frame of reference about substantive political, philosophical or moral ideas. Indeed there were certain respects in which political-theory writing of the 1890s and 1900s appeared more localised and culture-specific, less engaged with great universalist themes, than had been the case a century before. One reason for this, as indicated above, was simply that observers and theorists now knew far more about the sheer diversity and complexity of other people's cultures than in former times, thus making confident generalisation about statecraft and about social and political justice much more problematic. At the start of the nineteenth century a powerful focus for 'universalist' thought had been the still very recent American Declaration of Independence and the even more recent French Declaration of the Rights of Man, both of which had inspired (or provoked) political theorists and activists in many countries over a whole generation. Half a century later a similar impetus to universalist ideals among liberals, romantic nationalists and revolutionaries had been supplied by the intense political struggles of 1848 and the perception at that time that many peoples, movements and nations were sharing a unique common moment in world history (a perception dramatically symbolised by the great surge of international hero-worship bestowed on Garibaldi). The predictions made by Saint-Simon and Auguste Comte – that the countries of Western Europe would one day merge into a single unitary republic, regulated by 'law' rather than 'government' – were nowhere at the time seen as a practical proposition. But they nevertheless captured a certain spirit of cosmopolitan internationalism and universalism, which had characterised both elite and populist thinking in many Western countries at the mid-century (Comte 1865, pp. 66–101, 427–33; Saint-Simon 1976, pp. 83–98).

At the *fin de siècle*, however, the widespread pessimism and political unease that lurked in many quarters took a much more defensive and nationalistic turn, and the cross-national culture of shared political ideas seemed much more disparate and fragmented than in earlier decades of the nineteenth century. For all the rising concern about a European-wide 'arms-race', for example, the movement for promoting international peace through the Hague conventions remained largely a minority concern. It was supported by feminists and by a small handful of lawyers and liberal internationalists, but national governments unanimously rejected any suggestion of compulsory arbitration, particularly where questions of 'vital interests' and 'national honour' were involved (Holland 1908, pp. 76–9; Laity 2001, pp. 145–215; Swanwick 1915, pp. 3–11). Indeed many political commentators throughout Europe and beyond appeared much more preoccupied at this time by localised issues within their own national polities (in France, for example, by the Dreyfus case and endemic conflicts between the state and the Catholic Church, in Britain by the Boer War and the crisis of 'physical deterioration', in Germany by unresolved tensions within the imperial constitution).

Moreover, although since the 1870s 'political thought' or 'political science' had been taught under various labels in the world's leading universities, by the start of the new century the study of ideas about politics had not fully established itself as a major international discipline with a public voice and strong lines of communication between theorists in different countries. In Germany at the turn of the century there were many university chairs in political science, but these had become increasingly confined to candidates of a strongly 'nationalist' persuasion (with socialists and other critics of government, even of a purely 'ethical' kind, being largely excluded from university posts) (Mitzman 1987, pp. 114–18, 121–2). In Britain the subject had got off to an auspicious start in the 1870s and 1880s, with major philosophers like Sheldon Amos, T. H. Green, F. H. Bradley, Edward Caird, D. G. Ritchie, Henry Sidgwick, and even the young Bertrand Russell, lecturing to large audiences on aspects of political thought in London, Oxford, Cambridge and the Scottish universities (Amos 1883; Bradley 1988; Caird 1897; Green 1911; Russell 1896; Sidgwick 1891). During the 1900s, however, the cutting-edge in Anglo-Saxon philosophy appeared suddenly to move away from concern with problems in political theory, as several brilliant young practitioners of the subject switched their allegiance either to sociology or to more technical questions of language, mathematics and logic.[14] Thereafter, although political thought continued to be widely taught in British universities it was increasingly as a historical or cultural discipline rather than as a direct engagement with current political and philosophical issues. In France during the same period there was intense academic involvement with the political, philosophical and constitutional questions generated by the Third Republic, but this took place mainly under the auspices of faculties of law and sociology (Jones 1993, pp. 29–54, 149–50, 162–3; Lukes 1973, pp. 320–409). Only in the United States did the term 'political science' embrace a wide range of independent senior professorships, a nationwide professional organisation,

---

14 Thus Russell had lost interest in political theory as a formal philosophical discipline by around 1900. Two brilliant young Oxford graduates, E. J. Urwick and R. M. MacIver, set out on careers as would-be political philosophers, respectively at the LSE and the University of Aberdeen, in the early 1900s. But both soon migrated into sociology, and both moved to chairs of sociology at the University of Toronto.

specialist academic journals, and a body of young doctoral scholars some of whose work remains of interest to historians after more than a century (e.g. Calkins 1905; Kawakami 1903). But even in the USA much of the teaching of the subject remained strongly 'national' and even parochial in focus, having only limited contacts with wider international scholarship. This was in marked contrast to developments in the social sciences, which in the first decade of the twentieth century gave all the appearance of being the great new academic growth-area of the epoch, marked by a series of major conferences taking place in Chicago, St Louis, Hamburg, Frankfurt, Paris and Berlin. The meeting at St Louis in 1904 attracted the attendance of some of the great European 'founding fathers' of the modern social sciences, among them Max Weber, Wernher Sombart and Ferdinand Tönnies. But there were no comparable international gatherings in academic political theory.

A historical overview of new departures in political ideas at the start of the twentieth century must therefore look for portents of change largely beyond the confines of university-based faculties of political science or political philosophy. Instead, such developments were taking place, partly in non-academic and more 'activist' settings, and partly under the umbrella of other scholarly disciplines, such as history, law, psychology, economics, sociology and evolutionary biology. Not all such trends can be fully reviewed here, but a few of the most seminal for the future evolution of the subject may be highlighted. One of the most dramatic developments of the period was the almost simultaneous emergence (or re-emergence) in Britain, Europe, North America and the Far East of a much more politicised form of feminism, after several decades during which members of women's movements had been deeply involved in education, charities, local government and trade unionism, but had singularly failed in any country to gain the parliamentary vote.

Reasons for the sudden upsurge of female suffragist activism after 1900 remain contentious, and appear initially to have been more closely linked to contemporary crises in practical politics than to more abstract questions of political theory. But the fact that the Dreyfus case in France, the Boer War in Britain, and movements for legal and constitutional reform in Germany, Russia and China, all served to propel women into their various national suffrage movements, suggests that many were already attracted by wider questions of politics, quite apart from the core issue of the right to vote. Moreover, for English-speaking readers an important intellectual event of the early 1890s was the first republication for nearly half a century of the full text of Mary Wollstonecraft's *A Vindication of the Rights of Women*

(1792), a work that remained the single most powerful 'theoretical' statement by a female author, of the case for equality between the sexes and for women's full participation as citizens in the public sphere (Wollstonecraft 1892).[15] Another catalyst was the 1899 London congress of the (Washington-based) International Council of Women, which published seven volumes of papers on all aspects of the 'gender' question, highlighting particularly the political significance of women's subordinate economic position, and the key role that was being played by women's groups in current campaigns for international peace (Gordon 1900). And a further precipitating factor was the emergence in some quarters of a totally new kind of cross-national fin de siècle feminism that claimed for women exactly the same kind of personal freedoms as had long been enjoyed by men. This new feminism totally rejected the claim of many mid-nineteenth-century suffragists that women deserved the vote because of their superior moral qualities. Instead, like men – so argued the post-1900 'New Woman' in London, Paris, New York and Berlin – women should be enfranchised for their status as free adult persons and citizens, quite regardless of questions of devotion to civic duty, motherliness or private morality (Caine and Sluga 2000, pp. 117–42; Caird 1897, pp. 126, 190–1; Hamilton 1909). Indeed, it should not be forgotten that the *fin de siècle* was also the period of *la belle époque*, in which a small minority of women was transgressing settled boundaries of politics, art, religion, aesthetics and sexual identity, in ways that were still to remain contentious throughout the following century.

One effect of the ensuing debate on women's suffrage was to recapitulate some of the classic controversies which over many earlier centuries had characterised civic debate on the rights and duties of men. But it was also to bring into this debate certain generically new issues, which threatened to redefine the long-established boundaries of classic political thought. These new issues were partly about a total recasting of the conventional division of roles between the sexes; but more commonly they were concerned with the claim that some traditionally female functions, such as home-making and child-rearing, were no less significant for the flourishing of the wider body politic than more traditionally masculine ones. Arguments about property rights, taxation, the capacity to bear arms, the marriage relation, childbirth and motherhood, sexual psychology, and the very nature of the

15 Published in London with an informative introduction by the well-known art historian, Elisabeth Robins Pennell. Pennell also drew attention to the recent rediscovery of the works of 'the almost forgotten' seventeenth-century feminist political theorist and theologian, Mary Astell (Buhlbring 1891).

state: all were to be mobilised both by turn-of-the-century female suffragists and by their opponents, the latter often deeply embedded in the once-radical ideology of classical republicanism, which still heavily stressed the military, bread-winning, head-of-household, and tax-paying qualifications for full adult citizenship (Woolsey 1903, pp. 3–113; Wright 1913, pp. 13–14, 32–5). A full exploration of these debates is beyond the scope of this chapter, but some mention should be made of the many different ways in which feminist demands impinged upon the subject-matter of wider political theory. In France, Britain and North America, female suffragists were deeply divided on such questions as resort to civil disobedience, the use of violence, and the extent to which women activists should seek support from sympathetic males. And there were also widely varying visions of ultimate goals. To some women suffrage campaigners the vote was an end in itself, with attainment of formal civic equality being the main issue. To others, however, the vote was primarily a means to various more complex ends: either enhancement of the status of women's existing roles as home-makers, wives and mothers; or a transformation of those roles through the opening-up of education and wider influence in public life (Wills 1913). And to a significant minority in all countries the vote for women was primarily important as part of wider political engagement, whether in party politics, trade unionism, peace movements, or – particularly in Germany, China and Russia – in revolutionary political change (Caine and Sluga 2000, pp. 117–42; Hause and Kenney 1984; Reagin 1995; Soong 1995; Stites 1978).

The organised suffrage movement was merely the most dramatic and con-spicuous of the many turn-of-the-century movements that fused together previously disparate or antagonistic schools of thought and whose activi-ties challenged or redefined traditional theoretical conceptions of politics and the state. In Britain new ideas about the future of state and society could also be found in the rival literatures of imperialism, anti-imperialism and imperial federation (the latter in particular was deeply engrossed in the 1900s with promoting the contentious notion of a 'common citizen-ship' for the peoples of the British Empire (Bridger 1906; Parkin 1892)). In Germany ongoing debates between revisionist and revolutionary socialism were paralleled by various new forms of radical conservatism (often linked by little more than a shared hostility to market capitalism), that flourished among opponents of the imperial 'Civil Code', in agrarian, military and naval leagues (Coetzee 1990, pp. 30–43, 50–8; Herwig 1973, pp 7–8, 151–3; John 1989, pp. 108, 43; Steinberg 1964, pp. 102–10). And in France the

'Catholic royalism' of the disciples of Charles Maurras similarly converged with notions of patriotism, public spirit and 'civic virtue' that would once have been the characteristic province of the republican left (Weber 1962, pp. 6–16, 77–82).

New political ideas also abounded in the sphere of culture and aesthetics. The international 'modernist' movement of the early twentieth century stretched from Russia to Catalonia, from high art to the hard sciences; and under its auspices scarcely a poster, a poem, a papal encyclical or a prosaic scientific textbook failed to include some oblique reference to the sphere of political and social theory. Such works often included a great deal of ecstatic futurology, both benign and malign, linked together by common anticipation of a world both dominated and liberated by the impact of advanced technology. At one extreme they included the vision of Roger Fry and H. G. Wells, of the construction of a 'Great State' where toilsome labour would be largely abolished, unpleasant tasks that could not be mechanised would be discharged by universal conscription, and 'amateur' self-government would replace 'the trite omniscience of the stale official' (Fry 1920, pp. 39–54; Wells *et al.* 1912, pp. 31–41). And at the other extreme lay F. T. Marinetti's paean to the universal triumph of speed, violence, masculinity and the motor-car, outlined in the 1909 Futurist Manifesto. ('We want to glorify war – the only cure for the world . . . We want to demolish all museums and libraries, fight morality, feminism and all opportunist and utilitarian cowardice'; Marinetti 1983.) Modernism also bore witness to a very widely diffused sense of living in a newly unified world where – under pressure from massive industrial and intellectual change – all settled landmarks of social, economic and political identity were realigning or dissolving. And similar strains could be heard in the extensive war-scare literature of the period, where writers in many countries gave vent to the fear that advances in military technology were out of control, and had outrun the regulatory capacities of conventional politics and governments (Angell 1909, pp. 82–6, 98–114; Geppert 2008).

Developments in political thought under the umbrella of neighbouring academic disciplines likewise shared in this alternating culture of grandiose over-ambition and nervous apprehension about the future of the state, the world and of traditional socio-political arrangements. An influential work of social psychology published on the eve of the First World War, but composed several years earlier, was Graham Wallas' *The Great Society: A Psychological Analysis*, a study based primarily on American data, but used by its author to interpret what he saw as wider trends in international civilisation. Wallas reported on substantially rising living standards in many advanced countries, that coexisted with increasing alienation from work, mounting social and economic insecurity, disintegrating 'human material' and psychic 'malaise', leading to widespread breakdown of 'trust' in national and civic leaders, and violent political unrest. And, far from running itself with a minimum of state supervision (in the way classically envisaged by Adam Smith), the 'Great Society' of the early twentieth century seemed to be moving in exactly the opposite direction: in all countries it was generating demands for 'increased national armaments', 'increased internal coercive authority', and increased discretionary powers 'in the hands of an undemocratic executive'. Everywhere, in Wallas' view, there was a fundamental clash between the constraints and pressures of modern life and the inherited human psyche: expressed in a failure to harness 'Instinct' to 'Thought'. And everywhere there was a secret yearning for what he called 'the Extreme', by which he meant not necessarily extremist politics, but some kind of transcendent vision or principle of 'excellence' to counteract the shallowness and dreari- ness of life in the 'Great Society' (Wallas 1914, pp. 3–16, 171–6, 182–4, 236–45, 341–94).

New trends in economic thought taking place during the 1900s likewise impinged on political thought from a number of quite contrary direc- tions. On the one hand, classical-liberal notions of a slim-line, largely non- interventionist state – where questions of value and distribution were settled mainly by market choices – were seen by some as strongly reinforced by the theory of 'final' or 'marginal' utility, developed in the 1870s by theorists in Britain, Austria and Switzerland (Gide and Rist 1915, pp. 517–44; Hutchi- son 1953, pp. 1–17). But some decades later the notion that the 'utility' of material goods impinged with similar degrees of intensity upon ratio- nal individuals whether rich and poor was being deployed by reformers in support of graduated tax rates on wealth and income. It led to a strategy of using taxation, not just for the traditional purpose of 'raising revenue', but to relieve poverty, to stimulate consumer demand and to assert 'the supe- rior nobility of the collective over the private use of wealth' – outcomes that certainly had not been envisaged by the theory's original progenitors (Gide and Rist 1915, pp. 474, 521–8; Marshall 1926, pp. 130–1, 136–7, 247–9; Jackson 2004, p. 508). Similarly the arguments of French solidarists, 'revisionist' German socialists and English 'new liberals' and Fabians – that private wealth-creation was only possible within the supportive framework of a well-ordered political community, which was therefore entitled to levy a share of that 'social increment' – all pointed towards a relationship between state, economy and society quite different from that maintained by even the most 'interventionist' governments of the mid-nineteenth century (Baldwin 1990, pp. 1–31; Brouilhet 1910, pp. 71–82; Gide and Rist 1915, pp. 558–9; Hayward 1960, pp. 17–33; Hobson 1901, pp. 146–54). J. M. Keynes' early work on the Indian currency question likewise questioned orthodox convictions about the sovereignty of the market, by suggesting that monetary values were not part of a predetermined order of things, but the (somewhat precarious) product of subjective judgement, state intervention and positive law (Keynes 1912, pp. 15–36, 256–9). Such redistributive and interventionist arguments were only of limited impact before 1914. But they fundamentally challenged earlier liberal preconceptions about both the role of the state and the very nature of social and economic policy. And they implicitly drew up the battle-lines for the great economic Methodenstreit that was to dominate public policy in democratic countries for much of the twentieth century (Durbin 1949; Robbins 1932; Schumpeter 1944; Von Mises 2005).

Political thought in many contexts and in many countries was permeated even more closely by ideas borrowed from sociology; a relationship fostered by the fact that many prominent intellectuals of the turn-of-the-century period thought of themselves, and were seen by others, as practitioners of both disciplines (Weber, Durkheim, Tönnies, L. T. Hobhouse and Graham Wallas, were among the most prominent examples). The explosion of studies on the sociology of poverty in many Western European countries led to an enlarged conception of the state's role in relation to social welfare, even among theorists who were otherwise deeply averse to the growth of state power. The English 'new liberal', Charles Masterman, for example, strongly supported collectivist social welfare reforms whilst at the same time deploring the 'ant-heap or beehive' character of much modern state intervention (Masterman 1911, pp. 295–300, 1920, p. 28). Such interventionism was not usually sought on grounds of 'social justice' (though there were some arguments of that kind) but more often in terms of improving the health and safety of the wider 'body politic', with poverty itself being viewed in some quarters not just as a personal fault or social misfortune but as a symptom of 'inefficiency', malfunctioning and even 'degeneration' within the wider 'social organism' (Masterman 1902, pp. 1–17, 42–8; Simon 1897, pp. 434–50). The very term 'organism' signified both the impact of positivist social science, and a more intangible shift of the way in which collective social identity during the period was being subjectively conceived and imagined. It was accompanied throughout Europe, North America and much of the British Empire by a widespread vogue for remedial and reformatory institutions designed to assist, shelter, segregate or coerce those deemed unable or unwilling to cope with the encircling pressures of modern mass society (Dawson 1910; Pinker 1966). And sociology and political thought also shared certain increasingly close affinities to the biological sciences, with both Darwinian and Lamarckian models of evolution being invoked to explain the 'inherited' character of social 'problems' and the relative successes and failures of different individuals, families, classes and nation states. Social and political theorists from across Europe were present, along with many of the world's leading biological scientists, at the large-scale international celebrations in Cambridge in 1909 to celebrate the fiftieth anniversary of *The Origin of Species*; and although there was much sceptical disagreement among delegates about the exact nature of the biological parameters of politics and society, there appeared to be little doubt of their omnipresent salience and power (Seward 1909, pp. 152–70, 446–7, 529–42).

Sociologists also penetrated into what would earlier have been seen as the specifically 'political science' territory of the study of state institutions and public order. Max Weber's classic identification of the categorically 'coercive' role of the institution known as 'the state' (a view that directly linked him, as suggested above, to the lineage of Bentham and Hobbes) was not to be fully articulated until after the First World War (Weber 2005). But, though virtually unknown outside Germany until a much later period, Weber's earlier work on bureaucracy, rationality and administrative 'routinisation' – as processes peculiarly characteristic of 'modern' states and mass parties – underlined the fact that states were social and administrative 'systems', as well as clusters of abstract rules and powers (Weber 1998, pp. 361–6, 2005, pp. 150–234, 157–60, 753–5). And in a rather different sociological sphere, there had been since the early 1890s a stream of specialist investigations, particularly in France and Italy, into the phenomenon of the urban 'crowd' or 'mob' and the outbreaks of contagious 'hysteria' that were increasingly seen as dangerous and pathological attributes of modern mass societies (Le Bon 1908, pp. 25–88; Masterman 1902, pp. 1–8, 63–71; Tarde 1901, pp. 159–213). Émile Durkheim, supposedly the doyen of post-Comtean positivist social science and a critic of idealist and 'Hegelian' theories of the state, nevertheless diagnosed the malady in terms that bore marked affinities with both older and more recent traditions of idealist political thought. He ascribed it to the condition of anomie or normlessness brought about by disintegration of the functions, beliefs and authority systems that had once automatically (or 'mechanically') defined roles and identities for people living in more traditional communities: the set of guiding, intuitive, 'common-sense' assumptions that the English idealist F. H. Bradley had evocatively conjured up as 'my station and its duties' (Bradley 1988, pp. 160–206).

Durkheim's prescription for social estrangement was to reintegrate alienated individuals back into ordered social relationships, not 'mechanically' but 'organically', by restructuring modern societies on the basis of functional and vocational corporations. This strategy was to be supplemented by educational programmes of public and civic morality, designed to 'dispute the postulate that the rights of the individual are inherent'. It was to insist instead that 'the institution of these rights is in fact precisely the task of the State', whose main purpose was to 'liberate . . . individual personalities' (Durkheim 1933, pp. 1–31, 70–132, 1992, pp. 42–71). Durkheim's recipe for the social and political reintegration of both isolated individuals and the 'unattached' masses became for a time part of the semi-official public doctrine of the French Third Republic, and carried him and other 'corporatist' theorists of the period far beyond the confines of mere academic sociology (Hayward 1960, pp. 17–33, 185–202; Lukes 1973, 46–8, 320–7, 350–69, 376–7, 530–46). Very similar themes were to be echoed or paralleled in many other contexts and languages during the period between the 1890s and the First World War. Indeed throughout Europe the first decade of the twentieth century produced numerous ideas and experiments in what might be thought of as 'virtuous fascism', had not later events in history seemed to render any such notion a contradiction in terms. In Germany these included strategies for the systematic incorporation of workers (including many previously excluded and ostracised Social Democrats) into the management of municipal schools, labour bureaux, state social insurance and many other organs of civic life (Dawson 1912, pp. 72–4, 258–64, 278, 1914, pp. 76–80; HMSO Special Reports 1904; Steinmetz 1993, pp. 126–7, 132–3, 194–7). They could be found also in Sidney and Beatrice Webb's early vision of a trade union-based, self-governing, 'Industrial Democracy' that would supplement and in part replace the sphere of remote and unresponsive British parliamentary institutions (Webb and Webb 1902, pp. 806–50). And similar goals could be seen in Pope Leo XIII's proposals for the corporate reorganisation of work, welfare and family life set out in the famous papal encyclical, *Rerum Novarum*, of 1891 (Nitti 1895, pp. 399–422). All these programmes envisaged the reconstitution of civic and community life, and its reabsorption into the wider life of the nation, by means of a modernised version of medieval-style, self-governing vocational corporations: a model that Durkheim claimed also to have derived from the early

Roman republic (Durkheim 1992, pp. 17–35). And in many parts of Western Europe in the 1890s and 1900s very similar ideas were being promoted on a voluntary and philanthropic basis. They were the leitmotiv of many artists' and craftsmen's guilds, women's co-operative workshops, friendly societies, civic guilds, social-service organisations, and numerous other religious, secular and vocational 'corporate' bodies (Cole 1920, pp. 41–77, 103–6; Hobson 1920; Penty 1906).

Not all corporatist theorists, however, shared the Durkheimian vision of using vocational corporations to contain or counteract mass violence, or to reabsorb estranged citizens more closely into the structures of modern industry and the bureaucratic state. On the contrary, there were several rival strands within the 'corporatist' movement that aimed at just the opposite; they sought to defuse and downgrade the directive powers of the state and to encourage pluralism and functional autonomy. In Britain one of the most theoretically powerful defences of this latter model of 'corporatism' came from the legal historian, F. W. Maitland, and the Anglican theologian, J. N. Figgis. Both Maitland and Figgis denounced the Hobbes–Bentham model of unitary 'sovereignty' as enabling the modern state to swallow up and dictate to a wide range of communal, cultural and vocational activities (such as religion, local government, crafts, professions and higher learning): all of which in earlier times had been independently managed and self-regulated by participants and practitioners within those spheres. In the view of Figgis and Maitland, the proper role of the state itself was merely to act as one specialist corporation alongside many others. Its peculiar task was simply to maintain peace and public order so that all other bodies could perform their generic functions without fear of violent disruption (an approach which they portrayed as in direct opposition to the Hobbesian view that the state's peace-keeping functions took absolute priority over and above the rest). In Figgis' political thought, the main thrust of this argument was to defend the corporate autonomy of churches, which – alike in Bismarckian Germany, Third Republican France, Risorgimento Italy and Edwardian Britain – he saw as subject to continuous illegitimate constraints and encroachments from the secular power (Figgis 1914, pp. 3–93; Maitland 1911, pp. 110–11).

Very similar claims were being advanced in the 1900s from a variety of quarters – from trade unions, guild socialists, anarcho-syndicalists and other socio-political movements – which sought, not to absorb citizens more closely into the structures of state or church, but to limit or replace parliamentary government 'from above' by vocational or functional direct democracy 'from below' (Cole 1913, pp. 344–69). In Britain such pressures came primarily from trade unionists whose main objective was to resist legal restrictions upon the rights of workers to combine, strike or perform collectively any action that would have been legal if practised by a single individual – such as withdrawal of labour, mass picketing and peaceful persuasion and demonstration. Beyond these fairly limited objectives, British trade unionists before 1914 largely accepted, and in many cases strongly endorsed, the wider legal framework of conventional parliamentary democracy. It was far otherwise, however, in much of France, Italy, Spain and the USA, where a third powerful strand within the corporatist tradition took up the political doctrines associated with the French anarcho-syndicalist theorist George Sorel. Sorel, whose *Réflections sur la Violence* (1908) was one of the most eloquent and impassioned (if wholly utopian) theoretical works of the period, called for the dissolution of plutocracy by mass resort to the 'general strike'. This was to be a moment of secular 'theophany' (or divine visitation), whereby a single brief act of disinterested mass violence would purge both state and society of their endemic inequalities and corruption, and replace traditional politics by a state-free regime of direct workers' control (Sorel 1969, pp. 119–29, 151–215, 248–9).

5 Conclusion and postscript: rationality and violence

Political thought in the *fin-de-siècle* era therefore appeared as a discipline – if indeed 'discipline' it may be called – pulling simultaneously in many contrary directions. Far-reaching futuristic visions were everywhere floating in the air, ranging from the stateless apocalypse of post-revolutionary socialism, through to predictions of a world where unlimited state sovereignty would have given way to the universal dominion of abstract legal norms (the latter goal hinted at in the works of Kant, and more recently by the young Austrian legal philosopher, Hans Kelsen (Kant 1887, pp. 224–5; Kelsen 1911, pp. i–vii)).[16] In the world of real politics, by contrast, states were everywhere acquiring more extensive practical functions and discretionary powers. Yet, despite the global explosion of new political ideas, the nature of change both within and between nation states appeared to be widely eluding the grasp of much systematic political theory. Newer disciplines such as economics and sociology in part made up for this gap, by contributing

---

16 Hans Kelsen (1881–1973), one of the authors of the Austrian constitution of 1919, and subsequently the most influential jurisprudential theorist of the twentieth century.

substantially to debates about the functions of states in relation to economic and social policy. But neither discipline was able to explain or take account of the structural realities of political power, as embodied in such spheres as armaments programmes, imperialism, militant nationalism, disputed political identities, fiscal and constitutional crises and mass democracy. Thus in many contexts there appeared to be a deep hiatus between political systems as described by contemporary theorists and the ways in which those systems worked in everyday life (perhaps confirming Hegel's ironic aside of a hundred years earlier, that political philosophy was forever doomed to be wise only after the event). State governments as the embodiment of inherited power structures, for example, often seemed strangely at odds, both with contemporary visions of the state as an integrated 'moral community' and with more hedonistic notions of the citizenry as 'shareholders' in a 'company or business firm' (Bosanquet 1910, pp. 6, 298–91, 302; Mallock 1910, p. 1). So it was perhaps no coincidence that the early years of the twentieth century were marked by acute constitutional, territorial and ideological disputes and conflicts in many parts of the world – conflicts that ranged from Great Britain and Ireland, France, Germany, Austria-Hungary and Russia, through to China, Mexico, Latin America and the various constituent territories of the decaying Ottoman Empire (Harris *et al.* 2008).

Later historians have sometimes identified this cacophony of political thought during the *fin-de-siècle* era as a significant causal element in the sleep-walking of politicians and political actors in many nations into the avoidable tragedy of the Great War. In particular, the ideology of 'violence', common to radical protest movements of both left and right (and even to some degree in the usually law-abiding 'centre')[17] has often been cited as symptomatic of a much wider 'revolt against reason' that characterised Western society and culture during the pre-war decades. This revolt has been seen as directed against both the predominance of 'liberal-constitutionalism' in politics and law, and against 'rationalism' as a style of thought that had characterised the Europe-dominated world for much of the nineteenth century. A very extended spectrum of turn-of-the-century thinkers, ranging from die-hard defenders of the *ancien régime* through to anarcho-syndicalists, romantic nationalists and militant suffragettes, has been identified as

17 The support given in 1914 to potentially unconstitutional activities in Ulster by A. V. Dicey, the outstanding authority of the period on liberal constitutionalism and the 'rule of law', was a case in point.

complicit in this movement; whilst in the cultural sphere Freudians, intu-
itionists, religious visionaries and avant-garde intellectuals of many kinds
have all likewise been depicted as sharing in and stoking up a widely diffused anti-rationalist reaction (Burrow 2000, pp. xiii–xiv; Dangerfield 1936;
Stern 1974, pp. xvii–xix, 97–8; Sternhell 1996, pp. 11–29, 70–86, 365–71).
And an influence perceived as lurking behind those tendencies was the
thought of Friedrich Nietzsche, whose contempt for the rationalism of
Platonist and Enlightenment thought, and role in popularising the more
ecstatic and subliminal ideas of the 'pre-Socratic' Greek philosophers, have
often been pinpointed as a powerful element in the pre-history of European
fascism (Barker 1914; Stern 1974; Wolin 1989, pp. 133–7).

Addressing the full ramifications of this argument lies far beyond the scope
of this chapter. But, as suggested above, violence, irrationalism and social
disorder were certainly major concerns of several prominent turn-of-the-
century sociologists and social theorists, who in turn helped to shape and
define the anxieties and priorities of contemporary politics. The question
therefore arises of how far that anti-rationalist 'turn', seemingly so pervasive
in many spheres of early twentieth-century life and thought, was also part
of the culture and methodology of contemporary political theory.

This question is more multifaceted than it seems at first sight, and contains
several assumptions that invite closer attention. Just how far peaceful liberal-
constitutionalism as a form of government had in fact become the assumed
'norm' in Europe and elsewhere, over the course of a century shaped by
the French Revolution, the two Napoleons, the uprisings of 1848, the
Paris Commune, global imperialism and the autocratic constitutions of
Germany and Russia, seems at least open to question. And a similar point
may be made in the intellectual sphere. Despite the nineteenth-century
vogue for Positivism and political economy, earlier chapters in this book
have recorded many instances over the course of the whole century of total
or partial rejection of the ultra-rationalist inheritance of the Enlightenment
epoch. John Stuart Mill's famous 'mental crisis' of 1826 was one conspicuous
example; but such a reaction was not uncommon among intellectuals of
many different kinds throughout Europe over the course of the nineteenth
century (Mill 1960, 137–91; Berlin 1996, pp. 168–93).

A second point relates to the exact nature of the 'anti-rationalism' ascribed
to the political thought of the *fin-de-siècle* period. Whether the intellectual
culture of the 1890s and 1900s was in fact any more prone to 'irrationalist'
reaction than that of earlier decades seems at least open to question, particularly in view of the ultra-rationalist developments that were occurring

during precisely the same turn-of-the-century period in such related areas as jurisprudence, formal logic, neo-classical political economy and many areas of natural science. And, conversely, although many sociologists, nurtured in the positivist tradition, saw irrational thought and behaviour as something that was inherently deviant and abnormal, there were some spheres of intellectual enquiry and creative thought that took a quite different view. In music, poetry, psychoanalysis and Bergsonian philosophy, for example, 'intuition' and the 'subconscious' came increasingly to be seen as legitimate parts of the everyday subject-matter of these disciplines and as an authentic route into the discovery of deeper and different forms of truth. Similarly social anthropology had begun to shed its roots in evolutionary positivism, and to treat human behaviour, wherever found, as something to be studied on its own terms, rather than through the corrective lens of the detached and 'objective' social observer (Jane Harrison, in Seward 1909, pp. 494–511; Stocking 1996, pp. 63–83, 179–232).

Moreover, to some social and political theorists of the period it seemed that an element of the instinctive, transcendent or 'non-rational' was precisely what held complex political societies together. This was a view unexpectedly expressed by Graham Wallas himself a man of notoriously 'rationalist' outlook – both in his conclusion to *The Great Society*, and in his earlier study *Human Nature in Politics*. To Wallas it seemed that it was precisely the neglect of more 'instinctive' and 'customary' human traits by the rational imperatives of economic and administrative 'modernity' that was driving many early twentieth-century citizens into angst and social isolation. Moreover, the would-be political theorist was faced with the problem that his or her primary data was 'human experience', and that much of the experience of even the most 'rational' individuals was unique and varied and subjective and therefore irreducible to the kind of rationalist formulae suggested by either utilitarians or Kantians a hundred years before (Wallas 1914, pp. 376–94, 1962, pp. 138–82). A similar approach was to be found in the writings of J. A. Hobson, who throughout his career as an eclectic but nonetheless highly creative political thinker, struggled with the problem of how to reconcile rationalistic humanism with the burgeoning empirical evidence that human behaviour was also driven by instinct, intuition and subjectivity (Freeden 2005, pp. 107–28). And, most powerfully and persuasively, such a model was approved by Max Weber who unexpectedly portrayed eruptions of 'ecstasy' and 'charisma' in the leadership of social groups, not as inherently pathological, but as characteristic of recurrent patterns of political life throughout human history (Weber 1947, pp. 358–73, 2005, pp. 454–563).[18] Indeed, in Weber's view, what was commonly deemed 'irrationality' was not a deviant or abnormal symptom but an inescapable feature of human thought and action, and therefore of central concern to social and political science (Weber 1975, pp. 120–32, 191–2, 190–207).

A third problem relates to the implied (and often explicit) suggestion that irrationality was inherently linked to political extremism and 'violence', whereas rationality was the corollary of liberal constitutionalism and peaceful legal order. That some political activists of the 1890s and 1900s deliberately linked rejection of reason to their own strategies of violence cannot be denied, most notably in the cases of Sorel, the Futurists, many anti-Semites, and some militant suffragettes. Indeed, for Georges Sorel, the cult of the irrational was no mere strategy but an end in its own right – it was an intrinsically preferable alternative to what he perceived as the appalling cultural triumph of rationalistic humanism (Sorel 1916, pp. 61–2, 89–92, 101–5). Nevertheless, the suggestion that there was a generic and necessary link between interest in the 'irrational' and resort to political violence, or between constitutionalism and rejection of violence, seems very much open to question. Once again the writings of Max Weber, perhaps the greatest theorist of the power-politics of the *fin-de-siècle* epoch, are of relevance here. Weber focused upon the categorical element of systemic violence inherent in the inner structures of even the most legitimate, well-ordered and peaceful states; indeed the very existence of social and political order in Weber's view was predicated upon force and violence being exclusively at the state's disposal (Weber 1954, pp. 338–42). Lenin likewise offers an instructive, though rather different kind of, example. In his 1902 treatise *What is to be Done?* Lenin advanced the case for giving absolute priority in politics to exact science over muddled intuition and pragmatism, to 'organisation' rather than 'spontaneity', to precise calculation of the relation of means to ends, and to control of political strategy by a 'small, compact core' of highly trained political experts rather than by well-meaning democrats and blundering amateurs (Lenin 1961–6, V, pp. 370–5, 422–5, 430, 433–4, 459–65). This tightly reasoned, indeed ultra-rationalist, approach to politics was to be the hallmark of Lenin's lifelong career as a systematic political theorist (apparent in this earlier period no less than during the October Revolution of 1917) (Lenin 1961–6, XXVII, pp. 323–54, XXXI, pp. 17–118). The success of his analysis in winning away Russian social democratic and

---

18 More fully set out in Weber's *Wirtschaft und Gesellschaft* (1922–5), but central to his thought from a much earlier period (Weber 2005, pp. 454–9).

populist support from emerging movements for moderate and gradualist constitutional reforms must make *What is to be Done?* one of the most practically influential works in the long history of political theory. Yet the case of Lenin scarcely supports the view that 'reason' was the intimate partner of liberal constitutionalism, or that 'rational calculation' necessarily offered a virtuous alternative to revolutionary violence and terror. A more plausible assessment is that of the classic study of the period by H. Stuart Hughes, who concluded that the 'greatest' political thinkers of the turn-of-the-century epoch were those who, 'while fighting every step of the way to salvage as much as possible of the rationalist heritage', nevertheless took full account of 'the new definition of man as something more (or less) than a logically calculating animal' (Hughes 1979a, p. 17).

Biographies

ACTON, LORD JOHN

1834–1902. Born in Sicily, Acton was educated in England and Germany. He first gained public recognition writing for liberal Catholic journals. He was a Liberal MP from 1858–65 and was made a peer by Gladstone, his friend, in 1869. In 1895 he became Regius Professor of Modern History at Cambridge and in the years up to his death he planned the *Cambridge Modern History*. Acton never wrote a book, but was influential through his lectures and articles in periodicals. These are collected in *Essays on Church and State* (1952) and *Essays on Freedom and Power* (1948).
• Chadwick 1998.

ADAMS, HENRY

1838–1918. Born in Boston, Massachusetts, into one of the most prominent families in America: both his grandfather, John Quincy Adams and his great-grandfather, John Adams had been presidents of the United States. After graduating from Harvard, he served as private secretary to his father Charles Francis Adams, the American ambassador to Great Britain during the Civil War. Adams returned to the United States in 1868 and pursued a career in journalism. In 1870 he was appointed Assistant Professor at Harvard where he taught medieval, European and later American history. Resigning from Harvard in 1877, he pursued a life of independent scholarship, publishing biographies of Albert Gallatin and John Randolph, as well as the anonymous novel *Democracy* and the pseudonymous novel *Esther*. However, his most important achievement during this period was his monumental *History of the United States during the Administrations of Thomas Jefferson and James Madison* (1889–91).
• Decker 1990; Levenson 1957; Samuels 1948, 1958, 1964; Young 2001.

ANDREWS, STEPHEN PEARL

1812–86. Born in Templeton, Massachusetts, Andrews moved to Texas as a young man to practise law. Hoping to free the state's slaves by government purchase, he travelled to London in an unsuccessful effort to seek funds. Upon his return to the United States, he introduced the country to shorthand, believing it would become a universal language. In 1850 Andrews met Josiah Warren and embraced individualist anarchism. The following year, 1851, the two men founded the individualist utopian community Modern Times on Long Island; it survived until the 1860s. Also in 1851, Andrews wrote *The Science of Society*, a highly regarded scientific explanation of individualist anarchism. In the pages of the *New York Tribune*, Andrews caused a stir during a debate with Horace Greeley and Henry James by advocating free love.
• Johnpoll and Klehr 1986; Martin 1957; Stern 1968.

934

ANTHONY, SUSAN BROWNELL

1820–1906. A reformer and women's suffragist, born in Massachusetts, Susan Anthony was brought up a Quaker and allegedly started to read and write at the age of three. She was a teacher for fifteen years and then became active in the temperance movement; however, as a woman she was forbidden to speak at temperance rallies. In 1851 she met Elizabeth Cady Stanton and this friendship led her to join the women's rights movement and for the rest of her life she lectured and campaigned for women's suffrage and rights and the abolition of slavery. She compiled with Elizabeth Cady Stanton and Matilda Joslyn Gage the three-volume *History of Woman Suffrage* (1881–6).
• DuBois 1999; Kraditor 1981.

ARNOLD, MATTHEW

1822–88. Arnold was an English poet and cultural critic, educated at Rugby and Oxford. After graduating in 1844 he taught classics for a while at Rugby until he became an inspector of schools in 1851, a post he would occupy for 35 years. His reputation as a poet was established with *Empedocles on Etna* (1852) and *Poems* (1853) He was Professor of Poetry at Oxford from 1857–67. During this time he wrote his most famous critical works, *Essays in Criticism* (1865) and *Culture and Anarchy* (1869).
• Collini 1988; Honan 1981.

ARNOLD, THOMAS

1795–1842. Arnold was educated at Winchester and Oxford. After obtaining a first class degree, he was awarded a fellowship at Oriel. He was ordained deacon in 1818 and started a small school in Laleham. In 1827 he was invited to become a master at Rugby School and after his appointment as headmaster in 1828 he started a programme of regeneration at the school. His reforms were to have a lasting effect on the development of public school education in England. In his lifetime he wrote widely on social reform and also supported Catholic emancipation. His son was Matthew Arnold the poet. His main works are *Principles of Church Reform* (1833), *History of Rome* (1838) and *Christian Life* (1841).

AUSTIN, JOHN

1790–1859. One of five sons of an Ipswich industrialist, he entered the army but continued his studies in history and philosophy, and returning home in 1812 he began to read law, was called to the Bar in 1818 and the next year married Sarah Taylor (later translator of Ranke). Austin studied in German with Savigny and others and began lecturing in 1828 to a remarkable group of students including the young John Stuart Mill. In 1834 he lectured on 'the general principles of jurisprudence and international law', and later he was appointed Royal Commissioner to Malta. Austin's extensive influence in the philosophy of law, in which he distinguished between jurisprudence and morality, arose mainly from the second edition of his *Province of Jurisprudence*, published posthumously by his wife in 1861.
• Collini 1993; Kelley 1990; Morison 1982.

BAGEHOT, WALTER

1826–77. An economist and journalist, Bagehot was born in Somerset and educated in Bristol and University College, London. He was called to the Bar and then entered his father's business of shipping and banking. Bagehot wrote many articles for journals in the fields of economics, politics, history and literature and in 1855 founded the *National Review* with his friend Richard Holt. From 1860–77 he was the editor-in-chief of *The Economist*. Bagehot was one of the first to advocate the election of life peers to strengthen the House

of Lords. His most significant works are *The English Constitution* (1867), *Physics and Politics* (1872) and *Lombard Street* (1873).
• Irvine 1939; St John-Stevas 1959.

BAIN, ALEXANDER
1818–1903. Scottish philosopher and psychologist, born in Aberdeen. Bain was educated at Marischal College, Aberdeen where he later taught for three years. His acquaintance with John Stuart Mill began when he started contributing to *The Westminster Review* in 1840 and in 1842 he assisted Mill with the revision of the manuscript of his *System of Logic*. He became Professor of Logic at Aberdeen University (1860–81), and founded the journal *Mind* in 1876. His psychology was firmly based on physiology, and he sought to explain mind through a physical theory of the association of ideas.

BAKUNIN, MIKHAIL
1814–76. Born into the Russian gentry, Bakunin spent several years in artillery school and the army before deciding on a life of left-wing activism. During the 1830s and 1840s, Bakunin absorbed romantic sentimentalism and German idealism, then Left Hegelianism and finally anarchism. He agitated for Polish national independence and pan-Slavism, and took an active part in the revolutionary struggles in Prague in 1848 and in Dresden in 1849. Handed over to the Russian authorities, he spent over a decade imprisoned and in Siberian exile. In 1861, he escaped to Japan, then travelled via the United States to London. Until his death in 1876, he was particularly active in Italy and Switzerland, and it was from this regional base that he organised his secret sects, plotted revolutionary conspiracies, and confronted Marx with an anarchist theory that questioned the very basis of authority and political power.
• Berlin 1978; Carr 1961; Hepner 1950; Kelly 1982; Lehning 1974; Leier 2006; McLaughlin 2002; Mendel 1981; Pyziur 1968; Ravindranathan 1988; Venturi 1960.

BALLANCHE, PIERRE-SIMON
1776–1847. Born in Lyon and steeped in its culture of mysticism, Ballanche was a romantic thinker who, during the period of the Restoration and the July Monarchy, transformed the counter-revolutionary ideas of Maistre and Bonald into theories of expiation and progress. In *Du Sentiment* (1801), he placed the blame for the Revolution on Enlightenment rationalism, proposing sentiment instead as the safeguard of the foundations of religion and society. Ballanche's great work was the *Palingénésie Sociale* (1827–9), never entirely finished, in which he mapped out what he took to be the universal laws of human history. In the *Palingénésie*, Ballanche agrees with Bonald and Maistre that the individual cannot exist apart from society and that language and society are born together; but he departs from these traditionalists, in ascribing to humanity the capacity for rebirth thanks to a seed of 'palingenetic' progress contained in primitive man. Ballanche predicted that, through its sufferings, the human race would one day achieve perfection and unity.
• Bénichou 1977; McAlla 1998; Sainte-Beuve 1993.

BARKER, ERNEST
1874–1960. Born in Woodley, Cheshire, Barker was the son of a farm worker and former miner. He won a scholarship to Manchester Grammar School, and arrived at Balliol College, Oxford in 1893. Trained in classics and history, his first book examined *The Political Thought of Plato and Aristotle* (1906). His interests in idealism and pluralism informed his popular study of *Political Thought from Spencer to Today* (1915). After the First World War, he served as principal of King's College, London, before taking up the chair in political science at

Cambridge in 1927. His work combined both theoretical and institutional approaches to political science.
• Runciman 1997; Stapleton 1994.

BAUER, BRUNO

1808–82. Bauer read theology at Berlin University and between 1834 and 1839 he taught as a Privatdozent at Berlin and was counted as one of the most gifted of the orthodox Hegelians. He was appointed to edit Hegel's lectures on religion against the objections of Hegel's son who thought him too conservative. In the 1850s he became increasingly preoccupied with the growing power of Russia, seen from a German nationalistic perspective. At the same time his contempt for democracy and his hostility to Judaism became increasingly prominent and unrestrained, particularly once he became assistant to Hermann Wagener, editor of the ultra-conservative *Kreuzzeitung* (Journal of the Cross) between 1859 and 1866. From 1866 until his death in 1882, Bauer farmed in the Berlin suburb of Rixdorf.
• Moggach 2003, 2006; Tomba 2006.

BEBEL, (FERDINAND) AUGUST

1840–1913. Born in Cologne-Deutz, the son of a low-ranking army officer, Bebel attended the Volksschule and was trained as a wood turner and cabinet maker. He joined the Arbeit-erbildungsverein (1860) and rose quickly to prominence in the labour movement. A founder of the Social Democratic Workers' Party (1869), he explained its principles in *Unsere Ziele* (1869), and for several decades was the single most important leader of social democracy. He studied socialist thought seriously, especially Marxism, and presented his interpretation in the popular *Woman and Socialism* (1st edition 1879). His memoir, *Aus meinem Leben* (3 vols. 1910–14) is a rich source for his life and the labour movement.
• Herrmann and Emmrich 1989; Lopes and Roth 2000; Maehl 1980; Schraepler 1966; Seebacher-Brandt 1988.

BEESLEY, EDWARD SPENCER

1831–1915. The son of an evangelical minister, Beesley was educated at Wadham College, Oxford, where he met the other future leaders of Comtism in England (Richard Congreve, then a popular tutor, Frederic Harrison and John Henry Bridges). Soon after leaving Oxford, Beesley became converted to Positivism. Based on Comte's view of the proletariat and its 'historical destiny', he became very active in the labour movement during the 1860s and 1870s. He also held a series of academic appointments, including Professor of History at University College, London. In 1893 he became editor of the newly founded *Positivist Review*.
• Harrison 1959, 1965.

BELINSKII, VISSARION GRIGORIEVICH

1811–48. Born in Sveaborg (Finland), Belinskii was a literary critic whose writings exercised a powerful influence on several generations of the Russian intelligentsia. In the second half of the 1830s he was a Hegelian and preached the 'philosophical reconciliation with reality'. At the beginning of the 1840s he renounced his 'reconciliation', replaced conservative historicism with the Left Hegelian 'philosophy of action', and transformed the journal *Otechestvennye Zapiski* (Annals of the Fatherland) into the chief organ of democratic Westernism. In 1846 he joined the staff of *Sovremennik* (Contemporary) and engaged himself in polemics with the Slavophiles. In 1847 he made a trip to the West and as a result wrote his famous *Letter to N. V. Gogol* (1847).
• Berlin 1978; Masaryk 1955; Walicki 1975.

BELLAMY, EDWARD
1850–98. Born in Massachusetts, the son of a Baptist minister, Bellamy was an American journalist and political theorist who studied law and worked briefly in the newspaper industry. He wrote four novels and many articles in his lifetime; however, he is most remembered as author of the utopian *Looking Backward 2000 to 1887* (1889) which foretells many changes that have since become reality. The book achieved fame worldwide. In later life Bellamy lectured widely before dying of tuberculosis.
• Bowman 1958.

BENTHAM, JEREMY
1748–1832. Born in Spitalfields, London, Bentham entered Oxford at the age of twelve, and was admitted to Lincoln's Inn at the age of nineteen. He published copiously on penal and social reform, economics and politics and he is best known for his pioneering works *A Fragment on Government* (1776) and *Introduction to the Principles of Morals and Legislation* (1789), which argued that the proper objective of all conduct and legislation is 'the greatest happiness of the greatest number', and developed a 'hedonic calculus' to estimate the effects of different actions. He was made an honorary citizen of the French Republic in 1792.
• Baumgardt 1952; Conway 1990a, 1990b; Everett 1931; Harrison 1983; Kelly 1990; Ogden 1932; Rosen 1983, 1992.

BENZENBERG, JOHANN FRIEDRICH
1777–1846. Benzenberg studied theology and later natural sciences in Göttingen. A German liberal, he was in favour of provincial/regional (not national) government as the best representation of the public will. He published a treatise *Über Verfassung* (On the Constitution) in Düsseldorf in 1816 which claimed that the role of parliament must be to communicate and pressure government to rule in line with public opinion. The treatise formed the basis of the constitutional system in the southern German principalities in the nineteenth century which maintained the powerful position of the prince and his government while also demanding that a parliamentary majority should be secured for legislation, especially when it concerned taxation. In 1844 he founded his own observatory in Bilk, dying there two years later.
• Baum 2008.

BERNSTEIN, EDUARD
1850–1932. Born in Berlin, the son of a Jewish locomotive engineer, Bernstein joined the Social Democratic Workers' Party (Eisenachers) in 1872. He edited *Der Sozialdemokrat* (1879–90) in Zurich, until expelled in 1887, and then in London, where he formed a close relationship with Engels. Although a convinced Marxist for many years, contemporary developments in capitalism led him to question major principles of Marx's theory, a position he explicated in *The Preconditions of Socialism* (1899) and other publications. Bernstein's revisionism aroused a fierce debate among socialists; the immediate outcome was a formal rejection of his views in 1903. Since the Second World War the value of his ideas has been increasingly appreciated.
• Carsten 1993; Gay 1952; Meyer 1977; Steger 1997.

BICHAT, MARIE FRANÇOIS XAVIER
1771–1802. A French anatomist and physiologist, Bichat studied under M. A. Petit in Lyon and then with P. I. Dessault in Paris, where he began giving lectures in 1797. Appointed physician to the Hôtel-Dieu in 1801, he was the first to simplify anatomy and physiology by identifying tissues and classifying them into types. His larger speculations on human physiological types, especially in his *Recherches Physiologiques sur la Vie et la Mort* (1800),

influenced the development of French social thought away from an egalitarianism based on the sensationalist theory of mind. He also published the *Traité des Membranes* (1800), the *Traité d'Anatomie Descriptive* (5 vols. 1801–3) and the *Anatomie Générale* (1801).

• Dobo and Role 1989; Haigh 1984.

BLANC, LOUIS

1811–82. Blanc was born in Madrid where his father was inspector-general of finance for Joseph Bonaparte; he was therefore deeply affected by the fall of the Empire. He studied in Paris where he became a journalist and launched the *Revue du Progrès* in 1839. His political aspirations led him to write *L'Organisation du Travail* (Organisation of Labour) (1839) in which he defines his ideal of a new social order. He was a member of the provisional government of 1848 but was forced to flee to England when implicated in the workers' insurrection. In exile he wrote the twelve-volume *Histoire de la Révolution Française* (1847–62). He returned to France in 1871 and became a member of the Assemblée Nationale.

• Blanc 1982.

BLANQUI, AUGUSTE

1805–81. A French revolutionary and radical thinker and leader of the movement known as Blanquism. Blanqui was nicknamed *L'Enfermé* as he spent some 37 years of his life in prison. He was educated in Paris, studying law and medicine, and in 1824 became a member of the Carbonari, a revolutionary secret society. He took part in the July Revolution of 1830 and in 1839 he was condemned to life imprisonment for helping organise a failed insurrection against Louis Philippe; he was subsequently pardoned. Until his death he took part in every revolutionary activity in France and as a result spent much of his time behind bars. His most significant work is *Critique Social* (Social Criticism) (1885) which was published posthumously.

• Hayward 1991; Hutton 1981; Mariel 1971; Spitzer 1957.

BLATCHFORD, ROBERT

1851–1943. A socialist campaigner, Blatchford was born in Maidstone. Apprenticed as a brushmaker, he ran away to join the army. He left in 1878 and became a journalist in Manchester; this is said to have converted him to socialism. In 1890 he founded the Manchester Fabian Society and then in 1891 he founded the newspaper *The Clarion*. After the Boer War he became a fervent supporter of the British Empire and in the 1924 election he supported the Conservatives. His most significant book was *Merrie England* (1893), a collection of his socialist articles which sold extremely well. Other works include *Britain for the British* (1902) and *The Sorcery Shop* (1907).

BLYDEN, EDWARD

1832–1912. Blyden was a West Indian-born Christian preacher. He lived in both Liberia and Sierra Leone and became one of the earliest ideologues of pan-Africanism. In 1851 he emigrated to Liberia, and became tutor at Alexander High School and in 1862 Professor of Classics at Liberia College – a post he held until 1871. He held a variety of positions in Liberia and Sierra Leone, including secretary of state and ambassador to the Court of St James. His first pamphlet *A Voice from Bleeding Africa* was published in 1856, but his major work is *Christianity, Islam and the Negro Race* (1887) in which he argued that Islam suited African conditions better than Christianity, especially in its European missionary version.

• Blyden 1908.

BONALD, LOUIS-GABRIEL-AMBROISE, VICOMTE DE

1754–1840. Born into a family of provincial nobility, Bonald was the mayor of Millau in France from 1785–90. In 1791, having turned against the Revolution, Bonald emigrated from France to Coblenz (headquarters of the royal princes) and thence to Heidelberg, where he stayed until the autumn of 1795, writing *Théorie du Pouvoir Politique et Religieux* (1796). This work laid out his counter-revolutionary theory of power: a new science of society, in which families and society – a 'group of relationships' – were prior to the individual; likewise, language was prior to thought. Bonald insisted that power had a religious basis, and has therefore often been labelled as a 'theocrat', along with Joseph de Maistre. Through his work *Du Divorce* (1801), Bonald influenced the harshening of the terms of French divorce law (in 1802). He later lobbied successfully to repeal the divorce law altogether (in 1816). Admired by Napoleon I, Bonald was elected to the Chamber of Deputies and in 1823 he became a peer of France. After 1830, Bonald resigned his peerage in protest at the liberal revolution.
• Barclay 1967; Cohen 1969; Klinck 1996; Moulinié 1915; Nisbet 1944; Reedy 1983, 1993, 1995.

BOSANQUET, BERNARD

1848–1923. Born near Alnwick, Bosanquet was the son of a reverend. He attended Harrow and Balliol College, Oxford, where he encountered T. H. Green. Active in the Charity Organisation Society, Bosanquet wrote extensively about social work. Impressed by the work of F. H. Bradley, he produced a study of *Knowledge and Reality* (1885), followed by a work on *Logic* (1888). His most significant work of political theory, *The Philosophical Theory of the State* (1899), offered an elaborate idealist account of politics. It was metaphysics to which he devoted most subsequent attention, notably in *The Principle of Individuality and Value* (1912) and *The Value and Destiny of the Individual* (1913).
• Carter 2003; McBriar 1987; Morrow 2000; Nicholson 1990.

BRADLAUGH, CHARLES

1833–91. Born in London, the son of a solicitor's clerk, Bradlaugh left home in 1849 and joined the army; however, he obtained a discharge in 1853. In 1860 he founded *The National Reformer* with Joseph Barker. Bradlaugh led free thought and radical movements in Britain in the 1860s and wrote a series of pamphlets on politics and religion, founding the National Secular Society in 1866. In 1877 he published the controversial work by Charles Knowlton, *The Fruits of Philosophy*, a work which advocated birth control. He was convicted for publishing an 'obscene publication' but the case was dismissed on a technicality. He was the first atheist to become a Member of Parliament, serving Northampton from 1880–91.
• Bonner 1895; D'Arcy 1982.

BRANDES, ERNST

1758–1810. Brandes met Edmund Burke in 1785, on a journey to England, and later became one of Burke's chief Hanoverian followers, along with August Rehberg. In 1786, Brandes published an article praising the British constitution in the *Neue Deutsche Monatschrift*. In 1791, having read Burke's *Reflections*, he published a critique of the French Revolution, *Politische Betrachtungen über die Franzözische Revolution*. While conceding that some kind of revolution was inevitable, on account of the mistakes made by the French monarchy, Brandes argued that the constitution of 1791 – which he saw as the product of a 'Rousseau–American-economist clique' – was not appropriate for the French nation. He lamented that the French constitution was not more like the British one. By 1792, Brandes' hostility towards the Revolution had deepened, and his *Über einige bisherige Folgen der Französische*

Revolution in Rucksicht auf Deutschland urged Germans not to fall prey to the revolutionary spirit.
• Beiser 1992; Droz 1949; Godechot 1972; Raynaud 1989.

BRIGHT, JOHN

1811–89. A radical Quaker statesman, Bright was the son of a Rochdale cotton manufacturer and this Quaker heritage would define his life, campaigning for causes that would improve the lives of working people. Bright worked for a time in the family business and became involved in family politics. When the Anti-Corn League was created in 1839 he became a key member and together with his friend Richard Cobden, opposed the Corn Laws until they were repealed. In the 1840s he also opposed factory legislation. Bright promoted the reform movement that led to the introduction of free trade. As a fine orator he drew large crowds wherever he went. In 1843 he became Member of Parliament for Durham and subsequently held seats in Manchester and Birmingham.

BRISBANE, ALBERT

1809–90. A social theorist, Brisbane was born to wealthy parents. At eighteen he left for Paris to pursue his studies with the great social thinkers of Europe. He studied under François Guizot in Paris and G. W. F. Hegel in Berlin, although remained uninspired. When he returned to Paris he read a treatise of Charles Fourier and was greatly moved. He then studied with Fourier until 1834 when he returned to the United States as a disciple of the French socialists, an enthusiastic advocate of Fourierism. He started to lecture and wrote the *Social Destiny of Man* (1840) and *Association* (1843), both explaining Fourier's labour system. His subsequent column in the *New York Tribune* ensured a national audience for Fourierism.

BROUSSE, PAUL

1844–1912. Born in Montpellier, Brousse became an activist of the International Working Men's Association (IWA) in the Midi during 1871–2. Forced to take refuge in Spain and then Switzerland, he was a spokesman for the Bakuninist anti-authoritarians within the IWA and then an active member of the Jura Federation. He became a famous advocate of 'propaganda by the deed' (1877), which led to his expulsion from Switzerland. On return to France in the early 1880s, he broke with the anarchists and embraced a 'municipal socialism' that called for public assistance and practical local reform. As a leader of the so-called 'possibilist' wing of the Parti ouvrier français (POF), he led the opposition to Jules Guesde and the Marxists and became active in Parisian and national politics. When he died in 1912 he was part of the Jaurès wing of the Section Française de l'Internationale Ouvrière (SFIO).
• Guillaume 1985; Stafford 1971.

BRYCE, JAMES (FIRST VISCOUNT)

1838–1922. Bryce was a statesman and liberal, educated at Glasgow, Trinity College, Oxford and Heidelberg. He was called to the Bar in 1867 and served as Regius Professor of Civil Law at Oxford from 1870–93. Bryce gained recognition as a historian after publication of *The Holy Roman Empire* (1864). Later *The American Commonwealth* (1888) was the first book to discuss American institutions from the perspective of a historian and constitutional lawyer. A liberal, Bryce was elected to Parliament in 1880 and when the Liberals returned to government in 1905 he became Chief Secretary to Ireland. From 1907–12 he was Ambassador to the United States.

Biographies

BUONARROTI, PHILIPPE-MICHEL

1761–1837. Born in Pisa to an aristocratic family, Buonarroti was a French revolutionary. He studied literature and law at the University of Pisa and became a fervent admirer of Rousseau. This led him to publish the *Gazetta Universale* (1787) where he freely diffused his revolutionary ideas. As a Freemason and a member of the secret society the Illuminati de Bavière he was constantly under police surveillance. He fled to Paris in 1789 and joined the Jacobin Club, and was granted the title of French citizen by the Convention. He was later imprisoned as a follower of Robespierre. There he met Gracchus Babeuf and his work *History of Babeuf's Conspiracy* (1828) recounts their unsuccessful plot to overthrow the Directory Government of 1796.

• Bax 1911; Lehning 1956; Thomson 1947.

BYRON, LORD GEORGE GORDON

1788–1824. Born in London and educated at Harrow and Trinity College Cambridge, Byron took his seat in the House of Lords in 1809. His maiden speech in 1812 pleaded for the humane treatment of riotous weavers. The publication of the first two cantos of *Childe Harolde* in 1812 established Byron's reputation as a poet. Following the scandalous separation from his wife in 1816 Byron left England, settling finally in Italy. He died at Missolonghi while on a military expedition in support of Greek independence. There are many political references and allusions in Byron's poetry, and especially in *Don Juan* (1819), but the most developed statements of his aristocratic republicanism appeared in his two 'history plays', *Marino Faliero* (1820) and *The Two Foscari* (1821).

• Gross 2001; Kelsall 1987; Murphy 1985; Thorslev 1989; Watkins 1981; Woodring 1970.

CABANIS, PIERRE JEAN GEORGES

1757–1808. A student of the noted doctor Léon Dubreuil, Cabanis frequented the salon of Mme Helvétius in Auteuil until the outbreak of the Revolution. Doctor to Mirabeau and close friend of Condorcet, he survived the Terror to become a member of the Conseil des Cinq-Cents (in 1797) and then the Napoleonic Senate, which he refrained from attending because of opposition to Napoleon. He was a leading member of the Idéologues, among whom he was especially noted for his *Rapports du Physique et du Moral de l'Homme* (1802); this broke with Condillac's view that all psychic functions were transformations of sensations and emphasised sensibility in its physiological sense, with the aim of enabling medicine to become the basis of moral and social reform. He also wrote *Observations sur les Hôpitaux* (1790), *Du Degré de Certitude de la Médecine* (1798) and *Coup d'oeil sur les Révolutions et sur la Réforme de la Médecine* (1804).

• Gusdorf 1978; Staum 1980; Welch 1984.

CABET, ÉTIENNE

1788–1853. A communist lawyer, Cabet was elected to the Chambre des Députés in 1831. However, as a result of his embittered attacks on the French government, he was found guilty of treason and fled to England. There he came into contact with Robert Owen and started to develop a theory of communism. Shortly after his return to France in 1839 he wrote *Voyage en Icarie* (1840) setting out his picture of a utopian society which earned him many followers. Like Owen he sought to put his ideas into practice and founded the Icarian movement. In its wake several Icarian colonies were founded in the United States, which lasted until the early 1880s.

• C. Johnson 1974.

CAFIERO, CARLO

1846–92. Cafiero was born into a rich landowning family in Barletta and graduated in law from the University of Naples. Converted to Marxian socialism in 1870, he organised Italian sections of the International Working Men's Association (IWA) according to the tenets of Marx and Engels. In mid-1872, he was won over to Bakunin's anarchist collectivism and became a prominent advocate of what he termed 'permanent revolt'. He spent the money he inherited from his family for the anarchist cause, even buying a villa near Locarno for Bakunin. A leader of the insurrections of 1874 and 1877, he was forced into exile. He was mentally unstable in his final years (1882–92).
• Hostetter 1958; Pernicone 1993; Ravindranathan 1988.

CALHOUN, JOHN C.

1782–1850. Born in South Carolina, John C. Calhoun was first elected to Congress in 1810; he was secretary of war from 1817–25, vice-president from 1825–32, secretary of war from 1844–5 and, perhaps most importantly, senator for South Carolina from 1832–43 and from 1845–50. Calhoun began his political life as a fiery nationalist and ended it as a fiery sectionalist. His theories, developed over the years in a series of powerful speeches and in two posthumous theoretical works, the *Disquisition on Government* and the *Discourse on the Constitution and Government of the United States*, enjoyed a considerable vogue in the middle of the twentieth century, though they are less often celebrated today.
• Peterson 1987; Wiltse 1944–51.

CAMBACÉRÈS, JEAN-JACQUES-RÉGIS DE

1753–1824. Born in Montpellier in the nobility of the robe, he studied law and became a member of the National Convention, in which he occupied himself with the legislative work of the First Republic. In 1799 he became Second Consul of France behind Napoleon and later a Prince of the Empire and Duke of Parma, and before the Restoration he devoted himself to his major work, the redaction of the *Code Napoléon*.
• Bonnecase 1933; Gaudemet 1935; Kelley 1984a.

CARLYLE, THOMAS

1795–1881. Born at Ecclefechan, Scotland and educated at Annan Grammar School and the University of Edinburgh, Carlyle considered entering the church and the law before embarking on a literary career in the early 1820s. His first publications dealt with aspects of German literature, the anti-utilitarian and anti-materialist cast of which played an important role in *Sartor Resartus* (1833). Some of Carlyle's political ideas were sketched in *Signs of the Times* (1829); they were treated more fully in *Chartism* (1839). This work dealt with the condition of the lower classes and with problems of political leadership, themes that were also prominent in Carlyle's increasingly authoritarian politics presented in *On Heroes and Hero Worship* (1841), *Past and Present* (1843) and *Latter-Day Pamphlets* (1850).
• La Valley 1968; Lasch 1991; Lee 2004; Morrow 2006; Rosenberg 1974; Vanden Bossche 1991.

CHAADAEV, PËTR IAKOVLEVICH

1794–1856. Born into an aristocratic family in Moscow, Chaadaev served as an officer in the Russian army during the campaign against Napoleon and sympathised with the Decembrist movement. He gave a philosophical formulation to his world-view in the eight *Philosophical Letters*, written in French from 1828–31. The first of these letters, developing a view of Russia as a country 'Forgotten by the Providence', was published in the journal *Teleskop* (1836) and caused a violent reaction in official circles: Chaadaev was declared mad and put under medical surveillance. In the next year, Chaadaev wrote his *Apology of a Madman* which

943

showed that his view of Russia could be interpreted optimistically as a justification of belief in Russia's great future.
• Koyré 1950; Masaryk 1955; Walicki 1975.

CHAMBERS, ROBERT
1802–71. Born in Peebles, Scotland, Chambers was largely self-educated. From modest beginnings, selling books on an Edinburgh street, Robert and his brother successfully established a publishing firm in 1832. Chambers wrote mainly on Scottish folklore and history, supplying articles for *Chambers' Edinburgh Journal*, but by the 1840s his attention had turned to geology. His *Vestiges of the Natural History of Creation*, published anonymously in 1844, became a *succès de scandale*, due to its provocative evolutionary speculations. It offered hypotheses about human origins and suggested that nature had developed in stages from an original cloud of interstellar gas into a complex organic world. Its controversial reception was anxiously noted by Charles Darwin as he contemplated his own elaborate findings and speculations about evolution.
• Millhauser 1959; Secord 2000.

CHATEAUBRIAND, FRANÇOIS-RENÉ DE
1768–1848. Born at St Malo, Brittany and educated by the Jesuits at Rennes and Dinan, Chateaubriand served in the army from 1786–91. He visited North America in 1791–2, joined the émigré army on his return to France and went into exile in England until 1800. In 1802 he refused a diplomatic position in reaction to the execution of the Duc d'Enghien and became an implacable opponent of Napoleon. Made a peer of France in 1815 Chateaubriand was active in politics in the Restoration. He held diplomatic posts in Berlin, London and Rome, and was Minister of Foreign Affairs from 1822–4. He published *Essai sur les Révolutions* (1802), *De Bonaparte et des Bourbons* and *Réflexions Politiques* (1814) and *De la Monarchie selon la Charte* (1816).
• Aureau 2001; Beik 1956; Bénichou 1977; Benrekassa 1986; Clément 1998; Dupuis and Moreau 1967; Godechot 1972; Huet 2000; Loménie 1929; Sainte-Beuve 1993; Siegel 1970; Switzer 1971.

CHERNYSHEVSKII, NIKOLAI GAVRILOVICH
1828–89. Born in Saratov, Chernyshevskii was the main ideologist of the Russian democratic radicalism of the 1860s. As the editor-in-chief of the opposition journal *Sovremennik* (Contemporary) he exercised a formative influence on an entire generation of the newly emerged intelligentsia of non-gentry background. In his treatise *The Anthropological Principle in Philosophy* (1860) he developed an emancipatory, anthropocentric version of materialism; in his *Criticism of Philosophical Prejudice Against the Peasant Commune* (1859) he outlined a theory of Russia's direct transition to socialism. In 1862 he was arrested, accused of co-operation with the revolutionary organisation Land and Freedom and, despite insufficient evidence, condemned to lifetime exile in Siberia. In prison he wrote the novel *What is to be Done?* (1863) in which he described the 'new people' of Russia – 'rational egoists' – devoted to the cause of progress, and even a type of ascetic, self-sacrificing revolutionist.
• Masaryk 1955; Pereira 1975; Venturi 1960.

CHICHERIN, BORIS NIKOLAEVICH
1828–1904. Born in the province of Tambov, Chicherin was a historian, philosopher, jurist and the leading theorist of conservative liberalism in Russia. His book *On Popular Representation* (1866) clearly distinguished between civil rights and political rights. In his *Property and State* (1882–3) he defended private law and the free market, condemning socialism. The five

volumes of his *History of Political Doctrines* (1869–1902) belong to the best works of this kind produced in the nineteenth century. In *Russia on the Eve of the Twentieth Century* (published anonymously in Berlin in 1900) he argued that the only solution of Russia's problems would be a change from absolute to constitutional monarchy. In his *Philosophy of Law* (1900) he departed from Hegelianism and made a contribution to the revival of natural law in Russia.
• Hamburg 1992; Kelly 1998; Leontowitsch 1957; Walicki 1987.

CIESZKOWSKI, AUGUST
1814–94. Educated in Cracow then Berlin, where he was particularly influenced by the liberal Hegelians Eduard Gans and Karl-Ludwig Michelet. Apart from the *Prolegomena*, Cieszkowski participated in (old) Hegelian debates about the nature of God and immortality and in resistance to Schelling's 'philosophy of revelation'. In the decade before 1848, however, he spent most of his time in Paris, where his book on money, *Du Crédit et de la Circulation* (1839), became one of the sources of Proudhon's *Philosophie de la Misère*. After 1848 he returned to Posen, where he was active in local politics. His life work, *Our Father*, an attempt to build a utopian vision of the future upon an esoteric reading of the Lord's Prayer inspired by Joachimite prophecy, a millenarian reading of Hegel and Lessing's *Education of the Human Race*, remained unfinished at his death.
• Liebich 1979.

COBBETT, WILLIAM
1763–1835. Born near Farnham in Kent, Cobbett was a self-educated farmer's son who became a politician and radical journalist. From 1784–91 he served as a soldier in New Brunswick; when discharged he went first to France then America where he wrote the pro-British *The Life and Adventures of Peter Porcupine* (1796). He returned to England in 1800 and founded *Cobbett's Political Register* in 1802, where he freely voiced his radical views. He entered Parliament in 1832 but died in 1835. His most famous book is *Rural Rides* (1830) in which he admires the 'real' countryside, striking out against the changes brought on by the industrial revolution.
• Spater 1982.

COBDEN, RICHARD
1804–65. Cobden was born into a poor farming family, received very little formal education, and at fourteen he started to work in his uncle's London warehouse. In 1828 he entered into partnership with two friends selling calico in London and in 1831 they opened a calico printing works in Lancashire. Cobden subsequently travelled to America and the Levant and published *England, Ireland and America* (1835) and *Russia* (1836); these criticised British foreign policy and preached free trade. He stood as Member of Parliament for Stockport in 1837 on a free trade platform and failed, but was elected in 1840. Cobden was one of the seven founding members of the Anti-Corn Law League in 1838.

COLERIDGE, SAMUEL TAYLOR
1772–1834. Coleridge was educated at Christ's Hospital and Jesus College, Cambridge. Following a meeting with Robert Southey in 1794 the two men formed a plan for a communitarian settlement in America (Pantisocracy). In 1795 they lectured in Bristol to raise money for this settlement; Coleridge produced a large but disjointed and incomplete body of poems, journalism, and literary, philosophical and political criticism. *The Friend* (1809–10), *The Statesman's Manual* (1816), *A Lay Sermon* (1817) and *On the Constitution of the Church and State* (1829) expressed views that were broadly conservative in their political

bearing. There are extensive comments on politics in Coleridge's *Letters, Marginalia Notebooks* and *Table Talk*.

• Coleman 1988; Colmer 1959; Kennedy 1958; Leask 1988; Morrow 1990.

COMTE, ISIDORE AUGUSTE MARIE FRANÇOIS XAVIER

1798–1857. Born to a Catholic and royalist family, Comte was an intellectually gifted and rebellious youth. Expelled from the École Polytechnique in 1816 for subversive activities, he was from 1817 to 1823 the private secretary of Saint-Simon, a formative experience that decisively influenced his development of Positivism. He never acquired an academic post, and survived on money from lecture and examiner's fees, and from gifts from admirers (such as J. S. Mill and George Grote). The range of Comte's writings is remarkable: mathematics, philosophy of science, religion, morality and sociology. Particularly influential was his emphasis upon verification as the essential feature of the new positive methods in succession to the 'theological' and 'metaphysical' epochs. Among his important works are the *Calendrier Positiviste* (1849), *Catéchisme Positiviste* (1852), *Cours de Philosophie Positive* (6 vols. 1830–42), *Discours sur l'Ensemble du Positivisme* (1848) and *Système de Politique Positive* (4 vols. 1851–4).

• Arnaud 1969; Charlton 1959; Dale 1989; Frick 1990; Gouhier 1931, 1933–41; Lenzer 1975; Pickering 1993.

CONDORCET, MARIE JEAN ANTOINE NICOLAS CARITAT, MARQUIS DE

1743–94. At the outbreak of the French Revolution, Condorcet was inspector of the mint, permanent secretary of the Académie des Sciences, and a member of the Académie Française. Friend of d'Alembert and Turgot, he was an eminent *philosophe* with a reputation as a mathematician and as a scientific reformer. He published the important *Essai sur l'Application de l'Analyse à la Probabilité des Décisions Rendues à la Pluralité des Voix* (1785). Condorcet enthusiastically supported the early phase of the revolution, founding with Emmanuel Sieyès the Society of 1789, and serving as delegate to the Legislative Assembly and to the Convention. Associated with the Girondins, he shared in their proscription and went into hiding, where he wrote the influential *Esquisse d'un Tableau des Progrès de l'Esprit Humain*. After his arrest in March 1794, he was found dead in his cell, probably as the result of self-administered poison.

• Baker 1975; Gusdorf 1978; Welch 1984.

CONGREVE, RICHARD

1818–90. The official leader of the English Positivists, Congreve was educated at Rugby (under Arnold) and at Oxford. He resigned his fellowship at Wadham College in 1855 to devote himself to propagating Comte's positive philosophy, with which he had become acquainted during an earlier visit to Paris. A split in the ranks of English Positivism occurred in 1878, and Congreve became the leader of the more religious wing based in Chapel Street. His former students, Harrison, Beesley and Bridges, formed a separate society at Newton Hall.

• Simon 1963; Wright 1986.

CONSIDÉRANT, VICTOR

1808–93. Considérant was born in Salins and studied engineering at the École Polytechnique. As an engineer he collaborated with Fourier and became editor of the Fourierist journals *Le Phalanstère* and *La Phalange*. In 1848 he was elected member of the Assemblée Nationale but was forced to go into exile in Belgium when he organised the 1849 insurrection against Louis-Napoléon Bonaparte. In 1852 he emigrated to the United States where he tried and failed to establish a colony in Texas following Fourier's principles. His main publications are

the *Destinée Sociale* (1847–9), a digest of Fourier's writings, and the *Principes du Socialisme* (1847) which argues in support of Fourierism over other forms of socialism.
• Beecher 2001; Davidson 1988.

CONSTANT, BENJAMIN

1767–1830. Born in Lausanne and educated at the University of Edinburgh. In 1794 he met Anne Louise Germaine de Staël, daughter of Jacques Necker, former minister of France. In 1795 they arrived in Paris and remained there before going into exile from 1802–14. In the intervening years Constant published a series of justly famous pamphlets setting out his political views. Despite his opposition to Napoleon Bonaparte, on the latter's return from Elba he provided the Emperor with a new constitution. During the Restoration (1814–30) he combined the activities of journalist and parliamentary deputy, establishing himself as France's foremost liberal publicist. In addition to the many political writings he published during this period, Constant also published the semi-autobiographical novel *Adolphe* (1816), upon which for many years his reputation was based.
• Holmes 1984.

DAHLMANN, FRIEDRICH CHRISTOPH

1785–1860. Born in Wismar and trained as a classical philologist, Dahlmann became a historian and took up politics while Professor of History at Kiel University. In 1825 he was appointed professor at Göttingen, where he became the leading figure among the seven professors who protested against the abrogation of the constitution in 1837 and were subsequently dismissed. In 1842 Dahlmann accepted the chair of history and political science at Bonn. He was a member of the Frankfurt Parliament from 1848–9. His liberal views were influenced by British models, and his writings reflect the nationalism generated during the Napoleonic period. In his view a united Germany should not include Austria. This attitude underlies his *Quellenkunde der Deutschen Geschichte* (Sources on German history) (1830). He also wrote a *Geschichte von Dänemark* (History of Denmark, 3 vols. 1840–3).
• Heimpel 1962; Hubert 1937.

DANILEVSKII, NIKOLAI IAKOVLEVICH

1822–85. Born in the province of Orlovskaia, Danilevski was a naturalist and the main theorist of Russian pan-Slavism. In 1847 he received a master's degree in botany from St Petersburg University. For his activity in the Petrashevsky discussion group (seen by the authorities as a revolutionary circle) he was arrested in 1849 and exiled to Vologda. He resumed his scholarly activities in 1853, taking part in a number of scientific expeditions and becoming director of a botanical garden in 1879. His book *Russia and Europe* (1871) bases pan-Slavism on naturalistic foundations, developing the theory of 'historico-cultural types', similar to different biological species, and proclaiming the replacement of political idealism by self-conscious national egoism.
• Fadner 1961; Thaden 1964; Walicki 1975.

DARWIN, CHARLES

1809–82. Born in Shrewsbury, Darwin studied medicine at Edinburgh before moving, in 1827, to Christ's College, Cambridge. In 1831 he accepted an invitation to join a five-year scientific survey as a naturalist aboard HMS *Beagle*. The voyage took him to South America, the Galapagos, Tahiti, Australia and South Africa, and the papers he sent back ensured his reputation as a scientist on his return. This work, combined with research into the domestication of animals and a reading of Malthus' writings on population, led Darwin to write *On the Origin of Species* (1859). This provoked violent critical reactions as well as

enthusiasm, especially for its perceived atheistic implications. It was followed by *Variation of Animals and Plants under Domestication* (1868), *The Descent of Man* (1871) and *The Expression of the Emotions in Man and Animals* (1872). Darwin was buried in Westminster Abbey.
• Beer 1983; Bowlby 1990; Browne 1995; Clark 1984; Darwin 1958; Desmond and Moore 1991; Grubar 1974; Himmelfarb 1959; Levine 1988.

DESTUTT DE TRACY, ANTOINE-LOUIS-CLAUDE, COMTE DE
1754–1836. Of a noble family of Scottish descent, Destutt de Tracy served briefly as a cavalry leader under his friend Lafayette during the Revolution. Imprisoned during the Terror he studied Locke and Condillac and, upon his release, was named an associate of the National Institute in the Class of Moral and Political Sciences. He coined the term 'ideology' and was a leader of the Idéologue school during the Directory, Empire and Restoration. Author of a liberal treatise on economics (the third volume of his influential *Élémens d'Idéologie*), a utilitarian democrat and cautious constitutionalist in politics (as seen in his *Commentaire sur l'Esprit des Lois de Montesquieu*), Destutt de Tracy influenced the revival of liberal and republican thought in France after the Revolution.
• Gusdorf 1978; Kennedy 1978; Welch 1984.

DICEY, ALBERT VENN
1835–1922. Born near Lutterworth in Leicestershire, Dicey was the son of a newspaper proprietor. He went up to Balliol College, Oxford in 1858, and formed important friendships, notably with James Bryce. After over twenty years of legal practice and journalism, Dicey was elected to the Vinerian chair in English law at Oxford in 1882. In 1885, he published his *Introduction to the Study of the Law of the Constitution*, intended to demonstrate the importance of common law to the constitution. His most significant contribution to the history of political thought was his *Lectures on the Relation between Law and Public Opinion* (1905), originally given at Harvard in 1898. He became a prominent opponent of both Home Rule and votes for women.
• Collini 1993; Cosgrove 1980; Harvie 1976; Qvortrup 1999.

DILKE, SIR CHARLES WENTWORTH
1843–1911. A radical politician, Dilke was born in London and educated at Trinity Hall, Cambridge. He inherited the baronetcy when his father died in 1869 together with the *Atheneum* and *Notes and Queries*. He was Liberal Member of Parliament for Chelsea from 1868–86, losing his seat when he was cited as a co-respondent in a divorce case. Dilke had been called to the Bar in 1866 but never practised, instead embarking on travels through Canada, Australia, New Zealand and America. These formed the basis of his book *Greater Britain, A Record of Travel in English-Speaking Countries During 1866 and 1867* (1868), which ran to eight editions. This was followed by *The Problems of Greater Britain* (1890), a study of the problems of the British Empire.
• Jenkins 1958.

DISRAELI, BENJAMIN (EARL OF BEACONSFIELD)
1804–81. A politician and novelist, Disraeli was born in London. He was educated privately and then trained as a solicitor. When early business ventures failed he started writing and entered politics, becoming MP for Maidstone in 1837; in 1841 he was elected to represent Shrewsbury. Disraeli twice held the position of Chancellor of the Exchequer and when Lord Derby resigned in 1868 he became the first Prime Minister of Jewish parentage. He occupied this post again from 1874–80, a period marked by the conferment on Victoria of the title

of Empress of India. Disraeli's trilogy of novels, *Coningsby*, *Sybil* and *Tancred* (1844–7) roused the social conscience to the evils of industrial life and the class divide between rich and poor.
• Cain 2007b; Vincent 1990.

DOUGLASS, FREDERICK

1818–95. Born in Maryland, the son of a slave and probably a white father, he was originally named Frederick Baily. In 1835, after working for two brutal masters, he was sent to a new master but he won his freedom and took the name Douglass. By the 1840s he became associated with the radical anti-slavery position of William Lloyd Garrison and later John Brown. The publication of his first autobiography made him famous and, in general, he was an important writer and speaker on behalf of the anti-slavery cause and after the Civil War of liberal reconstruction policies. In time he became a strong supporter of Lincoln. Douglass was the most famous and influential black leader in the United States of his time.
• Blight 1989; Douglass 1994; Martin 1984; McFeely 1991; Stauffer 2001.

DU BOIS, W. E. B. (WILLIAM EDWARD BURGHARDT)

1868–1923. Black American civil rights leader, sociologist and activist, Du Bois was born in Massachusetts and educated at Fisk and then Harvard from where he received a doctorate in history in 1895 with the title *The Suppression of the African Slave Trade to the United States of America, 1638–1870* (1896). From 1897–1910 Du Bois taught economics and history at Atlanta University. In 1910 he became editor of *Crisis*, the official publication of the National Association for the Advancement of Colored People (NAACP), a post he held until 1934 when he returned to Atlanta. He wrote widely on race and African-American history, his most influential work being *The Souls of Black Folk* (1903). He became increasingly radical and anti-imperialist in later life.

DÜHRING, EUGEN

1833–1921. A German philosopher and political economist, trained in the law, Dühring practised in Berlin from 1856–9. However, an eye weakness (which led later to total blindness) forced him to abandon this career. In 1861 he took his doctorate in philosophy at the University of Berlin. He became a university lecturer in 1863 but he was dismissed in 1877 after feuding with his colleagues. From then until his death he lived the life of a private scholar. In his later years, Dühring's attacks on religion (*Asiatismus*), militarism, Marxism, the Bismarck state, the universities and Judaism became more and more virulent. Nevertheless, he retained a small group of loyal followers who founded a journal primarily devoted to his essays, the *Personalist und Emanzipator* (1899).

DUMONT, ÉTIENNE

1759–1829. Born in Geneva in 1759, Dumont originally trained as a clergyman, but he left Geneva in 1783 for political reasons and joined his sisters in St Petersburg. Two years later he left for England to work in the office of Prime Minister Lord Shelburne. There he was introduced to some of Bentham's manuscripts and as a result became an enthusiastic disciple, producing a series of works which made the new jurisprudence and political theory known in the world of letters. He translated, condensed and even supplied omissions, giving his style to the whole. In Bentham's collected *Works*, published posthumously, many of the important treatises are retranslations into English from Dumont's versions.
• Blamires 1990.

ELIOT, GEORGE (MARY ANN EVANS)

1819–80. Reared as an evangelical, Eliot rejected Christianity in the early 1840s. Her first published work was a translation of David Strauss' *Das Leben Jesus* (1846). In 1850 she moved to London and began to write for the *Westminster Review*, where she became part of a literary circle that included Herbert Spencer and George Henry Lewes. In 1854 her translation of Feuerbach's *Essence of Christianity* appeared. Unsurpassed in her ability to combine philosophical speculation with an evocation of the life and speech of the Midlands, Eliot gained immediate popularity and has achieved a lasting reputation. Her most important novels are *Adam Bede* (1859), *The Mill on the Floss* (1860), *Silas Marner* (1861), *Romola* (1863), *Felix Holt* (1866), *Middlemarch* (1872) and *Daniel Deronda* (1876).

• Beer 1986; Dale 1989; Paxton 1991; Wright 1981, 1986.

EMERSON, RALPH WALDO

1803–82. Born in Boston, Massachusetts, the son of a minister, Emerson attended Harvard College from 1817–21. In 1836 he started the Transcendental Club, whose members included Henry David Thoreau. During this time he emerged as an influential poet, essayist and lecturer on a wide range of topics, a major public intellectual whose influence spread to Europe, particularly in the work of Friedrich Nietzsche. He was bitterly opposed to the Fugitive Slave Law of 1850 and embraced the cause of the violent abolitionist John Brown. In spite of this, he had a deep reformist belief in the possibility of correcting the injustices of American politics and came to see Abraham Lincoln as the 'true representative' of the American continent. In his later years he continued to lecture widely until his health began to decline in 1872.

• Cavell 2003; Gougeon 1990; Kateb 1995; Lopez 1996; Richardson 1995; Teichgraber 1995.

ENGELS, FRIEDRICH

1820–95. Born into a prosperous industrial family in Barmen, Engels began his career in the family firm, but intellectually he was drawn to the radicals of his time, especially the Young Hegelians. He went to a branch in Manchester in 1842, the year he met Karl Marx, and, beginning in 1844, they collaborated closely until Marx's death in 1883. Engels was more of an interpreter and disseminator of Marxism than a creative theoretician. Nonetheless, his contributions were significant, including *The Condition of the Working Class in England in 1844* (1845), *The Origins of the Family, Private Property and the State* (1884) and the *Anti-Dühring* (1878).

• Carver 1989; Hunley 1991; Hunt 1975, 1984; Mayer 1934; Rigby 1992.

FADUMA, ORISHATUKEH

1857–1946. A Yoruba born in British Guyana, he was later christened William J. Davis in honour of the Welsh missionary. His parents later immigrated to Africa and settled in Sierra Leone. He was the first native African to enrol at Yale Divinity School from where he graduated in 1895. Subsequently, he accepted an American Missionary Association appointment to head the mission church and school at Troy, North Carolina. He served for nearly fifty years as a missionary educator in the American South and West Africa.

• Moore 1996.

FERRY, JULES FRANÇOIS CAMILLE

1832–93. A lawyer and deputy who was mayor of the city during the siege of Paris (1870–1), Jules Ferry later became an architect of the French school system (as minister of public instruction from 1879–82) and of the French Empire (as a cabinet minister in the early 1880s). Influenced by French revolutionary experiments in education and by positivist principles, he

tried to strengthen the foundations of the Republic and establish the moral unity of France by promoting free compulsory primary education, by sponsoring anti-clerical legislation, by expanding the secondary school curriculum and providing for state secondary education for girls, and by rebuilding the university system.
• Furet 1985; Furet and Ozouf 1993; Gaillard 1989; Nicolet 1982; Scott 1951.

FEUERBACH, LUDWIG

1804–72. Feuerbach was the son of a famous jurist. At first a supporter of romantic rationalism, he became a Hegelian and finally a student of Hegel in Berlin from 1824. Even at that time he expressed doubts about Hegel's reconciliation between philosophy and religion, which he expressed in his first anonymous publication in 1830, *Thoughts on Death and Immortality*. In the 1830s, he worked as a Privatdozent at the University of Erlangen in Bavaria, but the strongly fundamentalist, Pietist tone of the university made permanent employment unlikely. Eventually marriage to Berthe Löw, a woman of independent means, in 1837, made it possible for him to withdraw from university employment and assume the life of an independent scholar.
• Wartofsky 1977; Williams 2006.

FICHTE, JOHANN GOTTLIEB

1762–1814. Born in Rammenau, Saxony, Fichte studied theology and then philosophy at Jena, becoming an ardent disciple of Kant. As Professor of Philosophy at Jena he modified the Kantian system in his *Wissensschaftslehre* (1785), by substituting for the 'thing-in-itself' as the absolute reality, the more subjective *Ego*, the primitive act of consciousness. In 1805 he became professor at Erlangen, where he published the more popular versions of his philosophy. His historical importance is as the author of *Reden an die Deutsche Nation* (1807–8, Addresses to the German Nation), in which he invoked a metaphysical German nationalism as resistance against Napoleon. In 1810 the University of Berlin was opened, and Fichte, who had drawn up its constitution, became its first rector.
• La Vopa 2001; Neuhouser 1990; Rohs 1991.

FITZHUGH, GEORGE

1806–81. A lawyer, author and journalist, Fitzhugh was born in Virginia. He was largely self-educated and subsequently read law. He practised law for a while, but disliked the profession and turned to writing and journalism. Fitzhugh was in favour of slavery and defended it in his pamphlet *Slavery Justified* (1849). This theme was continued in subsequent articles and in his books *Sociology for the South: Or the Failure of Free Society* (1854) and *Cannibals All! Or, Slaves without Masters* (1857). These publications alarmed Northerners like Abraham Lincoln and encouraged Southerners to take a firmer stance in favour of slavery.
• Wish 1943.

FLORES MAGÓN, RICARDO

1873–1922. Born in San Antonio Eloxochitlán, Oaxaca, Mexico, Flores Magón participated in 1892 student demonstrations against the re-election of President Porfirio Díaz. He organised the anti-government newspapers *El Democrática* in 1893 and *Regeneración* in 1900. After repeated arrests, imprisonments and threats of death, he went into exile in the United States in 1904. In 1905, in St. Louis, Missouri, he helped form the Junta Organizadora del Partido Liberal Mexicano (PLM), which at first advocated Mexican economic nationalism, political freedom and revolution against the Díaz dictatorship. By 1911, the PLM endorsed communist anarchism. Hounded by the Mexican government, US federal agents and local and state authorities, Flores Magón spent half of the years between 1904 and 1922 in prison. He died in Leavenworth in 1922 from lack of treatment for diabetes.

• Day 1991; Hart 1978; MacLachlan 1991.

FONBLANQUE, ALBANY WILLIAM

1793–1872. Born in London and descended from a noble Huguenot family, he was sent to Woolwich Arsenal as preparation for a military career, but ill-health led him to suspend his studies. Once recovered, he studied law and at the age of nineteen began writing for newspapers. He went on to be employed by *The Times* and the *Morning Chronicle* and between 1830 and 1847, the *Examiner* newspaper was under his complete control and he brought in such contributors as John Stuart Mill, W. M. Thackeray and Charles Dickens. His best articles were republished as *England under Seven Administrations* (1837).

FOURIER, CHARLES

1772–1837. Born in Besançon, France, Fourier studied architecture and later worked as a commercial traveller. In his 1808 *Theory of the Four Movements*, Fourier developed his theory that men's natural passions would, if properly channelled, lead to social harmony. He condemned 'civilisation' as a distorting force, and spent his life attempting to theorise and raise money for the development of communities ('phalansteries') in which his ideas could be expressed. Within 'phalansteries', Fourier argued for the systematic expression of diverse passions, including sexual passions, and for work to be united with pleasure. Fourierite communities were tried in France and the United States, but none was long-lasting. He did, however, gain an extensive following, led after his death by Victor Considérant.

• Beecher 1986; Goldstein 1991; Wilson 2002.

FRIES, JAKOB FRIEDRICH

1773–1843. Born in Barby, Saxony, Fries studied theology at the academy of the Moravian brethren at Niesky, and philosophy at Leipzig and Jena and then in 1806 became Professor of Philosophy and Elementary Mathematics at Heidelberg. His most important treatise, the *Neue oder Anthropologische Kritik der Vernunft*, was an attempt to give a new foundation of psychological analysis to the critical theory of Kant. In 1816 he took on the chair of theoretical philosophy at Jena. Politically he was a strong Liberal and Unionist and he published his views in a brochure, *Von Deutschen Bund und Deutscher Staatsverfassung*, and his influence in turn gave powerful impetus to agitation which led in 1819 to the issue of the Carlsbad Decrees.

• Hubmann 1997.

FULLER, MARGARET

1810–50. Born in Massachusetts, Fuller received an intense scholarly education from her father Timothy Fuller. In Boston, she became famous for her philosophical writing and her 'conversations' – intellectual salons – which provided a rare scholarly space in which women might share ideas with men. She became editor of the Transcendentalist journal the *Dial* in 1839, and in 1845 she extended a *Dial* article into a book, *Woman in the Nineteenth Century*. In 1846 she began a tour of Europe; her visit to Italy coincided with the 1848 Revolution, and she became a fervent supporter of Guiseppe Mazzini. She met the Italian revolutionary Giovanni Angelo Ossoli and bore him a son in September 1848. While returning home with her new family to the United States in May 1850, their ship struck a sand-bar and all three drowned.

• Von Mehren 1994.

GALTON, FRANCIS

1822–1911. Galton grew up in Birmingham. He interrupted his medical studies in Birmingham to read mathematics at Cambridge (although he left without a degree). *Meteorographica* (1863) was a further change of direction, making a notable contribution to the science of meteorology, but it was Galton's reading of his cousin Darwin's *On the Origin of Species* that set the stage for his ambitious research into experimental and speculative psychology and resulting in *Hereditary Genius* (1869) and *Inquiries into Human Faculty and its Development* (1883). Among his many innovations were the application of statistical analyses to the question of inherited intelligence, the development of tools for anthropometric research and a system of fingerprint identification to be used by the police. The advancement of eugenics became the central mission of his later life. He was knighted in 1909.

• Blacker 1952; Bulmer 2003; Forrest 1974; Kevles 1985; Pearson 1914–30.

GAMBETTA, LÉON

1838–82. Genoese by birth, the future French statesman went to Paris in 1857 to study law. A popular orator, he fiercely opposed the imperial regime and was in 1869 elected deputy to the Corps Législatif. He was minister of the interior after the revolution of 4 September, and undertook a reorganisation of the French army. When he feared the forces of the monarchist right, Gambetta associated himself with the extreme left, but when these fears receded, he was instrumental in rallying all moderates to the idea of an inclusive French republic. Often characterised as a 'positivist' republican, Gambetta borrowed from the spirit and language of Comtism to legitimise a process-oriented republic.

• Bury 1973; Furet and Ozouf 1993; Nicolet 1982; Scott 1951.

GANS, EDUARD

1798–1839. Gans was a student and disciple of Thibaut at Heidelberg. In response to the increasingly conservative turn after the Carlsbad decrees in 1819, Gans and others founded the Union for the Culture and Science of Jews, to reconcile Judaism with a universal conception of science and culture. In 1822 he applied for the professorship of law in Berlin University. In response the king declared that Jews were no longer eligible. In 1825, he converted to Christianity, was appointed in Berlin in 1826 and became Hegel's closest companion. His great work, *Erbrecht in Weltgeschichtlicher Entwicklung* (1824–35), is of permanent value, not only for its extensive survey of facts, but for the admirable manner in which the general theory of the slow evolution of legal principles is presented.

• Moggach 2006; Waszek 2006.

GARIBALDI, GIUSEPPE

1807–82. Son of a sailor he joined the secret society Young Italy and took part in a failed insurrection in 1833, going into exile in 1834. He returned to Italy in 1848 and took control of the forces defending the Roman Republic in 1849. Following a second exile he decided to work with Piedmont in pursuit of national unification. He was given a command during the 1859 war against Austria. He subsequently took a small force to invade Sicily; this led to the collapse of the government of the Kingdom of the Two Sicilies, of which he was briefly ruler, and the rapid unification of the whole peninsula under Piedmontese leadership. Garibaldi thereafter belonged to the radical opposition to the new state, leading two unsuccessful invasions of Rome in 1862 and 1867.

• Riall 2007.

GARRISON, WILLIAM LLOYD

1805–79. American abolitionist, journalist and reformer, born in Newburyport, Massachusetts. Garrison had little formal education and supplemented this with newspaper work and later journalism. He moved to Baltimore in 1829 to assist Benjamin Lundy in publishing *The Genius of Universal Emancipation*, and in 1831 he launched the influential anti-slavery newspaper *The Liberator*. This journal stood for the immediate and total abolition of slavery and was published for thirty-five years. In 1833 he founded the American Antislavery Society of which he was president from 1843–65. Garrison also campaigned fervently for woman suffrage and prohibition.
• Dumond 1961; Kraditor 1969.

GENTZ, FRIEDRICH VON

1764–1832. Born in Breslau, Gentz entered the public service of Prussia in 1786, but in 1802 exchanged into that of Austria. From 1812 he was Metternich's secretary, and served as secretary-general at the Congresses of Vienna, Aachen, Laibach, Troppau and Verona, where he consistently supported the old orders against the new. In 1794 he translated Mallet du Pan's *Considérations sur la Révolution en France*. Gentz's political thought – expressed in such works as *Über den Ursprang und Charakter des Krieges gegen die Französische Revolution* – stressed the importance of the balance of power, both within states and without. An Anglophile, Gentz praised the British constitution for its internal equilibrium. He attacked the democratic concept of equality, in favour of a stable balance between estates. Consistent with his work with Metternich, Gentz also sought a European balance of power, condemning the notion of the individual nation in favour of European-wide alliances.
• Beiser 1992; Droz 1949; Godechot 1972; Kontler 1999; Paternò 1993; Reiff 1912.

GEORGE, HENRY

1839–97. A journalist and politician, George was born in Philadelphia. He left school at thirteen to try to make a living and worked as a sailor prior to moving to California to work as a printer and typesetter. It was this experience of life that led him to question in his works the nature of and reasons for poverty. By the 1860s he had entered into journalism, writing on political economy. His most famous book is *Progress and Poverty* (1879) which argued that all forms of taxation except that on land should be abolished, since land ownership was invariably a function of monopoly power. George's work had a great influence on the growth of the socialist movement in Britain.
• Andelson 1979.

GIERKE, OTTO VON

1841–1921. He studied at the University of Berlin, where he succeeded Georg Beseler to his Chair in 1887, and served in the wars against Austria and France. He wrote widely on legal and constitutional history and natural law, his masterpiece being *Das Genossenschaftsrecht* (1868–1913), which interpreted the history of German custom and law in terms of his theory of corporation, fellowship, and community and legal fictions. He also wrote on Althusius and early modern natural law theories.
• Gierke 1990; Lewis 1935.

GOBINEAU, JOSEPH ARTHUR, COMTE DE

1816–82. French diplomat, writer, ethnologist and social thinker whose controversial and long-since discredited theories of racial determinism and miscegenation were first little read, but came to have significant impact on anti-Semitic, Aryan and other anthropological and political theories in late nineteenth-century Europe. Gobineau came from an aristocratic

background and served as secretary to the writer and statesman Alexis de Tocqueville during the latter's brief term as foreign minister in 1849. Gobineau also had his own diplomatic career, which took him to posts in Bern, Hanover, Frankfurt, Tehran, Rio de Janeiro and Stockholm. He wrote short stories, works of history and literary criticism, but is best known for his *Essai sur l'Inégalité des Races Humaines* (Essay on the Inequality of Human Races) (4 vols. 1853–5).
• Gobineau 1970.

GODWIN, WILLIAM

1756–1836. Born in Wisbech, Cambridgeshire, the son of a Congregationalist minister, Godwin was educated by the strict Calvinist sect of the Sandemanians. After a brief period as a minister, he turned to writing and publishing. His most famous philosophical and political work was *Enquiry Concerning Political Justice* (1793), which insisted that men and women had moral and rational capacities that made government unnecessary. This view was also reflected in his novels *The Adventures of Caleb Williams* (1794), *St. Leon* (1799) and *Fleetwood* (1805). In 1797, Godwin married Mary Wollstonecraft, who died the same year giving birth to a daughter, Mary. He remarried in 1801 and in 1805 established a small publishing business specialising in children's books.
• Claeys 1983, 1984; Clark 1977; Marshall 1984; Monro 1953; Philp 1986; Rosen 1987; Stafford 1980; Woodcock 1989.

GOUGES, OLYMPE DE

1745–93. Born Marie Gouze to a petit bourgeois family in Montauban, France. After an unhappy early marriage, de Gouges moved to Paris and became a prolific writer of pamphlets and plays, on topics ranging from her opposition to slavery to gender equality. Her most controversial work on the 'woman question' was her response to the 1791 Declaration of the Rights of Man and of the Citizen, the *Déclaration des Droits de la Femme et de la Citoyenne* (Declaration of the Rights of Woman and the Female Citizen). She also drafted a civil contract for the equal rights of men and women in marriage. While she welcomed the Revolution, her opposition to the execution of Louis XVI led to her own execution in 1793.
• Scott 1996.

GRAVE, JEAN

1854–1939. Born in the Puy-de-Dôme but raised in Paris by working-class parents, Grave worked as a mechanic and a cobbler before becoming known as the 'high priest of anarchy'. He converted to communist anarchism in 1880 and in 1883 he moved to Geneva to take control of *Le Révolté*, founded in 1779 by Kropotkin and others. This journal changed its name twice in order to avoid prosecution (to *La Révolte* in 1887; to *Les Temps Nouveaux* in 1895). Grave's most famous book, *La Société Mourante et l'Anarchie* (1893), earned him a two-year prison sentence. Following Kropotkin during the First World War, Grave campaigned against Germany and for anarchist support of the Allied war effort, a stance that marginalised him in the post-war anarchist movement.
• Maitron 1975; Patsouras 1987; Reynaud-Paligot 1993; Vincent 1996.

GREEN, THOMAS HILL

1838–82. Born at Berkin in Yorkshire, Green was the son of a rector. From the age of fourteen, he attended Rugby School before going to Balliol College, Oxford, where he matriculated in 1855. As an undergraduate, Green was President of the Oxford Union and, along with A. V. Dicey and James Bryce, a member of the Old Mortality Society. In 1866, he became a tutor at Balliol, and in 1878 he won election to the Whyte professorship of moral philosophy. Green was an active campaigner for temperance reform, and served as a Liberal town councillor in Oxford. The bulk of his philosophical writings were edited and published posthumously by R. L. Nettleship in *The Works of Thomas Hill Green* (3 vols. 1885–8).

• Brink 2003; Carter 2003; De Sanctis 2005; Kelly 2006; Leighton 2004; Morrow 2007; Nicholson 1990; Plant 2006; Richter 1964; Thomas 1987; Tyler 2003; Vincent 1986; Wempe 2004.

GREENE, WILLIAM B.

1819–78. Born in Haverhill, Massachusetts, Greene was educated at West Point and served as an officer in the Indian and Civil Wars. Graduating from Harvard Divinity School in 1845, he became an outspoken clergyman in Brookfield, Massachusetts, supporting free speech, women's rights and labour reform. He is best known for advocating the elimination of the state from the economy, a position he outlined in his book *Mutual Banking* (1850). Along with Ezra Heywood he founded the New England Labor Reform League in 1869; later he served as president. During the last decade of his life, he was an influential anarchist philosopher.

• Martin 1957; Reichert 1976.

GUIZOT, FRANÇOIS

1787–1884. Born into a Protestant family of Nîmes and educated in Geneva in the revolutionary period and a student of law in Paris under Napoleon, he became a leading liberal politician as well as historian in Restoration France. Serving in the government at various times, especially during the July Monarchy after the revolution of 1830, he was in effect prime minister until his exile in 1848. Guizot also gave acclaimed lectures on civilisation in Europe and in France. After 1830 he founded the Society of French History, which published chronicles and records of French institutional history, especially of the medieval communes, and among his many other works were his laudatory studies of English government and of representative institutions.

• Johnson 1963; Kelley 2003; Mellon 1958; Rosanvallon 1985.

HAECKEL, ERNST HEINRICH

1834–1919. Born in Potsdam in Prussia and educated in Merseburg, Haeckel studied medicine at Würzburg and Berlin. His father, the physiologist and anatomist Johannes Müller, encouraged his interest in marine biology and in medicine. An encounter with Darwin's *On the Origin of Species* shifted his interests decisively towards zoology. By 1865 he had been offered a full professorship in comparative anatomy at the Zoological Institute in Jena. His work in the field of comparative embryology led to the theory for which he has became popularly known. Haeckel's popular book, *Anthropogenie* (1874), outlined his evolutionary ideas which he eventually extended into the realms of psychology and cosmology to arrive at a metaphysical monistic philosophy of nature. These ideas were summarised in *Die Welträtsel* (1899), translated as *The Riddle of the Universe*.

• Gasman 1971; Kelly 1981.

HALLAM, HENRY

1777–1859. Educated at Eton and Christ Church, Oxford, he practised law in Oxford before settling in Lincolnshire and turning to a literary career. Though associated with the Whigs and a supporter of various reforms, he was not involved in politics. His works included a survey of the European states in the Middle Ages, an introduction to European literature in the early modern period, and especially his *Constitutional History of England* (1827), which

carried the story from the Tudors down to the accession of George III and which for a long time remained the standard survey.
• Lang 1995; Macaulay n.d.b

HALLER, KARL LUDWIG VON

1768–1854. Born in Berne, Switzerland, Haller was the grandson of the poet Albrecht von Haller. A conservative – sometimes referred to as 'the restorer' – Haller is now mainly remembered as an intellectual adversary of Hegel (he was sharply attacked in Hegel's *Philosophy of Right*). From 1801–6 Haller served as a court secretary in Vienna. From 1806 he was Professor of Law at the newly formed academy of Berne, and became a member of the Sovereign Council of Berne. However, in 1821 he converted, sensationally, to Catholicism – something he described in a 'letter to his family' which ran to seventy editions and many translations – and this led to his dismissal from the Bernese government. His chief political work was the six-volume *Restauration der Staatswissenschaft oder Theorie des natürlich-geselligen Zustandes* (1816–34). In it, Haller rejects revolution (and Rousseau's concept of the social contract) and constructs a natural and juridical system of government.
• Breckman 1992; Pinkard 2000; Westerholt 1999.

HANSEMANN, DAVID

1790–1864. Born in Finkenwerder (now part of Hamburg), Hansemann was an economist and politician. Trained in commerce, he wrote a series of memoranda supporting the development of the railways and a new tax system. Especially significant are those on the domestic reform of Prussia (1830) and the question of the German and Prussian constitution (1848, 1850). In 1848 he was made Prussian Finance Minister. From 1848–51 he was head of the Prussian Bank prior to founding one of the first large German banks, the Berlin Disconto Company followed by the First Prussian Mortgage Bank in 1862–4.
• Angermann 1966; Malangré 1991.

HARRISON, FREDERIC

1831–1923. Reared as an Anglican, Harrison gradually became a convinced adherent of Comte's religion of humanity. In his long career as jurist, publicist and widely read man of letters, he was the most successful propagandist of positivism in England. Author of the minority report of the Royal Commission on Trades Unions, Harrison was instrumental in securing legal recognition for the unions in the 1870s. He also wrote many articles on international affairs, consistently opposing England's imperial expansion. Among his autobiographical writings, see especially *Creed of a Layman* (1907) and *Autobiographic Memoirs* (2 vols. 1911, with a bibliography of his writings). Some of his more important essays are collected in *National and Social Problems* (1908).
• Adelman 1971; Harrison 1965; Vogeler 1984; Wright 1986.

HAZLITT, WILLIAM

1778–1830. Born at Maidstone in Kent and educated at home and at Hackney, Hazlitt originally intended to follow his father into the Unitarian ministry. He gave up any thoughts of a clerical career in 1797 and subsequently studied painting; from 1805 he devoted his energies to literature and philosophy. Like Byron and Shelley, Hazlitt was a strident critic of post-war legitimism. His political ideas are scattered throughout his voluminous writings. *The Principles of Human Action* (1805), *Political Essays* (1819, collected from the *Morning Chronicle*) and *The Spirit of the Age* (1825) are particularly important.
• Brinton 1966; Cook 1981; Deane 1988; Grayling 2000; Mahoney 2002; Thorslev 1989.

Biographies

HECKER, FRIEDRICH

1811–81. Born in Eichtersheim, after studying law in Heidelberg and Munich, Hecker joined the Bavarian Civil Service and became a lawyer in Mannheim in 1838. In 1842 he was elected to the Baden Lower Chamber but soon became a radical democrat and republican under the influence of Gustav von Struve. They organised an unsuccessful armed rebellion in 1848, to be defeated by the Württemberg government troops. Hecker then fled to Switzerland and later emigrated to the USA, fighting on the side of the Union in the Civil War. His works include *Die Erhebung des Volkes in Baden für die Deutsche Republik* (The Uprising of the People in Baden for the German Republic) (1848) and *Reden and Vorlesungen* (Talks and Lectures) (1872).

• Freitag 1998.

HEGEL, GEORG WILHELM FRIEDRICH

1770–1831. Born in Stuttgart, Hegel attended the Theological Seminary in Tübingen, where he befriended Hölderlin and Schelling. After tutoring in Berne, where he published an anonymous critique of patriarchal rule, he lectured with Schelling in Jena. In 1801, he published a defence of Schelling against Fichte's subjectivism, but by 1807, when he completed his *Phenomenology*, had distanced himself from his former friend, and reassessed Fichte's contribution to modern understandings of freedom. Leaving Prussia after the battle of Jena, he was successively editor of a newspaper and rector of a secondary school in southern Germany. He taught at Heidelberg after publishing his *Science of Logic* (1812–16), and assumed the chair of philosophy in Berlin in 1818. He published *The Philosophy of Right* in 1820.

• Beiser 1993; Bubner 2003; Pippin 1989, 1997b.

HEINE, HEINRICH

1797–1856. A German lyric poet and journalist, Heine was born in Düsseldorf to Jewish parents. After failing in the family business and in banking he went to Göttingen to study law and gained a doctorate in 1825. He converted to Protestantism to improve his employment prospects but failed to find the appropriate position and turned to writing. Heine moved to Paris in 1831 to report for the *Allgemeine Zeitung*. His works were highly critical of conservative Germany, supporting the social ideals of the French Revolution, e.g. *Religion and Philosophy in Germany* (1833). The *Buch der Lieder* (1827) established his reputation as a lyric poet and *Reisebilder* (4 vols. 1826–31), a description of travels in poetry and prose, was widely read. He died in Paris in 1856.

HEINZEN, KARL

1809–80. A radical revolutionary, Heinzen was born in Grevenbroich, Germany. He started to study medicine in Bonn, but was suspended in 1829. Heinzen then served in the Prussian army prior to working as a civil servant. However he openly criticised the government and was forced to flee to Switzerland in 1844. He returned to take part in the 1848 German Revolution. Heinzen fled Germany in 1849 and immigrated to America as a 'Forty-Eighter', seeing it as an arena for the dissemination of his radical ideas. He edited *Der Pionier* (1859–79), championing the abolition of slavery, equal rights for workers and women and penal reform. His most significant work is *Der Mord* (Murder) (1849), seen by many as advocating terrorism.

• Wittke 1945; Zucker 1950.

HENRION DE PANSEY, PIERRE PAUL NICOLAS

1742–1829. He was a feudal lawyer under the Old Regime, an appeal judge under Napoleon, and an author who celebrated judicial, constitutional and professional tradition across the revolutionary interlude. Henrion's major work was *On Judicial Authority* (1812).
• Kelley 1984; Salmon 1995.

HERZEN, ALEXANDER IVANOVICH

1812–70. Born in Moscow, Ivan Iakovlev, Herzen was the chief intellectual of the Russian 'Remarkable Decade, 1838–48', advocating a Left Hegelian 'philosophy of action'. In January 1847 he left for Paris, never to return. He was deeply disillusioned by the revolutionary events in France, and his book *From the Other Shore* (1850) echoed this. In 1853, with the help of Polish émigrés, he founded The Free Russian Press in London and from 1857 published the periodical *Kolokol* (The Bell). In a number of booklets, he developed his conception of 'Russian socialism', presenting Russia as a country where socialism had better chances than in bourgeois Europe. In 1863 he supported the Polish uprising and paid for this by a sharp decline of his influence in Russia.
• Berlin 1978; Kelly 1998; Malia 1961.

HERZL, THEODOR

1860–1904. Born in Budapest, Herzl studied law in Vienna, working as a journalist and writer. At first his politics was oriented to German unity; however the rise of popular anti-Semitism in the early 1890s led him to the view that European societies would never assimilate Jews. In 1895 he wrote *Der Judenstaat*, translated and published in English under the title *The Jewish State* (1896). In this Herzl argued that Jews must found and possess a territorial state of their own. He devoted himself from then on to the Zionist cause, establishing the Congress of Zionists, of which he was president until his death. Herzl relied on diplomatic connections to the major Western powers and powerful individuals (such as the Rothschilds) as the best way of realising this goal.
• Vital 1999.

HESS, MOSES

1812–75. Born in Bonn, Hess studied philosophy but did not graduate. He became involved in radical and socialist politics, living as a journalist and writer. Hess was a close collaborator of Karl Marx and Friedrich Engels and later in his life his ethical concerns came to be expressed in terms of pantheism and race. He lived in Germany between 1861 and 1863 where there was some resurgence of intellectual, if not popular, anti-Semitism. Strongly influenced by the success of national movements, Hess advocated the creation of a territorial state for the Jewish nation in Palestine. He published the series of essays *Rome and Jerusalem* (1862). It was, however, only after Hess' death in Paris that his book and its arguments were taken up by the Zionist movement.
• Avineri 1985.

HOBHOUSE, LEONARD TRELAWNY

1864–1929. Born at St Ives in Cornwall, Hobhouse was educated at Corpus Christi College, Oxford, where he was president of the Russell Club. His interest in industrial affairs was apparent in his first book on *The Labour Movement* (1893). In 1896, he published *The Theory of Knowledge*, which was poorly received. Between 1897 and 1902, he worked full time for the *Manchester Guardian*, writing extensively about the labour question and the South African War. These concerns were combined in his 1904 study of *Democracy and Reaction*. His sociological work, especially *Morals in Evolution*, helped secure him the first chair in

959

sociology at the University of London, which he held until his death. His best-known work of political theory both then and now was *Liberalism* (1911).
• Clarke 1978; Collini 1979; Freeden 1978; Hobson and Ginsberg 1931; Meadowcroft 1995.

HOBSON, JOHN ATKINSON
1858–1940. Born in Derby, Hobson was the son of a local newspaper editor and proprietor. He was educated at Derby School and Lincoln College, Oxford. In 1889, he wrote a book with the businessman A. F. Mummery, entitled *The Physiology of Industry*. A series of under-consumptionist studies followed in the 1890s, including *The Evolution of Modern Capitalism* (1894). Hobson was an active member of the South Place Ethical Society and the Rainbow Circle. In 1899, he went to South Africa as special correspondent for the *Manchester Guardian*. This helped shape his *The Psychology of Jingoism* (1901) and its successor, *Imperialism* (1902). His most significant work of political theory, *The Crisis of Liberalism* (1909), began as lectures to the Christian Social Union in London.
• Allett 1981; Cain 2002; Clarke 1978; Freeden 1978, 1990; Gerson 2004a.

HODGSKIN, THOMAS
1787–1869. Born in Chatham, Hodgskin was sent to sea when he was twelve. He became a naval officer but left service when he got into a dispute concerning military discipline. After travelling on the continent of Europe and briefly staying in Edinburgh, Hodgskin moved to London to work on the *Morning Chronicle*. With I. C. Robertson, he founded the *Mechanics' Magazine*, dedicated to worker self-education, where he published his most famous work, *Labour Defended against the Claims of Capital* (1825). This argued that laws and the state should be eliminated so that the 'natural laws' of morality and the market could operate freely. During the 1830s, he wrote journal articles and became a popular speaker for Chartist electoral reform. Later, he embraced free trade and wrote for *The Economist*.
• Halévy 1956; Stack 1998.

HUGO, GUSTAV VON
1764–1844. Born in Baden, he studied at the University of Göttingen, took his degree at the University of Halle, taught law at Göttingen from 1792, and published a comprehensive textbook of civil law (1792–1821), in which he presented his historical method. As founder, before Savigny, of the 'historical school of law', he became the target, with Hegel, of Marx's early critique of social philosophy.
• Kelley 1984a, 1990; Whitman 1990; Wieacker 1967.

HUMBOLDT, WILHELM VON
1767–1835. Born in Potsdam, the son of an officer, Humboldt was co-founder of the now Humboldt University of Berlin. He was a great friend of Goethe and in particular Schiller. He attended Göttingen University where he studied classical languages and natural sciences and in 1789, in the company of his tutor, he travelled to revolutionary Paris. From 1802–8 he was a Prussian Ministerial Resident in the Vatican and from 1815–19 was the Prussian plenipotentiary at the Bundestag in Frankfurt am Main and an envoy in London. After he was dismissed he concentrated upon linguistic studies. His many works include books on language and history, in particular his *The Limits of State Action* (1854 [1792]) which made an impact on J. S. Mill.
• Borsche 1990; Petersen 2007; Spitta 2004.

HYNDMAN, H. M. (HENRY MAYERS)

1842–1921. A writer and politician, Hyndman was born in London and educated at Trinity College, Cambridge. He studied law for two years before turning to journalism, reporting for the *Pall Mall Gazette*. In 1869 he decided on a career in politics and stood as an independent candidate in the 1880 election, but was forced to stand down. In the aftermath he became fascinated by Lassalle and subsequently Karl Marx and founded the first Marxist political group in Britain, the Social Democratic Federation in 1884, which became the British Socialist Party in 1911. His significant works are *England for All* (1881), an attempt to explain the ideas of Marx, and *Socialism Made Plain* (1883), which explained the policies of the Social Democratic Federation.

JACKSON, ANDREW

1767–1845. An American general, Andrew Jackson was President of the United States from 1829–37. He was born in a backwoods settlement in the Carolinas and at thirteen took part in the Revolutionary War as a courier for the Continental army and was captured by the British. After reading law, he settled in Tennessee where he became a successful lawyer and ultimately entered politics – he was the first elected member from Tennessee to the House of Representatives. Jackson served as a major-general in the War of 1812, and became a hero after defeating the British at New Orleans. He lost his first bid for the presidency in 1824 to John Quincy Adams, but won in 1828 with an overwhelming majority. His presidency has come to be known as the 'Jacksonian Democracy'.

• Blau 1954; Meyers 1960; Reynolds 2008; Rogin 1975; Schlesinger 1945; Sellers 1991; Wilentz 1982.

JACOBY, JOHANN

1805–77. Born in Königsberg, the son of a Jewish merchant, Jacoby studied medicine but became politically active with the Parisian July Revolution of 1830, engaging himself for the rest of his life in the struggle to liberate the Polish people, emancipate the Jews and to overcome Prussian absolutism. He spoke out against Bismarck and as a result spent six months behind bars. In 1870 he protested against the annexation of Alsace-Lorraine for which he was again imprisoned. In 1872 he joined the Social Democratic Party and was subsequently elected to the Reichstag but in protest refused to take his seat. His works include *Vier Fragen, Beantwortet von einem Ostpreussen* (Four Questions Answered by an East Prussian) (1841) and *Gesammelte Schriften und Reden* (Collected Writings and Speeches) (1877).

• Herzfeld 1938; Jacoby 1841; Silberner 1976; Weber 1988.

JEFFERSON, THOMAS

1743–1826. Born in Albermarle County, Virginia, Jefferson attended the College of William and Mary from 1760–2 and then read law from 1762–7. Jefferson entered politics as a member of the Virginia House of Burgesses in 1769 and attracted attention by writing *A Summary View of the Rights of British America* (1774). He became ambassador to France in 1785 and in 1787 published his only major book, *Notes on the State of Virginia*. Returning to the United States in 1789, he became secretary of state in the first administration of George Washington. He was elected vice-president under John Adams in 1796 and in 1800 defeated Adams for the presidency. Jefferson wished to be remembered as the author of the Declaration of Independence, the Virginia Statute of Religious Liberty, and as the founder of the University of Virginia.

• Adams 1986; Banning 1978; Ellis 1997; Levy 1963; Malone 1948–81; Matthews 1984; Mayer 1994; McDonald 1976; Onuf 1993a, 1993b, 2000; Peterson 1986; Tucker and Hendrickson 1990; Wills 2003.

JEVONS, WILLIAM STANLEY

1835–82. Economist and logician, born in Liverpool. At sixteen he entered University College London from where he later graduated with honours in botany and chemistry. From 1854–9 he was assayer to the Mint in Sydney, Australia. Returning to London he studied logic under Augustus de Morgan, becoming Professor of Logic at Manchester (1866) and Professor of Political Economy at London (1876). He introduced mathematical methods into economics, was one of the first to use the concept of final or marginal utility as opposed to the classical cost of production theories, and wrote *Theory of Political Economy* (1871), a major work in the development of economic thought.
• Sigot 2002.

KARAMZIN, NIKOLAI MIKHAILOVICH

1766–1826. Born into a wealthy noble family in the province of Simbirsk, Karamazin was the leading representative of sentimentalism in Russian literature, the official historiographer of the Russian state, and a conservative political thinker. In 1784 he entered a Masonic lodge and from 1789–90 he made a European tour which he described in his *Letters of a Russian Traveller*. From 1802–3 he edited the journal *Vestnik Europy* (European Messenger) with the motto 'Russia is Europe'. In 1811 he presented to Alexander I his *Memoir on Ancient and Modern Russia* in which he claimed that the Russian monarch was not entitled to limit his autocratic power. His *History of the Russian State* (12 vols. 1816–29) greatly contributed to the formation of Russian national identity.
• Leontowitsch 1957; Pipes 1959; Walicki 1975.

KAUTSKY, KARL

1854–1938. Born in Prague, the son of a theatre painter, Kautsky joined the Austrian socialists while a student at the University of Vienna. He moved to Zurich in 1880, where he and Eduard Bernstein were close associates. But with the beginning of the revisionist controversy, they became public antagonists. As editor of the theoretical journal, *Die neue Zeit*, which he founded (1883), Kautsky emerged as the acknowledged expert on Marxist economic and historical thought. He solidified this status with the publication of *Karl Marx' Oekonomische Lehren* (1887), as the leading author and interpreter of the Erfurt programme (1891) and as an unyielding defender of orthodox Marxism.
• Geary 1987; Miller 1964; Pierson 1993; Salvadori 1979; Steenson 1978.

KEBLE, JOHN

1792–1866. Keble was an Anglican theologian and poet. He was educated at Oxford and was a fellow of Oriel College from 1811–23. He was ordained as a deacon in 1815 and as a priest in 1816. From 1831–41 he was Professor of Poetry at Oxford and from 1836 until his death he was priest in the parish of Hursley. On 14 July 1833 he preached the Assize Sermon at Oxford, with the title of 'National Apostasy', which is seen as the starting point of the Oxford Movement. His works include *The Christian Year* (1827), a volume of hymns and poetry, *Lyra Innocentium: Thoughts in Verse on Children* (1846) and a life of Bishop Wilson (1863). Keble College in Oxford was founded as a memorial to him.
• Chadwick 1960; Rowlands 1989.

KHOMIAKOV, ALEKSEI STEPANOVICH

1804–60. Born in Moscow, Khomiakov was the leading figure in the Slavophile movement. His main ideological contribution was the elaboration of the concept of *sobornost* as (allegedly) a distinctive feature not only of the Orthodox ecclesiology but of the Russian national life as well. During the Crimean War he advocated the aggressive policy of military pan-Slavism.

After the war he became involved in the preparation of the emancipation of the peasantry, suggesting that the peasants should receive only a part of their communal land. He did not hesitate to stress that the village commune should be preserved on the grounds of its convenience to the landlords and that in the case of the peasants' non-compliance with their obligations it should be possible to expel whole villages to Siberia.

• Christoff 1961; Gratieux 1939; Walicki 1975.

KOSSUTH, LOUIS (LAJOS)

1802–94. Born into minor Hungarian nobility, Kossuth was a lawyer and journalist whose writings made him the most prominent of the critics of the Habsburg government in the period immediately before 1848. A fine orator, his speech of 3 March 1848 at the Hungarian Diet helped start the Hungarian Revolution. He became the leader of the rebellion when war with the Habsburgs broke out in September 1848. By April 1849 he supported the overthrow of Habsburg rule. Once the Hungarian army was defeated by a combination of Habsburg and Russian armies as well as the mobilisation of non-Magyar nationalities, Kossuth went into exile. From there he enjoyed great support amongst radical circles and continued to advocate radical anti-Habsburg policies. He never returned to Austria.

• Deak 1979.

KROPOTKIN, PËTR ALEKSEEVICH

1842–1921. A member of an ancient princely family, born in Moscow, Kropotkin was an outstanding geographer and one of the chief theorists of international anarchism. In 1872 he joined the populist revolutionary movement and in 1874 he was arrested and imprisoned in the Peter and Paul Fortress in Petersburg. Two years later he planned a daring escape which his friends from outside helped him to put into effect. He settled in Switzerland and in 1879 founded the anarchist journal *Le Révolté*. His political philosophy is best expounded in *The Conquest of Bread* (1892), *Anarchism: Its Philosophy and Ideal* (1896) and *Mutual Aid: A Factor of Evolution* (1902).

• Avrich 1967; Cahm 1989; Miller 1976; Woodcock 1970; Woodcock and Avakumovic 1971.

LAMARCK, JEAN-BAPTISTE PIERRE ANTOINE DE MONET

1744–1829. Lamarck was from a military family in France, the youngest of eleven children. First educated for the priesthood, he enlisted in an infantry regiment, but then became increasingly interested in plants and produced an important three-volume study of the flora of France in 1778. A protégé of the great naturalist Buffon, Lamarck played a key role in the reorganisation during the 1790s of the Jardin des Plantes into the French Museum of Natural History. His publications were wide-ranging, including physics, meteorology and hydrology and over time he began to formulate new ideas about the transmutation of species. His transformist theory was first articulated publicly in lectures in 1800 and developed in *Philosophie Zoologique* (1809). He died blind and in poverty.

• Bowler 1983; Corsi and Weindling 1988; Jordanova 1984.

LAMARTINE, ALPHONSE-MARIE-LOUIS DE PRAT DE

1790–1869. Born at Mâconnais in Burgundy, Lamartine was educated in Lyon. Commissioned in the royal bodyguard in 1814 he went into exile with the Bourbons in 1815. Following a series of diplomatic appointments, Lamartine's election as deputy for Bergues in 1833 marked the beginning of a long parliamentary career which culminated with his appointment as Minister of Foreign Affairs just prior to the outbreak of the 1848 Revolution. Although he played a leading role in this event, Lamartine retired from politics in December 1848 following his defeat by Louis Napoleon for the presidency of the Republic.

Lamartine's most systematic presentation of his political ideas appeared in *Sur la Politique Rationnelle* (1831), but his *Voyage en Orient* (1835), *Histoire des Girondins* (1847) and *Histoire de la Révolution de 1848* are also important sources.
• Charlton 1984b; Dunn 1989; Fortesque 1983; Guillemin 1946; Harris 1932; Kelly 1992.

LAMENNAIS [LA MENNAIS], HUGUES-FÉLICITÉ ROBERT DE

1782–1854. Born at St Malo, Brittany, Lamennais was educated by his uncle Robert des Saudrais, later to be at the forefront of the revival of French Catholicism. Ordained in 1816 following his return from a brief exile in England, Lamennais became disenchanted with the alliance of church and state and increasingly critical of both these institutions. He was excommunicated in 1834 following publication of *Paroles d'un Croyant*. Elected to the National Assembly in 1848 and to the Constituent Assembly in the following year, Lamennais retired from politics on the accession to power of Louis Napoleon. Following the publication of *D'Avenir*, Lamennais' democratic and republican political ideas were presented in *Paroles d'un Croyant* (1834), *Livre du Peuple* (1838) and *Le Pays et le Gouvernement* (1840).
• Carcopino 1942; Evans 1951; Gurian 1947; Oldfield 1973; Vidler 1964b.

LASSALLE, FERDINAND

1825–64. Born in Breslau into a Jewish commercial family, Lassalle studied at the universities of Breslau and Berlin, and was deeply influenced by Hegel's philosophy. Attracted to radical democracy and socialism, he participated in the revolutions of 1848, collaborating for some time with Marx and Engels, with whom he shared many ideas. In the early 1860s he focused on the historical role of the working class, presented his ideas in a series of brilliant speeches and pamphlets, and founded the General Association of German Workingmen in 1863. His meteoric career as a charismatic leader was cut short when he was killed in a duel in August 1864.
• Bernstein 1893; Friederici 1985; Miller 1964; Na'aman 1970; Oncken 1912.

LAVROV, PËTR LAVROVICH

1823–1900. Born in the province of Pskov, Lavrov embarked upon a military career, reaching the rank of colonel. In 1862 he became a member of the underground group Land and Freedom which led to his arrest in 1866 and exile to Vologda. In 1868–9 he published (under the pseudonym P. Mirtov in the review *Nedelya*) *Historical Letters*, his most influential book, developing a theory of 'critically thinking individuals' who devote themselves to the struggle for social justice. In February 1878 he fled abroad and took part in the Paris Commune. From 1873–6 he published, in Zurich and in London, the revolutionary periodical *Vperëd* (Forward). In his numerous scholarly publications he laid the foundations for the so-called 'subjective sociology' stressing the role of the subjective factor in history.
• Masaryk 1955; Pomper 1972; Venturi 1960; Walicki 1969.

LEDRU-ROLLIN, ALEXANDRE AUGUSTE

1807–74. A French radical politician, Ledru-Rollin was born in Paris. Trained as a lawyer, he was elected to the Chamber of Deputies in 1841, representing the far left. He had an active role in the Banquets' Campaign, which led to the abdication of Louis Philippe in 1848 and was minister of the interior in the provisional government of May 1848. In the presidential elections of December 1848, Ledru-Rollin stood against Louis Napoleon but was then defeated in June 1849. He fled to England, exiled after a failed insurrection against the government. There he wrote many revolutionary pamphlets, which were published with his speeches in *Discours Politiques et Écrits Divers* (1879). When the Second Republic fell he returned to France.

LEONTIEV, KONSTANTIN NIKOLAEVICH
1831–91. Born into the gentry in the province of Kaluga, Leontiev became the most extreme religious and political conservative in Russia. From 1863–74 he served in the Russian consular service in various parts of the Ottoman Empire, frequently visiting the community of Orthodox monks on Mount Athos. After resigning from the diplomatic service (over disagreements with Russian policy towards Turkey), he worked as a censor, but after a few years handed in his resignation and settled in the Optina monastery, famous for its holy elders. In later life he took monastic vows.
• Berdiaev 1940; Masaryk 1955; Thaden 1964; Walicki 1975.

LEWES, GEORGE HENRY
1817–78. A prolific and acutely intelligent critic and author on many subjects, Lewes was editor of the *Leader* (1850–4) and of the *Fortnightly Review* (1865–6). He was responsible (along with John Stuart Mill) for the early popularisation of the ideas of Auguste Comte in England, particularly in his *Biographical History of Philosophy* (4 vols. 1845–6) and *Comte's Philosophy of the Sciences* (1853). Separated from his wife, in 1854 he entered into an unconventional lifelong union with George Eliot. The following year he published his most noted and successful work, the *Life of Goethe*. His later works combine his interests in philosophy and psychology; see *The Physiology of Common Life* (2 vols. 1859–60) and his final work, *Problems of Life and Mind* (5 vols. 1874–9).
• Ashton 1991; Dale 1989; Simon 1963.

LIEBKNECHT, WILHELM
1826–1900. Born into a Giesen family of pastors and officials, Liebknecht turned to socialism in his youth, studied at Marburg University, and participated in the revolutions of 1848–9. In London exile (1850–62) he became a friend and follower of Marx and Engels. When he returned to Germany (1862), he immediately joined the new labour movement, represented the First International and, along with Bebel, helped to found the Social Democratic Workers' Party (Eisenachers) in 1869. Although not an outstanding thinker, Liebknecht was an effective speaker, talented journalist (he edited several socialist newspapers), popular disseminator of socialist principles, and a Reichstag deputy almost without interruption from 1867 to 1900.
• Dominick 1982; Eisner 1906; Pelz 1994; Wendorff 1978.

LINCOLN, ABRAHAM
1809–65. Lincoln was born in Kentucky to illiterate parents and in the proverbial log cabin. His formal schooling was sporadic and he was largely self-educated. In 1834 Lincoln began to study law and was admitted to the Bar in 1836. In 1858 Lincoln ran for senator. He lost the election, but in debating he thus gained a national reputation that won him the Republican nomination for president in 1860. His anti-slavery reputation precipitated the secession of the Southern slaveholding states which led to American Civil War. In 1863 he delivered the Gettysburg address which provides the best short American definition of democracy as 'government of the people, by the people, for the people'. On 9 April 1865 the Southern forces surrendered. On 12 April Lincoln was assassinated by John Wilkes Booth.
• Borritt 1992; Donald 1995; Greenstone 1993; Jaffa 1959, 2000; McPherson 1990; Miller 2002; Paludan 1994; Wills 1992.

LITTRÉ, MAXIMILIEN PAUL ÉMILE
1801–81. Best known as the author of the impressive *Dictionnaire de la Langue Française* (5 vols. 1863–72), Littré was a philosopher, scholar and politician who originally trained as a

doctor. He fought on the barricades in 1830; was one of the editors of the republican journal, *National,* until 1851; and eventually became deeply involved in founding the republican, lay, centralised regime that became the Third Republic. From about 1840 he was associated with Auguste Comte and became his most distinguished and influential (though often wayward) disciple in France. Through his connections and his writings, he shaped the official philosophy of the Third Republic to a degree unmatched by any thinker, except perhaps the neo-Kantian Charles Renouvier.

• Charlton 1959; Hamburger 1988; Nicolet 1982; Scott 1951.

LLOYD, HENRY DEMAREST

1847–1903. Born in New York City, Lloyd was a journalist and social reformer, and a graduate of Columbia College. After attending Columbia Law School, he became a member of the New York Bar in 1869. Lloyd became editor of the *Chicago Tribune* in 1872 and remained there until 1885 when he resigned to devote himself to the cause of social reform. His most significant work was *Wealth Against Commonwealth* (1894) which begins and ends with an ethical critique of the new corporate economy.

• Destler 1963; Hofstadter 1955a; Lloyd 1912.

LOMBROSO, CESARE

1835–1909. Born in Verona into a Jewish family, Lombroso studied medicine, principally at Pavia. He served as doctor in the army, before becoming Professor of Psychiatry at the University of Turin in 1896. He is best known for *L'Uomo Delinquente* (The Criminal Man) (1876) which controversially argued for the biological determination of mental and moral character, and sought to identify the physical 'stigmata' of criminality. Lombroso rejected the Enlightenment and utilitarian theories of crime and punishment, arguing that criminality had an organic, hereditary basis. His work reflected and significantly shaped late nineteenth- and early twentieth-century attitudes to crime and punishment, criminology and scientific policing. Other important works included *Genio e Follia* (1877) (The Man of Genius, 1891) co-written with Guglielmo Ferrero, his son-in-law, and *La Donna Delinquente* (1893) (The Female Offender, 1895).

• Gibson 2002; Pick 1989.

LYELL, CHARLES

1797–1875. Lyell was born in Kinnordy, Scotland. While studying classics at Oxford he became interested in geology, which he pursued after his qualification as a lawyer in 1822. Throughout the 1820s Lyell compiled evidence for a theory of the formation of the earth and in 1831 he was appointed Professor of Geology at King's College London. The years 1830–3 saw the publication of his major work, *The Principles of Geology*, through which he popularised the notion of 'uniformitarianism'. In 1858 Lyell, with Joseph Hooker, presented Darwin and Wallace's papers on natural selection to the Linnaean Society, and in 1863 he turned his own attention to the origins of human life, examining the fossil record in *The Geological Evidence of the Antiquity of Man* (1863).

• Wilson 1998.

MACAULAY, THOMAS BABINGTON

1800–59. An English historian and politician, born in Leicestershire and educated at Cambridge. He was called to the Bar in 1826 and elected to Parliament in 1830 but he resigned in 1834 to become a member of the supreme council of the East India Company. There he was involved in the redrafting of the Indian penal code and in the instituting of an educational system, following the British model. He returned from India in 1838 and as

Member of Parliament for Edinburgh occupied the positions of war secretary and forces' paymaster. In 1857 he became Baron Macaulay of Rothley. His most significant work, *The History of England from the Accession of James the Second* (5 vols. 1849–61) was phenomenally successful.

MAINE, HENRY JAMES SUMNER

1822–88. A legal historian and jurist, Maine was educated at Pembroke College, Cambridge where he was considered one of the brightest classical scholars of the time and was subsequently appointed Regius Professor of Civil Law, a post he held until his death. In 1863 he went to India to advise the colonial government on the codification of a system of law. In 1869 he returned to Britain and took on the chair of historical and comparative jurisprudence at Oxford. His first work, *Ancient Law: Its Connection with the Early History of Society and its Relation to Modern Idea* (1861), was his most famous. His other works embodied his lectures on legal history. *Village Communities in the East and West* (1871) in particular was based on his experience in India.

MAISTRE, JOSEPH DE

1753–1821. Born an aristocrat in Chambéry in Savoy, and educated in Turin, Maistre turned against the Revolution as early as August 1789, after the voting of the Declaration of the Rights of Man and the Citizen. In 1792, he left for Turin and then Lausanne, where he wrote *Lettre d'un Royaliste Savoisien à ses Compatriotes* (1793) and *Les Bienfaits de la Révolution Française* (1795), a work in which he attacked the violence of the revolutionaries. He continued this theme in his most famous work, *Considérations sur la France* (1796) where he poured scorn on the concept of the social contract. From 1803, he was regent of Sardinia and from 1803–17, he served as Sardinian ambassador to the court of Tsar Alexander in St Petersburg. Maistre wrote many more books before his death in 1821, including *Du Pape* (1819) which attacked both Protestantism and Gallicanism and *Les Soirées de Saint-Petersbourg* (1821).
• Armenteros 2004; Berlin 1990; Bradley 1999; Darcel 1988a, 1988b; Dermenghem 1979; Faguet 1891; Garrard 1994; Lebrun 1965, 1972, 1988a, 1988b; Spektorowski 2002.

MALATESTA, ERRICO

1853–1932. Born in 1853 near Naples, Malatesta became involved in the Garibaldian republican movement while a medical student. He met Bakunin in 1872 and became an anarchist militant in Italy, helping to organise the insurrections of 1874 and 1877. By the mid-1870s, he had become a believer in Kropotkin's 'anarchist communism' and a proponent of 'propaganda by the deed'. Following the failure of the Benevento insurrection of 1877, Malatesta lived in London, Argentina and the United States. Returning to Italy in 1913, he participated in the Red Week general strike in June 1914; in 1920 he re-established the anarchist newspaper *Umanita Nova*. His most famous work was *Anarchy* (1891), which insisted that anarchism was not a set of blueprints, but rather a method of encouraging the free initiative of all after abolishing private property by revolution.
• Hostetter 1958; Pernicone 1993; Ravindranathan 1988; Richards 1965.

MALLET DU PAN, JACQUES

1749–1801. Born in Céligny, Mallet du Pan was a journalist, author and historian who was one of the first and most influential counter-revolutionary publicists. His first work was *Compte rendu de la Défense des Citoyens Bourgeois de Genève* (1771), a plea for compromise between the various factions in Genevan politics. From 1784, he was the editor of *Le Mercure de France*, where he defended enlightened despotism, adopting a position of moderation against excess. In 1789 he opposed the Revolution in its pages and in 1792 left France for

Frankfurt, Geneva and Berne. He became close to the group of deputies in the Constituent Assembly known as the 'monarchiens'. In August 1793, Mallet published *Considérations sur la Nature de la Révolution en France*, an attack on the Revolution admired by both Gentz and Maistre, although it rejected the view that revolution had been caused by philosophy or irreligion. For Mallet, the Revolution was essentially a displacement of power as the old regime imploded on itself. In 1798, in London, he founded *Le Mercure Britannique*. He died in a state of disappointment in 1801.

• Acomb 1973; Godechot 1972; Mallet 1902.

MARX, KARL

1818–83. Karl Marx was the son of a Jewish lawyer, recently converted to Christianity. As a student in Bonn and Berlin, Marx studied law and then philosophy. He joined with the Young Hegelians, the most radical of Hegel's followers, in denying that Hegel's philosophy could be reconciled with Christianity or the existing state. Forced out of university by his radicalism, he became a journalist and, soon after, a socialist. He left Prussia for Paris and then Brussels, where he stayed until 1848. In 1844 he began his collaboration with Friedrich Engels and developed a new theory of communism to be brought into being by a proletariat revolution, as outlined in *The Communist Manifesto*. Marx participated in the 1848 revolutions as a newspaper editor in Cologne. Exiled with his family to London, he tried to make a living writing for the *New York Herald Tribune* and other journals, but remained financially dependent on Engels. *Capital*, published in 1867, established him as the principal theorist of revolutionary socialism. He died in London in 1883.

• Avineri 1968; Cottier 1959; Elster 1985; Hunt 1974, 1984; Leopold 2007; Marx and Engels 2002; McLellan 1969, 1973; Rosdolsky 1977; Wheen 1999; Wood 1981.

MAZZINI, GIUSEPPE

1805–72. Mazzini joined the republican secret society, the Carbonari, at a young age. Dissatisfied with their ritual and poor organisation, he formed his own society, Young Italy, in 1831, committed to establishing a national republic by means of insurrection. Mazzini tirelessly recruited some thousands of members but every one of its planned uprisings was a failure and he was forced into exile in 1831. In 1848 he returned and advocated a policy of establishing republics in the various Italian states which together would wage war on Austria and establish national unity. He supported the establishment of a republic in Rome and became one of its leaders. Following its suppression he went once more into exile. He returned to Italy after unification but was a stern critic of the new state.

• Smith 1994.

MELLA, RICARDO

1861–1925. Born in Vigo (Galicia), Mella began working for a maritime agency when he was fourteen. At first an ardent Federalist, in 1881 he became a dedicated defender of the working classes, publishing with other young republicans the journal *La Propaganda*. In 1882, Mella converted to anarchism, moved to Madrid, and married the daughter of Juan Serrano y Oreiza, the anarchist editor of *La Revista Social*. Mella became a proponent of collectivist anarchism, translating Bakunin's *God and the State* into Spanish. In the 1880s, he advocated 'anarchism without adjectives' with Fernando Tarrida des Mármol, calling for greater tolerance within the anarchist movement regarding economic questions. His most famous work is a futuristic novella about the organisation of society entitled *La Nueva Utopia* (1889).

• Esenwein 1989.

MICHELET, JULES

1798–1874. Born in Paris, Michelet studied at the Collège Charlemagne and taught at the Collège Rollin before devoting himself to literary and historical studies as a younger member of the 'new history' of Restoration France. Later, with the support of Guizot, he took positions at the École Normale and the Collège de France as well as with the National Archives before his dismissal in the aftermath of the Revolution of 1848. After early works on Luther, Vico, a textbook on universal history, and the early volumes of his great history of France, Michelet published on the origins of French law (1837), which was a Vichian interpretation of the 'poetry of law' from its mythological beginnings. Other later works and especially his French history confirmed his position as the national historian of France.

• Kelley 1984a, 2003; Kippur 1981; Viallaneix 1998.

MIKHAILOVSKII, NIKOLAI KONSTANINOVICH

1842–1904. Born in Meshchëvsk in the province of Kaluga, Mikhailovskii was a literary critic, publicist and one of the main theorists of Russian populism. From 1868–84 he was the co-editor of *Otechestvennye Zapiski* (Annals of the Fatherland) and from 1892 until his death the chief editor of *Russkoe Bogatstvo* (Russian Wealth). In his treatise *What is Progress?* (1896) and *The Struggle for Individuality* (1875–6) he set forth his own variant of the populist 'subjective sociology' (see Lavrov), combining the ideal of 'the all-round individual' with a retrospective utopia and idealising the natural economy and pre-modern communalism. At the end of his life he engaged in philosophical and political polemics with the Russian Marxists.

• Masaryk 1955; Mendel 1961; Walicki 1969.

MILL, JOHN STUART

1806–73. Born in London, J. S. Mill was the eldest son of James Mill. After being educated by his father at home, he followed him into employment by the East India Company, where he remained until the Company was dissolved in 1858. He published his *System of Logic* in 1843, followed by his *Principles of Political Economy* (1848). His principal political writings were *On Liberty* (1859) and *Considerations on Representative Government* (1861). Mill was a Member of Parliament between 1865 and 1868. He died and was buried in Avignon, France, where he kept a house after his wife had died and been buried there in 1858.

• Berger 1984; Carlisle 1991; Cowling 1990; Crisp 1997; Donner 1991; Gray 1983; Hamburger 1999; Lyons 1997; Reeves 2007; Riley 1998; Robson 1968; Ryan 1987; Skorupski 1989, 1998, 2006; Ten 1980.

MIQUEL, JOHANNES (FROM 1897: VON MIGUEL)

1829–1901. Miquel read law at Göttingen and Heidelberg. Studying the writings of Karl Marx, he became an extreme revolutionary. He practised as a lawyer for a time in Göttingen, became a Liberal and co-founded the National Association. In 1864 he was elected to the Hanoverian Parliament and in 1867 he entered the Prussian Parliament, after accepting the annexation of Hannover. In 1879 he was elected Lord Mayor of Frankfurt and in 1887 he entered the Reichstag, where he would be Minister of Finance for ten years. He supported the Emperor's plans for colonial and naval expansion and carried out a radical reform of the tax system, but did not support the Emperor's canal schemes which led to him resigning in 1901.

• Aldenhoff 1994; Herzfeld 1938; Kassner 2001.

MOHL, ROBERT VON

1799–1875. Mohl was born in Stuttgart and studied law in Heidelberg and Berlin. He held in succession at Tübingen University, the assistant professorship of law, the professorship of political economy and the rectorship from 1836–44. From 1847–61 he taught in Heidelberg. He was member of the Upper Chamber of the Baden Landtag from 1857–73, serving as president from 1867. Mohl was Baden envoy to the German Confederation until 1866 and envoy in Bavaria from 1867–71 and from 1874–5 he sat in the Reichstag. His major works are *Die Geschichte und Literatur des Staatswissenschaften* (History and Literature of the State Sciences) (1855–8 [1960]) and *Staatsrecht, Völkerrecht and Politik* (Constitutional Law, International Law and Politics) (1860–9 [1962]).
• Angermann 1962; Stöcker 1992.

MOLESWORTH, SIR WILLIAM

1810–55. Born in London, he succeeded to the baronetcy at the age of thirteen. In 1832 he became Member of Parliament for the eastern division of Cornwall. Through the politician Charles Buller he met Grote and James Mill and subsequently founded, with John Roebuck, the *London Review*. After the publication of two volumes he purchased the *Westminster Review*, and for some time he and J. S. Mill edited the united magazines. He was Member of Parliament for Leeds from 1837–41 and from 1845 to his death in 1855 he represented Southwark.

MONTALEMBERT, COMTE CHARLES DE

1810–70. A French political leader and writer, Montalembert was born in London in 1810 (his father had left France after the Revolution to serve in the English army). He moved back to Paris in 1830 and acted as the editor of *Avenir* until 1831, collaborating with Jean-Baptiste Lacordaire and Félicité de Lamennais in the Catholic liberal movement. This journal was condemned by the Pope in 1832 and Montalembert started the newspaper *Correspondant* as a means of expressing his ideas of Catholic belief and liberal politics. He was a great exponent of the freedom of the press, became a Member of Parliament in 1837, and after the 1848 Revolution sat in the Chamber of Deputies. In 1851 he was named a member of the Académie Française.

MORRIS, WILLIAM

1834–96. Born into a prosperous family in Walthamstow. As a student at Oxford, he met Edward Burne-Jones, Swinburne and Rosetti, members of the Pre-Raphaelite circle. He practised architecture, art and poetry, and translated Icelandic sagas. In 1876 he founded the Society for the Protection of Ancient Buildings, and by 1883 was active in socialist politics, giving hundreds of public lectures, and later editing the journal of the Socialist League, *Commonweal*. He resisted both anarchist and authoritarian tendencies within the socialist movement. His publications include *Art and Socialism* (1884), *A Summary of the Principles of Socialism* (1884), *A Dream of John Ball* (1888), *Signs of Change* (1888) and *News from Nowhere* (1890; published serially in *Commonweal* in 1889). He died in London in 1896.
• Leopold 2003; Thompson 1977.

MOST, JOHANN

1846–1906. Born in Augsburg, Most had a miserable childhood. He moved to Vienna in 1867 where he joined the International Working Men's Association. A committed socialist, he was frequently arrested and jailed for his political activities. Most was deported from Austria in 1871 and returned to Germany to work as a journalist. He was elected to the Reichstag in 1874 but was forced to leave when anti-socialist laws were passed. He arrived in London in 1878, converted to anarchism and started publishing *Freiheit*; however, he was imprisoned for eighteen months when, in 1881, he published an article praising the assassination of Tsar Alexander II. Upon his release he emigrated to America where he continued to publish *Freiheit*.

MÜLLER, ADAM HEINRICH

1779–1829. Born in Berlin and educated at the University of Göttingen, Müller worked as a tutor in Poland and Saxe-Weimar. He was associated with the noble opposition to Hardenberg in 1810. In 1805 Müller was a secret convert to Roman Catholicism and in 1812 he went to Vienna and entered the imperial service. He served in a number of minor diplomatic positions and was created Ritter von Nittersdorf in 1826. Müller's political publications include *Elemente der Staatskunst* (1809) based on lectures given at Dresden in 1808–9, *Über König Friedrich II* (1810) and *Versuche einer neuen Theorie des Geldes* (1816).
• Aris 1936; Berdahl 1988; Hanisch 1978; Koehler 1980.

NEWMAN, JOHN HENRY (CARDINAL)

1801–90. Cardinal and theologian, Newman was born in London and educated at Oxford. He was elected to a Fellowship at Oriel College in 1822 and was ordained in the Church of England in 1824. In 1826 he was appointed Tutor at Oriel and in 1828 he became vicar of St Mary's Church, Oxford. Together with John Keble, Richard Froude and Edward Pusey he is considered as one of the founders of the Oxford Movement, which sought to link the Anglican Church more closely with the Roman Catholic Church. Newman's famous tracts earned this movement the title of Tractarians. By 1839, however, he had begun to lose faith in the cause. He converted to Catholicism and was ordained a priest in 1847, becoming Cardinal in 1879. His most famous work is *Apologia Pro Vita Sua* (1864).
• Ker 2010; Rowlands 1989.

NIEBUHR, BARTHOLD GEORG

1776–1831. Born in Copenhagen, the only son of the explorer Carsten Niebuhr. He left the University of Kiel to pursue a career in the Danish and later the Prussian Civil Service. He resigned from the latter in 1808 to become state historiographer. His *Römische Geschichte* (1811–32) marked an era in the study of its special subject and had a momentous influence on the general conception of history. From 1816–23 he was Prussian Ambassador to the Holy See and after this until his death in 1831 he was a professor in the University of Bonn.

NIETZSCHE, FRIEDRICH

1844–1900. Nietzsche came from a strongly religious family in Saxony. He was named Associate Professor of Classics at the University of Basel in 1869. His first notable work, *Die Geburt der Tragödie aus dem Geiste der Musik* (1873), reflects the influence of Schopenhauer and of Wagner, with whom Nietzsche maintained a close friendship between 1868 and 1876. He criticised Schopenhauer and the romantics for their self-abnegation and lack of vigour. Suffering from mental illness from 1876 onwards, he became incapacitated by 1889, dying in 1900. His works include *Unzeitgemäße Betrachtungen* (1873), *Menschliches Allzumenschliches* (1878), *Die fröhliche Wissenschaft* (1882), *Also sprach Zarathustra* (1883–91), *Jenseits von Gut und Böse* (1886), *Zur Genealogie der Moral* (1887) and a posthumous compilation of disputed validity, *Der Wille zur Macht* (1901).
• Bodei 2002; Tanner 1997.

NOVALIS (HARDENBERG, GEORG FRIEDRICH FREIHERR VON)

1772–1801. Born in Oberwiedstedt, Prussian Saxony, Novalis studied at the universities of Jena, Leipzig and Wittenberg. Having trained at Tennstedt, Novalis worked as an auditor at salt works at Weissenfels in 1796–7; he returned there as an inspector of mines in 1799 after studying mining at the Academy of Freiburg. Although his literary output is relatively slight and fragmentary Novalis is credited with playing a crucial inspirational role in romanticism in Germany. His political ideas appeared in aphorisms published in Schlegel's *Athenäum* (1799), in *Glauben und Liebe* (1798) and in *Christenheit oder Europa* (1799).
• Aris 1936; Beiser 1992; Kuhn 1961; O'Brien 1995.

O'BRIEN, JAMES (BRONTERRE O'BRIEN)

1805–64. Born in Ireland, O'Brien was educated at Trinity College, Dublin. He moved to London in 1829 and took up journalism, serving as editor of the *Poor Man's Guardian* and other radical journals, establishing his own *National Reformer* in 1837. When this failed he joined Feargus O'Connor at the *Northern Star*. He read widely the literature of the French Revolution and in 1836 his translated version of Buonarotti's *History of the Babeuf Conspiracy* was published, followed by the *Life of Robespierre* (1859). A prominent member of the Chartist cause from the outset, O'Brien was imprisoned from April 1840 to September 1841, for making a 'seditious speech' and when released he broke with O'Connor to advocate political and social reforms through the National Reform League.
• Chase 2006; Thompson 1986.

O'CONNELL, DANIEL

1775–1847. Irish nationalist, known as 'The Liberator', he was born in Ireland but educated in France and admitted to the Bar in Dublin in 1798. As a lawyer he dealt with many cases of Irish tenants against English landlords. O'Connell campaigned for the rights of Roman Catholics, founding the Roman Catholic Association in 1823, and was a member of the English Parliament for many years. His ardent wish was that the Act of Union be repealed and that an Irish Parliament be established. His meetings attracted hundreds of thousands and led to his imprisonment for three months for sedition. However, the potato famine of 1847 brought a halt to the movement's political momentum. His funeral was one of the largest ever seen in Ireland.
• O'Connell 1977.

OWEN, ROBERT

1771–1858. Born in Wales, Owen was apprenticed to drapers in Lincolnshire, London and Manchester, and went on to make his fortune in the cotton spinning trade. He ran his cotton spinning mill at New Lanark on a philanthropic basis, and became interested in ideas of rational education and its impact on the formation of character. Owen began to write and speak on welfare policy, and also against organised religion. In 1825 he began to develop the New Harmony community in Indiana, and to expound socialist ideas that would culminate in a secular millenarianism. After founding other communities but becoming disenchanted by their failure, he became increasingly involved in spiritualism and divorced from working-class politics and the socialist movement.
• Owen 1993; Taylor 1983.

PALACKÝ, FRANTIŠEK

1798–1876. Palacký came to prominence in 1848 when he opposed the holding of elections to the German National Assembly in Bohemia and Moravia which were within the German Confederation. Instead Palacký argued for the continuation of the Habsburg Empire; he

wanted it run on more decentralised and constitutional lines with autonomy for Czechs and other Slav nations. He went on to help organise the Prague Slav congress although he distanced himself from more radical elements. He also led the Czech party within the Austrian Constituent Assembly. However, defeat of the revolution also brought defeat of his decentralising ambitions and Palacký grew increasingly critical of the Habsburg monarchy, especially following the Austro-Hungarian Dualism of 1867.
• Zacek 1970.

PALEY, WILLIAM

1743–1805. Born in Peterborough, Paley was educated at Christ's College, Cambridge, where he became a tutor in 1768, lecturing on moral theology. Pursing a religious career alongside his academic one, he was ordained deacon in the Church of England in 1766 and archdeacon of Carlisle in 1782. *The Principles of Moral and Political Philosophy* (1785), developed from his lectures, became a key textbook at Cambridge. In the same period he campaigned as a vociferous opponent of the slave trade. His major work, *Natural Theology: or, Evidences of the Existence and Attributes of the Deity, Collected from the Appearances of Nature* (1802), sought to provide a teleological proof of the existence of God, and of His benevolence, by highlighting the complexity of biological organisation in the natural world.

PLEKHANOV, GEORGII VALENTINOVICH

1857–1918. Born in the province of Tambov, Plekhanov was the first theorist of Russian Marxism. In 1875 he joined the populist revolutionary movement and after the split in Land and Liberty (October 1879) he created his own organisation, the Black Repartition, which was opposed to the terrorist tactics of the People's Will Party. In 1880 he left Russia and in 1883 founded the social-democratic group the Emancipation of Labour in Geneva. His political programme was outlined in *Socialism and Political Struggle* (1883) and *Our Differences* (1885). His interpretation of Marxism, stressing the notion of 'objective laws of development', was best expounded in his *Development of the Monist View of History* (1895). After the February Revolution he returned to Russia. He saw the Bolshevik revolution as a fatal mistake but refused to endorse active struggle against Lenin's rule.
• Baron 1963; Schapiro 1986; Walicki 1969.

PORTALIS, JEAN ÉTIENNE MARIE

1746–1807. Born in Provence and educated at the University of Aix, Portalis was a lawyer for the *Parlement* of Aix-en-Provence. He moved to Paris at the time of the Revolution, was imprisoned, practised law briefly, and then left for Switzerland. Back in Paris he served Napoleon, was appointed Counsellor of State and Minister of Public Faith, and devoted himself to the redaction of the Napoleonic Code, on which he left extensive commentaries.
• Arnaud 1969; Kelley 1984.

PROUDHON, PIERRE-JOSEPH

1809–65. Proudhon was from humble origins and a printer by trade. He attained notoriety in 1840 for a short book, *What is Property?*, to which he answered 'It is theft'. During the next twenty-five years, he attacked idle property-owners and outlined a moral socio-political ideal which scorned politics and proposed to give workers direct control of the economy. He variously called this ideal 'anarchism', 'mutualism' and 'federalism'. He wrote many books; perhaps the most famous from his mature years was *De la Justice dans la Révolution et dans l'Église* (1858). He briefly held political office as a Deputy during the French Second Republic, but in 1849 was fined and imprisoned for three years because of his verbal attacks on Napoleon III. He went into exile in Brussels between 1858 and 1862 to avoid being imprisoned for the publication of *De la Justice*.

• Dolléans 1948; Halévy 1913; Haubtmann 1969, 1982; Hoffman 1972; Kelley 1994; Ritter 1969; Sainte-Beuve 1947; Vincent 1984; Woodcock 1956.

PUCHTA, GEORG FRIEDRICH

1790–1846. A member of an old Bohemian Protestant family and son of a judge, he studied in Nürnberg and Erlangen and fell under the influence of Savigny and Niebuhr; and he taught there as well as Munich, Marburg, Leipzig, and finally Berlin. His major works were devoted to the history of modern Roman law and especially customary law as an expression of the organic development of the German people.

• Whitman 1990; Wieacker 1967.

RECLUS, ELISÉE

1830–1905. Born in Saint-Foy-la-Grande into a pious Calvinist family, Reclus came to denounce religion and to espouse anarchist opposition to the state. He voluntarily left France after Napoleon III's coup of 1851, spending time in England, the United States and Colombia. Returning to Europe in 1857, he became involved first in Bakunin's International Brotherhood and then, during the 1860s, in the Parisian section of the International Working Men's Association (IWA). He was forced into exile following the Paris Commune of 1871, this time going to Switzerland and Belgium. His greatest fame was for geographical works, especially his huge *Nouvelle Géographie Universelle* (19 vols. 1872–95). He was also well known for works such as *L'Évolution, la Révolution et l'Idéal Anarchique* (1898), where he articulated a combative, strident anarchism.

• Fleming 1979; Sarrazin 2004.

REHBERG, AUGUST-GUILLAUME

1757–1836. A friend of Brandes, Rehberg helped to propagate the ideas of Burke in Germany and also contributed to the founding of the German Historical School of Law. In 1790, he became literary critic responsible for reviewing French books for the *Allgemeine Literature-Zeitung*, which led to him reviewing books dealing with the Revolution, of which he was critical. In 1793 Rehberg synthesised his ideas on the Revolution in *Untersuchungen über die Französische Revolution* (Enquiries into the French Revolution). He argued that man cannot be seen in isolation, but always as part of a particular society; that the French Constituent Assembly was wrong to place sovereignty in the will of the people, since the result would be 'only the will of some people', mass rule; and that the Constituent Assembly was wrong to try to stamp out Christianity. His critique of revolution was also a critique of pure Kantian reason. Rehberg did not attack the Revolution outright – as Maistre and Bonald would do – but argued that it had attempted to carry out reform in the wrong way.

• Beiser 1992; Droz 1949; Godechot 1972; Raynaud 1989.

REMUSAT, CHARLES FRANÇOIS MARIE DE
(COMTE DE REMUSAT)

1797–1875. Born in Paris and known as a leading member of the *Doctrinaires*. In 1830 he was elected deputy for the Haute Garonne and served intermittently in government until the fall of the July Monarchy in 1848. Re-elected in 1848 and 1849, he left France after the *coup d'état* of Louis-Napoleon in 1851 and did not re-enter political life until 1869. In 1871 he was appointed minister for foreign affairs and in 1873 was again elected to represent the Haute Garonne. Elected to the Académie Française in 1840, he wrote widely on literary, philosophical and political matters.

RITCHIE, DAVID GEORGE

1853–1903. Born in Jedburgh, Roxburghshire, Ritchie was a son of a minister. Educated at Edinburgh University and Balliol College, Oxford, he was active in a range of progressive causes and was a member of the Fabian Society from 1889–93. He was elected in 1894 to the chair of logic and metaphysics at St Andrews University. Ritchie's aim of combining idealism and evolutionary science was apparent in his studies of *Darwinism and Politics* (1889) and *Darwin and Hegel* (1893). He defended a range of state action in *Principles of State Interference* (1891) and sought to socialise *Natural Rights* (1895). His was a progressive brand of liberalism, which defended the congruence of idealism and modified utilitarianism.

• Den Otter 1996; Freeden 1978.

RODBERTUS, JOHANN KARL

1805–75. Born in Greifswald, the son of a professor of Roman law, Rodbertus studied law in Göttingen and Berlin. He served briefly in the Prussian justice ministry, but in 1830 turned to economics and history and first wrote on working-class conditions and needs in 1839. Although involved sporadically in public affairs until 1849, he lived the rest of his life on the Rittergut Jagetzow which he had purchased in 1835. He rejected liberal economic and political principles, as well as doctrines of class conflict, but argued for a monarchist state socialism that would improve the condition of workers. His publications appeared in diverse forms and there is still no systematic edition.

• Gonner 1899; Gottschalch 1969; Rudolph 1984.

ROSSI, PELLEGRINO

1787–1848. Born in Carrara in Tuscany and educated in the universities of Padua and Bologna, he left for France and Geneva, where he taught Roman law. With the support of Guizot he came to Paris to teach political economy as successor to J. B. Say in the Collège de France and later constitutional law in the law faculty. Later Guizot sent him to Rome as ambassador to Pius IX. He was assassinated because of his conservative views in 1848.

• Kelley 1984; Ledermann 1929.

ROTTECK, KARL VON

1775–1840. Born in Freiburg im Breisgau, Rotteck enrolled at the University of Freiburg at the age of fifteen. He obtained a doctorate in law and was appointed professor in 1798. In 1818 he became Professor of Political Science and Law. In the aftermath of the French Revolution of 1830 Rotteck fell under the spell of politics: in the 1831 elections he was elected to a seat in the lower chamber of the Baden Landtag, which he held for the rest of his life. He wrote prolifically, including the nine-volume *Allgemeine Geschichte vom Anfang der Historischen Kenntniss bis auf unsere Zeiten* (Universal History) (1812–26) which helped spread liberal and constitutional views of German history. In the 1830s and 1840s his main project was the *Staatslexicon oder Enzyklopädie der Staatswissenschaften* (1834–9) which he edited with Welcker.

• Kopf 1980.

ROY, RAJA RAM MOHUN

1774–1833. Born in Bengal, Roy came from a Persian-writing Mughal service family and was influenced by Muslim monotheism and Christian ethics. A religious reformer, he is still regarded as the first modern Indian political philosopher. He issued an English abridgement of the *Vedanta*, and published *The Precepts of Jesus* (1820) and pamphlets hostile to both Hinduism and Christian Trinitarianism. He read voraciously in English and later French and died in England in 1833 while upholding the 'rights' of the now powerless Mughal emperor and condemning the abuses of the East India Company. He argued for the freedom of the press and free trade, which, he believed, would banish the corruption associated with the Company's monopoly.

• Bayly 1998.

ROYER-COLLARD, PIERRE PAUL

1763–1845. Born in Sompuis (Marne) and educated by his Jansenist mother. In 1809 he was appointed to the chair of philosophy at the Sorbonne, where he opposed the sensationalism associated with Condillac. With the Restoration of the Bourbon monarchy he sat in the Chamber of Deputies almost continuously between 1815 and 1839, becoming President of the Chamber in 1828. In 1830 he presented Charles X with the so-called address of the 221 deputies, which effectively set the July Revolution under way. As leader of the *Doctrinaires* it was through his parliamentary discourses, especially those defending freedom of the press and representative government, that he established his reputation. He was elected to the Académie Française in 1827. Between 1835 and 1845 Royer-Collard was engaged in correspondence with Alexis de Tocqueville.

RUGE, ARNOLD

1802–80. Ruge was an activist in the student movement, the *Burschenschaft*, in the early 1820s, for which he was imprisoned for six years. In 1837 whilst at the University of Halle, he set up the *Hallische Jahrbücher*, the main journal of the Young Hegelian movement, followed from 1841–3 by the *Deutsche Jahrbücher*, once censorship had forced him to move the journal to Saxony. With the enforced closure of this journal in 1843 at the behest of the Prussian government, he moved to Paris. He broke with Marx over the question of socialism. In 1848 he was a radical member of the Frankfurt assembly, after which he stayed in exile in England, settling in Brighton, where he died in 1880.

RUSSWORM, JOHN BROWN

1799–1851. John Brown Russworm was born in Jamaica in 1799. He graduated from Bowdoin College, Brunswick, Maine, in 1826, the second African-American in the United States to earn a college degree. In the same year he celebrated the half-century of the American Revolution with a speech on the virtues of revolutionary transformation. He went on to participate in two abolitionist newspapers, *Freedom's Journal* and *Rights of All*. Frustrated by the thought that slavery would never be abolished in America, Russworm relocated to Liberia in 1829. There he served as superintendent of education, edited the *Liberia Herald*, became governor of the county of Maryland, and recruited American blacks to settle there until his death in 1851.

SAINT-SIMON, CLAUDE HENRI DE ROUVROY, COMTE DE

1760–1825. Saint-Simon fought for the American colonies in their revolt against Britain, and made and lost a fortune in land speculation during the French Revolution. For most of his later life he lived in abject poverty, surviving only through the generosity of a former valet and the income from a small family pension. In his brilliant but unsystematic and disorganised writings – for example, *Lettres d'un Habitant de Genève à ses Contemporains* (1802), *L'Industrie* (1817), *L'Organisateur* (1819), *Du Système Industriel* (1821), *Catéchisme des Industriels* (1823–4) and, finally, *Nouveau Christianisme* (1825) – Saint-Simon opposed the destructive spirit of the Revolution and proposed instead a positive reorganisation of society with leadership roles variously assigned to industrial leaders and scientists. The normative goal was the well-being of the 'poorest and most numerous classes'.

• Gouhier 1933–41; Manuel 1963; Manuel and Manuel 1979; Weill 1894.

SAVIGNY, FRIEDRICH KARL VON

1779–1861. Born in Frankfurt am Main, he attended the University of Marburg, where he took his doctorate in 1800. In 1810, after the publication of his seminal *Law of Possession*, he became Professor of Jurisprudence at the new University of Berlin, where he took an active political as well as academic role. In 1814 he published his manifesto on codification, *The Vocation of our Age for Legislation and Jurisprudence* and the first volume of his monumental history of Roman law in the Middle Ages, which established his leadership of the Historical School of Law. Later there appeared his eight-volume treatise on *The System of Contemporary Roman Law*. In 1842 he was appointed head of the Prussian juridical system, and before his retirement in 1848 he worked on legal reforms.

• Kelley 1990; Whitman 1990; Wieacker 1967.

SAY, JEAN-BAPTISTE

1767–1832. Of a Protestant Genevan family, Say was sent to England to begin a commercial career. On his return to Paris he read Adam Smith and decided to devote himself to economics and social reform. From 1794–1800 he edited the revolutionary periodical *La Décade Philosophique, Littéraire, et Politique*, which was closely associated with moderate republicanism and with the Idéologue philosophical school. He served in the Tribunate, but left after quarrelling with Napoleon, and devoted himself to cotton manufacture (at Auchy in the Pas de Calais). Say's most important work, the *Traité d'Économie Politique* (1803), went through many editions and was a primary text in spreading classical political economy on the continent. He also published a *Cours Complet d'Économie Politique Pratique* (1828–30), and in 1831 became Professor of Political Economy at the Collège de France.

• Blaug 1991; Guillaumont 1969; Hollander 2005; Sowell 1972; Welch 1984; Whatmore 2000.

SCHILLER, FRIEDRICH

1759–1805. Schiller was born into a medical family in Württemberg and studied medicine at the Karlsschule. He served briefly as an army doctor, but was arrested after the production of his play *Die Räuber* (1781), because of its stinging indictment of oppressive rule. This play figured in the *Sturm und Drang* movement, which attacked complacency, and stressed feeling and sensibility, contributing in various ways to romanticism and the Young German tendency. Escaping from Württemberg, Schiller met Goethe, and moved to Weimar in 1787. With Goethe's assistance, he was appointed Professor of History and Philosophy at Jena in 1789, and undertook an intensive study of Kant, notably the *Critique of Judgement*, leading to the publication of *Über Anmut und Würde* (1793), *Über Naïve und Sentimentale Dichtung* (1795–6), and his most famous philosophical work, *Über die Ästhetische Erziehung des Menschen* (1795).

• Sharpe 1995; Wilkinson and Willoughby 1967.

SCHLEGEL, KARL WILHELM FRIEDRICH (AFTER 1815: VON SCHLEGEL)

1772–1829. Born in Hannover, the son of a civil servant, Schlegel was educated at the universities of Göttingen and Leipzig. With his brother (A. W. Schlegel) he was at the core of the group of writers in Jena who were first identified as 'romantics'; the brothers Schlegel produced the important quarterly *Athenaeum* in 1799. After serving briefly as a Privatdozent at Jena in 1801 Schlegel continued his studies in Paris. In 1808 he became a Roman Catholic and from 1809 he served in the Vienna chancery. Statements of Schlegel's mature and generally conservative political ideas can be found in *Die Entwicklung der Philosophie* (1804–5), *Die Signatur des Zeitalters* (1820–3) and *Philosophie des Lebens* (1827).

• Aris 1936; Beiser 1992, 2003; Eichner 1970; Frank 1995; Hendrix 1962.

SCHLEIERMACHER, FRIEDRICH DANIEL

1768–1834. Born in Breslau, educated by the Moravian Brethren and at the University of Halle. Having been ordained in the Reformed Church Schleiermacher was appointed assistant pastor in Landsberg in 1794 and pastor to the Charité Hospital in Berlin in 1796. He was Professor of Theology at Halle from 1804–7 and at the University of Berlin from 1810. In 1797 Schleiermacher met Friedrich Schlegel (q.v.) and became closely attached to him. His nationalistic sermons during the war years attracted large audiences. Schleiermacher lectured on the state in Berlin in 1809, 1817, 1829 and 1833. A version of the 1829 lectures derived from student notes was published in 1845 as *Lehre vom Staat*.

• Dawson 1966; Holstein 1972; Hoover 1989, 1990; Redeker 1973; Schleiermacher 1988.

SCHOPENHAUER, ARTHUR

1788–1860. The son of a wealthy merchant family, Schopenhauer was born in Danzig, but moved to Weimar after the death of his father in 1805. After studying philosophy in Berlin from 1811 to 1813, he unsuccessfully rivalled Hegel as a university lecturer there, scheduling his classes at the same time. He moved to Frankfurt in 1831, living from his estate. Though published in 1819, his most important work, *Die Welt als Wille und Vorstellung*, went largely unnoticed until after the revolutions of 1848, when its profound pessimism struck a cultural chord, influencing Wagner and Nietzsche in different ways. His other writings include *Über die vierfache Wurzel des Satzes vom Zureichenden Grunde* (1813) and a miscellany, *Parerga und Paralipomena* (1851). He died in 1860 in Frankfurt.

• Janaway 1997; Luft 1988.

SCHULZE-DELITZSCH, HERMANN

1808–83. A German liberal politician and economist, born in Delitzsch in Prussian Saxony. Schulze-Delitzsch studied law in Leipzig and Halle. He entered the National Assembly in 1848 and adopted the name of Delitzsch to distinguish himself from other Schulzes. In 1851 he withdrew and returned to Delitzsch to devote himself to the social reform and the development of co-operation in Germany. He was responsible for the foundation of the system of *Vorschussvereine* (people's savings banks) and also mercantile and consumer co-operatives and in 1859 founded the *Genossenschaftstag*, a general association of German co-operatives. As a liberal nationalist he was one of the politicians behind the foundation of the *Nationalverein*, which supported German unification.

SEELEY, J. R. (SIR JOHN ROBERT)

1834–95. Seeley was an English historian, born in London and educated at Cambridge. In 1863 he was appointed Professor of Latin at University College London, and from 1869 until his death he served as Regius Professor of Modern History at Cambridge. Seeley first came to wide public attention with the anonymous publication of a religious polemic, *Ecce Homo* (1865). His most significant book was *The Expansion of England* (1883). In it he expounded his view of history as a 'school of statesmanship', and offered both a historical analysis of the rise of the British Empire and a defence of the value of the settler colonies. His other main publications are: *The Life and Times of Stein, or, Germany and Prussia in the Napoleonic Age* (3 vols. 1878), *Natural Religion* (1882) and, posthumously, *The Growth of English Policy* (1895) and *Introduction to Political Science* (1896).

• Bell 2007; Burrow, Collini and Winch 1983; Wormell 1980.

SHELLEY, PERCY BYSSHE

1792–1822. Born at Warnham in Sussex and educated at Eton and Oxford, Shelley was expelled from Oxford in 1811 for circulating a series of arguments on 'The Necessity of

Atheism'. Shelley was strongly influenced by William Godwin with whose daughter, later Mary Wollstonecraft Shelley, he eloped in 1814. Shelley left England in 1818 to settle in Italy where he was an intimate of Lord Byron. Shelley's political views appeared in many of his poetic works, especially in *Queen Mab* (1821), *The Revolt of Islam* (1818), *The Masque of Anarchy* (1832) and *Prometheus Unbound* (1820) and in a series of pamphlets written in connection with a visit to Ireland in 1812, but they were expounded most systematically in *A Philosophical View of Reform* (1819) and *In Defence of Poetry* (1821).
• Brinton 1966; Dawson 1980; Hoagwood 1988; Scrivener 1982; Thorslev 1989.

SIDGWICK, HENRY
1838–1900. Born at Skipton in Yorkshire, Sidgwick was the son of a headmaster. Educated at Rugby and Trinity College, Cambridge, he was elected a fellow in 1859. Concerned throughout the 1860s with the problem of belief, his growing doubts led him to resign his fellowship in 1869. His most enduring work, *The Methods of Ethics* (1874), examined the philosophical basis of morality. He was appointed to the Knightbridge chair of moral philosophy in 1872. In 1883 he published *The Principles of Political Economy* (1883), which, like *The Elements of Politics* (1891), was much concerned with the role of the state. Sidgwick was a determined campaigner for women's education and an active participant in the ethical societies movement.
• Collini 2001; Burrow, Collini and Winch 1983; Schultz 1992, 2004.

SISMONDI, JEAN CHARLES LÉONARD SIMONDE DE
1773–1842. A Swiss historian, critic and economist, Sismondi was a member of the 'Coppet circle' surrounding Mme de Staël, and he shared her political views. These are evident in his pioneering *Histoire des Républiques Italiennes du Moyen Âge* (1807–18). In his *De la Littérature du Midi de l'Europe* (1813), Sismondi was one of the first to portray literature as the result of social and political institutions. As an economist, he was at first a rather orthodox follower of Adam Smith, but his most important economic work, the pessimistic *Nouveaux Principes d'Économie Politique* (1819), contained a fundamental critique of the basic axioms of the classical economists. He argued that competition did not tend to establish an equilibrium between production and consumption, and that economic crises were produced by underconsumption on the part of the working classes, on whose behalf he demanded protections from the unacceptable consequences of the new industrial order.
• Guillaumont 1969; Leroy 1962; Procacci 1983.

SOLOVIEV, VLADIMIR SERGEEVICH
1853–1900. Born in Moscow, son of a famous historian, Soloviev was educated at Moscow University, where he later taught philosophy for a while. While teaching he started to work on the unfinished *Philosophical Principles of Integral Knowledge*. In 1877 he relinquished his university position due to his aversion to academic politics and moved to St Petersburg, where he gave the hugely successful lecture series on the theme of Godmanhood, later published as *Lectures on Divine Humanity*. In 1880 he defended his doctoral dissertation but spoilt any chances of obtaining a professorship by appealing to the Tsar to pardon the regicides of his father Alexander III. He encountered great opposition to his writings and in particular to his activity in promoting the union of Eastern Orthodoxy with the Roman Catholic Church.
• Losev 1990; Stremoukhoff 1979; Walicki 1987.

SORAI, OGYU
1666–1729. Born in Edo (now Tokyo), Ogyu Nabematsu took the pen name 'Sorai'. His father oversaw Sorai's study of the neo-Confucianism of Zhu Xi. Sorai gained attention

for his grasp of Zhu Xi's teachings and subsequently became grand chamberlain to Shogun Tsunayoshi. By 1717, Sorai had rejected neo-Confucianism in favour of his own brand of *kogaku* (ancient learning). He is most famous for his works, the *Bendō* (Discerning the Meaning of the Way) and *Bemmei* (Discerning the Meanings of Philosophical Terms), which called for a revival of the ancient Chinese philosophy of the six classics. His *Taiheisaku* (Plan for an Age of Great Peace) and *Seidan* (Discourses on Political Economy) advised that urban-based *samurai* be relocated in rural areas away from the vices of towns.

SOUTHEY, ROBERT

1774–1843. Born in Bristol and educated at Westminster School and at Balliol College, Oxford, Southey's early deism and Unitarianism prevented him from fulfilling his family's wish that he enter the Church of England. In 1794–5 he was associated with Coleridge on the Pantisocratic project. Thereafter, having toyed briefly with law and politics, he settled on a career in literature. Southey's literary output was vast; he wrote for the Tory *Quarterly Review* from 1808–39 and was appointed Poet Laureate in 1813. He was friendly with Wordsworth from 1795. Southey's mature political views were expressed in his poetry, but the most important statements appeared in his numerous contributions to the *Quarterly* (some of which were collected in 1832 as *Essays*) and in *Sir Thomas More* (1829).
• Carnall 1960; Eastwood 1989; Mendilow 1986; Story 1997.

SPENCER, HERBERT

1820–1903. A self-taught polymath, indefatigable writer and researcher, Spencer first worked as a civil engineer for the London and Birmingham Railway Company. His writings spanned an extraordinary range of topics in evolutionary philosophy, psychology, sociology, political ethics and educational theory. His energetic advocacy of individualism, powerful endorsement of progress and his championing of evolution made him one of the central intellectual figures of his age, whose ideas had far-reaching influence, perhaps most notably in the United States. He became one of the foremost ambassadors of science and the so-called scientific point of view theory during the second half of the nineteenth century. His landmark publications included *Social Statics* (1850), *Principles of Psychology* (1855), *First Principles* (1862), *Principles of Biology* (1864–7), *Man versus the State* (1884) and *Principles of Sociology* (1879–93).
• Ferri 1905; Francis 2007; Hofstadter 1955b; Jones and Peel 2004; Moore 2002b; Peel 1971; Spencer 1908; Wiltshire 1978.

STAHL, FRIEDRICH JULIUS

1802–61. Born in Munich of a Jewish family, he became a Lutheran and studied and taught law at various universities before becoming Professor of Ecclesiastical Law at Berlin in 1840. Under the influence of Schelling and Lutheran, Stahl wrote his great work *Die Philosophie des Rechts nach Geschictlicher Ansicht* (1830–7) (The Philosophy of Law from a Historical Standpoint). He retired after 1858.
• Whitman 1990.

STANTON, ELIZABETH CADY

1815–1902. Women's rights activist, feminist and writer, born in Johnstown, New York to a wealthy family, Elizabeth Cady Stanton was educated at the Troy Seminary School and married the abolitionist Henry B. Stanton in 1840. She organised with Lucretia Mott the Seneca Falls Convention of 1848, which was considered the founding moment of the American women's rights movement. From 1852 onwards she closely collaborated with Susan B. Anthony, promoting women's rights – particularly the right to vote – and in 1869 they formed the National Woman Suffrage Association. Her most significant work was the

three-volume *History of Woman Suffrage* (1881–6), compiled with Susan B. Anthony and Matilda Joslyn Gage.
• DuBois 1999; Kraditor 1981; Sigerman 2001.

STEPHEN, JAMES FITZJAMES

1829–94. A jurist and journalist and brother of Sir Leslie Stephen, he was educated at Eton and Cambridge and admitted to the Bar in 1854. From 1869–72 he was the legal member of the viceroy's council in India, and helped codify and reform Indian law. Stephen served as a judge of the High Court of Justice from 1879–91 and became a baronet in 1891. He wrote widely on ethics, literature and current topics for periodicals but his main interest was jurisprudence. His main works were the *General View of the Criminal Law* (1863), an attempt to explain the principles of English law, *Liberty, Equality, Fraternity* (1873) and the *History of the Criminal Law of England* (1883).
• Colaiaco 1983; Smith 1988; Stephen 1991.

STEPHEN, LESLIE

1832–1904. Born in London, Stephen was educated at Trinity Hall, Cambridge. An active Alpinist, much of his early writing was devoted to mountaineering. His career as a Cambridge don was curtailed by his growing agnosticism, which led eventually to resignation from his fellowship. He subsequently pursued an energetic path in journalism. His major works in intellectual history included his *History of English Thought in the Eighteenth Century* (1876). Best known now as Virginia Woolf's father and the first editor of the *Dictionary of National Biography*, works such as *The English Utilitarians* (1900) earned him a considerable contemporary reputation as a biographer and historian.
• Annan 1984; Collini 1993.

STIRNER, MAX (JOHANN CASPER SCHMIDT)

1806–56. Born in Bayreuth, Bavaria, Stirner studied philosophy at the University of Berlin under Schleiermacher, Marheineke and Hegel, completing his studies in 1834. He became a teacher in Berlin in 1839 and in 1842 published *Das unwahre Prinzip unserer Erziehung* (The False Principle of our Education) and *Kunst und Religion* (Art and Religion) in *der Rheinische Zeitung*. His magnum opus *Der Einzige und Sein Eigentum* (The Ego and Its Own) was published in 1844. Stirner translated Adam Smith's *The Wealth of Nations* into German in 1847. His last book, *Geschichte der Reaktion* (History of the Reaction), was published in 1852.

STRAUSS, DAVID FRIEDRICH

1808–74. A theologian, born in Ludwigsburg, Germany, Strauss studied for the Church at Tübingen, and lectured on philosophy as a disciple of Hegel. In his *Leben Jesu* (1835–6, translated by George Eliot, 1846) he argued that the supernatural element of the Gospels was a collection of historical myths created by popular legend. The book raised such a storm of controversy that he was dismissed, and also debarred from taking up a professorship at Zürich in 1839. His other major work was *Die Christliche Glaubenslehre* (1840–1), a review of Christian dogma. He later lived in Ludwigsburg and Darmstadt, where he worked as a legislator while continuing to write.
• Cromwell 1974; Harris 1982.

STRUVE, GUSTAV VON

1805–70. Republican lawyer and leader in the 1848 Baden uprising. Born in Munich, a descendant of minor Russian nobility, Struve became a lawyer in Mannheim (Baden). His

idea of radical democracy included demands for religious reform, Jewish emancipation, women's rights and vegetarianism. His *Grundzüge der Staatswissenschaft* (Outlines of Political Science) (1847) called for a federative and democratic republic, but when the Frankfurt pre-Parliament rejected these proposals, Struve – together with Hecker – proclaimed a republic in Konstanz and joined the uprising and in 1849 the Baden provisional republican government. In 1849 he published one of the first histories of the Baden Revolution (*Geschichte der drei Volkserhebungen in Baden*). In exile in New York he supported Abraham Lincoln and the North in the American Civil War.
• Reiß 2004.

SUMNER, WILLIAM GRAHAM
1840–1910. Born in Paterson, New Jersey, Sumner graduated in theology from Yale in 1863. In 1868 he was appointed to the faculty of Yale University where he remained for the rest of his life, becoming Professor of Political and Social Science in 1872. In the 1890s he turned to the pursuit of sociology, returning to politics to oppose the expansionist Spanish American War and the annexation of the Philippines. His major sociological contribution was *Folkways* (1906). This work was originally intended as part of a monumental *Science of Society*, which did not appear until seventeen years after his death with the joint authorship of Albert Keller. Sumner was a fiercely independent thinker who was quite capable of blunt criticism of the wealthy elites whose cause he usually championed.
• Hofstadter 1992; Keller 1933; Starr 1925.

TAINE, HIPPOLYTE
1828–93. A French philosopher, historian and critic born in Vouziers in the Ardennes, Taine was educated in Paris at the Collège Bourbon and then at the École Normale Supérieure. As a teacher of art and aesthetics at the École des Beaux-Arts from 1864–83, attempting to apply the scientific method to the study of the humanities, he became known as one of the most revered advocates of French positivism. Taine wrote many philosophical works, and also pieces that were highly critical of French, Italian and English art and literature at the time. He is most famous for his history of the French Revolution, *Les Origines de la France Contemporaine* (1876–99).

T'AO, WANG
1828–97. Born in the Kiangsu Province, he studied the Confucian classics in preparation for entry into the Civil Service but left for Shanghai in 1848 after failing the second examination. In 1849 he was appointed the Chinese editor of the London Missionary Society, but when accused of passing information to Taiping rebels in 1862 he fled to Hong Kong. Here he met the missionary James Legge and for over ten years he assisted him with the translation of Confucian classics. In the 1860s he became editor of the *Hong Kong News* and in 1873 he founded his own Chinese language newspaper. During the 1870s and 1880s Wang wrote prolifically, and his writings advocating the adoption in China of Western learning have ensured him of an enduring historical importance.
• Cohen 1974.

TAYLOR, HARRIET
1807–58. Taylor (born Harriet Hardy) sustained a long friendship and intellectual partnership with J. S. Mill during her marriage to John Taylor. Harriet bore three children by her husband, but eventually moved out of the family home in order to devote herself to Mill. After John Taylor's death in 1849, Mill and Taylor married in 1851. Mill attributed great intellectual powers and influence to Taylor, but their contemporaries (and some historians)

disagreed. Taylor certainly helped Mill to revise and edit his works, and Mill attributed to her the 'Enfranchisement of Women' article published in the *Westminster Review* in 1851. Mill also acknowledged her influence, and that of her daughter Helen Taylor Mill, on his 1869 *The Subjection of Women*. Harriet Taylor died in 1858 in Avignon.

• Jacobs 2002.

TAYLOR, JOHN 'OF CAROLINE'

1753–1824. A political philosopher born in Virginia, Taylor was orphaned at the age of ten and then sent by his uncle to the College of William and Mary where he studied law. He fought in the American Revolution, reaching the rank of major. Taylor was a member of the Senate from 1792–4, 1803 and 1822–24. He believed strongly in the rights of individual states and thus opposed the ratification of the constitution and in 1798 introduced the Virginia and Kentucky Resolutions in the Virginia legislature. Taylor's most famous work is *An Inquiry into the Principles and Policy of the Government of the United States* (1814), which opposed the growth of federal power and the damage it might cause to democracy and agriculture.

• Simms 1932.

THIERRY, AUGUSTIN

1795–1856. Journalist and then founder of the 'new history' in Restoration France, Thierry wrote on historical method and many aspects of French history, including the Norman Conquest, *Histoire de la Conquête de l'Angleterre par les Normands* (1825) and the rise of the Third Estate and its 'liberties', for which he published a collection of medieval documents in the series founded by Guizot.

• Gossman 1976; Mellon 1958; Smithson 1972.

THOMPSON, WILLIAM & WHEELER, ANNA

1775–1833. Born into a wealthy Anglo-Irish family, Thompson spent his life writing on the co-operative movement, socialism and political economy. He lived on his estate near Cork as a philanthropic and innovative landlord, as well as a supporter of Catholic emancipation. He never married, but sustained a long-standing friendship with Anna Doyle Wheeler (1785–1848). They had met through their involvement in utilitarian circles, and it was Wheeler's influence that Thompson claimed inspired his 1825 *Appeal of One-Half of the Human Race*. Wheeler had been unhappily married to Francis Massey Wheeler from the age of fifteen. Having raised two daughters, she left her husband and travelled to Guernsey and London, and then moved to France in 1823. The death of her husband in 1820 had forced her to support herself through translation work, including the work of Charles Fourier. She later became closely involved in the circle around the *Tribune des Femmes* journal in Paris.

• Dooley 1996.

THOREAU, HENRY DAVID

1817–62. Thoreau was born in Concord, Massachusetts and educated at Harvard College. In 1837 he commenced an extensive journal and began his friendship with Ralph Waldo Emerson. A naturalist, a believer in the simple life, and something of a hero to contemporary environmentalists, he became increasingly offended by the institution of slavery. In 1846 he was jailed overnight for failure to pay his poll tax in an anti-slavery protest and he published his essay *Resistance to Civil Government* (1858), in which his anti-slavery views drove him to the edge of anarchism. This article later became widely influential in the United States and abroad after it was republished in 1866 under the title *Civil Disobedience*. He was an ardent supporter of John Brown. He died of tuberculosis in 1862.

• Emerson 1966; Harding 1982; Richardson 1986; Taylor 1996; Teichgraber 1995.

TKACHEV, PËTR NIKITICH

1844–86. Born in Pskov province, Tkachev became the leading theorist of the Jacobin wing of Russian populism. From 1868–9 he was a close collaborator of Sergei Nechaev. He is said to have declared that the rebirth of Russia required the extermination of anyone over twenty-five. In 1869 he was arrested and sentenced to exile and in 1873 he escaped to Zurich where he tried to collaborate with Lavrov until he realised that differences between them were too great. In 1874 he wrote an 'Open Letter' to Frederick Engels, accusing him of giving up revolutionary ways and advocating only legal action. In 1875 he began to publish his own journal *Nabat* (Toscin), propagating the seizure of power by a revolutionary minority and the need for a strong centralised organisation.

• Hardy 1977; Venturi 1960; Walicki 1969; Weeks 1968.

TOCQUEVILLE, ALEXIS DE

1805–59. Born in Paris, Tocqueville trained in the law and visited America in 1830 to study prison reforms. In 1839 he was elected to the Chamber of Deputies where he positioned himself on the moderate left of the political spectrum. In 1848 he opposed the Revolution but with his election to the Constituent Assembly in that year participated in the writing of the constitution of the Second Republic. In 1849 he was elected to the Legislative Assembly, becoming its Vice-President and briefly Minister for Foreign Affairs. With the *coup d'état* of Louis-Napoleon he was briefly imprisoned and then barred from public office. Dogged by ill-health he retired from public life and devoted himself to his historical studies of France. He was elected to the Académie Française in 1841. His *Recollections* were published in 1893.

• Benoît 2005; Drolet 2003; Garnett 2003; Mancini 1994; Pierson 1996; Welch 2001.

TRISTAN, FLORA

1803–44. Born in Paris, the illegitimate daughter of a Peruvian aristocrat and a Frenchwoman. Her father's death brought a drastic decline in her family's standard of living, and Tristan began work at a lithography studio. She married her employer André Chazal in 1821, and had two children, but the marriage broke up in 1825. Unable to obtain a divorce, Tristan was pursued by the obsessive Chazal, who eventually wounded her in a shooting incident. She travelled to Peru in 1832 and spent two years trying unsuccessfully to claim her father's estate, and wrote of her experiences in *Peregrinations of a Pariah* (1838). Her other travel literature included *Promenades in London* (1840). She befriended Charles Fourier, and became interested in socialism. She died suddenly while touring France in 1844.

• Dijkstra 1992.

TUCKER, BENJAMIN R.

1854–1939. Tucker was born in South Dartmouth, Massachusetts, to radical Unitarian parents. A dedicated intellectual, he nonetheless refused to go to Harvard, instead enrolling in the Massachusetts Institute of Technology, from which he never graduated. At an early age, Tucker became a major spokesperson for individualist anarchism. In 1872 he was an associate editor of *The Word*; in 1876, he translated Pierre-Joseph Proudhon's *What is Property?* He is best known for his long editorship of *Liberty* (1875–1902), a broadsheet dedicated to anarchism, and especially to the individualist anarchist ideas of William B. Greene. In 1893, a collection of Tucker's writings was published as *Instead of a Book, by a Man too Busy to Write One*. He retired to France in 1908.

• DeLeon 1978; Martin 1957; Reichert 1976.

VIVEKANANDA, SWAMI

1863–1902. Born Narendranath Datta in Calcutta, he adopted the name Swami Vivekananda in later life. Vivekananda graduated from the Presidency College in Calcutta and in 1886 completed studies in law at the Metropolitan Institution. There he fell under the influence of Ramakrishna Paramahansa and became his chief disciple. After Ramakrishna's death in 1886, Vivekananda and others set up a monastery dedicated to his teachings. As a result Vivekananda became one of the most influential Hindu thinkers and publicists. He addressed the World Parliament of Religions in 1893 on Hinduism and then travelled in America and England spreading the Vedanta philosophy and religion, dying in India in 1902. His works have been collected in nine volumes.

• Ashrama 1960.

WALLACE, ALFRED RUSSEL

1823–1913. Born in Usk, Monmouthshire. Whilst teaching in Leicester, he came into contact with an entomologist with whom he mounted a research trip to the Amazon in 1848. Though Wallace lost his specimens through shipwreck, on his return voyage he made further explorations in the South Pacific region, where his examination of the difference between Australian and Asian fauna eventually led him towards a theory of evolution close to Darwin's. It was Wallace's paper 'On the Tendency of Varieties to Depart Indefinitely from the Original Type', sent to Darwin in 1858, which provoked Darwin into going public with his own ideas. *Contributions to the Theory of Natural Selection* (1870) promoted a spiritualistic belief in a metabiological agency, something that set him apart from Darwin, and Wallace also promoted socialism and was active in campaigning for women's suffrage.

• Loewenberg 1959.

WARREN, JOSIAH

1798–1874. Born in Boston, Warren moved to Cincinnati as a young man. In 1821, he obtained a patent for a lamp fuelled by lard and opened a factory to produce and sell his new invention. An admirer of Robert Owen, Warren moved his family to New Harmony, Indiana in 1825. When it failed, Warren founded two other colonies in Ohio. He is best known for his Time Store, a retail store where the sales price of each item was based on the cost of labour required to produce it. He detailed his economic philosophy in his book *Equitable Commerce* (1862). In 1851, Warren and Stephen Pearl Andrews founded the individualist utopian colony Modern Times on Long Island. When it collapsed in 1862, Warren moved back to Boston, where he continued to promote individualist anarchism through lectures and writing.

• Bailie 1972; DeLeon 1978; Johnpoll and Klehr 1986; Reichert 1976.

WEITLING, WILHELM

1808–71. Weitling was born in Magdeburg, Prussia and was a tailor by profession. He was the first early German socialist and Friedrich Engels saw him as the founder of German communism. A member of the secret revolutionary society, the League of the Just, Weitling moved to Paris in 1838 and joined the Parisian workers' street protests in 1839. Whilst staying in Switzerland he was arrested for revolutionary activities and extradited to Prussia, from which he was allowed to emigrate to the United States. His main work, *Guarantees of Harmony and Freedom* (1842), received praise from Bruno Bauer, Ludwig Feuerbach and Mikhail Bakunin.

• Wittke 1950.

WELCKER, CARL

1790–1869. A lawyer, writer and politician, educated in Giessen and Heidelberg. Welcker had chairs at both these universities before leaving to join the University of Bonn; however, he was forced to leave for Freiburg as he was suspected of taking part in 'demagogic intrigues' in the light of the Karlbad Decrees of 1819. A belief in an empire of the German nation and in federal constitutionalism dominated his political thought. *Kieler Blätter* (1815–19), compiled with Christoph Dahlmann, reflects this. In 1831 he was elected to a seat in the Upper Chamber of the Baden Landtag, which he held for twenty years. In the 1830s and 1840s his work concentrated on the *Staatslexicon oder Enzyklopädie der Staatswissenschaften* (1834–9) which he edited with Rotteck.
• Dippel 1990.

WELLS, H. G. (HERBERT GEORGE)

1866–1946. A novelist, Wells was born in Bromley, Kent. At fourteen he was apprenticed to a draper, and in 1884 he won a scholarship to the Royal College of Science in South Kensington, writing articles in his spare time. He joined the Fabian Society in 1903 and the works *New Worlds for Old* (1908) and *The Great State Essays in Construction* (1912) describe his aims in socialist terms. His faith in human progress was tested by the First World War and he was prompted to write *The Shape of Things to Come* (1933), an anti-fascist warning. Wells is perhaps most recognised for his early 'science fiction' works *The Time Machine* (1898), *The Invisible Man* (1897) and *The War of the Worlds* (1898) and his romantic novels *Kipps* (1905) and *The History of Mr Polly* (1910).
• Parrinder 1972; West 1984.

WOLLSTONECRAFT, MARY

1759–97. Born to a well-off London family who later suffered declining fortunes, Wollstonecraft received little formal education, but in 1784 she set up a school, and two years later began to write on girls' education. She went on to write travel books, fiction and works of philosophy and politics, and engaged in critical dialogues with the work of Rousseau and Burke. In 1792 she published *Vindication of the Rights of Woman*; her unfinished novel *The Wrongs of Women, or Maria* also dealt with the 'woman question'. The following year she had an illegitimate daughter by Gilbert Imlay; her unhappiness with Imlay led to an attempted suicide in 1795. She married William Godwin in 1797, only to die in childbirth later that year.
• Sapiro 1992; Shanley 1998; Taylor 2003.

WORDSWORTH, WILLIAM

1770–1850. Born at Cockermouth and educated at Hawkshead Grammar School and St John's College, Cambridge, Wordsworth visited France in 1790 and 1791–2 and became sympathetic towards the Girondist party. He and Coleridge issued the first version of their *Lyrical Ballads* (1798) and in 1798–9 they travelled to Germany. From 1802 Wordsworth settled at Grasmere and pursued a literary career. Wordsworth's early republican sympathies were formulated in an unpublished 'Letter to Llandaff' (1793). His mature views on the virtues of traditional society were conveyed through his poems, particularly *The Prelude* (1799–1805 but not published until after his death) and the *Excursion* (1814). Prose statements of Wordsworth's political ideas were presented in *On the Convention of Cintra* (1809), *Two Addresses to the Freeholders of Westmoreland* (1818) and in his *Postscript 1835* to *Yarrow Revisited and Other Poems*.
• Brinton 1966; Butler 1988; Chandler 1984; Friedman 1979; Roe 1988; Woodring 1970.

WRIGHT, FANNY

1795–1852. Born in Dundee, Scotland, Wright was orphaned early and raised by relatives including James Milne, the Scottish progressive philosopher. She visited the United States in 1818, and published a positive account of American political democracy in 1821. Influenced by Robert Owen's New Harmony, she founded her own Tennessee community of freed slaves in 1825. The sexual freedoms of her community caused great controversy, as did Wright's own 'rational dress' and support for socialism, sexual equality and universal suffrage. Her community failed in 1828, and she became a well-known public speaker. Wright married Guillaume d'Arusmont in 1831, a marriage which ended in divorce and a protracted battle for Wright to keep her income from lecturing and publishing.
• Bartlett 1994; Eckhardt 1984.

ZASULICH, VERA

1851–1919. Zasulich was born to an impoverished noble family. Involvement in radical politics and contacts with the revolutionary Sergei Nechaev led to her arrest and imprisonment from 1869–73. She achieved fame with her attempt to assassinate General Trepov, governor of St Petersburg, in 1878. Although acquitted, she fled abroad to escape rearrest and lived in political exile. She corresponded with Karl Marx, was a friend of Friedrich Engels, and was one of the founders of the first Russian Marxist organisation, the Liberation of Labour (*Osvobozhdenie Truda*) group in Geneva in 1883. Zasulich was commissioned by the Emancipation of Labour group to translate a number of Marx's works into Russian. With Lenin and Plekhanov she was a member of the editorial board of *Iskra*. She returned to Russia after the 1905 Revolution and died in 1919.
• Bergman 1983.

ZETKIN, CLARA

1857–1933. Born Clara Eissner in Saxony, Zetkin moved to Zurich in 1882 and later to Paris, to escape Bismarck's restrictions on socialist activism. She had two sons with Russian revolutionary Ossip Zetkin, and later married the artist, Georg Friedrich Zundel. Her political involvement was on the far left of the Social Democratic Party (SPD), and she suffered harassment and arrest for her anti-war stance during the First World War. From 1891 to 1917 she edited the SPD women's newspaper *Die Gleichheit* (Equality). In 1907 she became the leader of the SPD's Women's Bureau, and was influential in the establishment of International Women's Day. In 1919 she joined the German Communist Party; in 1933 she was forced into exile in the Soviet Union, where she died later that year.
• Coole 1993.

Bibliography

PRIMARY SOURCES

A Canterbury Tale of Fifty Years Ago Being the Story of the Extraordinary Career of Sir William Courtenay (1888), Canterbury

Acton, John Emerich Edward Dalberg (1907a). *The History of Freedom, and Other Essays*, ed. John Neville Figis and Reginald Vere Laurence, London

(1907b). 'Nationality', *Home and Foreign Review* (July 1862), reprinted in *The History of Freedom and Other Essays*, London, 270–300

(1952). *Essays on Church and State*, ed. Douglas Woodruff, London

(1958). *Essays on Freedom and Power*, ed. Gertrude Himmelfarb, Boston

Adams, Henry (1958). *The Great Secession Winter of 1860–61*, ed. George Hochfield, New York

(1963 [1907, 1918]). *The Education of Henry Adams*, ed. Ernest and Jayne Samuels, Boston

(1985). 'The German Schools of History', in J. Rufus Fears (ed.), *Essays in the Study and Writing of History*, Indianapolis

(1986 [1889–91]). *History of the United States during the Administrations of Thomas Jefferson and James Madison*, ed. Earl N. Harbert, New York

Adams, W. E. (1858). *Tyrannicide: Is It Justifiable?*, London

(1903). *Memoirs of a Social Atom*, 2 vols., London

Agathon (pseudonym of Alfred de Tarde and Henri Massis) (1911). *L'esprit de la Nouvelle Sorbonne: La Crise de la Culture Classique, la Crise du Français*, Paris

(1995 [1913]). *Les Jeunes Gens d'Aujourd'hui*, Paris

Allen, Ann Taylor (1991). *Feminism and Motherhood in Germany, 1800–1914*, New Brunswick

Amos, Sheldon (1883). *The Science of Politics*, London

An Essay on Civil Government (1793). London

Andrews, Stephen Pearl (1970 [1851]). *The Science of Society*, Weston

Argyll, George Douglas Campbell, Duke of (1869). *Primeval Man: An Examination of Some Recent Speculations*, London

Aristotle (1926). *The Art of Rhetoric* (Loeb Classical Library), trans. J. H. Freese, Cambridge, MA

(1971). *Metaphysics*, trans. Christopher Kirwan, Oxford

Arnold, Matthew (1861). *The Popular Education of France with Notices of that of Holland and Switzerland*, London

(1960 [1869]). *Culture and Anarchy*, Cambridge

(1960–77). *The Complete Prose Works of Matthew Arnold*, ed. R. H. Super, 11 vols., Ann Arbor, MI

(1993 [1869]). *Culture and Anarchy and Other Writings*, ed. Stefan Collini, Cambridge

(1998). *The Letters of Matthew Arnold: Volume* III, *1866–1870*, ed. Cecil Y. Lang, Charlottesville, VA

Arnold, Thomas (1874 [1833]). *Miscellaneous Works*, ed. A. P. Stanley, London

Ashley, Evelyn (1873). *A Monarchy and a Republic: A Lecture Delivered at the Mechanics' Institute, at Bradford, January 1873*, London

Ashley, W. J. (1894). 'Roscher's Programme of 1843', *Quarterly Journal of Economics*, 9: 99–105

(1907). 'The Present Position of Political Economy', *The Economic Journal*, 17: 467–89

Austen, Jane (1954 [1813]). *Pride and Prejudice*, London

(1985 [1814]). *Mansfield Park*, London

Austin, John (1873). *Lectures on Jurisprudence or the Philosophy of Positive Law*, 2 vols., London

(1965 [1832]). *The Province of Jurisprudence Determined*, ed. H. L. A. Hart, London

(1998). *The Province of Jurisprudence Determined*, Indianapolis

Aveling, Edward and Marx, Eleanor (1886). 'The Woman Question: From a Socialist Point of View', *The Westminster Review*, January

Bagehot, Walter (1860). 'Memoir of the Right Honourable James Wilson', *The Economist*, 17 November

(1867). *The English Constitution*, London

(1872). *Physics and Politics: or Thoughts on the Application of the Principles of 'Natural Selection' and 'Inheritance' to Political Society*, London

(1873). *Physics and Politics*, 2nd edition, London

(1876). *Physics and Politics: or, Thoughts on the Application of the Principles of 'Natural Selection' and 'Inheritance' to Political Society*, 4th edition, New York

(1908 [1880]). *Economic Studies*, London

(2001 [1867]). *The English Constitution*, ed. P. Smith, Cambridge

Bain, A. (1882a). *James Mill: A Biography*, London

(1882b). *John Stuart Mill. A Criticism: with Personal Recollections*, London

Bakunin, Mikhail (1932). *Confession*, Paris

(1953). *The Political Philosophy of Bakunin: Scientific Anarchism*, ed. G. P. Maximoff, Glencoe, IL

(1961–81). *Oeuvres Complètes de Bakounine*, 8 vols., Paris

(1965). 'Die Reaktion in Deutschland', in James M. Edie *et al.* (eds.), *Russian Philosophy*, Vol. I, Chicago

(1970). *God and the State*, New York (part of the larger, but never-completed, work *The Knouto-Germanic Empire and the Social Revolution*, written between 1870 and 1872)

(1971). *Bakunin on Anarchy*, ed. Sam Dolgoff, London

(1973). *Selected Writings*, ed. Arthur Lehning, New York

(1977). *The Confessions of Mikhail Bakunin*, trans. Robert C. Howes, Ithaca

(1990 [1873]). *Statism and Anarchy*, trans. and ed. Marshall S. Schatz, Cambridge

Balfour, Arthur (1908). *Decadence*, Henry Sidgwick Memorial Lecture, Cambridge

Ball, Sidney (1896). *The Moral Aspects of Socialism*, London

Ballanche, Pierre-Simon (1833). *Oeuvres*, 6 vols., Paris

[Balzac, H. de] Sand, Georges (1977 [1841]). 'Voyage d'un Moineau de Paris à la Recherche du Meilleur Gouvernment', in Grandville [J. I. I. Gérard], *La Vie Privée et Publique des Animaux*, Paris

Bancroft, George (1876). *History of the United States of America*, 8 vols., Boston

Barante, Prosper de (1821). *Des Communes et de l'Aristocratie*, Paris

Barker, Ernest (1906). *The Political Thought of Plato and Aristotle*, London

(1914). *Nietzsche and Treitschke: The Worship of Power in Modern Germany*, London

(1915a). 'The Discredited State', *Political Quarterly*, 2: 102–21

(1915b). *Political Thought in England from Herbert Spencer to the Present Day*, London

Bibliography

Barker, J. W. (1873). *Kidderminster Republican Club: An Address Delivered at the First Annual Dinner*

Barruel, Abbé (1798). *Proofs of a Conspiracy against Government and Religion by the Illuminati and the Freemasons*

Barwis, Jackson (1793). *A Fourth Dialogue Concerning Liberty*, London

Baudelaire, Charles (1964). *Baudelaire as a Literary Critic: Selected Essays*, ed. and trans. L. B. Hyslop and F. E. Hyslop Jr., University Park, PA

Bauer, Bruno (1840). *Die Evangelische Landeskirche Preußens und die Wissenschaft*, Leipzig
  (anon.) (1841). *Die Posaune des Jüngsten Gerichts über Hegel, den Atheisten und Antichristen. Ein Ultimatum*, Leipzig
  (anon.) (1842a). *Hegels Lehre von der Religion und Kunst von dem Standpunkte des Glaubens aus Beurtheilt*, Leipzig
  (1842b). 'Das Kölner Quartett', *Rheinische Zeitung*, No. 60, 1 March

Bauer, Otto (2000). *The Question of Nationalities and Social Democracy* 1908/1924, trans. J. O'Donnell, ed. Ephraim Nimni, London

Baumgarten, Alexander (1739). *Metaphysica* (3rd edition Halle, 1783)

Bax, Ernest Belfort (1887). *The Religion of Socialism*, London
  (1911). *The Last Episode of the French Revolution. Being a History of Gracchus Babeuf and the Conspiracy of the Equals*, London

Bax, Ernest Belfort, Dave, Victor and Morris, William (1886). *A Short Account of the Commune of Paris*, London

Baxter, John (1795). *Resistance to Oppression the Constitutional Right of Britons*, London

Bebel, August (1870). *Unsere Ziele. Eine Streitschrift gegen die 'Demokratische Correspondenz'*, Leipzig
  (1879). *Die Frau und der Sozialismus*, Zurich-Hottingen
  (1883). *Die Frau in der Vergangenheit, Gegenwart und Zukunft*, Zurich
  (1885). *Woman and Socialism*, trans. H. Adams Walther, London
  (1893). *Zukunftsstaat und Sozialdemokratie*, Berlin
  (1910). *Woman and Socialism*, trans. Meta L. Stern (Hebe), 50th edition, New York
  (1911–13). *Aus meinem Leben*, 3 vols., Stuttgart
  (1965). *August Bebels Briefwechsel mit Friedrich Engels*, ed. Werner Blumenberg, The Hague

Bell, T. (1859). Presidential Address, *Proceedings of the Linnean Society of London 1855–59*

Belloc, Hilaire (1912). *The Servile State*, London

Bentham, George (1827). *Outline of A New System of Logic, with a Critical Examination of Dr. Whately's "Elements of Logic"*, London
  (1997). *Autobiography, 1800–1834*, ed. M. Filipiuk, Toronto

Bentham, Jeremy (1789). *Draft of a New Plan for the Organisation of the Judicial Establishment in France*
  (1802). *Traités de Législation Civile et Pénale*, ed. E. Dumont, 3 vols., Paris
  (1811). *Théorie des Peines et des Récompenses*, ed. E. Dumont, 2 vols., London
  (1816). *Tactique des Assemblées Législatives, suivie d'un Traité des Sophismes Politiques*, ed. E. Dumont, 2 vols., Geneva and Paris
  (1817). *Plan of Parliamentary Reform, in the form of a Catechism, with Reasons For Each Article, with an Introduction, Shewing the Necessity of Radical, and the Inadequacy of Moderate Reform*, London
  (1818). *Church-of-Englandism and its Catechism Examined*, London
  (1822). *Codification Proposal . . . to all Nations Professing Liberal Opinions*, London
  (1823a). *Essai sur la Nomenclature et la Classification des Principales Branches d'Art-et-Science*, ed. G. Bentham, Paris
  (1823b). *Traité des Preuves Judiciaires*, ed. E. Dumont, 2 vols., Paris

(1824). *The Book of Fallacies: From Unfinished Papers of Jeremy Bentham. By a Friend* [P. Bingham], London

(1825). *A Treatise on Judicial Evidence*, ed. E. Dumont, London

(1827a). *Article Eight of the Westminster Review No. XII, for October, 1826, on Mr. Humphreys' Observations on the English Law of Real Property, with the Outline of a Code*, London

(1827b). *Rationale of Judicial Evidence, specially applied to English Practice*, ed. J. S. Mill, 5 vols., London

(1828). *De l'Organisation Judiciaire et de la Codification*, ed. E. Dumont, Paris

(1829–30). *Oeuvres de J. Bentham, Jurisconsulte Anglais*, ed. E. Dumont, 3 vols., Brussels

(1830). 'Emancipate Your Colonies!' in *Rights, Representation, and Reform: Nonsense Upon Stilts and Other Writings on the French Revolution*, ed. Philip Schofield, Catherine Pease-Watkin and Cyprian Blamires, Oxford (2002)

(1834). *Deontology; or, The Science of Morality*, ed. J. Bowring, 2 vols., London and Edinburgh

(1838–43). *The Works of Jeremy Bentham*, ed. J. Bowring, 11 vols., Edinburgh

(1932). *Bentham's Theory of Fictions*, ed. C. K. Ogden, London

(1952). *Handbook of Political Fallacies*, ed. Harold A. Larrabee, Baltimore

(1952–4 [1787]). Defence of Usury in *Jeremy Bentham's Economic Writings*, ed. W. Stark, 3 vols., London

(1970a [1789]). *An Introduction to the Principles of Morals and Legislation*, ed. J. H. Burns and H. L. A. Hart [*The Collected Works of Jeremy Bentham*, 1961–, henceforth *CW*], London

(1970b). *Of Laws in General*, ed. H. L. A. Hart, London

(1973). *Bentham's Political Thought*, ed. B. Parekh, London

(1981). *The Correspondence of Jeremy Bentham, Volume 5, January 1794 to December 1797*, ed. A. T. Milne, *CW*, London

(1983a [1817]). *Chrestomathia*, ed. M. J. Smith and W. H. Burston, *CW*, Oxford

(1983b [1830]). *Constitutional Code, Volume I*, ed. F. Rosen and J. H. Burns, *CW*, Oxford

(1983c). *Deontology together with A Table of the Springs of Action and Article on Utilitarianism*, ed. A. Goldworth, *CW*, Oxford

(1984). *The Correspondence of Jeremy Bentham, Volume 6, January 1798 to December 1801*, ed. J. R. Dinwiddy, *CW*, Oxford

(1988a). *The Correspondence of Jeremy Bentham, Volume 7, January 1802 to December 1808*, ed. J. R. Dinwiddy, *CW*, Oxford

(1988b). *The Correspondence of Jeremy Bentham, Volume 8, January 1809 to December 1816*, ed. S. Conway, *CW*, Oxford

(1988c [1776]). *A Fragment on Government*, ed. J. H. Burns and H. L. A. Hart, with an Introduction by R. Harrison, Cambridge

(1995 [1820–2]). 'Rid Yourselves of Ultramaria', in *Colonies, Commerce, and Constitutional Law: Rid Yourselves of Ultramaria and Other Writings on Spain and Spanish America*, ed. Philip Schofield, London

(1996 [1789]). *An Introduction to the Principles of Morals and Legislation*, ed. J. H. Burns and H. L. A. Hart, with a new introduction by F. Rosen, *CW*, Oxford

(1998). *'Legislator of the World': Writings on Codification, Law, and Education*, ed. P. Schofield and J. Harris, *CW*, Oxford

(1999). *Political Tactics*, ed. M. James, C. Blamires and C. Pease-Watkin, *CW*, Oxford

(2002a). *Rights, Representation, and Reform: Nonsense Upon Stilts and Other Writings on the French Revolution*, ed. P. Schofield, C. Pease-Watkin and C. Blamires, *CW*, Oxford

(2002b [1789]), 'Short Views on Economy, For the Use of the French Nation but not Inapplicable to the English', in *Rights, Representation, and Reform: Nonsense Upon Stilts and Other Writings on the French Revolution*, ed. Philip Schofield, Catherine Pease-Watkin and Cyprian Blamires, Oxford

(2008 [1823]). *A Comment on the Commentaries and a Fragment on Government*, ed. J. H. Burns, H. L. A. Hart and Philip Schofield, Oxford

Bentham, M. S. (1862). *The Life of Brigadier-General Sir Samuel Bentham, K.S.G.*, London

Bernardi, Joseph (1803). *Cours de Droit Civil Français*, Paris

Bernstein, Eduard (1893). *Ferdinand Lassalle as a Social Reformer*, trans. Eleanor Aveling, London

(1896). *Parlamentarismus und Sozialdemokratie*, Berlin

(1901a [1890]). 'Die Stellung der Sozialdemokratie in den Parlamenten', in Eduard Bernstein, *Zur Geschichte und Theorie des Socialismus. Gesammelte Abhandlungen*, 4th edition, Berlin-Bern

(1901b). *Wie ist Wissenschaftlicher Socialismus Möglich?*, Berlin

(1973 [1899]). *Die Voraussetzungen des Sozialismus und die Aufgaben der Sozialdemokratie*, Bonn-Bad Godesberg

(1993 [1899]). *The Preconditions of Socialism (The Prerequisites for Socialism and the Tasks of Social Democracy)*, ed. and trans. Henry Tudor, Cambridge

Bertoldi, Guiseppe (1821). *Memoirs of the Secret Societies of the South of Italy, Particularly the Carbonari*, London

Besant, Annie (1893). *Essays on Socialism*

Besant, Annie and Foote, G. W. (1887). *Is Socialism Sound?*, London

Beseler, Georg (1843). *Volksrecht und Juristenrecht*, Leipzig

Bexon, S. (1807). *Application de la Théorie de la Législation Penale, ou Code de la Sûreté Publique et Particulière . . . Rédigé en Projet Pour les États de sa Majesté Le Roi de Bavière*, Paris

Bichat, Xavier-Marie-François (1809). *Physiological Researches upon Life and Death*, trans. Tobias Watkins, Philadelphia

Bishop, Samuel (1796). *The Poetical Works of the Rev. Samuel Bishop*, 2 vols., London

Blackstone, William (1862). 'On the Study of Law', *Commentaries on the Laws of England*, ed. G. Sharswood, Philadelphia

Blanc, Louis (1848). *Threatened Social Disintegration of France. Louis Blanc on the Working Classes*, ed. James Ward, London

(1982). *Louis Blanc (1811–1882)*, ed. Jean-Michel Humilière, Paris

Blatchford, Robert (1902). *Britain for the British*, London

(1908 [1894]). *Merrie England*, London

(1909). *The Sorcery Shop*, London

Blau, Joseph L. (1954). *Social Theories of Jacksonian Democracy*, ed. Joseph Blau (American Heritage Series), Indianapolis

Bluntschli, Jacob (1885). *The Theory of the State*, trans. D. Ritchie *et al.*, Oxford

Böhm-Bawerk, Eugen von (1890). 'The Historical vs. the Deductive Method in Political Economy', *Annals of the American Academy of Political and Social Science*, 1: 244–71

(1949 [1896]). *Karl Marx and the Close of his System*, ed. P. Sweezy, New York

Bonald, Louis-Gabriel-Ambroise (1802). *Législation Primitive*, 2 vols., Paris

(1843). *Théorie du Pouvoir et Religieux dans la Société Civile, Démontré par le Raisonnement*, 3 vols., Paris

(1845). *Démonstration Philosophique du Principe Constitutive de la Société*, 4th edition, Brussels

(1859). *Oeuvres Complètes*, ed. J.-P. Migne, 3 vols., Paris

(1864). *Oeuvres Complètes de M. de Bonald*, 2 vols., Paris

Bonner, Hypatia Bradlaugh (1895). *Charles Bradlaugh. A Record of His Life and Work*, 2 vols., London

Bonnot de Mably, Gabriel (1849). *Théories Sociales et Politiques*, ed. Paul Rochery, Paris

Booth, A. J. (1869). *Robert Owen, the Founder of Socialism in England*, London
    (1871). *Saint-Simon and Saint-Simonism*, London
Booth, Charles (1902 [1889–1901]). *Life and Labour of the People in London*, 17 vols., London
Bosanquet, Bernard (1885). *Knowledge and Reality. A Criticism of Mr. F. H. Bradley's 'Principles of Logic'*, London
    (1888). *Logic, or the Morphology of Knowledge*, Oxford
    (1895). 'Character in its Bearing on Social Causation', in B. Bosanquet (ed.), *Aspects of the Social Problem*, London
    (1910 [1899]). *The Philosophical Theory of the State*, London
    (1912). *The Principle of Individuality and Value: The Gifford Lectures for 1911 Delivered in Edinburgh University*, London
    (1913). *The Value and Destiny of the Individual: The Gifford Lectures for 1912 Delivered in Edinburgh University*, London
    (1923). *The Philosophical Theory of the State*, 4th edition, London
Bradley, F. H. (1988 [1876]). *Ethical Studies*, Oxford
Bridger, Robert Lowther (1906). *Imperial Federation*, London
Brougham, Henry (1840). *Letter to the Queen, on the State of the Monarchy*, London
Brouilhet, Charles (1910). *Le Conflit des Doctrines dans l'Économie Politique Contemporaine*, Paris
Brousse, Paul (1877). 'La Propagande par le Fait', *Bulletin de La Fédération Jurassienne*, 5 August
Brown, Paul (1834). *The Radical, and Advocate of Equality*, Albany
Browne, G. Lathom (1888). *Wellington; or, the Public and Private Life of Arthur, First Duke of Wellington*, London
Bryan, William Jennings (1900). *The Second Battle, or the New Declaration of Independence*, Chicago
Bryce, James (1899). *The American Commonwealth*, 2 vols., London
Buckle, H. T. (1861 [1859]). *History of Civilisation in England*, 2 vols., London
Buhlbring, Karl D. (1891). 'Mary Astell: An Advocate of Woman's Rights Two Hundred Years Ago', *Journal of Education*, April/May, London
Bulwer, E. (1833). *England and the English*, 2 vols., London
Bunsen, Christian Carl Josias (1845). *Die Verfassung der Kirche der Zukunft*, Hamburg
Burckhardt, Jacob (1860). *Die Kultur der Renaissance in Italien*, Basel
    (1958 [1860]), *The Civilisation of the Renaissance in Italy*, New York
Burke, Edmund (1790). *Reflections on the Revolution in France*, London
    (1904). *Works of the Right Honourable Edmund Burke*, Vol. v, Boston
    (1969). *Reflections on the Revolution in France*, ed. Conor Cruise O'Brien, New York
    (1988). *Reflections on the Revolution in France*, ed. J. G. A. Pocock, Indianapolis
    (1991 [1796]). *The Writings and Speeches of Edmund Burke*, Vol. ix, ed. Paul Langford, Oxford
    (2003 [1790]). *Reflections on the Revolution in France*, ed. Frank M. Turner, New Haven and London
Buret, E. (1840). *De la Misère des Classes Labourieuses en Angleterre et en France*, Paris
Byrne, Miles (1910). *Some Notes of an Irish Exile of 1798*, Dublin
Byron, Lord (1912). *The Poetical Works of Lord Byron*, London
    (1980–6). *The Complete Poetical Works*, ed. Jerome J. McGann, 5 vols., London
Cabanis, P.-J.-G. (1956 [1802]). *Rapports du Physique et du Moral de l'Homme*, 2 vols., in *Oeuvres philosophiques*, ed. Claude Lehec and Jean Cazeneuve, Paris
Caird, A. Mona (1897 [1907]). *The Morality of Marriage, and Other Essays on the Status and Destiny of Woman*, London
    (1913). *Personal Rights*, London

Caird, Edward (2002 [1883]). *Hegel*, Edinburgh

Calhoun, John C. (1992 [1811]). *Union and Liberty: The Political Philosophy of John C. Calhoun*, ed. Ross M. Lence, Indianapolis

Calkins, M. W. (1905). *The Metaphysical System of Hobbes as Contained in Twelve Chapters from his 'Elements of Philosophy Concerning Body'*, Chicago

Cambacérès, Jean-Jacques-Régis de (1789). *Discours sur la Science Social*, Paris

Campbell, John (1848). *A Theory of Equality; or, the Way to Make Every Man Act Honestly*, Philadelphia

Carey, Henry C. (1864). *Financial Crises: Their Causes and Effects*, Philadelphia

Carlyle, Thomas (1849). 'Occasional Discourse on the Nigger Question', *Fraser's Magazine*, 40: 670–9

    (1893a). *Critical and Miscellaneous Essays*, 8 vols., London

    (1893b [1839]). *Chartism*, London

    (1893c [1850]). *Latter-Day Pamphlets*, London

    (1893d [1829]). 'Novalis', in Carlyle, *Critical and Miscellaneous Essays*, Vol. III, London

    (1893e [1841]). *On Heroes, Hero-Worship, and the Heroic in History*, London

    (1893f [1843]). *Past and Present*, London

    (1893g [1831]). *Sartor Resartus. The Life and Opinions of Herr Teufelsdröckh*, London

    (1893h [1829]). 'Signs of the Times', in Carlyle, *Critical and Miscellaneous Essays*, Vol. III, London

    (1893i [1851]). *The Life of John Sterling*, London

    (1893j [1837]). *Sartor Resartus*, London

    (1903 [1843]). *Past and Present*, London

    (1904 [1839]). *Chartism*, London

    (1953). *An Anthology*, ed. G. M. Trevelyan, London

    (1971 [1840]). 'Chartism', in *Thomas Carlyle: Selected Writings*, ed. Alan Shelston, Harmondsworth

    (1977 [1843]). *Past and Present*, ed. Richard D. Altick, New York

    (2000 [1838]). *Sartor Resartus*, ed. Kerry McSweeney and Peter Sabor, Oxford

Carpenter, Edward (1890). *Civilisation: Its Cause and Cure*, London

    (1916). *My Days and Dreams*, London

Carruthers, John (1894). *Socialism and Radicalism*, Hammersmith

Chaadaev, Pëtr (1991). *Philosophical Works of Peter Chaadaev*, ed. Raymond T. McNally and Richard Tempest, Boston

Chalmers, Thomas (1883). *Select Sermons*, Edinburgh

Chamberlain, Joseph (1885). *The Radical Programme*, London

    (1897). 'The True Conception of the Empire', in *Mr Chamberlain's Speeches*, ed. Charles Boyd, Vol. II, London

Charcot, J.-M. and Richer, P. (1887). *Les Démoniaques dans l'Art*, Paris

Charléty, Sébastien (1896). *Histoire du Saint-Simonisme*, Paris

The Chartist Riots at Newport (2nd edition, 1889). Newport

Chateaubriand, François René de (1815 [1798]). *An Historical, Political and Moral Essay on Revolutions, Ancient and Modern*, no trans. given, London

    (1838a). *Oeuvres Complètes de Chateaubriand*, ed. M. Sainte-Beuve, 12 vols., Paris

    (1838b [1814]). *De Bonaparte et des Bourbons*, in Chateaubriand, *Oeuvres Complètes*, Paris

    (1838c [1816]). *De la Monarchie selon la Charte*, in Chateaubriand, *Oeuvres Complètes*, Paris

    (1838d [1823]). *De La Presse*, in Chateaubriand, *Oeuvres Complètes*, Paris

    (1838e [1814]). *Réflexions Politiques*, in Chateaubriand, *Oeuvres Complètes*, Paris

    (1856). *The Genius of Christianity, or the Spirit and Beauty of the Christian Religion*, trans. C. I. White, New York

(1859). 'Études Historiques', in Chateaubriand, *Oeuvres Complètes*, Vol. IX, Paris

(1902 [1848–50]). *The Memoirs of François René, Vicomte de Chateaubriand [Mémoires D'Outre Tombe]*, trans. Alexander Teixeira de Mattos, 6 vols., London

(1973 [1849]). *Mémoires d'Outre-tombe*, 3 vols., Paris

(1978 [1797]). *Le Génie du Christianisme ou Beautés de la Religion Chrétienne*, in Chateaubriand, *Essai sur les Révolution. Génie du Christianisme*, ed. Maurice Regard, Paris

Cherbuliez, A.-E. (1853). *Étude sur les Causes de la Misère tant Morale que Physique*, Paris

Chicherin, Boris (1998). *Liberty, Equality, and the Market* (Russian Literature and Thought), trans. and ed. G. M. Hamburg, New Haven and London

Christie, Thomas (1995 [1791]). *Letters on the Revolution in France*, in *Political Writings of the 1790s*, ed. G. Claeys, 8 vols., London

Chunder, Bholanauth (1869). *The Travels of a Hindoo to Various Parts of Bengal and Upper India*, 2 vols., London

Clarke, William (1908). *William Clarke: A Collection of His Writings*, ed. H. Burrow and J. A. Hobson, London

Cliffe Leslie, T. E. (1870). *Land Systems and Industrial Economy of Ireland, England, and Continental Countries*, London

(1879 [1860]). 'The Question of the Age – Is it Peace?', in Cliffe Leslie, *Essays in Political and Moral Philosophy*, Dublin

Cobbe, Frances Power (1870). *Our Policy: An Address to Women Concerning the Suffrage*, London

Cobbett, William (1817). *Cobbett's Opinion of Tom Paine as published by Cobbett Himself in 1797*, Fulham

(1830). *Rural Rides*, London

(1831). *Cobbett's Two-Penny Trash*, 2 vols., London

(1836). *Cobbett's Legacy to Peel*, London

Cobden, Richard (1835). *England, Ireland and America*, London

Coleridge, Samuel Taylor (1956–71). *Collected Letters*, ed. Earl Leslie Griggs, 6 vols., Oxford

(1969 [1809–10]). *The Friend*, ed. Barbara E. Rooke, 2 vols., Princeton

(1971) [1795]). *Lectures 1795 on Politics and Religion*, ed. Lewis Patton and Peter Mann, Princeton

(1972 [1816–17]). *Lay Sermons*, ed. R. J. White, Princeton

(1973). *The Notebooks of Samuel Taylor Coleridge, 1808–1819*, 5 vols., ed. Kathleen Coburn, Princeton

(1976 [1830]). *On the Constitution of the Church and State, According to the Idea of Each*, ed. John Colmer (Vol. X in *The Collected Works of Samuel Taylor Coleridge*), ed. K. Coburn, Princeton

(1980–). *Marginalia*, ed. George Whalley, 3 vols., Princeton

(1983 [1817]). *Biographia Literaria*, ed. James Engell and W. Jackson Bate, 2 vols., Princeton

(1987). *Lectures 1808–1819*, ed. R. A. Foakes, 2 vols., Princeton

(1990). *Table Talk. Recorded by Henry Nelson Coleridge (and John Taylor Coleridge)*, ed. Carl Woodring, 2 vols., Princeton

Comte, Auguste (1851–3). *A Discourse on the Positive Spirit*, trans. E. S. Beesley, London

(1853). *The Positive Philosophy of Auguste Comte*, 2 vols., trans. Harriet Martineau, London

(1865 [1848]). *A General View of Positivism*, trans. J. H. Bridges, London

(1875–7). *System of Positive Polity*, 4 vols., trans. J. H. Bridges *et al.*, London

(1877). *A General View of Positivism*, trans. J. H. Bridges, London

(1968). *Oeuvres d'Auguste Comte*, 12 vols., Paris

(1975). *Auguste Comte and Positivism: The Essential Writings*, ed. Gertrud Lenzer, New York

(1998 [1830–42]). *Cours de Philosophie Positive*, Paris

Condorcet, Jean-Antoine-Nicolas Caritat (1847). *Oeuvres de Condorcet*, 12 vols., Paris

(1912 [1790]). 'On the Admission of Women to the Rights of Citizenship', in *The First Essay on the Political Rights of Women*, ed. A. D. Vickery, Letchworth

Constant, Benjamin (1797). *Des Effets de la Terreur*, Paris

(1988a). *Political Writings*, ed. and intro. Biancamaria Fontana, Cambridge

(1988b [1819]). 'The Liberty of the Ancients Compared with that of the Moderns', in *Political Writings*, ed. Biancamaria Fontana, Cambridge

(1988c [1814]). 'The Spirit of Conquest and Usurpation and their Relation to European Civilisation', in *Political Writings*, ed. Biancamaria Fontana, Cambridge

(2004 [1822]). *Commentaire sur l'Ouvrage de Filangieri*, Paris

Conway, Moncure (1872). *Republican Superstitions as Illustrated in the Political History of America*, London

Cornewall Lewis, George (1832). *Remarks on the Use and Abuse of Some Political Terms*, London

(1841). *An Essay on the Government of Dependencies*, London

Courtney, Sir William (1834). *The Eccentric and Singular Productions of Sir William Courtney*, London

Cox, Harold (1902). *American Progress and British Commerce*, London

Cox, Homersham (1854). *The British Commonwealth: Or a Commentary on the Institutions and Principles of British Government*, London

Croly, Herbert (1965 [1909]). *The Promise of American Life*, ed. Arthur M. Schlesinger, Jr., Cambridge, MA

Crummell, Alexander (1856). *The Duty of a Rising Christian State*, London

(1861). *The Negro Race not under a Curse*, London

Dalberg, Carl von (1791). *Grundsätze der Ästhetik, deren Anwendung und Künftige Entwicklung*, Erfurt

Daly, J. Bowles (1892). *The Dawn of Radicalism*, London

Darwin, Charles (1871). *The Descent of Man and Selection in Relation to Sex*, 2 vols., London

(1945). *Charles Darwin and the Voyage of the Beagle*, ed. and intro. Nora Barlow

(1964 [1859]). *On the Origin of Species*, intro. E. Mayr, Cambridge, MA

(1985). *A Calendar of the Correspondence of Charles Darwin, 1821–1882*, ed. F. Burckhardt and S. Smith, New York and London

(1989). *The Correspondence of Charles Darwin*, Vol. v, ed. F. Burkhardt and S. Smith, Cambridge

(1990). *The Correspondence of Charles Darwin*, Vol. vi, ed. F. Burkhardt and S. Smith, Cambridge

Darwin, Erasmus (1804). *The Temple of Nature; or, The Origin of Society*, New York

Darwin. F. (ed.) (1887). *The Life and Letters of Charles Darwin including an Autobiographical Chapter*, 3 vols., London

(1958 [1892]). *The Autobiography of Charles Darwin and Selected Letters*, unabridged reprint of *Charles Darwin: His Life Told in an Autobiographical Chapter and in a Selected Series of his Published Letters*, New York

Darwin, F. and Seward A. C. (eds.) (1903). *More Letters of Charles Darwin*, 2 vols., London

Davidson, J. Morrison (1899). *The Annals of Toil*, London

(n.d.). *Anarchist Socialism vs. State Socialism*.

Davies, Emil (1914). *The Collectivist State in the Making*, London

Davis, Thomas (1890). *Prose Writings of Thomas Davis*, ed. T. W. Rolleston, London

Davitt, Michael (1885). *Leaves from a Prison Diary*, 2 vols., London

(1902). *The Boer Fight for Freedom*, New York and London

(1904). *The Fall of Feudalism in Ireland*, London

Dawson, W. H. (1910). *The Vagrancy Problem; with a Study of Continental Detention Colonies and Labour Houses*, London

(1912). *Social Insurance in Germany 1883–1911*, London

(1914). *Municipal Life and Government in Germany*, London

De Potter, Louis Joseph A. (1859). *Dictionnaire Rationnel des Mots les plus Usités en Science, en Philosophie, en Politique, en Morale et en Religion avec leur Signification Déterminée et leur Rapport aux Questions d'Ordre Social*, Brussels and Leipzig

DeGérando, J. M. (1839). *De la Bienfaisance Publique*, 2 vols., Brussels

Destutt de Tracy, Antoine-Louis-Claude (1817). *Élémens d'Idéologie*. 4 vols., Paris

(1926) *De l'Amour*, trans. Gilbert Chinard, Paris

(1958). *Doctrine of Saint-Simon: An Exposition, First Year, 1828–1829*, trans. George G. Iggers, New York

Devyr, Thomas Ainge (1882). *The Odd Book of the Nineteenth Century*, New York

Dewey, John and Tufts, James (1910). *Ethics*, London

Dicey, Albert Venn (1885). *Lectures Introductory to the Study of the Law of the Constitution*, London

(1886). *England's Case against Home Rule*, London

(1909). *Letters to a Friend on Votes for Women*, London

(1914 [1905]). *Lectures on the Relation between Law and Public Opinion in England during the Nineteenth Century*, London

(1915). *Introduction to the Study of the Law of the Constitution*, 8th edition, London

(1981 [1914]). *Lectures on the Relation between Law and Public Opinion*, New Brunswick

Dilke, Charles (1868). *Greater Britain, A Record of Travel in English-Speaking Countries During 1866 and 1867*, 2 vols., London

Dillon, William (1888). *Life of John Mitchel*, 2 vols., London

Dohrn, A. (1982). *Charles Darwin, Anton Dohrn. Correspondence*, ed. Christine Groeber, Naples

Dostoevsky, Fyodor M. (1965 [1863]). *Winter Notes on Summer Impressions*, ed. Saul Bellow, New York

(1994). *A Writer's Diary*, trans. Kenneth Lanz, Evanston, IL

Douglass, Frederick (1976). *Frederick Douglass on Women's Rights*, ed. Philip S. Foner, Westport, CT

(1994 [1845, 1855, 1881]). *Autobiographies*, ed. Henry Louis Gates, Jr., New York

Dowe, Dieter (ed.) (1980). *Berichte über die Verhandlungen der Vereinstag Deutscher Arbeitervereine 1863 bis 1869*, reprint, Berlin, Bonn

Drage, Geoffrey (1904). *Russian Affairs*, London

Drummond, Henry (1894). *The Lowell Lectures on the Ascent of Man*, London

Du Bois, W. E. B. (1897). 'Review of Frederick L. Hoffman, Race Traits and Tendencies of the American Negro', *Annals of the American Academy of Political and Social Science*, Vol. IX: 127–33

(1903). 'Review of Joseph Alexander Tillinghast, The Negro in Africa and America', *Political Science Quarterly*, 18: 695–7

(1986 [1903]). *Writings*, ed. Nathan Huggins, New York

(1992 [1935]). *Black Reconstruction in America: 1860–1880*, intro. David Levering Lewis, New York

Dufau, P. A. (1860). 'Mémoire sur la Conciliation de l'Économie Politique et de l'Économie Charitable ou d'Assistance', *Séances et Travaux de l'Académie des Sciences Morales*, 51: 89–117

Duffy, Charles Gavan (1896). *Young Ireland. A Fragment of Irish History*, London
    (1898). *My Life in Two Hemispheres*, 2 vols., London
Dumont, E. (1832). *Recollections of Mirabeau and of the Two First Legislative Assemblies of France*, London
Duncan, David (1908). *The Life and Letters of Herbert Spencer*, 2 vols., London
Durkheim, Émile (1933 [1893]). *The Division of Labour in Society*, trans. George Simpson, New York
    (1959). *Socialism and Saint-Simon*, London
    (1960). *Montesquieu and Rousseau*, Ann Arbor
    (1992 [1947]). *Professional Ethics and Civic Morals*, trans. Cornelia Brookfield, London and New York
Edgeworth, F. Y. (1881). *Mathematical Psychics: An Essay on the Application of Mathematics to the Moral Sciences*, London
Edie, J. M., Scanlan, J. P. and Zeldin, M. B. (eds.) (1966). *Russian Philosophy*, 3 vols., Chicago
Edwards, H. Sutherland (1865). *The Private History of a Polish Insurrection*, 2 vols., London
Elm, Ludwig (1968). 'Deutsche Volkspartei (DtVp) 1868–1910', in Dieter Fricke (ed.), *Die Bürgerlichen Parteien in Deutschland*, 2 vols. Leipzig, Vol. 1
Ely, Richard Theodore (1883). *French and German Socialism in Modern Times*, New York
    (1884). *Recent American Socialism*, Baltimore
    (1894). *Socialism*, London
Emerson, Ralph Waldo (1966 [1862]). 'Thoreau', in Owen Thomas (ed.), *Walden and Civil Disobedience*, New York
    (1983). *Essays and Lectures*, ed. Joel Porte, New York
    (1995). *Emerson's Antislavery Writings*, ed. Len Gougeon and Joel Myerson, New Haven
    (2008). *Political Writings*, ed. Kenneth Sacks (Cambridge Texts in the History of Political Thought), Cambridge
Emminghaus, Arwen (1870). *Das Armenwesen und die Armengesetzgebung in Europaischen Staat*, Berlin
Engels, Friedrich (1901/02). 'Zur Kritik des Sozialdemokratischen Programmentwurfes 1891', *Die Neue Zeit*, 20, Part 1
    (1940a). *Dialectics of Nature* (written 1873–83, first published 1925), trans. C. Dutt, London
    (1940b [1884]). *Origin of the Family, Private Property and the State*, London
    (1962 [1878]). *Anti-Dühring. Herr Eugen Dühring's Revolution in Science*, 3rd edition, Moscow
    (1972a [1847]). 'Deutscher Sozialismus in Versen und Prosa', in Karl Marx and Friedrich Engels, *Werke*, Vol. IV, Berlin
    (1972b). *Socialism: Utopian and Scientific*, New York
    (1999 [1845]). *The Condition of the Working Classes in England*. Oxford and New York
Ethelmer, Ellis (1898). 'Feminism', *Westminster Review*, January
Faguet, Émile (1891). *Politiques et Moralistes du Dix-Neuvième Siècle*, Paris
Farr, F. (1910). *Modern Woman: Her Intentions*, London
Faust, Drew Gilpin (1981). *The Ideology of Slavery: Proslavery Thought in the Antebellum South, 1830–1860*, ed. Faust, Baton Rouge
Feiling, Keith (1913). *Toryism, a Political Dialogue*, London
Fenet, P. A. (ed.) (1827). *Recueil Complet des Travaux Préparatoires du Code Civil I*, Paris
The Fenian's Progress: A Vision (1865)
Ferri, E. (1905 [1896]). *Socialism and Positive Science: Darwin, Spencer and Marx*, trans. E. C. Harvey, London
Ferry, Jules (1884/1893). 'Speech before the French Chamber of Deputies, March 28, 1884', in *Discours et Opinions de Jules Ferry*, ed. Paul Robiquet, Paris
Feuerbach, Ludwig (1841). *Das Wesen des Christentums*, Leipzig

(1843). *Grundsätze der Philosophie der Zukunft*, Zürich

(1957 [1841]). *The Essence of Christianity*, trans. George Eliot, New York

(1972). 'Preliminary Theses on the Reform of Philosophy', in Z. Hanfi (ed.), *The Fiery Brook*, New York

Fichte, Johann Gottlieb (1845). *Reden an die Deutsche Nation* (1808) in *Sämmtliche Werke*, Vol. VII, *Zur Politik, Moral, und Philosophie der Geschichte*, ed. J. H. Fichte, Leipzig

(1965 [1794–95]). *Grundlage der Gesammten Wissenschaftslehre, Gesamtausgabe*, Vol. 1/2, Stuttgart

(1971 [1808]). *Reden an die Deutsche Nation, Werke*, Vol. VII, Berlin

(2008). *Addresses to the German Nation* (Cambridge Texts in the History of Political Thought), ed. Gregory Moore, Cambridge

Figgis, J. N. (1914 [1913]). *Churches in the Modern State*, London

Fiske, J. (1885). *American Political Ideas Viewed from the Standpoint of Universal History*, London

Fitzhugh, George (1854). *Sociology for the South; or, the Failure of Free Society*, Richmond, VA

(1960 [1856]). *Cannibals All! Or, Slaves Without Masters*, ed. C. Vann Woodward, Cambridge, MA

Flint, Robert (1895). *Socialism*, London

Fonblanque, A. (1837). *England under Seven Administrations*, 3 vols., London

(1874). *The Life and Labours of Albany Fonblanque*, ed. E. B. de Fonblanque, London

Forbes-Mitchell, William (1893). *Reminiscences of the Great Mutiny*, London

Fourier, Charles (1851). *The Passions of the Human Soul*, 2 vols., trans. Hugh Doherty, London

(1889). *Oeuvres Choisies*, ed. Charles Gide, Paris

(1901 [1971]). *Selections from the Works of Fourier*, ed. Charles Gide (reprinted as *Design for Utopia: Selected Writings of Charles Fourier*), New York

(1966–8). *Oeuvres Complètes*, 12 vols., Paris

(1971a). *Harmonian Man: Selected Writings of Charles Fourier*, ed. M. Poster, New York

(1971b). *The Utopian Vision of Charles Fourier: Selected Texts on Work, Love, and Passionate Attraction*, ed. Jonathan Beecher and Richard Bienvenu, Boston

(1977). *Aus der Neuen Liebeswelt*, ed. Marion Luckow, Berlin

(1996 [1808]). *Theory of the Four Movements*, ed. G. Stedman Jones, trans. Ian Patterson, Cambridge

Fox, Charles James (1815). *The Speeches of the Right Honourable Charles James Fox*, 6 vols., London

Frégier, H.-A. (1840). *Des Classes Dangereuses de la Population dans les Grandes Villes et des Moyens de les Rendre Meilleures*, Paris

Frost, Thomas (1876). *The Secret Societies of the European Revolution 1776–1876*, 2 vols., London

Froude, J. A. (1882–4). *Thomas Carlyle*, 4 vols., London

(1886). *Oceana, or England and Her Colonies*, London

Fry, Roger (1920 [1981]). 'Art and Socialism', in J. B. Bullen (ed.), *Vision and Design*, London

Fuller, Margaret (1971 [1845]). *Woman in the Nineteenth Century*, New York

Gammage, R. G. (1854). *History of the Chartist Movement*, London

Gandhi, Mahatma (1997 [1909]). *Hind Swaraj and Other Writings*, ed. Anthony J. Parel, Cambridge

Gans, Eduard (1995 [1836]). *Rückblicke auf Personen und Zustände*, reprint, ed. N. Waszek, Stuttgart

Geddes, P. (1886). 'On the Application of Biology to Economics', *Report of the Fifty Fifth Meeting of the British Association for the Advancement of Science*

Gentz, Friedrich von (1802). *De l'État de l'Europe avant et après la Révolution Française: pour Servir de Réponse à l'Écrit Intitulé: De l'État de la France à la Fin de l'An VIII*, London

(1909). *Briefe von und an Friedrich von Gentz*, ed. Friedrich Carl Wittichen, 2 vols., Munich

(1977). *The Origin and Principles of the American Revolution Compared with the Origin and Principles of the French Revolution*, trans. John Quincy Adams, New York

George, Henry (1879). *Progress and Poverty: An Inquiry into the Cause of Industrial Depression and of Increase of Want with Increase of Wealth. The Remedy*, New York

Ghose, J.C. (1887). *The English Works of Raja Ram Mohun Roy*, 2 vols., Calcutta

Gide, Charles and Rist, Charles (1915 [1913]). *A History of Economic Doctrines from the Time of the Physiocrats to the Present Day*, trans. W. Smart and R. Richards, London

Gierke, Otto (1934). *Natural Law and the Theory of Society, 1500 to 1800*, trans. Ernest Barker, Cambridge

(1990). *Community in Historical Perspective*, ed. Antony Black, trans. Mary Fischer, Cambridge

Giffen, Robert (1891 [1880]). 'Bagehot as an Economist', in Forrest Morgan (ed.), *The Works of Walter Bagehot*, 5 vols., Vol. I, Hartford, CT

Gladstone, William Ewart (1838). *The State in its Relations with the Church*, London

(1855). *Our Colonies*, London

(1879). *Gleanings of Past Years*, 7 vols., London

(1885). *Speech . . . on the War and the Negotiations, in the House of Commons, on the 3rd of August, 1855*, London

(1971 [1879]). *Midlothian Speeches, 1879*, ed. M. R. D. Foot, Leicester

Gobineau, Joseph Arthur (1915 [1853–5]). *Essai sur L'Inégalité des Races Humaines*, abridged and translated into English as *The Inequality of Human Races*, trans. A. Collins, London

(1970). *Gobineau: Selected Political Writings*, ed. and intro. Michael Denis Biddiss, London

Godard, André (1900). *Le Positivisme Chrétien*, Paris

Godwin, William (1820). *Of Population: An Enquiry Concerning the Power of Increase in the Numbers of Mankind, Being an Answer to Mr. Malthus's Essay on that Subject*, London

(1976 [1795]). *Enquiry Concerning Political Justice*, 3rd edition, ed. I. Kramnick, London

(1980 [1794]). *Caleb Williams*, Oxford

(1993). *Political and Philosophical Writings of William Godwin*, ed. Mark Philp, 7 vols., London

Goethe, Johann Wolfgang von (1790). *An Attempt to Interpret the Metamorphosis of Plants* in *Goethe's Botany*, republished from *Chronica Botanica: An International Collection of Studies in the Method and History of Biology and Agriculture*, ed. F. Verdoorn, Vol. X, no. 2, 1946,

(1993 [1774]). *Die Leiden des Jungen Werther*, London

(1994 [1808–33]). *Faust*, trans. David Luke, Oxford

Goldman, E. (1969a [1910]). *Anarchism and Other Essays*, New York

(1969b). 'The Psychology of Political Violence', in *Anarchism and Other Essays*, New York

(1983). *Red Emma Speaks: An Emma Goldman Reader*, ed. Alix Kates Shulman, New York

Gonner, E. C. K. (1895). *The Socialist State*, London

(1899). *The Social Philosophy of Rodbertus*, London

Gordon, Ishbel, Countess of Aberdeen (ed.) (1900). *International Congress of Women of 1899*, 7 vols., London

Gore, Charles (1913). *Property: Its Duties and Rights, Historically, Philosophically and Religiously Regarded. Essays by Various Writers*, London

Graham, William (1890). *Socialism Old and New*, London

Grave, Jean (1893). *La Société Mourante et l'Anarchie*, Paris

(1899). *L'Anarchie: Son But, Ses Moyens*, 4th edition, Paris

Green, Thomas Hill (1885–8), *Works*, ed. R. L. Nettleship, 3 vols., London

(1911 [1886]). *Lectures on the Principles of Political Obligation*, London

(1986). *Lectures on the Principles of Political Obligation and Other Writings*, ed. Paul Harris and John Morrow, Cambridge

(1997), *Collected Works of T. H. Green*, ed. P. Nicholson, 5 vols., Bristol

Greene, William B. (1870). *Mutual Banking* (n.p.: New England Labour Reform League)

Greg, W. R. (1862). 'Why Are Women Redundant?' *National Review*, 14: 433–5

Grimké, Sarah (1988 [1838]). *Letters on the Equality of the Sexes, and Other Essays*, ed. Elizabeth Bartlett, New Haven

Gronlund, Laurence (1886). *The Co-operative Commonwealth: An Exposition of Modern Socialism*, London

Grote, H. (1866). *The Philosophical Radicals of 1832, comprising The Life of Sir William Molesworth, and Some Incidents Connected with the Reform Movement from 1832 to 1842*, London

Guizot, François (1821). *Des Moyens de Gouvernement et d'Opposition dans l'État Actuel de la France*, Paris

(1823). *Essais sur l'Histoire de France*, Paris

(1826–7). *Histoire de la Révolution en Angleterre depuis l'Avènement de Charles I jusqu'à la Restauration de Charles II*, Paris

(1849). *De la Démocratie en France*, Paris

(1850). *Pourquoi la Révolution d'Angleterre a-t-elle Réussi?*, Paris

(1851). *Histoire des Origines du Gouvernement Représentatif en Europe*, 2 vols., Paris

(1852 [1820]). *History of the Origins of Representative Government in Europe*, trans. A. Scoble, London

(1858–9). *Mémoires*, 8 vols., London

(1863). *Histoire Parlementaire de France*, Paris

(1985 [1846]). *Histoire de la Civilisation en Europe: Depuis la Chute de l'Empire Romain jusqu'à la Révolution Française; suivie de Philosophie Politique: De la Souveraineté*, Paris

(1997 [1846]). *The History of Civilisation in Europe*, trans. William Hazlitt, ed. and intro. Larry Siedentop, London

(2002). *The History of the Origins of Representative Government in Europe*, Indianapolis

Guttsman, W. L. (1967 [1867]). *A Plea for Democracy*, London

Hadley, Arthur T. (1899). 'The Relation between Economics and Politics', *Yale Law Journal*, 8: 194–206

Haigh, Arthur E. (1878). *The Political Theories of Dante*, Oxford

Hallam, Henry (1827). *Constitutional History of England*, 4 vols., London

Haller, Karl Ludwig von (1821). *Letter of Charles Louis de Haller, Member of the Supreme Council of Berne, Announcing his Abjuration of Lutheranism*, Dublin

(1824–75). *Restauration de la Science Politique ou Théorie de l'État Social Natural*, translated from the German, 6 vols., Lyon

(1839). *Mélanges de Droit Public et de Haute Politique*, 2 vols., Lyon

Hamilton, Alexander (2001). *Writings*, ed. Joanne Freeman, New York

Hamilton, Cicely (1909). *Marriage as a Trade*. London

Hansard's Parliamentary Debates (1838). 3rd series, XL, 23 January, London

Harding, C. G. (ed.) (1848). *The Republican: A Magazine*, London

Hare, Thomas (1858). *The Election of Representatives, Parliamentary and Municipal*, London

Harris, William (1885). *The History of the Radical Party in Parliament*, London

Harrison, Frederic (1875). *Order and Progress*, London

(1901). *George Washington and Other American Addresses*, London.

(1908). *National and Social Problems*, London

(1911). *Autobiographic Memoirs*, 2 vols., London

Bibliography

Hartley, D. (1749). *Observations on Man, His Frame, His Duty, and His Expectations*, 2 vols., London

Hauterive, Alexandre de (1800). *De l'État de la France, à la Fin de l'An VIII*, Paris

Haym, Rudolf (1857). *Hegel und seine Zeit*, Berlin

Hazlitt, William (1819). *Political Essays*, London

(1828 [1825]). *The Spirit of the Age, or Contemporary Portraits*, London

(1931–4a). *The Complete Works of William Hazlitt*, ed. P. P. Howe, 21 vols., London

(1931–4b [1819]). *A Letter to William Gifford Esq.*, in Hazlitt, *Complete Works*, Vol. IX, London

(1931–4c [1826]). 'On Reason and Imagination', *The Plain Speaker*, in Hazlitt, *Complete Works*, Vol. XII, London

(1931–4d [1836]). 'Project for a New Theory of Civil and Criminal Legislation', *Literary and Political Criticism*, in Hazlitt, *Complete Works*, Vol. XIX, London

(1931–4e [1825]). *The Spirit of the Age, or Contemporary Portraits*, in Hazlitt, *Complete Works*, Vol. XI, London

(1969 [1825]). *The Spirit of the Age or Contemporary Portraits*, ed. E. D. Mackerness, London and Glasgow

Heckethorn, Charles William (1875). *The Secret Societies of All Ages and Countries*, 2 vols., London

Hegel, Georg Friedrich Wilhelm (1952). *The Philosophy of Right*, trans. T. M. Knox, Oxford

(1956 [1837]). *The Philosophy of History*, trans. J. Sibree, New York

(1961). *Briefe von und an Hegel*, Bd. III, ed. J. Hoffmeister, Hamburg

(1964 [1835–8]). *Vorlesungen über die Ästhetik*, 3 vols., *Sämtliche Werke*, ed. H. Glockner, Vols. XII–XIV, Stuttgart

(1967a [1807]). *Phenomenology of Mind*, trans. J. B. Baillie, New York

(1967b). *The Philosophy of Right*, trans. T. M. Knox, New York

(1970). *Werke in Zwanzig Bänden. Werkausgabe*, ed. Eva Moldenhauer and Karl Michel, Frankfurt

(1971 [1833]). *Vorlesungen über die Geschichte der Philosophie*, III, *Werke*, Vol. XX, Frankfurt am Main

(1975a). *Lectures on the Philosophy of World History (1827–31)*, trans. H. B. Nisbet, Cambridge

(1975b [1837]). *Lectures on the Philosophy of World History. Introduction: Reason in History*, trans. H. B. Nisbet, Cambridge

(1975c [1830]). *Logic, Encyclopedia of the Philosophical Sciences*, Part I, trans. William Wallace, Oxford

(1980 [1822–31]). *Lectures on the Philosophy of World History. Introduction: Reason in History*, trans. H. B. Nisbet, Cambridge

(1989 [1827]). *Enzyklopädie der Philosophischen Wissenschaften im Grundrisse*, *Gesammelte Werke*, Vol. XIX, Hamburg

(1991 [1821]). *Elements of the Philosophy of Right*, ed. Allen W. Wood, trans. H. B. Nisbet, Cambridge

Heine, H (1959 [1833]). *Religion and Philosophy in Germany*, ed. L. Marcuse, Boston

Heinzen, Karl (1881 [1853]). *Murder and Liberty*. Reprinted as a contribution for the 'Peace League' of Geneva, Indianapolis

Henrion de Pansey, P. P. N. (1843). *De l'Autorité Judiciaire*, in *Oeuvres*, ed. L. Rozet, Paris

Herbert, Auberon (1893). 'Free Life', *Voluntary State Papers*, 1 July: 1–8

Herder, Johann Gottfried (1877 [1774]). *Auch eine Philosophie der Geschichte zur Bildung der Menschheit*, *Sämtliche Werke*, Vol. V, Berlin

(1878). *Sämtliche Werke*, Bd. IV, Berlin

(1892). *Sämtliche Werke*, Bd. VIII, Berlin

(1965 [1784–91]). *Ideen zu einer Philosophie der Geschichte der Menschheit*, Vol. I, Berlin

(2004 [1744]). *Another Philosophy of History and Selected Political Writings*, trans. and intro. Ioanis Evrrigenis and Daniel Pellerin, Indianapolis and Cambridge

Herzen, Alexander (1956 [1850]). *From the Other Shore and the Russian People and Socialism* (Library of Ideas), intro. Isaiah Berlin, London

Hess, Moses (1958 [1862]) *Rome and Jerusalem*, ed. and trans. Rabbi Maurice J. Bloom, New York

(1961 [1837–1850]). 'Die Heilige Geschichte der Menschheit. Von einem Jünger Spinozas', in *Philosophische und Sozialistische Schriften*, ed. W. Monke, Berlin

(1962 [1862]). *Rom und Jerusalem*, in Horst Lademacher (ed.), *Ausgewählte Schriften*, Cologne

Hildebrand, Bruno (1848). *Die Nationalökonomie der Gegenwart und Zukunft*, Frankfurt

(1863). 'Vorwort', *Jahrbücher für Nationalökonomie und Statistik*, 1: 1–4

History of the Irish Invincibles (1883), London

HMSO Special Reports on Educational Subjects (1904). *The Gemeindeschulen of Berlin and Charlottenburg*, British Parliamentary Papers, Vol. XXII, London

(1910). *The Teaching of Classics in Secondary Schools in Germany*, British Parliamentary Papers, Vol. XXIII, London

Hobhouse, Leonard Trelawny (1893). *The Labour Movement*, London

(1896). *The Theory of Knowledge. A Contribution to Some Problems of Logic and Metaphysics*, London

(1904). *Democracy and Reaction*, London

(1906). *Morals and Ethics: A Study in Comparative Evolution*, London

(1911). *Liberalism*, London

(1913). 'The Historical Evolution of Property, in Fact and in Idea', in Charles Gore (ed.), *Property: Its Duties and Rights, Historically, Philosophically and Religiously Regarded. Essays by Various Writers*, London

(1918). *The Metaphysical Theory of the State: A Criticism*, London

(1972 [1904]). *Democracy and Reaction*, ed. Peter Clarke, Brighton

(1974 [3rd edition, 1912]). *The Labour Movement*, ed. Philip P. Poirier, Brighton

Hobson, John Atkinson (1894). *The Evolution of Modern Capitalism. A Study of Machine Production*, London

(1898). 'Free Trade and Foreign Policy', *Contemporary Review*, 74: 167–80

(1901a). *The Psychology of Jingoism*, London

(1901b). *The Social Problem: Life and Work*, London

(1901c). *The War in South Africa: Its Causes and Effects*, London

(1909). *The Crisis of Liberalism: New Issues of Democracy*, London

(1910). *A Modern Outlook: Studies of English and American Tendencies*, London

(1968 [1918]). *Cobden: The International Man*, ed. Neville Masterman, London

(1974 [1909]). *The Crisis of Liberalism: New Issues of Democracy*, ed. P. F. Clarke, Hassocks

(1997 [1902]). *Imperialism: A Study*, ed. Philip Siegelman, Ann Arbor

Hobson, J. A. and Ginsberg, Morris (1931). *L. T. Hobhouse, his Life and Work; with Selected Essays and Articles*, London

Hobson, S. G. (1920). *National Guilds and the State*, London

Hodde, Lucien de la (1864). *The Cradle of Rebellions. A History of the Secret Societies of France*, New York

Hodgskin, Thomas (1922 [1825]). *Labour Defended Against the Claims of Capital*, ed. G. D. H. Cole, London

(1966 [1827]). *Popular Political Economy*, New York

(1973 [1832]). *The Natural and Artificial Right of Property Contrasted*, New York

Hodson, W. S. R. (1859). *Twelve Years of a Soldier's Life in India*, London

Hoffman, Frederick L. (1896). 'The Race Traits and Tendencies of the American Negro', *Publications of the American Economic Association*, 11: 1–329

Holland, T. E. (1908). 'The Hague Conference of 1907', *Law Quarterly Review*, 93

Holt, Joseph (1838). *Memoirs of Joseph Holt*, 2 vols., London

Holyoake, Austin (1873). *Would a Republican Form of Government Be Suitable to England?* London

Holyoake, George Jacob (1893). *Sixty Years of an Agitator's Life*, 2 vols., London
  (1905). *Bygones Worth Remembering*, London

Hook, Madison (1891). *Human Rights*, Iowa

Hucko, Elmar M. (ed.) (1987 [1849]). 'Verfassung des Deutschen Reiches', in *The Democratic Tradition: Four German Constitutions*, ed. and trans. E. M. Hucko, Leamington Spa

Hugo, Gustav (1819 [1798]). *Lehrbuch des Naturrechts*, Berlin

Hugo, Victor (1854). *The Prospects of Republicanism*, London

Hume, David (1994a [1748]). 'Of National Characters', in Knud Haakonssen (ed.), *Hume: Political Essays*, Cambridge, 78–92
  (1994b). 'Of the Original Contract', in Knud Haakonssen (ed.), *Hume: Political Essays*, Cambridge

Humphreys, J. (1826). *Observations on the Actual State of the English Laws of Real Property; with the Outlines of a Code*, London

Hunt, Henry (1820). *Memoirs of Henry Hunt*, 3 vols., London

Huxley, L. (1900). *Life and Letters of Thomas Henry Huxley*, 2 vols., London

Huxley, T. H. (1865). 'Emancipation – Black and White', in *Lay Sermons, Addresses and Reviews*, London, 1895
  (1891). *Social Diseases and Worse Remedies. Letters to The Times on Mr Booth's Scheme*, London
  (1894). *Evolution and Ethics, Collected Essays*, Vol. IX, London

Ingram, John Kells (1967 [1888]). *A History of Political Economy*, New York

Jacoby, Johan (1841). *Vier Fragen Beantwortet von einem Ostpreußen*, Mannheim

Janet, Paul (1878). *Saint-Simon et le Saint-Simonisme*, Paris

Jefferson, Thomas (1984). *Writings*, ed. Merrill D. Peterson, New York
  (1999). *Political Writings*, ed. Joyce Appleby and Terrence Ball (Cambridge Texts in the History of Political Thought), Cambridge

Jenkyns, Henry (1902). *British Rule and Jurisdiction Beyond the Seas*, Oxford

Jevons, W. Stanley (1882). *The State in Relation to Labour*, London
  (1888). *The Theory of Political Economy*, London
  (1972–81). *Papers and Correspondence of William Stanley Jevons*, ed. R. D. Collison Black and Rosamond Könekamp, 7 vols., London

Jones, Lloyd (1889). *The Life, Times, and Labours of Robert Owen*, 2 vols., London

Kant, Immanuel (1887). *The Philosophy of Law*, trans. W. Hastie, Edinburgh
  (1902). *Gesammelte Schriften*, ed. Preußischen Akademie der Wissenschaften, Berlin
  (1970). *Kant's Political Writings*, ed. Hans Reiss, Cambridge
  (1985 [1777]). *Critique of Practical Reason*, trans. Lewis White Beck, London
  (1987 [1790]). *Critique of Judgment*, trans. Werner S. Pluhar, Indianapolis
  (1991a [1797]). *Metaphysics of Morals*, trans. Mary Gregor, Cambridge
  (1991b [1795]). 'Perpetual Peace', in Hans Reiss (ed.), *Kant's Political Writings*, Cambridge
  (1997 [1781/87]). *Critique of Pure Reason*, ed. and trans. Paul Guyer and Allen W. Wood, Cambridge
  (1998/9 [1797]). *Metaphysical Elements of Justice; Part One of the Metaphysics of Morals*, ed. and trans. John Ladd, Indianapolis and Cambridge

(2002 [1785]). *Groundwork of the Metaphysics of Morals*, in *Practical Philosophy*, trans. Mary Gregor, Cambridge
Kaufmann, M. (1888). *Christian Socialism*, London
Kautsky, Karl (1893). *Der Parliamentarismus, die Volksgesetzgebung und die Sozialdemokratie*, Stuttgart
  (1910 [1892]). *The Class Struggle (Erfurt Program)*, trans. William E. Bohn, Chicago
  (1926 [1921]). *Are the Jews a Race?*, trans. from *Rasse und Judentum*, London
  (1960). *Erinnerungen und Erörterungen*, ed. Benedikt Kautsky, The Hague
  (1979 [1887]). *The Economic Doctrines of Karl Marx*, trans. H. J. Stenning, Westport, CT
  (1983). *Karl Kautsky: Selected Political Writings*, ed. and trans. Patrick Goode, New York
  (1988 [1927]). *The Materialist Conception of History*, ed. J. H. Kautsky, trans. R. Meyer with J. H. Kautsky, New Haven and London
  (1996 [1909]). *The Road to Power: Political Reflections on Growing into the Revolution*, Atlantic Highlands, NJ
Kawakami, K. (1903). *The Political Ideas of Modern Japan*, Iowa
Kelsen, Hans (1911). *Hauptprobleme der Staatrechtslehre Entwickelt aus der Lehre von Rechtssatz*, Tubingen
Kent, C. B. Roylance (1899). *The English Radicals*, London
Key, E. (1912). *The Woman Movement*, trans. M. B. Borthwick, London
Keynes, John Maynard (1912). *Indian Currency and Finance*, London
Khan, Sayyid Ahmad (1858). *Causes of the Indian Revolt*, London
Kidd, Benjamin (1894). *Social Evolution*, London
Kingsley, Charles (1877). *Charles Kingsley: Letters and Memories of His Life*, 2 vols., London
Kirkup, Thomas (1892). *A History of Socialism*, London
  (1908). *A Primer of Socialism*, London
  (1913). *A History of Socialism*, London
Kollontai, Alexandra (1977). *Selected Writings of Alexandra Kollontai*, ed. Alix Holt, London
Kovalevsky, M. M. (1902). *Russian Political Institutions, the Growth and Development of these Institutions*, Chicago
Kropotkin, Peter (1899). *Memoirs of a Revolutionist*, 2 vols., London
  (1924). *Ethics: Origin and Development*, New York
  (1930 [1899]). *Memoirs of a Revolutionist*, Boston
  (1970a). *Selected Writings on Anarchism and Revolution*, ed. M. A. Miller, Cambridge, MA
  (1970b). 'The Spirit of Revolt', in *Kropotkin's Revolutionary Pamphlets*, ed. Roger N. Baldwin, New York
  (1972). *The Conquest of Bread*, London
  (1992 [1885]). *Words of a Rebel*, trans. G. Woodcock, Montreal
Laboulaye, Édouard (1848). *Considérations sur la Constitution*, Paris
  (1850). *De la Constitution Américaine et de l'Utilité de son Étude*, Paris
  (1863a). *L'État et ses Limites*, Paris
  (1863b). *Le Parti Libéral, Son Programme, Son Avenir*, Paris
Lafargue, Paul (1890). *The Evolution of Property from Savagery to Civilisation*, London
Lamartine, Alphonse de (1848). *History of the Girondists; or Personal Memoirs of the Patriots of the French Revolution*, trans. H. T. Ryde, 3 vols., London
  (1856). 'Résumé politique du Voyage en Orient', *Souvenirs, Impressions, Pensées et Paysages pendant un Voyage en Orient 1832–1833*, Paris
  (1860–6 [1831]). *Sur la Politique Rationnelle, Oeuvres Complètes*, Vol. XXXVII, Paris
  (1862). *Travels in the East, Including a Journey to the Holy Land*, 2 vols., Edinburgh
Lamennais, Félicité de (1817–23). *Essai sur l'Indifférence en Matière de Religion*, 4 vols., Paris
  (1820). *Essai sur l'Indifférence en Matière de Religion*, 6th edition, 4 vols., Paris

(1825–6). *Religion Considered in its Relations with the Political and Civil Order*, Paris

(1830–1a). *Articles de l'Avenir*, 7 vols., Louvain

(1830–1b). 'De l'Avenir de la Société', in Lamennais, *Articles de l'Avenir*, Vol. v, Louvain

(1830–1c). 'Le Pape', in Lamennais, *Articles de l'Avenir*, Vol. i, Louvain

(1834). *Paroles d'un Croyant*, Paris

(1837). *Book of the People*, Paris

Lang, John Dunmore (1852). *Freedom and Independence for the Golden Lands of Australia*, London

Lange, F. A. (1925 [1865]). *A History of Materialism and Criticism of its Present Importance*, trans. E. C. Thomas, intro. B. Russell, International Library of Psychology, Philosophy and Scientific Method, 3 vols., London [original title: *Geschichte des Materialismus und Kritik seiner Bedeutung in der Gegenwart*, Iserlohn]

Lankester, E. R. (1880). *Degeneration: A Chapter in Darwinism*, London

Las Cases, Comte de (1968 [1842]). *Le Mémorial de Sainte-Hélène*, ed. Joël Schmidt, Paris

Laski, Harold J. (1917). *Studies in the Problem of Sovereignty*, Yale

Lassalle, Ferdinand (1919–20). *Gesammelte Reden und Schriften*, ed. Eduard Bernstein, 12 vols., Berlin

Laveleye, Émile de (1878). *Primitive Property*, London

(1885). *The Socialism of Today*, London

Lavollée, R. (1884, 1896). *Les Classes Ouvrières en Europe*, 3 vols., Paris

Lavrov, Peter (1967). *Historical Letters*, ed. James P. Scanlan, Berkeley

Le Bon, Gustave (1895). *The Crowd: A Study of the Popular Mind*, London

(1898). *Psychologie du Socialisme*, Paris

(1899). *The Psychology of Socialism*, London

(1908 [1895]). *The Crowd: A Study of the Popular Mind*, London

(1913). *The Psychology of Revolution*, London

(1979 [1895]). *Psychologie des Foules*, Paris

Le Conservateur, 5 October 1818: 7

Leibniz, G. W. (1993). *Leibniz–Thomasius. Correspondance (1663–1672)*, ed. Richard Bodéus, Paris

Leidigkeit, Karl-Heinz (ed.) (1960 [1872]). *Der Leipziger Hochverratsprozess vom Jahre 1872*, Berlin

Lenin, Vladimir Ilyich (1899). *Development of Capitalism in Russia*, Moscow

(1917). *Imperialism: The Highest Stage of Capitalism: A Popular Outline*, Petrograd

(1961–6 [1902]). *Collected Works*, Vols. v, xxvii and xxxi, Moscow

(1968). 'Notebooks on Imperialism', *Collected Works*, Vol. xxxix, Moscow, 405–36

Leroy-Beaulieu, Paul (1874). *De la Colonisation chez Peuples Modernes*, Paris

Lessing, Gotthold Ephraim (2003 [1770]). 'Laocoön', in J. M. Bernstein (ed.), *Classic and Romantic German Aesthetics*, Cambridge

Levy-Bruhl L. (1903). *The Philosophy of Auguste Comte*, trans. Frederic Harrison, London

Lewes, George Henry (1845–6). *The Biographical History of Philosophy*, 2 vols., London

(1853). *Comte's Philosophy of the Sciences*, London

Lewis, Sarah (1839). *Woman's Mission*, London

Lezardière, Mlle. de (1844 [1792]). *Théorie des Lois Politiques de la Monarchie Française*, Paris

Liebknecht, Wilhelm (1883 [1871]). *Zu Trutz und Schutz*, 5th edition, Hottingen-Zurich

(1890). *Umsturz und Parlementarismus*, in Vetter Niemand [pseudonym for Liebknecht], *Trutz-Eisenstirn*, Part 3, London

(1959 [1869]). *On the Political Position of Social-Democracy. Particularly with Respect to the Reichstag*, Moscow

Lincoln, Abraham (1989a) *Speeches and Writings: 1832–1858*, ed. Don E. Fehrenbacher, New York

(1989b). *Speeches and Writings: 1859–1865*, ed. Don E. Fehrenbacher, New York

Linguet, Simon-Nicolas-Henri (1767). *Théorie des Loix Civiles*, Paris

Linton, W. J. (1893). *European Republicans: Recollections of Mazzini and His Friends*, London

(n.d.). *Republican Tracts No. 1: Republican Organisation*

Lissagaray, Prosper Olivier (1886). *History of the Commune of 1871*, London

List, Friedrich (1841). *Das Nationale System der Politischen Oekonomie*, 2 vols., Stuttgart and Tübingen

(1909 [1841]). *The National System of Political Economy*, trans. Sampson S. Lloyd, London

Littré, Maximilien Paul Émile (1852). *Conservation, Révolution, Positivisme*, 5 vols. Paris

(1864). *Auguste Comte et la Philosophie Positive*, Paris

(1867–83) (ed.). *La Philosophie Positive*, Paris

(1880). *De l'Établissement de la Troisième République*, Paris

Lloyd, Caro (1912). *Henry Demarest Lloyd, 1847–1903, a Biography*, New York

Lloyd, Henry Demarest (1894). *Wealth Against Commonwealth*, New York

Lombroso, Cesar (1896). *Die Anarchisten. Eine Kriminal-psychologische und Sociologische Studie*, Hamburg

Louis, Paul (1905). *Le Colonialisme*, Paris

Lowance, Mason (2000). *Against Slavery: An Abolitionist Reader*, New York

Lowes Dickinson, G. (1905). *A Modern Symposium*, London

Lyell, Charles (1863). *The Geological Evidences of the Antiquity of Man with Remarks on Theories of The Origin of Species by Variation*, London

Macaulay, Thomas Babington (1833/1898), 'Speech on the Renewal of the East India Company Charter' (10 July), reprinted in Macaulay, *Complete Works*, Vol. XI, London

(1864 [1848]). 'Peculiar Character of the English Revolution', in *The History of England from the Accession of James the Second*, Vol. II, London

(n.d. [a]). *Critical, Historical and Miscellaneous Essays and Poems*, New York

(n.d. [b]). *The History of England from the Accession of James II*, New York

MacDonald, J. Ramsay (1909). *Socialism and Government*, 2 vols., London

(1910). *The Awakening of India*, London

Madden, Richard (1858). *The United Irishmen*, 3 vols., Dublin

Madison, James (1999). *Writings*, ed. Jack N. Rakove, New York

Madison, James, Hamilton, Alexander and Jay, John (1987 [1787]). *The Federalist Papers*, ed. Isaac Kramnick, Harmondsworth and New York

Mahan, Alfred Thayer (1890). *The Influence of Sea Power Upon History, 1663–1783*, London

Maine, Henry Sumner (1871). *Village Communities in the East and West*, London

(1881). *Village Communities in the East and West*, London

(1885). *Popular Government: Four Essays*, London

(1893 [1861]). *Ancient Law: Its Connection with the Early History of Society and its Relation to Modern Ideas*, London

Maistre, Joseph de (1843). *Du Pape*, Paris (Charpentier)

(1852 [1819]). *Du Pape*, Lyon

(1870). *Oeuvres Inédites de Joseph de Maistre*, Paris

(1884). *Oeuvres Complètes . . . Nouvelle Édition*, 14 vols., Lyon

(1971). *The Works of Joseph de Maistre*, ed. Jack Lively, New York

(1994). *Considerations on France*, ed. and trans. Richard Lebrun, Cambridge

Maitland, F.W. (1911). *The Collected Papers of Frederic William Maitland*, ed. H. A. L. Fisher, 3 vols., Cambridge

Bibliography

Malatesta, Errico (1974 [1891]). *Anarchy*, London
Malebranche, Nicholas (1945 [1674–75]). *De la Recherche de la Vérité*, Paris
Mallet du Pan, Jacques (1793). *Considérations sur la Nature de la Révolution de France: et sur les Causes qui en Prolongent la Durée*, Brussels
Mallock, W. H. (1910). *The Nation as a Business Firm*, London
   (1975 [1877]). *The New Republic; or, Culture, Faith and Philosophy in an English Country House*, Leicester
Malthus, Thomas Robert (1798). *An Essay on the Principle of Population*, London
   (1826). *An Essay on the Principle of Population*, 2 vols., London.
   (1988). *An Essay on the Principle of Population and A Summary View of the Principle of Population*, Harmondsworth
Marchand, Louis-Joseph. Letters, Bibliothèque Nationale de France, Reserve P. R. 379
Marinetti, F. T. (1983 [1909]). *Manifesto of Futurism: Published in Le Figaro, 20 February 1909*, New Haven
Marshall, Alfred (1890). *Principles of Economics*, London
   (1897). 'The Old Generation of Economists and the New', *Quarterly Journal of Economics*, 11: 115–35
   (1925). *Memorials of Alfred Marshall*, ed. A. C. Pigou, London
   (1926). *Official Papers*, ed. J. M. Keynes, London
Martineau, Harriet (1859). Letter to George Holyoake, British Library Manuscript, Add Ms 42, 726 f. 26.
Marx, Karl (n.d. [1847]). *The Poverty of Philosophy*, trans. C. P. Dutt and V. Chattopadhyaya, London
   (1954a [1867]). *Capital, A Critical Analysis of Capitalist Production, Volume I, Collected Works*, Vol. xxxv, London
   (1954b [1867]). *Capital, A Critical Analysis of Capitalist Production, Volume I*, Moscow
   (1966 [1848–1883]). *Later Political Writings*, ed. Terrell Carver, Cambridge
   (1972 [1880–2]). 'Marx's Excerpts from Henry Sumner Maine, *Lectures on the Early History of Institutions*', reprinted in L. Krader (ed.), *The Ethnological Notebooks of Karl Marx*, Assen
   (1973 [1847–50]). *The Revolutions of 1848*, Harmondsworth
   (1973 [1848–50]). *Surveys from Exile*, intro. David Fernbach, Harmondsworth
   (1974 [1843–4]). *Early Writings*, intro. Lucio Colletti, Harmondsworth
   (1975 [1844]). 'Economic and Philosophical Manuscripts,' in Karl Marx and Friedrich Engels, *Collected Works*, Vol. iii, 270–82
Marx, Karl and Engels, Friedrich (1936). *Selected Correspondence*, London
   (1955). *Selected Works in Two Volumes*, 2 vols., Moscow
   (1960a [1853a]). 'The British Rule in India', *New York Daily Tribune* (25 June 1853), reprinted in *Karl Marx and Friedrich Engels On Colonialism*, Moscow
   (1960b [1853b]). 'The Future Results of the British Rule in India', *New York Daily Tribune* (8 August 1853), reprinted in *Karl Marx and Friedrich Engels On Colonialism*, Moscow
   (1971). *Writings on the Paris Commune*, ed. Hal Draper, New York
   (1975–2005) *Karl Marx and Friedrich Engels Collected Works (MECW)*, 50 vols., Moscow, London and New York
   (1976 [1845–46]). *The German Ideology, in Collected Works*, Vol. v, New York
   (1978a). *Collected Works*, Vol. x, London
   (1978b). *The German Ideology*, ed. C. J. Arthur, New York
   (1987). *Collected Works*, Vol. xlii, London
   (1993a). *Collected Works*, Vol. xlvi, London
   (1993b). *Collected Works*, Vol. xlvii, London

(1989–) *Karl Marx/Friedrich Engels/Gesamtausgabe* (*MEGA*), begun in Moscow and Frankfurt in the 1920s, under David Ryazanov, but discontinued under Stalin; resumed in Berlin by Dietz Verlag. 1975–98, then refounded under the Internationale Marx-Engels Stiftung (IMES) and published in Berlin by Akademie Verlag (1998–).

(2002 [1848]). *The Communist Manifesto*, ed. and intro. Gareth Stedman Jones, Harmondsworth

Masterman, C. F. G. (1902 [1892]). *From the Abyss; or its Inhabitants, By One of Them*, London

(1911). *The Condition of England*, London

(1920). *The New Liberalism*, London

May, Thomas Erskine (1871). *The Constitutional History of England since the Accession of George III 1760–1860*, 3rd edition, 2 vols., London

Mayreder, R. (1913). *A Survey of the Woman Problem*, trans. Herman Scheffauer, London

Mazzini, Joseph (1861). *The Italian Question and the Republicans*, London

(1864). *Life and Writings of Joseph Mazzini*, 6 vols., London

(1907). *The Duties of Man and Other Essays*, London

McCarthy, Justin (1871). 'Republicanism in England', *The Galaxy*, New York

Menger, Carl (1883). *Untersuchungen über die Methode der Socialwissenschaften, u. der Politischen Oekonomie Insbesondere*, Leipzig

(1884). *Die Irrthümer des Historismus in der Deutschen Nationalökonomie*, Vienna

(1976 [1871]). *Principles of Economics*, trans. James Dingwall and Bert F. Hoselitz, New York

(1985 [1883]). *Problems of Economics and Sociology*, trans. F. J. Nock, New York

Merriam, Charles E. (1900). *History of the Theory of Sovereignty since Rousseau*, London

(1903). *A History of American Political Theories*, New York

Merz, John Theodore (1896–1914). *A History of European Thought in the Nineteenth Century*, 4 vols., Edinburgh

Meyer, Rudolf (1882). *Der Emanzipationskampf des Vierten Standes*, 2nd edition, 2 vols., Berlin

Meyer, Thomas (1977). *Bernsteins Konstruktiver Sozialismus: Eduard Bernsteins Beitrag zur Theorie des Sozialismus*, Berlin

Michelet, Jules (1847–53). *Histoire de la Révolution Française*, 7 vols., Paris

(1972). *Oeuvres Complètes*, 6 vols., ed. P. Viallaneix, Paris

Mill, James (1810). 'Review of *Voyage aux Indes Orientales*, by Le P. Paulin De S. Barthélemy', *Edinburgh Review*, 15: 363–84

(1817). *The History of British India*, 3 vols., London

(1824). 'Government', in *Essays*, London

(1829). *Analysis of the Phenomena of the Human Mind*, 2 vols., London

(1835). *A Fragment on Mackintosh: being Strictures on Some Passages in the Dissertation by Sir James Mackintosh, Prefixed to the Encyclopaedia Britannica*, London

(1992a [1828]). 'Colonies', in 'Essays from the Supplement to the Encyclopaedia Britannica', in *Collected Works of James Mill*, London

(1992b [1824]). 'Education', in T. Ball (ed.), *Political Writings*, Cambridge

Mill, John Stuart (1834). 'The New Colony' [1], *The Examiner*, 29 June. Reprinted in *Collected Works of John Stuart Mill* (ed. J. M. Robson, 33 vols., London and Toronto, 1963–1991, henceforth *CWM*), Vol. XXIII

(1836a). 'Civilisation', *CWM*, Vol. XVIII. London and Toronto

(1836b). 'On the Definition of Political Economy; and on the Method of Investigation Proper to it', *CWM*, Vol. IV, London and Toronto

(1843). 'Wakefield's "The New British Province of South Australia"', *CWM*, Vol. XXIII. London and Toronto

(1844). *Essays on Some Unsettled Questions of Political Economy, CWM*, Vol. IV, London and Toronto

(1849). 'Vindication of the French Revolution of February 1848', *CWM*, Vol. XX, London and Toronto

(1850). 'The Negro Question', *Fraser's Magazine*, 41: 25–31

(1859a). 'A Few Words on Non-Intervention', *CWM*, Vol. XXI, London and Toronto

(1859b). *Thoughts on Parliamentary Reform*, London

(1862 [1843]). *A System of Logic, Ratiocinative and Inductive, Being a Connected View of the Principles of Evidence, and the Methods of Scientific Investigation*, 5th edition, 2 vols., London

(1865). *Auguste Comte and Positivism*, London

(1874a). *Autobiography*, London

(1874b). *Three Essays on Religion*, London

(1960 [1861]) *Considerations on Representative Government*, London

(1963–91). *Collected Works of John Stuart Mill (CWM)*, ed. J. M. Robson, 33 vols., London and Toronto

(1963a) *The Earlier Letters of John Stuart Mill 1812–1848*, Part I, *CWM*, Volume XII, London and Toronto

(1963b). *The Earlier Letters of John Stuart Mill 1812–1848*, Part II, *CWM*, Vol. XIII. London and Toronto

(1965a [1848]). *Principles of Political Economy with Some of Their Applications to Social Philosophy, CWM*, Vol. II, London and Toronto

(1965b [1843]). *A System of Logic Ratiocinative and Inductive*, London

(1968 [1865]). *Auguste Comte and Positivism*, Ann Arbor

(1969). *Essays on Ethics, Religion and Society, CWM*, Vol. X, London and Toronto

(1972a). *The Later Letters of John Stuart Mill, 1849–1873*, Part I, *CWM*, Vol. XIV, London and Toronto

(1972b). *The Later Letters of John Stuart Mill, 1849–1873*, Part II, *CWM*, Vol. XV, London and Toronto

(1972c). *The Later Letters of John Stuart Mill, 1849–1873*, Part III, *CWM*, Vol. XVI, London and Toronto

(1972d). *The Later Letters of John Stuart Mill, 1849–1873*, Part IV, *CWM*, Vol. XVII, London and Toronto

(1974 [1843]). *A System of Logic, Ratiocinative and Inductive, Being a Connected View of the Principles of Evidence, and the Methods of Scientific Investigation*, Parts I and II, *CWM*, Vols. VII–VIII, London and Toronto

(1977a). *Essays on Politics and Society*, Part I, *On Liberty, CWM*, Vol. XVIII, London and Toronto

(1977b). *Essays on Politics and Society*, Part II, *Considerations on Representative Government, CWM*, Vol. XIX, London and Toronto

(1979 [1865]). *An Examination of Sir William Hamilton's Philosophy, CWM*, Vol. IX, London and Toronto

(1980 [1838 and 1840]). *Mill on Bentham and Coleridge*, intro. F. R. Leavis, Cambridge

(1981). *Autobiography and Literary Essays, CWM*, Vol. I, London and Toronto

(1982). *Essays on England, Ireland and the Empire, CWM*, Vol. VI, London and Toronto

(1988). *Journals and Debating Speeches*, Parts I and II, *CWM*, Vols. XXVI–XXVII, London and Toronto

(1989a), *Autobiography*, London

(1989b). *On Liberty and Other Writings*, ed. Stefan Collini, Cambridge

Mill, John Stuart and Bentham, Jeremy (1987 [1861]). *Utilitarianism and Other Essays*, ed. Alan Ryan, London

Mill, John Stuart and Mill, Harriet Taylor (1970). *Essays on Sex Equality*, ed. A. Rossi, Chicago

Miller, Samuel (1805). *Brief Retrospect of the Eighteenth Century*, 3 vols., London

Mills, Arthur (1856). *Colonial Constitutions: An Outline of the Constitutional History and Existing Government of the British Dependencies*, London

Miquel, Johannes von (1911). *Johannes von Miquel's Reden*, ed. W. Schultze and F. Thimme, Halle, Vol. I, p. 198

Mises, Ludwig von (2005 [1990]). *Economic Freedom and Interventionism: An Anthology of Articles and Essays*, ed. B. Greaves, Indianapolis

Mitzakis, J. (1911). *The Russian Oil Fields and Petroleum Industry*, London

Mittermaier, C. J. A. (1839). *Zeitschrift für Deutsches Recht und Deutsche Rechtswissenschaft*, Leipzig

Mivart, St. George Jackson (1871). *The Genesis of Species*, London

Mohl, Robert von (1855). *Die Geschichte und Literatur der Staatswissenschaften*, Erlangen

Mommsen, Theodor (2007 [1854–6]). *History of Rome*, ed. and trans. W. P. Dickson, London

Money, Leo Chiozza (1905). *Riches and Poverty*, London

Montesquieu, Charles de Secondat (1951 [1748]). *De l'Esprit des Lois*, Paris

  (1989 [1748]). *The Spirit of the Laws*, ed A. M. Cohler, B. C. Miller and H. S. Stone, Cambridge

Moore, Thomas (1831). *The Life of Lord Edward Fitzgerald*, 2 vols., London

Moran, D. P. (2006 [1906]). *The Philosophy of Irish Ireland*, ed. P. Maume, Dublin

Morgan, L. H. (1877). *Ancient Society or Researches in the Lines of Human Progress from Savagery through Barbarism to Civilisation*, London

Morley, John (1873). 'Mr Mill's Doctrine of Liberty', *Fortnightly Review*, 14: 234–56

  (1874). *On Compromise*, London

  (1910/1881). *The Life of Richard Cobden*, London

Morley, John (1917). *Recollections*, 2 vols., London

Morris, William (1884). *Art and Socialism*, London

  (1888). *A Dream of John Ball*, London

  (1896–7 [1868]). *The Earthly Paradise*, London

  (1899 [1890]). *News from Nowhere or an Epoch of Rest. Being Some Chapters from a Utopian Romance*, London

  (2003 [1890]). *News from Nowhere*, ed. David Leopold, Oxford

Mühlenbruch, C. F. (1838). *Doctrina Pandectarum: Scholarum in Usum*, Brussels

Müller, Adam (1804). *Die Lehre vom Gegensatz*, Berlin

  (1810). *Über König Friedrich II und die Natur, Würde und Bestimmung der Preussichen Monarchie*, Berlin

  (1817). 'Der Staat, als Nützliche Enterprise', in Adam Müller, *Vermischte Schriften über Staat, Philosophie und Kunst*, 2 vols., Vienna, Vol. I

  (1922 [1809]). *Elemente der Staatskunst*, ed. Jakob Baxa, 2 vols., Leipzig

  (1923). *Adam Müller: Schriften zur Staatsphilosophie*, ed. Rudolf Kohler, Munich

  (1931 [1810]). 'Fragmente', in Adam Müller, *Ausgewählte Abhandlungen*, ed. Jakob Baxa, Jena

  (1936 [1809]). *Die Elemente der Staatskunst*, Leipzig

  (1978). *Twelve Lectures on Rhetoric*, ed. and trans. Dennis R. Borman and Elizabeth Leinfellner, Lincoln, NE

Mummery, A. F. and Hobson, J. A. (1889). *The Physiology of Industry: Being an Exposure of Certain Fallacies in Existing Theories of Economics*, London

Naumann, Franz (1905). *Demokratie und Kaisertum: Ein Handbuch für Innenpolitik*, Berlin

Neale, E. V. (1851). *The Characteristic Features of Some of the Principal Systems of Socialism*, London

Newman, John Henry Cardinal (1870). *An Essay in the Aid of a Grammar of Assent*, London

(1956). *Autobiographical Writings*, ed. H. Tristram, London

(1961–2008). *The Letters and Diaries of John Henry Newman*, eds. C. S. Dessain *et al.*, 32 vols., London

(1967 [1873]). *Apologia pro Vita Sua*, ed. Martin J. Svaglic, Oxford

Niebuhr, Barthold Georg (1926). *Die Briefe Barthold Georg Niebuhrs*, ed. Dietrich Gerhard and William Norvin, 2 vols., Berlin

Niebuhr, Reinhold (1961). 'Reply to Interpretation and Criticism', in Charles W. Kegley and Robert W. Bretalln (eds.), *Reinhold Niebuhr: His Religious, Social, and Political Thought*, New York

Nietzsche, Friedrich (1903). *The Dawn of Day*, London

(1910). *The Genealogy of Morals*, London

(1921a [1882]). *Die Fröhliche Wissenschaft. Werke*, Bd. 5, Stuttgart

(1921b [1872]). *Die Geburt der Tragödie aus dem Geiste der Musik. Werke*, Bd. 1, Stuttgart

(1954). *The Portable Nietzsche*, ed. Walter Kaufmann, New York

(1968a [1883]). *Also Sprach Zarathustra. Werke*, Abt. VI, Bd. 1, Berlin

(1968b [1887]). *Zur Genealogie der Moral. Eine Streitschrift. Werke*, Abt. VI, Bd. 2, Berlin

(1994a). *Écrits Autobiographiques 1856–1869*, trans. Marc Crépon, Paris

(1994b [1887]). *On the Genealogy of Morality*, trans. Carol Diethe, Cambridge

(2001 [1882]) *The Gay Science with a Prelude in German Rhymes and an Appendix of Songs*, ed. B. Williams, Cambridge

(2003). *Writings from the Late Notebooks*, Cambridge

Nitti, Francesco S. (1895 [1890]). *Catholic Socialism*, trans. Mary Mackintosh, London

(1911). *Catholic Socialism*, London

Novalis [Friedrich von Hardenberg] (1929). 'Randbemerkungen zu Fr. Schlegel's Ideen', in P. Kluckhohn (ed.) *Schriften*, Vol. III, Leipzig

(1969a). *Novalis Werke*, ed. Gerhard Schulz, Munich

(1969b [1799]). 'Die Christenheit oder Europa', in *Novalis Werke*, ed. Gerhard Schulz, Munich

(1969c [1798]). 'Glauben und Liebe oder der König und die Königin', in *Novalis Werke*, ed. Gerhard Schulz, Munich

(1969d [1798]). 'Politische Aphorism', in *Novalis Werke*, ed. Gerhard Schulz, Munich

(1969e [1797–8]). 'Vermischte Bemerkungen', in *Novalis Werke*, ed. Gerhard Schulz, Munich

(1996 [1799]). 'Christianity or Europe: A Fragment', in Frederick C. Beiser (ed. and trans.) *The Early Political Writings of the German Romantics*, Cambridge

Noyes, John Humphrey (1870). *History of American Socialisms*, London

O'Brien, James Bronterre (1859). *A Dissertation and Elegy, on the Life and Death of the Immortal Maximilian Robespierre*, London

O'Connell, Daniel (1846). *The Life and Speeches of Daniel O'Connell*, ed. John O'Connell, 2 vols., Dublin

O'Connell, Maurice R. (ed.) (1977). *The Correspondence of Daniel O'Connell*, Vol. IV, 1829–32, Dublin

O'Connor, Arthur, Emmett, T. A. and McNeven, W. J. (1798). *Memoir [on the objects of the Societies of United Irishmen] With the Substance of their Examination before the Secret Committee of the House of Lords*, London

O'Meara, Barry E. (1824). *Napoléon en Exil*, 2 vols., Paris

Orsini, Felice (1857). *Memoirs and Adventures of Felice Orsini*, Edinburgh

Bibliography

Owen, Robert (1858). *The Life of Robert Owen*, 2 vols., London
  (1991 [1813]). *A New View of Society*, ed. Gregory Claeys, London
  (1993). *Selected Works of Robert Owen*, 4 vols., ed. Gregory Claeys, London
Paine, Thomas (1908). *The Writings of Thomas Paine*, ed. Moncure Conway, 4 vols., New York
  (1989a [1776–97]). *Political Writings*, ed. Bruce Kuklick, Cambridge
  (1989b). *The Rights of Man, Part I, Political Writings*, ed. Bruce Kuklick, Cambridge
  (1992). *Rights of Man*, ed. G. Claeys, Indianapolis
Paley, William (1785). *Principles of Moral and Political Philosophy*, London
  (1802). *Natural Theology: or, Evidences of the Existence and Attributes of the Deity Collected from the Appearances of Nature*, London
Palgrave, R. H. I. (1899). *Dictionary of Political Economy*, 3 vols., London
Pankhurst, Christabel (n.d.). *The Militant Methods of the N.W.S.P.U.*, London
Parkin, George (1892). *Imperial Federation and the Problem of National Unity*, London
Pater, Walter (1974). *Selected Writings*, ed. Howard Bloom, New York
Pearson, Karl (1887a). *The Moral Basis of Socialism*, London
  (1887b). *Socialism, Its Theory and Practice*, London
  (1905 [1901]). *National Life from the Standpoint of Science*, London
  (1912). *Darwinism, Medical Progress and Eugenics, The Cavendish Lecture 1912*, London
  (1914–1930), *The Life, Letters and Labours of Francis Galton*, 3 vols., Cambridge
Pease, William H. and Pease, Jane H. (1965). *The Antislavery Argument*, ed. Pease and Pease (American Heritage Series), Indianapolis
Pelz, William A. (ed.) (1994). *Wilhelm Liebknecht and German Social Democracy: A Documentary History*, trans. Erich Hahn, Westport, CT
Penty, A. P (1906). *The Restoration of the Gild System*, London
Pigott, Richard (1883). *Personal Recollections of an Irish National Journalist*, Dublin
Place, Francis. Place Papers, British Library, Add. Mss. 35153
Plato (1888). *The Republic of Plato*, trans. and intro. Benjamin Jowett, 3rd edition, Oxford
Playfair, William (1805). 'The Life of Dr. Adam Smith', in Adam Smith, *An Inquiry into the Nature and Causes of the Wealth of Nations*, 11th edition, 3 vols., London, Vol. 1
Plekhanov, G.V. (1934). *Essays in the History of Materialism*, London
  (1969 [1897]). 'The Materialist Conception of History', published as an appendix to his *Fundamental Problems of Marxism*, London
Poincaré, Henri (1960 [1901]). 'Lettre à M. Leon Walras', in Walras, 'Économique et Mécanique', *Metroeconomica*, 12 (1960): 3–11.
Pollack, Norman (1977). *The Populist Mind*, ed. Norman Pollack (American Heritage Series), Indianapolis
Pollock, Frederick (1896). *A First Book of Jurisprudence*, London
Pollock, Frederick and Maitland, F. W. (1895). *A History of English Law before the Time of Edward I*, Cambridge
Portalis, J. E. M. (1827). *De l'Usage et de l'Abus de l'Esprit Philosophique durant le Dix-huitième Siècle*, Paris
  (1840). *Discours sur la Science Sociale*, Paris
  (1844). *Discours*, Paris
Producteur, Le Journal de l'Industrie des Sciences et des Beaux Arts, 5 vols. (1826), Paris
Proudhon, Pierre-Joseph (1868 [1848]). 'Solution du Problème Social', in *Oeuvres Complètes de P.-J. Proudhon*, Paris
  (1875). *Correspondance de P.-J. Proudhon*, 14 vols., Paris
  (1923a [1851]). *General Idea of the Revolution in the Nineteenth Century*, London

(1923b [1851]). *Idée Générale de la Révolution au XIXe Siècle*, Paris
(1923c [1846]). *Système des Contradictions Économiques*, 2 vols., Paris
(1924 [1865]). *De la Capacité Politique des Classes Ouvrières*, Paris
(1926a [1839]). *De la Célébration du Dimanche*, Paris
(1926b [1840]). *Qu'est-ce que la Propriété*, Paris
(1927 [1843]). *De la Création de l'Ordre dans l'Humanité*, Paris
(1929 [1863]). *Du Principe Fédératif*, Paris
(1930 [1858]). *De la Justice dans la Révolution et dans l'Eglise*, 2 vols., Paris
(1960). *Carnets de P.-J. Proudhon*, 4 vols., ed. Pierre Haubtmann, Paris
(1994 [1840]). *Qu'est-ce que la Propriété? Ou Recherches sur le Principe du Droit et du Gouvernement*, ed. Donald R. Kelley and Bonnie G. Smith, Cambridge
Pryme, George (1823). *An Introductory Lecture and Syllabus, to a Course Delivered in the University of Cambridge, on the Principles of Political Economy*, Cambridge
Puchta, G. F. (1828). *Das Gewohnheitsrecht*, Marburg
Pufendorf, S. (1672). *De Jure Belli ac Pacis* (On the Law of Nature and Nations)
Rae, John (1891). *Contemporary Socialism*, 2nd edition, London
Ranade, Mahadev Govind (1906 [1892]). *Essays on Indian Economics*, 2nd edition, Madras
Ranke, Leopold von (1824). *Geschichte der Romanischen und Germanischen Voelker*, Berlin
(1827). *Die Osmanen und die Spanische Monarchie im 16. und 17. Jahrhundert*, Berlin
(1867–90). *Sämtliche Werke*, 54 vols., Leipzig
(1901). *The History of the Popes*, 3 vols., trans. E. Fowler, New York
(1925–6). *Deutsche Geschichte im Zeitalter der Reformation*, 6 vols., ed. P. Joachimsen, Munich
(1949). *Das Briefwerk*, ed. W. P. Fuchs, Hamburg
(1964–75). *Aus Werk und Nachlass*, 4 vols., Munich
Rathbone, E. (1924). *The Disinherited Family*, London
Read, D. B. (1896). *The Canadian Rebellion of 1837*, Toronto
Reclus, Elisée (1925 [1851]). 'Développement de la Liberté dans le Monde', *Le Libertaire* (28 August–1 December 1925)
Rémusat, Charles de (1860). *Politique Libérale ou Fragments pour Servir à la Défense de la Révolution Française*, Paris
(2003). *La Pensée Politique Doctrinaire sous la Restauration*, ed. Darío Roldán, Paris
The Republican, Vol. 1, No. 1 (27 August 1819), London
Reybaud, Louis (1840). *Études sur les Réformateurs ou Socialistes Modernes*, Paris
(1864). *Études sur les Réformateurs Modernes*, 7th edition, Paris
Reynolds, Sir Joshua (1778). *Seven Discourses Delivered in the Royal Academy by the President*, London
R. H. (1865). *The Insurrection in Jamaica*, London
Ricardo, David (1817). *On the Principles of Political Economy and Taxation*, London
(1819). *On the Principles of Political Economy and Taxation*, 2nd edition, London
(1951–73). *The Works and Correspondence of David Ricardo*, ed. Piero Sraffa, 11 vols., Cambridge
(1973 [1817]). *The Principles of Political Economy and Taxation*, ed. Donald Winch, New York
Riehl, Wilhelm Heinrich (1897 [1851]). *Die Bürgerliche Gesellschaft*, 9th edition, Stuttgart
Ritchie, David George (1889). *Darwinism and Politics*, London
(1891). *The Principles of State Interference: Four Essays on the Political Philosophy of Mr Herbert Spencer, J. S. Mill, and T. H. Green*, London
(1893). *Darwin and Hegel: With Other Philosophical Studies*, London
(1895). *Natural Rights: A Criticism of Some Political and Ethical Conceptions*, London
Ritter, Constantin, (1910). *Platon, sein Leben, seine Schriften, seine Lehre*, Munich

Robertson, J. P. and Robertson, W. P. (1839). *Francia's Reign of Terror. Being the Continuation of the Letters on Paraguay*, 3 vols., London

Rodbertus-Jagetzow, Johann Karl (1880). *Briefe und Socialpolitische Aufsätze*, ed. Rudolf Meyer, 2 vols., Berlin

Roebuck, J. A. (1897). *Life and Letters of John Arthur Roebuck P.C., Q.C., M.P. with Chapters of Autobiography*, ed. Robert Eadon Leader, London and New York

Roesler, Hermann (1871). *Über die Grundlehren der von Adam Smith begründeten Volkwirthschaftstheorie*, 2nd edition, Erlangen

Rogers, J. E. Thorold (1885). *The British Citizen: His Rights and Privileges. A Short History*, London

Roscher, Wilhelm (1843). *Grundriß zu Vorlesungen über die Staatswirthschaft nach Geschichtlicher Methode*, Göttingen

(1882). *Principles of Political Economy*, trans. John J. Lalor, 2 vols., Chicago

Roscher, Wilhelm and Robert Jannasch (1885). *Kolonien, Kolonialpolitik und Auswanderung*, Leipzig

Rosenkranz, Karl (1972 [1844]). *G.W.F. Hegels Leben*, Darmstadt

Rossi, Pellegrino (1840). *Cours d'Économie Politique*, Paris

Rotteck, Karl von and Welcker, Carl Theodor (eds.) (1834–39). *Staats-Lexicon oder Encyclopädie der Staatswissenschaften*, 15 vols., Altona

Rousseau, Jean-Jacques (1970). *Oeuvres Complètes de Jean-Jacques Rousseau*, ed. Bernard Gagnebin and Marcel Raymond, 4 vols., Paris

Rowntree, B. S. (1901). *Poverty: A Study of Town Life*, London

Royer-Collard, Pierre-Paul (1861). *La Vie Politique de M. Royer-Collard: Ses Discours et ses Écrits*, 2 vols., Paris

Ruge, Arnold (1832). *Die Platonische Ästhetik*, Halle

(1837). *Neue Vorschule der Ästhetik: Das Komische*, Halle

Ruskin, John (1849). *The Seven Lamps of Architecture*, London

(1853). *The Stones of Venice*, London

(n.d. [1865]). *Sesames and Lilies*, London

(1872). *The Works of John Ruskin*, 11 vols., London

(1903–12). *The Works of John Ruskin*, 39 vols., ed. E. T. Cook and Alexander Wedderburn, London

(1906 [1856]). *Modern Painters IV, Works*, Vol. VI, ed. E. T. Cook and Alexander Wedderburn, London

Russell, Bertrand (1896). *German Social Democracy: Six Lectures*, London

(1956). *Portraits from Memory and other Essays*, London

(1983–). *Collected Papers*, Vols. I, VII, VIII, XII, London

Rutherford, John (1877). *The Secret History of the Fenian Conspiracy*, 2 vols., London

Saint-Simon, Henri de (1865–78). *Oeuvres de Saint-Simon et d'Enfantin*, 47 vols., Paris

(1958 [1828–9]). *The Doctrine of Saint-Simon: An Exposition, First Year, 1828–1829*, ed. Georg G. Iggers, Boston

(1964). *Henri de Saint-Simon: Social Organization, the Science of Man, and Other Writings*, ed. Felix Markham, New York

(1975). *Henri Saint-Simon: Selected Writings on Science, Industry, and Social Organisation*, ed. Keith Taylor, London

(1976). *The Political Thought of Saint-Simon*, ed. Ghita Ionescu, Oxford

Saint-Simon, Henri de and Comte, Auguste (1966 [1823–4]). 'Catéchisme des Industriels', in *Oeuvres de Claude-Henri de Saint-Simon*, Paris

Sainte-Beuve, Charles-Augustin (1947 [1872]). *P.-J. Proudhon, Sa Vie et Sa Correspondance, 1838–1848*, Paris

(1993). *Portraits Littéraires*, ed. Gérald Antoine, Paris

Salat, Jakob (1802). *Auch ein Paar Worte über die Frage: Führt die Aufklärung zur Revolution*, Munich

Samuel, Herbert (1902). *Liberalism: An Attempt to State the Principles and Proposals of Contemporary Liberalism in England*, London

(1904). 'The Cobden Centenary and Modern Liberalism', *Nineteenth Century*, 55: 898–909

Sand, Georges (1964–95). *Correspondance*, ed. Georges Lubin, 26 vols., Paris

Saraswati, Swami Dayananda (1927 [1874]). *The Light of Truth (Satyarth Prakash)*, trans. G. Bharadwaja, Lahore

Sargant, W. L. (1860). *Robert Owen and his Philosophy*, London

Savigny, Karl Friedrich (1831). *On the Vocation of our Age for Legislation and Jurisprudence*, trans. A. Hayward, London

(1840). *System des Heutigen Römischen Rechts*, Berlin

Say, Jean-Baptiste (1803). *Traité d'Économie Politique, ou Simple Exposition de la Manière dont se Forment, se Distribuent, et se Consomment les Richesses*, 2 vols., Paris

(1807). *Abhandlung über die National-Oekonomie*, 2 vols., Halle and Leipzig

Schaack, Michael J. (1889). *Anarchy and Anarchists: A History of the Red Terror and the Social Revolution in America and Europe*, Chicago

Schaeffle, A. (1889). *The Quintessence of Socialism*, London

Schiller, Friedrich (1793). *Über Anmut und Würde*, Leipzig

(1967 [1795]). *On the Aesthetic Education of Man: In a Series of Letters*, ed. and trans. Elizabeth Wilkinson and L. A. Willoughby, Oxford

(1982). *On the Aesthetic Education of Man*, trans. E. M. Wilkinson and L. A. Willoughby, Oxford

(1984 [1795–6]). 'Über Naïve und Sentimentale Dichtung', in Gerhard Fricke and Herbert G. Gopfert (eds.), *Über das Schöne und die Kunst. Schriften zur Ästhetik*, Munich

Schlegel, A.W. (1808). *Über das Verhältnis der Bildenden Künste zur Natur*, Landshut

Schlegel, Friedrich (1964 [1804–5]). *Die Entwicklung der Philosophie in Zwölf Buchern*, in *Philosophische Vorlesungen*, ed. Jean-Jacques Ansttett, *Kritsche Friedrich-Schlegel-Ausgabe*, 22 vols., Vol. xiii, Munich

(1966 [1820–3]). *Die Signatur des Zeitalters*, in *Studien zur Geschichte und Politik*, ed. Ernst Behler, *Kritsche Friedrich-Schlegel-Ausgabe*, 22 vols., Vol. vii, Munich

(1968 [1799–1800]). *Dialogue on Poetry and Literary Aphorisms*, trans. E. Behler and R. Struc, University Park, PA

(1969 [1827]). *Philosophie des Lebens. In fünfzehn Vorlesungen zu Wien im Jahre 1827*, ed. Ernst Behler, *Kritsche Friedrich-Schlegel-Ausgabe*, 22 vols., Vol. x, Munich

(1996a [1796]). 'Essay on the Concept of Republicanism Occasioned by the Kantian Tract Perpetual Peace', in Frederick Beiser (ed. and trans.), *The Early Political Writings of the German Romantics*, Cambridge

(1996b [1800]). 'Ideas', in Frederick Beiser (ed. and trans.), *The Early Political Writings of the German Romantics*, Cambridge

(2003 [1797–9]). 'Critical Fragments', 'Athenaeum Fragments', 'Ideas', in J. M. Bernstein (ed.), *Classic and Romantic German Aesthetics*, Cambridge

Schleiermacher, Friedrich (1845). *Lehre vom Staat*, ed. G. Wolde, *Fr. Schleiermachers Sämmtliche Werke*, ed. Chr. Brandis, 30 vols., Vol. viii, Berlin

(1967). *Schleiermachers Werke: Auswahl in vier Bänden*, 4 vols., ed. Otto Braun and Johannes Bauer, Aalen

(1984 [1799]). *Über die Religion. Reden an die Gebildeten unter ihren Verächtern*, in Günter Meckenstock (ed.), *Schriften aus der Berliner Zeit, 1796–1799*, Berlin and New York

(1988 [1796–9]). *On Religion: Speeches to its Cultured Despisers*, trans. Richard Crouter, Cambridge

Schopenhauer, Arthur (1818). *Die Welt als Wille und Vorstellung*

Schramm, C. A. (1885). *Rodbertus, Marx, Lassalle*, Munich

Seeley, J. R. (1870). 'The English Revolution of the Nineteenth Century', *MacMillan's Magazine*, 22: 241–51, 347–58, 444–51

(1883). *The Expansion of England: Two Courses of Lectures*, London

(1885). 'Our Insular Ignorance', *The Nineteenth Century*, 18: 861–73

Senior, Nassau W. (1965 [1836]). *An Outline of the Science of Political Economy*, London

Seton-Watson, R.W. (1915). *The Spirit of the Serb*, London

(1917). *The Rise of Nationality in the Balkans*, London

Seward, A. C. (ed.) (1909). *Darwin and Modern Science: Essays in Commemoration of the Fiftieth Anniversary of the Publication of The Origin of Species*, Cambridge

Shaw, George Bernard (1900). *Fabianism and the Empire: A Manifesto by the Fabian Society*, London

Shelley, Percy Bysshe (1965a). *The Complete Works of Percy Bysshe Shelley*, ed. Roger Ingpen and Walter E. Peck, 10 vols., New York

(1965b [1819]). *A Philosophical View of Reform*, in Shelley, *Complete Works*, Vol. VII, New York

(1965c [1821]). *In Defence of Poetry*, in Shelley, *Complete Works*, Vol. VII, New York

(1965d [1812]). *Queen Mab*, in Shelley, *Complete Works*, Vol. I, New York

(1965e [1815–19?]). *Speculation of Morals*, in Shelley, *Complete Works*, Vol. VII, New York

Sidgwick, Henry (1874). *The Methods of Ethics*, London

(1883). *The Principles of Political Economy*, London

(1886). 'The Historical Method', *Mind*, 11: 203–19

(1891). *The Elements of Politics*, London

(1902). *Lectures on the Ethics of T. H. Green, Mr. Herbert Spencer and J. Martineau*, London

(1904 [1885]). *Miscellaneous Essays and Addresses*, London

Sieyès, Emmanuel Joseph (2003). *Political Writings*, ed. Michael Sonenscher, Indianapolis

Silbey, Joel H. (ed.) (1999). *The American Party Battle: Election Campaign Pamphlets: 1828–76*, 2 vols., Harvard

Simmel, Georg (1971). *On Individuality and Social Forms: Selected Writings*, ed. Donald N. Levine, Chicago

Simon, John (1897 [1890]). *English Sanitary Institutions, Reviewed in their Course of Development and in some of their Political and Social Relations*, London

Sinclair, M. (1912). *Feminism*. London: The Women Writers' Suffrage Society

(1922). *The New Idealism*, London

Sismondi, Jean Charles Leonard Simonde de (1832 [1826]). *A History of the Italian Republics, Being a View of the Origin, Progress and Fall of Italian Freedom*, London

(1975 [1827]). *Nouveaux Principes d'Économie Politique*, 2nd edition, Tome II, Paris

(1991 [1819] English trans.). *New Principles of Political Economy*, ed. R. Hyse and R. Heilbroner, New Brunswick

Smith, Adam (1809). *The Theory of Moral Sentiments*, 12th edition, London

(1974 [1759]). *The Theory of Moral Sentiments*, ed. D. D. Raphael and A. L. Macfie, Oxford

Soloviev, Vladimir (1888). *L'Idée Russe*, Paris

(1889). *La Russie et L'Église Universelle*, Paris

(1915 [1900]). *Three Conversations on War, Progress, and the End of Universal History*, trans. A. Bakshy, St Petersburg

(2000). *Politics, Law, Morality* (Russian Literature and Thought), ed. and trans. V. Wozniuk, New Haven and London.

Sombart, Werner (1906). *Warum Gibt es in den Vereinigten Staaten keinen Sozialismus? [Why is there no Socialism in the United States?]*, Tübingen

Sombart, Wernher (1909 [1913]). *The Jews and Modern Capitalism*, trans. M. Epstein, London
    (1913 [1909]). *Socialism and the Social Movement*, London

Sorel Georges (1916 [1908]). *Reflections on Violence*, trans. T. E. Hulme, London
    (1969). *Reflections on Violence*, New York

Sotheran, Charles (1892). *Horace Greeley; and other Pioneers of American Socialism*, New York

Southey, Robert (1812). 'Inquiry into the Poor Laws, &c.', *The Quarterly Review*, 8: 319–56
    (1825). *The Book of the Church*, London
    (1829). *Sir Thomas More: or Colloquies on the Progress of Society*, 2 vols., London
    (1832a). *Essays, Moral and Political*, 2 vols., London
    (1832b [1828]). 'On the Catholic Question', in Southey, *Essays, Moral and Political*, Vol. II, London
    (1832c [1818]). 'On the Means of Improving the People', in Southey, *Essays, Moral and Political*, Vol. II, London
    (1832d [1817]). 'On the Rise and Progress of Popular Disaffection', in Southey, *Essays, Moral and Political*, Vol. II, London
    (1832e [1816]). 'On the State of the Poor and the Means Pursued by the Society for Bettering their Condition', in Southey, *Essays, Moral and Political*, Vol. I, London
    (1832f [1812]). 'On the State of the Poor, the Principles of Mr. Malthus' Essay on Population, and the Manufacturing System', in Southey, *Essays, Moral and Political*, Vol. I, London
    (1832g [1822, 1824]). 'Two Letters Concerning Lord Byron', in Southey, *Essays, Moral and Political*, Vol. II, London
    (1844). *Poetical Works*, London
    (1856). *Selections from the Letters of Robert Southey*, 4 vols., London
    (1996 [1882]). *Political Institutions, Being Part V of The Principles of Sociology*, in Herbert Spencer, *Collected Writings*, ed. Michael Taylor, Vol. VIII, London

Spencer, Herbert (1876–96). *The Principles of Sociology*, 3 vols., London
    (1902a). 'Imperialism and Slavery', in *Facts and Comments*, London
    (1902b). 'Re-barbarisation', in *Facts and Comments*, London
    (1902c). 'Regimentation', in *Facts and Comments*, London
    (1908). *Life and Letters*, ed. David Duncan, London
    (1969 [1884]). *The Man versus the State*, ed. Donald Macrae, London
    (1982 [1884]). *The Man versus the State, with Six Essays on Government, Society and Freedom*, ed. E. Mack and A. J. Nock, Indianapolis
    (1992 [1842]). 'The Proper Sphere of Government', in *The Man Versus the State, With Six Essays on Government, Society, and Freedom*, Indianapolis

Spinoza, Benedict [Baruch] (2000 [1677]). *Ethics*, ed. and trans. G. H. R. Parkinson, Oxford

Staël, Germaine de (2008 [1818]). *Considerations on the Principal Events of the French Revolution*, ed. A. Craiutu, Indianapolis

Stahl, Friedrich Julius (1830). *Die Philosophie des Rechts nach Geschichtlicher Ansicht*, Heidelberg
    (1833). *Die Philosophie des Rechts*, Hildesheim
    (1840). *Die Kirchenverfassung und Lehre und Recht der Protestanten*, Erlangen

Stanton, Elizabeth Cady and others (1881). *History of Woman Suffrage*, New York

Steevens, G. W. (1899). *In India*, London

Stein, Lorenz von (1848). *Der Sozialismus und Communismus des Heutigen Frankreichs*, 2nd edition, 2 vols., Leipzig
    (1956 [1856]). *Begriff und Wesen der Gesellschaft*, originally published as part of *Die Gesellschaftslehre*, Vol. II, Cologne and Opladen

(1962 [1886–1884]). *Die Verwaltungslehre*, Stuttgart

(1964 [1850]). *The History of the Social Movement in France, 1789–1850*, trans. Kaethe Mengelberg, Totowa, NJ

(2002 [1850]). *Le Concept de Société*, ed. Norbert Waszek, trans. Marc Béghin, Grenoble

Stephen, James Fitzjames (1862). 'Liberalism', *Cornhill Magazine*, 5: 70–83

(1873a). *Liberty, Equality, Fraternity*, London

(1873b). 'Parliamentary Government', *Contemporary Review*, 23: 1–19 and 168–81

(1892 [1874]). *Horae Sabbaticae*, second series, London

(1978 [1879–93]). *The Principles of Ethics*, 2 vols., Indianapolis

(1991 [1873]). *Liberty, Equality, Fraternity, and Three Brief Essays*, with a new foreword by Richard A. Posner and notes by R. J. White, Chicago

Stephen, Leslie (1875). 'The Machinery of Government', *Fortnightly Review*, 18: 836–52

(1876). *History of English Thought in the Eighteenth Century*, 2 vols., London

(1894). 'Mill, John Stuart (1806–73)', *Dictionary of National Biography*, Oxford

(1900). *The English Utilitarians*, 3 vols., London

Stirner, Max [Johann Caspar Schmidt] (1845). *Der Einzige und sein Eigentum*, Leipzig

(1995 [1845]). *The Ego and Its Own*, ed. D. Leopold, Cambridge

Stopes, Charlotte (1907a). *British Freewomen: Their Historical Privilege*, London

(1907b). *The Sphere of 'Man' in Relation to That of 'Woman' in the Constitution*, London

Strauss, David Friedrich (1840–1). *The Christian Faith in its Historical Development and Battle with Modern Science*, Tübingen

(1841). *Streitschriften zur Vertheidigung meiner Schrift über das Leben Jesu und zur Charakteristik der gegenwärtigen Theologie*, 3 vols., Tübingen

Stutfield, Hugh (1897). 'The Psychology of Feminism', *Blackwood's Edinburgh Magazine*, January: 104–17

Sumner, William Graham (1911). *War and Other Essays*, ed. A. G. Keller, New Haven and London

(1963). *Social Darwinism: Selected Essays*, ed. Stow Persons, New York

(1989 [1883]). *What Social Classes Owe to Each Other*, Caldwell, ID

Swanwick, Helena (1915). *Women and War*, London

Tacitus (1970). *The Agricola and the Germania*, trans. and intro. H. Mattingly, Harmondsworth

Taine, Hippolyte Adolphe (1872). *Notes sur L'Angleterre*, Paris

(1878–85). *The Revolution*, 3 vols., trans. J. Durand, London

(1962 [1881]). *The Origins of Contemporary France: The French Revolution*, trans. John Durand, 3 vols., Gloucester, MA

Tarde, Jean Gabriel de (1901). *L'Opinion et la Foule*, Paris

(1905). *Underground Man*, trans. C. Breton, London

Taylor, Harriet (1998). *The Complete Works of Harriet Taylor Mill*, ed. J. E. Jacobs, Bloomington, IN

Temple, F. *et al.* (1861 [1860]). *Essays and Reviews*, 4th edition, London

Thierry, Augustin (1866). *Essai sur l'Histoire de la Formation et des Progrès du Tiers État*, Paris

Thompson, C. Bradley (2004). *Antislavery Political Writings, 1833–1860*, New York

Thompson, George Carslake (1886). *Public Opinion and Lord Beaconsfield, 1875–1880*, 2 vols., London

Thompson, Herbert M. (1896). *Russian Politics*, London

Thompson, William (1827). *Labour Rewarded, or the Claims of Capital and Labour reconciled through Co-operation*, London

(1997 [1825]). *Appeal of One Half of the Human Race, Women, Against the Pretensions of the Other Half, Men*, Cork

Bibliography

Thompson, W. F. (1839). *The Practical Philosophy of the Muhammadan People* (a translation of the 'Akhlaq-I-Jalali'), London

Thoreau, Henry David (1996). *Political Writings*, ed. Nancy Rosenblum (Cambridge Texts in the History of Political Thought), Cambridge

Thorold Rogers, J. E. (1885). *The British Citizen: His Rights and Privileges. A Short History*, London

The Times-Parnell Commission Speech (1890), London

Tocqueville, Alexis de (1835–40). *Democracy in America*, 2 vols., New York

(1837a). 'First Letter on Algeria', republished in *Writings on Empire and Slavery* (2001), ed. J. Pitts, Baltimore

(1837b). 'Second Letter on Algeria', republished in *Writings on Empire and Slavery* (2001), ed. J. Pitts, Baltimore

(1841). 'Essay on Algeria', republished in *Writings on Empire and Slavery* (2001), ed. J. Pitts, Baltimore

(1846). 'Intervention in the Debate over the Appropriation of Special Funding', republished in *Writings on Empire and Slavery* (2001), ed. J. Pitts, Baltimore

(1847a). 'First Report on Algeria', republished in *Writings on Empire and Slavery* (2001), ed. J. Pitts, Baltimore

(1847b). 'Second Report on Algeria', republished in *Writings on Empire and Slavery* (2001), ed. J. Pitts, Baltimore

(1945 [1835, 1840]). *Democracy in America*, ed. Phillips Bradley, New York

(1951 [1835, 1840]) (1–2). *De la Démocratie en Amérique, Oeuvres Complètes*, Vol. I, Paris

(1952 [1856]). *L'Ancien Régime et la Révolution, Oeuvres Complètes*, Vol. II, Paris

(1959a). *'The European Revolution' and Correspondence with Gobineau*, ed. John Lukacs, New York

(1959b). *Oeuvres, Papiers et Correspondances*, Vol. IX, *Correspondance d'Alexis de Tocqueville et d'Arthur de Gobineau*, Paris

(1959c). *Recollections*, ed. J. P. Mayer, trans. Alexander Teixeira de Mattos, New York

(1968 [1835]). *Democracy in America*, 2 vols., ed. J. P. Mayer, trans. George Lawrence, New York

(1971 [1893]). *Recollections*, ed. J. P. Mayer and A. P. Kerr, New York

(1985). *Selected Letters on Politics and Society*, ed. R. Boesche, Berkeley and London.

(1986). *Correspondance Étrangère d'Alexis de Tocqueville, Oeuvres Complètes*, Vol. VII, Paris

(1990). *Écrits et Discours Politiques, Oeuvres Complètes*, Vol. III, Paris

(1998 [1856]). *The Old Regime and the Revolution*, Chicago

(2000 [1835 and 1840]). *Democracy in America*, ed. and trans. Harvey Mansfield and Debra Winthrop, Chicago

(2001). *Writings on Slavery and Empire*, ed. Jennifer Pitts, Baltimore

(2005). *Textes Économiques*, ed. Jean-Louis Benoît and Eric Keslassy, Paris

Tone, Wolfe (1827). *Memoirs of Theobald Wolfe Tone*, 2 vols., London

Tönnies, Ferdinand (1914). 'Rechtsstaat und Wolfahrtsstaat', *Archiv für Rechts- und Wirtschaftsphilosophie*, Berlin and Leipzig, Vol. VIII, 1, 65–70

(1974). *On Social Ideas and Ideologies*, ed. and trans. E. G. Jacoby, New York

(2001 [1887]). *Gemeinschaft und Gesellschaft*, ed. and trans. J. Harris and M. Hollis as *Community and Civil Society*, Cambridge

Treitschke, Heinrich von (1971 [1870]). 'Das Constitutionelle Königtum in Deutschland', *Preußische Jahrbücher*, reprinted in Treitschke, *Historisch-Politische Aufsätze*, Bd. 3, 427ff.

Tucker, Benjamin R. (1969 [1897]). *Instead of a Book. A Fragmentary Exposition of Philosophical Anarchism*, New York

Tuckwell, Rev. W. (1889). *Christian Socialism*, London

Bibliography

'The Twelfth Annual Meeting' (1899) in *Publications of the American Economic Association*, 3rd series, 1: 37–43

Urwick, E. J. (1912). *A Philosophy of Social Progress*, London

Veblen, T. (1912 [1899]). *The Theory of the Leisure Class*, New York

Villeneuve-Bargemont, J. P. A. (1834). *Économie Politique Chrétienne, ou Recherches sur la Nature et les Causes du Paupérisme en France et en Europe*, 3 vols., Paris

Villermé, Louis René (1840). *Tableau de l'État Physique et Moral des Ouvriers*, 2 vols., Paris

Vollgraf, C. E. and Roth R. (2003). *Manuskripte und Redaktionelle Texte zum dritten Buch des 'Kapitals'*, MEGA 11/14, Berlin

Von Mohl, Robert (1855). *Die Geschichte und Literatur der Staatswissenschaften*, Erlangen

Von Rosen, Baron A. (1872). *Russian Conspirators in Siberia: A Personal Narrative*, London

Wagner, Richard (1974). *Ausgewählte Schriften*, ed. Dietrich Mack, Frankfurt am Main

  (1993). *The Art Work of the Future and Other Writings*, trans. W. Ashton Ellis, Lincoln and London

  (1994). *Religion and Art*, trans. W. Ashton Ellis, Lincoln and London

Wakefield, Edward Gibbon (1968 [1829]). 'Outline of a System of Colonisation', in *The Collected Works of Edward Gibbon Wakefield*, ed. M. F. Lloyd Prichard, Glasgow

Wallace, A. R. (1882). *Land Nationalisation: Its Necessity and its Aims*, London

  (1891). *Natural Selection and Tropical Nature: Essays on Descriptive and Theoretical Biology*, London

  (1903). *Man's Place in the Universe: A Study of the Results of Scientific Research in Relation to the Unity or Plurality of Worlds*, London

Wallas, Graham (1914). *The Great Society. A Psychological Study*, London

  (1951 [1898]). *The Life of Francis Place*, 4th edition, London

  (1962 [1908]). *Human Nature in Politics*, London

Walras, Léon (1858). *Francis Sauveur*, Paris

  (1896). *Études d'Économie Sociale*, Paris

  (1926). *Éléments d'Économie Politique Pure*, Lausanne

Warren, Josiah (1852). *Equitable Commerce*, New York

Watson, Robert Spence (1871). 'On the Best Method of Providing Higher Education in the Boroughs', in *Transactions of the National Association for the Promotion of Social Science 1870*, London

Watts, Charles (1873). *The English Monarchy and American Republicanism*, London

Webb, Beatrice (1886). 'The History of English Economics', Passfield MSS, London School of Economics

  (1886–7). 'Diary', typescript, Vol. X, Passfield MSS, London School of Economics

Webb, Sidney (1910). 'Social Movements', in G. P. Gooch (ed.), *Cambridge Modern History*, Vol. XII: *The Latest Age*, Cambridge

  (n.d.). *Difficulties of Individualism*, Fabian Tract no. 69

Webb, Sidney and Webb, Beatrice (1902 [1899]). *Industrial Democracy*, London

Weber, Max (1947 [1925]). *The Theory of Social and Economic Organisation*, ed. Talcott Parsons, New York

  (1948). *From Max Weber: Essays in Sociology*, ed. H. H. Gerth and C. Wright Mills, Chicago and London

  (1954 [1925]). *Max Weber on Law in Economy and Society*, Harvard

  (1962 [1864–1920]). *Basic Concepts in Sociology*, trans. H. P. Secher, New York

  (1975 [1902]). *Roscher and Knies: The Logical Problems of Historical Economics*, ed. Guy Oakes, New York

  (1978). 'Ethnic Groups', in Guenther Roth and Claus Wittich (eds.), *Economy and Society* (1921), Vol. I, Berkeley and Los Angeles

(1984a [1895]). 'Der Nationalstaat und die Volkswirtschaftspolitik', in Wolfgang J. Momm-sen (ed.), *Landarbeiterfrage, Nationalstaat und Volkswirtschaftspolitik. Schriften und Reden 1892–1899*, Max Weber Gesamtausgabe Bd. 4, 2

(1984b). *Zur Politik im Weltkrieg. Schriften und Reden 1914–1918*, ed. Wolfgang J. Mommsen, Max Weber Gesamtausgabe, Vol. xv, Tübingen

(1994a). 'The Nation State and Economic Policy' (Inaugural Lecture 1895), in Peter Lassmann and Ronald Speirs (eds.), *Weber: Political Writings*, Cambridge

(1994b). *Political Writings*, ed. Peter Lassman and Ronald Speirs, Cambridge

(1998). *Gesamtausgabe, Band 8. Wirtschaft, Staat und Socialpolitik. Schriften und Reden 1900–1912*, ed. Wolfgang Schlucter, Peter Kurth and Birgit Moorgenbrod, Tübingen

(2005). *Gesamtausgabe, Band 22–4. Wirtschaft und Gesellschaft*, ed. Edith Hanke and Thomas Kroll, Tübingen

Weill, Georges (1896). *L'École Saint-Simonienne*, Paris

Weitling, Wilhelm (1844). *Young Germany. An Account of the Rise, Progress, and Present Position of German Communism; with a Memoir of Wilhelm Weitling*, London

(1969). *The Poor Sinner's Gospel*, London

Weld, Theodore Dwight (1838). *American Slavery As It Is: Testimony of a Thousand Witnesses*, New York

Wells, H. G. (1905). *A Modern Utopia*, London

(1906). *The Future in America*, London

(1908). *New Worlds for Old*, London

(1933). *The Shape of Things to Come*, London

Wells, H. G. et al. (1912). *The Great State: Essays in Construction*, ed. H. G. Wells, London

Whately, R. (1826). *Elements of Logic*, London

Wilde, Oscar (1895). *The Importance of Being Earnest*, London

(1962 [1891]). *The Picture of Dorian Gray and Selected Stories*, New York

Wills, Rose Mary (1913). *Personality and Womanhood*, London

Wilson, Woodrow (1893). *An Old Master and Other Political Essays*, New York

Winckelmann, J. J. (1755). *Gedanken über die Nachahmung der Griechischen Werke in der Mahlerei und Bildhauer Kunst*, Leipzig [?]

(1764). *Geschichte der Kunst des Alterthums*, Darmstadt

Wollstonecraft, Mary (1892 [1792]). *A Vindication of the Rights of Woman*, ed. Elisabeth Pennell, London

(1993 [1792]). *A Vindication of the Rights of Woman*, ed. Janet Todd, Oxford

Woolsey, Kate (1903). *Republics Versus Woman*, New York

Wordsworth, William (1946 [1820]). 'After-Thought', *River Duddon. A Series of Sonnets*, in *The Poetical Works of William Wordsworth*, ed. Ernest de Selincourt and Helen Darbishire, 5 vols., Vol. iii, Oxford

(1974a). *The Prose Works of William Wordsworth*, ed. W. J. B. Owen and Jane Worthington Symser, 3 vols., Oxford

(1974b [1809]). *Concerning the Relations of Great Britain, Spain, and Portugal, to each other, and to the Common Enemy, at This Crisis; and Specifically as Affected by the Convention of Cintra*, in Wordsworth, *Prose Works*, Oxford, Vol. i

(1974c [1798]). 'Essay on Morals', in Wordsworth, *Prose Works*, Vol. i, Oxford

(1974d [1835]). 'Postscript 1835', in Wordsworth, *Prose Works*, Vol. iii, Oxford

(1974e [1800]). 'Preface to Lyrical Ballads', in Wordsworth, *Prose Works*, Vol. i, Oxford

(1974f [1818]). 'Two Addresses to the Freeholders of Westmoreland', in Wordsworth *Prose Works*, Vol. iii, Oxford

(1979 [1799–1805]). *The Prelude*, ed. J. Wordsworth, M. H. Abrams and S. Gill, New York

(1991 [1798?]). *The Thirteen Book Prelude* (The Cornell Wordsworth), ed. Mark L. Reed, 2 vols., Ithaca

(1992 [*c*.1797–1800]). *Lyrical Ballads and Other Poems*, ed. James Butler and Karen Green, Ithaca

Wright, Almoth (1913). *The Unexpurgated Case against Woman Suffrage*, London

Zenker, E. V. (1898). *Anarchism: A Criticism and History of the Anarchist Theory*, London

Zetkin, Clara (1983 [1889]). 'Gotha Speech', in S. Bell and K. Offen (eds.), *Women, the Family and Freedom*, Vol. II: *1880–1950*, Stanford

SECONDARY SOURCES

Aaron, Daniel (1951). *Men of Good Hope: A Story of American Progressivism*, New York

Abizadeh, Arash (2005). 'Was Fichte an Ethnic Nationalist? On Cultural Nationalism and its Double', *History of Political Thought* 26(2): 334–59

Abrams, M. H. (1971). *Natural Supernaturalism: Tradition and Revolution in Romantic Literature*, New York

Abrams, P. (1968). *The Origins of British Sociology: 1834–1914*, Chicago

Acomb, Frances (1973). *Mallet du Pan: A Career in Political Journalism*, Durham, NC

Adas, Michael (1987). *Prophets of Rebellion: Millenarian Protest Movements against the European Colonial Order*, Cambridge

Adelman, P. (1971). 'Frederic Harrison and the "Positivist" Attack on Orthodox Political Economy', *History of Political Economy*, 3: 170–89

(1984). *Victorian Radicalism. The Middle Class Experience 1830–1914*, London

Adorno, T. W. (1974). *Minima Moralia*, London

Agulhon, Maurice (1983). *The Republican Experiment 1848–1852*, trans. J. Lloyd, Cambridge

Alcock, Susan *et al.* (eds.) (2001). *Empires: Perspectives from History and Archaeology*, Cambridge

Aldenhoff, Rita (1994). 'Miquel, Johannes von', in *Neue Deutsche Biographie (NDB)*, Vol. XVII, Berlin

Allen, Ann Taylor (1991). *Feminism and Motherhood in Germany, 1800–1914*, New Brunswick

Allen, Peter (1985). 'S. T. Coleridge's *Church and State* and the Idea of an Intellectual Establishment', *JHI*, 46: 89–106

Allett, John (1981). *New Liberalism: The Political Economy of J. A. Hobson*, Toronto and London

Al-Rashid, Madawi (2002). *A History of Saudi Arabia*, Cambridge

Ambirajan, S. (1978). *Classical Political Economy and British Policy in India*, Cambridge

Ameriks, Karl (ed.) (2000). *The Cambridge Companion to German Idealism*, Cambridge

Andelson, Robert V. (ed.) (1979). *Critics of Henry George*, London

Anderson, Benedict (1991). *Imagined Communities: Reflections on the Origins and Spread of Nationalism*, 2nd edition, London

Anderson, W. P. (2002). *The Cultivation of Whiteness, Science, Health and Racial Destiny in Australia*, Melbourne

Andrew, Edward G. (2001). *Conscience and Its Critics: Protestant Conscience, Enlightenment Reason, and Modern Subjectivity*, Toronto

Andrews, Naomi J. (2006). *Socialism's Muse: Gender in the Intellectual Landscape of French Romantic Socialism*, Oxford

Angell, Norman (1909). *The Great Illusion*, London

Angermann, Erich (1962). *Robert von Mohl*, Neuwied

(1966). 'Hansemann, David Justus Ludwig', in *Neue Deutsche Biographie (NDB)*, Vol. VII, Berlin

Anghie, Anthony (2005). *Imperialism, Sovereignty, and the Making of International Law*, Cambridge

Annan, Noel (1959). *The Curious Strength of Positivism in English Political Thought*, London
    (1984). *Leslie Stephen: The Godless Victorian*, London

Ansart, Pierre (1970). *Naissance de l'Anarchisme: Esquisse d'une Explication Sociologique du Proudhonisme*, Paris

Anthony, P. D. (1983). *John Ruskin's Labour: A Study of Ruskin's Social Theory*, Cambridge

Antoine, Agnès (2003). *L'Impensé de la Démocratie: Tocqueville, la Citoyenneté et la Religion*, Paris

Appleby, Joyce (1984). *Capitalism and a New Social Order: The Republican Vision of the 1790s*, New York
    (2000). *Inheriting the Revolution*, Cambridge, MA

Arendt, Hannah (1963). *On Revolution*, London
    (1969). *On Violence*, New York

Argov, Daniel (1967). *Moderates and Extremists in the Indian Nationalist Movement 1883–1920*, London

Aris, Reinhold (1936). *History of Political Thought in Germany from 1789 to 1815*, London

Armenteros, Carolina Renata (2004). 'Joseph de Maistre and the Idea of History, 1794–1820', Ph.D. dissertation, University of Cambridge

Armitage, David (2000). *The Ideological Origins of the British Empire*, Cambridge
    (2002). 'Empire and Liberty: A Republican Dilemma', in Martin van Gelderen and Quentin Skinner (eds.), *Republicanism: A Shared European Heritage, Vol. II: The Values of Republicanism in Early Modern Europe*, Cambridge
    (2007). *The Declaration of Independence: A Global History*, Cambridge, MA

Arnaud, A.-J. (1969). *Les Origines Doctrinales du Code Civil Français*, Paris
    (1973). *Essai d'Analyse Structurale du Code Civil Français: la Règle du Jeu dans la Paix Bourgeois*, Paris

Arnaud, P. (1969). *La Pensée d'Auguste Comte*, Paris

Ashrama, Advaita (1960). *The Life of Swami Vivekananda*, Calcutta

Ashton, R. (1991). *George Henry Lewes: A Life*, Oxford

Ashton, Rosemary (1980). *The German Idea: Four English Writers and the Reception of German Thought, 1800–1860*, Cambridge

August, H. (1975). *John Stuart Mill: A Mind at Large*, London

Aureau, Bertrand (2001). *Chateaubriand: Penseur de la Révolution*, Paris

Aurobindo, Sri (1958). *The Foundations of Indian Culture*, Pondicherry

Avineri, Shlomo (1968). *The Social and Political Thought of Karl Marx*, Cambridge
    (1972). *Hegel's Theory of the Modern State*, Cambridge
    (1985). *Moses Hess: Prophet of Communism and Zionism*, New York

Avrich, Paul (1967). *The Russian Anarchists*, Princeton
    (1978). *An American Anarchist: The Life of Voltairine de Cleyre*, Princeton
    (1988). *Anarchist Portraits*, Princeton

Baar, Monika (2010). *Historians and Nationalism: East-central Europe in the Nineteenth Century*, Oxford

Badawi, M. A. Zaki (1978). *The Reformers of Egypt*, London

Badrawi, Malak (2000). *Political Violence in Egypt 1910–1924: Secret Societies, Plots and Assassinations*, Richmond, Surrey

Bagchi, Nirmalya (2005). *Rammohun: A Study*, trans. Kalyan Kumar Das, Kolkata

Bagge, Dominique (1952). *Les Idées Politiques en France sous la Restauration*, Paris

Bailie, William (1972 [1906]). *Josiah Warren: The First American Anarchist*, New York

Bailyn, Bernard (1967). *The Ideology of the American Revolution*, Cambridge, MA

(1992 [1967]). *Ideological Sources of the American Revolution*, expanded edition, Cambridge, MA

Baker, Keith Michael (1964). 'The Early History of the Term "Social Science"', *Annals of Science*, 20: 211–26

(1975). *Condorcet: From Natural Philosophy to Social Mathematics*, Chicago

(1987). *The French Revolution and the Creation of Modern Political Culture*, 4 vols., Oxford

Bakshi, S. R. (1988). *Revolutionaries and the British Raj*, New Delhi

Baldwin, Peter (1990). *The Politics of Social Solidarity: Class Bases of the European Welfare State 1875–1975*, Cambridge

Bann, Stephen (1988). 'Romanticism in France', in Ray Porter and Mikuláš Teich (eds.), *Romanticism in National Context*, Cambridge

Banning, Lance (1978). *The Jeffersonian Persuasion: Evolution of a Party Ideology*, Ithaca

Bannister, R. C. (1979). *Social Darwinism, Science and Myth in Anglo-American Social Thought*, Philadelphia

Banton, Michael (1998). *Racial Theories*, 2nd edition, Cambridge

Barany, G (1968). *Stephen Szechenyi and the Awakening of Hungarian Nationalism, 1791–1841*, Princeton

Barclay, L (1967). 'Louis de Bonald, Prophet of the Past', *Studies on Voltaire and the Eighteenth Century*, 4: 167–204

Barnard, F. M (1965). *Herder's Social and Political Thought: From Enlightenment to Nationalism*, Oxford

(2003). *Herder on Nationality, Humanity and History*, Montreal

Barnett, Randy E. (2004). *Restoring the Constitution: The Presumptions of Liberty*, Princeton

Baron, Samuel H. (1963). *Plekhanov: The Father of Russian Marxism*, London

Barrell, John (1986). *The Political Theory of Painting from Reynolds to Hazlitt: 'The Body of the Public'*, New Haven

Barrow, Logie and Bullock, Ian (1996). *Democratic Ideas and the British Labour Movement, 1880–1914*, Cambridge

Barrows, S. (1981). *Distorting Mirrors: Visions of the Crowd in Late Nineteenth-Century France*, New Haven

Bartlett, E. A. (1994). *Liberty, Equality, Sorority: The Origins and Interpretation of American Feminist Thought: Frances Wright, Sarah Grimké, and Margaret Fuller*, Brooklyn

Bary, Wm. Theodore de, *et al.* (eds.) (1960). *Sources of Chinese Tradition*, Vol. II, New York

Bate, Jonathan (1991). *Romantic Ecology, Wordsworth and the Environmental Tradition*, London

Bate, Walter Jackson (1949). *Premises of Taste in Eighteenth-Century England*, Cambridge, MA

Baum, Dajana (2008). *Johann Friedrich Benzenberg (1777–1846)*, Essen

Baumgardt, D. (1952). *Bentham and the Ethics of Today with Bentham Manuscripts Hitherto Unpublished*, Princeton

Baycroft, Timothy and Hewitson, Mark (eds.) (2006). *What is a Nation? Europe, 1789–1914*, Oxford

Bayly, C. A. (1998). *The Origins of Nationality in South Asia: Patriotism and Ethical Government in the Making of Modern India*, Delhi

(2004). *The Birth of the Modern World, 1780–1914*, Oxford

Beasley, W. G. (1987). *Japanese Imperialism 1894–1945*, Oxford

Beck, H. (1995). *The Origins of the Authoritarian Welfare State in Prussia: Conservatives, Bureaucracy and the Social Question, 1815–70*, Ann Arbor

Becker, Carl L. (1958 [1922]). *The Declaration of Independence: A Study in the History of Ideas*, New York

Becq, Annie (1984). *Genèse de l'Esthétique Française Moderne*, 2 vols., Pisa

Bédé, Jean-Albert (1970). 'Chateaubriand as a Constitutional and Political Strategist', in Richard Switzer (ed.), *Chateaubriand Today*, Madison, WI

Beecher, Jonathan (1986). *Charles Fourier: The Visionary and His World*, Berkeley

  (2001). *Victor Considérant and the Rise and Fall of French Romantic Socialism*, Berkeley

Beer, G. (1983). *Darwin's Plots: Evolutionary Narrative in Darwin, George Eliot and Nineteenth-century Fiction*, London

  (1986). *George Eliot*, Bloomington

Beer, Max (1948). *A History of British Socialism*, London

Beer, Max (ed.) (1920). *The Pioneers of Land Reform: Thomas Spence. William Ogilvie. Thomas Paine*, London

Beer, Samuel H. (1993). *To Make a Nation: The Rediscovery of American Federalism*, Cambridge, MA

Behler, Ernst (1992). *Frühromantik*, Berlin

  (1996). 'Nietzsche in the Twentieth Century', in Bernd Magnus and Kathleen M. Higgins (eds.), *The Cambridge Companion to Nietzsche* (Cambridge Companions to Philosophy), Cambridge

Beik, Paul (1956). 'The French Revolution Seen from the Right: Social Theories in Motion, 1789–1799', *Transactions of the American Philosophical Society*, 46(1)

Beiser, Frederick C. (1992). *Enlightenment, Revolution and Romanticism: The Genesis of Modern German Political Thought, 1790–1800*, Cambridge, MA

  (2002). *German Idealism*, Cambridge, MA

  (2003). *The Romantic Imperative: The Concept of Early German Romanticism*, Cambridge, MA

  (2005). *Hegel*, London

Beiser, Frederick C. (ed.) (1993). *The Cambridge Companion to Hegel* (Cambridge Companions to Philosophy), Cambridge

  (ed. and trans.) (1996). *The Early Political Writings of the German Romantics,* Cambridge

Belaúnde, Victor (1938). *Bolivar and the Political Thought of Spanish American Revolution*, Baltimore and Oxford

Belchem, John (1986). *Popular Radicalism in Nineteenth Century Britain*, Basingstoke

Belich, James (1996). *Making Peoples: A History of the New Zealanders*, Auckland

Bell, David A. (2001). *The Cult of the Nation in France: Inventing Nationalism 1680–1800*, Cambridge MA.

Bell, Duncan (2007). *The Idea of Greater Britain: Empire and the Future of World Order, c.1860–1900*, Princeton

  (2009). 'Republican Imperialism: J. A. Froude and the Virtue of Empire', *History of Political Thought*, 30(1): 166–191

Bell, Duncan (2010). 'John Stuart Mill on Colonies', *Political Theory*, 38(1): 34–64

Bell, Duncan and Sylvest, Casper (2006). 'International Society in Victorian Political Thought: Herbert Spencer, T. H. Green, and Henry Sidgwick', *Modern Intellectual History*, 3: 1–32

Bellamy, Richard (2003). 'The Advent of the Masses and the Making of Modern Democracy', in Terence Ball and Bellamy (eds.), *The Cambridge History of Twentieth Century Political Thought*, Cambridge

Bello, Andres (1997). *Selected Writings of Andres Bello*, ed. I. Jacsik, trans. F. M. Lopez-Morillas, New York and Oxford

Bénichou, Paul (1977). *Le Temps des Prophètes: Doctrines de l'Âge Romantique*, Paris

Benjamin, Walter (1986). *Le Concept de Critique Esthétique dans le Romantisme Allemand*, trans. Philippe Lacoue-Labarthe and Anne-Marie Lang, Paris

Bennett, Jane (1994). *Thoreau's Nature: Ethics, Politics, and the Wild*, Thousand Oaks

Benoît, Jean-Louis (2005). *Tocqueville: Un Destin Paradoxal*, Paris

Benrekassa, Georges (1986). 'Chateaubriand et le Refus du Politique: Le Moment de l' Essai sur les Révolutions', *Romantisme*, 51: 5–16

Benton, Lauren (2002). *Law and Colonial Cultures: Legal Regimes in World History 1400–1800*, Cambridge

Beramendi, J., Máiz, R. and Núñez, X. (eds.) (1993). *Nationalism in Europe: Past and Present*, Santiago de Compostela

Berdahl, Robert M. (1988). *The Politics of the Prussian Nobility: The Development of a Conservative Ideology 1770–1848*, Princeton

Berdiaev, Nikolai (1940). *Leontiev*, London

Berend, Ivan (2003). *History Derailed: Central and Eastern Europe in the Long Nineteenth Century*, Berkeley

Berenson, Edward (1989). 'A New Religion of the Left: Christianity and Social Radicalism in France, 1815–1848', in François Furet and Mona Ozouf (eds.), *The French Revolution and the Creation of Modern Political Culture*, London

Berger, F. R. (1984). *Happiness, Justice, and Freedom: The Moral and Political Theory of John Stuart Mill*, Berkeley

Bergman, Jay (1983). *Vera Zasulich: A Biography*, Stanford, CA

Berkman, Alexander (1912). *Prison Memoirs of an Anarchist*, New York

Berkowitz, P. (1998). 'Mill: Liberty, Virtue, and the Discipline of Individuality', in E. Eisenach (ed.), *Mill and the Moral Character of Liberalism*, University Park, PA

Berlin, Isaiah (1959). *The Life and Opinions of Moses Hess*, Cambridge

(1965). 'The Thought of de Tocqueville', *History*, 50: 199–206

(1969). 'Two Concepts of Liberty', in *Four Essays on Liberty*, New York

(1970). *The Hedgehog and the Fox: An Essay on Tolstoy's View of History*, New York

(1978). *Russian Thinkers*, London

(1990). 'Joseph de Maistre and the Origins of Fascism', *New York Review of Books*, 37(16) (25 October 25)

(1994) 'Introduction' to Joseph de Maistre's *Considerations on France*, Cambridge

(1996 [1960]). 'The Romantic Revolution: A Crisis in the History of Modern Thought', in Berlin, *The Sense of Reality: Studies in Ideas and their History*, ed. Henry Hardy, London

(1998 [1958]). 'Two Concepts of Liberty', in Berlin, *The Proper Study of Mankind: An Anthology of Essays*, ed. Henry Hardy and Roger Hausheer, London

(2002a). *Freedom and its Betrayal*, Princeton

(2002b). *Liberty*, ed. Henry Hardy, Oxford

Bernal, Martin (1976). *Chinese Socialism to 1907*, Cornell

Bernstein, J. M. (1992). *The Fate of Art: Aesthetic Alienation from Kant to Derrida and Adorno*, Cambridge

Bernstein, J. M. (ed.) (2003). *Classic and Romantic German Aesthetics*, Cambridge

Best, Otto (ed.) (1974). *Ästhetische Schriften in Auswahl*, Darmstadt

Bestor, A. E. (1950). *Backwoods Utopias: The Sectarian and Owenite Phases of Communitarian Socialism in America, 1663–1829*, Philadelphia

Bevir, Mark (1989). 'Fabianism and the Theory of Rent', *History of Political Thought*, 10: 313–27

(1996). 'Review Article: English Political Thought in the Nineteenth Century', *History of Political Thought*, 17(1) (Spring)

Biagini, Eugenio F. (1992). *Liberty, Retrenchment and Reform: Popular Liberalism in the Age of Gladstone, 1860–80*, Cambridge

(1996a). *Citizenship and Community: Liberals, Radicals and Collective Identities in the British Isles, 1865–1931*, Cambridge

(1996b). 'Liberalism and Direct Democracy: John Stuart Mill and the Model of Ancient Athens', in Eugenio F. Biagini (ed.), *Citizenship and Community: Liberals, Radicals and Collective Identities in the British Isles*, Cambridge

(2003). 'Neo-Roman Liberalism: "Republican" Values and British Liberalism, ca.1860–1875', *History of European Ideas*, 29: 55–72

(2007). *British Democracy and Irish Nationalism 1876–1906*, Cambridge

Biagini, Eugenio F. and Reid, Alastair J. (eds.) (1991). *Currents of Radicalism: Popular Radicalism, Organised Labour and Party Politics in Britain, 1850–1914*, Cambridge

Bibliography of Robert Owen, the Socialist (1914). 2nd edition, 1925, Aberystwyth

Biddiss, Michael (1970). *Father of Racist Ideology: The Social and Political Thought of Count Gobineau*, London

(1977). *The Age of the Masses: Ideas and Society in Europe Since 1870*, Harmondsworth

Biefang, Andreas (ed.) (1995). *Der Deutsche Nationalverein*, Düsseldorf

Billig, Michael (1995). *Banal Nationalism*, London

Billington, L. and Billington, R. (1987). '"A Burning Zeal for Righteousness": Women in the British Anti–Slavery Movement, 1820–1860', in J. Rendall (ed.), *Equal or Different: Women's Politics 1800–1914*, Oxford

Binyon, Gilbert C. (1931). *The Christian Socialist Movement in England*, London

Birchall, Ian H. (1997). *The Spectre of Babeuf*, Basingstoke

Birker, Karl (1973). *Die Deutschen Arbeiterbildungsvereine 1840–1870*, Berlin

Birtsch, Günter (1978). 'Aspekte und Wandlungen des Freiheitsbegriffs in der Deutschen Romantik zwischen Naturrechtlichem Rationalismus und Traditionalismus', in Richard Brinkmann (ed.), *Romantik in Deutschland. Ein Interdisziplinäres Symposion*, Stuttgart

Bishop, Paul (ed.) (2004). *Nietzsche and Antiquity: His Reaction and Response to the Classical Tradition*, Studies in German Literature, Linguistics and Culture, Rochester, NY

Blackbourn, David (1980). *Class, Religion and Local Politics in Wilhelmine Germany: The Centre Party in Württemberg before 1914*, Wiesbaden

(2006). *The Conquest of Nature: Water, Landscape and the Making of Modern Germany*, London

Blacker, C. P. (1952). *Eugenics: Galton and After*, London

Blake, Robert (1966). *Disraeli*, London

(1985). *The Conservative Party from Peel to Thatcher*, London

Blakemore, Steven (1988). *Burke and the Fall of Language: The French Revolution as Linguistic Event*, Hannover, NH

Blamires, C. (1990). 'Etienne Dumont, Genevan Apostle of Utility', *Utilitas*, 2: 55–70

(2008). *The French Revolution and the Creation of Benthamism*, Basingstoke

Blanke, Horst Walter (1992). *Historiographiegeschichte als Historik*, Stuttgart

Blanning, T. C. W. (1983). *The French Revolution in Germany: Occupation and Resistance in the Rhineland, 1792–1802*, Oxford

Blaug, Mark (ed.) (1991). *Jean-Baptiste Say (1776–1832)*, Aldershot

Blight, David A. (1989). *Frederick Douglass' Civil War: Keeping Faith in Jubilee*, Amherst

(2001). *Race and Reunion: The Civil War in American Memory*, Cambridge, MA

Blit, Lucjan (1971). *The Origins of Polish Socialism: The History and Ideas of the First Polish Socialist Party, 1878–1886*, Cambridge

Block, James E. (2003). *A Nation of Agents: The American Path to a Modern Self and Society*, Cambridge, MA

Blyden, Edward (1908). *African Life and Customs*, London

Bodei, Remo (2002). *Destini Personali. L'età della Colonizzazione delle Coscienze*, Milan

Bibliography

Boesche, Roger (2005). 'The Dark Side of Tocqueville: On War and Empire', *Review of Politics*, 67(4): 737–52

(2006). *Tocqueville's Road Map: Methodology, Liberalism, Revolution and Despotism*, Lanham, MD

Boffa, Massimo (1989). 'Counterrevolution', in François Furet and Mona Ozouf (eds.), *A Critical Dictionary of the French Revolution*, trans. Arthur Goldhammer, Cambridge, MA

Bohrer, Karl Heinz (1998). *Die Grenzen des Ästhetischen*, Munich

Bolt, C. (1995). *Feminist Ferment: 'The Woman Question' in the USA and England, 1870–1940*, London

(2004). *Sisterhood Questioned? Race, Class and Internationalism in the American and British Women's Movements, c.1800s–1970s*, London

Bongie, Laurence (1965). *David Hume: Prophet of the Counter-Revolution*, Oxford

Bonham, Barbara (1970). *Battle of Wounded Knee: The Ghost Dance Uprising*, Chicago

Bonnecase, J. (1933). *La Pensée Juridique Française*, Bordeaux

Borritt, Gabor S. (1992). *Lincoln the War President*, ed. Gabor Borritt, New York

Borsche, Tilman (1990). *Wilhelm von Humboldt*, München

Bose, Sugata (1997). 'Nation as Mother: Representations and Contestations of "India" in Bengali Literature and Culture', in Sugata Bose and Ayesha Jalal (eds.), *Nationalism, Democracy and Development: State and Politics in India*, Delhi

Boucher, David and Vincent, Andrew (2001). *British Idealism and Political Theory*, Edinburgh

Bowie, Andrew (1990). *Aesthetics and Subjectivity: From Kant to Nietzsche*, Manchester

(2000). 'German Idealism and the Arts', in Karl Ameriks (ed.), *Cambridge Companion to German Idealism*, Cambridge

Bowlby, J. (1990). *Charles Darwin: A Biography*, London

Bowler, P. (1983). *The Eclipse of Darwinism: Anti–Darwinian Evolution Theories in the Decades around 1900*, Baltimore and London

(1989). *The Invention of Progress: The Victorians and the Past*, Oxford

Bowman, Sylvia (1958). *The Year 2000: A Critical Biography of Edward Bellamy*, London

Boxer, Charles Ralph (1963). *Race Relations and the Portuguese Colonial Empire, 1415–1825*, Oxford

Boyle, Nicholas (1991). *Goethe: The Poet and the Age*, Vol. 1, Oxford

Brading, D. A. (1991). *The First America: The Spanish Monarchy, Creole Patriots and the Liberal State 1492–1867*, Cambridge

Bradley, Owen (1999). *A Modern Maistre: The Social and Political Thought of Joseph de Maistre*, London and Lincoln, NE

Brady, Edward M. (1925). *Ireland's Secret Service in England*, Dublin and Cork

Brantlinger, Patrick (2003). *Dark Vanishings: Discourse on the Extinction of Primitive Races, 1800–1930*, Ithaca

Brazill, William (1970). *The Young Hegelians*, New Haven

Brebner, J. B. (1948). 'Laissez Faire and State Intervention in Nineteenth-century Britain', *Journal of Economic History*, 8: 59–73

Breckman, Warren (1992). 'Ludwig Feuerbach and the Political Theology of Restoration', *History of Political Thought*, 13: 437–62

(1999). *Marx, the Young Hegelians, and the Origins of Radical Social Theory*, Cambridge

Bredin, Jean-Denis (1987 [1983]). *The Affair: The Case of Alfred Dreyfus*, London

Breuilly, John (1993). *Nationalism and the State*, 2nd edition, Manchester

(1994). 'Culture, Doctrine, Politics: Three Ways of Constructing Nationalism', in J. Beramendi, R. Máiz and X. Núñez (eds.), *Nationalism in Europe. Past and Present*, Santiago de Compostela

Bibliography

(1996). *The Formation of the First German Nation-State 1800–1871*, London

(1998a). 'Mass Politics and the Revolutions of 1848' (TLTP History Courseware Consortium), University of Glasgow

(1998b), 'Nationalbewegung und Revolution', in Christof Dipper and Ulrich Speck (eds.), *1848: Revolution in Deutschland*, Frankfurt

(2000). 'Nationalism and the History of Ideas', *Proceeedings of the British Academy*, 105: 187–223

Briefs, Goetz A. (1941). 'The Economic Philosophy of Romanticism', *JHI*, 2: 279–300

Brink, David O. (2003). *Perfectionism and the Common Good: Themes in the Philosophy of T. H. Green*, Oxford

Brinkmann, Richard (ed.) (1978). *Romantik in Deutschland. Ein Interdisziplinäres Symposion*, (ed.), Stuttgart

Brinton, Crane (1966 [1926]). *The Political Ideas of the English Romanticists*, Ann Arbor

Brock, Peter (1977). *Polish Revolutionary Populism: A Study in Agrarian Socialist Thought from the 1830s to the 1850s*, Toronto

Bromwich, David (2001). 'Lincoln's Constitutional Necessity', *Raritan* (Winter): 1–33

Bronstein, Jamie (1999). *Land Reform and Working-class Experience in Britain and the United States, 1800–1862*, Stanford

Brooke, John Hedley (1991). 'Indications of a Creator: Whewell as Apologist and Priest', in M. Fisch and S. Schaffer (eds.), *William Whewell: A Composite Portrait*, Oxford

Brooks, John I. (1998). *The Eclectic Legacy: Academic Philosophy and the Human Sciences in Nineteenth Century France*, Newark

Brown, Delmer M. (1955). *Nationalism in Japan*, Berkeley

Brown, R. (1984). *The Nature of Social Laws: Machiavelli to Mill*, Cambridge

Brown, Stewart J. (1982). *Thomas Chalmers and the Godly Commonwealth in Scotland*, Oxford

Browne, Janet (1995). *Charles Darwin*, New York

Brubacker, Rogers (2004). *Ethnicity without Groups*, Cambridge, MA

Bruford, W. H. (1975). *The German Tradition of Self-Cultivation: 'Bildung' from Humboldt to Thomas Mann*, Cambridge

Brunschwig, Henri (1974 [1947]). *Enlightenment and Romanticism in Eighteenth-Century Prussia*, trans. Frank Jellinck, Chicago

Bubner, Rüdiger (1971). 'Einführung', in G. W. F. Hegel, *Vorlesungen über die Ästhetik, Erster und Zweiter Teil*, Stuttgart

(2003). *The Innovations of Idealism*, Cambridge

Buche, Joseph (1935). *L'École Mystique de Lyon, 1776–1847*, Paris

Buckler, F. W. (1922). 'The Political Theory of the Indian Mutiny', *Transactions of the Royal Historical Society*, 5: 71–100

Bulmer, M. G. (2003). *Francis Galton: Pioneer of Heredity and Biometry*, Baltimore

Burbank, Jane and Cooper, Frederick (2010). *Empires in World History: Power and the Politics of Difference*, Princeton

Burnham, Scott (1995). *Beethoven Hero*, Princeton

Burns, J. H. (1957 [1969]). 'J. S. Mill and Democracy, 1829–61', in J. B. Schneewind (ed.), *Mill: A Collection of Critical Essays*, London

(1966). 'Bentham and the French Revolution', *Transactions of the Royal Historical Society*, 5th Series, 16: 95–114

Burrow, John W. (1979 [1966]). *Evolution and Society: A Study in Victorian Social Theory*, Cambridge

(1981). *A Liberal Descent: Victorian Historians and the English Past*, Cambridge

(1988). *Whigs and Liberals: Continuity and Change in English Political Thought*, Oxford

(2000). *The Crisis of Reason: European Thought, 1848–1914*, New Haven

Burrow, John, Collini, Stefan and Winch, Donald (1983). *That Noble Science of Politics: A Study in Nineteenth-Century Intellectual History*, Cambridge

Burt, John (1999). 'Liberalism's Hope and Despair: Lincoln's Peoria Speech of 1854', *Social Research* (Summer): 679–7

Bury, J. P. T. (1965). *Napoleon III and the Second Empire*, London
  (1973). *Gambetta and the Making of the Third Republic*, London

Bush, Julia (2007). *Woman Against the Vote: Female Anti-Suffragism in Britain*, Oxford

Bussy, Frederick Moir (1910). *Irish Conspiracies: Recollections of John Mallon (The Great Irish Detective) and Other Reminiscences*, London

Butler, E. M. (1926). *The Saint-Simonian Religion in Germany*, Cambridge

Butler, Marilyn (1981). *Romantics, Rebels and Reactionaries: English Literature and its Background 1760–1830*, Oxford
  (1988). 'Romanticism in England', in Porter and Teich (eds.), *Romanticism in National Context*, Cambridge

Butler, Perry (1982). *Gladstone: Church, State and Tractarianism*, Oxford

Butt, John (ed.) (1971). *Robert Owen. Prince of the Cotton-Spinners*, London

Butterfield, Herbert (1955). *Man on his Past*, Cambridge

Byrnes, Robert F. (1968). *Pobedonostse: His Life and Thought*. Bloomington and London

Cahm, Caroline (1989). *Peter Kropotkin and the Rise of Revolutionary Anarchism 1872–1886*, Cambridge and New York

Cain, Peter J. (2002). *Hobson and Imperialism: Radicalism, New Liberalism and Finance 1887–1938*, Oxford
  (2007a). 'Empire and the Language of Character and Virtue in Later Victorian and Edwardian Britain', *Modern Intellectual History*, 4(2): 249–73
  (2007b). 'Radicalism, Gladstone, and the Liberal Critique of Disraelian "Imperialism"', in Duncan Bell (ed.), *Victorian Visions of Global Order: Empire and International Relations in Nineteenth-Century Political Thought*, Cambridge

Caine, Barbara (1992). *Victorian Feminists*, Oxford
  (1997). *English Feminism 1780–1980*, Oxford

Caine, Barbara and Sluga, Glenda (2000). *Gendering European History 1780–1920*, London

Callot, E. (1971). *La Philosophie Biologique de Goethe*, Paris

Calloway, Stephen (1997). 'Wilde and the Dandyism of the Senses', in Peter Raby (ed.), *The Cambridge Companion to Oscar Wilde*, Cambridge

Campbell, Ian (1993) *Thomas Carlyle*, 2nd edition, Edinburgh

Cappellini, Paolo (1984–5). *Systema Iuris*, 2 vols., Milan

Carcassonne, E. (ed.) (1927). *Écrits Inédits de Mlle. de Lezardière*, Paris

Carcopino, C. (1942). *Les Doctrines Sociales de Lamennais*, Paris

Carlisle, Janice (1991). *John Stuart Mill and the Writing of Character*, Athens

Carlisle, Robert B. (1987). *The Proferred Crown: Saint-Simonianism and the Doctrine of Hope*, Baltimore

Carlson, Andrew R. (1972). *Anarchism in Germany, Vol. I: The Early Movement*, Metuchen

Carnall, Geoffrey (1960). *Robert Southey and his Age*, Oxford

Carr, Edward Hallett (1961 [1937]). *Michael Bakunin*, New York

Carr, Reg (1977). *Anarchism in France: The Case of Octave Mirbeau*, Manchester

Carsten, Francis Ludwig (1993). *Eduard Bernstein 1850–1932. Eine politische Biographie*, Munich

Carter, April (1971). *The Political Theory of Anarchism*, London

Carter, Matt (2003). *T. H. Green and the Development of Ethical Socialism*, Exeter

Carver, Terrell (1982). *Marx's Social Theory*, Oxford
  (1989). *Friedrich Engels. His Life and Thought*, Basingstoke

Cash, Wilbur J. (1991 [1941]). *The Mind of the South*, New York

Cashdollar, C. D. (1989). *The Transformation of Theology, 1830–1890: Positivism and Protestant Thought in Britain and America*, Princeton

Cassirer, Ernst (1946). *The Myth of the State*, New Haven

Castiglione, Dario and Hampsher-Monk, Iain (2001). *The History of Political Thought in National Context*, Cambridge

Cavell, Stanley (1981). *The Senses of Walden*, expanded edition, San Francisco
  (2003). *Emerson's Transcendental Etudes*, Stanford, CA
  (2004). *Cities of Words: Pedagogical Letters of a Register of the Moral Life*, Cambridge, MA

Cesa, Claudio (2000). '"L'antico, Buon Paganesimo": Delle *Divinità di Samotracia*', in Carlo Tatasciore (ed.), *Dalla Materia della Coscienza. Studi su Schelling in Ricordo di Giuseppe Semerari*, Naples

Chace, James (2004). *1912: Wilson, Roosevelt, Taft, and Debs – The Election that Changed the Country*, New York

Chadwick, Andrew (1999). *Augmenting Democracy: Political Movements and Constitutional Reform during the Rise of Labour, 1900–1924*, Aldershot

Chadwick, Owen (1960). *The Mind of the Oxford Movement*, London
  (1998). *Acton and History*, Cambridge

Chamley, Paul (1963). *Économie Politique chez Stuart et Hegel*, Paris

Chandler, James K. (1984) *Wordsworth's Second Nature: A Study of the Poetry and Politics*, Chicago

Charlton, D. G. (1959). *Positivist Thought in France During the Second Empire 1852–1870*, Oxford
  (1983). *Secular Religions in France, 1815–1870*, London and New York
  (1984a). 'The French Romantic Movement', in D. G. Charlton (ed.), *The French Romantics*, Cambridge, Vol. I
  (1984b). 'Religious and Political Thought', in D. G. Charlton (ed.), *The French Romantics*, Cambridge, Vol. I

Charlton, D. G. (ed.) (1984c). *The French Romantics*, 2 vols., Cambridge

Chase, Malcolm (1988). *The People's Farm: English Radical Agrarianism 1775–1840*, Oxford
  (2006). *Chartism: A New History*, Manchester

Chernock, Arianne (2010). *Men and the Making of Modern British Feminism*, Stanford

Chevalier, L. (1973 [1958]). *Labouring Classes and Dangerous Classes*, trans. Frank Jellinek, New York

Chikeka, Charles (2004). *European Hegemony and African Resistance 1880–1990*, Lampeter

Chirol, Valentine (1910). *Indian Unrest*, London

Chowdhury, S. B. (1965). *Theories of the Indian Mutiny*, Calcutta

Christoff, Peter (1961). *An Introduction to Nineteenth-Century Russian Slavophilism, Vol. I: A. S. Xomjakov*, The Hague

Chytry, Josef (1989). *The Aesthetic State: A Quest in Modern German Thought*, Berkeley

Cioran, E. M. (1987). *Aveux et Anathèmes*, Paris

Claeys, Gregory (1983). 'The Concept of "Political Justice" in Godwin's *Political Justice*: A Reconsideration', *Political Theory*, 11: 565–84.
  (1984). 'The Effects of Property on Godwin's Theory of Justice', *Journal of the History of Philosophy*, 22: 81–101.
  (1987). *Machinery, Money and the Millennium, From Moral Economy to Socialism, 1815–1860*, Princeton
  (1989a). *Citizens and Saints: Politics and Anti-Politics in Early British Socialism*, Cambridge

(1989b). *Thomas Paine: Social and Political Thought*, London

(1996). 'The Example of America a Warning to Britain? The Transformation of America in Early British Radicalism and Socialism, 1790–1860', in Malcolm Chase and Ian Dyck (eds.), *Living and Learning: Essays for J. F. C. Harrison*, London

(1997a). "Justice, Independence and Industrial Democracy: The Development of John Stuart Mill's Views on Socialism", *Journal of Politics*, 49: 122–147 [Reprinted in Geoff Smith (ed.), *John Stuart Mill: Critical Assessments*, London]

(1998). 'From "Polite Manners" to "Rational Character": The Critique of Culture in Owenite Socialism, 1800–1850', in Herman Diedrichs, Frits van Holthoon and Lex Heerma van Voss (eds.), *Working Class and Popular Culture in Britain and Holland*, Amsterdam

(2003). '"Individualism", "Socialism", and "Social Science": Further Notes on a Process of Conceptual Formation 1800–1850', *Journal of the History of Ideas*, 47: 81–93 [Reprinted in Jeremy Jennings (ed.), *Socialism: Critical Concepts in the Social Science*, Baltimore]

(2007a). *The French Revolution Debate in Britain*, Basingstoke

(2007b). 'The "Left" and the Critique of Empire c.1865–1900: Three Roots of Humanitarian Foreign Policy', in Duncan Bell (ed.), *Victorian Visions of Global Order: Empire and International Relations in Nineteenth-Century Political Thought*, Cambridge

(2010). *Imperial Sceptics: British Critics of Empire, 1850–1920*, Cambridge

Claeys, Gregory (ed.) (1994). *Utopias of the British Enlightenment*, Cambridge

(ed.) (1995). *Political Writings of the 1790s*, 8 vols., London

(ed.) (1997b). *Modern British Utopias*, 8 vols., London

(ed.) (2005). *The Owenite Socialist Movement: Pamphlets and Correspondence*, 10 vols., London

Clark, A. (1995). *The Struggle for the Breeches: Gender and the Making of the British Working Class*, Berkeley

Clark, John P. (1984). *The Anarchist Moment: Reflections on Culture, Nature and Power*, Montreal

(1977). *The Philosophical Anarchism of William Godwin*, Princeton

Clark, L. (1984). *Social Darwinism in France*, Alabama

Clark, S. and Donnelly, J. S. (eds.) (1983) *Irish Peasants: Violence and Political Unrest, 1780–1914*, Manchester

Clarke, P. F. (1971). *Lancashire and the New Liberalism*, London

(1978). *Liberals and Social Democrats*, Cambridge

Clarke, Prescott and Gregory, J. S. (eds.) (1982) *Western Reports on the Taiping: A Selection of Documents*, London

Clément, Jean-Paul (1998). *Chateaubriand: Biographie Morale et Intellectuelle*, Paris

Clive, John (1973). *Macaulay: The Shaping of the Historian*. New York

Coates, J. D. (1977). 'Coleridge's Debt to Harrington: A Discussion of *Zapolya*', *JHI*, 38: 501–8

Cobban, Alfred (1960 [1929]). *Edmund Burke and the Revolt Against the Eighteenth Century*, 2nd edition, London

Cockram, Gill (2007). *Ruskin and Social Reform: Ethics and Economics in the Victorian Age*, London

Coetzee, Marilyn (1990). *The German Army League: Popular Nationalism in Wilhelmine Germany*, London

Cofer, David (1931). *Saint-Simonism in the Radicalism of Thomas Carlyle*, Austin

Cohen, D. K. (1969). 'The Viscomte de Bonald's Critique of Individualism', *Journal of Modern History*, 41: 475–84

Cohen, G. A. (1978). *Karl Marx's Theory of History: A Defence*, Oxford

(1988). *History, Labour and Freedom: Themes from Marx*, Oxford

Cohen, Gary (1981). *The Politics of Ethnic Survival: Germans in Prague, 1861–1914*, Princeton

Cohen, Nancy (2002). *The Reconstruction of American Liberalism: 1865–1914*, Chapel Hill

Cohen, Paul A. (1965). *China and Christianity: The Missionary Movement and the Growth of Chinese Anti-foreignism, 1860–1870*, Cambridge, MA

(1974). *Between Tradition and Modernity: Wang T'ao and Reform in Late Ch'ing China*, Cambridge, MA

Colaiaco, James A. (1983). *Sir James Fitzjames Stephen and the Crisis of Victorian Thought*, New York

Cole, G. D. H. (1913). *The World of Labour*, London

(1920). *Guild Socialism Re-stated*, London

(1943). *Fabian Socialism*, London

(1954). *Socialist Thought. Marxism and Anarchism, 1850–1890*, London

(1962). *A History of Socialist Thought, Vol. 1: The Forerunners*, London

(1965). *The Life of Robert Owen*, London

Cole, Margaret (1961). *The Story of Fabian Socialism*, London

Coleman, Deidre (1988). *Coleridge and 'The Friend' (1809–10)*, Oxford

Collier, Simon (2003). *Chile, the Making of a Republic, 1830–1865: Politics and Ideas*, Cambridge

Collini, Stefan (1977). 'Liberalism and the Legacy of Mill', *Historical Journal*, 20: 237–54

(1979). *Liberalism and Sociology: L. T. Hobhouse and Political Argument in England, 1880–1914*, Cambridge

(1988). *Matthew Arnold: A Critical Portrait*, Oxford

(1993). *Public Moralists: Political Thought and Intellectual Life in Britain, 1850–1930*, revised edition, Oxford

(2001). 'My Roles and Their Duties: Sidgwick as Philosopher, Professor and Public Moralist', *Proceedings of the British Academy*, 109: 9–50

Collini, Stefan, Whatmore, Richard and Young, Brian (eds.) (2000). *History, Religion, and Culture: British Intellectual History, 1750–1950*, Cambridge

Collini, Stefan, Winch, Donald and Burrow, John (1983). *That Noble Science of Politics: A Study in Nineteenth-Century Intellectual History*, Cambridge

Collins, Henry, and Abramsky, Chimen (1965). *Karl Marx and the British Labour Movement: Years of the First International*, London

Colmer, John (1959). *Coleridge: Critic of Society*, Oxford

(1976). 'Editor's Introduction', in S. T. Coleridge, *On the Constitution of the Church and State* [*The Collected Works of Samuel Taylor Coleridge*, Vol. x], Princeton and London

Colp, Jr., R. (1977). *To be an Invalid: The Illness of Charles Darwin*, Chicago

(1987). '"Confessing a Murder": Darwin's First Revelations about Transmutation', *Isis*, 77: 9–32

Comerford. R. V. (1998). *Fenianism: Irish Politics and Society, 1848–1882*, Dublin

Conan-Doyle, Arthur (1900). *The Great Boer War*, London

Confino, Michael (1973). *Daughter of a Revolutionary: Natalie Herzen and the Bakunin-Nachayev Circle*, Lasalle, IL

Conklin, Alice (1997). *A Mission to Civilise: The Republican Idea of Empire in France and West Africa, 1895–1914*, Stanford

Connelly, William (1989). *Political Theory and Modernity*, Cambridge, MA.

Conner, Clifford D. (2000). *Colonel Despard: The Life and Times of an Anglo-Irish Rebel*, Conshohocken

Connolly, James (1917). *Labour in Ireland. Labour in Irish History. The Reconquest of Ireland*, Dublin

Connolly, S. J. (ed.) (2000). *Political Ideas in Eighteenth Century Ireland*, Dublin

Conry, Y. (1974). *L'introduction du Darwinisme en France au XIXe siècle*, Paris

Conway, S. (1990a). 'Bentham and the Nineteenth century Revolution in Government', in R. Bellamy (ed.), *Victorian Liberalism: Nineteenth-Century Political Thought and Practice*, London

(1990b). 'Bentham, the Benthamites, and the Nineteenth-Century Peace Movement', *Utilitas*, 2: 221–43

(1991). 'John Bowring and the Nineteenth-Century Peace Movement', *Historical Research*, 64: 344–58

Cook, Jonathan (1981). 'Hazlitt: Criticism and Ideology', in David Aers, Jonathan Cook and David Panter, *Romanticism and Ideology: Studies in English Writing, 1765–1830*, London

Coole, D. (1993). *Women in Political Theory: From Ancient Misogyny to Contemporary Feminism*, Hemel Hempstead

Coppa, Frank J. (1998). *The Modern Papacy since 1789*, Harlow

Cornford, James, (1963). 'The Transformation of Conservatism in the Late Nineteenth Century', *Victorian Studies*, 7

Cornwall, Mark (ed.) (1990). *The Last Years of Austria-Hungary: Essays in Political and Military History 1908–1918*, Exeter

Corpus, Revue de Philosophie, No. 47 (2004), *Proudhon*, Paris

Corsi, P. and Weindling, P. (1988). 'Darwinism in Germany, France and Italy', in David Kohn (ed.) *The Darwinian Heritage*, Princeton

Corwin, Edward S. (1950). 'The Impact of the Idea of Evolution on the American Political and Constitutional Tradition', in Stow Persons (ed.), *Evolutionary Thought in America*, New Haven

Cosgrove, Richard A. (1980). *The Rule of Law: Albert Venn Dicey, Victorian Jurist*, London

Cott, N. (1987). *The Grounding of Modern Feminism*, New Haven

Cottier, G, M, M (1959) *L'Athéisme du Jeune Marx: Ses Origines Hégéliennes*, Paris

Cowling, Maurice (1990). *Mill and Liberalism*, 2nd edition, Cambridge

Craig, David M. (2003). 'The Crowned Republic? Monarchy and Anti-monarchy in Britain, 1760–1901', *Historical Journal*, 46: 167–85

(2007a). 'Bagehot's Republicanism', in Andrzej Olechnowicz (ed.), *The Monarchy and the British Nation, 1780 to the Present*, Cambridge

(2007b). *Robert Southey and Romantic Apostasy: Political Argument in Britain, 1780–1840*, Woodbridge

Craig, Gordon (1978). *Germany 1866–1945*, Oxford

Crais, Clifton C. (1991). *White Supremacy and Black Resistance in Pre-Industrial South Africa*, Cambridge

Craiutu, Aurelian (2003). *Liberalism Under Siege: The Political Thought of the French Doctrinaires*, Lanham, MD

Craiutu, Aurelian and Jennings, Jeremy (2004). 'The Third Democracy: Tocqueville's Views of America after 1840', *American Political Science Review*, 3: 391–405

(2009) *Tocqueville on America after 1840: Letters and other Writings*, Cambridge

Crick, Bernard, (1955). 'The Strange Quest for an American Conservatism', *The Review of Politics*, 17: 359–76

Crimmins, J. (1994). 'Bentham's Political Radicalism Reexamined', *Journal of the History of Ideas*, 54: 259–81

Crisp, Roger (1997). *Mill on Utilitarianism*, London

Cromwell, Richard S. (1974). *David Friedrich Strauss and his Place in Modern Thought*, Fair Lawn, NJ

Cromwell, V. (1966). 'Interpretations of Nineteenth-Century Administration: An Analysis', *Victorian Studies*, 9: 245–55

Cronin, Richard (2002). *Romantic Victorians: English Literature, 1824–1840*, Basingstoke

Crook, D. P. (1984). *Benjamin Kidd: Portrait of a Social Darwinist*, Cambridge
    (1994). *Darwinism, War and History: The Debate over the Biology of War from 'The Origin of Species' to the First World War*, Cambridge
    (2007). *Darwin's Coat-Tails: Essays on Social Darwinism*, New York
Crossick, Geoffrey and Jaumain, Serge (eds.) (1999). *Cathedrals of Consumption: The European Department Store, 1850–1939*, Aldershot
Crossley, Ceri (1993). *French Historians and Romanticism: Thierry, Guizot, the Saint-Simonians, Quinet, Michelet*, London
Crowder, George (1991). *Classical Anarchism: The Political Thought of Godwin, Proudhon, Bakunin, and Kropotkin*, Oxford
Crowder, Michael (ed.) (1978). *West African Resistance: The Military Response to Colonial Occupation*, London
Cummins, Ian (1980). *Marx, Engels and National Movements*, London
Curtin, Nancy J. (1994) *United Irishmen: Popular Politics in Ulster and Dublin, 1791–98*, Oxford
Curtis, L. P (1971). *Apes and Angels: the Irishman in Victorian Caricature*, London
Dahl, Robert A. (2003). *How Democratic is the American Constitution?*, 2nd edition, New Haven
Dain, Bruce (2002). *A Hideous Monster of the Mind: American Race Theory in the New Republic*, Cambridge, MA
Dale, P. A. (1989). *In Pursuit of a Scientific Culture: Science, Art and Society in the Victorian Age*, Madison
Daley, Caroline and Nolan, Melanie (1994). 'Between Old Worlds and New: International Feminist Perspectives', in Caroline Daley and Melanie Nolan (eds.), *Suffrage and Beyond: International Feminist Perspectives*, Auckland
Dangerfield, George (1936). *The Strange Death of Liberal England*, London
Dann, Otto and Dinwiddy, John (eds.) (1987). *Nationalism in Europe in the Age of the French Revolution*, London
Darcel, Jean Louis (1988a). 'Maistre and the French Revolution', in Richard Lebrun (ed.), *Maistre Studies*, Lanham
    (1988b). 'Maistre's Libraries', in Richard Lebrun (ed.), *Maistre Studies*, Lanham
D'Arcy, F. A. (1982). 'Charles Bradlaugh and the English Republican Movement 1868–78', *Historical Journal*, 25, London
Dart, Gregory (1999). *Rousseau, Robespierre and English Romanticism*, Cambridge
David, Saul (2002). *The Indian Mutiny 1857*, London
Davidoff, L. (1995). *Worlds Between: Historical Perspectives on Class and Gender*, New York
Davidoff, L. and Hall, Catherine (1987). *Family Fortunes: Men and Women of the English Middle Class, 1780–1850*, London
Davidson, Rondel Van (1988). *Did We Think Victory Great? The Life and Ideas of Victor Considérant*, Lanham
Davies, Norman (1962). *God's Playground: A History of Poland, Vol. II: 1792 to Present*, New York
Davies, Peter (2002). *The Extreme Right in France, 1789 to the Present: From de Maistre to Le Pen*, London
Davis, David Brion (1975). *The Problem of Slavery in Western Culture, 1770–1823*, Ithaca
    (2001). *In the Image of God: Religion, Moral Values, and Our Heritage of Slavery*, New Haven
    (2003). *Challenging the Boundaries of Slavery*, Harvard
Davis, H. W. C. (1973 [1914]). *The Political Thought of Heinrich von Treitschke*, Westport
Davis, R. P. (1974). *Arthur Griffith and Non-Violent Sinn Féin*, Dublin
Davis, Richard (1987). *The Young Ireland Movement*, Dublin

Dawley, Alan (1991). *Struggles for Justice: Social Responsibility and the Liberal State*, Cambridge (2003). *Challenging the Boundaries of Slavery*, Cambridge, MA

Dawson, Jerry (1966). *Friedrich Schleiermacher: The Evolution of a Nationalist*, Texas

Dawson. P. M. S. (1980). *The Unacknowledged Legislator: Shelley and Politics*, Oxford

Day, Douglas (1991). *The Prison Notebooks of Ricardo Flores Magón*, New York

De Man, Henry (1928). *The Psychology of Socialism*, London

De Mattei, Roberto (2004). *Blessed Pius IX*, trans. John Laughland, London

De Sanctis, Alberto (2005). *The 'Puritan' Democracy of Thomas Hill Green: With some Unpublished Writings*, Exeter

De Silva, D. M. (1981). 'Byron's Politics and the History Plays', in Erwin A. Sturzl and James Hogg (eds.), *Byron: Poetry and Politics*, Saltzburg

De Vos, Lu (2000). 'Das Ideal. Anmerkungen zum Spekulativen Begriff des Schönen', *Hegel-Jahrbuch*: 13–19

Deak, Istvan (1979). *The Lawful Revolution. Louis Kossuth and the Hungarians, 1848–1849*, New York

Deane, P. (1989). *The State and the Economic System: An Introduction to the History of Political Economy*, Oxford

Deane, Seamus (1988). *The French Revolution and Enlightenment in England (1789–1832)*, Cambridge, MA

Debout, Simone (1979). *L'Utopie de Charles Fourier*, Paris

Decker, William Merrill (1990). *The Literary Vocation of Henry Adams*, Chapel Hill

Delap, L. (2004). 'The Superwoman: Theories of Gender and Genius in Edwardian Britain', *The Historical Journal*, 47: 101–26

(2005). 'Feminist and Anti-Feminist Encounters in Edwardian Britain', *Historical Research*, 78: 377–99

(2007). *The Feminist Avant-Garde: Transatlantic Encounters of the Early Twentieth Century*, Cambridge

Delbanco, Andrew (1997). *Required Reading: Why Our American Classics Matter*, New York

(2005). *Melville: His World and Work*, New York

DeLeon, David (1978). *The American as Anarchist: Reflections on Indigenous Radicalism*, Baltimore

Deme, Laszlo (1976). *The Radical Left in the Hungarian Revolution of 1848*, Boulder

Demetriou, K. (1999). *George Grote on Plato and Athenian Democracy: A Study in Classical Reception*, Frankfurt

Den Otter, S. (1996). *British Idealism and Social Explanation: A Study in Late Victorian Thought*, Oxford

Denes, Ivan Zoltan, (ed.) (2006). *Liberty and the Search for Identity: Liberal Nationalisms and the Legacy of Empires*, Budapest

Denieffe, Joseph (1906). *A Personal Narrative of the Irish Revolutionary Brotherhood*, New York

Dermenghem, Émile (1979). *Joseph de Maistre, Mystique: Ses Rapports avec le Martinisme, l'Illuminisme, et la Franc–maçonnerie*, Paris

Desai, M. (1979). *Marxian Economics*, Oxford

(2002). *Marx's Revenge: The Resurgence of Capitalism and the Death of Statist Socialism*, London

Desmond, A. and Moore, J. (1991). *Darwin: The Life of a Tormented Evolutionist*, London

Desmond, William (1988). 'Schopenhauer, Art, and the Dark Origin', in Eric v. d. Luft (ed.), *Schopenhauer: New Essays in Honour of His 200th Birthday*, Lewiston

Destler, Chester McArthur (1963). *Henry Demarest Lloyd and the Empire of Reform*, Philadelphia

Detwiler, Bruce (1990). *Nietzsche and the Politics of Aristocratic Radicalism*, Chicago

Deutsch, Karl (1966). *Nationalism and Social Communication*, Cambridge, MA

Devigne, Robert (2006). 'Reforming Reformed Religion: J. S. Mill's Critique of the Enlightenment's Natural Religion', *American Political Science Review*, 100: 15–27

D'Hondt, Jacques (1968a). *Hegel Secret*, Paris

(1968b). *Hegel en son Temps (Berlin 1818–1831)*, Paris

Di Gregorio, M. (1984). *T. H. Huxley's Place in Nature*, Cambridge

Di Scala, S. M. and Mastellone, S. (1998). *European Political Thought, 1815–1980*, Colorado

Diamond, Alan (ed.) (1991). *The Victorian Achievement of Sir Henry Maine*, Cambridge

Diamond, Martin (1957). 'American Political Thought and the Study of Politics: Comment on McCloskey', *American Political Science Review*, 51: 130–4

Dicey, Albert Venn (1905). *Lectures on the Relation between Law and Public Opinion in England During the Nineteenth Century*, London

Dickens, Peter (2000). *Social Darwinism: Linking Evolutionary Thought to Social Theory*, Buckingham

Dickey, Laurence (1987). *Hegel: Religion, Economics, and Politics of Spirit, 1770–1807*, Cambridge

(1993). 'Hegel on Religion and Philosophy', in F. C. Beiser (ed.), *The Cambridge Companion to Hegel*, Cambridge

(1999). 'General Introduction', *Hegel, Political Writings*, Cambridge

Diggins, John Patrick (1984). *The Lost Soul of American Politics: Virtue, Self-Interest, and the Foundations of Liberalism*, New York

(2000). *On Hallowed Ground: Abraham Lincoln and the Foundations of American History*, New Haven

Dijkstra, S. (1992). *Flora Tristan: Feminism in the Age of George Sand*, London

Dijn, Annelien de (2008). *French Political Thought from Montesquieu to Tocqueville: Liberty in a Levelled Society?*, Cambridge

Dikötter, F. (1992). *The Discourse of Race in Modern China*, London

Dinwiddy, J. R. (1975). 'Bentham's Transition to Political Radicalism', *Journal of the History of Ideas*, 36: 683–700

(1992a). 'Conceptions of Revolution in the English Radicalism of the 1790s', in J. R. Dinwiddy, *Radicalism and Reform in Britain, 1780–1850*, London

(1992b). *Radicalism and Reform in Britain, 1780–1850*, London

Dippel, Wolfgang D. (1990). *Wissenschaftsverständnis, Rechtsphilosophie und Vertragslehre im vormärzlichen Konstitutionalismus bei Rotteck und Welcker*, Münster

Dixon, S. (1999). *Modernisation in Russia, 1676–1825*, Cambridge

Dobo, N. and Role, A. (1989). *Bichat: La Vie Fulgurante d'un Génie*, Paris

Dollard, C. L. (2000). 'The Female Surplus: Constructing the Unmarried Woman in Imperial Germany, 1871–1914', Ph.D. dissertation, University of North Carolina

Dolléans, Edouard (1948). *Proudhon*, Paris

Dominick, Raymond H. III (1982). *Wilhelm Liebknecht and the Founding of the German Social Democratic Party*, Chapel Hill

Dominquez, Jorge I. (1980). *Insurrection or Loyalty: The Breakdown of the Spanish American Empire*, Cambridge, MA

Donald, David Herbert (1995). *Lincoln*, New York

Donnachie, Ian (2000). *Robert Owen. Owen of New Lanark and New Harmony*, East Linton

Donner, Wendy (1991). *The Liberal Self: John Stuart Mill's Moral and Political Philosophy*, Ithaca

Donoghue, Denis (2005). *The American Classics*, New Haven

Dooley, Dolores (1996). *Equality in Community: Sexual Equality in the Writings of William Thompson and Anna Doyle Wheeler*, Cork

Dorpalen, Andreas (1957). *Heinrich von Treitschke*, New Haven

Dostian, I. S. (1979). 'Evropeiskaia Utopia V. F. Malinovskogo', *Voprosy Filosofii*, 6: 32–46.

Doty, C. S. (1976). *From Cultural Rebellion to Counter-Revolution: The Politics of Maurice Barrès*, Ohio

Dowe, Dieter, et al. (eds.) (2001). *Europe in 1848: Revolution and Reform*, New York and Oxford

Draper, A. J. (1997). 'Bentham's Theory of Punishment', Ph.D. dissertation, University of London

(2000). 'Cesare Beccaria's Influence on English Discussions of Punishment, 1764–1789', *History of European Ideas*, 26: 177–99

(2001). 'William Eden and Leniency in Punishment', *History of Political Thought*, 22: 106–30

Draper, H. (1977). *Karl Marx's Theory of Revolution*, 2 vols., New York

Draus, Franciszek (1989). 'Burke et les Français', in François Furet and Mona Ozouf (eds.), *The French Revolution and the Creation of Modern Political Culture*, London

Drescher, Seymour (1964). 'Tocqueville's Two Democracies', *Journal of the History of Ideas*, 25: 117–27

(1968). *Dilemmas of Democracy: Tocqueville and Moderation*, Pittsburgh

Drolet, Michael (2003). *Tocqueville, Democracy and Social Reform*, Basingstoke

Droz, Jacques (1949). *L'Allemagne et la Révolution Française*, Paris

(1963). 'Présentation', in Jacques Droz (ed.), *Le Romantisme Politique En Allemagne*, Paris

DuBois, Ellen Carol (1987). 'The Radicalism of the Woman Suffrage Movement', in Anne Phillips (ed.), *Feminism and Equality*, New York, 127–38

(1999 [1978]). *Feminism and Suffrage: The Emergence of an Independent Women's Movement in America, 1848–1869*, with a new Preface, Ithaca

Dugard, John (1989). 'International Terrorism and the Just War', in David C. Rapoport and Yonah Alexander (eds.), *The Morality of Terrorism: Religious and Secular Justifications*, New York

Dumond, D. L. (1961). *Antislavery: The Crusade for Freedom in America*, Ann Arbor

Dunn, Susan (1989). 'Michelet and Lamartine: Regicide, Passion, and Compassion', *History and Theory*, 28: 275–95

Dupuis, G., Georgel, J. and Moreau, J. (1967). *Politique de Chateaubriand*, Paris

Durant, J. R. (1977). 'The Meaning of Evolution: Post-Darwinian Debates on the Significance for Man of the Theory of Evolution, 1858–1908', Ph.D. dissertation, Cambridge

Durant, J. R. (ed.) (1985). *Darwinism and Divinity*, Oxford

Durbin, Evan (1949). *The Politics of Democratic Socialism: An Essay on Social Policy*, London

Duverger, Maurice (ed.) (1980). *Le Concept d'Empire*, Paris

Eagleton, Terry (1990). *The Ideology of the Aesthetic*, Oxford

Eastwood, David (1989). 'Robert Southey and the Intellectual Origins of Romantic Conservatism', *English Historical Review*, 104: 308–31

Eckhardt, Celia Morris (1984). *Fanny Wright: Rebel in America*, Harvard

Eckstein, A. M. (1991). 'Is There a "Hobson–Lenin Thesis" on Late Nineteenth-Century Colonial Expansion?', *Economic History Review*, 44: 297–318

Eddy, J. and D. Schreuder (1998). *The Rise of Colonial Nationalism, 1880–1914*, London

Edwards, P. (1995). 'Liberty and Continuity in the Political Thought of Samuel Taylor Coleridge, 1794–1834', Ph.D. dissertation, University of London

Edwards, Ruth Dudley (1993). *The Pursuit of Reason: The Economist, 1843–1993*, London

Eichner, Hans (1970). *Friedrich Schlegel*, New York

Einaudi, Luca (2001). *Money and Politics: European Monetary Unification and the International Gold Standard, 1865–1873*, Oxford

Bibliography

Eisfeld, Gerhard (1969). *Die Entstehung der Liberalen Parteien in Deutschland 1858–1870*, Hannover

Eisner, Kurt (1906). *Wilhelm Liebknecht: Sein Leben und Wirken*, 2nd edition, Berlin

Eley, Geoff (1991a [1980]). *Reshaping the German Right: Radical Nationalism and Political Change after Bismarck*, Michigan

  (1991b). *Wilhelminismus, Nationalismus, Faschismus. Zur historischen Kontinuität in Deutschland*, Münster

Elkins, Stanley and McKitrick, Eric (1971). 'The Founding Fathers: Young Men of the Revolution', *Political Science Quarterly*, 76(2): 181–216

  (1993). *The Age of Federalism: The Early American Republic, 1788–1800*, New York

Ellis, Joseph J. (1997). *American Sphinx: The Character of Thomas Jefferson*, New York

  (2000). *Founding Brothers: The Revolutionary Generation*, New York

Ellis, P. Berresford and Mac A'Ghobhainn, Seumas (1970). *The Scottish Insurrection of 1820*, London

Elm, Ludwig (1968). 'Deutsche Volkspartei (DtVp) 1868–1910', in Dieter Fricke (ed.), *Die Bürgerlichen Parteien in Deutschland*, 2 vols., Vol. 1, Leipzig

Elster, J. (1985). *Making Sense of Marx*, Cambridge

Eltzbacher, Paul (1908). *Anarchism*, London

Ely, Richard T. (1910). 'The American Economic Association, 1885–1909', *American Economic Association Quarterly*, 3rd series, 11: 47–111

Engelhardt, Dietrich von (1988). 'Romanticism in Germany', in R. Porter and M. Teich (eds.), *Romanticism in National Context*, Cambridge

Engelstein, L. (1992). *The Keys to Happiness: Sex and the Search for Modernity in Fin-de-Siècle Russia*, Ithaca

Englander. D. and O'Day, R. (1995). *Retrieved Riches: Social Investigation in Britain*

Engs, R. C. (2005). *The Eugenics Movement: An Encyclopedia*, London

Epstein, Klaus (1966). *The Genesis of German Conservatism*, Princeton

  (1975 [1966]). *The Genesis of German Conservatism*, 2nd edition, Princeton

Esenwein, George R. (1989). *Anarchist Ideology and the Working-Class Movement in Spain, 1868–1898*, Berkeley

'Essays in Colonial Finance' (1900). *American Economic Association Quarterly*, 3rd series, 1: 393–691

Etzler, John Adolphus (1977). *The Collected Works of John Adolphus Etzler*, ed. Joel Nydahl, Delmar, NJ

Evans, D. (1951). *Social Romanticism in France, 1830–1848*, Oxford

Evans, Richard J. (1977). *The Feminists: Women's Emancipation Movements in Europe, America and Australasia, 1840–1920*, London

  (1987a). *Comrades and Sisters: Feminism, Socialism and Pacifism, 1870–1915*, Brighton

  (1987b). *Rethinking German History: Nineteenth-Century Germany and the Origins of the Third Reich*, London

Evans, R. J. W. and von Strandmann, H. P. (eds.) (2000). *The Revolutions in Europe 1848–1849: From Reform to Reaction*, Oxford

Everett, C. W. (1931). *The Education of Jeremy Bentham*, New York

Everson, S. (ed.) (1996). *Aristotle, The Politics and the Constitution of Athens*, Cambridge

Ewald, F. (1986). *L'État-Providence*, Paris

Faber, Karl-Georg (1978). 'Zur Machttheorie der Politischen Romantik und der Restauration', in Richard Brinkmann (ed.), *Romantik in Deutschland. Ein Interdisziplinäres Symposion*, Stuttgart

Faber, Richard (1987). *Young England*, London

Fadner, Frank (1961). *Seventy Years of Panslavism in Russia: Karazin to Danilevskii, 1800–1870*, Washington, DC

Fanon, Frantz (1969). *The Wretched of the Earth*, Harmondsworth

Fassò, Guico (1974). *Storia della Filosofia del Diritto*, 3 vols., Bologna

Faure, C. (1986). 'The Utopia of the New Woman in the Work of Alexandra Kollontai and its Impact on the French Feminist and Communist Press', in Freidlander *et al.* (eds.), *Women in Culture and Politics*, Bloomington

Feeley, Francis (1991). *The French Anarchist Labour Movement and 'La Vie Ouvrière', 1909–1914*, New York

Fehrenbach, Elisabeth (1986). 'Nation', in Rolf Reichardt and Eberhard Schmitt (eds.), *Handbuch Politisch-sozialer Grundbegriffe in Frankreich 1680–1820*, Heft 7, Munich

Femia, Joseph V. (2001). *Against the Masses: Varieties of Anti-Democratic Thoughts since the French Revolution*, Oxford

Fenton, Steve (2003). *Ethnicity*, Cambridge

  (2006). 'Race and the Nation', in Gerard Delanty and Krishan Kumar (eds.), *The Sage Handbook of Nations and Nationalism*, London

Ferry, Luc (1990). *Homo Aestheticus: L'Invention du Goût à l'Âge Démocratique*, Paris

Fetter, Frank A. (1901). 'The Next Decade of Economic Theory', *American Economic Association Quarterly*, 3rd series, 2: 236–46

Fiala, Andrew G. (2000). 'Aesthetic Education and the Aesthetic State', in William Maker (ed.), *Hegel and Aesthetics*, Albany

Fine, Sidney (1956). *Laissez Faire and the General-Welfare State: A Study of Conflict in American Thought, 1865–1901*, Ann Arbor

Finer, S. E. (1972). 'The Transmission of Benthamite Ideas, 1820–50', in G. Sutherland (ed.), *Studies in the Growth of Nineteenth-century Government*, London

Finley, M. I. (1976). 'Colonies – An Attempt at a Typology', *Transactions of the Royal Historical Society*, 26: 167–88

Finn, Margot (1993). *After Chartism: Class and Nation in English Radical Politics, 1848–1874*, Cambridge

Fischer, George (1958). *Russian Liberals: From Gentry to Intelligentsia*, Cambridge, MA

Fisher, H. A. L. (1911). *The Republican Tradition in Europe*, London

Fisher, Philip (1999). *Still the New World: American Literature in a State of Creative Destruction*, Cambridge, MA

Fishman, Joshua (1973). *Language and Nationalism*, Rowley, MA

Fitzmaurice, Andrew (2007). 'A Genealogy of Terra Nullius', *Australian Historical Review*, April

Fitzsimmons, Michael P. (1987). *The Parisian Order of Barristers and the French Revolution*, Cambridge

Flaig, Egon (1987). 'Ästhetischer Historismus. Zur Ästhetisierung der Historie bei Humboldt und Burckhardt', *Philosophisches Jahrbuch*, 94: 79–95

Flanagan, Frances (2006). 'At Home in the Balkans: Narratives of Care and Responsibility in the Writings of M. E. Durham and H. N. Brailsford', Master's thesis, University of Oxford

Fleming, Marie (1979). *The Anarchist Way to Socialism: Elisée Reclus and Nineteenth Century European Anarchism*, London

  (1982). 'Propaganda by the Deed: Terrorism and Anarchist Theory in Late Nineteenth Century Europe', in Yohah Alexander and Kenneth A. Myers (eds.), *Terrorism in Europe*, London

  (1988). *The Geography of Freedom*, Montreal

Florida, Nancy K. (1995). *Writing the Past, Inscribing the Future. History as Prophecy in Colonial Java*, Durham, NC

Foner, Eric (1970). *Free Soil, Free Labour, Free Men: The Ideology of the Republican Party before the Civil War*, New York

    (1980). *Politics and Ideology in the Age of the Civil War*, New York

    (1988). *Reconstruction: America's Unfinished Revolution, 1863–77*, New York

Forbes, Geraldine (1998). *Positivism in Bengal: A Study in the Transmission and Transformation of an Ideology*, Delhi

Ford, Caroline (1993). *Creating the Nation in Provincial France: Religion and Political Identity in Britanny*, Princeton, NJ

Ford, Franklin L. (1985). *Political Murder: From Tyrannicide to Terrorism*, Cambridge

Forget, Evelyn L. (2001). 'Saint-Simonian Feminism', *Feminist Economics*, 7(1): 79–96

Forrest, D. W. (1974). *Francis Galton. The Life and Work of a Victorian Genius*, London

Fortesque, William (1983). *Alphonse de Lamartine: A Political Biography*, London

Foster, Michael (1935). *The Political Philosophies of Plato and Hegel*, Oxford

Foucault, M. (1966). *Les Mots et les Choses: Une Archéologie des Sciences Humaines*, Paris

    (1971). *The Order of Things: Archaeology of the Human Sciences*, New York

Fouchard, Jean (1989). *The Haitian Maroons*, New York

France, P. (1992). *Politeness and its Discontent: Problems in French Classical Culture*, Cambridge

Francis, E. (2002). *The Secret Treachery of Words: Feminism and Modernism in America*, Minneapolis

Francis, Mark (1992). *Governors and Settlers: Images of Authority in the British Colonies 1820–1860*, London

    (2002). 'The Domestication of the Male? Recent Research on Nineteenth- and Twentieth-Century British Masculinity', *Historical Journal*, 45: 637–52

    (2007). *Herbert Spencer and the Invention of Modern Life*, Ithaca

Francis, Mark and Morrow, J. (1994). *A History of English Political Thought in the Nineteenth Century*, London

Franco, Paul (1999). *Hegel's Philosophy of Freedom*, New Haven

Frank, Joseph (1995). *Dostoevsky: The Miraculous Years, 1865–1871*, Princeton

    (2002). *The Mantle of the Prophet, 1871–1881*, Princeton

Frank, Manfred (1995). 'Philosophical Foundations of Early Romanticism', in Karl Ameriks and Dieter Sturma (eds.), *The Modern Subject*, Albany

Freeden, Michael (1978). *The New Liberalism. An Ideology of Social Reform*, Oxford

    (2005). *Liberal Languages: Ideological Imaginations and Twentieth-Century Progressive Thought*, Princeton

Freeden, Michael (ed.) (1990). *Reappraising J. A. Hobson: Humanism and Welfare*, London

Freitag, Sabine (1998). *Friedrich Hecker: Biographie eines Republikaners*, Stuttgart

Freund, Michael (ed.) (1965). *Der Liberalismus*, Stuttgart

Frick, Jean-Paul (1990). *Auguste Comte ou la République Positive*, Nancy

Friederici, Hans Jürgen (1985). *Ferdinand Lassalle: Eine Politische Biographie*, Berlin

Friedman, Michael H. (1979). *The Making of a Tory Humanist: William Wordsworth and the Idea of Community*, New York

Furet, François (1992). *Marx et La Révolution Française*, Paris

Furet, François (ed.) (1985). *Jules Ferry, Fondateur de la République: Actes du Colloque*, Paris

Furet, François and Ozouf, Mona (eds.) (1989). *The Transformation of Political Culture, 1789–1848*, Oxford

    (1993). *Le Siècle de l'Avènement Républicain*, Paris

Gagnier, Regenia (2000). *On the Insatiability of Human Wants: Economics and Aesthetics in Market Society*, Chicago

Bibliography

Gaillard, J.-M. (l989). *Jules Ferry*, Paris

Gall, Lothar (1975). 'Liberalismus und "Bürgerliche Gesellschaft": Zu Charakter und Entwicklung der Liberalen Bewegung in Deutschland', *Historische Zeitschrift*, 220: 324–56

Gall, Lothar (ed.) (1978). *Liberalismus*, Köln

(1985). *Liberalismus*, 3rd edition, Königstein

(1990). *Stadt und Bürgertum im 19. Jahrhundert*, München

(1993). *Stadt und Bürgertum im Übergang von der Traditionalen zur Modernen Gesellschaft*, München

(1997) *Bürgertum und Bürgerlich-Liberale Bewegung in Mitteleuropa seit dem 18. Jahrhundert*, Historische Zeitschrift, Sonderheft 17, München

Gall, Lothar and Koch, Rainer (eds.) (1981). *Der Europäische Liberalismus im 19. Jahrhundert*, 4 vols., Frankfurt

Gall, Lothar and Langewiesche, Dieter (eds.) (1995). *Liberalismus und Region*, Historische Zeitschrift Beiheft 19, München

Gammon, Martin (2000). 'Modernity and the Crisis of Aesthetic Representation in Hegel's Early Writings', in William Maker (ed.), *Hegel and Aesthetics*, Albany

Garnett, R. G. (1972). *Co-operation and the Owenite Socialist Communities in Britain, 1825–45*, Manchester

Garnett, Robert T. (2003). *Tocqueville Unveiled: The Historian and His Sources for the Old Regime and the Revolution*, Chicago

Garrard, G. (1994). 'Rousseau, Maistre and the Counter-Enlightenment', *History of Political Thought*, 15: 97–120

(1996). 'Joseph de Maistre's Civilisation and its Discontents', *Journal of the History of Ideas*, 57: 429–46

Garvin, Tom (1987). *Nationalist Revolutionaries in Ireland, 1858–1928*, Oxford

Gasman, D. (1971). *The Scientific Origins of National Socialism: Social Darwinism in Ernest Haeckel and the German Monist League*, London

Gaudemet, F. (1904). *Le Code Civil 1804–1904: Livre du Centenaire*, Paris

(1935). *L'Interprétation du Code Civil en France depuis 1804*, Basel

Gay, Peter (1952). *The Dilemma of Democratic Socialism: Eduard Bernstein's Challenge to Marx*, New York

(1994). *The Cultivation of Hatred*, London

Geary, Dick (1987). *Karl Kautsky*, Manchester

(2003). 'The Second International: Socialism and Social Democracy', in Terence Ball and Richard Bellamy (eds.), *The Cambridge History of Twentieth-Century Political Thought*, Cambridge

Geertz, Clifford (2000). *Available Light: Anthropological Reflections on Philosophical Topics*, Princeton

Geggus, David P. (ed.) (2001). *The Impact of the Haitian Revolution in the Atlantic World*, Columbia, SC

Geifman, Anna (1993). *Thou Shalt Kill. Revolutionary Terrorism in Russia, 1894–1917*, Princeton

Gellner, Ernest (2006). *Nations and Nationalism*, 2nd edition, Oxford

Genovese, Eugene (1969). *The World the Slaveholders Made: Two Essays in Interpretation*, New York

(1979). *From Rebellion to Revolution: Afro-American Slave Revolts in the Making of the Modern World*, Baton Rouge

(1988). *The World the Slaveholders Made*, New introduction, Middletown

(1992). *The Slaveholders' Dilemma: Freedom and Progress in Southern Conservative Thought, 1820–1860*, Columbia

(1996). *The Southern Tradition: The Achievement and Limitations of Southern Conservatism*, Cambridge, MA

George, Albert Joseph (1940). *Lamartine and Romantic Unanimism*, New York

(1945). *Pierre-Simon Ballanche: Precursor of Romanticism*, Syracuse

Geppert, Dominik (2008). 'Between Warmongering and International Co-operation: The Popular Press in British–German Relations', in D. Geppert and R. Gerwarth (eds.), *Edwardian Britain and Wilhelmine Germany*, Oxford

Gerson, Gal (2004a). 'Liberalism, Welfare and the Crowd in J. A. Hobson', *History of European Ideas*, 30: 197–215

(2004b). *Margins of Disorder: New Liberalism and the Crisis of the European Consciousness*, Albany, NY

Gethmann-Siefert, Anne-Marie (1981). 'Die Idee des Schönen', in O. Pöggeler *et al.* (eds.), *Hegel in Berlin: Preußische Kulturpolitik und Idealistische Ästhetik*, Berlin

(1983). 'H. G. Hotho: Kunst als Bildungserlebnis und Kunsttheorie in Systematischer Absicht- oder die Entpolitisierte Version der Ästhetischen Erziehung des Menschen', in Otto Pöggeler and A. M. Gethmann-Siefert (eds.), *Kunsterfahrung und Kulturpolitik im Berlin Hegels*, Bonn

(1984). *Die Funktion der Kunst in der Geschichte, Untersuchungen zu Hegels Ästhetik*, Bonn

(1986a). 'Die Rolle der Kunst im Staat', *Hegel-Studien*, Beiheft 27: 69–72

(1986b). 'Einleitung', in A. Gethmann-Siefert and Otto Pöggeler (eds.), *Welt und Wirkung von Hegels Ästhetik*, Bonn, Vols. XI–XIII, XXVIII

(1991). 'Ästhetik oder Philosophie der Kunst', *Hegel-Studien*, 26: 92–110

Gethmann-Siefert, Anne-Marie (ed.) (1992). *Phänomen versus System. Zum Verhältnis von Philosophischer Systematik und Kunsturteil in Hegels Berliner Vorlesungen über Ästhetik oder Philosophie der Kunst*, Bonn

Geuss, Raymond (2002). 'Liberalism and its Discontents', *Political Theory*, 30: 320–38

Geyer, Dietrich (1987). *Russian Imperialism: The Interaction of Domestic and Foreign Policy, 1860–1914*, Leamington Spa

Gibson, Mary (2002). *Born to Crime: Cesare Lombroso and the Origins of Biological Criminology* (Italian and Italian American Studies), Westport, CT

Gide, Charles (1928). *Communist and Co-operative Colonies*, New York

Gill, A. (1974). *Die Polnische Revolution, 1846*, Munich

Gillespie, Frances Elma (1927). *Labor and Politics in England, 1850–1867*, Durham, NC

Gillespie, Michael Patrick (1996). *Oscar Wilde and the Poetics of Ambiguity*, Gainesville, FL

Gilmartin, Kevin (2007). *Writing Against Revolution: Literary Conservatism in Britain, 1790–1832*, Cambridge

Ginneken, J. van (1992). *Crowds, Psychology and Politics, 1871–1899*, Cambridge

Giradet, Raoul (1972). *L'Idée Coloniale en France de 1871 à 1962*, Paris

Glasier, J. Bruce (1919). *The Meaning of Socialism*, London

Glick, T. (ed.) (1972). *The Comparative Reception of Darwinism*, Austin, TX

Gluck, Carol (1985). *Japan's Modern Myths: Ideology in the Late Meiji Period*, Princeton

Godechot, Jacques (1956). *La Grande Nation; l'Expansion Révolutionnaire de la France dans le Monde de 1789 à 1799*, Paris

(1970). *The Counter-Revolution: Doctrine and Action, 1789–1804*, Princeton

(1972). *Counter-Revolution: Doctrine and Action, 1789–1804*, trans. Salvator Attanasio, London

(1995). *Les Constitutions de la France*, Paris

Goldman, Eric (1956). *Rendezvous with Destiny*, New York

Goldman, Lawrence (1999). 'John Ruskin, Oxford, and the British Labour Movement, 1880–1914', in Dinah Birch (ed.), *Ruskin and the Dawn of the Modern*, Oxford

Bibliography

(2000). 'Republicanism, Radicalism and Sectionalism: Land Reform and the Languages of American Working Men, 1820–1860', in Rebecca Starr (ed.), *Articulating America: Fashioning a National Political Culture in Early America*, Maryland

(2002). *Science, Reform and Politics in Victorian Britain: The Social Science Association, 1857–1886*, Cambridge

(2003). 'Civil Society in Nineteenth-Century Britain and Germany: J. M. Ludlow, Lujo Brentano, and the Labour Question', in José Harris (ed.), *Civil Society in British History. Ideas, Identities, Institutions*, Oxford

Goldstein, L. (1991). 'Early Feminist Themes in French Utopian Socialism', in M. C. Horowitz (ed.), *Race, Class and Gender in Nineteenth Century Culture*, New York

Goldstein, Marc A. (1988). *The People in French Counter-revolutionary Thought*, New York

Goldwell, Francis (1918). *Guild Socialism* (n.p.)

Gombin, Richard (1978). *The Radical Tradition*, London

Gooch, G. P. (1913). *History and Historians in the Nineteenth Century*, London

(1927). *Germany and the French Revolution*, London and New York

(1965). *Germany and the French Revolution*, 2nd edn, London

Goodwin, Doris Kearns (2006). *Team of Rivals: The Political Genius of Abraham Lincoln*, New York

Gordon, D. (1994). *Citizens without Sovereignty*, Princeton

Gordon, F. and Cross, Máire (1996). *Early French Feminisms: A Passion for Liberty*, Cheltenham

Gordon-Reed, Annette (2008). *The Hemmingses of Monticello: An American Family*, New York

Gosewinkel, Dieter (2004). 'Rückwirkungen des Kolonialen Rasserechts? Deutsche Staatsangehörigkeit zwischen Rassestaat und Rechtsstaat', in Sebastian Conrad and Jürgen Osterhammel (eds.), *Das Kaiserreich Transnational: Deutschland in der Welt 1871–1914*, Göttingen

Gossman, Lionel (1976). 'Augustine Thierry and Liberal Historiography', *History and Theory*, 15: 3–6.

Gossman, Norbert J. (1962). 'Republicanism in Nineteenth Century England', *International Review of Social History*, 7: 47–60

Goswami, Manu (2004). *Producing India: From Colonial Economy to National Space*, Chicago

Goto, Shigeru (1932–4). *Robert Owen, 1771–1858: A New Bibliographical Study*, 2 vols., Osaka

Gottfried, Paul (1967). 'German Romanticism and Natural Law', *Studies in Romanticism*, 7: 231–42

Gottschalch, Wilfried (1969). 'Ideengeschichte des Sozialismus in Deutschland', in Helga Grebing (ed.), *Geschichte der Sozialen Ideen in Deutschland*, Munich and Vienna

Gougeon, Len (1990). *Virtue's Hero: Emerson, Antislavery, and Reform*, Athens, GA

Gouhier, H. G. (1931). *La Vie d'Auguste Comte*, Paris

(1933–41). *La Jeunesse d'Auguste Comte: La Formation du Positivisme*, 3 vols., Paris

Gould, Andrew C. (1999). *Origins of Liberal Dominance: State, Church and Party in Nineteenth-Century Europe*, Ann Arbor

Gould, Robert (1931). *Gould's History of Freemasonry*, 5 vols., ed. Dudley Wright, London

Graber, Mark (2006). *Dred Scott and the Problem of Constitutional Evil*, Cambridge

Graham, Richard (1972). *Britain and the Onset of Modernisation in Brazil, 1850–1914*, Cambridge

Grainger, J. H. (1979). 'The View from Britain II: the Moralising Island', in E. Kamenka and F. B. Smith (eds.), *Intellectuals and Revolution: Socialism and the Experience of 1848*

Gratieux, A. (1939). *A. S. Khomiakov et le Mouvement Slavophile*, 2 vols., Paris

Gray, John (1983). *Mill on Liberty: a Defence*, London

Gray, Tim S. (1996). *The Political Philosophy of Herbert Spencer: Individualism and Organicism*, Aldershot

Bibliography

Grayling, A. C. (2000). *The Quarrel of the Age: The Life and Times of William Hazlitt*, London

Green, E. H. H. (2002). *Ideologies of Conservatism: Conservative Political Ideas in the Twentieth Century*, Oxford

Green, M. (1989). 'Sympathy and Self-Interest: The Crisis in Mill's Mental History', *Utilitas*, 1: 259–77

Greenstone, J. David (1993). *The Lincoln Persuasion: Remaking American Liberalism*, Princeton

Greg, W. R. (1862). 'Why are Women Redundant?', *National Review*, 14: 433–5

Griffin, Ben (2011). *Feminism, Masculinity and Politics in Victorian Britain*, Cambridge

Griffith, Arthur (1918). *The Resurrection of Hungary*, Dublin

Grimmer-Solem, Eric (2003). *The Rise of Historical Economics and Social Reform in Germany, 1864–1894*, Oxford

Grimmer-Solem, Eric and Romani, Roberto (1998). 'The Historical School, 1870–1900: A Cross-national Reassessment', *History of European Ideas*, 24: 267–99

(1999). 'In Search of Full Empirical Reality: Historical Political Economy, 1870–1900', *European Journal of the History of Economic Thought*, 6: 333–64

Grimsley, Ronald (1973). *The Philosophy of Rousseau*, London

Gross, Jonathan David (2001). *Byron: The Erotic Liberal*, Lanham, MD

Grubar, H. E. (1974). *Darwin on Man: A Psychological Study of Scientific Creativity together with Darwin's Early and Unpublished Notebooks*, London

Gruber, J. W. (1960). *A Conscience in Conflict: The Life of St. George Jackson Mivart*, New York

Guarneri, Carl J. (1991). *The Utopian Alternative: Fourierism in Nineteenth-Century America*, Ithaca

Gubar, S. (1994). 'Feminist Misogyny: Mary Wollstonecraft and the Paradox of "It Takes One to Know One"', *Feminist Studies*, 20: 452–73

Guérin, Daniel (1970). *Anarchism: From Theory to Practice*, trans. M. Klopper, New York

Guillard, Antoine (1915). *Modern Germany and her Historians*, London

Guillaume, James (1985 [1905–10]). *L'Internationale: Documents et Souvenirs*, Paris

Guillaumont, P. (1969). *La Pensée Demo-économique de Jean-Baptiste Say et de Sismondi*, Paris

Guillemin, H. (1946). *Lamartine et la Question Sociale*, Paris

Guillou, Louis Le (1969). 'Politique et Religion: Lamennais et Les Révolution de 1830', in *Romantisme et Politique* (Colloque de l'École Normale Supérieure de Saint-Cloud), Paris

(1992). 'Révolution Française, Rupture ou Continuité le Cas Lamennais', *History of European Ideas*, 14(1): 5–12

Gurian, W. (1947). 'Lamennais', *Review of Politics*, 9: 205–29

Gurr, Ted (1970). *Why Men Rebel*, Princeton

Gurvitch, Georges (1932). *L'Idée du Droit Social*, Paris

Gusdorf, Georges (1978). *Les Sciences Humaines, et la Pensée Occidentale*, 13 vols., Paris

Gustafson, Richard F. (1986). *Leo Tolstoy, Resident and Stranger: A Study in Fiction and Theology*, Princeton

Guyot, Yves (1914). 'Préface', in R. Schüller, *Les Économistes Classiques et Leurs Adversaires. L'Économie Politique et la Politique Sociale depuis Adam Smith*, Paris

Habermas, Jürgen (1987). *The Philosophical Discourse of Modernity: Twelve Lectures*, trans. Frederick Lawrence, Cambridge, MA.

Hacking, Ian (1998). *Mad Travellers: Reflections on the Reality of Transient Mental Illnesses*, Charlottesville

Hagemann, Karen (2002). '*Männlicher Muth und Teutsche Ehre*'. *Nation, Militär und Geschlecht zur Zeit der Antinapoleonischen Kriege Preußens*, Paderborn

Hagen, William (1980). *Germans, Poles, and Jews: the Nationality Conflict in the Prussian East, 1772–1914*, Chicago

Haigh, E. (1984). *Xavier Bichat and the Medical Theory of the Eighteenth Century*, London

Hale, C. A. (1968). *Mexican Liberalism in the Age of Mora, 1821–53*, New Haven

Hales, E. E. Y. (1956). *Mazzini and the Secret Societies: The Making of a Myth*, London

Halévy, Daniel (1913). *La Jeunesse de Proudhon*, Paris

Halévy, Elie (1901–4). *La Formation du Radicalisme Philosophique*, 3 vols., Paris

   (1928). *The Growth of Philosophic Radicalism*, trans. Mary Morris, London

   (1955). *The Growth of Philosophic Radicalism*, trans. Mary Morris, Boston

   (1956). *Thomas Hodgskin*, trans. A. J. Taylor, London

Hall, B. N. (1974). 'The Economic Ideas of Josiah Warren, First American Anarchist', *History of Political Economy*, 6: 94–108.

Hall, Catherine (2002). *Civilising Subjects: Metropole and Colony in the English Imagination, 1830–1867*, Oxford

Hall, Raymond L. (1978). *Black Separatism in the United States*, Hanover, NH

Halldenius, Lena (2007). 'The Primacy of Right: On the Triad of Liberty, Equality, and Virtue in Wollstonecraft's Political Thought', *British Journal for the History of Philosophy*, 15: 75–99

Hallowell, John (1950). *Main Currents in Political Thought*, New York

Hamburg, Gary (1992). *Boris Chicherin and Early Russian Liberalism, 1828–1866*, Stanford

Hamburger, Jean (1988). *Monsieur Littré*, Paris

Hamburger, Joseph (1965). *Intellectuals in Politics: John Stuart Mill and the Philosophic Radicals*, New Haven and London

   (1999). *John Stuart Mill on Liberty and Control*, Princeton

Hamilton, S. and Schroeder, J. (2010). 'Nineteenth-Century Feminisms: Press and Platform', *Nineteenth-Century Gender Studies*, 6(2)

Hanisch, Ernst von (1978). 'Der "vormoderne" Antikapitalismus der Politischen Romantik. Des Beispiel Adam Müller', in Richard Brinkmann (ed.), *Romantik in Deutschland. Ein Interdisziplinäres Symposion*, Stuttgart

Hansen, J. (ed.) (1919). *Rheinische Briefe und Akten zur Geschichte der Politischen Bewegung 1830–1850*, Vol. 1, Essen

Hanson, Russell L. (1985). *The Democratic Imagination in America: Conversations with our Past*, Princeton

Hardie, James Keir (1907). *From Serfdom to Socialism*, London

   (n.d.). *Keir Hardie's Speeches and Writings*, London

Hardimon, Michael (1994). *Hegel's Social Philosophy*, Cambridge

Harding, Anthony John (1986). *Coleridge and the Inspired Word*, Kingston and Montreal

Harding, Walter (1952). 'South Carolina vs. the United States', in Daniel Aaron (ed.), *America in Crisis: Fourteen Crucial Episodes in American History*, New York

   (1982). *The Days of Henry Thoreau*, Princeton

Hardy, Deborah (1977). *Petr Tkachev: The Critic as Jacobin*, Seattle and London

   (1987). *Land and Freedom: The Origins of Russian Terrorism, 1876–1879*, New York

Harp, Gillis J. (1995). *Positivist Republic: Auguste Comte and the Reconstruction of American Liberalism, 1865–1920*, Pennsylvania

Harré, Rom (2003). 'Positivist Thought in the Nineteenth Century', in Thomas Baldwin (ed.), *The Cambridge History of Philosophy, 1870–1945*, Cambridge

Harris, David (1966). *Socialist Origins in the United States: American Forerunners of Marx, 1817–32*, Assen

Harris, E. (1932). *Lamartine et le Peuple*, Paris

Harris, H. S. (1972). *Hegel's Development: Toward the Sunlight, 1770–1801*, Oxford

   (1993). 'Hegel's Intellectual Development to 1807', in F. C. Beiser (ed.), *The Cambridge Companion to Hegel*, Cambridge

Harris, Horton (1982). *David Friedrich Strauss and His Theology*, Cambridge

Harris, Jose (1972). *Unemployment and Politics: A Study in English Social Policy, 1886–1914*, Oxford

(1993). *Private Lives, Public Spirit: A Social History of Britain, 1870–1914*, Oxford

(2004a) 'Nationality, Rights and Virtue', in R. Bellamy (ed.), *Languages of European Citizenship: Rights, Belonging and Participation in Eleven Nation States*, Basingstoke

(2004b). 'Victorian Interpretations of Thomas Hobbes', in P. Ghosh and L. Goldman (eds.), *Politics and Culture in Victorian Britain*. Oxford

Harris, Jose (ed.) (2003). *Civil Society in British History: Ideas, Identities, Institutions*, Oxford

Harris, Jose, Gerwarth, Robert and Nehring, Holger (eds.) (2008). 'Constitutions, Civility, and Violence in European history from the Mid-eighteenth Century to the Present', *Journal of Modern European History*, 6(1)

Harrison, Brian (1978). *Separate Spheres: The Opposition to Women's Suffrage in Britain*, London

(1982). 'The Act of Militancy: Violence and the Suffragettes, 1904–1914', in *Peaceable Kingdom: Stability and Change in Modern Britain*, Oxford

Harrison, J. F. C. (1969). *Robert Owen and the Owenites in Britain and America*, London

Harrison, P. G. (2000). *Connecting Links: The British and American Woman Suffrage Movements, 1900–1914*, Connecticut

Harrison, Royden (1959). 'E. S. Beesly and Karl Marx', *International Review of Social History*, 4: 22–58; 208–38.

(1962). 'The 10 April of Spencer Walpole: The Problem of Revolution in Relation to Reform, 1865–1867', *International Review of Social History*, 7: 354–6

(1965). *Before the Socialists: Studies in Labour and Politics 1861–1881*, London

(1983). *Bentham*, London

Harrold, Charles Frederick (1963 [1934]). *Carlyle and German Thought: 1819–1834*, Hamden, CT

Hart, H. L. A. (1982). *Essays on Bentham, Studies in Jurisprudence and Political Theory*, Oxford

Hart, J. (1965). 'Nineteenth-Century Social Reform: A Tory Interpretation of History', *Past and Present*, 31: 39–61

Hart, John M. (1978). *Anarchism and the Mexican Working Class, 1860–1931*, Austin

Hartz, Louis (1952). 'South Carolina vs. the United States', in Daniel Aaron (ed.), *America in Crisis: Fourteen Crucial Episodes in American History*, New York

(1955). *The Liberal Tradition in America: An Interpretation of American Political Thought Since the Revolution*, New York

Harvey, R. H. (1949). *Robert Owen: Social Idealist*, Berkeley

Harvie, Christopher (1976). *The Lights of Liberalism: University Liberals and the Challenge of Democracy, 1860–86*, London

Haubtmann, Pierre (1969). *P.-J. Proudhon: Genèse d'un Anti-Théiste*, Paris

(1982). *Pierre-Joseph Proudhon: Sa Vie et Sa Pensée (1809–1949)*, Paris

Haupt, Heinz-Gerhard and Langewiesche, Dieter (eds.) (2001). *Nation und Religion in der Deutsche Geschichte*, Frankfurt and New York

Hause, Stephen C. and Kenney, Anne R. (1984). *Women's Suffrage and Social Politics in the French Third Republic*, Princeton

Havránek, Jan (2004). 'Bohemian Spring 1848 – Conflict of Loyalties and its Picture in Historiography', in Axel Körner (ed.), *1848: A European Revolution: International Ideas and National Memories of 1848*, London

Hawkins, Angus (1989). '"Parliamentary Government" and Victorian Political Parties, c.1830–1880', *English Historical Review*, 104: 638–69

Hawkins, Mike (1997). *Social Darwinism in European and American Thought 1860–1945: Nature as Model and Nature as Threat*, Cambridge

Hayek, F. A. von (1934). 'Carl Menger', in Carl Menger, *Grundsätze der Volkswirthschaftslehre*, London
(1952). *The Counter-Revolution of Science: Studies on the Abuse of Reason*, Glencoe
Hayward, J. E. S. (1959). 'Solidarity: The Social History of an Idea in Nineteenth Century France', *International Review of Social History*, 4: 17–33
(1960). 'Solidarist Syndicalism: Durkheim and Duguit', *Sociological Review*, 8: 17–33; 185–202
(1961). 'The Official Social Philosophy of the French Third Republic: Leon Bourgeois and Solidarism', *International Review of Social History*, 6: 19–48
(1991). *After the French Revolution: Six Critics of Democracy and Nationalism*, London
(2007). *Fragmented France: Two Centuries of Disputed Identity*. Oxford
Hazareesingh, Sudhir (1998). *From Subject to Citizen: The Second Empire and the Emergence of Modern French Democracy*, Princeton
(2001). *Intellectual Founders of the Republic: Five Studies in Nineteenth-Century French Republican Political Thought*, Oxford
Hazareesingh, Sudhir and Wright, Vincent (2001). *Francs-maçons sous le Second Empire: les Loges Provinciales du Grand-Orient à la Veille de la Troisième République*, Rennes
Head, B. W. (1985). *Ideology and Social Science: Destutt de Tracy and French Liberalism*, The Hague
Heidegger, Martin (1991). *Nietzsche*, 2 vols. in 1, trans. David Farrell Krell, San Francisco
Heimpel, Hermann (1962). *Zwei Historiker: Friedrich Christoph Dahlmann und Jacob Burckhardt*, Göttingen
Helfer, Martha (1990). 'Herder, Fichte, and Humboldt's "Thinking and Speaking"', in Kurt Mueller-Vollmer (ed.), *Herder Today*, Berlin
Heller, Hermann (1921). *Hegel und der Nationale Machtstaatsgedanke in Deutschland*, Leipzig
Helmstadter, Richard J. (1985). 'Conscience and Politics: Gladstone's First Book', in Bruce L. Kinzer (ed.), *The Gladstonian Turn of Mind: Essays Presented to J. B. Conacher*, Toronto
Helsinger, E., *et al.* (1983). *The Woman Question: Society and Literature in Britain and America, 1837–1883*, Manchester
Henckmann, Wolfhart (1990). 'Symbolische und allegorische Kunst bei K.W.F. Solger', in Walter Jaeschke and Helmut Holzhey (eds.), *Früher Idealismus und Frühromantik. Der Streit um die Grundlagen der Ästhetik (1795–1805)*, Hamburg
Henderson, Willie (2000). *John Ruskin's Political Economy*, London
Hendrix, G. (1962). *Das Politische Weltbild Friedrich Schlegels*, Bonn
Henrich, Dieter (1974). 'Zur Aktualität von Hegels Ästhetik', *Hegel-Studien*, Beiheft 11: 295–301
(1983). 'Einleitung' to *Philosophie des Rechts: Die Vorlesung von 1819/20 in einer Nachschrift*, Frankfurt
(2003). *Between Kant and Hegel: Lectures on German Idealism*, ed. David Pacini, Cambridge, MA
Henry, Robert Mitchell (1920). *The Evolution of Sinn Fein*, Dublin
Hepner, Benoît-P. (1950). *Bakounine et le Panslavisme Révolutionnaire*, Paris
Herrmann, Ursula and Emmrich, Volker (eds.) (1989). *August Bebel: Eine Biographie*, Berlin
Herwig, Holger H. (1973). *The German Naval Officer Corps: A Social and Political History, 1890–1918*, Oxford
Herzfeld, Hans (1938). *Johannes von Miquel. Sein Anteil am Ausbau des Deutschen Eiches*, 2 vols., Detmold
Hewitson, Mark (2006). 'Conclusion', in T. Baycroft and M. Hewitson, *What is a Nation? Europe, 1789–1914*, Oxford

Hewitt, Nancy (2010). 'From Seneca Falls to Suffrage? Reimagining a "Master" Narrative in U.S. Women's History', in Nancy Hewitt (ed.), *No Permanent Waves: Recasting Histories of U.S. Feminism*, Rutgers

Hewitt, Regina (1997). *The Possibilities of Society: Wordsworth, Coleridge, and the Sociological Viewpoint of English Romanticism*, Albany, NY

Heyderhoff, Julius (ed.) (1925). *Deutscher Liberalismus im Zeitalter Bismarcks*, 2 vols., Bonn

Higonnet, Patrice (1988). *Sister Republics: The Origins of French and American Republicanism*, Cambridge, MA

Hillquit, Morris (1903). *History of Socialism in the United States*, London

Hilton, Boyd (1988). *The Age of Atonement: The Influence of Evangelicalism on Social and Economic Thought, 1795–1865*, Oxford

Hilton, Tim (1985). *John Ruskin: The Early Years 1819–1859*, New Haven and London

Himmelfarb, Gertrude (1952). *Victorian Minds*, London

(1959). *Darwin and the Darwinian Revolution*, New York

(1984). *The Idea of Poverty*, New York

(1990). *On Liberty and Liberalism: The Case of John Stuart Mill*, San Francisco

Hinsley, F. H. (1986). *Sovereignty*, Cambridge

Hinton, Thomas R. (1951). *Liberation, Nationalism and the German Intellectuals*, Cambridge

Hirschhausen, Ulrich von and Leonhard, Jörn (eds.) (2001). *Nationalismen in Europa. West- und Osteuropa im Vergleich*, Göttingen

Hitchins, Keith (1969). *The Rumanian National Movement in Transylvania, 1780–1849*, Cambridge, MA

(1977). *Orthodoxy and Nationalism: Andreu Saguna and the Rumanians of Transylvania, 1846–1873*, Cambridge, MA

Hoagwood, Terence Allan (1988). *Skepticism and Ideology: Shelley's Political Prose and Its Philosophical Context from Bacon to Marx*, Iowa City

Hobsbawm, Eric (1959). *Primitive Rebels: Studies in Archaic Forms of Social Movement in the 19th and 20th Centuries*, New York

(1972). *Bandits*, Harmondsworth

(1975). *The Age of Capital, 1848–1875*, London

(1987). *The Age of Empire, 1875–1914*, London

(1990). *Nations and Nationalism since 1780: Programme, Myth, Reality*, Cambridge

Hobsbawm, Eric and Rudé, George (1973). *Captain Swing*, Harmondsworth

Hoffman, Robert (1972). *Revolutionary Justice: The Social and Political Theory of P.-J. Proudhon*, Urbana

Hoffmeister, Gerhart (1989). 'Rhetorics of Revolution in Western European Romanticism', in Gerhart Hoffmeister (ed.), *The French Revolution and the Age of Goethe*, Hildesheim

Hofmann, Hasso (1971). 'Jacob Burckhardt und Friedrich Nietzsche als Kritiker des Bismarckreiches', *Der Staat* 4: 433–53

Hofstadter, A. (1974). 'Die Kunst: Tod und Verklärung', *Hegel-Studien*, Beiheft 11: 271–85

Hofstadter, Richard (1955a). *The Age of Reform from Bryan to FDR*, New York

(1955b [1944]). *Social Darwinism in American Thought*, New York

(1968). *The Progressive Historians: Turner, Beard, Parrington*, New York

(1969). *The Idea of a Party System: The Rise of Legitimate Opposition in the United States*, Berkeley

(1973 [1948]). *The American Political Tradition and the Men Who Made It*, Twenty-fifth Anniversary Edition, New York

(1992 [1955, 1944]). *Social Darwinism in American Thought*, intro. Eric Foner, Boston

Holcombe, L. (1983). *Wives and Property: Reform of the Married Women's Property Law in Nineteenth-Century England*, Toronto and Buffalo

Hollander, Samuel (2005). *Jean-Baptiste Say and the Classical Canon in Economics: The British Connection in French Classicism*, London

Hollis, Martin (1983). 'The Social Liberty Game', in A. Phillips Griffiths (ed.), *Of Liberty*, Cambridge

Holmes, Stephen (1984). *Benjamin Constant and the Making of Modern Liberalism*, New Haven
 (1993). *The Anatomy of Antiliberalism*, Cambridge, MA

Holstein, Günther (1972). *Die Staatsphilosphie Schleiermacher's*, Aalen

Holt, Peter M. (1970). *The Mahdist State in the Sudan, 1881–1898*, Oxford

Holton, S. S. (1986). *Feminism and Democracy: Women's Suffrage and Reform Politics in Britain, 1900–1918*, Cambridge

Holzheuer, Walter (1972). *Karl Kautsky's Werk als Weltanschauung*, Munich

Honan, Park (1981). *Matthew Arnold: A Life*, London

Honold, Alexander (2004). 'Ausstellung des Fremden – Menschen und Völkerschau um 1900', in Sebastian Conrad and Jürgen Oesterhammel (eds.), *Das Kaiserreich Transnational*. Göttingen

Hont, Istvan (1989). 'Negative Community: The Natural Law Heritage from Pufendorf to Marx', *John N. Olin Programme in the History of Political Culture 1989*, Chicago
 (2005). *Jealousy of Trade: International Competition and the Nation-State in Historical Perspective*, Harvard

Hont, I. and Ignatieff, M. (eds.) (1983). *Wealth and Virtue: The Shaping of Political Economy in the Scottish Enlightenment*, Cambridge

Hook, Sidney (1970). 'Hegel Rehabilitated?', in Walter Kaufmann (ed.), *Hegel's Political Philosophy*, New York

Hoover, Jeffrey (1989). 'The Foundations of the Communitarian State in the Thought of Friedrich Schleiermacher', *History of Political Thought*, 10: 295–312
 (1990). 'Friedrich Schleiermacher's Theory of the Limited Communitarian State', *Canadian Journal of Philosophy*, 20: 241–60

Hostetter, Richard (1958). *The Italian Socialist Movement, Vol. I: Origins (1860–1882)*, Princeton

Houghton, Walter E. (ed.) (1966). *The Wellesley Index to Victorian Periodicals, 1824–1900*, 5 vols., Toronto and London

Hourani, Albert (1970). *Arabic Thought in the Liberal Age, 1789–1939*, Oxford

Howard, Thomas Albert (2006). *Protestant Theology and the Making of the Modern German University*, Oxford

Howe, Anthony (1997). *Free Trade and Liberal England, 1846–1946*, Oxford

Howe, Anthony and Morgan, Simon (eds.) (2006). *Rethinking Nineteenth-Century Liberalism: Richard Cobden Bicentenary Essays*, Aldershot

Howe, Daniel Walker (2007). *What Hath God Wrought: The Transformation of America, 1815–1848* (Oxford History of the United States), New York

Hroch, Miroslav (1985). *Social Preconditions of National Revival in Europe: A Comparative Analysis of the Social Composition of Patriotic Groups among the Smaller European Nations*, Cambridge
 (1996). 'From National Movement to the Fully-Formed Nation: The Nation-Building Process in Europe', in Gopal Balakrishnan (ed.), *Mapping the Nation*, London

Hubert, Ernst Rudolf (1937). *Friedrich Christoph Dahlmann und die Deutsche Verfassungsbewegung*, Hamburg

Hubert, Ernst Rudolf (ed.) (1961). *Dokumente zur Deutschen Verfassungsgeschichte*, Vol. I, Stuttgart
 (1986). *Dokumente zur Deutschen Vertassungsgeschichte*, Vol. II, Stuttgart.

Hübinger, Gangolf (1994). *Kulturprotestantismus und Politik. Zum Verhältnis von Liberalismus und Protestantismus im Wilhelminischen Deutschland*, Tübingen

Hubmann, Gerald (1997). *Ethische Überzeugung und Politische Gesinnungsethik: Jakob Fries und die Deutsche Tradition der Gesinnungsethik*, Heidelberg

Huet, Marie Helene (2000). 'Chateaubriand and the Politics of (Im)mortality', *Diacritics*, 30: 28–39

Hughan, Jessie Wallace (1912). *American Socialism of the Present Day*, London

Hughes, H. Stuart (1958). *Consciousness and Society: The Reorientation of European Social Thought 1890–1930*, London and New York

   (1979a [1958]). *Consciousness and Society: The Reorientation of European Social Thought, 1890–1930*, Brighton

   (1979b). *The United States and Italy*, Harvard

Hughes, Spencer Leigh (1918). *Press, Platform and Parliament*, London

Hulliung, Mark (2002). *Citizens and Citoyens: Republicans and Liberals in America and France*, Cambridge, MA

Hume, L. J. (1967). 'Jeremy Bentham and the Nineteenth-Century Revolution in Government', *Historical Journal*, 10: 361–75

Hundert, Edward (1998). 'Performing the Passions in Commercial Society: Bernard Mandeville and the Theatricality of Eighteenth-Century Thought', in Kevin Sharpe and Steven Zwicker (eds.), *Refiguring Revolutions: Aesthetics and Politics from the English Revolution to the Romantic Revolution*, Berkeley

Hunley, J. D. (1991). *The Life and Thought of Friedrich Engels*, New Haven and London

Hunt, John Dixon (1982). *The Wider Sea: A Life of John Ruskin*, New York

Hunt, R. N. (1975). *The Political Ideas of Marx and Engels, Vol. I: Marxism and Totalitarian Democracy, 1818–1850*, London

   (1984). *The Political Ideas of Marx and Engels*, Vol. II: *Classical Marxism, 1830–1895*, London

Huntingdon, Samuel P. (1957). 'Conservatism as an Ideology', *American Political Science Review*, 51(2): 454–73

Hutchinson, John (2005). *Nations as Zones of Conflict*, London

Hutchison, T. W. (1953). *A Review of Economic Doctrines, 1870–1929*, Oxford

Hutton, Patrick (1981). *The Cult of the Revolutionary Tradition: The Blanquists in French Politics, 1864–1893*, Berkeley

Hyams, Edward (1969). *Killing No Murder: A Study of Assassination as a Political Means*, London

   (1974). *Terrorists and Terrorism*, London

Hyde, Lewis (2002). 'Henry Thoreau, John Brown, and the Problem of Prophetic Action', *Raritan* (Fall): 125–44

Iggers, Georg G. (1958). *The Cult of Authority: The Political Philosophy of the Saint-Simonians*, The Hague

Iggers, Georg (ed.) (1972). *The Doctrine of Saint-Simon: An Exposition. First Year, 1828–1829*, New York

Ikeda, S., Otonashi, M. and Shigemori, T. (1989). *A Bibliographical Catalogue of the Works of Jeremy Bentham*, Tokyo

Immerwahr, Raymond (1970). 'The Word "*Romantisch*" and its History', in Siegbert Prawer (ed.), *The Romantic Period in Germany*, London

Ireson, J. C. (1969). *Lamartine: A Revaluation* (University of Hull Occasional Papers in Modern Languages), Hull

Irvine, William (1939). *Walter Bagehot*, London

Isenberg, N. (1998). *Sex and Citizenship in Antebellum America*, Chapel Hill

Izenberg, Gerald W. (1992). *Impossible Individuality: Romanticism, Revolution, and the Origins of Modern Selfhood*, Princeton

(1998). 'The Politics of Song in Wordsworth's *Lyrical Ballads*', in Kevin Sharpe and Steven Zwicker (eds.), *Refiguring Revolutions: Aesthetics and Politics from the English Revolution to the Romantic Revolution*, Berkeley

Jabarri, Eric (1999). 'Pierre Laroque and the Origins of French Social Security', Oxford D.Phil. thesis

Jackson, Anna and Jaffer, Amin (eds.) (2004). *Encounters: The Meeting of Asia and Europe 1500–1800*, London

Jackson, Ben (2004). 'The Uses of Utilitarianism: Social Justice, Welfare Economics and British Socialism, 1931–48', *History of Political Thought*, 25(3)

(2007). *Equality and the British Left: A Study in Progressive Political Thought, 1900–64*, Manchester

Jacobs, J. (2002). *The Voice of Harriet Taylor Mill*, Bloomington, IN

Jaeschke, Walter (1990). 'Ästhetische Revolution: Stichworte zur Einführung', in Walter Jaeschke and Helmut Holzhey (eds.), *Früher Idealismus und Frühromantik. Der Streit um die Grundlagen der Ästhetik (1795–1805)*, Hamburg

Jaffa, Harry V. (1959). *Crisis of the House Divided*, Garden City

(2000). *A New Birth of Freedom*, Lanham, MD

Jaffe, Hosea (1994). *European Colonial Despotism: A History of Oppression and Resistance in South Africa*, London

Jaffé, William and Walker, Donald A. (1983). *William Jaffé's Essays on Walras*, Cambridge

Jahn, Beate (2005) 'Barbarian Thoughts: Imperialism in the Philosophy of John Stuart Mill', *Review of International Studies*, 31: 599–618

Jähnig, Dieter (1979). 'Jacob Burckhardts Bedeutung für die Ästhetik', *Deutsche Vierteljahrschrift für Literaturwissenschaft und Geistesgeschichte*, 53: 173–90

Jaksic, I. (2001). *Andres Bello, Scholarship and Nation-Building in Nineteenth-Century Latin America*, Cambridge

James, C. L. R. (1963 [1938]). *The Black Jacobins: Toussaint l'Ouverture and the San Domingo Revolution*, New York

(1989). *The Black Jacobins: Toussaint l'Ouverture and the San Domingo Revolution*, London

James, M. (1986). 'Bentham's Democratic Theory at the Time of the French Revolution', *The Bentham Newsletter*, 10: 5–16

Janaway, Christopher (1997). 'Schopenhauer', in Roger Scruton *et al.*, *German Philosophers: Kant, Hegel, Schopenhauer, Nietzsche* (Past Masters), Oxford

Jarausch, Konrad A. and Jones, Larry E. (eds.) (1990). *In Search of a Liberal Germany*, Oxford

Jardin, André (1985). *Histoire du Libéralisme Politique de la Crise de l'Absolutisme à la Constitution de 1875*, Paris

(1988). *Tocqueville: A Biography*, New York

Jaszi, Oscar and Lewis, John D. (1957). *Against the Tyrant: The Tradition and Theory of Tyrannicide*, Glencoe, IL

Jaume, Lucien (1997). *L'Individu Effacé ou le Paradoxe du Libéralisme Français*, Paris

(2008). *Tocqueville*, Paris

Jay, Mike (2004). *The Unfortunate Colonel Despard*, London

Jenkins, Roy (1958). *Sir Charles Dilke: A Victorian Tragedy*, London

Jenkyns, Richard (1980). *The Victorians and Ancient Greece*, Oxford and Harvard

Jennings, Jeremy (1990). *Syndicalism in France: A Study of Ideas*, London and New York

Jessop, Ralph (1997). *Carlyle and Scottish Thought*, Basingstoke

John, Michael (1989). *Politics and Law in Late-Nineteenth-Century Germany: The Origins of the Civil Code*, Oxford

Johnpoll, Bernard (1981). *The Impossible Dream: The Rise and Demise of the American Left*, London

Johnpoll, Bernard K. and Klehr, Harvey (eds.) (1986). *Biographical Dictionary of the American Left*, New York

Johnson, Christopher (1974). *Utopian Communism in France: Cabet and the Icarians, 1839–1851*, Ithaca

Johnson, David (1974). *Regency Revolution: The Case of Arthur Thistlewood*, Salisbury

Johnson, Douglas (1963). *Guizot: Aspect of French History, 1787–1874*, London

  (1966). *France and the Dreyfus Affair*, London

Johnston, R. M. (1904). *The Napoleonic Empire in Southern Italy and the Rise of the Secret Societies*, 2 vols., London

Joll, James (1964). *The Anarchist*, New York

Jones, David J. V. (1985). *The Last Rising: The Newport Insurrection of 1839*, Oxford

Jones, Greta (1980). *Social Darwinism and English Thought*. Brighton

Jones, Greta and Peel, Robert A. (eds.) (2004). *Herbert Spencer: The Intellectual Legacy*, London

Jones, H. S. (1993). *The French State in Question: Public Law and Political Argument in the French Third Republic*, Cambridge

  (2000). *Victorian Political Thought*, London

Jones, Peter d'A. (1968). *The Christian Socialist Revival 1877–1914*, Princeton

  (1991). *Henry George and British Socialism*, London

Jordan, Winthrop (1968). *White Over Black: American Attitudes Toward the Negro, 1550–1812*, Baltimore

Jordanova, L. (1984). *Lamarck*, Oxford

Josephson, Matthew (1963 [1934]). *The Robber Barons*, New York

'Julius S. Scott on John Brown Russworm, Africans to Americans', www.pbs.org/wgbh/aia/part 3/3i3131.html

Julliard, Jacques (1988). *Autonomie Ouvrière: Études sur le Syndicalisme d'Action Directe*, Paris

Jullien, Jean (1926). *Saint-Simon et le Socialisme*, Bordeaux

Kadish, Alon and Tribe, Keith (1993). *The Market for Political Economy: The Advent of Economics in British University Culture, 1850–1905*, London

Kammen, Michael (1997). 'The Problem of American Exceptionalism: A Reconsideration', in Kammen, *In the Past Lane: Historical Perspectives on American Culture*, New York

Kane, P. V. (1960–8). *A History of Dharmasastra*, 8 vols., Pune

Kapila, Shruti (2011). 'Gandhi before Mahatma', *Public Culture*, forthcoming

Kapila, Shruti (ed.) (2009). *An Intellectual History for India*, New Delhi, reprint of *Modern Intellectual History*, 4(1) (April 2007)

Kaplan, F. (1983). *Thomas Carlyle: A Biography*, Cambridge

Kaplan, Temma (1977). *The Anarchists of Andalusia, 1868–1903*, Princeton

Karkama, Pertti (2003). 'Mythische Geschichte und Nationale Identität. Die Bedeutung *Kalevalas* in Finnland', unpublished communication, Convent für europäische Philosophie und Ideengeschichte, Oulu, Finland, August

Karl, Barry D. (1974). *Charles E. Merriam and the Study of Politics*, Chicago

Kassner, Thorsten (2001). *Der Steuerreformer Johannes von Miquel. Leben und Werk. Zum 100. Todestag des Preußichen Finanzministers. Ein Beitrag*, Osnabrück

Kateb, George (1992). *The Inner Ocean: Individualism and Democratic Culture*, Ithaca

  (1995). *Emerson and Self-Reliance*, Thousand Oaks

  (2003). 'Undermining the Constitution', *Social Research* (Summer): 579–604

Katznelson, Ira (2003). 'The Possibilities of Analytical Political History', in Meg Jacobs *et al.* (eds.), *The Democratic Experiment: New Directions in American Political History*, Princeton

Kauder, Emil (1965). *A History of Marginal Utility Theory*, Princeton

Kaufmann, Eric (ed.) (2004). *Rethinking Ethnicity: Majority Groups and Dominant Minorities*, London

Kaufmann, M. (1906). *Socialism and Modern Thought*, London

Kazin, Michael (2006). *A Godly Hero: The Life of William Jennings Bryan*, New York

Keach, William (1996). 'Shelley and the Constitution of Political Authority', in Betty T. Bennett and Stuart Curran (eds.), *Shelley: Poet and Legislator of the World*, Baltimore

Kedourie, Elie (1966). *Nationalism*, 2nd edition, London

Keller, Albert G. (1933). *Reminiscences of William Graham Sumner*, New Haven

Kelley, Donald R. (1978). 'The Metaphysics of Law: An Essay on the Very Young Marx', *American Historical Review*, 83: 350–67; reprinted in Kelley (1984), *History, Law and the Human Sciences*, London

  (1984a). *Historians and the Law in Post Revolutionary France*, Princeton

  (1984b). 'The Science of Anthropology: An Essay on the Very Old Marx', *Journal of the History of Ideas*, 45: 245–62

  (1987). 'Ancient Verses on New Ideas: Legal Tradition and the French Historical School', *History and Theory*, 26: 319–38

  (1990). '"Second Nature": The Idea of Law in European Law, Society, and Culture', in A. Grafton and A. Blair (eds.), *The Transmission of Culture in Early Modern Europe*, Philadelphia

  (1991). *The Human Measure: Social Thought in the Western Legal Tradition*, Cambridge, MA

  (1994). 'Men of Law and the French Revolution', in Adrianna E. Bakos (ed.), *Politics, Ideology and the Law in Early Modern Europe*, Rochester

  (2001). 'What Pleases the Prince', *History of Political Thought*, 23: 288–302

  (2003). *Fortunes of History: Historical Inquiry from Herder to Huizinga*, New Haven

Kelley, Donald R. and Smith, Bonnie G. (1984). 'What Was Property? Legal Dimensions of the Social Question in France 1789–1848', *American Philosophical Society, Proceedings*: 200–30

Kelly, Aileen (1982). *Mikhail Bakunin: A Study in the Psychology and Politics of Utopianism*, Oxford

  (1998). *Towards Another Shore: Russian Thinkers between Necessity and Chance*, New Haven and London

Kelly, Alfred (1981). *The Descent of Darwin: The Popularisation of Darwinism in Germany, 1860–1914*, Chapel Hill

Kelly, D. (2006). 'Idealism and Revolution: T. H. Green's *Four Lectures on the English Commonwealth*', *History of Political Thought*, 27: 505–42

Kelly, Duncan (2010). *The Propriety of Liberty: Persons, Passions & Judgement in Modern Political Thought*, Princeton

Kelly, George Armstrong (1992). *The Humane Comedy: Constant, Tocqueville and French Liberalism*, Cambridge

Kelly, P. J. (1990). *Utilitarianism and Distributive Justice: Jeremy Bentham and the Civil Law*, Oxford

Kelsall, Malcolm (1987). *Byron's Politics*, Brighton

Kendall, W. (1969). *The Revolutionary Movement in Britain, 1900–21: The Origins of British Communism*, London

Kennedy, E. (1978). *A Philosophe in the Age of Revolution: Destutt de Tracy and the Origins of 'Ideology'*, Philadelphia

Kennedy, Michael and Suny, Ronald (eds.) (1999). *Intellectuals and the Articulation of the Nation*, Ann Arbor

Kennedy, Paul (1980). *The Rise of Anglo-German Antagonism, 1860–1914*, London
(1987). *The Rise and Fall of the Great Powers*, New York

Kennedy, Paul and Nicholls, Anthony (eds.) (1981). *Nationalist and Racialist Movements in Britain and Germany before 1914*, London

Kennedy, William F. (1958). *Humanist versus Economist: The Economic Thought of Samuel Taylor Coleridge*, Berkeley

Keown-Boyd, Henry (1991). *The Fists of Righteous Harmony: A History of the Boxer Uprising in China in the Year 1900*, Barnsley

Kepp, Kevin (2000). *Reformers, Cities and the Paths of German Modernity. Anti-Politics and the Search for Alternatives, 1890–1914*, Harvard

Ker, Ian (2010). *John Henry Newman: A Biography*, Oxford

Kerber, L. K. (1980). *Women of the Republic: Intellect and Ideology in Revolutionary America*, Chapel Hill

Kevles, D. (1985). *In the Name of Eugenics: Genetics and the Uses of Human Heredity*, Harmondsworth

Key, E. (1912). *The Woman Movement*, trans. M. B. Borthwick, London

Key, V. O. Jr. (1964). *Politics, Parties, and Pressure Groups*, 5th edition, New York

Keyssar, Alexander (2000). *The Right to Vote: The Contested History of Democracy in the United States*, New York

Kim, C. T. E. (1967). *Korea and the Politics of Imperialism*, Cambridge

Kimmel, M. S. (1987). 'The "Crisis" in Masculinity in Historical Perspective', in Harry Brod (ed.), *The Making of Masculinities: The New Men's Studies*, Boston

Kimmerle, Heinz (1999). 'Die Freie une Versöhnte Totalität der Kunst. Die Bedeutung des Gemeinsinns für Ästhetische und Politische Urteile bei Hegel, Kant und in Interkulturell Philosophischer Perspektive', *Hegel-Jahrbuch* 1999: 91–9

King, Jeremy (2002). *Budweisers into Czechs and Germans: A Local History of Bohemian Politics, 1848–1948*, Princeton

Kinzer, Bruce L. (1982). *The Ballot Question in Nineteenth-Century English Politics*, New York
(1991). 'John Stuart Mill and the Experience of Political Engagement', in M. Laine (ed.), *A Cultivated Mind, Essays on J. S. Mill Presented to John M. Robson*, Toronto

Kippur, Stephen A. (1981). *Jules Michelet: A Study of Mind and Sensibility*, New York

Kirkpatrick, Jennet (2008). *Uncivil Disobedience: Studies in Violence and Democratic Politics*, Princeton

Kitchin, J. (1966). *Un Journal Philosophique: La Décade (1794–1807)*, Paris

Klaus, Peter (1985). 'Einleitung', in Peter Klaus (ed.), *Die politische Romantik in Deutschland*, Stuttgart

Klein, L. E. (1995). 'Gender and the Public/Private Distinction in the Eighteenth Century: Some Questions about Evidence and Analytic Procedure', *Eighteenth Century Studies*, 29: 97–109

Klinck, David (1996). *The French Counter-revolutionary Theorist, Louis de Bonald (1754–1840)*, New York

Kline, Wm. Gary (1987). *The Individualist Anarchists: A Critique of Liberalism*, Lanham

Klinger, Cornelia (1990). 'Ästhetik als Philosophie – Ästhetik als Kunsttheorie', in Walter Jaeschke and Helmut Holzhey (eds.), *Früher Idealismus und Frühromantik. Der Streit um die Grundlagen der Ästhetik (1795–1805)*, Hamburg

Kloppenberg, James T. (1986). *Uncertain Victory: Social Democracy and Progressivism in European and American Thought, 1870–1920*, New York
(2003). 'From Hartz to Tocqueville: Shifting the Focus from Liberalism to Democracy in America', in Meg Jacobs *et al*. (eds.), *The Democratic Experiment: New Directions in American Political History*, Princeton
Knights, Ben (1978). *The Idea of the Clerisy in the Nineteenth Century*, Cambridge
Knox, Israel (1958). *The Aesthetic Theories of Kant, Hegel, and Schopenhauer*, London
Knox, T. M. (1980). 'The Puzzle of Hegel's Aesthetics', in W. E. Steinkraus and K. I. Schmitz (eds.), *Art and Logic in Hegel's Philosophy*, Brighton
Koebner, Richard and Schmidt, Helmut Dan (1964). *Imperialism: The Story and Significance of a Political Word, 1840–1960*, Cambridge
Koehler, Benedikt (1980). *Ästhetik des Politik. Adam Müller und die Politische Romantik*, Stuttgart
Kohn D. (ed.) (1986). *The Darwinian Heritage*, Princeton
Kohn, Hans (1953). *Pan-Slavism: Its History and Ideology*, Notre Dame
(1968). *The Age of Nationalism: The First Era of Global History*, New York
Kohn, Marek (2004). *A Reason for Everything: Natural Selection and the English Imagination*, London
Kohn, Margaret and O'Neill, Daniel (2006). 'A Tale of Two Indias: Burke and Mill on Empire and Slavery in the West Indies and America', *Political Theory* 34: 192–228
Kolakowski, Leszek (1978). *Main Currents of Marxism*, 2 vols., Oxford
Kollontai, A. (1977). *Selected Writings of Alexandra Kollontai*, ed. Alix Holt, London
Kolmerten, Carol (1990). *Women in Utopia: The Ideology of Gender in the American Owenite Communities*, Syracuse
Kontler, Lázló (1999). 'Superstition, Enthusiasm and Propagandism: Burke and Gentz on the French Revolution', in B. Taithe and T. Thornton (eds.), *Propaganda, Political Rhetoric and Identity*, Stroud
Kopf, Hermann (1980). *Karl von Rotteck zwischen Revolution und Restauration*, Freiburg
Koselleck, Reinhart (1967). *Preussen zwischen Reform und Revolution, Allgemeines Landrecht, Verwaltung und Soziale Bewegung von 1791 bis 1848*, Stuttgart
Koskenniemi, Martti (2001). *The Gentle Civiliser of Nations: The Rise and Fall of International Law, 1870–1960*, Cambridge
Kostal, R. W. (2005). *A Jurisprudence of Power: Victorian Empire and the Rule of Law*, Oxford
Koyré, Alexandre (1950). *Études sur l'Histoire de la Pensée Philosophique en Russie*, Paris
Krader, L. (1972). *The Ethnological Notebooks of Karl Marx (Studies of Morgan, Phear, Maine, Lubbock)*, Assen
Kraditor, Aileen S. (1969). *Means and Ends in American Abolitionism: Garrison and his Critics on Strategy and Tactics, 1834–1850*, New York
(1981 [1965]). *The Ideas of the Woman Suffrage Movement, 1890–1920*, New York
Kramnick, Isaac (1977). *The Rage of Edmund Burke*, New York
(1990). *Republicanism and Bourgeois Radicalism: Political Ideology in Late Eighteenth-century England and America*, Ithaca
Kraus, Peter (2004). 'History and Moral Imperatives: The Contradictions of German Romanticism', in Dennis F. Murphy (ed.), *The Literature of German Romanticism* (The Camden House History of German Romanticism, 8), Rochester, NY
Kreml, William P. (1977). *The Anti-Authoritarian Personality*, Oxford
Krieger, Leonard (1972 [1957]). *The German Idea of Freedom: History of a Political Tradition from the Reformation to 1871*, Chicago

Kubitz, O. A. (1932). *Development of John Stuart Mill's 'System of Logic'* (Illinois Studies in the Social Sciences, Vol. XVIII), Urbana

Kuhn, H. (1974). 'Die Gegenwärtigkeit der Kunst nach Hegels Vorlesungen über Ästhetik', *Hegel-Studien*, Beiheft 11: 251–69

Kuhn, Hans Wolfgang (1961). *Der Apoklyptiker und die Politik. Studien zur Staatsphilosophie des Novalis*, Freiburg

Kuitenbrouwer, Maarten (1991). *The Netherlands and the Rise of Modern Imperialism: Colonies and Foreign Policy, 1870–1902*, Oxford

Kumar, Krishan (ed.) (1970). *Revolution: The Theory and Practice of a European Idea*, London

Kwame Anthony Appiah, 'The Black World', 'Pan Africanism', www.africana.com/Articles/tt_658.htm

La Valley, Albert J. (1968). *Carlyle and the Idea of the Modern*, New Haven

La Vergata, A. (1990). *L'Equilibrio e la Guerra della Natura. Dalla Teologia Naturale al Darwinismo*, Naples

La Vopa, Anthony (2001). *Fichte: The Self and the Calling of Philosophy, 1762–1799*, Cambridge

LaCapra, Dominick (1983). *Rethinking Intellectual History*, Ithaca

Laity, Paul (2001). *The British Peace Movement, 1870–1914*, Oxford

Lalor, James Fintan (1918). *James Fintan Lalor: Collected Writings*, ed. Nathaniel Marlowe, Dublin and London

Lamberti, Jean-Claude (1989). *Tocqueville and the Two Democracies*, Cambridge, MA

Landsberg, E. (1912). *Geschichte der Deutschen Rechtswisenschaft*, 3 vols., Munich

Landucci, G. (1981). 'Darwinismo e Nazionalismo', *La Cultura Italiana tra '800 e '900 e le Origini del Nazionalismo*, Florence

Lang, Timothy (1995). 'Henry Hallam and Early Nineteenth-Century Whiggism', in *The Victorians and the Stuart Heritage: Interpretations of a Discordant Past*, Cambridge

Langewiesche, Dieter (1988a). 'German Liberalism in the Second Empire, 1871–1914', in Dieter Langewiesche (ed.), *Liberalismus im 19. Jahrhundert*, Göttingen

  (1992). 'Germany and the National Question in 1848', in John Breuilly (ed.), *The State of Germany: The National Idea in the Making, Unmaking and Remaking of a Modern Nation-state*, London

  (1997). 'Frühliberalismus und Bürgertum 1815–1849', in Lothar Gall (ed.), *Bürgertum und Bürgerlich-Liberale Idee Bewegung in Mitteleuropa seit dem 18. Jahrhundert*, Munich

Langewiesche, Dieter (ed.) (1988b). *Liberalismus in Deutschland. Deutschland im Europäischen Vergleich*, Frankfurt

Langley, J. Ayo (1979). *Ideologies of Political Liberation in Black Africa, 1856–1970: Documents on Modern African Political Thought from Colonial Times to the Present*, London

Lapp, Robert Keith (1999). *Contest for Cultural Authority: Hazlitt, Coleridge and the Distresses of the Regency*, Detroit

Laqueur, Walter (1977). *Terrorism*, Boston

Laqueur, Walter (ed.) (1979). *The Terrorism Reader: A Historical Anthology*, New York

Laremont, Ricardo R. (1999). *Islam and the Politics of Resistance in Algeria, 1783–1992*, Trenton, NJ

Large, D. A. (2000). '"Our Greatest Teacher": Nietzsche, Burckhardt, and the Concept of Culture', *International Studies in Philosophy*, 32(3): 3–23

Larrabee, Harold A. (ed.) (1952). *Handbook of Political Fallacies*, Baltimore

Lasch, Christopher (1991). *The True and Only Heaven: Progress and Its Critics*, New York

Laski, Harold (1917). *Studies in the Problems of Modern Sovereignty*, New Haven

Lattek, Christine (1988). 'The Beginnings of Socialist Internationalism in the 1840s: The "Democratic Friends of All Nations" in London', in Frits van Holthoon and Marcel van der Linden (eds.), *Internationalism in the Labour Movement 1830–1940*, Leiden

(2006). *Revolutionary Refugees. German Socialism in Britain, 1840–1860*, London

Laven, David (2006). 'Italy', in T. Baycroft and M. Hewitson, *What is a Nation? Europe, 1789–1914*, Oxford

Lawrence, Jon (1998). *Speaking for the People: Party, Language and Popular Politics in England, 1867–1914*, Cambridge

(2009). *Electing our Masters: The Hustings in British Politics from Hogarth to Blair*, Oxford

Lawson, Philip (1993). *The East India Company: A History*, New York

Layet, Louise (2005). 'Le Société de Saint-Vincent de Paul en Angleterre, 1869–1914. Un Modèle de Charité Catholique', Maîtrise d'Histoire, Université Paris X – Nanterre

Lazarus, Simon (2004). 'The Constitution in Play', *American Prospect* (21 April): 60–2

Le Rossignol, James Edward (1911). *State Socialism in New Zealand*, London

Leask, Nigel (1988). *The Politics of Imagination in Coleridge's Critical Thought*, London

Lebrun, G. (1970). *Kant et la Fin de la Métaphysique*, Paris

Lebrun, Richard (1965). *Throne and Altar: The Political and Religious Thought of Joseph de Maistre*, Ottawa

(1972). 'Joseph de Maistre and Rousseau', *Studies in Voltaire and the Eighteenth Century*, 88: 881–98

(1988b). *Joseph de Maistre: An Intellectual Militant*, Kingston

Lebrun, Richard (trans and ed.) (1988a). *Maistre Studies*, Lanham, MD

Lebrun, Richard A. (ed.) (2001). *Joseph de Maistre's Life, Thought, and Influence: Selected Studies*, Montreal and Kingston

Lecky, W. E. H. (1913). *A History of Ireland in the Eighteenth Century*, 5 vols., London

Ledermann, László (1929). *Pellegrino Rossi, L'homme et L'économiste, 1787–1848, une Grande Carrière Internationale au XIXe Siècle, avec de Nombreux Documents Inédits*, Paris

Ledger, A. St. (1909). *Australian Socialism: An Historical Sketch of Its Origin and Developments*, London

Lee, John A. (1938). *Socialism in New Zealand*, London

Lee, Yoon Sun (2004). *Nationalism and Irony*, New York

Leersen, Joep (2006). *National Thought in Europe: A Cultural History*, Amsterdam

Lehning, Arthur (1956). 'Buonarroti and His International Secret Societies', *International Review of Social History*, 1: 112–40

(1974). 'Bakunin's Conceptions of Revolutionary Organisations and their Role: A Study of his "Secret Societies"', in C. Abramsky (ed.), *Essays in Honor of E. H. Carr*, London

Lehning, James (1995). *Peasant and French: Cultural Contact in Rural France during the Nineteenth Century*, Cambridge

Lehouck, Émile (1978). *Vie de Charles Fourier*, Paris

Leier, Mark (2006). *Bakunin: The Creative Passion*, New York

Leighton, Denys P. (2004). *The Greenian Moment: T. H. Green, Religion and Political Argument in Victorian Britain*, Exeter

Lenzer, G. (ed. and intro.) (1975). *Auguste Comte and Positivism: The Essential Writings*, New York

Leonard, Jörn (2001). *Liberalismus. Zur Historischen Semantik eines Europäischen Deutungsmusters*, München

Leontowitsch, Victor (1957). *Geschichte des Liberalismus in Russland*, Frankfurt am Main

Leopardi, Giacomo (1993). *Tutte le Opere*, ed. Walter Binni, 2 vols., Milan

Leopold, David (2003). 'Introduction', in William Morris, *News from Nowhere*, Oxford

(2007). *The Young Karl Marx: German Philosophy, Modern Politics and Human Flourishing*, Cambridge

Lepper, John Heron (1932). *Famous Secret Societies*, London

Lepsius, M. Rainer (1966). 'Parteiensystem und Sozialstruktur: Zum Problem der Demokratisierung der Deutschen Gesellschaft', in Wilhelm Abel, Knut Borchardt, Hermann Kellenbenz and Wolfgang Zorn (eds.), *Wirtschaft, Geschichte und Wirtschaftsgeschichte. Festschrift zum 65. Geburtstag von Friedrich Lütge*, Stuttgart

Lerner, G., and Grimké, Sarah Moore (1998). *The Feminist Thought of Sarah Grimké*, New York

Leroy, M. (1962). *Histoire des Idées Sociales en France*, 3 vols., Paris

Levenson, J. C. (1957). *The Mind and Art of Henry Adams*, Stanford

Levine, G. (1988). *Darwin and the Novelists: Patterns of Science in Victorian Fiction*, Cambridge MA

Levine, P. (1994). *Victorian Feminism 1850–1900*, Gainesville, FL

Levy, Leonard W. (1963). *Jefferson and Civil Liberties: The Darker Side*, Cambridge, MA

Lewis, A. D. E. (1990). 'The Background to Bentham on Evidence', *Utilitas*, 2: 195–219

Lewis, Bernard (2002). *What Went Wrong? Western Impact and Middle Eastern Response*, Oxford

Lewis, J. (1987). *Before the Vote was Won: Arguments For and Against Women's Suffrage*, London

Lewis, J., Kessler-Harris, A., and Wikander, U. (eds.) (1995). *Protecting Women. Labour Legislation in Europe, the United States, and Australia, 1880–1920*, Urbana

Lewis, John D. (1935). *The Genossenschaft-theory of Otto von Gierke: A Study in Political Thought*, Madison

Lichtheim, George (1969). *The Origins of Socialism*, London

Lidtke, Vernon L. (1964). 'German Social Democracy and German State Socialism, 1876–1884', *International Review of Social History*, 9, Part 2: 202–25

 (1966). *The Outlawed Party: Social Democracy in Germany, 1878–1890*, Princeton

Lieberman, David. (1985). 'Bentham's Digest', *The Bentham Newsletter*, 9: 7–20

 (1989). *The Province of Legislation Determined, Legal Theory in Eighteenth-Century Britain*, Cambridge

 (2000). 'Economy and Polity in Bentham's Science of Legislation', in S. Collini, R. Whatmore and B. Young (eds.), *Economy, Polity, and Society: British Intellectual History 1750–1950*, Cambridge

Liebich A. (ed.) (1979). *Selected Writings of A. Cieszkowski*, Cambridge

Lieven, Dominic (2000). *Empire: The Russian Empire and Its Rivals*, London

Lillibridge, G. D. (1954). *Beacon of Freedom: The Impact of American Democracy upon Great Britain, 1830–70*, Philadelphia

Lindemann, Albert S. (1983). *A History of European Socialism*, New Haven

Lindenfeld, David F. (1997). *The Practical Imagination: The German Sciences of State in the Nineteenth Century*, Chicago and London

Linton, W. H. (n.d.). *Are the Socialists Republicans?*

Lipow, Arthur (1982). *Authoritarian Socialism in America: Edward Bellamy and the Nationalist Movement*, Berkeley

Lipset, Seymour Martin and Marx, Gary (2000). *It Didn't Happen Here: Why Socialism Failed in the United States*, New York

Lively Jack and Rees, John (eds.) (1984). *Utilitarian Logic and Politics: James Mill's 'Essay on Government', Macaulay's Critique, and the Ensuing Debate*, Oxford

Livesey, James (2001). *Making Democracy in the French Revolution*, Harvard

Loewenberg, B. J. (1959). *Darwin, Wallace and the Theory of Natural Selection including the Linnean Society Papers*, Cambridge, MA

Logue, William (1983). *From Philosophy to Sociology: The Evolution of French Liberalism, 1870–1914*, Dekalb, IL

Lombard, Charles M. (1973). *Lamartine* (Twayne World Author Series), New York

Loménie, E. Beau de (1929). *La Carrière Politique de Chateaubriand de 1814 à 1830*, 2 vols., Paris

Long, David (1996). *Towards a New Liberal Internationalism: The International Theory of J. A. Hobson*, Cambridge

Lopes, Anne and Roth, Gary (eds.) (2000). *Men's Feminism: August Bebel and the German Socialist Movement*, Amherst, NY

Lopez, Michael (1996). *Emerson and Power: Creative Antagonism in the Nineteenth Century*, DeKalb

Lorenz, Ina Susanna (1980). *Eugen Richter. Der Entschiedene Liberalismus in Wilhelminischer Zeit 1871 bis 1906*, Husum

Lorimer, D. (1988). 'Theoretical Racism in later Victorian Anthropology', *Victorian Studies*, 31: 405–30

Losev, Aleksei (1990). *Vladimir Soloviev i Ego Vremia*, Moscow

Losurdo, Domenico (2002). *Nietzsche. Il Rebelle Aristocratico*, Turin

Loubère, Leo (1974). *Radicalism in Mediterranean France: Its Rise and Decline, 1848–1914*, Albany

Lougee, Robert W. (1959). 'German Romanticism and Political Thought', *Review of Politics*, 21: 631–45

Lovett, Clara M. (1982). *The Democratic Movement in Italy, 1830–1876*, Cambridge, MA

Lovett, Sir Verney (1920). *A History of the Indian Nationalist Movement*, London

Löwy, M. (2003). *The Theory of Revolution in the Young Marx*, Leiden

Lucas, Colin (1989). 'Edmund Burke and the Emigrés', in François Furet and Mona Ozouf (eds.), *The Transformation of Political Culture, 1789–1848*, Oxford

Lucas, Colin (ed.) (1988). *The French Revolution and the Creation of Modern Political Culture, Vol. II: The Political Culture of the French Revolution*, Oxford

Lucas, H.-C. and Pöggeler, O. (eds.) (1986). *Hegels Rechtsphilosophie in Zusammenhang der Europäischen Verfassungsgeschichte*, Stuttgart

Lucas, J. R. (1979). 'Wilberforce and Huxley: A Legendary Encounter', *Historical Journal*, 22: 313–30

Ludovici, Anthony (1915). *A Defence of Aristocracy: A Text Book for the Tories*, London

Luft, Eric v. d. (2006). 'Edgar Bauer and the Origins of the Theory of Terrorism', in Douglas Moggach (ed.), *The New Hegelians. Politics and Philosophy in the Hegelian School*, Cambridge

Luft, Eric v. d. (2008). *Schopenhauer: New Essays in Honor of His 200th Birthday*, New York

Lukács, Georg (1954). 'Zur Ästhetik Schillers', *Beiträge zur Geschichte der Ästhetik*, Berlin

(1973). *Der Junge Hegel*, 2 vols., Frankfurt

(1980). *The Destruction of Reason*, trans. Peter Palmer, London

Lukes, Steven (1973). *Emile Durkheim: His Life and Work*, Harmondsworth

Lustig, A., Richards, R. J. and Ruse, M. (eds.) (2004). *Darwinian Heresies*, Cambridge

Lutz, H. L. (1913). 'Theorie des Geldes und der Umlaufsmittel', *American Economic Review*, 3: 144–6

Lynch, John (1986). *The Spanish American Revolutions, 1808–1826*, New York

(2006). *Simón Bolívar: A Life*, New Haven

Lynd, Robert (1912). *Rambles in Ireland*, London

Lyons, David (ed.) (1997). *Mill's Utilitarianism: Critical Essays*, Lanham

Lyons, F. S. L. (1979). *Culture and Anarchy in Ireland, 1890–1939*, Oxford

Lyons, Martin (2006). *Post-Revolutionary Europe, 1815–1856*, London

Lypp, Bernhard (1972). *Ästhetischer Absolutismus und Politische Vernunft. Zum Widerstreit von Reflexion und Sittlichkeit im Deutschen Idealismus*, Frankfurt am Main

(1990). 'Idealismus und Philosophie der Kunst', in H.-F. Fulda and R.-P. Horstmann (eds.), *Hegel und die Kritik der Urteilskraft*, Stuttgart

MacDonagh, O. (1958). 'The Nineteenth-Century Revolution in Government: A Reappraisal', *Historical Journal*, 1: 52–67

Macfarlane, Anthony and Posada-Carbó, Eduardo (eds.) (1999). *Independence and Revolution in Spanish America: Perspectives and Problems*, London

Macfie, Alec (1998). *The End of the Ottoman Empire, 1908–1923*, New York

MacIver, R. M. (1917). *Community: A Sociological Study*, London and Toronto

Mack, M. (1962). *Jeremy Bentham: An Odyssey of Ideas, 1748–92*, London

Mackenzie, Norman and Mackenzie, Jean (1979). *The First Fabians*, London

MacLachlan, Colin M. (1991). *Anarchism and the Mexican Revolution: The Political Trials of Ricardo Flores Magón in the United States*, Berkeley

MacMann, George (1935). *Turmoil and Tragedy in India*, London

MacMaster, Neil (2001). *Racism in Europe, 1870–2000*, Basingstoke

MacNair, Everett (1957). *Edward Bellamy and the Nationalist Movement*, London

Maehl, William Harvey (1980). *August Bebel: Shadow Emperor of the German Workers*, Philadelphia

Magee, Bryan (2000). *The Tristan Chord. Wagner and Philosophy*, New York

Magnus, R. (1949 [1906]). *Goethe as a Scientist*, trans. H. Norden, New York

Maguire, J. M. (1978). *Marx's Theory of Politics*, Cambridge

Mahoney, Charles (2002). *Romantics and Renegades: The Poetics of Political Reaction*, New York

Maier, Pauline (1997). *American Scripture: Making the Declaration of Independence*, New York

Maitron, Jean (1964). *Ravachol et les Anarchistes*, Paris

  (1975). *Le Mouvement Anarchiste en France*, 2 vols., Paris

  (1985). *Paul Delesalle: Un Anarchiste de la Belle Époque*, Paris

Majeed, Javed (1992). *Ungoverned Imaginings: James Mill's 'The History of British India' and Orientalism*, Oxford

Majumdar, B. B. (1934). *A History of Political Thought from Rammohun to Dayananda (1821–84)*, Calcutta

Majumedar, R. C. (1962). *History of the Freedom Movement in India*, 3 vols., Calcutta

Malangré, Heinz (1991). *David Hansemann*, Aachen

Mali, Joseph and Wokler, Robert (2003). 'Isaiah Berlin's Counter-Enlightenment', *Transactions of the American Philosophical Society*, Philadelphia

Malia, Martin (1961). *Alexander Herzen and the Birth of Russian Socialism 1812–1855*, Cambridge, MA

Mallet, Bernard (1902). *Mallet Du Pan and the French Revolution*, London

Malone, C. (1998). 'Gendered Discourses and the Making of Protective Labour Legislation in England, 1830–1914', *Journal of British Studies*, 37: 166–91

Malone, Dumas (1948–81). *Jefferson and his Time*, 6 vols., Boston

Mancini, Matthew (1994). *Alexis de Tocqueville*, New York

Mandler, Peter (2000). '"Race" and "Nation" in mid-Victorian Thought', in S. Collini *et al.* (eds.), *History, Religion, and Culture: British Intellectual History, 1750–1950*, Cambridge

  (2006). *The English National Character: The History of an Idea from Edmund Burke to Tony Blair*, New Haven

Manin, Bernard (1992). 'Montesquieu', in François Furet and Mona Ozouf (eds.), *Dictionnaire Critique de la Révolution Française*, Paris

Mannheim, Karl (1971 [1927]). 'Conservative Thought', in Kurt H. Wolff (ed.), *From Karl Mannheim*, New York

Manninen, Juha (1996). *Feuer am Pol. Zum Aufbau der Vernunft im Europäischen Norden*, Frankfurt am Main

Mansfield, Harvey C. and Winthrop, Delba (2000). 'Editors' Introduction', in Alexis de Tocqueville, *Democracy in America*, Chicago

Mantena, Karuna (2010). *Alibis of Empire: Henry Maine and the Ends of Liberal Imperialism*, Princeton

Manuel, Frank E. (1956). *The New World of Henri de Saint-Simon*, 2nd edition, Notre Dame 1963, Cambridge, MA

  (1962). *The Prophets of Paris*, Cambridge

  (1965). *The Prophets of Paris*, New York

Manuel, Frank E. and Manuel, F. P. (1979). *Utopian Thought in the Western World*, Cambridge, MA

Marcuse, Herbert (1955). *Eros and Civilisation*, Boston

Mariel, Pierre (1971). *Les Carbonari*, Paris

Marino, Giuliano (1969). *L'Opera di Gustav Hugo*, Milan

  (1978). *Friedrich Karl von Savigny*, Milan

Marr, David G. (1971). *Vietnamese Anticolonialism, 1885–1925*, Berkeley

Marshall, Byron K. (1977). 'Professors and Politics: The Meiji Academic Elite', *Journal of Japanese Studies*, 3: 71–97

Marshall, Peter H. (1984). *William Godwin*, New Haven

Marshall, T. H. (1977). *Class Citizenship and Social Development*, Chicago

Martin, Alexander M. (1997). *Romantics, Reformers, Reactionaries: Russian Conservative Thought and Politics in the Reign of Alexander I*, Dekalb

Martin, James J. (1957). *Men Against the State: The Expositors of Individualist Anarchism in America, 1827–1908*, New York

Martin, Waldo E. (1984). *The Mind of Frederick Douglass*, Chapel Hill, NC

Masaryk, Thomas Garrigue (1955 [1919]). *The Spirit of Russia: Studies in History, Literature and Philosophy*, London and New York

Masterman, C. F. G. (1920). *The New Liberalism*, London

Masterman, Lucy (1939). *C. F. G. Masterman: A Biography*, London

Masur, Louis P. (2001). *1831: Year of Eclipse*, New York

Mathers, H. (2002). 'Evangelicalism and Feminism: Josephine Butler, 1828–1906', in S. Morgan (ed.), *Women, Religion and Feminism in Britain, 1750–1900*, Basingstoke

Mathurin, Owen Charles (1976). *Henry Sylvester Williams and the Origins of the Pan-Africanist Movement, 1869–1911*, Westport

Mathy, Dietrich (1994). *Von der Metaphysik zur Ästhetik, oder Das Exil der Philosophie. Untersuchungen zum Prozess der Ästhetischen Moderne*, Hamburg

Matthews, R. C. O. (1954). *A Study in Trade Cycle History: Economic Fluctuations in Great Britain, 1833–1842*, Cambridge

Matthews, Richard K. (1984). *The Radical Politics of Thomas Jefferson: A Revisionist View*, Lawrence

Mauduit, Roger (1929). *Auguste Comte et la Science Économique*, Paris

Maurer, G. L. (1854). *Einleitung zur Geschichte der Mark-, Hof-, Dorf- und Stadt-Verfassung und der öffentlichen Gewalt*, Munich

Maximoff, G. P. (ed.) (1964). *The Political Philosophy of Bakunin: Scientific Anarchism*, New York

Mayer, David N. (1994). *The Constitutional Thought of Thomas Jefferson*, Charlottesville

Mayer, Gustav (1912). 'Die Trennung der Proletarischen von der Bürgerlichen Demokratie in Duetschland (1863–1970)', *Archiv für die Geschichte des Sozialismus und der Arbeiterbewegung*, Vol. II

  (1934). *Friedrich Engels: Eine Biographie*, 2 vols., The Hague

Maza, Sarah (2002). 'The Social Imaginary of the Revolution: The Third Estate, the National Guard, and the Absent Bourgeoisie', in Colin Jones and Dror Wahrman (eds.), *The Age of Cultural Revolutions. Britain and France, 1750–1820*, Berkeley

Mazower, Mark (2000). *Dark Continent: Europe's Twentieth Century*, New York

(2004). *Salonica, City of Ghosts: Christians, Muslims and Jews, 1430–1950*, London

McAdoo, Bill (1983). *Pre-Civil War Black Nationalism*, New York

McAlla, Arthur (1998). *A Romantic Historiosophy: The Philosophy of History of Pierre-Simon Ballanche*, Leiden

McBriar, A. M. (1962). *Fabian Socialism and English Politics 1884–1918*, Cambridge

(1987). *An Edwardian Mixed Doubles: The Bosanquets versus the Webbs: A Study in English Social Policy, 1890–1929*, Oxford

McBride, Ian (2000). 'The Harp without the Crown: Nationalism and Republicanism in the 1790s', in S. J. Connolly (ed.), *Political Ideas in Eighteenth-Century Ireland*, Dublin

McCalman, Iain (1988). *Radical Underworld: Prophets, Revolutionaries and Pornographers in London, 1795–1840*, Cambridge

McCloskey, Robert Green (1951). *American Conservatism in the Age of Enterprise, 1865–1910: A Study of William Graham Sumner, Stephen J. Field, and Andrew Carnegie*, Cambridge, MA

(1957). 'American Political Thought and the Study of Politics', *American Political Science Review*, 51: 115–29

McCracken, C. J. (1983). *Malebranche and British Philosophy*, Oxford

McDonald, Forrest (1976). *The Presidency of Thomas Jefferson*, Lawrence

(2000). *States' Rights and the Union: Imperium in Imperio, 1776–1876* (American Political Thought), Lawrence

McFadden, M. (1996). 'Anna Doyle Wheeler (1785–1848): Philosopher, Socialist, Feminist', in L. L. McAlister (ed.), *Hypatia's Daughters: Fifteen Hundred Years of Women Philosophers*, Bloomington

(1999). *Golden Cables of Sympathy: The Transatlantic Sources of Nineteenth-century Feminism*, Kentucky

McFeely, William S. (1991). *Frederick Douglass*, New York

McKenna, Mark (1996). *The Captive Republic: A History of Republicanism in Australia, 1788–1996*, Cambridge

McKenna, Mark and Hudson, Wayne (eds.) (2003). *Australian Republicanism: A Reader*, Melbourne

McKibbin, Ross (1974). *The Evolution of the Labour Party, 1910–24*, Oxford

(1998). *Classes and Cultures: England, 1918–51*, Oxford

McLaughlin, Paul (2002). *Mikhail Bakunin: The Philosophical Basis of His Anarchism*, New York

McLellan, David (1969). *The Young Hegelians and Karl Marx*, London

(1973). *Karl Marx: His Life and Thought*, London

Mclloyd, J. (1995). 'Raising Lilies: Ruskin and Women', *Journal of British Studies*, 34: 325–50

McMahon, Darrin (2001). *Enemies of the Enlightenment*, Oxford

McNeil, G (1953). 'The Anti-revolutionary Rousseau', *American Historical Review*, 58(4): 808–23

McPherson, James M. (1990). *Abraham Lincoln and the Second American Revolution*, New York

(2003). *Battle Cry of Freedom: The Civil War Era*, Oxford

McWilliams, Wilson Carey (1973). *The Idea of Fraternity in America*, Berkeley

Meadowcroft, James (1995). *Conceptualising the State: Innovation and Dispute in British Political Thought, 1880–1914*, Oxford

Meek, Ronald (1976). *Social Science and the Ignoble Savage*, Cambridge

Mehta, Uday Singh (1999). *Liberalism and Empire: A Study in Nineteenth-Century British Liberal Thought*, 1999.

Meinecke, Friedrich (1924). *Die Idee der Staatsräson in der neueren Geschichte*, Munich (1970 [1963]). *Cosmopolitanism and the National State*, trans Robert B. Kimber, Princeton

Melder, K. (1977). *The Beginnings of Sisterhood: The American Woman's Rights Movement, 1800–1850*, New York

Mellon, Stanley (1958). *The Political Uses of History*, Stanford

Melman, B. (1991). 'Claiming the Nation's Past: The Invention of an Anglo-Saxon Tradition', *Journal of Contemporary History*, 26: 575–95

Mélonio, Françoise (1993). *Tocqueville et les Français*, Paris

Melzer, Arthur (1996). 'The Origin of the Counter-Enlightenment: Rousseau and the New Religion of Sincerity', *American Political Science Review* 90: 344–60

Menand, Louis (2001). *The Metaphysical Club: A Story of Ideas in America*, New York (2002). 'John Brown's Body', *Raritan* (Fall): 53–61

Mendel, Arthur P. (1961). *Dilemmas of Progress in Tsarist Russia: Legal Marxism and Legal Populism*, Cambridge, MA

(1981). *Michael Bakunin: Roots of Apocalypse*, New York

Mendilow, Jonathan (1986). *The Romantic Tradition in British Political Thought*, London

Menke, Christoph (1999). 'Ästhetische Subjektivität. Zu einem Grundbegriff Moderner Ästhetik', in Gerhart von Graevenitz (ed.), *Konzepte der Moderne*, Stuttgart

Merchior, J. G. (1991). *Liberalism Old and New*, Boston

Meredith, Isabel (1903) *A Girl Among Anarchists*, London

Merriam, Charles E. (1923 [1920]). *American Political Ideas: Studies in the Development of American Political Thought, 1865–1917*, New York

Merton, Robert K. (1963). 'Introduction: The Ambivalences of Le Bon's *The Crowd*', in Gustave Le Bon, *The Crowd: A Study of the Popular Mind*, New York

Metcalfe, Charles Theophilus (ed.) (1974). *Two Native Narratives of the Mutiny in Delhi*, Delhi

Meyers, Marvin (1960 [1957]). *The Jacksonian Persuasion: Politics and Belief*, Stanford

Michael, Franz (1966). *The Taiping Rebellion*, 3 vols., Seattle

Michels, R. (1930). 'Conservatism', in E. R. Seligman (ed.), *International Encyclopaedia of the Social Sciences*, Vol. IV, New York

Mielke, Siegfried (1976). *Der Hansa-Bund für Gewerbe, Handel und Industrie 1909–1914. Der Gescheiterte Versuch einer Antifeudalen Sammlungspolitik*, Göttingen

Milgate, Murray and Stimson, Shannon (1991). *Ricardian Politics*, Princeton

Miller, David (1984). *Anarchism*, London (1995). *On Nationality*, Oxford

Miller, John Chester (1977). *The Wolf by the Ears: Thomas Jefferson and Slavery*, New York

Miller, Martin A. (1976). *Kropotkin*, Chicago

Miller, Susanne (1964). *Das Problem der Freiheit im Sozialismus. Freiheit, Staat und Revolution in der Programmatik der Sozialdemokratie von Lassalle bis zum Revisionismusstreit*, Frankfurt am Main

Miller, William Ian (1993). *Humiliation*, Ithaca (2002). *Lincoln's Virtues: An Ethical Biography*, New York

Millhauser, Milton (1959). *Just Before Darwin: Robert Chambers and Vestiges*, Middletown, CT

Milner, Anthony (1994). *The Invention of Politics in Colonial Malaya: Contesting Nationalism and the Expansion of the Public Sphere*, Cambridge

Mitzman, Arthur (1987). *Sociology and Estrangement: Three Sociologists of Imperial Germany*, New Brunswick

Moggach, D. (2000). 'New Goals and New Ways: Republicanism and Socialism in 1848', in D. Moggach and P. L. Browne (eds.), *The Social Question and the Democratic Revolution*, Ottawa
   (2003). *The Philosophy and Politics of Bruno Bauer*, Cambridge
   (2007). 'Schiller's Aesthetic Republicanism', *History of Political Thought*, 28(3): 520–41
Moggach, D. (ed.) (2006). *The New Hegelians: Politics and Philosophy in the Hegelian School*, Cambridge
Moggach, D. and Browne, P. L. (eds.) (2000). *The Social Question and the Democratic Revolution: Marx and the Legacy of 1848*, Ottawa
Molnar, Laszlo (2000). 'Der Staat Vereinigt die beiden Seiten des Subjektiven und Objektiven Kunstwerks', *Hegel-Jahrbuch*: 149–53
Mommsen, Wilhelm (ed.) (1971). *Deutsche Parteiprogramme*, München
Mommsen, Wolfgang J. (1975). Wandlungen der Liberalen Idee im Zeitalter des Imperialismus', in Karl Holl and Deiter List (eds.), *Liberalismus und Imperialistischer Staat*, Göttingen
   (1978) 'Der deutsche Liberalismus zwischen "Klassenloser Bürgergesellschaft" und "Organisiertem Kapitalismus"', *Geschichte und Gesellschaft*, 4: 77–90
   (1984). *Max Weber and German Politics, 1890–1920*, Chicago
   (2000). *Die ungewollte Revolution*, Frankfurt
Monro, D. H. (1953). *Godwin's Moral Philosophy*, Oxford
Moody, T. W. (1981). *Davitt and Irish Revolution*, Oxford
Moore, Barrington, Jr. (1966). *Social Origins of Dictatorship and Democracy: Lord and Peasant in the Making of the Modern World*, Boston
Moore, G. (2002a). *Nietzsche, Biology and Metaphor*, Cambridge
   (2002b). 'Nietzsche, Spencer and the Ethics of Evolution', *Journal of Nietzsche Studies*, 23: 1–20
Moore, G. and Brobjer, T. H. (2004). *Nietzsche and Science*, Aldershot
Moore, J. and Silverthorne, M. (1983). 'Gershom Carmichael and the Natural Jurisprudence Tradition in Eighteenth-Century Scotland', in I. Hont and M. Ignatieff (eds.), *Wealth and Virtue: The Shaping of Political Economy in the Scottish Enlightenment*, Cambridge
Moore, Moses N. (1996). *Orishatukeh Faduma: Liberal Theology and Evangelical Pan-Africanism, 1857–1946*, Lanham, MD
Moravia, Sergio (1974). *Il Pensiero degli Idéologues: Scienza e Filosofia in Francia (1780–1815)*, Florence
   (1980). 'Su Federico Carlo di Savigny', *Quaderni Fiorentini per la Storia del Pensiero Giuridico Moderno*, 9: 451–4
Moreau, Pierre (1935). *L'Histoire en France au XIXe Siècle*, Paris
Morel, E. D. (1906). *Red Rubber: The Story of the Rubber Slave Trade Flourishing on the Congo in the Year of Grace 1906*, London
Mori, M. I., Peers, D. M. and Zastoupil, L. (eds.) (1999). *John Stuart Mill's Encounter with India*, Toronto
Morison, W. L. (1982). *John Austin*, London
Morone, James A. (2003). *Hellfire Nation: The Politics of Sin in American History*, New Haven
Morrow, John (1988). 'Coleridge and the English Revolution', *Political Science*, 40: 128–41
   (1990). *Coleridge's Political Thought, Property, Morality and the Limits of Traditional Discourse*, Basingstoke
   (1997). 'The Paradox of Carlyle as Caslylean Hero', *Historical Journal*, 40: 97–110
   (2000). 'Community, Class and Bosanquet's "New State"', *History of Political Thought*, 21: 485–99
   (2006). *Thomas Carlyle*, London

Morrow, John (ed.) (2007). *T. H. Green*, Aldershot

Mortensen, Preben (1997). *Art in the Social Order: The Making of the Modern Conception of Art*, Albany

Moses, Claire Goldberg (1984). *French Feminism in the 19th Century*, Albany

(1993). *Feminism, Socialism, and French Romanticism*, Bloomington

Moss, Bernard (1976). *The Origins of the French Labor Movement, 1830–1914*, Berkeley

Mosse, George L. (1966). *The Crisis of German Ideology: Intellectual Origins of the Third Reich*, London

(1975). *The Nationalisation of the Masses*, New York

Moulinié, Henri (1915). *De Bonald*, Paris

Mueller Lehning, Arthur (1970). *From Buonarotti to Bakunin: Studies in International Socialism*, Leiden

Muirhead, J. H. (1915). *German Philosophy in Relation to the War*, London

Muldoon, James (1999). *Empire and Order: The Concept of Empire, 800–1800*, Basingstoke

Muller, Jerry Z. (1997). 'Introduction', in Jerry Z. Muller (ed.), *Conservatism. An Anthology of Social and Political Thought from David Hume to the Present*, Princeton

Murphy, Peter T. (1985). 'Visions of Success: Byron and Southey', *Studies in Romanticism*, 24: 355–73

Muthu, Sankar (2003). *Enlightenment Against Empire*, Princeton

Na'aman, Shlomo (1970). *Lassalle*, Hanover.

Naimark, Norman M. (1983). *Terrorists and Social Democrats: The Russian Revolutionary Movement under Alexander III*, Cambridge, MA

Namier, L. B. (1940). *1848: The Revolution of the Intellectuals*, London

Nash, David and Taylor, Antony (2000). *Republicanism in Victorian Society*, Stroud.

Naumann, Friedrich (1964). *Politische Schriften*, 4 vols., Opladen

Nehamas, Alexander (1996). 'Nietzsche, Modernity, Aestheticism', in Bernd Magnus and Kathleen M. Higgins (eds.), *The Cambridge Companion to Nietzsche*, Cambridge

Nelson, Eric (2004). *The Greek Tradition in Republican Thought*, Cambridge

New Formations (2007). 'Eugenics: Old and New', Special Issue, No. 60

Neuhouser, Frederick (1990). *Fichte's Theory of Subjectivity*, Cambridge

Newbury, Paul W. (ed.) (1999). *Aboriginal Heroes of the Resistance: From Pemulwuy to Mabo*, Surry Hills

Newsinger, John (1994). *Fenianism in Mid-Victorian Britain*, London

Nicholson, Peter P. (1990). *The Political Philosophy of the British Idealists: Selected Studies*, Cambridge

Nicolet, C. (1982). *L'Idée Républicaine en France (1789–1924): Essai d'Histoire Critique*, Paris

Nicoll, Fergus (2004). *The Mahdi of Sudan and the Death of General Gordon*, Stroud

Nimni, Ephraim (1991). *Marxism and Nationalism: Theoretical Origins of the Political Crisis*, London

Nisbet, Robert (1944). 'De Bonald and the Concept of the Social Group', *Journal of the History of Ideas*, 5: 315–31

(1978). 'Conservatism', in Tom Bottomore and Robert Nisbet (eds.), *A History of Sociological Analysis*, London

Niven, John (1988). *John C. Calhoun and the Price of Union: A Biography*, Baton Rouge

Nomad, Max (1966). 'The Anarchist Tradition', in M. M. Drachkovitch (ed.), *The Revolutionary Internationals, 1864–1943*. Stanford

Nonini, Donald M. (1992). *British Colonial Rule and the Resistance of the Malay Peasantry, 1900–1957*, New Haven

Bibliography

Nord, Philip (1995). *The Republican Moment: Struggles for Democracy in Nineteenth-Century France*, Cambridge, MA

Nordhoff, Charles (1966 [1875]). *The Communistic Societies of the United States*, London

Norman, Judith (2000). 'Squaring the Romantic Circle: Hegel's Critique of Schlegel's Theories of Art', in William Maker (ed.), *Hegel and Aesthetics*, Albany

Noyes, P. H. (1966). *Organization und Revolution: Working-Class Associations in the German Revolutions of 1848–1849*, Princeton

Nugent, Walter (2008). *Habits of Empire: A History of American Expansion*, New York

Nye, R. A. (1975). *The Origins of Crowd Psychology: Gustave Le Bon and the Crisis of Mass Democracy in the Third Republic*, London

  (1994). *Crime, Madness and Politics in Modern France: The Medical Concept of National Decline*, Princeton

O'Brien, Karen (2001). 'Poetry Against Empire: Milton to Shelley', *Proceedings of the British Academy*, 117: 269–96

O'Brien, Patrick (2006). 'Historiographical Traditions and Modern Imperatives for the Restoration of Global History', *Journal of Global History*, 1: 3–39

O'Brien, William Arctander (1995). *Novalis: Signs of Revolution*, Durham, NC

O'Brion, Leon (1973). 'The Invincibles', in T. Desmond Williams (ed.), *Secret Societies in Ireland*, Dublin

O'Donoghue, D. J. (1902). *Life of Robert Emmet*, Dublin

O'Gorman, Frank (1973). *Edmund Burke: His Political Philosophy*, London

O'Hanlon, Rosalind (1985). *Caste, Conflict and Ideology*, Cambridge

O'Hegarty, P. S. (1919). *Sinn Fein: An Illumination*, Dublin

  (1924). *The Victory of Sinn Fein*, Dublin

O'Rourke, K. (2001). *John Stuart Mill and Freedom of Expression: The Genesis of a Theory*, London

Oakeshott, Michael (1962). 'On Being Conservative', in *Rationalism in Politics and Other Essays*, London

Obermann, Karl (1947). *Joseph Weydemeyer: Pioneer of American Socialism*, New York

Offen, K. (2000). *European Feminisms, 1700–1950: A Political History*, Stanford

  (2010). *Globalising Feminisms, 1789–1945*, London

Ogden, C. K. (1932). *Jeremy Bentham, 1832–2032*, London

Okey, Robin (2000). *The Habsburg Monarchy, c.1765–1918*, London

Oldfield, John J. (1973). *The Problem of Tolerance and Social Existence in the Writings of Félicité Lamennais, 1809–1831*, Leiden

Oldroyd, D. R. (1980). *Darwinian Impacts: An Introduction to the Darwinian Revolution*, London

Oliver, Hermia (1983). *The International Anarchist Movement in Late Victorian London*, London

Oncken, Hermann (1912). *Lassalle*, 2nd edition, Stuttgart.

Onuf, Peter S. (1993b). 'The Scholar's Jefferson', *William and Mary Quarterly*, 3rd Series (October)

  (2000). *Jefferson's Empire: The Language of American Nationhood*, Charlottesville

Onuf, Peter S. (ed.) (1993a). *Jeffersonian Legacies*, Charlottesville

Orisini, G. (1969). *Coleridge and German Idealism*, Carbondale, IL

Osofsky, Stephen (1979). *Peter Kropotkin*, Boston

Ospovat, D. (1980). 'God and Natural Selection: The Darwinian Idea of Design', *Journal of the History of Biology*, 13: 169–94

Owen, James (2008). 'Triangular Contests and Caucus Rhetoric at the 1885 General Election', *Parliamentary History*, 27: 215–35

Owen, Nicholas (2003). 'British Progressives and Civil Society in India, 1905–1914', in Jose Harris (ed.), *Civil Society in British History*, Oxford

Bibliography

Owen, Roger (2004). *Lord Cromer: Victorian Imperialist, Edwardian Proconsul*, Oxford

Ozouf, Mona (1989). *L'Homme Régénéré: Essais sur la Révolution Française*, Paris

Packe, Michael St. John (1954). *The Life of John Stuart Mill*, London

(1957). *The Bombs of Orsini*, London

Packer, Ian (2003). 'Religion and the New Liberalism: The Rowntree Family, Quakerism, and Social Reform', *Journal of British Studies*, 42: 236–57

Paetzold, Heinz (1992). 'Rhetorik-Kritik und Theorie der Künste in der Philosophischen Ästhetik von Baumgarten bis Kant', in Gérard Raulet (ed.), *Von der Rhetorik zur Ästhetik. Studien zur Entstehung der Modernen Ästhetik im Achtzehnten Jahrhundert*, Rennes

Pagden, Anthony (1995). *Lords of All the World: Ideologies of Empire in Spain, Britain and France, c.1500–c.1800*, New Haven

(1998). *Spanish Imperialism and the Political Imagination: Studies in European and Spanish-American Social and Political Theory*, New Haven

Pal, Satyendranth (1991). *Rise of Radicalism in Bengal in the Nineteenth Century*, Calcutta

Palmegiano, E. M. (1976). *Women and British Periodicals, 1832–1867*, New York

Palsdottir, Sigrun (2001). 'Icelandic Culture in Victorian Thought', D.Phil. thesis, University of Oxford

Paludan, Philip Shaw (1994). *The Presidency of Abraham Lincoln* (American Presidency Series), Lawrenceville

Pancaldi, G. (1983). *Darwin in Italia: Impresa Scientifica e Frontiere Culturali*, Bologna

Pankhurst, Richard (1957). *The Saint-Simonians, Mill and Carlyle*, London

Pappe, H. O. (1951). 'Wakefield and Marx', *Economic History Review*, 4: 88–97

Pareyson, Luigi (1974). *Estetica. Teoria della Formatività*, 3rd edition, Florence

Parrinder, Patrick (1972). *H. G. Wells*, Edinburgh

Parris, H. (1960). 'The Nineteenth-Century Revolution in Government: A Reappraisal Reappraised', *Historical Journal*, 3: 17–37

Parry, Albert (1976). *Terrorism: From Robespierre to Arafat*, New York

Parry, J. P. (1986). *Democracy and Religion: Gladstone and the Liberal Party, 1867–75*, Cambridge

(1993). *The Rise and Fall of Liberal Government in Victorian Britain*, New Haven and London

(2001). 'The Impact of Napoleon III on British Politics, 1851–1880', *Transactions of the Royal Historical Society*, 11: 147–75

(2006). *The Politics of Patriotism: English Liberalism, National Identity and Europe, 1830–86*, Cambridge

Parvi, Jerzy (1992). *Révolution, Indépendance, Romantisme*, Warsaw

Paternò, Maria Pia (1993). *Friedrich Gentz e la Rivoluzione Francese*, Rome

Patsouras, Louis (1987). 'Jean Grave and the French Anarchist Tradition', in Louis Patsouras (ed.), *Crucible of Socialism*, Atlantic Highlands

Patten, Alan (1999). *Hegel's Idea of Freedom*, Oxford

Paul, H. W. (1972). 'Religion and Darwinism: Varieties of Catholic Reaction', in T. Glick (ed.), *The Comparative Reception of Darwinism*, Austin, TX

Paul, Leslie (1951). *The Age of Terror*, Boston

Paulin, Tom (1998). *The Day-star of Liberty: William Hazlitt's Radical Style*, London

Pawlikova-Vilhanova, Vera (1988). *History of Anti-Colonial Resistance and Protest in the Kingdoms of Buganda and Bunyoro, 1890–1899*, Prague

Paxton, N. L. (1991). *George Eliot and Herbert Spencer: Feminism, Evolutionism, and the Reconstruction of Gender*, Princeton

Peacock, A. J. (1965). *Bread or Blood: A Study of the Agrarian Riots in East Anglia in 1816*, London

Peel, J. D. Y. (1971). *Herbert Spencer. The Evolution of a Sociologist*, London and New York

(2000). *Religious Encounter and the Making of the Yoruba*, Bloomington

Pelczynski, Z. A. (1971). 'The Hegelian Conception of the State', in Pelczynski, *Hegel's Political Philosophy: Problems and Perspectives*, Cambridge

Pelczynski, Z. A. (ed.) (1984). *The State and Civil Society: Studies in Hegel's Political Philosophy*, Cambridge

Peperzak, Adrian (2001). *Modern Freedom: Hegel's Legal, Moral, and Political Philosophy*, Dordrecht

Pereira, Norman (1975). *The Thought and Teaching of N. G. Cernysevskij*, The Hague

Perinbam, B. M. (1982). *Holy Violence: The Revolutionary Thought of Frantz Fanon*, Washington, DC

Pernicone, Nunzio (1993). *Italian Anarchism, 1864–1892*, Princeton

Perras, Arne (2004). *Carl Peters and German Imperialism, 1856–1918: A Political Biography*, Oxford

Petersen, Jens (2007). *Wilhelm von Humboldts Rechtsphilosophie*, Berlin

Peterson, Merrill D. (1960). *The Jefferson Image in the American Mind*, Indianapolis,
  (1986). *Thomas Jefferson and the New Nation: A Biography*, New York
  (1987). *The Great Triumvirate: Webster, Clay, Calhoun*, New York

Petitjean, Patrick (2004). 'Science and the "Civilising Mission": France and the Colonial Enterprise', in Benedikt Stuchtey (ed.), *Science Across the European Empires, 1800–1950*, Oxford

Petrovich, Michael Boro (1956). *The Emergence of Russian Panslavism, 1856–1870*, New York

Pettit, Philip (1997). *Republicanism: A Theory of Freedom and Government*, Oxford

Phillips, R. (1991). *Untying the Knot: A Short History of Divorce*, Cambridge

Philp, Mark (1986). *Godwin's Political Justice*, Ithaca
  (1998). 'English Republicanism in the 1790s', *Journal of Political Philosophy*, 6: 235–62

Pick, Daniel (1989). *Faces of Degeneration: A European Disorder, c.1848–c.1918*, Cambridge
  (2003). *War Machine: The Rationalisation of Slaughter in the Modern Age*, New Haven and London

Pickering, M. (1993). *Auguste Comte: An Intellectual Biography*, Vol. 1, Cambridge

Picon, Antoine (2002). *Les Saint-Simoniens: Raison, Imaginaire et Utopia*, London

Pierson, George Wilson (1996). *Tocqueville in America*, Baltimore

Pierson, Stanley (1993). *Marxist Intellectuals and the Working-class Mentality in Germany, 1887–91*, Cambridge, MA

Pilbeam, Pamela (1995). *Republicanism in Nineteenth Century France, 1814–1871*, Basingstoke
  (2000). *French Socialism Before Marx: Workers, Women and the Social Question in France*, Teddington

Pinkard, Terry (2000). *Hegel: A Biography*, Cambridge
  (2002). *German Philosophy, 1760–1860*, Cambridge

Pinker, Robert (1966). *English Hospital Statistics, 1861–1938*, London

Pipes, Richard (1959). *Karamzin's Memoir on Ancient and Modern Russia: A Translation and Analysis*, Cambridge, MA

Pippin, Robert B. (1989). *Hegel's Idealism: The Satisfactions of Self-Consciousness*, Cambridge
  (1991). *Modernism as a Philosophical Problem: On the Dissatisfactions of European High Culture*, Oxford
  (1996). 'Nietzsche's Alleged Farewell: The Premodern, Modern, and Postmodern Nietzsche', in Bernd Magnus and Kathleen M. Higgins (eds.), *The Cambridge Companion to Nietzsche*, Cambridge
  (1997a). 'Hegel's Ethical Rationalism', in Pippin, *Idealism as Modernism: Hegelian Variations*, Cambridge
  (1997b). *Idealism as Modernism: Hegelian Variations*, Cambridge

Pitts, Jennifer (2005). *A Turn to Empire: The Rise of Imperial Liberalism in Britain and France*, Princeton

(2007). 'The Boundaries of Victorian International Law', in Duncan Bell (ed.), *Victorian Visions of Global Order: Empire and International Relations in Nineteenth-Century Political Thought*, Cambridge

Plamenatz, John (1952). *The Revolutionary Movement in France, 1815–71*, London

(1963). *Man and Society*, 2 vols., London

Plant, Raymond (1973). *Hegel*, London

(2006). 'T. H. Green: Citizenship, Education and the Law', *Oxford Review of Education*, 32: 23–37

Plessis, Alain (1985 [1979]). *The Rise and Fall of the Second Empire, 1852–71*, Cambridge

Pluhar, Werner S. (1987). 'Translator's Introduction', in Immanuel Kant, *Critique of Judgement*, Indianapolis

Pocock, J. G. A. (1975). *The Machiavellian Moment: Florentine Political Thought and the Atlantic Republican Tradition*, Princeton

(1982). 'The Political Economy of Burke's Analysis of the French Revolution', *Historical Journal*, 25: 331–49

(1985). *Virtue, Commerce, and History*, Cambridge

(1990/2005). 'Empire, State and Confederation: The War of American Independence as a Crisis in Multiple Monarchy', in Pocock, *The Discovery of Islands: Essays in British History*, Cambridge

(2005). *Barbarism and Religion*, Vol. IV: *Barbarians, Savages, and Empires*, Cambridge

Pohl, Karl Heinrich (1995). 'Die Nationalliberalen in Sachsen vor 1914. Eine Partei der Konservativen Honoratiorenschicht auf dem Wege zur Partei der Industrie', in Lothar Gall and Dieter Langewiesche (eds.), *Liberalismus und Region*, Historische Zeitschrift Beiheft 19, München

Poliakov, Leon (1974). *The Aryan Myth: A History of Racist and Nationalist Ideas in Europe*, London

Polkinghorn, Bette (1993). *Jane Marcet: An Uncommon Woman*, Aldermaston

Pollard, Sidney and Salt, John (eds.) (1971). *Robert Owen: Prophet of the Poor*, London

Pomper, Philip (1972). *Peter Lavrov and the Russian Revolutionary Movement*, Chicago and London

Poole, Steve (2000). *The Politics of Regicide in England, 1760–1850*, Manchester

Poovey, M. (1988). *Uneven Developments: The Ideological Work of Gender in Mid-Victorian England*, Chicago

Pope, Daniel (ed.) (2001). *American Radicalism*, Oxford

Popitz, Heinrich (1953). *Der Entfremdete Mensch*, Basel

Popper, Karl (1945). *The Open Society and its Enemies*, 2 vols., London

Porter, Andrew (ed.) (1999). *The Oxford History of the British Empire, Vol III: The Nineteenth Century*, Oxford

Porter, Bernard (2004). *The Absent-minded Imperialists: Empire, Society, and Culture in Britain*, Oxford.

Porter, Ray and Teich, Mikuláš (eds.) (1988). *Romanticism in National Context*, Cambridge

Posada-Carbo, Eduardo (ed.) (1998). *In Search of a New Order: Essays on the Politics and Society of Latin America*, London

Postgate, R. W. (1926). *Out of the Past: Some Revolutionary Sketches*, New York

Pott, Hans-Georg (1980). *Die Schöne Freiheit*, Munich

Pozzetta, George E. (ed.) (1981). *Immigrant Radicals: The View from the Left*, London

Préposiet, Jean (1993). *Histoire de l'Anarchisme*, Paris

Price, Roger (1988). *The Revolutions of 1848*, London

Prickett, Stephen (1976). *Romanticism and Religion: The Tradition of Coleridge and Wordsworth in the Victorian Church*, Cambridge

Pringle-Pattison, A. S. (1907). *The Philosophical Radicals and Other Essays with Chapters Reprinted on the Philosophy of Religion in Kant and Hegel*, Edinburgh

Procacci, G. (1993). *Gouverner Le misère: la Question Sociale en France, 1789–1848*, Paris.

Prothero, I. J. (1974). 'William Benbow and the Concept of the 'General Strike', *Past and Present*, 63: 132–71

Pugh, Martin (2002). *The Making of Modern British Politics, 1867–1945*, 3rd edition, Oxford

Puntambekar, S. V. (1929). 'The "Ajnapatra" or Royal Edict Relating to the Principles of Maratha State Policy', *Journal of Indian History*, 8: 81–105, 207–33

Purcell, Victor (1963). *The Boxer Uprising*, Cambridge, MA

Pusey, J. R. (1983). *China and Charles Darwin*, Cambridge, MA

Pyle, A. (1994). *Liberty: Contemporary Responses to John Stuart Mill*, Bristol

Pyle, Kenneth B. (1974). 'Advantages of Followership: German Economics and Japanese Bureaucrats, 1890–1925', *Journal of Japanese Studies*, 1: 127–64

Pyziur, Eugene (1968). *The Doctrine of Anarchism of Michael A. Bakunin*, Chicago

Quagliariello, G. (1996). *Politics without Parties: Moisei Ostrogorski and the Debate on Political Parties on the Eve of the Twentieth Century*, Aldershot

Quail, John (1978). *The Slow Burning Fuse*, London

Quataert, Jean (1979). *Reluctant Feminists in German Social Democracy, 1885–1917*, Princeton

Quentin-Bauchart, Paul (1903). *Lamartine, Homme Politique*, Paris

Quine, W. V. (1995). *From Stimulus to Science*, Cambridge, MA

Quinlan, Mary Hall (1953). *The Historical Thought of the Vicomte de Bonald: A Dissertation*, Washington, DC

Quinlivan, Patrick and Rose, Paul (1982). *The Fenians in England, 1865–1872*, London

Quint, Howard (1953). *The Forging of American Socialism: Origins of the Modern Movement*, Charleston

Quinton, Anthony (1978). *The Politics of Imperfection: The Religious and Secular Traditions of Conservative Thought from Hooker to Oakeshott*, London

Qvortrup, Mads (1999). 'A. V. Dicey: The Referendum as the People's Veto', *History of Political Thought*, 20: 531–46

Raeburn, Antonia (1973). *The Militant Suffragettes*, London

Raeff, Marc (1957). *Michael Speransky: Statesman of Imperial Russia*, The Hague

Randolph, John (2007). *The House in the Garden: The Bakunin Family and the Romance of Russian Idealism*, Ithaca

Rapoport, David C. and Alexander, Yonah (eds.) (1989). *The Morality of Terrorism: Religious and Secular Justifications*, New York

Rathbone, E. (1924). *The Disinherited Family*, London

Raulet, Gérard (1992). 'Von der Allegorie zur Geschichte. Säkularisierung und Ornament im 18. Jahrhundert', in Gérard Raulet (ed.), *Von der Rhetorik zur Ästhetik. Studien zur Entstehung der Modernen Ästhetik im Achtzehnten Jahrhundert*, Rennes

Raven, C. E. (1920). *Christian Socialism 1848–54*, London

Ravindranathan, T. R. (1988). *Bakunin and the Italians*, Kingston and Montreal

Rawls, John (2000). *Lectures on the History of Moral Philosophy*. Cambridge, MA

Raynaud, Philippe (1989). 'Burke et les Allemands', in François Furet and Mona Ozouf (eds.), *The Transformation of Political Culture, 1789–1848*, Oxford

Readman, Paul (2008). *Land and Nation in England: Patriotism, National Identity and the Politics of Land, 1880–1914*, Woodbridge

Reagin, Nancy R. (1995). *A German Women's Movement*, Chapel Hill, NC

Reardon, Bernard M. G. (1975). *Liberalism and Tradition: Aspects of Catholic Thought in Nineteenth-century France*, Cambridge

(1985). *Religion in the Age of Romanticism: Studies in Early Nineteenth-Century Thought*, Cambridge

Reddy, W. M. (1984). *The Rise of Market Culture: The Textile Trade and French Society, 1750–1900*, Cambridge

Redeker, Martin (1973 [1968]). *Schleiermacher: Life and Thought*, trans. John Wallhauser, Philadelphia

Reed, T. J. (1984). *Goethe*, Oxford

Reedy, W. Jay (1983). 'Language, Counterrevolution and the "Two Cultures": Bonald's Traditionalist Scientism', *Journal of the History of Ideas*, 44: 579–97

(1993). 'History, Authority and the Ideological Representation of Tradition in Louis de Bonald's Science of Society', *Studies on Voltaire and the Eighteenth Century*, 311: 143–77

(1995). 'The Traditionalist Critique of Individualism in Post-Revolutionary France: The Case of Louis de Bonald', *History of Political Thought*, 16(1): 49–75

Rees, John (1978). *Mill and His Early Critics*, Leicester

Reeves, Richard (2007). *John Stuart Mill: Victorian Firebrand*, London

Reeves, William Pember (1901). 'Review of Essays in Colonial Finance', *The Economic Journal*, 11: 60–3

(1902). *State Experiments in Australia and New Zealand*, 2 vols., London

Reichert, William O. (1976). *Partisans of Freedom: A Study in American Anarchism*, Bowling Green

(1984). 'Natural Right in the Political Philosophy of P.-J. Proudhon', in T. Holterman and H. van Maarseveen (eds.), *Law and Anarchism*, Montreal

Reiff, Paul Friedrich (1912). *Friedrich Gentz: An Opponent of the French Revolution and Napoleon*, Urbana-Champaign

Reill, Peter Hanns (1975). *The German Enlightenment and the Rise of Historicism*, Berkeley

Reis, João José (1993). *Slave Rebellion in Brazil: The Muslim Uprising of 1835 in Bahia*, Baltimore

Reiß, Ansgar (2004). *Radikalismus und Exil: Gustav Struve und die Demokratie in Deutschland und Amerika*, Stuttgart

Reiss, Hans Siegbert (ed. and trans.) (1955). *Political Thought of the German Romantics, 1793–1815*, Oxford

Reizov, B. (n.d.). *L'Historiographie Romantique Française, 1815–1830*, Moscow

Rémond, René (1969). *The Right Wing in France: From 1815 to de Gaulle [La Droite en France (1954)]*, trans. James M. Laux, 2nd edition, Philadelphia

Rendall, J. (1985). *The Origins of Modern Feminism: Women in Britain, France and the United States, 1780–1860*, London

Repp, Kevin (2000). *Reformers, Critics, and the Paths of German Modernity: Anti-Politics and the Search for Alternatives, 1890–1914*, Cambridge, MA

Retallack, James (1988). *Notables of the Right: The Conservative Party and Political Mobilisation in Germany, 1876–1918*, London

Reynaud-Paligot, Carole (1993). *'Les Temps Nouveaux' 1895–1914*, Pantin

Reynolds, David S. (2005). *John Brown: Abolitionist*, New York

(2008). *Waking Giant: America in the Age of Jackson*, New York

Reynolds, Henry (1982). *The Other Side of the Frontier: Aboriginal Resistance to the European Invasion of Australia*, Harmondsworth

Riall, Lucy (1994). *The Italian Risorgimento: State, Society and National Unification*, London

(2007) *Garibaldi: Invention of a Hero*, Basingstoke

Riasanovsky, Nicholas V. (1969). *Nicholas I and Official Nationality in Russia, 1825–1855*, Berkeley

(1969). *The Teaching of Charles Fourier*, Berkeley

Rich, Paul (1986). *Race and Empire in British Politics*, Cambridge

Richards, E. (1989). 'Huxley and Woman's Place in Science', in James Moore (ed.), *History, Humanity and Evolution*, Cambridge

Richards, R. J. (1982). 'Darwin and the Biologising of Moral Behaviour', in W. R. Woodward and T. Ash (eds.), *The Problematic Science: Psychology in Nineteenth-Century Thought*, New York

Richards, Vernon (ed.) (1965). *Errico Malatesta: His Life and Ideas*, London

Richardson, A. (2003). *Love and Eugenics in the Late Nineteenth Century: Rational Reproduction and the New Woman*, Oxford

Richardson, Heather Cox (2001). *The Death of Reconstruction: Race, Labour, and Politics in the Post-Civil War North, 1865–1901*, Cambridge, MA

(2007). *West from Appomattox: The Reconstruction of America*, New Haven

Richardson, J. (2004). *Nietzsche's New Darwinism*, Oxford

Richardson, J. S. (1991). '*Imperium Romanum*: Empire and the Language of Power', *Journal of Roman Studies*, 81: 1–9

Richardson, R. (1986). 'Bentham and "Bodies for Dissection"', *The Bentham Newsletter*, 10: 22–33

(2001 [1988]). *Death, Dissection and the Destitute*, 2nd edition, London

Richardson, Jr., Robert D. (1986). *Henry Thoreau: A Life of the Mind*, Berkeley

(1995). *Emerson: The Mind on Fire*, Berkeley

Richter, Melvin (1963). 'Tocqueville on Algeria', *Review of Politics*, 25: 60–77

(1964). *The Politics of Conscience: T. H. Green and His Age*, London

Ridley, F. F. (1970). *Revolutionary Syndicalism in France*, Cambridge

Riedel, Manfred (1973). *System und Geschichte: Studien zum Historischen Standort von Hegels Philosophie*, Frankfurt

(1984). *Between Tradition and Revolution: The Hegelian Transformation of Political Philosophy*, trans. Walter Wright, Cambridge

Rigby, S. H. (1992). *Engels and the Formation of Marxism: History, Dialectics and Revolution*, Manchester

Rihs, Charles (1978). *L'École des Jeunes Hégéliens et les Penseurs Socialistes Français*, Paris

Riley, Jonathan (1998). *Mill on Liberty*, London

Riley, Patrick (1982). *Will and Political Legitimacy*, Cambridge, MA

(1986). *The General Will before Rousseau*, Princeton

Ripoli, M. (1998). 'The Return of James Mill', *Utilitas*, 10: 105–21

Ritter, Alan (1969). *The Political Thought of Pierre-Joseph Proudhon*, Princeton

(1980). *Anarchism: A Theoretical Analysis*, Cambridge

Ritter, Joachim (1965). *Hegel und die Franzöische Revolution*, Frankfurt

Ritvo, Lucille (1990). *Darwin's Influence on Freud*, New Haven

Rivers, W. H. R. (1923). *Psychology and Politics*, London

Rizvi, S. A. A. (1980). *Shah Wali-allah and his Times*, Canberra

(1982). *Shah Abd al-Aziz, Puritanism, Sectarian Politics and Jihad*, Canberra

Robbins, Lionel (1932). *An Essay on the Nature and Significance of Economic Science*, London

Roberts, D. (1959). 'Jeremy Bentham and the Victorian Administrative State', *Victorian Studies*, 2: 193–210

Roberts, J. M. (1973). 'The French Origins of the "Right"', *Transactions of the Royal Historical Society*, 23: 27–53

Roberts, M. J. D. (2004). *Making English Morals: Voluntary Association and Moral Reform in England, 1787–1886*, Cambridge

Roberts, M. L. (2002). *Disruptive Acts: The New Woman in Fin-de-Siècle France*, Chicago

Robinson, Dean (2001). *Black Nationalism in American Politics and Thought*, Cambridge

Robinson, Fergus and York, Barry (1977). *The Black Resistance: An Introduction to the History of the Aborigines' Struggle against British Colonialism*, Camberwell

Robson, J. M. (1964). 'John Stuart Mill and Jeremy Bentham, with some Observations on James Mill', in M. MacLure and F. Watt (eds.), *Essays in English Literature from the Renaissance to the Victorian Age Presented to A. S. P. Woodhouse*, Toronto

   (1968). *The Improvement of Mankind: The Social and Political Thought of John Stuart Mill*, Toronto

   (1993 [1983]). 'Which Bentham was Mill's Bentham?', in B. Parekh (ed.), *Jeremy Bentham: Critical Assessments*, 4 vols., London

Rocker, Rudolf (1949). *Pioneers of American Freedom*, Los Angeles

Rodgers, Daniel T. (1992). 'Republicanism: The Career of a Concept', *Journal of American History* (June): 11–38

   (1998a). *Atlantic Politics: Social Politics in a Progressive Age*, Cambridge, MA

   (1998b). 'Exceptionalism', in Anthony Molho and Gordon S. Wood (eds.), *Imagined Histories: American Historians Interpret the Past*, Princeton

Rodriguez, Jaime E. (1997). *The Independence of Spanish America*, Cambridge

Roe, Nicholas (1988). *Wordsworth and Coleridge: The Radical Years*, Oxford

Roe, W. G. (1966). *Lamennais and England*, Oxford

Rogers, H. (2000). *Women and the People: Authority, Authorship and the Radical Tradition in Nineteenth-Century England*, Aldershot

Rogers, P. G. (1962). *Battle in Bossenden Wood: The Strange Story of Sir William Courtenay*, Oxford

Rogger, Hans and Weber, Eugen (eds.) (1966). *The European Right*, Berkeley

Rogin, Michael Paul (1975). *Fathers and Children: Andrew Jackson and the Subjugation of the American Indian*, New York

   (1983). *Subversive Genealogies: The Politics and Art of Herman Melville*, New York

Rohs, Peter (1991). *Johann Gottlieb Fichte*, Munich

Romani, Roberto (2002). *National Character and Public Spirit in Britain and France, 1750–1914*, Cambridge

Ronsin, F. (1980). *La Grève des Ventres: Propagande Néo-Malthusienne et Baisse de la Natalité Française, xixe–xxe Siècles*, Paris

Roosevelt, Priscilla R. (1986). *Apostle of Russian Liberalism: Timofei Granovsky*, Newtonville, MA

Roper, Jon (1989). *Democracy and its Critics: Anglo-American Democratic Thought in the Nineteenth Century*, London

Rosanvallon, Pierre (1985). *Le Moment Guizot*, Paris

   (1994). *La Monarchie Impossible: Les Chartes de 1814 et de 1830*, Paris

Rosdolsky, Roman (1977). *The Making of Marx's 'Capital'*, London

   (1986). *Engels and the 'Nonhistoric' Peoples: The National Question in the Revolution of 1848*, ed., trans. and intro. John-Paul Himka, Glasgow

Rose, R. B. (1978). *Gracchus Babeuf: The First Revolutionary Communist*, Stanford

Rose, S. *et al.* (1984). *Not in our Genes: Biology, Ideology and Human Nature*, Harmondsworth

Rosen, Frederick (1983). *Jeremy Bentham and Representative Democracy: A Study of the Constitutional Code*, Oxford

   (1987). *Progress and Democracy: William Godwin's Contribution to Political Philosophy*, New York

(1992). *Bentham, Byron, and Greece: Constitutionalism, Nationalism, and Early Liberal Political Thought*, Oxford

(2003). *Classical Utilitarianism from Hume to Mill*, London

(2004). 'Jeremy Bentham's Radicalism', in G. Burgess and M. Festenstein (eds.), *English Radicalism 1550–1850*, Cambridge

Rosenberg, Philip (1974). *The Seventh Hero: Thomas Carlyle and the Theory of Radical Activism*, Cambridge, MA

Rosenzweig, Franz (1920). *Hegel und der Staat*, 2 vols., Munich. Reprint (1982), Aalen

Ross, Ronald J. (1998). *The Failure of Bismarck's Kulturkampf: Catholicism and State Power in Imperial Germany, 1871–1887*, Washington

Rossiter, Clinton (1968). 'Conservatism', in D. Sills (ed.), *International Encyclopaedia of Social Science*, New York

Roth, Ralf (1998). 'Bürger und Workers: Liberalism and the Labour Movement in Germany, 1848 to 1914', in David E. Barclay and Eric D. Weitz (eds.), *Between Reform and Revolution: German Socialism and Communism from 1840 to 1990*, New York and Oxford

Roth, Regina and Moseley, Fred (2002). 'Marx, Engels, and the Text of Book 3 of *Capital*', *International Journal of Political Economy*, 32

Rothschild, Emma (1998). '*Smithianismus* and Enlightenment in Nineteenth-Century Europe', Working Paper, Centre for History and Economics, King's College, Cambridge

(2001). *Economic Sentiments: Adam Smith, Condorcet and the Enlightenment*, Cambridge, MA

Rowe, Michael (ed.) (2003). *Collaboration and Resistance in Napoleonic Europe: State Formation in an Age of Upheaval, c.1800–1815*, London

Rowlands, J. H. L. (1989). *Church, State and Society: The Attitudes of John Keble, Richard Hurrel Froude and John Henry Newman, 1827–1845*, Worthing

Royer, J.-P. (1979). *La Société Judiciaire depuis le XVIIIe Siècle*, Paris

Royle, Edward (1974). *Victorian Infidels: The Origins of the British Secularist Movement 1791–1866*, Manchester

(1980). *Radicals, Secularists and Republicans: Popular Freethought in Britain, 1866–1915*, Manchester

(1998). *Robert Owen and the Commencement of the Millennium: A Study of the Harmony Community*, Manchester

(2000). *Revolutionary Britannia? Reflections on the Threat of Revolution in Britain, 1789–1848*, Manchester

Rubinstein, Richard E. (1987). *Alchemists of Revolution: Terrorism in the Modern World*, New York.

Rudolph, Günter (1984). *Karl Rodbertus und die Grundrententheorie: Politische Ökonomie aus dem Deutschen Vormärz*, Berlin

Rüsen, Jörn (1976). *Ästhetik und Geschichte*, Stuttgart

Runciman, David (1997). *Pluralism and the Personality of the State*, Cambridge

Ryan, Alan (1975). *J. S. Mill*, London

(1984). *Property and Political Theory*, Oxford

(1987 [1970]). *The Philosophy of John Stuart Mill*, 2nd edition, Basingstoke

(1998). 'Mill in a Liberal Landscape', in John Skorupski (ed.), *The Cambridge Companion to Mill*, Cambridge

Ryan, Tim and Parham, Bill (2002). *The Colonial New Zealand Wars*, Wellington

Ryusaku, Tsunoda *et al.* (eds.) (1964). *Sources of Japanese Tradition*, Vol. II, New York

Sacks, Kenneth S. (2003). *Understanding Emerson: 'The American Scholar' and his Struggle for Self-Reliance*, Princeton

Salmon, J. H. M. (1995). 'Constitutions Old and New: Henrion de Pansey before and after the French Revolution', *The Historical Journal*, 38: 907–31.

Salvadori, Massimo (1979 [1976]). *Karl Kautsky and the Socialist Revolution, 1880–1938*, trans. Jon Rothschild, London

Samuels, Arthur Warren (1911). *Home Rule: Fenian Home Rule: Home Rule All Round: Devolution: What Do They Mean?*, Dublin

Samuels, Ernest (1948). *The Young Henry Adams*, Boston
   (1958). *Henry Adams: The Middle Years*, Boston
   (1964). *Henry Adams: The Major Phase*. Boston

Sandel, Michael J. (1996). *Democracy's Discontent: America in Search of a Public Philosophy*, Cambridge, MA

Sanders, V. (1996). *Eve's Renegades: Victorian Anti-Feminist Women Novelists*, Basingstoke

Sanderson, S. K. (1990). *Social Evolutionism: A Critical History*, Oxford

Sapiro, Virginia (1992). *A Vindication of Political Virtue: The Political Theory of Mary Wollstonecraft*, Chicago

Sarrazin, H. (2004). *Elisée Reclus ou la Passion du Monde*, Paris

Sartori, Andrew (2008). *Bengal in Global Concept History: Culturalism in the Age of Capital*, Chicago

Saye, Robert and Löwry, Michael (1984). 'Figures of Romantic Anti-Capitalism', *New German Criticism*, 32: 42–92

Scales, Len and Zimmer, Oliver (eds.) (2005). *Power and the Nation in European History*, Cambridge

Scanlan, James P. (2002). *Dostoevsky the Thinker*, Ithaca

Schomber, Ellie Nower (1984). *The Artist as Politician: The Relationship between the Arts and the Politics of the French Romantics*, Lanham, MD

Schapiro, Leonard (1967). *Rationalism and Nationalism in Russian Nineteenth-Century Political Thought*, New Haven and London
   (1986). *Russian Studies*, ed. Ellen Dahrendorf, London

Schattschneider, E. E. (1960). *The Semi-Sovereign People*, New York

Schenk, H. G. (1979 [1966]). *The Mind of the European Romantics: An Essay in Cultural History*, Oxford

Scheuner, Ulrich (1978). 'Staatsbild und Politische Form in der Romantischen Anschauung in Deutschland', in Richard Brinkmann (ed.), *Romantik in Deutschland. Ein Interdisziplinäres Symposion*, Stuttgart
   (1980). *Der Beitrag des Deutschen Romantik zur Politschen Theorie*, Opladen

Schimséwitsch, L. (1936). *Portalis et son Temps*, Paris

Schleiffer, James T. (1980). *The Making of Tocqueville's Democracy in America*, Chapel Hill

Schlesinger, Arthur M., Jr. (1945). *The Age of Jackson*, Boston
   (2000). *A Life in the Twentieth Century: Innocent Beginnings, 1917–1950*, Boston

Schmitt, Carl (1924). *Die Politische Romantik*, 2nd edition, Munich
   (1986 [1919]). *Political Romanticism*, trans. Guy Oakes, Cambridge, MA
   (2007). *The Concept of the Political*, expanded edition translated with introduction and notes by George Schwab, Chicago

Schneewind, J. B. (1977). *Sidgwick's Ethics and Victorian Moral Philosophy*, Oxford

Schofield, P. (1999a). 'Jeremy Bentham, the French Revolution, and Electoral Reform', unpublished paper
   (1999b). Jeremy Bentham, the French Revolution, and Parliamentary Reform in Britain', unpublished paper
   (2003). 'Jeremy Bentham, the Principle of Utility, and Legal Positivism', *Current Legal Problems*, 56: 1–39

(2004). 'Jeremy Bentham, the French Revolution and Political Radicalism', *History of European Ideas*, 30: 381–401

(2006). *Utility and Democracy: The Political Thought of Jeremy Bentham*, Oxford

Scholtz, Gunter (1990). 'Der Weg zum Kunstsystem des Deutschen Idealismus', in Walter Jaeschke and Helmut Holzhey (eds.), *Früher Idealismus und Frühromantik. Der Streit um die Grundlagen der Ästhetik (1795–1805)*, Hamburg

Schönemann, Bernd (1997 [1978]). 'Volk, Nation', in Otto Brunner *et al.* (eds.), *Geschichtliche Grundbegriffe: Historisches Lexikon zur Politisch-sozialen Sprache in Deutschland*, Vol. VII, Stuttgart

Schorske, Carl (1981). *Fin-de-siècle Vienna: Politics and Culture*, New York and Cambridge

Schraepler, Ernst (1966). *August Bebel: Sozialdemokrat im Kaiserreich*, Frankfurt am Main and Zürich

Schroeder, Susan (ed.) (1998). *Native Resistance and the Pax Colonial in New Spain*, Lincoln

Schüle, Christian (2000). 'Zur Möglichkeit einer Ästhetischen Ethik', *Hegel-Jahrbuch*: 128–33

Schüller, Richard (1914). *Les Économistes Classiques et leurs Adversaires*, Paris

Schultz, Bart (1992). *Essays on Henry Sidgwick*, Cambridge

(2004). *Henry Sidgwick, Eye of the Universe: An Intellectual Biography*, Cambridge

Schumpeter, Joseph (1919). *Zur Soziologie der Imperialismen*, Tübingen

(1944). *Capitalism, Socialism and Democracy*, New York and London

Scott, Edith Hope (1931). *Ruskin's Guild of St. George*, London

Scott, J. A. (1951). *Republican Ideas and the Liberal Tradition in France*, New York

Scott, J. W. (1996). *Only Paradoxes to Offer: French Feminists and the Rights of Man*, Cambridge, MA

Scrivener, Michael Henry (1982). *Radical Shelley: The Philosophical Anarchism and Utopian Thought of Percy Bysshe Shelley*, Princeton

Scruton, Roger (1980). *The Meaning of Conservatism*, London

(1991). 'Introduction: What is Conservatism?', in Scruton (ed.), *Conservative Texts: An Anthology*, Basingstoke

Scruton, Roger (ed.) (1991), *Conservative Texts: An Anthology*, Basingstoke

Searle, G. R. (1976). *Eugenics and Politics in Britain 1900–1914*, Leyden

(1981). 'Eugenics and Class', in Charles Webster (ed.), *Biology, Medicine and Society 1840–1940*, Cambridge

Secord, James A. (2000). *Victorian Sensation: The Extraordinary Publication, Reception and Secret Authorship of Vestiges of the Natural History of Creation*, Chicago

Seebacher-Brandt, Brigitte (1988). *Bebel: Künder und Kärrner im Kaiserreich*, Berlin, Bonn

Seigel, Jules (1983). 'Carlyle and Peel: The Prophet's Search for a Heroic Politician and an Unpublished Fragment', *Victorian Studies*, 26: 181–95

Sellers, Charles (1991). *The Market Revolution: Jacksonian American, 1815–1846*, New York

Semmel, Bernard (1960). *Imperialism and Social Reform: English Social-Imperial Thought, 1895–1914*, London

(1962). *The Governor Eyre Controversy*, London

(1970). *The Rise of Free Trade Imperialism: Classical Political Economy, the Empire of Free Trade and Imperialism, 1750–1850*, Cambridge

(1998). 'John Stuart Mill's Coleridgean Neoradicalism', in E. Eisenach (ed.), *Mill and the Moral Character of Liberalism*, University Park, PA

Semple, J. (1993). *Bentham's Prison: A Study of the Panopticon Penitentiary*, Oxford

Sengupta, Kalyan Kumar (1975). *Recent Writings on the Revolt of 1857: A Survey*, New Delhi

Seth, Ronald (1966). *The Russian Terrorists: The Story of the Narodniki*, London

Shalhope, Robert (1976). 'Thomas Jefferson's Republicanism and Antebellum Southern Thought', *Journal of Southern History*, 42: 529–56

Shanahan, T. (1991). 'Chance in Evolutionary Biology', *History and Philosophy of the Life Sciences*, 13: 249–68

Shanley, M. L. (1989). *Feminism, Marriage and the Law in Victorian England*, Princeton

——(1998). 'Mary Wollstonecraft on Sensibility, Women's Rights, and Patriarchal Power', in H. L. Smith (ed.), *Women Writers and Early Modern British Political Tradition*, Cambridge

Sharp, Alan (1991). *The Versailles Settlement: Peacemaking in Paris, 1919*, Basingstoke

Sharpe, Lesley (1995). *Schiller's Aesthetic Essays: Two Centuries of Criticism*, Columbia, SC

Sheehan, James J. (1966). *The Career of Lujo Brentano: A Study of Liberalism and Social Reform in Imperial Germany*, Chicago.

——(1978). *German Liberalism in the Nineteenth Century*, Chicago

——(1988). 'Wie Bürgerlich war der Deutsche Liberalismus?', in Dieter Langewiesche (ed.), *Liberalismus im 19. Jahrhundert. Deutschland im Europäischen Vergleich.*, Göttingen

——(1989). *German History, 1770–1866*, Oxford

Sheehy-Skeffington, F. (1908). *Michael Davitt*, London

Sherren, J. A. (1914). *Dorset Masonic Calender*, Weymouth

Shine, Hill (1941). *Carlyle and the Saint-Simonians*, Baltimore

Shklar, Judith N. (1984). 'The Renaissance American', *New Republic*, 191 (5 November): 29–35

——(1991). *American Citizenship: The Quest for Inclusion*, Cambridge, MA

——(1998). *Redeeming American Political Thought*, ed. Stanley Hoffman and Dennis F. Thompson, intro. Dennis F. Thompson, Chicago

Showalter, E. (1992). *Sexual Anarchy: Gender and Culture at the Fin de Siècle*, London

Shulman, George (2008). *American Prophecy: Race and Redemption in American Political Culture*, Minneapolis

Siedentop, L. (1979). 'Two Liberal Traditions', in A. Ryan (ed.), *The Idea of Freedom Essays in Honour of Isaiah Berlin*, Oxford

——(2001). *Democracy in Europe*, London

Siegel, Patricia Joan (1970). 'Chateaubriand, Révolutionnaire Politique', in Richard Switzer (ed.), *Chateaubriand Today*, Madison, WI

Siegfried, André (1914). *Democracy in New Zealand*, London

Siemes, Johannes (1968). *Hermann Roesler and the Making of the Meiji State: An Examination of his Background and his Influence on the Founders of Modern Japan*, Tokyo

Siep, Ludwig (ed.) (1997). *G. W. F Hegel. Grundlinien der Philosophie des Rechts*, Berlin

Sigerman, Harriet (2001). *Elizabeth Cady Stanton: The Right is Ours* (Oxford Portraits), Oxford

Sigot, N. (2002). 'Jevons's Debt to Bentham: Mathematical Economy, Morals and Psychology', *The Manchester School*, 70: 262–78

Sigurdson, Richard F. (1990). 'Jacob Burckhardt: The Cultural Historian as Political Thinker', *Review of Politics* 52: 417–40

Silberner, Edmund (1976). *Johann Jacoby: Politiker und Mensch*, Bonn-Bad Godesberg

Silva, Noenoe K. (2004). *Aloha Betrayed: Native Hawaiian Resistance to American Colonialism*, Durham, NC

Simhony, Avital and Weinstein, D. (2001). *The New Liberalism: Reconciling Liberty and Community*, Cambridge

Simms, Henry (1932). *Life of John Taylor: The Story of a Brilliant Leader in the Early Virginia State Rights School*, Richmond

Simon, W. M. (1963). *European Positivism in the Nineteenth Century: An Essay in Intellectual History*, Ithaca

Simpson, David (1984). 'Introduction', in Simpson, *German Aesthetic and Literary Criticism*, Cambridge

Simpson, Dwight J. (1951). 'Carlyle as a Political Theorist: Natural Law', *Midwest Journal of Political Science*, 3: 263–76

Sinclair, May (1912). *Feminism*, London

(1922). *The New Idealism*, London

Skaria, Ajay (2002). 'Gandhi's Politics: Liberalism and the Question of the Ashram', *South Atlantic Quarterly*, 101(4): 955–86

Sked, Alan (1979). *The Survival of the Habsburg Empire: Radetzky, the Imperial Army and the Class War, 1848*, London

Skinner, Quentin (1998). *Liberty before Liberalism*, Cambridge

(2001). 'A Third Concept of Liberty', *Proceedings of the British Academy*, 117, London

(2002). 'Visions of Civil Liberty', in Peter Martland (ed.), *The Future of the Past: Big Questions in History*, London

Skinner, Simon (2004). *Tractarians and the 'Condition of England': The Social and Political Thought of the Oxford Movement*, Oxford

Sklar, Martin (1988). *The Corporate Reconstruction of American Capitalism: 1890–1916*, New York

Skorupski, John (1989). *John Stuart Mill*, London

(1998). *John Stuart Mill*, London

(2006). *Why Read Mill Today?*, London

Skorupski, John (ed.) (1998). *The Cambridge Companion to Mill*, Cambridge

Small, Stephen (2002). *Political Thought in Ireland 1776–1798: Republicanism, Patriotism, and Radicalism*, Oxford

Smith, Anthony D. (1971). *Theories of Nationalism*, London

(1998). *Nationalism and Modernism*, London

Smith, Denis Mack (1994). *Mazzini*, New Haven

Smith, Helmut Walser (1995). *German Nationalism and Religious Conflict: Culture, Ideology and Politics, 1870–1914*, Princeton

Smith, Jeremy (1999). *The Bolsheviks and the National Question, 1917–1923*, New York

Smith, K. J. M. (1988). *James Fitzjames Stephen: Portrait of a Victorian Rationalist*, Cambridge

Smith, Rogers (1993). 'Judith Shklar and the Pleasures of American Political Thought', *Yale Journal of Law and Humanities*, 51: 187–9

(1996). 'The Unfinished Tasks of Liberalism', in Bernard Yack (ed.), *Liberalism without Illusions: Essays on Liberalism and the Political Vision of Judith N. Shklar*, Chicago

(1997). *Civic Ideals: Conflicting Visions of Citizenship in US History*, New Haven

Smith, Steven (1989). *Hegel's Critique of Liberalism*, Chicago

Smith-Rosenberg, C. (1985). *Disorderly Conduct: Visions of Gender in Victorian America*, New York

Smithson, R. (1972). *Augustin Thierry*, Geneva

Snowden, Philip (1934). *Autobiography*, 2 vols., London

Snyder, A. D. (1929). *Coleridge on Logic and Learning with Selections from the Unpublished Manuscripts*, New Haven

Snyder, Timothy (2003). *The Reconstruction of Nations: Poland, Ukraine, Lithuania, Belarus, 1569–1999*, New Haven

Soffer, Reba (1978). *Ethics and Society in England: The Revolution in the Social Sciences, 1870–1914*, Berkeley

Sokol, M. (1992). 'Jeremy Bentham and the Real Property Commission of 1828', *Utilitas*, 4: 225–45

Solomon, Robert C. and Higgins, Kathleen M. (2000). *What Nietzsche Really Said*, New York

Soltau, Roger (1931). *French Political Thought in the Nineteenth Century*, New Haven

Sonn, Richard D. (1989). *Anarchism and Cultural Politics in Fin de Siècle France*, Lincoln
    (1992). *Anarchism*, New York
Soong, Ching Ling (Madame Sun Yatsen) (1995). *Woman in World History*, Beijing
Sowell, Thomas (1972). *Say's Law: An Historical Aanalysis*, Princeton
Spain, August O. (1951). *The Political Theory of John C. Calhoun*, New York
Spater, George (1982). *William Cobbett: The Poor Man's Friend*, Cambridge
Spektorowski, Alberto (2002). 'Maistre, Donoso Cortés and the Legacy of Catholic Author-
    itarianism', *Journal of the History of Ideas*, 63: 283–302
Spence, J. (1999). *In Search of Modern China*, New York
Spence, Peter (1996). *The Birth of Romantic Radicalism: War, Popular Politics, and English Radical
    Reformism, 1800–1815*, Aldershot
Spencer, M. C. (1981). *Charles Fourier*, Boston
Sperber, Jonathan (1991). *Rhineland Radicals: The Democratic Movement and the Revolution of
    1848–1849*, Princeton
    (2005). *The European Revolutions, 1848–1851*, 2nd edition, Cambridge
Spitta, Dietrich (2004). *Die Staatsidee Wilhelm von Humboldts*, Berlin
Spitzer, Alan B. (1957). *The Revolutionary Theories of Louis Auguste Blanqui*, New York
    (1971). *Old Hatreds and Young Hopes: The French Carbonari against the Bourbon Restoration*,
    Cambridge, MA
Srivastava, M. P. (1997). *Freedom Fighters of the Indian Mutiny 1857*, Allahabad
St John-Stevas, Norman (1959). *Walter Bagehot: A Study of his Life and Thought, together with
    a Selection from his Political Writings*, London
Stack, David (1998). *Nature and Artifice: The Life and Thought of Thomas Hodgskin (1787–1869)*,
    Woodbridge
    (2003). *The First Darwinian Left: Socialism and Darwinism, 1859–1914*, Cheltenham
Stack, G. J. (1983). *Lange and Nietzche*, Berlin and New York
Stadter, P. (1948). *Geschichtschreibung und Historischen Denken in Frankreich 1789–1871*, Zurich
Stafford, David (1971). *From Anarchism to Reformism: A Study of the Political Activities of
    Paul Brousse within the First International and the French Socialist Movement, 1870–90*,
    Toronto
Stafford, William (1980). 'Dissenting Religion Translated into Politics: Godwin's *Political
    Justice*', *History of Political Thought*, 1: 279–99.
    (1987). *Socialism, Radicalism, and Nostalgia*, Cambridge
Stanslowski, Volker (1978). 'Bürgerliche Gesellschaft als Organismus. Zum Verhältnis
    von Staats-und Naturwissenschaften in der "Politischen Romantik"', in Richard
    Brinkmann (ed.), *Romantik in Deutschland*, Stuttgart
Stapleton, Julia (1994). *Englishness and the Study of Politics*, Cambridge
Stark, W. (1946). 'Jeremy Bentham as an Economist', *Economic Journal*, 56: 583–608
Starobinski, Jean (1964). *L'Invention de la Liberté (1700–1789)*, Geneva
Starr, Harris E. (1925). *William Graham Sumner*, New York
Stauffer, John (2001). *The Black Hearts of Men: Radical Abolitionists and the Transformation of
    Race*, Cambridge, MA
Staum, Martin S. (1980). *Cabanis: Enlightenment and Medical Philosophy in the French Revolution*,
    Princeton
Stears, M. (2002). *Progressives, Pluralists and the Problems of the State: Ideologies of Reform in the
    United States and Britain, 1909–1926*, Oxford
Stedman Jones, Gareth (1983a). *Languages of Class: Studies in English Working Class History
    1832–1982*, Cambridge
    (1983b). 'Rethinking Chartism', in *Languages of Class: Studies in English Working Class
    History 1832–1982*, Cambridge

(1983c). 'What was Chartism?' in *Languages of Class: Studies in English Working Class History 1832–1982*, Cambridge

(2002a). 'National Bankruptcy and Social Revolution: European Observers on Britain, 1813–1844', in D. Winch and P. K. O'Brien (eds.), *The Political Economy of British Historical Experience, 1688–1914*, Oxford

(2004). *An End to Poverty?*, London

(2006). 'Engels and the Invention of the Catastrophist Conception of the Industrial Revolution', in D. Moggach (ed.), *The New Hegelians: Politics and Philosophy in the Hegelian School*, Cambridge

(2007). 'Radicalism and the Extra-European World: The Case of Karl Marx', in Duncan Bell (ed.), *Victorian Visions of Global Order: Empire and International Relations in Nineteenth-Century Political Thought*, Cambridge

Stedman Jones, G. (ed.) (2002b). *Karl Marx and Friedrich Engels: The Communist Manifesto*, London

Steenson, Gary P. (1978). *Karl Kautsky, 1854–1938: Marxism in the Classical Year*, Pittsburgh

Steger, Manfred (1997). *The Quest for Evolutionary Socialism: Eduard Bernstein and Social Democracy*, Cambridge

Stein, Peter (1980). *Legal Evolution: The Story of an Idea*, Cambridge

(1999). *Roman Law in European History*, Cambridge

Steinberg, Jonathan (1964). 'The Kaiser's Navy and German Society', *Past and Present*, 28/1: 102–10

Steinmetz, George (1993). *Regulating the Social: The Welfare State and Local Politics in Imperial Germany*, Princeton

Stepan, N. (1982). *The Idea of Race in Science: Britain, 1800–1960*, London

(1987). '"Nature's Pruning Hook": War, Race and Evolution, 1914–18', in J. M. W. Bean (ed.), *The Political Culture of Modern Britain: Studies in Memory of Stephen Koss*, London

Stepelevich, Lawrence (1983). *The Young Hegelians*, Cambridge

Stern, Fritz (1974 [1961]. *The Politics of Cultural Despair: A Study in the Rise of the Germanic Ideology*, Berkeley and Los Angeles

Stern, J. (1959). *Thibaut und Savigny*, Darmstadt

Stern, Madeleine B. (1968). *The Pantarch: A Biography of Stephen Pearl Andrews*, Austin

Sternhell, Zeev (ed.) (1996). *The Intellectual Revolt against Liberal Democracy, 1870–1914*, Jerusalem

Stites, Richard (1978). *The Women's Liberation Movement in Russia: Feminism, Nihilism, and Bolshevism, 1860–1930*, Princeton

Stöcker, Birgit (1992). *Die Gemeinwohltheorie Robert von Mohls als ein Früher Ansatz des Sozialen Rechtsstaatsprinzips*, München

Stocking, George (1968). *Race, Culture and Evolution*, New York

(1987). *Victorian Anthropology*, New York

(1996). *After Tylor: British Social Anthropology, 1888–1951*, London

Stoecker, Helmuth (ed.) (1987). *German Imperialism in Africa: From the Beginnings until the Second World War*, London

Stokes, Eric (1959). *The English Utilitarians and India*, Oxford

(1989). *The English Utilitarians and India*, Delhi

Stone, Dan (2002). *Breeding Superman: Nietzsche, Race and Eugenics in Edwardian and Interwar Britain*, Liverpool

Story, Mark (1997). *Robert Southey: A Life*, Oxford

Strachey, R. (1928). *The Cause: A Short History of the Women's Movement in Great Britain*, London

Strasser, S. *et al.* (1998). *Social Justice Feminists in the United States and Germany: A Dialogue in Documents, 1885–1933*, Ithaca

Stremoukhoff, Dimitri (1979). *Vladimir Soloviev and his Messianic Work*, Belmont, MA

Stresemann, Gustav (1911). *Wirtschaftspolitische Zeitfragen*, Dresden

Strong, Tracy (1996). 'Nietzsche's Political Misappropriation', in Bernd Magnus and Kathleen M. Higgins (eds.), *The Cambridge Companion to Nietzsche*, Cambridge

Studenski, Paul (1958). *The Income of Nations: Theory, Measurement, and Analysis*, New York

Sukehiro, H. (1989). 'Japan's Turn to the West', in Marius B. Jansen (ed.), *Cambridge History of Japan*, Vol. v, Cambridge

Sullivan, Eileen P. (1983). 'Liberalism and Imperialism: J. S. Mill's Defense of the British Empire', *Journal of the History of Ideas*, 44: 599–617

Sullivan, T. D. (1905). *Recollections of Troubled Times in Irish Politics*, Dublin

Susman, W. (1996). *Culture as History: The Transformation of American Society in the Twentieth Century*, New York

Sutton, Robert P. (1994). *Les Icariens: The Utopian Dream in Europe and America*, Urbana

Sutton-Ramspeck, B. (1999). 'Shot Out of the Canon: Mary Ward and the Claims of Conflicting Feminism', in Nicola D. Thompson (ed.), *Victorian Women Writers and the Woman Question*, Cambridge

Suzuki, Yasuzo (1941). 'Hermann Roesler und die Japanische Verfassung', trans. J. Siemes, *Monumenta Nipponica*, 4: 53–87

Sweet, Paul, R. (1941). *Friedrich von Gentz: Defender of the Old Order*, Madison, WI

Switzer, Richard (1971). *Chateaubriand* (Twayne World Author Series), New York

Talmon, Jacob (1960). *The Origins of Totalitarian Democracy*, New York

Tanner, Michael (1997). 'Nietzsche', in Roger Scruton *et al.*, *German Philosophers*, Oxford

Tarello, Giovanni (1976). *Storia della Cultura Giuridica Moderna, Vol. 1: Assolutismo e Codificazione del Diritto*, Bologna

Taylor, A. J. P. (1965). *English History, 1914–45*, Oxford

Taylor, Antony (1996). 'Republicanism Reappraised: Anti-Monarchism and the English Radical Tradition, 1850–1872', in James Vernon (ed.), *Re-reading the Constitution: New Narratives in the Political History of England's Long Nineteenth Century*, Cambridge

(1999). *'Down with the Crown': British Anti-monarchism and Debates about Royalty since 1790*, London

(2004). *Lords of Misrule: Hostility to Aristocracy in Late Nineteenth- and Early Twentieth-Century Britain*, Basingstoke

Taylor, Barbara (1983). *Eve and the New Jerusalem: Socialism and Feminism in the Nineteenth Century*, London

(2003). *Mary Wollstonecraft and the Feminist Imagination*, Cambridge

Taylor, Bob Pepperman (1996). *America's Bachelor Uncle: Thoreau and the American Polity* (American Political Thought), Lawrence

Taylor, Charles (1989). *Sources of the Self: The Making of the Modern Identity*, Cambridge MA

(1991). *The Malaise of Modernity*, Concord, Ontario.

Taylor, Keith (1982). *The Political Ideas of the Utopian Socialists*, London

Taylor, M. A. (1991). *Feminism and Motherhood in Germany, 1800–1914*, Rutgers

Taylor, M. W. (1992). *Man Versus the State: Herbert Spencer and Late Victorian Individualism*, Oxford

Taylor, Miles (1991). 'Imperium et Libertas? Rethinking the Radical Critique of Imperialism during the Nineteenth Century', *Journal of Imperial and Commonwealth History*, 19: 1–23

(1995). *The Decline of British Radicalism, 1847–1860*, Oxford

(2000). 'Republics versus Empires: Charles Dilke's Republicanism Reconsidered', in David Nash and Antony Taylor (eds.), *Republicanism in Victorian Society*, Stroud

Taylor, Raymond (1970). *The Romantic Tradition in Germany*, London

Teichgraber III, Richard F. (1995). *Sublime Thoughts/Penny Wisdom*, Baltimore

Ten, C. L. (1980). *Mill on Liberty*, Oxford

Thaden, Edward (1964). *Conservative Nationalism in Nineteenth-Century Russia*, Seattle

Theiner, Peter (1983). *Sozialer Liberalismus und Deutsche Weltpolitik. Friedrich Naumann im Wilhelminischen Deutschland (1860–1919)*, Baden-Baden

Thérien, Claude (1997). 'De la Beauté comme Symbole de la Paix Perpetuelle', *Dialogue*, 36(4): 753–70

Thieme, Hans (1936). 'Der Zeit der Späten Naturrechts', *Zeitschrift der Savigny-Stiftung für Rechtsgeschichte*, Ger. Abt., 56

Tholfsen, Trygve R. (1967). *Historical Thinking: An Introduction*, New York

Thomas, Geoffrey (1987). *The Moral Philosophy of T. H. Green*, Oxford

Thomas, John L. (1983). *Alternative America: Henry George, Edward Bellamy, Henry Demarest Lloyd and the Adversary Tradition*, Cambridge, MA

Thomas, Paul (1980). *Karl Marx and the Anarchists*, London

Thomas, W. (1974). 'The Philosophic Radicals', in P. Hollis (ed.), *Pressure from Without in Early Victorian England*, London

(1979). *The Philosophic Radicals: Nine Studies in Theory and Practice, 1817–41*, Oxford

(1985). *Mill* (Past Masters), Oxford

Thomis, Malcolm (1972). *The Luddites: Machine-Breaking in Regency England*, New York

Thomis, Malcolm and Holt, Peter (1977). *Threats of Revolution in Britain 1789–1848*, London

Thompson, Dorothy (1986). *The Chartists*, Aldershot

Thompson, E. P. (1977). *William Morris: Romantic to Revolutionary*, 2nd edition, London

Thompson, J. (1998). 'The Genesis of the 1906 Trades Disputes Act: Liberalism, Trade Unions, and the Law', *Twentieth Century British History*, 9: 175–200

(2000). '*The Idea of "Public Opinion" in Britain, 1870–1914*', Ph.D. dissertation, Cambridge

(2007). 'Political Economy, the Labour Movement and the Minimum Wage, 1880–1914', in E. H. H. Green and D. Tanner (eds.), *The Strange Survival of Liberal England: Political Leaders, Moral Values and the Reception of Economic Debate*, Cambridge

Thompson, Noel (1984). *The People's Science: The Popular Political Economy of Exploitation and Crisis, 1816–34*, Cambridge

Thompson, R. C. (1980). *Australian Imperialism in the Pacific: The Expansionist Era, 1820–1920*, Melbourne

Thomson, David (1947). *The Babeuf Plot: The Making of a Republican Legend*, London

Thomson, Guy (ed.) (2002). *The European Revolutions of 1848 and the Americas*, London

Thorslev, Peter (1989). 'Post-Waterloo Liberalism: The Second Generation', *Studies in Romanticism*, 28: 437–61

Thrupp, Sylvia L. (ed.) (1970). *Millennial Dreams in Action: Studies in Revolutionary Religious Movements*, New York

Tillinghast, Joseph Alexander (1902). 'The Negro in Africa and America', *Publications of the American Economic Association*, 3rd series, 3: 1–231

Tiryakian, Edward A. (1978). 'Emile Durkheim', in Tom Bottomore and Robert Nisbet (eds.), *A History of Sociological Analysis*, London

Tober, Holger J. (1999). *Deutscher Liberalismus und Sozialpolitik in der Ära des Wilhelminismus*, Husung

Todd, David (2008a). *L'identité Économique de la France: Libre-échange et Protectionnisme, 1814–1851*, Paris

(2008b). 'John Bowring and the Global Dissemination of Free Trade', *The Historical Journal*, 51: 373–97

(2009). 'The Second Global Empire: Michel Chevalier and the French "Imperialism of Free Trade"', Working paper, Centre for History and Economics, King's College, Cambridge

(2011). 'A French Imperial Meridian, 1814–1870', *Past and Present*, 210: 156–86

Todorova, Maria (ed.) (2004). *Balkan Identities: Nation and Memory*, London.

Toesca, Maurice (1969). *Lamartine ou l'Amour de la Vie*, Paris

Toews, John E. (1980). *Hegelianism: The Path toward Dialectical Humanism, 1805–1841*, Cambridge

(1993). 'Transformation of Hegelianism', in F. C. Beiser (ed.), *The Cambridge Companion to Hegel*, Cambridge

Tomba, Massimiliano (2006). 'Exclusiveness and Political Universalism in Bruno Bauer', in D. Moggach (ed.), *The New Hegelians: Politics and Philosophy in the Hegelian School*, Cambridge

Tort, P. (ed.) (1992). *Darwinisme et Société*, Paris

Tosh, J. (1999). *A Man's Place: Masculinity and the Middle-Class Home in Victorian England*, New Haven

Totman, Conrad (2000). *A History of Japan*, Oxford

Towers, Frank (2006), 'Civic Nationalism Restored: The Politics of Race and Ethnicity in the Civil-War Era United States', European Social Science Conference, Amsterdam

Toye, Richard (2008) 'H. G. Wells and the New Liberalism', *20th Century British History*, 19: 156–85

Toynbee, Arnold (1927). 'Are Radicals Socialists?', in *Lectures on the Industrial Revolution*, London

Trainor, L. (ed.) (1996). *Republicanism in New Zealand*, Palmerstown

Traugott, M. (1985). *Armies of the Poor*, Princeton

Trentmann, Frank (2008). *Free Trade Nation: Commerce, Consumption and Civil Society in Modern Britain*, Oxford

Trung, Buu Lam (1967). *Patterns of Vietnamese Response to Foreign Intervention, 1858–1900*, New Haven

Tsunoda, R. *et al.* (eds.) (1958). *Sources of the Japanese Tradition*, New York

Tsuzuki, Chushichi (1980). *Edward Carpenter, 1844–1929: Prophet of Human Fellowship*, Cambridge

Tsuzuki, Chushichi (ed.) (1992). *Robert Owen and the World of Co-operation*, Tokyo

Tuck, Richard (1979). *Natural Rights Theories: Their Origins and Development*, Cambridge

(1993). 'The Contribution of History', in R. Goodin and P. Pettit (eds.), *A Companion to Contemporary Political Philosophy*, Oxford

(1999). *The Rights of War and Peace: Political Thought and International Order from Grotius to Kant*, Oxford

Tucker, Robert W. and Hendrickson, David C. (1990). *Empire of Liberty: The Statecraft of Thomas Jefferson*, New York

Tudor, H. and Tudor, J. M. (eds.) (1988). *Marxism and Social Democracy: The Revisionist Debate, 1896–1896*, Cambridge

Tulloch, H. A. (1977). 'Changing British Attitudes to the United States in the 1880s', *Historical Journal*, 20: 825–40

(1988). *Acton*, London

Tully, James (1993). 'Rediscovering America: The Two Treatises and Aboriginal Rights', in Tully, *An Approach to Political Philosophy: Locke in Context*, Cambridge

Tunick, Mark (1992). *Hegel's Political Philosophy*, Princeton

Turner, Frank (1981). *The Greek Heritage in Victorian Britain*, Yale

Tusi, Nasiruddin (1969). *The Nasirean Ethics*, trans. G. M. Wickens, London

Twelve Southerners (1930). *I'll Take My Stand: The South and the Agrarian Tradition*, New York

Twining, W. (1985). *Theories of Evidence: Bentham and Wigmore*, London.

Twomey, Richard (1989). *Jacobins and Jeffersonians: Anglo-American Radicalism in the United States, 1790–1820*, New York

Tyler, C. (2003). 'T. H. Green, Advanced Liberalism and the Reform Question 1865–1876', *History of European Ideas*, 29: 437–58.

Ullmann, Hans-Peter (1976). *Der Bund der Industriellen. Organisation, Einfluß und Politik Klein- und-Mittelbetrieblicher Industrieller im Deutschen Kaiserreich, 1895–1914*, Göttingen

Ullmann, Walter (1961). *Principles of Government and Politics in the Middle Ages*, London

Urbinati, Nadia (2002). *Mill on Democracy: From the Athenian Polis to Representative Government*, Chicago

Urbinati, Nadia and Zakaras, Alex (eds.) (2007). *John Stuart Mill's Political Thought: A Bicentennial Reassessment*, Cambridge

Utechin, Sergei V. (1964). *Russian Political Thought: A Concise History*, New York and London.

Vanden Bossche, Chris R. (1991). *Carlyle and the Search for Authority*, Columbus, OH

Varnhagen, Rahel (1966). *Briefwechsel mit Alexander von der Marwitz, Karl von Finckenstein, Wilhelm Bokelmann, Raphael d'Urquijo*, ed. Friedrich Kemp, Munich

Varouxakis, Georgios (1998). 'National Character in John Stuart Mill's Thought', *History of European Ideas*, 24: 375–91

   (2002a). *Mill on Nationality*, London

   (2002b). *Victorian Political Thought on France and the French*, Basingstoke

Varouxakis, Georgios and Schultz, Bart (eds.) (2005). *Utilitarianism and Empire*, Lanham

Veblen, Thorstein (1970). *The Theory of the Leisure Class*, London

Venturi, Franco (1960). *Roots of Revolution: A History of the Populist and Socialist Movements in Nineteenth-Century Russia*, trans. Francis Haskell, London and New York

Vernadsky G. *et al.* (eds) (1972). *A Source Book for Russian History from Early Times to 1917*, Vol. II, New Haven

Vial, Theodor (2005). 'Schleiermacher and the State', in Jacqueline Marina (ed.), *The Cambridge Companion to Friedrich Schleiermacher*, Cambridge

Viallaneix, Paul (1998). *Michelet, les Travaux et les Jours, 1798–1874*, Paris

Vicinus, M. (1985). *Independent Women: Work and Community for Single Women, 1850–1920*, London

Vick, Brian (2002). *Defining German: The 1848 Frankfurt Parliamentarians and National Identity*, Cambridge, MA

Vickery, A. (1993). 'Golden Age to Separate Spheres? A Review of the Categories and Chronology of English Women's History', *Historical Journal*, 36: 383–414

Vidler, A. R. (1964a). *A Century of Social Catholicism*, London

   (1964b). *Prophecy and Papacy: A Study of Lamennais, the Church and the Revolution*, London

Vierhaus, Rudolf (1973). 'Conservatism', in Philip W. Wiener (ed.), *Dictionary of the History of Ideas*, 5 vols., New York

Vile, M. J. (1967). *Constitutionalism and the Separation of Powers*, Oxford

Villiers, Brougham (pseud. F. J. Shaw) (1908). *The Socialist Movement in England*, London

Vincent, Andrew (ed.) (1986). *The Philosophy of T. H. Green*, Aldershot

Vincent, Andrew and Plant, Raymond (1984). *Philosophy, Politics and Citizenship: The Life and Thought of British Idealists*, Oxford

Vincent, John Russell (1990). *Disraeli*, Oxford

Vincent, K. Steven (1984). *Pierre-Joseph Proudhon and the Rise of French Republican Socialism*, Oxford and New York

   (1992). *Between Marxism and Anarchism: Benoît Malon and French Reformist Socialism*, Berkeley

   (1996). 'Jean Grave and French Communist Anarchism', *Proceedings of the Western Society for French History*, 23: 244–55

Vital, David (1975). *The Origins of Zionism*, Oxford

   (1999). *A People Apart: The Jews in Europe, 1789–1939*, Oxford

Vivekananda, Swami (1960). *The Life of Swami Vivekananda by his Eastern and Western Disciples*, Calcutta

Vivian, Herbert (1927). *Secret Societies Old and New*, London

Vizetelly, Ernest Alfred (1911). *The Anarchists: Their Faith and Their Record*, London

Vogeler, M. S. (1984). *Frederic Harrison: The Vocations of a Positivist*, Oxford

Vollgraf, C.-E. and Jungnickel, J. (2002). '"Marx in Marx's Words"? On Engels's Edition of the Main Manuscript of Book Three of *Capital*', *International Journal of Political Economy*, 32

Von Arx, Jeffrey Paul (1985). *Progress and Pessimism: Religion, Politics and History in late Nineteenth-century Britain*, Cambridge, MA

Von Mehren, Joan (1994). *Minerva and the Muse: A Life of Margaret Fuller*, Amherst

Vorenberg, Michael (2001). *Final Freedom: The Civil War, the Abolition of Slavery, and the Thirteenth Amendment*, Cambridge

Vucinich, A. (1988). *Darwin in Russian Thought*, Los Angeles

Wada, H. (1983). 'Marx and Revolutionary Russia', in T. Shanin (ed.), *The Late Marx and the Russian Road*, London

Walch, Jean (1967). *Bibliographie du Saint-Simonisme*, Paris

   (1986). *Les Maîtres de l'Histoire, 1815–1850*, Geneva

Walicki, Andrzej (1969). *The Controversy over Capitalism: Studies in the Social Philosophy of the Russian Populists*, Oxford

   (1975). *The Slavophile Controversy: History of a Conservative Utopia in Nineteenth-Century Russian Thought*, Oxford

   (1987). *Legal Philosophies of Russian Liberalism*, Oxford

   (1989). *The Enlightenment and the Birth of Modern Nationhood: Polish Political Thought from Noble Republicanism to Tadeusz Kościuszko*, Notre Dame, IN

Walker, Mabel Gregory (1969). *The Fenian Movement*, Colorado Springs

Walkowitz, J. R. (1992). *City of Dreadful Delight: Narratives of Sexual Danger in Late-Victorian London*, London

Walzer, Michael (1983). *Spheres of Justice*, New York

   (1986). *Interpretation and Social Criticism*, Cambridge, MA

   (1988). *The Company of Critics: Social Criticism and Political Commitment in the Twentieth Century*, New York

   (1994). *Thick and Thin: Moral Argument at Home and Abroad*, South Bend

Wardlaw, Grant (1982). *Political Terrorism: Theory, Tactics, Counter-Measures*, Cambridge

Wartofsky, Marx (1977). *Feuerbach*, Cambridge

Waszek, N. (1988). *The Scottish Enlightenment and Hegel's Account of Civil Society*, Dordrecht

   (2006). 'Eduard Gans on Poverty and on the Constitutional Debate', in D. Moggach (ed.), *The New Hegelians: Politics and Philosophy in the Hegelian School*, Cambridge

Watkins, Daniel P. (1981). 'Violence, Class Consciousness, and Ideology in Byron's History Plays', *ELH*, 48: 799–816

Watson, George (ed.) (1994). *Lord Acton's History of Liberty: A Study of his Library, with an Edited Text of his History of Liberty Notes*, Aldershot

Wawn, Andrew (2000). *The Vikings and the Victorians*, Woodbridge

Wawn, Andrew (ed.) (1994). *Northern Antiquity: The Post-Medieval Reception of Edda and Saga*, Enfield

Webb, Darren (2000). *Marx, Marxism and Utopia*, London

Weber, Eugen (1959). *The Nationalist Revival in France, 1905–1914*, Berkeley

— (1976). *Peasants into Frenchmen: The Modernisation of Rural France, 1870–1914*, London

Weber, Rolf (1968). 'Demokratische Volkspartei 1863–1966', in Dieter Fricke (ed.), *Die Bürgerlichen Parteien in Deutschland*, 2 vols., Vol. I, Leipzig

— (1988). *Johann Jacoby*, Köln

Wedderburn, William (1974 [1913]). *Allan Octavian Hume, CBE*, Delhi

Weeks, Albert L. (1968). *The First Russian Bolshevik: A Political Biography of Peter Tkachev*, New York

Wehler, Hans-Ulrich (1985 [1973]). *Das Deutsche Kaiserreich, 1871–1918, Göttingen*. Published in English as *The German Empire, 1871–1918* (1985), Leamington Spa

Weil, Eric (1950). *Hegel et l'État*, Paris

Weill, G. (1894). *Un Précurseur du Socialisme: Saint-Simon et son Oeuvre*, Paris

Weiming, Tu (1996). *Confucian Traditions in East Asian Modernity: Exploring Moral Education and Economic Culture in Japan and the Four Mini-Dragons*, Harvard

Weinstein David (1998). *Equal Freedom and Utility: Herbert Spencer's Liberal Utilitarianism*, Cambridge

— (2005). 'Imagining Darwinism', in G. Varouxakis and B. Schultz (eds.), *Utilitarianism and Empire*, Lanham

— (2007). *Utilitarianism and the New Liberalism*, Cambridge

Weiss, Horace John (1960). *Moses Hess, Utopian Socialist*, Detroit

Weiss, John (1977). *Conservatism in Europe 1770–1945*, London

Welch, Cheryl B. (1984). *Liberty and Utility: The French Idéologues and the Transformation of Liberalism*, New York

— (1989). 'Liberalism and Social Rights', in M. Milgate and C. Welch (eds.), *Critical Issues in Social Thought*, London

— (2001). *De Tocqueville*, Oxford

— (2003). 'Colonial Violence and the Rhetoric of Evasion: Tocqueville on Algeria', *Political Theory*, 31: 235–64

Welch, Cheryl B. (ed.) (2006). *The Cambridge Companion to Tocqueville*, Cambridge

Wells, Roger (1986). *Insurrection: The British Experience, 1795–1803*, Gloucester

Welskopp, Thomas (2000). *Das Banner der Brüderlichkeit: Die Deutsche Sozialdemokratie vom Vormärz bis zum Sozialistengesetz*, Bonn

Welter, B. (1966). 'The Cult of True Womanhood, 1820–1860', *American Quarterly*, 18(2): 151–74

Wempe, B. (2004). *T. H. Green's Theory of Positive Freedom: From Metaphysics to Political Theory*, Exeter

Wendorff, Werner (1978). *Schule und Bildung in der Politik von Wilhelm Liebknecht*, Berlin

Wesseling, H. L. (ed.) (1978). *Expansion and Reaction: Essays on European Expansions and Reactions in Asia and Africa*, Leiden

West, Anthony (1984). *H. G. Wells: Aspects of a Life*, London

Westerholt, Burchard, Graf von (1999). *Patrimonialismus und Konstitutionalismus in der Rechts- und Staatstheorie Karl Ludwig von Hallers*, Berlin

Whale, John (2000). *Imagination Under Pressure, 1789–1832: Aesthetics, Politics, and Utility*, Cambridge

Whatmore, Richard (2000). *Republicanism and the French Revolution: An Intellectual History of Jean-Baptiste Say's Political Economy*, Oxford

Wheen, F. (1999). *Karl Marx*, London

Whelan, Kevin (1996). *The Tree of Liberty: Radicalism, Catholicism and the Construction of Irish Identity, 1760–1830*, Cork

White, Albert C. (1913). *The Irish Free State*, London

White, Dan S. (1976). *The Splintered Party: National Liberalism in Hessen and in the Reich, 1876–1918*, Cambridge, MA

White, J. D. (1996). *Karl Marx and the Intellectual Origins of Dialectical Materialism*, London

Whitman, James Q. (1990). *The Legacy of Roman Law in the German Romantic Era: Historical Vision and Legal Change*, Princeton

Wieacker, Franz (1967). *Privatrechtsgeschichte der Neuzeit*, Göttingen

Wiebe, Robert H. (1967). *The Search for Order, 1877–1920*, New York

Wilentz, Sean (1982). 'On Class and Politics in Jacksonian America', in Stanley I. Kutler and Stanley N. Katz (eds.), *The Promise of American History: Progress and Prospects*, Baltimore

(1997). 'Society, Politics, and the Market Revolution: 1815–1848', in Eric Foner (ed.), *The New American History: Revised and Expanded Edition*, Philadelphia

(2004). 'The Details of Greatness: American Historians versus the American Founders', *The New Republic* (29 March): 27–35

(2005). *The Rise of American Democracy: Jefferson to Lincoln*, New York

Wilkinson, Elizabeth and Willoughby, L. A. (1967). 'Introduction', in Friedrich Schiller, *On the Aesthetic Education of Man in a Series of Letters*, ed. and trans. E. Wilkinson and L. A. Willoughby, Oxford

Wilkinson, Paul (1974). *Political Terrorism*, London

Williams, Bernard (1995 [1982]). 'The Point of View of the Universe: Sidgwick and the Ambitions of Ethics', in Williams, *Making Sense of Humanity, and Other Philosophical Papers, 1982–1993*, Cambridge

Williams, Howard (2006). 'Ludwig Feuerbach's Critique of Religion and the End of Moral Philosophy', in D. Moggach (ed.), *The New Hegelians: Politics and Philosophy in the Hegelian School*, Cambridge

Williams, Raymond (1958). *Culture and Society: 1780–1950, Part 1, 'A Nineteenth Century Tradition'*, London

Williams, Richard (1997). *The Contentious Crown: Public Discussion of the British Monarchy in the Age of Victoria*, Aldershot

Williams, T. Desmond (ed.) (1973). *Secret Societies in Ireland*, Dublin

Williamson, George S. (2004). *The Longing for Myth in Germany: Religion and Aesthetic Culture from Romanticism to Nietzsche*, Chicago and London

Wills, Garry (1992). *Lincoln at Gettysburg: The Words that Remade America*, New York

(2003). *A Negro President: Jefferson and the Slave Power*, Boston

(2004). 'Did Tocqueville "Get" America?', *The New York Review of Books*, 51 (29 April)

Wilson, B. (2002). '*Charles Fourier (1772–1837) and Questions of Women*', Ph.D. dissertation, University of Cambridge

Wilson, Leonard G. (1998). *Lyell in America: Transatlantic Geology, 1841–1853*, Baltimore

Wiltse, Charles M. (1944–51). *John C. Calhoun*, 3 vols., Indianapolis

Wiltshire, D. (1978). *The Social and Political Thought of Herbert Spencer*, Oxford

Winch, Donald (1987). *Malthus*, Oxford

(1996). *Riches and Poverty: An Intellectual History of Political Economy in Britain, 1750–1834*, Cambridge

Bibliography

(2009). *Wealth and Life: Essays on the Intellectual History of Political Economy in Britain, 1848–1914*, Cambridge

Winfield, R. D. (1993). 'Rethinking the Particular Forms of Art: Prolegomena to a Rational Reconstruction of Hegel's Theory of the Artforms', *Owl of Minerva*, 24(2): 131–44

Wingate, Francis R. (1968). *Mahdiism and the Egyptian Sudan*, London

Wingfield, Nancy (2003). *Creating the Other: Ethnic Conflict and Nationalism in Habsburg Central Europe*, New York

Winkler, Heinrich August (1978). *Vom Linken zum Rechten Nationalismus. Der Deutsche Liberalismus in der Krise von 1878/79*, in *Geschichte und Gesellschaft*, 4: 5–28

Wisdom, J. (1931). *Interpretation and Analysis in Relation to Bentham's Theory of Definition*, London

Wish, Harvey (1943). *George Fitzhugh: Propagandist of the Old South*, Baton Rouge

Wisner, David A. (1997). *The Cult of the Legislator in France 1750–1850: A Study in the Political Theology of the French Enlightenment*, Oxford

Wittke, Carl (1945). *Against the Current: The Life of Karl Heinzen*, Chicago

(1950). *The Utopian Communist: A Biography of Wilhelm Weitling*, Baton Rouge

(1952). *Refugees of Revolution: The German Forty-Eighters in America*, Philadelphia

Wokler, R. (1987). 'Saint-Simon and the Passage from Political to Social Science', in A. Pagden (ed.), *The Languages of Political Theory in Early-Modern Europe*, Cambridge

Wolfe, Willard (1975). *From Radicalism to Socialism: Men and Ideas in the Formation of Fabian Socialist Doctrines, 1881–1889*, New Haven

Wolin, Sheldon S. (1961). *Politics and Vision: Continuity and Innovation in Western Political Thought*, London

(1981). 'The King's Two Bodies', *Democracy* (January): 9–24

(1989). *The Presence of the Past: Essays on the State and the Constitution*, Baltimore

(2001). *Tocqueville between Two Worlds: The Making of a Political and Theoretical Life*, Princeton

(2004). *Politics and Vision: Continuity and Innovation in Western Political Thought*, expanded edition, Princeton

Wood, Allen (1981). *Karl Marx*, London

(1990). *Hegel's Ethical Thought*, Cambridge

Wood, Gordon S. (1969). *The Creation of the American Republic, 1776–1787*, Chapel Hill, NC

(1992). *The Radicalism of the American Revolution*, New York

(2001). 'Tocqueville's Lesson', *New York Review of Books*, 48 (17 May): 46–9

Woodcock, George (1956). *Pierre-Joseph Proudhon: His Life and Work*, New York

(1970). *Anarchism: A History of Libertarian Ideas and Movements*, Harmondsworth

(1989 [1946]). *William Godwin: A Biographical Study*, Montreal

Woodcock, George and Avakumovic, Ivan (1971 [1950]). *The Anarchist Prince: A Biographical Study of Peter Kropotkin*, New York

Woodring, Carl (1970). *Politics in English Romantic Poetry*, Cambridge, MA

Woodward, C. Vann (1966 [1951]). *Reunion and Reaction: The Compromise of 1877 and the End of Reconstruction*, New York

(1971). *American Counterpoint: Slavery and Racism in the North–South Dialogue*, Boston

Woodworth, Arthur (1903). *Christian Socialism in England*, London

Woolf, S. J. (1979). *A History of Italy: The Social Constraints of Political Change*, London

Woolf, S. J. (ed.) (1996). *Nationalism in Europe: 1815 to the Present*, London

Woolf, Virginia (1996). *A Room of One's Own and Three Guineas*, London

Wormell, Deborah (1980). *Sir John Seeley and the Uses of History*, Cambridge

Wootton, David (1994). 'The Republican Tradition: From Commonwealth to Common Sense', in Wootton (ed.), *Republicanism, Liberty and Commercial Society, 1649–1776*, Stanford

Wright, D. G. (1988). *Popular Radicalism: The Working Class Experience 1780–1880*, London

Wright, T. R. (1981). 'George Eliot and Positivism: A Reassessment', *Modern Language Review*, 76: 257–72

(1986). *The Religion of Humanity: The Impact of Comtean Positivism on Victorian Britain*, Cambridge

Yarmolinsky, Avraham (1957). *Road to Revolution: A Century of Russian Radicalism*, London

Yashinaga, Toshinobu (1992). *Ando Shoeki: Social and Ecological Philosopher in Eighteenth-Century Japan*, New York

Yeol, Ku Dae (1985). *Korea under Colonialism: The March First Movement and Anglo-Japanese Relations*, Seoul

Yoast, Richard A. (1975). 'The Development of Argentine Anarchism: A Socio-Ideological Analysis', Ph.D. dissertation, University of Wisconsin

Young, James P. (1996). *Reconsidering American Liberalism: The Troubled Odyssey of the Liberal Idea*, Boulder

(2001). *Henry Adams: The Historian as Political Theorist* (American Political Thought), Lawrence

Young, R. (1985). *Darwin's Metaphor: Nature's Place in Victorian Culture*, Cambridge

Yovel, Yirmiahu (1996). 'Hegel's Dictum that the Rational is the Actual and the Actual is the Rational: Its Ontological Content and its Function in Discourse', in Jon Stewart (ed.), *Hegel Myths and Legends*, Chicago

Zacek, Joseph Frederick (1970). *Palacký: The Historian as Scholar and Nationalist*, The Hague

Zastoupil, Lynn (1994). *John Stuart Mill and India, 1806–73*, Stanford

Zeldin, David (1969). *The Educational Ideas of Charles Fourier*, London

Zeldin, Theodore (1958). *The Political System of Napoleon III*, London

(1977). *France 1848–1945, Vol.* II: *Intellect, Taste and Anxiety*, Oxford

Zimmer, Oliver (2003). 'Boundary Mechanisms and Symbolic Resources: Towards a Process-Oriented Approach to National Identity', *Nations and Nationalism*, 9(2): 173–93.

Zimmermann, Andrew (2004). 'Ethnologie im Kaiserreich. Natur, Kultur und "Rasse" in Deutschland und seinen Kolonien', in Sebastian Conrad and Jürgen Osterhammel (eds.), *Das Kaiserreich Transnational: Deutschland in der Welt 1871–1914*, Göttingen

Ziolkowski, Theodore (1990). *German Romanticism and its Institutions*, Princeton

Zucker, Adolf (1950). *The Forty-Eighters: Political Refugees of the German Revolution of 1848*, New York

Zuckert, Michael (1996). *The Natural Rights Republic*, South Bend

(1998). 'A Work of Our Hands', *Review of Politics*, 60: 355–60

Index

Index

education
  aesthetic (Schiller) 490–1, 492–3
  anarchism and 439, 472
  apprenticeships (Proudhon) 458
  Bell's 'Madras system' 47
  as ethical guide 703
  French secular 195, 197
  and national history 107
  public (Comte) 191
  role of clerisy 51
  state provision 734
  of women 319, 338, 742, 921
Education Act (1902) 734
Egypt
  African influence in 861
  Napoleon in 876, 877
  political violence in 247
  and women's franchise 850
Eichhorn, Karl Friedrich 158, 161
elections, indirect 74
Eliot, George (Mary Ann Evans) 83, 189,
    189n13, 190n14, **950**
elite nationalism, linked with popular resistance
    80
elites
  and nationality 83
  responsibilities of 68
  and role of tutelage 845
  Saint-Simon's assumption of rule by 540
Elizabeth of Austria, Empress 247
Ely, Richard 528n2, 762
emancipation
  of individual 603
  Marx's concept of 568
  of serfs (Russia) 101, 230, 819
  of slaves 391, 395, 859
  see also franchise; freedom; women's suffrage
Emancipation of Labour Group (Russian) 830,
    833
Emerson, Ralph Waldo 394, 395–6, **950**
emigrés, anti-revolutionary 10, 11
Emmett, Robert 233
empire
  definitions 864
  Marx's view of 593
  see also British Empire; Habsburg Empire;
    imperialism; Ottoman Empire
empiricism
  ethical 114
  Mill and 295
Employers' Liability Act (1881) 720, 721
employment
  Mill on 298, 301
  for women 335, 340, 343, 794
  see also unemployment

energy, and development (Mill) 308, 309–10
Enfantin, (Barthélemy-)Prosper 329, 541, 542
Engels, Friedrich 142, 216, 557, 590–2, **950**
  Anti-Dühring 588n39, 590, 591, 792
  and Capital 588n39
  The Condition of the Working Class in England
    557, 574, 761
  essay in Deutsch-Französische Jahrbücher 572
  and Gotha programme 790
  Herr Eugen Dühring's Revolution in Science 792
  Ludwig Feuerbach und der Ausgang der klassischen
    deutschen Philosophie 143
  and Marxism 590
  and nationalism 85
  Origin of the Family 342–3
  and political reform in England 574n17, 591
  republicanism 804
  on Schiller 489
  and Social Democrats 796
  and terrorism 238
England
  church reform movements 631–5
  conservative romanticism 41–52
  constitution (unwritten) 165, 166
    French interest in 350, 353, 361, 363
  Glorious Revolution (1688), French references
    to 354, 364
  Guizot on representative government 363
  history and law in 162–6
  influence of Comtism 188–92, 198
  as nation 78
  nature of state (Marx) 579, 580
  pauperism in 182
  political economy in
  social reformers 183
  see also Great Britain
Enlightenment, the
  counter-revolutionaries and 11
  French Romantic view of 69
  German Romantic view of 52
  Godwin and 443
  intellectual legacy 479
  and national idea 78
  and neo-classicism 487
  romantic view of 41, 42
  see also reason
Epicureanism 287
'episodic citizenship' (Kateb) 396
equality
  in America 367, 399, 401
  before the law 27
  communistic egalitarianism 522
  Fourier's view of 534
  in German liberalism 411, 424
  of opportunity 119, 125

Index

Index

Janet, Pierre 180*n*6
Jansenism 17
Japan 107, 905
   assassination of Prime Minister 247
   concept of civilisation 869
   and concept of rights 841, 846
   influence of Comte in 851
   and Korea 220
   Meiji government 749, 844, 846
   political economy in 749, 763, 849
   political norms 841
Jaume, Lucien, *L'Individu Effacé . . .* 360
Jaurès, Jean 437, 548
Java 220
Jefferson, Thomas 217, 859, **961**
   and decentralisation 385*n*18
   Declaration of Independence (1775) 379
   liberalism 407
   Notes on the State of Virginia 382, 384, 387, 710
   as president 382
   and rebellion 384*n*17
   republicanism 379–89
   and slavery 383*n*15, 387–9
   and women's rights 394
Jevons, William Stanley 272, 751, 767, 773, **962**
   The Theory of Political Economy 765, 766
Jewish nationalism 95–6
   Zionism 96, 96*n*29
Jews 908
   pogroms in Russia 105
   see also anti-Semitism; Judaism
Johnson, Joseph 324
Jones, Ernest 207
Journal politique national 12
Judaism 95*n*28
   Marx and 569
   see also anti-Semitism; Jews
judiciary 148
   American model 368
   independence (Constant) 358
   liberal views of 737
Jura Federation 436
   Kropotkin and 470, 471
'just war', concept of 249
justice
   immanent (Proudhon) 435, 456
   and liberalism 731
   social 899
Justinian, *Corpus Juris Justiniani* (AD 529–33) 147

Kammick, Isaac 378
Kanai Noburu 763
Kane, P. V., *History of Dharmasastra* 836
Kang Youwei 848, 850, 851
Kant, Immanuel 160, 487, 557

aesthetic theory 485–6
   and constitutional reforms 410
   Critique of Judgement 486, 502
   Critique of Pure Reason 502
   determinability 492
   freedom of will 486
   Hegel on 502
   intuitive intellect 494
   laws of reason 134
   Metaphysics of Morals 494
   subjective idealism 115
   'Theory-Practice' essay 113
'Kantian paradox' 482
Karamzin, Nikolai Mikhailovich **962**
   Memoir on Ancient and Modern Russia 812
Karlsbad Decrees (1819) 117
Kateb, George 396
Katkov, Mikhail 825
Kautsky, Karl 679, **962**
   and Darwin 801–2
   interpretation of Marxism 800–2, 805
   and parliamentary participation 803–4
   and social democracy 792
Kavelin, Konstantin 818
   Dvoriastvo i Osvobozhdenie Krestian 819
   Survey of Juridical Relations in Ancient Russia 816
Keble, John 632, **962**
Kedourie, Elie 109
Kelly, George 179
Kelsen, Hans 928, 928*n*16
Ketteler, Baron von 546
Key, Ellen 348
Keynes, John Maynard 924
Khan, Sir Sayyid Ahmad 853
Khomiakov, Aleksei Stephanovich 815, **962**
Kidd, Benjamin, *Social Evolution* 680
Killing No Murder 237
kingship *see* monarchy
Kingsley, Charles 546, 658
Kinnear, John Boyd 726
Kireevskii, Ivan 815
knowledge
   accumulation of 903, 904–5
   Bentham's work on 269
   communal 614
   historical 644, 904–5
   of non-European civilisations 905
   'scientific' (Hegel) 622
   as utilitarian good 311, 313, 315
Knox, Robert, *The Races of Men* 673
Kogălniceanu, Mihail, Romanian historian 93
Kollontai, Alexandra 341, 341*n*12
Kolokol (*The Bell*), journal 230, 818, 825
Korea 220

1116

Index

Index

Index